LITERATURE
An Introduction to
Critical Reading

LITERATURE
An Introduction to Critical Reading

William Vesterman

Rutgers University

Harcourt Brace Jovanovich College Publishers

Fort Worth • Philadelphia • San Diego
New York • Orlando • Austin • San Antonio
Toronto • Montreal • London • Sydney • Tokyo

Publisher	Ted Buchholz
Acquisitions Editor	Michael Rosenberg
Developmental Editors	Christine Caperton, Karl Yambert
Project Editor	Mark Hobbs
Senior Production Manager	Ken Dunaway
Senior Book Designer	Terry Rasberry
Permissions Editor	Van Strength

Requests for permission to make copies of any part of the work should be mailed to the Permissions Department, Harcourt Brace Jovanovich, Publishers, 8th Floor, 6277 Sea Harbor Drive, Orlando, Florida 32887.

Address for Editorial Correspondence: Harcourt Brace Jovanovich College Publishers, 301 Commerce Street, Suite 3700, Fort Worth, TX 76102.

Address for Orders: Harcourt Brace Jovanovich, Publishers, 6277 Sea Harbor Drive, Orlando, Florida 32887. 1-800-782-4479, or 1-800-433-0001 (in Florida).

ISBN: 0-03-046914-7

Library of Congress Catalog Card Number: 92-073554

CREDITS: The literary credits are found on page 971.

Printed in the United States of America

2 3 4 5 6 7 8 9 0 1 016 9 8 7 6 5 4 3 2 1

Brief Contents

PART ONE: FICTION

PART TWO: POETRY

PART THREE: DRAMA

Preface: To the Instructor

Purpose and Principles

An Introduction to Critical Reading contains 30 stories, 140 poems, and 8 plays. It is distinguished most clearly from other text-anthologies designed for introductory courses by its combination of classic and contemporary selections with introductions to some of the critical approaches most widely used by today's teachers of literature. Further, those critical approaches are represented by twenty-eight detailed accounts of practical criticism of the individual works of fiction, poetry, and drama included herein.

The accounts summarize, paraphrase, and quote from the critical essays, thus avoiding difficulties of implied context, unexplained references, and specialized vocabulary—matters that might make reading so many differing published essays needlessly difficult and confusing for the beginning student. Naturally, full bibliographic information makes it possible to assign any or all of the original critical essays if desired. In addition, Appendix I provides four critical essays, in their original forms, along with student writing exercises based on those essays.

This book is based on the assumption that undergraduates are best introduced to the study of literature by becoming acquainted not only with a wide range of literary material but also with the actual range of views and practices among professional students of literature—their teachers and their teachers' colleagues. The book thereby explicitly seeks to do some justice to the great diversity that unquestionably exists today among those views and practices. Many teachers of literature have themselves been trained as students in critical methods now generally associated with the New Criticism, and its emphasis on "close reading" continues to be a part of any careful professional instruction in literature. Yet very few teachers of any background would now deny the importance of the interest in other critical theories, nor would many teachers endorse the false impression made by most introductory text-anthologies of a professional unanimity or scholarly consensus about literary theory. In a world with differing views of literature, the real range now entertained by professional students should be acknowledged; and the present volume is an attempt to take some account of that critical variety.

The anticipated difficulty of critical theory for undergraduates has proved to be as illusory as the fear of computers felt by non-technical students before word processing so quickly became almost universal among almost all students. Given that all text-anthologies in literature attempt to introduce the complexities of writers like Shakespeare, the relatively minor mysteries of contemporary literary theory seem easily attained. The following pages attempt to act on that assumption in order to foster greater instructional flexibility in one of the most important courses in any college curriculum.

Using the Book

The text does not pretend to completeness, or to great depth, or to be anything other than an introduction to critical reading for beginning students. It does claim to make explicit by its account of critical theories and examples of critical practice the importance of the values and assumptions that every reader brings to literature.

The first major division of the book focuses on fiction. An introduction containing two short stories—James Joyce's "Araby" and Alice Munro's "Eskimo"—illustrates some commonly used critical terms. Chapters on eight major critical approaches follow. Each approach is introduced by a brief overview followed by a famous short story and an account of a critical essay that uses the approach. In each case, questions on the story include issues of "close reading" and theoretical concerns. A collection of stories concludes the section on fiction.

In the poetry and drama sections, the book offers two accounts of different approaches to each of five featured poems and five featured plays. Again, questions invite the student to a consideration of basic matters of close reading and larger issues of theory.

The organization of the book provides flexibility for teaching each of the literary genres and the critical approaches to them. Though most introductory courses begin with fiction, the instructor may start the book with any genre, since the introductions to the various modes of criticism are independent of the stories. Even a course that follows the structure of the book can naturally give greater or lesser emphasis to any genre or featured author. Several suggested syllabi for semester, quarter, and two-semester courses are included in the Instructor's Manual.

Acknowledgments

Many people helped in many ways with this book. I thank Robert Atwan, Daniel Moran, and Nancy Miller for help in planning and production. Sean Fletcher, Ron Quade, and Pawna Aulani assisted with the word processing. I am grateful to the people at HBJ College Publishers who worked diligently on converting ideas and manuscript into a book: Michael Rosenberg, Christine Caperton, Karl Yambert, Mark Hobbs, Ken Dunaway, and Terry Rasberry.

My very special thanks are due to Bonnie Klomp Stevens (Augustana College) and Larry Stewart (College of Wooster), who offered numerous valuable suggestions that are now incorporated into the book.

Finally, I thank the many other scholars who helped shape the book by their readings at various stages: Louis Burkhardt, University of Colorado, Boulder; Joseph Childers, University of California, Riverside; L. Leon Duke, Montgomery College; Richard Dunn, University of Washington; Donella Eberle, Mesa Community College; Laurie Finke, Lewis and Clark College; Marjorie Garber, Harvard University; Stephen Hahn, William Paterson College; Milo Kaufmann, University of Illinois; Mary Klayder, University of Kansas; Don Kleine, University of Maryland; Leland Krauth, University of Colorado, Boulder; Helen Marlborough, DePaul University; Ann Matthews, Princeton University; Della W. Paul, Valencia Community College; Merry Pawlowski, California State University, Bakersfield; Paul Rogalus, Plymouth State College; Carole Shaffer-Koros, Kean College of New Jersey; and Kathleen Vogt, Wheaton College.

Contents

PART TWO: POETRY

PART THREE: DRAMA

LITERATURE
An Introduction to
Critical Reading

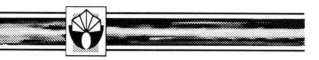

Introduction: Increasing Your Enjoyment and Understanding of Literature Through Critical Theory and Practice

L iterature" is a word that generally describes language used for imaginative purposes and is even more broadly understood as a term of praise for writing of any purpose that has excited admiration for its imaginative qualities—Gibbons' *Decline and Fall of the Roman Empire* or Darwin's *Origin of Species,* for example.

For most people the emotion of admiration for anything—a building, an animal, an athletic team—overflows into language at some point. We are fond of praising and discussing what moves us to feeling and gives us insight. Because what moves us in literature is itself composed of words, the praise and the discussion become particularly interesting. The mutual interaction of critical discussion and our experience of literature is especially productive, as discussion leads to further insights and the power of insight to further pleasure and understanding.

In any activity, knowledge of a subject enhances the experience of that subject. When botanists walk through a meadow, they receive with the rest of us the same light rays that convey what they see, but they also *perceive* through their knowledge of botany a vastly richer world than many of the rest of us do. By knowing the names of plants and the structures of those plants, by knowing the interrelations among them and the variation of the plants with elements of the environment (moisture for example), the enhanced world illuminated by their previous studies is brighter than the world illuminated for all of us by the sun alone. We see ordinary "grass"; the botanist sees a complex and interesting bio-system. In a similar way, knowledge about literature increases our perceptions and hence our possibilities for enjoyment and insight.

This book seeks to bring a reader to the richness in criticism that lies beyond easy positive or negative judgments. It seeks to introduce the critical knowledge of literature that may be gained by improving on initial reactions through further inquiries that themselves lead to further reactions in a productive cycle of continuing illumination. In other words, it seeks to enhance your enjoyment and to expand your insights through knowledge and to enhance your knowledge through enjoyment and insight.

In attempting to initiate such a cycle, this book offers an introduction to the *study* of literature. It assumes, along with most professional critics, that the first major activity of criticism is an inquiry into the nature of the story, poem, or play and that this inquiry is necessary before any reasonable judgment may be made or argued. Also, greater knowledge leads to *better* judgments, just as an American's ability to judge the quality of British cricket or the British ability to distinguish great baseball are matters that clearly depend not on innate "good taste" but upon knowledge gained through experience.

Part of that knowledge may be called "theory," and part of that experience may have modified and developed that theory—the theory of how a play in a game should *best* be handled or how the lyrics of a song should *best* be orchestrated and sung. Should "The Star Spangled Banner," for example, be sung in the manner of a sultry love song? "Why?" or "Why not?" are in fact questions of literary theory.

Everyone mentally carries innumerable theories around, and it would be impossible to function in life without them. In fact, no one could perform any "practical" acts of the kind often carelessly contrasted with "theory." Here for example is a common theory: "All things using mechanical threads, like bottle caps and nuts and bolts, will unscrew in a counterclockwise direction." Yet, is this theory true? Many people have broken the lugnuts on the wheels of Chrysler Corporation products when trying to change a tire on the left side of the car because of a conflicting theory held—for good reasons—by Chrysler engineers.

One reason for the bad reputation of the word *theory* may be that many people hold a false belief of what theory is. You may have often heard: "That's all very well in *theory*" and "They may teach you that *theoretical* stuff in school, but when you get out in the real world, you'll find that, practically speaking, it's all useless." Yet even when, and if, these objections prove to be true, they are not objections to "theory" but to *bad* theory or *incorrect* theories that do not match or explain the facts. A theory rightly understood is designed to explain facts and to generalize about their relations to one another. Theories attempt to generalize about a great many facts, and if they do not successfully do so, they must be abandoned or revised. In this way, newly observed facts about the planets led to the replacement of the earth-centered theory of the solar system by a sun-centered theory, with one practical result being better predictions of planetary motions.

Theories of literary criticism are efforts to illuminate literature. No one denies the real complexity of literature, since it derives from the complexity of the human imagination expressed in the language that produces literature. But human creations should be understandable by human beings, and illuminating through criticism even some parts of the vast domains of imagination and language has been found by generations of readers to be a highly pleasurable and informative activity.

Many theories of literary criticism have been attempted and, as stated earlier, this book aims to introduce you to some of the more widely used modern methods. Those methods are themselves introduced—both as theory and as practice—in the hope that you may learn by example and imitation to further your own understanding of the variety of approaches that make up literary criticism.

Yet the student may well ask, "If theories are supposed to explain facts, why then is there more than *one* theory of literary criticism?" The answer involves both the complexity of literature itself and the many different ways in which it may be approached. Literary historian and critic Myer Abrams has offered an account of the differences among theories that provides a way of understanding their relations to literature and to one another in the following map:

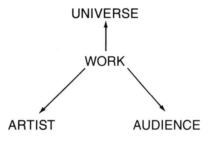

While every critical theory tries to explain in some way all these aspects of literature, each particular approach emphasizes or focuses on one or another aspect. Thus perhaps the most widely used theoretical approach today is that associated with what is called the New Criticism (see p. 29). This approach initially focuses on the work as a *verbal* construction and seeks to understand its complexities and to resolve its puzzles and contradictions by maintaining attention on the words of the text itself as much as possible. Again, this focus is a matter only of emphasis, and the leading adherents of this approach have insisted that they never meant to deny the importance of (say) the historical context of the text or the life of the author who wrote it.

The New Criticism is the first approach introduced in this book, after a brief introduction to some general critical terms. As with the others that follow it, the section on the New Criticism offers a brief introduction to the approach, presents a classic story, and gives an account of a professional critic who uses the approach to read the story. When the book turns to poetry and drama, it gives accounts of critical essays that use two of the critical approaches introduced in the fiction section to read each of five major poems and five major plays. Thus, by leading you not only to great examples of literature but also to examples of contemporary criticism in both its theoretical and practical aspects, the book attempts to show you how the art of criticism becomes clearer as the nature of literature becomes more richly explored.

PART ONE

FICTION

Chapter One

Introduction to Fiction

T his chapter aims to introduce you to some of the common terms used in discussing fiction. You should first read two short stories: "Araby," by Irish writer James Joyce (1882–1941), and a more recent story, "Eskimo" by the widely read Canadian writer, Alice Munro, who was born in 1931. An introduction to some critical terms will follow the stories, with illustrations taken from those stories. The terms, it is hoped, will enable you to describe and discuss your experiences as a reader and will serve as the basis for further introductions to critical methods later in the book.

JAMES JOYCE (1882–1941) was born in Dublin on February 2, 1882, the son of an Irish landowner. Although educated at Jesuit schools to prepare him for a possible life in the priesthood, Joyce rebelled against Catholicism and, in 1902, left Dublin and spent the rest of his life in Paris, Zurich, Rome, and Trieste. However, Ireland and its people lie at the core of Joyce's entire literary output.

While living in self-imposed exile, Joyce earned meager salaries teaching foreign languages and doing clerical work. In 1912, Joyce briefly returned to Dublin to arrange *Dubliners* for publication, a collection of short stories about the city and its inhabitants. Because of fears of censorship, however, the book was not published until 1914, when it came under attack for mentioning actual Dublin persons and places.

In 1916, with the help of Ezra Pound, Joyce published *A Portrait of the Artist as a Young Man*, a largely autobiographical novel which details his rebellion against family ties, Catholicism, and Irish nationalism. During 1914–1921, he composed *Ulysses*, widely considered Joyce's greatest achievement. Like *Dubliners*, *Ulysses* met great opposition from publishers due to obscenity charges; the book was finally published in Paris in 1922 and was banned in the United States until 1933. Joyce published his most experimental novel, *Finnegans Wake*, in 1939, a project which took him seventeen years to complete.

"Araby" is taken from *Dubliners*, wherein Joyce provides a panorama of the Dublin from which he fled. Most of the stories concern ordinary Catholic middle-class life. In each of the stories, Joyce uses a device he named the *epiphany:* a sudden event, remark, moment, or symbol which clarifies and redefines the meaning of a complex or jarring experience.

JAMES JOYCE
Araby
(1914)

North Richmond Street, being blind, was a quiet street except at the hour when the Christian Brothers' School set the boys free. An uninhabited house of two storeys stood at the blind end, detached from its neighbours in a square ground. The other houses of the street, conscious of decent lives within them, gazed at one another with brown imperturbable faces.

The former tenant of our house, a priest, had died in the back drawing-room. Air, musty from having been long enclosed, hung in all the rooms, and the waste room behind the kitchen was littered with 10 old useless papers. Among these I found a few paper-covered books, the pages of which were curled and damp: *The Abbot*, by Walter Scott, *The Devout Communicant* and *The Memoirs of Vidocq*. I liked the last best because its leaves were yellow. The wild garden behind the house contained a central apple-tree and a few straggling bushes under one of which I found the late tenant's rusty bicycle-pump. He had been a very charitable priest; in his will he had left all his money to institutions and the furniture of his house to his sister.

When the short days of winter came dusk fell before we had well eaten our dinners. When we met in the street the houses had grown som- 20 bre. The space of sky above us was the colour of ever-changing violet and towards it the lamps of the street lifted their feeble lanterns. The cold air stung us and we played till our bodies glowed. Our shouts echoed in the silent street. The career of our play brought us through the dark muddy lanes behind the houses where we ran the gauntlet of the rough tribes from the cottages, to the back doors of the dark dripping gardens where odours arose from the ashpits, to the dark odorous stables where a coachman smoothed and combed the horse or shook music from the buckled harness. When we returned to the street light from the kitchen windows had filled the areas. If my uncle was seen turning the corner we hid in the 30 shadow until we had seen him safely housed. Or if Mangan's sister came out on the doorstep to call her brother in to his tea we watched her from our shadow peer up and down the street. We waited to see whether she would remain or go in and, if she remained, we left our shadow and walked up to Mangan's steps resignedly. She was waiting for us, her figure defined by the light from the half-opened door. Her brother always teased her before he obeyed and I stood by the railings looking at her. Her dress swung as she moved her body and the soft rope of her hair tossed from side to side.

Every morning I lay on the floor in the front parlour watching her 40 door. The blind was pulled down to within an inch of the sash so that I could not be seen. When she came out on the doorstep my heart leaped. I ran to the hall, seized my books and followed her. I kept her brown figure

always in my eye and, when we came near the point at which our ways di-
verged, I quickened my pace and passed her. This happened morning after
morning. I had never spoken to her, except for a few casual words, and yet
her name was like a summons to all my foolish blood.

Her image accompanied me even in places the most hostile to romance. On Saturday evenings when my aunt went marketing I had to go
to carry some of the parcels. We walked through the flaring streets, jos-
50 tled by drunken men and bargaining women, amid the curses of labourers, the shrill litanies of shop-boys who stood on guard by the barrels of
pigs' cheeks, the nasal chanting of street-singers, who sang a *come-all-
you* about O'Donovan Rossa, or a ballad about the troubles in our native
land. These noises converged in a single sensation of life for me: I imagined that I bore my chalice safely through a throng of foes. Her name
sprang to my lips at moments in strange prayers and praises which I
myself did not understand. My eyes were often full of tears (I could not
tell why) and at times a flood from my heart seemed to pour itself out
into my bosom. I thought little of the future. I did not know whether I
60 would ever speak to her or not or, if I spoke to her, how I could tell her
of my confused adoration. But my body was like a harp and her words
and gestures were like fingers running upon the wires.

One evening I went into the back drawing-room in which the priest
had died. It was a dark rainy evening and there was no sound in the
house. Through one of the broken panes I heard the rain impinge upon
the earth, the fine incessant needles of water playing in the sodden
beds. Some distant lamp or lighted window gleamed below me. I was
thankful that I could see so little. All my senses seemed to desire to veil
themselves and, feeling that I was about to slip from them, I pressed the
70 palms of my hands together until they trembled, murmuring: "*O love!
O love!*" many times.

At last she spoke to me. When she addressed the first words to me I
was so confused that I did not know what to answer. She asked me was
I going to *Araby.* I forgot whether I answered yes or no. It would be a
splendid bazaar, she said she would love to go.

"And why can't you?" I asked.

While she spoke she turned a silver bracelet round and round her
wrist. She could not go, she said, because there would be a retreat that
week in her convent. Her brother and two other boys were fighting for
80 their caps and I was alone at the railings. She held one of the spikes, bowing her head towards me. The light from the lamp opposite our door
caught the white curve of her neck, lit up her hair that rested there and,
falling, lit up the hand upon the railing. It fell over one side of her dress
and caught the white border of a petticoat, just visible as she stood at ease.

"It's well for you," she said.

"If I go," I said, "I will bring you something."

What innumerable follies laid waste my waking and sleeping
thoughts after that evening! I wished to annihilate the tedious interven-
ing days. I chafed against the work of school. At night in my bedroom

90 and by day in the classroom her image came between me and the page I
strove to read. The syllables of the word *Araby* were called to me
through the silence in which my soul luxuriated and cast an Eastern enchantment over me. I asked for leave to go to the bazaar on Saturday
night. My aunt was surprised and hoped it was not some Freemason affair. I answered few questions in class. I watched my master's face pass
from amiability to sternness; he hoped I was not beginning to idle. I
could not call my wandering thoughts together. I had hardly any patience with the serious work of life which, now that it stood between me
and my desire, seemed to me child's play, ugly monotonous child's play.

100   On Saturday morning I reminded my uncle that I wished to go to
the bazaar in the evening. He was fussing at the hallstand, looking for the
hatbrush, and answered me curtly:

"Yes, boy, I know."

As he was in the hall I could not go into the front parlour and lie
at the window. I left the house in bad humour and walked slowly towards the school. The air was pitilessly raw and already my heart mis-
gave me.

When I came home to dinner my uncle had not yet been home. Still it
was early. I sat staring at the clock for some time and, when its ticking
110 began to irritate me, I left the room. I mounted the staircase and gained
the upper part of the house. The high cold empty gloomy rooms liberated
me and I went from room to room singing. From the front window I saw
my companions playing below in the street. Their cries reached me weakened and indistinct and, leaning my forehead against the cool glass, I
looked over at the dark house where she lived. I may have stood there for
an hour, seeing nothing but the brown-clad figure cast by my imagination, touched discreetly by the lamplight at the curved neck, at the hand
upon the railings and at the border below the dress.

When I came downstairs again I found Mrs. Mercer sitting at the fire.
120 She was an old garrulous woman, a pawnbroker's widow, who collected
used stamps for some pious purpose. I had to endure the gossip of the
tea-table. The meal was prolonged beyond an hour and still my uncle did
not come. Mrs. Mercer stood up to go: she was sorry she couldn't wait any
longer, but it was after eight o'clock and she did not like to be out late, as
the night air was bad for her. When she had gone I began to walk up and
down the room, clenching my fists. My aunt said:

"I'm afraid you may put off your bazaar for this night of Our Lord."

At nine o'clock I heard my uncle's latchkey in the halldoor. I heard
him talking to himself and heard the hallstand rocking when it had re-
130 ceived the weight of his overcoat. I could interpret these signs. When he
was midway through his dinner I asked him to give me the money to go
to the bazaar. He had forgotten.

"The people are in bed and after their first sleep now," he said.

I did not smile. My aunt said to him energetically:

"Can't you give him the money and let him go? You've kept him late
enough as it is."

My uncle said he was very sorry he had forgotten. He said he believed in the old saying: "All work and no play makes Jack a dull boy."
He asked me where I was going and, when I had told him a second
140 time he asked me did I know *The Arab's Farewell to his Steed*. When I left
the kitchen he was about to recite the opening lines of the piece to
my aunt.

I held a florin tightly in my hand as I strode down Buckingham
Street towards the station. The sight of the streets thronged with buyers
and glaring with gas recalled to me the purpose of my journey. I took
my seat in a third-class carriage of a deserted train. After an intolerable
delay the train moved out of the station slowly. It crept onward among
ruinous houses and over the twinkling river. At Westland Row Station a
crowd of people pressed to the carriage doors; but the porters moved
150 them back, saying that it was a special train for the bazaar. I remained
alone in the bare carriage. In a few minutes the train drew up beside an
improvised wooden platform. I passed out on to the road and saw by the
lighted dial of a clock that it was ten minutes to ten. In front of me was
a large building which displayed the magical name.

I could not find any sixpenny entrance and, fearing that the bazaar
would be closed, I passed in quickly through a turnstile, handing a
shilling to a weary-looking man. I found myself in a big hall girdled at
half its height by a gallery. Nearly all the stalls were closed and the
greater part of the hall was in darkness. I recognised a silence like that
160 which pervades a church after a service. I walked into the centre of the
bazaar timidly. A few people were gathered about the stalls which were
still open. Before a curtain, over which the words *Café Chantant* were
written in coloured lamps, two men were counting money on a salver. I
listened to the fall of the coins.

Remembering with difficulty why I had come I went over to one of
the stalls and examined porcelain vases and flowered tea-sets. At the
door of the stall a young lady was talking and laughing with two young
gentlemen. I remarked their English accents and listened vaguely to
their conversation.

170   "O, I never said such a thing!"

"O, but you did!"

"O, but I didn't!"

"Didn't she say that?"

"Yes. I heard her."

"O, there's a . . . fib!"

Observing me the young lady came over and asked me did I wish
to buy anything. The tone of her voice was not encouraging; she
seemed to have spoken to me out of a sense of duty. I looked humbly at
the great jars that stood like eastern guards at either side of the dark
180 entrance to the stall and murmured:

"No, thank you."

The young lady changed the position of one of the vases and went back
to the two young men. They began to talk of the same subject. Once or
twice the young lady glanced at me over her shoulder.

I lingered before her stall, though I knew my stay was useless, to make my interest in her wares seem the more real. Then I turned away slowly and walked down the middle of the bazaar. I allowed the two pennies to fall against the sixpence in my pocket. I heard a voice call from one end of the gallery that the light was out. The upper part of the hall was now com-
190 pletely dark.

Gazing up into the darkness I saw myself as a creature driven and derided by vanity; and my eyes burned with anguish and anger.

ALICE MUNRO (née Eric) (1931–   ) was born on July 10, 1931, in Wingham, Ontario. In 1949 she graduated from Wingham District High School and enrolled in the University of Western Ontario. In 1968 her first collection of short stories, *Dance of the Happy Shades* was published, and the collection was awarded the Governor General's Award. The title story concerns a set of snobbish mothers trying to parade the musical skill of their daughters, only to have their pride thwarted by the true talent of a retarded child. Her next work, *Lives of Girls and Women: A Novel*, received the Canadian Booksellers Association International Book Year Award. In 1972, Munro returned to Ontario where she became a writer-in-residence at the University of Western Ontario. *Something I've Been Meaning to Tell You* was published in 1974, the same year in which she received the Great Lakes College Association Award for *Dance of the Happy Shades*. Munro's other critically acclaimed and popular works include *Who Do You Think You Are?* (1978), *The Moons of Jupiter* (1982), and *The Progress of Love* (1986).

ALICE MUNRO
Eskimo
(from *The Progress of Love*, 1986)

Mary Jo can hear what Dr. Streeter would have to say.

"Regular little United Nations back here."

Mary Jo, knowing how to handle him, would remark that there was always first class.

He would say that he didn't propose paying an arm and a leg for the privilege of swilling free champagne.

"Anyway, you know what's up in first class? Japs. Japanese business-men on their way home from buying up some more of the country."

Mary Jo might say then that Japanese hardly seemed foreign to her
10 anymore. She would say this thoughtfully, as if she was wondering about it, almost talking to herself.

"I mean, they hardly seem like a foreign race."

"Well, you seem foreign to them, and you better not forget it."

When he had got these remarks off his chest, Dr. Streeter would not be displeased. He would settle down beside her, glad they had these front seats where there was room for his legs. A tall, bulky man, florid and white-haired, he would stand out here—a slightly clumsy but noble-headed giant—among the darker skins, the more compact and fine-boned races, in their flashy or picturesque clothes. He would settle
20 down as if he had a right to be here, as if he had a right to be on this earth—which only other men of his age and race, dressed and thinking like him, could really match.

But he isn't stretching his legs out beside her, grumbling and content. She is off to Tahiti by herself. His Christmas present to her, this holiday. She has an aisle seat, and the window seat is empty.

"He has the mind of a dinosaur, that's all," said Dr. Streeter's daughter, Rhea, not long ago, talking to Mary Jo about what seems to be her favorite subject—her father. She has a list of favorite subjects, favorite serious subjects—nuclear proliferation, acid rain, unemployment, as 30 well as racial bigotry and the situation of women—but the road into them always appears to be through her father. Her father is not far from being the cause of all this, in Rhea's mind. He is behind bombs and pollution and poverty and discrimination. And Mary Jo has to admit that there are things he says that would lead you to this conclusion.

"That's just his opinions," Mary Jo said. She pictured a certain kind of dinosaur, the one with the frill of bony plates along its spine—a showy armor, almost like decoration. "Men have to have their opinions."

What a stupid thing to say, especially to Rhea. Rhea is twenty-five years old, unemployed, a fat, breezy, pretty girl who rides around on a 40 motorcycle. When Mary Jo said that, Rhea just stared at her for a minute, smiling her fat leisurely smile. Then she said softly, "Why, Mary Jo? Why do men have to have their opinions? So women can sit around clicking their tongues while men wreck the world?"

She had taken off her motorcycle helmet and set it down, wet from the rain, on Mary Jo's desk. She was shaking out her long, dark, tangled hair.

"No man is wrecking my world," said Mary Jo spiritedly, picking up the helmet and setting it on the floor. She didn't feel as equal to this conversation as she sounded. What was it Rhea wanted, really, when she came into her father's office and started up on these rambling com-50 plaints? She surely didn't expect Mary Jo to agree with her. No. She wanted and expected Mary Jo to defend her father, so that she could be amused and scornful (Oh, sure, Mary Jo, you think he's God!), and at the same time reassured. Mary Jo was supposed to do the work this girl's mother should have done—making her understand her father, and forgive and admire him. But Dr. Streeter's wife is not one for forgiving or admiring anybody, least of all her husband. She is a drinker, and thinks herself a wit. Sometimes she will phone the office and ask if she may speak to the Great Healer. A big, loud, untidy woman, with wild white hair, who likes to spend her time with actors—she is on the board of the local theater 60 —and so-called poets—English professors from the university, where she has been working on her Ph.D. for the last several years.

"A man like your father, who saves lives every day," said Mary Jo to Rhea—making a point she had often made before—"can hardly be said to be wrecking the world." Mary Jo did not defend Dr. Streeter just because he was a man, and a father, not at all; it was not for those reasons she thought his wife should have instilled some respect for him in his children. It was because he was the best cardiologist in that part of the

country, because he gave himself over every day to the gray-faced people
in his waiting room, the heart cases, people living in fear, in pain. His
70 life was given over.

In spite of the helmet, some of Rhea's hair had got wet, and she was
shaking raindrops over Mary Jo's desk.

"Rhea, watch it, please."

"What is your world, Mary Jo?"

"I haven't got time to tell you."

"You're so busy helping my dad."

Mary Jo has been working for Dr. Streeter for twelve years, living in
the apartment upstairs for ten. When Rhea was younger—a boisterous,
overweight, strenuous, but likable teenager—she used to like to visit
80 Mary Jo in the apartment, and Mary Jo would have to be sure that all
signs of Dr. Streeter's regular, though not lengthy, times there were out of
the way. Now Rhea must know all about that, but does not make direct
investigations. She often seems to be probing, skirting the subject. Mary
Jo remains bland and unforthcoming, but sometimes the effort tires her.

"It's nice you're going to Tahiti, though," said Rhea, still smiling in
her dangerous way, her hair and eyes sparkling. "Have you always wanted
to go there?"

"Of course," said Mary Jo. "Who wouldn't?"

"Not that he doesn't owe it to you. It's about time he paid you back
90 some of your devotion, I think."

Mary Jo, without answering, went on writing up her records. After
a while, Rhea calmed down and began to discuss the possibility of getting some money out of her father for repairs to her motorcycle—which
was what she had come into the office for in the first place.

Why is it that Rhea always knows the tricky question to ask, in spite
of her predictable mockery, lectures, and propaganda? "Have you always
wanted to go there?" Tahiti is, in fact, a place where Mary Jo has never
thought of going. Tahiti to her means palm trees, red flowers, curling
turquoise waves, and the sort of tropical luxuriance and indolence that
100 has never interested her. The gift has something unimaginative but touching about it, like the chocolates on St. Valentine's Day.

A winter holiday in Tahiti! I bet you're excited about it!

Well, I certainly am!

She has told patients, and her friends, and her sisters—whom she suspects of thinking she doesn't have much of a life—how excited she is. And
she couldn't sleep last night, if that counts for anything. Before six o'clock
this morning—it seems a long time ago—she stood at the window of her
apartment, wearing new clothes from the skin out, waiting for the taxi to
take her to the airport. A short, bumpy flight to Toronto, a longer flight
110 from Toronto to Vancouver, and here she is, launched over the Pacific
Ocean. A stop at Honolulu, then Tahiti. She can't go back on it.

Greece would have been better. Or Scandinavia. Well, perhaps not
Scandinavia at this time of year. Ireland. Last summer, Dr. Streeter and

his wife went to Ireland. His wife is "working on" some Irish poet. Mary Jo does not for a minute suppose that they had a good time. Who could have a good time with such an unkempt, capricious, disruptive woman? She believes they drank quite a bit. He went salmon-fishing. They stayed in a castle. Their holidays—and his holidays alone, usually fishing trips—are always expensive, and seem to Mary Jo ritualized and burdensome.
120 His house, too, his social life and family life—it's all like that, she thinks, all prescribed, bleak, and costly.

When Mary Jo started working for Dr. Streeter, she had had her nursing degree for three years, but she had never had any extra money, because she was paying back money borrowed for her education and helping her sisters with theirs. She came from a small town in Huron County. Her father worked on the town maintenance crew. Her mother had died of what was called "heart disease"—something Mary Jo later knew was a heart problem that Dr. Streeter could have detected and recommended surgery for.
130   As soon as she had enough money, Mary Jo started getting some work done on her teeth. She was self-conscious about them; she never wore lipstick and was careful of how she smiled. She had her eyeteeth pulled and the front teeth filed. She still didn't like the way they looked, so she got braces. She planned to lighten her hair—which was plain brown—and buy some new clothes, perhaps even move away and get a different sort of job once the braces came off. By the time they did, her life was changed without these stratagems.
      Some of the other changes came, in the course of time. From a serious-looking thick-waisted girl with an attentive manner, a gentle voice, a
140 heavy bosom, she has become a slender well-dressed woman with short blond-streaked hair—prettier now than other women of her age who were so much prettier than she when they were all young—and an agreeable but decisive way of talking. It's hard to tell how much difference any of this makes to Dr. Streeter. He used to tell her not to get too glamorous or somebody would spot her and grab her away from him. She was uneasy with this talk, finding a discouraging message in it. He stopped saying such things, and she was glad. Just recently he has started up again, with reference to her trip to Tahiti. But she thinks she knows better now how to deal with him, and she teases him, saying, You never know, and,
150 Stranger things have happened.
      He liked her when the braces were still on. They were on the first time he made love to her. She turned her head aside, conscious that a mouthful of metal might not be pleasing. He shut his eyes, and she wondered if it might be for that reason. Later she learned that he always closed his eyes. He doesn't want to be reminded of himself at such times, and probably not of her, either. His is a fierce but solitary relish.

Across the aisle from Mary Jo are two empty seats and then a young family, mother and father and baby and a little girl about two years old. Italian or Greek or Spanish, Mary Jo thinks, and she soon finds out from

160 their conversation with the stewardess that they are Greek, but living now in Perth, Australia. Their row of seats under the movie screen is the only place on the plane that could have provided room for their equipment and family operations. Insulated bags, plastic food dishes, baby-sized pillows, the folding cot that makes into a seat, milk bottles, juice bottles, and an enormous panda bear for the consolation of the little girl. Both parents busy themselves continually with the children—changing them into pastel pajamas, feeding them, joggling them, singing to them. Yes, they tell the admiring stewardess, very close, only fourteen months between them. The baby is a boy. He has a slight teething problem. She has occa-
170 sional fits of jealousy. Both are very fond of bananas. Hers whole, his mashed. Get his bib, dear, out of the blue bag. The washcloth, too, he's drooling a bit. No, the washcloth isn't there, it's in the plastic. Hurry. There it is. Hurry. Good.

Mary Jo is surprised at how ill-disposed she feels toward this harmless family. Why are you shovelling food into him? she feels like saying (for they have mixed up some cereal in a blue bowl). Solid food is a total waste at his age; it just gives you more to mop up at both ends. What a fuss, what accumulation and display and satisfaction, just because they have managed to reproduce. Also, they are delaying the stewardess
180 when she might be serving the drinks.

In the row behind them is another sort of young family, Indian. The mother wears a gold-embroidered red sari, the father a tight cream-colored suit. Slim, silent, gold-laden mother; well-fed, indolent-looking father, listening to the rock channel on his headphones. You can tell it's the rock channel by the movement of his fingers on the cream cloth stretched over his full thighs. Between these two parents sit two little girls, all in red, with gold bracelets and earrings and patent-leather shoes, and a younger brother, maybe as old as the little Greek girl in front, dressed up in a suit that is a miniature copy of his father's—vest, fly, pockets, and all. The
190 stewardess offers crayons and coloring books, but the little girls, glistening with gold, just giggle and hide their faces. She brings them glasses of ginger ale. The little brother shakes his head at the ginger ale. He climbs on his mother's lap, and she fetches out of her sari a shadowy, serviceable breast. He settles there, lolls and sucks, with his eyes open, looking blissful and commanding.

This way of going on doesn't suit Mary Jo any better. She is not used to feeling such aversion; she knows it is not reasonable. She is never like this in the office. No matter what difficulties develop there, or how tired she is, she deals easily with any sort of strange or rude behavior, with un-
200 pleasant habits, sour smells, impossible questions. Something is wrong with her. She didn't sleep. Her throat feels slightly raw and her head heavy. There is a hum in her head. She may be getting a fever. But it's more likely that her body is protesting its removal too quickly, by ever-increasing distance, from its place of habitual attachment and rest. This morning, she could see from her window a corner of Victoria Park, the snow under the streetlights and the bare trees. The apartment and the office are in a handsome old brick house owned by Dr. Streeter, in a row

of similar houses given over to such uses. Mary Jo looked at the slushy
streets, the dirty February snow, the gray walls of these houses, a tall of-
210　fice block, with its night lights on, that she could see beyond the park. She
wanted nothing so much as to stay. She wanted to cancel the taxi, change
her new suede suit for her uniform, go downstairs and put on coffee and
water the plants, prepare for another long day of problems and routine,
fear and reassurance, dread to be held in check—some of the time—by
talk about the dismal weather. She loves the office, the waiting room, the
lights on in the darkening icy afternoons; she loves the challenge and the
monotony. At the end of the day, Dr. Streeter sometimes comes upstairs
with her; she makes supper, and he stays for part of the evening. His wife
is out at meetings, classes, poetry readings; she is out drinking or has
220　come home and gone straight to bed.

When the stewardess gets around to asking her, Mary Jo orders a
vodka martini. She always chooses vodka, hoping it's true that you can't
smell it. For obvious reasons, Dr. Streeter dislikes the smell of liquor on
a woman.

Here come two new people down the aisle, changing their seats, evidently, creating problems with the drinks cart. Another stewardess
comes fussing behind them. She and the woman of the pair are carrying
shopping bags, a travelling bag, an umbrella. The man walks ahead and
doesn't carry anything. They take the seats directly across from Mary
230　Jo, beside the Greek family. They try to stow their paraphernalia under
the seat, but it won't go.

The stewardess says that there is lots of room in the overhead bins.

No. Low growls of protest from the man, muttered apologies from
the woman. The stewardess is given to understand that they intend to
keep an eye on all their belongings. Now that the drinks cart has moved
on, they can see a place where things might go—in front of Mary Jo, and
behind the little jump seat used by a stewardess at takeoff and landing.

The stewardess says she hopes that won't be too much in the lady's
way. Her bright voice suggests a certain amount of difficulty already
240　undergone with these passengers. Mary Jo says no, it will be quite all
right. The couple settle down then, the man in the aisle seat. He gives another growl, peremptory but not ill-humored, and the stewardess brings
two whiskeys. He raises his glass slightly, in Mary Jo's direction. A lordly
gesture that might be a thank-you. It is certainly not an apology.

He is a corpulent man, probably older than Dr. Streeter, but more
buoyant. An incautious, unpredictable-looking man, with rather long gray
hair and new, expensive clothes. Sandals over brown socks, rust-colored
trousers, bright yellow shirt, a handsome gold suede jacket with many little tabs and pleats and pockets. His skin is brown and his eyes are slightly
250　slanted. Not Japanese or Chinese—what is he? Mary Jo has a feeling that
she has seen him before. Not as a patient, not in the office. Where?

The woman peers around his shoulder, smiling with her lips closed,
pleasantly creasing her broad face. Her eyes have a more definite slant
than his, and her skin is paler. Her black hair is parted in the middle and
held with an elastic band in a childish ponytail. Her clothes are cheap

and decent and maybe fairly new—brown slacks, flowered blouse—but not in keeping with his. When she came along the aisle with the shopping bags, she looked middle-aged—thick-waisted and round-shouldered. But now, smiling at Mary Jo around the man's bulky shoulder, she looks quite
260 young. There is something odd about the smile itself. What that is becomes apparent when she opens her mouth and says something to the man. Her front teeth are missing, all across the top. That is what gives the smile such a secretive yet innocent look—a look of sly, durable merriment such as an old woman's smile might have, or a baby's.

Now Mary Jo thinks she has an idea about where she might have seen the man across the aisle before. A few weeks ago, she watched a television program about a tribe that lived in one of the high valleys of Afghanistan, near the Tibetan border. The film had been shot a few years ago, before the Russians came in. The people of the tribe lived in skin houses, and
270 their wealth was in herds of sheep and goats and in fine horses. One man seemed to have cornered most of this wealth, and had become the ruler of the tribe, not through hereditary right but through force of personality and financial power. He was called "the Khan." He had beautiful rugs in his skin house, and a radio, and several wives or concubines.

That's who this man reminds her of—the Khan. And isn't it possible, isn't it really possible, that that's who he might be? He might have left his country, got out before the Russians came, with his rugs and women and perhaps a horde of gold, though not likely his goats and sheep and horses. If you travel the world in great airliners, aren't you bound to see, sooner
280 or later, somebody you have seen on television? And it could easily be an exotic ruler, just as easily as an entertainer or a politician or a faith healer. In these days of upheaval, it could be somebody who had been photographed as a curiosity, a relic even, in a shut-off country, and is now turned loose like everybody else.

The woman must be one of his wives. The youngest, maybe the favorite, to be taken on a trip like this. He has taken her to Canada or the United States, where he has put his sons in school. He has taken her to a dentist to get her fitted with false teeth. Perhaps she has the teeth in her handbag, is just getting used to them, doesn't wear them yet all the time.
290 Mary Jo feels cheered up by her own invention, and perhaps also by the vodka. In her head, she starts to compose a letter describing these two, and mentioning the television program. Of course the letter is to Dr. Streeter, who was sitting on the couch beside her—but had fallen asleep—while she watched it. She mentions the woman's teeth and the possibility that they might have been removed on purpose, to comply with some strange notion of improving a female's appearance.

"If he asks me to join his harem, I promise I won't agree to any such weird procedures!"

The movie screen is being lowered. Mary Jo obediently turns out her
300 light. She thinks of ordering another drink but decides against it. Alcohol is more potent at this altitude. She tries to watch the movie, but the images are much elongated from this angle. They seem doleful and absurd. There is murder in the first two minutes—some girl with marvellous sil-

very hair is being stalked through empty corridors and apparently shot, right behind the credits. Mary Jo almost immediately loses interest, and after a while takes off her headphones. When she does so, she becomes aware of some sort of argument going on across the aisle.

The woman, or girl, seems to be trying to get up. The man pushes her down. He grumbles at her. She replies in a voice that wanders from com-
310 plaint to reassurance and back to complaint. He appears to lose interest, tilts his head back to watch the figures on the screen. The girl eases her way out of the seat and stumbles over him. He growls in earnest now, and grabs her leg. To Mary Jo's surprise, the girl speaks to him in English.

"I am not," she says stubbornly. "I am not. Drunk." She says this in the passionate, hopeless tone that drunk people will often use when arguing that they are not.

The man releases her with a sound of disgust.

"You can't boss me," she says, and there are tears now in her voice and eyes. "You're not my father." Instead of going down the aisle to the wash-
320 room—if that was what she had in mind—she remains standing within his reach, looking mournfully down at him. He makes a feint to grab at her again, a swift, brutal movement, as if this time, next time, he intends really to hurt her. She stumbles aside. He turns his attention back to the screen.

Still the girl doesn't move off down the aisle. She leans over Mary Jo.

"Excuse me," she says. She smiles with her eyes full of tears. Her baffled, offended face is creased with this wide, closed-mouthed smile, of apology or conspiracy. "Excuse me."

"That's all right," says Mary Jo, thinking the girl is apologizing for
330 the quarrel. Then she sees that "Excuse me" means "May I get past?" The girl wants to step over Mary Jo's legs, which are stretched out for comfort, crossed at the ankles. She wants to sit down in the window seat.

Mary Jo makes way. The girl sits down, wipes her eyes with a straight-across movement of her forefinger, and gives a loud snuffle that sounds businesslike and conclusive. What now?

"Don't tell nobody," the girl says. "Don't tell nobody."

She lays her broad hand on Mary Jo's knee, then takes it away.

"No," says Mary Jo. But who would she tell and why would she tell about such a formless bit of a quarrel?
340 "Don't tell nobody. I am Eskimo."

Of course Mary Jo has known ever since the girl got into the aisle and opened her mouth that it was all nonsense about the Khan and the favorite wife. She nods, but the word "Eskimo" bothers her more than the fact. That isn't the word to use anymore, is it? "Inuit." That's the word they use now.

"He is Métis. I am Eskimo."

All right, then. Métis and Eskimo. Fellow-Canadians. A joke on me, thinks Mary Jo. In her head, she'll have to start a different sort of letter.

"Don't tell nobody."
350 The girl behaves as if she is confessing something—a shameful

secret, a damaging mistake. She is frightened but trying to be dignified. She says again, "Don't tell nobody," and she puts her fingers for a few seconds across Mary Jo's mouth. Mary Jo can feel the heat of her skin and the tremor that runs through the girl's fingers and her whole body. She is like an animal in an entirely uncommunicable panic.

"No. No, I won't," says Mary Jo again. The best thing to do, she thinks, is to pretend to understand everything contained in this request.

"Are you going to Tahiti?" she says conversationally. She knows how an ordinary question at a moment like this can provide a bridge over
360 somebody's terror.

The girl's smile breaks open as if she appreciates the purpose of the question, its kindness, though in her case it can hardly be enough. "He's going to Hawaii," the girl says. "Me, too."

Mary Jo glances across the aisle. The man's head is lolling. He may have dozed off. Even when she has turned away, she can feel the girl's heat and quivering.

"How old are you?" says Mary Jo. She doesn't really know why she asks this.

The girl shakes her head, as if her age is indeed an absurd and de-
370 plorable fact. "I am Eskimo."

What has that to do with it? She says it as if it might be a code word, which Mary Jo would eventually understand.

"Yes. But how old are you?" says Mary Jo more confidently. Are you twenty? Are you over twenty? Eighteen?"

More headshaking and embarrassment, more smiling. "Don't tell nobody."

"How old?"

"I am Eskimo. I am sixteen."

Mary Jo looks across the aisle again to make sure the man isn't lis-
380 tening. He seems to be asleep.

"Sixteen?"

The girl wags her head heavily, almost laughing. And doesn't stop trembling.

"Are you? No? Yes? Yes."

Again those thick fingers passed like feathers over Mary Jo's mouth.

"Do you want to go to Hawaii with him? Is it all right?"

"He is going to Hawaii. Me, too."

"Listen," says Mary Jo, speaking softly and carefully. "I am going to get up and walk to the back of the plane. I am going to where the wash-
390 rooms are. The toilets. I'll wait for you back there. After a moment, you get up and come back. You come to the back of the plane where the toilets are and we'll talk there. It's better to talk there. All right? Do you understand me? All right."

She gets up unhurriedly, retrieves her jacket, which has slipped down on the seat, rearranges it. The man rolls his head on the cushion, gives her a glazed, gloomy look, the look of a dog half-asleep. His eyes slide under the lids and his head turns away.

"All right?" Mary Jo mouths the words at the girl without a sound.

The girl presses her fingers over her own mouth, her smile.

400   Mary Jo walks to the back of the plane. Earlier, she removed her boots and put on slippers. Now she pads along comfortably, but misses the feeling of competence and resolution that boots can give.

She has to get in the lineup for the toilets, because there is nowhere else to stand. The line extends into the little space by the window where she intended to wait. She keeps looking around, waiting for the girl to come up behind her. Not yet. Other, taller people join the line and she has to keep peering around them, wanting to make sure the girl can see where she is. She has to move forward with the line, and when it's her turn she has no choice but to go in. It's time she went, anyway.

410   She gets out as quickly as possible. The girl is still not there. Not in the lineup. Not hanging around the galley or sitting in any of the back seats. The line is shorter now and there is room for Mary Jo to stand by the window. She waits there, shivering, wishing she had brought her jacket.

In the washroom, she didn't take time to put on fresh lipstick. She does so now, looking at her reflection in the dark window. Suppose she decided to speak to somebody about the girl—what would they think of her? She could speak to somebody now—that older, rather grim-looking stewardess with the coppery eye makeup, who seems to be in charge, or

420 the steward, who looks distracted but more approachable. She could tell them what the girl had said, and about her trembling. She could voice her suspicions. But what do those amount to? The girl has not really said anything that suspicions can be firmly based on. She is Eskimo, she is sixteen, she is going to Hawaii with a much older man who is not her father. Is sixteen underage? Is taking a girl to Hawaii a crime? She may be more than sixteen after all; she certainly looks it. She may be drunk and lying. She may be his wife, though she doesn't wear a ring. He may certainly be some sort of relative. If Mary Jo says anything now, she will be seen as a meddling woman, who has had one drink and may have

430 had more. She may be seen as someone trying to get hold of the girl for her own purposes.

The girl herself will have to say more if anything is to be done.

You can't be helped if you don't ask for it.

You will have to say what you want.

You will have to say.

Mary Jo walks slowly back to her seat, checking on the way to see if the girl has moved, if she is sitting somewhere else. She looks for the large docile head with its black ponytail.

Nowhere.

440   But when she is nearly back to her seat she sees that the girl has moved. She has moved back to where she was sitting before beside the man. They have been provided with two more whiskeys.

Perhaps he grabbed her when she got up, and forced her to sit down with him. Mary Jo should have seen that the girl went first. But could she have persuaded her, made her understand? Did the girl really understand that help was being offered?

Mary Jo stands in the aisle putting on her jacket. She looks down at the couple, but they don't look at her. She sits down and snaps on her reading light, then turns it off. Nobody is watching the movie anymore. 450 The Greek baby is crying, and the father is walking it up and down the aisle. The little Indian girls have toppled over on each other, and their brother is asleep in his mother's narrow lap.

Dr. Streeter would soon put Mary Jo straight about this. Some kinds of concern—he has made her admit this—are little more than frivolity and self-indulgence. With their self-indulgent good intentions, people are apt to do more harm than good. And that is what she might do in this case.

Yes. But he could always turn to what was inside people, inside their chests. If this girl had a faulty heart, even if she was twenty years older, 460 forty years older, than she is, even if her life was totally muddled and useless and her brain half-rotted with drink—even then he would put himself completely at her service. He withheld nothing, he used himself up in such rescues or attempted rescues. If it was a problem of the real heart, the bloody, pumping, burdened heart inside a person's chest.

Dr. Streeter's voice has an underlying sadness. It's not only his voice. His breathing is sad. An incurable, calm, and decent sadness is what he breathes out over the phone before you even hear his voice. He would be displeased if you told him that. Not that he particularly wishes to be thought jolly. But he would think it unnecessary, impertinent, for any- 470 body to assume that he is sad.

This sadness seems to come from obedience. Mary Jo can just recog- nize that, never understand it. She thinks there is an obedience about men that women can't understand. (What would Rhea say to that?) It's not the things he knows about—Mary Jo could manage that—but the things he accepts that make a difference. He baffles her, and compels her. She loves this man with a baffled, cautious, permanent love.

When she pictures him, she always sees him wearing his brown three- piece suit, an old-fashioned suit that makes him look like a doctor from his classically poor and rural childhood. He has good-looking casual clothes 480 and she has seen him in them, but she thinks he isn't at ease in them. He isn't at ease with being rich, she thinks, though he feels an obligation to be so and a hatred for any government that would prevent him. All obedi- ence, acceptance, sadness.

He wouldn't believe her if she told him that. Nobody would.

She is shivering, even with her jacket on. She seems to have caught something of the girl's persistent and peculiar agitation. Perhaps she re- ally is sick, has a fever. She twists around, trying to compose herself. She closes her eyes but cannot keep them closed. She cannot stop herself from watching what is going on across the aisle.

490   What is going on is something she should have the sense and de- cency to turn away from. But she hasn't, and she doesn't.

The whiskey glasses are empty. The girl has leaned forward and is kissing the man's face. His head is resting against the cushion and he does not stir. She leans over him, her eyes closed, or almost closed, her face broad and pale and impassive, a true moon face. She kisses his lips, his cheeks, his eyelids, his forehead. He offers himself to her; he permits her. She kisses him and licks him. She licks his nose, the faint stubble of his cheeks and neck and chin. She licks him all over his face, then takes a breath and resumes her kissing.

500   This is unhurried, not greedy. It is not mechanical, either. There is no trace of compulsion. The girl is in earnest; she is in a trance of devotion. True devotion. Nothing so presumptuous as forgiveness or consolation. A ritual that takes every bit of her concentration and her self but in which her self is lost. It could go on forever.

Even when the girl's eyes open and she looks straight out across the aisle, with an expression that is not dazed and unaware but direct and shocking—even then, Mary Jo has to keep looking. Only with a jolting effort, and after an immeasurable amount of time, is she able to pull her own eyes away.

510   If anybody was to ask her what she was feeling while she watched this, Mary Jo would have said that she felt sick. And she would have meant it. Not just sick with the beginnings of a fever or whatever it is that's making her dull and shivery, but sick with revulsion, as if she could feel the slow journeys of the warm, thick tongue over her face. Then, when she takes her eyes away, something else is released, and that is desire—sudden and punishing as a rush of loose earth down a mountainside.

At the same time, she is listening to Dr. Streeter's voice, and it says clearly, "You know, that girl's teeth were probably knocked out. In some brawl."

520   This is Dr. Streeter's familiar, reasonable voice, asking that some facts, some conditions, should be recognized. But she has put something new into it—a sly and natural satisfaction. He is not just sad, not just accepting; he is satisfied that some things should be so. The satisfaction far back in his voice matches the loosening feeling in her body. She feels a physical shame and aversion, a heat that seems to spread from her stomach. This passes, the wave of it passes, but the aversion remains. Aversion, disgust, dislike spreading out from you can be worse than pain. It would be a worse condition to live in. Once she has thought this, and put some sort of name to what she is feeling, she is a little steadier. It must be the

530 strangeness of being on the flight, and the drink, and the confusion offered by that girl, and perhaps a virus, that she is struggling with. Dr. Streeter's voice is next thing to a real delusion, but it isn't a delusion; she knows she manufactured it herself. Manufactured what she could then turn away from, so purely hating him. If such a feeling became real, if a delusion like that got the better of her, she would be in a state too dreary to think about.

She sets about deliberately to calm herself down. She breathes deeply and pretends that she is going to sleep. She starts telling herself a story in which things work out better. Suppose the girl had followed

540 her to the back of the plane a while ago; suppose they had been able to talk? The story slips ahead, somehow, to the waiting room in Honolulu.

Mary Jo sees herself sitting there in a room with stunted, potted palm trees, on a padded bench. The man and the girl walk past her. The girl is walking ahead, carrying the shopping bags. The man has the travelling bag slung over his shoulder and he is carrying the umbrella. With the end of the furled umbrella, he gives the girl a poke. Nothing to hurt her or even surprise her. A joke. The girl scurries and giggles and looks around her with an expression of endless apology, embarrassment, helplessness, good humor. Then Mary Jo catches her eye, without the man's
550 noticing. Mary Jo gets up and walks across the waiting room and reaches the bright, tiled refuge of the ladies' washroom.

And this time the girl does follow her.

Mary Jo runs the cold water. She splashes it over her own face, in a gesture of encouragement.

She urges the girl to do the same.

She speaks to her calmly and irresistibly.

"That's right. Cool your face off. Get your head clear. You have to think clearly. You have to think very clearly. Now. What is it? What is it you want? What are you afraid of? Don't be afraid. He can't come in
560 here. We've got time. You can tell me what you want and I can help you. I can get in touch with the authorities."

But the story halts at this point. Mary Jo has hit a dry spot, and her dream—for she is dreaming by now—translates this in its unsubtle way into an irregular, surprising patch of rust where the enamel has worn away at the bottom of the sink.

What a badly maintained ladies' room.

"Is it always like this in the tropics?" says Mary Jo to the woman standing beside her at the next sink, and this woman covers her sink with her hands as if she doesn't want Mary Jo to look at or use it. (Not that
570 Mary Jo was intending to.) She is a large, white-haired woman in a red sari, and she seems to have some authority in the ladies' room. Mary Jo looks around for the Eskimo girl and is bewildered to see her lying on the floor. She has shrunk, and has a rubbery look, a crude face like a doll's. But the real shock is that her head has come loose from her body, though it is still attached by an internal elastic band.

"You'll get a chance to choose your own," says the white-haired woman, and Mary Jo thinks this means your own punishment. She knows she is in no danger of that—she is not responsible, she didn't hit the girl or push her to the floor. The woman is crazy.
580 "I'm sorry," she says, "but I have to get back to the plane."

But this is later, and they are no longer in the ladies' room. They are back in Dr. Streeter's office and Mary Jo has a sense of a dim scramble of events she can't keep track of, of lapses in time she hasn't noted. She still thinks about getting back on the plane, but how is she to find the waiting room, let alone get to Honolulu?

A large figure entirely wrapped up in bandages is carried past, and Mary Jo means to find out who it is, what has happened, why they are bringing a victim of burns in here.

The woman in the red sari is there, too. She says to Mary Jo, in quite
590 a friendly way, "The court is in the garden?"

This may mean that Mary Jo is still to be accused of something, and
that there is a court being conducted in the garden. On the other hand, the
word "court" may refer to Dr. Streeter. The woman may mean "count," being mixed up in her spelling. If that's so, she intends to mock him. Calling
him the count is a joke, and "in the garden" means something else, too,
which Mary Jo will have to concentrate hard on to figure out.

But the woman opens her hand and shows Mary Jo some small blue
flowers—like snowdrops, but blue—and explains that these are "court"
and that "court" means flowers.

600   A ruse, and Mary Jo knows it, but she can't concentrate because she's
waking up. In a jumbo jet over the Pacific Ocean, with the movie screen
furled and the lights mostly out and even the baby asleep. She can't get
back through the various curtains of the dream to the clear part, in the
ladies' room, when the cold water was streaming down their faces and
she—Mary Jo—was telling the girl how she could save herself. She can't
get back there. People all around her are sleeping under blankets, with
their heads on small orange pillows. Somehow a pillow and a blanket have
been provided for her as well. The man and the girl across the aisle are
asleep with their mouths open, and Mary Jo is lifted to the surface by
610 their duet of eloquent, innocent snores.

This is the beginning of her holiday.

COMMON TERMS OF CRITICAL DISCOURSE ON FICTION

You have now read two quite different short stories and may have
some questions of your own, but certainly "What is it about?" is the most
common question asked of anyone who mentions having read any work of
fiction. So let us begin there, as if someone had asked that question of you
about "Araby" or "Eskimo," and you were wondering how to reply.

Any attempt to answer the literary question "What is it about?" involves a critical vocabulary of some sort, however much it may rely on
more or less commonly known words, and our first goal will be to introduce some basic terms. Other chapters in this book will show you that
particular critical approaches also employ a few easily learned special
terms as well. But it is the purpose of this initial section to introduce
you to some of the words used generally in critical discussions of fiction
(and of other genres like poetry and drama) so that you may engage
yourself more productively as a reader of literature—that is, as a practicing critic. For one thing, knowing a few general and traditional terms
will allow you to notice more easily in subsequent chapters how different critical theories focus on different aspects of the general and traditional concerns of readers.

Answering the question "What is it about?" usually begins with the issue of **plot**. A series of events in your life may occur at random and without any very meaningful connections among different daily happenings. But like real "plots" in real life (plots to defraud companies or to assassinate political figures, for example), fictional plots are arrangements of events planned with particular purposes in mind. In the case of literature, the purpose is more benign—to create through language effects in a reader's heart and mind. To these ends, the arrangement of events in a plot usually includes **conflict** for the **protagonist**, or leading character. *Protagonist* provides a neutral term and is therefore useful in discussing any story, including those with unattractive leading figures whom one would hesitate to call a "hero" or a "heroine." Further, most plots can be described as having a **beginning** (where **exposition**, or the unfolding of the fictional background and the story's issues, takes place); a **middle** (where **complication** of the issues occurs with **rising action** leading to a **crisis** or **climax**); and an **end** with **falling action** leading to a **resolution** or **"dénouement"**—a French word for "untying the knot."

In "Araby," for example, the exposition includes what we learn of the protagonist's youthful emotional state centered on Mangan's sister. The conflict in the plot involves first his inability to find satisfactory expression for those emotions and then his difficulty in getting to Araby when the bazaar becomes the focus of his attempts to act in some way that is expressive of his feelings, which themselves were not very clear to him. Next, the crisis of the story takes place when the protagonist finds the reality of the bazaar disappointingly incapable of satisfying the expectations his imagination has brought to it. He resolves this crisis by changing how he thinks about his young life and by scorning the self that had indulged in what he now sees as romantic dreaming. In this way, the protagonist thus becomes his own **antagonist**, or opponent in the plot. Or rather, this account describes the resolution the protagonist *himself* finds. But how Joyce really invites us to see the new attitude—whether as an achievement of sensible clarification or as the sign of a deadening paralysis of spirit—is a good question for a critical discussion. This example of ambiguity in Joyce's fiction points out why the **narrator**, or teller of the story, should not necessarily be associated with the **author** even, or perhaps especially, in stories told by an "I." This distinction is related to some other important issues of narration that will be taken up in a moment.

In reading stories we may generally tend to expect the common pattern of plot described above—one with some resolution (however debatable) to its conflicts. But "Eskimo" shows that the common pattern is not always employed. The problematic situation of the protagonist there is *unresolved,* whether her situation be viewed in particular (on the airplane) or more generally (her relations with her lover). This story might be said to *end* with "rising action," if one were to describe it in traditional terms. "Eskimo" also shows in another way how careful one should be in avoiding the imposition of any critical pattern on a story, especially in order to judge an author's performance by reference to that pattern. It is not fair to blame an author for lacking something like "resolution of conflict" that he or she might never have intended to supply. But even here you may agree that "rising action" allows us to discuss something unusual about the story.

In the case of "Eskimo," Mary Jo's involvement with her fellow passengers may be seen as the **main plot** of the story, but it is clearly a **subplot** in the larger story of her life. On the other hand, her interactions with Rhea, Dr. Streeter's daughter, clearly make a subplot in both senses. In the case of even more-highly plotted stories, such as detective mysteries, a story may contain many subplots which come together at the end.

Plots involve **characters**, and the word *character* comes basically from the language of morals. The fact that *character* is the word most often used to describe the figures of fiction perhaps shows how fond we are of judging other people, whether real or imaginary. Yet, while no full answer to the question "What's it about?" would necessarily exclude judgments about the moral "character" of the **characters** involved in the plot, the most memorable creations of fiction have been those most resistent to quick and easy moral categorization. The enrichment of reading as an artistic experience in itself involves a search for *understanding* how the literary evidence of the text interacts with our values and assumptions about life (and about reading) to create our sense of what a character is like. The search for such understanding often requires surrendering the false confidence and superior, dismissive attitude that easy moral judgments can foster ("He's just a jerk, that's all"). Seeking to understand the literary evidence in the most complete way can help us to construe the little black and white marks on a page into some of the most moving of emotional and intellectual experiences—that is, experiences in which judgment plays only a part. Such an enrichment of reading is the principle focus and goal of all the critical methods represented later in this book.

Characters act out a plot in imaginary time, but they also exist in imaginary space or in a **setting** which may be said to have an **atmosphere** that influences our sense of the issues involved in a story. The literally dreary and chilly atmosphere that the young boys of Joyce's Dublin strive to overcome by the exuberance of their animal spirits may make the emotional atmosphere of the protagonist's life seem figuratively dreary and chilly as well. In a similar way, his street may seem "blind" in more than the Irish sense of "dead end." Analogously, the potentially dangerous setting of an airplane—including its forced and often undesired intimacy with strangers—helps to create the atmosphere of "Eskimo" and contributes to Mary Jo's anxious mood. The atmosphere on the plane may also serve to suggest a comparison with, as well as a contrast to, the atmosphere of her life at home, her "place of habitual attachment and rest."

Similarly, literary **symbols** are images invested with qualities that lead us to feel more meaning is being expressed than those same images would express in ordinary uses of language. Of course, authors employ the symbols of ordinary language like flags and wedding rings, but literary symbols can have special, private, and sometimes changing meaning. For example, to the narrator of Joyce's story, the whole idea of Araby first becomes a symbol of all that is romantic and exotic and then a symbol of vain imaginings. For Alice Munro's character, the image of the Eskimo woman may be said to become a symbol of Mary Jo's own situation with her lover, yet it is a symbol not yet fully conscious and is perceived only in dreams during the time of the story.

The **point of view** taken on the events of a story makes a part of our sense of atmosphere and mood. For example, the narrator of "Eskimo" seems tacitly in sympathy with the protagonist's own generally lukewarm attitude toward the projected pleasures of her vacation. On the other hand, the narrator of "Araby" *now* sees that Mangan's sister's name (which he never reveals to us) was "a summons to all my foolish blood" and that he was wrong to neglect his school work. Yet his point of view *at the time* was quite different, and the intensity of the emotions of first love was the only reality he cared for then.

Both points of view in "Araby" are created by a **first-person narrator** who gives us the character's own perspective looking back on the events of his youth, while the story in "Eskimo" is told by a **third-person narrator.** Such a narrator is sometimes said to have a **limited-omniscient** point of view, since the narrator apparently knows all the thoughts and history of the protagonist, but tells us about *other* characters only what that protagonist herself knows or surmises. This contrasts to the **omniscient narrator** who often appears in early prose fiction and who sometimes still appears in modern fiction—as in Willa Cather's "Paul's Case" included later in the book. Another story, Ernest Hemingway's "Hills Like White Elephants," shows still another technique: that of the **objective narrator** who tells us *nothing* about the inner lives of the characters, but instead reports only what an objective observer on the scene could have observed—the point of view of the proverbial "fly on the wall."

Narrators, and especially first-person narrators, are said to be **reliable** or **unreliable** according to the degree that they seem to have the author's backing for what they tell us. A satire, for example, may involve an unreliable narrator whose motives the author wishes us to suspect. Trying to decide on the basis of the evidence in the story which kind of narrator Joyce provides for "Araby" has been one of the issues for readers of that narrative since the story's first publication.

Another way to put the issue is to ask whether Joyce is employing **irony.** Unlike "sarcasm," which clearly says one thing and means another, irony is often a delicate and difficult matter to understand, and different readers may understand the same words differently just as different characters do. How, for example, do you and your classmates think Joyce intended his character's words at the end to be understood, and why do you think so?

The words discussed in this brief introduction are the names of some general concepts used in talking about fiction and other literary forms. There are many other common terms defined in the glossary at the end of the book, and your instructor will no doubt introduce you to still more of them. Remember that any critical terms are meant to advance your progress toward a richer and more interesting experience of reading literature. Knowing a general critical vocabulary will also help make the particular critical approaches that follow more clear in their concerns and operations. But the goal is not so much the accumulation of special vocabularies as the help the vocabularies may give you in articulating richer answers to the most basic critical questions such as "What is it about?"

Chapter Two

The New Criticism: Literature as a Verbal Construction

A BRIEF INTRODUCTION TO THE NEW CRITICISM

The New Criticism has been one of the most influential critical movements of our century. During the 1930s, 1940s, and 1950s, many of the most respected critics in the country were to some extent identified with the New Criticism; and, although the approach is no longer in favor with many critical journals, generations of professors shaped by the New Criticism continue to put its principles into practice in the classroom. Yet the label (like the labels attached to the other critical theories introduced later in this book) has been pasted on an extremely large collection of critical views, even from the very first use of the term. And today the New Criticism often may be used *too* conveniently to cover every critical analysis that does not explicitly align itself with one of the more recent critical methods.

In one sense, the vagueness about exactly to what the New Criticism refers might be attributed to its very success. For example, close reading of the text and an intense interest in the forms of literary works have long been associated with the leading figures of the New Criticism. Today, however, these characteristics of the New Criticism no longer seem distinctive: Almost no contemporary critic would say that the texts of literature should *not* receive close attention or that form can be ignored. And since the New Criticism was from the first an activity largely manifested in practical interpretation—exactly what every teacher does in class and what most do in their own critical writing as well—defining the New Criticism so broadly by those practical activities may seem needlessly to evoke a theory to name obvious and universal facts.

Given disagreement on exactly what the New Criticism stands for, the question of how it came to be perceived as virtually synonymous with the establishment of North American literary criticism is perhaps best answered by looking at what criticism was before the New Criticism came along. The fact is that the New Criticism was at first more of a rallying cry than a critical strategy. And the rallying cry was sounded in a rebellion against what was *then* considered to be the academic literary establishment.

The kind of literary study that the New Criticism offered to replace was itself a critical reaction that took the form of scientific scholarship. This ideal of scholarship was part of a rational response in the late nineteenth century, not only to a kind of romantic and often flowery impressionistic criticism (e.g., "One feels on reading the poem that one hears a vibrant, thought-tormented music. . ."), but to the astounding triumphs of nineteenth-century natural science. Those triumphs had confirmed the rapid progress of knowledge in a relatively short time. In a few centuries, explanations of the natural world had changed from being what they largely had been from the dawn of history—matters largely of faith, opinion, and speculation—and had apparently become matters of demonstrable *fact*. The new understanding of physical nature and the immense powers derived from that understanding seemed to turn literary study—for thousands of years almost the entire content of Western education—into a poor and outcast relation of the natural sciences, which now claimed the right to define what real knowledge meant. Partly in an effort to learn from the success of science, many scholars proposed to put the study of literature itself onto a scientific footing. Such a study was to base itself in facts and rigorous "scientific" logical deduction from facts and would leave the ineffable and the debatable to those less willing or able to understand the nature of the modern age. Increasingly, literary scholars emphasized those matters about which facts could be gathered—the textual history of a literary work, or its author's biography, or the historical period during which it was written.

Yet the results of such scientific literary research often made the environment of literature in the world of higher education a dry and thirsty land for those other than future specialists. For example, when the great editor of Shakespeare, George Lyman Kittredge, taught Shakespeare at Harvard at the beginning of this century, his method of instruction began with a stack of index cards on his desk. As the class went through the text of a play, he would announce from one or more of these cards the *sources* of a plot or a situation or an allusion, or a word, tracing any of these facts back through all of European literature, to classical literature and finally, if possible, to anthropological origins. Needless to say, this did not explain to many young people why they had been so moved by their reading of Shakespeare.

It was therefore partly in reaction to the factual dryness of professional literary study that the New Criticism arose. Poet and critic John Crowe Ransom gave the movement a name when he published *The New Criticism* in 1941. It could be argued, however, that this approach to literary criticism had already been defined and set into motion by a remarkable and widely used 1938 college textbook, *Understanding Poetry*, by Cleanth Brooks and Robert Penn Warren; in 1943, a second Brooks and Warren textbook, *Understanding Fiction,* further extended the movement's influence. Probably more than any theoretical works, these practical applications of the New Criticism's principles and methods helped to make it the dominant approach to literary study in classrooms across the country.

Central to this approach is a close focus on the text of a literary work, on the complexities of meaning found in the words on the page. The New Criticism tends to regard biographical matters external to the text as likely to be more distracting than illuminating: Trying to interpret an author's words by the presumed light of the facts in his or her biography as a person too often leads the critic away from the text and, therefore, from the real work of interpretation. Thus, in his analysis of "The Fall of the House of Usher," summarized later in this chapter, Allen Tate does not try to explain Poe's strangeness as a writer by discussing his difficult childhood or his drinking habits. Instead, Tate focuses on the formal patterns of Poe's imagery and their implications, arguing that these implications result from the author's highly logical metaphysical despair, rather than (say) an alcoholic muddle.

In addition to focusing on imagery, a New Critic interpreting a short story might well consider plot, character, setting, point of view, and the other elements of fiction discussed in Chapter 1. Analyzing such elements prepares the critic to comment on *form.* For the New Critic, the analysis of form involves far more than assigning a work to a pre-existing category. In a sense, the form of each literary work is unique, a particular combination of elements arranged for a particular purpose. As Brooks and Warren point out in *Understanding Fiction,* "Form is not to be thought of merely as a sort of container for the story; it is, rather, the total principle of organization and affects every aspect of the composition." Since this term encompasses so much for the New Critics, they are often called *formalists,* and their judgment of a literary work's merits often rests heavily on considerations of form. "It may be said," Brooks and Warren write in *Understanding Fiction,* "that a story is successful—that it has achieved form—when all of the elements are functionally related to each other, when each part contributes to the intended effect."

Brooks and Warren's comments on James Joyce's "Araby" provide an example of New Critical analysis. The critics begin by noting that the story contains many elements not explicitly related to the narrator's romantic disappointment—"the description of his street, the information about the dead priest and his abandoned belongings, the relations with the aunt and uncle," and so on. If these elements amount to no more than "mere atmosphere," Brooks and Warren write, then the story is "obviously overloaded with nonfunctional material." Analyzing the story therefore involves trying to determine "in what way these apparently irrelevant items in 'Araby' are related to each other and to the disappointment of the boy." After a painstaking examination of the story, Brooks and Warren conclude that all of these elements are indeed related, that everything from imagery to point of view helps to develop a central theme having to do with the narrator's first awareness of "the discrepancy between the real and the ideal." Thus, by the New Criticism's standards, the story is successful—it has "achieved form."

For most New Critics, a technically complex literary work such as "Araby" is far more interesting and impressive than a simple one. For example, an O. Henry story might achieve a simple effect—surprising the reader—by manipulating a single element—the plot twist. Analyzing such a story is not likely to be very rewarding for either the reader or the critic of literary technique. Typically, the New Critic favors works that offer more of a challenge. As David Richter comments in *The Critical Tradition* (1989), the New Critic identifies "oppositions and conflicts" within a literary work, then explains how these are "resolved into a harmonious balance." Often, this balance is achieved through *ambiguity,* "the capacity of language to carry multiple meanings." For American New Critics, Richter says, *irony* also becomes a centrally important concept, "defined not in its strict sense—saying the opposite of what is intended—but very broadly, as occurring whenever a statement is undercut or qualified by its context." Such an understanding of irony is evident in Brooks and Warren's comments on the final scene of "Araby." Brooks and Warren point out several elements that they consider ironic—for example, the bazaar's "magical name" is juxtaposed with its ordinary, rather shabby appearance; the young lady at the stall is, for the boy, both a symbol of the world of romance and a part of the "inimical world" of crude, trivial conversation. These implicit ironies, Brooks and Warren argue, help to prepare the reader for the narrator's final disillusionment.

By identifying such elements as irony and ambiguity, the New Critics hope to "open up" a literary text, to show how it works as well as what it says. Their emphasis on getting the text clear implies using the clearest possible language in discussion. The New Critics show disdain for any specialized jargon that might be a needless, pseudoscientific barrier between the critic's understanding and the reader's.

Most of the *explicit* theoretical statements associated with the New Criticism seem to be about what *not* to do as a reader. Many important essays have "heresy" or "fallacy" in their titles. For example, William K. Wimsatt argued against "The Intentional Fallacy." Wimsatt said that since we could never know with absolute certainty the "true intentions" of authors (they lie, they forget, they act on subconscious promptings, etc.), we should pay attention only to the text, the meaning discernible in what Wimsatt called the "verbal icon."

Yet Wimsatt's view seemed needlessly extreme to many people associated with the New Criticism and positively pernicious to one of its founders, William Empson. Empson thought that Wimsatt's ideas undermined the very justification for studying literature in the first place, and he argued against it vigorously in print and in public on many occasions for over forty years. So, as this example may suggest, since the New Criticism became known as a coherent theory largely through the most extreme statements associated with that label, and since many of those statements were disavowed or ignored by many of the people who found the leading critics and their general focus useful, "theory" itself became a word of ill omen to most readers trained on the "theoretical" basis of the New Criticism.

Today, the New Criticism has in many ways been challenged by the critical approaches discussed later in this book. Some have charged that because their methods are best suited to the analysis of such elements as irony and ambiguity, the New Critics tend to overrate literary works rich in those qualities and to underrate more straightforward works that may be extremely rich in ideas or in moral or historical significance. Moreover, because of their emphasis on language and form, the New Critics may seem to isolate the literary text too much, to remove it from the world in which authors and readers live. Yet no major adherent of the New Criticism (including Tate, as you will see from the analysis of Poe that follows) ever really argued that a text exists in the absence of historical context or of the ideas that it dramatizes. As Brooks and Warren argue in *Understanding Fiction,* a strong interest in form need not lead to a distorted, incomplete appreciation of a work's meaning and significance:

> Another and more specific objection which may be raised [to our methods] concerns the apparent emphasis on formal considerations in the evaluation of fiction—what may be thought the editors' failure to give adequate heed to the importance, on ethical, religious, philosophical, or sociological grounds, of the "ideas" in a piece of fiction. In attempting to reply to such an objection the editors would first say that idea or theme is one of the elements in the fictional structure, but that the structure is not to be set over against the idea in any mechanical fashion. Rather it is their first article of faith that the structure of a piece of fiction, in so far as that piece of fiction is successful, must involve a vital and functional relationship between the idea and the other elements in that structure—plot, style, character and the like.

This sort of emphasis on structure or form is still very evident in much of the literary criticism being written today. Even though few people now publishing in critical journals would identify themselves as New Critics, most would admit that they are at least to some extent indebted to the New Criticism. For example, most contemporary critics take for granted the necessity of beginning with a close reading of the text. They may well disagree with the New Critics—and with each other—about *how* a text should be read and about the purpose and even the possibility of interpretation. But in developing and defending their theories, most are exploring directions that were first opened up by the New Criticism and relying on methods they learned from such books as *Understanding Fiction.*

EDGAR ALLAN POE (1809–1849) once hailed by the French poet Paul Valéry as "that great literary engineer," was born the son of traveling actors on January 19, 1809. After the desertion of the family by his father and the subsequent death of his mother, Poe was taken into the home of Mr. and Mrs. John Allan, from who he derived his middle name. From 1815 to 1820 the Allans lived in England, where Poe studied at a classical academy; after their return to the United States, he attended the University of Virginia. He accumulated considerable gambling debts, however, and after just one year Allan withdrew him from the University.

Poe then traveled to Boston and, in 1827, published his first book of poetry, *Tamerlane and Other Poems*. After a brief attempt at a career in the army, Poe for a time supported himself by magazine writing, first in New York and then in Baltimore. His first short stories were published in 1832. In the years that followed, Poe worked as an editor on several magazines, becoming known as a literary critic as well as an author of poems and short stories. In 1845, the publication of "The Raven" established his national reputation. His career came to an abrupt and still-mysterious end in 1849, when he disappeared for several days, was found unconscious on the streets of Baltimore, and died soon after.

Although critics have always disagreed about the quality of his work, Poe's influence on modern literature is undeniable. Essays such as "The Philosophy of Composition" made important contributions to the development of analytical literary criticism in America; his poetry had a profound influence on many symbolist poets, both in this country and in France. Perhaps even more important are Poe's contributions to the development of the modern short story. As the author of such stories as "The Purloined Letter" (see p. 198 and the essays on the story, pp. 917–936) and "The Murders in the Rue Morgue," Poe may be seen as the inventor of the detective story. As the author of such stories as "The Fall of the House of Usher," Poe proved himself a master of the horror story and contributed to the development of modern science fiction. His life was short and in many respects tragic, but Poe's accomplishments are remarkably varied, remarkably significant.

EDGAR ALLAN POE
The Fall of the House of Usher
(1839)

Son coeur est un luth suspendu;
Sitôt qu'on le touche il résonne.
—*DE BÉRANGER*

During the whole of a dull, dark, and soundless day in the autumn of the year, when the clouds hung oppressively low in the heavens, I had been passing alone, on horseback, through a singularly dreary tract of country; and at length found myself, as the shades of the evening drew on, within view of the melancholy House of Usher. I knew not how it was—but, with the first glimpse of the building, a sense of insufferable gloom pervaded my spirit. I say insufferable; for the feeling was unrelieved by any of that half-pleasurable, because poetic, sentiment with which the mind usually receives even the sternest natural images of the
10 desolate or terrible. I looked upon the scene before me—upon the mere house, and the simple landscape features of the domain, upon the bleak walls, upon the vacant eye-like windows, upon a few rank sedges, and upon a few white trunks of decayed trees—with an utter depression of soul which I can compare to no earthly sensation more properly than to

the afterdream of the reveler upon opium; the bitter lapse into everyday life, the hideous dropping off of the veil. There was an iciness, a sinking, a sickening of the heart, an unredeemed dreariness of thought which no goading of the imagination could torture into aught of the sublime. What was it—I paused to think—what was it that so unnerved me in the
20 contemplation of the House of Usher? It was a mystery all insoluble; nor could I grapple with the shadowy fancies that crowded upon me as I pondered. I was forced to fall back upon the unsatisfactory conclusion, that while, beyond doubt, there *are* combinations of very simple natural objects which have the power of thus affecting us, still the analysis of this power lies among considerations beyond our depth. It was possible, I reflected, that a mere different arrangement of the particulars of the scene, of the details of the picture, would be sufficient to modify, or perhaps to annihilate, its capacity for sorrowful impression; and, acting upon this idea, I reined my horse to the precipitous brink of a black and
30 lurid tarn that lay in unruffled luster by the dwelling, and gazed down—but with a shudder even more thrilling than before—upon the remodeled and inverted images of the gray sedge, and the ghastly tree stems, and the vacant and eye-like windows.

Nevertheless, in this mansion of gloom I now proposed to myself a sojourn of some weeks. Its proprietor, Roderick Usher, had been one of my boon companions in boyhood; but many years had elapsed since our last meeting. A letter, however, had lately reached me in a distant part of the country—a letter from him—which in its wildly importunate nature had admitted of no other than a personal reply. The MS. gave evidence of nerv-
40 ous agitation. The writer spoke of acute bodily illness, of a mental disorder which oppressed him, and of an earnest desire to see me, as his best and indeed his only personal friend, with a view of attempting, by the cheerfulness of my society, some alleviation of his malady. It was the manner in which all this, and much more, was said—it was the apparent *heart* that went with his request—which allowed me no room for hesitation; and I accordingly obeyed forthwith what I still considered a very singular summons.

Although as boys we had been even intimate associates, yet I really knew little of my friend. His reserve had been always excessive and habit-
50 ual. I was aware, however, that his very ancient family had been noted, time out of mind, for a peculiar sensibility of temperament, displaying itself, through long ages, in many works of exalted art, and manifested of late in repeated deeds of munificent yet unobtrusive charity, as well as in a passionate devotion of the intricacies, perhaps even more than to the orthodox and easily recognizable beauties, of musical science. I had learned, too, the very remarkable fact that the stem of the Usher race, all time-honored as it was, had put forth at no period any enduring branch; in other words, that the entire family lay in the direct line of descent, and had always, with very trifling and very temporary variation, so lain. It
60 was this deficiency, I considered, while running over in thought the perfect keeping of the character of the premises with the accredited character

of the people, and while speculating upon the possible influence which
the one, in the long lapse of centuries, might have exercised upon the
other—it was this deficiency, perhaps, of collateral issue, and the consequent undeviating transmission from sire to son of the patrimony with
the name, which had, at length, so identified the two as to merge the original title of the estate in the quaint and equivocal appellation of the
"House of Usher"—an appellation which seemed to include, in the minds
of the peasantry who used it, both the family and the family mansion.

70   I have said that the sole effect of my somewhat childish experiment,
that of looking down within the tarn, had been to deepen the first singular
impression. There can be no doubt that the consciousness of the rapid
increase of my superstition—for why should I not so term it?—served
mainly to accelerate the increase itself. Such, I have long known, is the
paradoxical law of all sentiments having terror as a basis. And it might
have been for this reason only, that, when I again uplifted my eyes to the
house itself, from its image in the pool, there grew in my mind a strange
fancy—a fancy so ridiculous, indeed, that I but mention it to show the
vivid force of the sensations which oppressed me. I had so worked upon
80 my imagination as really to believe that about the whole mansion and domain there hung an atmosphere peculiar to themselves and their immediate vicinity: an atmosphere which had no affinity with the air of heaven,
but which had reeked up from the decayed trees, and the gray wall, and
the silent tarn: a pestilent and mystic vapor, dull, sluggish, faintly discernible, and leaden-hued.

Shaking off from my spirit what *must* have been a dream, I scanned
more narrowly the real aspect of the building. Its principal feature
seemed to be that of an excessive antiquity. The discoloration of ages
had been great. Minute fungi overspread the whole exterior, hanging in
90 a fine tangled webwork from the eaves. Yet all this was apart from any
extraordinary dilapidation. No portion of the masonry had fallen; and
there appeared to be a wild inconsistency between its still perfect adap-
tion of parts and the crumbling condition of the individual stones. In
this there was much that reminded me of the specious totality of old
woodwork which has rotted for long years in some neglected vault, with
no disturbance from the breath of the external air. Beyond this indication of excessive decay, however, the fabric gave little token of instability.
Perhaps the eye of a scrutinizing observer might have discovered a
barely perceptible fissure, which, extending from the roof of the build-
100 ing in front, made its way down the wall in a zigzag direction, until it
became lost in the sullen waters of the tarn.

Noticing these things, I rode over a short causeway to the house. A
servant in waiting took my horse, and I entered the Gothic archway of
the hall. A valet, of stealthy step, thence conducted me, in silence,
through many dark and intricate passages in my progress to the studio
of his master. Much that I encountered on the way contributed, I know
not how, to heighten the vague sentiments of which I have already

spoken. While the objects around me—while the carvings of the ceil-
ings, the somber tapestries of the walls, the ebon blackness of the floors,
110 and the phantasmagoric armorial trophies which rattled as I strode,
were but matters to which, or to such as which, I had been accustomed
from my infancy—while I hesitated not to acknowledge how familiar
was all this—I still wondered to find how unfamiliar were the fancies
which ordinary images were stirring up. On one of the staircases, I met
the physician of the family. His countenance, I thought, wore a mingled
expression of low cunning and perplexity. He accosted me with trepida-
tion and passed on. The valet now threw open a door and ushered me
into the presence of his master.

The room in which I found myself was very large and lofty. The
120 windows were long, narrow, and pointed, and at so vast a distance from
the black oaken floor as to be altogether inaccessible from within. Feeble gleams of encrimsoned light made their way through the trellised
panes, and served to render sufficiently distinct the more prominent objects around; the eye, however, struggled in vain to reach the remoter
angles of the chamber, or the recesses of the vaulted and fretted ceiling.
Dark draperies hung upon the walls. The general furniture was profuse,
comfortless, antique, and tattered. Many books and musical instruments lay scattered about, but failed to give any vitality to the scene. I
felt that I breathed an atmosphere of sorrow. An air of stern, deep, and
130 irredeemable gloom hung over and pervaded all.

Upon my entrance, Usher arose from a sofa on which he had been lying at full length, and greeted me with a vivacious warmth which had
much in it, I at first thought, of an overdone cordiality—of the constrained
effort of the *ennuyé* man of the world. A glance, however, at his countenance, convinced me of his perfect sincerity. We sat down; and for some
moments, while he spoke not, I gazed upon him with a feeling half of
pity, half of awe. Surely man had never before so terribly altered in so
brief a period as had Roderick Usher! It was with difficulty that I could
bring myself to admit the identity of the wan being before me with the
140 companion of my boyhood. Yet the character of his face had been at all
times remarkable. A cadaverousness of complexion; an eye large, liquid,
and luminous beyond comparison; lips somewhat thin and very pallid,
but of a surpassingly beautiful curve; a nose of a delicate Hebrew model,
but with a breadth of nostril unusual in similar formations; a finely
molded chin, speaking, in its want of prominence, of a want of moral energy; hair of a more than weblike softness and tenuity; these features,
with an inordinate expansion above the regions of the temple, made up
altogether a countenance not easily to be forgotten. And now in the mere
exaggeration of the prevailing character of these features, and of the ex-
150 pression they were wont to convey, lay so much of change that I doubted
to whom I spoke. The now ghostly pallor of the skin, and the now miraculous luster of the eye, above all things startled and even awed me. The
silken hair, too, had been suffered to grow all unheeded, and as, in its

wild gossamer texture, it floated rather than fell about the face, I could not, even with effort, connect its arabesque expression with any idea of simple humanity.

In the manner of my friend I was at once struck with an incoherence, an inconsistency; and I soon found this to arise from a series of feeble and futile struggles to overcome an habitual trepidancy, an excessive ner-
160 vous agitation. For something of this nature I had indeed been prepared, no less by his letter than by reminiscences of certain boyish traits, and by conclusions deduced from his peculiar physical conformation and temperament. His action was alternatively vivacious and sullen. His voice varied rapidly from a tremulous indecision (when the animal spirits seemed utterly in abeyance) to that species of energetic concision—that abrupt, weighty, unhurried, and hollow-sounding enunciation—that leaden, self-balanced and perfectly modulated guttural utterance—which may be observed in the lost drunkard, or the irreclaimable eater of opium, during the periods of his most intense excitement.
170   It was thus that he spoke of the object of my visit, of his earnest desire to see me, and of the solace he expected me to afford him. He entered, at some length, into what he conceived to be the nature of his malady. It was, he said, a constitutional and a family evil, and one for which he despaired to find a remedy—a mere nervous affection, he immediately added, which would undoubtedly soon pass off. It displayed itself in a host of unnatural sensations. Some of these, as he detailed them, interested and bewildered me: although, perhaps, the terms and the general manner of the narration had their weight. He suffered much from a morbid acuteness of the senses; the most insipid food was alone endurable; he
180 could wear only garments of a certain texture; the odors of all flowers were oppressive; his eyes were tortured by even a faint light; and there were but peculiar sounds, and these from stringed instruments, which did not inspire him with horror.

To an anomalous species of terror I found him a bounden slave. "I shall perish," said he, "I *must* perish in this deplorable folly. Thus, thus, and not otherwise, shall I be lost. I dread the events of the future, not in themselves, but in their results. I shudder at the thought of any, even the most trivial, incident, which may operate upon this intolerable agitation of soul. I have, indeed, no abhorrence of danger, except in its absolute
190 effect—in terror. In this unnerved—in this pitiable condition—I feel that the period will sooner or later arrive when I must abandon life and reason together, in some struggle with the grim phantasm, FEAR."

I learned moreover at intervals, and through broken and equivocal hints, another singular feature of his mental condition. He was enchained by certain superstitious impressions in regard to the dwelling which he tenanted, and whence, for many years, he had never ventured forth—in regard to an influence whose suppositious force was conveyed in terms too shadowy here to be restated—an influence which some peculiarities in the mere form and substance of his family mansion, had,
200 by dint of long sufferance, he said, obtained over his spirit—an effect

which the physique of the gray walls and turrets, and of the dim tarn
into which they all looked down, had, at length, brought about upon the
morale of his existence.

He admitted, however, although with hesitation, that much of the peculiar gloom which thus afflicted him could be traced to a more natural
and far more palpable origin—to the severe and long-continued illness,
indeed to the evidently approaching dissolution, of a tenderly beloved sister—his sole companion for long years, his last and only relative on earth.
"Her decease," he said, with a bitterness which I can never forget, "would
210 leave him (him the hopeless and the frail) the last of the ancient race of
the Ushers." While he spoke, the lady Madeline (for so was she called)
passed slowly through a remote portion of the apartment, and, without
having noticed my presence, disappeared. I regarded her with an utter astonishment not unmingled with dread, and yet I found it impossible to
account for such feelings. A sensation of stupor oppressed me, as my eyes
followed her retreating steps. When a door, at length, closed upon her, my
glance sought instinctively and eagerly the countenance of the brother,
but he had buried his face in his hands, and I could only perceive that a
far more than ordinary wanness had overspread the emaciated fingers
220 through which trickled many passionate tears.

The disease of the lady Madeline had long baffled the skill of her
physicians. A settled apathy, a gradual wasting away of the person, and
frequent although transient affections of a partially cataleptical character,
were the unusual diagnosis. Hitherto she had steadily borne up against the
pressure of her malady, and had not betaken herself finally to bed; but, on
the closing in of the evening of my arrival at the house, she succumbed (as
her brother told me at night with inexpressible agitation) to the prostrating
power of the destroyer; and I learned that the glimpse I had obtained of
her person would thus probably be the last I should obtain—that the lady,
230 at least while living, would be seen by me no more.

For several days ensuing, her name was unmentioned by either Usher
or myself; and during this period I was busied in earnest endeavors to al-
leviate the melancholy of my friend. We painted and read together; or I
listened, as if in a dream, to the wild improvisation of his speaking guitar. And thus, as a closer and still closer intimacy admitted me more unreservedly into the recesses of his spirit, the more bitterly did I perceive
the futility of all attempt at cheering a mind from which darkness, as if
an inherent positive quality, poured forth upon all objects of the moral
and physical universe, in one unceasing radiation of gloom.

240 I shall ever bear about me a memory of the many solemn hours I thus
spent alone with the master of the House of Usher. Yet I should fail in any
attempt to convey an idea of the exact character of the studies, or of the
occupations, in which he involved me, or led me the way. An excited and
highly distempered ideality threw a sulphurous luster over all. His long
improvised dirges will ring forever in my ears. Among other things, I
hold painfully in mind a certain singular perversion and amplification of
the wild air of the last waltz of Von Weber. From the paintings over which

his elaborate fancy brooded, and which grew, touch by touch, into vagueness at which I shuddered the more thrillingly because I shuddered
250 knowing not why;—from these paintings (vivid as their images now are
before me) I would in vain endeavor to educe more than a small portion
which should lie within the compass of merely written words. By the utter simplicity, by the nakedness of his designs, he arrested and overawed
attention. If ever mortal painted an idea, that mortal was Roderick Usher.
For me at least, in the circumstances then surrounding me, there arose,
out of the pure abstractions which the hypochondriac contrived to throw
upon his canvas, an intensity of intolerable awe, no shadow of which felt I
ever yet in the contemplation of the certainly glowing yet too concrete
reveries of Fuseli.
260   One of the phantasmagoric conceptions of my friend, partaking not so
rigidly of the spirit of abstraction, may be shadowed forth, although feebly, in words. A small picture presented the interior of an immensely
long and rectangular vault or tunnel, with low walls, smooth, white, and
without interruption or device. Certain accessory points of the design
served well to convey the idea that this excavation lay at an exceeding
depth below the surface of the earth. No outlet was observed in any portion of its vast extent, and no torch or other artificial source of light was
discernible; yet a flood of intense rays rolled throughout, and bathed the
whole in a ghastly and inappropriate splendor.
270   I have just spoken of that morbid condition of the auditory nerve
which rendered all music intolerable to the sufferer, with the exception of
certain effects of stringed instruments. It was, perhaps, the narrow limits
to which he thus confined himself upon the guitar, which gave birth, in
great measure, to the fantastic character of his performances. But the fervid *facility* of his *impromptus* could not be so accounted for. They must have
been, and were, in the notes, as well as in the words of his wild fantasias
(for he not infrequently accompanied himself with rhymed verbal improvi-
sations), the result of that intense mental collectedness and concentration
to which I have previously alluded as observable only in particular mo-
280 ments of the highest artificial excitement. The words of one of these rhap-
sodies I have easily remembered. I was, perhaps, the more forcibly impressed with it, as he gave it, because, in the under or mystic current of its
meaning, I fancied that I perceived, and for the first time, a full consciousness, on the part of Usher, of the tottering of his lofty reason upon her
throne. The verses, which were entitled "The Haunted Palace," ran very
nearly, if not accurately, thus:

I

In the greenest of our valleys,
By good angels tenanted,
290   Once a fair and stately palace—
Radiant palace—reared its head.
In the monarch Thought's dominion,
It stood there!

Never seraph spread a pinion
Over fabric half so fair.

                                        II
Banners yellow, glorious, golden,
On its roof did float and flow,
(This—all this—was in the olden
300   Time long ago)
And every gentle air that dallied,
In that sweet day,
Along the ramparts plumed and pallid,
A wingèd odor went away.

                                        III
Wanderers in that happy valley
Through two luminous windows saw
Spirits moving musically
To a lute's well-tunèd law,
310   Round about a throne where, sitting,
(Porphyrogene!)
In state his glory well befitting,
The ruler of the realm was seen.

                                        IV
And all with pearl and ruby glowing
Was the fair palace door,
Through which came flowing, flowing, flowing,
And sparkling evermore,
A troop of Echoes whose sweet duty
320   Was but to sing.
In voices of surpassing beauty,
The wit and wisdom of their king.

                                        V
But evil things, in robes of sorrow,
Assailed the monarch's high estate;
(Ah, let us mourn, for never morrow
Shall dawn upon him, desolate!)
And round about his home the glory
That blushed and bloomed
330   Is but a dim-remembered story
Of the old time entombed.

                                        VI
And travellers now within that valley
Through the red-litten windows see
Vast forms that move fantastically

> To a discordant melody;
> While, like a rapid ghastly river,
> Through the pale door,
> A hideous throng rush out forever,
> And laugh—but smile no more.

340

I well remember that suggestions arising from this ballad led us into a train of thought, wherein there became manifest an opinion of Usher's which I mention not so much on account of its novelty (for other men have thought thus) as on account of the pertinacity with which he maintained it. This opinion, in its general form, was that of the sentience of all vegetable things. But in his disordered fancy the idea had assumed a more daring character, and trespassed, under certain conditions, upon the kingdom of inorganization. I lack words to express the full extent, or the earnest *abandon* of his persuasion. The belief, however, was connected
350 (as I have previously hinted) with the gray stones of the home of his forefathers. The conditions of the sentience had been here, he imagined, fulfilled in the method of collocation of these stones—in the order of their arrangement, as well as in that of the many fungi which overspread them, and of the decayed trees which stood around—above all, in the long undisturbed endurance of this arrangement, and in its reduplication in the still waters of the tarn. Its evidence—the evidence of the sentience— was to be seen, he said (and I here started as he spoke), in the gradual yet certain condensation of an atmosphere of their own about the waters and the walls. The result was discoverable, he added, in that silent, yet impor-
360 tunate and terrible influence which for centuries had molded the destinies of his family, and which made *him* what I now saw him—what he was. Such opinions need no comment, and I will make none.

Our books—the books which, for years, had formed no small portion of the mental existence of the invalid—were, as might be supposed, in strict keeping with this character of phantasm. We pored together over such works as the Ververt and Chartreuse of Gresset; the Belphegor of Machiavelli; the Heaven and Hell of Swedenborg; the Subterranean Voyage of Nicholas Klimm by Holberg; the Chiromancy of Robert Flud, of Jean D'Indaginé, and of De la Chambre; the Journey
370 into the Blue Distance of Tieck; and the City of the Sun of Campanella. One favorite volume was a small octavo edition of the *Directorium Inquisitorium,* by the Dominican Eymeric de Gironne; and there were passages in Pomponius Mela, about the old African Satyrs and Ægipans, over which Usher would sit dreaming for hours. His chief delight, however, was found in the perusal of an exceedingly rare and curious book in quarto Gothic—the manual of a forgotten church—the *Vigiliæ Mortuorum Secundum Chorum Ecclesiæ Maguntinæ.*

I could not help thinking of the wild ritual of this work, and of its probable influence upon the hypochondriac, when one evening, having in-
380 formed me abruptly that the lady Madeline was no more, he stated his intention of preserving her corpse for a fortnight (previously to its final

interment) in one of the numerous vaults within the main walls of the building. The worldly reason, however, assigned for this singular proceeding was one which I did not feel at liberty to dispute. The brother had been led to his resolution (so he told me) by consideration of the unusual character of the malady of the deceased, of certain obtrusive and eager inquiries on the part of her medical men, and of the remote and exposed situation of the burialground of the family. I will not deny that when I called to mind the sinister countenance of the person whom I met
390 upon the staircase, on the day of my arrival at the house, I had no desire to oppose what I regarded as at best but a harmless, and by no means an unnatural, precaution.

At the request of Usher, I personally aided him in the arrangements for the temporary entombment. The body having been encoffined, we two alone bore it to its rest. The vault in which we placed it (and which had been so long unopened that our torches, half smothered in its oppressive atmosphere, gave us little opportunity for investigation) was small, damp, and entirely without means of admission for light; lying, at great depth, immediately beneath that portion of the building in which was my own
400 sleeping apartment. It had been used, apparently, in remote feudal times, for the worst purposes of a donjon-keep, and in later days as a place of deposit for powder, or some other highly combustible substance, as a portion of its floor, and the whole interior of a long archway through which we reached it, were carefully sheathed with copper. The door, of massive iron, had been also similarly protected. Its immense weight caused an unusually sharp grating sound, as it moved upon its hinges.

Having deposited our mournful burden upon trestles within this region of horror, we partially turned aside the yet unscrewed lid of the coffin, and looked upon the face of the tenant. A striking similitude be-
410 tween the brother and sister now first arrested my attention; and Usher divining, perhaps, my thoughts, murmured out some few words from which I learned that the deceased and himself had been twins, and that sympathies of a scarcely intelligible nature had always existed between them. Our glances, however, rested not long upon the dead—for we could not regard her unawed. The disease which had thus entombed the lady in the maturity of youth, had left, as usual in all maladies of a strictly cataleptical character, the mockery of a faint blush upon the bosom and the face, and that suspiciously lingering smile upon the lip which is so terrible in death. We replaced and screwed down the lid, and, having se-
420 cured the door of iron, made our way, with toil, into the scarcely less gloomy apartments of the upper portion of the house.

And now, some days of bitter grief having elapsed, an observable change came over the features of the mental disorder of my friend. His ordinary manner had vanished. His ordinary occupations were neglected or forgotten. He roamed from chamber to chamber with hurried, unequal, and objectless step. The pallor of his countenance had assumed, if possible, a more ghastly hue—but the luminousness of his eye had utterly gone out. The once occasional huskiness of his tone was heard no more; and a

tremulous quaver, as if of extreme terror, habitually characterized his ut-
430 terance. There were times, indeed, when I thought his unceasingly agitated mind was laboring with some oppressive secret, to divulge which he
struggled for the necessary courage. At times, again, I was obliged to resolve all into the mere inexplicable vagaries of madness, for I beheld him
gazing upon vacancy for long hours, in an attitude of the profoundest attention, as if listening to some imaginary sound. It was no wonder that his
condition terrified—that it infected me. I felt creeping upon me, by slow
yet certain degrees, the wild influences of his own fantastic yet impressive
superstitions.

It was, especially, upon retiring to bed late in the night of the seventh
440 or eighth day after the placing of the lady Madeline within the donjon,
that I experienced the full power of such feelings. Sleep came not near my
couch, while the hours waned and waned away. I struggled to reason off
the nervousness which had dominion over me. I endeavored to believe
that much, if not all, of what I felt was due to the bewildering influence of
the gloomy furniture of the room—of the dark and tattered draperies
which, tortured into motion by the breath of a rising tempest, swayed fitfully to and fro upon the walls, and rustled uneasily about the decorations of the bed. But my efforts were fruitless. An irrepressible tremor
gradually pervaded my frame; and at length there sat upon my very heart
450 an incubus of utterly causeless alarm. Shaking this off with a gasp and a
struggle, I uplifted myself upon the pillows, and, peering earnestly
within the intense darkness of the chamber, hearkened—I know not why,
except that an instinctive spirit prompted me—to certain low and indefinite sounds which came, through the pauses of the storm, at long intervals, I knew not whence. Overpowered by an intense sentiment of horror,
unaccountable yet unendurable, I threw on my clothes with haste (for I
felt that I should sleep no more during the night) and endeavored to
arouse myself from the pitiable condition into which I had fallen, by pacing rapidly to and fro through the apartment.

460   I had taken but few turns in this manner, when a light step on an
adjoining staircase arrested my attention. I presently recognized it as
that of Usher. In an instant afterward he rapped with a gentle touch at
my door, and entered, bearing a lamp. His countenance was, as usual,
cadaverously wan—but, moreover, there was a species of mad hilarity in
his eyes—an evidently restrained *hysteria* in his whole demeanor. His air
appalled me—but anything was preferable to the solitude which I had so
long endured, and I even welcomed his presence as a relief.

"And you have not seen it?" he said abruptly, after having stared
about him for some moments in silence—"you have not then seen it?
470 but, stay! you shall." Thus speaking, and having carefully shaded his
lamp, he hurried to one of the casements, and threw it freely open to
the storm.

The impetuous fury of the entering gust nearly lifted us from our
feet. It was, indeed, a tempestuous yet sternly beautiful night, and one
wildly singular in its terror and its beauty. A whirlwind had apparently

collected its force in our vicinity; for there were frequent and violent alterations in the direction of the wind; and the exceeding density of the clouds (which hung so low as to press upon the turrets of the house) did not prevent our perceiving the lifelike velocity with which they flew
480 careening from all points against each other, without passing away into the distance. I say that even their exceeding density did not prevent our perceiving this; yet we had no glimpse of the moon or stars, nor was there any flashing forth of the lightning. But the under surfaces of the huge masses of agitated vapor, as well as all terrestrial objects immediately around us, were glowing in the unnatural light of a faintly luminous and distinctly visible gaseous exhalation which hung about and enshrouded the mansion.

"You must not—you shall not behold this!" said I, shudderingly, to Usher, as I led him with a gentle violence from the window to a seat.
490 "These appearances, which bewilder you, are merely electrical phenomena not uncommon—or it may be that they have their ghastly origin in the rank miasma of the tarn. Let us close this casement; the air is chilling and dangerous to your frame. Here is one of your favorite romances. I will read, and you shall listen;—and so we will pass away this terrible night together."

The antique volume which I had taken up was the *Mad Trist* of Sir Launcelot Canning; but I had called it a favorite of Usher's more in sad jest than in earnest; for, in truth, there is little in its uncouth and unimaginative prolixity which could have had interest for the lofty
500 and spiritual ideality of my friend. It was, however, the only book immediately at hand; and I indulged a vague hope that the excitement which now agitated the hypochondriac might find relief (for the history of mental disorder is full of similar anomalies) even in the extremeness of the folly which I should read. Could I have judged, indeed, by the wild overstrained air of vivacity with which he hearkened, or apparently hearkened, to the words of the tale, I might well have congratulated myself upon the success of my design.

I had arrived at that well-known portion of the story where Ethelred, the hero of the Trist, having sought in vain for peaceable ad-
510 mission into the dwelling of the hermit, proceeds to make good an entrance by force. Here, it will be remembered, the words of the narrative run thus:

"And Ethelred, who was by nature of a doughty heart, and who was now mighty withal, on account of the powerfulness of the wine which he had drunken, waited no longer to hold parley with the hermit, who, in sooth, was of an obstinate and maliceful turn, but, feeling the rain upon his shoulders, and fearing the rising of the tempest, uplifted his mace outright, and, with blows, made quickly room in the plankings of the door for his gauntleted hand; and now pulling therewith sturdily, he so cracked,
520   and ripped, and tore all asunder, that the noise of the dry and hollow-sounding wood alarummed and reverberated throughout the forest."

At the termination of this sentence I started, and for a moment paused; for it appeared to me (although I at once concluded that my excited fancy had deceived me)—it appeared to me that from some very remote portion of the mansion there came, indistinctly, to my ears, what might have been, in its exact similarity of character, the echo (but a stifled and dull one certainly) of the very cracking and ripping sound which Sir Launcelot had so particularly described. It was, beyond doubt, the coincidence alone which had arrested my attention; for, amid the rattling of
530 the sashes of the casements, and the ordinary commingled noises of the still increasing storm, the sound, in itself, had nothing, surely, which should have interested or disturbed me. I continued the story:

> "But the good champion Ethelred, now entering within the door, was sore enraged and amazed to perceive no signal of the maliceful hermit; but, in the stead thereof, a dragon of a scaly and prodigious demeanor, and of a fiery tongue, which sate in guard before a palace of gold, with a floor of silver; and upon the wall there hung a shield of shining brass with this legend enwritten—
> Who entereth herein, a conqueror hath bin;
540   Who slayeth the dragon, the shield he shall win
> And Ethelred uplifted his mace, and struck upon the head of the dragon, which fell before him, and gave up his pesty breath, with a shriek so horrid and harsh, and withal so piercing, that Ethelred had fain to close his ears with his hands against the dreadful noise of it, the like whereof was never before heard."

Here again I paused abruptly, and now with a feeling of wild amazement; for there could be no doubt whatever that, in this instance, I did actually hear (although from what direction it proceeded I found it impossible to say) a low and apparently distant, but harsh, protracted,
550 and most unusual screaming or grating sound—the exact counterpart of what my fancy had already conjured up for the dragon's unnatural shriek as described by the romancer.

Oppressed, as I certainly was, upon the occurrence of this second and most extraordinary coincidence, by a thousand conflicting sensations, in which wonder and extreme terror were predominant, I still retained sufficient presence of mind to avoid exciting, by any observation, the sensitive nervousness of my companion. I was by no means certain that he had noticed the sounds in question; although, assuredly, a strange alteration had during the last few minutes taken place in his demeanor. From a po-
560 sition fronting my own, he had gradually brought round his chair, so as to sit with his face to the door of the chamber; and thus I could but partially perceive his features, although I saw that his lips trembled as if he were murmuring inaudibly. His head had dropped upon his breast—yet I knew that he was not asleep, from the wide and rigid opening of the eye as I caught a glance of it in profile. The motion of his body, too, was at variance with this idea—for he rocked from side to side with a gentle yet

constant and uniform sway. Having rapidly taken notice of all this, I resumed the narrative of Sir Launcelot, which thus proceeded:

570 "And now, the champion having escaped from the terrible fury of the dragon, bethinking himself of the brazen shield, and of the breaking up of the enchantment which was upon it, removed the carcass from out of the way before him, and approached valorously over the silver pavement of the castle to where the shield was upon the wall; which in sooth tarried not for his full coming, but fell down at his feet upon the silver floor, with a mighty great and terrible ringing sound."

No sooner had these syllables passed my lips, than—as if a shield of brass had indeed, at the moment, fallen heavily upon a floor of silver—I became aware of a distinct, hollow, metallic and clangorous, yet apparently muffled reverberation. Completely unnerved, I leaped to my feet;
580 but the measured rocking movement of Usher was undisturbed. I rushed to the chair in which he sat. His eyes were bent fixedly before him, and throughout his whole countenance there reigned a stony rigidity. But, as I placed my hand upon his shoulder, there came a strong shudder over his whole person; a sickly smile quivered about his lips; and I saw that he spoke in a low, hurried, and gibbering murmur, as if unconscious of my presence. Bending closely over him, I at length drank in the hideous import of his words.

"Not hear it?—yes, I hear it, and *have* heard it. Long—long—long—many minutes, many hours, many days, have I heard it—yet I dared
590 not—oh, pity me, miserable wretch that I am!—I dared not—*I dared not speak! We have put her living in the tomb!* Said I not that my senses were acute? I *now* tell you that I heard her first feeble movements in the hollow coffin. I heard them—many, many days ago—yet I dared not—*I dared not speak!* And now—tonight—Ethelred—ha! ha!—the breaking of the hermit's door, and the death-cry of the dragon, and the clangor of the shield—say, rather, the rending of her coffin, and the grating of the iron hinges of her prison, and her struggles within the coppered archway of the vault! Oh, whither shall I fly? Will she not be here anon? Is she not hurrying to upbraid me for my haste? Have I not heard her
600 footsteps on the stair? Do I not distinguish that heavy and horrible beating of her heart? Madman!"—here he sprang furiously to his feet, and shrieked out his syllables, as if in the effort he were giving up his soul—*"Madman! I tell you that she now stands without the door!"*

As if in the superhuman energy of his utterance there had been found the potency of a spell, the huge antique panels to which the speaker pointed drew slowly back, upon the instant, their ponderous and ebony jaws. It was the work of the rushing gust—but then without the doors there *did* stand the lofty and enshrouded figure of the lady Madeline of Usher. There was blood upon her white robes, and the evi-
610 dence of some bitter struggle upon every portion of her emaciated frame. For a moment she remained trembling and reeling to and fro

upon the threshold—then, with a low moaning cry, fell heavily inward upon the person of her brother, and, in her violent and now final death-agonies, bore him to the floor a corpse, and a victim to the terrors he had anticipated.

From that chamber, and from that mansion, I fled aghast. The storm was still abroad in all its wrath as I found myself crossing the old cause-way. Suddenly there shot along the path a wild light, and I turned to see whence a gleam so unusual could have issued; for the vast house and its
620 shadows were alone behind me. The radiance was that of a full, setting, and blood-red moon, which now shone vividly through that once barely discernible fissure, of which I have before spoken as extending from the roof of the building, in a zigzag direction, to the base. While I gazed, this fissure rapidly widened—there came a fierce breath of the whirl-wind—the entire orb of the satellite burst at once upon my sight—my brain reeled as I saw the mighty walls rushing asunder—there was a long tumultuous shouting sound like the voice of a thousand waters—and the deep and dank tarn at my feet closed sullenly and silently over the fragments of the House of Usher.

ACCOUNT: ALLEN TATE ON "OUR COUSIN, MR. POE"

Tate explains that his use of the word "cousin" is partly meant to express the *familiarity* of Poe's writing to American readers. Poe has long been a household name, and many people in Tate's generation grew up in houses that contained Poe's books, often in volumes that had belonged to their grandparents. However, the familiarity of Poe's writing may serve to mask just how *odd* his imagination was, precisely because the wildness of his stories is like the oddness of a long-known cousin who may be "placed" in various unattractive categories of strangeness, but never denied a place in the family. Yet, it is not enough merely to acknowledge or to tolerate Poe's oddity, Tate says: "We must avoid the trap of a mere abstract evaluation, and try to reproduce the actual conditions of our relations to him."

Tate goes on to argue that, though odd, Poe's imagination in his writing was consistent. Poe's texts surround us with what T.S. Eliot called "a wilderness of mirrors." That is, in all his work we see "a sub-liminal self endlessly repeated or, turning a new posture of the same figure." That figure always has the *desperation* seen in the famous photograph of Poe. In that photograph (as in the title of Tate's book containing this essay) Poe seems a "forlorn demon."

What is the source of the desperation and the demonic quality in the stories themselves? First of all, a strange fire is Poe's leading visual

From Allen Tate, *The Forlorn Demon: Didactic and Critical Essays* (Chicago: Regnery, 1953).

symbol. We see it in the eyes of the Raven, in "those eyes! those large, those shining, those divine orbs" of the Lady Lygia, and in "an eye large, liquid, and luminous beyond comparison" of Roderick Usher in "The Fall of the House of Usher." Poe's heroes and heroines always burn with this fierce but *bodiless* exaltation.

For this fire is not an indication of sensuality—the fires are (in the words of another story) "not the fires of Eros." And readers seem always to have agreed on the absence of the sexual in Poe, since in no nineteenth- or twentieth-century criticism is there any sense of shock or even surprise that Roderick Usher is so in love with his sister. Since their relation is not physical, it was seen as "pure."

In fact, Poe's fire is the fire of the abstract, bodiless intellect seen in the heightened sensitivity and consciousness that burns in Roderick Usher. Poe's morbidity in that story and elsewhere is felt through the intellectual compulsion to *know* "that drives through, and beyond, physical incest toward the extinction of the beloved's will in complete possession, not of her body, but of her being." It also becomes a reciprocal force, returning on the lover as self-destruction, and Madeline Usher falls upon Roderick in the end killing him with the half sexual embrace of a vampire.

Tate points out that D.H. Lawrence was the first to notice the implicit vampirism in Poe, and Tate enlarges on its implications:

> If a writer ambiguously exalts the "spirit" over the "body," and the spirit must live wholly upon another spirit, some version of the vampire legend is likely to issue as the symbolic situation.
>
> Although the action is reported by a narrator, the fictional point of view is that of Usher: it is all seen through his eyes. But has Madeline herself not also been moving towards the cataclysmic end in the enveloping action outside the frame of the story? Has not her *will to know* done its reciprocal work upon the inner being of her brother? Their very birth had violated their unity of being. They must achieve spiritual identity in mutual destruction. The physical symbolism of the fissured house, of the miasmic air, and of the special order of nature surrounding the House of Usher and conforming to the laws of the spirits inhabiting it—all this supports the central dramatic situation which moves toward spiritual unity through disintegration.

In this way, Poe's characters are not really sexual in their desire for possession. They are dead to the world and hence *like* vampires: the "undead." Yet Poe does not use traditional vampire images explicitly, because the horrors displayed by his vision are in fact the *reverse* of the "supernatural" associated with the vampire legends. Poe's implications are particularly modern in avoiding traditional images of the supernatural, and his modernity is therefore another sense in which Poe may be seen as our cousin. For the images of Poe's language are those of modern man dehumanized in the traditional sense of "humanity," because our humanity is seen as *without* its traditional supernatural aspect. In the scientific, "rational" view of life that Poe was so fascinated by in so many ways, the body is a mere machine of sensation, a physical bundle of particles and reflexes which, however complexly responsive to "stimuli" chemical and electrical, is nevertheless without a soul. Poe's literary language is odd because of the horrifying implications of the modern view that life exists in an entirely physical universe without the traditional supernatural complement of a universe of spirit: "everything in Poe is dead: the houses, the rooms, the furniture, to say nothing of nature and of human beings."

Tate adds:

> Does it explain anything to say that this is necrophilism? I think not. Poe's prose style as well as certain qualities of his verse, expresses the kind of "reality" to which he had access: I believe I have indicated that it is a reality sufficiently terrible. In spite of an early classical education and a Christian upbringing, he wrote as if the experience of these traditions had been lost: he was well ahead of his time. . . . No other writer in England or the United States, or, so far as I know, in France, went so far as Poe in his vision of dehumanized man.

In this way (Tate concludes) Poe's art was like much modern art: "From the literary point of view he combined the primitive and the decadent: primitive, because he had neither history nor the historical sense; decadent, because he was the conscious artist of an intensity which lacked moral perspective." Morality cannot exist for Poe, since morals are not based on the physical, but rather depend upon the *spiritual* traditions in which he like other "moderns" no longer believed. This "scientific" lack of supernatural belief was far from liberating or comforting—and hence his desperation. The vision expressed in the language of his stories in general and in "The Fall of the House of Usher" in particular is therefore like the modern vision of the ultimate fate of human life, of the earth, and of the universe: a vision of "inevitable annihilation."

As with all the critical approaches introduced in this section on fiction, the New Criticism will be represented later on. Other examples of the New Criticism will be found in the poetry section with accounts of Cleanth Brooks on William Butler Yeats's "Among School Children" and Maria K. Mootry on Gwendolyn Brooks's sonnets. In the drama section are included accounts of Cleanth Brooks and Robert Heilman on Sophocles' *Oedipus the King* and Richard Hornby on Henrik Ibsen's *A Doll House.* Further, in both the poetry and the drama sections, two critical approaches are given on each featured work, giving you a chance through comparison and contrast to understand more fully some of the distinctive characteristics of a given theoretical position.

SUGGESTIONS FOR DISCUSSION AND WRITING

1. Tate points out a conflict between the ostensible narrative technique and the **point of view** in the story. What kind of **narrator** does Poe employ? How does the author maintain a point of view different from that of his narrator? What keeps him from using Usher himself as the narrator?

2. How does Tate's analysis illuminate the story's **rising action, crisis, resolution, and falling action**? What do you notice about the proportions of material in each case? What do you think of the **pacing** of Poe's **plot**? Does he, in your view, employ a **subplot** in that pacing?

3. Tate speaks of a "wilderness of mirrors." What **images** in the story support that critical image? Make a list. How, for example, may brother and sister be said to "mirror" one another?

4. Compare and contrast Poe's story to Ralph Ellison's "The King of the Bingo Game." In what similar and different ways does each author create "an outward and visible sign of an inward and spiritual state," like that suggested by Tate's analysis?

5. Write an essay in which you support or oppose—with analysis, evidence, and demonstration—Tate's contention that Poe's fictional universe is a universe of "deadness."

6. Make some notes (for discussion in class or for an essay) on the aspects of the New Criticism you see in Tate's view of Poe. How (for example) does he see the story as expressive of a complex human view of the world organized and unified in some way by a sensibility? How well does the approach apply to Melville's "Bartleby the Scrivener?" Make some notes on that story that could be expanded into an essay using the approach of the New Criticism.

Chapter Three

Psychoanalytic Criticism: Mind and Emotion in Literature

A BRIEF INTRODUCTION TO PSYCHOANALYTIC CRITICISM

The word *psychology* comes from ancient Greek words meaning "the study of the soul," and psychology has been a topic of inquiry in many forms before modern times—forms that may nowadays be considered unscientific because they focused on the unprovable. Yet by the late nineteenth century, the wide ambitions of modern science ceased to be limited to the physical universe and were extended to the "analytic" study of the mind, most famously by the work of Sigmund Freud.

What Freud found was in general terms familiar enough and resembled what Plato had seen and what the Judeo-Christian tradition had found—a struggle of good and evil principles striving for control of the self. But with the moral objectivity and relativism of science, a new factor was added—the contending forces were no longer seen in the moral terms of "good" and "evil," but as impersonal forces parallel to those of the physical universe. In fact, these psychic forces (according to Freud) created the human sense of morals.

Like the Marxist criticism and the Feminist criticism covered in chapters to come, psychoanalytic criticism may focus on the relation of its topic to the outside world reflected in literature, to the work of literature itself (including the characters within the work), on the author of the work, or on the audience that reads it. Psychological motivations in any or all of these areas may be explored and interpreted in the light of psychoanalytic theory.

Yet the process of analysis by psychology also works in a reciprocal way as far as literature is concerned. That is, Freud both searched literature for knowledge of the mind as instinctively anticipated and revealed by poets and authors *and* used what he discovered there along with his own ideas to analyze other works of literature. From his studies of both real and imaginary people, Freud formed a map of the mind which evolved over time. Because of its changing nature, no summary can do full justice to Freud's "thought," and whether his early or late views are considered the most illuminating is a matter of debate. For our purposes, however, a crude map may be drawn while keeping the conceptual limitations of all brief introductions in mind.

Freud proposed three parts or agencies within the mind: the *id*, the *ego*, and the *superego*. The id is the location of the primary and largely unconscious human drives for pleasure and aggression. The ego, a more conscious part of the mind, acts to control these drives in their desire for instant gratification (the *Pleasure Principle* and the *Reality Principle*). The superego represents parental and institutional values, usually learned in childhood. In Freud's view, these agencies within the mind are not autonomous and independent but act on each other dynamically.

The ego, for example, uses various tactics, sometimes called *defenses*, to control the lower impulses of the id. Among these defenses, *repression*, *projection*, and *symbolization* are all methods employed by the ego to keep disagreeable drives from coming to consciousness in their original and disturbing form. Repression, in some sense the more straightforward of these, simply keeps offensive feelings buried in the unconscious. Although these repressed desires are not recognized by the conscious mind, they may surface in numerous ways. For instance, dreams or slips of the tongue—Freudian slips as they are sometimes called—may be evidence of a repressed impulse. Projection is the act of *imagining* that one's own hidden desires and impulses are held by someone else. For example, a son who unconsciously hates his mother may accuse others of disliking her or may accuse her of disliking him, thus projecting his own feelings upon another person. Symbolization shifts the goal or object of the drive onto someone or something that makes a symbolic substitute for the original goal. The phallic symbol is a well-known example. A disturbing or unmentionable object is symbolized by a more innocent or proper one.

The superego is both a product of the ego and an influence on the ego. The superego begins as a result of the Oedipus Complex, a stage in psychological development through which Freud believed all children pass between their third and sixth years. Freud theorized that both boys and girls focus the desires for pleasure of their infant sexuality on their mothers and their aggressive drives on the fathers who stand in the way of their fully possessing those mothers. The ego struggles to keep these motives from being acted out, in part by evoking not only the child's love for the father but also a fear of his retaliation.

Yet the experiences of the sexes are not entirely the same. In the long and agonizing process of the Oedipal stage, boys differ from girls through the functioning of the *castration process*. In this stage boys fear castration as retaliation and girls shift the object of their desires from mothers to fathers, who possess the penis they want and envy. Eventually, girls "reidentify" with their mothers as psychic preparation for possessing men like their fathers.

However, the guilts and conflicts involved in the Oedipal stage produce the superego, the seat of the ideal image and standards of perfection against which adults will compare their actual performances in life. The superego becomes the agency which keeps the forbidden desires of the Oedipal phase from surfacing. In Norman Holland's phrase, the superego threatens the ego with guilt (*The Dynamics of Literary Response*) and causes it to act upon the id in the name of higher social values and restrictions.

Freudian psychoanalysis has long been used in literary interpretation. Freud himself believed that literature is like dreams insofar as it expresses disguised wishes through a manifest content that conceals the latent or real meaning. As dreams do, literature may take disturbing impulses or feelings from the id and translate or symbolize them in acceptable forms. As noted, psychoanalytic critics may concentrate on the text itself and what meanings can be found in its symbolizations; they may consider particularly what a literary text tells us about the author or they may focus on the response of readers to the disguised wishes.

For example, in considering a short story with a dispute between two male characters, the psychoanalytic interpreter might discover an Oedipal conflict with one of the characters in the role of an authority or father figure and then trace through the implications of that discovery for the story. However, the critic might be more interested in what the Oedipal conflict tells about the author's feelings or in what the conflict suggests about reasons for readers responding as they do to the story. How critics actually work with Freudian psychology will be exemplified in the account of Frederick Crews' analysis of Hawthorne's "Young Goodman Brown" that appears later in this chapter, as well as in the account of Geoffrey Hartman on a poem by Wordsworth. See also the essay on original form by Maria Bonaparte in the Appendix, where she discusses another story by Hawthorne, "The Birthmark" (p. 917).

While Freud's psychoanalytic views and their literary implications are perhaps the views most widely known, an Oedipal process of sorts occurred within his own movement through the rivalry of Carl Jung. Jung eventually proposed a different way of understanding the operations of the mind in life and art. An early colleague and favorite pupil of Freud when his Oedipal revolt took place, Jung posited that the unconscious of Freud, the "personal unconscious," did exist but was relatively less powerful than the "collective unconscious" of racial memories carried by all human beings.

Longstanding myths show stories particularly successful in satisfying the needs of the unconscious. Their original particular content has been worn away to reveal the true core of basic images which stimulate the human mind and form its collective unconscious. Jung thus explains the similarity among many myths produced by widely separated cultures. One major paradigm that appears in Jungian criticism may be exemplified by Alice Munro's story "Eskimo" that appears in the section introducing fiction (see p. 11). In that work, Mary Jo almost literally (like Joyce's narrator more figuratively) undertakes a Jungian "night sea-journey from life through symbolic death to a new rebirth."

The scope of this book does not permit even a brief account of the wide variety of other psychological theories of literary criticism that have been advanced even in modern times. Yet one famous example may be pointed to—the work of Northrop Frye, who proposed that literature divided itself into differing "archetypes" as described in his *Anatomy of Criticism* (1957). Further, in addition to views that rival Freud's, the modifications, critiques, reinterpretations, and continuations of Freudian theory continue today. Perhaps the best-known contemporary exemplar of these scholars, who see themselves not only as heirs to but as developers of the means of inquiry pioneered by Freud, is the French critic, Jacques Lacan, whose views on *Hamlet* appear in the section on drama.

NATHANIEL HAWTHORNE (1804–1864) was born on July 4, 1804, in Salem, Massachusetts, where earlier members of his family once participated in the Salem witch trials and Quaker persecutions. Hawthorne attended Bowdoin College in Maine, where he befriended Franklin Pierce, later president of the United States, and the poet Henry Wadsworth Longfellow. After graduating in 1825, he lived in near seclusion, writing sketches and stories for magazines and newspapers. His first novel, *Fanshawe*, was based on his college life and published anonymously in 1829. Feeling ashamed of his work, however, Hawthorne withdrew most of the copies and burned them. His first important work was *Twice-Told Tales*, a collection of short stories published in 1837. During the same year, Hawthorne worked at a Boston Customs House and invested his savings in the Transcendentalist community Brook Farm. In 1841 he left Brook Farm (due to disillusionment with communal life), married Sophia Peabody, and moved to the Old Manse in Concord, Massachusetts, the one-time home of Ralph Waldo Emerson. 1846 saw the publication of his second volume of short stories, *Mosses from an Old Manse*, which was reviewed by Herman Melville and established a friendship between the two writers.

In 1849, Hawthorne (having returned to Salem and his job at the Customs House) began work on his masterpiece, *The Scarlet Letter*. Published in 1850, the highly successful novel was followed by *The House of the Seven Gables* (1851) and *The Blithedale Romance* (1852). Hawthorne also wrote a campaign biography for his college friend Franklin Pierce; when Pierce became president in 1853, Hawthorne was appointed consul to Liverpool. The position allowed Hawthorne to travel extensively in Europe, where he completed his last published novel, *The Marble Faun* (1860). Hawthorne died on May 18, 1864, in Plymouth, New Hampshire, leaving four unfinished novels. Like his contemporary Edgar Allan Poe, Hawthorne elevated and transformed the short story from magazine filler to legitimate art form. First published in *Mosses from an Old Manse*, "Young Goodman Brown" exemplifies Hawthorne's use of Puritan New England as a setting for his works. Hawthorne's "The Birthmark" also appears later in the book (p. 212) and is one subject of two analyses in Appendix I (p. 936).

NATHANIEL HAWTHORNE
Young Goodman Brown
(1835)

Young Goodman Brown came forth at sunset into the street of Salem village; but put his head back, after crossing the threshold, to exchange a parting kiss with his young wife. And Faith, as the wife was aptly named, thrust her own pretty head into the street, letting the wind play with the pink ribbons of her cap while she called to Goodman Brown.

"Dearest heart," whispered she, softly and rather sadly, when her lips were close to his ear, "prithee put off your journey until sunrise and sleep in your own bed to-night. A lone woman is troubled with dreams and such thoughts that she's afeared of herself sometimes. Pray
10 tarry with me this night, dear husband, of all nights in the year."

"My love and my Faith," replied young Goodman Brown, "of all nights in the year, this one night must I tarry away from thee. My journey, as thou callest it, forth and back again, must needs be done 'twixt now and sunrise. What, my sweet, pretty wife, dost thou doubt me already, and we but three months married?"

"Then God bless you!" said Faith, with the pink ribbons; "and may you find all well when you come back."

"Amen!" cried Goodman Brown. "Say thy prayers, dear Faith, and go to bed at dusk, and no harm will come to thee."
20   So they parted; and the young man pursued his way until, being about to turn the corner by the meeting-house, he looked back and saw the head of Faith still peeping after him with a melancholy air, in spite of her pink ribbons.

"Poor little Faith!" thought he, for his heart smote him. "What a wretch am I to leave her on such an errand! She talks of dreams, too. Methought as she spoke there was trouble in her face, as if a dream had warned her what work is to be done tonight. But no, no; 't would kill her to think it. Well, she's a blessed angel on earth; and after this one night I'll cling to her skirts and follow her to heaven."
30   With this excellent resolve for the future, Goodman Brown felt himself justified in making more haste on his present evil purpose. He had taken a dreary road, darkened by all the gloomiest trees of the forest, which barely stood aside to let the narrow path creep through, and closed immediately behind. It was all as lonely as could be; and there is this peculiarity in such solitude, that the traveller knows not who may be concealed by the innumerable trunks and the thick boughs overhead; so that with lonely footsteps he may yet be passing through an unseen multitude.

"There may be a devilish Indian behind every tree," said Goodman
40 Brown to himself; and he glanced fearfully behind him as he added, "What if the devil himself should be at my very elbow!"

His head turned back, he passed a crook of the road, and, looking forward again, beheld the figure of a man, in grave and decent attire, seated at the foot of an old tree. He arose at Goodman Brown's approach and walked onward side by side with him.

"You are late, Goodman Brown," said he. "The clock of the Old South was striking as I came through Boston, and that is full fifteen minutes agone."

"Faith kept me back a while," replied the young man, with a tremor
50 in his voice, caused by the sudden appearance of his companion, though
not wholly unexpected.

It was now deep dusk in the forest, and deepest in that part of it
where these two were journeying. As nearly as could be discerned, the
second traveller was about fifty years old, apparently in the same rank
of life as Goodman Brown, and bearing a considerable resemblance to
him, though perhaps more in expression than features. Still they might
have been taken for father and son. And yet, though the elder person
was as simply clad as the younger, and as simple in manner too, he had
an indescribable air of one who knew the world, and who would not
60 have felt abashed at the governor's dinner table or in King William's
court, were it possible that his affairs should call him thither. But the
only thing about him that could be fixed upon as remarkable was his
staff, which bore the likeness of a great black snake, so curiously
wrought that it might almost be seen to twist and wriggle itself like a
living serpent. This, of course, must have been an ocular deception, assisted by the uncertain light.

"Come, Goodman Brown," cried his fellow-traveller, "this is a dull
pace for the beginning of a journey. Take my staff, if you are so soon
weary."
70   "Friend," said the other, exchanging his slow pace for a full stop,
"having kept covenant by meeting thee here, it is my purpose now to return whence I came. I have scruples touching the matter thou wot'st of."

"Sayest thou so?" replied he of the serpent, smiling apart. "Let us walk
on, nevertheless, reasoning as we go; and if I convince thee not thou shalt
turn back. We are but a little way in the forest yet."

"Too far! too far!" exclaimed the goodman, unconsciously resuming
his walk. "My father never went into the woods on such an errand, nor
his father before him. We have been a race of honest men and good
Christians since the days of the martyrs; and shall I be the first of the
80 name of Brown that ever took this path and kept—"

"Such company, thou wouldst say," observed the elder person, interpreting his pause. "Well said, Goodman Brown! I have been as well acquainted with your family as with ever a one among the Puritans; and
that's no trifle to say. I helped your grandfather, the constable, when he
lashed the Quaker woman so smartly through the streets of Salem; and
it was I that brought your father a pitch-pine knot, kindled at my own
hearth, to set fire to an Indian village, in King Philip's war. They were
my good friends, both; and many a pleasant walk have we had along
this path, returned merrily after midnight. I would fain be friends with
90 you for their sake."

"If it be as thou sayest," replied Goodman Brown, "I marvel they
never spoke of these matters; or, verily, I marvel not, seeing that the least
rumor of the sort would have driven them from New England. We are a
people of prayer, and good works to boot, and abide no such wickedness."

"Wickedness or not," said the traveller with the twisted staff, "I have a very general acquaintance here in New England. The deacons of many a church have drunk the communion wine with me; the selectmen of divers towns make me their chairman; and a majority of the Great and General Court are firm supporters of my interest. The governor and
100 I, too—But these are state secrets."

"Can this be so?" cried Goodman Brown, with a stare of amazement at his undisturbed companion. "Howbeit, I have nothing to do with the governor and council; they have their own ways, and are no rule for a simple husbandman like me. But, were I to go on with thee, how should I meet the eye of that good old man, our minister, at Salem village? Oh, his voice would make me tremble both Sabbath day and lecture day."

Thus far the elder traveller had listened with due gravity; but now burst into a fit of irrepressible mirth, shaking himself so violently that his snakelike staff actually seemed to wriggle in sympathy.
110   "Ha! ha! ha!" shouted he again and again; then composing himself, "Well, go on, Goodman Brown, go on; but, prithee, don't kill me with laughing."

"Well, then, to end the matter at once," said Goodman Brown, considerably nettled, "there is my wife, Faith. It would break her dear little heart; and I'd rather break my own."

"Nay, if that be the case," answered the other, "e'en go thy ways, Goodman Brown. I would not for twenty old women like the one hobbling before us that Faith should come to any harm."

As he spoke he pointed his staff at a female figure on the path, in
120 whom Goodman Brown recognized a very pious and exemplary dame, who had taught him his catechism in youth, and was still his moral and spiritual adviser, jointly with the minister and Deacon Gookin.

"A marvel, truly, that Goody Cloyse should be so far in the wilderness at nightfall," said he. "But with your leave, friend, I shall take a cut through the woods until we have left this Christian woman behind. Being a stranger to you, she might ask whom I was consorting with and whither I was going."

"Be it so," said his fellow-traveller. "Betake you to the woods, and let me keep the path."
130   Accordingly the young man turned aside, but took care to watch his companion, who advanced softly along the road until he had come within a staff's length of the old dame. She, meanwhile, was making the best of her way, with singular speed for so aged a woman, and mumbling some indistinct words—a prayer, doubtless—as she went. The traveller put forth his staff and touched her withered neck with what seemed the serpent's tail.

"The devil!" screamed the pious old lady.

"Then Goody Cloyse knows her old friend?" observed the traveller, confronting her and leaning on his writhing stick.
140   "Ah, forsooth, and is it your worship indeed?" cried the good dame. "Yea, truly is it, and in the very image of my old gossip, Goodman Brown,

the grandfather of the silly fellow that now is. But—would your worship believe it?—my broomstick hath strangely disappeared, stolen, as I suspect, by that unhanged witch, Goody Cory, and that, too, when I was all anointed with the juice of smallage, and cinquefoil, and wolf's bane—"

"Mingled with fine wheat and the fat of a new-born babe," said the shape of old Goodman Brown.

"Ah, your worship knows the recipe," cried the old lady, cackling aloud. "So, as I was saying, being all ready for the meeting, and no horse
150 to ride on, I made up my mind to foot it; for they tell me there is a nice young man to be taken into communion tonight. But now your good worship will lend me your arm, and we shall be there in a twinkling."

"That can hardly be," answered her friend. "I may not spare you my arm, Goody Cloyse; but here is my staff, if you will."

So saying, he threw it down at her feet, where, perhaps, it assumed life, being one of the rods which its owner had formerly lent to the Egyptian magi. Of this fact, however, Goodman Brown could not take cognizance. He had cast up his eyes in astonishment, and, looking down again, beheld neither Goody Cloyse nor the serpentine staff, but his fellow
160 traveller alone, who waited for him as calmly as if nothing had happened.

"That old woman taught me my catechism," said the young man; and there was a world of meaning in this simple comment.

They continued to walk onward, while the elder traveller exhorted his companion to make good speed and persevere in the path, discoursing so aptly that his arguments seemed rather to spring up in the bosom of his auditor than to be suggested by himself. As they went, he plucked a branch of maple to serve for a walking stick, and began to strip it of the twigs and little boughs, which were wet with evening dew. The moment his fingers touched them they became strangely withered and
170 dried up as with a week's sunshine. Thus the pair proceeded, at a good free pace, until suddenly, in a gloomy hollow of the road, Goodman Brown sat himself down on the stump of a tree and refused to go any farther.

"Friend," said he, stubbornly, "my mind is made up. Not another step will I budge on this errand. What if a wretched old woman do choose to go to the devil when I thought she was going to heaven: is that any reason why I should quit my dear Faith and go after her?"

"You will think better of this by and by," said his acquaintance, composedly. "Sit here and rest yourself a while; and when you feel like
180 moving again, there is my staff to help you along."

Without more words, he threw his companion the maple stick, and was as speedily out of sight as if he had vanished into the deepening gloom. The young man sat a few moments by the roadside, applauding himself greatly, and thinking with how clear a conscience he should meet the minister in his morning walk, nor shrink from the eye of good old Deacon Gookin. And what calm sleep would be his that very night, which was to have been spent so wickedly, but so purely and sweetly now, in the arms of Faith! Amidst these pleasant and praiseworthy

meditations, Goodman Brown heard the tramp of horses along the road,
190 and deemed it advisable to conceal himself within the verge of the
forest, conscious of the guilty purpose that had brought him thither,
though now so happily turned from it.

On came the hoof tramps and the voices of the riders, two grave old
voices, conversing soberly as they drew near. These mingled sounds appeared to pass along the road, within a few yards of the young man's
hiding-place; but, owing doubtless to the depth of the gloom at that particular spot, neither the travellers nor their steeds were visible. Though
their figures brushed the small boughs by the wayside, it could not be
seen that they intercepted, even for a moment, the faint gleam from
200 the strip of bright sky athwart which they must have passed. Goodman
Brown alternately crouched and stood on tiptoe, pulling aside the
branches and thrusting forth his head as far as he durst without dis-
cerning so much as a shadow. It vexed him the more, because he could
have sworn, were such a thing possible, that he recognized the voices of
the minister and Deacon Gookin, jogging along quietly, as they were
wont to do, when bound to some ordination or ecclesiastical council.
While yet within hearing, one of the riders stopped to pluck a switch.

"Of the two, reverend sir," said the voice like the deacon's, "I had
rather miss an ordination dinner than to-night's meeting. They tell me
210 that some of our community are to be here from Falmouth and beyond,
and others from Connecticut and Rhode Island, besides several of the
Indian powwows, who, after their fashion, know almost as much deviltry as the best of us. Moreover, there is a goodly young woman to be
taken into communion."

"Mighty well, Deacon Gookin!" replied the solemn old tones of the
minister. "Spur up, or we shall be late. Nothing can be done, you know,
until I get on the ground."

The hoofs clattered again; and the voices, talking so strangely in the
empty air, passed on through the forest, where no church had ever been
220 gathered or solitary Christian prayed. Whither, then, could these holy
men be journeying so deep into the heathen wilderness? Young Goodman Brown caught hold of a tree for support, being ready to sink down
on the ground, faint and overburdened with the heavy sickness of his
heart. He looked up to the sky, doubting whether there really was a
heaven above him. Yet there was the blue arch, and the stars brightening
in it.

"With heaven above and Faith below, I will yet stand firm against
the devil!" cried Goodman Brown.

While he still gazed upward into the deep arch of the firmament and
230 had lifted his hands to pray, a cloud, though no wind was stirring, hurried across the zenith and hid the brightening stars. The blue sky was
still visible, except directly overhead, where this black mass of cloud was
sweeping swiftly northward. Aloft in the air, as if from the depths of the
cloud, came a confused and doubtful sound of voices. Once the listener
fancied that he could distinguish the accents of towns-people of his own,

men and women, both pious and ungodly, many of whom he had met at
the communion table, and had seen others rioting at the tavern. The next
moment, so indistinct were the sounds, he doubted whether he had heard
aught but the murmur of the old forest, whispering without a wind. Then
240 came a stronger swell of those familiar tones, heard daily in the sunshine
at Salem village, but never until now from a cloud of night. There was one
voice of a young woman, uttering lamentations, yet with an uncertain
sorrow, and entreating for some favor, which, perhaps, it would grieve her
to obtain; and all the unseen multitude, both saints and sinners, seemed
to encourage her onward.

"Faith!" shouted Goodman Brown, in a voice of agony and desperation; and the echoes of the forest mocked him, crying, "Faith! Faith!" as
if bewildered wretches were seeking her all through the wilderness.

The cry of grief, rage, and terror was yet piercing the night, when the
250 unhappy husband held his breath for a response. There was a scream,
drowned immediately in a louder murmur of voices, fading into far-off
laughter, as the dark cloud swept away, leaving the clear and silent sky
above Goodman Brown. But something fluttered lightly down through
the air and caught on the branch of a tree. The young man seized it, and
beheld a pink ribbon.

"My Faith is gone!" cried he, after one stupefied moment. "There is
no good on earth; and sin is but a name. Come, devil; for to thee is this
world given."

And, maddened with despair, so that he laughed loud and long, did
260 Goodman Brown grasp his staff and set forth again, at such a rate that
he seemed to fly along the forest path rather than to walk or run. The
road grew wilder and drearier and more faintly traced, and vanished at
length, leaving him in the heart of the dark wilderness, still rushing onward with the instinct that guides mortal men to evil. The whole forest
was peopled with frightful sounds—the creaking of the trees, the howling of wild beasts, and the yell of Indians; while sometimes the wind
tolled like a distant church bell, and sometimes gave a broad roar
around the traveller, as if all Nature were laughing him to scorn. But he
was himself the chief horror of the scene, and shrank not from its other
270 horrors.

"Ha! ha! ha!" roared Goodman Brown when the wind laughed at him.
"Let us hear which will laugh loudest. Think not to frighten me with
your deviltry. Come witch, come wizard, come Indian powwow, come
devil himself, and here comes Goodman Brown. You may as well fear him
as he fear you."

In truth, all through the haunted forest there could be nothing more
frightful than the figure of Goodman Brown. On he flew among the
black pines, brandishing his staff with frenzied gestures, now giving
vent to an inspiration of horrid blasphemy, and now shouting forth such
280 laughter as set all the echoes of the forest laughing like demons around
him. The fiend in his own shape is less hideous than when he rages in
the breast of man. Thus sped the demoniac on his course, until, quivering

among the trees, he saw a red light before him, as when the felled trunks and branches of a clearing have been set on fire, and throw up their lurid blaze against the sky, at the hour of midnight. He paused, in a lull of the tempest that had driven him onward, and heard the swell of what seemed a hymn, rolling solemnly from a distance with the weight of many voices. He knew the tune; it was a familiar one in the choir of the village meeting-house. The verse died heavily away, and was length-
290 ened by a chorus, not of human voices, but of all the sounds of the be-nighted wilderness pealing in awful harmony together. Goodman Brown cried out, and his cry was lost to his own ear by its unison with the cry of the desert.

In the interval of silence he stole forward until the light glared full upon his eyes. At one extremity of an open space, hemmed in by the dark wall of the forest, arose a rock, bearing some rude, natural resemblance either to an altar or a pulpit, and surrounded by four blazing pines, their tops aflame, their stems untouched, like candles at an evening meeting. The mass of foliage that had overgrown the summit of the rock was all on
300 fire, blazing high into the night and fitfully illuminating the whole field. Each pendent twig and leafy festoon was in a blaze. As the red light arose and fell, a numerous congregation alternately shone forth, then disap-peared in shadow, and again grew, as it were, out of the darkness, peo-pling the heart of the solitary woods at once.

"A grave and dark-clad company," quoth Goodman Brown.

In truth they were such. Among them, quivering to and fro between gloom and splendor, appeared faces that would be seen next day at the council board of the province, and others which, Sabbath after Sabbath, looked devoutly heavenward, and benignantly over the crowded pews,
310 from the holiest pulpits in the land. Some affirm that the lady of the gov-ernor was there. At least there were high dames well known to her, and wives of honored husbands, and widows, a great multitude, and ancient maidens, all of excellent repute, and fair young girls, who trembled lest their mothers should espy them. Either the sudden gleams of light flash-ing over the obscure field bedazzled Goodman Brown, or he recognized a score of the church members of Salem village famous for their especial sanctity. Good old Deacon Gookin had arrived, and waited at the skirts of that venerable saint, his revered pastor. But, irreverently consorting with these grave, reputable, and pious people, these elders of the church, these
320 chaste dames and dewy virgins, there were men of dissolute lives and women of spotted fame, wretches given over to all mean and filthy vice, and suspected even of horrid crimes. It was strange to see that the good shrank not from the wicked, nor were the sinners abashed by the saints. Scattered also among their pale-faced enemies were the Indian priests, or powwows, who had often scared their native forest with more hideous in-cantations than any known to English witchcraft.

"But where is Faith?" thought Goodman Brown; and, as hope came into his heart, he trembled.

Another verse of the hymn arose, a slow and mournful strain, such
330 as the pious love, but joined to words which expressed all that our nature can conceive of sin, and darkly hinted at far more. Unfathomable to
mere mortals is the lore of fiends. Verse after verse was sung; and still
the chorus of the desert swelled between like the deepest tone of a
mighty organ; and with the final peal of that dreadful anthem there
came a sound, as if the roaring wind, the rushing streams, the howling
beasts, and every other voice of the unconcerted wilderness were mingling and according with the voice of guilty man in homage to the
prince of all. The four blazing pines threw up a loftier flame, and obscurely discovered shapes and visages of horror on the smoke wreaths
340 above the impious assembly. At the same moment the fire on the rock
shot redly forth and formed a glowing arch above its base, where now
appeared a figure. With reverence be it spoken, the figure bore no slight
similitude, both in garb and manner, to some grave divine of the New
England churches.

"Bring forth the converts!" cried a voice that echoed through the
field and rolled into the forest.

At the word, Goodman Brown stepped forth from the shadow of the
trees and approached the congregation, with whom he felt a loathful
brotherhood by the sympathy of all that was wicked in his heart. He could
350 have well-nigh sworn that the shape of his own dead father beckoned him
to advance, looking downward from a smoke wreath, while a woman, with
dim features of despair, threw out her hand to warn him back. Was it his
mother? But he had no power to retreat one step, nor to resist, even in
thought, when the minister and good old Deacon Gookin seized his arms
and led him to the blazing rock. Thither came also the slender form of a
veiled female, led between Goody Cloyse, that pious teacher of the catechism, and Martha Carrier, who had received the devil's promise to be
queen of hell. A rampant hag was she. And there stood the proselytes beneath the canopy of fire.

360 "Welcome, my children," said the dark figure, "to the communion
of your race. Ye have found thus young your nature and your destiny.
My children, look behind you!"

They turned; and flashing forth, as it were, in a sheet of flame, the
fiend worshippers were seen; the smile of welcome gleamed darkly on
every visage.

"There," resumed the sable form, "are all whom ye have reverenced
from youth. Ye deemed them holier than yourselves, and shrank from
your own sin, contrasting it with their lives of righteousness and prayerful aspirations heavenward. Yet here are they all in my worshipping as-
370 sembly. This night it shall be granted you to know their secret deeds;
how hoary-bearded elders of the church have whispered wanton words
to the young maids of their households; how many a woman, eager for
widows' weeds, has given her husband a drink at bedtime and let him
sleep his last sleep in her bosom; how beardless youths have made haste

to inherit their fathers' wealth; and how fair damsels—blush not, sweet ones—have dug little graves in the garden, and bidden me, the sole guest, to an infant's funeral. By the sympathy of your human hearts for sin ye shall scent out all the places—whether in church, bedchamber, street, field, or forest—where crime has been committed, and shall exult
380 to behold the whole earth one stain of guilt, one mighty blood spot. Far more than this. It shall be yours to penetrate, in every bosom, the deep mystery of sin, the fountain of all wicked arts, and which inexhaustibly supplies more evil impulses than human power—than my power at its utmost—can make manifest in deeds. And now, my children, look upon each other."

They did so; and, by the blaze of the hell-kindled torches, the wretched man beheld his Faith, and the wife her husband, trembling before that unhallowed altar.

"Lo, there ye stand, my children," said the figure, in a deep and
390 solemn tone, almost sad with its despairing awfulness, as if his once angelic nature could yet mourn for our miserable race. "Depending upon one another's hearts, ye had still hoped that virtue were not all a dream. Now are ye undeceived. Evil is the nature of mankind. Evil must be your only happiness. Welcome again, my children, to the communion of your race."

"Welcome," repeated the fiend worshippers, in one cry of despair and triumph.

And there they stood, the only pair, as it seemed, who were yet hesitating on the verge of wickedness in this dark world. A basin was hol-
400 lowed, naturally, in the rock. Did it contain water, reddened by the lurid light? or was it blood? or, perchance, a liquid flame? Herein did the shape of evil dip his hand and prepare to lay the mark of baptism upon their foreheads, that they might be partakers of the mystery of sin, more conscious of the secret guilt of others, both in deed and thought, than they could now be of their own. The husband cast one look at his pale wife, and Faith at him. What polluted wretches would the next glance show them to each other, shuddering alike at what they disclosed and what they saw!

"Faith! Faith!" cried the husband, "look up to heaven, and resist the
410 wicked one."

Whether Faith obeyed he knew not. Hardly had he spoken when he found himself amid calm night and solitude, listening to a roar of the wind which died heavily away through the forest. He staggered against the rock, and felt it chill and damp; while a hanging twig, that had been all on fire, besprinkled his cheek with the coldest dew.

The next morning young Goodman Brown came slowly into the street of Salem village, staring around him like a bewildered man. The good old minister was taking a walk along the graveyard to get an appetite for breakfast and meditate his sermon, and bestowed a blessing,
420 as he passed, on Goodman Brown. He shrank from the venerable saint as if to avoid an anathema. Old Deacon Gookin was at domestic worship,

and the holy words of his prayer were heard through the open window. "What God doth the wizard pray to?" quoth Goodman Brown. Goody Cloyse, that excellent old Christian, stood in the early sunshine at her own lattice catechizing a little girl who had brought her a pint of morning's milk. Goodman Brown snatched away the child as from the grasp of the fiend himself. Turning the corner by the meeting-house, he spied the head of Faith, with the pink ribbons, gazing anxiously forth, and bursting into such joy at sight of him that she skipped along the
430 street and almost kissed her husband before the whole village. But Goodman Brown looked sternly and sadly into her face, and passed on without a greeting.

Had Goodman Brown fallen asleep in the forest and only dreamed a wild dream of a witch-meeting?

Be it so if you will; but, alas! it was a dream of evil omen for young Goodman Brown. A stern, a sad, a darkly meditative, a distrustful, if not a desperate man did he become from the night of that fearful dream. On the Sabbath day, when the congregation were singing a holy psalm, he could not listen because an anthem of sin rushed loudly upon his ear
440 and drowned all the blessed strain. When the minister spoke from the pulpit with power and fervid eloquence, and, with his hand on the open Bible, of the sacred truths of our religion, and of saint-like lives and triumphant deaths, and of future bliss or misery unutterable, then did Goodman Brown turn pale, dreading lest the roof should thunder down upon the gray blasphemer and his hearers. Often, waking suddenly at midnight, he shrank from the bosom of Faith; and at morning or eventide, when the family knelt down at prayer, he scowled and muttered to himself, and gazed sternly at his wife, and turned away. And when he had lived long, and was borne to his grave a hoary corpse, followed by
450 Faith, an aged woman, and children and grandchildren, a goodly procession, besides neighbors not a few, they carved no hopeful verse upon his tombstone, for his dying hour was gloom.

ACCOUNT: FREDERICK CREWS ON ESCAPISM IN "YOUNG GOODMAN BROWN"

In the first chapter of *The Sins of the Fathers: Hawthorne's Psychological Themes*, the book from which this essay comes, Crews speaks of what he believes to be errors of understanding on the part of both Hawthorne's biographers and his critics. Thus, his interpretation of "Young Goodman Brown" attempts to shed light on Hawthorne's biography and on the work itself. His account is aimed both at understanding the psychological roots

---

From Chapter VI of *The Sins of the Fathers: Hawthorne's Psychological Themes* (Oxford University Press: New York, 1966).

of Hawthorne's own ambiguity and at bringing to the surface the latent meaning of the apparently ambiguous story.

Crews begins his analysis by admitting that Hawthorne's plots are notoriously ambiguous. But is this ambiguity a matter of Hawthorne's acting on the reader with double explanations and omitted information? Or does it come from real uncertainties of attitude on Hawthorne's own part? Above all, how are we to understand the moral purport of his work in conjunction with its ambiguity?

Young Goodman Brown is an example of a character type in Hawthorne, a type who embodies the whole problem of moral ambiguity:

> This is the idealist who has determined to learn or do something that will set him apart from the mass of ignorant men. Moral interpretations of Hawthorne's purpose invariably turn upon analysis of this figure, for he always seems to teach a lesson. Since he usually comes to a sorry end, and is sometimes explicitly criticized for his pride and isolation, he is most often interpreted as a cautionary example; in his death or madness or chagrin we are meant to see that the bonds of common humanity are not to be severed. Yet Hawthorne sometimes lends encouragement to an exactly contrary reading.

Crews finds the contradiction to be based in Hawthorne's own mixed feelings. As a writer, the basis of his professional activity was the exploration of morbid natures, yet as a man he aspired to normal happiness. The result of the personal and professional conflict is a sense of reality that can be called "neurotic": the idealist character becomes obsessed with ideas like Hawthorne's own, but for that reason he has a claim on Hawthorne's sympathy.

First of all, Crews says, the idealist is always an "escapist" who seeks to avoid the challenges of normal adult life:

> As Richard P. Adams says of the early Hawthornian hero, 'incest, parricide, and fear of castration' stalk him wherever he chooses to flee. And yet all Hawthorne's irony of characterization cannot prevent him from secretly agreeing with what his escapists discover about the 'foul cavern' of the human heart. His plots enact a return of the repressed, and the repressed is the truth. Neurotic terror, for Hawthorne, underlies every placid mental surface, but it reaches consciousness and corrodes sanity only when summoned forth by intolerable conflicts.

Thus, Young Goodman Brown undergoes a dreamlike (or dreamed) experience that turns him into "a sad, a darkly meditative, a distrustful, if not a desperate man."

If the main character loses his "faith" in mankind or religious salvation, he does so by fleeing a normal, loving wife named "Faith." The very arbitrariness and absoluteness of his decision to leave her makes us question its psychological motivation, and Young Goodman Brown is seen to meet the embodiments of his own thoughts in the forest. The haunted forest frightens him, "but he himself was the chief horror of the scene" and "he felt a loathful brotherhood by the sympathy of all that was wicked in his heart."

What the Devil offers Young Goodman Brown is far from ambiguous. All the people of the village assembled are secret sinners:

> Knowledge of sin, then, and most often of sexual sin is the prize for which Goodman Brown seems tempted to barter his soul. In this version of the Faustian pact, the offered power is unrelated to any practical influence in the world; what Brown aspires to, if we can take this bargain as emanating from his own wishes, is an acme of voyeurism, a prurience so effective in its ferreting for scandal that it can uncover wicked thoughts before they have been enacted.

> Thus Goodman Brown, a curiously preoccupied bridegroom, escapes from his wife's embraces to a vision of general nastiness. The accusation that Brown's Devil makes against all mankind, and then more pointedly against Faith, clearly issues from Brown's own horror of adulthood, his inability to accept the place of sexuality in married love. Brown remains the little boy who has heard rumors about the polluted pleasures of adults, and who wants to learn more about them despite or because of the fact that he finds them disgusting. His forest journey, in fact, amounts to a vicarious and lurid sexual adventure.

The Oedipal theme is further implied in other ways, since the Devil who proposes the carnal initiation happens to look exactly like Brown's grandfather and he and Brown "might have been taken for father and son." The whole experience in fact follows the classical Oedipal pattern with a combination of ambiguous sexual temptation and a resentment of parental authority. Women are generally suspect and all the reputable women of Brown's society turn out to be sinners in his forest. His mother is conspicuously absent, but his wife does turn up—only to disappear at the key moment, as if Brown finally could not stand facing his suspicions about her:

> The general pattern of "Young Goodman Brown" is that fathers are degraded to devils and mothers to witches (both attributions, of course, are confirmed in psychoanalysis). Yet the outcome of that pattern, as is always true in Hawthorne's plots, is not simple degradation but a perpetuated ambivalence. Brown lives out a long life with Faith and has children by her, but entertains continual suspicions about her virtue. In retrospect we can say that the source of his uncertainty has been discernible from the beginning—namely, his insistence upon seeing Faith more as an idealized mother than as a wife.

Whether the forest experience was "dreamed" or "real," it has served Young Goodman Brown's need to make lurid sexual complaints against mankind as a whole. The sure point is that *he* has become different and his case if no other proves depravity secretly exists in people. In looking into his own mind (Crews says) Hawthorne may have found other convincing reasons to confirm the conclusion.

SUGGESTIONS FOR DISCUSSION AND WRITING

1. Crews argues that the ambiguity of the story has its basis in Hawthorne the author. But how is that ambiguity created by Hawthorne through the **narrator** in the story? Pick an instance that seems representative of that narrator's manner. In what ways is it ambiguous in **tone**? Are we to assume **irony** in that tone, for example? How does the meaning of what is told change if we do? Does the narrator sound knowing or naive? Describe his manner as fully as you can.

2. Locate what you think Crews would find to be an ambiguity of **plot** in the story. Is it possible that Young Goodman Brown dreamed the events? Where does the dream begin? How can you tell? What effect does the narrator's dismissal of the issue have?

3. What might another psychoanalytic critic find interesting about Hawthorne's *setting*? Nighttime can produce ambiguous visual impressions. Make a list of the **images** that, like the general **setting** of nighttime, contribute to the ambiguity of the story in some way.

4. Using Crews' approach as a model, compare this story to Melville's "Bartleby the Scrivener" with regard to the ambiguity of the **protagonist** in each case. In what similar and different ways do Hawthorne and Melville dramatize the issue?

5. Given your own sense of Hawthorne's psychology as dramatized in the story, write an essay in which you either describe with supporting evidence what really happened to Young Goodman Brown or show with supporting evidence how it is impossible for a reader to tell "what really happened."

6. What does the psychoanalytic approach illuminate for you about any episode in "Bartleby the Scrivener?" Make some notes for discussion or as the basis for an essay on the psychoanalytic implications of the story. For example, does the narrator appear in any way as a father figure?

Chapter Four

Rhetoric and Reader-Response Criticism: Reading as Reaction

A BRIEF INTRODUCTION TO RHETORIC AND READER-RESPONSE CRITICISM

As its name implies, the focus of reader-response criticism is on the audience of literature. Its emphasis thereby differs both from the New Criticism's focus on the text in the twentieth century and from Romantic criticism's focus on the author as a supreme, god-like creator in the nineteenth century. Yet, attending to the role of the audience is far from a modern idea, and, in fact, for most of literary history, the audience was the major focus of systematic inquiry into the effects of language.

Rhetoric is the name of the oldest formal study of how linguistic techniques may move the hearts and minds of an audience. The study began in the West in ancient Greece and Rome, where the effective use of language made such an important element of political power through public debate that it was naturally given great educational attention. However, in modern times, an association in the popular mind of the word "rhetoric" with an *overemphasis* of technique at the expense of content has given the word the implication of "empty talk" in common speech. This negative implication was not at all the meaning rhetoric held for antiquity, and neither is it the implication of the term for contemporary criticism.

Modern rhetorical and reader-response criticism takes seriously the relation between the text and the reader but with varying emphases. Some critics focus on the way literary works control the reading of the audience; some examine the influence of what readers bring to a text; and some emphasize the relationship between the reader and the text. That is, some look most closely at the text, some at the reader, and some at the dynamics between the two.

Twentieth-century students of rhetoric like Kenneth Burke and Wayne C. Booth have attempted to explain what is communicated to the reader and how that reader is invited to receive communication in the way the author intended. These rhetoricians look at the strategies used in literary works to guide the reader's understanding and response. For example, Booth, in the *Rhetoric of Fiction,* has such section titles as "Molding Beliefs," "Heightening the Significance of Events," and "Manipulating Mood," titles which indicate his interest in the way authors and works attempt to shape their readers' reactions. How, for instance, can an author influence readers to sympathize with a character whose actions, at times, are disagreeable and offensive? In an examination of the novel *Emma,* Booth suggests that Jane Austen solves this problem by taking an "inside view." She so narrates the novel that readers see Emma's feelings and thoughts as well as her actions. If the story were narrated in a more objective fashion, with only the actions of the character being shown, readers would probably be less sympathetic. Thus, the decision about how to narrate the novel becomes a strategy designed to control the reader's understanding of the text.

Of course, as rhetorical critics are well aware, techniques and strategies do not exist in a vacuum but must take the reader into account. When (to use a crude example) an author of children's books needs pathos, something like an injured or abused animal may be introduced to produce the desired effect of distress on the reader. But such techniques are not automatically productive of the emotion intended and more sophisticated audiences may be moved to quite different feelings by an obvious contrivance of literary technique. A reader may in fact be moved to scorn for the crudity of the technique itself, as when Oscar Wilde said of a famous Dickensian scene, "That man must have a heart of stone who does not laugh at the death of Little Nell!"

Recognizing the significant role of the reader, recent critics have begun looking closely at how the background or makeup of individual readers affects their understanding of meaning in literary works. In the previous example, readers who share with Wilde a background of relatively wide reading and a knowledge of the means by which writers can manipulate readers may also share his disdain for Dickens' deathbed scene. However, other readers may be moved to the feelings apparently intended by Dickens. That different people may respond in opposite ways to the same passage or that varying interpretations may be proposed for a single text might seem to suggest complete relativism, a belief that each person has her or his own meaning regardless of the text.

In fact, however, there is frequently remarkable agreement about texts; and, when there is not, reader-response critics can often point to elements in a reader's background to explain the discrepancies. Stanley Fish accounts for both agreement and disagreement by the concept of "Interpretive Communities" whose values and assumptions are shared by its members. One interpretive community might be composed of those trained in literature in American colleges and universities. Such persons would share many broad assumptions and probably a number of more specific ones. They would, at the very least, know enough about the conventions of fiction not to look in obituaries for news of Little

Nell's passing, a seemingly obvious recognition until we think of death threats to soap opera villains, presumably from those who do not distinguish between fiction and nonfiction. Elizabeth A. Flynn notes another interpretive community in her study of the ways students read "Araby." Flynn finds primarily that gender seems to influence to a great degree what a given reader focuses on and how that reader interprets his or her focus. Thus, assumptions shared within genders are important to the forming of an interpretive community.

Reader-response critics recognize that both the individual psychological makeup of the reader and the reader's social background influence her or his response to a text. For instance, Norman Holland combines a knowledge of psychology and an interest in reader-response to suggest that individuals read according to their own identities, identities composed of everything from the person's understanding of literary conventions to his or her own fantasies and needs. A person with deep feelings of inadequacy may understand a literary passage very differently from the way it is understood by a confident and assured individual. Or a person's own experiences of youthful love and infatuation may influence the individual's interpretation of "Araby." Similarly, the reader's social and class background may be significant. Marxist critics, for instance, look at the economic makeup of an audience to understand what it likes and dislikes and therefore what determines its "canonical" list of texts— the group of books regarded as important and worthy of reading by a given group.

The distinction between those who look particularly at how texts govern readers and those who examine ways in which readers construe texts recognizes a difference of emphasis, but all critics noted in this chapter are aware of the interplay between the reader and the literary work. In fact, the word *transaction*, stressing the dynamic interplay between reader and text, is used both by Holland and by Louise Rosenblatt, one of the earliest of reader-response critics. However, an important approach with special focus on the transaction between author and reader is the phenomenological approach of Roman Ingarden and Wolfgang Iser. This approach views reading as a dynamic between the reader *imagined* by an author and the author *imagined* by a reader. For instance, a writer wanting to demonstrate the worth of a particular character's action might show another character acting in a disagreeable way, thus using contrast to emphasize the first character's goodness. According to phenomenological criticism, the author would have to imagine a reader who could recognize that contrast was being purposely used. The reader would have to imagine an author who would use contrast in order to make a point. To take another example, if Joyce intends "Araby" to be satirical, he must imagine that good readers see through the self-image of his narrator, the man ashamed of his past. Yet that narrator seems to imagine a reader who shares his views of what is serious and what is foolish in life. The reader must imagine an author behind the narrative voice, an author using language in ways that satirize the speaking voice of the narrator. How does

Joyce create such subtle illusions and conflicts? And how are we to decide among the possibilities created?

As this brief survey indicates, reader-response criticism may refer to a range of critical enterprises. A good example of both variety and similarity in the ways readers respond to texts is shown by the critical account of Faulkner's "A Rose for Emily." Among readers of that story, the critic George L. Dillon has found what he calls three "styles" of reading. Dillon's Reader-Response approach is probably closest to that of Norman Holland, and, in fact, Dillon's essay uses as part of its evidence material from one of Holland's studies. Dillon does not investigate strategies used by Faulkner to guide the reader but focuses on how the personality and background of readers influence their reactions to the text. Because reading is usually such a private matter, the student may find Dillon's study of other students enlightening and his concrete examples may demonstrate why the study of audiences has recently attracted the interest of so many different critics.

WILLIAM FAULKNER (1897–1962) was born in New Albany, Mississippi, on September 25, 1897; as a young boy he moved to Oxford, Mississippi, where he would reside for most of his life. After only a brief flirtation with formal education (two years of high school), Faulkner decided to join the Army's Aviation Unit to serve in World War I. However, he was rejected because he was too short and enlisted instead in the Royal Canadian Air Force. The war ended before Faulkner received his commission, and he again attempted a formal education, this time at the University of Mississippi. Faulkner withdrew from the University after only one year and worked in a variety of places, including his grandfather's bank in Oxford, an arms plant in Connecticut, and a bookstore in New York City.

In 1925, Faulkner met Sherwood Anderson, author of *Winesburg, Ohio*, who encouraged him to begin his first novel, *Soldier's Pay*, which was published in 1926. Although *Soldier's Pay* received favorable reviews, it was not until 1929, with the publication of *The Sound and the Fury*, that Faulkner's literary reputation blossomed. He was awarded the Nobel Prize in Literature in 1949, and was also awarded two National Book Awards and two Pulitzer Prizes. It was only after he received these awards, however, that Faulkner's books began to sell in large quantities; to augment his income during their composition, Faulkner spent periods of time in Hollywood writing film scripts. His most famous novels include *As I Lay Dying* (1930), *Sanctuary* (1931), *Light in August* (1932), and *Absalom! Absalom!* (1936). Although known primarily as a novelist, Faulkner also penned almost a hundred short stories. He died in Byhalia on July 6, 1962.

WILLIAM FAULKNER

A Rose for Emily
(1930)

I

When Miss Emily Grierson died, our whole town went to her funeral: the men through a sort of respectful affection for a fallen monument, the women mostly out of curiosity to see the inside of her house, which no one save an old manservant—a combined gardener and cook—had seen in at least ten years.

It was a big, squarish frame house that had once been white, decorated with cupolas and spires and scrolled balconies in the heavily lightsome style of the seventies, set on what had once been our most select street. But garages and cotton gins had encroached and obliterated even
10 the august names of that neighborhood; only Miss Emily's house was left, lifting its stubborn and coquettish decay above the cotton wagons and the gasoline pumps—an eyesore among eyesores. And now Miss Emily had gone to join the representatives of those august names where they lay in the cedar-bemused cemetery among the ranked and anonymous graves of Union and Confederate soldiers who fell at the battle of Jefferson.

Alive, Miss Emily had been a tradition, a duty, and a care; a sort of hereditary obligation upon the town, dating from that day in 1894 when Colonel Sartoris, the mayor—he who fathered the edict that no Negro
20 woman should appear on the streets without an apron—remitted her taxes, the dispensation dating from the death of her father on into perpetuity. Not that Miss Emily would have accepted charity. Colonel Sartoris invented an involved tale to the effect that Miss Emily's father had loaned money to the town, which the town, as a matter of business, preferred this way of repaying. Only a man of Colonel Sartoris' generation and thought could have invented it, and only a woman could have believed it.

When the next generation, with its more modern ideas, became mayors and aldermen, this arrangement created some little dissatisfaction.
30 On the first of the year they mailed her a tax notice. February came, and there was no reply. They wrote her a formal letter, asking her to call at the sheriff's office at her convenience. A week later the mayor wrote her himself, offering to call or to send his car for her, and received in reply a note on paper of an archaic shape, in a thin, flowing calligraphy in faded ink, to the effect that she no longer went out at all. The tax notice was also enclosed, without comment.

They called a special meeting of the Board of Aldermen. A deputation waited upon her, knocked at the door through which no visitor had passed since she ceased giving china-painting lessons eight or ten years
40 earlier. They were admitted by the old Negro into a dim hall from which a stairway mounted into still more shadow. It smelled of dust and disuse—a close, dank smell. The Negro led them into the parlor. It was furnished in heavy, leather-covered furniture. When the Negro opened the blinds of one window, they could see that the leather was cracked; and when they sat down, a faint dust rose sluggishly about their thighs, spinning with slow motes in the single sun-ray. On a tarnished gilt easel before the fireplace stood a crayon portrait of Miss Emily's father.

They rose when she entered—a small, fat woman in black, with a thin gold chain descending to her waist and vanishing into her belt,
50 leaning on an ebony cane with a tarnished gold head. Her skeleton was small and spare; perhaps that was why what would have been merely plumpness in another was obesity in her. She looked bloated, like a body long submerged in motionless water, and of that pallid hue. Her eyes,

lost in the fatty ridges of her face, looked like two small pieces of coal pressed into a lump of dough as they moved from one face to another while the visitors stated their errand.

She did not ask them to sit. She just stood in the door and listened quietly until the spokesman came to a stumbling halt. Then they could hear the invisible watch ticking at the end of the gold chain.

60   Her voice was dry and cold. "I have no taxes in Jefferson. Colonel Sartoris explained it to me. Perhaps one of you can gain access to the city records and satisfy yourselves."

"But we have. We are the city authorities, Miss Emily. Didn't you get a notice from the sheriff, signed by him?"

"I received a paper, yes," Miss Emily said. "Perhaps he considers himself the sheriff . . . I have no taxes in Jefferson."

"But there is nothing on the books to show that, you see. We must go by the—"

"See Colonel Sartoris. I have no taxes in Jefferson."

70   "But, Miss Emily—"

"See Colonel Sartoris." (Colonel Sartoris had been dead almost ten years.) "I have no taxes in Jefferson. Tobe!" The Negro appeared. "Show these gentlemen out."

II

So she vanquished them, horse and foot, just as she had vanquished their fathers thirty years before about the smell. That was two years after her father's death and a short time after her sweetheart—the one we believed would marry her—had deserted her. After her father's death she went out very little; after her sweetheart went away, people hardly saw her at all. A few of the ladies had the temerity to call, but were not

80   received, and the only sign of life about the place was the Negro man—a young man then—going in and out with a market basket.

"Just as if a man—any man—could keep a kitchen properly," the ladies said; so they were not surprised when the smell developed. It was another link between the gross, teeming world and the high and mighty Griersons.

A neighbor, a woman, complained to the mayor, Judge Stevens, eighty years old.

"But what will you have me do about it, madam?" he said.

"Why, send her word to stop it," the woman said. "Isn't there a law?"

90   "I'm sure that won't be necessary," Judge Stevens said. "It's probably just a snake or a rat that nigger of hers killed in the yard. I'll speak to him about it."

The next day he received two more complaints, one from a man who came in diffident deprecation. "We really must do something about it, Judge. I'd be the last one in the world to bother Miss Emily, but we've got to do something." That night the Board of Aldermen met—three graybeards and one younger man, a member of the rising generation.

"It's simple enough," he said. "Send her word to have her place cleaned up. Give her a certain time to do it in, and if she don't . . ."

100 "Dammit, sir," Judge Stevens said, "will you accuse a lady to her face of smelling bad?"

So the next night, after midnight, four men crossed Miss Emily's lawn and slunk about the house like burglars, sniffing along the base of the brickwork and at the cellar openings while one of them performed a regular sowing motion with his hand out of a sack slung from his shoulder. They broke open the cellar door and sprinkled lime there, and in all the outbuildings. As they recrossed the lawn, a window that had been dark was lighted and Miss Emily sat in it, the light behind her, and her upright torso motionless as that of an idol. They crept quietly across the 110 lawn and into the shadow of the locusts that lined the street. After a week or two the smell went away.

That was when people had begun to feel really sorry for her. People in our town, remembering how old lady Wyatt, her great-aunt, had gone completely crazy at last, believed that the Griersons held themselves a little too high for what they really were. None of the young men were quite good enough for Miss Emily and such. We had long thought of them as a tableau, Miss Emily a slender figure in white in the background, her father a spraddled silhouette in the foreground, his back to her and clutching a horsewhip, the two of them framed by the back-flung front door. So 120 when she got to be thirty and was still single, we were not pleased exactly, but vindicated; even with insanity in the family she wouldn't have turned down all of her chances if they had really materialized.

When her father died, it got about that the house was all that was left to her; and in a way, people were glad. At last they could pity Miss Emily. Being left alone, and a pauper, she had become humanized. Now she too would know the old thrill and the old despair of a penny more or less.

The day after his death all the ladies prepared to call at the house and offer condolence and aid, as is our custom. Miss Emily met them at 130 the door, dressed as usual and with no trace of grief on her face. She told them that her father was not dead. She did that for three days, with the ministers calling on her, and the doctors, trying to persuade her to let them dispose of the body. Just as they were about to resort to law and force, she broke down, and they buried her father quickly.

We did not say she was crazy then. We believed she had to do that. We remembered all the young men her father had driven away, and we knew that with nothing left, she would have to cling to that which had robbed her, as people will.

III

She was sick for a long time. When we saw her again, her hair was 140 cut short, making her look like a girl, with a vague resemblance to those angels in colored church windows—sort of tragic and serene.

The town had just let the contracts for paving the sidewalks, and in the summer after her father's death they began the work. The construction company came with niggers and mules and machinery, and a foreman named Homer Barron, a Yankee—a big, dark, ready man, with a big voice and eyes lighter than his face. The little boys would follow in groups to hear him cuss the niggers, and the niggers singing in time to the rise and fall of picks. Pretty soon he knew everybody in town. Whenever you heard a lot of laughing anywhere about the square, Homer Barron would 150 be in the center of the group. Presently we began to see him and Miss Emily on Sunday afternoons driving in the yellow-wheeled buggy and the matched team of bays from the livery stable.

At first we were glad that Miss Emily would have an interest, because the ladies all said, "Of course a Grierson would not think seriously of a Northerner, a day laborer." But there were still others, older people, who said that even grief could not cause a real lady to forget *noblesse oblige*—without calling it *noblesse oblige.* They just said, "Poor Emily. Her kinsfolk should come to her." She had some kin in Alabama; but years ago her father had fallen out with them over the estate of old 160 lady Wyatt, the crazy woman, and there was no communication between the two families. They had not even been represented at the funeral.

And as soon as the old people said, "Poor Emily," the whispering began. "Do you suppose it's really so?" they said to one another. "Of course it is. What else could . . ." This behind their hands; rustling of craned silk and satin behind jalousies closed upon the sun of Sunday afternoon as the thin, swift clop-clop-clop of the matched team passed: "Poor Emily."

She carried her head high enough—even when we believed that she was fallen. It was as if she demanded more than ever the recognition of 170 her dignity as the last Grierson; as if it had wanted that touch of earthiness to reaffirm her imperviousness. Like when she bought the rat poison, the arsenic. That was over a year after they had begun to say "Poor Emily," and while the two female cousins were visiting her.

"I want some poison," she said to the druggist. She was over thirty then, still a slight woman, though thinner than usual, with cold, haughty black eyes in a face the flesh of which was strained across the temples and about the eyesockets as you imagine a lighthouse-keeper's face ought to look. "I want some poison," she said.

"Yes, Miss Emily. What kind? For rats and such? I'd recom—" 180   "I want the best you have. I don't care what kind."

The druggist named several. "They'll kill anything up to an elephant. But what you want is—"

"Arsenic," Miss Emily said. "Is that a good one?"

"Is . . . arsenic? Yes, ma'am. But what you want—"

"I want arsenic."

The druggist looked down at her. She looked back at him, erect, her face like a strained flag. "Why, of course," the druggist said. "If that's what you want. But the law requires you to tell what you are going to use it for."

190   Miss Emily just stared at him, her head tilted back in order to look him eye for eye, until he looked away and went and got the arsenic and wrapped it up. The Negro delivery boy brought her the package; the druggist didn't come back. When she opened the package at home there was written on the box, under the skull and bones: "For rats."

IV

    So the next day we all said, "She will kill herself"; and we said it would be the best thing. When she had first begun to be seen with Homer Barron, we had said, "She will marry him." Then we said, "She will persuade him yet," because Homer himself had remarked—he liked men, and it was known that he drank with the younger men in the Elks' Club
200 that he was not a marrying man. Later we said, "Poor Emily" behind the jalousies as they passed on Sunday afternoon in the glittering buggy, Miss Emily with her head high and Homer Barron with his hat cocked and a cigar in his teeth, reins and whip in a yellow glove.

    Then some of the ladies began to say that it was a disgrace to the town and a bad example to the young people. The men did not want to interfere, but at last the ladies forced the Baptist minister—Miss Emily's people were Episcopal—to call upon her. He would never divulge what happened during that interview, but he refused to go back again. The next Sunday they again drove about the streets, and the following day the min-
210 ister's wife wrote to Miss Emily's relations in Alabama.

    So she had blood-kin under her roof again and we sat back to watch developments. At first nothing happened. Then we were sure that they were to be married. We learned that Miss Emily had been to the jeweler's and ordered a man's toilet set in silver, with the letters H. B. on each piece. Two days later we learned that she had bought a complete outfit of men's clothing, including a nightshirt, and we said, "They are married." We were really glad. We were glad because the two female cousins were even more Grierson than Miss Emily had ever been.

    So we were not surprised when Homer Barron—the streets had been
220 finished some time since—was gone. We were a little disappointed that there was not a public blowing-off, but we believed that he had gone on to prepare for Miss Emily's coming, or to give her a chance to get rid of the cousins. (By that time it was a cabal, and we were all Miss Emily's allies to help circumvent the cousins.) Sure enough, after another week they departed. And, as we had expected all along, within three days Homer Barron was back in town. A neighbor saw the Negro man admit him at the kitchen door at dusk one evening.

    And that was the last we saw of Homer Barron. And of Miss Emily for some time. The Negro man went in and out with the market basket,
230 but the front door remained closed. Now and then we would see her at a window for a moment, as the men did that night when they sprinkled the lime, but for almost six months she did not appear on the streets. Then we knew that this was to be expected too; as if that quality of her

father which had thwarted her woman's life so many times had been too virulent and too furious to die.

When we next saw Miss Emily, she had grown fat and her hair was turning gray. During the next few years it grew grayer and grayer until it attained an even pepper-and-salt iron-gray, when it ceased turning. Up to the day of her death at seventy-four it was still that vigorous iron
240 gray, like the hair of an active man.

From that time on her front door remained closed, save for a period of six or seven years, when she was about forty, during which she gave lessons in china-painting. She fitted up a studio in one of the downstairs rooms, where the daughters and granddaughters of Colonel Sartoris' contemporaries were sent to her with the same regularity and in the same spirit that they were sent to church on Sundays with a twenty-five cent piece for the collection plate. Meanwhile her taxes had been remitted.

Then the newer generation became the backbone and the spirit of the town, and the painting pupils grew up and fell away and did not
250 send their children to her with boxes of color and tedious brushes and pictures cut from the ladies' magazines. The front door closed upon the last one and remained closed for good. When the town got free postal delivery, Miss Emily alone refused to let them fasten the metal numbers above her door and attach a mailbox to it. She would not listen to them.

Daily, monthly, yearly we watched the Negro grow grayer and more stooped, going in and out with the market basket. Each December we sent her a tax notice, which would be returned by the post office a week later, unclaimed. Now and then we would see her in one of the downstairs windows—she had evidently shut up the top floor of the house—like the car-
260 ven torso of an idol in a niche, looking or not looking at us, we could never tell which. Thus she passed from generation to generation—dear, inescapable, impervious, tranquil, and perverse.

And so she died. Fell ill in the house filled with dust and shadows, with only a doddering Negro man to wait on her. We did not even know she was sick; we had long since given up trying to get any information from the Negro. He talked to no one, probably not even to her, for his voice had grown harsh and rusty, as if from disuse.

She died in one of the downstairs rooms, in a heavy walnut bed with a curtain, her gray head propped on a pillow yellow and moldy with age
270 and lack of sunlight.

V

The Negro met the first of the ladies at the front door and let them in, with their hushed, sibilant voices and their quick, curious glances, and then he disappeared. He walked right through the house and out the back and was not seen again.

The two female cousins came at once. They held the funeral on the second day, with the town coming to look at Miss Emily beneath a mass of bought flowers, with the crayon face of her father musing profoundly

above the bier and the ladies sibilant and macabre; and the very old men—some in their brushed Confederate uniforms—on the porch and the
280 lawn, talking of Miss Emily as if she had been a contemporary of theirs, believing that they had danced with her and courted her perhaps, confusing time with its mathematical progression, as the old do, to whom all the past is not a diminishing road but, instead, a huge meadow which no winter ever quite touches, divided from them now by the narrow bottle-neck of the most recent decade of years.

Already we knew that there was one room in that region above stairs which no one had seen in forty years, and which would have to be forced. They waited until Miss Emily was decently in the ground before they opened it.
290 The violence of breaking down the door seemed to fill this room with pervading dust. A thin, acrid pall as of the tomb seemed to lie everywhere upon this room decked and furnished as for a bridal: upon the valance curtains of faded rose color, upon the rose-shaded lights, upon the dressing table, upon the delicate array of crystal and the man's toilet things backed with tarnished silver, silver so tarnished that the monogram was obscured. Among them lay a collar and tie, as if they had just been removed, which, lifted, left upon the surface a pale crescent in the dust. Upon a chair hung the suit, carefully folded; beneath it the two mute shoes and the discarded socks.
300 The man himself lay in the bed.

For a long while we just stood there, looking down at the profound and fleshless grin. The body had apparently once lain in the attitude of an embrace, but now the long sleep that outlasts love, that conquers even the grimace of love, had cuckolded him. What was left of him, rotten beneath what was left of the nightshirt, had become inextricable from the bed in which he lay; and upon him and upon the pillow beside him lay that even coating of the patient and biding dust.

Then we noticed that in the second pillow was the indentation of a head. One of us lifted something from it, and leaning forward, that faint
310 and invisible dust dry and acrid in the nostrils, we saw a long strand of iron-gray hair.

ACCOUNT: GEORGE L. DILLON ON STYLES OF READING "A ROSE FOR EMILY"

Surveying the responses of readers to "A Rose for Emily" made by both professional critics and college students, Dillon finds that the interpretations all fall into three distinct "styles" distinguishable by the ways a given reader sees both literature and life. Just as a particular

From *Poetics Today*, 3, no.2 (1982), 77–88.

musician or band habitually performs a musical text in a characteristic style, readers also might be said to "perform" the text of a story in ways that suit their habits of mind and training. The variety of styles in which the National anthem is performed at sporting events is thus comparable to the ways in which different readers read.

The differences among styles of reading may be clearly seen in a process Dillon calls "event chaining"—the ways in which different readers make different connections between events and infer the causes of those connections. Dillon offers a list of all the questions raised about the chain of the events by the readers he has surveyed:

1. Why weren't there suitable suitors for Emily?
2. How does Emily respond to being denied suitors?
3. Why does Emily take up with Homer Barron?
4. What happened when he left? Did he abandon her? Why did he come back?
5. Why did she kill him?
6. Why did the smell disappear after only one week?
7. What did Miss Emily think of the men scattering lime around her house?
8. How did the hair come to be on the pillow? How much hair is a *strand?*
9. What was her relationship to Tobe?
10. Did she lie beside the corpse? How often, for what period of years?
11. Why did she not leave the house for the last decade of her life?
12. Did she not know Colonel Sartoris had been dead ten years when she faced down the Aldermen?
13. How crazy was she (unable to distinguish fantasy from reality)?
14. Why does she allow so much dust in her house?

To be sure, no reader answers all these questions or perceives the issues of the story in terms of exactly the same set of questions. But Dillon says that three *patterns* of reading emerge that allow grouping of both professional critics (as known from their published articles and books) and student readers (as reported in Norman Holland's study *5 Readers Reading*). Dillon classifies the patterns into three modes:

1. The Character–Action–Moral style (CAM)
2. The Digger for Secrets style
3. The Anthropologist style

The first mode of reading—the Character–Action–Moral style—differs from the other two by assuming that the meaning or significance of the story is evident in the text. Character–Action–Moral readers are said to treat the world of the text as an extension or portion of the real world, the characters as real persons, so that we will recognize the experience of characters as being like our own experience; hence it can be understood or explained just as we would understand our own experience.

In CAM readings there are often speculations on alternatives to the story as actually written—for example, "The outcome could have been happy if Homer Barron had been a marrying man." Such speculations affirm a CAM reader's sense of characters as free to choose and to act. Stories are therefore treated as collisions between characters and situations—as *tragedies* in the traditional sense of irreconcilable difficulties—or as events from which we too can learn a moral lesson concerning how to behave when faced with conflict. Perhaps it is for this reason that CAM readers seem to talk about characters in terms the characters themselves might use: "'She lost her honor, and what else could she do but keep him [Homer] forever, make him hers in the only way she possibly could?'" The clear and logical nature of characters as seen by CAM readers goes along with their desire to draw a moral to guide their own behavior. As Dillon says, "Even lines of inference that would attribute dark or complex motives are avoided or treated as normal."

Dillon goes on to contrast this straightforward style of reading with another style:

> For Diggers of Secrets, however, the story enwraps secrets, the narrator hides them—much as Miss Emily, and the narrator, conceal the body of Homer Barron—and the reader must uncover them.

Such readers do not treat the story as a part of their own world, but take an analytic distance from it as something to be probed for what is behind what the story says about its events. Accordingly, when Diggers for Secrets explain the motives of characters:

> . . . they employ the categories of depth and abnormal psychology
> . . . and frequently 'diagnose' motives that characters would not be aware of and in terms they might well not accept.

Such students confidently use terms like "obsession," "necrophilia," or "erotic gratification." In the same way, the concept of "symbols" is commonly employed by Diggers for Secrets. Miss Emily's house is thus "an isolated fortress, a forbidden majestic stronghold."

Dillon says that his third group—The Anthropologists—differ in their approach from the other two groups:

> . . . the Anthropologists, have much less to say about events than either of the first two groups. Their interest, rather, is in identifying the

cultural norms and values that explain what characters indisputably do and say. Like Diggers for Secrets, these readers go beneath the surface and state things that are implicit and not said, though what they bring out is not a secret, but the general principles and values which the story illustrates as an example.

For these readers, the story may be seen to exemplify a struggle between Northern and Southern civilizations or between classes, races, or genders, or a general struggle between true and false values. As one example, Dillon quotes a student who writes on the class conflict that the student sees behind Miss Emily's situation. Dillon also quotes Judith Fetterly in her book, *The Resisting Reader,* which emphasizes the ways in which gender roles in the story itself are acted out:

> Having been consumed by her father, Emily in turn feeds off Homer Barron, becoming, after his death, suspiciously fat. Or, to put it another way, it is as if, after her father's death, she has reversed his act of incorporating her by incorporating and becoming him, metamorphosed from the slender figure in white to the obese figure in black whose hair is "a vigorous iron-gray, like the hair of an active man." She has taken into herself the violence in him which thwarted her and has reenacted it upon Homer Barron.

From his survey of the three groups of readers, Dillon concludes that styles of reading seem indeed to be related to styles of living that all people may recognize:

> We think of ourselves and others as conscious, moral agents shaping our destinies in situations benign and hostile, but also as mysteries to ourselves and others, and/or as enacting typical social roles and attitudes. There is some basis for concluding that we understand literature and life in the same or similar ways, and that some of the ways we read literature will be applied in reading others of life's texts.

In this way, Dillon expresses some of the literary values and assumptions that begin to define a widely employed contemporary critical approach.

Another example of this approach may be found in a later section of the book when Kate Beaird Meyers uses it to read Alexander Pope's poem "The Rape of the Lock" (see p. 394). Further, Kenneth Burke uses the related Rhetorical approach to understand William Shakespeare's *Hamlet* in the drama section (see p. 712).

SUGGESTIONS FOR DISCUSSION AND WRITING

1. What kind of **narrator** does the story employ? What seems to be the **narrative point of view** taken on the story in general? On Miss Emily in particular? On the townspeople?

2. Does the **narrator** seem to be characterized by any of the types of *reader* Dillon describes—The Character–Action–Moral, The Digger for Secrets, or The Anthropologist? If you think any one of these characterizations pertinent, explain why with examples. If you think not, characterize the way the narrator seems to "read" the story in your own terms. How would you characterize the townspeople as readers of the story's events?

3. What **images** or **symbols** besides the strand of hair seem to operate in an important way in the story? In what similar and differing ways are those images or symbols read by the different groups of readers Dillon describes? How do you read them?

4. Compare this story with "A Hunger Artist" by Franz Kafka. What similar and differing values and assumptions seem to define the sense of what is normal and abnormal in each story? What techniques does each author employ in creating the sense of the two standards of behavior?

5. One student quoted by Dillon explains Emily's actions as inevitable given that she had lost her "honor." Write an essay in which you describe the differing ways in which "honor" operates as a theme a reader responds to in "A Rose for Emily." Try to identify the group or groups with which Dillon would associate your points. How do assumptions about what is normal and abnormal differ among the groups of readers that Dillon describes?

6. Which of Dillon's groups of readers seem to read in ways that most resemble your own way of reading? Make some notes for discussion or an essay on the way one or more groups of readers would read some of the events in Melville's "Bartleby the Scrivener" (p. 224).

Chapter Five

Feminist Criticism: Gender in Literature

A BRIEF INTRODUCTION TO FEMINIST CRITICISM

Feminism began as a general social and political movement and came to include literary theorists and critics as the movement continued. At that time, literary feminists began to see, both in books and in the larger social context that produces and consumes books, the need for a critique of a culture they called *patriarchal*—that is, dominated by the patriarch or father, based on the assumptions that men are superior and that women should therefore be relegated to subordinate roles. Rejecting these assumptions, feminists have offered arguments such as the ones Annette Barnes identifies as some "minimal criteria for feminism":

> . . . all feminists, I argue, would agree that women are not automatically or necessarily inferior to men, that role models for men and women in the current Western societies are inadequate, that equal rights for women are necessary, that it is unclear what by nature either men or women are. . . .

Feminist literary critics have opposed such beliefs to the male biases which, they argue, have pervaded both literature and criticism. In the latter part of our century, feminist critics have built up a body of criticism that focuses on women as characters in literature, writers of literature, and readers of literature.

When they examine works by male authors, feminist critics often conclude that throughout history the female characters in these works have more nearly reflected the authors' hopes and fears about women than they have real women in a real world. In the early, highly influential *The Second Sex* (1949), French writer Simone de Beauvoir finds both in myth and in literature patterns that glorify men and degrade women. One familiar pattern portrays men as strong and active, women as weak, passive objects:

Woman is a special prize which the hero, the adventurer and the rugged individualist are destined to win. In antiquity, we see Perseus delivering Andromeda, Orpheus seeking Eurydice in the underworld, and Troy fighting to protect fair Helen. The novels of chivalry are concerned chiefly with such prowess as the delivery of captive princesses. What would Prince Charming have for occupation if he had not to awaken Sleeping Beauty?

De Beauvoir continues with analyses of works by such authors as D.H. Lawrence and Stendhal. Here too, she argues, man is the powerful figure and the center of interest, and woman is merely the "Other"—sometimes feared, sometimes desired or loathed or idolized, but always secondary, never recognized as a complete human being. Later feminist critics have built on de Beauvoir's insights. For example, in her 1970 book, *Sexual Politics,* Kate Millett charges that even some authors widely regarded as liberal or advanced—for example, D.H. Lawrence, Henry Miller, and Norman Mailer—describe sex as an act through which men prove their superiority by subduing and often showing contempt for women. Other feminist critics have concentrated on examining works that, in their view, portray women in a more positive, truthful way. These critics argue that Chaucer and Shakespeare, for example, offer us female characters who are stronger and more admirable than most male critics have realized.

For many feminist critics, however, the study of works by male authors is ultimately less interesting than the study of works by women. Traditionally, male authors have dominated the *canon,* the group of works widely recognized as outstanding, important, and worthy of study. In a famous 1924 essay, "A Room of One's Own," Virginia Woolf asks why so few women writers have claimed places in the canon. She describes the woman writer's need for "room," both in the sense of a literal room in which to write and also in the sense of a figurative space in which female discourse can take place without the "shadow across the page," the imposition of ego that she sees as characteristic of writing by men. Economically dependent on men, barred from most means of education, exhausted by menial tasks, held back by prejudices that denied their intelligence and sometimes even their humanity, women could seldom, Woolf says, attain the freedom and inner peace needed for creative work.

Although later feminist critics have generally accepted Woolf's analysis, they have also argued that, despite all the disadvantages they have faced, many women have in fact written excellent literary works. Too often, however, these works have been misinterpreted, undervalued, or completely ignored. Elaine Showalter uses the term *gynocritics* to describe the branch of feminist criticism devoted to the study of literature by women. Sometimes, gynocritics involves calling attention to the merits of neglected women writers or arguing that women usually regarded as minor figures rightfully deserve a place in the canon. Kate Chopin is one example of a writer who has benefitted from these efforts. When she published *The Awakening* in 1899, her frank portrayal of a woman's sexuality and independence was condemned as scandalous. The book was censored, and Chopin could not find publishers for her later works. Today, thanks largely to the efforts of feminist critics who have pointed out the book's literary and social importance, *The Awakening* is widely regarded as a major novel. The story included in this chapter, Charlotte Perkins Gilman's "The Yellow Wall-paper," has had a similar history. First published in 1892, the story did not find many readers or attract serious critical attention until Elaine Hedges and several other critics offered feminist interpretations of it in the early 1970s. Now, the story is widely anthologized and almost universally praised.

Others interested in gynocritics have called for reinterpretations of works by women already recognized as major figures. According to these critics, important feminist elements in these works have often been over-looked or denied, sometimes because they made male critics uncomfortable. For example, in *The Madwoman in the Attic: The Woman Writer and the Nineteenth-Century Literary Imagination,* Sandra M. Gilbert and Susan Gubar argue that many women writers have been angered and frustrated by Milton's portrayal of Eve in *Paradise Lost.* Gilbert and Gubar list authors as diverse as Mary Shelley, the Brontes, Emily Dickinson, George Eliot, and Sylvia Plath as among those who have, explicitly or implicitly, responded to Milton's view of woman as "inferior and Satanically inspired." And authors such as Jane Austen, Gilbert and Gubar argue, challenge male domination and assumptions in ways far more radical than most critics have realized. For example, they describe Austen's *Persuasion* as an exploration of "the effects on women of submission to authority"; its protagonist has "deteriorated into a ghostly insubstantiality" at least partly because "she is a dependent female in a world symbolized by her vain and selfish aristocratic father." Although Austen is not usually seen as a feminist author, novels such as *Persuasion* may in fact imply a condemnation of patriarchal society.

By urging us to see classic texts in new ways, feminist critics have drawn attention to women as readers of literature. Elaine Showalter, in the introduction to her collection *The New Feminist Criticism: Essays on Women, Literature, and Theory* (1985), argues that "the assumptions of literary study have been profoundly altered" by the recent contributions of feminist criticism: "Whereas it had always been taken for granted that the representative reader, writer, and critic of Western literature is male, feminist criticism has shown that women readers and critics bring different perceptions and expectations to their literary experience. . . ." As critics, feminists have employed a wide range of methods, both traditional ones and those that have developed contemporaneously with feminist inquiry. In the essay summarized in this chapter, for example, Jean E. Kennard draws on the insights of reader-response criticism to provide a context for her feminist interpretation of "The Yellow Wall-paper." In many ways, then, "feminist criticism" as a term describes less a critical approach than it does a collection of interdisciplinary studies commonly informed by a concern for literature by and about women. Insofar as this literature tells a story of discrimination, the interdisciplinary aspects may also include issues of "multiple marginality"—the literary situation of black women's writing, for example. Other feminist critics have focused on the relationship between gender and language. For example, influential French feminists such as Julia Kristeva and Luce Irigray have argued that language, far from being neutral or objective, has been shaped by men in ways that exclude and alienate women. For these critics, discovering—or creating—a more open, inclusive language is a central part of the feminist endeavor.

CHARLOTTE ANNE PERKINS (1860–1935) was born in Hartford, Connecticut; her father, who also enjoyed a career as a writer, left his wife soon after this event. He never returned to his family, and, as a result, Charlotte's childhood was marked by poverty and instability. At the age of twenty-four, after studying art and working as an art teacher, Charlotte Perkins married Charles Stetson, an artist.

When her only child was born in 1885, Charlotte fell into a period of deep depression. She then became a patient of S. Weir Mitchell, a famous Philadelphia physician who was famous for treating female nervous disorders in the 1870s. Mitchell had Charlotte confined to bed and isolated from all activities, mental and physical. His treatment almost drove Charlotte insane, which she avoided by escaping to California, abandoning both her well-meaning but domineering doctor and her husband.

In 1892 she was able to convert her experience into "The Yellow Wall-paper." In 1900 she married again, this time to her first cousin, George Gilman. Although best known for "The Yellow Wall-paper," her works include *Women and Economics* (1899), *The Home: Its Work and Influence* (1903), and *The Man-Made World, or Our Androcentric Culture* (1911). Her autobiography, *The Living of Charlotte Perkins Gilman*, was published posthumously in 1935, the year in which she committed suicide after discovering that she suffered from inoperable cancer.

CHARLOTTE PERKINS GILMAN
The Yellow Wall-paper
(1892)

It is very seldom that mere ordinary people like John and myself secure ancestral halls for the summer.

A colonial mansion, a hereditary estate, I would say a haunted house, and reach the height of romantic felicity—but that would be asking too much of fate!

Still I will proudly declare that there is something queer about it.

Else, why should it be let so cheaply? And why have stood so long untenanted?

John laughs at me, of course, but one expects that in marriage.

10   John is practical in the extreme. He has no patience with faith, an intense horror of superstition, and he scoffs openly at any talk of things not to be felt and seen and put down in figures.

John is a physician, and *perhaps*—(I would not say it to a living soul, of course, but this is dead paper and a great relief to my mind—) *perhaps* that is one reason I do not get well faster.

You see he does not believe I am sick!

And what can one do?

If a physician of high standing, and one's own husband, assures friends and relatives that there is really nothing the matter with one but
20 temporary nervous depression—a slight hysterical tendency—what is one to do?

My brother is also a physician, and also of high standing, and he says the same thing.

So I take phosphates or phosphites—whichever it is, and tonics, and journeys, and air, and exercise, and am absolutely forbidden to "work" until I am well again.

Personally, I disagree with their ideas.

Personally, I believe that congenial work, with excitement and change, would do me good.

30   But what is one to do?

I did write for a while in spite of them; but it *does* exhaust me a good deal—having to be so sly about it, or else meet with heavy opposition.

I sometimes fancy that in my condition if I had less opposition and more society and stimulus—but John says the very worst thing I can do is to think about my condition, and I confess it always makes me feel bad.

So I will let it alone and talk about the house.

The most beautiful place! It is quite alone, standing well back from the road, quite three miles from the village. It makes me think of English places that you read about, for there are hedges and walls and gates that
40 lock, and lots of separate little houses for the gardeners and people.

There is a *delicious* garden! I never saw such a garden—large and shady, full of box-bordered paths, and lined with long grape-covered arbors with seats under them.

There were greenhouses, too, but they are all broken now.

There was some legal trouble, I believe, something about the heirs and coheirs; anyhow, the place has been empty for years.

That spoils my ghostliness, I am afraid, but I don't care—there is something strange about the house—I can feel it.

I even said so to John one moonlight evening, but he said what I felt
50 was a *draught,* and shut the window.

I get unreasonably angry with John sometimes. I'm sure I never used to be so sensitive. I think it is due to this nervous condition.

But John says if I feel so, I shall neglect proper self-control; so I take pains to control myself—before him, at least, and that makes me very tired.

I don't like our room a bit. I wanted one downstairs that opened on the piazza and had roses all over the window, and such pretty old-fashioned chintz hangings! but John would not hear of it.

He said there was only one window and not room for two beds, and
60 no near room for him if he took another.

He is very careful and loving, and hardly lets me stir without special direction.

I have a schedule prescription for each hour in the day; he takes all care from me, and so I feel basely ungrateful not to value it more.

He said we came here solely on my account, that I was to have perfect rest and all the air I could get. "Your exercise depends on your strength, my dear," said he, "and your food somewhat on your appetite; but air you can absorb all the time." So we took the nursery at the top of the house.

70   It is a big, airy room, the whole floor nearly, with windows that look all ways, and air and sunshine galore. It was nursery first and then playroom and gymnasium, I should judge; for the windows are barred for little children, and there are rings and things in the walls.

The paint and paper look as if a boys' school had used it. It is stripped off—the paper—in great patches all around the head of my bed, about as far as I can reach, and in a great place on the other side of the room low down. I never saw a worse paper in my life.

One of those sprawling flamboyant patterns committing every artistic sin.

80   It is dull enough to confuse the eye in following, pronounced enough to constantly irritate and provoke study, and when you follow the lame uncertain curves for a little distance they suddenly commit suicide—plunge off at outrageous angles, destroy themselves in unheard of contradictions.

The color is repellent, almost revolting; a smouldering unclean yellow, strangely faded by the slow-turning sunlight.

It is a dull yet lurid orange in some places, a sickly sulphur tint in others.

No wonder the children hated it! I should hate it myself if I had to
90 live in this room long.

There comes John, and I must put this away,—he hates to have me write a word.

*

We have been here two weeks, and I haven't felt like writing before, since that first day.

I am sitting by the window now, up in this atrocious nursery, and there is nothing to hinder my writing as much as I please, save lack of strength.

John is away all day, and even some nights when his cases are serious.

I am glad my case is not serious!

100   But these nervous troubles are dreadfully depressing.

John does not know how much I really suffer. He knows there is no *reason* to suffer, and that satisfies him.

Of course it is only nervousness. It does weigh on me so not to do my duty in any way!

I meant to be such a help to John, such a real rest and comfort, and here I am a comparative burden already!

Nobody would believe what an effort it is to do what little I am able,—to dress and entertain, and order things.

It is fortunate Mary is so good with the baby. Such a dear baby!

110   And yet I *cannot* be with him, it makes me so nervous.

I suppose John never was nervous in his life. He laughs at me so about this wall-paper!

At first he meant to repaper the room, but afterwards he said that I was letting it get the better of me, and that nothing was worse for a nervous patient than to give way to such fancies.

He said that after the wall-paper was changed it would be the heavy bedstead, and then the barred windows, and then that gate at the head of the stairs, and so on.

"You know the place is doing you good," he said, "and really, dear, 120 I don't care to renovate the house just for a three months' rental."

"Then do let us go downstairs," I said, "there are such pretty rooms there."

Then he took me in his arms and called me a blessed little goose, and said he would go down cellar, if I wished, and have it whitewashed into the bargain.

But he is right enough about the beds and windows and things.

It is an airy and comfortable room as any one need wish, and, of course, I would not be so silly as to make him uncomfortable just for a whim.

130   I'm really getting quite fond of the big room, all but that horrid paper.

Out of one window I can see the garden, those mysterious deep-shaded arbors, the riotous old-fashioned flowers, and bushes and gnarly trees.

Out of another I get a lovely view of the bay and a little private wharf belonging to the estate. There is a beautiful shaded lane that runs down there from the house. I always fancy I see people walking in these numerous paths and arbors, but John has cautioned me not to give way to fancy in the least. He says that with my imaginative power and habit of story-making, a nervous weakness like mine is sure to lead to all 140 manner of excited fancies, and that I ought to use my will and good sense to check the tendency. So I try.

I think sometimes that if I were only well enough to write a little it would relieve the press of ideas and rest me.

But I find I get pretty tired when I try.

It is so discouraging not to have any advice and companionship about my work. When I get really well, John says we will ask Cousin Henry and Julia down for a long visit; but he says he would as soon put fireworks in my pillowcase as to let me have those stimulating people about now.

150   I wish I could get well faster.

But I must not think about that. This paper looks to me as if it *knew* what a vicious influence it had!

There is a recurrent spot where the pattern lolls like a broken neck and two bulbous eyes stare at you upside down.

I get positively angry with the impertinence of it and the everlastingness. Up and down and sideways they crawl, and those absurd, unblinking eyes are everywhere. There is one place where two breadths didn't match, and the eyes go all up and down the line, one a little higher than the other.

160   I never saw so much expression in an inanimate thing before, and we all know how much expression they have! I used to lie awake as a child and get more entertainment and terror out of blank walls and plain furniture than most children could find in a toy-store.

I remember what a kindly wink the knobs of our big, old bureau used to have, and there was one chair that always seemed like a strong friend.

I used to feel that if any of the other things looked too fierce I could always hop into that chair and be safe.

The furniture in this room is no worse than inharmonious, however,
170 for we had to bring it all from downstairs. I suppose when this was used as a playroom they had to take the nursery things out, and no wonder! I never saw such ravages as the children have made here.

The wall-paper, as I said before, is torn off in spots, and it sticketh closer than a brother—they must have had perseverance as well as hatred.

Then the floor is scratched and gouged and splintered, the plaster itself is dug out here and there, and this great heavy bed which is all we found in the room, looks as if it had been through the wars.

But I don't mind it a bit—only the paper.

180   There comes John's sister. Such a dear girl as she is, and so careful of me! I must not let her find me writing.

She is a perfect and enthusiastic housekeeper, and hopes for no better profession. I verily believe she thinks it is the writing which made me sick!

But I can write when she is out, and see her a long way off from these windows.

There is one that commands the road, a lovely shaded winding road, and one that just looks off over the country. A lovely country, too, full of great elms and velvet meadows.

190   This wall-paper has a kind of subpattern in a different shade, a particularly irritating one, for you can only see it in certain lights, and not clearly then.

But in the places where it isn't faded and where the sun is just so—I can see a strange, provoking, formless sort of figure, that seems to skulk about behind that silly and conspicuous front design.

There's sister on the stairs!

*

Well, the Fourth of July is over! The people are all gone and I am tired out. John thought it might do me good to see a little company, so we just had mother and Nellie and the children down for a week.

200   Of course I didn't do a thing. Jennie sees to everything now.

But it tired me all the same.

John says if I don't pick up faster he shall send me to Weir Mitchell[1] in the fall.

But I don't want to go there at all. I had a friend who was in his hands once, and she says he is just like John and my brother, only more so!

Besides, it is such an undertaking to go so far.

I don't feel as if it was worth while to turn my hand over for anything, and I'm getting dreadfully fretful and querulous.

I cry at nothing, and cry most of the time.

210   Of course I don't when John is here, or anybody else, but when I am alone.

And I am alone a good deal just now. John is kept in town very often by serious cases, and Jennie is good and lets me alone when I want her to.

So I walk a little in the garden or down that lovely lane, sit on the porch under the roses, and lie down up here a good deal.

I'm getting really fond of the room in spite of the wall-paper. Perhaps *because* of the wall-paper.

It dwells in my mind so!

I lie here on this great immovable bed—it is nailed down, I believe—
220   and follow that pattern about by the hour. It is as good as gymnastics, I assure you. I start, we'll say, at the bottom, down in the corner over there where it has not been touched, and I determine for the thousandth time that I *will* follow that pointless pattern to some sort of a conclusion.

I know a little of the principle of design, and I know this thing was not arranged on any laws of radiation, or alternation, or repetition, or symmetry, or anything else that I ever heard of.

It is repeated, of course, by the breadths, but not otherwise.

Looked at in one way each breadth stands alone, the bloated curves and flourishes—a kind of "debased Romanesque" with *delirium tremens* go
230   waddling up and down in isolated columns of fatuity.

But, on the other hand, they connect diagonally, and the sprawling outlines run off in great slanting waves of optic horror, like a lot of wallowing seaweeds in full chase.

The whole thing goes horizontally, too, at least it seems so, and I exhaust myself in trying to distinguish the order of its going in that direction.

They have used a horizontal breadth for a frieze, and that adds wonderfully to the confusion.

There is one end of the room where it is almost intact, and there,
240   when the crosslights fade and the low sun shines directly upon it, I can almost fancy radiation after all,—the interminable grotesques seem to

form around a common centre and rush off in headlong plunges of equal distraction.

It makes me tired to follow it. I will take a nap I guess.

*

I don't know why I should write this.

I don't want to.

I don't feel able.

And I know John would think it absurd. But I *must* say what I feel and think in some way—it is such a relief!

250 But the effort is getting to be greater than the relief.

Half the time now I am awfully lazy, and lie down ever so much.

John says I mustn't lose my strength, and has me take cod liver oil and lots of tonics and things, to say nothing of ale and wine and rare meat.

Dear John! He loves me very dearly, and hates to have me sick. I tried to have a real earnest reasonable talk with him the other day, and tell him how I wish he would let me go and make a visit to Cousin Henry and Julia.

But he said I wasn't able to go, nor able to stand it after I got there; 260 and I did not make out a very good case for myself, for I was crying before I had finished.

It is getting to be a great effort for me to think straight. Just this nervous weakness I suppose.

And dear John gathered me up in his arms, and just carried me upstairs and laid me on the bed, and sat by me and read to me till it tired my head.

He said I was his darling and his comfort and all he had, and that I must take care of myself for his sake, and keep well.

He says no one but myself can help me out of it, that I must use my 270 will and self-control and not let any silly fancies run away with me.

There's one comfort, the baby is well and happy, and does not have to occupy this nursery with the horrid wall-paper.

If we had not used it, that blessed child would have! What a fortunate escape! Why, I wouldn't have a child of mine, an impressionable little thing, live in such a room for worlds.

I never thought of it before, but it is lucky that John kept me here after all, I can stand it so much easier than a baby, you see.

Of course I never mention it to them any more—I am too wise,—but I keep watch of it all the same.

280 There are things in that paper that nobody knows but me, or ever will.

Behind that outside pattern the dim shapes get clearer every day.

It is always the same shape, only very numerous.

And it is like a woman stooping down and creeping about behind that pattern. I don't like it a bit. I wonder—I begin to think—I wish John would take me away from here!

*

It is so hard to talk with John about my case, because he is so wise, and because he loves me so.

But I tried it last night.

290   It was moonlight. The moon shines in all around just as the sun does.

I hate to see it sometimes, it creeps so slowly, and always comes in by one window or another.

John was asleep and I hated to waken him, so I kept still and watched the moonlight on that undulating wall-paper till I felt creepy.

The faint figure behind seemed to shake the pattern, just as if she wanted to get out.

I got up softly and went to feel and see if the paper *did* move, and when I came back John was awake.

300   "What is it, little girl?" he said. "Don't go walking about like that—you'll get cold."

I thought it was a good time to talk, so I told him that I really was not gaining here, and that I wished he would take me away.

"Why, darling!" said he, "our lease will be up in three weeks, and I can't see how to leave before."

"The repairs are not done at home, and I cannot possibly leave town just now. Of course if you were in any danger, I could and would, but you really are better, dear, whether you can see it or not. I am a doctor, dear, and I know. You are gaining flesh and color, your appetite is bet-

310   ter, I feel really much easier about you."

"I don't weigh a bit more," said I, "nor as much; and my appetite may be better in the evening when you are here, but it is worse in the morning when you are away!"

"Bless her little heart!" said he with a big hug, "she shall be as sick as she pleases! But now let's improve the shining hours by going to sleep, and talk about it in the morning!"

"And you won't go away?" I asked gloomily.

"Why, how can I, dear? It is only three weeks more and then we will take a nice little trip of a few days while Jennie is getting the house

320   ready. Really dear you are better!"

"Better in body perhaps—" I began, and stopped short, for he sat up straight and looked at me with such a stern, reproachful look that I could not say another word.

"My darling," said he, "I beg of you, for my sake and for our child's sake, as well as for your own, that you will never for one instant let that idea enter your mind! There is nothing so dangerous, so fascinating, to a temperament like yours. It is a false and foolish fancy. Can you not trust me as a physician when I tell you so?"

So of course I said no more on that score, and we went to sleep be-
330 fore long. He thought I was asleep first, but I wasn't, and lay there for hours trying to decide whether that front pattern and the back pattern really did move together or separately.

*

On a pattern like this, by daylight, there is a lack of sequence, a defiance of law, that is a constant irritant to a normal mind.

The color is hideous enough, and unreliable enough, and infuriating enough, but the pattern is torturing.

You think you have mastered it, but just as you get well underway in following, it turns a back-somersault and there you are. It slaps you in the face, knocks you down, and tramples upon you. It is like a bad
340 dream.

The outside pattern is a florid arabesque, reminding one of a fungus. If you can imagine a toadstool in joints, an interminable string of toadstools, budding and sprouting in endless convolutions—why, that is something like it.

That is, sometimes!

There is one marked peculiarity about this paper, a thing nobody seems to notice but myself, and that is that it changes as the light changes.

When the sun shoots in through the east windows—I always watch
350 for that first long, straight ray—it changes so quickly that I never can quite believe it.

That is why I watch it always.

By moonlight—the moon shines in all night when there is a moon—I wouldn't know it was the same paper.

At night in any kind of light, in twilight, candlelight, lamplight, and worst of all by moonlight, it becomes bars! The outside pattern I mean, and the woman behind it is as plain as can be.

I didn't realize for a long time what the thing was that showed behind, that dim subpattern, but now I am quite sure it is a woman.
360 By daylight she is subdued, quiet. I fancy it is the pattern that keeps her so still. It is so puzzling. It keeps me quiet by the hour.

I lie down ever so much now. John says it is good for me, and to sleep all I can.

Indeed he started the habit by making me lie down for an hour after each meal.

It is a very bad habit I am convinced, for you see I don't sleep.

And that cultivates deceit, for I don't tell them I'm awake—O no!

The fact is I am getting a little afraid of John.

370   He seems very queer sometimes, and even Jennie has an inexplicable look.

It strikes me occasionally, just as a scientific hypothesis,—that perhaps it is the paper!

I have watched John when he did not know I was looking, and come into the room suddenly on the most innocent excuses, and I've caught him several times *looking at the paper!* And Jennie too. I caught Jennie with her hand on it once.

She didn't know I was in the room, and when I asked her in a quiet, a very quiet voice, with the most restrained manner possible, what she was doing with the paper—she turned around as if she had been caught steal-
380 ing, and looked quite angry—asked me why I should frighten her so!

Then she said that the paper stained everything it touched, that she had found yellow smooches on all my clothes and John's, and she wished we would be more careful!

Did not that sound innocent? But I know she was studying that pattern, and I am determined that nobody shall find it out but myself!

                                                    *

Life is very much more exciting now than it used to be. You see I have something more to expect, to look forward to, to watch. I really do eat better, and am more quiet than I was.

John is so pleased to see me improve! He laughed a little the other
390 day, and said I seemed to be flourishing in spite of my wall-paper.

I turned it off with a laugh. I had no intention of telling him it was *because* of the wall-paper—he would make fun of me. He might even want to take me away.

I don't want to leave now until I have found it out. There is a week more, and I think that will be enough.

                                                    *

I'm feeling ever so much better! I don't sleep much at night, for it is so interesting to watch developments; but I sleep a good deal in the daytime.

In the daytime it is tiresome and perplexing.

There are always new shoots on the fungus, and new shades of yel-
400 low all over it. I cannot keep count of them, though I have tried consci-
entiously.

It is the strangest yellow, that wall-paper! It makes me think of all the yellow things I ever saw—not beautiful ones like buttercups, but old foul, bad yellow things.

But there is something else about that paper—the smell! I noticed it the moment we came into the room, but with so much air and sun it was not bad. Now we have had a week of fog and rain, and whether the windows are open or not, the smell is here.

It creeps all over the house.

410   I find it hovering in the dining-room, skulking in the parlor, hiding in the hall, lying in wait for me on the stairs.

It gets into my hair.

Even when I go to ride, if I turn my head suddenly and surprise it—there is that smell!

Such a peculiar odor, too! I have spent hours in trying to analyze it, to find what it smelled like.

It is not bad—at first, and very gentle, but quite the subtlest, most enduring odor I ever met.

In this damp weather it is awful, I wake up in the night and find it
420 hanging over me.

It used to disturb me at first. I thought seriously of burning the house—to reach the smell.

But now I am used to it. The only thing I can think of that it is like is the *color* of the paper! A yellow smell.

There is a very funny mark on this wall, low down, near the mop-board. A streak that runs round the room. It goes behind every piece of furniture, except the bed, a long, straight, even *smooch*, as if it had been rubbed over and over.

I wonder how it was done and who did it, and what they did it for.
430 Round and round and round—round and round and round!—it makes me dizzy!

*

I really have discovered something at last.

Through watching so much at night when it changes so, I have finally found out.

The front pattern *does* move—and no wonder! The woman behind shakes it!

Sometimes I think there are a great many women behind, and sometimes only one, and she crawls around fast, and her crawling shakes it all over.

440   Then in the very bright spots she keeps still, and in the very shady spots she just takes hold of the bars and shakes them hard.

And she is all the time trying to climb through. But nobody could climb through that pattern—it strangles so; I think that is why it has so many heads.

They get through, and then the pattern strangles them off and turns them upside down, and makes their eyes white!

If those heads were covered or taken off it would not be half so bad.

*

I think that woman gets out in the daytime!

And I'll tell you why—privately—I've seen her!
450   I can see her out of every one of my windows!

It is the same woman, I know, for she is always creeping, and most women do not creep by daylight.

I see her in that long shaded lane, creeping up and down. I see her in those dark grape arbors, creeping all around the garden.

I see her on that long road under the trees, creeping along, and when a carriage comes she hides under the blackberry vines.

I don't blame her a bit. It must be very humiliating to be caught creeping by daylight!

I always lock the door when I creep by daylight. I can't do it at night, for I know John would suspect something at once.

And John is so queer now, that I don't want to irritate him. I wish he would take another room! Besides, I don't want anybody to get that woman out at night but myself.

I often wonder if I could see her out of all the windows at once.

But, turn as fast as I can, I can only see out of one at one time.

And though I always see her, she *may* be able to creep faster than I can turn!

I have watched her sometimes away off in the open country, creeping as fast as a cloud shadow in a high wind.

*

If only that top pattern could be gotten off from the under one! I mean to try it, little by little.

I have found out another funny thing, but I shan't tell it this time! It does not do to trust people too much.

There are only two more days to get this paper off, and I believe John is beginning to notice. I don't like the look in his eyes.

And I heard him ask Jennie a lot of professional questions about me. She had a very good report to give.

She said I slept a good deal in the daytime.

John knows I don't sleep very well at night, for all I'm so quiet!

He asked me all sorts of questions, too, and pretended to be very loving and kind.

As if I couldn't see through him!

Still, I don't wonder he acts so, sleeping under this paper for three months.

It only interests me, but I feel sure John and Jennie are secretly affected by it.

*

Hurrah! This is the last day, but it is enough. John to stay in town over night, and won't be out until this evening.

Jennie wanted to sleep with me—the sly thing! but I told her I should undoubtedly rest better for a night all alone.

That was clever, for really I wasn't alone a bit! As soon as it was moonlight and that poor thing began to crawl and shake the pattern, I got up and ran to help her.

I pulled and she shook, I shook and she pulled, and before morning we had peeled off yards of that paper.

A strip about as high as my head and half around the room.

And then when the sun came and that awful pattern began to laugh at me, I declared I would finish it to-day!

500 We go away to-morrow, and they are moving all my furniture down again to leave things as they were before.

Jennie looked at the wall in amazement, but I told her merrily that I did it out of pure spite at the vicious thing.

She laughed and said she wouldn't mind doing it herself, but I must not get tired.

How she betrayed herself that time!

But I am here, and no person touches this paper but me,—not *alive!*

She tried to get me out of the room—it was too patent! But I said it was so quiet and empty and clean now that I believed I would lie down again and sleep all I could; and not to wake me even for dinner—I

510 would call when I woke.

So now she is gone, and the servants are gone, and the things are gone, and there is nothing left but that great bedstead nailed down, with the canvas mattress we found on it.

We shall sleep downstairs to-night, and take the boat home to-morrow.

I quite enjoy the room, now it is bare again.

How those children did tear about here!

This bedstead is fairly gnawed!

But I must get to work.

I have locked the door and thrown the key down into the front path.

520 I don't want to go out, and I don't want to have anybody come in, till John comes.

I want to astonish him.

I've got a rope up here that even Jennie did not find. If that woman does get out, and tries to get away, I can tie her!

But I forgot I could not reach far without anything to stand on!

This bed will *not* move!

I tried to lift and push it until I was lame, and then I got so angry I bit off a little piece at one corner—but it hurt my teeth.

Then I peeled off all the paper I could reach standing on the floor. It

530 sticks horribly and the pattern just enjoys it! All those strangled heads and bulbous eyes and waddling fungus growths just shriek with derision!

I am getting angry enough to do something desperate. To jump out of the window would be admirable exercise, but the bars are too strong even to try.

Besides I wouldn't do it. Of course not. I know well enough that a step like that is improper and might be misconstrued.

I don't like to *look* out of the windows even—there are so many of those creeping women, and they creep so fast.

I wonder if they all come out of that wall-paper as I did?

540   But I am securely fastened now by my well-hidden rope—you don't get *me* out in the road there!

I suppose I shall have to get back behind the pattern when it comes night, and that is hard!

It is so pleasant to be out in this great room and creep around as I please!

I don't want to go outside. I won't, even if Jennie asks me to.

For outside you have to creep on the ground, and everything is green instead of yellow.

But here I can creep smoothly on the floor, and my shoulder just fits
550 in that long smooch around the wall, so I cannot lose my way.

Why there's John at the door!

It is no use, young man, you can't open it!

How he does call and pound!

Now he's crying for an axe.

It would be a shame to break down that beautiful door!

"John dear!" said I in the gentlest voice, "the key is down by the front steps, under a plantain leaf!"

That silenced him for a few moments.

Then he said—very quietly indeed, "Open the door, my darling!"
560   "I can't," said I. "The key is down by the front door under a plantain leaf!"

And then I said it again, several times, very gently and slowly, and said it so often that he had to go and see, and he got it of course, and came in. He stopped short by the door.

"What is the matter?" he cried. "For God's sake, what are you doing!"

I kept on creeping just the same, but I looked at him over my shoulder.

"I've got out at last," said I, "in spite of you and Jane! And I've pulled off most of the paper, so you can't put me back!"

Now why should that man have fainted? But he did, and right across
570 my path by the wall, so that I had to creep over him every time!

ACCOUNT: JEAN E. KENNARD ON HOW TO READ YOUR OWN LIFE IN "THE YELLOW WALL-PAPER"

As noted earlier, feminist criticism focuses on women as characters in literature, writers of literature, and readers of literature. Jean E. Kennard's "Convention Coverage or How to Read Your Own Life"

From Jean E. Kennard, "Convention Coverage or How to Read Your Own Life," *New Literary History*, 8 (1981), 69–88.

reflects all three of these interests. As Kennard notes, "feminist critics approach "The Yellow Wall-paper" from the point of view of the narrator," seeing her as "the victim of an oppressive patriarchal social system which restricts women and prevents their functioning as full human beings." As a study of a once-neglected work by a woman author, Kennard's article is also a contribution to gynocritics; Kennard comments that for feminist critics, "one of our major tasks [is] the rereading of earlier works, both those well established in the traditional literary canon and those previously excluded from it." Kennard's primary emphasis in this article, however, is on women as readers of literature. Just as many other feminist critics have employed a variety of critical methods in their work, Kennard draws on the insights and terminology of reader-response criticism to explain why feminist readings of "The Yellow Wall-paper" differ so sharply from earlier responses to the story.

Kennard begins with definitions of concepts central to reader-response criticism. For critics such as Northrop Frye and Jonathan Culler, she explains, literary *conventions* are best seen as positive agreements among readers about their shared values in life and their expectations in reading. These common assumptions enable readers to read texts in the ways that they in fact do—readers who share a set of conventions will tend to read a literary work in more or less similar ways. Kennard also uses reader-response critic Stanley Fish's term *interpretive communities* to identify "groups of readers who share certain interpretive strategies (who agree to apply particular literary conventions)." Psychoanalytic critics provide one example of an interpretive community; feminist critics provide another. The conventions accepted by an interpretive community may change over time. Kennard argues that feminist rereadings of works such as "The Yellow Wall-paper" offer important insights into why these changes occur.

The critical history of "The Yellow Wall-paper," Kennard says, can help us understand how the same works get read differently in different periods. When Gilman wrote "The Yellow Wall-paper" late in the nineteenth century, the few readers who took any interest in it at all saw it only as a psychological horror story. No early reader, Kennard says, saw the story as "in any way positive":

> When Horace Scudder rejected it for publication in *The Atlantic Monthly,* he explained that he did not wish to make his readers as miserable as the story had made him. As Elaine Hedges points out, "No one seems to have made the connection between insanity and the sex, or sexual role of the victim, no one explored the story's implications for male–female relationships in the nineteenth century."

In the 1970s, however, Hedges and several other feminist critics found more positive ways of interpreting the story by approaching it from the narrator's point of view. For these critics, the narrator is not a psychological oddity, a hysterical woman suffering from bizarre delusions. Rather,

her situation reflects the condition of women in a patriarchal society. For example, Kennard says, "the restrictions on women are symbolized by the narrator's imprisonment in a room with bars on the window, an image the narrator sees echoed in the patterns of the room's yellow wallpaper." The narrator's husband, John, emerges as a "representative of the repressive patriarchal society": "The description of John as rational rather than emotional, as a man who laughs at what cannot be put down in figures, emphasizes his position as representative of a male power which excludes feeling and imagination."

Feminist critics generally identify John and the society he represents as the forces that drive the narrator into madness and keep her from recovering:

> The narrator experiences her victimization as a conflict between her own personal feelings, perceived by feminist critics as healthy and positive, and the patriarchal society's view of what is proper behavior for women. Since, like so many women up to the present day, she has internalized society's expectations of women, this conflict is felt as a split within herself. Early in the story the words "Personally, I" are twice set against the views of John and her brother. Nevertheless, she also continues to judge her own behavior as John does. "I get unreasonably angry with John sometimes," she explains. "I cry at nothing, and cry most of the time." As Hedges points out, this split is symbolized by the woman behind the wallpaper: "By rejecting that woman, she might free the other imprisoned woman within herself." The narrator's madness is perceived by Hedges and others as a direct result of societally induced confusion over personal identity.

A still more radical view introduced by some feminist critics sees the narrator's madness as a "higher form of sanity" and a positive representation of a guest for her own identity.

All this is a long way from the early responses to the story. Why is it that the readers of Gilman's own day apparently did not consider, even as possibilities, interpretations that strike most contemporary readers as natural and plausible? According to Kennard, the different responses stem from different sets of conventions:

> . . . the ability to read the narrator's confinement in a room as symbolic of the situation of women in a patriarchal society depends on an agreement, on a literary convention, which, I suggest, was formed from contemporary experience—both literary and extraliterary. The feminist reading of "The Yellow Wall-paper" depends on the knowledge of a series of "associative clusters" of meaning which have been employed sufficiently frequently in contemporary literature for us to accept them as conventions. The existence of these conventions in the 1970s accounts both for the new reading and for its widespread acceptance.

The literary experiences that contribute to a feminist reading of "The Yellow Wall-paper" include familiarity with relatively recent women's fiction; as Kennard points out, "In seventies fiction by women, madness or some form of mental disturbance became a conventional representation of the situation of women in a patriarchal society." Reading such fiction prepares the critic to see "The Yellow Wall-paper" narrator's madness as symbolic, not merely aberrant. "Extraliterary" experiences may also lead some readers to this conclusion. Many women, Kennard writes, feel a "split" similar to the one the narrator experiences "because their own reality/feeling is in conflict with society's expectations." Thus, readers' actual experiences in a patriarchal society can help guide them toward a feminist interpretation of works such as "The Yellow Wall-paper."

Kennard concludes with some suggestions about why critical conventions change. In the case of "The Yellow Wall-paper," she suggests, earlier conventions were rejected because they "had become oppressive to the feminist 'interpretive community.' By oppressive I mean both dishonest, suggesting an idea contrary to the view of experience called reality by the interpretive community, and inadequate, not able to provide a form in which to express that view of experience." The conventions that support a feminist reading of the story seem far more honest and adequate—at least for the time being, at least for this particular interpretive community. Inevitably, Kennard writes, these conventions too will change, and new readings will be proposed; she does not see any interpretation as completely objective, as eternal and beyond challenge. But recognizing the influence of conventions on all readers can, she says, help feminist critics reply to those who accuse them of bias: "Feminists and other clearly defined interpretive communities are no more biased than any other readers; our biases are simply more readily identifiable and often more acknowledged."

A feminist reading of poetry will be found in the account of Adrienne Rich's approach to Emily Dickinson's "My Life Had Stood—A Loaded Gun" (p. 420), and Declar Kiberd offers a feminist reading of Ibsen's play *A Doll House* (p. 843). See also Appendix I for Judith Fetterley on Hawthorne's "The Birthmark."

SUGGESTIONS FOR DISCUSSION AND WRITING

1. What kind of **narrator** does the story have? How would you characterize that narrator's **tone of voice**? What literary techniques work to create your impression of tone? For example, what effect do the very short paragraphs create?

2. What kinds of **images** does the story use besides the visual? To what senses do these images appeal? What, for example, is the effect of odor, described and undescribed, in the story? In what ways does the narrator "analyze" the images? Do you as a reader analyze them in the same way? According to the evidence in the account of Kennard, what kinds of images seem to interest feminist critics? What kinds, if any, seem not to interest them?

3. "Confinement" and "freedom" are words that might name **themes** in the story. What literary techniques does the author use to dramatize those themes? In what ways are they important themes for feminist critics, according to the account of Kennard? In what ways have the themes changed for feminist criticism since the story's first publication?

4. Compare this story with "Cloud, Castle, Lake" by Vladimir Nabokov. How does each story differently dramatize similar themes— oppression and insanity, for example. Like its author, the protagonist of "Cloud, Castle, Lake" is a man. Nevertheless, does Kennard's account suggest for you any ways in which the story might be of interest to feminist critics? Explain your answer.

5. Kennard says that readers "invent" rather than "discover" literary meanings. Consider the main character as a reader of her world and write an essay in which you show how it makes a difference whether we consider her as an inventor or a discoverer.

6. Make some notes for a discussion or an essay on a feminist reading of Alice Munro's "Eskimo" (p. 11). Make clear the different senses in which Kennard's ideas about "conventions" operate in your reading of that story.

Chapter Six

Marxist Criticism: Economic Struggle in Literature

A BRIEF INTRODUCTION TO MARXIST CRITICISM

If, like art and music, literature artistically expresses the spirit of a general culture, the question still remains: "On what is the spirit of that general culture based?" For nineteenth-century German social thinker Karl Marx, history was the story, not of the manifestation of a Divine will or of human wills manifested in the great figures of the past, but the story of an evolving general culture in which the material economic relations among people were the basic forces of change.

One implication of this view is that artistic styles have changed over time because everything in general culture has changed, and general culture has changed as a function of economic developments. For example, feudal art, with its poetic tales of valiant knights and ladies in need of that valor, was understandable as the result of an economic system whose "means of production" were primarily units of land owned by nobles who formed a military class that highly valued personal courage. Similarly, when the bourgeois capitalists of the industrial revolution came to own the machines that made the new means of economic production, a new bourgeois literature was one of the results. This literature naturally included, for example, the flowering of the novel which dealt with stories of middle-class lives and values.

In Marxian terms, the economic "base" of any age determined its cultural "superstructure," which included everything from table manners to metaphysics as reflections of that base. But how did the history of the base arrive at any given stage? Marx answered this question by modifying the dialectical process of the German philosopher Hegel to form the concept of "dialectical materialism." In Marx's view, world history showed a continuing economic or material struggle in which any particular victory—say, that of the bourgeois class over the old nobility—made a "thesis," or new status quo. But any thesis inevitably calls opposing forces the "antithesis"—for example, the alienation and opposition of the proletariat or working class in the age of capitalism. The result of the ensuing class struggle is a "synthesis" of the conflicting forces. In its turn, any synthesis becomes the new thesis for the next stage of historical development where it will inevitably be met by a new antithesis.

For Marxist criticism, the historical conflicts in the universe and their results, like the psychological conflicts and their results for Freudian criticism, could be reflected in an author or in a work; but in either case a close study would reveal a connection of content to economic cause. Literature could therefore be read as expressing the conflicting dialectical ideologies of the historical period in which it was written. For Marxist criticism, then, the study of economic history makes the favored focus of literary inquiry.

Yet the critical discourse of Marxism has itself evolved and is far from settled today. Because history is so vast, and economic relations are so complicated, **Marxism** has been a term evoked to name a wide, disparate, and sometimes contradictory set of assumptions about both literature and the functions of a critic in relation to it. For, true to its idea of history in general, the history of Marxist criticism has shown dialectical features of its own, with older views being attacked and discredited and new views taking their places.

The most general example of this process may be seen in the example of Marx's ideas themselves. Today's view of Marx sees him as some contemporary psychologists see Freud—as an illuminating philosopher with a powerful analytical method, but no longer as a sage who completely understood the topic of history once and for all. In this spirit, any crude cause-and-effect relation of history to literature has come to seem overly determined and an example of "vulgar Marxism." Increasingly, literature has come to be seen as helping to create history as well as to reflect it—and this applies to economic history. In this way, the so-called "muckraking" American novels that helped frame anti-monopoly legislation early in this century (Upton Sinclair's exposé of the meatpacking industry, *The Jungle*, is an example) may be seen as one instance of literature's taking on an active political and economic role.

In another dialectical process, modern Marxist criticism has acted on and reacted with other contemporary approaches. Perhaps most important today are the "structuralist" views of the French Marxist philosopher Louis Althusser and his student Pierre Macherey (for Structuralism see p. 156). For Althusser and Macherey, history itself is a "text," a symbolic structure written by people and therefore readable by them in turn. In this situation, criticism becomes a political act that can change history by changing the way history in general, and economic history in particular, is read. Ideology, in this view, is, in the words of Michael Ryan, "the beliefs, attitudes, and habits of feeling and behavior that a society inculcates in order to generate an automatic reproduction of its structuring premises." That is, society promotes beliefs that will maintain that society's structure. Literature portrays these beliefs and attitudes, and literary criticism can discover the ideological basis of them. Marxist critics, then, seek to uncover the political implications that they claim traditional criticism has tended to cover up either by ignoring the issues or by falsely considering them as immutable facts of nature.

In looking at history as a language to be interpreted, contemporary Marxist critics are like other critics who may differ in ideological bent. For example, they may be seen to resemble some contemporary psychoanalytic critics who read the mind as a "text" or some contemporary Feminists who "read" the "text" of gender. In this way, too, many contemporary Feminist critics may consider themselves Marxists as well as Feminists.

However, the precise relation of Marxist criticism to other approaches is a matter of debate. Fredric Jameson, for instance, views Marxism as the primary or fundamental approach to which all other approaches are simply supplementary. For Jameson, Marxism is "the absolute horizon of all reading and all interpretation" (*The Political Unconscious*). On the other hand, Terry Eagleton, among the most influential of contemporary Marxist critics, prefaces one of his books by suggesting that his study "conjointly uses" three approaches: the perspectives of poststructuralism, of feminism and psychoanalysis, and of historical materialism or Marxism (*The Rape of Clarissa*).

On the level of individual Marxist criticisms, the ideological issues are less clear than any overview can do justice to, yet perhaps Peter Kosenko's Marxist analysis of Shirley Jackson's "The Lottery" in this chapter will illustrate the spirit of a critical enterprise that seeks revealing connections between the material facts of economics and other aspects of human life. Certainly, Kosenko's analysis reflects Althusser's understanding of ideology by attempting to uncover the underlying beliefs, attitudes, and habits of the lottery and the village society. As well, he sees these beliefs, as represented in the lottery, as reinforcing "the village's hierarchical social order." Kosenko also makes use of other critical approaches but uses them in service of his Marxist view. For example, in noting that one character wears the jeans of the common person but the white shirt of the businessman, Kosenko is reading as closely as any formalist critic. However, the point of observing this detail is to clarify the way the character preserves an illusion of democracy.

Other Marxist criticism based on later developments in theory may be found in Tom Bowden's reading of Pope's poem, "The Rape of the Lock," and in Stephen Watt's reading of Samuel Beckett's play, *Happy Days* (p. 872). See also the essay by Eric Mottram in the Appendix I, where he discusses Poe's "Purloined Letter."

SHIRLEY JACKSON (1919–1965) was born in San Francisco and moved in her teens to Rochester, New York. Her experiences on the West Coast are the subject of her first book, *The Road Through the Wall* (1948). She began college at the University of Rochester, but dropped out due to severe depression, a problem which would torment her throughout her life. She eventually graduated from Syracuse University in 1940 and, in the same year, married literary critic Stanley Edgar Hyman. When he became a faculty member at Bennington College in Vermont, the couple settled there permanently in a nineteenth-century house; "Our major exports," Jackson once said of this house, "are books and children, both of which we produce in abundance."

Two of Jackson's books, *Life Among the Savages* (1953) and *Raising Demons* (1957) are comic accounts of Bennington family life. Despite the lighhearted subject matter of these works, as well as those books which she wrote for children, Jackson is primarily known for her preoccupation with horror, psychological disturbances, the supernatural, and the nature of evil; these themes are explored in *Hangsaman* (1951), *The Bird's Nest* (1954), *The Haunting of Hill House* (1959), and *We Have Always Lived in the Castle* (1963). Jackson died of heart failure in 1965.

SHIRLEY JACKSON
The Lottery
(1948)

The morning of June 27th was clear and sunny, with the fresh warmth of a full-summer day; the flowers were blossoming profusely and the grass was richly green. The people of the village began to gather in the square, between the post office and the bank, around ten o'clock; in some towns there were so many people that the lottery took two days and had to be started on June 26th, but in this village, where there were only about three hundred people, the whole lottery took less than two hours, so it could begin at ten o'clock in the morning and still be through in time to allow the villagers to get home for noon dinner.

10   The children assembled first, of course. School was recently over for the summer, and the feeling of liberty sat uneasily on most of them; they tended to gather together quietly for a while before they broke into boisterous play, and their talk was still of the classroom and the teacher, of books and reprimands. Bobby Martin had already stuffed his pockets full of stones, and the other boys soon followed his example, selecting the smoothest and roundest stones; Bobby and Harry Jones and Dickie Delacroix—the villagers pronounced his name "Dellacroy"—eventually made a great pile of stones in one corner of the square and guarded it against the raids of the other boys. The girls stood aside, talking among
20 themselves, looking over their shoulders at the boys, and the very small children rolled in the dust or clung to the hands of their older brothers or sisters.

Soon the men began to gather, surveying their own children, speaking of planting and rain, tractors and taxes. They stood together, away from the pile of stones in the corner, and their jokes were quiet and they smiled rather than laughed. The women, wearing faded house dresses and sweaters, came shortly after their menfolk. They greeted one another and exchanged bits of gossip as they went to join their husbands. Soon the women, standing by their husbands, began to call to their chil-
30 dren, and the children came reluctantly, having to be called four or five times. Bobby Martin ducked under his mother's grasping hand and ran,

laughing, back to the pile of stones. His father spoke up sharply, and Bobby came quickly and took his place between his father and his oldest brother.

The lottery was conducted—as were the square dances, the teenage club, the Halloween program—by Mr. Summers, who had time and energy to devote to civic activities. He was a round-faced, jovial man and he ran the coal business, and people were sorry for him, because he had no children and his wife was a scold. When he arrived in the square,
40 carrying the black wooden box, there was a murmur of conversation among the villagers, and he waved and called, "Little late today, folks." The postmaster, Mr. Graves, followed him, carrying a three-legged stool, and the stool was put in the center of the square and Mr. Summers set the black box down on it. The villagers kept their distance, leaving a space between themselves and the stool, and when Mr. Summers said, "Some of you fellows want to give me a hand?" there was a hesitation before two men, Mr. Martin and his oldest son, Baxter, came forward to hold the box steady on the stool while Mr. Summers stirred up the papers inside it.

50 The original paraphernalia for the lottery had been lost long ago, and the black box now resting on the stool had been put into use even before Old Man Warner, the oldest man in town, was born. Mr. Summers spoke frequently to the villagers about making a new box, but no one liked to upset even as much tradition as was represented by the black box. There was a story that the present box had been made with some pieces of the box that had preceded it, the one that had been constructed when the first people settled down to make a village here. Every year, after the lottery, Mr. Summers began talking again about a new box, but every year the subject was allowed to fade off without any-
60 thing's being done. The black box grew shabbier each year; by now it was no longer completely black but splintered badly along one side to show the original wood color, and in some places faded or stained.

Mr. Martin and his oldest son, Baxter, held the black box securely on the stool until Mr. Summers had stirred the papers thoroughly with his hand. Because so much of the ritual had been forgotten or discarded, Mr. Summers had been successful in having slips of paper substituted for the chips of wood that had been used for generations. Chips of wood, Mr. Summers had argued, had been all very well when the village was tiny, but now that the population was more than three hundred and likely to
70 keep on growing, it was necessary to use something that would fit more easily into the black box. The night before the lottery, Mr. Summers and Mr. Graves made up the slips of paper and put them in the box, and it was then taken to the safe of Mr. Summers' coal company and locked up until Mr. Summers was ready to take it to the square next morning. The rest of the year, the box was put away, sometimes one place, sometimes another; it had spent one year in Mr. Graves's barn and another year underfoot in the post office, and sometimes it was set on a shelf in the Martin grocery and left there.

There was a great deal of fussing to be done before Mr. Summers
80 declared the lottery open. There were the lists to make up—of heads of
families, heads of households in each family, members of each household
in each family. There was the proper swearing-in of Mr. Summers by the
postmaster, as the official of the lottery; at one time, some people remembered, there had been a recital of some sort, performed by the official of the lottery, a perfunctory, tuneless chant that had been rattled off
duly each year; some people believed that the official of the lottery used
to stand just so when he said or sang it, others believed that he was supposed to walk among the people, but years and years ago this part of the
ritual had been allowed to lapse. There had been, also, a ritual salute,
90 which the official of the lottery had had to use in addressing each person who came up to draw from the box, but this also had changed with
time, until now it was felt necessary only for the official to speak to
each person approaching. Mr. Summers was very good at all this; in his
clean white shirt and blue jeans, with one hand resting carelessly on the
black box, he seemed very proper and important as he talked interminably to Mr. Graves and the Martins.

Just as Mr. Summers finally left off talking and turned to the assembled villagers, Mrs. Hutchinson came hurriedly along the path to the
square, her sweater thrown over her shoulders, and slid into place in
100 the back of the crowd. "Clean forgot what day it was," she said to Mrs.
Delacroix, who stood next to her, and they both laughed softly. "Thought
my old man was out back stacking wood," Mrs. Hutchinson went on, "and
then I looked out the window and the kids were gone, and then I remembered it was the twenty-seventh and came a-running." She dried her
hands on her apron, and Mrs. Delacroix said, "You're in time, though.
They're still talking away up there."

Mrs. Hutchinson craned her neck to see through the crowd and found
her husband and children standing near the front. She tapped Mrs.
Delacroix on the arm as a farewell and began to make her way through
110 the crowd. The people separated good-humoredly to let her through; two
or three people said, in voices just loud enough to be heard across the
crowd, "Here comes your Missus, Hutchinson," and "Bill, she made it after all." Mrs. Hutchinson reached her husband, and Mr. Summers, who
had been waiting, said cheerfully, "Thought we were going to have to get
on without you, Tessie." Mrs. Hutchinson said, grinning, "Wouldn't have
me leave m'dishes in the sink, now, would you, Joe?," and soft laughter
ran through the crowd as the people stirred back into position after Mrs.
Hutchinson's arrival.

"Well, now," Mr. Summers said soberly, "guess we better get started,
120 get this over with, so's we can go back to work. Anybody ain't here?"

"Dunbar," several people said. "Dunbar, Dunbar."

Mr. Summers consulted his list. "Clyde Dunbar," he said. "That's
right. He's broke his leg, hasn't he? Who's drawing for him?"

"Me, I guess," a woman said, and Mr. Summers turned to look at her.
"Wife draws for her husband," Mr. Summers said. "Don't you have a

grown boy to do it for you, Janey?" Although Mr. Summers and everyone else in the village knew the answer perfectly well, it was the business of the official of the lottery to ask such questions formally. Mr. Summers waited with an expression of polite interest while Mrs. Dunbar answered.

130   "Horace's not but sixteen yet," Mrs. Dunbar said regretfully. "Guess I gotta fill in for the old man this year."

"Right," Mr. Summers said. He made a note on the list he was holding. Then he asked, "Watson boy drawing this year?"

A tall boy in the crowd raised his hand. "Here," he said. "I'm drawing for m'mother and me." He blinked his eyes nervously and ducked his head as several voices in the crowd said things like "Good fellow, Jack," and "Glad to see your mother's got a man to do it."

"Well," Mr. Summers said, "guess that's everyone. Old Man Warner make it?"

140   "Here," a voice said, and Mr. Summers nodded.

A sudden hush fell on the crowd as Mr. Summers cleared his throat and looked at the list. "All ready?" he called. "Now, I'll read the names—heads of families first—and the men come up and take a paper out of the box. Keep the paper folded in your hand without looking at it until everyone has had a turn. Everything clear?"

The people had done it so many times that they only half listened to the directions; most of them were quiet, wetting their lips, not looking around. Then Mr. Summers raised one hand high and said, "Adams." A man disengaged himself from the crowd and came forward: "Hi, Steve,"
150 Mr. Summers said, and Mr. Adams said, "Hi, Joe." They grinned at one another humorlessly and nervously. Then Mr. Adams reached into the black box and took out a folded paper. He held it firmly by one corner as he turned and went hastily back to his place in the crowd, where he stood a little apart from his family, not looking down at his hand.

"Allen." Mr. Summers said, "Anderson. . . . Bentham."

"Seems like there's no time at all between lotteries any more," Mrs. Delacroix said to Mrs. Graves in the back row. "Seems like we got through with the last one only last week."

"Time sure goes fast," Mrs. Graves said.

160   "Clark. . . . Delacroix."

"There goes my old man," Mrs. Delacroix said. She held her breath while her husband went forward.

"Dunbar," Mr. Summers said, and Mrs. Dunbar went steadily to the box while one of the women said, "Go on, Janey," and another said, "There she goes."

"We're next," Mrs. Graves said. She watched while Mr. Graves came around from the side of the box, greeted Mr. Summers gravely, and selected a slip of paper from the box. By now, all through the crowd there were men holding the small folded papers in their large hands, turning
170 them over and over nervously. Mrs. Dunbar and her two sons stood together, Mrs. Dunbar holding the slip of paper.

"Harburt. . . . Hutchinson."

"Get up there, Bill," Mrs. Hutchinson said, and the people near her laughed.

"Jones."

"They do say," Mr. Adams said to Old Man Warner, who stood next to him, "that over in the north village they're talking of giving up the lottery."

Old Man Warner snorted. "Pack of crazy fools," he said. "Listening
180 to the young folks, nothing's good enough for *them*. Next thing you know, they'll be wanting to go back to living in caves, nobody work any more, live *that* way for a while. Used to be a saying about 'Lottery in June, corn be heavy soon.' First thing you know, we'd all be eating stewed chickweed and acorns. There's *always* been a lottery," he added petulantly. "Bad enough to see young Joe Summers up there joking with everybody."

"Some places have already quit lotteries," Mrs. Adams said.

"Nothing but trouble in *that*," Old Man Warner said stoutly. "Pack of young fools."

190   "Martin." And Bobby Martin watched his father go forward. "Overdyke. . . . Percy."

"I wish they'd hurry," Mrs. Dunbar said to her older son. "I wish they'd hurry."

"They're almost through," her son said.

"You get ready to run tell Dad," Mrs. Dunbar said.

Mr. Summers called his own name and then stepped forward precisely and selected a slip from the box. Then he called, "Warner."

"Seventy-seventh year I been in the lottery," Old Man Warner said as he went through the crowd. "Seventy-seventh time."

200   "Watson." The tall boy came awkwardly through the crowd. Someone said, "Don't be nervous, Jack," and Mr. Summers said, "Take your time, son."

"Zanini."

After that, there was a long pause, a breathless pause, until Mr. Summers, holding his slip of paper in the air, said, "All right, fellows." For a minute, no one moved, and then all the slips of paper were opened. Suddenly, all the women began to speak at once, saying, "Who is it?," "Who's got it?," "Is it the Dunbars?," "Is it the Watsons?" Then the voices began to say, "It's Hutchinson. It's Bill," "Bill Hutchinson's got it."

210   "Go tell your father," Mrs. Dunbar said to her older son.

People began to look around to see the Hutchinsons. Bill Hutchinson was standing quiet, staring down at the paper in his hand. Suddenly, Tessie Hutchinson shouted to Mr. Summers, "You didn't give him time enough to take any paper he wanted. I saw you. It wasn't fair!"

"Be a good sport, Tessie," Mrs. Delacroix called, and Mrs. Graves said, "All of us took the same chance."

"Shut up, Tessie," Bill Hutchinson said.

"Well, everyone," Mr. Summers said, "that was done pretty fast, and now we've got to be hurrying a little more to get it done in time." He consulted his next list. "Bill," he said, "you draw for the Hutchinson family. You got any other households in the Hutchinsons?"

"There's Don and Eva," Mrs. Hutchinson yelled. "Make *them* take their chance!"

"Daughters draw with their husbands' families, Tessie," Mr. Summers said gently. "You know that as well as anyone else."

"It wasn't *fair*," Tessie said.

"I guess not, Joe," Bill Hutchinson said regretfully. "My daughter draws with her husband's family, that's only fair. And I've got no other family except the kids."

"Then, as far as drawing for families is concerned, it's you," Mr. Summers said in explanation, "and as far as drawing for households is concerned, that's you, too. Right?"

"Right," Bill Hutchinson said.

"How many kids, Bill?" Mr. Summers asked formally.

"Three," Bill Hutchinson said. "There's Bill, Jr., and Nancy, and little Dave. And Tessie and me."

"All right, then," Mr. Summers said. "Harry, you got their tickets back?"

Mr. Graves nodded and held up the slips of paper. "Put them in the box, then," Mr. Summers directed. "Take Bill's and put it in."

"I think we ought to start over," Mrs. Hutchinson said, as quietly as she could. "I tell you it wasn't *fair*. You didn't give him time enough to choose. *Every*body saw that."

Mr. Graves had selected the five slips and put them in the box, and he dropped all the papers but those onto the ground, where the breeze caught them and lifted them off.

"Listen, everybody," Mrs. Hutchinson was saying to the people around her.

"Ready, Bill?" Mr. Summers asked, and Bill Hutchinson, with one quick glance around at his wife and children, nodded.

"Remember," Mr. Summers said, "take the slips and keep them folded until each person has taken one. Harry, you help little Dave." Mr. Graves took the hand of the little boy, who came willingly with him up to the box. "Take a paper out of the box, Davy," Mr. Summers said. Davy put his hand into the box and laughed. "Take just *one* paper," Mr. Summers said. "Harry, you hold it for him." Mr. Graves took the child's hand and removed the folded paper from the tight fist and held it while little Dave stood next to him and looked up at him wonderingly.

"Nancy next," Mr. Summers said. Nancy was twelve, and her school friends breathed heavily as she went forward, switching her skirt, and took a slip daintily from the box. "Bill, Jr.," Mr. Summers said, and Billy, his face red and his feet over-large, nearly knocked the box over as he got a paper out. "Tessie," Mr. Summers said. She hesitated for a minute, looking around defiantly, and then set her lips and went up to the box. She snatched a paper out and held it behind her.

"Bill," Mr. Summers said, and Bill Hutchinson reached into the box and felt around, bringing his hand out at last with the slip of paper in it.

The crowd was quiet. A girl whispered, "I hope it's not Nancy," and the sound of the whisper reached the edges of the crowd.

270   "It's not the way it used to be," Old Man Warner said clearly. "People ain't the way they used to be."

"All right," Mr. Summers said. "Open the papers. Harry, you open little Dave's."

Mr. Graves opened the slip of paper and there was a general sigh through the crowd as he held it up and everyone could see that it was blank. Nancy and Bill, Jr., opened theirs at the same time, and both beamed and laughed, turning around to the crowd and holding their slips of paper above their heads.

"Tessie," Mr. Summers said. There was a pause, and then Mr.
280 Summers looked at Bill Hutchinson, and Bill unfolded his paper and showed it. It was blank.

"It's Tessie," Mr. Summers said, and his voice was hushed. "Show us her paper, Bill."

Bill Hutchinson went over to his wife and forced the slip of paper out of her hand. It had a black spot on it, the black spot Mr. Summers had made the night before with the heavy pencil in the coal-company office. Bill Hutchinson held it up, and there was a stir in the crowd.

"All right, folks," Mr. Summers said. "Let's finish quickly."

Although the villagers had forgotten the ritual and lost the original
290 black box, they still remembered to use stones. The pile of stones the boys had made earlier was ready; there were stones on the ground with the blowing scraps of paper that had come out of the box. Mrs. Delacroix selected a stone so large she had to pick it with both hands and turned to Mrs. Dunbar. "Come on," she said. "Hurry up."

Mrs. Dunbar had small stones in both hands, and she said, gasping for breath, "I can't run at all. You'll have to go ahead and I'll catch up with you."

The children had stones already, and someone gave little Davy Hutchinson a few pebbles.

300   Tessie Hutchinson was in the center of a cleared space by now, and she held her hands out desperately as the villagers moved in on her. "It isn't fair," she said. A stone hit her on the side of the head.

Old Man Warner was saying, "Come on, come on, everyone." Steve Adams was in the front of the crowd of villagers, with Mrs. Graves beside him.

"It isn't fair, it isn't right," Mrs. Hutchinson screamed, and then they were upon her.

ACCOUNT: PETER KOSENKO ON A
MARXIST READING OF "THE LOTTERY"

Kosenko begins by describing the original response of readers to the story—a reaction of "bewilderment, speculation, and good old fashioned abuse." He reports that the story had an effect like no other before published by *The New Yorker* when it appeared in the June 28, 1948, edition. Though Shirley Jackson rarely commented on her work and had no desire to be "the pundit of the Sunday supplements," she did respond to persistent inquiries about her intentions in this case as follows:

> I suppose, I hoped, by setting a particularly brutal ancient rite in the present and in my own village to shock the story's readers with a graphic dramatization of the pointless violence and general inhumanity in their own lives.

Kosenko argues that these remarks have wrongly and unduly influenced critics and that the story's shock has been hitherto explained in two ways: as an examination of "man's ineradicable primitive aggressivity" or as an example of "man's victimization" by "unexamined and unchanging traditions which he could easily change if only he realized their implications."

Kosenko finds these explanations unsatisfactory for several reasons, as he goes on to say:

> Missing from both of these approaches, however, is a careful analysis of the abundance of social detail that links the lottery to the ordinary social practices of the village. No mere "irrational" tradition, the lottery is an *ideological mechanism*. It serves to reinforce the village's hierarchical social order by instilling the villagers with an unconscious fear that if they resist the order they might be selected in the next lottery. In the process of creating this fear, it also reproduces the ideology necessary for the smooth functioning of that social order, despite its inherent inequality.

Kosenko sees the village setting as a small-scale example of modern capitalist socioeconomic stratification. First, he points to the occupations of some principal citizens:

> The village's most powerful man, Mr. Summers, owns the village's largest business (a coal concern) and is also its mayor, since he has, Jackson writes, more "time and energy [read money and leisure] to devote to civic activities" than others. (Summers' very name suggests that he has become

Peter Kosenko, "A Marxist/Feminist Reading of Shirley Jackson's 'The Lottery' *The New Orleans Review* 12, no. 1 (Spring 1985), 27–32.

a man of leisure through his wealth.) Next in line in the social hierarchy is Mr. Graves, the village's second most powerful government official—its postmaster. (His name may suggest the gravity of officialism.) And beneath Mr. Graves is Mr. Martin, who has the economically advantageous position of being the grocer in a village of three hundred.

The most powerful men in the village control not only the town but the lottery itself, which is held in a space between the post office and the bank—between "two buildings which represent government and finance, the institutions from which Summers, Graves, and Martin derive their power." How then is the evil of the lottery tied to the disorder of capitalist social organization?

> First the lottery's rules of participation reflect and *codify* a rigid social hierarchy based upon an inequitable social division of labor. Second, the fact that everyone participates in the lottery and understands *consciously* that its outcome is pure chance gives it a certain "democratic" aura that obscures its first codifying function. Third, the villagers believe *unconsciously* that their commitment to a work ethic will grant them some magical immunity from selection. Fourth, this work ethic prevents them from understanding that the lottery's actual function is not to encourage work *per se* but to reinforce an inequitable social *division* of labor. Finally, after working through these points, it will be easier to explain how Jackson's choice of Tessie Hutchinson as the lottery's victim/scapegoat reveals the lottery to be an ideological mechanism which serves to defuse the average villager's deep, inarticulate dissatisfaction with the social order in which he lives by channeling it into anger directed at the victims of that social order.

Though the lottery appears to be a matter of universal or democratic participation, the *rules* it is founded on suggest a different basis. Besides being controlled by the town's most powerful men, the patriarchal organization of both the village and the lottery is based on a distinction between labor for wages and the disenfranchised labor of women, who work outside the wage economy. Again, though Mr. Summers wears jeans, as if to identify himself with the common people, he also wears a businessman's white shirt and is seen to talk mainly with his social equals. Further, his apparently general appeal for help in conducting the drawing is actually met by Mr. Martin, the third most powerful man in the village. In this way, the lottery functions as an illusion of democracy to keep the villagers from criticizing the real class structure of their society. At the same time, the lottery also reinforces a work ethic that, among other things "keeps women powerless in their homes and Mr. Summers powerful in his coal company office."

Among the other characters, Old Man Warner functions as a spokesman for a superstitious view of the work ethic that keeps everyone in his or her place in the general subordination to finance capitalism. On the other hand, Tessie Hutchinson makes an unconscious rebellion first manifested in her being "unintentionally" late. The village's singling out of the Dunbars and Watsons indicate the villagers' unconscious commitment to the work ethic and opposition to those who don't follow it or who rebel against it:

> In stoning Tessie, the villagers treat her as a scapegoat onto which they can project and through which they can "purge"—actually, the term *repress* is better, since the impulse is conserved rather than eliminated—their own temptations to rebel. The only places we can see these rebellion impulses are in Tessie, in Mr. and Mrs. Adams' suggestion, squelched by Warner, that the lottery might be given up, and in the laughter of the crowd. (The crowd's nervous laughter is ambivalent: It expresses uncertainty about the validity of the taboo that Tessie breaks.) But ultimately, these rebellious impulses are channeled by the lottery and its attendant ideology away from their proper objects—capitalism and capitalist patriarchs—into anger at the rebellious victims of capitalist social organization. Like Tessie, the villagers cannot articulate their rebellion because the massive force of ideology stands in the way.
>
> The lottery functions, then, to terrorize the village into accepting, in the *name* of work and democracy, the inequitable social division of labor and power on which its social order depends.

Kosenko concludes by wondering how we are to take the story's pessimistic view of possibilities for social change. He allows that capitalism has many subtle means of keeping the frustrations it creates from turning into a critique of the capitalist system. Nevertheless, "pockets of resistance" are bound to become formed among the disillusioned:

> Perhaps it is not Jackson's intention to deny this, but to shock her complacent readers with an exaggerated image of the ideological *modus operandi* of capitalism: accusing those whom it cannot or will not employ of being lazy, promoting "the family" as the essential social unit in order to discourage broader associations and identifications, offering men power over their wives as a consolation for their powerlessness in the labor market, and pitting workers against each other and against the unemployed. It is our fault as readers if our own complacent pessimism makes us *read* Jackson's story pessimistically as a parable of man's innate depravity.

SUGGESTIONS FOR DISCUSSION AND WRITING

1. How would you characterize the **narrator's attitude** or **point of view** taken toward the events described in the first few paragraphs? Do

you understand a different attitude when you reread those paragraphs in the context of having finished the story? Describe the ways in which reading the account of a Marxist approach did or did not change your sense of the story's narrative attitude. Explain and exemplify your answers.

2. What are some of the **subplots** in the story? What do they contribute to its **atmosphere** and **setting?** What, for example, do the differences in behavior of young and old people contribute? In what ways does Kosenko use the evidence of subplots, atmosphere, and setting in his analysis?

3. Which of his central points do you think Kosenko makes most convincingly? Which least? Explain and exemplify your answers by particular reference to the text.

4. Compare this story with "Cloud, Castle, Lake" by Vladimir Nabokov (p. 301). In what similar and what different ways does each author work to preserve the ending as a surprise without artistic cheating? What function, or functions, does the surprise ending perform, implicitly or explicitly, in Kosenko's Marxist analysis?

5. Write an essay describing the ways in which Shirley Jackson maintains an **atmosphere** of ordinary normality in her story. Be sure to address the function of the atmosphere claimed by Kosenko, whether you agree or disagree with his analysis.

6. Note the economic implications of Melville's subtitle in his story, "Bartleby the Scrivener: A Story of Wall Street" (p. 224). Make some notes for discussion or an essay on a Marxist reading of that story.

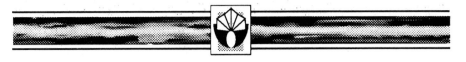

Chapter Seven

Racial and Ethnic Criticism: Toward Multiculturalism

A BRIEF INTRODUCTION TO RACIAL AND ETHNIC CRITICISM

Unlike the New Criticism, which emphasizes close analysis of literary texts considered more or less in isolation, most other current critical approaches draw attention to various elements in the cultural contexts that influence authors and readers. A Marxist critic, for example, might focus on economic forces, and a Feminist critic might stress the importance of gender. Similarly, race and ethnicity provide another basis from which to examine literature. This perspective assumes particular importance in the study of American literature, since Americans are famously such a richly mixed lot of various racial, ethnic, and national groups. In recent years, many critics have called for greater attention both to the way members of minority groups are portrayed in literature and, especially, to works written by minority authors.

Some critics have focused on what is sometimes called *stereotypical* criticism, on the way members of various racial and ethnic groups are portrayed both in "mainstream" literature and in works by minority authors. In an essay in *Studies in American Indian Literature*, for example, Joseph M. Backus argues that affection for Mark Twain should not keep us from recognizing the hostility toward Indians that taints even some of his greatest works. "In Twain," Backus writes, "there would seem to be an inherited puritanical blindness that causes him to see all Indians as agents of Satan." Twain's "only fully developed Indian character," the villainous Injun Joe of *Adventures of Tom Sawyer*, reflects several widespread prejudices against Indians—he is a drunkard and a liar, he is consumed by a desire for revenge, he is bloodthirsty and brutal. Critical assessments of Twain, Backus says, should include an acknowledgment of his bigotry; similarly, studies of Walt Whitman should note his far more positive portrayals of Indians and his possible indebtedness to the rhythms of Indian poetry. Stereotypical criticism can thus focus the reader's attention on issues that might otherwise be overlooked in the study of classic American works.

Other critics of racial and ethnic literature have concentrated on challenging traditional ideas about which works deserve to be regarded as "classic." In *Minority Language and Literature: Retrospective and Perspective,* Dexter Fisher maintains that important literary works by Asian Americans, Blacks, Chicanos, Native Americans, and Puerto Ricans have unjustly been excluded from the canon, and that our understanding of American literature has been impoverished as a result:

> It is the juxtaposition of ideas, world views, and linguistic variations through literature that revitalizes our notions of man and culture, making such terms as "dominant" and "minority" ultimately irrelevant. By revising the canon of American literature, we challenge some values and affirm others, with the result that our understanding of tradition is deepened, our appreciation of neglected literatures refined, and our concept of genre expanded.

Critics who share Fisher's convictions have brought recognition to a number of works by minority authors. For example, Marion Wilson Starling and other scholars have shown that slave narratives deserve a place in the study of American literature. Other critics have worked to show that minority novelists such as Nora Zeale Hurston, once dismissed as of minor importance, in fact are artistically accomplished and socially significant. The success of such critical endeavors is to some extent reflected in the pages of scholarly journals and literature anthologies and in the curricula of schools and colleges across the nation. It seems safe to say that minority literature is now far more widely read and far more highly regarded than it was just a few decades ago.

In addition to arguing that the canon should include a broader range of works, many critics of ethnic and minority literature have argued that our standards of literary merit should be re-examined. In *Blues, Ideology, and Afro-American Literature,* for example, Houston A. Baker, Jr., argues that "historical and literary-critical discourse in the United States have been powerfully arrested for generations among (and by) New England male Brahmins"; only literature that fits the tastes and expectations of such "Brahmins" was seen as having any value or importance. Rejecting such narrow criteria, Baker and others have explored the aesthetics of minority traditions in literature, maintaining that such traditions reflect values, assumptions, and standards other than those of the dominant Anglo-American tradition. In the article summarized later in this chapter, for example, John E. Loftis takes issue with those critics who have dismissed Richard Wright's fiction as "crude and careless" or "technically unpolished." On the contrary, Loftis argues, a story such as "The Man Who Was Almost a Man" can best be seen as a highly sophisticated parody of some traditional elements found in many works by white American authors. A reader who assumes that Wright is merely attempting to mimic those elements will fundamentally misinterpret the story—and will fail to appreciate its artistry. Similarly, Charles T. Davis points out, in "Black Literature and the Critic," that black literature often incorporates "matter defying easy ordering, matter that often has a source in popular culture." Black writers may draw on "folk materials" such as sermons, worksongs, and jazz; they may engage in "bold and rewarding experimentation" that reflects the political and social unrest of recent years. To understand such literature, critics must adjust to "the realities of history, form and language in the black world, seek an appreciation for a music, indeed, for a literary performance, that is off as well as on the beat."

Recently, some critics of racial and ethnic literature have called for changes in critical methods, as well as in critical standards. In an essay in *Afro-American Literary Study in the 1990s*, Henry Louis Gates, Jr., says that mastering the methods and languages of such approaches as New Criticism, structuralism, feminism, and new historicism has been "an act of empowerment" for black critics of his generation, helping them to win wider recognition and respect for minority literature. Now, however, critics must move beyond applying existing approaches, must "turn to the black tradition itself to develop theories of criticism indigenous to our literatures." His comments serve as another indication that the study of minority literatures is a critical area still changing and expanding.

One enduring characteristic of many studies of minority literature is an interest in interdisciplinary approaches. Arguing that such literature can be understood only in the context of the cultures that produced it, critics frequently draw upon the insights and methods of fields such as history, anthropology, and the arts. Paula Gunn Allen, in the introductory essay to *Studies in American Indian Literature*, points out that understanding works from minority cultures often requires special preparation:

> Universality of meaning may necessarily be required of all works of literature, but it may be that such universality must be got at from a very particular point of view. If this is so, the critic in American Indian literature becomes important—not as a scholarly adjunct to the creating and re-creating that are always the component parts of the synergy between teller and listener, but as a mediator who allows teller and listener to share a particular understanding even though they come from widely divergent traditions.

Thus, Allen says, the critic of Indian literature must become familiar with tribal history and traditions, as well as with the present-day situation of the tribe; since Indian literature was traditionally sung or chanted, knowledge of musicology is also important. Similarly, Kenneth Lincoln, in *Native American Renaissance*, argues that "Art is not on the decorative edges of Indian cultures, but alive at the functional heart: in blankets that warm bodies, potteries that store food, songs that gather power, stories that bond people, ceremonies that heal, disciplines that

strengthen spirits." Therefore, critics must move beyond narrow definitions and incorporate considerations of "folklore, history, religion, hand-
craft, and the expressive arts" in their attempts to understand Native
American literature.

As a relatively recent and rapidly evolving field, studies of racial
and ethnic literature take on many and various manifestations. Other
examples of such studies will be found in the account of Gladys
Margaret Williams's reading of Gwendolyn Brooks's sonnets (p. 444)
and the account of Rob Nixon on Shakespeare's *The Tempest* (p. 781).

RICHARD WRIGHT (1908–1960) was born to a sharecropper father and schoolteacher
mother. When Wright was very young, his family moved to Memphis, Tennessee;
shortly after this relocation, Richard's father deserted his family. Because of the family's lack of money, Wright spent most of his youth moving from town to town with his
mother, who was constantly searching for work although she was in ill health. Wright
was often forced to live in foster homes, orphanages, and with his grandmother in Jackson, Mississippi. The experiences of his early life are chronicled in *Black Boy,* first published in 1945.

His graduation (as valedictorian) from the ninth grade marked the end of Wright's
formal education. In 1927 he set off for Chicago, where he later became a member of the
Communist Party and began writing. In the early 1930s he was employed writing guide-
books for the Depression-era Federal Writer's Project. During these years in Chicago,
Wright wrote *Uncle Tom's Children* (1938), a collection of four novellas which brought him
some success and recognition. In 1940 Wright's first novel, *Native Son,* was published, bringing Wright international acclaim. In 1942 Wright became disillusioned with the Communist
Party over racial issues. In 1947 he left the United States and moved to Paris, where he became acquainted with Andre Gide, Gertrude Stein, Jean Paul Sartre, and Simon de Beauvoir.
He traveled throughout Europe, always returning to France, and died in Paris in 1960. His
other works include *Twelve Million Black Voices* (1941), *The Outsider* (1953), *Savage Holiday*
(1954), *Pagan Spain* (1957), and *The Long Dream* (1958).

RICHARD WRIGHT

The Man Who Was Almost a Man
(1940)

Dave struck out across the fields, looking homeward through paling
light. Whuts the usa talkin wid em niggers in the field? Anyhow, his
mother was putting supper on the table. Them niggers can't understand
nothing. One of these days he was going to get a gun and practice shooting, then they can't talk to him as though he were a little boy. He
slowed, looking at the ground. Shucks, Ah ain scareda them even ef they
are biggern me! Aw, Ah know whut Ahma do. . . . Ahm going by ol
Joe's sto n git that Sears Roebuck catlog n look at them guns. Mabbe Ma
will lemme buy one when she gits mah pay from ol man Hawkins.
10 Ahma beg her t gimme some money. Ahm ol enough to hava gun. Ahm
seventeen. Almost a man. He strode, feeling his long, loose-jointed
limbs. Shucks, a man oughta hava little gun aftah he done worked hard
all day. . . .

He came in sight of Joe's store. A yellow lantern glowed on the front porch. He mounted steps and went through the screen door, hearing it bang behind him. There was a strong smell of coal oil and mackerel fish. He felt very confident until he saw fat Joe walk in through the rear door, then his courage began to ooze.

'Howdy, Dave! Whutcha want?'

20 'How yuh, Mistah Joe? Aw, Ah don wanna buy nothing. Ah jus wanted t see ef yuhd lemme look at tha ol catlog erwhile.'

'Sure! You wanna see it here?'

'Nawsuh. Ah wans t take it home wid me. Ahll bring it back termorrow when Ah come in from the fiels.'

'You plannin on buyin something?'

'Yessuh.'

'Your ma letting you have your own money now?'

'Shucks. Mistah Joe, Ahm gittin t be a man like anybody else!'

Joe laughed and wiped his greasy white face with a red bandanna.

30 'Whut you plannin on buyin?'

Dave looked at the floor, scratched his head, scratched his thigh, and smiled. Then he looked up shyly.

'Ahll tell yuh, Mistah Joe, ef yuh promise yuh won't tell.'

'I promise.'

'Waal, Ahma buy a gun.'

'A gun? Whut you want with a gun?'

'Ah wanna keep it.'

'You ain't nothing but a boy. You don't need a gun.'

'Aw, lemme have the catalog, Mistah Joe. Ahll bring it back.'

40 Joe walked through the rear door. Dave was elated. He looked around at barrels of sugar and flour. He heard Joe coming back. He craned his neck to see if he were bringing the book. Yeah, he's got it! Gawddog, he's got it!

'Here; but be sure you bring it back. It's the only one I got.'

'Sho, Mistah Joe.'

'Say, if you wanna buy a gun, why don't you buy one from me. I gotta gun to sell.'

'Will it shoot?'

'Sure it'll shoot.'

50 'Whut kind is it?'

'Oh, it's kinda old. . . . A Lefthand Wheeler. A pistol. A big one.'

'Is it got bullets in it?'

'It's loaded.'

'Kin Ah see it?'

'Where's your money?'

'Whut yuh wan fer it?'

'I'll let you have it for two dollars.'

'Just *two* dollahs? Shucks, Ah could buy tha when Ah git mah pay.'

'I'll have it here when you want it.'

60 'Awright, suh. Ah be in fer it.'

He went through the door, hearing it slam again behind him. Ahma git some money from Ma n buy me a gun! Only *two* dollahs! He tucked the thick catalogue under his arm and hurried.

'Where yuh been, boy?' His mother held a steaming dish of black-eyed peas.

'Aw, Ma, Ah jus stopped down the road t talk wid th boys.'

'Yuh know bettah than t keep suppah waitin.'

He sat down, resting the catalogue on the edge of the table.

70 'Yuh git up from there and git to the well n wash yosef! Ah ain feedin no hogs in mah house!'

She grabbed his shoulder and pushed him. He stumbled out of the room, then came back to get the catalogue.

'Whut this?'

'Aw, Ma, it's jusa catlog.'

'Who yuh git it from?'

'From Joe, down at the sto.'

'Waal, thas good. We kin use it around the house.'

'Naw, Ma.' He grabbed for it. 'Gimme mah catlog, Ma.'

She held onto it and glared at him.

80 'Quit hollerin at me! Whuts wrong wid yuh? Yuh crazy?'

'But Ma, please. It ain mine! It's Joe's! He tol me t bring it back t im termorrow.'

She gave up the book. He stumbled down the back steps, hugging the thick book under his arm. When he had splashed water on his face and hands, he groped back to the kitchen and fumbled in a corner for the towel. He bumped into a chair; it clattered to the floor. The catalogue sprawled at his feet. When he had dried his eyes he snatched up the book and held it again under his arm. His mother stood watching him.

'Now, ef yuh gonna acka fool over that ol book, Ahll take it n burn
90 it up.'

'Naw, Ma, please.'

'Waal, set down n be still!'

He sat and drew the oil lamp close. He thumbed page after page, unaware of the food his mother set on the table. His father came in. Then his small brother.

'Whutcha got there, Dave?' his father asked.

'Jusa catlog,' he answered, not looking up.

'Ywah, here they is!' His eyes glowed at blue and black revolvers. He glanced up, feeling sudden guilt. His father was watching him. He eased
100 the book under the table and rested it on his knees. After the blessing was asked, he ate. He scooped up peas and swallowed fat meat without chewing. Buttermilk helped to wash it down. He did not want to mention money before his father. He would do much better by cornering his mother when she was alone. He looked at his father uneasily out of the edge of his eye.

'Boy, how come yuh don quit foolin wid tha book n eat yo suppah?'

'Yessuh.'

'How yuh n ol man Hawkins gittin erlong?'

'Suh?'

110 'Can't yuh hear? Why don yuh lissen? Ah ast yuh how wuz yuh n ol man Hawkins gittin erlong?'

'Oh, swell, Pa. Ah plows mo lan than anybody over there.'

'Waal, yuh oughta keep yo min on whut yuh doin.'

'Yessuh.'

He poured his plate full of molasses and sopped at it slowly with a chunk of cornbread. When all but his mother had left the kitchen, he still sat and looked again at the guns in the catalogue. Lawd, ef Ah only had tha pretty one! He could almost feel the slickness of the weapon with his fingers. If he had a gun like that he would polish it and keep it shining so 120 it would never rust. N Ahd keep it loaded, by Gawd!

'Ma?'

'Hunh?'

'Ol man Hawkins give yuh mah money yit?'

'Yeah, but ain no usa yuh thinkin bout thowin nona it erway. Ahm keepin tha money sos yuh kin have cloes t go to school this winter.'

He rose and went to her side with the open catalogue in his palms. She was washing dishes, her head bent low over a pan. Shyly he raised the open book. When he spoke his voice was husky, faint.

'Ma, Gawd knows Ah wans one of these.'

130 'One of whut?' she asked, not raising her eyes.

'One of *these,*' he said again, not daring even to point. She glanced up at the page, then at him with wide eyes.

'Nigger is yuh gone plum crazy?'

'Ah, Ma—'

'Git outta here! Don yuh talk t me bout no gun! Yuh a fool!'

'Ma, Ah kin buy one fer *two* dollahs.'

'Not ef Ah knows it yuh ain!'

'But yuh promised me one—'

'Ah don care whut Ah promised! Yuh ain nothing but a boy yit!'

140 'Ma, ef yuh lemme buy one Ahll *never* ast yuh fer nothing no mo.'

'Ah tol yuh t git outta here! Yuh ain gonna toucha penny of tha money fer no gun! Thas how come Ah has Mistah Hawkins t pay yo wages t me, cause Ah knows yuh ain got no sense.'

'But Ma, we needa gun. Pa ain got no gun. We needa gun in the house. Yuh kin never tell whut might happen.'

'Now don yuh try to maka fool outta me, boy! Ef we did hava gun yuh wouldn't have it!'

He laid the catalogue down and slipped his arm around her waist.

'Aw, Ma, Ah done worked hard alla summer n ain ast yuh fer 150 nothin, is Ah, now?'

'Thas whut yuh spose t do!'

'But Ma, Ah wans a gun. Yuh kin lemme have two dollahs outta mah money. Please, Ma. I kin give it to Pa . . . Please, Ma! Ah loves yuh, Ma.'

When she spoke her voice came soft and low.

'Whut yuh wan wida gun, Dave? Yuh don need no gun. Yuhll git in trouble. N ef yo Pa jus *thought* Ah let yuh have money t buy a gun he'd hava fit.'

'Ahll hide it, Ma, it ain but two dollahs.'

'Lawd, chil, whuts wrong wid yuh?'

160   'Ain nothing wrong, Ma. Ahm almos a man now. Ah wans a gun.'

'Who gonna sell yuh a gun?'

'Ol Joe at the sto.'

'N it don cos but two dollahs?'

'Thas all, Ma. Just two dollahs. Please, Ma.'

She was stacking the plates away; her hands moved slowly, reflectively. Dave kept an anxious silence. Finally, she turned to him.

'Ahll let yuh git tha gun ef yuh promise me one thing.'

'Whuts tha, Ma?'

'Yuh bring it straight back t *me,* yuh hear? Itll be fer Pa.'

170   'Yessum! Lemme go now, Ma.'

She stooped, turned slightly to one side, raised the hem of her dress, rolled down the top of her stocking, and came up with a slender wad of bills.

'Here,' she said. 'Lawd knows yuh don need no gun. But yer Pa does. Yuh bring it right back t *me,* yuh hear? Ahma put it up. Now ef yuh don, Ahma have yuh Pa lick yuh so hard yuh won ferget it.'

'Yessum.'

He took the money, ran down the steps, and across the yard.

'Dave! Yuuuuuh Daaaaave!'

180   He heard, but he was not going to stop now. 'Naw, Lawd!'

The first movement he made the following morning was to reach under his pillow for the gun. In the gray light of dawn he held it loosely, feeling a sense of power. Could killa man wida gun like this. Kill anybody, black er white. And if he were holding his gun in his hand nobody could run over him; they would have to respect him. It was a big gun, with a long barrel and a heavy handle. He raised and lowered it in his hand, marveling at its weight.

He had not come straight home with it as his mother had asked; instead he had stayed out in the fields, holding the weapon in his hand,
190 aiming it now and then at some imaginary foe. But he had not fired it; he had been afraid that his father might hear. Also he was not sure he knew how to fire it.

To avoid surrendering the pistol he had not come into the house until he knew that all were asleep. When his mother had tiptoed to his bedside late that night and demanded the gun, he had first played 'possum; then he had told her that the gun was hidden outdoors, that he would bring it to her in the morning. Now he lay turning it slowly in his hands. He broke it, took out the cartridges, felt them, and then put them back.

He slid out of bed, got a long strip of old flannel from a trunk,
200 wrapped the gun in it, and tied it to his naked thigh while it was still

loaded. He did not go in to breakfast. Even though it was not yet day-light, he started for Jim Hawkins' plantation. Just as the sun was rising he reached the barns where the mules and plows were kept.

'Hey! That you, Dave?'

He turned. Jim Hawkins stood eying him suspiciously.

'Whatre yuh doing here so early?'

'Ah didn't know Ah wuz gittin up so early, Mistah Hawkins. Ah wuz fixin t hitch up ol Jenny n take her t the fiels.'

'Good. Since you're here so early, how about plowing that stretch
210 down by the woods?'

'Suits me, Mistah Hawkins.'

'O.K. Go to it!'

He hitched Jenny to a plow and started across the fields. Hot dog! This was just what he wanted. If he could get down by the woods, he could shoot his gun and nobody would hear. He walked behind the plow, hearing the traces creaking, feeling the gun tied tight to his thigh.

When he reached the woods, he plowed two whole rows before he decided to take out the gun. Finally, he stopped, looked in all direc-tions, then untied the gun and held it in his hand. He turned to the
220 mule and smiled.

'Know whut this is, Jenny? Naw, yuh wouldn't know! Yuhs jusa ol mule! Anyhow, this is a gun, n it kin shoot, by Gawd!'

He held the gun at arm's length. Whut t hell, Ahma shoot this thing! He looked at Jenny again.

'Lissen here, Jenny! When Ah pull this ol trigger Ah don wan yuh t run n acka fool now.'

Jenny stood with head down, her short ears pricked straight. Dave walked off about twenty feet, held the gun far out from him, at arm's length, and turned his head. Hell, he told himself, Ah ain afraid. The gun
230 felt loose in his fingers; he waved it wildly for a moment. Then he shut his eyes and tightened his forefinger. *Blooom!* A report half-deafened him and he thought his right hand was torn from his arm. He heard Jenny whin-nying and galloping over the field, and he found himself on his knees, squeezing his fingers hard between his legs. His hand was numb; he jammed it into his mouth, trying to warm it, trying to stop the pain. The gun lay at his feet. He did not quite know what had happened. He stood up and stared at the gun as though it were a live thing. He gritted his teeth and kicked the gun. Yuh almos broke mah arm! He turned to look for Jenny; she was far over the fields, tossing her head and kicking wildly.
240 'Hol on there, ol mule!'

When he caught up with her she stood trembling, walling her big white eyes at him. The plow was far away; the traces had broken. Then Dave stopped short, looking, not believing. Jenny was bleeding. Her left side was red and wet with blood. He went closer. Lawd have mercy! Won-dah did Ah shoot this mule? He grabbed for Jenny's mane. She flinched, snorted, whirled, tossing her head.

'Hol on now! Hol on.'

Then he saw the hole in Jenny's side, right between the ribs. It was round, wet, red. A crimson stream streaked down the front leg, flowing 250 fast. Good Gawd! Ah wuznt shootin at tha mule. . . . He felt panic. He knew he had to stop that blood, or Jenny would bleed to death. He had never seen so much blood in all his life. He ran the mule for half a mile, trying to catch her. Finally she stopped, breathing hard, stumpy tail half arched. He caught her mane and led her back to where the plow and gun lay. Then he stopped and grabbed handfuls of damp black earth and tried to plug the bullet hole. Jenny shuddered, whinnied, and broke from him.

'Hol on! Hol on now!'

He tried to plug it again, but blood came anyhow. His fingers were 260 hot and sticky. He rubbed dirt hard into his palms, trying to dry them. Then again he attempted to plug the bullet hole, but Jenny shied away, kicking her heels high. He stood helpless. He had to do something. He ran at Jenny; she dodged him. He watched a red stream of blood flow down Jenny's leg and form a bright pool at her feet.

'Jenny . . . Jenny . . .' he called weakly.

His lips trembled. She's bleeding t death! He looked in the direction of home, wanting to go back, wanting to get help. But he saw the pistol lying in the damp black clay. He had a queer feeling that if he only did something, this would not be; Jenny would not be there bleeding to death. 270   When he went to her this time, she did not move. She stood with sleepy, dreamy eyes; and when he touched her she gave a low-pitched whinny and knelt to the ground, her front knees slopping in blood.

'Jenny . . . Jenny . . .' he whispered.

For a long time she held her neck erect; then her head sank, slowly. Her ribs swelled with a mighty heave and she went over.

Dave's stomach felt empty, very empty. He picked up the gun and held it gingerly between his thumb and forefinger. He buried it at the foot of a tree. He took a stick and tried to cover the pool of blood with dirt—but what was the use? There was Jenny lying with her mouth open 280 and her eyes walled and glassy. He could not tell Jim Hawkins he had shot his mule. But he had to tell something. Yeah, Ahll tell em Jenny started gittin wil n fell on the joint of the plow. . . . But that would hardly happen to a mule. He walked across the field slowly, head down.

It was sunset. Two of Jim Hawkins' men were over near the edge of the woods digging a hole in which to bury Jenny. Dave was surrounded by a knot of people; all of them were looking down at the dead mule.

'I don't see how in the world it happened,' said Jim Hawkins for the tenth time.

The crowd parted and Dave's mother, father, and small brother 290 pushed into the center.

'Where Dave?' his mother called.

'There he is,' said Jim Hawkins.

His mother grabbed him.

'Whut happened, Dave? Whut yuh done?'

'Nothing.'

'C'mon, boy, talk,' his father said.

Dave took a deep breath and told the story he knew nobody believed.

'Waal,' he drawled, 'Ah brung ol Jenny down here sos Ah could do mah plowin. Ah plowed bout two rows, just like yuh see.' He stopped
300 and pointed at the long rows of upturned earth. 'Then something musta been wrong wid ol Jenny. She wouldn't ack right atall. She started snortin n kickin her heels. Ah tried to hol her, but she pulled erway, rearin n goin on. Then when the point of the plow was stickin up in the air, she swung erroun n twisted hersef back on it. . . . She stuck hersef n started t bleed. N fo Ah could do anything, she wuz dead.'

'Did you ever hear of anything like that in all your life?' asked Jim Hawkins.

There were white and black standing in the crowd. They murmured. Dave's mother came close to him and looked hard into his face.
310   'Tell the truth, Dave,' she said.

'Looks like a bullet hole ter me,' said one man.

'Dave, whut yuh do wid tha gun?' his mother asked.

The crowd surged in, looking at him. He jammed his hands into his pockets, shook his head slowly from left to right, and backed away. His eyes were wide and painful.

'Did he hava gun?' asked Jim Hawkins.

'By Gawd, Ah tol yuh tha wuz a *gun* wound,' said a man, slapping his thigh.

His father caught his shoulders and shook him till his teeth rattled.
320   'Tell whut happened, yuh rascal! Tell whut . . .'

Dave looked at Jenny's stiff legs and began to cry.

'Whut yuh do wid tha gun?' his mother asked.

'Whut wuz he doin wida gun?' his father asked.

'Come on and tell the truth,' said Hawkins. 'Ain't nobody going to hurt you . . .'

His mother crowded close to him.

'Did yuh shoot tha mule, Dave?'

Dave cried, seeing blurred white and black faces.

'Ahh ddinnt gggo tt sshoooot hher. . . . Ah sssswear off Gawd Ahh
330 ddint. . . . Ah wuz a-tryin t sssee ef the ol gggun would sshoot—'

'Where yuh git the gun from?' his father asked.

'Ah got it from Joe, at the sto.'

'Where yuh git the money?'

'Ma give it t me.'

'He kept worryin me, Bob. . . . Ah had t. . . . Ah tol im t bring the gun right back t me. . . . It was fer yuh, the gun.'

'But how yuh happen to shoot that mule?' asked Jim Hawkins.

'Ah wuznt shootin at the mule, Mistah Hawkins. The gun jumped when Ah pulled the trigger . . . N fo Ah knowed anything Jenny wuz
340 there a-bleedin.'

Somebody in the crowd laughed. Jim Hawkins walked close to Dave and looked into his face.

'Well, looks like you have bought you a mule, Dave.'

'Ah swear fo Gawd, Ah didn't go t kill the mule, Mistah Hawkins!'

'But you killed her!'

All the crowd was laughing now. They stood on tiptoe and poked heads over one another's shoulders.

'Well, boy, looks like yuh done bought a dead mule! Hahaha!'

'Ain tha ershame.'

350   'Hohohohoho.'

Dave stood head down, twisting his feet in the dirt.

'Well, you needn't worry about it, Bob,' said Jim Hawkins to Dave's father. 'Just let the boy keep on working and pay me two dollars a month.'

'Whut yuh wan fer yo mule, Mistah Hawkins?'

Jim Hawkins screwed up his eyes.

'Fifty dollars.'

'Whut yuh do wid tha gun?' Dave's father demanded.

Dave said nothing.

'Yuh wan me t take a tree lim n beat yuh till yuh talk!'

360   'Nawsuh!'

'Whut yuh do wid it?'

'Ah throwed it erway.'

'Where?'

'Ah . . . Ah throwed it in the creek.'

'Waal, c'mon home. N firs thing in the mawnin git to tha creek n fin tha gun.'

'Yessuh.'

'Whut yuh pay fer it?'

'Two dollahs.'

370   'Take tha gun n git yo money back n carry it t Mistah Hawkins, yuh hear? N don fergit Ahma lam yo black bottom good fer this! Now march yosef on home, suh!'

Dave turned and walked slowly. He heard people laughing. Dave glared, his eyes welling with tears. Hot anger bubbled in him. Then he swallowed and stumbled on.

That night Dave did not sleep. He was glad that he had gotten out of killing the mule so easily, but he was hurt. Something hot seemed to turn over inside him each time he remembered how they had laughed. He tossed on his bed, feeling his hard pillow. N Pa says he's gonna beat

380   me. . . . He remembered other beatings, and his back quivered. Naw, naw, Ah sho don wan im t beat me tha way no mo. . . . Dam em *all!* Nobody ever gave him anything. All he did was work. They treat me lika mule. . . . N then they beat me. . . . He gritted his teeth. N Ma had t tell on me.

Well, if he had to, he would take old man Hawkins that two dollars.

But that meant selling the gun. And he wanted to keep that gun. Fifty dollahs fer a dead mule.

190 He turned over, thinking of how he had fired the gun. He had an itch to fire it again. Ef other men kin shoota gun, by Gawd, Ah kin! He was still listening. Mebbe they all sleepin now. . . . The house was still. He heard the soft breathing of his brother. Yes, now! He would go down and get that gun and see if he could fire it! He eased out of bed and slipped into overalls.

The moon was bright. He ran almost all the way to the edge of the woods. He stumbled over the ground, looking for the spot where he had buried the gun. Yeah, here it is. Like a hungry dog scratching for a bone he pawed it up. He puffed his black cheeks and blew dirt from the trigger and barrel. He broke it and found four cartridges unshot. He looked around; the fields were filled with silence and moonlight. He clutched
400 the gun stiff and hard in his fingers. But as soon as he wanted to pull the trigger, he shut his eyes and turned his head. Naw, Ah can't shoot wid mah eyes closed n mah head turned. With effort he held his eyes open; then he squeezed. *Blooooom!* He was stiff, not breathing. The gun was still in his hands. Dammit, he'd done it! He fired again. *Blooooom!* He smiled. *Blooooom! Blooooom! Click, click.* There! It was empty. If anybody could shoot a gun, he could. He put the gun into his hip pocket and started across the fields.

When he reached the top of a ridge he stood straight and proud in the moonlight, looking at Jim Hawkins' big white house, feeling the gun
410 sagging in his pocket. Lawd, ef Ah had jus one mo bullet Ahd taka shot at tha house. Ahd like t scare ol man Hawkins jusa little. . . . Jussa enough t let im know Dave Sanders is a man.

To his left the road curved, running to the tracks of the Illinois Central. He jerked his head, listening. From far off came a faint *hoooof-hoooof; hoooof-hoooof; hoooof-hoooof* . . . Tha's number eight. He took a swift look at Jim Hawkins' white house; he thought of pa, of ma, of his little brother, and the boys. He thought of the dead mule and heard *hoooof-hoooof; hoooof-hoooof; hoooof-hoooof* . . . He stood rigid. Two dollahs a mont. Les see now . . . Tha means itll take bout two years. Shucks! Ahll be dam!

420 He started down the road, toward the tracks. Yeah, here she comes! He stood beside the track and held himself stiffly. Here she comes, erroun the ben. . . . C'mon, yuh slow poke! C mon! He had his hand on his gun; something quivered in his stomach. Then the train thundered past, the gray and brown box cars rumbling and clinking. He gripped the gun tightly; then he jerked his hand out of his pocket. Ah betcha Bill wouldn't do it! Ah betcha. . . . The cars slid past, steel grinding upon steel. Ahm riding yuh ternight so hep me Gawd! He was hot all over. He hesitated just a moment; then he grabbed, pulled atop of a car, and lay flat. He felt his pocket; the gun was still there. Ahead the long
430 rails were glinting in the moonlight, stretching away, away to somewhere, somewhere where he could be a man. . . .

ACCOUNT: JOHN E. LOFTIS ON "THE MAN WHO WAS ALMOST A MAN" AS A PARODY OF THE HUNT TRADITION

John E. Loftis begins "Domestic Prey: Richard Wright's Parody of the Hunt Tradition in 'The Man Who Was Almost a Man'" by discussing an apparent dilemma confronting the black American writer. In "a new and unsettled land," Loftis says, the hunt became a popular literary theme, especially in initiation stories featuring a "young hero who achieves manhood by hunting and slaying a wild beast." James Fenimore Cooper, Herman Melville, Ernest Hemingway, and William Faulkner are among the many writers who have used the hunt in this way. "In American literature, however," Loftis writes, "the hunt is a European and thus a white tradition, and its heroic and mythic dimensions hardly seem available to black American writers—unless used ironically to underscore the gulf between the chivalrous white hero and the black field hand or urban outcast." Richard Wright, however, has found a way to turn this "problematic theme" into an "artistic asset," using the hunt to "embody the hero's maturation at the same time that its parodic implications dramatize the distance between black and white possibilities of growth and development in American society." At times, Loftis says, critics have dismissed Wright's fiction as "crude and careless," as "technically unpolished." Through his analysis of "The Man Who Was Almost a Man," Loftis hopes to demonstrate that Wright is in fact a highly skillful writer, one who "succeeds in a sophisticated manipulation, parody, of a complex literary tradition, the hunt, to embody his vision." Like many other critics who focus on racial and ethnic issues, then, Loftis attempts to guide his readers toward a fuller appreciation of a sometimes underrated work by a minority author.

Loftis uses Faulkner's short story "The Old People" as an example of a white author's treatment of the hunt as a theme. For Faulkner's young hero, Ike McCaslin, the shooting of his first buck "solidifies a complex of relationships to family, community, and heritage." Guns have been "a natural part" of Ike's life since he was a very small boy: "It is part of Ike's heritage to own guns and to use them to prove his manhood." Further, as Ike prepares for his initiation, he is guided by Sam Fathers, "whose very name suggests his relationship to Ike, to teach him to hunt and become a man." When Ike sees the buck, Sam Fathers is at his side to tell him just when and how to shoot and, afterwards, to slit the buck's throat and ritualistically mark Ike's face with its blood "to signal his achieved manhood." Ike's initiation is "fairly straightforward," Loftis says, "a conscious act that marks a normal stage of development."

John E. Loftis, "Domestic Prey: Richard Wright's Parody of the Hunt Tradition in 'The Man Who Was Almost a Man,'" *Studies in Short Fiction* 23 (Fall, 1986): 437–442.

Dave's initiation in "The Man Who Was Almost a Man" is radically different. Unlike Ike McCaslin, Dave has no experience with guns and no recognized claim to owning one. "His desire for a gun and his equating ownership of the gun with manhood seem almost pathetic," Loftis writes. To get his mother to give him the money for the gun, Dave must act like a child—"he whines, wheedles, and begs, and his mother responds as if he were a child." She finally gives him the money only when they agree that the gun will really be for his father, not for him. Their bargain suggests that in Dave's culture, as in Ike's, there is "a tacit association . . . between manhood and owning a gun." But Dave's right to this symbol of manhood is never actually acknowledged: "His family and immediate social environment do not allow for him what was so natural for Ike McCaslin."

Dave also lacks a teacher comparable to Sam Fathers: he "has no adult black males to guide him or even to serve as models that could allow him to define his manhood":

> He is surrounded daily by anonymous black field hands; he lives in a matriarchal family; and his larger social setting is obviously dominated by white men, Joe at the store and especially Jim Hawkins, his employer. His father is virtually a phantom figure in the story, appearing at supper where he asks Dave what he is reading and again in the scene when Dave is being brought to account for the mule he killed. In that scene Dave's father promises to beat him, but he offers no support for Dave or resistance to Jim Hawkins about the settlement for the mule. . . . If anything, Dave's adults are threats and exploiters, virtually the opposite of the guides with which Ike McCaslin is so abundantly supplied.

In all, Dave "lacks the familial and cultural mechanisms and personal supports that make growing up a natural journey with identifiable ritual milestones."

It is therefore hardly surprising that Dave's first shot is a solitary attempt that goes horribly wrong. He must hide the gun when he goes to the fields, pretending that he plans only to do his plowing. Not knowing how to fire a gun or even how to hold one, Dave shuts his eyes when he pulls the trigger. The shot deafens him, knocks him to his knees, and hurts his hand. "The gun is as much in control of Dave as Dave is of the gun in this scene," Loftis writes. Unlike Ike McCaslin, who consciously chooses to shoot the buck and feels proud when he succeeds, Dave has no intention of shooting anything; when he realizes that he has shot the mule, he is horrified. Desperately, he tries to stop the bleeding, to hide the bullethole, to lie about what happened. When the truth is discovered, Jim Hawkins and the field hands erupt into laughter, and Dave is utterly humiliated. It is hard to imagine anything more distant from the solemn moment when Sam Fathers marks Ike McCaslin's face with the buck's blood.

Despite all these differences, Loftis argues, "The Man Who Was Almost a Man" is also an initiation story. Although the shooting of the mule is "a childish error that means nothing in itself," it "forces the development that Dave could not otherwise achieve":

> His rejection of his bondage to Jim Hawkins to pay for the mule motivates Dave to return to the hidden gun and to assert his manhood by successfully firing it. This success in turn provides the confidence he needs to reject his childhood, turn his back on his family, and board the freight train headed "away, away to somewhere, somewhere where he could be a man . . . "

Although Wright's story is not a direct parody of Faulkner's, Loftis says, it is a parody of "the tradition that informs Faulkner's version of the hunt with much of its significance." Loftis notes that the mule Dave shoots is named Jenny, "short for Jennifer which derives from Guinevere which in turn derives from the Welsh 'gwen,' white." By killing Jenny, Dave symbolically frees himself from the whites who dominate his society and "refuse to allow any black male to truly mature." Further, the fact that Dave kills a domestic animal rather than a wild one again reminds the reader that his initiation "lies outside" the tradition of the hunt. Wright thus uses, manipulates, and transforms various elements in the hunt story. By doing so, he both parodies the tradition and "shapes a convincing and moving account of the black experience of growing up in the rural South in the second quarter of the twentieth century."

SUGGESTIONS FOR DISCUSSION AND WRITING

1. How does Wright establish the **point of view** of his **protagonist** in the beginning of the story? In particular, how does he invite you to understand the last sentence of the first paragraph: "Shucks, a man oughta have a little gun afta he done worked hard all day. . . ." What context do the events *before* the narrative opens provide here? How does the analysis made by Loftis take into account the protagonist's point of view and the changes it undergoes?

2. What seems to be the rationale behind Wright's "phonetic" spelling? What do you make of those words spelled in the *usual* way as "little" in the last sentence of the first paragraph? In what ways does *accent* differ from **tone of voice** as a literary matter? Explain and exemplify your answer. What points do you imagine might be made about your evidence by an approach like that Loftis takes?

3. In what ways does Wright work to make the issue of *blame* for killing the mule a complicated one? What part does intent play in the

various views of blame taken within the story by the protagonist and by the white characters? What part does blame play in the account of the story by Loftis?

4. One critic talks about several of Wright's characters as "displaced persons." In what various ways does Wright create this sense in the **protagonist** of this story? Compare "The Misfit" in Flannery O'Connor's "A Good Man Is Hard To Find" (p. 181). What use does Loftis make of this theme in his analysis?

5. Write an essay in which you try to separate what significant aspects of "The Man Who Was Almost a Man" are black, which are southern, and which are generally American.

6. Make some notes for discussion or an essay toward a racial or ethnic reading of Alice Munro's "Eskimo" (p. 11).

Chapter Eight

Structuralist Criticism: Language as a Critical Method

A BRIEF INTRODUCTION TO STRUCTURALIST CRITICISM

Structuralism is a critical approach that began with the work of philosophers and linguists and came to be employed as a method of analyzing any product of the human imagination. It has been used to understand not only "primitive" myth and highly "sophisticated" literature but also the cultures that produce myth and literature. The structuralist movement began and first flourished in Europe, particularly in France, before coming to the United States in the 1960s with the force of an intellectual revolution in literary criticism.

By using the tools, techniques, and terminologies of modern linguistics to describe literature, structuralism appears not so much a set of beliefs as an activity that first seeks to analyze an imaginative work into its smallest meaningful component parts, much as a grammarian analyzes a sentence or as a philologist a word. Then, like the grammarian, the structuralist critic tries to understand the structure of, or *relations* among, those parts—their syntax or grammar, as it were. Thus, a structuralist approach differs from many others insofar as it does not try to reach an interpretation of a given literary work but to explain the common elements or structures of literary works. A grammarian might point out the shared subject–verb–direct object structure of two clauses: "The writer opened a window" and "The president declared war." Similarly, a structuralist critic might point to such shared elements in two short stories as a protagonist leaving home, followed by a villain gaining information about the protagonist, followed in turn by the protagonist being duped by the villain. The structuralist would not be trying to interpret these stories but would be trying to determine their underlying structure. The structuralist critic, then, is less interested in the meaning of works than in the way in which the parts of the work create meaning. All in all, as Roland Barthes said in "The Structuralist Activity" (1964), the structuralist pays attention more to the process of meaning than its product.

Tzvetan Todorov, whose discussion of Henry James's "The Beast in the Jungle" is summarized in this chapter, has developed a general theory of narrative which he calls "the grammar of narrative." Using some traditional parts of speech to name what he sees as the basic categories of any story, he defines narrative structure as the relation among them, just as a sentence creates a relation among parts of speech to give them a collective meaning. Thus, characters become "proper nouns," qualities as "adjectives," and actions in the plot as "verbs."

A somewhat similar attempt to view the grammar or syntax of narratives is given by Vladimir Propp in *The Morphology of the Folktale*. In studying a group of Russian folktales, Propp found them all to be composed of certain elements, thirty-one in total, which occurred in certain sequences. These elements included such plot actions as absentation (a person absents him or herself from home), interdiction (a hero or heroine is given a warning), violation (the hero or heroine violates the interdiction), reconnaissance (the villain finds information about the hero), etc. Not all elements occurred in any tale, but those elements which were present always followed a certain order. Thus, a tale might jump from absentation to reconnaissance, but reconnaissance would never precede violation. Using this system, Propp was able to plot the syntax or, as he called it, the morphology of each of the tales. The morphology did not lead to an interpretation of the tales but to a comparison of their underlying structures.

It is relatively easy to see how narrative elements can be viewed as analogous to grammatical elements and to understand why structuralists might want to determine certain types of narratives just as linguists determine types of sentences. However, structuralism goes far beyond the study of narrative grammar and is probably better defined by its concern with even larger relations between language and meaning, a concern very much at the heart of modern structural linguistics.

Two insights from modern linguistics became especially important to literary structuralism. The first concerns a distinction between what the Swiss linguist Ferdinand de Saussure called *langue* and *parole. Langue* is the system of language, the conventions, rules, and principles which govern the construction of speech. *Parole* consists of individual speech in a language, the actual utterances of each person. "A mauve parrot residing on Mars eats blue cheese" is a statement probably never before said or written, yet speakers of English recognize it as a grammatical English utterance. That each of us can make grammatical statements (*parole*) we have never heard or seen suggests there is a system or set of rules (*langue*) that we have assimilated.

Structuralists have transferred this understanding of language to the study of literature. As linguists distinguish between individual utterances or statements and the principles governing the construction of these statements, structuralist critics distinguish between individual stories or poems and the conventions or principles underlying them. Individual works of literature are analogous to *parole,* and the structuralist critic attempts to study the *langue,* the system that makes possible both the creation and the understanding of the works. The studies of Todorov and Propp cited above are attempts to determine the *langue,* the underlying structures, of the texts they are examining.

For structuralism, the second crucial insight of modern linguistics is based on the study of relations between "signs" (which include words) and the meaning that signs convey, matters explored around the turn of the century not only by Saussure but by the American philosopher Charles Sanders Pierce. It is easy to think of signs or words as having a one-to-one relationship to meaning or to an object in the world. The word "car" seems to point to a particular kind of vehicle; car seems to *mean* automobile. However, Saussure and Pierce suggested the relations between sign and meaning were less obvious than they first appear. In languages other than English, car does not mean automobile. In no other language than English would it be possible for the sentence "I drove my car" to be generated or understood.

Thus, Saussure saw that signs may organize the world into meaning for the humans who use them, but signs themselves do not have a direct one-to-one relation to the things of the world. Signs in fact consist of two parts: the "signifier" (a set of speech sounds or black and white marks on a page, for example) and the "signified," which is a concept, not a thing out in the world. Signifiers are arbitrary (as the existence of the multitude of human languages suggests) and the relation of signifiers to signifieds are matters of convention or agreement among the users of the sign system. The users agree that shaking the head in one way or making a particular sound signifies a negative expression, for example. Yet they could have agreed otherwise.

To take another example, what is the signified of the signifier "Yankee"? In Europe, all Americans are Yankees; in the southern United States, all Northerners; for Northerners, New Englanders; for New Englanders, someone from rural Vermont; in Vermont, someone who eats apple pie for breakfast! Another example: Is the difference between a "weed" and a "flower" a matter in nature or a matter of agreement among people? Or again, does *voiture* signify for most Americans the vehicle they drive to work?

These matters of *langue* and *parole* and of signs may seem far removed from reading and studying literary texts. However, they are crucial in understanding the fundamental assumptions of structuralism: first, that literary works are individual expressions produced from an underlying set of principles or conventions and second, that these conventions are tied to a particular culture or community and have meaning only for those who have learned or assimilated this particular set of conventions or, as structuralists might say, the "system" in which the work participates.

However, this system varies depending on the kind of text or "speech act" being considered. Jonathan Culler, one of the foremost

American writers on structuralism, points out not only the different conventions that govern the creation of a poem as against, for example, a newspaper article or a personal note but also the different expectations of readers. For instance, a student returning to her dormitory might find a note from her roommate saying, "I've gone to the dance. Don't wait up for me." The note would probably call for little speculation, and the student would go to bed if she wished. The same student encountering the same words in an anthology of poetry would probably think about them quite differently:

> I've gone
> To the dance.
> Don't wait
> Up
> For me.

Once the student assumes the words to be a poem rather than a personal communication, she will likely apply the conventions of poetry to her reading, conventions such as the likelihood of universal significance and the use of symbols and form to express meaning. Does "I've gone" refer to death; is there an allusion to the "dance of death"? How does the form function: Should "Don't wait" be read as a clause in itself; why is "Up" separated from the lines above and below; with which does it go or is the placement deliberately ambiguous to allow two readings? These questions are quite legitimate and suggest that we all assume that different conventions operate in different reading situations. There is one system of conventions for poems and another for informal personal communication.

Another way to describe the emphasis of the Structuralist approach is to think of it as contrasted to the emphasis a Rhetorical approach places on the communicative functions of language and therefore on techniques of persuasiveness. Structuralism focuses not so much on such results of language as on the conditions through which language and literature become meaningful or persuasive in the first place. In other words, structuralists study how meaning is created rather than how it is most effectively expressed. To use an analogy from linguistics: If etymology studies the history of words *over time*—their "diachronic" aspects—structuralism focuses on the "synchronic" structure of language *at a given moment in time* or within a given work or group of works.

It is important to recognize, however, that structuralism is defined by fundamental assumptions about the nature of language and literature and not by a specific vocabulary or technique. Not all, or even most, structural studies will speak of grammars of narrative or of signs and signifiers. For example, the account of Tzvetan Todorov's essay on Henry James's "The Beast in the Jungle" later in this chapter makes little use of terminology from linguistics. Clearly, however, Todorov is attempting to determine the underlying structure of the quest in James's tales, and therefore, he is working from a synchronic perspective. He is not studying the different particular goals of the quest in James's stories or the differing ways in which those quests develop. Rather, he contends that the stories are always structured around a quest, which is always of the same kind.

Todorov suggests a set of conventions which underlie these quest stories, conventions having to do with presence and absence. Todorov believes the basic common form of James's tales to be "the quest for the absolute and absent cause" of the events in the story. In his formula, Todorov uses "absence" and "presence" to differentiate between matters that appear within the story and those that do not appear immediately or never appear at all. To use an example from an earlier chapter of this book, during most of "Araby," the bazaar is "absent," though of great significance to the narrator. When the bazaar does become "present," it takes on quite a different significance for the narrator and for the reader. Further, Todorov's belief that James's style is no different than his theme, that "form and content all say the same thing," though reminiscent of formalist criticism, demonstrates the structuralist's interest in *how* meaning is created.

In summary, as a method of literary criticism, structuralism seeks to uncover the signs and codes that make up the functioning system of a literary work, and that system includes the cultural values and assumptions that define the rules under which it is written and read. Structuralism thus shifted the goal of literary study from the explication of individual literary works to the exploration of the basis of interpretation itself.

At the same time, and by the same means, structuralists made the "language" of culture available to literary analysis, and the advent of structuralism saw more and more literary scholars emerging as general cultural critics. Yet the great promise of structuralism—to offer a rational analysis of the humanities that match for the human world the intellectual status and rigor of science's exploration of the physical world—was itself soon critiqued by the activities of the "post-structuralism" explored in the next chapter. Surprisingly, that critique was undertaken partly through the methods of close reading that were fostered so successfully by the very New Criticism that structuralism had at first seemed destined to replace.

HENRY JAMES (1843–1916) was born in New York City on April 15, 1843. His grandfather was one of America's first millionaires, his father was a writer and philosopher, and his older brother William was to become an eminent philosopher. James spent long periods of his childhood in London and Paris, where he received most of his formal education. He enrolled at Harvard Law School in 1862, but withdrew after one year to focus his attention on writing.

In 1864, his first story, "A Tragedy of Error," appeared in the *North American Review*; in 1871, his first novel, *Watch and Ward,* was published serially in the *Atlantic Monthly.* In 1869 James had returned, as an adult, to Europe, where he became fascinated with the theme of the American abroad that is explored in many of his works. He became friends with many prominent literary figures such as Guy de Maupassant, Gustave Flaubert, and Ivan Turgenev.

In 1876 James decided to establish permanent residence in England. He lived in London from 1876 to 1897; this period in James's career marked the publication of *The American* (1877), *Daisy Miller* (1874), *The Portrait of a Lady* (1881), and *The Princess Casamassima* (1896). In the early 1890s, James took to writing plays, but found very little, if any, commercial success. In 1896 he relocated to Rye, Sussex, a peaceful locale whose solitude contributed to his most fruitful and creative period; his most important novels of this time include *The Turn of the Screw* (1898), *The Wings of the Dove* (1902), *The Ambassadors* (1902), and *The Golden Bowl* (1904).

In 1904, James visited the United States, producing on his return to England a travelogue, *The American Scene* (1907). At this time, James also undertook a complete revision of every novel and short story he had written, resulting in the twenty-six volume New York Edition of his work. After his brother William's death in 1910, James wrote three autobiographical works. In 1915, James became a British subject to show his support for the Allied cause in World War I. He died of a stroke on February 28, 1916.

HENRY JAMES

The Beast in the Jungle
(1903)

1

What determined the speech that startled him in the course of their encounter scarcely matters, being probably but some words spoken by himself quite without intention—spoken as they lingered and slowly moved together after their renewal of acquaintance. He had been conveyed by friends an hour or two before to the house at which she was staying; the party of visitors at the other house, of whom he was one, and thanks to whom it was his theory, as always, that he was lost in the crowd, had been invited over to luncheon. There had been after luncheon much dispersal, all in the interest of the original move, a view of Weatherend itself and
10 the fine things, intrinsic features, pictures, heirlooms, treasures of all the arts, that made the place almost famous; and the great rooms were so numerous that guests could wander at their will, hang back from the principal group and in cases where they took such matters with the least seriousness give themselves up to mysterious appreciations and measurements. There were persons to be observed, singly or in couples, bending toward objects in out-of-the-way corners with their hands on their knees and their heads nodding quite as with the emphasis of an excited sense of smell. When they were two they either mingled their sounds of ecstasy or melted into silences of even deeper import, so that there were aspects of
20 the occasion that gave it for Marcher much the air of the "look round," previous to a sale highly advertised, that excites or quenches, as may be, the dream of acquisition. The dream of acquisition at Weatherend would have had to be wild indeed, and John Marcher found himself, among such suggestions, disconcerted almost equally by the presence of those who knew too much and by that of those who knew nothing. The great rooms caused so much poetry and history to press upon him that he needed some straying apart to feel in a proper relation with them, though this impulse was not, as happened, like the gloating of some of his companions,

to be compared to the movements of a dog sniffing a cupboard. It
30 had an issue promptly enough in a direction that was not to have been
calculated.

It led, briefly, in the course of the October afternoon, to his closer
meeting with May Bartram, whose face, a reminder, yet not quite a remembrance, as they sat much separated at a very long table, had begun
merely by troubling him rather pleasantly. It affected him as the sequel
of something of which he had lost the beginning. He knew it, and for
the time quite welcomed it, as a continuation, but didn't know what it
continued, which was an interest or an amusement the greater as he was
also somehow aware—yet without a direct sign from her—that the
40 young woman herself hadn't lost the thread. She hadn't lost it, but she
wouldn't give it back to him, he saw, without some putting forth of his
hand for it; and he not only saw that, but saw several things more,
things odd enough in the light of the fact that at the moment some accident of grouping brought them face to face he was still merely fumbling
with the idea that any contact between them in the past would have had
no importance. If it had had no importance he scarcely knew why his
actual impression of her should so seem to have so much; the answer to
which, however, was that in such a life as they all appeared to be leading for the moment one could but take things as they came. He was sat-
50 isfied, without in the least being able to say why, that this young lady
might roughly have ranked in the house as a poor relation; satisfied also
that she was not there on a brief visit, but was more or less a part of the
establishment—almost a working, a remunerated part. Didn't she enjoy
at periods a protection that she paid for by helping, among other services, to show the place and explain it, deal with the tiresome people,
answer questions about the dates of the building, the styles of the furniture, the authorship of the pictures, the favourite haunts of the ghost? It
wasn't that she looked as if you could have given her shillings—it was
impossible to look less so. Yet when she finally drifted toward him, dis-
60 tinctly handsome, though ever so much older—older than when he had
seen her before—it might have been as an effect of her guessing that he
had, within the couple of hours, devoted more imagination to her than
to all the others put together, and had thereby penetrated to a kind of
truth that the others were too stupid for. She *was* there on harder terms
than any one; she was there as a consequence of things suffered, one
way and another, in the interval of years; and she remembered him very
much as she was remembered—only a good deal better.

By the time they at last thus came to speech they were alone in one of
the rooms—remarkable for a fine portrait over the chimneyplace—out of
70 which their friends had passed, and the charm of it was that even before
they had spoken they had practically arranged with each other to stay behind to talk. The charm, happily, was in other things too—partly in there
being scarce a spot at Weatherend without something to stay behind
for. It was in the way the autumn day looked into the high windows as
it waned; the way the red light, breaking at the close from under a low

sombre sky, reached out in a long shaft and played over old wainscots, old tapestry, old gold, old colour. It was most of all perhaps in the way she came to him as if, since she had been turned on to deal with the simpler sort, he might, should he choose to keep the whole thing down, just take
80 her mild attention for a part of her general business. As soon as he heard her voice, however, the gap was filled up and the missing link supplied; the slight irony he divined in her attitude lost its advantage. He almost jumped at it to get there before her. "I met you years and years ago in Rome. I remember all about it." She confessed to disappointment—she had been so sure he didn't; and to prove how well he did he began to pour forth the particular recollections that popped up as he called for them. Her face and her voice, all at his service now, worked the miracle—the impression operating like the torch of a lamplighter who touches into flame, one by one, a long row of gas-jets. Marcher flattered himself the
90 illumination was brilliant, yet he was really still more pleased on her showing him, with amusement, that in his haste to make everything right he had got most things rather wrong. It hadn't been at Rome—it had been at Naples; and it hadn't been eight years before—it had been more nearly ten. She hadn't been, either, with her uncle and aunt, but with her mother and her brother; in addition to which it was not with the Pembles *he* had been, but with the Boyers, coming down in their company from Rome—a point on which she insisted, a little to his confusion, and as to which she had her evidence in hand. The Boyers she had known, but didn't know the Pembles, though she had heard of them, and it was the people he was
100 with who had made them acquainted. The incident of the thunderstorm that had raged round them with such violence as to drive them for refuge into an excavation—this incident had not occurred at the Palace of the Caesars, but at Pompeii, on an occasion when they had been present there at an important find.

He accepted her amendments, he enjoyed her corrections, though the moral of them was, she pointed out, that he *really* didn't remember the least thing about her; and he only felt it as a drawback that when all was made strictly historic there didn't appear much of anything left. They lingered together still, she neglecting her office—for from the moment he
110 was so clever she had no proper right to him—and both neglecting the house, just waiting as to see if a memory or two more wouldn't again breathe on them. It hadn't taken them many minutes, after all, to put down on the table, like the cards of a pack, those that constituted their respective hands; only what came out was that the pack was unfortunately not perfect—that the past, invoked, invited, encouraged, could give them, naturally, no more than it had. It had made them anciently meet—her at twenty, him at twenty-five; but nothing was so strange, they seemed to say to each other, as that, while so occupied, it hadn't done a little more for them. They looked at each other as with the feeling of an
120 occasion missed; the present would have been so much better if the other, in the far distance, in the foreign land, hadn't been so stupidly meagre. There weren't apparently, all counted, more than a dozen little old things

that had succeeded in coming to pass between them; trivialities of youth, simplicities of freshness, stupidities of ignorance, small possible germs, but too deeply buried—too deeply (didn't it seem?) to sprout after so many years. Marcher could only feel he ought to have rendered her some service—saved her from a capsized boat in the Bay or at least recovered her dressing-bag, filched from her cab in the streets of Naples by a laz-zarone with a stiletto. Or it would have been nice if he could have been
130 taken with fever all alone at his hotel, and she could have come to look after him, to write to his people, to drive him out in convalescence. *Then* they would be in possession of the something or other that their actual show seemed to lack. It yet somehow presented itself, this show, as too good to be spoiled; so that they were reduced for a few minutes more to wondering a little helplessly why—since they seemed to know a certain number of the same people—their reunion had been so long averted. They didn't use that name for it, but their delay from minute to minute to join the others was a kind of confession that they didn't quite want it to be a failure. Their attempted supposition of reasons for their not having met
140 but showed how little they knew of each other. There came in fact a mo-ment when Marcher felt a positive pang. It was vain to pretend she was an old friend, for all the communities were wanting, in spite of which it was as an old friend that he saw she would have suited him. He had new ones enough—was surrounded with them for instance on the stage of the other house; as a new one he probably wouldn't have so much as noticed her. He would have liked to invent something, get her to make-believe with him that some passage of a romantic or critical kind *had* originally occurred. He was really almost reaching out in imagination—as against time—for something that would do, and saying to himself that if it didn't
150 come this sketch of a fresh start would show for quite awkwardly bun-gled. They would separate, and now for no second or no third chance. They would have tried and not succeeded. Then it was, just at the turn, as he afterwards made it out to himself, that, everything else failing, she her-self decided to take up the case and, as it were, save the situation. He felt as soon as she spoke that she had been consciously keeping back what she said and hoping to get on without it; a scruple in her that immensely touched him when, by the end of three or four minutes more, he was able to measure it. What she brought out, at any rate, quite cleared the air and supplied the link—the link it was so odd he should frivolously have man-
160 aged to lose.

"You know you told me something I've never forgotten and that again and again has made me think of you since; it was that tremen-dously hot day when we went to Sorrento, across the bay, for the breeze. What I allude to was what you said to me, on the way back, as we sat under the awning of the boat enjoying the cool. Have you forgotten?"

He had forgotten and was even more surprised than ashamed. But the great thing was that he saw in this no vulgar reminder of any "sweet" speech. The vanity of women had long memories, but she was making no claim on him of a compliment or a mistake. With another

170 woman, a totally different one, he might have feared the recall possibly even some imbecile "offer." So, in having to say that he had indeed forgotten, he was conscious rather of a loss than of a gain; he already saw an interest in the matter of her mention. "I try to think—but I give it up. Yet I remember the Sorrento day."

"I'm not very sure you do," May Bartram after a moment said; "and I'm not very sure I ought to want you to. It's dreadful to bring a person back at any time to what he was ten years before. If you've lived away from it," she smiled, "so much the better."

"And if *you* haven't why should I?" he asked.

180 "Lived away, you mean, from what I myself was?"

"From what *I* was. I was of course an ass," Marcher went on; "but I would rather know from you just the sort of ass I was than—from the moment you have something in your mind—not know anything."

Still, however, she hesitated. "But if you've completely ceased to be that sort—?"

"Why I can then all the more bear to know. Besides, perhaps I haven't."

"Perhaps. Yet if you haven't," she added, "I should suppose you'd remember. Not indeed that *I* in the least connect with my impression the 190 invidious name you use. If I had only thought you foolish," she explained, "the thing I speak of wouldn't so have remained with me. It was about yourself." She waited as if it might come to him; but as, only meeting her eyes in wonder, he gave no sign, she burnt her ships. "Has it ever happened?"

Then it was that, while he continued to stare, a light broke for him and the blood slowly came to his face, which began to burn with recognition. "Do you mean I told you—?" But he faltered, lest what came to him shouldn't be right, lest he should only give himself away.

"It was something about yourself that it was natural one shouldn't 200 forget—that is if one remembered you at all. That's why I ask you," she smiled, "if the thing you then spoke of has ever come to pass?"

Oh then he saw, but he was lost in wonder and found himself embarrassed. This, he also saw, made her sorry for him, as if her allusion had been a mistake. It took him but a moment, however, to feel it hadn't been, much as it had been a surprise. After the first little shock of it her knowledge on the contrary began, even if rather strangely, to taste sweet to him. She was the only other person in the world then who would have it, and she had had it all these years, while the fact of his having so breathed his secret had unaccountably faded from him. No wonder they 210 couldn't have met as if nothing had happened. "I judge," he finally said, "that I know what you mean. Only I had strangely enough lost any sense of having taken you so far into my confidence."

"Is it because you've taken so many others as well?"

"I've taken nobody. Not a creature since then."

"So that I'm the only person who knows?"

"The only person in the world."

"Well," she quickly replied, "I myself have never spoken. I've never, never repeated of you what you told me." She looked at him so that he perfectly believed her. Their eyes met over it in such a way that he was
220 without a doubt. "And I never will."

She spoke with an earnestness that, as if almost excessive, put him at ease about her possible derision. Somehow the whole question was a new luxury to him—that is from the moment she was in possession. If she didn't take the sarcastic view she clearly took the sympathetic, and that was what he had had, in all the long time, from no one whomsoever. What he felt was that he couldn't at present have begun to tell her, and yet could profit perhaps exquisitely by the accident of having done so of old. "Please don't then. We're just right as it is."

"Oh I am," she laughed, "if you are!" To which she added: "Then
230 you do still feel in the same way?"

It was impossible he shouldn't take to himself that she was really interested, though it all kept coming as perfect surprise. He had thought of himself so long as abominably alone, and lo he wasn't alone a bit. He hadn't been, it appeared, for an hour—since those moments on the Sorrento boat. It was *she* who had been, he seemed to see as he looked at her—she who had been made so by the graceless fact of his lapse of fidelity. To tell her what he had told her—what had it been but to ask something of her? something that she had given, in her charity, without his having, by a remembrance, by a return of the spirit, failing another
240 encounter, so much as thanked her. What he had asked of her had been simply at first not to laugh at him. She had beautifully not done so for ten years, and she was not doing so now. So he had endless gratitude to make up. Only for that he must see just how he had figured to her. "What, exactly, was the account I gave—?"

"Of the way you did feel? Well, it was very simple. You said you had had from your earliest time, as the deepest thing within you, the sense of being kept for something rare and strange, possibly prodigious and terrible, that was sooner or later to happen to you, that you had in your bones the foreboding and the conviction of, and that would perhaps
250 overwhelm you."

"Do you call that very simple?" John Marcher asked.

She thought a moment. "It was perhaps because I seemed, as you spoke, to understand it."

"You do understand it?" he eagerly asked.

Again she kept her kind eyes on him. "You still have the belief?"

"Oh!" he exclaimed helplessly. There was too much to say.

"Whatever it's to be," she clearly made out, "it hasn't yet come."

He shook his head in complete surrender now. "It hasn't yet come. Only, you know, it isn't anything I'm to *do,* to achieve in the world, to be
260 distinguished or admired for. I'm not such an ass as *that.* It would be much better, no doubt, if I were."

"It's to be something you're merely to suffer?"

"Well, say to wait for—to have to meet, to face, to see suddenly break out in my life; possibly destroying all further consciousness, possibly annihilating me; possibly, on the other hand, only altering everything, striking at the root of all my world and leaving me to the consequences, however they shape themselves."

She took this in, but the light in her eyes continued for him not to be that of mockery. "Isn't what you describe perhaps but the expecta-
270 tion—or at any rate the sense of danger, familiar to so many people—of falling in love?"

John Marcher wondered. "Did you ask me that before?"

"No—I wasn't so free-and-easy then. But it's what strikes me now."

"Of course," he said after a moment, "it strikes you. Of course it strikes *me*. Of course what's in store for me may be no more than that. The only thing is," he went on, "that I think if it had been that I should by this time know."

"Do you mean because you've *been* in love?" And then as he but looked at her in silence: "You've been in love, and it hasn't meant such
280 a cataclysm, hasn't proved the great affair?"

"Here I am, you see. It hasn't been overwhelming."

"Then it hasn't been love," said May Bartram.

"Well, I at least thought it was. I took it for that—I've taken it till now. It was agreeable, it was delightful, it was miserable," he explained. "But it wasn't strange. It wasn't what *my* affair's to be."

"You want something all to yourself—something that nobody else knows or *has* known?"

"It isn't a question of what I 'want'—God knows I don't want anything. It's only a question of the apprehension that haunts me—that I
290 live with day by day."

He said this so lucidly and consistently that he could see it further impose itself. If she hadn't been interested before she'd have been interested now. "Is it a sense of coming violence?"

Evidently now too again he liked to talk of it. "I don't think of it as—when it does come—necessarily violent. I only think of it as natural and as of course above all unmistakable. I think of it simply as *the* thing. *The* thing will of itself appear natural."

"Then how will it appear strange?"

Marcher bethought himself. "It won't—to *me*."
300   "To whom then?"

"Well," he replied, smiling at last, "say to you."

"Oh then I'm to be present?"

"Why you *are* present—since you know."

"I see." She turned it over. "But I mean at the catastrophe."

At this, for a minute, their lightness gave way to their gravity; it was as if the long look they exchanged held them together. "It will only depend on yourself—if you'll watch with me."

"Are you afraid?" she asked.

"Don't leave me *now*," he went on.
310   "Are you afraid?" she repeated.

"Do you think me simply out of my mind?" he pursued instead of answering. "Do I merely strike you as a harmless lunatic?"

"No," said May Bartram. "I understand you. I believe you."

"You mean you feel how my obsession—poor old thing!—may correspond to some possible reality?"

"To some possible reality."

"Then you *will* watch with me?"

She hesitated, then for the third time put her question. "Are you afraid?"

320   "Did I tell you I was—at Naples?"

"No, you said nothing about it."

"Then I don't know. And I should *like* to know," said John Marcher. "You'll tell me yourself whether you think so. If you'll watch with me you'll see."

"Very good then." They had been moving by this time across the room, and at the door, before passing out, they paused as for the full wind-up of their understanding. "I'll watch with you," said May Bartram.

2

The fact that she "knew"—knew and yet neither chaffed him nor betrayed him—had in a short time begun to constitute between them a
330 goodly bond, which became more marked when, within the year that followed their afternoon at Weatherend, the opportunities for meeting multiplied. The event that thus promoted these occasions was the death of the ancient lady her great-aunt, under whose wing, since losing her mother, she had to such an extent found shelter, and who, though but the widowed mother of the new successor to the property, had succeeded—thanks to a high tone and a high temper—in not forfeiting the supreme position at the great house. The deposition of this personage arrived but with her death, which, followed by many changes, made in particular a difference for the young woman in whom Marcher's expert
340 attention had recognised from the first a dependent with a pride that might ache though it didn't bristle. Nothing for a long time had made him easier than the thought that the aching must have been much soothed by Miss Bartram's now finding herself able to set up a small home in London. She had acquired property, to an amount that made that luxury just possible, under her aunt's extremely complicated will, and when the whole matter began to be straightened out, which indeed took time, she let him know that the happy issue was at last in view. He had seen her again before that day, both because she had more than once accompanied the ancient lady to town and because he had paid an-
350 other visit to the friends who so conveniently made of Weatherend one of the charms of their own hospitality. These friends had taken him back there; he had achieved there again with Miss Bartram some quiet detachment; and he had in London succeeded in persuading her to more than one brief absence from her aunt. They went together, on these latter occasions, to the National Gallery and the South Kensington Museum, where, among vivid reminders, they talked of Italy at large— not now attempting to recover, as at first, the taste of their youth and

their ignorance. That recovery, the first day at Weatherend, had served its purpose well, had given them quite enough; so that they were, to
360 Marcher's sense, no longer hovering about the headwaters of their stream, but had felt their boat pushed sharply off and down the current.

They were literally afloat together; for our gentleman this was marked, quite as marked as that the fortunate cause of it was just the buried treasure of her knowledge. He had with his own hands dug up this little hoard, brought to light—that is to within reach of the dim day constituted by their discretions and privacies—the object of value the hiding-place of which he had, after putting it into the ground himself, so strangely, so long forgotten. The rare luck of his having again just stumbled on the spot made him indifferent to any other question; he would
370 doubtless have devoted more time to the odd accident of his lapse of memory if he hadn't been moved to devote so much to the sweetness, the comfort, as he felt, for the future, that this accident itself had helped to keep fresh. It had never entered into his plan that any one should "know," and mainly for the reason that it wasn't in him to tell any one. That would have been impossible, for nothing but the amusement of a cold world would have waited on it. Since, however, a mysterious fate had opened his mouth betimes, in spite of him, he would count that a compensation and profit by it to the utmost. That the right person *should* know tempered the asperity of his secret more even than his shyness had permitted him to imagine;
380 and May Bartram was clearly right, because—well, because there she was. Her knowledge simply settled it; he would have been sure enough by this time had she been wrong. There was that in his situation, no doubt, that disposed him too much to see her as a mere confidant, taking all her light for him from the fact—the fact only—of her interest in his predicament; from her mercy, sympathy, seriousness, her consent not to regard him as the funniest of the funny. Aware, in fine, that her price for him was just in her giving him this constant sense of his being admirably spared, he was careful to remember that she had also a life of her own, with things that might happen to *her*, things that in friendship one should likewise take ac-
390 count of. Something fairly remarkable came to pass with him, for that matter, in this connexion—something represented by a certain passage of his consciousness, in the suddenest way, from one extreme to the other.

He had thought himself, so long as nobody knew, the most disinterested person in the world, carrying his concentrated burden, his perpetual suspense, ever so quietly, holding his tongue about it, giving others no glimpse of it nor of its effect upon his life, asking of them no allowance and only making on his side all those that were asked. He hadn't disturbed people with the queerness of their having to know a haunted man, though he had had moments of rather special temptation on hearing them
400 say they were forsooth "unsettled." If they were as unsettled as he was— he who had never been settled for an hour in his life—they would know what it meant. Yet it wasn't, all the same, for him to make them, and he listened to them civilly enough. This was why he had such good—though possibly such rather colourless—manners; this was why, above all, he

could regard himself, in a greedy world, as decently—as in fact perhaps even a little sublimely—unselfish. Our point is accordingly that he valued this character quite sufficiently to measure his present danger of letting it lapse, against which he promised himself to be much on his guard. He was quite ready, none the less, to be selfish just a little, since surely no more
410 charming occasion for it had come to him. "Just a little," in a word, was just as much as Miss Bartram, taking one day with another, would let him. He never would be in the least coercive, and would keep well before him the lines on which consideration for her—the very highest—ought to proceed. He would thoroughly establish the heads under which her affairs, her requirements, her peculiarities—he went so far as to give them the latitude of that name—would come into their intercourse. All this naturally was a sign of how much he took the intercourse itself for granted. There was nothing more to be done about *that*. It simply existed; had sprung into being with her first penetrating question to him in the autumn light there
420 at Weatherend. The real form it should have taken on the basis that stood out large was the form of their marrying. But the devil in this was that the very basis itself put marrying out of the question. His conviction, his apprehension, his obsession, in short, wasn't a privilege he could invite a woman to share; and that consequence of it was precisely what was the matter with him. Something or other lay in wait for him, amid the twists and the turns of the months and the years, like a crouching beast in the jungle. It signified little whether the crouching beast were destined to slay him or to be slain. The definite point was the inevitable spring of the creature; and the definite lesson from that was that a man of feeling didn't
430 cause himself to be accompanied by a lady on a tiger-hunt. Such was the image under which he had ended by figuring his life.
     They had at first, none the less, in the scattered hours spent together, made no allusion to that view of it; which was a sign he was handsomely alert to give that he didn't expect, that he in fact didn't care, always to be talking about it. Such a feature in one's outlook was really like a hump on one's back. The differences it made every minute of the day existed quite independently of discussion. One discussed of course *like* a hunchback, for there was always, if nothing else, the hunchback face. That remained, and she was watching him; but people
440 watched best, as a general thing, in silence, so that such would be predominantly the manner of their vigil. Yet he didn't want, at the same time, to be tense and solemn; tense and solemn was what he imagined he too much showed for with other people. The thing to be, with the one person who knew, was easy and natural—to make the reference rather than be seeming to avoid it, to avoid it rather than be seeming to make it, and to keep it, in any case, familiar, facetious even, rather than pedantic and portentous. Some such consideration as the latter was doubtless in his mind for instance when he wrote pleasantly to Miss Bartram that perhaps the great thing he had so long felt as in the lap of
450 the gods was no more than this circumstance, which touched him so nearly, of her acquiring a house in London. It was the first allusion they

had yet again made, needing any other hitherto so little; but when she replied, after having given him the news, that she was by no means satisfied with such a trifle as the climax to so special a suspense, she almost set him wondering if she hadn't even a larger conception of singularity for him than he had for himself. He was at all events destined to become aware little by little, as time went by, that she was all the while looking at his life, judging it, measuring it, in the light of the thing she knew, which grew to be at last, with the consecration of the
460 years, never mentioned between them save as "the real truth" about him. That had always been his own form of reference to it, but she adopted the form so quietly that, looking back at the end of a period, he knew there was no moment at which it was traceable that she had, as he might say, got inside his idea, or exchanged the attitude of beautifully indulging for that of still more beautifully believing him.

It was always open to him to accuse her of seeing him but as the most harmless of maniacs, and this, in the long run—since it covered so much ground—was his easiest description of their friendship. He had a screw loose for her, but she liked him in spite of it and was practically,
470 against the rest of the world, his kind wise keeper, unremunerated but fairly amused and, in the absence of other near ties, not disreputably occupied. The rest of the world of course thought him queer, but she, she only, knew how, and above all why, queer; which was precisely what enabled her to dispose the concealing veil in the right folds. She took his gaiety from him—since it had to pass with them for gaiety—as she took everything else; but she certainly so far justified by her unerring touch his finer sense of the degree to which he had ended by convincing her. *She* at least never spoke of the secret of his life except as "the real truth about you," and she had in fact a wonderful way of making it seem, as
480 such, the secret of her own life too. That was in fine how he so constantly felt her as allowing for him; he couldn't on the whole call it anything else. He allowed for himself, but she, exactly, allowed still more; partly because, better placed for a sight of the matter, she traced his unhappy perversion through reaches of its course into which he could scarce follow it. He knew how he felt, but, besides knowing that, she knew how he *looked* as well; he knew each of the things of importance he was insidiously kept from doing, but she could add up the amount they made, understand how much, with a lighter weight on his spirit, he might have done, and thereby establish how, clever as he was, he fell
490 short. Above all she was in the secret of the difference between the forms he went through—those of his little office under Government, those of caring for his modest patrimony, for his library, for his garden in the country, for the people in London whose invitations he accepted and repaid—and the detachment that reigned beneath them and that made of all behaviour, all that could in the least be called behaviour, a long act of dissimulation. What it had come to was that he wore a mask painted with the social simper, out of the eye-holes of which there looked eyes of an expression not in the least matching the other

features. This the stupid world, even after years, had never more than
500 half-discovered. It was only May Bartram who had, and she achieved, by
an art indescribable, the feat of at once—or perhaps it was only alternately—meeting the eyes from in front and mingling her own vision, as
from over his shoulder, with their peep through the apertures.

So while they grew older together she did watch with him, and so she
let this association give shape and colour to her own existence. Beneath
her forms as well detachment had learned to sit, and behaviour had become for her, in the social sense, a false account of herself. There was but
one account of her that would have been true all the while and that she
could give straight to nobody, least of all to John Marcher. Her whole atti-
510 tude was a virtual statement, but the perception of that only seemed
called to take its place for him as one of the many things necessarily
crowded out of his consciousness. If she had moreover, like himself, to
make sacrifices to their real truth, it was to be granted that her compensation might have affected her as more prompt and more natural. They
had long periods, in this London time, during which, when they were together, a stranger might have listened to them without in the least pricking up his ears; on the other hand the real truth was equally liable at any
moment to rise to the surface, and the auditor would then have wondered
indeed what they were talking about. They had from an early hour made
520 up their mind that society was, luckily, unintelligent, and the margin allowed them by this had fairly become one of their commonplaces. Yet
there were still moments when the situation turned almost fresh—usually under the effect of some expression drawn from herself. Her expressions doubtless repeated themselves, but her intervals were generous.
"What saves us, you know, is that we answer so completely to so usual an
appearance: that of the man and woman whose friendship has become
such a daily habit—or almost—as to be at last indispensable." That for instance was a remark she had frequently enough had occasion to make,
though she had given it at different times different developments. What
530 we are especially concerned with is the turn it happened to take from her
one afternoon when he had come to see her in honour of her birthday.
This anniversary had fallen on a Sunday, at a season of thick fog and general outward gloom; but he had brought her his customary offering, having known her now long enough to have established a hundred small
traditions. It was one of his proofs to himself, the present he made her on
her birthday, that he hadn't sunk into real selfishness. It was mostly nothing more than a small trinket, but it was always fine of its kind, and he
was regularly careful to pay for it more than he thought he could afford.
"Our habit saves you at least, don't you see? because it makes you, after
540 all, for the vulgar, indistinguishable from other men. What's the most inveterate mark of men in general? Why the capacity to spend endless time
with dull women—to spend it I won't say without being bored, but without minding that they are, without being driven off at a tangent by it;
which comes to the same thing. I'm your dull woman, a part of the daily

bread for which you pray at church. That covers your tracks more than anything."

"And what covers yours?" asked Marcher, whom his dull woman could mostly to this extent amuse. "I see of course what you mean by your saving me, in this way and that, so far as other people are concerned—I've 550 seen it all along. Only what is it that saves *you?* I often think, you know, of that."

She looked as if she sometimes thought of that too, but rather in a different way. "Where other people, you mean, are concerned?"

"Well, you're really so in with me, you know—as a sort of result of my being so in with yourself. I mean of my having such an immense regard for you, being so tremendously mindful of all you've done for me. I sometimes ask myself if it's quite fair. Fair I mean to have so involved and— since one may say it—interested you. I almost feel as if you hadn't really had time to do anything else."

560   "Anything else but be interested?" she asked. "Ah what else does one ever want to be? If I've been 'watching' with you, as we long ago agreed I was to do, watching's always in itself an absorption."

"Oh certainly," John Marcher said, "if you hadn't had your curiosity—! Only doesn't it sometimes come to you as time goes on that your curiosity isn't being particularly repaid?"

May Bartram had a pause. "Do you ask that, by any chance, because you feel at all that yours isn't? I mean because you have to wait so long."

Oh he understood what she meant! "For the thing to happen that never does happen? For the beast to jump out? No, I'm just where I was 570 about it. It isn't a matter as to which I can *choose,* I can decide for a change. It isn't one as to which there *can* be a change. It's in the lap of the gods. One's in the hands of one's law—there one is. As to the form the law will take, the way it will operate, that's its own affair."

"Yes," Miss Bartram replied; "of course one's fate's coming, of course it *has* come in its own form and its own way, all the while. Only, you know, the form and the way in your case were to have been—well, something so exceptional and, as one may say, so particularly *your* own."

Something in this made him look at her with suspicion. "You say 'were to *have* been,' as if in your heart you had begun to doubt."

580   "Oh!" she vaguely protested.

"As if you believed," he went on, "that nothing will now take place."

She shook her head slowly but rather inscrutably. "You're far from my thought."

He continued to look at her. "What then is the matter with you?"

"Well," she said after another wait, "the matter with me is simply that I'm more sure than ever my curiosity, as you call it, will be but too well repaid."

They were frankly grave now; he had got up from his seat, had turned once more about the little drawing-room to which, year after 590 year, he brought his inevitable topic; in which he had, as he might have said, tasted their intimate community with every sauce, where every object was as familiar to him as the things of his own house and the very carpets were worn with his fitful walk very much as the desks in old counting-houses are worn by the elbows of generations of clerks. The generations of his nervous moods had been at work there, and the place was the written history of his whole middle life. Under the impression of what his friend had just said he knew himself, for some reason, more aware of these things; which made him, after a moment, stop again before her. "Is it possibly that you've grown afraid?"

600   "Afraid?" He thought, as she repeated the word, that his question had made her, a little, change colour; so that, lest he should have touched on a truth, he explained very kindly: "You remember that that was what you asked *me* long ago—that first day at Weatherend."

"Oh yes, and you told me you didn't know—that I was to see for myself. We've said little about it since, even in so long a time."

"Precisely," Marcher interposed—"quite as if it were too delicate a matter for us to make free with. Quite as if we might find, on pressure, that I *am* afraid. For then," he said, "we shouldn't, should we? quite know what to do."

610   She had for the time no answer to this question. "There have been days when I thought you were. Only, of course," she added, "there have been days when we have thought almost anything."

"Everything. Oh!" Marcher softly groaned as with a gasp, half-spent, at the face, more uncovered just then than it had been for a long while, of the imagination always with them. It had always had its incalculable moments of glaring out, quite as with the very eyes of the very Beast, and, used as he was to them, they could still draw from him the tribute of a sigh that rose from the depths of his being. All they had thought, first and last, rolled over him; the past seemed to have been

620   reduced to mere barren speculation. This in fact was what the place had just struck him as so full of—the simplification of everything but the state of suspense. That remained only by seeming to hang in the void surrounding it. Even his original fear, if fear it had been, had lost itself in the desert. "I judge, however," he continued, "that you see I'm not afraid now."

"What I see, as I make it out, is that you've achieved something almost unprecedented in the way of getting used to danger. Living with it so long and so closely you've lost your sense of it; you know it's there, but you're indifferent, and you cease even, as of old, to have to whistle

630   in the dark. Considering what the danger is," May Bartram wound up, "I'm bound to say I don't think your attitude could well be surpassed."

John Marcher faintly smiled. "It's heroic?"

"Certainly—call it that."

It was what he would have liked indeed to call it. "I *am* then a man of courage?"

"That's what you were to show me."

He still, however, wondered. "But doesn't the man of courage know what he's afraid of—or *not* afraid of? I don't know *that*, you see. I don't focus it. I can't name it. I only know I'm exposed."

640 "Yes, but exposed—how shall I say?—so directly. So intimately. That's surely enough."

"Enough to make you feel then—as what we may call the end and the upshot of our watch—that I'm not afraid?"

"You're not afraid. But it isn't," she said, "the end of our watch. That is it isn't the end of yours. You've everything still to see."

"Then why haven't *you?*" he asked. He had had, all along, to-day, the sense of her keeping something back, and he still had it. As this was his first impression of that it quite made a date. The case was the more marked as she didn't at first answer; which in turn made him go on. "You 650 know something I don't." Then his voice, for that of a man of courage, trembled a little. "You know what's to happen." Her silence, with the face she showed, was almost a confession—it made him sure. "You know, and you're afraid to tell me. It's so bad that you're afraid I'll find out."

All this might be true, for she did look as if, unexpectedly to her, he had crossed some mystic line that she had secretly drawn round her. Yet she might, after all, not have worried; and the real climax was that he himself, at all events, needn't. "You'll never find out."

3

It was all to have made, none the less, as I have said, a date; which came out in the fact that again and again, even after long intervals, other things 660 that passed between them wore in relation to this hour but the character of recalls and results. Its immediate effect had been indeed rather to lighten insistence—almost to provoke a reaction; as if their topic had dropped by its own weight and as if moreover, for that matter, Marcher had been visited by one of his occasional warnings against egotism. He had kept up, he felt, and very decently on the whole, his consciousness of the importance of not being selfish, and it was true that he had never sinned in that direction without promptly enough trying to press the scales the other way. He often repaired his fault, the season permitting, by inviting his friend to accompany him to the opera; and it not infre-670 quently thus happened that, to show he didn't wish her to have but one sort of food for her mind, he was the cause of her appearing there with him a dozen nights in the month. It even happened that, seeing her home at such times, he occasionally went in with her to finish, as he called it, the evening, and, the better to make his point, sat down to the frugal but always careful little supper that awaited his pleasure. His point was made, he thought, by his not eternally insisting with her on himself; made for instance, at such hours, when it befell that, her piano at hand and each of them familiar with it, they went over passages of the opera together. It chanced to be on one of these occasions, however, that he reminded her of 680 her not having answered a certain question he had put to her during the talk that had taken place between them on her last birthday. "What is it that saves *you?*"—saved her, he meant, from that appearance of variation from the usual human type. If he had practically escaped remark, as she pretended, by doing, in the most important particular, what most men do—find the answer to life in patching up an alliance of a sort with a woman no better than himself—how had she escaped it, and how could the alliance, such as it was, since they must suppose it had been more or less noticed, have failed to make her rather positively talked about?

"I never said," May Bartram replied, "that it hadn't made me a good
690 deal talked about."

"Ah well then you're not 'saved.'"

"It hasn't been a question for me. If you've had your woman I've had," she said, "my man."

"And you mean that makes you all right?"

Oh it was always as if there were so much to say! "I don't know why it shouldn't make me—humanly, which is what we're speaking of—as right as it makes you."

"I see," Marcher returned. "'Humanly,' no doubt, as showing that you're living for something. Not, that is, just for me and my secret."
700   May Bartram smiled. "I don't pretend it exactly shows that I'm not living for you. It's my intimacy with you that's in question."

He laughed as he saw what she meant. "Yes, but since, as you say, I'm only, so far as people make out, ordinary, you're—aren't you?—no more than ordinary either. You help me to pass for a man like another. So if I *am*, as I understand you, you're not compromised. Is that it?"

She had another of her waits, but she spoke clearly enough. "That's it. It's all that concerns me—to help you to pass for a man like another."

He was careful to acknowledge the remark handsomely. "How kind, how beautiful, you are to me! How shall I ever repay you?"
710   She had her last grave pause, as if there might be a choice of ways. But she chose. "By going on as you are."

It was into this going on as he was that they relapsed, and really for so long a time that the day inevitably came for a further sounding of their depths. These depths, constantly bridged over by a structure firm enough in spite of its lightness and of its occasional oscillation in the somewhat vertiginous air, invited on occasion, in the interest of their nerves, a dropping of the plummet and a measurement of the abyss. A difference had been made moreover, once for all, by the fact that she had all the while not appeared to feel the need of rebutting his charge of an idea within
720 her that she didn't dare to express—a charge uttered just before one of the fullest of their later discussions ended. It had come up for him then that she "knew" something and that what she knew was bad—too bad to tell him. When he had spoken of it as visibly so bad that she was afraid he might find it out, her reply had left the matter too equivocal to be let alone and yet, for Marcher's special sensibility, almost too formidable again to touch. He circled about it at a distance that alternately narrowed and widened and that still wasn't much affected by the consciousness in

him that there was nothing she could "know," after all, any better than he did. She had no source of knowledge he hadn't equally—except of course 730 that she might have finer nerves. That was what women had where they were interested; they made out things, where people were concerned, that the people often couldn't have made out for themselves. Their nerves, their sensibility, their imagination, were conductors and revealers, and the beauty of May Bartram was in particular that she had given herself so to his case. He felt in these days what, oddly enough, he had never felt before, the growth of a dread of losing her by some catastrophe—some catastrophe that yet wouldn't at all be *the* catastrophe: partly because she had almost of a sudden begun to strike him as more useful to him than ever yet, and partly by reason of an appearance of uncertainty in her health, coinci740 dent and equally new. It was characteristic of the inner detachment he had hitherto so successfully cultivated and to which our whole account of him is a reference, it was characteristic that his complications, such as they were, had never yet seemed so as at this crisis to thicken about him, even to the point of making him ask himself if he were, by any chance, of a truth, within sight or sound, within touch or reach, within the immediate jurisdiction, of the thing that waited.

When the day came, as come it had to, that his friend confessed to him her fear of a deep disorder in her blood, he felt somehow the shadow of a change and the chill of a shock. He immediately began to 750 imagine aggravations and disasters, and above all to think of her peril as the direct menace for himself of personal privation. This indeed gave him one of those partial recoveries of equanimity that were agreeable to him—it showed him that what was still first in his mind was the loss she herself might suffer. "What if she should have to die before knowing, before seeing—?" It would have been brutal, in the early stages of her trouble, to put that question to her; but it had immediately sounded for him to his own concern, and the possibility was what most made him sorry for her. If she did "know," moreover, in the sense of her having had some—what should he think?—mystical irresistible light, this 760 would make the matter not better, but worse, inasmuch as her original adoption of his own curiosity had quite become the basis of her life. She had been living to see what would *be* to be seen, and it would quite lacerate her to have to give up before the accomplishment of the vision. These reflexions, as I say, quickened his generosity; yet, make them as he might, he saw himself, with the lapse of the period, more and more disconcerted. It lapsed for him with a strange steady sweep, and the oddest oddity was that it gave him, independently of the threat of much inconvenience, almost the only positive surprise his career, if career it could be called, had yet offered him. She kept to the house as she had 770 never done; he had to go to her to see her—she could meet him nowhere now, though there was scarce a corner of their loved old London in which she hadn't in the past, at one time or another, done so; and he found her always seated by her fire in the deep old-fashioned chair she was less and less able to leave. He had been struck one day, after an

absence exceeding his usual measure, with her suddenly looking much older to him than he had ever thought of her being; then he recognized that the suddenness was all on his side—he had just simply and suddenly noticed. She looked older because inevitably, after so many years, she *was* old, or almost; which was of course true in still greater measure
780 of her companion. If she was old, or almost, John Marcher assuredly was, and yet it was her showing of the lesson, not his own, that brought the truth home to him. His surprises began here; when once they had begun they multiplied; they came rather with a rush: it was as if, in the oddest way in the world, they had all been kept back, sown in a thick cluster, for the late afternoon of life, the time at which for people in general the unexpected has died out.

One of them was that he should have caught himself—for he *had* so done—*really* wondering if the great accident would take form now as nothing more than his being condemned to see this charming woman,
790 this admirable friend, pass away from him. He had never so unreservedly qualified her as while confronted in thought with such a possibility; in spite of which there was small doubt for him that as an answer to his long riddle the mere effacement of even so fine a feature of his situation would be an abject anticlimax. It would represent, as connected with his past attitude, a drop of dignity under the shadow of which his existence could only become the most grotesque of failures. He had been far from holding it a failure—long as he had waited for the appearance that was to make it a success. He had waited for quite another thing, not for such a thing as that. The breath of his good faith
800 came short, however, as he recognised how long he had waited, or how long at least his companion had. That she, at all events, might be recorded as having waited in vain—this affected him sharply, and all the more because of his at first having done little more than amuse himself with the idea. It grew more grave as the gravity of her condition grew, and the state of mind it produced in him, which he himself ended by watching as if it had been some definite disfigurement of his outer person, may pass for another of his surprises. This conjoined itself still with another, the really stupefying consciousness of a question that he would have allowed to shape itself had he dared. What did everything
810 mean—what, that is, did *she* mean, she and her vain waiting and her probable death and the soundless admonition of it all—unless that, at this time of day, it was simply, it was overwhelmingly too late? He had never at any stage of his queer consciousness admitted the whisper of such a correction; he had never till within these last few months been so false to his conviction as not to hold that what was to come to him had time, whether *he* struck himself as having it or not. That at last, at last, he certainly hadn't it, to speak of, or had it but in the scantiest measure—such, soon enough, as things went with him, became the inference with which his old obsession had to reckon: and this it was not
820 helped to do by the more and more confirmed appearance that the great vagueness casting the long shadow in which he had lived had, to attest

itself, almost no margin left. Since it was in Time that he was to have met his fate, so it was in Time that his fate was to have acted; and as he waked up to the sense of no longer being young, which was exactly the sense of being stale, just as that, in turn, was the sense of being weak, he waked up to another matter beside. It all hung together; they were subject, he and the great vagueness, to an equal and indivisible law. When the possibilities themselves had accordingly turned stale, when the secret of the gods had grown faint, had perhaps even quite evapo-
830 rated, that, and that only, was failure. It wouldn't have been failure to be bankrupt, dishonoured, pilloried, hanged; it was failure not to be any-thing. And so, in the dark valley into which his path had taken its un-looked-for twist, he wondered not a little as he groped. He didn't care what awful crash might overtake him, with what ignominy or what monstrosity he might yet be associated—since he wasn't after all too ut-terly old to suffer—if it would only be decently proportionate to the posture he had kept, all his life, in the threatened presence of it. He had but one desire left—that he shouldn't have been "sold."

4

Then it was that, one afternoon, while the spring of the year was young
840 and new she met all in her own way his frankest betrayal of these alarms. He had gone in late to see her, but evening hadn't settled and she was presented to him in that long fresh light of waning April days which affects us often with a sadness sharper than the greyest hours of autumn. The week had been warm, the spring was supposed to have be-gun early, and May Bartram sat, for the first time in the year, without a fire; a fact that, to Marcher's sense, gave the scene of which she formed part a smooth and ultimate look, an air of knowing, in its immaculate order and cold meaningless cheer, that it would never see a fire again. Her own aspect—he could scarce have said why—intensified this note.
850 Almost as white as wax, with the marks and signs in her face as numer-ous and as fine as if they had been etched by a needle, with soft white draperies relieved by a faded green scarf on the delicate tone of which the years had further refined, she was the picture of a serene and exquisite but impenetrable sphinx, whose head, or indeed all whose per-son, might have been powdered with silver. She was a sphinx, yet with her white petals and green fronds she might have been a lily too—only an artificial lily, wonderfully imitated and constantly kept, without dust or stain, though not exempt from a slight droop and a complexity of faint creases, under some clear glass bell. The perfection of household
860 care, of high polish and finish, always reigned in her rooms, but they now looked most as if everything had been wound up, tucked in, put away, so that she might sit with folded hands and with nothing more to do. She was "out of it," to Marcher's vision; her work was over; she com-municated with him as across some gulf or from some island of rest that she had already reached, and it made him feel strangely abandoned. Was it—or rather wasn't it—that if for so long she had been watching with

him the answer to their question must have swum into her ken and taken on its name, so that her occupation was verily gone? He had as much as charged her with this in saying to her, many months before, 870 that she even then knew something she was keeping from him. It was a point he had never since ventured to press, vaguely fearing as he did that it might become a difference, perhaps a disagreement, between them. He had in this later time turned nervous, which was what he in all the other years had never been; and the oddity was that his nervousness should have waited till he had begun to doubt, should have held off so long as he was sure. There was something, it seemed to him, that the wrong word would bring down on his head, something that would so at least ease off his tension. But he wanted not to speak the wrong word; that would make everything ugly. He wanted the knowledge he lacked 880 to drop on him, if drop it could, by its own august weight. If she was to forsake him it was surely for her to take leave. This was why he didn't directly ask her again what she knew; but it was also why, approaching the matter from another side, he said to her in the course of his visit: "What do you regard as the very worst that at this time of day *can* happen to me?"

He had asked her that in the past often enough; they had, with the odd irregular rhythm of their intensities and avoidances, exchanged ideas about it and then had seen the ideas washed away by cool intervals, washed like figures traced in sea-sand. It had ever been the mark of their 890 talk that the oldest allusions in it required but a little dismissal and reaction to come out again, sounding for the hour as new. She could thus at present meet his enquiry quite freshly and patiently. "Oh yes, I've repeatedly thought, only it always seemed to me of old that I couldn't quite make up my mind. I thought of dreadful things, between which it was difficult to choose; and so must you have done."

"Rather! I feel now as if I had scarce done anything else. I appear to myself to have spent my life in thinking of nothing *but* dreadful things. A great many of them I've at different times named to you, but there were others I couldn't name."

900   "They were too, too dreadful?"

"Too, too dreadful—some of them."

She looked at him a minute, and there came to him as he met it an inconsequent sense that her eyes, when one got their full clearness, were still as beautiful as they had been in youth, only beautiful with a strange cold light—a light that somehow was a part of the effect, if it wasn't rather a part of the cause, of the pale hard sweetness of the season and the hour. "And yet," she said at last, "there are horrors we've mentioned."

It deepened the strangeness to see her, as such a figure in such a picture, talk of "horrors," but she was to do in a few minutes something 910 stranger yet—though even of this he was to take the full measure but afterwards—and the note of it already trembled. It was, for the matter of that, one of the signs that her eyes were having again the high flicker of their prime. He had to admit, however, what she said. "Oh yes, there were times when we did go far." He caught himself in the act of speaking as if it all were over. Well, he wished it were; and the consummation depended for him clearly more and more on his friend.

But she had now a soft smile. "Oh far—!"

It was oddly ironic. "Do you mean you're prepared to go further?"

She was frail and ancient and charming as she continued to look at him, yet it was rather as if she had lost the thread. "Do you consider that we went far?"

"Why I thought it the point you were just making—that we *had* looked most things in the face."

"Including each other?" She still smiled. "But you're quite right. We've had together great imaginations, often great fears; but some of them have been unspoken."

"Then the worst—we haven't faced that. I *could* face it, I believe, if I knew what you think it. I feel," he explained, "as if I had lost my power to conceive such things." And he wondered if he looked as blank as he sounded. "It's spent."

"Then why do you assume," she asked, "that mine isn't?"

"Because you've given me signs to the contrary. It isn't a question for you of conceiving, imagining, comparing. It isn't a question now of choosing." At last he came out with it. "You know something I don't. You've shown me that before."

These last words had affected her, he made out in a moment, exceedingly, and she spoke with firmness. "I've shown you, my dear, nothing."

He shook his head. "You can't hide it."

"Oh, oh!" May Bartram sounded over what she couldn't hide. It was almost a smothered groan.

"You admitted it months ago, when I spoke of it to you as of something you were afraid I should find out. Your answer was that I couldn't, that I wouldn't, and I don't pretend I have. But you had something therefore in mind, and I now see how it must have been, how it still is, the possibility that, of all possibilities, has settled itself for you as the worst. This," he went on, "is why I appeal to you. I'm only afraid of ignorance to-day—I'm not afraid of knowledge." And then as for a while she said nothing: "What makes me sure is that I see in your face and feel here, in this air and amid these appearances, that you're out of it. You've done. You've had your experience. You leave me to my fate."

Well, she listened, motionless and white in her chair, as on a decision to be made, so that her manner was fairly an avowal, though still, with a small fine inner stiffness, an imperfect surrender. "It *would* be the worst," she finally let herself say. "I mean the thing I've never said."

It hushed him a moment. "More monstrous than all the monstrosities we've named?"

"More monstrous. Isn't that what you sufficiently express," she asked, "in calling it the worst?"

Marcher thought. "Assuredly—if you mean, as I do, something that includes all the loss and all the shame that are thinkable."

"It would if it *should* happen," said May Bartram. "What we're speaking of, remember, is only my idea."

"It's your belief," Marcher returned. "That's enough for me. I feel your beliefs are right. Therefore if, having this one, you give me no more light on it, you abandon me."

"No, no!" she repeated. "I'm with you—don't you see?—still." And as to make it more vivid to him she rose from her chair—a movement she seldom risked in these days—and showed herself, all draped and all soft, in her fairness and slimness. "I haven't forsaken you."

970   It was really, in its effort against weakness, a generous assurance, and had the success of the impulse not, happily, been great, it would have touched him to pain more than to pleasure. But the cold charm in her eyes had spread, as she hovered before him, to all the rest of her person, so that it was for the minute almost a recovery of youth. He couldn't pity her for that; he could only take her as she showed—as capable even yet of helping him. It was as if, at the same time, her light might at any instant go out; wherefore he must make the most of it. There passed before him with intensity the three or four things he wanted most to know; but the question that came of itself to his lips re-

980   ally covered the others. "Then tell me if I shall consciously suffer."

She promptly shook her head. "Never!"

It confirmed the authority he imputed to her, and it produced on him an extraordinary effect. "Well, what's better than that? Do you call that the worst?"

"You think nothing is better?" she asked.

She seemed to mean something so special that he again sharply wondered, though still with the dawn of a prospect of relief. "Why not, if one doesn't *know?*" After which, as their eyes, over his question, met in a silence, the dawn deepened and something to his purpose came

990   prodigiously out of her very face. His own, as he took it in, suddenly flushed to the forehead, and he gasped with the force of a perception to which, on the instant, everything fitted. The sound of his gasp filled the air; then he became articulate. "I see—if I don't suffer!"

In her own look, however, was doubt. "You see what?"

"Why what you mean—what you've always meant."

She again shook her head. "What I mean isn't what I've always meant. It's different."

"It's something new?"

She hung back from it a little. "Something new. It's not what you

1000   think. I see what you think."

His divination drew breath then; only her correction might be wrong. "It isn't that I *am* a blockhead?" he asked between faintness and grimness. "It isn't that it's all a mistake?"

"A mistake?" she pityingly echoed. *That* possibility, for her, he saw, would be monstrous; and if she guaranteed him the immunity from pain it would accordingly not be what she had in mind. "Oh no," she declared; "it's nothing of that sort. You've been right."

Yet he couldn't help asking himself if she weren't, thus pressed, speaking but to save him. It seemed to him he should be most in a hole if his
1010 history should prove all a platitude. "Are you telling me the truth, so that I shan't have been a bigger idiot than I can bear to know? I *haven't* lived with a vain imagination, in the most besotted illusion? I haven't waited but to see the door shut in my face?"

She shook her head again. "However the case stands *that* isn't the truth. Whatever the reality, it *is* a reality. The door isn't shut. The door's open," said May Bartram.

"Then something's to come?"

She waited once again, always with her cold sweet eyes on him. "It's never too late." She had, with her gliding step, diminished the distance
1020 between them, and she stood nearer to him, close to him, a minute, as if still charged with the unspoken. Her movement might have been for some finer emphasis on what she was at once hesitating and deciding to say. He had been standing by the chimney-piece, fireless and sparely adorned, a small perfect old French clock and two morsels of rosy Dresden constituting all its furniture; and her hand grasped the shelf while she kept him waiting, grasped it a little as for support and encouragement. She only kept him waiting, however; that is he only waited. It had become suddenly, from her movement and attitude, beautiful and vivid to him that she had something more to give him; her wasted face delicately shone
1030 with it—it glittered almost as with the white lustre of silver in her expression. She was right, incontestably, for what he saw in her face was the truth, and strangely, without consequence, while their talk of it as dreadful was still in the air, she appeared to present it as inordinately soft. This, prompting bewilderment, made him but gape the more gratefully for her revelation, so that they continued for some minutes silent, her face shining at him, her contact imponderably pressing, and his stare all kind but all expectant. The end, none the less, was that what he had expected failed to come to him. Something else took place instead, which seemed to consist at first in the mere closing of her eyes. She gave way at the same
1040 instant to a slow fine shudder, and though he remained staring—though he stared in fact but the harder—turned off and regained her chair. It was the end of what she had been intending, but it left him thinking only of that.

"Well, you don't say—?"

She had touched in her passage a bell near the chimney and had sunk back strangely pale. "I'm afraid I'm too ill."

"Too ill to tell me?" It sprang up sharp to him, and almost to his lips, the fear she might die without giving him light. He checked himself in time from so expressing his question, but she answered as if she
1050 had heard the words.

"Don't you know—now?"

"'Now'—?" She had spoken as if some difference had been made within the moment. But her maid, quickly obedient to her bell, was already with them. "I know nothing." And he was afterwards to say to himself that he must have spoken with odious impatience, such an impatience as to show that, supremely disconcerted, he washed his hands of the whole question.

"Oh!" said May Bartram.

"Are you in pain?" he asked as the woman went to her.

1060   "No," said May Bartram.

Her maid, who had put an arm round her as if to take her to her room, fixed on him eyes that appealingly contradicted her; in spite of which, however, he showed once more his mystification. "What then has happened?"

She was once more, with her companion's help, on her feet, and, feeling withdrawal imposed on him, he had blankly found his hat and gloves and had reached the door. Yet he waited for her answer. "What *was* to," she said.

5

He came back the next day, but she was then unable to see him, and as
1070   it was literally the first time this had occurred in the long stretch of their acquaintance he turned away, defeated and sore, almost angry—or feeling at least that such a break in their custom was really the beginning of the end—and wandered alone with his thoughts, especially with the one he was least able to keep down. She was dying and he would lose her; she was dying and his life would end. He stopped in the Park, into which he had passed, and stared before him at his recurrent doubt. Away from her the doubt pressed again; in her presence he had believed her, but as he felt his forlornness he threw himself into the explanation that, nearest at hand, had most of a miserable warmth for him
1080   and least of a cold torment. She had deceived him to save him—to put him off with something in which he should be able to rest. What could the thing that was to happen to him be, after all, but just this thing that had begun to happen? Her dying, her death, his consequent solitude—
that was what he had figured as the Beast in the Jungle, that was what had been in the lap of the gods. He had had her word for it as he left her—what else on earth could she have meant? It wasn't a thing of a monstrous order; not a fate rare and distinguished; not a stroke of fortune that overwhelmed and immortalised; it had only the stamp of the common doom. But poor Marcher at this hour judged the common doom
1090   sufficient. It would serve his turn, and even as the consummation of infinite waiting he would bend his pride to accept it. He sat down on a bench in the twilight. He hadn't been a fool. Something had *been,* as she had said, to come. Before he rose indeed it had quite struck him that the final fact really matched with the long avenue through which he had had to reach it. As sharing his suspense and as giving herself all, giving her life, to bring it to an end, she had come with him every step of the way. He had lived by her aid, and to leave her behind would be cruelly, damnably to miss her. What could be more overwhelming than that?

Well, he was to know within the week, for though she kept him a
while at bay, left him restless and wretched during a series of days on
each of which he asked about her only again to have to turn away, she
ended his trial by receiving him where she had always received him. Yet
she had been brought out at some hazard into the presence of so many
things that were, consciously, vainly, half their past, and there was scant
service left in the gentleness of her mere desire, all too visible, to check
his obsession and wind up his long trouble. That was clearly what she
wanted, the one thing more for her own peace while she could still put
out her hand. He was so affected by her state that, once seated by her
chair, he was moved to let everything go; it was she herself therefore
who brought him back, took up again, before she dismissed him, her
last word of the other time. She showed how she wished to leave their
business in order. "I'm not sure you understood. You've nothing to wait
for more. It *has* come."

Oh how he looked at her! "Really?"

"Really."

"The thing that, as you said, *was* to?"

"The thing that we began in our youth to watch for."

Face to face with her once more he believed her; it was a claim to
which he had so abjectly little to oppose. "You mean that it has come as
a positive definite occurrence, with a name and a date?"

"Positive. Definite. I don't know about the 'name,' but oh with a date!"

He found himself again too helplessly at sea. "But come in the night—
come and passed me by?"

May Bartram had her strange faint smile. "Oh no, it hasn't passed
you by!"

"But if I haven't been aware of it and it hasn't touched me—?"

"Ah your not being aware of it"—and she seemed to hesitate an instant
to deal with this—"your not being aware of it is the strangeness *in* the
strangeness. It's the wonder *of* the wonder." She spoke as with the softness
almost of a sick child, yet now at last, at the end of all, with the perfect
straightness of a sibyl. She visibly knew that she knew, and the effect on
him was of something co-ordinate, in its high character, with the law that
had ruled him. It was the true voice of the law; so on her lips would the
law itself have sounded. "It *has* touched you," she went on. "It has done its
office. It has made you all its own."

"So utterly without my knowing it?"

"So utterly without your knowing it." His hand, as he leaned to her,
was on the arm of her chair, and, dimly smiling always now, she placed
her own on it. "It's enough if *I* know it."

"Oh!" he confusedly breathed, as she herself of late so often had
done.

"What I long ago said is true. You'll never know now, and I think
you ought to be content. You've *had* it," said May Bartram.

"But had what?"

"Why what was to have marked you out. The proof of your law. It has acted. I'm too glad," she then bravely added, "to have been able to see what it's *not.*"

He continued to attach his eyes to her, and with the sense that it was all beyond him, and that *she* was too, he would still have sharply chal-
1150 lenged her hadn't he so felt it an abuse of her weakness to do more than take devoutly what she gave him, take it hushed as to a revelation. If he did speak, it was out of the foreknowledge of his loneliness to come. "If you're glad of what it's 'not' it might then have been worse?"

She turned her eyes away, she looked straight before her; with which after a moment: "Well, you know our fears."

He wondered. "It's something then we never feared?"

On this slowly she turned to him. "Did we ever dream, with all our dreams, that we should sit and talk of it thus?"

He tried for a little to make out that they had; but it was as if their
1160 dreams, numberless enough, were in solution in some thick cold mist through which thought lost itself. "It might have been that we couldn't talk?"

"Well"—she did her best for him—"not from this side. This, you see," she said, "is the *other* side."

"I think" poor Marcher returned, "that all sides are the same to me." Then, however, as she gently shook her head in correction: "We mightn't, as it were, have got across—?"

"To where we are—no. We're *here*"—she made her weak emphasis.

"And much good does it do us!" was her friend's frank comment.

1170   "It does us the good it can. It does us the good that *it* isn't here. It's past, it's behind," said May Bartram. "Before—" but her voice dropped.

He had got up, not to tire her, but it was hard to combat his yearning. She after all told him nothing but that his light had failed—which he knew well enough without her. "Before—?" he blankly echoed.

"Before, you see, it was always to *come.* That kept it present."

"Oh I don't care what comes now! Besides," Marcher added, "it seems to me I liked it better present, as you say, than I can like it absent with *your* absence."

"Oh mine!"—and her pale hands made light of it.

1180   "With the absence of everything." He had a dreadful sense of standing there before her for—so far as anything but this proved, this bottomless drop was concerned—the last time of their life. It rested on him with a weight he felt he could scarce bear, and this weight it apparently was that still pressed out what remained in him of speakable protest. "I believe you; but I can't begin to pretend I understand. *Nothing,* for me, is past; nothing *will* pass till I pass myself, which I pray my stars may be as soon as possible. Say, however," he added, "that I've eaten my cake, as you contend, to the last crumb—how can the thing I've never felt at all be the thing I was marked out to feel?"

1190   She met him perhaps less directly, but she met him unperturbed. "You take your 'feelings' for granted. You were to suffer your fate. That was not necessarily to know it."

"How in the world—when what is such knowledge but suffering?"

She looked up at him a while in silence. "No—you don't understand."

"I suffer," said John Marcher.

"Don't, don't!"

"How can I help at least *that?*"

"*Don't!*" May Bartram repeated.

1200   She spoke it in a tone so special, in spite of her weakness, that he stared an instant—stared as if some light, hitherto hidden, had shimmered across his vision. Darkness again closed over it, but the gleam had already become for him an idea. "Because I haven't the right—?"

"Don't *know*—when you needn't," she mercifully urged. "You needn't—for we shouldn't."

"Shouldn't?" If he could but know what she meant!

"No—it's too much."

"Too much?" he still asked but, with a mystification that was the next moment of a sudden to give way. Her words, if they meant some-
1210 thing, affected him in this light—the light also of her wasted face—as meaning *all*, and the sense of what knowledge had been for herself came over him with a rush which broke through into a question. "Is it of that then you're dying?"

She but watched him, gravely at first, as to see, with this, where he was, and she might have seen something or feared something that moved her sympathy. "I would live for you still—if I could." Her eyes closed for a little, as if, withdrawn into herself, she were for a last time trying. "But I can't!" she said as she raised them again to take leave of him.

She couldn't indeed, as but too promptly and sharply appeared, and
1220 he had no vision of her after this that was anything but darkness and doom. They had parted for ever in that strange talk; access to her chamber of pain, rigidly guarded, was almost wholly forbidden him; he was feeling now moreover, in the face of doctors, nurses, the two or three relatives attracted doubtless by the presumption of what she had to "leave," how few were the rights, as they were called in such cases, that he had to put forward, and how odd it might even seem that their intimacy shouldn't have given him more of them. The stupidest fourth cousin had more, even though she had been nothing in such a person's life. She had been a feature of features in *his*, for what else was it to have been so indis-
1230 pensable? Strange beyond saying were the ways of existence, baffling for him the anomaly of his lack, as he felt it to be, of producible claim. A woman might have been, as it were, everything to him, and it might yet present him in no connexion that any one seemed held to recognise. If this was the case in these closing weeks it was the case more sharply on

the occasion of the last offices rendered, in the great grey London cemetery, to what had been mortal, to what had been precious, in his friend.
The concourse at her grave was not numerous, but he saw himself treated
as scarce more nearly concerned with it than if there had been a thousand
others. He was in short from this moment face to face with the fact that
1240 he was to profit extraordinarily little by the interest May Bartram had
taken in him. He couldn't quite have said what he expected, but he hadn't
surely expected this approach to a double privation. Not only had her
interest failed him, but he seemed to feel himself unattended—and for a
reason he couldn't seize—by the distinction, the dignity, the propriety,
if nothing else, of the man markedly bereaved. It was as if in the view of
society he had not *been* markedly bereaved, as if there still failed some
sign or proof of it, and as if none the less his character could never be affirmed nor the deficiency ever made up. There were moments as the
weeks went by when he would have liked, by some almost aggressive act,
1250 to take his stand on the intimacy of his loss, in order that it *might* be questioned and his retort, to the relief of his spirit, so recorded; but the moments of an irritation more helpless followed fast on these, the moments
during which, turning things over with a good conscience but with a bare
horizon, he found himself wondering if he oughtn't to have begun, so to
speak, further back.

He found himself wondering indeed at many things, and this last
speculation had others to keep it company. What could he have done, after all, in her lifetime, without giving them both, as it were, away? He
couldn't have made known she was watching him, for that would have
1260 published the superstition of the Beast. This was what closed his mouth
now—now that the Jungle had been threshed to vacancy and that the
Beast had stolen away. It sounded too foolish and too flat; the difference
for him in this particular, the extinction in his life of the element of suspense, was such as in fact to surprise him. He could scarce have said
what the effect resembled; the abrupt cessation, the positive prohibition,
of music perhaps, more than anything else, in some place all adjusted
and all accustomed to sonority and to attention. If he could at any rate
have conceived lifting the veil from his image at some moment of the
past (what had he done, after all, if not lift it to *her?*) so to do this to-
1270 day, to talk to people at large of the Jungle cleared and confide to them
that he now felt it as safe, would have been not only to see them listen
as to a goodwife's tale, but really to hear himself tell one. What it
presently came to in truth was that poor Marcher waded through his
beaten grass, where no life stirred, where no breath sounded, where no
evil eye seemed to gleam from a possible lair, very much as if vaguely
looking for the Beast, and still more as if acutely missing it. He walked
about in an existence that had grown strangely more spacious, and,
stopping fitfully in places where the undergrowth of life struck him as
closer, asked himself yearningly, wondered secretly and sorely, if it
1280 would have lurked here or there. It would have at all events *sprung;* what

was at least complete was his belief in the truth itself of the assurance given him. The change from his old sense to his new was absolute and final: what was to happen *had* so absolutely and finally happened that he was as little able to know a fear for his future as to know a hope; so absent in short was any question of anything still to come. He was to live entirely with the other question, that of his unidentified past, that of his having to see his fortune impenetrably muffled and masked.

The torment of this vision became then his occupation; he couldn't perhaps have consented to live but for the possibility of guessing. She had told him, his friend, not to guess; she had forbidden him, so far as he might, to know, and she had even in a sort denied the power in him to learn: which were so many things, precisely, to deprive him of rest. It wasn't that he wanted, he argued for fairness, that anything past and done should repeat itself; it was only that he shouldn't, as an anticlimax, have been taken sleeping so sound as not to be able to win back by an effort of thought the lost stuff of consciousness. He declared to himself at moments that he would either win it back or have done with consciousness for ever; he made this idea his one motive in fine, made it so much his passion that none other, to compare with it, seemed ever to have touched him. The lost stuff of consciousness became thus for him as a strayed or stolen child to an unappeasable father; he hunted it up and down very much as if he were knocking at doors and enquiring of the police. This was the spirit in which, inevitably, he set himself to travel; he started on a journey that was to be as long as he could make it; it danced before him that, as the other side of the globe couldn't possibly have less to say to him, it might, by a possibility of suggestion, have more. Before he quitted London, however, he made a pilgrimage to May Bartram's grave, took his way to it through the endless avenues of the grim suburban metropolis, sought it out in the wilderness of tombs, and, though he had come but for the renewal of the act of farewell, found himself, when he had at last stood by it, beguiled into long intensities. He stood for an hour, powerless to turn away and yet powerless to penetrate the darkness of death; fixing with his eyes her inscribed name and date, beating his forehead against the fact of the secret they kept, drawing his breath, while he waited, as if some sense would in pity of him rise from the stones. He kneeled on the stones, however, in vain; they kept what they concealed; and if the face of the tomb did become a face for him it was because her two names became a pair of eyes that didn't know him. He gave them a last long look, but no palest light broke.

6

He stayed away, after this, for a year; he visited the depths of Asia, spending himself on scenes of romantic interest, of superlative sanctity; but what was present to him everywhere was that for a man who had known what *he* had known the world was vulgar and vain. The state of mind in which he had lived for so many years shone out to him, in reflexion, as a light that coloured and refined, a light beside which the glow of the East was garish, cheap and thin. The terrible truth was that he had lost—with everything else—a distinction as well; the things he saw couldn't help being common when he had become common to look at them. He was simply now one of them himself—he was in the dust, without a peg for the sense of difference; and there were hours when, before the temples of gods and the sepulchres of kings, his spirit turned for nobleness of association to the barely discriminated slab in the London suburb. That had become for him, and more intensely with time and distance, his one witness of a past glory. It was all that was left to him for proof or pride, yet the past glories of Pharaohs were nothing to him as he thought of it. Small wonder then that he came back to it on the morrow of his return. He was drawn there this time as irresistibly as the other, yet with a confidence, almost, that was doubtless the effect of the many months that had elapsed. He had lived, in spite of himself, into his change of feeling, and in wandering over the earth had wandered, as might be said, from the circumference to the centre of his desert. He had settled to his safety and accepted perforce his extinction; figuring to himself, with some colour, in the likeness of certain little old men he remembered to have seen, of whom, all meagre and wizened as they might look, it was related that they had in their time fought twenty duels or been loved by ten princesses. They indeed had been wondrous for others while he was but wondrous for himself; which, however, was exactly the cause of his haste to renew the wonder by getting back, as he might put it, into his own presence. That had quickened his steps and checked his delay. If his visit was prompt it was because he had been separated so long from the part of himself that alone he now valued.

It's accordingly not false to say that he reached his goal with a certain elation and stood there again with a certain assurance. The creature beneath the sod *knew* of his rare experience, so that, strangely now, the place had lost for him its mere blankness of expression. It met him in mildness—not, as before, in mockery; it wore for him the air of conscious greeting that we find, after absence, in things that have closely belonged to us and which seem to confess of themselves to the connexion. The plot of ground, the graven tablet, the tended flowers affected him so as belonging to him that he resembled for the hour a contented landlord reviewing a piece of property. Whatever had happened—well, had happened. He had not come back this time with the vanity of that question, his former worrying "What, *what?*" now practically so spent. Yet he would none the less never again so cut himself off from the spot; he would come back to it every month, for if he did nothing else by its aid he at least held up his head. It thus grew for him, in the oddest way, a positive resource; he carried out his idea of periodical returns, which took their place at last among the most inveterate of his habits. What it all amounted to, oddly enough, was that in his finally so simplified world this garden of death gave him the few square feet of earth on which he could still most live. It was as if, being nothing anywhere else for any one, nothing even for himself, he were just everything here, and if not for a crowd of witnesses or indeed for any witness but John Marcher, then by clear right of the register that he could scan like an open page. The open page was the tomb of his friend, and *there* were the facts of the past, there the truth of his life, there the backward reaches in which he could lose himself. He did this from time to time with such effect that he seemed to wander through the old years with his hand in the arm of a companion who was, in the most extraordinary manner, his other, his younger self; and to wander, which was more extraordinary yet, round and round a third presence—not wandering she, but stationary, still, whose eyes, turning with his revolution, never ceased to follow him, and whose seat was his point, so to speak, of orientation. Thus in short he settled to live—feeding all on the sense that he once *had* lived, and dependent on it not alone for a support but for an identity.

It sufficed him in its way for months and the year elapsed; it would doubtless even have carried him further but for an accident, superficially slight, which moved him, quite in another direction, with a force beyond any of his impressions of Egypt or of India. It was a thing of the merest chance—the turn, as he afterwards felt, of a hair, though he was indeed to live to believe that if light hadn't come to him in this particular fashion it would still have come in another. He was to live to believe this, I say, though he was not to live, I may not less definitely mention, to do much else. We allow him at any rate the benefit of the conviction, struggling up for him at the end, that, whatever might have happened or not happened, he would have come round of himself to the light. The incident of an autumn day had put the match to the train laid from of old by his misery. With the light before him he knew that even of late his ache had only been smothered. It was strangely drugged, but it throbbed; at the touch it began to bleed. And the touch, in the event, was the face of a fellow mortal. This face, one grey afternoon when the leaves were thick in the alleys, looked into Marcher's own, at the cemetery, with an expression like the cut of a blade. He felt it, that is, so deep down that he winced at the steady thrust. The person who so mutely assaulted him was a figure he had noticed, on reaching his own goals, absorbed by a grave a short distance away, a grave apparently fresh, so that the emotion of the visitor would probably match it for frankness. This fact alone forbade further attention, though during the time he stayed he remained vaguely conscious of his neighbour, a middle-aged man apparently, in mourning, whose bowed back, among the clustered monuments and mortuary yews, was constantly presented. Marcher's theory that these were elements in contact with which he himself revived, had suffered, on this occasion, it may be granted, a marked, an excessive check. The autumn day was dire for him as none had recently been, and he rested with a heaviness he had not yet known on the low stone table that bore May Bartram's name. He rested without power to

move, as if some spring in him, some spell vouchsafed, had suddenly been broken for ever. If he could have done that moment as he wanted he would simply have stretched himself on the slab that was ready to
1420 take him, treating it as a place prepared to receive his last sleep. What in all the wide world had he now to keep awake for? He stared before him with the question, and it was then that, as one of the cemetery walks passed near him, he caught the shock of the face.

His neighbour at the other grave had withdrawn, as he himself, with force enough in him, would have done by now, and was advancing along the path on his way to one of the gates. This brought him close, and his pace was slow, so that—and all the more as there was a kind of hunger on his look—the two men were for a minute directly confronted. Marcher knew him at once for one of the deeply stricken—a perception so sharp
1430 that nothing else in the picture comparatively lived, neither his dress, his age, nor his presumable character and class; nothing lived but the deep ravage of the features he showed. He *showed* them—that was the point; he was moved, as he passed, by some impulse that was either a signal for sympathy or, more possibly, a challenge to an opposed sorrow. He might already have been aware of our friend, might at some previous hour have noticed in him the smooth habit of the scene, with which the state of his own senses so scantly consorted, and might thereby have been stirred as by an overt discord. What Marcher was at all events conscious of was in the first place that the image of scarred passion presented to him was con-
1440 scious too—of something that profaned the air; and in the second that, roused, startled, shocked, he was yet the next moment looking after it, as it went, with envy. The most extraordinary thing that had happened to him—though he had given that name to other matters as well—took place, after his immediate vague stare, as a consequence of this impression. The stranger passed, but the raw glare of his grief remained, making our friend wonder in pity what wrong, what wound it expressed, what injury not to be healed. What had the man *had*, to make him by the loss of it so bleed and yet live?

Something—and this reached him with a pang—that *he*, John Marcher,
1450 hadn't; the proof of which was precisely John Marcher's arid end. No passion had ever touched him, for this was what passion meant; he had survived and maundered and pined, but where had been *his* deep ravage? The extraordinary thing we speak of was the sudden rush of the result of this question. The sight that had just met his eyes named to him, as in letters of quick flame, something he had utterly, insanely missed, and what he had missed made these things a train of fire, made them mark themselves in an anguish of inward throbs. He had seen *outside* of his life, not learned it within, the way a woman was mourned when she had been loved for herself: such was the force of his conviction of the meaning of the stranger's
1460 face, which still flared for him as a smoky torch. It hadn't come to him, the knowledge, on the wings of experience; it had brushed him, jostled him, upset him, with the disrespect of chance, the insolence of accident. Now

that the illumination had begun, however, it blazed to the zenith, and what he presently stood there gazing at was the sounded void of his life. He gazed, he drew breath, in pain; he turned in his dismay, and, turning, he had before him in sharper incision than ever the open page of his story. The name on the table smote him as the passage of his neighbour had done, and what it said to him, full in the face, was that *she* was what he had missed. This was the awful thought, the answer to all the past, the vi-
1470 sion at the dread clearness of which he grew as cold as the stone beneath him. Everything fell together, confessed, explained, overwhelmed; leaving him most of all stupefied at the blindness he had cherished. The fate he had been marked for he had met with a vengeance—he had emptied the cup to the lees; he had been the man of his time, *the* man, to whom nothing on earth was to have happened. That was the rare stroke—that was his vis-itation. So he saw it, as we say, in pale horror, while the pieces fitted and fitted. So *she* had seen it while he didn't, and so she served at this hour to drive the truth home. It was the truth, vivid and monstrous, that all the while he had waited the wait was itself his portion. This the companion of
1480 his vigil had at a given moment made out, and she had then offered him the chance to baffle his doom. One's doom, however, was never baffled, and on the day she told him his own had come down she had seen him but stupidly stare at the escape she offered him.

The escape would have been to love her; then, *then* he would have lived. *She* had lived—who could say now with what passion?—since she had loved him for himself; whereas he had never thought of her (ah how it hugely glared at him!) but in the chill of his egotism and the light of her use. Her spoken words came back to him—the chain stretched and stretched. The Beast had lurked indeed, and the Beast, at its hour, had
1490 sprung; it had sprung in that twilight of the cold April when, pale, ill, wasted, but all beautiful, and perhaps even then recoverable, she had risen from her chair to stand before him and let him imaginably guess. It had sprung as he didn't guess; it had sprung as she hopelessly turned from him, and the mark, by the time he left her, had fallen where it *was* to fall. He had justified his fear and achieved his fate; he had failed, with the last exactitude, of all he was to fail of; and a moan now rose to his lips as he remembered she had prayed he mightn't know. This hor-ror of waking—*this* was knowledge, knowledge under the breath of which the very tears in his eyes seemed to freeze. Through them, none
1500 the less, he tried to fix it and hold it; he kept it there before him so that he might feel the pain. That at least, belated and bitter, had something of the taste of life. But the bitterness suddenly sickened him, and it was as if, horribly, he saw, in the truth, in the cruelty of his image, what had been appointed and done. He saw the Jungle of his life and saw the lurking Beast; then, while he looked, perceived it, as by a stir of the air, rise, huge and hideous, for the leap that was to settle him. His eyes darkened—it was close; and, instinctively turning, in his hallucination, to avoid it, he flung himself, face down, on the tomb.

ACCOUNT: TZVETAN TODOROV ON
THE STRUCTURE OF HENRY JAMES'S TALES

Todorov argues that most of Henry James's short stories are organized by a similar structure and that the structure manifests itself particularly in works written during the period from 1892–1903 when James (then in his fifties) wrote almost half of his tales. In two of the stories from this period, the organizing principle becomes itself an explicit theme: They thus become "metaliterary" tales, tales beyond or above the other stories in the same sense that metaphysics is beyond or above physics. That is, their subject is James's *method* of writing his tales. The first of these stories, "The Figure in the Carpet" (1896), is plainly plotted around the life's work of a writer of fiction. The second, "The Beast in the Jungle" (1903), is overtly about the life of a man who is not a writer, yet his life in fact becomes one organized like a story by Henry James, with a similar "climax" to a similar "plot."

As explained in the Introduction to this chapter, Todorov uses the terms "absence" and "presence" to differentiate between matters that appear within a story and those that do not appear immediately or never appear at all. In the case of Henry James, Todorov describes the general pattern of a story as follows:

> James's tales are based on the quest for an absolute and absent cause. Let me explain one by one the terms of this formula. There exists a cause—to be understood in a very broad sense. It is often a character, but sometimes also an event or an object. Its effect is the tale, the story which we are told. The cause is absolute: everything in the story owes its presence, in the last analysis, to it. But it is absent and we set off in quest of it. And it is not only absent but for most of the time unknown as well; only its existence, not its nature, is suspected. There is a quest: that is, the story consists in the search for, the pursuit of this initial cause, this primary essence. The story stops if it is found. On the one hand then, there is an absence (of the cause, of the essence, of the truth) but this absence determines everything; on the other hand, there is a presence (of the quest) which is simply the pursuit of the absence. The secret of James's tales is therefore, precisely this existence of an essential secret, of something which is not named, of an absent overwhelming force which puts the whole present machinery of the narrative into motion.

Because the movement of James's stories is such a double one or even a contradictory one, it is inexhaustible. The narrative exerts all its effort in a quest to find the secret cause. But the appearance of the

Based on a translation by David Robey in *Structuralism: An Introduction*, ed. David Robey (Oxford University Press, 1973).

secret cause of the whole story brings the story to an end, when the "figure in the carpet," the pattern or design we have been trying to perceive, at last becomes clear. With that appearance the mystery is solved, yet there is therefore nothing left to say about it, and so the story must end: "The presence of the truth is possible, but it is incompatible with the tale."

The pattern of the plot also has an equivalence in Henry James's narrative technique. That is, every event is described from and limited to a particular and single point of view. We never respond to an omniscient narrator who could tell us the thoughts and feelings of everyone in the story. Rather, we know only the thoughts and feelings of a particular person, who may or may not be a narrator within the story. In other words, we are never presented with a certified "truth" in itself, but only with a particular perception or interpretation of a truth. In this way, we see only a character's vision of the truth, not the truth itself. We often come upon such sentences as: "He knew I really couldn't help him and that I knew he knew I couldn't."

But looked at structurally, Henry James's famous style is no different from his theme. It is like a translation into another form of the quest for the absolute and absent cause: "The style and sentiments, the form and the content all say the same thing."

In "The Beast in the Jungle," Todorov's formula describes John Marcher's life. Both May Bartram and Marcher come to realize the fact of this pattern, though they do so at different times. May discovers it first—the secret of her life was loving Marcher and she asked for nothing more. But Marcher finds too late that her absence is "the absence of everything."

Todorov concludes that the theme that is the story's structure finds its ultimate form in "The Beast in the Jungle." There, the "dialectical negation" of the theme is equal and opposite, the "present" content of a life like that May Bartram defines by her love is "absent" for Marcher. This is *not* to say that for Marcher the quest is its own reward. Marcher's quest was May's own reward. Similarly, for Henry James, his life as a writer was filled by his writing rather than by any fame or material reward for that writing. As a dedicated artist, his art *was* his life—for better and for worse. And this is the fact that he acknowledges and dramatizes in the content and style of his tales.

———————————

Other examples of the structuralist approach to literature will be found in the sections on poetry and drama. Helmut Bonheim examines the significance of form in Emily Dickinson's "My Life Had Stood a Loaded Gun" and Margorie Garber looks at the relation of the structures within Shakespeare's *The Tempest* to those within other literary works.

SUGGESTIONS FOR DISCUSSION AND WRITING

1. The manner of James's **narrator** in this and other of his stories has often been called difficult. Find a moment that, at least on first reading, seems difficult to you. Try to locate as completely as you can the sources of this difficulty. Is it, for example, a matter of missing information or context? In what ways does rereading the passage help? In what ways do Todorov's views of the structure of plot and style help?

2. What literary effects does Henry James achieve by his **dialogue**? Pick a passage containing dialogue that seems to you important and representative. Do Todorov's terms of "quest," "presence," and "absence" help you to describe the ways in which dialogue appears to its reader? Explain and exemplify what seem to you to be the leading characteristics of the dialogue using any other terms that seem helpful. It may be illuminating to compare the dialogue here to that in another story—"Hills Like White Elephants" by Ernest Hemingway (p. 297), for example.

3. Is the intimacy between the two central characters dramatized as well as asserted by the narrative? How do the relations of Marcher and May compare in this regard with those of other couples in fiction? Again, you might use "Hills Like White Elephants" as an example. How might Todorov's insights apply to this story?

4. Given the nature of the story, what other critical approaches besides that of structuralism strike you as likely to be most fruitful? Pick an approach and try to understand the ending here by its light.

5. Write an essay showing how Todorov's claims about the quest for an absent cause is or is not dramatized within any important conversational sequence in the story.

6. Make some notes for discussion or an essay on the "structure" of Ernest Hemingway's "Hills Like White Elephants" (p. 297). What is "absent" and "present" in that story for the characters? For the reader? How does the plot move toward a change in what is absent and what present? Which of Todorov's insights seem most pertinent? Which least?

Chapter Nine

Post-Structuralist Criticism: Critical Method as a Language

A BRIEF INTRODUCTION TO POST-STRUCTURALIST CRITICISM

In one way, *post-structuralist criticism* is an easy term to define: It undeniably refers to the methods of criticism that have emerged since the flourishing of structuralism in the 1960s. But those methods are many and various, and contemporary critics often draw simultaneously on critical approaches that were introduced earlier in this book as separate methods. For example, Marxist–Feminist readings that depend in part on psychoanalytic theory are widely represented in today's critical journals. Usually, however, post-structuralism is defined more narrowly, to refer specifically to deconstructionist criticism. Deconstruction is post-structuralist in a double sense—it builds upon structuralism's insights while at the same time rejecting some of its assumptions.

Structuralism bases its name on a spatial metaphor. Only something that exists in space—a building, for example—can *literally* have a structure. Thus, linguistic or mental phenomena like myths and novels are described *figuratively* by structuralism as if they existed in space. The name *deconstruction* seems to continue the spatial metaphor as a description of literature, but it announces that it does so only in order to destroy the basis of the metaphor altogether by taking apart any structure or "construction" and thus showing it to be really unstable. That is, structuralism seeks in the so-called structures of language a way of understanding the nature of literature. But does literature really have a structure? Does either literature or language that exists in time and in a changing world have even the figurative stability that the term *structure* implies? Deconstruction sets out to prove that they do not. As Steven Lynn says in a 1990 essay in *College English,* "If structuralism shows how the conventions of a text work, then post-structuralism, in a sense, points out how they fail."

Deconstruction challenges the assumptions that a text has a single, stable meaning, that an author has full control over a text and all of its elements, and that the critic's task is to guide the reader toward the meaning the author intends. In rejecting these assumptions, deconstruction goes far beyond the commonplace observations that more than one interpretation of a text is often possible or that authors sometimes fail to make their meanings clear. Deconstruction's claims are far more radical. Like the New Critics, deconstructionists often focus on a text's ambiguities. The New Critics, however, argue that in an excellent literary work, ambiguities can be resolved, and a skillful critic can show how all the apparently discordant or irrelevant elements in a text in fact work together to reveal a central theme, to create a unifying form. Deconstructionists, on the other hand, maintain that such views of the text and of the critic's role are illusory and undesirable. Partly because language itself has, at best, a tenuous relationship to reality, no text can consistently sustain a single meaning. Any text contains elements that undermine the author's intentions. Thus, any text is open to any number of interpretations, and the critic is not bound by an obligation to try to discover the author's meaning. Rather, the critic can freely use the text to create new meanings.

For example, an author may write a story designed to express certain ideas about men and women, about innocence and experience, or about skepticism and belief; the author may see one of these elements as superior to the other—or, to borrow a term deconstructionists frequently use, as *privileged*. At some point, however, the meaning the author intends breaks down, the hierarchies the author sets up reverse—the text deconstructs. Commenting upon this breakdown and showing that the text can support meanings other than the one the author intended become the particular tasks of the deconstructionist critic. Even if the author has stated his or her theme explicitly, in the story itself or in a separate commentary, the critic need not feel bound by the author's view of the text. For example, Flannery O'Connor has written essays and letters explaining the ideas she expresses in various short stories, including "A Good Man Is Hard to Find." Most critics would accept O'Connor's statements as authoritative, commenting on how successfully or unsuccessfully she presents her ideas but not challenging her interpretation of her own story. In the article summarized later in this chapter, however, deconstructionist critic Mary Jane Schenck acknowledges O'Connor's ideas about the story as one possible interpretation but grants them no special status. Despite O'Connor's insistence that the story's themes are essentially religious, Schenck argues that the story can also—and just as legitimately—be read as an exploration of ideas about language.

Deconstruction has become a very influential movement in recent years, and critics such as Jacques Derrida, Paul de Man, and Jonathan Culler have been widely read, admired, and emulated. Acceptance has not been universal, however. Critics who favor more traditional approaches to literature have charged that deconstructionist commentaries are often absurd and merely willful, an imposition of the critic's ego on the text; they argue that deconstruction gives critics an opportunity to indulge in pointless cleverness, while putting at risk the very idea that language communicates, that literature gives readers an opportunity to share writers' ideas about life. Barbara Johnson, in "Teaching Deconstructively," defends the approach against such accusations. Deconstruction, she says, is not merely "textual vandalism or generalized skepticism designed to show that meaning is impossible":

> Rather, it is a careful teasing out of the conflicting forces of signification that are at work within the text itself. If anything is destroyed in a deconstructive reading, it is not meaning per se but the claim to unequivocal domination of one mode of signifying over another. This implies that a text signifies in more than one way, that it can signify something more, something less, or something other than it claims to, or that it signifies in different degrees of explicitness, effectiveness, or coherence. A deconstructive reading makes evident the ways in which a text works out its complex disagreements with itself.

Thus, deconstructive analysis is very much grounded in the text—like the New Critics, deconstructionists are close readers. Since deconstructionists do not feel in any sense bound by the author's intentions, however, or by the idea that any single interpretation can be "privileged," their commentaries may strike many readers as far-fetched or even playful—adjectives that many deconstructionist critics might be quite willing to accept. Deconstructionists generally do not hesitate to seize upon textual details that may seem minor or even accidental, to build whole interpretations around them, and to propose more than one interpretation within a single article.

Barbara Johnson's 1980 analysis of Melville's short story "Billy Budd," in *The Critical Difference*, illustrates several characteristics of deconstructionist criticism. The story might at first seem to dramatize a conflict between good, embodied in the innocent but naive sailor Billy Budd, and evil, embodied in John Claggart, the master-at-arms who falsely accuses Billy of mutiny. But, Johnson points out, this dichotomy reverses itself when Billy strikes out at Claggart and kills him—the innocent man becomes guilty, and the villain becomes a victim. Thus, Johnson concludes, the "real opposition" in the story "is less the static opposition between evil and good than the dynamic opposition between a man's 'nature' and his acts . . . the relation between human 'being' and human 'doing.'" To this point, Johnson may seem to be doing essentially what many traditionalist critics do, arguing that the standard interpretation of a story is inadequate, that the story is really more complex than most readers realize. Johnson does not stop here, however. She suggests that the story may also be about different ways of reading: The illiterate, trusting Billy represents the "literal reader," and the suspicious Claggart represents the "ironic reader." At another point, Johnson notes that Melville describes

Claggart as approaching Billy with "the calm collected air of an asylum physician"; thus, she says, Claggart can be seen as a psychoanalyst, Billy as a patient. When Billy kills Claggart, he is lashing out "against the very process of analysis itself." Further, the narrator at one point says that he will attempt to draw Claggart's portrait "but shall never hit it." This remark, Johnson says, implies a dichotomy between "speaking and killing"—the narrator uses words and thus "shall never hit" Claggart, but Billy, who cannot defend himself verbally, does hit and kill his accuser. Thus, instead of arguing that "Billy Budd" *should* be read in one particular way, Johnson seems intent on demonstrating that it *can* be read in various ways and that all these readings can be seen as valid and significant.

As noted earlier, deconstruction begins with a challenge to some fundamental assumptions of structuralist criticism. Other approaches to literary criticism have also faced radical challenges in recent years, as critics reexamine and remake the very bases or grounds of the discourses they employ. Only the briefest sketch of some of these new critical developments is possible here.

Marxist criticism today, for example, may focus on the *late* writings of Marx, rather than on those earlier texts traditionally referred to by Marxist critics. Some sense of the current directions in Marxist criticism may be gained by comparing Steven Watt's analysis of Samuel Beckett's *Happy Days*, presented later in this book, with Peter Kosenko's critique of Shirley Jackson's "The Lottery." Similarly, psychoanalytical criticism may today begin from Lacan's critique of Freud. One of the manifestations of that critique appears in Lacan's essay on *Hamlet* later in this book. Another important contemporary approach, known as the New Historicism, questions traditional notions of historical criticism, arguing that greater attention must be paid to a literary work's full cultural context, to the role that readers play in determining a work's meaning and significance. Along with feminist critics and critics of minority literature, the New Historicists have also challenged traditional ideas about the literary canon—should some works be seen as "masterpieces," as more important and worthy of study than others? If so, on what basis should works be admitted to the canon? Later in this book, Rob Nixon's approach to history in his study of Shakespeare's *The Tempest* serves as an example of some recent directions in historical criticism.

To sum up: If structuralists seek to understand literature by determining not so much the meaning of a text as the conditions that allow it to express meaning, deconstruction questions the very activity of *seeking* those conditions in some final and "structured" form. It also questions whether language really allows for such understandings and determinings. While admitting that structuralism follows the tradition of rational Western thought in creating knowledge by creating a model through which a subject may be understood, the very nature of "models" (another spatial metaphor) may be considered suspect as a way of doing justice to the real diversity and complexity of the terrain it describes. Maps may even *distort* the reality of the terrain, as (for example) maps using the Mercator projection method of translating distances from a three-dimensional world to a two-dimensional surface greatly enlarge the relative size of Canada. Questioning the reality displayed by maps or systems of any kind is the constant and defining activity of post-structuralist criticism.

MARY FLANNERY O'CONNOR (1925–1964) was born in Savannah, Georgia, on March 25, 1925. During her childhood, she moved to a farm in Milledgeville, Georgia, where she attended Catholic schools. O'Connor began writing at an early age; her chief hobby (as listed in her high school yearbook) was "collecting rejection slips." She graduated from Georgia State College for Women in 1945 and in 1946 received her M.F.A. from the University of Iowa.

In 1950, after completing the preliminary draft of her first novel, *Wise Blood*, O'Connor learned that she was afflicted with lupus erythematosus, the incurable blood disease which had taken the life of her father. She returned to Milledgeville and devoted herself to writing for the remaining thirteen years of her life. O'Connor wrote a second novel, *The Violent Bear It Away* (1960), and numerous short stories, which are collected in *A Good Man Is Hard to Find* (1955), *Everything That Rises Must Converge* (1965), and *The Complete Stories of Flannery O'Connor* (1971).

As a child, O'Connor had a pet chicken that could walk either backward or forward; her interest in this animal, O'Connor later said, marked the beginning of her fascination with the deformed and the grotesque, shown in her irreverent, often violent comedy. As she explained, "Southern writers are fond of writing about freaks because we are still able to recognize one."

FLANNERY O'CONNOR
A Good Man Is Hard to Find
(1953)

The grandmother didn't want to go to Florida. She wanted to visit some of her connections in east Tennessee and she was seizing at every chance to change Bailey's mind. Bailey was the son she lived with, her only boy. He was sitting on the edge of his chair at the table, bent over the orange sports section of the *Journal*. "Now look here, Bailey," she said, "see here, read this," and she stood with one hand on her thin hip and the other rattling the newspaper at his bald head. "Here this fellow that calls himself The Misfit is aloose from the Federal Pen and headed toward Florida and you read here what it says he did to these people. Just you read it. I
10 wouldn't take my children in any direction with a criminal like that aloose in it. I couldn't answer to my conscience if I did."

Bailey didn't look up from his reading so she wheeled around then and faced the children's mother, a young woman in slacks, whose face was as broad and innocent as a cabbage and was tied round with a green head-kerchief that had two points on the top like rabbit's ears. She was sitting on the sofa, feeding the baby his apricots out of a jar. "The children have been to Florida before," the old lady said. "You all ought to take them somewhere else for a change so they would see different parts of the world and be broad. They never have been to east
20 Tennessee."

The children's mother didn't seem to hear her but the eight-year-old boy, John Wesley, a stocky child with glasses, said, "If you don't want to go to Florida, why dontcha stay at home?" He and the little girl, June Star, were reading the funny papers on the floor.

"She wouldn't stay at home to be queen for a day," June Star said without raising her yellow head.

"Yes and what would you do if this fellow, The Misfit, caught you?" the grandmother asked.

"I'd smack his face," John Wesley said.

30   "She wouldn't stay at home for a million bucks," June Star said. "Afraid she'd miss something. She has to go everywhere we go."

"All right, Miss," the grandmother said. "Just remember that the next time you want me to curl your hair."

June Star said her hair was naturally curly.

The next morning the grandmother was the first one in the car, ready to go. She had her big black valise that looked like the head of a hippopotamus in one corner, and underneath it she was hiding a basket with Pitty Sing, the cat, in it. She didn't intend for the cat to be left alone in the house for three days because he would miss her too much

40 and she was afraid he might brush against one of the gas burners and accidentally asphyxiate himself. Her son, Bailey, didn't like to arrive at a motel with a cat.

She sat in the middle of the back seat with John Wesley and June Star on either side of her. Bailey and the children's mother and the baby sat in the front and they left Atlanta at eight forty-five with the mileage on the car at 55890. The grandmother wrote this down because she thought it would be interesting to say how many miles they had been when they got back. It took them twenty minutes to reach the outskirts of the city.

50   The old lady settled herself comfortably, removing her white cotton gloves and putting them up with her purse on the shelf in front of the back window. The children's mother still had on slacks and still had her head tied up in a green kerchief, but the grandmother had on a navy blue straw sailor hat with a bunch of white violets on the brim and a navy blue dress with a small white dot in the print. Her collar and cuffs were white organdy trimmed with lace and at her neckline she had pinned a purple spray of cloth violets containing a sachet. In case of an accident, anyone seeing her dead on the highway would know at once that she was a lady.

60   She said she thought it was going to be a good day for driving, neither too hot nor too cold, and she cautioned Bailey that the speed limit was fifty-five miles an hour and that the patrolmen hid themselves behind billboards and small clumps of trees and sped out after you before you had a chance to slow down. She pointed out interesting details of the scenery: Stone Mountain; the blue granite that in some places came up to both sides of the highway; the brilliant red clay banks slightly streaked with purple; and the various crops that made rows of green

lace-work on the ground. The trees were full of silver-white sunlight and the meanest of them sparkled. The children were reading comic

70 magazines and their mother had gone back to sleep.

"Let's go through Georgia fast so we won't have to look at it much," John Wesley said.

"If I were a little boy," said the grandmother, "I wouldn't talk about my native state that way. Tennessee has the mountains and Georgia has the hills."

"Tennessee is just a hillbilly dumping ground," John Wesley said, "and Georgia is a lousy state too."

"You said it," June Star said.

"In my time," said the grandmother, folding her thin veined fingers,

80 "children were more respectful of their native states and their parents and everything else. People did right then. Oh look at the cute little pickaninny!" she said and pointed to a Negro child standing in the door of a shack. "Wouldn't that make a picture, now?" she asked and they all turned and looked at the little Negro out of the back window. He waved.

"He didn't have any britches on," June said.

"He probably didn't have any," the grandmother explained. "Little niggers in the country don't have things like we do. If I could paint, I'd paint that picture," she said.

90 The children exchanged comic books.

The grandmother offered to hold the baby and the children's mother passed him over the front seat to her. She set him on her knee and bounced him and told him about the things they were passing. She rolled her eyes and screwed up her mouth and stuck her leathery thin face into his smooth bland one. Occasionally he gave her a faraway smile. They passed a large cotton field with five or six graves fenced in the middle of it, like a small island. "Look at the graveyard!" the grandmother said, pointing it out. "That was the old family burying ground. That belonged to the plantation."

100 "Where's the plantation?" John Wesley asked.

"Gone With the Wind," said the grandmother. "Ha. Ha."

When the children finished all the comic books they had brought, they opened the lunch and ate it. The grandmother ate a peanut butter sandwich and an olive and would not let the children throw the box and the paper napkins out the window. When there was nothing else to do they played a game by choosing a cloud and making the other two guess what shape it suggested. John Wesley took one the shape of a cow and June Star guessed a cow and John Wesley said, no, an automobile, and June Star said he didn't play fair, and they began to slap

110 each other over the grandmother.

The grandmother said she would tell them a story if they would keep quiet. When she told a story, she rolled her eyes and waved her head and was very dramatic. She said once when she was a maiden lady she had been courted by a Mr. Edgar Atkins Teagarden from Jasper, Georgia. She

said he was a very good-looking man and a gentleman and that he brought her a watermelon every Saturday afternoon with his initials cut in it, E. A. T. Well, one Saturday, she said, Mr. Teagarden brought the watermelon and there was nobody at home and he left it on the front porch and returned in his buggy to Jasper, but she never got the watermelon,
120 she said, because a nigger boy ate it when he saw the initials, E. A. T.! This story tickled John Wesley's funny bone and he giggled and giggled but June Star didn't think it was any good. She said she wouldn't marry a man that just brought her a watermelon on Saturday. The grandmother said she would have done well to marry Mr. Teagarden because he was a gentleman and had bought Coca-Cola stock when it first came out and that he had died only a few years ago, a very wealthy man.

They stopped at The Tower for barbecued sandwiches. The Tower was a part stucco and part wood filling station and dance hall set in a clearing outside of Timothy. A fat man named Red Sammy Butts ran it
130 and there were signs stuck here and there on the building and for miles up and down the highway saying, TRY RED SAMMY'S FAMOUS BARBECUE. NONE LIKE FAMOUS RED SAMMY'S! RED SAM! THE FAT BOY WITH THE HAPPY LAUGH. A VETERAN! SAMMY'S YOUR MAN!

Red Sammy was lying on the bare ground outside The Tower with his head under a truck while a gray monkey about a foot high, chained to a small chinaberry tree, chattered nearby. The monkey sprang back into the tree and got on the highest limb as soon as he saw the children jump out of the car and run toward him.

Inside, The Tower was a long dark room with a counter at one end and
140 tables at the other and dancing space in the middle. They all sat down at a broad table next to the nickelodeon and Red Sam's wife, a tall burnt-brown woman with hair and eyes lighter than her skin, came and took their order. The children's mother put a dime in the machine and played, "The Tennessee Waltz," and the grandmother said that tune always made her want to dance. She asked Bailey if he would like to dance but he only glared at her. He didn't have a naturally sunny disposition like she did and trips made him nervous. The grandmother's brown eyes were very bright. She swayed her head from side to side and pretended she was dancing in her chair. June Star said play something she could tap to so the chil-
150 dren's mother put in another dime and played a fast number and June Star stepped out onto the dance floor and did her tap routine.

"Ain't she cute?" Red Sam's wife said, leaning over the counter. "Would you like to come be my little girl?"

"No I certainly wouldn't," June Star said. "I wouldn't live in a broken-down place like this for a million bucks!" and she ran back to the table.

"Ain't she cute?" the woman repeated, stretching her mouth politely.

"Aren't you ashamed?" hissed the grandmother.

Red Sam came in and told his wife to quit lounging on the counter and hurry with these people's order. His khaki trousers reached just to
160 his hip bones and his stomach hung over them like a sack of meal swaying under his shirt. He came over and sat down at a table nearby and let

out a combination sigh and yodel. "You can't win," he said. "You can't win," and he wiped his sweating red face off with a gray handkerchief. "These days you don't know who to trust," he said. "Ain't that the truth?"

"People are certainly not nice like they used to be," said the grandmother.

"Two fellers come in here last week," Red Sammy said, "driving a Chrysler. It was a old beat-up car but it was a good one and these boys looked all right to me. Said they worked at the mill and you know I let them fellers charge the gas they bought? Now why did I do that?"

"Because you're a good man!" the grandmother said at once.

"Yes'm, I suppose so," Red Sam said as if he were struck with the answer.

His wife brought the orders, carrying the five plates all at once without a tray, two in each hand and one balanced on her arm. "It isn't a soul in this green world of God's that you can trust," she said. "And I don't count anybody out of that, not nobody," she repeated, looking at Red Sammy.

"Did you read about that criminal, The Misfit, that's escaped?" asked the grandmother.

"I wouldn't be a bit surprised if he didn't attact this place right here," said the woman. "If he hears about it being here, I wouldn't be none surprised to see him. If he hears it's two cent in the cash register, I wouldn't be a tall surprised if he . . ."

"That'll do," Red Sam said. "Go bring these people their Co'-Colas," and the woman went off to get the rest of the order.

"A good man is hard to find," Red Sammy said. "Everything is getting terrible. I remember the day you could go off and leave your screen door unlatched. Not no more."

He and the grandmother discussed better times. The old lady said that in her opinion Europe was entirely to blame for the way things were now. She said the way Europe acted you would think we were made of money and Red Sam said it was no use talking about it, she was exactly right. The children ran outside into the white sunlight and looked at the monkey in the lacy chinaberry tree. He was busy catching fleas on himself and biting each one carefully between his teeth as if it were a delicacy.

They drove off again into the hot afternoon. The grandmother took cat naps and woke up every few minutes with her own snoring. Outside of Toombsboro she woke up and recalled an old plantation that she had visited in this neighborhood once when she was a young lady. She said the house had six white columns across the front and that there was an avenue of oaks leading up to it and two little wooden trellis arbors on either side in front where you sat down with your suitor after a stroll in the garden. She recalled exactly which road to turn off to get to it. She knew that Bailey would not be willing to lose any time looking at an old house, but the more she talked about it, the more she wanted to see it

once again and find out if the little twin arbors were still standing.
210 "There was a secret panel in this house," she said craftily, not telling
the truth but wishing that she were, "and the story went that all the
family silver was hidden in it when Sherman came through but it was
never found . . ."

"Hey!" John Wesley said. "Let's go see it! We'll find it! We'll poke all
the woodwork and find it! Who lives there? Where do you turn off at?
Hey, Pop, can't we turn off there?"

"We never have seen a house with a secret panel!" June Star
shrieked. "Let's go to the house with the secret panel! Hey, Pop, can't
we go see the house with the secret panel!"

220   "It's not far from here, I know," the grandmother said. "It wouldn't
take over twenty minutes."

Bailey was looking straight ahead. His jaw was as rigid as a horse-
shoe. "No," he said.

The children began to yell and scream that they wanted to see the
house with the secret panel. John Wesley kicked the back of the front
seat and June Star hung over her mother's shoulder and whined desperately into her ear that they never had any fun even on their vacation,
and that they could never do what THEY wanted to do. The baby began
to scream and John Wesley kicked the back of the seat so hard that his
230 father could feel the blows in his kidney.

"All right!" he shouted, and drew the car to a stop at the side of the
road. "Will you all shut up? Will you all just shut up for one second? If
you don't shut up, we won't go anywhere."

"It would be very educational for them," the grandmother murmured.

"All right," Bailey said, "but get this: this is the only time we're going to stop for anything like this. This is the one and only time."

"The dirt road that you have to turn down is about a mile back," the
grandmother directed. "I marked it when we passed."

"A dirt road," Bailey groaned.

240   After they had turned around and were headed toward the dirt road,
the grandmother recalled other points about the house, the beautiful
glass over the front doorway and the candle-lamp in the hall. John Wesley
said that the secret panel was probably in the fireplace.

"You can't go inside this house," Bailey said. "You don't know who
lives there."

"While you all talk to the people in front, I'll run around behind
and get in a window," John Wesley suggested.

"We'll all stay in the car," his mother said.

They turned onto the dirt road and the car raced roughly along in a
250 swirl of pink dust. The grandmother recalled the times when there were
no paved roads and thirty miles was a day's journey. The dirt road was
hilly and there were sudden washes in it and sharp curves on dangerous
embankments. All at once they would be on a hill, looking down over the
blue tops of trees for miles around, then the next minute, they would be
in a red depression with the dust-coated trees looking down on them.

"This place had better turn up in a minute," Bailey said, "or I'm going to turn around."

The road looked as if no one had traveled on it in months.

"It's not much farther," the grandmother said and just as she said it, a
260 horrible thought came to her. The thought was so embarrassing that she turned red in the face and her eyes dilated and her feet jumped up, upsetting her valise in the corner. The instant the valise moved, the newspaper top she had over the basket under it rose with a snarl and Pitty Sing, the cat, sprang onto Bailey's shoulder.

The children were thrown to the floor and their mother, clutching the baby, was thrown out the door onto the ground, the old lady was thrown into the front seat. The car turned over once and landed right-side-up in a gulch on the side of the road. Bailey remained in the driver's seat with the cat—gray-striped with a broad white face and an orange nose—cling-
270 ing to his neck like a caterpillar.

As soon as the children saw they could move their arms and legs, they scrambled out of the car, shouting. "We've had an ACCIDENT!" The grandmother was curled up under the dashboard, hoping she was injured so that Bailey's wrath would not come down on her all at once. The horrible thought she had had before the accident was that the house she had remembered so vividly was not in Georgia but in Tennessee.

Bailey removed the cat from his neck with both hands and flung it out the window against the side of a pine tree. Then he got out of the car and started looking for the children's mother. She was sitting against the
280 side of the red gutted ditch, holding the screaming baby, but she only had a cut down her face and a broken shoulder. "We've had an ACCIDENT!" the children screamed in a frenzy of delight.

"But nobody's killed," June Star said with disappointment as the grandmother limped out of the car, her hat still pinned to her head but the broken front brim standing up at a jaunty angle and the violet spray hanging off the side. They all sat down in the ditch, except the children, to recover from the shock. They were all shaking.

"Maybe a car will come along," said the children's mother hoarsely.

"I believe I have injured an organ," said the grandmother, pressing her
290 side, but no one answered her. Bailey's teeth were clattering. He had on a yellow sport shirt with bright blue parrots designed in it and his face was as yellow as the shirt. The grandmother decided that she would not mention that the house was in Tennessee.

The road was about ten feet above and they could see only the tops of the trees on the other side of it. Behind the ditch they were sitting in there were more woods, tall and dark and deep. In a few minutes they saw a car some distance away on top of a hill, coming slowly as if the occupants were watching them. The grandmother stood up and waved both arms dramatically to attract their attention. The car continued to come on
300 slowly, disappeared around a bend and appeared again, moving even slower, on top of the hill they had gone over. It was a big black battered hearse-like automobile. There were three men in it.

It came to a stop just over them and for some minutes, the driver looked down with a steady expressionless gaze to where they were sitting, and didn't speak. Then he turned his head and muttered something to the other two and they got out. One was a fat boy in black trousers and a red sweat shirt with a silver stallion embossed on the front of it. He moved around on the right side of them and stood staring, his mouth partly open in a kind of loose grin. The other had on
310   khaki pants and a blue striped coat and a gray hat pulled down very low, hiding most of his face. He came around slowly on the left side. Neither spoke.

The driver got out of the car and stood by the side of it, looking down at them. He was an older man than the other two. His hair was just beginning to gray and he wore silver-rimmed spectacles that gave him a scholarly look. He had a long creased face and didn't have on any shirt or undershirt. He had on blue jeans that were too tight for him and was holding a black hat and a gun. The two boys also had guns.

"We've had an ACCIDENT!" the children screamed.

320   The grandmother had the peculiar feeling that the bespectacled man was someone she knew. His face was as familiar to her as if she had known him all her life but she could not recall who he was. He moved away from the car and began to come down the embankment, placing his feet carefully so that he wouldn't slip. He had on tan and white shoes and no socks, and his ankles were red and thin. "Good afternoon," he said. "I see you all had you a little spill."

"We turned over twice!" said the grandmother.

"Oncet," he corrected. "We seen it happen. Try their car and see will it run, Hiram," he said quietly to the boy with the gray hat.

330   "What you got that gun for?" John Wesley asked. "Whatcha gonna do with that gun?"

"Lady," the man said to the children's mother, "would you mind calling them children to sit down by you? Children make me nervous. I want all you all to sit down right together there where you're at."

"What are you telling us what to do for?" June Star asked.

Behind them the line of woods gaped like a dark open mouth. "Come here," said their mother.

"Look here now," Bailey began suddenly, "we're in a predicament! We're in . . . ."

340   The grandmother shrieked. She scrambled to her feet and stood staring. "You're The Misfit!" she said. "I recognized you at once."

"Yes'm," the man said, smiling slightly as if he were pleased in spite of himself to be known, "but it would have been better for all of you, lady, if you hadn't of reckernized me."

Bailey turned his head sharply and said something to his mother that shocked even the children. The old lady began to cry and The Misfit reddened.

"Lady," he said, "don't you get upset. Sometimes a man says things he don't mean. I don't reckon he meant to talk to you thataway."

350   "You wouldn't shoot a lady, would you?" the grandmother said and removed a clean handkerchief from her cuff and began to slap at her eyes with it.

    The Misfit pointed the toe of his shoe into the ground and made a little hole and then covered it up again. "I would hate to have to," he said.

    "Listen," the grandmother almost screamed, "I know you're a good man. You don't look a bit like you have common blood. I know you must come from nice people!"

    "Yes mam," he said, "finest people in the world." When he smiled he showed a row of strong white teeth. "God never made a finer woman

360 than my mother and my daddy's heart was pure gold," he said. The boy with the red sweat shirt had come around behind them and was standing with his gun at his hip. The Misfit squatted down on the ground. "Watch them children, Bobby Lee," he said. "You know they make me nervous." He looked at the six of them huddled together in front of him and he seemed to be embarrassed as if he couldn't think of anything to say. "Ain't a cloud in the sky," he remarked, looking up at it. "Don't see no sun but don't see no cloud neither."

    "Yes, it's a beautiful day," said the grandmother. "Listen," she said, "you shouldn't call yourself The Misfit because I know you're a good

370 man at heart. I can just look at you and tell."

    "Hush!" Bailey yelled. "Hush! Everybody shut up and let me handle this!" He was squatting in the position of a runner about to spring forward but he didn't move.

    "I pre-chate that, lady," The Misfit said and drew a little circle in the ground with the butt of his gun.

    "It'll take a half a hour to fix this here car," Hiram called, looking over the raised hood of it.

    "Well, first you and Bobby Lee get him and that little boy to step over yonder with you," The Misfit said, pointing to Bailey and John Wesley.

380 "The boys want to ask you something," he said to Bailey. "Would you mind stepping back in them woods there with them?"

    "Listen," Bailey began, "we're in a terrible predicament. Nobody realizes what this is," and his voice cracked. His eyes were as blue and intense as the parrots in his shirt and he remained perfectly still.

    The grandmother reached up to adjust her hat brim as if she were going to the woods with him but it came off in her hand. She stood staring at it and after a second she let it fall on the ground. Hiram pulled Bailey up by the arm as if he were assisting an old man. John Wesley caught hold of his father's hand and Bobby Lee followed. They went off toward the

390 woods and just as they reached the dark edge, Bailey turned and supporting himself against a gray naked pine trunk, he shouted, "I'll be back in a minute, Mamma, wait on me!"

    "Come back this instant!" his mother shrilled but they all disappeared into the woods.

    "Bailey Boy!" the grandmother called in a tragic voice but she found she was looking at The Misfit squatting on the ground in front of her. "I just know you're a good man," she said desperately. "You're not a bit common!"

"Nome, I ain't a good man," The Misfit said after a second as if he had
400 considered her statement carefully, "but I ain't the worst in the world nei-
ther. My daddy said I was different breed of dog from my brothers and sisters. 'You know,' Daddy said, 'it's some that can live their whole life out without asking about it and it's others has to know why it is, and this boy is one of the latters. He's going to be into everything!'" He put on his black hat and looked up suddenly and then away deep into the woods as if he were embarrassed again. "I'm sorry I don't have on a shirt before you ladies," he said, hunching his shoulders slightly. "We buried our clothes that we had on when we escaped and we're just making do until we can get better. We borrowed these from some folks we met," he explained.
410   "That's perfectly all right," the grandmother said. "Maybe Bailey has an extra shirt in his suitcase."

"I'll look and see terrectly," The Misfit said.

"Where are they taking him?" the children's mother screamed.

"Daddy was a card himself," The Misfit said. "You couldn't put any-
thing over on him. He never got in trouble with the Authorities though. Just had the knack of handling them."

"You could be honest too if you'd only try," said the grandmother. "Think how wonderful it would be to settle down and live a comfortable life and not have to think about somebody chasing you all the time."
420   The Misfit kept scratching in the ground with the butt of his gun as if he were thinking about it. "Yes'm, somebody is always after you," he murmured.

The grandmother noticed how thin his shoulder blades were just be-
hind his hat because she was standing up looking down on him. "Do you ever pray?" she asked.

He shook his head. All she saw was the black hat wiggle between his shoulder blades. "Nome," he said.

There was a pistol shot from the woods, followed closely by another. Then silence. The old lady's head jerked around. She could hear the
430 wind move through the tree tops like a long satisfied insuck of breath. "Bailey Boy!" she called.

"I was a gospel singer for a while," The Misfit said. "I been most everything. Been in the arm service, both land and sea, at home and abroad, been twict married, been an undertaker, been with the rail-
roads, plowed Mother Earth, been in a tornado, seen a man burnt alive oncet," and he looked up at the children's mother and the little girl who were sitting close together, their faces white and their eyes glassy; "I even seen a woman flogged," he said.

"Pray, pray," the grandmother began, "pray, pray . . ."
440   "I never was a bad boy that I remember of," The Misfit said in an almost dreamy voice, "but somewheres along the line I done something wrong and got sent to the penitentiary. I was buried alive," and he looked up and held her attention to him by a steady stare.

"That's when you should have started to pray," she said. "What did you do to get sent to the penitentiary that first time?"

"Turn to the right, it was a wall," The Misfit said, looking up again at the cloudless sky. "Turn to the left, it was a wall. Look up it was a ceiling, look down it was a floor. I forgot what I done, lady. I set there and set there, trying to remember what it was I done and I ain't recalled
450 it to this day. Oncet in a while, I would think it was coming to me, but it never come."

"Maybe they put you in by mistake," the old lady said vaguely.

"Nome," he said. "It wasn't no mistake. They had the papers on me."

"You must have stolen something," she said.

The Misfit sneered slightly. "Nobody had nothing I wanted," he said. "It was a head-doctor at the penitentiary said what I had done was kill my daddy but I know that for a lie. My daddy died in nineteen ought nineteen of the epidemic flu and I never had a thing to do with it. He was buried in the Mount Hopewell Baptist churchyard and you can
460 go there and see for yourself."

"If you would pray," the old lady said, "Jesus would help you."

"That's right," The Misfit said.

"Well then, why don't you pray?" she asked trembling with delight suddenly.

"I don't want no hep," he said. "I'm doing all right by myself."

Bobby Lee and Hiram came ambling back from the woods. Bobby Lee was dragging a yellow shirt with bright blue parrots in it.

"Throw me that shirt, Bobby Lee," The Misfit said. The shirt came flying at him and landed on his shoulder and he put it on. The grandmother
470 couldn't name what the shirt reminded her of. "No, lady," The Misfit said while he was buttoning it up. "I found out the crime don't matter. You can do one thing or you can do another, kill a man or take a tire off his car, because sooner or later you're going to forget what it was you done and just be punished for it."

The children's mother had begun to make heaving noises as if she couldn't get her breath. "Lady," he asked, "would you and that little girl like to step off yonder with Bobby Lee and Hiram and join your husband?"

"Yes, thank you," the mother said faintly. Her left arm dangled helplessly and she was holding the baby, who had gone to sleep, in the other.
480 "Hep that lady up, Hiram," The Misfit said as she struggled to climb out of the ditch, "and Bobby Lee, you hold onto that little girl's hand."

"I don't want to hold hands with him," June Star said. "He reminds me of a pig."

The fat boy blushed and laughed and caught her by the arm and pulled her off into the woods after Hiram and her mother.

Alone with The Misfit, the grandmother found that she had lost her voice. There was not a cloud in the sky nor any sun. There was nothing around her but woods. She wanted to tell him that he must pray. She opened and closed her mouth several times before anything came out. Fi-
490 nally she found herself saying, "Jesus, Jesus," meaning Jesus will help

you, but the way she was saying it, it sounded as if she might be cursing.

"Yes'm," The Misfit said as if he agreed. "Jesus thown everything off balance. It was the same case with Him as with me except He hadn't committed any crime and they could prove I had committed one because they had papers on me. Of course," he said, "they never shown me any papers. That's why I sign myself now. I said long ago, you get you a signature and sign everything you do and keep a copy of it. Then you'll know what you done and you can hold up the crime to the punishment and see do they match and in the end you'll have something to prove you ain't been treated right. I call myself The Misfit," he said, "because I can't make what all I done wrong fit what all I gone through in punishment."

There was a piercing scream from the woods, followed closely by a pistol report. "Does it seem right to you, lady, that one is punished a heap and another ain't punished at all?"

"Jesus!" the old lady cried. "You've got good blood! I know you wouldn't shoot a lady! I know you come from nice people! Pray! Jesus, you ought not to shoot a lady. I'll give you all the money I've got!"

"Lady," The Misfit said, looking beyond her far into the woods, "there never was a body that give the undertaker a tip."

There were two more pistol reports and the grandmother raised her head like a parched old turkey hen crying for water and called, "Bailey Boy, Bailey Boy!" as if her heart would break.

"Jesus was the only One that ever raised the dead," The Misfit continued, "and He shouldn't have done it. He thown everything off balance. If He did what He said, then it's nothing for you to do but thow away everything and follow Him, and if He didn't, then it's nothing for you to do but enjoy the few minutes you got left the best way you can—by killing somebody or burning down his house or doing some other meanness to him. No pleasure but meanness," he said and his voice had become almost a snarl.

"Maybe He didn't raise the dead," the old lady mumbled, not knowing what she was saying and feeling so dizzy that she sank down in the ditch with her legs twisted under her.

"I wasn't there so I can't say He didn't," The Misfit said. "I wisht I had of been there," he said, hitting the ground with his fist. "It ain't right I wasn't there because if I had of been there I would of known. Listen lady," he said in a high voice, "if I had of been there I would of known and I wouldn't be like I am now." His voice seemed about to crack and the grandmother's head cleared for an instant. She saw the man's face twisted close to her own as if he were going to cry and she murmured, "Why you're one of my babies. You're one of my own children!" She reached out and touched him on the shoulder. The Misfit sprang back as if a snake had bitten him and shot her three times through the chest. Then he put his gun down on the ground and took off his glasses and began to clean them.

Hiram and Bobby Lee returned from the woods and stood over the ditch, looking down at the grandmother who half sat and half lay in a puddle of blood with her legs crossed under her like a child's and her face smiling up at the cloudless sky.

540   Without his glasses, The Misfit's eyes were red-rimmed and pale and defenseless-looking. "Take her off and thow her where you thown the others," he said, picking up the cat that was rubbing itself against his leg.

"She was a talker, wasn't she?" Bobby Lee said, sliding down the ditch with a yodel.

"She would of been a good woman," The Misfit said, "if it had been somebody there to shoot her every minute of her life."

"Some fun!" Bobby Lee said.

"Shut up, Bobby Lee," The Misfit said. "It's no real pleasure in life."

ACCOUNT: MARY JANE SCHENCK ON DECONSTRUCTED MEANING IN "A GOOD MAN IS HARD TO FIND"

Schenck begins by saying that though contemporary criticism pays less attention to the issue of authorial intention than did criticism in the past, the issue is still very much alive in the case of Flannery O'Connor. Further, since that author commented so fully on her own art and since moreover those comments were expressed in the terms of her own deeply held faith as a Roman Catholic, critics may seem presumptuous who interpret the intentions of her fiction in other ways.

Though the grotesque and brutal elements of her stories seem at odds with at least the conventional understanding of Christian doctrine, O'Connor explained her themes by the need to shock the complacent reader into an awareness of the real nature of the world and the need for Divine grace. Yet, since her stories are so ironic, they do not operate as straightforward moral parables, and her irony tends to create ambiguities that may seem to undercut O'Connor's own interpretations and (as several critics have suggested) even to create the opposite of what was intended.

Schenck considers the operations of irony in the light of the deconstructionist critic Paul de Man's remarks on the French poet, Baudelaire, who also was a writer concerned with using irony as a mode of language. Irony's doubleness—its saying one thing and meaning another—seems to allow a person a double existence through *language*. First, by using human language, one acknowledges a self like all others immersed in the empirical facts of the physical world. But irony also posits another self, one that refuses the limitations of the first, as a person

---

From *Ambiguities in Literature and Film: Selected Papers from the Seventh Annual FSU Conference on Literature and Film.* Ed. Hans P. Braendlin (Tallahassee: FSUP, 1988).

tries to do by lying about his or her past, for example. By purely linguistic means, including lying and irony, the second self seeks to separate its identity as a spiritual consciousness, one that can *control* its destiny, one *superior* to everyday realities, and so on. The result is a person defined not only by one self known by evidence and facts, an "empirical" self, but also by another self created in ironic, lying, or fictional uses of language, a "linguistic" self.

Schenck says that de Man's "ironic consciousness" depicts the method by which O'Connor's characters are created and by which they create themselves. The characters use spoken words and written text to escape their empirical selves, and (to the extent they succeed) they create reality rather than reflect it. The trouble comes in the disastrous climaxes when they fail to understand the arbitrary nature of their unreal language, and the conflicts are often between the two selves as well as between "empirical" characters in the story.

The unmasking of language to reveal it as *only* language leads to violence if not to madness:

> From the outset, the grandmother relies on "texts" to structure her reality. The newspaper article about The Misfit mentioned in the opening paragraph of the story is a written text which has a particular status in the narrative. It refers to events outside and prior to the primary *recit* [or tale], but it stands as an unrecognized prophecy of the events which occur at the end. For Bailey, the newspaper story is not important or meaningful, and for the grandmother it does not represent a real threat but is part of a ploy to get her own way. It is thus the first one of her "fictions," one which ironically comes true. The grandmother's whole personality is built upon the fictions she tells herself and her family.

On the trip, the grandmother continues her fictions by telling the children stories and by making up stories of her own about the graveyard and about the hidden panel. This last fiction and the implicit former lie about her cat's whereabouts lead to the terrible ending. The more she talks about the treasure, the more she and her language constitute it as a reality, and the more its mere linguistic existence affects the reality of the car. The children kick and scream, and the father changes his plans, all because of something that has no real existence outside of words:

> The scene with The Misfit is the apogee of the grandmother's use of "fictions" to explain and control reality, attempts that are thwarted by her encounter with a character who understands there is no reality behind her words. When the grandmother recognizes The Misfit, he tells her it would have been better if she hadn't, but she has *named* him, thus forcing him to become what is behind his self selected name. In a desperate attempt to cope with the threat posed by the murder, the grandmother runs through her litany of convenient fictions. She believes that there are class distinctions ("I know you're a good man. You don't look a

bit like you have common blood"), that appearance reflects reality ("You shouldn't call yourself The Misfit because I know you're a good man at heart. I can just look at you and tell"), that redemption can be achieved through work ("You could be honest too if you'd only try. . . . Think how wonderful it would be to settle down . . ."), and finally that prayer will change him ("'Pray, pray,' she commanded him").

Unlike the grandmother's flood of words in questions, explanations, and exhortations, the other family members seem deprived of language and react only physically in an empirical world of objects. Even the grandmother starts to lose her voice and her human, linguistically created identity. When she tries to tell The Misfit to pray, her language is "fractured" and she can hardly speak at all. At the point she loses control of language, she may also lose the myths that have sustained her, as she mumbles "Maybe He didn't raise the dead."

Her final linguistic fantasy is the direct cause of her death when she reaches out to touch The Misfit and tells him he is one of her own babies. Does she confuse him with her son because of the shirt, or is this a final ingratiating appeal for sympathy?

O'Connor's interpretation of this line is that at this moment the grandmother realizes, "even in her limited way, that she is responsible for the man before her and joined to him by ties of kinship which have their roots deep in the mystery she has been merely prattling about so far."

Schenck acknowledges that this reading is a possible one—even the generally accepted one—but suggests that we could also say the grandmother is simply wrong again. Not knowing what she means allows us to witness "the moment when a clash of language creates the vertiginous moment of irony into violence and madness." When The Misfit rejects her language, her fictions are revealed as "just talk," and both her selves—the linguistic and the empirical—are destroyed.

Schenck contrasts the failure of the grandmother's fictional language to affect reality with The Misfit's successful use of words to relate events literally ("'We turned over twice!' said the grandmother. 'Oncet,' he corrected. 'We seen it happen'"). At the same time, he is aware of the great and mysterious powers of words. He knows that words (in the "papers" that keep him in prison, for example) have in part created him.

Given his relation to language, The Misfit has the apparent ability to deal with reality as he sees it—a world without religious sanctions and hence one in which the rational course is to act in whatever way gives him the most pleasure: "It's nothing for you to do but enjoy the few minutes you got left the best way you can—by killing somebody or burning down his house or doing some other meanness to him. No pleasure but meanness." Yet with the very last line of the story, The Misfit deconstructs even that self: "Shut up, Bobby Lee," The Misfit said, "It's no real pleasure in life." Schenck comments:

His strange alterations between polite talk and cold blooded murder and his last statement demonstrate the radical shifting back and forth between selves that cancel each other figuratively as he has canceled the shifting consciousness of the grandmother.

Schenck concludes that the personalities of the characters are created by the language they use and the fictions of self they employ, but that language finally fails them. The ironic effects of language are thus like "falling through a trap door into nothingness." Further, this happens not only to characters but to the reader's sense of the stories as well. Whatever O'Connor says she intended, we might therefore justifiably feel that we are both witnessing and experiencing the disintegration of linguistic selves as they fall through that trap door.

———————

Other examples of deconstructionist criticism will be found in the poetry section, with the accounts of J. Hillis Miller's reading of Wordsworth's "A Slumber Did My Spirit Seal" and of Paul de Man's analysis of William Butler Yeats's "Among School Children." Further on, the drama section offers an account of Phyllis Carey's post-structuralist approach to Samuel Beckett's *Happy Days*.

SUGGESTIONS FOR DISCUSSION AND WRITING

1. How would you characterize the **narrator's** attitude toward the people in the family as the story opens? What techniques does Flannery O'Connor employ to create the sense you get? How, for example, does calling a character "the" grandmother affect your idea of the degree of intimacy between narrator and character? Between narrator and reader? Among the characters? Does the narrator seem "ironic" in Schenck's sense?

2. What, for you, is the most striking characteristic of The Misfit's speaking style? What about the things he says and doesn't say define him for you? In what ways does his style act to "deconstruct" language, according to Schenck?

3. The story's title is also that of a blues song. In what registers other than that of romantic love do the implications of the phrase resonate for you? For example, in the religious terms of Christianity that operate in the story, *how* hard has it been to find a good man in the history of the world?

4. How do the various reactions of the family members to the threat of death differ? How are they similar? Pick one character and describe

how his or her reaction is "characteristic" of the figure earlier created. How do Schenck's insights apply to this character?

5. Using Schenck's insights into the differing ways in which The Misfit and the grandmother use language, write an essay analyzing the values and assumptions about language that seem to characterize Flannery O'Connor's **narrator**.

6. Make some notes for discussion or for an essay on a "deconstruction" of the language used by the characters in Ernest Hemingway's "Hills Like White Elephants" (p. 297). In what ways do Schenck's ideas about deconstructing language apply to this story?

A Collection of Stories

EDGAR ALLAN POE (1809–1849)
The Purloined Letter
(1836)

Nil sapienatiae odiosius acumine nimio.[1]
—*SENECA*

At Paris, just after dark one gusty evening in the autumn of 18____, I was enjoying the twofold luxury of meditation and a meerschaum, in company with my friend, C. Auguste Dupin, in his little back library, or book-closet, *au troisième*, No. 33 *Rue Dunôt, Faubourg St. Germain.*[2] For one hour at least we had maintained a profound silence; while each, to any casual observer, might have seemed intently and exclusively occupied with the curling eddies of smoke that oppressed the atmosphere of the chamber. For myself, however, I was mentally discussing certain topics which had formed matter for conversation between us at an ear-
10 lier period of the evening; I mean the affair of the Rue Morgue, and the mystery attending the murder of Marie Rogêt.[3] I looked upon it, there-fore, as something of a coincidence, when the door of our apartment was thrown open and admitted our old acquaintance, Monsieur G____, the Prefect of the Parisian police.

We gave him a hearty welcome; for there was nearly half as much of the entertaining as of the contemptible about the man, and we had not seen him for several years. We had been sitting in the dark, and Dupin now arose for the purpose of lighting a lamp, but sat down again, with-out doing so, upon G.'s saying that he had called to consult us, or rather
20 to ask the opinion of my friend, about some official business which had occasioned a great deal of trouble.

---

[1] Nothing is more offensive to the wise than an excess of trickery.
[2] On the third floor above the ground in a fashionable district in Paris.
[3] These are the subjects of previous detective stories by Poe.

"If it is any point requiring reflection," observed Dupin, as he forbore to enkindle the wick, "we shall examine it to better purpose in the dark."

"That is another of your odd notions," said the Prefect, who had the fashion of calling everything "odd" that was beyond his comprehension, and thus lived amid an absolute legion of "oddities."

"Very true," said Dupin, as he supplied his visitor with a pipe, and rolled toward him a comfortable chair.

"And what is the difficulty now?" I asked. "Nothing more in the as-
30 sassination way I hope?"

"Oh, no; nothing of that nature. The fact is, the business is *very* simple indeed, and I make no doubt that we can manage it sufficiently well ourselves; but then I thought Dupin would like to hear the details of it because it is so excessively *odd.*"

"Simple and odd," said Dupin.

"Why, yes; and not exactly that either. The fact is, we have all been a good deal puzzled because the affair *is* so simple, and yet baffles us altogether."

"Perhaps it is the very simplicity of the thing which puts you at
40 fault," said my friend.

"What nonsense you *do* talk!" replied the Prefect, laughing heartily.

"Perhaps the mystery is a little *too* plain," said Dupin.

"Oh, good heavens! who ever heard of such an idea?"

"A little *too* self-evident."

"Ha! ha! ha!—ha! ha! ha!—ho! ho! ho!" roared our visitor, profoundly amused, "oh, Dupin, you will be the death of me yet."

"And what, after all, *is* the matter on hand?" I asked.

"Why, I will tell you," replied the Prefect, as he gave a long, steady, and contemplative puff, and settled himself in his chair. "I will tell you in
50 a few words; but, before I begin, let me caution you that this is an affair demanding the greatest secrecy, and that I should most probably lose the position I now hold, were it known that I confided it to any one."

"Proceed," said I.

"Or not," said Dupin.

"Well, then; I have received personal information, from a very high quarter, that a certain document of the last importance has been purloined from the royal apartments. The individual who purloined it is known; this beyond a doubt; he was seen to take it. It is known, also, that it still remains in his possession."

60 "How is this known?" asked Dupin.

"It is clearly inferred," replied the Prefect, "from the nature of the document, and from the non-appearance of certain results which would at once arise from its passing *out* of the robber's possession—that is to say, from his employing it as he must design in the end to employ it."

"Be a little more explicit," I said.

"Well, I may venture so far as to say that the paper gives its holder a certain power in a certain quarter where such power is immensely valuable." The Prefect was fond of the cant of diplomacy.

"Still I do not quite understand," said Dupin.

70 "No? Well; the disclosure of the document to a third person, who shall be nameless, would bring in question the honor of a personage of most exalted station; and this fact gives the holder of the document an ascendancy over the illustrious personage whose honor and peace are so jeopardized."

"But this ascendancy," I interposed, "would depend upon the robber's knowledge of the loser's knowledge of the robber. Who would dare—"

"The thief," said G____, "is the Minister D____, who dares all things, those unbecoming as well as those becoming a man. The method of the theft was not less ingenious than bold. The document in ques-
80 tion—a letter, to be frank—had been received by the personage robbed while in the royal *boudoir*. During its perusal she was suddenly interrupted by the entrance of the other exalted personage from whom especially it was her wish to conceal it. After a hurried and vain endeavor to thrust it in a drawer, she was forced to place it, open as it was, upon a table. The address, however, was uppermost, and, the contents thus unexposed, the letter escaped notice. At this juncture enters the Minister D____. His lynx eye immediately perceives the paper, recognizes the handwriting of the address, observes the confusion of the personage addressed, and fathoms her secret. After some business transactions, hur-
90 ried through in his ordinary manner, he produces a letter somewhat similar to the one in question, opens it, pretends to read it, and then places it in close juxtaposition to the other. Again he converses, for some fifteen minutes, upon the public affairs. At length, in taking leave, he takes also from the table the letter to which he had no claim. Its rightful owner saw, but, of course, dared not call attention to the act, in the presence of the third personage who stood at her elbow. The minister decamped; leaving his own letter—one of no importance—upon the table."

"Here, then," said Dupin to me, "you have precisely what you demand to make the ascendancy complete—the robber's knowledge of the
100 loser's knowledge of the robber."

"Yes," replied the Prefect; "and the power thus attained has, for some months past, been wielded, for political purposes, to a very dangerous extent. The personage robbed is more thoroughly convinced, every day, of the necessity of reclaiming her letter. But this, of course, cannot be done openly. In fine, driven to despair, she has committed the matter to me."

"Than whom," said Dupin, amid a perfect whirlwind of smoke, "no more sagacious agent could, I suppose, be desired, or even imagined."

"You flatter me," replied the Prefect; "but it is possible that some
110 such opinion may have been entertained."

"It is clear," said I, "as you observe, that the letter is still in the possession of the minister; since it is this possession, and not any employment of the letter, which bestows the power. With the employment the power departs."

"True," said G____; "and upon this conviction I proceeded. My first care was to make thorough search of the minister's hotel;[4] and here my chief embarrassment lay in the necessity of searching without his knowledge. Beyond all things, I have been warned of the danger which would result from giving him reason to suspect our design."

120   "But," said I, "you are quite *au fait* in these investigations. The Parisian police have done this thing often before."

"Oh, yes; and for this reason I did not despair. The habits of the minister gave me, too, a great advantage. He is frequently absent from home all night. His servants are by no means numerous. They sleep at a distance from their master's apartment, and, being chiefly Neapolitans, are readily made drunk. I have keys, as you know, with which I can open any chamber or cabinet in Paris. For three months a night has not passed, during the greater part of which I have not been engaged, personally, in ransacking the D____ Hotel. My honor is interested, and, to

130 mention a great secret, the reward is enormous. So I did not abandon the search until I had become fully satisfied that the thief is a more astute man than myself. I fancy that I have investigated every nook and corner of the premises in which it is possible that the paper can be concealed."

"But is it not possible," I suggested, "that although the letter may be in possession of the minister, as it unquestionably is, he may have concealed it elsewhere than upon his own premises?"

"This is barely possible," said Dupin. "The present peculiar condition of affairs at court, and especially of those intrigues in which D____ is

140 known to be involved, would render the instant availability of the document—its susceptibility of being produced at a moment's notice—a point of nearly equal importance with its possession."

"Its susceptibility of being produced?" said I.

"That is to say, of being *destroyed*," said Dupin.

"True," I observed; "the paper is clearly then upon the premises. As for its being upon the person of the minister, we may consider that as out of the question."

"Entirely," said the Prefect. "He has been twice waylaid, as if by footpads, and his person rigidly searched under my own inspection."

150   "You might have spared yourself this trouble," said Dupin. "D____, I presume, is not altogether a fool, and, if not, must have anticipated these waylayings, as a matter of course."

"Not *altogether* a fool," said G., "but then he is a poet, which I take to be only one remove from a fool."

"True," said Dupin, after a long and thoughtful whiff from his meerschaum, "although I have been guilty of certain doggerel myself."

"Suppose you detail," said I, "the particulars of your search."

---

[4] "Hotel" in the French sense: a large building; in this case a private house in the city.

"Why, the fact is, we took our time, and we searched *everywhere*. I have had long experience in these affairs, I took the entire building, room
160 by room; devoting the nights of a whole week to each. We examined, first, the furniture of each apartment. We opened every possible drawer; and I presume you know that, to a properly trained police-agent, such a thing as a 'secret' drawer is impossible. Any man is a dolt who permits a 'secret' drawer to escape him in a search of this kind. The thing is *so* plain. There is a certain amount of bulk—of space—to be accounted for in every cabinet. Then we have accurate rules. The fiftieth part of a line could not escape us. After the cabinets we took the chairs. The cushions we probed with the fine long needles you have seen me employ. From the tables we removed the tops."
170   "Why so?"

"Sometimes the top of a table, or other similarly arranged piece of furniture, is removed by the person wishing to conceal an article; then the leg is excavated, the article deposited within the cavity, and the top replaced. The bottoms and tops of bedposts are employed in the same way."

"But could not the cavity be detected by sounding?" I asked.

"By no means, if, when the article is deposited, a sufficient wadding of cotton be placed around it. Besides, in our case, we were obliged to proceed without noise."

"But you could not have removed—you could not have taken to pieces
180 *all* articles of furniture in which it would have been possible to make a deposit in the manner you mention. A letter may be compressed into a thin spiral roll, not differing much in shape or bulk from a large knitting-needle, and in this form it might be inserted into the rung of a chair, for example. You did not take to pieces all the chairs?"

"Certainly not; but we did better—we examined the rungs of every chair in the hotel, and, indeed, the jointings of every description of furniture, by the aid of a most powerful microscope. Had there been any traces of recent disturbance we should not have failed to detect it instantly. A single grain of gimlet-dust, for example, would have been as obvious as
190 an apple. Any disorder in the gluing—any unusual gaping in the joints—would have sufficed to insure detection."

"I presume you looked to the mirrors, between the boards and the plates, and you probed the beds and the bedclothes, as well as the curtains and carpets."

"That of course; and when we had absolutely completed every particle of furniture in this way, then we examined the house itself. We divided its entire surface into compartments, which we numbered, so that none might be missed; then we scrutinized each individual square inch throughout the premises, including the two houses immediately adjoin-
200 ing, with the microscope, as before."

"The two houses adjoining!" I exclaimed; "you must have had a great deal of trouble."

"We had; but the reward offered is prodigious."

"You included the *grounds* about the houses?"

"All the grounds are paved with brick. They gave us comparatively little trouble. We examined the moss between the bricks, and found it undisturbed."

"You looked among D——'s papers, of course, and into the books of the library?"

210 "Certainly; we opened every package and parcel; we not only opened every book, but we turned over every leaf in each volume, not contenting ourselves with a mere shake, according to the fashion of some of our police officers. We also measured the thickness of every book-*cover*, with the most accurate admeasurement, and applied to each the most jealous scrutiny of the microscope. Had any of the bindings been recently meddled with, it would have been utterly impossible that the fact should have escaped observation. Some five or six volumes, just from the hands of the binder, we carefully probed, longitudinally, with needles."

"You explored the floors beneath the carpets?"

220 "Beyond doubt. We removed every carpet, and examined the boards with the microscope."

"And the paper on the walls?"

"Yes."

"You looked into the cellars?"

"We did."

"Then," I said, "you have been making a miscalculation, and the letter is *not* upon the premises, as you suppose."

"I fear you are right there," said the Prefect. "And now, Dupin, what would you advise me to do?"

230 "To make a thorough research of the premises."

"That is absolutely needless," replied G——. "I am not more sure that I breathe than I am that the letter is not at the hotel."

"I have no better advice to give you," said Dupin. "You have, of course, an accurate description of the letter?"

"Oh, yes!"—And here the Prefect, producing a memorandum-book, proceeded to read aloud a minute account of the internal, and especially of the external, appearance of the missing document. Soon after finishing the perusal of this description, he took his departure, more entirely depressed in spirits than I had ever known the good gentleman before.

240 In about a month afterward he paid us another visit, and found us occupied very nearly as before. He took a pipe and a chair and entered into some ordinary conversation. At length I said:

"Well, but G——, what of the purloined letter? I presume you have at last made up your mind that there is no such thing as overreaching the Minister?"

"Confound him, say I—yes; I made the re-examination, however, as Dupin suggested—but it was all labor lost, as I knew it would be."

"How much was the reward offered, did you say?" asked Dupin.

"Why, a very great deal—a *very* liberal reward—I don't like to say 250 how much, precisely; but one thing I *will* say, that I wouldn't mind giving my individual check for fifty thousand francs to any one who could obtain me that letter. The fact is, it is becoming of more and more importance every day; and the reward has been lately doubled. If it were trebled, however, I could do no more than I have done."

"Why, yes," said Dupin, drawlingly, between the whiffs of his meerschaum, "I really—think, G——, you have not exerted yourself—to the utmost in this matter. You might—do a little more, I think, eh?"

"How?—in what way?"

"Why—puff, puff—you might—puff, puff—employ counsel in the
260 matter, eh?—puff, puff, puff. Do you remember the story they tell of Abernethy?"

"No; hang Abernethy!"

"To be sure! hang him and welcome. But, once upon a time, a certain rich miser conceived the design of spunging upon this Abernethy for a medical opinion. Getting up, for this purpose, an ordinary conversation in a private company, he insinuated his case to the physician, as that of an imaginary individual.

"'We will suppose,' said the miser, 'that his symptoms are such and such; now, doctor, what would *you* have directed him to take?'

270   "'Take!' said Abernethy, 'why, take *advice*, to be sure.'"

"But," said the Prefect, a little discomposed, "I am *perfectly* willing to take advice, and to pay for it. I would *really* give fifty thousand francs to any one who would aid me in the matter."

"In that case," replied Dupin, opening a drawer, and producing a check-book, "you may as well fill me up a check for the amount mentioned. When you have signed it, I will hand you the letter."

I was astounded. The Prefect appeared absolutely thunderstricken. For some minutes he remained speechless and motionless, looking incredulously at my friend with open mouth, and eyes that seemed start-
280 ing from their sockets; then apparently recovering himself in some measure, he seized a pen, and after several pauses and vacant stares, finally filled up and signed a check for fifty thousand francs, and handed it across the table to Dupin. The latter examined it carefully and deposited it in his pocket-book; then, unlocking an *escritoire*, took thence a letter and gave it to the prefect. This functionary grasped it in a perfect agony of joy, opened it with a trembling hand, cast a rapid glance at its contents, and then, scrambling and struggling to the door, rushed at length unceremoniously from the room and from the house, without having uttered a syllable since Dupin had requested him to fill up the
290 check.

When he had gone, my friend entered into some explanations.

"The Parisian police," he said, "are exceedingly able in their way. They are persevering, ingenious, cunning, and thoroughly versed in the knowledge which their duties seem chiefly to demand. Thus, when G—— detailed to us his mode of searching the premises at the Hotel D——, I felt entire confidence in his having made a satisfactory investigation—so far as his labors extended."

"So far as his labors extended?" said I.

"Yes," said Dupin. "The measures adopted were not only the best of their kind, but carried out to absolute perfection. Had the letter been deposited within the range of their search, these fellows would, beyond a question, have found it."

I merely laughed—but he seemed quite serious in all that he said.

"The measures, then," he continued, "were good in their kind, and well executed; their defect lay in their being inapplicable to the case and to the man. A certain set of highly ingenious resources are, with the Prefect, a sort of Procrustean bed, to which he forcibly adapts his designs. But he perpetually errs by being too deep or too shallow for the matter in hand; and many a school-boy is a better reasoner than he. I knew one about eight years of age, whose success at guessing in the game of 'even and odd' attracted universal admiration. This game is simple, and is played with marbles. One player holds in his hand a number of these toys, and demands of another whether that number is even or odd. If the guess is right, the guesser wins one; if wrong, he loses one. The boy to whom I allude won all the marbles of the school. Of course he had some principle of guessing; and this lay in mere observation and admeasurements of the astuteness of his opponents. For example, an arrant simpleton is his opponent, and holding up his closed hand, asks, 'Are they even or odd?' Our school-boy replies, 'Odd,' and loses; but upon the second trial he wins, for he then says to himself: 'The simpleton had them even upon the first trial, and his amount of cunning is just sufficient to make him have them odd upon the second; I will therefore guess odd';—he guesses odd, and wins. Now, with a simpleton a degree above the first, he would have reasoned thus: 'This fellow finds that in the first instance I guessed odd, and, in the second, he will propose to himself, upon the first impulse, a simple variation from even to odd, as did the first simpleton; but then a second thought will suggest that this is too simple a variation, and finally he will decide upon putting it even as before. I will therefore guess even';—he guesses even, and wins. Now this mode of reasoning in the school-boy, whom his fellows termed 'lucky,'—what, in its last analysis, is it?"

"It is merely," I said, "an identification of the reasoner's intellect with that of his opponent."

"It is," said Dupin; "and, upon inquiring of the boy by what means he effected the *thorough* identification in which his success consisted, I received answer as follows; 'When I wish to find out how wise, or how stupid or how good, or how wicked is any one, or what are his thoughts at the moment, I fashion the expression of my face, as accurately as possible, in accordance with the expression of his, and then wait to see what thoughts or sentiments arise in my mind or heart, as if to match or correspond with the expression.' This response of the school-boy lies at the bottom of all the spurious profundity which has been attributed to Rochefoucault, to La Bougive, to Machiavelli, and to Campanella."

"And the identification," I said, "of the reasoner's intellect with that of his opponent, depends, if I understand you aright, upon the accuracy with which the opponent's intellect is admeasured."

"For its practical value it depends upon this," replied Dupin; "and the Prefect and his cohort fail so frequently, first, by default of this identification and, secondly, by ill-admeasurement, or rather through non-admeasurement, of the intellect with which they are engaged.
350 They consider only their *own* ideas of ingenuity; and, in searching for any thing hidden, advert only to the modes, in which *they* would have hidden it. They are right in this much—that their own ingenuity is a faithful representative of that of the *mass*; but when the cunning of the individual felon is diverse in character from their own, the felon foils them, of course. This always happens when it is above their own, and very usually when it is below. They have no variation of principle in their investigations; at best, when urged by some unusual emergency— by some extraordinary reward—they extend or exaggerate their old modes of *practice,* without touching their principles. What, for example,
360 in this case of D____, has been done to vary the principle of action? What is all this boring, and probing, and sounding, and scrutinizing with the microscope, and dividing the surface of the building into registered square inches—what is it all but an exaggeration *of the application* of the one principle or set of principles of search, which are based upon the one set of notions regarding human ingenuity, to which the Prefect, in the long routine of his duty, has been accustomed? Do you not see he has taken it for granted that *all* men proceed to conceal a letter, not exactly in a gimlet-hole bored in a chair-leg, but, at least, in *some* out-of-the-way hole or corner suggested by the same tenor of
370 thought which would urge a man to secrete a letter in a gimlet-hole bored in a chair-leg? And do you not see also, that such *recherchés* nooks for concealment are adapted only for ordinary occasions, and would be adopted only by ordinary intellects; for, in all cases of concealment, a disposal of the article concealed—a disposal of it in this *recherché* manner,—is, in the very first instance, presumable and presumed; and thus its discovery depends, not at all upon the acumen, but altogether upon the mere care, patience, and determination of the seekers; and where the case is of importance—or, what amounts to the same thing in the political eyes, when the reward is of magnitude,—
380 the qualities in question have *never* been known to fail. You will now understand what I meant in suggesting that, had the purloined letter been hidden anywhere within the limits of the Prefect's examination— in other words, had the principle of its concealment been comprehended within the principles of the Prefect—its discovery would have been a matter altogether beyond question. This functionary, however, has been thoroughly mystified; and the remote source of his defeat lies in the supposition that the Minister is a fool, because he has acquired renown as a poet. All fools are poets; this the Prefect *feels*; and he is merely guilty of a *non distributio medii* in thence inferring that all poets
390 are fools."

"But is this really the poet?" I asked. "There are two brothers, I know; and both have attained reputation in letters. The Minister I believe has written learnedly on the Differential Calculus. He is a mathematician, and no poet."

"You are mistaken; I know him well; he is both. As poet *and* mathematician, he would reason well; as mere mathematician, he could not have reasoned at all, and thus would have been at the mercy of the Prefect."

"You surprise me," I said, "by these opinions, which have been contradicted by the voice of the world. You do not mean to set at naught the
400 well-digested idea of centuries. The mathematical reason has long been regarded as *the* reason *par excellence.*"

"'*Il y a à parier,'*" replied Dupin, quoting from Chamfort, "'*que toute idée publique, toute convention reçue, est une sottise, car elle a convenu au plus grand nombre.'*[5] The mathematicians, I grant you, have done their best to promulgate the popular error to which you allude, and which is none the less an error for its promulgation as truth. With an art worthy a better cause, for example, they have insinuated the term 'analysis' into application to algebra. The French are the originators of this particular deception; but if a term is of any importance—if words derive any value from
410 applicability—then 'analysis' conveys 'algebra' about as much as, in Latin, '*ambitus*' implies ambition, '*religio*' 'religion,' or '*homines honesti*' a set of *honorable* men."

"You have a quarrel on hand, I see," said I, "with some of the algebraists of Paris; but proceed."

"I dispute the availability, and thus the value, of that reason which is cultivated in any especial form other than the abstractly logical. I dispute, in particular, the reason educed by mathematical study. The mathematics are the science of form and quantity; mathematical reasoning is merely logic applied to observation upon form and quantity. The great
420 error lies in supposing that even the truths of what is called *pure* algebra are abstract or general truths. And this error is so egregious that I am confounded at the universality with which it has been received. Mathematical axioms are *not* axioms of general truth. What is true of *relation*—of form and quantity—is often grossly false in regard to morals, for example. In this latter science it is very usually *un*true that the aggregated parts are equal to the whole. In chemistry also the axiom fails. In the consideration of motive it fails; for two motives, each of a given value, have not, necessarily, a value when united, equal to the sum of their values apart. There are numerous other mathematical truths which
430 are only truths within the limits of *relation*. But the mathematician argues from his *finite truths*, through habit, as if they were of an absolutely general applicability—as the world indeed imagines them to be. Bryant, in his very learned 'Mythology,' mentions an analogous source of error, when he says that 'although the pagan fables are not believed, yet we forget ourselves continually, and make inferences from them as existing realities.' With the algebraists, however, who are pagans themselves, the

---

[5] "The odds are that any public idea or accepted opinion is stupid, because it has suited the majority of people."

'pagan fables' *are* believed and the inferences are made, not so much through lapse of memory as through an unaccountable addling of the brains. In short, I never yet encountered the mere mathematician who
440 would be trusted out of equal roots, or one who did not clandestinely hold it as a point of his faith that $x2 + px$ was absolutely and unconditionally equal to q. Say to one of these gentlemen, by way of experiment, if you please, that you believe occasions may occur where $x2 + px$ is *not* altogether equal to q, and, having made him understand what you mean, get out of his reach as speedily as convenient, for, beyond doubt, he will endeavor to knock you down.

"I mean to say," continued Dupin, while I merely laughed at his last observations, "that if the Minister had been no more than a mathematician, the Prefect would have been under no necessity of giving me this
450 check. I knew him, however, as both mathematician and poet, and my measures were adapted to his capacity, with reference to the circumstances by which he was surrounded. I knew him as a courtier, too, and as a bold *intriguant*. Such a man, I considered, could not fail to be aware of the ordinary policial modes of action. He could not have failed to anticipate—and events have proved that he did not fail to anticipate—the waylayings to which he was subjected. He must have foreseen, I reflected, the secret investigations of his premises. His frequent absences from home at night, which were hailed by the Prefect as certain aids to his success, I regarded only as *ruses*, to afford opportunity for thorough
460 search to the police, and thus the sooner to impress them with the conviction to which G____, in fact, did finally arrive—the conviction that the letter was not upon the premises. I felt, also, that the whole train of thought, which I was at some pains in detailing to you just now, concerning the invariable principle of policial action in searches for articles concealed—I felt that this whole train of thought would necessarily pass through the mind of the minister. It would imperatively lead him to despise all the ordinary *nooks* of concealment. *He* could not, I reflected, be so weak as not to see that the most intricate and remote recess of his hotel would be as open as his commonest closets to the eyes, to the
470 probes, to the gimlets, and to the microscopes of the Prefect. I saw, in fine, that he would be driven, as a matter of course, to *simplicity*, if not deliberately induced to it as a matter of choice. You will remember, perhaps, how desperately the Prefect laughed when I suggested, upon our first interview, that it was just possible this mystery troubled him so much on account of its being so *very* self-evident."

"Yes," said I, "I remember his merriment well. I really thought he would have fallen into convulsions."

"The material world," continued Dupin, "abounds with very strict analogies to the immaterial; and thus some color of truth has been
480 given to the rhetorical dogma, that metaphor, or simile, may be made to strengthen an argument as well as to embellish a description. The principle of the *vis inertiae*, for example, seems to be identical in physics and metaphysics. It is not more true in the former, that a large body is with

more difficulty set in motion than a smaller one, and that its subsequent *momentum* is commensurate with this difficulty, than it is, in the latter, that intellects of the vaster capacity, while more forcible, more constant, and more eventful in their movements than those of inferior grade, are yet the less readily moved, and more embarrassed, and full of hesitation in the first few steps of their progress. Again: have you ever noticed
490 which of the street signs, over the shop doors, are the most attractive of attention?"

"I have never given the matter a thought," I said.

"There is a game of puzzles," he resumed, "which is played upon a map. One party playing requires another to find a given word—the name of town, river, state, or empire—any word, in short, upon the motley and perplexed surface of the chart. A novice in the game generally seeks to embarrass his opponents by giving them the most minutely lettered names; but the adept selects such words as stretch, in large characters, from one end of the chart to the other. These, like the over-largely lettered
500 signs and placards of the street, escape observation by dint of being excessively obvious; and here the physical oversight is precisely analogous with the moral inapprehension by which the intellect suffers to pass unnoticed those considerations which are too obtrusively and too palpably self-evident. But this is a point, it appears, somewhat above or beneath the understanding of the Prefect. He never once thought it probable, or possible, that the minister had deposited the letter immediately beneath the nose of the whole world, by way of best preventing any portion of that world from perceiving it.

"But the more I reflected upon the daring, dashing, and discriminat-
510 ing ingenuity of D——; upon the fact that the document must always have been *at hand,* if he intended to use it to good purpose; and upon the decisive evidence, obtained by the Prefect, that it was not hidden within the limits of the dignitary's ordinary search—the more satisfied I became that, to conceal this letter, the minister had resorted to the comprehensive and sagacious expedient of not attempting to conceal it at all.

"Full of these ideas, I prepared myself with a pair of green spectacles, and called one fine morning, quite by accident, at the Ministerial hotel. I found D—— at home, yawning, lounging, and dawdling, as usual, and pretending to be in the last extremity of *ennui.* He is, perhaps, the most
520 really energetic human being now alive—but that is only when nobody sees him.

"To be even with him, I complained of my weak eyes, and lamented the necessity of the spectacles, under cover of which I cautiously and thoroughly surveyed the whole apartment, while seemingly intent only upon the conversation of my host.

"I paid especial attention to a large writing-table near which he sat, and upon which lay confusedly, some miscellaneous letters and other papers, with one or two musical instruments and a few books. Here, however, after a long and very deliberate scrutiny, I saw nothing to ex-
530 cite particular suspicion.

"At length my eyes, in going the circuit of the room, fell upon a trumpery filigree card-rack of pasteboard, that hung dangling by a dirty blue ribbon, from a little brass knob just beneath the middle of the mantelpiece. In this rack, which had three or four compartments, were five or six visiting cards and a solitary letter. This last was much soiled and crumpled. It was torn nearly in two, across the middle—as if a design, in the first instance, to tear it entirely up as worthless, had been altered, or stayed, in the second. It had a large black seal, bearing the D⸻ cipher *very* conspicuously, and was addressed, in a diminutive female hand, to
540 D⸻, the minister himself. It was thrust carelessly, and even, as it seemed, contemptuously, into one of the uppermost divisions of the rack.

"No sooner had I glanced at this letter than I concluded it to be that of which I was in search. To be sure, it was, to all appearance, radically different from the one of which the Prefect had read us so minute a description. Here the seal was large and black, with the D⸻ cipher; there it was small and red, with the ducal arms of the S⸻ family. Here, the address, to the minister, was diminutive and feminine; there the superscription, to a certain royal personage, was markedly bold and decided; the size alone formed a point of correspondence. But, then, the *radicalness* of
550 these differences, which was excessive; the dirt; the soiled and torn condition of the paper, so inconsistent with the *true* methodical habits of D⸻, and so suggestive of a design to delude the beholder into an idea of the worthlessness of the document;—these things, together with the hyperobtrusive situation of this document, full in the view of every visitor, and thus exactly in accordance with the conclusions to which I had previously arrived; these things, I say were strongly corroborative of suspicion, in one who came with the intention to suspect.

"I protracted my visit as long as possible, and, while I maintained a most animated discussion with the minister, upon a topic which I knew
560 well had never failed to interest and excite him, I kept my attention really riveted upon the letter. In this examination, I committed to memory its external appearance and arrangement in the rack; and also fell, at length, upon a discovery which set at rest whatever trivial doubt I might have entertained. In scrutinizing the edges of the paper, I observed them to be more *chafed* than seemed necessary. They presented the *broken* appearance which is manifested when a stiff paper, having been once folded and pressed with a folder, is refolded in a reversed direction, in the same creases or edges which had formed the original fold. This discovery was sufficient. It was clear to me that the letter had been turned, as a glove,
570 inside out, re-directed and re-sealed. I bade the minister good-morning, and took my departure at once, leaving a gold snuff-box upon the table.

"The next morning I called for the snuff-box, when we resumed, quite eagerly, the conversation of the preceding day. While thus engaged, however, a loud report, as if of a pistol, was heard immediately beneath the windows of the hotel, and was succeeded by a series of fearful screams, and the shoutings of a terrified mob. D⸻ rushed to a casement, threw it open, and looked out. In the meantime I stepped to the card-rack, took the letter, put it in my pocket, and replaced it by a *fac-simile*, (so far as

regards externals) which I had carefully prepared at my lodgings—imitat-
580 ing the D____ cipher, very readily, by means of a seal formed of bread.

"The disturbance in the street had been occasioned by the frantic behavior of a man with a musket. He had fired it among a crowd of women and children. It proved, however, to have been without ball, and the fellow was suffered to go his way as a lunatic or a drunkard. When he had gone, D____ came from the window, whither I had followed him immediately upon securing the object in view. Soon afterward I bade him farewell. The pretended lunatic was a man in my own pay."

"But what purpose had you," I asked, "in replacing the letter by a *fac-simile?* Would it not have been better, at the first visit, to have seized
590 it openly, and departed?"

"D____," replied Dupin, "is a desperate man, and a man of nerve. His hotel, too, is not without attendants devoted to his interests. Had I made the wild attempt you suggest, I might never have left the Ministerial presence alive. The good people of Paris might have heard of me no more. But I had an object apart from these considerations. You know my political prepossessions. In this matter, I act as a partisan of the lady concerned. For eighteen months the Minister has had her in his power. She has now him in hers—since, being unaware that the letter is not in his possession, he will proceed with his exactions as if it was. Thus will he inevitably
600 commit himself, at once, to his political destruction. His downfall, too, will not be more precipitate than awkward. It is all very well to talk about the *facilis descensus Averni;*[6] but in all kinds of climbing, as Catalani said of singing, it is far more easy to get up than to come down. In the present instance I have no sympathy—at least no pity—for him who descends. He is that *monstrum horrendum,* an unprincipled man of genius. I confess, however, that I should like very well to know the precise character of his thoughts, when, being defied by her whom the Prefect terms 'a certain personage,' he is reduced to opening the letter which I left for him in the card-rack."

610   "How?" did you put any thing particular in it?"

"Why—it did not seem altogether right to leave the interior blank—that would have been insulting. D____, at Vienna once, did me an evil turn, which I told him, quite good-humoredly, that I should remember. So, as I knew he would feel some curiosity in regard to the identity of the person who had outwitted him, I thought it a pity not to give him a clew. He is well acquainted with my MS.,[7] and I just copied into the middle of the blank sheet the words—

    "'_____ Un dessein si funeste,
        S'il n'est digne d'Atrée, est digne de Thyeste.'[8]

620 They are to be found in Crébillon's 'Atrée.'"

---

[6] "The easy descent to Hell" as described by Vergil in *The Aeneid.*
[7] MS—handwriting.
[8] "A scheme so horrible,/If it is unworthy of Atreus, is worthy of Thyestes." The allusion is to a particularly revolting episode of revenge in Greek mythology.

NATHANIEL HAWTHORNE (1804–1864)

The Birthmark

(1843)

In the latter part of the last century there lived a man of science, and eminent proficient in every branch of natural philosophy, who not long before our story opens had made experience of a spiritual affinity more attractive than any chemical one. He had left his laboratory to the care of an assistant, cleared his fine countenance from the furnace smoke, washed the stain of acids from his fingers, and persuaded a beautiful woman to become his wife. In those days when the comparatively recent discovery of electricity and other kindred mysteries of Nature seemed to open paths into the region of miracle, it was not unusual for the love of
10 science to rival the love of woman in its depth and absorbing energy. The higher intellect, the imagination, the spirit, and even the heart might all find their congenial ailment in pursuits which, as some of their ardent votaries believed, would ascend from one step of powerful intelligence to another, until the philosopher should lay his hand on the secret of creative force and perhaps make new worlds for himself. We know not whether Aylmer possessed this degree of faith in man's ultimate control over Nature. He had devoted himself, however, too unreservedly to scientific studies ever to be weaned from them by any second passion. His love for his young wife might prove the stronger of the two; but it could only
20 be by intertwining itself with his love of science, and uniting the strength of the latter to his own.

Such a union accordingly took place, and was attended with truly remarkable consequences and a deeply impressive moral. One day, very soon after their marriage, Aylmer sat gazing at his wife with a trouble in his countenance that grew stronger until he spoke.

"Georgiana," said he, "has it never occurred to you that the mark upon your cheek might be removed?"

"No, indeed," said she, smiling; but perceiving the seriousness of his manner, she blushed deeply. "To tell you the truth it has been so of-
30 ten called a charm that I was simple enough to imagine it might be so."

"Ah, upon another face perhaps it might," replied her husband; "but never on yours. No, dearest Georgiana, you came so nearly perfect from the hand of Nature that this slightest possible defect, which we hesitate whether to term a defect or a beauty, shocks me, as being the visible mark of earthly imperfection."

"Shocks you, my husband!" cried Georgiana, deeply hurt; at first reddening with momentary anger, but then bursting into tears. "Then why did you take me from my mother's side? You cannot love what shocks you!"

40   To explain this conversation it must be mentioned that in the center of Georgiana's left cheek there was a singular mark, deeply interwoven, as it were, with the texture and substance of her face. In the usual state of her

complexion—a healthy though delicate bloom—the mark wore a tint of deeper crimson, which imperfectly defined its shape amid the surrounding rosiness. When she blushed it gradually became more indistinct, and finally vanished amid the triumphant rush of blood that bathed the whole cheek with its brilliant glow. But if any shifting motion caused her to turn pale, there was the mark again, a crimson stain upon the snow, in what Aylmer sometimes deemed an almost fearful distinctness. Its shape
50 bore not a little similarity to the human hand, though of the smallest pygmy size. Georgiana's lovers were wont to say that some fairy at her birth hour had laid her tiny hand upon the infant's cheek, and left this impress there in token of the magic endowments that were to give her such sway over all hearts. Many a desperate swain would have risked life for the privilege of pressing his lips to the mysterious hand. It must not be concealed, however, that the impression wrought by this fairy sign manual varied exceedingly, according to the difference of temperament in the beholders. Some fastidious persons—but they were exclusively of her own sex—affirmed that the bloody hand, as they chose to call it, quite de-
60 stroyed the effect of Georgiana's beauty, and rendered her countenance even hideous. But it would be as reasonable to say that one of those small blue stains which sometimes occur in the purest statuary marble would convert the Eve of Powers to a monster. Masculine observers, if the birthmark did not heighten their admiration, contented themselves with wishing it away, that the world might posses one living specimen of ideal loveliness without the semblance of a flaw. After his marriage,—for he thought little or nothing of the matter before,—Aylmer discovered that this was the case with himself.

Had she been less beautiful,—if Envy's self could have found aught
70 else to sneer at,—he might have felt his affection heightened by the prettiness of this mimic hand, now vaguely portrayed, now lost, now stealing forth again and glimmering to and fro with every pulse of emotion that throbbed within her heart; but seeing her otherwise so perfect, he found this one defect grow more and more intolerable with every moment of their united lives. It was the fatal flaw of humanity which Nature, in one shape or another, stamps ineffaceably on all her productions, either to imply that they are temporary and finite, or that their perfection must be wrought by toil and pain. The crimson hand expressed the ineludible gripe in which mortality clutches the highest and purest of earthly mold,
80 degrading them into kindred with the lowest, and even with the very brutes, like whom their visible frames return to dust. In this manner, selecting it as the symbol of his wife's liability to sin, sorrow, decay, and death, Aylmer's somber imagination was not long in rendering the birthmark a frightful object, causing him more trouble and horror than ever Georgiana's beauty, whether of soul or sense, had given him delight.

At all the seasons which should have been their happiest, he invariably and without intending it, nay, in spite of a purpose to the contrary, reverted to this one disastrous topic. Trifling as it at first appeared, it so connected itself with innumerable trains of thought and modes of feeling

90 that it became the central point of all. With the morning twilight Aylmer opened his eyes upon his wife's face and recognized the symbol of imperfection; and when they sat together at the evening hearth his eyes wandered stealthily to her cheek, and beheld, flickering with the blaze of the wood fire, the spectral hand that wrote mortality where he would fain have worshipped. Georgiana soon learned to shudder at his gaze. It needed but a glance with the peculiar expression that his face often wore to change the roses of her cheek into a deathlike paleness, amid which the crimson hand was brought strongly out, like a bas-relief of ruby on the whitest marble.

100   Late one night when the lights were growing dim, so as hardly to betray the stain on the poor wife's cheek, she herself, for the first time, voluntarily took up the subject.

"Do you remember, my dear Aylmer," said she, with a feeble attempt at a smile, "have you any recollection of a dream last night about this odious hand?"

"None! none whatever!" replied Aylmer, starting; but then he added, in a dry, cold tone, affected for the sake of concealing the real depth of his emotion, "I might well dream of it; for before I fell asleep it had taken a pretty firm hold of my fancy."

110   "And you did dream of it?" continued Georgiana hastily, for she dreaded lest a gush of tears should interrupt what she had to say. "A terrible dream! I wonder that you can forget it. Is it possible to forget this one expression?—'It is in her heart now; we must have it out!' Reflect, my husband; for by all means I would have you recall that dream."

The mind is in a sad state when Sleep, the all-involving, cannot confine her specters within the dim region of her sway, but suffers them to break forth, affrighting this actual life with secrets that perchance belong to a deeper one. Aylmer now remembered his dream. He had fancied himself with his servant Aminadab, attempting an operation for
120 the removal of the birthmark; but the deeper went the knife, the deeper sank the hand, until at length its tiny grasp appeared to have caught hold of Georgiana's heart; whence, however, her husband was inexorably resolved to cut or wrench it away.

When the dream had shaped itself perfectly in his memory, Aylmer sat in his wife's presence with a guilty feeling. Truth often finds its way to the mind close muffled in robes of sleep, and then speaks with uncompromising directness of matters in regard to which we practice an unconscious self-deception during our waking moments. Until now he had not been aware of the tyrannizing influence acquired by one idea over his
130 mind, and of the lengths which he might find in his heart to go for the sake of giving himself peace.

"Aylmer," resumed Georgiana solemnly, "I know not what may be the cost to both of us to rid me of this fatal birthmark. Perhaps its removal may cause cureless deformity; or it may be the stain goes as deep as life itself. Again: do we know that there is a possibility, on any terms, of unclasping the firm gripe of this little hand which was laid upon me before I came into the world?"

"Dearest Georgiana, I have spent much thought upon the subject," hastily interrupted Aylmer. "I am convinced of the perfect practicability
140 of its removal."

"If there be the remotest possibility of it," continued Georgiana, "let the attempt be made at whatever risk. Danger is nothing to me; for life, while this hateful mark makes me the object of your horror and disgust,— life is a burden which I would fling down with joy. Either remove this dreadful hand, or take my wretched life! You have deep science. All the world bears witness of it. You have achieved great wonders. Cannot you remove this little, little mark, which I cover with the tips of two small fingers? Is this beyond your power, for the sake of your own peace, and to save your poor wife from madness?"

150   "Noblest, dearest, tenderest wife," cried Aylmer rapturously, "doubt not my power. I have already given this matter the deepest thought— thought which might almost have enlightened me to create a being less perfect than yourself. Georgiana, you have led me deeper than ever into the heart of science. I feel myself fully competent to render this dear cheek as faultless as its fellow; and then, most beloved, what will be my triumph when I shall have corrected what Nature left imperfect in her fairest work! Even Pygmalion, when his sculptured woman assumed life, felt not greater ecstasy than mine will be."

"It is resolved, then," said Georgiana, faintly smiling. "And, Aylmer,
160 spare me not, though you should find the birthmark take refuge in my heart at last."

Her husband tenderly kissed her cheek—her right cheek—not that which bore the impress of the crimson hand.

The next day Aylmer apprised his wife of a plan that he had formed whereby he might have opportunity for the intense thought and constant watchfulness which the proposed operation would require; while Georgiana, likewise, would enjoy the perfect repose essential to its success. They were to seclude themselves in the extensive apartments occupied by Aylmer as a laboratory, and where, during his toilsome youth,
170 he had made discoveries in the elemental powers of Nature that had roused the admiration of all the learned societies in Europe. Seated calmly in this laboratory, the pale philosopher had investigated the secrets of the highest cloud region and of the profoundest mines; he had satisfied himself of the causes that kindled and kept alive the fires of the volcano; and had explained the mystery of fountains, and how it is that they gush forth, some so bright and pure, and others with such rich medicinal virtues, from the dark bosom of the earth. Here, too, at an earlier period, he had studied the wonders of the human frame, and attempted to fathom the very process by which Nature assimilates all her
180 precious influences from earth and air, and from the spiritual world, to create and foster man, her masterpiece. The latter pursuit, however,

Aylmer had long laid aside in unwilling recognition of the truth—
against which all seekers sooner or later stumble—that our great creative Mother, while she amuses us with apparently working in the
broadest sunshine, is yet severely careful to keep her own secrets, and,
in spite of her pretended openness, shows us nothing but results. She
permits us, indeed, to mar, but seldom to mend, and, like a jealous
patentee, on no account to make. Now, however, Aylmer resumed these
half-forgotten investigations,—not, of course, with such hopes or wishes
190 as first suggested them, but because they involved much physiological
truth and lay in the path of his proposed scheme for the treatment of
Georgiana.

As he led her over the threshold of the laboratory, Georgiana was
cold and tremulous. Aylmer looked cheerfully into her face, with intent
to reassure her, but was so startled with the intense glow of the birthmark upon the whiteness of her cheek that he could not restrain a
strong convulsive shudder. His wife fainted.

"Aminadab! Aminadab!" shouted Aylmer, stamping violently on the
floor.

200   Forthwith there issued from an inner apartment a man of low
stature, but bulk frame, with shaggy hair hanging about his visage,
which was grimed with the vapors of the furnace. This personage had
been Aylmer's underworker during his whole scientific career, and was
admirably fitted for that office by his great mechanical readiness, and
the skill with which, while incapable of comprehending a single principle, he executed all the details of his master's experiments. With his
vast strength, his shaggy hair, his smoky aspect, and the indescribable
earthiness that encrusted him, he seemed to represent man's physical
nature; while Aylmer's slender figure, and pale, intellectual face, were
210 no less apt a type of the spiritual element.

"Throw open the door of the boudoir, Aminadab," said Aylmer,
"and burn a pastille."

"Yes, master," answered Aminadab, looking intently at the lifeless
form of Georgiana; and then he muttered to himself, "If she were my
wife, I'd never part with that birthmark."

When Georgiana recovered consciousness she found herself breathing
an atmosphere of penetrating fragrance, the gentle potency of which had
recalled her from her deathlike faintness. The scene around her looked
like enchantment. Aylmer had converted those smoky, dingy, somber
220 rooms, where he had spent his brightest years in recondite pursuits, into
a series of beautiful apartments not unfit to be the secluded abode of a
lovely woman. The walls were hung with gorgeous curtains, which imparted the combination of grandeur and grace that no other species of
adornment can achieve; and as they fell from the ceiling to the floor, their
rich and ponderous folds, concealing all angles and straight lines, appeared to shut in the scene from infinite space. For aught Georgiana
knew, it might be a pavilion among the clouds. And Aylmer, excluding

the sunshine, which would have interfered with his chemical processes, had supplied its place with perfumed lamps, emitting flames of various
230 hue, but all uniting in a soft, empurpled radiance. He now knelt by his wife's side, watching her earnestly, but without alarm; for he was confident in his science, and felt that he could draw a magic circle round her within which no evil might intrude.

"Where am I? Ah, I remember," said Georgiana faintly; and she placed her hand over her cheek to hide the terrible mark from her husband's eyes.

"Fear not, dearest!" exclaimed he. "Do not shrink from me! Believe me, Georgiana, I even rejoice in this single imperfection, since it will be such a rapture to remove it."

240 "Oh, spare me!" sadly replied his wife. "Pray do not look at it again. I never can forget that convulsive shudder."

In order to soothe Georgiana, and, as it were, to release her mind from the burden of actual things, Aylmer now put in practice some of the light and playful secrets which science had taught him among its profounder lore. Airy figures, absolutely bodiless ideas, and forms of unsubstantial beauty came and danced before her, imprinting their momentary footsteps on beams of light. Though she had some indistinct idea of the method of these optical phenomena, still the illusion was almost perfect enough to warrant the belief that her husband possessed
250 sway over the spiritual world. Then again, when she felt a wish to look forth from her seclusion, immediately, as if her thoughts were answered, the procession of external existence flitted across a screen. The scenery and figures of actual life were perfectly represented, but with that bewitching, yet indescribable difference which always makes a picture, an image, or a shadow so much more attractive than the original. When wearied of this, Aylmer bade her cast her eyes upon a vessel containing a quantity of earth. She did so, with little interest at first; but was soon startled to perceive the germ of a plant shooting upward from the soil. Then came the slender stalk; the leaves gradually unfolded
260 themselves; and amid them was a perfect and lovely flower.

"It is magical!" cried Georgiana. "I dare not touch it."

"Nay, pluck it," answered Aylmer: "pluck it, and inhale its brief perfume while you may. The flower will wither in a few moments and leave nothing save its brown seed vessels; but thence may be perpetuated a race as ephemeral as itself."

But Georgiana had no sooner touched the flower than the whole plant suffered a blight, its leaves turning coal-black as if by the agency of fire.

"There was too powerful a stimulus," said Aylmer thoughtfully.

270 To make up for this abortive experiment, he proposed to take her portrait by a scientific process of his own invention. It was to be effected by rays of light striking upon a polished plate of metal. Georgiana assented; but, on looking at the result, was affrighted to find the

features of the portrait blurred and indefinable; while the minute figure of a hand appeared where the cheek should have been. Aylmer snatched the metallic plate and threw it into a jar of corrosive acid.

Soon, however, he forgot these mortifying failures. In the intervals of study and chemical experiment he came to her flushed and exhausted, but seemed invigorated by her presence, and spoke in glowing
280 language of the resources of his art. He gave a history of the long dynasty of the alchemists, who spent so many ages in quest of the universal solvent by which the golden principle might be elicited from all things vile and base. Aylmer appeared to believe that, by the plainest scientific logic, it was altogether within the limits of possibility to discover this long-sought medium; "but," he added, "a philosopher who should go deep enough to acquire the power would attain too lofty a wisdom to stoop to the exercise of it." Not less singular were his opinions in regard to the elixir vitae. He more than intimated that it was at his option to concoct a liquid that should prolong life for years, perhaps
290 interminably; but that it would produce a discord in Nature which all the world, and chiefly the quaffer of the immortal nostrum, would find cause to curse.

"Aylmer, are you in earnest?" asked Georgiana, looking at him with amazement and fear. "It is terrible to possess such power, or even to dream of possessing it."

"Oh, do not tremble, my love," said her husband. "I would not wrong either you or myself by working such inharmonious effects upon our lives; but I would have you consider how trifling, in comparison, is the skill requisite to remove this little hand."
300   At the mention of the birthmark, Georgiana, as usual, shrank as if a red-hot iron had touched her cheek.

Again Aylmer applied himself to his labors. She could hear his voice in the distant furnace-room giving directions to Aminadab, whose harsh, uncouth, misshapen tones were audible in response, more like the grunt or growl of a brute than human speech. After hours of absence, Aylmer reappeared and proposed that she should now examine his cabinet of chemical products and natural treasures of the earth. Among the former he showed her a small vial, in which, he remarked, was contained a gentle yet most powerful fragrance, capable of impregnating all the breezes that
310 blow across a kingdom. They were of inestimable value, the contents of that little vial; and, as he said so, he threw some of the perfume into the air and filled the room with piercing and invigorating delight.

"And what is this?" asked Georgiana, pointing to a small crystal globe containing a gold-colored liquid. "It is so beautiful to the eye that I could imagine it the elixir of life."

"In one sense it is," relied Aylmer; "or rather, the elixir of immortality. It is the most precious poison that ever was concocted in this world. By its aid I could apportion the lifetime of any mortal at whom you might point your finger. The strength of the dose would determine whether he
320 were to linger out years, or drop dead in the midst of a breath. No king on

his guarded throne could keep his life if I, in my private station, should deem that the welfare of millions justified me in depriving him of it."

"Why do you keep such a terrific drug?" inquired Georgiana in horror.

"Do not mistrust me, dearest," said her husband, smiling; "its virtuous potency is yet greater than its harmful one. But see! here is a powerful cosmetic. With a few drops of this in a vase of water, freckles may be washed away as easily as the hands are cleansed. A stronger infusion would take the blood out of the cheek, and leave the rosiest beauty a
330 pale ghost."

"Is it with this lotion that you intend to bathe my cheek?" asked Georgiana, anxiously.

"Oh, no," hastily replied her husband; "this is merely superficial. Your case demands a remedy that shall go deeper."

In his interviews with Georgiana, Aylmer generally made minute inquiries as to her sensations and whether the confinement of the rooms and the temperature of the atmosphere agreed with her. These questions had such a particular drift that Georgiana began to conjecture that she was already subjected to certain physical influences, either breathed
340 in with the fragrant air or taken with her food. She fancied likewise, but it might be altogether fancy, that there was a stirring up of her system— a strange, indefinite sensation creeping through her veins, and tingling, half painfully, half pleasurably, at her heart. Still, whenever she dared to look into the mirror, there she beheld herself pale as a white rose and with the crimson birthmark stamped upon her cheek. Not even Aylmer now hated it so much as she.

To dispel the tedium of the hours which her husband found it necessary to devote to the processes of combination and analysis, Georgiana turned over the volumes of his scientific library. In many dark old tomes
350 she met with chapters full of romance and poetry. They were the works of the philosophers of the middle ages, such as Albertus Magnus, Cornelius Agrippa, Paracelsus, and the famous friar who created the prophetic Brazen Head. All these antique naturalists stood in advance of their centuries, yet were imbued with some of their credulity, and therefore were believed, and perhaps imagined themselves to have acquired from the investigation of Nature a power above Nature, and from physics a sway over the spiritual world. Hardly less curious and imaginative were the early volumes of the Transactions of the Royal Society, in which the members, knowing little of the limits of natural possibility, were continually record-
360 ing wonders or proposing methods whereby wonders might be wrought.

But to Georgiana the most engrossing volume was a large folio from her husband's own hand, in which he had recorded every experiment of his scientific career, its original aim, the methods adopted for its development, and its final success or failure, with the circumstances to which either event was attributable. The book, in truth, was both the history and emblem of his ardent, ambitious, imaginative, yet practical and laborious life. He handled physical details as if there were nothing beyond them;

yet spiritualized them all, and redeemed himself from materialism by his
strong and eager aspiration towards the infinite. In his grasp the veriest
370 clod of earth assumed a soul. Georgiana, as she read, reverenced Aylmer
and loved him more profoundly than ever, but with a less entire dependence on his judgment than heretofore. Much as he had accomplished, she
could not but observe that his most splendid successes were almost invariably failures, if compared with the ideal at which he aimed. His brightest
diamonds were the merest pebbles, and felt to be so by himself, in comparison with the inestimable gems which lay hidden beyond his reach.
The volume, rich with achievements that had won renown for its author,
was yet as melancholy a record as ever mortal hand had penned. It was
the sad confession and continual exemplification of the shortcomings of
380 the composite man, the spirit burdened with clay and working in matter,
and of the despair that assails the higher nature at finding itself so miserably thwarted by the earthly part. Perhaps every man of genius in whatever sphere might recognize the image of his own experience in Aylmer's
journal.

So deeply did these reflections affect Georgiana that she laid her
face upon the open volume and burst into tears. In this situation she
was found by her husband.

"It is dangerous to read in a sorcerer's books," said he with a smile,
though his countenance was uneasy and displeased. "Georgiana, there
390 are pages in that volume which I can scarcely glance over and keep my
senses. Take heed lest it prove as detrimental to you."

"It has made me worship you more than ever," said she.

"Ah, wait for this one success," rejoined he, "then worship me if you
will. I shall deem myself hardly unworthy of it. But come, I have sought
you for the luxury of your voice. Sing to me, dearest."

So she poured out the liquid music of her voice to quench the thirst of
his spirit. He then took his leave with a boyish exuberance of gaiety, as-
suring her that her seclusion would endure but a little longer, and that
the result was already certain. Scarcely had he departed when Georgiana
400 felt irresistibly impelled to follow him. She had forgotten to inform
Aylmer of a symptom which for two or three hours past had begun to excite her attention. It was a sensation in the fatal birthmark, not painful,
but which induced a restlessness throughout her system. Hastening after
her husband, she intruded for the first time into the laboratory.

The first thing that struck her eye was the furnace, that hot and feverish worker, with the intense glow of its fire, which by the quantities of
soot clustered above it seemed to have been burning for ages. There was a
distilling apparatus in full operation. Around the room were retorts,
tubes, cylinders, crucibles, and other apparatus of chemical research. An
410 electrical machine stood ready for immediate use. The atmosphere felt
oppressively close, and was tainted with gaseous odors which had been
tormented forth by the processes of science. The severe and homely simplicity of the apartment, with its naked walls and brick pavement, looked
strange, accustomed as Georgiana had become to the fantastic elegance of

her boudoir. But what chiefly, indeed almost solely, drew her attention, was the aspect of Aylmer himself.

He was pale as death, anxious and absorbed, and hung over the furnace as if it depended upon his utmost watchfulness whether the liquid which it was distilling should be the draught of immortal happiness or 420 misery. How different from the sanguine and joyous mien that he had assumed for Georgiana's encouragement!

"Carefully now, Aminadab; carefully, thou human machine; carefully, thou man of clay!" muttered Aylmer, more to himself than his assistant. "Now, if there be a thought too much or too little, it is all over."

"Ho! ho!" mumbled Aminadab. "Look, master! look!"

Aylmer raised his eyes hastily, and at first reddened, then grew paler than ever, on beholding Georgiana. He rushed towards her and seized her arm with a gripe that left the print of his fingers upon it.

"Why do you come hither? Have you no trust in your husband?" 430 cried he impetuously. "Would you throw the blight of that fatal birthmark over my labors? It is not well done. Go, prying woman, go!"

"Nay, Aylmer," said Georgiana with the firmness of which she possessed no stinted endowment, "it is not you that have a right to complain. You mistrust your wife; you have concealed the anxiety with which you watch the development of this experiment. Think not so unworthily of me, my husband. Tell me all the risk we run, and fear not that I shall shrink; for my share in it is far less than your own."

"No, no, Georgiana!" said Aylmer impatiently; "it must not be."

"I submit," replied she calmly. "And, Aylmer, I shall quaff whatever 440 draught you bring me; but it will be on the same principle that would induce me to take a dose of poison if offered by your hand."

"My noble wife," said Aylmer, deeply moved, "I knew not the height and depth of your nature until now. Nothing shall be concealed. Know, then, that this crimson hand, superficial as it seems, has clutched its grasp into your being with a strength of which I had no previous conception. I have already administered agents powerful enough to do aught except to change your entire physical system. Only one thing remains to be tried. If that fail us we are ruined."

"Why did you hesitate to tell me this?" asked she.

450   "Because, Georgiana," said Aylmer in a low voice, "there is danger."

"Danger? There is but one danger—that this horrible stigma shall be left upon my cheek!" cried Georgiana. "Remove it, remove it, whatever be the cost, or we shall both go mad!"

"Heaven knows your words are too true," said Aylmer sadly. "And now, dearest, return to your boudoir. In a little while all will be tested."

He conducted her back and took leave of her with a solemn tenderness which spoke far more than his words how much was now at stake. After his departure Georgiana became rapt in musings. She considered the character of Aylmer, and did it completer justice than at any previ-
460 ous moment. Her heart exulted, while it trembled, at his honorable love—so pure and lofty that it would accept nothing less than perfection

nor miserably make itself contented with an earthlier nature than he had dreamed of. She felt how much more precious was such a sentiment than that meaner kind which would have borne with the imperfection for her sake, and have been guilty of treason to holy love by degrading its perfect idea to the level of the actual; and with her whole spirit she prayed that, for a single moment, she might satisfy his highest and deepest conception. Longer than one moment she well knew it could not be; for his spirit was ever on the march, ever ascending, and each instant
470 required something that was beyond the scope of the instant before.

The sound of her husband's footsteps aroused her. He bore a crystal goblet containing a liquor colorless as water, but bright enough to be the draught of immortality. Aylmer was pale; but it seemed rather the consequence of a highly wrought state of mind and tension of spirit than of fear or doubt.

"The concoction of the draught has been perfect," said he, in answer to Georgiana's look. "Unless all my science have deceived me, it cannot fail."

"Save on your account, my dearest Aylmer," observed his wife, "I
480 might wish to put off this birthmark of mortality by relinquishing mortality itself in preference to any other mode. Life is but a sad possession to those who have attained precisely the degree of moral advancement at which I stand. Were I weaker and blinder it might be happiness. Were I stronger, it might be endured hopefully. But, being what I find myself, methinks I am of all mortals the most fit to die."

"You are fit for heaven without tasting death!" replied her husband. "But why do we speak of dying? The draught cannot fail. Behold its effect upon this plant."

On the window seat there stood a geranium diseased with yellow
490 blotches, which had overspread all its leaves. Aylmer poured a small quantity of the liquid upon the soil in which it grew. In a little time, when the roots of the plant had taken up the moisture, the unsightly blotches began to be extinguished in a living verdure.

"There needed no proof," said Georgiana quietly. "Give me the goblet. I joyfully stake all upon your word."

"Drink, then, thou lofty creature!" exclaimed Aylmer, with fervid admiration. "There is no taint of imperfection on thy spirit. Thy sensible frame, too, shall soon be all perfect."

She quaffed the liquid and returned the goblet to his hand.
500   "It is grateful," said she, with a placid smile. "Methinks it is like water from a heavenly fountain; for it contains I know not what of unobtrusive fragrance and deliciousness. It allays a feverish thirst that had parched me for many days. Now, dearest, let me sleep. My earthly senses are closing over my spirit like the leaves around the heart of a rose at sunset."

She spoke the last words with a gentle reluctance, as if it required almost more energy than she could command to pronounce the faint and lingering syllables. Scarcely had they loitered through her lips ere she was lost in slumber. Aylmer sat by her side, watching her aspect

with the emotions proper to a man the whole value of whose existence
510 was involved in the process now to be tested. Mingled with this mood,
however, was the philosophic investigation characteristic of the man of
science. Not the minutest symptom escaped him. A heightened flush of
the cheek, a slight irregularity of breath, a quiver of the eyelid, a hardly
perceptible tremor through the frame,—such were the details which, as
the moments passed, he wrote down in his folio volume. Intense
thought had set its stamp upon every previous page of that volume, but
the thoughts of years were all concentrated upon the last.

While thus employed, he failed not to gaze often at the fatal hand,
and not without a shudder. Yet once, by a strange and unaccountable
520 impulse, he pressed it with his lips. His spirit recoiled, however, in the
very act; and Georgiana, out of the midst of her deep sleep, moved uneasily and murmured as if in remonstrance. Again Aylmer resumed his
watch. Nor was it without avail. The crimson hand, which at first had
been strongly visible upon the marble paleness of Georgiana's cheek,
now grew more faintly outlined. She remained not less pale than ever;
but the birthmark, with every breath that came and went, lost somewhat
of it former distinctness. Its presence had been awful; its departure was
more awful still. Watch the stain of the rainbow fading out of the sky,
and you will know how that mysterious symbol passed away.
530 "By Heaven! it is well-nigh gone!" said Aylmer to himself, in almost
irrepressible ecstasy. "I can scarcely trace it now. Success! success! And
now it is like the faintest rose color. The lightest flush of blood across
her cheek would overcome it. But she is so pale!"

He drew aside the window curtain and suffered the light of natural
day to fall into the room and rest upon her cheek. At the same time he
heard a gross, hoarse chuckle, which he had long known as his servant
Aminadab's expression of delight.

"Ah, clod! ah, earthly mass!" cried Aylmer, laughing in a sort of
frenzy, "you have served me well! Matter and spirit—earth and heaven—
540 have both done their part in this! Laugh, thing of the senses! You have
earned the right to laugh."

These exclamations broke Georgiana's sleep. She slowly unclosed her
eyes and gazed into the mirror which her husband had arranged for that
purpose. A faint smile flitted over her lips when she recognized how
barely perceptible was now that crimson hand which had once blazed
forth with such disastrous brilliancy as to scare away all their happiness. But then her eyes sought Aylmer's face with a trouble and anxiety
that he could by no means account for.

"My poor Aylmer!" murmured she.
550 "Poor? Nay, richest, happiest, most favored!" exclaimed he. "My
peerless bride, it is successful! You are perfect!"

"My poor Aylmer," she repeated, with a more than human tenderness, "you have aimed loftily; you have done nobly. Do not repent that
with so high and pure a feeling, you have rejected the best the earth
could offer. Aylmer, dearest Aylmer, I am dying!"

Alas! it was too true! The fatal hand had grappled with the mystery of life, and was the bond by which an angelic spirit kept itself in union with a mortal frame. As the last crimson tint of the birthmark—that sole token of human imperfection—faded from her cheek, the parting breath
560 of the now perfect woman passed into the atmosphere, and her soul, lingering a moment near her husband, took its heavenward flight. Then a hoarse, chuckling laugh was heard again! Thus ever does the gross fatality of earth exult in its invariable triumph over the immortal essence which, in this dim sphere of half development, demands the completeness of a higher state. Yet, had Aylmer reached a profounder wisdom, he need not thus have flung away the happiness which would have woven his mortal life of the selfsame texture with the celestial. The momentary circumstance was too strong for him; he failed to look beyond the shadowy scope of time, and, living once for all in eternity, to find the perfect
570 future in the present.

HERMAN MELVILLE (1819–1891)

Bartleby the Scrivener
A Story of Wall Street
(1853)

I am a rather elderly man. The nature of my avocations, for the last thirty years, has brought me into more than ordinary contact with what would seem an interesting and somewhat singular set of men, of whom, as yet, nothing, that I know of, has ever been written—I mean, the law-copyists, or scriveners. I have known very many of them, professionally and privately, and, if I pleased, could relate divers histories, at which good-natured gentlemen might smile, and sentimental souls might weep. But I waive the biographies of all other scriveners, for a few passages in the life of Bartleby, who was a scrivener, the strangest I ever saw, or heard of.
10 While, of other law-copyists, I might write the complete life, of Bartleby nothing of that sort can be done. I believe that no materials exist for a full and satisfactory biography of this man. It is an irreparable loss to literature. Bartleby was one of those beings of whom nothing is ascertainable, except from the original sources, and, in his case, those are very small. What my own astonished eyes saw of Bartleby, *that* is all I know of him, except, indeed, one vague report, which will appear in the sequel.

Ere introducing the scrivener, as he first appeared to me, it is fit I make some mention of myself, my employees, my business, my chambers, and general surroundings; because some such description is indispens-
20 able to an adequate understanding of the chief character about to be presented. Imprimis: I am a man who, from his youth upwards, has been filled with a profound conviction that the easiest way of life is the best. Hence, though I belong to a profession proverbially energetic and nervous, even to turbulence, at times, yet nothing of that sort have I ever suffered to invade my peace. I am one of those unambitious lawyers who

never addresses a jury, or in any way draws down public applause; but, in the cool tranquillity of a snug retreat, do a snug business among rich men's bonds, and mortgages, and title-deeds. All who know me, consider me an eminently *safe* man. The late John Jacob Astor, a personage little
30 given to poetic enthusiasm, had no hesitation in pronouncing my first grand point to be prudence; my next, method. I do not speak it in vanity, but simply record the fact, that I was not unemployed in my profession by the late John Jacob Astor; a name which, I admit, I love to repeat; for it hath a rounded and orbicular sound to it, and rings like unto bullion. I will freely add, that I was not insensible to the late John Jacob Astor's good opinion.

Some time prior to the period at which this little history begins, my avocations had been largely increased. The good old office, now extinct in the State of New York, of a Master in Chancery, had been conferred upon
40 me. It was not a very arduous office, but very pleasantly remunerative. I seldom lose my temper; much more seldom indulge in dangerous indignation at wrongs and outrages; but, I must be permitted to be rash here, and declare that I consider the sudden and violent abrogation of the office of Master in Chancery, by the new Constitution, as a—premature act; inasmuch as I had counted upon a life-lease of the profits, whereas I only received those of a few short years. But this is by the way.

My chambers were up stairs, at No._____ Wall Street. At one end, they looked upon the white wall of the interior of a spacious skylight shaft, penetrating the building from top to bottom.
50 This view might have been considered rather tame than otherwise, deficient in what landscape painters call "life." But, if so, the view from the other end of my chambers offered, at least, a contrast, if nothing more. In that direction, my windows commanded an unobstructed view of a lofty brick wall, black by age and everlasting shade; which wall required no spyglass to bring out its lurking beauties, but, for the benefit of all near-sighted spectators, was pushed up to within ten feet of my window panes. Owing to the great height of the surrounding buildings, and my chambers being on the second floor, the interval between this wall and mine not a little resembled a huge square cistern.
60 At the period just preceding the advent of Bartleby, I had two persons as copyists in my employment, and a promising lad as an office-boy. First, Turkey; second, Nippers; third, Ginger Nut. These may seem names, the like of which are not usually found in the Directory. In truth, they were nicknames, mutually conferred upon each other by my three clerks, and were deemed expressive of their respective persons or characters. Turkey was a short, pursy Englishman, of about my own age—that is, somewhere not far from sixty. In the morning, one might say, his face was of a fine florid hue, but after twelve o'clock, meridian—his dinner hour—it blazed like a grate full of Christmas coals; and continued blazing—but, as it
70 were, with a gradual wane—till six o'clock P.M., or thereabouts; after which, I saw no more of the proprietor of the face, which, gaining its meridian with the sun, seemed to set with it, to rise, culminate, and decline

the following day, with the like regularity and undiminished glory. There
are many singular coincidences I have known in the course of my life, not
the least among which was the fact, that, exactly when Turkey displayed
his fullest beams from his red and radiant countenance, just then, too, at
that critical moment, began the daily period when I considered his business capacities as seriously disturbed for the remainder of the twenty-
four hours. Not that he was absolutely idle, or averse to business, then; far
80 from it. The difficulty was, he was apt to be altogether too energetic.
There was a strange, inflamed, flurried, flighty recklessness of activity
about him. He would be incautious in dipping his pen into his inkstand.
All his blots upon my documents were dropped there after twelve o'clock
meridian. Indeed, not only would he be reckless, and sadly given to making blots in the afternoon, but, some days, he went further, and was rather
noisy. At such times, too, his face flamed with augmented blazonry, as if
cannel coal had been heaped on anthracite. He made an unpleasant racket
with his chair; spilled his sand-box; in mending his pens, impatiently
split them all to pieces, and threw them on the floor in a sudden passion;
90 stood up, and leaned over his table, boxing his papers about in a most in-
decorous manner, very sad to behold in an elderly man like him. Nevertheless, as he was in many ways a most valuable person to me, and all
the time before twelve o'clock meridian, was the quickest, steadiest creature, too, accomplishing a great deal of work in a style not easily to be
matched—for these reasons, I was willing to overlook his eccentricities,
though, indeed, occasionally, I remonstrated with him. I did this very
gently, however, because, though the civilest, nay, the blandest and most
reverential of men in the morning, yet, in the afternoon, he was disposed,
upon provocation, to be slightly rash with his tongue—in fact, insolent.
100 Now, valuing his morning services as I did, and resolved not to lose
them—yet, at the same time, made uncomfortable by his inflamed ways
after twelve o'clock—and being a man of peace, unwilling by my admoni-
tions to call forth unseemly retorts from him, I took upon me, one Saturday noon (he was always worse on Saturdays) to hint to him, very kindly,
that, perhaps, now that he was growing old, it might be well to abridge
his labors; in short, he need not come to my chambers after twelve
o'clock, but, dinner over, had best go home to his lodgings, and rest himself till tea-time. But no; he insisted upon his afternoon devotions. His
countenance became intolerably fervid, as he oratorically assured me—
110 gesticulating with a long ruler at the other end of the room—that if
his services in the morning were useful, how indispensable, then, in the
afternoon?

   "With submission, sir," said Turkey, on this occasion, "I consider myself your right-hand man. In the morning I but marshal and deploy
my columns; but in the afternoon I put myself at their head, and gallantly
charge the foe, thus"—and he made a violent thrust with the ruler.

   "But the blots, Turkey," intimated I.

   "True; but, with submission, sir, behold these hairs! I am getting
old. Surely, sir, a blot or two of a warm afternoon is not to be severely

120 urged against gray hairs. Old age—even if it blot the page—is honorable. With submission, sir, we *both* are getting old."

This appeal to my fellow-feeling was hardly to be resisted. At all events, I saw that go he would not. So, I made up my mind to let him stay, resolving, nevertheless, to see to it that, during the afternoon, he had to do with my less important papers.

Nippers, the second on my list, was a whiskered, sallow, and, upon the whole, rather piratical-looking young man, of about five and twenty. I always deemed him the victim of two evil powers—ambition and indigestion.

130 The ambition was evinced by a certain impatience of the duties of a mere copyist, an unwarrantable usurpation of strictly professional affairs, such as the original drawing up of legal documents. The indigestion seemed betokened in an occasional nervous testiness and grinning irritability, causing the teeth to audibly grind together over mistakes committed in copying; unnecessary maledictions, hissed, rather than spoken, in the heat of business; and especially by a continual discontent with the height of the table where he worked. Though of a very ingenious, mechanical turn, Nippers could never get this table to suit him. He put chips under it, blocks of various sorts, bits of pasteboard, and at last went so far as to attempt an exquisite adjustment, by final pieces of folded blotting-

140 paper. But no invention would answer. If, for the sake of easing his back, he brought the table lid at a sharp angle well up towards his chin, and wrote there like a man using the steep roof of a Dutch house for his desk, then he declared that it stopped the circulation in his arms. If now he lowered the table to his waistbands, and stooped over it in writing, then there was a sore aching in his back. In short, the truth of the matter was, Nippers knew not what he wanted. Or, if he wanted anything, it was to be rid of a scrivener's table altogether. Among the manifestations of his diseased ambition was a fondness he had for receiving visits from certain ambiguous-looking fellows in seedy coats, whom he called his clients. In-

150 deed, I was aware that not only was he, at times, considerable of a ward-politician, but he occasionally did a little business at the Justices' courts, and was not unknown on the steps of the Tombs. I have good reason to believe, however, that one individual who called upon him at my chambers, and who, with a grand air, he insisted was his client, was no other than a dun, and the alleged title-deed, a bill. But, with all his failings, and the annoyances he caused me, Nippers, like his compatriot Turkey, was a very useful man to me; wrote a neat, swift hand; and, when he chose, was not deficient in a gentlemanly sort of deportment. Added to this, he always dressed in a gentlemanly sort of way; and so, incidentally,

160 reflected credit upon my chambers. Whereas, with respect to Turkey, I had much ado to keep him from being a reproach to me. His clothes were apt to look oily, and smell of eating houses. He wore his pantaloons very loose and baggy in summer. His coats were execrable; his hat not to be handled. But while the hat was a thing of indifference to me, inasmuch as his natural civility and deference, as a dependent Englishman, always led him to doff it the moment he entered the room, yet his coat was another

matter. Concerning his coats, I reasoned with him; but with no effect. The truth was, I suppose, that a man with so small an income could not afford to sport such a lustrous face and a lustrous coat at one and the same time.
170 As Nippers once observed, Turkey's money went chiefly for red ink. One winter day, I presented Turkey with a highly respectable-looking coat of my own—a padded gray coat, of a most comfortable warmth, and which buttoned straight up from the knee to the neck. I thought Turkey would appreciate the favor, and abate his rashness and obstreperousness of afternoons. But no; I verily believe that buttoning himself up in so downy and blanket-like a coat had a pernicious effect upon him—upon the same principle that too much oats are bad for horses. In fact, precisely as a rash, restive horse is said to feel his oats, so Turkey felt his coat. It made him insolent. He was a man whom prosperity harmed.
180   Though, concerning the self-indulgent habits of Turkey, I had my own private surmises, yet, touching Nippers, I was well persuaded that, whatever might be his faults in other respects, he was, at least, a temperate young man. But, indeed, nature herself seemed to have been his vintner, and, at his birth, charged him so thoroughly with an irritable, brandy-like disposition, that all subsequent potations were needless. When I consider how, amid the stillness of my chambers, Nippers would sometimes impatiently rise from his seat, and stooping over his table, spread his arms wide apart, seize the whole desk, and move it, and jerk it, with a grim, grinding motion on the floor, as if the table were a perverse voluntary
190 agent and vexing him, I plainly perceive that, for Nippers, brandy-and-water were altogether superfluous.
    It was fortunate for me that, owing to its peculiar cause—indigestion—the irritability and consequent nervousness of Nippers were mainly observable in the morning, while in the afternoon he was comparatively mild. So that, Turkey's paroxysms only coming on about twelve o'clock, I never had to do with their eccentricities at one time. Their fits relieved each other, like guards. When Nipper's was on, Turkey's was off; and *vice versa.* This was a good natural arrangement, under the circumstances.
    Ginger Nut, the third on my list, was a lad, some twelve years old. His
200 father was a car-man, ambitious of seeing his son on the bench instead of a cart, before he died. So he sent him to my office, as student at law, errand-boy, cleaner and sweeper, at the rate of one dollar a week. He had a little desk to himself; but he did not use it much. Upon inspection, the drawer exhibited a great array of the shells of various sorts of nuts. Indeed, to this quick-witted youth, the whole noble science of the law was contained in a nutshell. Not the least among the employments of Ginger Nut, as well as one which he discharged with the alacrity, was his duty as cake and apple purveyor for Turkey and Nippers. Copying law-papers being proverbially a dry, husky sort of business, my two scriveners were
210 fain to moisten their mouths very often with Spitzenbergs, to be had at the numerous stalls nigh the Custom House and Post Office. Also, they sent Ginger Nut very frequently for that peculiar cake—small, flat, round, and very spicy—after which he had been named by them. Of a cold

morning, when business was but dull, Turkey would gobble up scores of these cakes, as if they were mere wafers—indeed, they sell them at the rate of six or eight for a penny—the scrape of his pen blending with the crunching of the crisp particles in his mouth. Rashest of all the fiery afternoon blunders and flurried rashnesses of Turkey, was his once moistening a ginger-cake between his lips, and clapping it on to a mortgage, for
220 a seal. I came within an ace of dismissing him then. But he mollified me by making an oriental bow, and saying—

"With submission, sir, it was generous of me to find you in stationery on my own account."

Now my original business—that of a conveyancer and title hunter, and drawer-up of recondite documents of all sorts—was considerably increased by receiving the master's office. There was now great work for scriveners. Not only must I push the clerks already with me, but I must have additional help.

In answer to my advertisement, a motionless young man one morning
230 stood upon my office threshold, the door being open, for it was summer. I can see that figure now—pallidly neat, pitiably respectable, incurably forlorn! It was Bartleby.

After a few words touching his qualifications, I engaged him, glad to have among my corps of copyists a man of so singularly sedate an aspect, which I thought might operate beneficially upon the flighty temper of Turkey, and the fiery one of Nippers.

I should have stated before that ground glass folding-doors divided my premises into two parts, one of which was occupied by my scriveners, the other by myself. According to my humor, I threw open these doors, or
240 closed them. I resolved to assign Bartleby a corner by the folding-doors, but on my side of them, so as to have this quiet man within easy call, in case any trifling thing was to be done. I placed his desk close up to a small side-window in that part of the room, a window which originally had afforded a lateral view of certain grimy backyards and bricks, but which, owing to subsequent erections, commanded at present no view at all, though it gave some light. Within three feet of the panes was a wall, and the light came down from far above, between two lofty buildings, as from a very small opening in a dome. Still further to a satisfactory arrangement, I procured a high green folding screen, which might entirely
250 isolate Bartleby from my sight, though not remove him from my voice. And thus, in a manner, privacy and society were conjoined.

At first, Bartleby did an extraordinary quantity of writing. As if long famishing for something to copy, he seemed to gorge himself on my documents. There was no pause for digestion. He ran a day and night line, copying by sun-light and by candle-light. I should have been quite delighted with his application, had he been cheerfully industrious. But he wrote on silently, palely, mechanically.

It is, of course, an indispensable part of a scrivener's business to verify the accuracy of his copy, word by word. Where there are two or more
260 scriveners in an office, they assist each other in this examination, one

reading from the copy, the other holding the original. It is a very dull, wearisome, and lethargic affair. I can readily imagine that, to some sanguine temperaments, it would be altogether intolerable. For example, I cannot credit that the mettlesome poet, Byron, would have contentedly sat down with Bartleby to examine a law document of, say five hundred pages, closely written in a crimpy hand.

Now and then, in the haste of business, it had been my habit to assist in comparing some brief document myself, calling Turkey or Nippers for this purpose. One object I had, in placing Bartleby so handy to me behind
270 the screen, was to avail myself of his services on such trivial occasions. It was on the third day, I think, of his being with me, and before any necessity had arisen for having his own writing examined, that, being much hurried to complete a small affair I had in hand, I abruptly called to Bartleby. In my haste and natural expectancy of instant compliance, I sat with my head bent over the original on my desk, and my right hand sideways, and somewhat nervously extended with the copy, so that, immediately upon emerging from his retreat, Bartleby might snatch it and proceed to business without the least delay.

In this very attitude did I sit when I called to him, rapidly stating
280 what it was I wanted him to do—namely, to examine a small paper with me. Imagine my surprise, nay, my consternation, when, without moving from his privacy, Bartleby, in a singularly mild, firm voice, replied, "I would prefer not to."

I sat awhile in perfect silence, rallying my stunned faculties. Immediately it occurred to me that my ears had deceived me, or Bartleby had entirely misunderstood my meaning. I repeated my request in the clearest tone I could assume; but in quite as clear a one came the previous reply, "I would prefer not to."

"Prefer not to," echoed I, rising in high excitement, and crossing the
290 room with a stride. "What do you mean? Are you moon-struck? I want you to help me compare this sheet here—take it," and I thrust it towards him.

"I would prefer not to," said he.

I looked at him steadfastly. His face was leanly composed; his gray eye dimly calm. Not a wrinkle of agitation rippled him. Had there been the least uneasiness, anger, impatience, or impertinence in his manner; in other words, had there been any thing ordinarily human about him, doubtless I should have violently dismissed him from the premises. But as it was, I should have as soon thought of turning my pale plaster-of-paris
300 bust of Cicero out of doors. I stood gazing at him awhile, as he went on with his own writing, and then reseated myself at my desk. This is very strange, thought I. What had one best do? But my business hurried me. I concluded to forget the matter for the present, reserving it for my future leisure. So calling Nippers from the other room, the paper was speedily examined.

A few days after this, Bartleby concluded four lengthy documents, being quadruplicates of a week's testimony taken before me in my High

Court of Chancery. It became necessary to examine them. It was an important suit, and great accuracy was imperative. Having all things arranged, I called Turkey, Nippers, and Ginger Nut from the next room, meaning to place the four copies in the hands of my four clerks, while I should read from the original. Accordingly, Turkey, Nippers, and Ginger Nut had taken their seats in a row, each with his document in his hand, when I called to Bartleby to join this interesting group.

"Bartleby! quick, I am waiting."

I heard a slow scrape of his chair legs on the uncarpeted floor, and soon he appeared standing at the entrance of his hermitage.

"What is wanted?" said he, mildly.

"The copies, the copies," said I, hurriedly. "We are going to examine them. There—" and I held towards him the fourth quadruplicate.

"I would prefer not to," he said, and gently disappeared behind the screen.

For a few moments I was turned into a pillar of salt, standing at the head of my seated column of clerks. Recovering myself, I advanced towards the screen, and demanded the reason for such extraordinary conduct.

"*Why* do you refuse?"

"I would prefer not to."

With any other man I should have flown outright into a dreadful passion, scorned all further words, and thrust him ignominiously from my presence. But there was something about Bartleby that not only strangely disarmed me, but in a wonderful manner, touched and disconcerted me. I began to reason with him.

"These are your own copies we are about to examine. It is labor saving to you, because one examination will answer for your four papers. It is common usage. Every copyist is bound to help examine his copy. Is it not so? Will you not speak? Answer!"

"I prefer not to," he replied in a flutelike tone. It seemed to me that, while I had been addressing him, he carefully revolved every statement that I made; fully comprehended the meaning; could not gainsay the irresistible conclusion; but, at the same time, some paramount consideration prevailed with him to reply as he did.

"You are decided, then, not to comply with my request—a request made according to common usage and common sense?"

He briefly gave me to understand, that on that point my judgment was sound. Yes: his decision was irreversible.

It is not seldom the case that, when a man is browbeaten in some unprecedented and violently unreasonable way, he begins to stagger in his own plainest faith. He begins, as it were, vaguely to surmise that, wonderful as it may be, all the justice and all the reason is on the other side. Accordingly, if any disinterested persons are present, he turns to them for some reinforcement of his own faltering mind.

"Turkey," said I, "what do you think of this? Am I not right?"

"With submission, sir," said Turkey, in his blandest tone, "I think that you are."

"Nippers," said I, "what do *you* think of it?"

"I think I should kick him out of the office."

(The reader, of nice perceptions, will here perceive that, it being morning, Turkey's answer is couched in polite and tranquil terms, but Nippers replies in ill-tempered ones. Or, to repeat a previous sen-
360 tence, Nipper's ugly mood was on duty, and Turkey's off.)

"Ginger Nut," said I, willing to enlist the smallest suffrage in my behalf, "what do *you* think of it?"

"I think, sir, he's a little *luny*," replied Ginger Nut, with a grin.

"You hear what they say," said I, turning towards the screen, "come forth and do your duty."

But he vouchsafed no reply. I pondered a moment in sore perplexity. But once more business hurried me. I determined again to postpone the consideration of this dilemma to my future leisure. With a little trouble we made out to examine the papers without Bartleby, though at every
370 page or two Turkey deferentially dropped his opinion, that this proceeding was quite out of the common; while Nippers, twitching in his chair with a dyspeptic nervousness, ground out, between his set teeth, occasional hissing maledictions against the stubborn oaf behind the screen. And for his (Nipper's) part, this was the first and the last time he would do another man's business without pay.

Meanwhile Bartleby sat in his hermitage, oblivious to everything but his own peculiar business there.

Some days passed, the scrivener being employed upon another lengthy work. His late remarkable conduct led me to regard his ways nar-
380 rowly. I observed that he never went to dinner; indeed, that he never went anywhere. As yet I had never, of my personal knowledge, known him to be outside of my office. He was a perpetual sentry in the corner. At about eleven o'clock though, in the morning, I noticed that Ginger Nut would advance toward the opening in Bartleby's screen, as if silently beckoned thither by a gesture invisible to me where I sat. The boy would then leave the office, jingling a few pence, and reappear with a handful of ginger-nuts, which he delivered in the hermitage, receiving two of the cakes for his trouble.

He lives, then, on ginger-nuts, thought I; never eats a dinner, properly
390 speaking; he must be a vegetarian, then; but no; he never eats even vegetables; he eats nothing but ginger-nuts. My mind then ran on in reveries concerning the probable effects upon the human constitution of living entirely on ginger-nuts. Ginger-nuts are so called, because they contain ginger as one of their peculiar constituents, and the final flavoring one. Now, what was ginger? A hot, spicy thing. Was Bartleby hot and spicy? Not at all. Ginger, then, had no effect upon Bartleby. Probably he preferred it should have none.

Nothing so aggravates an earnest person as a passive resistance. If the individual so resisted be of a not inhumane temper, and the resisting one
400 perfectly harmless in his passivity, then, in the better moods of the former, he will endeavor charitably to construe to his imagination what proves impossible to be solved by his judgment. Even so, for the most part,

I regarded Bartleby and his ways. Poor fellow! thought I, he means no mischief; it is plain he intends no insolence; his aspect sufficiently evinces that his eccentricities are involuntary. He is useful to me. I can get along with him. If I turn him away, the chances are he will fall in with some less-indulgent employer, and then he will be rudely treated, and perhaps driven forth miserably to starve. Yes. Here I can cheaply purchase a delicious self-approval. To befriend Bartleby; to humor him in his
410 strange willfulness, will cost me little or nothing, while I lay up in my soul what will eventually prove a sweet morsel for my conscience. But this mood was not invariable with me. The passiveness of Bartleby sometimes irritated me. I felt strangely goaded on to encounter him in new opposition—to elicit some angry spark from him answerable to my own. But, indeed, I might as well have essayed to strike fire with my knuckles against a bit of Windsor soap. But one afternoon the evil impulse in me mastered me, and the following little scene ensued:

"Bartleby," said I, "when those papers are all copied, I will compare them with you."
420 "I would prefer not to."

"How? Surely you do not mean to persist in that mulish vagary?"

No answer.

I threw open the folding-doors near by, and, turning upon Turkey and Nippers, exclaimed:

"Bartleby a second time says, he won't examine his papers. What do you think of it, Turkey?"

It was afternoon, be it remembered. Turkey sat glowing like a brass boiler; his bald head steaming; his hands reeling among his blotted papers.

"Think of it?" roared Turkey; "I think I'll just step behind his
430 screen, and black his eyes for him!"

So saying, Turkey rose to his feet and threw his arms into a pugilistic position. He was hurrying away to make good his promise, when I detained him, alarmed at the effect of incautiously rousing Turkey's combativeness after dinner.

"Sit down, Turkey," said I, "and hear what Nippers has to say. What do you think of it, Nippers? Would I not be justified in immediately dismissing Bartleby?"

"Excuse me, that is for you to decide, sir. I think his conduct quite unusual, and, indeed, unjust, as regards Turkey and myself. But it may
440 only be a passing whim."

"Ah," exclaimed I, "you have strangely changed your mind, then—you speak very gently of him now."

"All beer," cried Turkey; "gentleness is effects of beer—Nippers and I dined together to-day. You see how gentle *I* am, sir. Shall I go and black his eyes?"

"You refer to Bartleby, I suppose. No, not to-day, Turkey," I replied; "pray, put up your fists."

I closed the doors, and again advanced towards Bartleby. I felt additional incentives tempting me to my fate. I burned to be rebelled against
450 again. I remembered that Bartleby never left the office.

"Bartleby," said I,"Ginger Nut is away; just step around to the Post Office, won't you? (it was but a three minutes' walk), and see if there is anything for me."

"I would prefer not to."

"You *will* not?"

"I *prefer* not."

I staggered to my desk, and sat there in a deep study. My blind inveteracy returned. Was there any other thing in which I could procure myself to be ignominiously repulsed by this lean, penniless wight?—my
460 hired clerk? What added thing is there, perfectly reasonable, that he will be sure to refuse to do? "Bartleby!"

No answer.

"Bartleby," in a louder tone.

No answer.

"Bartleby," I roared.

Like a very ghost, agreeably to the laws of magical invocation, at the third summons, he appeared at the entrance of his hermitage.

"Go to the next room, and tell Nippers to come to me."

"I prefer not to," he respectfully and slowly said and mildly disap-
470 peared.

"Very good, Bartleby," said I, in a quiet sort of serenely-severe, self-possessed tone, intimating the unalterable purpose of some terrible retribution very close at hand. At the moment I half intended something of the kind. But upon the whole, as it was drawing towards my dinner-hour, I thought it best to put on my hat and walk home for the day, suffering much from perplexity and distress of mind.

Shall I acknowledge it? The conclusion of this whole business was, that it soon became a fixed fact of my chambers, that a pale young scrivener, by the name of Bartleby, had a desk there; that he copied for me at the usual
480 rate of four cents a folio (one hundred words); but he was permanently exempt from examining the work done by him, that duty being transferred to Turkey and Nippers, out of compliment, doubtless, to their superior acuteness; moreover, said Bartleby was never, on any account, to be dispatched on the most trivial errand of any sort; and that even if entreated to take upon him such a matter, it was generally understood that he would "prefer not to"—in other words, that he would refuse point-blank.

As days passed on, I became considerably reconciled to Bartleby. His steadiness, his freedom from all dissipation, his incessant industry (except when he chose to throw himself into a standing revery behind his
490 screen), his great stillness, his unalterableness of demeanor under all circumstances, made him a valuable acquisition. One prime thing was this— *he was always there*—first in the morning, continually through the day, and the last at night. I had a singular confidence in his honesty. I felt my most precious papers perfectly safe in his hands. Sometimes, to be sure, I could not, for the very soul of me, avoid falling into sudden spasmodic passions with him. For it was exceeding difficult to bear in mind all the time those strange peculiarities, privileges, and unheard of exemptions, forming the

tacit stipulations on Bartleby's part under which he remained in my office. Now and then, in the eagerness of dispatching pressing business, I
500 would inadvertently summon Bartleby, in a short, rapid tone, to put his finger, say, on the incipient tie of a bit of red tape with which I was about compressing some papers. Of course, from behind the screen the usual answer, "I prefer not to," was sure to come; and then, how could a human creature, with the common infirmities of our nature, refrain from bitterly exclaiming upon such perverseness—such unreasonableness. However, every added repulse of this sort which I received only tended to lessen the probability of my repeating the inadvertence.

Here it must be said, that according to the custom of most legal gentlemen occupying chambers in densely-populated law buildings, there
510 were several keys to my door. One was kept by a woman residing in the attic, which person weekly scrubbed and daily swept and dusted my apartments. Another was kept by Turkey for convenience sake. The third I sometimes carried in my own pocket. The fourth I knew not who had.

Now, one Sunday morning I happened to go to Trinity Church, to hear a celebrated preacher, and finding myself rather early on the ground I thought I would walk around to my chambers for a while. Luckily I had my key with me; but upon applying it to the lock, I found it resisted by something inserted from the inside. Quite surprised, I called out; when to my consternation a key was turned from within;
520 and thrusting his lean visage at me, and holding the door ajar, the apparition of Bartleby appeared, in his shirt sleeves, and otherwise in a strangely tattered *déshabillé,* saying quietly that he was sorry, but he was deeply engaged just then, and—preferred not admitting me at present. In a brief word or two, he moreover added, that perhaps I had better walk around the block two or three times, and by that time he would probably have concluded his affairs.

Now, the utterly unsurmised appearance of Bartleby, tenanting my law-chambers of a Sunday morning, with his cadaverously gentlemanly *nonchalance,* yet withal firm and self-possessed, had such a strange effect
530 upon me, that incontinently I slunk away from my own door, and did as desired. But not without sundry twinges of impotent rebellion against the mild effrontery of this unaccountable scrivener. Indeed, it was his wonderful mildness chiefly, which not only disarmed me, but unmanned me as it were. For I consider that one, for the time, is somehow unmanned when he tranquilly permits his hired clerk to dictate to him, and order him away from his own premises. Furthermore, I was full of uneasiness as to what Bartleby could possibly be doing in my office in his shirt sleeves, and in an otherwise dismantled condition of a Sunday morning. Was anything amiss going on? Nay, that was out of the
540 question. It was not to be thought of for a moment that Bartleby was an immoral person. But what could he be doing there?—copying? Nay again, whatever might be his eccentricities, Bartleby was an eminently decorous person. He would be the last man to sit down to his desk in any state approaching to nudity. Besides, it was Sunday; and there was

something about Bartleby that forbade the supposition that he would by any secular occupation violate the proprieties of the day.

Nevertheless, my mind was not pacified; and full of a restless curiosity, at last I returned to the door. Without hindrance I inserted my key, opened it, and entered. Bartleby was not to be seen. I looked round anx-
550 iously, peeped behind his screen; but it was very plain that he was gone. Upon more closely examining the place, I surmised that for an indefinite period Bartleby must have eaten, dressed, and slept in my office, and that, too, without plate, mirror, or bed. The cushioned seat of a rickety old sofa in one corner bore the faint impress of a lean, reclining form. Rolled away under his desk, I found a blanket; under the empty grate, a blacking box and brush; on a chair, a tin basin, with soap and a ragged towel; in a newspaper a few crumbs of ginger-nuts and a morsel of cheese. Yes, thought I, it is evident enough that Bartleby has been making his home here, keeping bachelor's hall all by himself. Immediately then the thought came sweep-
560 ing across me, what miserable friendlessness and loneliness are here revealed! His poverty is great; but his solitude, how horrible! Think of it. Of a Sunday, Wall Street is deserted as Petra, and every night of every day it is an emptiness. This building, too, which of week-days hums with industry and life, at nightfall echoes with sheer vacancy, and all through Sunday is forlorn. And here Bartleby makes his home; sole spectator of a solitude which he has seen all populous—a sort of innocent and transformed Marius brooding among the ruins of Carthage!

For the first time in my life a feeling of over-powering stinging melancholy seized me. Before, I had never experienced aught but a not unpleas-
570 ing sadness. The bond of a common humanity now drew me irresistibly to gloom. A fraternal melancholy! For both I and Bartleby were sons of Adam. I remembered the bright silks and sparkling faces I had seen that day, in gala trim, swan-like sailing down the Mississippi of Broadway; and I contrasted them with the pallid copyist, and thought to myself, Ah, happiness courts the light, so we deem the world is gay; but misery hides aloof, so we deem that misery there is none. These sad fancyings— chimeras, doubtless, of a sick and silly brain—led on to other and more special thoughts, concerning the eccentricities of Bartleby. Presentiments of strange discoveries hovered round me. The scrivener's pale form ap-
580 peared to me laid out, among uncaring strangers, in its shivering winding sheet.

Suddenly I was attracted by Bartleby's closed desk, the key in open sight left in the lock.

I mean no mischief, seek the gratification of no heartless curiosity, thought I; besides, the desk is mine, and its contents, too, so I will make bold to look within. Everything was methodically arranged, the papers smoothly placed. The pigeon holes were deep, and removing the files of documents, I groped into their recesses. Presently I felt something there, and dragged it out. It was an old bandanna handkerchief, heavy
590 and knotted. I opened it, and saw it was a savings bank.

I now recalled all the quiet mysteries which I had noted in the man. I remembered that he never spoke but to answer; that, though at intervals he had considerable time to himself, yet I had never seen him reading— no, not even a newspaper; that for long periods he would stand looking out, at his pale window behind the screen, upon the dead brick wall; I was quite sure he never visited any refectory or eating house; while his pale face clearly indicated that he never drank beer like Turkey, or tea and coffee even, like other men; that he never went anywhere in particular that I could learn; never went out for a walk, unless, indeed, that was 600 the case at present; that he had declined telling who he was, or whence he came, or whether he had any relatives in the world; that though so thin and pale, he never complained of ill health. And more than all, I remembered a certain unconscious air of pallid—how shall I call it?—of pallid haughtiness, say, or rather an austere reserve about him, which had positively awed me into my tame compliance with his eccentricities, when I had feared to ask him to do the slightest incidental thing for me, even though I might know, from his long-continued motionlessness, that behind his screen he must be standing in one of those dead-wall reveries of his.

Revolving all these things, and coupling them with the recently dis- 610 covered fact, that he made my office his constant abiding place and home, and not forgetful of his morbid moodiness; revolving all these things, a prudential feeling began to steal over me. My first emotions had been those of pure melancholy and sincerest pity; but just in proportion as the forlornness of Bartleby grew and grew to my imagination, did that same melancholy merge into fear, that pity into repulsion. So true it is, and so terrible, too, that up to a certain point the thought or sight of misery enlists our best affections; but, in certain special cases, beyond that point it does not. They err who would assert that invariably this is owing to the inherent selfishness of the human heart. It rather proceeds from a certain 620 hopelessness of remedying excessive and organic ill. To a sensitive being, pity is not seldom pain. And when at last it is perceived that such pity cannot lead to effectual succor, common sense bids the soul be rid of it. What I saw that morning persuaded me that the scrivener was the victim of innate and incurable disorder. I might give alms to his body; but his body did not pain him; it was his soul that suffered, and his soul I could not reach.

I did not accomplish the purpose of going to Trinity Church that morning. Somehow, the thing I had seen disqualified me for the time from churchgoing. I walked homeward, thinking what I would do with 630 Bartleby. Finally, I resolved upon this—I would put certain calm questions to him the next morning, touching his history, etc., and if he declined to answer them openly and unreservedly (and I supposed he would prefer not), then to give him a twenty dollar bill over and above whatever I might owe him, and tell him his services were no longer required; but that if in any other way I could assist him, I would be happy to do so, especially if he desired to return to his native place, wherever that might be, I would willingly help to defray the expenses. Moreover, if, after reaching home, he found himself at any time in want of aid, a letter from him would be sure of a reply.

640   The next morning came.

"Bartleby," said I, gently calling to him behind his screen.

No reply.

"Bartleby," said I, in a still gentler tone, "come here; I am not going to ask you to do anything you would prefer not to do—I simply wish to speak to you."

Upon this he noiselessly slid into view.

"Will you tell me, Bartleby, where you were born?"

"I would prefer not to."

"Will you tell me *anything* about yourself?"

650   "I would prefer not to."

"But what reasonable objection can you have to speak to me? I feel friendly towards you."

He did not look at me while I spoke, but kept his glance fixed upon my bust of Cicero, which, as I then sat, was directly behind me, some six inches above my head.

"What is your answer, Bartleby," said I, after waiting a considerable time for a reply, during which his countenance remained immovable, only there was the faintest conceivable tremor of the white attenuated mouth.

"At present I prefer to give no answer," he said, and retired into his

660   hermitage.

It was rather weak in me I confess, but his manner, on this occasion, nettled me. Not only did there seem to lurk in it a certain calm disdain, but his perverseness seemed ungrateful, considering the undeniable good usage and indulgence he had received from me.

Again I sat ruminating what I should do. Mortified as I was at his behavior, and resolved as I had been to dismiss him when I entered my office, nevertheless I strangely felt something superstitious knocking at my heart, and forbidding me to carry out my purpose, and denouncing me for a villain if I dared to breathe one bitter word against this forlornest of

670   mankind. At last, familiarly drawing my chair behind his screen, I sat down and said: "Bartleby, never mind, then, about revealing your history; but let me entreat you, as a friend, to comply as far as may be with the usages of this office. Say now, you will help to examine papers to-morrow or next day: in short, say now, that in a day or two you will begin to be a little reasonable:—say so, Bartleby."

"At present I would prefer not to be a little reasonable," was his mildly cadaverous reply.

Just then the folding-doors opened, and Nippers approached. He seemed suffering from an unusually bad night's rest, induced by severer

680   indigestion than common. He overheard those final words of Bartleby.

"*Prefer not*, eh?" gritted Nippers—"I'd *prefer* him, if I were you, sir," addressing me—"I'd *prefer* him; I'd give him preferences, the stubborn mule! What is it, sir, pray, that he *prefers* not to do now?"

Bartleby moved not a limb.

"Mr. Nippers," said I, "I'd prefer that you would withdraw for the present."

Somehow, of late, I had got into the way of involuntarily using this word "prefer" upon all sorts of not exactly suitable occasions. And I trembled to think that my contact with the scrivener had already and se-
690 riously affected me in a mental way. And what further and deeper aberration might it not yet produce? This apprehension had not been without efficacy in determining me to summary measures.

As Nippers, looking very sour and sulky, was departing, Turkey blandly and deferentially approached.

"With submission, sir," said he, "yesterday I was thinking about Bartleby here, and I think that if he would but prefer to take a quart of good ale every day, it would do much towards mending him, and enabling him to assist in examining his papers."

"So you have got the word, too," said I, slightly excited.
700   "With submission, what word, sir," asked Turkey, respectfully crowding himself into the contracted space behind the screen, and by so doing, making me jostle the scrivener. "What word, sir?"

"I would prefer to be left alone here," said Bartleby, as if offended at being mobbed in his privacy.

"*That's* the word, Turkey," said I—"*that's* it."

"Oh, *prefer?* oh yes—queer word. I never use it myself. But, sir, as I was saying, if he would but prefer—"

"Turkey," interrupted I, "you will please withdraw."

"Oh certainly, sir, if you prefer that I should."
710   As he opened the folding-door to retire, Nippers at his desk caught a glimpse of me, and asked whether I would prefer to have a certain paper copied on blue paper or white. He did not in the least roguishly accent the word prefer. It was plain that it involuntarily rolled from his tongue. I thought to myself, surely I must get rid of a demented man, who already has in some degree turned the tongues, if not the heads of myself and clerks. But I thought it prudent not to break the dismission at once.

The next day I noticed that Bartleby did nothing but stand at his window in his dead-wall revery. Upon asking him why he did not write, he said that he had decided upon doing no more writing.
720   "Why, how now? what next?" exclaimed I, "do no more writing?"

"No more."

"And what is the reason?"

"Do you not see the reason for yourself," he indifferently replied.

I looked steadfastly at him, and perceived that his eyes looked dull and glazed. Instantly it occurred to me, that his unexampled diligence in copying by his dim window for the first few weeks of his stay with me might have temporarily impaired his vision.

I was touched. I said something in condolence with him. I hinted that of course he did wisely in abstaining from writing for a while; and urged
730 him to embrace that opportunity of taking wholesome exercise in the

open air. This, however, he did not do. A few days after this, my other clerks being absent, and being in a great hurry to dispatch certain letters by the mail, I thought that, having nothing else earthly to do, Bartleby would surely be less inflexible than usual, and carry these letters to the post-office. But he blankly declined. So, much to my inconvenience, I went myself.

Still added days went by. Whether Bartleby's eyes improved or not, I could not say. To all appearance I thought they did. But when I asked him if they did, he vouchsafed no answer. At all events, he would do no 740 copying. At last, in reply to my urgings, he informed me that he had permanently given up copying.

"What!" exclaimed I; "suppose your eyes should get entirely well— better than ever before—would you not copy then?"

"I have given up copying," he answered, and slid aside.

He remained as ever, a fixture in my chamber. Nay—if that were possible—he became still more of a fixture than before. What was to be done? He would do nothing in the office; why should he stay there? In plain fact, he had now become a millstone to me, not only useless as a necklace, but afflictive to bear. Yet I was sorry for him. I speak less than 750 truth when I say that, on his own account, he occasioned me uneasiness. If he would but have named a single relative or friend, I would instantly have written, and urged their taking the poor fellow away to some convenient retreat. But he seemed alone, absolutely alone in the universe. A bit of wreck in the mid Atlantic. At length, necessities connected with my business tyrannized over all other considerations. Decently as I could, I told Bartleby that in six days time he must unconditionally leave the office. I warned him to take measures, in the interval, for procuring some other abode. I offered to assist him in his endeavor, if he himself would but take the first step towards a removal. "And when you finally 760 quit me, Bartleby," added I, "I shall see that you go not away entirely unprovided. Six days from this hour, remember."

At the expiration of that period, I peeped behind the screen, and lo! Bartleby was there.

I buttoned up my coat, balanced myself; advanced slowly towards him, touched his shoulder, and said, "The time has come; you must quit this place; I am sorry for you; here is money; but you must go."

"I would prefer not," he replied, with his back still towards me.

"You *must*."

He remained silent.

770   Now I had an unbounded confidence in this man's common honesty. He had frequently restored to me sixpences and shillings carelessly dropped upon the floor, for I am apt to be very reckless in such shirt-button affairs. The proceeding, then, which followed will not be deemed extraordinary.

"Bartleby," said I, "I owe you twelve dollars on account; here are thirty-two; the odd twenty are yours—Will you take it?" and I handed the bills towards him.

But he made no motion.

"I will leave them here, then," putting them under a weight on the
780 table. Then taking my hat and cane and going to the door, I tranquilly
turned and added—"After you have removed your things from these offices, Bartleby, you will of course lock the door—since every one is now
gone for the day but you—and if you please, slip your key underneath
the mat, so that I may have it in the morning. I shall not see you again;
so good-by to you. If, hereafter, in your new place of abode, I can be of
any service to you, do not fail to advise me by letter. Good-by, Bartleby,
and fare you well."

But he answered not a word; like the last column of some ruined
temple, he remained standing mute and solitary in the middle of the
790 otherwise deserted room.

As I walked home in a pensive mood, my vanity got the better of my
pity. I could not but highly plume myself on my masterly management in
getting rid of Bartleby. Masterly I call it, and such it must appear to any
dispassionate thinker. The beauty of my procedure seemed to consist in
its perfect quietness. There was no vulgar bullying, no bravado of any
sort, no choleric hectoring, and striding to and fro across the apartment,
jerking out vehement commands for Bartleby to bundle himself off with
his beggarly traps. Nothing of the kind. Without loudly bidding Bartleby
depart—as an inferior genius might have done—I *assumed* the ground that
800 depart he must; and upon that assumption built all I had to say. The more
I thought over my procedure, the more I was charmed with it. Nevertheless, next morning, upon awakening, I had my doubts—I had somehow
slept off the fumes of vanity. One of the coolest and wisest hours a man
has, is just after he awakes in the morning. My procedure seemed as sagacious as ever—but only in theory. How it would prove in practice—there
was the rub. It was truly a beautiful thought to have assumed Bartleby's
departure; but, after all, that assumption was simply my own, and none
of Bartleby's. The great point was, not whether I had assumed that he
would quit me, but whether he would prefer so to do. He was more a man
810 of preferences than assumptions.

After breakfast, I walked down town, arguing the probabilities *pro*
and *con*. One moment I thought it would prove a miserable failure, and
Bartleby would be found all alive at my office as usual; the next moment it
seemed certain that I should find his chair empty. And so I kept veering
about. At the corner of Broadway and Canal Street, I saw quite an excited
group of people standing in earnest conversation.

"I'll take odds he doesn't," said a voice as I passed.

"Doesn't go?—done!" said I; "put up your money."

I was instinctively putting my hand in my pocket to produce my own,
820 when I remembered that this was an election day. The words I had overheard bore no reference to Bartleby, but to the success or non-success of
some candidate for the mayoralty. In my intent frame of mind, I had, as it
were, imagined that all Broadway shared in my excitement, and were de-
bating the same question with me. I passed on, very thankful that the uproar of the street screened my momentary absent-mindedness.

As I had intended, I was earlier than usual at my office door. I stood

listening for a moment. All was still. He must be gone. I tried the knob. The door was locked. Yes, my procedure had worked to a charm; he indeed must be vanished. Yet a certain melancholy mixed with this: I
830　was almost sorry for my brilliant success. I was fumbling under the door mat for the key, which Bartleby was to have left there for me, when accidentally my knee knocked against a panel, producing a summoning sound, and in response a voice came to me from within—"Not yet; I am occupied."

　　It was Bartleby.

　　I was thunderstruck. For an instant I stood like the man who, pipe in mouth, was killed one cloudless afternoon long ago in Virginia, by summer lightning; at his own warm open window he was killed, and remained leaning out there upon the dreamy afternoon, till some one touched him,
840　when he fell.

　　"Not gone!" I murmured at last. But again obeying that wondrous ascendancy which the inscrutable scrivener had over me, and from which ascendancy, for all my chafing, I could not completely escape, I slowly went down stairs and out into the street, and while walking round the block, considered what I should next do in this unheard-of perplexity. Turn the man out by an actual thrusting I could not; to drive him away by calling him hard names would not do; calling in the police was an unpleasant idea; and yet, permit him to enjoy his cadaverous triumph over me—this, too, I could not think of. What was to be done? or, if nothing
850　could be done, was there anything further that I could *assume* in the matter? Yes, as before I had prospectively assumed that Bartleby would depart, so now I might retrospectively assume that departed he was. In the legitimate carrying out of this assumption, I might enter my office in a great hurry, and pretending not to see Bartleby at all, walk straight against him as if he were air. Such a proceeding would in a singular degree have the appearance of a home-thrust. It was hardly possible that Bartleby could withstand such an application of the doctrine of assumptions. But upon second thoughts the success of the plan seemed rather dubious. I resolved to argue the matter over with him again.
860　　"Bartleby," said I, entering the office, with a quietly severe expression, "I am seriously displeased. I am pained, Bartleby. I had thought better of you. I had imagined you of such a gentlemanly organization, that in any delicate dilemma a slight hint would suffice—in short, an assumption. But it appears I am deceived. Why," I added, unaffectedly starting, "you have not even touched that money yet," pointing to it, just where I had left it the evening previous.

　　He answered nothing.

　　"Will you, or will you not, quit me?" I now demanded in a sudden passion, advancing close to him.
870　　"I would prefer *not* to quit you," he replied, gently emphasizing the *not*.

　　"What earthly right have you to stay here? Do you pay any rent? Do you pay my taxes? Or is this property yours?"

　　He answered nothing.

"Are you ready to go on and write now? Are your eyes recovered? Could you copy a small paper for me this morning? or help examine a few lines? or step round to the post-office? In a word, will you do anything at all, to give a coloring to your refusal to depart the premises?"

He silently retired into his hermitage.

880   I was now in such a state of nervous resentment that I thought it but prudent to check myself at present from further demonstrations. Bartleby and I were alone. I remembered the tragedy of the unfortunate Adams and the still more unfortunate Colt in the solitary office of the latter; and how poor Colt, being dreadfully incensed by Adams, and imprudently permitting himself to get wildly excited, was at unawares hurried into his fatal act—an act which certainly no man could possibly deplore more than the actor himself. Often it had occurred to me in my ponderings upon the subject, that had that altercation taken place in the public street, or at a private residence, it would not have terminated as it did. It was the
890 circumstance of being alone in a solitary office, up stairs, of a building entirely unhallowed by humanizing domestic associations—an uncarpeted office, doubtless, of a dusty, haggard sort of appearance—this it must have been, which greatly helped to enhance the irritable desperation of the hapless Colt.

But when this old Adam of resentment rose in me and tempted me concerning Bartleby, I grappled him and threw him. How? Why, simply by recalling the divine injunction: "A new commandment give I unto you, that ye love one another." Yes, this it was that saved me. Aside from higher considerations, charity often operates as a vastly wise and pru-
900 dent principle—a great safeguard to its possessor. Men have committed murder for jealousy's sake, and anger's sake, and hatred's sake, and selfishness' sake, and spiritual pride's sake; but no man, that ever I heard of, ever committed a diabolical murder for sweet charity's sake. Mere self-interest, then, if no better motive can be enlisted, should, especially with high-tempered men, prompt all beings to charity and philanthropy. At any rate, upon the occasion in question, I strove to drown my exasperated feelings towards the scrivener by benevolently construing his conduct. Poor fellow, poor fellow! thought I, he don't mean anything; and besides, he has seen hard times, and ought to be indulged.

910   I endeavored, also, immediately to occupy myself, and at the same time to comfort my despondency. I tried to fancy, that in the course of the morning, at such time as might prove agreeable to him, Bartleby, of his own free accord, would emerge from his hermitage and take up some decided line of march in the direction of the door. But no. Half-past twelve o'clock came; Turkey began to glow in the face, overturn his inkstand, and become generally obstreperous; Nippers abated down into quietude and courtesy; Ginger Nut munched his noon apple; and Bartleby remained standing at his window in one of his profoundest dead-wall reveries. Will it be credited? Ought I to acknowledge it? That afternoon I left
920 the office without saying one further word to him.

Some days now passed, during which, at leisure intervals I looked a little into "Edwards on the Will," and "Priestley on Necessity." Under the circumstances, those books induced a salutary feeling. Gradually I slid into the persuasion that these troubles of mine, touching the scrivener, had been all predestined from eternity, and Bartleby was billeted upon me for some mysterious purpose of an all-wise Providence, which it was not for a mere mortal like me to fathom. Yes, Bartleby, stay there behind your screen, thought I; I shall persecute you no more; you are harmless and noiseless as any of these old chairs; in short, I never feel so private as when I know you are here. At last I see it, I feel it; I penetrate to the pre-destinated purpose of my life. I am content. Others may have loftier parts to enact; but my mission in this world, Bartleby, is to furnish you with office-room for such period as you may see fit to remain.

I believe that this wise and blessed frame of mind would have contin-ued with me, had it not been for the unsolicited and uncharitable remarks obtruded upon me by my professional friends who visited the rooms. But thus it often is, that the constant friction of illiberal minds wears out at last the best resolves of the more generous. Though to be sure, when I re-flected upon it, it was not strange that people entering my office should be struck by the peculiar aspect of the unaccountable Bartleby, and so be tempted to throw out some sinister observations concerning him. Some-times an attorney, having business with me, and calling at my office, and finding no one but the scrivener there, would undertake to obtain some sort of precise information from him touching my whereabouts; but with-out heeding his idle talk, Bartleby would remain standing immovable in the middle of the room. So after contemplating him in that position for a time, the attorney would depart, no wiser than he came.

Also, when a reference was going on, and the room full of lawyers and witnesses, and business driving fast, some deeply-occupied legal gentleman present, seeing Bartleby wholly unemployed, would request him to run round to his (the legal gentleman's) office and fetch some pa-pers for him. Thereupon, Bartleby would tranquilly decline, and yet re-main idle as before. Then the lawyer would give a great stare, and turn to me. And what could I say? At last I was made aware that all through the circle of my professional acquaintance, a whisper of wonder was running round, having reference to the strange creature I kept at my office. This worried me very much. And as the idea came upon me of his possibly turning out a long-lived man, and keep occupying my chambers, and denying my authority; and perplexing my visitors; and scandalizing my professional reputation; and casting a general gloom over the premises; keeping soul and body together to the last upon his savings (for doubtless he spent but half a dime a day), and in the end perhaps outlive me, and claim possession of my office by right of his perpetual occupancy: as all these dark anticipations crowded upon me more and more, and my friends continually intruded their relentless remarks upon the apparition in my room; a great change was wrought in me. I resolved to gather all my faculties together, and forever rid me of this intolerable incubus.

Ere revolving any complicated project, however, adapted to this end, I first simply suggested to Bartleby the propriety of his permanent

970 departure. In a calm and serious tone, I commended the idea to his careful and mature consideration. But, having taken three days to meditate upon it, he apprised me, that his original determination remained the same; in short, that he still preferred to abide with me.

What shall I do? I now said to myself, buttoning up my coat to the last button. What shall I do? what ought I to do? what does conscience say I *should* do with this man, or, rather, ghost. Rid myself of him, I must; go, he shall. But how? You will not thrust him, the poor, pale, passive mortal—you will not thrust such a helpless creature out of your door? you will not dishonor yourself by such cruelty? No, I will not, I cannot do 980 that. Rather would I let him live and die here, and then mason up his remains in the wall. What, then, will you do? For all your coaxing, he will not budge. Bribes he leaves under your own paper-weight on your table; in short, it is quite plain that he prefers to cling to you.

Then something severe, something unusual must be done. What! surely you will not have him collared by a constable, and commit his innocent pallor to the common jail? And upon what ground could you procure such a thing to be done?—a vagrant, is he? What! he a vagrant, a wanderer, who refuses to budge? It is because he will *not* be a vagrant, then, that you seek to count him *as* a vagrant. This is too absurd. No visa- 990 ble means of support: there I have him. Wrong again: for indubitably he *does* support himself, and that is the only unanswerable proof that any man can show of his possessing the means so to do. No more, then. Since he will not quit me, I must quit him. I will change my offices; I will move elsewhere, and give him fair notice, that if I find him on my new premises I will then proceed against him as a common trespasser.

Acting according, next day I thus addressed him: "I find these chambers too far from the City Hall; the air is unwholesome. In a word, I propose to remove my offices next week, and shall no longer require your services. I tell you this now, in order that you may seek another 1000 place."

He made no reply; and nothing more was said.

On the appointed day I engaged carts and men, proceeded to my chambers, and, having but little furniture, everything was removed in a few hours. Throughout, the scrivener remained standing behind the screen, which I directed to be removed the last thing. It was withdrawn; and, being folded up like a huge folio, left him the motionless occupant of a naked room. I stood in the entry watching him a moment, while something from within me upbraided me.

I re-entered, with my hand in my pocket—and—and my heart in my 1010 mouth.

"Good-by, Bartleby; I am going—good-by, and God some way bless you; and take that," slipping something in his hand. But it dropped upon the floor, and then—strange to say—I tore myself from him whom I had so longed to be rid of.

Established in my new quarters, for a day or two I kept the door locked, and started at every footfall in the passages. When I returned to my rooms, after any little absence, I would pause at the threshold for an instant, and attentively listen, ere applying my key. But these fears were needless. Bartleby never came nigh me.

1020   I thought all was going well, when a perturbed-looking stranger visited me, inquiring whether I was the person who had recently occupied rooms at No._____ Wall Street.

Full of forebodings, I replied that I was.

"Then, sir," said the stranger, who proved a lawyer, "you are responsible for the man you left there. He refuses to do any copying; he refuses to do anything; he says he prefers not to; and he refuses to quit the premises."

"I am very sorry, sir," said I, with assumed tranquillity, but an inward tremor, "but, really, the man you allude to is nothing to me—he is
1030 no relation or apprentice of mine, that you should hold me responsible for him."

"In mercy's name, who is he?"

"I certainly cannot inform you. I know nothing about him. Formerly I employed him as a copyist; but he has done nothing for me now for some time past."

"I shall settle him, then—good morning, sir."

Several days passed, and I heard nothing more; and, though I often felt a charitable prompting to call at the place and see poor Bartleby, yet a certain squeamishness, of I know not what, withheld me.

1040   All is over with him, by this time, thought I, at last, when, through another week, no further intelligence reached me. But, coming to my room the day after, I found several persons waiting at my door in a high state of nervous excitement.

"That's the man—here he comes," cried the foremost one, whom I recognized as the lawyer who had previously called upon me alone.

"You must take him away, sir, at once," cried a portly person among them, advancing upon me, and whom I knew to be the landlord of No._____ Wall Street. "These gentlemen, my tenants, cannot stand it any longer; Mr. B____," pointing to the lawyer, "has turned him out of his
1050 room, and he now persists in haunting the building generally, sitting upon the banisters of the stairs by day, and sleeping in the entry by night. Everybody is concerned; clients are leaving the offices; some fears are entertained of a mob; something you must do, and that without delay."

Aghast at this torrent, I fell back before it, and would fain have locked myself in my new quarters. In vain I persisted that Bartleby was nothing to me—no more than to any one else. In vain—I was the last person known to have anything to do with him, and they held me to the terrible account. Fearful, then, of being exposed in the papers (as one person present obscurely threatened), I considered the matter, and, at
1060 length, said, that if the lawyer would give me a confidential interview with the scrivener, in his (the lawyer's) own room, I would, that afternoon, strive my best to rid them of the nuisance they complained of.

Going up stairs to my old haunt, there was Bartleby silently sitting upon the banister at the landing.

"What are you doing here, Bartleby?" said I.

"Sitting upon the banister," he mildly replied.

I motioned him into the lawyer's room, who then left us.

"Bartleby," said I, "are you aware that you are the cause of great tribu-
lation to me, by persisting in occupying the entry after being dismissed
1070 from the office?"

No answer.

"Now one of two things must take place. Either you must do something, or something must be done to you. Now what sort of business would
you like to engage in? Would you like to re-engage in copying for some
one?"

"No; I would prefer not to make any change."

"Would you like a clerkship in a dry-goods store?"

"There is too much confinement about that. No, I would not like a
clerkship; but I am not particular."

1080   "Too much confinement," I cried, "why you keep yourself confined
all the time!"

"I would prefer not to take a clerkship," he rejoined, as if to settle
that little item at once.

"How would a bar-tender's business suit you? There is no trying of
the eye-sight in that."

"I would not like it at all; though, as I said before, I am not particular."

His unwonted wordiness inspirited me. I returned to the charge.

"Well, then, would you like to travel through the country collecting
bills for the merchants? That would improve your health."

1090   "No, I would prefer to be doing something else."

"How, then, would going as a companion to Europe, to entertain
some young gentleman with your conversation—how would that suit
you?"

"Not at all. It does not strike me that there is anything definite
about that. I like to be stationary. But I am not particular."

"Stationary you shall be, then," I cried, now losing all patience, and,
for the first time in all my exasperating connection with him, fairly flying
into a passion. "If you do not go away from these premises before night, I
shall feel bound—indeed, I *am* bound—to—to—to quit the premises my-
1100 self!" I rather absurdly concluded, knowing not with what possible threat
to try to frighten his immobility into compliance. Despairing of all further efforts, I was precipitately leaving him, when a final thought occurred to me—one which had not been wholly unindulged before.

"Bartleby," said I, in the kindest tone I could assume under such exciting circumstances, "will you go home with me now—not to my office,
but my dwelling—and remain there till we can conclude upon some convenient arrangement for you at our leisure? Come, let us start now, right
away."

"No: at present I would prefer not to make any change at all."

1110   I answered nothing; but, effectually dodging every one by the suddenness and rapidity of my flight, rushed from the building, ran up Wall
Street towards Broadway, and, jumping into the first omnibus, was soon

removed from pursuit. As soon as tranquillity returned, I distinctly perceived that I had now done all that I possibly could, both in respect to the
demands of the landlord and his tenants, and with regard to my own desire and sense of duty, to benefit Bartleby, and shield him from rude persecution. I now strove to be entirely care-free and quiescent; and my
conscience justified me in the attempt; though, indeed, it was not so successful as I could have wished. So fearful was I of being again hunted out
1120 by the incensed landlord and his exasperated tenants, that, surrendering
my business to Nippers, for a few days, I drove about the upper part
of the town and through the suburbs, in my rockaway; crossed over to
Jersey City and Hoboken, and paid fugitive visits to Manhattanville and
Astoria. In fact, I almost lived in my rockaway for the time.

When again I entered my office, lo, a note from the landlord lay upon
the desk. I opened it with trembling hands. It informed me that the
writer had sent to the police, and had Bartleby removed to the Tombs as a
vagrant. Moreover, since I knew more about him than any one else, he
wished me to appear at that place, and make a suitable statement of the
1130 facts. These tidings had a conflicting effect upon me. At first I was indignant; but, at last, almost approved. The landlord's energetic, summary disposition, had led him to adopt a procedure which I do not think I would
have decided upon myself; and yet, as a last resort, under such peculiar
circumstances, it seemed the only plan.

As I afterwards learned, the poor scrivener, when told that he must
be conducted to the Tombs, offered not the slightest obstacle, but, in his
pale, unmoving way, silently acquiesced.

Some of the compassionate and curious bystanders joined the party;
and headed by one of the constables arm in arm with Bartleby, the silent
1140 procession filed its way through all the noise, and heat, and joy of the
roaring thoroughfares at noon.

The same day I received the note, I went to the Tombs, or, to speak
more properly, the Halls of Justice. Seeking the right officer, I stated the
purpose of my call, and was informed that the individual I described was,
indeed, within. I then assured the functionary that Bartleby was a perfectly honest man, and greatly to be compassionated, however unaccountably eccentric. I narrated all I knew, and closed by suggesting the idea of
letting him remain in as indulgent confinement as possible, till something
less harsh might be done—though, indeed, I hardly knew what. At all
1150 events, if nothing else could be decided upon, the alms-house must receive him. I then begged to have an interview.

Being under no disgraceful charge, and quite serene and harmless in
all his ways, they had permitted him freely to wander about the prison,
and, especially, in the inclosed grass-platted yards thereof. And so I found
him there, standing all alone in the quietest of the yards, his face towards
a high wall, while all around, from the narrow slits of the jail windows, I
thought I saw peering out upon him the eyes of murderers and thieves.

"Bartleby!"

"I know you," he said, without looking round— "and I want noth-
1160 ing to say to you."

"It was not I that brought you here, Bartleby," said I, keenly pained at his implied suspicion. "And to you, this should not be so vile a place. Nothing reproachful attaches to you by being here. And see, it is not so sad a place as one might think. Look, there is the sky, and here is the grass."

"I know where I am," he replied, but would say nothing more, and so I left him.

As I entered the corridor again, a broad meat-like man, in an apron, accosted me, and, jerking his thumb over his shoulder, said—"Is that your friend?"

1170 "Yes."

"Does he want to starve? If he does, let him live on the prison fare, that's all."

"Who are you?" asked I, not knowing what to make of such an unofficially speaking person in such a place.

"I am the grub-man. Such gentlemen as have friends here, hire me to provide them with something good to eat."

"Is this so?" said I, turning to the turnkey.

He said it was.

"Well, then," said I, slipping some silver into the grub-man's hands
1180 (for so they called him), "I want you to give particular attention to my friend there; let him have the best dinner you can get. And you must be as polite to him as possible."

"Introduce me, will you?" said the grub-man, looking at me with an expression which seemed to say he was all impatience for an opportunity to give a specimen of his breeding.

Thinking it would prove of benefit to the scrivener, I acquiesced; and, asking the grub-man his name, went up with him to Bartleby.

"Bartleby, this is a friend; you will find him very useful to you."

"Your sarvant, sir, your sarvant," said the grub-man, making a low
1190 salutation behind his apron. "Hope you find it pleasant here, sir; nice grounds—cool apartment—hope you'll stay with us sometime—try to make it agreeable. What will you have for dinner to-day?"

"I prefer not to dine to-day," said Bartleby, turning away. "It would disagree with me; I am unused to dinners." So saying, he slowly moved to the other side of the inclosure, and took up a position fronting the dead-wall.

"How's this?" said the grub-man, addressing me with a stare of astonishment. "He's odd, ain't he?"

"I think he is a little deranged," said I, sadly.

1200 "Deranged? deranged is it? Well, now, upon my word, I thought that friend of yours was a gentleman forger; they are always pale and genteel-like, them forgers. I can't help pity 'em—can't help it, sir. Did you know Monroe Edwards?" he added, touchingly, and paused. Then, laying his hand piteously on my shoulder, sighed, "He died of consumption at Sing-Sing. So you weren't acquainted with Monroe?"

"No, I was never socially acquainted with any forgers. But I cannot stop longer. Look to my friend yonder. You will not lose by it. I will see you again."

Some few days after this, I again obtained admission to the Tombs,
1210 and went through the corridors in quest of Bartleby; but without finding
him.

"I saw him coming from his cell not long ago," said a turnkey, "may
be he's gone to loiter in the yards."

So I went in that direction.

"Are you looking for the silent man?" said another turnkey, passing
me. "Yonder he lies—sleeping in the yard there. 'Tis not twenty minutes
since I saw him lie down."

The yard was entirely quiet. It was not accessible to the common prisoners. The surrounding walls of amazing thickness, kept off all sounds
1220 behind them. The Egyptian character of the masonry weighed upon me
with its gloom. But a soft imprisoned turf grew under foot. The heart of
the eternal pyramids, it seemed, wherein, by some strange magic, through
the clefts, grass-seed, dropped by birds, had sprung.

Strangely huddled at the base of the wall, his knees drawn up, and lying on his side, his head touching the cold stones, I saw the wasted
Bartleby. But nothing stirred. I paused; then went close up to him; stooped
over, and saw that his dim eyes were open; otherwise he seemed profoundly sleeping. Something prompted me to touch him. I felt his hand,
when a tingling shiver ran up my arm and down my spine to my feet.

1230   The round face of the grub-man peered upon me now. "His dinner
is ready. Won't he dine to-day, either? Or does he live without dining?"

"Lives without dining," said I, and closed the eyes.

"Eh!—He's asleep, ain't he?"

"With kings and counselors," murmured I.

There would seem little need for proceeding further in this history.
Imagination will readily supply the meager recital of poor Bartleby's interment. But, ere parting with the reader, let me say, that if this little narrative has sufficiently interested him, to awaken curiosity as to who
Bartleby was, and what manner of life he led prior to the present narra-
1240 tor's making his acquaintance, I can only reply, that in such curiosity I
fully share, but am wholly unable to gratify it. Yet here I hardly know
whether I should divulge one little item of rumor, which came to my ear
a few months after the scrivener's decease. Upon what basis it rested, I
could never ascertain; and hence, how true it is I cannot now tell. But,
inasmuch as this vague report has not been without a certain suggestive
interest to me, however said, it may prove the same with some others; and
so I will briefly mention it. The report was this: that Bartleby had been a
subordinate clerk in the Dead Letter Office at Washington, from which he
had been suddenly removed by a change in the administration. When I
1250 think over this rumor, hardly can I express the emotions which seize me.
Dead letters! does it not sound like dead men? Conceive a man by nature
and misfortune prone to a pallid hopelessness, can any business seem
more fitted to heighten it than that of continually handling these dead
letters, and assorting them for the flames? For by the cart-load they are

annually burned. Some times from out the folded paper the pale clerk takes a ring—the finger it was meant for, perhaps, moulders in the grave; a bank-note sent in swiftest charity—he whom it would relieve, nor eats nor hungers any more; pardon for those who died despairing; hope for those who died unhoping; good tidings for those who died stifled by un-
1260 relieved calamities. On errands of life, these letters speed to death.

Ah, Bartleby! Ah, humanity!

STEPHEN CRANE (1871–1900)
The Bride Comes to Yellow Sky
(1898)

I

The great Pullman was whirling onward with such dignity of motion that a glance from the window seemed simply to prove that the plains of Texas were pouring eastward. Vast flats of green grass, dull-hued spaces of mesquit and cactus, little groups of frame houses, woods of light and tender trees, all were sweeping into the east, sweeping over the horizon, a precipice.

A newly married pair had boarded this coach at San Antonio. The man's face was reddened from many days in the wind and sun, and a direct result of his new black clothes was that his brick-coloured hands
10 were constantly performing in a most conscious fashion. From time to time he looked down respectfully at his attire. He sat with a hand on each knee, like a man waiting in a barber's shop. The glances he devoted to other passengers were furtive and shy.

The bride was not pretty, nor was she very young. She wore a dress of blue cashmere, with small reservations of velvet here and there, and with steel buttons abounding. She continually twisted her head to regard her puff sleeves, very stiff, straight, and high. They embarrassed her. It was quite apparent that she had cooked, and that she expected to cook, dutifully. The blushes caused by the careless scrutiny of some pas-
20 sengers as she had entered the car were strange to see upon this plain, under-class countenance, which was drawn in placid, almost emotionless lines.

They were evidently very happy. "Ever been in a parlour-car before?" he asked, smiling with delight.

"No," she answered; "I never was. It's fine, ain't it?"

"Great! And then after a while we'll go forward to the diner, and get a big lay-out. Finest meal in the world. Charge a dollar."

"Oh, do they?" cried the bride. "Charge a dollar? Why, that's too much—for us—ain't it, Jack?"

30 "Not this trip, anyhow," he answered bravely. "We're going to go the whole thing."

Later he explained to her about the trains. "You see, it's a thousand miles from one end of Texas to the other; and this train runs right

across it, and never stops but four times." He had the pride of an owner. He pointed out to her the dazzling fittings of the coach; and in truth her eyes opened wider as she contemplated the sea-green figured velvet, the shining brass, silver, and glass, the wood that gleamed as darkly brilliant as the surface of a pool of oil. At one end a bronze figure sturdily held a support for a separated chamber, and at convenient places on the
40 ceiling were frescos in olive and silver.

To the minds of the pair, their surroundings reflected the glory of their marriage that morning in San Antonio; this was the environment of their new estate; and the man's face in particular beamed with an elation that made him appear ridiculous to the negro porter. This individual at times surveyed them from afar with an amused and superior grin. On other occasions he bullied them with skill in ways that did not make it exactly plain to them that they were being bullied. He subtly used all the manners of the most unconquerable kind of snobbery. He oppressed them; but of this oppression they had small knowledge, and
50 they speedily forgot that infrequently a number of travellers covered them with stares of derisive enjoyment. Historically there was supposed to be something infinitely humorous in their situation.

"We are due in Yellow Sky at 3:42," he said, looking tenderly into her eyes.

"Oh, are we?" she said, as if she had not been aware of it. To evince surprise at her husband's statement was part of her wifely amiability. She took from a pocket a little silver watch; and as she held it before her, and stared at it with a frown of attention, the new husband's face shone.

"I bought it in San Anton' from a friend of mine," he told her gleefully.
60   "It's seventeen minutes past twelve," she said, looking up at him with a kind of shy and clumsy coquetry. A passenger, noting this play, grew excessively sardonic, and winked at himself in one of the numerous mirrors.

At last they went to the dining-car. Two rows of negro waiters, in glowing white suits, surveyed their entrance with the interest, and also the equanimity, of men who had been forewarned. The pair fell to the lot of a waiter who happened to feel pleasure in steering them through their meal. He viewed them with the manner of a fatherly pilot, his countenance radiant with benevolence. The patronage, entwined with the ordi-
70 nary deference, was not plain to them. And yet, as they returned to their coach, they showed in their faces a sense of escape.

To the left, miles down a long purple slope, was a little ribbon of mist where moved the keening Rio Grande. The train was approaching it at an angle, and the apex was Yellow Sky. Presently it was apparent that, as the distance from Yellow Sky grew shorter, the husband became commensurately restless. His brick-red hands were most insistent in their prominence. Occasionally he was even rather absent-minded and far-away when the bride leaned forward and addressed him.

As a matter of truth, Jack Potter was beginning to find the shadow of
80 a deed weigh upon him like a leaden slab. He, the town marshal of Yellow Sky, a man known, liked, and feared in his corner, a prominent person,

had gone to San Antonio to meet a girl he believed he loved, and there, after the usual prayers, had actually induced her to marry him, without consulting Yellow Sky for any part of the transaction. He was now bringing his bride before an innocent and unsuspecting community.

Of course people in Yellow Sky married as it pleased them, in accordance with a general custom; but such was Potter's thought of his duty to his friends, or of their idea of his duty, or of an unspoken form which does not control men in these matters, that he felt he was heinous. He had committed an extraordinary crime. Face to face with this girl in San Antonio, and spurred by his sharp impulse, he had gone headlong over all the social hedges. At San Antonio he was like a man hidden in the dark. A knife to sever any friendly duty, any form, was easy to his hand in that remote city. But the hour of Yellow Sky—the hour of daylight— was approaching.

He knew full well that his marriage was an important thing to his town. It could only be exceeded by the burning of the new hotel. His friends could not forgive him. Frequently he had reflected on the advisability of telling them by telegraph, but a new cowardice had been upon him. He feared to do it. And now the train was hurrying him toward a scene of amazement, glee, and reproach. He glanced out of the window at the line of haze swinging slowly in toward the train.

Yellow Sky had a kind of brass band, which played painfully, to the delight of the populace. He laughed without heart as he thought of it. If the citizens could dream of his prospective arrival with his bride, they would parade the band at the station and escort them, amid cheers and laughing congratulations, to his adobe home.

He resolved that he would use all the devices of speed and plainscraft in making the journey from the station to his house. Once within that safe citadel, he could issue some sort of vocal bulletin, and then not go among the citizens until they had time to wear off a little of their enthusiasm.

The bride looked anxiously at him. "What's worrying you, Jack?"

He laughed again. "I'm not worrying, girl; I'm only thinking of Yellow Sky."

She flushed in comprehension.

A sense of mutual guilt invaded their minds and developed a finer tenderness. They looked at each other with eyes softly aglow. But Potter often laughed the same nervous laugh; the flush upon the bride's face seemed quite permanent.

The traitor to the feelings of Yellow Sky narrowly watched the speeding landscape. "We're nearly there," he said.

Presently the porter came and announced the proximity of Potter's home. He held a brush in his hand, and, with all his airy superiority gone, he brushed Potter's new clothes as the latter slowly turned this way and that way. Potter fumbled out a coin and gave it to the porter, as he had seen others do. It was a heavy and muscle-bound business, as that of a man shoeing his first horse.

The porter took their bag, and as the train began to slow they

130 moved forward to the hooded platform of the car. Presently the two engines and their string of coaches rushed into the station of Yellow Sky.

"They have to take water here," said Potter, from a constricted throat and in mournful cadence, as one announcing death. Before the train stopped his eye had swept the length of the platform, and he was glad and astonished to see there was none upon it but the station-agent, who, with a slightly hurried and anxious air, was walking toward the water-tanks. When the train had halted, the porter alighted first, and placed in position a little temporary step.

"Come on, girl," said Potter, hoarsely. As he helped her down they
140 each laughed on a false note. He took the bag from the negro, and bade his wife cling to his arm. As they slunk rapidly away, his hang-dog glance perceived that they were unloading the two trunks, and also that the station-agent, far ahead near the baggage-car, had turned and was running toward him, making gestures. He laughed, and groaned as he laughed, when he noted the first effect of his marital bliss upon Yellow Sky. He gripped his wife's arm firmly to his side, and they fled. Behind them the porter stood, chuckling fatuously.

II

The California express on the Southern Railway was due at Yellow Sky in twenty-one minutes. There were six men at the bar of the Weary
150 Gentleman saloon. One was a drummer who talked a great deal and rapidly; three were Texans who did not care to talk at that time; and two were Mexican sheepherders, who did not talk as a general practice in the Weary Gentleman saloon. The barkeeper's dog lay on the board walk that crossed in front of the door. His head was on his paws, and he glanced drowsily here and there with the constant vigilance of a dog that is kicked on occasion. Across the sandy street were some vivid green grass-plots, so wonderful in appearance, amid the sands that burned near them in a blazing sun, that they caused a doubt in the mind. They exactly resembled the grass mats used to represent lawns
160 on the stage. At the cooler end of the railway station, a man without a coat sat in a tilted chair and smoked his pipe. The fresh-cut bank of the Rio Grande circled near the town, and there could be seen beyond it a great plum-coloured plain of mesquit.

Save for the busy drummer and his companions in the saloon, Yellow Sky was dozing. The new-comer leaned gracefully upon the bar, and recited many tales with the confidence of a bard who has come upon a new field.

"—and at the moment that the old man fell downstairs with the bureau in his arms, the old woman was coming up with two scuttles of
170 coal, and of course—"

The drummer's tale was interrupted by a young man who suddenly appeared in the open door. He cried: "Scratchy Wilson's drunk, and has turned loose with both hands." The two Mexicans at once set down their glasses and faded out of the rear entrance of the saloon.

The drummer, innocent and jocular, answered: "All right, old man. S'pose he has? Come in and have a drink, anyhow."

But the information had made such an obvious cleft in every skull in the room that the drummer was obliged to see its importance. All had become instantly solemn. "Say," said he, mystified, "what is this?" His
180 three companions made the introductory gesture of eloquent speech; but the young man at the door forestalled them.

"It means, my friend," he answered, as he came into the saloon, "that for the next two hours this town won't be a health resort."

The barkeeper went to the door, and locked and barred it; reaching out of the window, he pulled in heavy wooden shutters, and barred them. Immediately a solemn, chapel-like gloom was upon the place. The drummer was looking from one to another.

"But say," he cried, "what is this, anyhow? You don't mean there is going to be a gun-fight?"
190   "Don't know whether there'll be a fight or not," answered one man grimly; "but there'll be some shootin'—some good shootin'."

The young man who had warned them waved his hand. "Oh, there'll be a fight fast enough, if anyone wants it. Anybody can get a fight out there in the street. There's a fight just waiting."

The drummer seemed to be swayed between the interest of a foreigner and a perception of personal danger.

"What did you say his name was?" he asked.

"Scratchy Wilson," they answered in chorus.

"And will he kill anybody? What are you going to do? Does this
200 happen often? Does he rampage around like this once a week or so? Can he break in that door?"

"No; he can't break down that door," replied the barkeeper. "He's tried it three times. But when he comes you'd better lay down on the floor, stranger. He's dead sure to shoot at it, and a bullet may come through."

Thereafter the drummer kept a strict eye upon the door. The time had not yet been called for him to hug the floor, but, as a minor precaution, he sidled near to the wall. "Will he kill anybody?" he said again.

The men laughed low and scornfully at the question.

"He's out to shoot, and he's out for trouble. Don't see any good in
210 experimentin' with him."

"But what do you do in a case like this? What do you do?"

A man responded: "Why, he and Jack Potter—"

"But," in chorus the other men interrupted, "Jack Potter's in San Anton'."

"Well, who is he? What's he got to do with it?"

"Oh, he's the town marshal. He goes out and fights Scratchy when he gets on one of these tears."

"Wow!" said the drummer, mopping his brow. "Nice job he's got."

The voices had toned away to mere whisperings. The drummer
220 wished to ask further questions, which were born of an increasing anxiety and bewilderment; but when he attempted them, the men merely

looked at him in irritation and motioned him to remain silent. A tense waiting hush was upon them. In the deep shadows of the room their eyes shone as they listened for sounds from the street. One man made three gestures at the barkeeper; and the latter, moving like a ghost, handed him a glass and a bottle. The man poured a full glass of whisky, and set down the bottle noiselessly. He gulped the whisky in a swallow, and turned again toward the door in immovable silence. The drummer saw that the barkeeper, without a sound, had taken a Winchester from
230 beneath the bar. Later he saw this individual beckoning to him, so he tiptoed across the room.

"You better come with me back of the bar."

"No, thanks," said the drummer, perspiring; "I'd rather be where I can make a break for the back door."

Whereupon the man of bottles made a kindly but peremptory gesture. The drummer obeyed it, and, finding himself seated on a box with his head below the level of the bar, balm was laid upon his soul at sight of various zinc and copper fittings that bore a resemblance to armour-plate. The barkeeper took a seat comfortably upon an adjacent box.

240   "You see," he whispered, "this here Scratchy Wilson is a wonder with a gun—a perfect wonder; and when he goes on the war-trail, we hunt our holes—naturally. He's about the last one of the old gang that used to hang out along the river here. He's a terror when he's drunk. When he's sober he's all right—kind of simple—wouldn't hurt a fly—nicest fellow in town. But when he's drunk—whoo!"

There were periods of stillness. "I wish Jack Potter was back from San Anton'," said the barkeeper. "He shot Wilson up once—in the leg—and he would sail in and pull out the kinks in this thing."

Presently they heard from a distance the sound of a shot, followed
250 by three wild yowls. It instantly removed a bond from the men in the darkened saloon. There was a shuffling of feet. They looked at each other. "Here he comes," they said.

III

A man in a maroon-coloured flannel shirt, which had been purchased for purposes of decoration, and made principally by some Jewish women on the East Side of New York, rounded a corner and walked into the middle of the main street of Yellow Sky. In either hand the man held a long, heavy, blue-black revolver. Often he yelled, and these cries rang through a semblance of a deserted village, shrilly flying over the roofs in a volume that seemed to have no relation to the ordinary vocal strength of a man. It
260 was as if the surrounding stillness formed the arch of a tomb over him. These cries of ferocious challenge rang against walls of silence. And his boots had red tops with gilded imprints, of the kind beloved in winter by little sledding boys on the hillsides of New England.

The man's face flamed in a rage begot of whisky. He eyes, rolling, and yet keen for ambush, hunted the still doorways and windows. He

walked with the creeping movement of the midnight cat. As it occurred
to him, he roared menacing information. The long revolvers in his hands
were as easy as straws; they were moved with an electric swiftness. The
little fingers of each hand played sometimes in a musician's way. Plain
270 from the low collar of the shirt, the cords of his neck straightened and
sank, straightened and sank, as passion moved him. The only sounds
were his terrible invitations. The calm adobes preserved their de-
meanour at the passing of this small thing in the middle of the street.

There was no offer of fight—no offer of fight. The man called to the
sky. There were no attractions. He bellowed and fumed and swayed his
revolvers here and everywhere.

The dog of the barkeeper of the Weary Gentleman saloon had not appreciated the advance of events. He yet lay dozing in front of his master's
door. At sight of the dog, the man paused and raised his revolver humor-
280 ously. At sight of the man, the dog sprang up and walked diagonally
away, with a sullen head, and growling. The man yelled, and the dog
broke into a gallop. As it was about to enter an alley, there was a loud
noise, a whistling, and something spat the ground directly before it. The
dog screamed, and, wheeling in terror, galloped headlong in a new direction. Again there was a noise, a whistling, and sand was kicked viciously
before it. Fear-stricken, the dog turned and flurried like an animal in a
pen. The man stood laughing, his weapons at his hips.

Ultimately the man was attracted by the closed door of the Weary
Gentleman saloon. He went to it and, hammering with a revolver, de-
290 manded drink.

The door remaining imperturbable, he picked a bit of paper from the
walk, and nailed it to the framework with a knife. He then turned his
back contemptuously upon this popular resort and, walking to the opposite side of the street and spinning there on his heel quickly and
lithely, fired at the bit of paper. He missed it by a half-inch. He swore at
himself, and went away. Later he comfortably fusilladed the windows of
his most intimate friend. The man was playing with this town; it was a
toy for him.

But still there was no offer of fight. The name of Jack Potter, his an-
300 cient antagonist, entered his mind, and he concluded that it would be a
glad thing if he should go to Potter's house, and by bombardment induce
him to come out and fight. He moved in the direction of his desire,
chanting Apache scalp-music.

When he arrived at it, Potter's house presented the same still front
as had the other adobes. Taking up a strategic position, the man howled
a challenge. But this house regarded him as might a great stone god. It
gave no sign. After a decent wait, the man howled further challenges,
mingling with them wonderful epithets.

Presently there came the spectacle of a man churning himself into
310 deepest rage over the immobility of a house. He fumed at it as the winter
wind attacks a prairie cabin in the North. To the distance there should

have gone the sound of a tumult like the fighting of two hundred Mexicans. As necessity bade him, he paused for breath or to reload his revolvers.

IV

Potter and his bride walked sheepishly and with speed. Sometimes they laughed together shamefacedly and low.

"Next corner, dear," he said finally.

They put forth the efforts of a pair walking bowed against a strong wind. Potter was about to raise a finger to point the first appearance of
320 the new home when, as they circled the corner, they came face to face with a man in a maroon-coloured shirt, who was feverishly pushing cartridges into a large revolver. Upon the instant the man dropped his revolver to the ground and, like lightning, whipped another from its holster. The second weapon was aimed at the bridegroom's chest.

There was a silence. Potter's mouth seemed to be merely a grave for his tongue. He exhibited an instinct to at once loosen his arm from the woman's grip, and he dropped the bag to the sand. As for the bride, her face had gone as yellow as old cloth. She was a slave to hideous rites, gazing at the apparitional snake.
330   The two men faced each other at a distance of three paces. He of the revolver smiled with a new and quiet ferocity.

"Tried to sneak up on me," he said. "Tried to sneak up on me!" His eyes grew more baleful. As Potter made a slight movement, the man thrust his revolver venomously forward. "No; don't you do it, Jack Potter. Don't you move a finger toward a gun just yet. Don't you move an eyelash. The time has come for me to settle with you, and I'm goin' to do it my own way, and loaf along with no interferin'. So if you don't want a gun bent on you, just mind what I tell you."

Potter looked at his enemy. "I ain't got a gun on me, Scratchy," he said.
340 "Honest, I ain't." He was stiffening and steadying, but yet somewhere at the back of his mind a vision of the Pullman floated: the sea-green figured velvet, the shining brass, silver, and glass, the wood that gleamed as darkly brilliant as the surface of a pool of oil—all the glory of the marriage, the environment of the new estate. "You know I fight when it comes to fighting, Scratchy Wilson; but I ain't got a gun on me. You'll have to do all the shootin' yourself."

His enemy's face went livid. He stepped forward, and lashed his weapon to and fro before Potter's chest. "Don't you tell me you ain't got no gun on you, you whelp. Don't tell me no lie like that. There ain't a
350 man in Texas ever seen you without no gun. Don't take me for no kid." His eyes blazed with light, and his throat worked like a pump.

"I ain't takin' you for no kid," answered Potter. His heels had not moved an inch backward. "I'm takin' you for a damn fool. I tell you I ain't got a gun, and I ain't. If you're goin' to shoot me up, you better begin now; you'll never get a chance like this again."

So much enforced reasoning had told on Wilson's rage; he was calmer. "If you ain't got a gun, why ain't you got a gun?" he sneered. "Been to Sunday-school?"

"I ain't got a gun because I've just come from San Anton' with my 360 wife. I'm married," said Potter. "And if I'd thought there was going to be any galoots like you prowling around when I brought my wife home, I'd had a gun, and don't you forget it."

"Married!" said Scratchy, not at all comprehending.

"Yes, married. I'm married," said Potter, distinctly.

"Married?" said Scratchy. Seemingly for the first time, he saw the drooping, drowning woman at the other man's side. "No!" he said. He was like a creature allowed a glimpse of another world. He moved a pace backward, and his arm, with the revolver, dropped to his side. "Is this the lady?" he asked.

370 "Yes; this is the lady," answered Potter.

There was another period of silence.

"Well," said Wilson at last, slowly, "I s'pose it's all off now."

"It's all off if you say so, Scratchy. You know I didn't make the trouble." Potter lifted his valise.

"Well, I 'low it's off, Jack," said Wilson. He was looking at the ground. "Married!" He was not a student of chivalry; it was merely that in the presence of this foreign condition he was a simple child of the earlier plains. He picked up his starboard revolver, and, placing both weapons in their holsters, he went away. His feet made funnel-shaped 380 tracks in the heavy sand.

WILLA CATHER (1873–1947)

Paul's Case
(1905)

It was Paul's afternoon to appear before the faculty of the Pittsburgh High School to account for his various misdemeanors. He had been suspended a week ago, and his father had called at the Principal's office and confessed his perplexity about his son. Paul entered the faculty room suave and smiling. His clothes were a trifle outgrown, and the tan velvet on the collar of his open overcoat was frayed and worn; but for all that there was something of the dandy about him, and he wore an opal pin in his neatly knotted black four-in-hand, and a red carnation in his buttonhole. This latter adornment the faculty somehow felt was not properly significant of 10 the contrite spirit befitting a boy under the ban of suspension.

Paul was tall for his age and very thin, with high, cramped shoulders and a narrow chest. His eyes were remarkable for a certain hysterical brilliancy, and he continually used them in a conscious, theatrical sort of way, peculiarly offensive in a boy. The pupils were abnormally large, as though he were addicted to belladonna, but there was a glassy glitter about them which that drug does not produce.

When questioned by the Principal as to why he was there, Paul
stated, politely enough, that he wanted to come back to school. This was a
lie, but Paul was quite accustomed to lying; found it, indeed, indispens-
20 able for overcoming friction. His teachers were asked to state their respective charges against him, which they did with such a rancour and ag-
grievedness as evinced that this was not a usual case. Disorder and
impertinence were among the offences named, yet each of his instructors
felt that it was scarcely possible to put into words the real cause of the
trouble, which lay in a sort of hysterically defiant manner of the boy's; in
the contempt which they all knew he felt for them, and which he seemingly made not the least effort to conceal. Once, when he had been making a synopsis of a paragraph at the blackboard, his English teacher had
stepped to his side and attempted to guide his hand. Paul had started
30 back with a shudder and thrust his hands violently behind him. The astonished woman could scarcely have been more hurt and embarrassed
had he struck at her. The insult was so involuntary and definitely personal as to be unforgettable. In one way and another, he had made all his
teachers, men and women alike, conscious of the same feeling of physical
aversion. In one class he habitually sat with his hand shading his eyes; in
another he always looked out of the window during the recitation; in
another he made a running commentary on the lecture, with humorous
intent.

His teachers felt this afternoon that his whole attitude was symbol-
40 ized by his shrug and his flippantly red carnation flower, and they fell
upon him without mercy, his English teacher leading the pack. He stood
through it smiling, his pale lips parted over his white teeth. (His lips were
continually twitching, and he had a habit of raising his eyebrows that was
contemptuous and irritating to the last degree.) Older boys than Paul had
broken down and shed tears under that ordeal, but his set smile did not
once desert him, and his only sign of discomfort was the nervous trembling of the fingers that toyed with the buttons of his overcoat, and an occasional jerking of the other hand which held his hat. Paul was always
smiling, always glancing about him, seeming to feel that people might be
50 watching him and trying to detect something. This conscious expression,
since it was as far as possible from boyish mirthfulness, was usually attributed to insolence or "smartness."

As the inquisition proceeded, one of his instructors repeated an impertinent remark of the boy's, and the Principal asked him whether he
thought that a courteous speech to make to a woman. Paul shrugged his
shoulders slightly and his eyebrows twitched.

"I don't know," he replied. "I didn't mean to be polite or impolite,
either. I guess it's a sort of way I have, of saying things regardless."

The Principal asked him whether he didn't think that a way it
60 would be well to get rid of. Paul grinned and said he guessed so. When
he was told that he could go, he bowed gracefully and went out. His bow
was like a repetition of the scandalous red carnation.

His teachers were in despair, and his drawing-master voiced the
feeling of them all when he declared there was something about the boy

which none of them understood. He added: "I don't really believe that smile of his comes altogether from insolence; there's something sort of haunted about it. The boy is not strong, for one thing. There is something wrong about the fellow."

The drawing-master had come to realize that, in looking at Paul, one 70 saw only his white teeth and the forced animation of his eyes. One warm afternoon the boy had gone to sleep at his drawing-board, and his master had noted with amazement what a white, blue-veined face it was; drawn and wrinkled like an old man's about the eyes, the lips twitching even in his sleep.

His teachers left the building dissatisfied and unhappy; humiliated to have felt so vindictive toward a mere boy, to have uttered this feeling in cutting terms, and to have set each other on, as it were, in the gruesome game of intemperate reproach. One of them remembered having seen a miserable street cat set at bay by a ring of tormentors.

80 As for Paul, he ran down the hill whistling the Soldiers' Chorus from "Faust," looking behind him now and then to see whether some of his teachers were not there to witness his light-heartedness. As it was now late in the afternoon and Paul was on duty that evening as usher at Carnegie Hall, he decided that he would not go home to supper.

When he reached the concert hall, the doors were not yet open. It was chilly outside, and he decided to go up into the picture gallery— always deserted at this hour—where there were some of Raffelli's gay studies of Paris streets and an airy blue Venetian scene or two that always exhilarated him. He was delighted to find no one in the gallery 90 but the old guard, who sat in the corner, a newspaper on his knee, a black patch over one eye and the other closed. Paul possessed himself of the place and walked confidently up and down, whistling under his breath. After a while he sat down before a blue Rico and lost himself. When he bethought him to look at his watch, it was after seven o'clock, and he rose with a start and ran downstairs, making a face at Augustus Caesar, peering out from the cast-room, and an evil gesture at the Venus of Milo as he passed her on the stairway.

When Paul reached the ushers' dressing-room, half a dozen boys were there already, and he began excitedly to tumble into his uniform. It was 100 one of the few that at all approached fitting, and Paul thought it very becoming—though he knew the tight, straight coat accentuated his narrow chest, about which he was exceedingly sensitive. He was always excited while he dressed, twanging all over to the tuning of the strings and the preliminary flourishes of the horns in the music-room; but tonight he seemed quite beside himself, and he teased and plagued the boys until, telling him that he was crazy, they put him down on the floor and sat on him.

Somewhat calmed by his suppression, Paul dashed out to the front of the house to seat the early comers. He was a model usher. Gracious and 110 smiling he ran up and down the aisles. Nothing was too much trouble for him; he carried messages and brought programmes as though it were his greatest pleasure in life, and all the people in his section thought him a

charming boy, feeling that he remembered and admired them. As the house filled, he grew more and more vivacious and animated, and the colour came to his cheeks and lips. It was very much as though this were a great reception and Paul were the host. Just as the musicians came out to take their places, his English teacher arrived with cheques for the seats which a prominent manufacturer had taken for the season. She betrayed some embarrassment when she handed Paul the tickets, and a hauteur
120 which subsequently made her feel very foolish. Paul was startled for a moment, and had the feeling of wanting to put her out; what business had she here among all these fine people and gay colours? He looked her over and decided that she was not appropriately dressed and must be a fool to sit downstairs in such togs. The tickets had probably been sent her out of kindness, he reflected, as he put down a seat for her, and she had about as much right to sit there as he had.

When the symphony began, Paul sank into one of the rear seats with a long sigh of relief, and lost himself as he had done before the Rico. It was not that symphonies, as such, meant anything in particular to Paul,
130 but the first sight of the instruments seemed to free some hilarious spirit within him; something that struggled there like the Genius in the bottle found by the Arab fisherman. He felt a sudden zest of life; the lights danced before his eyes and the concert hall blazed into unimaginable splendour. When the soprano soloist came on, Paul forgot even the nastiness of his teacher's being there, and gave himself up to the peculiar intoxication such personages always had for him. The soloist chanced to be a German woman, by no means in her first youth, and the mother of many children; but she wore a satin gown and a tiara, and she had that indefinable air of achievement, that world-shine upon her, which always
140 blinded Paul to any possible defects.

After a concert was over, Paul was often irritable and wretched until he got to sleep—and to-night he was even more than usually restless. He had the feeling of not being able to let down; of its being impossible to give up his delicious excitement which was the only thing that could be called living at all. During the last number he withdrew and, after hastily changing his clothes in the dressing-room, slipped out to the side door where the singer's carriage stood. Here he began pacing rapidly up and down the walk, waiting to see her come out.

Over yonder the Schenley, in its vacant stretch, loomed big and
150 square through the fine rain, the windows of its twelve stories glowing like those of a lighted cardboard house under a Christmas tree. All the actors and singers of any importance stayed there when they were in Pittsburgh, and a number of the big manufacturers of the place lived there in the winter. Paul had often hung about the hotel, watching the people go in and out, longing to enter and leave schoolmasters and dull care behind him forever.

At last the singer came out, accompanied by the conductor, who helped her into her carriage and closed the door with a cordial *auf wiedersehen*—which set Paul to wondering whether she were not an old

160 sweetheart of his. Paul followed the carriage over to the hotel, walking so rapidly as not to be far from the entrance when the singer alighted and disappeared behind the swinging glass doors which were opened by a Negro in a tall hat and a long coat. In the moment that the door was ajar, it seemed to Paul that he, too, entered. He seemed to feel himself go after her up the steps, into the warm, lighted building, into an exotic, a tropical world of shiny, glistening surfaces and basking ease. He reflected upon the mysterious dishes that were brought into the dining-room, the green bottles in buckets of ice, as he had seen them in the supper-party pictures of the Sunday supplement. A quick gust of wind brought the rain down

170 with sudden vehemence, and Paul was startled to find that he was still outside in the slush of the gravel driveway; that his boots were letting in the water and his scanty overcoat was clinging wet about him; that the lights in front of the concert hall were out, and that the rain was driving in sheets between him and the orange glow of the windows above him. There it was, what he wanted—tangibly before him, like the fairy world of a Christmas pantomime; as the rain beat in his face, Paul wondered whether he were destined always to shiver in the black night outside, looking up at it.

He turned and walked reluctantly toward the car tracks. The end had

180 to come sometime; his father in his night-clothes at the top of the stairs, explanations that did not explain, hastily improvised fictions that were forever tripping him up, his upstairs room and its horrible yellow wallpaper, the creaking bureau with the greasy plush collar-box, and over his painted wooden bed the pictures of George Washington and John Calvin, and the framed motto, 'Feed my Lambs,' which had been worked in red worsted by his mother, whom Paul could not remember.

Half an hour later, Paul alighted from the Negley Avenue car and went slowly down one of the side streets off the main thoroughfare. It was a highly respectable street, where all the houses were exactly alike,

190 and where business men of moderate means begot and reared large families of children, all of whom went to Sabbath School and learned the shorter catechism, and were interested in arithmetic; all of whom were as exactly alike as their homes, and of a piece with the monotony in which they lived. Paul never went up Cordelia Street without a shudder of loathing. His home was next the house of the Cumberland minister. He approached it to-night with the nerveless sense of defeat, the hopeless feeling of sinking back forever into ugliness and commonness that he had always had when he came home. The moment he turned into Cordelia Street he felt the waters close above his head. After each of

200 these orgies of living, he experienced all the physical depression which follows a debauch; the loathing of respectful beds, of common food, of a house permeated by kitchen odours; a shuddering repulsion for the flavourless, colourless mass of every-day existence; a morbid desire for cool things and soft lights and fresh flowers.

The nearer he approached the house, the more absolutely unequal Paul felt to the sight of it all: his ugly sleeping chamber; the old bathroom

with the grimy zinc tub, the cracked mirror, the dripping spigots; his father, at the top of the stairs, his hairy legs sticking out from his night-shirt, his feet thrust into carpet slippers. He was so much later than usual
210 that there would certainly be enquiries and reproaches. Paul stopped short before the door. He felt that he could not be accosted by his father to-night; that he could not toss again on that miserable bed. He would not go in. He would tell his father that he had no car-fare, and it was raining so hard he had gone home with one of the boys and stayed all night.

Meanwhile, he was wet and cold. He went around to the back of the house and tried one of the basement windows, found it open, and raised it cautiously, and scrambled down the cellar wall to the floor. There he stood, holding his breath, terrified by the noise he had made; but the floor above him was silent, and there was no creak on the stairs. He found
220 a soap-box, and carried it over to the soft ring of light that streamed from the furnace door, and sat down. He was horribly afraid of rats, so he did not try to sleep, but sat looking distrustfully at the dark, still terrified lest he might have awakened his father.

In such reactions, after one of the experiences which made days and nights out of the dreary blanks of the calendar, when his senses were deadened, Paul's head was always singularly clear. Suppose his father had heard him getting in at the window and had come down and shot him for a burglar? Then again, suppose his father had come down, pistol in hand, and he had cried out in time to save himself, and his father had been hor-
230 rified to think how nearly he had killed him? Then again, suppose a day should come when his father would remember that night, and wish there had been no warning cry to stay his hand? With this last supposition Paul entertained himself until daybreak.

The following Sunday was fine; the sodden November chill was broken by the last flash of autumnal summer. In the morning Paul had to go to church and Sabbath School, as always. On seasonable Sunday afternoons the burghers of Cordelia Street usually sat out on their front "stoops," and talked to their neighbours on the next stoop, or called to those across the street in neighbourly fashion. The men sat placidly on gay cushions
240 placed upon the steps that led down to the sidewalk, while the women, in their Sunday "waists," sat in rockers on the cramped porches, pretending to be greatly at their ease. The children played in the streets; there were so many of them that the place resembled the recreation grounds of a kindergarten. The men on the steps, all in their shirt-sleeves, their vests unbuttoned, sat with their legs well apart, their stomachs comfortably protruding, and talked of the prices of things, or told anecdotes of the sagacity of their various chiefs and overlords. They occasionally looked over the multitude of squabbling children, listened affectionately to their high-pitched, nasal voices, smiling to see their own proclivities repro-
250 duced in their offspring, and interspersed their legends of the iron kings with remarks about their sons' progress at school, their grades in arithmetic, and the amounts they had saved in their toy banks.

On this last Sunday of November, Paul sat all afternoon on the lowest step of his "stoop," staring into the street, while his sisters, in their rockers, were talking to the minister's daughters next door about how many shirtwaists they had made in the last week, and how many waffles someone had eaten at the last church supper. When the weather was warm, and his father was in a particularly jovial frame of mind, the girls made lemonade, which was always brought out in a red-glass pitcher, ornamented with forget-me-nots in blue enamel. This the girls thought very fine, and the neighbours joked about the suspicious colour of the pitcher.

To-day Paul's father, on the top step, was talking to a young man who shifted a restless baby from knee to knee. He happened to be the young man who was daily held up to Paul as a model, and after whom it was his father's dearest hope that he would pattern. This young man was of a ruddy complexion, with a compressed, red mouth, and faded, nearsighted eyes, over which he wore thick spectacles, with gold bows that curved about his ears. He was clerk to one of the magnates of a great steel corporation, and was looked upon in Cordelia Street as a young man with a future. There was a story that, some five years ago—he was now barely twenty-six—he had been a trifle "dissipated," but in order to curb his appetites and save the loss of time and strength that a sowing of wild oats might have entailed, he had taken his chief's advice, oft reiterated to his employees, and at twenty-one had married the first woman whom he could persuade to share his fortunes. She happened to be an angular schoolmistress, much older than he, who also wore thick glasses, and who had now borne him four children, all nearsighted like herself.

The young man was relating how his chief, now cruising in the Mediterranean, kept in touch with all the details of the business, arranging his office hours on his yacht just as though he were at home, and "knocking off work enough to keep two stenographers busy." His father told, in turn, the plan his corporation was considering, of putting in an electric railway plant at Cairo. Paul snapped his teeth; he had an awful apprehension that they might spoil it all before he got there. Yet he rather liked to hear these legends of the iron kings, that were told and retold on Sundays and holidays; these stories of palaces in Venice, yachts on the Mediterranean, and high play at Monte Carlo appealed to his fancy, and he was interested in the triumphs of cash-boys who had become famous, though he had no mind for the cash-boy stage.

After supper was over, and he had helped to dry the dishes, Paul nervously asked his father whether he could go to George's to get some help in his geometry, and still more nervously asked for car-fare. This latter request he had to repeat, as his father, on principle, did not like to hear requests for money, whether much or little. He asked Paul whether he could not go to some boy who lived nearer, and told him that he ought not to leave his school work until Sunday; but he gave him the dime. He was not a poor man, but he had a worthy ambition to come up in the world.

His only reason for allowing Paul to usher was that he thought a boy
300 ought to be earning a little.

Paul bounded upstairs, scrubbed the greasy odour of the dishwater
from his hands with the ill-smelling soap he hated, and then shook over
his fingers a few drops of violet water from the bottle he kept hidden in
his drawer. He left the house with his geometry conspicuously under
this arm, and the moment he got out of Cordelia Street and boarded a
downtown car, he shook off the lethargy of two deadening days, and began to live again.

The leading juvenile of the permanent stock company which played at
one of the downtown theatres was an acquaintance of Paul's, and the boy
310 had been invited to drop in at the Sunday-night rehearsals whenever he
could. For more than a year Paul had spent every available moment loitering about Charley Edwards's dressing-room. He had won a place among
Edwards's following not only because the young actor, who could not afford to employ a dresser, often found him useful, but because he recognized in Paul something akin to what churchmen term "vocation."

It was at the theatre and at Carnegie Hall that Paul really lived; the
rest was but sleep and a forgetting. This was Paul's fairy tale, and it had
for him all the allurement of a secret love. The moment he inhaled the
gassy, painty, dusty odour behind the scenes, he breathed like a prisoner
320 set free, and felt within him the possibility of doing or saying splendid,
brilliant things. The moment the cracked orchestra beat out the overture
from "Martha," or jerked at the serenade from "Rigoletto," all stupid and
ugly things slid from him, and his senses were deliciously, yet delicately
fired.

Perhaps it was because, in Paul's world, the natural nearly always
wore the guise of ugliness, that a certain element of artificiality seemed
to him necessary in beauty. Perhaps it was because his experience of life
elsewhere was so full of Sabbath-School picnics, petty economies, wholesome advice as to how to succeed in life, and the unescapable odours of
330 cooking, that he found this existence so alluring, these smartly clad men
and women so attractive, that he was so moved by these starry apple orchards that bloomed perennially under the limelight. It would be difficult
to put it strongly enough how convincingly the stage entrance of the theatre was for Paul the actual portal of Romance, Certainly none of the company ever suspected it, least of all Charley Edwards. It was very like the
old stories that used to float about London of fabulously rich Jews, who
had subterranean halls, with palms, and fountains, and soft lamps
and richly apparelled women who never saw the disenchanting light of
London day. So, in the midst of that smoke-palled city, enamoured of fig-
340 ures and grimy toil, Paul had his secret temple, his wishing-carpet, his bit
of blue-and-white Mediterranean shore bathed in perpetual sunshine.

Several of Paul's teachers had a theory that his imagination had been
perverted by garish fiction; but the truth was he scarcely ever read at
all. The books at home were not such as would either tempt or corrupt a

youthful mind, and as for reading the novels that some of his friends urged upon him—well, he got what he wanted much more quickly from music; any sort of music, from an orchestra to a barrel-organ. He needed only the spark, the indescribable thrill that made his imagination master of his senses, and he could make plots and pictures enough of his own. It 350 was equally true that he was not stage-struck—not, at any rate, in the usual acceptation of that expression. He had no desire to become an actor, any more than he had to become a musician. He felt no necessity to do any of these things; what he wanted was to see, to be in the atmosphere, float on the wave of it, to be carried out, blue league after league, away from everything.

After a night behind the scenes, Paul found the schoolroom more than ever repulsive; the bare floors and naked walls; the prosy men who never wore frock coats, or violets in their buttonholes; the women with their dull gowns, shrill voices, and pitiful seriousness about preposi-360 tions that govern the dative. He could not bear to have the other pupils think, for a moment, that he took these people seriously; he must convey to them that he considered it all trivial, and was there only by way of a joke, anyway. He had autographed pictures of all the members of the stock company which he showed his classmates, telling them the most incredible stories of his familiarity with these people, of his acquaintance with the soloists who came to Carnegie Hall, his suppers with them and the flowers he sent them. When these stories lost their effect, and his audience grew listless, he would bid all the boys goodbye, announcing that he was going to travel for a while; going to Naples, to 370 California, to Egypt. Then, next Monday, he would slip back, conscious and nervously smiling; his sister was ill, and he would have to defer his voyage until spring.

Matters went steadily worse with Paul at school. In the itch to let his instructors know how heartily he despised them, and how thoroughly he was appreciated elsewhere, he mentioned once or twice that he had no time to fool with theorems; adding—with a twitch of the eyebrows and a touch of that nervous bravado which so perplexed them—that he was helping the people down at the stock company; they were old friends of his.

380 The upshot of the matter was that the Principal went to Paul's father, and Paul was taken out of school and put to work. The manager at Carnegie Hall was told to get another usher in his stead; the doorkeeper at the theatre was warned not to admit him to the house; and Charley Edwards remorsefully promised the boy's father not to see him again.

The members of the stock company were vastly amused when some of Paul's stories reached them—especially the women. They were hardworking women, most of them supporting indolent husbands or brothers, and they laughed rather bitterly at having stirred the boy to such fervid and florid inventions. They agreed with the faculty and with his 390 father, that Paul's was a bad case.

The east-bound train was ploughing through a January snowstorm; the dull dawn was beginning to show grey when the engine whistled a mile out of Newark. Paul started up from the seat where he had lain curled in uneasy slumber, rubbed the breath-misted window-glass with his hand, and peered out. The snow was whirling in curling eddies above the white bottom lands, and the drifts lay already deep in the fields and along the fences, while here and there the tall dead grass and dried weed stalks protruded black above it. Lights shone from the scattered houses, and a gang of labourers who stood beside the track waved 400 their lanterns.

Paul had slept very little, and he felt grimy and uncomfortable. He had made the all-night journey in a day coach because he was afraid if he took a Pullman he might be seen by some Pittsburgh business man who had noticed him in Denny and Carson's office. When the whistle woke him, he clutched quickly at his breast pocket, glancing about him with an uncertain smile. But the little, clay-bespattered Italians were still sleeping, the slatternly women across the aisle were in open-mouthed oblivion, and even the crumby, crying babies were for the time stilled. Paul settled back to struggle with his impatience as best he could.

410   When he arrived at the Jersey City station, he hurried through his breakfast, manifestly ill at ease and keeping a sharp eye about him. After he reached the Twenty-Third Street station, he consulted a cabman, and had himself driven to a men's furnishing establishment which was just opening for the day. He spent upward of two hours there, buying with endless reconsidering and great care. His new street suit he put on in the fitting-room; the frock coat and dress clothes he had bundled into the cab with his new shirts. Then he drove to a hatter's and a shoe house. His next errand was at Tiffany's, where he selected silver-mounted brushes and a scarf-pin. He would not wait to have his silver marked, he said. 420 Lastly, he stopped at a trunk shop on Broadway, and had his purchases packed into various travelling-bags.

It was a little after one o'clock when he drove up to the Waldorf, and, after settling with the cabman, went into the office. He registered from Washington; said his mother and father had been abroad, and that he had come down to await the arrival of their steamer. He told his story plausibly and had no trouble, since he offered to pay for them in advance, in engaging his rooms; a sleeping-room, sitting-room, and bath.

Not once, but a hundred times Paul had planned this entry into New York. He had gone over every detail of it with Charley Edwards, and in 430 his scrapbook at home there were pages of description about New York hotels, cut from the Sunday papers.

When he was shown to his sitting-room on the eighth floor, he saw at a glance that everything was as it should be; there was but one detail in his mental picture that the place did not realize, so he rang for the bell-boy and sent him down for flowers. He moved about nervously until the boy returned, putting away his new linen and fingering it delightedly

as he did so. When the flowers came, he put them hastily into water, and then tumbled into a hot bath. Presently he came out of his white bath-room, resplendent in his new silk underwear, and playing with the tassels
440 of his red robe. The snow was whirling so fiercely outside his windows that he could scarcely see across the street; but within, the air was deli-ciously soft and fragrant. He put the violets and jonquils on the tabouret beside the couch, and threw himself down with a long sigh, covering him-self with a Roman blanket. He was thoroughly tired; he had been in such haste, he had stood up to such a strain, covered so much ground in the last twenty-four hours, that he wanted to think how it had all come about. Lulled by the sound of the wind, the warm air, and the cool fragrance of the flowers, he sank into deep, drowsy retrospection.

It had been wonderfully simple; when they had shut him out of the
450 theatre and concert hall, when they had taken away his bone, the whole thing was virtually determined. The rest was a mere matter of opportu-nity. The only thing that at all surprised him was his own courage—for he realized well enough that he had always been tormented by fear, a sort of apprehensive dread which, of late years, as the meshes of the lies he had told closed about him, had been pulling the muscles of his body tighter and tighter. Until now, he could not remember a time when he had not been dreading something. Even when he was a little boy, it was always there—behind him, or before, or on either side. There had always been the shadowed corner, the dark place into which he dared not look, but
460 from which something seemed always to be watching him—and Paul had done things that were not pretty to watch, he knew.

But now he had a curious sense of relief, as though he had at last thrown down the gauntlet to the thing in the corner.

Yet it was but a day since he had been sulking in the traces; but yesterday afternoon that he had been sent to the bank with Denny and Carson's deposit, as usual—but this time he was instructed to leave the book to be balanced. There was above two thousand dollars in cheques, and nearly a thousand in the banknotes which he had taken from the book and quietly transferred to his pocket. At the bank he had made out
470 a new deposit slip. His nerves had been steady enough to permit of his returning to the office, where he had finished his work and asked for a full day's holiday to-morrow, Saturday, giving a perfectly reasonable pre-text. The bank book, he knew, would not be returned before Monday or Tuesday, and his father would be out of town for the next week. From the time he slipped the banknotes into his pocket until he boarded the night train for New York, he had not known a moment's hesitation.

How astonishingly easy it had all been; here he was, the thing done; and this time there would be no awakening, no figure at the top of the stairs. He watched the snowflakes whirling by his window until he fell
480 asleep.

When he awoke, it was four o'clock in the afternoon. He bounded up with a start; one of his precious days gone already! He spent nearly an hour in dressing, watching every stage of his toilet carefully in the mirror. Everything was quite perfect; he was exactly the kind of boy he had always wanted to be.

When he went downstairs, Paul took a carriage and drove up Fifth Avenue toward the Park. The snow had somewhat abated; carriages and tradesmen's wagons were hurrying soundlessly to and fro in the winter twilight; boys in woollen mufflers were shovelling off the doorsteps; the 490 Avenue stages made fine spots of colour against the white sheet. Here and there on the corners whole flower gardens blooming behind glass windows, against which the snowflakes stuck and melted; violets, roses, carnations, lilies-of-the-valley—somehow vastly more lovely and alluring that they blossomed thus unnaturally in the snow. The Park itself was a wonderful stage winter-piece.

When he returned, the pause of the twilight had ceased, and the tune of the streets had changed. The snow was falling faster, lights streamed from the hotels that reared their many stories fearlessly up into the storm, defying the raging Atlantic winds. A long, black stream of car- 500 riages poured down the Avenue, intersected here and there by other streams, tending horizontally. There were a score of cabs about the entrance of his hotel, and his driver had to wait. Boys in livery were running in and out of the awning stretched across the sidewalk, up and down the red velvet carpet laid from the door to the street. Above, about, within it all, was the rumble and roar, the hurry and toss of thousands of human beings as hot for pleasure as himself, and on every side of him towered the glaring affirmation of the omnipotence of wealth.

The boy set his teeth and drew his shoulders together in a spasm of realization; the plot of all dramas, the text of all romances, the nerve- 510 stuff of all sensations was whirling about him like the snowflakes. He burnt like a fagot in a tempest.

When Paul came down to dinner, the music of the orchestra floated up the elevator shaft to greet him. As he stepped into the thronged corridor, he sank back into one of the chairs against the wall to get his breath. The lights, the chatter, the perfumes, the bewildering medley of colour—he had, for a moment, the feeling of not being able to stand it. But only for a moment; these were his own people, he told himself. He went slowly about the corridors, through the writing-rooms, smoking-rooms, reception-rooms, as though he were exploring the chambers of an enchanted palace, 520 built and peopled for him alone.

When he reached the dining-room he sat down at a table near a window. The flowers, the white linen, the many-coloured wine-glasses, the gay toilettes of the women, the low popping of corks, the undulating repetitions of the "Blue Danube" from the orchestra, all flooded Paul's dream with bewildering radiance. When the roseate tinge of his champagne was added—that cold, precious, bubbling stuff that creamed and foamed in his glass—Paul wondered that there were honest men in the world at all. This was what all the world was fighting for, he reflected; this was what all the struggle was about. He doubted the reality of his past. Had he ever

530 known a place called Cordelia Street, a place where fagged-looking business men boarded the early car? Mere rivets in a machine they seemed to Paul—sickening men, with combings of children's hair always hanging to their coats, and the smell of cooking in their clothes. Cordelia Street—Ah, that belonged to another time and country! Had he not always been thus, had he not sat here night after night, from as far back as he could remember, looking pensively over just such shimmering textures, and slowly twirling the stem of a glass like this one between his thumb and middle finger? He rather thought he had.

He was not in the least abashed or lonely. He had no especial desire to
540 meet or to know any of these people; all he demanded was the right to look on and conjecture, to watch the pageant. The mere stage properties were all he contended for. Nor was he lonely later in the evening, in his loge at the Opera. He was entirely rid of his nervous misgivings, of his forced aggressiveness, of the imperative desire to show himself different from his surroundings. He felt now that his surroundings explained him. Nobody questioned the purple; he had only to wear it passively. He had only to glance down at his dress coat to reassure himself that here it would be impossible for anyone to humiliate him.

He found it hard to leave his beautiful sitting-room to go to bed that
550 night, and sat long watching the raging storm from his turret window. When he went to sleep, it was with the lights turned on in his bedroom; partly because of his old timidity, and partly so that, if he should wake in the night, there would be no wretched moment of doubt, no horrible suspicion of yellow wallpaper, or of Washington and Calvin above his bed.

On Sunday morning the city was practically snowbound. Paul breakfasted late, and in the afternoon he fell in with a wild San Francisco boy, a freshman at Yale, who said he had run down for a "little flyer" over Sunday. The young man offered to show Paul the night side of the town, and the two boys went off together after dinner, not returning to the
560 hotel until seven o'clock the next morning. They had started out in the confiding warmth of a champagne friendship, but their parting in the elevator was singularly cool. The freshman pulled himself together to make his train, and Paul went to bed. He awoke at two o'clock in the afternoon, very thirsty and dizzy, and rang for ice-water, coffee, and the Pittsburgh papers.

On the part of the hotel management, Paul excited no suspicion. There was this to be said for him, that he wore his spoils with dignity and in no way made himself conspicuous. His chief greediness lay in his ears and eyes, and his excesses were not offensive ones. His dearest
570 pleasures were the grey winter twilights in his sitting-room; his quiet enjoyment of his flowers, his clothes, his wide divan, his cigarette, and his sense of power. He could not remember a time when he had felt so at peace with himself. The mere release from the necessity of petty lying, lying every day and every day, restored his self-respect. He had never lied for pleasure, even at school; but to make himself noticed and admired, to assert his difference from other Cordelia Street boys; and he

felt a good deal more manly, more honest, even, now that he had no need for boastful pretensions, now that he could, as his actor friends used to say, "dress the part." It was characteristic that remorse did not occur to
580 him. His golden days went by without a shadow, and he made each as perfect as he could.

On the eighth day after his arrival in New York, he found the whole affair exploited in the Pittsburgh papers, exploited with a wealth of detail which indicated that local news of a sensational nature was at a low ebb. The firm of Denny and Carson announced that the boy's father had re-funded the full amount of his theft, and that they had no intention of prosecuting. The Cumberland minister had been interviewed, and ex-pressed his hope of yet reclaiming the motherless lad, and Paul's Sabbath-School teacher declared that she would spare no effort to that end. The
590 rumour had reached Pittsburgh that the boy had been seen in a New York hotel, and his father had gone East to find him and bring him home.

Paul had just come in to dress for dinner; he sank into the chair, weak in the knees, and clasped his head in his hands. It was to be worse than jail, even; the tepid waters of Cordelia Street were to close over him fi-nally and forever. The grey monotony stretched before him in hopeless, unrelieved years;—Sabbath-School, Young People's Meeting, the yellow-papered room, the damp dish-towels; it all rushed back upon him with sickening vividness. He had the old feeling that the orchestra had sud-denly stopped, the sinking sensation that the play was over. The sweat
600 broke out on his face, and he sprang to his feet, looked about him with his white, conscious smile, and winked at himself in the mirror. With some-thing of the childish belief in miracles with which he had so often gone to class, all his lessons unlearned, Paul dressed and dashed whistling down the corridor to the elevator.

He had no sooner entered the dining-room and caught the measure of the music than his remembrance was lightened by his old elastic power of claiming the moment, mounting with it, and finding it all-sufficient. The glare and glitter about him, the mere scenic accessories had again, and for the last time, their old potency. He would show him-
610 self that he was game, he would finish the thing splendidly. He doubted, more than ever, the existence of Cordelia Street, and for the first time he drank his wine recklessly. Was he not, after all, one of these fortunate beings? Was he not still himself, and in his own place? He drummed a nervous accompaniment to the music and looked about him, telling himself over and over that it had paid.

He reflected drowsily, to the swell of the violin and the chill sweet-ness of his wine, that he might have done it more wisely. He might have caught an outbound steamer and been well out of their clutches before now. But the other side of the world had seemed too far away and too un-
620 certain then; he could not have waited for it; his need had been too sharp. If he had to choose over again, he would do the same thing to-morrow. He looked affectionately about the dining-room, now gilded with a soft mist. Ah, it had paid indeed!

Paul was awakened next morning by a painful throbbing in his head and feet. He had thrown himself across the bed without undressing, and had slept with his shoes on. His limbs and hands were lead-heavy, and his tongue and throat were parched. There came upon him one of those fateful attacks of clear-headedness that never occurred except when he was physically exhausted and his nerves hung loose. He lay still and closed his 630 eyes and let the tide of realities wash over him.

His father was in New York; "stopping at some joint or other," he told himself. The memory of successive summers on the front stoop fell upon him like a weight of black water. He had not a hundred dollars left; and he knew now, more than ever, that money was everything, the wall that stood between all he loathed and all he wanted. The thing was winding itself up; he had thought of that on his first glorious day in New York, and had even provided a way to snap the thread. It lay on his dressing-table now; he had got it out last night when he came blindly up from dinner—but the shiny metal hurt his eyes, and he disliked the 640 look of it, anyway.

He rose and moved about with a painful effort, succumbing now and again to attacks of nausea. It was the old depression exaggerated; all the world had become Cordelia Street. Yet somehow he was not afraid of anything, was absolutely calm; perhaps because he had looked into the dark corner at last, and knew. It was bad enough, what he saw there; but somehow not so bad as his long fear of it had been. He saw everything clearly now. He had a feeling that he had made the best of it, that he had lived the sort of life he was meant to live, and for half an hour he sat staring at the revolver. But he told himself that was not the way, so he 650 went downstairs and took a cab to the ferry.

When Paul arrived at Newark, he got off the train and took another cab, directing the driver to follow the Pennsylvania tracks out of the town. The snow lay heavy on the roadways and had drifted deep in the open fields. Only here and there the dead grass or dried weed stalks projected, singularly black, above it.

Once well into the country, Paul dismissed the carriage and walked, floundering along the tracks, his mind a medley of irrelevant things. He seemed to hold in his brain an actual picture of everything he had seen that morning. He remembered every feature of both his drivers, the 660 toothless old woman from whom he had bought the red flowers in his coat, the agent from whom he had got his ticket, and all of his fellow-passengers on the ferry. His mind, unable to cope with vital matters near at hand, worked feverishly and deftly at sorting and grouping these images. They made for him a part of the ugliness of the world, of the ache in his head, and the bitter burning on his tongue. He stooped and put a handful of snow into his mouth as he walked, but that, too, seemed hot. When he reached a little hillside, where the tracks ran through a cut some twenty feet below him, he stopped and sat down.

The carnations in his coat were drooping with the cold, he noticed; 670 their red glory over. It occurred to him that all the flowers he had seen in the show windows that first night must have gone the same way, long before this. It was only one splendid breath they had, in spite of their brave mockery at the winter outside the glass. It was a losing game in the end, it seemed, this revolt against the homilies by which the world is run. Paul took one of the blossoms carefully from his coat and scooped a little hole in the snow, where he covered it up. Then he dozed awhile, from his weak condition, seeming insensible to the cold.

The sound of an approaching train woke him and he started to his feet, remembering only his resolution, and afraid lest he should be too
680 late. He stood watching the approaching locomotive, his teeth chattering, his lips drawn away from them in a frightened smile; once or twice he glanced nervously sidewise, as though he were being watched. When the right moment came, he jumped. As he fell, the folly of his haste occurred to him with merciless clearness, the vastness of what he had left undone. There flashed through his brain, clearer than ever before, the blue of Adriatic water, the yellow of Algerian sands.

He felt something strike his chest—his body was being thrown swiftly through the air, on and on, immeasurably far and fast, while his limbs gently relaxed. Then, because the picture-making mechanism was
690 crushed, the disturbing visions flashed into black, and Paul dropped back into the immense design of things.

VIRGINIA WOOLF (1882–1941)

Kew Gardens
(1919)

From the oval-shaped flower-bed there rose perhaps a hundred stalks spreading into heart-shaped or tongue-shaped leaves half-way up and unfurling at the tip red or blue or yellow petals marked with spots of colour raised upon the surface; and from the red, blue or yellow gloom of the throat emerged a straight bar, rough with gold dust and slightly clubbed at the end. The petals were voluminous enough to be stirred by the summer breeze, and when they moved, the red, blue and yellow lights passed one over the other, staining an inch of the brown earth beneath with a spot of the most intricate colour. The light fell either upon the smooth,
10 grey back of a pebble, or, the shell of a snail with its brown, circular veins, or falling into a raindrop, it expanded with such intensity of red, blue and yellow the thin walls of water that one expected them to burst and disappear. Instead, the drop was left in a second silver grey once more, and the light now settled upon the flesh of a leaf, revealing the branching thread of fibre beneath the surface, and again it moved on and spread its illumination in the vast green spaces beneath the dome of the heart-shaped and tongue-shaped leaves. Then the breeze stirred rather more briskly overhead and the colour was flashed into the air above, into the eyes of the men and women who walk in Kew Gardens in July.

20   The figures of these men and women straggled past the flower-bed with a curiously irregular movement not unlike that of the white and blue butterflies who crossed the turf in zig-zag flights from bed to bed. The man was about six inches in front of the woman, strolling carelessly, while she bore on with greater purpose, only turning her head now and then to see that the children were not too far behind. The man kept this distance in front of the woman purposely, though perhaps unconsciously, for he wished to go on with his thoughts.

"Fifteen years ago I came here with Lily," he thought. "We sat some-where over there by a lake and I begged her to marry me all through the
30 hot afternoon. How the dragonfly kept circling round us: how clearly I see the dragonfly and her shoe with the square silver buckle at the toe. All the time I spoke I saw her shoe and when it moved impatiently I knew without looking up what she was going to say: the whole of her seemed to be in her shoe. And my love, my desire, were in the dragon-fly; for some reason I thought that if it settled there, on that leaf, the broad one with the red flower in the middle of it, if the dragonfly set-tled on the leaf she would say 'Yes' at once. But the dragonfly went round and round: it never settled anywhere—of course not, happily not, or I shouldn't be walking here with Eleanor and the children. Tell me,
40 Eleanor. D'you ever think of the past?"

"Why do you ask, Simon?"

"Because I've been thinking of the past. I've been thinking of Lily, the woman I might have married. . . . Well, why are you silent? Do you mind my thinking of the past?"

"Why should I mind, Simon? Doesn't one always think of the past, in a garden with men and women lying under the trees. Aren't they one's past, all that remains of it, those men and women, those ghosts lying under the trees, . . . one's happiness, one's reality?"

"For me, a square silver shoe buckle and a dragonfly—"
50   "For me, a kiss. Imagine six little girls sitting before their easels twenty years ago, down by the side of a lake, painting the water-lilies, the first red water-lilies I'd ever seen. And suddenly a kiss, there on the back of my neck. And my hand shook all the afternoon so that I couldn't paint. I took out my watch and marked the hour when I would allow myself to think of the kiss for five minutes only—it was so precious—the kiss of an old grey-haired woman with a wart on her nose, the mother of all my kisses all my life. Come, Caroline, come, Hubert."

They walked on past the flower-bed, now walking four abreast, and soon diminished in size among the trees and looked half transparent as
60 the sunlight and shade swam over their backs in large trembling irregu-lar patches.

In the oval flower-bed the snail, whose shell had been stained red, blue and yellow for the space of two minutes or so, now appeared to be moving very slightly in its shell, and next began to labour over the crumbs of loose earth which broke away and rolled down as it passed

over them. It appeared to have a definite goal in front of it, differing in
this respect from the singular high stepping angular green insect who
attempted to cross in front of it, and waited for a second with its anten-
nae trembling as if in deliberation, and then stepped off as rapidly and
70 strangely in the opposite direction. Brown cliffs with deep green lakes
in the hollows, flat, blade-like trees that waved from root to tip, round
boulders of grey stone, vast crumpled surfaces of a thin crackling
texture—all these objects lay across the snail's progress between one
stalk and another to his goal. Before he had decided whether to circumvent the arched tent of a dead leaf or to breast it there came past the bed
the feet of other human beings.

This time they were both men. The younger of the two wore an expression of perhaps unnatural calm; he raised his eyes and fixed them
very steadily in front of him while his companion spoke, and directly his
80 companion had done speaking he looked on the ground again and sometimes opened his lips only after a long pause and sometimes did not open
them at all. The elder man had a curiously uneven and shaky method of
walking, jerking his hand forward and throwing up his head abruptly,
rather in the manner of an impatient carriage horse tired of waiting outside a house; but in the man these gestures were irresolute and pointless.
He talked almost incessantly; he smiled to himself and again began to
talk, as if the smile had been an answer. He was talking about spirits—the
spirits of the dead, who, according to him, were even now telling him all
sorts of odd things about their experiences in Heaven.
90 "Heaven was known to the ancients as Thessaly, William, and now,
with this war, the spirit matter is rolling between the hills like thunder."
He paused, seemed to listen, smiled, jerked his head and continued:
"You have a small electric battery and a piece of rubber to insulate
the wire—isolate?—insulate?—well, we'll skip the details, no good going into details that wouldn't be understood—and in short the little machine stands in any convenient position by the head of the bed, we will
say, on a neat mahogany stand. All arrangements being properly fixed
by workmen under my direction, the widow applies her ear and summons the spirit by sign as agreed. Women! Widows! Women in black—"
100 Here he seemed to have caught sight of a woman's dress in the distance, which in the shade looked a purple black. He took off his hat,
placed his hand upon his heart, and hurried towards her muttering and
gesticulating feverishly. But William caught him by the sleeve and
touched a flower with the tip of his walking-stick in order to divert the
old man's attention. After looking at it for a moment in some confusion
the old man bent his ear to it and seemed to answer a voice speaking
from it, for he began talking about the forests of Uruguay which he had
visited hundreds of years ago in company with the most beautiful
young woman in Europe. He could be heard murmuring about forests in
110 Uruguay blanketed with the wax petals of tropical roses, nightingales,
sea beaches, mermaids, and women drowned at sea, as he suffered

himself to be moved on by William, upon whose face the look of stoical patience grew slowly deeper and deeper.

Following his steps so closely as to be slightly puzzled by his gestures came two elderly women of the lower middle class, one stout and ponderous, the other rosy cheeked and nimble. Like most people of their station they were frankly fascinated by other signs of eccentricity betokening a disordered brain, especially in the well-to-do; but they were too far off to be certain whether the gestures were merely eccentric or
120 genuinely mad. After they had scrutinized the old man's back in silence for a moment and given each other a queer, sly look, they went on energetically piecing together their very complicated dialogue:

"Nell, Bert, Lot, Cess, Phil, Pa, he says, I says, she says, I says, I says—"

"My Bert, Sis, Bill, Grandad, the old man, sugar,
Sugar, flour, kippers, greens,
Sugar, sugar, sugar."

The ponderous woman looked through the pattern of falling words at the flowers standing cool, firm, and upright in the earth, with a curi-
130 ous expression. She saw them as a sleeper waking from a heavy sleep sees a brass candlestick reflecting the light in an unfamiliar way, and closes his eyes and opens them, and seeing the brass candlestick again, finally starts broad awake and stares at the candlestick with all his powers. So the heavy woman came to a standstill opposite the oval-shaped flower-bed, and ceased even to pretend to listen to what the other woman was saying. She stood there letting the words fall over her, swaying the top part of her body slowly backwards and forwards, looking at the flowers. Then she suggested that they should find a seat and have their tea.

140 The snail had now considered every possible method of reaching his goal without going round the dead leaf or climbing over it. Let alone the effort needed for climbing, a leaf, he was doubtful whether the thin texture which vibrated with such an alarming crackle when touched even by the tips of his horns would bear his weight; and this determined him finally to creep beneath it, for there was a point where the leaf curved high enough from the ground to admit him. He had just inserted his head in the opening and was taking stock of the high brown roof and was getting used to the cool brown light when two other people came past outside on the turf. This time they were both young, a young man
150 and a young woman. They were both in the prime of youth, the season before the smooth pink folds of the flower have burst their gummy case, when the wings of the butterfly, though fully grown, are motionless in the sun.

"Lucky it isn't Friday," he observed.

"Why? D'you believe in luck?"

"They make you pay sixpence on Friday."

"What's a sixpence anyway? Isn't it worth sixpence?"

"What's 'it'—what do you mean by 'it'?"

"O, anything—I mean—you know what I mean."

160   Long pauses came between each of these remarks; they were uttered in toneless and monotonous voices. The couple stood still on the edge of the flower-bed, and together pressed the end of her parasol deep down into the soft earth. The action and the fact that his hand rested on the top of hers expressed their feelings in a strange way, as these short insignificant words also expressed something, words with short wings for their heavy body of meaning, inadequate to carry them far and thus alighting awkwardly upon the very common objects that surrounded them, and were to their inexperienced touch so massive; but who knows (so they thought as they pressed the parasol into the earth) what

170 precipices aren't concealed in them, or what slopes of ice don't shine in the sun on the other side? Who knows? Who has ever seen this before? Even when she wondered what sort of tea they gave you at Kew, he felt that something loomed up behind her words, and stood vast and solid behind them; and the mist very slowly rose and uncovered—O, Heavens, what were those shapes?—little white tables, and waitresses who looked first at her and then at him; and there was a bill that he would pay with a real two-shilling piece, and it was real, all real, he assured himself, fingering the coin in his pocket, real to everyone except to him and to her; even to him it began to seem real; and then—but it was too

180 exciting to stand and think any longer, and he pulled the parasol out of the earth with a jerk and was impatient to find the place where one had tea with other people, like other people.

"Come along, Trissie; it's time we had our tea."

"Wherever *does* one have one's tea?" she asked with the oddest thrill of excitement in her voice, looking vaguely round and letting herself be drawn on down the grass path, trailing her parasol; turning her head this way and that way forgetting her tea, wishing to go down there and then down there, remembering orchids and cranes among wild flowers, a Chinese pagoda and a crimson crested bird; but he bore her on.

190   Thus one couple after another with much the same irregular and aimless movement passed the flower-bed and were enveloped in layer after layer of green-blue vapour, in which at first their bodies had substance and a dash of colour, but later both substance and colour dissolved in the green-blue atmosphere. How hot it was! So hot that even the thrush chose to hop, like a mechanical bird, in the shadow of the flowers, with long pauses between one movement and the next; instead of rambling vaguely the white butterflies danced one above another, making with their white shifting flakes the outline of a shattered marble column above the tallest flowers; the glass roofs of the palm house

200 shone as if a whole market full of shiny green umbrellas had opened in the sun; and in the drone of the aeroplane the voice of the summer sky murmured its fierce soul. Yellow and black, pink and snow white, shapes of all these colours, men, women, and children were spotted for a second upon the horizon, and then, seeing the breadth of yellow that

lay upon the grass, they wavered and sought shade beneath the trees, dissolving like drops of water in the yellow and green atmosphere, staining it faintly with red and blue. It seemed as if all gross and heavy bodies had sunk down in the heat motionless and lay huddled upon the ground, but their voices went wavering from them as if they were
210 flames lolling from the thick waxen bodies of candles. Voices. Yes, voices. Wordless voices, breaking the silence suddenly with such depth of contentment, such passion of desire, or, in the voices of children, such freshness of surprise; breaking the silence? But there was no silence; all the time the motor omnibuses were turning their wheels and changing their gear; like a vast nest of Chinese boxes all of wrought steel turning ceaselessly one within another the city murmured; on the top of which the voices cried aloud and the petals of myriads of flowers flashed their colours into the air.

FRANZ KAFKA (1883–1924)
A Hunger Artist*
(1922)

During these last decades the interest in professional fasting has markedly diminished. It used to pay very well to stage such great performances under one's own management, but today that is quite impossible. We live in a different world now. At one time the whole town took a lively interest in the hunger artist; from day to day of his fast the excitement mounted; everybody wanted to see him at least once a day; there were people who bought season tickets for the last few days and sat from morning till night in front of his small barred cage; even in the nighttime there were visiting hours, when the whole effect was heightened by torch flares; on fine days
10 the cage was set out in the open air, and then it was the children's special treat to see the hunger artist; for their elders he was often just a joke that happened to be in fashion, but the children stood open-mouthed, holding each other's hands for greater security, marveling at him as he sat there pallid in black tights, with his ribs sticking out so prominently, not even on a seat but down among straw on the ground, sometimes giving a courteous nod, answering questions with a constrained smile, or perhaps stretching an arm through the bars so that one might feel how thin it was, and then again withdrawing deep into himself, paying no attention to anyone or anything, not even to the all-important striking of the clock that
20 was the only piece of furniture in his cage, but merely staring into vacancy with half-shut eyes, now and then taking a sip from a tiny glass of water to moisten his lips.

Besides casual onlookers there were also relays of permanent watchers selected by the public, usually butchers, strangely enough, and it was their task to watch the hunger artist day and night, three of them at a

---

* Translated by Edwin and Willa Muir.

time, in case he should have some secret recourse to nourishment. This was nothing but a formality, instituted to reassure the masses, for the initiates knew well enough that during his fast the artist would never in any circumstances, not even under forcible compulsion, swallow the smallest
30 morsel of food; the honor of his profession forbade it. Not every watcher, of course, was capable of understanding this; there were often groups of night watchers who were very lax in carrying out their duties and deliberately huddled together in a retired corner to play cards with great absorption, obviously intending to give the hunger artist the chance of a little refreshment, which they supposed he could draw from some private hoard. Nothing annoyed the artist more than such watchers; they made him miserable; they made his fast seem unendurable; sometimes he mastered his feebleness sufficiently to sing during their watch for as long as he could keep going, to show them how unjust their suspicions were. But
40 that was of little use; they only wondered at his cleverness in being able to fill his mouth even while singing. Much more to his taste were the watchers who sat close up to the bars, who were not content with the dim night lighting of the hall but focused him in the full glare of the electric pocket torch given them by the impresario. The harsh light did not trouble him at all, in any case he could never sleep properly, and he could always drowse a little, whatever the light, at any hour, even when the hall was thronged with noisy onlookers. He was quite happy at the prospect of spending a sleepless night with such watchers; he was ready to exchange jokes with them, to tell them stories out of his nomadic life, anything at
50 all to keep them awake and demonstrate to them again that he had no eatables in his cage and that he was fasting as not one of them could fast. But his happiest moment was when the morning came and an enormous breakfast was brought them, at his expense, on which they flung themselves with the keen appetite of healthy men after a weary night of wakefulness. Of course there were people who argued that this breakfast was an unfair attempt to bribe the watchers, but that was going rather too far, and when they were invited to take on a night's vigil without a breakfast, merely for the sake of the cause, they made themselves scarce, although they stuck stubbornly to their suspicions.
60   Such suspicions, anyhow, were a necessary accompaniment to the profession of fasting. No one could possibly watch the hunger artist continuously, day and night, and so no one could produce first-hand evidence that the fast had really been rigorous and continuous; only the artist himself could know that, he was therefore bound to be the sole completely satisfied spectator of his own fast. Yet for other reasons he was never satisfied; it was not perhaps mere fasting that had brought him to such skeleton thinness that many people had regretfully to keep away from his exhibitions, because the sight of him was too much for them, perhaps it was dissatisfaction with himself that had worn him
70 down. For he alone knew, what no other initiate knew, how easy it was to fast. It was the easiest thing in the world. He made no secret of this, yet people did not believe him, at the best they set him down as modest,

most of them, however, thought he was out for publicity or else was some kind of cheat who found it easy to fast because he had discovered a way of making it easy, and then had the impudence to admit the fact, more or less. He had to put up with all that, and in the course of time had got used to it, but his inner dissatisfaction always rankled, and never yet, after any term of fasting—this must be granted to his credit— had he left the cage of his own free will. The longest period of fasting
80 was fixed by his impresario at forty days, beyond that term he was not allowed to go, not even in great cities, and there was good reason for it, too. Experience had proved that for about forty days the interest of the public could be stimulated by a steadily increasing pressure of adver- tisement, but after that the town began to lose interest, sympathetic support began notably to fall off; there were of course local variations as between one town and another or one country and another, but as a general rule forty days marked the limit. So on the fortieth day the flower bedecked cage was opened, enthusiastic spectators filled the hall, a military band played, two doctors entered the cage to measure
90 the results of the fast, which were announced through a megaphone, and finally two young ladies appeared, blissful at having been selected for the honor, to help the hunger artist down the few steps leading to a small table on which was spread a carefully chosen invalid repast. And at this very moment the artist always turned stubborn. True, he would entrust his bony arms to the outstretched helping hands of the ladies bending over him, but stand up he would not. Why stop fasting at this particular moment, after forty days of it? He had held out for a long time, an illimitably long time; why stop now, when he was in his best fasting form, or rather, not yet quite in his best fasting form? Why
100 should he be cheated of the fame he would get for fasting longer, for be- ing not only the record hunger artist of all time, which presumably he was already, but for beating his own record by a performance beyond human imagination, since he felt that there were no limits to his capac- ity for fasting? His public pretended to admire him so much, why should it have so little patience with him; if he could endure fasting longer, why shouldn't the public endure it? Besides, he was tired, he was comfortable sitting in the straw, and now he was supposed to lift him- self to his full height and go down to a meal the very thought of which gave him a nausea that only the presence of the ladies kept him from
110 betraying, and even that with an effort. And he looked up into the eyes of the ladies who were apparently so friendly and in reality so cruel, and shook his head, which felt too heavy on its strengthless neck. But then there happened yet again what always happened. The impresario came forward, without a word—for the band made speech impossible— lifted his arms in the air above the artist, as if inviting Heaven to look down upon its creature here in the straw, this suffering martyr, which indeed he was, although in quite another sense; grasped him round the emaciated waist, with exaggerated caution, so that the frail condition he was in might be appreciated; and committed him to the care of the

120 blenching ladies, not without secretly giving him a shaking so that his
legs and body tottered and swayed. The artist now submitted completely; his head lolled on his breast as if it had landed there by chance;
his body was hollowed out; his legs in a spasm of self-preservation clung
close to each other at the knees, yet scraped on the ground as if it were
not really solid ground, as if they were only trying to find solid ground;
and the whole weight of his body, a feather-weight after all, relapsed
onto one of the ladies, who, looking round for help and panting a little—this post of honor was not at all what she had expected it to be—
first stretched her neck as far as she could to keep her face at least free
130 from contact with the artist, when finding this impossible, and her more
fortunate companion not coming to her aid but merely holding extended
on her own trembling hand the little bunch of knucklebones that was
the artist's, to the great delight of the spectators burst into tears and
had to be replaced by an attendant who had long been stationed in
readiness. Then came the food, a little of which the impresario managed
to get between the artist's lips, while he sat in a kind of half-fainting
trance, to the accompaniment of cheerful patter designed to distract the
public's attention from the artist's condition; after that, a toast was
drunk to the public, supposedly prompted by a whisper from the artist
140 in the impresario's ear; the band confirmed it with a mighty flourish,
the spectators melted away, and no one had any cause to be dissatisfied
with the proceedings, no one except the hunger artist himself, he only,
as always.

So he lived for many years, with small regular intervals of recupera-
tion, in visible glory, honored by the world, yet in spite of that troubled
in spirit, and all the more troubled because no one would take his trouble seriously. What comfort could he possible need? What more could he
possibly wish for? And if some good-natured person, feeling sorry for
him, tried to console him by pointing out that his melancholy was prob-
150 ably caused by fasting, it could happen, especially when he had been
fasting for some time, that he reacted with an outburst of fury and to
the general alarm began to shake the bars of his cage like a wild animal.
Yet the impresario had a way of punishing these outbreaks which he
rather enjoyed putting into operation. He would apologize publicly for
the artist's behavior, which was only to be excused, he admitted, because of the irritability caused by fasting; a condition hardly to be understood by well-fed people; then by natural transition he went on to
mention the artist's equally incomprehensible boast that he could fast
for much longer than he was doing; he praised the high ambition, the
160 good will, the great self-denial undoubtedly implicit in such a statement; and then quite simply countered it by bringing out photographs,
which were also on sale to the public, showing the artist on the fortieth
day of a fast lying in bed almost dead from exhaustion. This perversion
of the truth, familiar to the artist though it was, always unnerved him
afresh and proved too much for him. What was a consequence of the
premature ending of his fast was here presented as the cause of it! To

fight against this lack of understanding, against a whole world of non-understanding, was impossible. Time and again in good faith he stood by the bars listening to the impresario, but as soon as the photographs
170 appeared he always let go and sank with a groan back on to his straw, and the reassured public could once more come close and gaze at him.

A few years later when the witnesses of such scenes called them to mind, they often failed to understand themselves at all. For meanwhile the aforementioned change in public interest had set in; it seemed to happen almost overnight; there may have been profound causes for it, but who was going to bother about that; at any rate the pampered hunger artist suddenly found himself deserted one fine day by the amusement seekers, who went streaming past him to other more favored attractions. For the last time the impresario hurried him over half Europe to discover
180 whether the old interest might still survive here and there; all in vain; everywhere as if by secret agreement, a positive revulsion from professional fasting was in evidence. Of course it could not really have sprung up so suddenly as all that, and many premonitory symptoms which had not been sufficiently remarked or suppressed during the rush and glitter of success now came retrospectively to mind, but it was now too late to take any countermeasures. Fasting would surely come into fashion again at some future date, yet that was no comfort for those living in the present. What, then, was the hunger artist to do? He had been applauded by thousands in his time and could hardly come down to showing himself
190 in a street booth at village fairs, and as for adopting another profession, he was not only too old for that but too fanatically devoted to fasting. So he took leave of the impresario, his partner in an unparalleled career, and hired himself to a large circus; in order to spare his own feelings he avoided reading the conditions of his contract.

A large circus with its enormous traffic in replacing and recruiting men, animals and apparatus can always find a use for people at any time, even for a hunger artist, provided of course that he does not ask too much, and in this particular case anyhow it was not only the artist who was taken on but his famous and long-known name as well, indeed con-
200 sidering the peculiar nature of his performance, which was not impaired by advancing age, it could not be objected that here was an artist past his prime, no longer at the height of his professional skill, seeking a refuge in some quiet corner of a circus; on the contrary, the hunger artist averred that he could fast as well as ever, which was entirely credible, he even alleged that if he were allowed to fast as he liked, and this was at once promised him without more ado, he could astound the world by establishing a record never yet achieved, a statement which certainly provoked a smile among the other professionals, since it left out of account the change in public opinion, which the hunger artist in his zeal conveniently
210 forgot.

He had not, however, actually lost his sense of the real situation and took it as a matter of course that he and his cage should be stationed, not in the middle of the ring as a main attraction, but outside, near the animal

cages, on a site that was after all easily accessible. Large and gaily painted placards made a frame for the cage and announced what was to be seen inside it. When the public came thronging out in the intervals to see the animals, they could hardly avoid passing the hunger artist's cage and stopping there for a moment, perhaps they might even have stayed longer had not those pressing behind them in the narrow gangway, who did not un-
220 derstand why they should be held up on their way toward the excitements of the menagerie, made it impossible for anyone to stand gazing quietly for any length of time. And that was the reason why the hunger artist, who had of course been looking forward to these visiting hours as the main achievement of his life, began instead to shrink from them. At first he could hardly wait for the intervals; it was exhilarating to watch the crowds come streaming his way, until only too soon—not even the most obstinate self-deception, clung to almost consciously, could hold out against the fact—the conviction was borne in upon him that these people, most of them, to judge from their actions, again and again, without exception,
230 were all on their way to the menagerie. And the first sight of them from the distance remained the best. For when they reached his cage he was at once deafened by the storm of shouting and abuse that arose from the two contending factions, which renewed themselves continuously, of those who wanted to stop and stare at him—he soon began to dislike them more than the others—not out of real interest but only out of obstinate self-assertiveness, and those who wanted to go straight on to the animals. When the first great rush was past, the stragglers came along, and these, whom nothing could have prevented from stopping to look at him as long as they had breath, raced past with long strides, hardly even glancing
240 at him, in their haste to get to the menagerie in time. And all too rarely did it happen that he had a stroke of luck, when some father of a family fetched up before him with his children, pointed a finger at the hunger artist and explained at length what the phenomenon meant, telling stories of earlier years when he himself had watched similar but much more thrilling performances, and the children, still rather uncomprehending, since neither inside nor outside school had they been sufficiently prepared for this lesson—what did they care about fasting?—yet showed by the brightness of their intent eyes that new and better times might be coming. Perhaps, said the hunger artist to himself many a time, things would be a
250 little better if his cage were set not quite so near the menagerie. That made it too easy for people to make their choice, to say nothing of what he suffered from the stench of the menagerie, the animals' restlessness by night, the carrying past of raw lumps of flesh for the beasts of prey, the roaring at feeding times, which depressed him continually. But he did not dare to lodge a complaint with the management; after all, he had the animals to thank for the troops of people who passed his cage, among whom there might always be one here and there to take an interest in him, and who could tell where they might seclude him if he called attention to his existence and thereby to the fact that, strictly speaking, he was only an imped-
260 iment on the way to the menagerie.

A small impediment, to be sure, one that grew steadily less. People grew familiar with the strange idea that they could be expected, in times like these, to take an interest in a hunger artist, and with this familiarity the verdict went out against him. He might fast as much as he could, and he did so; but nothing could save him now, people passed him by. Just try to explain to anyone the art of fasting! Anyone who has no feeling for it cannot be made to understand it. The fine placards grew dirty and illegible, they were torn down; the little notice board telling the number of fast days achieved, which at first was changed carefully every day, had long

270 stayed at the same figure, for after the first few weeks even this small task seemed pointless to the staff; and so the artist simply fasted on and on, as he had once dreamed of doing, and it was no trouble to him, just as he had always foretold, but no one counted the days, no one, not even the artist himself, knew what records he was already breaking, and his heart grew heavy. And when once in a time some leisurely passer-by stopped, made merry over the old figure on the board and spoke of swindling, that was in its way the stupidest lie ever invented by indifference and inborn malice, since it was not the hunger artist who was cheating; he was working honestly, but the world was cheating him of his reward.

280 Many more days went by, however, and that too came to an end. An overseer's eye fell on the cage one day and asked the attendants why this perfectly good cage should be left standing there unused with dirty straw inside it; nobody knew, until one man, helped out by the notice board, remembered about the hunger artist. They poked into the straw with sticks and found him in it. "Are you still fasting?" asked the overseer. "When on earth do you mean to stop?" "Forgive me, everybody," whispered the hunger artist; only the overseer, who had his ear to the bars, understood him. "Of course," said the overseer, and tapped his forehead with a finger to let the attendants know what state the man was in, "we forgive

290 you." "I always wanted you to admire my fasting," said the hunger artist. "We do admire it," said the overseer, affably. "But you shouldn't admire it," said the hunger artist. "Well, then we don't admire it," said the overseer, "but why shouldn't we admire it?" "Because I have to fast, I can't help it," said the hunger artist. "What a fellow you are," said the overseer, "and why can't you help it?" "Because," said the hunger artist, lifting his head a little and speaking, with his lips pursed, as if for a kiss, right into the overseer's ear, so that no syllable might be lost, "because I couldn't find the food I liked. If I had found it, believe me, I should have made no fuss and stuffed myself like you or anyone else." These were his

300 last words, but in his dimming eyes remained the firm though no longer proud persuasion that he was still continuing to fast.

"Well, clear this out now!" said the overseer, and they buried the hunger artist, straw and all. Into the cage they put a young panther. Even the most insensitive felt it refreshing to see this wild creature leaping around the cage that had so long been dreary. The panther was all right. The food he liked was brought him without hesitation by the attendants;

he seemed not even to miss his freedom; his noble body, furnished almost to the bursting point with all that it needed, seemed to carry freedom around with it too; somewhere in his jaws it seemed to lurk; and the joy
310 of life streamed with such ardent passion from this throat that for the on-lookers it was not easy to stand the shock of it. But they braced themselves, crowded around the cage, and did not want ever to move away.

JAMES THURBER (1894–1961)
The Secret Life of Walter Mitty
(1942)

"We're going through!" The Commander's voice was like thin ice breaking. He wore his full-dress uniform, with the heavily braided white cap pulled down rakishly over one cold gray eye. "We can't make it, sir. It's spoiling for a hurricane, if you ask me." "I'm not asking you, Lieutenant Berg," said the Commander. "Throw on the power lights! Rev her up to 8,500! We're going through!" The pounding of the cylinders increased: ta-pocketa-pocketa-pocketa-*pocketa-pocketa*. The Commander stared at the ice forming on the pilot window. He walked over and twisted a row of complicated dials. "Switch on No. 8 auxiliary!" he shouted. "Switch
10 on No. 8 auxiliary!" repeated Lieutenant Berg. "Full strength in No. 3 turret!" shouted the Commander. "Full strength in No. 3 turret!" The crew, bending to their various tasks in the huge, hurtling eight-engined Navy hydroplane, looked at each other and grinned. "The Old Man'll get us through," they said to one another. "The Old Man ain't afraid of Hell!" . . .

"No so fast! You're driving too fast!" said Mrs. Mitty. "What are you driving so fast for?"

"Hmm?" said Walter Mitty. He looked at his wife, in the seat beside him, with shocked astonishment. She seemed grossly unfamiliar, like a
20 strange woman who had yelled at him in a crowd. "You were up to fifty-five," she said. "You know I don't like to go more than forty. You were up to fifty-five." Walter Mitty drove on toward Waterbury in silence, the roaring of the SN202 through the worst storm in twenty years of Navy flying fading in the remote, intimate airways of his mind. "You're tensed up again," said Mrs. Mitty. "It's one of your days. I wish you'd let Dr. Renshaw look you over."

Walter Mitty stopped the car in front of the building where his wife went to have her hair done. "Remember to get those overshoes while I'm having my hair done," she said. "I don't need overshoes," said Mitty.
30 She put her mirror back into her bag. "We've been all through that," she said, getting out of the car. "You're not a young man any longer." He raced the engine a little. "Why don't you wear your gloves? Have you lost your gloves?" Walter Mitty reached in a pocket and brought out the gloves. He put them on, but after she had turned and gone into the building and he had driven on to a red light, he took them off again.

"Pick it up, brother!" snapped a cop as the light changed, and Mitty hastily pulled on his gloves and lurched ahead. He drove around the streets aimlessly for a time, and then he drove past the hospital on his way to the parking lot.

40   . . . "It's the millionaire banker, Wellington McMillan," said the pretty nurse. "Yes?" said Walter Mitty, removing his gloves slowly. "Who has the case?" "Dr. Renshaw and Dr. Benbow, but there are two specialists here, Dr. Remington from New York and Mr. Pritchard-Mitford from London. He flew over." A door opened down a long, cool corridor and Dr. Renshaw came out. He looked distraught and haggard. "Hello, Mitty," he said. "We're having the devil's own time with McMillan, the millionaire banker and close personal friend of Roosevelt. Obstreosis of the ductal tract. Tertiary. Wish you'd take a look at him." "Glad to," said Mitty.

In the operating room there were whispered introductions: "Dr.
50 Remington, Dr. Mitty. Mr. Pritchard-Mitford, Dr. Mitty." "I've read your book on streptothricosis," said Pritchard-Mitford, shaking hands. "A brilliant performance, sir." "Thank you," said Walter Mitty. "Didn't know you were in the States, Mitty," grumbled Remington. "Coals to Newcastle, bringing Mitford and me here for a tertiary." "You are very kind," said Mitty. A huge, complicated machine, connected to the operating table, with many tubes and wires, began at this moment to go pocketa-pocketa-pocketa. "The new anesthetizer is giving way!" shouted an interne. "There is no one in the East who knows how to fix it!" "Quiet, man!" said Mitty, in a low, cool voice. He sprang to the machine, which
60 was now going pocketa-pocketa-queep-pocketa-queep. He began fingering delicately a row of glistening dials. "Give me a fountain pen!" he snapped. Someone handed him a fountain pen. He pulled a faulty piston out of the machine and inserted the pen in its place. "That will hold for ten minutes," he said. "Get on with the operation." A nurse hurried over and whispered to Renshaw, and Mitty saw the man turn pale. "Coreopsis has set in," said Renshaw nervously. "If you would take over, Mitty?" Mitty looked at him and at the craven figure of Benbow, who drank, and at the grave, uncertain faces of the two great specialists. "If you wish," he said. They slipped a white gown on him; he adjusted a mask and drew on
70 thin gloves; nurses handed him shining. . . .

"Back it up, Mac! Look out for that Buick!" Walter Mitty jammed on the brakes. "Wrong lane, Mac," said the parking-lot attendant, looking at Mitty closely. "Gee. Yeh," muttered Mitty. He began cautiously to back out of the lane marked "Exit Only." "Leave her sit there," said the attendant. "I'll put her away." Mitty got out of the car. "Hey, better leave the key." "Oh," said Mitty, handing the man the ignition key. The attendant vaulted into the car, backed it up with insolent skill, and put it where it belonged.

They're so damn cocky, thought Walter Mitty, walking along Main
80 Street; they think they know everything. Once he had tried to take his chains off, outside New Milford, and he had got them wound around the axles. A man had had to come out in a wrecking car and unwind them, a

young, grinning garageman. Since then Mrs. Mitty always made him drive to a garage to have the chains taken off. The next time, he thought, I'll wear my right arm in a sling; they won't grin at me then. I'll have my right arm in a sling and they'll see I couldn't possibly take the chains off myself. He kicked at the slush on the sidewalk. "Overshoes," he said to himself, and he began looking for a shoe store.

90   When he came out into the street again, with the overshoes in a box under his arm, Walter Mitty began to wonder what the other thing was his wife had told him to get. She had told him twice, before they set out from their house for Waterbury. In a way he hated these weekly trips to town—he was always getting something wrong. Kleenex, he thought, Squibb's, razor blades? No. Toothpaste, toothbrush, bicarbonate, carborundum, initiative and referendum? He gave it up. But she would remember it. "Where's the what's-its-name?" she would ask. "Don't tell me you forgot the what's-its-name?" A newsboy went by shouting something about the Waterbury trial.

100   . . ."Perhaps this will refresh your memory." The District Attorney suddenly thrust a heavy automatic at the quiet figure on the witness stand. "Have you ever seen this before?" Walter Mitty took the gun and examined it expertly. "This is my Webley-Vickers 50.80," he said calmly. An excited buzz ran around the courtroom. The judge rapped for order. "You are a crack shot with any sort of firearms, I believe?" said the District Attorney, insinuatingly. "Objection!" shouted Mitty's attorney. "We have shown that the defendant could not have fired the shot. We have shown that he wore his right arm in a sling on the night of the fourteenth of July." Walter Mitty raised his hand briefly and the bickering attorneys were stilled. "With any known make of gun," he said evenly, "I could
110 have killed Gregory Fitzhurst at three hundred feet *with my left hand.*" Pandemonium broke loose in the courtroom. A woman's scream rose above the bedlam and suddenly a lovely, dark-haired girl was in Walter Mitty's arms. The District Attorney struck at her savagely. Without rising from his chair, Mitty let the man have it on the point of the chin. "You miserable cur!" . . .

    "Puppy biscuit," said Walter Mitty. He stopped walking and the buildings of Waterbury rose up out of the misty courtroom and surrounded him again. A woman who was passing laughed. "He said 'Puppy biscuit,'" she said to her companion. "That man said 'Puppy bis-
120 cuit' to himself." Walter Mitty hurried on. He went into an A & P, not the first one he came to but a smaller one farther up the street. "I want some biscuit for small, young dogs," he said to the clerk. "Any special abrand, sir?" The greatest pistol shot in the world thought a moment. "It says 'Puppies Bark for It' on the box," said Walter Mitty.

    His wife would be through at the hairdresser's in fifteen minutes, Mitty saw in looking at his watch, unless they had trouble drying it; sometimes they had trouble drying it. She didn't like to get to the hotel first; she would want him to be there waiting for her as usual. He found a big leather chair in the lobby, facing a window, and he put the

130 overshoes and the puppy biscuit on the floor beside it. He picked up an
old copy of *Liberty* and sank down into the chair. "Can Germany Conquer the World Through the Air?" Walter Mitty looked at the pictures
of bombing planes and of ruined streets.

. . . "The cannonading has got the wind up in young Raleigh, sir,"
said the sergeant. Captain Mitty looked up at him through tousled hair.
"Get him to bed," he said wearily. "With the others. I'll fly alone." "But
you can't, sir," said the sergeant anxiously. "It takes two men to handle
that bomber and the Archies are pounding hell out of the air. Von Richt-
man's circus is between here and Saulier." "Somebody's got to get that
140 ammunition dump," said Mitty. "I'm going over. Spot of brandy?" He
poured a drink for the sergeant and one for himself. War thundered and
whined around the dugout and battered at the door. There was a rending of wood and splinters flew through the room. "A bit of a near
thing," said Captain Mitty carelessly. "The box barrage is closing in,"
said the sergeant. "We only live once, Sergeant," said Mitty, with his
faint, fleeting smile. "Or do we?" He poured another brandy and tossed
it off. "I never see a man could hold his brandy like you, sir," said the
sergeant. "Begging your pardon, sir." Captain Mitty stood up and
strapped on his huge Webley-Vickers automatic. "It's forty kilometers
150 through hell, sir," said the sergeant. Mitty finished one last brandy.
"After all," he said softly, "what isn't?" The pounding of the cannon
increased; there was the rat-tat-tatting of machine guns, and from
somewhere came the menacing pocketa-pocketa-pocketa of the new
flame-throwers. Walter Mitty walked to the door of the dugout humming "Auprès de Ma Blonde." He turned and waved to the sergeant.
"Cheerio!" he said. . . .

Something struck his shoulder. "I've been looking all over this hotel
for you," said Mrs. Mitty. "Why do you have to hide in this old chair?
How did you expect me to find you?" "Things close in," said Walter
160 Mitty vaguely. "What?" Mrs. Mitty said. "Did you get the what's-its-
name? The puppy biscuit? What's in the box?" "Overshoes," said Mitty.
"Couldn't you have put them on in the store?" "I was thinking," said
Walter Mitty. "Does it ever occur to you that I am sometimes thinking?"
She looked at him. "I'm going to take your temperature when I get you
home," she said.

They went out through the revolving doors that made a faintly derisive whistling sound when you pushed them. It was two blocks to the
parking lot. At the drugstore on the corner she said, "Wait here for me.
I forgot something. I won't be a minute." She was more than a minute.
170 Walter Mitty lighted a cigarette. It began to rain, rain with sleet in it.
He stood up against the wall of the drugstore, smoking. . . . He put his
shoulders back and his heels together. "To hell with the handkerchief,"
said Walter Mitty scornfully. He took one last drag on his cigarette and
snapped it away. Then, with that faint, fleeting smile playing about his
lips, he faced the firing squad; erect and motionless, proud and disdainful, Walter Mitty the Undefeated, inscrutable to the last.

JORGE LUIS BORGES (1899–1986)
The Garden of Forking Paths*
(1941)

On page 22 of Liddell Hart's *History of World War I* you will read that an attack against the Serre-Montauban line by thirteen British divisions (supported by 1,400 artillery pieces), planned for the 24th of July, 1916, had to be postponed until the morning of the 29th. The torrential rains, Captain Liddell Hart comments, caused this delay, an insignificant one, to be sure.

The following statement, dictated, reread and signed by Dr. Yu Tsun, former professor of English at the *Hochschule* at Tsingtao, throws an unsuspected light over the whole affair. The first two pages of the
10 document are missing.

". . . and I hung up the receiver. Immediately afterwards, I recognized the voice that had answered in German. It was that of Captain Richard Madden. Madden's presence in Viktor Runeberg's apartment meant the end of our anxieties and—but this seemed, *or should have seemed*, very secondary to me—also the end of our lives. It meant that Runeberg had been arrested or murdered.[†] Before the sun set on that day, I would encounter the same fate. Madden was implacable. Or rather, he was obliged to be so. An Irishman at the service of England, a man accused of laxity and perhaps of treason, how could he fail to seize
20 and be thankful for such a miraculous opportunity: the discovery, capture, maybe even the death of two agents of the German Reich? I went up to my room; absurdly I locked the door and threw myself on my back on the narrow iron cot. Through the window I saw the familiar roofs and the cloud-shaded six o'clock sun. It seemed incredible to me that that day without premonitions or symbols should be the one of my inexorable death. In spite of my dead father, in spite of having been a child in a symmetrical garden of Hia Feng, was I—now—going to die? Then I reflected that everything happens to a man precisely, precisely *now*. Centuries of centuries and only in the present do things happen;
30 countless men in the air, on the face of the earth and the sea, and all that really is happening is happening to me . . . The almost intolerable recollection of Madden's horselike face banished these wanderings. In the midst of my hatred and terror (it means nothing to me now to speak of terror, now that I have mocked Richard Madden, now that my throat yearns for the noose) it occurred to me that that tumultuous and doubtless happy warrior did not suspect that I possessed the Secret. The name of the exact location of the new British artillery park on the River

---

* *Translated by Donald A. Yates.*
    [†] An hypothesis both hateful and odd. The Prussian spy Hans Rabener, alias Viktor Runeberg, attacked with drawn automatic the bearer of the warrant for his arrest, Captain Richard Madden. The latter, in self-defense, inflicted the wound which brought about Runeberg's death. (Note supplied by Borges' "Editor.")

Ancre. A bird streaked across the gray sky and blindly I translated it into an airplane and that airplane into many (against the French sky) 40 annihilating the artillery station with vertical bombs. If only my mouth, before a bullet shattered it, could cry out that secret name so it could be heard in Germany . . . My human voice was very weak. How might I make it carry to the ear of the Chief? To the ear of that sick and hateful man who knew nothing of Runeberg and me save that we were in Staffordshire and who was waiting in vain for our report in his arid office in Berlin, endlessly examining newpapers . . . I said out loud: *I must flee.* I sat up noiselessly, in useless perfection of silence, as if Madden were already lying in wait for me. Something—perhaps the mere vain ostentation of proving my resources were nil—made me look 50 through my pockets. I found what I knew I would find. The American watch, the nickel chain and the square coin, the key ring with the incriminating useless keys to Runeberg's apartment, the notebook, a letter which I resolved to destroy immediately (and which I did not destroy), a crown, two shillings and a few pence, the red and blue pencil, the handkerchief, the revolver with one bullet. Absurdly, I took it in my hand and weighed it in order to inspire courage within myself. Vaguely I thought that a pistol report can be heard at a great distance. In ten minutes my plan was perfected. The telephone book listed the name of the only person capable of transmitting the message; he lived in a sub- 60 urb of Fenton, less than a half hour's train ride away.

I am a cowardly man. I say it now, now that I have carried to its end a plan whose perilous nature no one can deny. I know its execution was terrible. I didn't do it for Germany, no. I care nothing for a barbarous country which imposed upon me the abjection of being a spy. Besides, I know of a man from England—a modest man—who for me is no less great than Goethe. I talked with him for scarcely an hour, but during that hour he was Goethe . . . I did it because I sensed that the Chief somehow feared people of my race—for the innumerable ancestors who merge within me. I wanted to prove to him that a yellow man could save his armies. Be- 70 sides, I had to flee from Captain Madden. His hands and his voice could call at my door at any moment. I dressed silently, bade farewell to myself in the mirror, went downstairs, scrutinized the peaceful street and went out. The station was not far from my home, but I judged it wise to take a cab. I argued that in this way I ran less risk of being recognized; the fact is that in the deserted street I felt myself visible and vulnerable, infinitely so. I remember that I told the cab driver to stop a short distance before the main entrance. I got out with voluntary, almost painful slowness; I was going to the village of Ashgrove but I bought a ticket for a more distant station. The train left within a very few minutes, at eighty-fifty. I 80 hurried; the next one would leave at nine-thirty. There was hardly a soul on the platform. I went through the coaches; I remember a few farmers, a woman dressed in mourning, a young boy who was reading with fervor the *Annals* of Tacitus, a wounded and happy soldier. The coaches jerked forward at last. A man whom I recognized ran in vain to the end of the platform. It was Captain Richard Madden. Shattered, trembling, I shrank into the far corner of the seat, away from the dreaded window.

From this broken state I passed into an almost abject felicity. I told myself that the duel had already begun and that I had won the first encounter by frustrating, even if for forty minutes, even if by a stroke of
90 fate, the attack of my adversary. I argued that this slightest of victories foreshadowed a total victory. I argued (no less fallaciously) that my cowardly felicity proved that I was a man capable of carrying out the adventure successfully. From this weakness I took strength that did not abandon me. I foresee that man will resign himself each day to more atrocious undertakings; soon there will be no one but warriors and brigands; I give them this counsel: *The author of an atrocious undertaking ought to imagine that he has already accomplished it, ought to impose upon himself a future as irrevocable as the past.* Thus I proceeded as my eyes of a man already dead registered the elapsing of that day, which was per-
100 haps the last, and the diffusion of the night. The train ran gently along, amid ash trees. It stopped, almost in the middle of the fields. No one announced the name of the station. "Ashgrove?" I asked a few lads on the platform. "Ashgrove," they replied. I got off.

A lamp enlightened the platform but the faces of the boys were in shadow. One questioned me, "Are you going to Dr. Stephen Albert's house?" Without waiting for my answer, another said, "The house is a long way from here, but you won't get lost if you take this road to the left and at every crossroads turn again to your left." I tossed them a coin (my last), descended a few stone steps and started down the soli-
110 tary road. It went downhill, slowly. It was of elemental earth; overhead the branches were tangled; the low, full moon seemed to accompany me.

For an instant, I thought that Richard Madden in some way had penetrated my desperate plan. Very quickly, I understood that that was impossible. The instructions to turn always to the left reminded me that such was the common procedure for discovering the central point of certain labyrinths. I have some understanding of labyrinths: not for nothing am I the great grandson of that Ts'ui Pên who was governor of Yunnan and who renounced wordly power in order to write a novel that might be even more populous than the *Hung Lu Meng* and to construct a labyrinth in
120 which all men would become lost. Thirteen years he dedicated to these heterogeneous tasks, but the hand of a stranger murdered him—and his novel was incoherent and no one found the labyrinth. Beneath English trees I meditated on that lost maze: I imagined it inviolate and perfect at the secret crest of a mountain; I imagined it erased by rice fields or beneath the water; I imagined it infinite, no longer composed of octagonal kiosks and returning paths, but of rivers and provinces and kingdoms . . . I thought of a labyrinth of labyrinths, of one sinuous spreading labyrinth that would encompass the past and the future and in some way involve the stars. Absorbed in these illusory images, I forgot my destiny of
130 one pursued. I felt myself to be, for an unknown period of time, an abstract perceiver of the world. The vague, living countryside, the moon, the

remains of the day worked on me, as well as the slope of the road which eliminated any possibility of weariness. The afternoon was intimate, infinite. The road descended and forked among the now confused meadows. A high-pitched, almost syllabic music approached and receded in the shifting of the wind, dimmed by leaves and distance. I thought that a man can be an enemy of other men, of the moments of other men, but not of a country: not of fireflies, words, gardens, streams of water, sunsets. Thus I arrived before a tall, rusty gate. Between the iron bars I made out 140 a poplar grove and a pavilion. I understood suddenly two things, the first trivial, the second almost unbelievable: the music came from the pavilion, and the music was Chinese. For precisely that reason I had openly accepted it without paying it any heed. I do not remember whether there was a bell or whether I knocked with my hand. The sparkling of the music continued.

From the rear of the house within a lantern approached: a lantern that the trees sometimes striped and sometimes eclipsed, a paper lantern that had the form of a drum and the color of the moon. A tall man bore it. I didn't see his face for the light blinded me. He opened the door and said 150 slowly, in my own language: "I see that the pious Hsi P'êng persists in correcting my solitude. You no doubt wish to see the garden?"

I recognized the name of one of our consuls and I replied, disconcerted, "The garden?"

"The garden of forking paths."

Something stirred in my memory and I uttered with incomprehensible certainty, "The garden of my ancestor Ts'ui Pên."

"Your ancestor? Your illustrious ancestor? Come in."

The damp path zigzagged like those of my childhood. We came to a library of Eastern and Western books. I recognized bound in yellow silk 160 several volumes of the Lost Encyclopedia, edited by the Third Emperor of the Luminous Dynasty but never printed. The record on the phonograph revolved next to a bronze phoenix. I also recall a *famille rose* vase and another, many centuries older, of that shade of blue which our craftsmen copied from the potters of Persia . . .

Stephen Albert observed me with a smile. He was, as I have said, very tall, sharp-featured, with gray eyes and a gray beard. He told me that he had been a missionary in Tientsin "before aspiring to become a Sinologist."

We sat down—I on a long, low divan, he with his back to the win-170 dow and a tall circular clock. I calculated that my pursuer, Richard Madden, could not arrive for at least an hour. My irrevocable determination could wait.

"An astounding fate, that of Ts'ui Pên," Stephen Albert said. "Governor of his native province, learned in astronomy, in astrology and in the tireless interpretation of the canonical books, chess player, famous poet and calligrapher—he abandoned all this in order to compose a book and a maze. He renounced the pleasures of both tyranny and justice, of his populous couch, of his banquets and even of erudition—all to close

himself up for thirteen years in the Pavilion of the Limpid Solitude. When
180 he died, his heirs found nothing save chaotic manuscripts. His family, as
you may be aware, wished to condemn them to the fire; but his executor—
a Taoist or Buddhist monk—insisted on their publication."

"We descendants of Ts'ui Pên," I replied, "continue to curse that
monk. Their publication was senseless. The book is an indeterminate
heap of contradictory drafts. I examined it once: in the third chapter the
hero dies, in the fourth he is alive. As for the other undertaking of Ts'ui
Pên, his labyrinth . . ."

"Here is Ts'ui Pên's labyrinth," he said, indicating a tall lacquered
desk.

190   "An ivory labyrinth!" I exclaimed. "A minimum labyrinth."

"A labyrinth of symbols," he corrected. "An invisible labyrinth of
time. To me, a barbarous Englishman, has been entrusted the revelation
of this diaphanous mystery. After more than a hundred years, the details are irretrievable; but it is not hard to conjecture what happened.
Ts'ui Pên must have said once: *I am withdrawing to write a book.* And another time: *I am withdrawing to construct a labyrinth.* Every one imagined
two works; to no one did it occur that the book and the maze were one
and the same thing. The Pavilion of the Limpid Solitude stood in the
center of a garden that was perhaps intricate; that circumstance could
200 have suggested to the heirs a physical labyrinth. Ts'ui Pên died; no one
in the vast territories that were his came upon the labyrinth; the confusion of the novel suggested to me that *it* was the maze. Two circumstances gave me the correct solution of the problem. One: the curious
legend that Ts'ui Pên had planned to create a labyrinth which would be
strictly infinite. The other: a fragment of a letter I discovered."

Albert rose. He turned his back on me for a moment; he opened a
drawer of the black and gold desk. He faced me and in his hands he held
a sheet of paper that had once been crimson, but was now pink and tenuous and cross-sectioned. The fame of Ts'ui Pên as a calligrapher had
210 been justly won. I read, uncomprehendingly and with fervor, these
words written with a minute brush by a man of my blood: *I leave to the
various futures (not to all) my garden of forking paths.* Wordlessly, I returned
the sheet. Albert continued:

Before unearthing this letter, I had questioned myself about the ways
in which a book can be infinite. I could think of nothing other than a cyclic
volume, a circular one. A book whose last page was identical with the first,
a book which had the possibility of continuing indefinitely. I remembered
too that night which is at the middle of the Thousand and One Nights
when Scheherazade (through a magical oversight of the copyist) begins to
220 relate word for word the story of the Thousand and One Nights, establishing the risk of coming once again to the night when she must repeat it, and
thus on to infinity. I imagined as well a Platonic, hereditary work, transmitted from father to son, in which each new individual adds a chapter or
corrects with pious care the pages of his elders. These conjectures diverted

me; but none seemed to correspond, not even remotely, to the contradictory chapters of Ts'ui Pên. In the midst of this perplexity, I received from Oxford the manuscript you have examined. I lingered, naturally, on the sentence: *I leave to the various futures (not to all) my garden of forking paths.* Almost instantly, I understood: 'the garden of forking paths' was the chaotic novel; the phrase 'the various futures (not to all)' suggested to me the forking in time, not in space. A broad rereading of the work confirmed the theory. In all fictional works, each time a man is confronted with several alternatives, he chooses one and eliminates the others; in the fiction of Ts'ui Pên, he chooses—simultaneously—all of them. *He creates,* in this way, diverse futures, diverse times which themselves also proliferate and fork. Here, then, is the explanation of the novel's contradictions. Fang, let us say, has a secret; a stranger calls at his door; Fang resolves to kill him. Naturally, there are several possible outcomes: Fang can kill the intruder, the intruder can kill Fang, they both can escape, they both can die, and so forth. In the work of Ts'ui Pên, all possible outcomes occur; each one is the point of departure for other forkings. Sometimes, the paths of this labyrinth converge: for example, you arrive at this house, but in one of the possible pasts you are my enemy, in another, my friend. If you will resign yourself to my incurable pronunciation, we shall read a few pages."

His face, within the vivid circle of the lamplight, was unquestionably that of an old man, but with something unalterable about it, even immortal. He read with slow precision two versions of the same epic chapter. In the first, an army marches to a battle across a lonely mountain; the horror of the rocks and shadows makes the men undervalue their lives and they gain an easy victory. In the second, the same army traverses a palace where a great festival is taking place; the resplendent battle seems to them a continuation of the celebration and they win the victory. I listened with proper veneration to these ancient narratives, perhaps less admirable in themselves than the fact that they had been created by my blood and were being restored to me by a man of a remote empire, in the course of a desperate adventure, on a Western isle. I remember the last words, repeated in each version like a secret commandment: *Thus fought the heroes, tranquil their admirable hearts, violent their swords, resigned to kill and to die.*

From that moment on, I felt about me and within my dark body an invisible, intangible swarming. Not the swarming of the divergent, parallel and finally coalescent armies, but a more inaccessible, more intimate agitation that they in some manner prefigured. Stephen Albert continued:

"I don't believe that your illustrious ancestor played idly with these variations. I don't consider it credible that he would sacrifice thirteen years to the infinite execution of a rhetorical experiment. In your country, the novel is a subsidiary form of literature; in Ts'ui Pên's time it was a despicable form. Ts'ui Pên was a brilliant novelist, but he was also a man of letters who doubtless did not consider himself a mere novelist. The testimony of his contemporaries proclaims—and his life fully confirms—his metaphysical and mystical interests. Philosophic controversy usurps a good part of the novel. I know that of all problems, none disturbed him so greatly nor worked upon him so much as the abysmal problem of time. Now then, the latter is the only problem that does not figure in the pages of the *Garden.* He does not even use the word that signifies *time.* How do you explain this voluntary omission?"

I proposed several solutions—all unsatisfactory. We discussed them. Finally, Stephen Albert said to me:

"In a riddle whose answer is chess, what is the only prohibited word?"

280   I thought a moment and replied, "The word *chess.*"

"Precisely," said Albert. *"The Garden of Forking Paths* is an enormous riddle, or parable, whose theme is time; this recondite cause prohibits its mention. To omit a word always, to resort to inept metaphors and obvious periphrases, is perhaps the most emphatic way of stressing it. That is the tortuous method preferred, in each of the meanderings of his indefatigable novel, by the oblique Ts'ui Pên. I have compared hundreds of manuscripts, I have corrected the errors that the negligence of the copyists has introduced, I have guessed the plan of this chaos, I have re-established—I believe I have re-established—the primordial organiza-

290   tion, I have translated the entire work: it is clear to me that not once does he employ the word 'time.' The explanation is obvious: *The Garden of Forking Paths* is an incomplete, but not false, image of the universe as Ts'ui Pên conceived it. In contrast to Newton and Schopenhauer, your ancestor did not believe in a uniform, absolute time. He believed in an infinite series of times, in a growing, dizzying net of divergent, convergent and parallel times. This network of times which approached one another, forked, broke off, or were unaware of one another for centuries, embraces *all* possibilities of time. We do not exist in the majority of these times; in some you exist, and not I; in others I, and not you; in

300   others, both of us. In the present one, which a favorable fate has granted me, you have arrived at my house; in another, while crossing the garden, you found me dead; in still another, I utter these same words, but I am a mistake, a ghost."

"In every one," I pronounced, not without a tremble to my voice, "I am grateful to you and revere you for your re-creation of the garden of Ts'ui Pên."

"Not in all," he murmured with a smile. "Time forks perpetually toward innumerable futures. In one of them I am your enemy."

Once again I felt the swarming sensation of which I have spoken. It

310   seemed to me that the humid garden that surrounded the house was infinitely saturated with invisible persons. Those persons were Albert and I, secret, busy and multi-form in other dimensions of time. I raised my eyes and the tenuous nightmare dissolved. In the yellow and black garden there was only one man; but this man was as strong as a statue . . . this man was approaching along the path and he was Captain Richard Madden.

"The future already exists," I replied, "but I am your friend. Could I see the letter again?"

Albert rose. Standing tall, he opened the drawer of the tall desk; for
the moment his back was to me. I had readied the revolver. I fired with
320 extreme caution. Albert fell uncomplainingly, immediately. I swear his
death was instantaneous—a lightning stroke.

The rest is unreal, insignificant. Madden broke in, arrested me. I
have been condemned to the gallows. I have won out abominably; I have
communicated to Berlin the secret name of the city they must attack.
They bombed it yesterday; I read it in the same papers that offered to
England the mystery of the learned Sinologist Stephen Albert who was
murdered by a stranger, one Yu Tsun. The Chief had deciphered this
mystery. He knew my problem was to indicate (through the uproar of
the war) the city called Albert, and that I had found no other means
330 to do so than to kill a man of that name. He does not know (no one can
know) my innumerable contrition and weariness.

ERNEST HEMINGWAY (1899-1961)
Hills Like White Elephants
(1927)

The hills across the valley of the Ebro were long and white. On this side
there was no shade and no trees and the station was between two lines of
rails in the sun. Close against the side of the station there was the warm
shadow of the building and a curtain, made of strings of bamboo beads,
hung across the open door into the bar, to keep out flies. The American
and the girl with him sat at a table in the shade, outside the building. It
was very hot and the express from Barcelona would come in forty minutes. It stopped at this junction for two minutes and went on to Madrid.

"What should we drink?" the girl asked. She had taken off her hat
10 and put it on the table.

"It's pretty hot," the man said.

"Let's drink beer."

"Dos cervezas," the man said into the curtain.

"Big ones?" a woman asked from the doorway.

"Yes. Two big ones."

The woman brought two glasses of beer and two felt pads. She put the
felt pads and the beer glasses on the table and looked at the man and
the girl. The girl was looking off at the line of hills. They were white in
the sun and the country was brown and dry.

20   "They look like white elephants," she said.

"I've never seen one," the man drank his beer.

"No, you wouldn't have."

"I might have," the man said. "Just because you say I wouldn't have
doesn't prove anything."

The girl looked at the bead curtain. "They've painted something on
it," she said. "What does it say?"

"Anis del Toro. It's a drink."

"Could we try it?"

The man called "Listen" through the curtain. The woman came out
30 from the bar.

"Four reales."

"We want two Anis del Toro."

"With water?"

"Do you want it with water?"

"I don't know," the girl said. "Is it good with water?"

"It's all right."

"You want them with water?" asked the woman.

"Yes, with water."

"It tastes like licorice," the girl said and put the glass down.
40   "That's the way with everything."

"Yes," said the girl. "Everything tastes of licorice. Especially all the
things you've waited so long for, like absinthe."

"Oh, cut it out."

"You started it," the girl said. "I was being amused. I was having a
fine time."

"Well, let's try and have a fine time."

"All right. I was trying. I said the mountains looked like white elephants. Wasn't that bright?"

"That was bright."

50   "I wanted to try this new drink. That's all we do, isn't it—look at
things and try new drinks?"

"I guess so."

The girl looked across at the hills.

"They're lovely hills," she said. "They don't really look like white
elephants. I just meant the coloring of their skin through the trees."

"Should we have another drink?"

"All right."

The warm wind blew the bead curtain against the table.

"The beer's nice and cool," the man said.
60   "It's lovely," the girl said.

"It's really an awfully simple operation, Jig," the man said. "It's not
really an operation at all."

The girl looked at the ground the table legs rested on.

"I know you wouldn't mind it, Jig. It's really not anything. It's just
to let the air in."

The girl did not say anything.

"I'll go with you and I'll stay with you all the time. They just let the
air in and then it's all perfectly natural."

"Then what will we do afterward?"
70   "We'll be fine afterward. Just like we were before."

"What makes you think so?"

"That's the only thing that bothers us. It's the only thing that's
made us unhappy."

The girl looked at the bead curtain, put her hand out and took hold of two of the strings of beads.

"And you think then we'll be all right and be happy."

"I know we will. You don't have to be afraid. I've known lots of people that have done it."

"So have I," said the girl. "And afterward they were all so happy."

80 "Well," the man said, "if you don't want to you don't have to. I wouldn't have you do it if you didn't want to. But I know it's perfectly simple."

"And you really want to?"

"I think it's the best thing to do. But I don't want you to do it if you don't really want to."

"And if I do it you'll be happy and things will be like they were and you'll love me?"

"I love you now. You know I love you."

"I know. But if I do it, then it will be nice again if I say things are
90 like white elephants, and you'll like it?"

"I'll love it. I love it now but I just can't think about it. You know how I get when I worry."

"If I do it you won't ever worry?"

"I won't worry about that because it's perfectly simple."

"Then I'll do it. Because I don't care about me."

"What do you mean?"

"I don't care about me."

"Well, I care about you."

"Oh, yes. But I don't care about me. And I'll do it and then every-
100 thing will be fine."

"I don't want you to do it if you feel that way."

The girl stood up and walked to the end of the station. Across, on the other side, were fields of grain and trees along the banks of the Ebro. Far away, beyond the river, were mountains. The shadow of a cloud moved across the field of grain and she saw the river through the trees.

"And we could have all this," she said. "And we could have everything and every day we make it more impossible."

"What did you say?"

"I said we could have everything."

110 "We can have everything."

"No, we can't."

"We can have the whole world."

"No, we can't."

"We can go everywhere."

"No, we can't. It isn't ours any more."

"It's ours."

"No, it isn't. And once they take it away, you never get it back."

"But they haven't taken it away."

"We'll wait and see."

120   "Come on back in the shade," he said. "You mustn't feel that way."
          "I don't feel any way," the girl said. "I just know things."
          "I don't want you to do anything that you don't want to do—"
          "Nor that isn't good for me," she said. "I know. Could we have an-
other beer?"
          "All right. But you've got to realize—"
          "I realize," the girl said. "Can't we maybe stop talking?"
          They sat down at the table and the girl looked across at the hills on
the dry side of the valley and the man looked at her and at the table.
          "You've got to realize," he said, "that I don't want you to do it if you
130 don't want to. I'm perfectly willing to go through with it if it means
anything to you."
          "Doesn't it mean anything to you? We could get along."
          "Of course it does. But I don't want anybody but you. I don't want
any one else. And I know it's perfectly simple."
          "Yes, you know it's perfectly simple."
          "It's all right for you to say that, but I do know it."
          "Would you do something for me now?"
          "I'd do anything for you."
          "Would you please please please please please please please stop
140 talking?"
          He did not say anything but looked at the bags against the wall of
the station. There were labels on them from all the hotels where they
had spent nights.
          "But I don't want you to," he said, "I don't care anything about it."
          "I'll scream," the girl said.
          The woman came out through the curtains with two glasses of beer
and put them down on the damp felt pads. "The train comes in five minutes," she said.
          "What did she say?" asked the girl.
150   "That the train is coming in five minutes."
          The girl smiled brightly at the woman, to thank her.
          "I'd better take the bags over to the other side of the station," the
man said. She smiled at him.
          "All right. Then come back and we'll finish the beer."
          He picked up the two heavy bags and carried them around the station
to the other tracks. He looked up the tracks but could not see the train.
Coming back, he walked through the barroom, where people waiting for
the train were drinking. He drank an Anis at the bar and looked at the
people. They were all waiting reasonably for the train. He went out
160 through the bead curtain. She was sitting at the table and smiled at him.
          "Do you feel better?" he asked.
          "I feel fine," she said. "There's nothing wrong with me. I feel fine."

VLADIMIR NABOKOV (1899–1977)

Cloud, Castle, Lake
(1937)

One of my representatives—a modest, mild bachelor, very efficient—happened to win a pleasure trip at a charity ball given by Russian refugees. That was in 1936 or 1937. The Berlin summer was in full flood (it was the second week of damp and cold, so that it was a pity to look at everything which had turned green in vain, and only the sparrows kept cheerful); he did not care to go anywhere, but when he tried to sell his ticket at the office of the Bureau of Pleasantrips he was told that to do so he would have to have special permission from the Ministry of Transportation; when he tried them, it turned out that first he would
10 have to draw up a complicated petition at a notary's on stamped paper; and besides, a so-called "certificate of non-absence from the city for the summertime" had to be obtained from the police.

So he sighed a little, and decided to go. He borrowed an aluminum flask from friends, repaired his soles, bought a belt and a fancy-style flannel shirt—one of those cowardly things which shrink in the first wash. Incidentally, it was too large for that likable little man, his hair always neatly trimmed, his eyes so intelligent and kind. I cannot remember his name at the moment. I think it was Vasili Ivanovich.

He slept badly the night before the departure. And why? Because he
20 had to get up unusually early, and hence took along into his dreams the delicate face of the watch ticking on his night table; but mainly because that very night, for no reason at all, he began to imagine that this trip, thrust upon him by a feminine Fate in a low-cut gown, this trip which he had accepted so reluctantly, would bring him some wonderful, tremulous happiness. This happiness would have something in common with his childhood, and with the excitement aroused in him by Russian lyrical poetry, and with some evening sky line once seen in a dream, and with that lady, another man's wife, whom he had hopelessly loved for seven years—but it would be even fuller and more significant than
30 all that. And besides, he felt that the really good life must be oriented toward something or someone.

The morning was dull, but steam-warm and close, with an inner sun, and it was quite pleasant to rattle in a streetcar to the distant railway station where the gathering place was: several people, alas, were taking part in the excursion. Who would they be, these drowsy beings, drowsy as seem all creatures still unknown to us? By Window No. 6, at 7 A.M., as was indicated in the directions appended to the ticket, he saw them (they were already waiting; he had managed to be late by about three minutes).

40   A lanky blond young man in Tyrolese garb stood out at once. He was burned the color of a cockscomb, had huge brick-red knees with golden hairs, and his nose looked lacquered. He was the leader furnished by the

Bureau, and as soon as the newcomer had joined the group (which consisted of four women and as many men) he led it off toward a train lurking behind other trains, carrying his monstrous knapsack with terrifying ease, and firmly clanking with his hobnailed boots.

Everyone found a place in an empty car, unmistakably third-class, and Vasili Ivanovich, having sat down by himself and put a peppermint into his mouth, opened a little volume of Tyutchev, whom he had long in-
50 tended to reread; but he was requested to put the book aside and join the group. An elderly bespectacled post-office clerk, with skull, chin, and upper lip a bristly blue as if he had shaved off some extraordinarily luxuriant and tough growth especially for this trip, immediately announced that he had been to Russia and knew some Russian—for instance, *pat-zlui*—and, recalling philanderings in Tsaritsyn, winked in such a manner that his fat wife sketched out in the air the outline of a backhand box on the ear. The company was getting noisy. Four employees of the same building firm were tossing each other heavy-weight jokes: a middle-aged man, Schultz; a younger man, Schultz also, and two fidgety young
60 women with big mouths and big rumps. The red-headed, rather burlesque widow in a sport skirt knew something too about Russia (the Riga beaches). There was also a dark young man by the name of Schramm, with lusterless eyes and a vague velvety vileness about his person and manners, who constantly switched the conversation to this or that attractive aspect of the excursion, and who gave the first signal for rapturous appreciation; he was, as it turned out later, a special stimulator from the Bureau of Pleasantrips.

The locomotive, working rapidly with its elbows, hurried through a pine forest, then—with relief—among fields. Only dimly realizing as yet
70 all the absurdity and horror of the situation, and perhaps attempting to persuade himself that everything was very nice, Vasili Ivanovich contrived to enjoy the fleeting gifts of the road. And indeed, how enticing it all is, what charm the world acquires when it is wound up and moving like a merry-go-round! The sun crept toward a corner of the window and suddenly spilled over the yellow bench. The badly pressed shadow of the car sped madly along the grassy bank, where flowers blended into colored streaks. A crossing: a cyclist was waiting, one foot resting on the ground. Trees appeared in groups and singly, revolving coolly and blandly, displaying the latest fashions. The blue dampness of a ravine. A memory of
80 love, disguised as a meadow. Wispy clouds—greyhounds of heaven.

We both, Vasili Ivanovich and I, have always been impressed by the anonymity of all the parts of a landscape, so dangerous for the soul, the impossibility of ever finding out where that path you see leads—and look, what tempting thicket! It happened that on a distant slope or in a gap in the trees there would appear and, as it were, stop for an instant, like air retained in the lungs, a spot so enchanting—a lawn, a terrace—such perfect expression of tender well-meaning beauty—that it seemed that if one could stop the train and go thither, forever, to you, my love . . . But a

thousand beech trunks were already madly leaping by, whirling in a siz-
zling sun pool, and again the chance for happiness was gone.

At the stations, Vasili Ivanovich would look at the configuration of
some entirely insignificant objects—a smear on the platform, a cherry
stone, a cigarette butt—and would say to himself that never, never
would he remember these three little things here in that particular in-
terrelation, this pattern, which he now could see with such deathless
precision; or again, looking at a group of children waiting for a train, he
would try with all his might to single out at least one remarkable destiny—in the form of a violin or a crown, a propeller or a lyre—and
would gaze until the whole party of village schoolboys appeared as on
an old photograph, now reproduced with a little white cross above the
face of the last boy on the right: the hero's childhood.

But one could look out of the window only by snatches. All had been
given sheet music with verses from the Bureau:

> Stop that worrying and moping,
> Take a knotted stick and rise,
> Come a-tramping in the open
> With the good, the hearty guys!
> Tramp your country's grass and stubble,
> With the good, the hearty guys,
> Kill the hermit and his trouble
> And to hell with doubts and sighs!
> In a paradise of heather
> Where the field mouse screams and dies,
> Let us march and sweat together
> With the steel-and-leather guys!

This was to be sung in chorus: Vasili Ivanovich, who not only could
not sing but could not even pronounce German words clearly, took advantage of the drowning roar of mingling voices and merely opened his
mouth while swaying slightly, as if he were really singing—but the
leader, at a sign from the subtle Schramm, suddenly stopped the general
singing and, squinting askance at Vasili Ivanovich, demanded that he
sing solo. Vasili Ivanovich cleared his throat, timidly began, and after a
minute of solitary torment all joined in; but he did not dare thereafter to
drop out.

He had with him his favorite cucumber from the Russian store, a
loaf of bread, and three eggs. When evening came, and the low crimson
sun entered wholly the soiled seasick car, stunned by its own din, all
were invited to hand over their provisions, in order to divide them
evenly—this was particularly easy, as all except Vasili Ivanovich had the
same things. The cucumber amused everybody, was pronounced inedi-
ble, and was thrown out of the window. In view of the insufficiency of
his contribution, Vasili Ivanovich got a smaller portion of sausage.

He was made to play cards. They pulled him about, questioned him, verified whether he could show the route of the trip on a map—in a word, all busied themselves with him, at first good-naturedly, then with malevolence, which grew with the approach of night. Both girls were called Greta; the red-headed widow somehow resembled the rooster-leader; Schramm, Schultz, and the other Schultz, the post-office clerk and his wife, all gradually melted together, merged together, forming one collective, wobbly, many-handed being, from which one could not escape. It pressed upon him from all sides. But suddenly at some station all climbed out, and it was already dark, although in the west there still hung a very long, very pink cloud, and farther along the track, with a soul-piercing light, the star of a lamp trembled through the slow smoke of the engine, and crickets chirped in the dark, and from somewhere there came the odor of jasmine and hay, my love.

They spent the night in a tumble-down inn. A mature bedbug is awful, but there is a certain grace in the motions of silky silverfish. The post-office clerk was separated from his wife, who was put with the widow; he was given to Vasili Ivanovich for the night. The two beds took up the whole room. Quilt on top, chamber pot below. The clerk said that somehow he did not feel sleepy, and began to talk of his Russian adventures, rather more circumstantially than in the train. He was a great bully of a man, thorough and obstinate, clad in long cotton drawers, with mother-of-pearl claws on his dirty toes, and bear's fur between fat breasts. A moth dashed about the ceiling, hobnobbing with its shadow. "In Tsaritsyn," the clerk was saying, "there are now three schools, a German, a Czech, and a Chinese one. At any rate, that is what my brother-in-law says; he went there to build tractors."

Next day, from early morning to five o'clock in the afternoon, they raised dust along a highway, which undulated from hill to hill; then they took a green road through a dense fir wood. Vasili Ivanovich, as the least burdened, was given an enormous round loaf of bread to carry under his arm. How I hate you, our daily! But still his precious, experienced eyes noted what was necessary. Against the background of fir-tree gloom a dry needle was hanging vertically on an invisible thread.

Again they piled into a train, and again the small partitionless car was empty. The other Schultz began to teach Vasili Ivanovich how to play the mandolin. There was much laughter. When they got tired of that, they thought up a capital game, which was supervised by Schramm. It consisted of the following: the women would lie down on the benches they chose, under which the men were already hidden, and when from under one of the benches there would emerge a ruddy face with ears, or a big outspread hand, with a skirt-lifting curve of the fingers (which would provoke much squealing), then it would be revealed who was paired off with whom. Three times Vasili Ivanovich lay down in filthy darkness, and three times it turned out that there was no one on the bench when he crawled out from under. He was acknowledged the loser and was forced to eat a cigarette butt.

180   They spent the night on straw mattresses in a barn, and early in the morning set out again on foot. Firs, ravines, foamy streams. From the heat, from the songs which one had constantly to bawl, Vasili Ivanovich became so exhausted that during the midday halt he fell asleep at once, and awoke only when they began to slap at imaginary horseflies on him. But after another hour of marching, that very happiness of which he had once half dreamt was suddenly discovered.

It was a pure, blue lake, with an unusual expression of its water. In the middle, a large cloud was reflected in its entirety. On the other side, on a hill thickly covered with verdure (and the darker the verdure, the

190   more poetic it is), towered, arising from dactyl to dactyl, an ancient black castle. Of course, there are plenty of such views in Central Europe, but just this one—in the inexpressible and unique harmoniousness of its three principal parts, in its smile, in some mysterious innocence it had, my love! my obedient one!—was something so unique, and so familiar, and so long-promised, and it so *understood* the beholder that Vasili Ivanovich even pressed his hand to his heart, as if to see whether his heart was there in order to give it away.

At some distance, Schramm, poking into the air with the leader's alpenstock, was calling the attention of the excursionists to something

200   or other; they had settled themselves around on the grass in poses seen in amateur snapshots, while the leader sat on a stump, his behind to the lake, and was having a snack. Quietly, concealing himself in his own shadow, Vasili Ivanovich followed the shore, and came to a kind of inn. A dog still quite young greeted him; it crept on its belly, its jaws laughing, its tail fervently beating the ground. Vasili Ivanovich accompanied the dog into the house, a piebald two-storied dwelling with a winking window beneath a convex tiled eyelid; and he found the owner, a tall old man vaguely resembling a Russian war veteran, who spoke German so poorly and with such a soft drawl that Vasili Ivanovich changed to

210   his own tongue, but the man understood as in a dream and continued in the language of his environment, his family.

Upstairs was a room for travelers. "You know, I shall take it for the rest of my life," Vasili Ivanovich is reported to have said as soon as he had entered it. The room itself had nothing remarkable about it. On the contrary, it was a most ordinary room, with a red floor, daisies daubed on the white walls, and a small mirror half filled with the yellow infusion of the reflected flowers—but from the window one could clearly see the lake with its cloud and its castle, in a motionless and perfect correlation of happiness. Without reasoning, without considering, only entirely surrender-

220   ing to an attraction the truth of which consisted in its own strength, a strength which he had never experienced before, Vasili Ivanovich in one radiant second realized that here in this little room with that view, beautiful to the verge of tears, life would at last be what he had always wished it to be. What exactly it would be like, what would take place here, that of course he did not know, but all around him were help, promise, and consolation—so that there could not be any doubt that he must live here. In a

moment he figured out how he would manage it so as not to have to return to Berlin again, how to get the few possessions that he had—books, the blue suit, her photograph. How simple it was turning out! As my represen-
230 tative, he was earning enough for the modest life of a refugee Russian.

"My friends," he cried, having run down again to the meadow by the shore, "my friends, good-by. I shall remain for good in that house over there. We can't travel together any longer. I shall go no farther. I am not going anywhere. Good-by!"

"How is that?" said the leader in a queer voice, after a short pause, during which the smile on the lips of Vasili Ivanovich slowly faded, while the people who had been sitting on the grass half rose and stared at him with stony eyes.

"But why?" he faltered. "It is here that . . ."
240 "Silence!" the post-office clerk suddenly bellowed with extraordinary force. "Come to your senses, you drunken swine!"

"Wait a moment, gentlemen," said the leader, and, having passed his tongue over his lips, he turned to Vasili Ivanovich.

"You probably have been drinking," he said quietly. "Or have gone out of your mind. You are taking a pleasure trip with us. Tomorrow, according to the appointed itinerary—look at your ticket—we are all returning to Berlin. There can be no question of anyone—in this case you—refusing to continue this communal journey. We were singing today a certain song—try and remember what it said. That's enough now! Come, children,
250 we are going on."

"There will be beer at Ewald," said Schramm in a caressing voice. "Five hours by train. Hikes. A hunting lodge. Coal mines. Lots of interesting things."

"I shall complain," wailed Vasili Ivanovich. "Give me back my bag. I have the right to remain where I want. Oh, but this is nothing less than an invitation to a beheading"—he told me he cried when they seized him by the arms.

"If necessary we shall carry you," said the leader grimly, "but that is not likely to be pleasant. I am responsible for each of you, and shall
260 bring back each of you, alive or dead."

Swept along a forest as in a hideous fairy tale, squeezed, twisted, Vasili Ivanovich could not even turn around, and only felt how the radiance behind his back receded, fractured by trees, and then it was no longer there, and all around the dark firs fretted but could not interfere. As soon as everyone had got into the car and the train had pulled off, they began to beat him—they beat him a long time, and with a good deal of inventiveness. It occurred to them, among other things, to use a corkscrew on his palms; then on his feet. The post-office clerk, who had been to Russia, fashioned a knout out of a stick and a belt, and began to
270 use it with devilish dexterity. Atta boy! The other men relied more on their iron heels, whereas the women were satisfied to pinch and slap. All had a wonderful time.

After returning to Berlin, he called on me, was much changed, sat down quietly, putting his hands on his knees, told his story; kept on repeating that he must resign his position, begged me to let him go, insisted that he could not continue, that he had not the strength to belong to mankind any longer. Of course, I let him go.

TILLIE OLSEN (1913–   )

I Stand Here Ironing
(1953–1954)

I stand here ironing, and what you asked me moves tormented back and forth with the iron.

"I wish you would manage the time to come in and talk with me about your daughter. I'm sure you can help me understand her. She's a youngster who needs help and whom I'm deeply interested in helping."

"Who needs help." Even if I came, what good would it do? You think because I am her mother I have a key, or that in some way you could use me as a key? She has lived for nineteen years. There is all that life that has happened outside of me, beyond me.

10   And when is there time to remember, to sift, to weight, to estimate, to total? I will start and there will be an interruption and I will have to gather it all together again. Or I will become engulfed with all I did or did not do, with what should have been and what cannot be helped.

She was a beautiful baby. The first and only one of our five that was beautiful at birth. You do not guess how new and uneasy her tenancy in her now-loveliness. You did not know her all those years she was thought homely, or see her poring over her baby pictures, making me tell her over and over how beautiful she had been—and would be, I would tell her— and was now, to the seeing eye. But the seeing eyes

20 were few or nonexistent. Including mine.

I nursed her. They feel that's important nowadays. I nursed all the children, but with her, with all the fierce rigidity of first motherhood, I did like the books then said. Though her cries battered me to trembling and my breasts ached with swollenness, I waited till the clock decreed.

Why do I put that first? I do not even know if it matters, or if it explains anything.

She was a beautiful baby. She blew shining bubbles of sound. She loved motion, loved light, loved color and music and textures. She would lie on the floor in her blue overalls patting the surface so hard in ecstasy

30 her hands and feet would blur. She was a miracle to me, but when she was eight months old I had to leave her daytimes with the woman downstairs to whom she was no miracle at all, for I worked or looked for work and for Emily's father, who "could no longer endure" (he wrote in his goodbye note) "sharing want with us."

I was nineteen. It was the pre-relief, pre-WPA world of the depression. I would start running as soon as I got off the streetcar, running up the stairs, the place smelling sour, and awake or asleep to startle awake, when she saw me she would break into a clogged weeping that could not be comforted, a weeping I can hear yet.

40   After a while I found a job hashing at night so I could be with her days, and it was better. But it came to where I had to bring her to his family and leave her.

It took a long time to raise the money for her fare back. Then she got chicken pox and I had to wait longer. When she finally came, I hardly knew her, walking quick and nervous like her father, looking like her father, thin, and dressed in a shoddy red that yellowed her skin and glared at the pockmarks. All the baby loveliness gone.

She was two. Old enough for nursery school they said, and I did not know then what I know now—the fatigue of the long day, and the lacera-
50 tions of group life in nurseries that are only parking places for children.

Except that it would have made no difference if I had known. It was the only place there was. It was the only way we could be together, the only way I could hold a job.

And even without knowing, I knew. I knew the teacher that was evil because all these years it has curdled into my memory, the little boy hunched in the corner, her rasp, "why aren't you outside, because Alvin hits you? that's no reason, go out, scaredy." I knew Emily hated it even if she did not clutch and implore "don't go Mommy" like the other children, mornings.

60   She always had a reason why we should stay home. Momma, you look sick. Momma, I feel sick. Momma, the teachers aren't there today, they're sick. Momma, we can't go, there was a fire there last night. Momma, it's a holiday today, no school, they told me.

But never a direct protest, never rebellion. I think of our others in their three-, four-year-oldness—the explosions, the tempers, the denunci-ations, the demands—and I feel suddenly ill. I put the iron down. What in me demanded that goodness in her? And what was the cost, the cost to her of such goodness?

The old man living in the back once said in his gentle way: "You
70 should smile at Emily more when you look at her." What *was* in my face when I looked at her? I loved her. There were all the acts of love.

It was only with the others I remembered what he said, and it was the face of joy, and not of care or tightness or worry I turned to them—too late for Emily. She does not smile easily, let alone almost always as her brothers and sisters do. Her face is closed and sombre, but when she wants, how fluid. You must have seen it in her pantomimes, you spoke of her rare gift for comedy on the stage that rouses a laughter out of the au-dience so dear they applaud and applaud and do not want to let her go.

Where does it come from, that comedy? There was none of it in her
80 when she came back to me that second time, after I had had to send her away again. She had a new daddy now to learn to love, and I think perhaps it was a better time.

Except when we left her alone nights, telling ourselves she was old enough.

"Can't you go some other time, Mommy, like tomorrow?" she would ask. "Will it be just a little while you'll be gone? Do you promise?"

The time we came back, the front door open, the clock on the floor in the hall. She rigid awake. "It wasn't just a little while. I didn't cry. Three times I called you, just three times, and then I ran downstairs to 90 open the door so you could come faster. The clock talked loud. I threw it away, it scared me what it talked."

She said the clock talked loud again that night I went to the hospital to have Susan. She was delirious with the fever that comes before red measles, but she was fully conscious all the week I was gone and the week after we were home when she could not come near the new baby or me.

She did not get well. She stayed skeleton thin, not wanting to eat, and night after night she had nightmares. She would call for me, and I would rouse from exhaustion to sleepily call back: "You're all right, darling, go to sleep, it's just a dream," and if she still called, in a sterner 100 voice, "now go to sleep, Emily, there's nothing to hurt you." Twice, only twice, when I had to get up for Susan anyhow, I went in to sit with her.

Now when it is too late (as if she would let me hold and comfort her like I do the others) I get up and go to her at once at her moan or restless stirring. "Are you awake, Emily? Can I get you something?" And the answer is always the same: "No, I'm all right, go back to sleep, Mother."

They persuaded me at the clinic to send her away to a convalescent home in the country where "she can have the kind of food and care you can't manage for her, and you'll be free to concentrate on the new baby." They still send children to that place. I see pictures on the society page 110 of sleek young women planning affairs to raise money for it, or dancing at the affairs, or decorating Easter eggs or filling Christmas stockings for the children.

They never have a picture of the children so I do not know if the girls still wear those gigantic red bows and the ravaged looks on the every other Sunday when parents can come to visit "unless otherwise notified"—as we were notified the first six weeks.

Oh it is a handsome place, green lawns and tall trees and fluted flower beds. High up on the balconies of each cottage the children stand, the girls in their red bows and white dresses, the boys in white suits and 120 giant red ties. The parents stand below shrieking up to be heard and the children shriek down to be heard, and between them the invisible wall "Not To Be Contaminated by Parental Germs or Physical Affection."

There was a tiny girl who always stood hand in hand with Emily. Her parents never came. One visit she was gone. "They moved her to Rose College," Emily shouted in explanation. "They don't like you to love anybody here."

She wrote once a week, the labored writing of a seven-year-old. "I am fine. How is the baby. If I write my leter nicly I will have a star. Love." There never was a star. We wrote every other day, letters she could never 130 hold or keep but only hear read—once. "We simply do not have room for children to keep any personal possessions," they patiently explained when we pieced one Sunday's shrieking together to plead how much it would mean to Emily, who loved so to keep things, to be allowed to keep her letters and cards.

Each visit she looked frailer. "She isn't eating," they told us.

(They had runny eggs for breakfast or mush with lumps, Emily said later, I'd hold it in my mouth and not swallow. Nothing ever tasted good, just when they had chicken.)

It took us eight months to get her released home, and only the fact 140 that she gained back so little of her seven lost pounds convinced the social worker.

I used to try to hold and love her after she came back, but her body would stay stiff, and after a while she'd push away. She ate little. Food sickened her, and I think much of life too. Oh she had physical lightness and brightness, twinkling by on skates, bouncing like a ball up and down up and down over the jump rope, skimming over the hill; but these were momentary.

She fretted about her appearance, thin and dark and foreign-looking at a time when every little girl was supposed to look or thought she should 150 look a chubby blonde replica of Shirley Temple. The doorbell sometimes rang for her, but no one seemed to come and play in the house or be a best friend. Maybe because we moved so much.

There was a boy she loved painfully through two school semesters. Months later she told me how she had taken pennies from my purse to buy him candy. "Licorice was his favorite and I brought him some every day, but he still liked Jennifer better'n me. Why, Mommy?" The kind of question for which there is no answer.

School was a worry to her. She was not glib or quick in a world where glibness and quickness were easily confused with ability to learn. To her 160 overworked and exasperated teachers she was an over-conscientious "slow learner" who kept trying to catch up and was absent entirely too often.

I let her be absent, though sometimes the illness was imaginary. How different from my now-strictness about attendance with the others. I wasn't working. We had a new baby, I was home anyhow. Sometimes, after Susan grew old enough, I would keep her home from school, too, to have them all together.

Mostly Emily had asthma, and her breathing, harsh and labored, would fill the house with a curiously tranquil sound. I would bring the 170 two old dresser mirrors and her boxes of collections to her bed. She would select beads and single earrings, bottle tops and shells, dried flowers and pebbles, old postcards and scraps, all sorts of oddments; then she and Susan would play Kingdom, setting up landscapes and furniture, peopling them with action.

Those were the only times of peaceful companionship between her and Susan. I have edged away from it, that poisonous feeling between them, that terrible balancing of hurts and needs I had to do between the two, and did so badly, those earlier years.

Oh there are conflicts between the others too, each one human, need-
180 ing, demanding, hurting, taking—but only between Emily and Susan, no,
Emily toward Susan that corroding resentment. It seems so obvious on the
surface, yet it is not obvious. Susan, the second child, Susan, golden- and
curly-haired and chubby, quick and articulate and assured, everything in
appearance and manner Emily was not; Susan, not able to resist Emily's
precious things, losing or sometimes clumsily breaking them; Susan
telling jokes and riddles to company for applause while Emily sat silent (to
say to me later: that was *my* riddle, Mother, I told it to Susan); Susan, who
for all the five years' difference in age was just a year behind Emily in developing physically.
190   I am glad for that slow physical development that widened the difference between her and her contemporaries, though she suffered over it.
She was too vulnerable for that terrible world of youthful competition, of
preening and parading, of constant measuring of yourself against every
other, of envy, "If I had that copper hair," "If I had that skin. . . ." She
tormented herself enough about not looking like the others, there was
enough of the unsureness, and having to be conscious of words before
you speak, the constant caring—what are they thinking of me? without
having it all magnified by the merciless physical drives.
     Ronnie is calling. He is wet and I change him. It is rare there is such a
200 cry now. That time of motherhood is almost behind me when the ear is
not one's own but must always be racked and listening for the child cry,
the child call. We sit for a while and I hold him, looking out over the city
spread in charcoal with its soft aisles of light. *"Shoogily,"* he breathes and
curls closer. I carry him back to bed, asleep. *Shoogily.* A funny word, a
family word, inherited from Emily, invented by her to say: *comfort.*
     In this and other ways she leaves her seal, I say aloud. And startle at
my saying it. What do I mean? What did I start to gather together, to try
and make coherent? I was at the terrible, growing years. Way years. I do
not remember them well. I was working, there were four smaller ones
210 now, there was not time for her. She had to help be a mother, and housekeeper, and shopper. She had to set her seal. Mornings of crisis and near
hysteria trying to get lunches packed, hair combed, coats and shoes
found, everyone to school or Child Care on time, the baby ready for transportation. And always the paper scribbled on by a smaller one, the book
looked at by Susan then mislaid, the homework not done. Running out to
that huge school where she was one, she was lost, she was a drop; suffering over the unpreparedness, stammering and unsure in her classes.
     There was so little time left at night after the kids were bedded down.
She would struggle over books, always eating (it was in those years she
220 developed her enormous appetite that is legendary in our family) and I
would be ironing, or preparing food for the next day, or writing V-mail to
Bill, or tending the baby. Sometimes, to make me laugh, or out of her despair, she would imitate happenings or types at school.
     I think I said once: "Why don't you do something like this in the
school amateur show?" One morning she phoned me at work, hardly

understandable through the weeping: "Mother, I did it. I won, I won; they gave me first prize; they clapped and clapped and wouldn't let me go."

Now suddenly she was Somebody, and as imprisoned in her difference as she had been in anonymity.

230   She began to be asked to perform at other high schools, even in colleges, then at city and statewide affairs. The first one we went to, I only recognized her that first moment when thin, shy, she almost drowned herself into the curtains. Then: Was this Emily? The control, the command, the convulsing and deadly clowning, the spell, then the roaring, stamping audience, unwilling to let this rare and precious laughter out of their lives.

Afterwards: You ought to do something about her with a gift like that—but without money or knowing how, what does one do? We have left it all to her, and the gift has an often eddied inside, clogged and
240   clotted, as been used and growing.

She is coming. She runs up the stairs two at a time with her light graceful step, and I know she is happy tonight. Whatever it was that occasioned your call did not happen today.

"Aren't you ever going to finish the ironing, Mother? Whistler painted his mother in a rocker. I'd have to paint mine standing over an ironing board." This is one of her communicative nights and she tells me everything and nothing as she fixes herself a plate of food out of the icebox.

She is so lovely. Why did you want me to come in at all? Why were you concerned? She will find her way.

250   She starts up the stairs to bed. "Don't get me up with the rest in the morning." "But I thought you were having midterms." "Oh, those," she comes back in, kisses me, and says quite lightly, "in a couple of years when we'll all be atom-dead they won't matter a bit."

She has said it before. She *believes* it. But because I have been dredging the past, and all that compounds a human being is so heavy and meaningful in me, I cannot endure it tonight.

I will never total it all. I will never come in to say: She was a child seldom smiled at. Her father left me before she was a year old. I had to work her first six years when there was work, or I sent her home and to
260   his relatives. There were years she had care she hated. She was dark and thin and foreign-looking in a world where the prestige went to blondeness and curly hair and dimples, she was slow where glibness was prized. She was a child of anxious, not proud, love. We were poor and could not afford for her the soil of easy growth. I was a young mother, I was a distracted mother. There were the other children pushing up, demanding. Her younger sister seemed all that she was not. There were years she did not let me touch her. She kept too much in herself, her life was such she had to keep too much in herself. My wisdom came too late. She has much to her and probably little will come of it. She is a
270   child of her age, of depression, of war, of fear.

Let her be. So all that is in her will not bloom—but in how many does it? There is still enough left to live by. Only help her to know—

help make it so there is cause for her to know—that she is more than this dress on the ironing board, helpless before the iron.

RALPH ELLISON (1914–   )

King of the Bingo Game
(1944)

The woman in front of him was eating roasted peanuts that smelled so good that he could barely contain his hunger. He could not even sleep and wished they'd hurry and begin the bingo game. There, on his right, two fellows were drinking wine out of a bottle wrapped in a paper bag, and he could hear soft gurgling in the dark. His stomach gave a low, gnawing growl. "If this was down South," he thought, "all I'd have to do is lean over and say, 'Lady, gimme a few of those peanuts, please ma'm,' and she'd pass me the bag and never think nothing of it." Or he could ask the fellows for a drink in the same way. Folks down South stuck to-
10 gether that way; they didn't even have to know you. But up here it was different. Ask somebody for something, and they'd think you were crazy. Well, I ain't crazy. I'm just broke, 'cause I got no birth certificate to get a job, and Laura 'bout to die 'cause we got no money for a doctor. But I ain't crazy. And yet a pinpoint of doubt was focused in his mind as he glanced toward the screen and saw the hero stealthily entering a dark room and sending the beam of a flashlight along a wall of book-cases. This is where he finds the trapdoor, he remembered. The man would pass abruptly through the wall and find the girl tied to a bed, her legs and arms spread wide, and her clothing torn to rags. He
20 laughed softly to himself. He had seen the picture three times, and this was one of the best scenes.

On his right the fellow whispered wide-eyed to his companion. "Man, look a-yonder!"

"Damn!"

Wouldn't I like to have her tied up like that . . ."

"Hey! That fool's letting her loose!"

"Aw, man, he loves her."

"Love or no love!"

The man moved impatiently beside him, and he tried to involve him-
30 self in the scene. But Laura was on his mind. Tiring quickly of watching the picture he looked back to where the white beam filtered from the projection room above the balcony. It started small and grew large, specks of dust dancing in its whiteness as it reached the screen. It was strange how the beam always landed right on the screen and didn't mess up and fall somewhere else. But they had it all fixed. Everything was fixed. Now suppose when they showed that girl with her dress torn the girl started taking off the rest of her clothes, and when the guy came in he didn't untie her but kept her there and went to taking off his own clothes? *That* would be something to see. If a picture got out of

40 hand like that those guys up there would go nuts. Yeah, and there'd be so many folks in here you couldn't find a seat for nine months! A strange sensation played over his skin. He shuddered. Yesterday he'd seen a bedbug on a woman's neck as they walked out into the bright street. But exploring his thigh through a hole in his pocket he found only goose pimples and old scars.

The bottle gurgled again. He closed his eyes. Now a dreamy music was accompanying the film and train whistles were sounding in the distance, and he was a boy again walking along a railroad trestle down South, and seeing the train coming, and running back as fast as he
50 could go, and hearing the whistle blowing, and getting off the trestle to solid ground just in time, with the earth trembling beneath his feet, and feeling relieved as he ran down the cinder-strewn embankment onto the highway, and looking back and seeing with terror that the train had left the track and was following him right down the middle of the street, and all the white people laughing as he ran screaming . . .

"Wake up there, buddy! What the hell do you mean hollering like that! Can't you see we trying to enjoy this here picture?"

He stared at the man with gratitude.

"I'm sorry, old man," he said. "I musta been dreaming."
60   "Well, here, have a drink. And don't be making no noise like that, damn!"

His hands trembled as he tilted his head. It was not wine, but whiskey. Cold rye whiskey. He took a deep swoller, decided it was better not to take another, and handed the bottle back to its owner.

"Thanks, old man," he said.

Now he felt the cold whiskey breaking a warm path straight through the middle of him, growing hotter and sharper as it moved. He had not eaten all day, and it made him light-headed. The smell of the peanuts stabbed him like a knife, and he got up and found a seat in the middle
70 aisle. But no sooner did he sit that he saw a row of intense-faced young girls, and got up again, thinking, "You chicks musta been Lindy-hopping somewhere." He found a seat several rows ahead as the lights came on, and he saw the screen disappear behind a heavy red and gold curtain; then the curtain rising, and the man with the microphone and a uniformed attendant coming on the stage.

He felt for his bingo cards, smiling. The guy at the door wouldn't like it if he knew about his having *five* cards. Well, not everyone played the bingo game; and even with five cards he didn't have much of a chance. For Laura, though, he had to have faith. He studied the cards, each with its
80 different numerals, punching the free center hole in each and spreading them neatly across his lap; and when the lights faded he sat slouched in his seat so that he could look from his cards to the bingo wheel with but a quick shifting of his eyes.

Ahead, at the end of the darkness, the man with the microphone was pressing a button attached to a long cord and spinning the bingo wheel and calling out the number each time the wheel came to rest. And each

time the voice rang out his finger raced over the cards for the number. With five cards he had to move fast. He became nervous; there were too many cards, and the man went too fast with his grating voice. Perhaps he
90 should just select one and throw the others away. But he was afraid. He became warm. Wonder how much Laura's doctor would cost? Damn that, watch the cards! And with despair he heard the man call three in a row which he missed on all five cards. This way he'd never win . . .

When he saw the row of holes punched across the third card, he sat paralyzed and heard the man call three more numbers before he stumbled forward, screaming.

"Bingo! Bingo!"

"Let that fool up there," someone called.

"Get up there, man!"

100 He stumbled down the aisle and up the steps to the stage into a light so sharp and bright that for a moment it blinded him, and he felt that he had moved into the spell of some strange, mysterious power. Yet it was as familiar as the sun, and he knew it was the perfectly familiar bingo.

The man with the microphone was saying something to the audience as he held out his card. A cold light flashed from the man's finger as the card left his hand. His knees trembled. The man stepped closer, checking the card against the numbers chalked on the board. Suppose he had made a mistake? The pomade on the man's hair made him feel faint, and he backed away. But the man was checking the card over the micro-
110 phone now, and he had to stay. He stood tense, listening.

"Under the O, forty-four," the man chanted. "Under the I, seven. Under the G, three. Under the B, ninety-six. Under the N, thirteen!"

His breath came easier as the man smiled at the audience.

"Yessir, ladies and gentlemen, he's one of the chosen people!"

The audience rippled with laughter and applause.

"Step right up to the front of the stage."

He moved slowly forward, wishing that the light was not so bright.

"To win tonight's jackpot of $36.90 the wheel must stop between the double zero, understand?"

120 He nodded, knowing the ritual from the many days and nights he had watched the winners march across the stage to press the button that controlled the spinning wheel and receive the prizes. And now he followed the instructions as though he'd crossed the slippery stage a million prize-winning times.

The man was making some kind of a joke, and he nodded vacantly. So tense had he become that he felt a sudden desire to cry and shook it away. He felt vaguely that his whole life was determined by the bingo wheel; not only that which would happen now that he was at last before it, but all that had gone before, since his birth, and his mother's birth and the birth
130 of his father. It had always been there, even though he had not been aware of it, handing out the unlucky cards and numbers of his days. The feeling persisted, and he started quickly away. I better get down from here before I make a fool of myself, he thought.

"Here, boy," the man called. "You haven't started yet."

Someone laughed as he went hesitantly back.

"Are you all reet?"

He grinned at the man's jive talk, but no words would come, and he knew it was not a convincing grin. For suddenly he knew that he stood on the slippery brink of some terrible embarrassment.

140   "Where are you from, boy?" the man asked.

"Down South."

"He's from down South, ladies and gentlemen," the man said. "Where from? Speak right into the mike."

"Rocky Mont," he said. "Rock' Mont, North Car'lina."

"So you decided to come down off that mountain to the U.S.," the man laughed. He felt that the man was making a fool of him, but then something cold was placed in his hand, and the lights were no longer behind him.

Standing before the wheel he felt alone, but that was somehow right,
150 and he remembered his plan. He would give the wheel a short quick twirl. Just a touch of the button. He had watched it many times, and always it came close to double zero when it was short and quick. He steeled himself; the fear had left, and he felt a profound sense of promise, as though he were about to be repaid for all the things he'd suffered all his life. Trembling, he pressed the button. There was a whirl of lights, and in a second he realized with finality that though he wanted to, he could not stop. It was as though he held a high-powered line in his naked hand. His nerves tightened. As the wheel increased its speed it seemed to draw him more and more into its power, as though it held his fate; and with it came
160 a deep need to submit, to whirl, to lose himself in its swirl of color. He could not stop it now, he knew. So let it be.

The button rested snugly in his palm where the man had placed it. And now he became aware of the man beside him, advising him through the microphone, while behind the shadowy audience hummed with noisy voices. He shifted his feet. There was still that feeling of helplessness within him, making part of him desire to turn back, even now that the jackpot was right in his hand. He squeezed the button until his fist ached. Then, like the sudden shriek of a subway whistle, a doubt tore through his head. Suppose he did not spin the wheel long enough? What could he
170 do, and how could he tell? And then he knew, even as he wondered, that as long as he pressed the button, he could control the jackpot. He and only he could determine whether or not it was to be his. Not even the man with the microphone could do anything about it now. He felt drunk. Then, as though he had come down from a high hill into a valley of people, he heard the audience yelling.

"Come down from there, you jerk!"

"Let somebody else have a chance . . ."

"Ole Jack thinks he done found the end of the rainbow . . ."

The last voice was not unfriendly, and he turned and smiled dreamily
180 into the yelling mouths. Then he turned his back squarely on them.

"Don't take too long, boy," a voice said.

He nodded. They were yelling behind him. Those folks did not understand what had happened to him. They had been playing the bingo game
day in and night out for years, trying to win rent money or hamburger
change. But not one of those wise guys had discovered this wonderful
thing. He watched the wheel whirling past the numbers and experienced
a burst of exaltation: This is God! This is the really truly God! He said it
aloud, "This is God!"

He said it with such absolute conviction that he feared he would fall
190 fainting into the footlights. But the crowd yelled so loud that they could
not hear. Those fools, he thought. I'm here trying to tell them the most
wonderful secret in the world, and they're yelling like they gone crazy. A
hand fell upon his shoulder.

"You'll have to make a choice now, boy. You've taken too long."

He brushed the hand violently away.

"Leave me alone, man. I know what I'm doing!"

The man looked surprised and held on to the microphone for support.
And because he did not wish to hurt the man's feelings he smiled, realizing with a sudden pang that there was no way of explaining to the man
200 just why he had to stand there pressing the button forever.

"Come here," he called tiredly.

The man approached, rolling the heavy microphone across the stage.

"Anybody can play this bingo game, right?" he said.

"Sure, but . . ."

He smiled, feeling inclined to be patient with this slick looking
white man with his blue sport shirt and his sharp gabardine suit.

"That's what I thought," he said. "Anybody can win the jackpot as
long as they get the lucky number, right?"

"That's the rule, but after all . . ."

210   "That's what I thought," he said. "And the big prize goes to the man
who knows how to win it?"

The man nodded speechlessly.

"Well then, go on over there and watch me win like I want to. I ain't
going to hurt nobody," he said, "and I'll show you how to win. I mean to
show the whole world how it's got to be done."

And because he understood, he smiled again to let the man know
that he held nothing against him for being white and impatient. Then
he refused to see the man any longer and stood pressing the button, the
voices of the crowd reaching him like sounds in distant streets. Let
220 them yell. All the Negroes down there were just ashamed because he
was black like them. He smiled inwardly, knowing how it was. Most of
the time he was ashamed of what Negroes did himself. Well, let them be
ashamed for something this time. Like him. He was like a long thin
black wire that was being stretched and wound upon the bingo wheel;
wound until he wanted to scream; wound, but this time himself controlling the winding and the sadness and the shame, and because he did,
Laura would be all right. Suddenly the lights flickered. He staggered

backwards. Had something gone wrong? All this noise. Didn't they
know that although he controlled the wheel, it also controlled him,
230 and unless he pressed the button forever and forever and ever it would
stop, leaving him high and dry, dry and high on this hard high slippery
hill and Laura dead? There was only one chance; he had to do whatever
the wheel demanded. And gripping the button in despair, he discovered
with surprise that it imparted a nervous energy. His spine tingled. He
felt a certain power.

Now he faced the raging crowd with defiance, its screams penetrating his eardrums like trumpets shrieking from a jukebox. The vague
faces glowing in the bingo lights gave him a sense of himself that he had
never known before. He was running the show, by God! They had to re-
240 act to him, for he was their luck. This is *me*, he thought. Let the bastards
yell. Then someone was laughing inside him, and he realized that somehow he had forgotten his own name. It was a sad, lost feeling to lose
your name, and a crazy thing to do. That name had been given him by
the white man who had owned his grandfather a long lost time ago
down South. But maybe those wise guys knew his name.

"Who am I?" he screamed.

"Hurry up and bingo, you jerk!"

They didn't know either, he thought sadly. They didn't even know
their own names, they were all poor nameless bastards. Well, he didn't
250 need that old name; he was reborn. For as long as he pressed the button
he was The-man-who-pressed-the-button-who-held-the-prize-who-was-
the-King-of-Bingo. That was the way it was, and he'd have to press the
button even if nobody understood, even though Laura did not understand.

"Live!" he shouted.

The audience quieted like the dying of a huge fan.

"Live, Laura, baby. I got holt of it now, sugar. Live!"

He screamed it, tears streaming down his face. "I got nobody but
YOU!"

260   The screams tore from his very guts. He felt as though the rush of
blood to his head would burst out in baseball seams of small red droplets,
like a head beaten by police clubs. Bending over he saw a trickle of blood
splashing the toe of his shoe. With his free hand he searched his head. It
was his nose. God, suppose something has gone wrong? He felt that the
whole audience had somehow entered him and was stamping its feet in
his stomach, and he was unable to throw them out. They wanted the
prize, that was it. They wanted the secret for themselves. But they'd never
get it; he would keep the bingo wheel whirling forever, and Laura would
be safe in the wheel. But would she? It had to be, because if she were not
270 safe the wheel would cease to turn; it could not go on. He had to get away,
vomit all, and his mind formed an image of himself running with Laura in
his arms down the tracks of the subway just ahead of an A train, running
desperately *vomit* with people screaming for him to come out but knowing no way of leaving the tracks because to stop would bring the train

crushing down upon him and to attempt to leave across the other tracks would mean to run into a hot third rail as high as his waist which threw blue sparks that blinded his eyes until he could hardly see.

He heard singing and the audience was clapping its hands.

280

Shoot the liquor to him, Jim, boy!
Clap-clap-clap
Well a-calla the cop
He's blowing his top!
Shoot the liquor to him, Jim, boy!

Bitter anger grew within him at the singing. They think I'm crazy. Well let 'em laugh. I'll do what I got to do.

He was standing in an attitude of intense listening when he saw that they were watching something on the stage behind him. He felt weak. But when he turned he saw no one. If only his thumb did not ache so. Now they were applauding. And for a moment he thought that the
290 wheel had stopped. But that was impossible, his thumb still pressed the button. Then he saw them. Two men in uniform beckoned from the end of the stage. They were coming toward him, walking in step, slowly, like a tap-dance team returning for a third encore. But their shoulders shot forward, and he backed away, looking wildly about. There was nothing to fight them with. He had only the long black cord which led to a plug somewhere back stage, and he couldn't use that because it operated the bingo wheel. He backed slowly, fixing the men with his eyes as his lips stretched over his teeth in a tight, fixed grin; moved toward the end of the stage and realizing that he couldn't go much further, for suddenly
300 the cord became taut and he couldn't afford to break the cord. But he had to do something. The audience was howling. Suddenly he stopped dead, seeing the men halt, their legs lifted as in an interrupted step of a slow-motion dance. There was nothing to do but run in the other direction and he dashed forward, slipping and sliding. The men fell back, surprised. He struck out violently going past.

"Grab him!"

He ran, but all too quickly the cord tightened, resistingly, and he turned and ran back again. This time he slipped them, and discovered by running in a circle before the wheel he could keep the cord from
310 tightening. But this way he had to flail his arms to keep the men away. Why couldn't they leave a man alone? He ran, circling.

"Ring down the curtain," someone yelled. But they couldn't do that. If they did the wheel flashing from the projection room would be cut off. But they had him before he could tell them so, trying to pry open his fist, and he was wrestling and trying to bring his knees into the fight and holding on to the button, for it was his life. And now he was down, seeing a foot coming down, crushing his wrist cruelly, down, as he saw the wheel whirling serenely above.

"I can't give it up," he screamed. Then quietly, in a confidential
320 tone, "Boys, I really can't give it up."

It landed hard against his head. And in the blank moment they had it away from him, completely now. He fought them trying to pull him up from the stage as he watched the wheel spin slowly to a stop. Without surprise he saw it rest at double zero.

"You see," he pointed bitterly.

"Sure, boy, sure, it's O.K.," one of the men said smiling.

And seeing the man bow his head to someone he could not see, he felt very, very happy; he would receive what all the winners received.

But as he warmed in the justice of the man's tight smile he did not
330 see the man's slow wink, nor see the bow-legged man behind him step clear of the swiftly descending curtain and set himself for a blow. He only felt the dull pain exploding in his skull, and he knew even as it slipped out of him that his luck had run out on the stage.

DORIS LESSING (1919–   )

Wine

(1957)

A man and woman walked towards the boulevard from a little hotel in a side street.

The trees were still leafless, black, cold; but the fine twigs were swelling towards spring, so that looking upward it was with an expectation of the first glimmering greenness. Yet everything was calm, and the sky was a calm, classic blue.

The couple drifted slowly along. Effort, after days of laziness, seemed impossible; and almost at once they turned into a cafe and sank down, as if exhausted, in the glass-walled space that was thrust forward into the
10 street.

The place was empty. People were seeking the midday meal in the restaurants. Not all: that morning crowds had been demonstrating, a procession had just passed, and its straggling end could still be seen. The sounds of violence, shouted slogans and singing, no longer absorbed the din of Paris traffic; but it was these sounds that had roused the couple from sleep.

A waiter leaned at the door, looking after the crowds, and he reluctantly took an order for coffee.

The man yawned; the woman caught the infection; and they laughed
20 with an affectation of guilt and exchanged glances before their eyes, without regret, parted. When the coffee came, it remained untouched. Neither spoke. After some time the woman yawned again; and this time the man turned and looked at her critically, and she looked back. Desire asleep, they looked. This remained: that while everything which drove them slept, they accepted from each other a sad irony; they could look at each other without illusion, steady-eyed.

And then, inevitably, the sadness deepened in her till she consciously resisted it; and into him came the flicker of cruelty.

"Your nose needs powdering," he said.

30 "You need a whipping boy."

But always he refused to feel sad. She shrugged, and, leaving him to it, turned to look out. So did he. At the far end of the boulevard there was a faint agitation, like stirred ants, and she heard him mutter, "Yes, and it still goes on. . . ."

Mocking, she said, "Nothing changes, everything always the same. . . ."

But he had flushed. "I remember," he began, in a different voice. He stopped, and she did not press him, for he was gazing at the distant demonstrators with a bitterly nostalgic face.

40 Outside drifted the lovers, the married couples, the students, the old people. There the stark trees; there the blue, quiet sky. In a month the trees would be vivid green; the sun would pour down heat; the people would be brown, laughing, bare-limbed. No, no, she said to herself, at this vision of activity. Better the static sadness. And, all at once, unhappiness welled up in her, catching her throat, and she was back fifteen years in another country. She stood in blazing tropical moonlight, stretching her arms to a landscape that offered her nothing but silence; and then she was running down a path where small stones glinted sharp underfoot, till at last she fell spent in a swath of glistening grass. Fifteen years.

50 It was at this moment that the man turned abruptly and called the waiter and ordered wine.

"What," she said humorously, "already?"

"Why not?"

For the moment she loved him completely and maternally, till she suppressed the counterfeit and watched him wait, fidgeting, for the wine, pour it, and then set the two glasses before them beside the still-brimming coffee cups. But she was again remembering that night, envying the girl ecstatic with moonlight, who ran crazily through the trees in an unsharable desire for—but what was the point.

60 "What are you thinking of?" he asked, still a little cruel.

"Ohhh," she protested humorously.

"That's the trouble, that's the trouble." He lifted his glass, glanced at her, and set it down. "Don't you want to drink?"

"Not yet."

He left his glass untouched and began to smoke.

These movements demanded some kind of gesture—something slight, even casual, but still an acknowledgement of the separateness of those two people in each of them; the one seen, perhaps, as a soft-staring never-closing eye, observing, always observing, with a tired compassion; the 70 other, a shape of violence that struggled on in the cycle of desire and rest, creation and achievement.

He gave it to her. Again their eyes met in the grave irony, before he turned away, flicking his fingers irritably against the table; and she turned also, to note the black branches where the sap was tingling.

"I remember," he began; and again she said, in protest, "Ohhh!"

He checked himself. "Darling," he said dryly, "you're the only woman I've ever loved." They laughed.

"It must have been this street. Perhaps this cafe—only they change so. When I went back yesterday to see the place where I came every summer, it was a *pâtisserie*,[1] and the woman had forgotten me. There was a whole crowd of us—we used to go around together—and I met a girl here, I think, for the first time. There were recognized places for contacts; people coming from Vienna or Prague, or wherever it was, knew the places—it couldn't be this cafe, unless they've smartened it up. We didn't have the money for all this leather and chromium."

"Well, go on."

"I keep remembering her, for some reason. Haven't thought of her for years. She was about sixteen, I suppose. Very pretty—no, you're quite wrong. We used to study together. She used to bring her books to my room. I liked her, but I had my own girl, only she was studying something else, I forget what." He paused again, and again his face was twisted with nostalgia, and involuntarily she glanced over her shoulder down the street. The procession had completely disappeared; not even the sounds of singing and shouting remained.

"I remember her because . . ." And after a preoccupied silence: "Perhaps it is always the fate of the virgin who comes and offers herself, naked, to be refused."

"What!" she exclaimed, startled. Also, anger stirred in her. She noted it, and sighed. "Go on."

"I never made love to her. We studied together all that summer. Then, one weekend, we all went off in a bunch. None of us had any money, of course, and we used to stand on the pavements and beg lifts, and meet up again in some village. I was with my own girl, but that night we were helping the farmer get in his fruit, in payment for using his barn to sleep in, and I found this girl Marie was beside me. It was moonlight, a lovely night, and we were all singing and making love. I kissed her, but that was all. That night she came to me. I was sleeping up in the loft with another lad. He was asleep. I sent her back down to the others. They were all together down in the hay. I told her she was too young. But she was no younger than my own girl." He stopped; and after all these years his face was rueful and puzzled. "I don't know," he said. "I don't know why I sent her back." Then he laughed. "Not that it matters, I suppose."

"Shameless hussy," she said. The anger was strong now. "You had kissed her, hadn't you?"

He shrugged. "But we were all playing the fool. It was a glorious night—gathering apples, the farmer shouting and swearing at us because we were making love more than working, and singing and drinking wine. Besides, it was that time: the youth movement. We regarded faithfulness and jealousy and all that sort of thing as remnants of bourgeois morality." He laughed again, rather painfully. "I kissed her. There she was, beside me, and she knew my girl was with me that weekend."

---

[1] A bakery specializing in pastry.

"You kissed her," she said accusingly.

He fingered the stem of his wine glass, looking over at her and grinning. "Yes, darling," he almost crooned at her. "I kissed her."

She snapped over into anger. "There's a girl all ready for love. You make use of her for working. Then you kiss her. You know quite well . . ."

"What do I know quite well?"

"It was a cruel thing to do."

130 "I was a kid myself. . . ."

"Doesn't matter." She noted, with discomfort, that she was almost crying. "Working with her! Working with a girl of sixteen, all summer!"

"But we all studied very seriously. She was a doctor afterwards, in Vienna. She managed to get out when the Nazis came in, but . . ."

She said impatiently, "Then you kiss her, on *that* night. Imagine her, waiting till the others were asleep, then she climbed up the ladder to the loft, terrified the other man might wake up, then she stood watching you sleep, and she slowly took off her dress and . . ."

"Oh, I wasn't asleep. I pretended to be. She came up dressed. Shorts
140 and sweater—our girls didn't wear dresses and lipstick—more bourgeois morality. I watched her strip. The loft was full of moonlight. She put her hand over my mouth and came down beside me." Again, his face was filled with rueful amazement. "God knows, I can't understand it myself. She was a beautiful creature. I don't know why I remember it. It's been coming into my mind the last few days." After a pause, slowly twirling the wine glass: "I've been a failure in many things, but not with . . ." He quickly lifted her hand, kissed it, and said sincerely: "I don't know why I remember it now, when . . ." Their eyes met, and they sighed.

150 She said slowly, her hand lying in his: "And so you turned her away."

He laughed. "Next morning she wouldn't speak to me. She started a love affair with my best friend—the man who'd been beside me that night in the loft, as a matter of fact. She hated my guts, and I suppose she was right."

"Think of her. Think of her at that moment. She picked up her clothes, hardly daring to look at you. . . ."

"As a matter of fact, she was furious. She called me all the names she could think of; I had to keep telling her to shut up, she'd wake the
160 whole crowd."

"She climbed down the ladder and dressed again, in the dark. Then she went out of the barn, unable to go back to the others. She went into the orchard. It was still brilliant moonlight. Everything was silent and deserted, and she remembered how you'd all been singing and laughing and making love. She went to the tree where you'd kissed her. The moon was shining on the apples. She'll never forget it, never, never!"

He looked at her curiously. The tears were pouring down her face.

"It's terrible," she said. "Terrible. Nothing could ever make up to her for that. Nothing, as long as she lived. Just when everything was

170 most perfect, all her life, she'd suddenly remember that night, standing alone, not a soul anywhere, miles of damned empty moonlight. . . ."

He looked at her shrewdly. Then, with a sort of humorous, deprecating grimace, he bent over and kissed her and said: "Darling, it's not my fault; it just isn't my fault."

"No," she said.

He put the wine glass into her hands; and she lifted it, looked at the small crimson globule of warming liquid, and drank with him.

DONALD BARTHELME (1931–1989)

The Indian Uprising
(1967)

We defended the city as best we could. The arrows of the Comanches came in clouds. The war clubs of the Comanches clattered on the soft, yellow pavements. There were earthworks along the Boulevard Mark Clark and the hedges had been laced with sparkling wire. People were trying to understand. I spoke to Sylvia. "Do you think this is a good life?" The table held apples, books, long-playing records. She looked up. "No."

Patrols of paras and volunteers with armbands guarded the tall, flat buildings. We interrogated the captured Comanche. Two of us forced his head back while another poured water into his nostrils. His body jerked,
10 he choked and wept. Not believing a hurried, careless and exaggerated report of the number of casualties in the outer districts where trees, lamps, swans had been reduced to clear fields of fire we issued entrenching tools to those who seemed trustworthy and turned the heavy-weapons companies so that we could not be surprised from that direction. And I sat there getting drunker and drunker and more in love and more in love. We talked.

"Do you know Fauré's 'Dolly'?"

"Would that be Gabriel Fauré?"

"It would."
20 "Then I know it," she said. "May I say that I play it at certain times, when I am sad, or happy, although it requires four hands."

"How is that managed?"

"I accelerate," she said, "ignoring the time signature."

And when they shot the scene in the bed I wondered how you felt under the eyes of the cameramen, grips, juicers, men in the mixing booth: excited? stimulated? And when they shot the scene in the shower I sanded a hollow-core door working carefully against the illustrations in texts and whispered instructions from one who had already solved the problem. I had made after all other tables, one while living with
30 Nancy, one while living with Alice, one while living with Eunice, one while living with Marianne.

Red men in waves like people scattering in a square startled by something tragic or a sudden, loud noise accumulated against the barricades

we had made of window dummies, silk, thoughtfully planned job descriptions (including scales for the orderly progress of other colors), wine in demijohns, and robes. I analyzed the composition of the barricade nearest me and found two ashtrays, ceramic, one dark brown and one dark brown with an orange blur at the lip; a tin frying pan; two-liter bottles of red wine; three-quarter-liter bottles of Black & White, aquavit,
40 cognac, vodka, gin, Fad #6 sherry; a hollow-core door in birch veneer on black wrought-iron legs; a blanket, red-orange with faint blue stripes; a red pillow and a blue pillow; a woven straw wastebasket; two glass jars for flowers; corkscrews and can openers; two plates and two cups, ceramic, dark brown; a yellow-and-purple poster; a Yugoslavian carved flute, wood, dark brown; and other items. I decided I knew nothing.

The hospitals dusted wounds with powders the worth of which was not quite established, other supplies having been exhausted early in the first day. I decided I knew nothing. Friends put me in touch with a Miss R., a teacher, unorthodox they said, excellent they said, successful with
50 difficult cases, steel shutters on the windows made the house safe. I had just learned via an International Distress Coupon that Jane had been beaten up by a dwarf in a bar on Tenerife but Miss R. did not allow me to speak of it. "You know nothing," she said, "you feel nothing, you are locked in a most savage and terrible ignorance, I despise you, my boy, *mon cher*, my heart. You may attend but you must not attend now, you must attend later, a day or a week or an hour, you are making me ill. . . ." I nonevaluated these remarks as Korzybski instructed. But it was difficult. Then they pulled back in a feint near the river and we rushed into that sector with a reinforced battalion hastily formed among the Zouaves and
60 cabdrivers. This unit was crushed in the afternoon of a day that began with spoons and letters in hallways and under windows where men tasted the history of the heart, cone-shaped muscular organ that maintains *circulation of the blood.*

But it is you I want now, here in the middle of this Uprising, with the streets yellow and threatening, short, ugly lances with fur at the throat and inexplicable shell money lying in the grass. It is when I am with you that I am happiest, and it is for you that I am making this hollow-core door table with black wrought-iron legs. I held Sylvia by her bear-claw necklace. "Call off your braves," I said. "We have many years
70 left to live." There was a sort of muck running in the gutters, yellowish, filthy stream suggesting excrement, or nervousness, a city that does not know what it has done to deserve baldness, errors, infidelity. "With luck you will survive until matins," Sylvia said. She ran off down the Rue Chester Nimitz, uttering shrill cries.

Then it was learned that they had infiltrated our ghetto and that the people of the ghetto instead of resisting had joined the smooth, well-coordinated attack with zip guns, telegrams, lockets, causing that portion of the line held by the IRA to swell and collapse. We sent more heroin into the ghetto, and hyacinths, ordering another hundred thousand of
80 the pale, delicate flowers. On the map we considered the situation with

its strung-out inhabitants and merely personal emotions. Our parts were blue and their parts were green. I showed the blue-and-green map to Sylvia. "Your parts are green," I said. "You gave me heroin first a year ago," Sylvia said. She ran off down George C. Marshall Allée, uttering shrill cries. Miss R. pushed me into a large room painted white (jolting and dancing in the soft light, and I was excited! and there were people watching!) in which there were two chairs. I sat in one chair and Miss R. sat in the other. She wore a blue dress containing a red figure. There was nothing exceptional about her. I was disappointed by her 90 plainness, by the bareness of the room, by the absence of books.

The girls of my quarter wore long blue mufflers that reached to their knees. Sometimes the girls hid Comanches in their rooms, the blue mufflers together in a room creating a great blue fog. Block opened the door. He was carrying weapons, flowers, loaves of bread. And he was friendly, kind, enthusiastic, so I related a little of the history of torture, reviewing the technical literature quoting the best modern sources, French, German, and American, and pointing out the flies which had gathered in anticipation of some new, cool color.

"What is the situation?" I asked.

100   "The situation is liquid," he said. "We hold the south quarter and they hold the north quarter. The rest is silence."

"And Kenneth?"

"That girl is not in love with Kenneth," Block said frankly. "She is in love with his coat. When she is not wearing it she is huddling under it. Once I caught it going down the stairs by itself. I looked inside. Sylvia."

Once I caught Kenneth's coat going down the stairs by itself but the coat was a trap and inside a Comanche who made a thrust with his short, ugly knife at my leg which buckled and tossed me over the balustrade 110 through a window and into another situation. Not believing that your body brilliant as it was and your fat, liquid spirit distinguished and angry as it was were stable quantities to which one could return on wires more than once, twice, or another number of times I said: "See the table?"

In Skinny Wainwright Square the forces of green and blue swayed and struggled. The referees ran out on the field trailing chains. And then the blue part would be enlarged, the green diminished. Miss R. began to speak. "A former king of Spain, a Bonaparte, lived for a time in Bordentown, New Jersey. But that's no good." She paused. "The ardor aroused in men by the beauty of women can only be satisfied by God. 120 That is *very* good (it is Valéry) but it is not what I have to teach you, goat, muck, filth, heart of my heart." I showed the table to Nancy. "See the table?" She stuck out her tongue red as a blood test. "I made such a table once," Block said frankly. "People all over America have made such tables. I doubt very much whether one can enter an American home without finding at least one such table, or traces of its having been there, such as faded places in the carpet." And afterward in the garden the men of the 7th Cavalry played Gabrieli, Albinoni, Marcello,

Vivaldi, Boccherini. I saw Sylvia. She wore a yellow ribbon, under a long
blue muffler. "Which side are you on," I cried, "after all?"

130   "The only form of discourse of which I approve," Miss R. said in her
dry, tense voice, "is the litany. I believe our masters and teachers as well
as plain citizens should confine themselves to what can safely be said.
Thus when I hear the words *pewter, snake, tea, Fad #6 sherry, serviette, fenes-
tration, crown, blue* coming from the mouth of some public official, or some
raw youth, I am not disappointed. Vertical organization is also possible,"
Miss R. said, "as in

> pewter
> snake
> tea
140   Fad #6 sherry
> serviette
> fenestration
> crown
> blue.

I run to liquids and colors," she said, "but you, you may run to something else, my virgin, my darling, my thistle, my poppet, my own.
Young people," Miss R. said, "run to more and more unpleasant combinations as they sense the nature of our society. Some people," Miss R.
said, "run to conceits or wisdom but I hold to the hard, brown, nutlike
150 word. I might point out that there is enough aesthetic excitement here to
satisfy anyone but a damned fool." I sat in solemn silence.

Fire arrows lit my way to the post office in Patton Place where members of the Abraham Lincoln Brigade offered their last, exhausted letters, postcards, calendars. I opened a letter but inside was a Comanche
flint arrowhead played by Frank Wedekind in an elegant gold chain and
congratulations. Your earring rattled against my spectacles when I
leaned forward to touch the soft, ruined place where the hearing aid
had been. "Pack it in! Pack it in!" I urged, but the men in charge of the
Uprising refused to listen to reason or to understand that it was real
160 and that our water supply had evaporated and that our credit was no
longer what it had been, once.

We attached wires to the testicles of the captured Comanche. And I
sat there getting drunker and drunker and more in love and more in
love. When we threw the switch he spoke. His name, he said, was Gustave Aschenbach. He was born at L——, a country town in the province
of Silesia. He was the son of an upper official in the judicature, and his
forebears had all been officers, judges, departmental functionaries.
. . . And you can never touch a girl in the same way more than once,
twice, or another number of times however much you may wish to hold,
170 wrap, or otherwise fix her hand, or look, or some other quality, or incident, known to you previously. In Sweden the little Swedish children
cheered when we managed nothing more remarkable than getting off a

bus burdened with packages, bread and liver paste and beer. We went to an old church and sat in the royal box. The organist was practicing. And then into the graveyard next to the church. *Here lies Anna Pedersen, a good woman.* I threw a mushroom on the grave. The officer commanding the garbage dump reported by radio that the garbage had begun to move.

Jane! I heard via an International Distress Coupon that you were beaten up by a dwarf in a bar on Tenerife. That doesn't sound like you,
180 Jane. Mostly you kick the dwarf in his little dwarf groin before he can get his teeth into your tasty and nice-looking leg, don't you, Jane? Your affair with Harold is reprehensible, you know that, don't you, Jane? Harold is married to Nancy. And there is Paula to think about (Harold's kid), and Billy (Harold's other kid). I think your values are peculiar, Jane! Strings of language extend in every direction to bind the world into a rushing, ribald whole.

And you can never return to felicities in the same way, the brilliant body, the distinguished spirit recapitulating moments that occur once, twice, or another number of times in rebellions, or water. The rolling con-
190 sensus of the Comanche nation smashed our inner defenses on three sides. Block was firing a grease gun from the upper floor of a building designed by Emery Roth & Sons. "See the table?" "Oh, pack it in with your bloody table!" The city officials were tied to trees. Dusky warriors padded with their forest tread into the mouth of the mayor. "Who do you want to be?" I asked Kenneth and he said he wanted to be Jean-Luc Go-dard but later when time permitted conversations in large, lighted rooms, whispering galleries with black-and-white Spanish rugs and problematic sculpture on calm, red catafalques. The sickness of the quarrel lay thick in the bed. I touched your back, the white, raised scars.
200   We killed a great many in the south suddenly with helicopters and rockets but we found that those we had killed were children and more came from the north and from the east and from other places where there are children preparing to live. "Skin," Miss R. said softly in the white, yellow room. "This is the Clemency Committee. And would you remove your belt and shoelaces." I removed my belt and shoelaces and looked (rain shattering from a great height the prospects of silence and clear, neat rows of houses in the subdivisions) into their savage black eyes, paint, feathers, beads.

JOHN UPDIKE (1932–   )

A & P
(1961)

In walks these three girls in nothing but bathing suits. I'm in the third checkout slot, with my back to the door, so I don't see them until they're over by the bread. The one that caught my eye first was the one in the plaid green two-piece. She was a chunky kid, with a good tan and a sweet broad soft-looking can with those two crescents of white just under it, where the sun never seems to hit, at the top of the backs of her legs. I stood there with my hand on a box of HiHo crackers trying to remember if I rang it up or not. I ring it up again and the customer starts giving me hell. She's one of these cash-register-watchers, a witch about fifty with rouge on her cheekbones and no eyebrows, and I know it made her day to trip me up. She'd been watching cash registers for fifty years and probably never seen a mistake before.

By the time I got her feathers smoothed and her goodies into a bag— she gives me a little snort in passing, if she'd been born at the right time they would have burned her over in Salem—by the time I get her on her way the girls had circled around the bread and were coming back, without a pushcart, back my way along the counters, in the aisle between the checkouts and the Special bins. They didn't even have shoes on. There was this chunky one, with the two-piece—it was bright green and the seams on the bra were still sharp and her belly was still pretty pale so I guessed she just got it (the suit)—there was this one, with one of those chubby berry-faces, the lips all bunched together under her nose, this one, and a tall one, with black hair that hadn't quite frizzed right, and one of these sunburns right across under the eyes, and a chin that was too long—you know, the kind of girl other girls think is very "striking" and "attractive" but never quite makes it, as they very well know, which is why they like her so much—and then the third one, that wasn't quite so tall. She was the queen. She kind of led them, the other two peeking around and making their shoulders round. She didn't look around, not this queen, she just walked straight on slowly, on these long white prima-donna legs. She came down a little hard on her heels, as if she didn't walk in her bare feet that much, putting down her heels and then letting the weight move along to her toes as if she was testing the floor with every step, putting a little deliberate extra action into it. You never know for sure how girls' minds work (do you really think it's a mind in there or just a little buzz like a bee in a glass jar?) but you got the idea she had talked the other two into coming in here with her, and now she was showing them how to do it, walk slow and hold yourself straight.

She had on a kind of dirty-pink—beige maybe, I don't know—bathing suit with a little nubble all over it, and what got me, the straps were down. They were off her shoulders looped loose around the cool tops of her arms, and I guess as a result the suit had slipped a little on her, so all around the top of the cloth there was this shining rim. If it hadn't been there you wouldn't have known there could have been anything whiter than those shoulders. With the straps pushed off, there was nothing between the top of the suit and the top of her head except just *her*, this clean bare plane of the top of her chest down from the shoulder bones like a dented sheet of metal tilted in the light. I mean, it was more than pretty.

She had sort of oaky hair that the sun and salt had bleached, done up in a bun that was unravelling, and a kind of prim face. Walking into the A & P with your straps down, I suppose it's the only kind of face you *can* have. She held her head so high her neck, coming up out of those white shoulders, looked kind of stretched, but I didn't mind. The longer her neck was, the more of her there was.

She must have felt in the corner of her eye me and over my shoulder Stokesie in the second slot watching, but she didn't tip. Not this queen. She kept her eyes moving across the racks, and stopped, and turned so slow it made my stomach rub the inside of my apron, and buzzed to the other two, who kind of huddled against her for relief, and then they all 60 three of them went up the cat-and-dog-food-breakfast-cereal-macaroni-rice-raisins-seasonings-spreads-spaghetti-soft-drinks-crackers-and-cookies aisle. From the third slot I look straight up this aisle to the meat counter, and I watched them all the way. The fat one with the tan sort of fumbled with the cookies, but on second thought she put the package back. The sheep pushing their carts down the aisle—the girls were walking against the usual traffic (not that we have one-way signs or anything)—were pretty hilarious. You could see them, when Queenie's white shoulders dawned on them, kind of jerk, or hop, or hiccup, but their eyes snapped back to their own baskets and on they pushed. I bet 70 you could set off dynamite in an A & P and the people would by and large keep reaching and checking oatmeal off their lists and muttering "Let me see, there was a third thing, began with A, asparagus, no, ah, yes, applesauce!" or whatever it is they do mutter. But there was no doubt, this jiggled them. A few house-slaves in pin curlers even looked around after pushing their carts past to make sure what they had seen was correct.

You know, it's one thing to have a girl in a bathing suit down on the beach, where what with the glare nobody can look at each other much anyway, and another thing in the cool of the A & P, under the fluores- 80 cent lights, against all those stacked packages, with her feet paddling along naked over our checkerboard green-and-cream rubber-tile floor.

"Oh Daddy," Stokesie said beside me. "I feel so faint."

"Darling," I said. "Hold me tight." Stokesie's married, with two babies chalked up on his fuselage already, but as far as I can tell that's the only difference. He's twenty-two, and I was nineteen this April.

"Is it done?" he asks, the responsible married man finding his voice. I forgot to say he thinks he's going to be manager some sunny day, maybe in 1990 when it's called the Great Alexandrov and Petrooshki Tea Company or something.

90   What he meant was, our town is five miles from a beach, with a big summer colony out on the Point, but we're right in the middle of town, and the women generally put on a shirt or shorts or something before they get out of the car into the street. And anyway these are usually women with six children and varicose veins mapping their legs and nobody, including them, could care less. As I say, we're right in the middle of town, and if you stand at our front doors you can see two banks and the Congregational church and the newspaper store and three real-estate offices and about twenty-seven old freeloaders tearing up Central Street because the sewer broke again. It's not as if we're on the Cape; we're north

100 of Boston and there's people in this town haven't seen the ocean for twenty years.

The girls had reached the meat counter and were asking McMahon something. He pointed, they pointed, and they shuffled out of sight behind a pyramid of Diet Delight peaches. All that was left for us to see was old McMahon patting his mouth and looking after them sizing up their joints. Poor kids, I began to feel sorry for them, they couldn't help it.

Now here comes the sad part of the story, at least my family says it's sad, but I don't think it's so sad myself. The store's pretty empty, it being Thursday afternoon, so there was nothing much to do except lean on
110 the register and wait for the girls to show up again. The whole store was like a pinball machine and I didn't know which tunnel they'd come out of. After a while they came around out of the far aisle, around the light bulbs, records at discount of the Caribbean Six or Tony Martin Sings or some such gunk you wonder they waste the wax on, sixpacks of candy bars, and plastic toys done up in cellophane that fall apart when a kid looks at them anyway. Around they come, Queenie still leading the way, and holding a little gray jar in her hand. Slots Three through Seven are unmanned and I could see her wondering between Stokes and me, but Stokesie with his usual luck draws an old party in baggy gray pants
120 who stumbles up with four giant cans of pineapple juice (what do these bums *do* with all that pineapple juice? I've often asked myself) so the girls come to me. Queenie puts down the jar and I take it into my fingers icy cold. Kingfish Fancy Herring Snacks in Pure Sour Cream: 49¢. Now her hands are empty, not a ring or a bracelet, bare as God made them, and I wonder where the money's coming from. Still with that prim look she lifts a folded dollar bill out of the hollow at the center of her nubbled pink top. The jar went heavy in my hand. Really, I thought that was so cute.

Then everybody's luck begins to run out. Lengel comes in from hag-
130 gling with a truck full of cabbages on the lot and is about to scuttle into that door marked MANAGER behind which he hides all day when the girls touch his eye. Lengel's pretty dreary, teaches Sunday school and the rest, but he doesn't miss that much. He comes over and says, "Girls, this isn't the beach."

Queenie blushes, though maybe it's just a brush of sunburn I was noticing for the first time, now that she was so close. "My mother asked me to pick up a jar of herring snacks." Her voice kind of startled me, the way voices do when you see the people first, coming out so flat and dumb yet kind of tony, too, the way it ticked over "pick up" and "snacks." All of
140 a sudden I slid right down her voice into her living room. Her father and the other men were standing around in ice-cream coats and bow ties and the women were in sandals picking up herring snacks on toothpicks off a big glass plate and they were all holding drinks the color of water with olives and sprigs of mint in them. When my parents have somebody over they get lemonade and if it's a real racy affair Schlitz in tall glasses with "They'll Do It Every Time" cartoons stencilled on.

"That's all right," Lengel said. "But this isn't the beach." His repeating this struck me as funny, as if it had just occurred to him, and he had been thinking all these years the A & P was a great big sand dune and he was the head lifeguard. He didn't like my smiling—as I say he doesn't miss much—but he concentrates on giving the girls that sad Sunday-school-superintendent stare.

Queenie's blush is no sunburn now, and the plump one in plaid, that I liked better from the back—a really sweet can—pipes up, "We weren't doing any shopping. We just came in for the one thing."

"That makes no difference," Lengel tells her, and I could see from the way his eyes went that he hadn't noticed she was wearing a two-piece before. "We want you decently dressed when you come in here."

"We *are* decent," Queenie says suddenly, her lower lip pushing, getting sore now that she remembers her place, a place from which the crowd that runs the A & P must look pretty crummy. Fancy Herring Snacks flashed in her very blue eyes.

"Girls, I don't want to argue with you. After this come in here with your shoulders covered. It's our policy." He turns his back. That's policy for you. Policy is what the kingpins want. What the others want is juvenile delinquency.

All this while, the customers had been showing up with their carts but, you know, sheep, seeing a scene, they had all bunched up on Stokesie, who shook open a paper bag as gently as peeling a peach, not wanting to miss a word. I could feel in the silence everybody getting nervous, most of all Lengel, who asks me, "Sammy, have you rung up their purchase?"

I thought and said "No" but it wasn't about that I was thinking. I go through the punches, 4, 9, GROC, TOT—it's more complicated than you think, and after you do it often enough, it begins to make a little song, that you hear words to, in my case "Hello (*bing*) there, you (*gung*) hap-py *pee*-pul (*splat*)!"—the *splat* being the drawer flying out. I uncrease the bill, tenderly as you may imagine, it just having come from between the two smoothest scoops of vanilla I had ever known were there, and pass a half and a penny into her narrow pink palm, and nestle the herrings in a bag and twist its neck and hand it over, all the time thinking.

The girls, and who'd blame them, are in a hurry to get out, so I say "I quit" to Lengel quick enough for them to hear, hoping they'll stop and watch me, their unsuspected hero. They keep right on going, into the electric eye; the door flies open and they flicker across the lot to their car, Queenie and Plaid and Big Tall Goony-Goony (not that as raw material she was so bad), leaving me with Lengel and a kink in his eyebrow.

"Did you say something, Sammy?"

"I said I quit."

"I thought you did."

"You didn't have to embarrass them."

"It was they who were embarrassing us."

I started to say something that came out "Fiddle-de-doo." It's a saying of my grandmother's, and I know she would have been pleased.

"I don't think you know what you're saying," Lengel said.

"I know you don't," I said. "But I do." I pull the bow at the back of my apron and start shrugging it off my shoulders. A couple customers that had been heading for my slot begin to knock against each other, like scared pigs in a chute.

200 Lengel sighs and begins to look very patient and old and gray. He's been a friend of my parents for years. "Sammy, you don't want to do this to your Mom and Dad," he tells me. It's true, I don't. But it seems to me that once you begin a gesture it's fatal not to go through with it. I fold the apron, "Sammy" stitched in red on the pocket, and put it on the counter, and drop the bow tie on top of it. The bow tie is theirs, if you've ever wondered. "You'll feel this for the rest of your life," Lengel says, and I know that's true, too, but remembering how he made that pretty girl blush makes me so scrunchy inside I punch the No Sale tab and the machine whirs "pee-pul" and the drawer splats out. One advan-
210 tage to this scene taking place in summer, I can follow this up with a clean exit, there's no fumbling around getting your coat and galoshes, I just saunter into the electric eye in my white shirt that my mother ironed the night before, and the door heaves itself open, and outside the sunshine is skating around on the asphalt.

I look around for my girls, but they're gone, of course. There wasn't anybody but some young married screaming with her children about some candy they didn't get by the door of a powder-blue Falcon station wagon. Looking back in the big windows, over the bags of peat moss and aluminum lawn furniture stacked on the pavement, I could see Lengel in my
220 place in the slot, checking the sheep through. His face was dark gray and his back stiff, as if he'd just had an injection of iron, and my stomach kind of fell as I felt how hard the world was going to be to me hereafter.

RAYMOND CARVER (1939–1988)

Cathedral
(1981)

This blind man, an old friend of my wife's, he was on his way to spend the night. His wife had died. So he was visiting the dead wife's relatives in Connecticut. He called my wife from his in-laws'. Arrangements were made. He would come by train, a five-hour trip, and my wife would meet him at the station. She hadn't seen him since she worked for him one summer in Seattle ten years ago. But she and the blind man had kept in touch. They made tapes and mailed them back and forth. I wasn't enthusiastic about his visit. He was no one I knew. And his being blind bothered me. My idea of blindness came from the movies. In the
10 movies, the blind moved slowly and never laughed. Sometimes they

were led by seeing-eye dogs. A blind man in my house was not something I looked forward to.

That summer in Seattle she had needed a job. She didn't have any money. The man she was going to marry at the end of the summer was in officers' training school. He didn't have any money, either. But she was in love with the guy, and he was in love with her, etc. She'd seen something in the paper: HELP WANTED—*Reading to Blind Man*, and a telephone number. She phoned and went over, was hired on the spot. She'd worked with this blind man all summer. She read stuff to him,
20 case studies, reports, that sort of thing. She helped him organize his little office in the county social-service department. They'd become good friends, my wife and the blind man. How do I know these things? She told me. And she told me something else. On her last day in the office, the blind man asked if he could touch her face. She agreed to this. She told me he touched his fingers to every part of her face, her nose—even her neck! She never forgot it. She even tried to write a poem about it. She was always trying to write a poem. She wrote a poem or two every year, usually after something really important had happened to her.

When we first started going out together, she showed me the poem.
30 In the poem, she recalled his fingers and the way they had moved around over her face. In the poem, she talked about what she had felt at the time, about what went through her mind when the blind man touched her nose and lips. I can remember I didn't think much of the poem. Of course, I didn't tell her that. Maybe I just don't understand poetry. I admit it's not the first thing I reach for when I pick up something to read.

Anyway, this man who'd first enjoyed her favors, the officer-to-be, he'd been her childhood sweetheart. So okay. I'm saying that at the end of the summer she let the blind man run his hands over her face, said good-
40 bye to him, married her childhood etc., who was now a commissioned officer, and she moved away from Seattle. But they'd kept in touch, she and the blind man. She made the first contact after a year or so. She called him up one night from an Air Force base in Alabama. She wanted to talk. They talked. He asked her to send him a tape and tell him about her life. She did this. She sent the tape. On the tape, she told the blind man about her husband and about their life together in the military. She told the blind man she loved her husband but she didn't like it where they lived and she didn't like it that he was a part of the military–industrial thing. She told the blind man she'd written a poem and he was in it. She told
50 him that she was writing a poem about what it was like to be an Air Force officer's wife. The poem wasn't finished yet. She was still writing it. The blind man made a tape. He sent her the tape. She made a tape. This went on for years. My wife's officer was posted to one base and then another. She sent tapes from Moody AFB, McGuire, McConnell, and finally Travis, near Sacramento, where one night she got to feeling lonely and cut off from people she kept losing in that moving-around life. She got to feeling she couldn't go it another step. She went in and swallowed all the pills

and capsules in the medicine chest and washed them down with a bottle of gin. Then she got into a hot bath and passed out.

60   But instead of dying, she got sick. She threw up. Her officer—why should he have a name? he was the childhood sweetheart, and what more does he want?—came home from somewhere, found her, and called the ambulance. In time, she put it all on a tape and sent the tape to the blind man. Over the years, she put all kinds of stuff on tapes and sent the tapes off lickety-split. Next to writing a poem every year, I think it was her chief means of recreation. On one tape, she told the blind man she'd decided to live away from her officer for a time. On another tape, she told him about her divorce. She and I began going out, and of course she told her blind man about it. She told him everything, or so it seemed to me. Once she

70 asked me if I'd like to hear the latest tape from the blind man. This was a year ago. I was on the tape, she said. So I said okay, I'd listen to it. I got us drinks and we settled down in the living room. We made ready to listen. First she inserted the tape into the player and adjusted a couple of dials. Then she pushed a lever. The tape squeaked and someone began to talk in this loud voice. She lowered the volume. After a few minutes of harmless chitchat, I heard my own name in the mouth of this stranger, this blind man I didn't even know! And then this: "From all you've said about him, I can only conclude—" But we were interrupted, a knock at the door, something, and we didn't ever get back to the tape. Maybe it was just as well, I'd

80 heard all I wanted to.

Now this same blind man was coming to sleep in my house.

"Maybe I could take him bowling," I said to my wife. She was at the draining board doing scalloped potatoes. She put down the knife she was using and turned around.

"If you love me," she said, "you can do this for me. If you don't love me, okay. But if you had a friend, any friend, and the friend came to visit, I'd make him feel comfortable." She wiped her hands with the dish towel.

"I don't have any blind friends," I said.

90   "You don't have *any* friends," she said. "Period. Besides," she said, "goddamn it, his wife's just died! Don't you understand that? The man's lost his wife!"

I didn't answer. She'd told me a little about the blind man's wife. Her name was Beulah, Beulah! That's a name for a colored woman.

"Was his wife a Negro?" I asked.

"Are you crazy?" my wife said. "Have you just flipped or something?" She picked up a potato. I saw it hit the floor, then roll under the stove. "What's wrong with you?" she said. "Are you drunk?"

"I'm just asking," I said.

100   Right then my wife filled me in with more detail than I cared to know. I made a drink and sat at the kitchen table to listen. Pieces of the story began to fall into place.

Beulah had gone to work for the blind man the summer after my wife had stopped working for him. Pretty soon Beulah and the blind man had

themselves a church wedding. It was a little wedding—who'd want to go
to such a wedding in the first place?—just the two of them, plus the minister and the minister's wife. But it was a church wedding just the same. It
was what Beulah had wanted, he'd said. But even then Beulah must have
been carrying the cancer in her glands. After they had been inseparable
110 for eight years—my wife's word, *inseparable*—Beulah's health went into a
rapid decline. She died in a Seattle hospital room, the blind man sitting
beside the bed and holding on to her hand. They'd married, lived and
worked together, slept together—had sex, sure—and then the blind man
had to bury her. All this without his having ever seen what the goddamned woman looked like. It was beyond my understanding. Hearing
this, I felt sorry for the blind man for a little bit. And then I found myself
thinking what a pitiful life this woman must have led. Imagine a woman
who could never see herself as she was seen in the eyes of her loved one.
A woman who could go on day after day and never receive the smallest
120 compliment from her beloved. A woman whose husband could never read
the expression on her face, be it misery or something better. Someone
who could wear makeup or not—what difference to him? She could, if she
wanted, wear green eye-shadow around one eye, a straight pin in her
nostril, yellow slacks and purple shoes, no matter. And then to slip off
into death, the blind man's hand on her hand, his blind eyes streaming
tears—I'm imagining now—her last thought maybe this: that he never
even knew what she looked like, and she on an express to the grave.
Robert was left with a small insurance policy and half of a twenty-peso
Mexican coin. The other half of the coin went into the box with her.
130 Pathetic.

So when the time rolled around, my wife went to the depot to pick
him up. With nothing to do but wait—sure, I blamed him for that—I
was having a drink and watching the TV when I heard the car pull into
the drive. I got up from the sofa with my drink and went to the window
to have a look.

I saw my wife laughing as she parked the car. I saw her get out of
the car and shut the door. She was still wearing a smile. Just amazing.
She went around to the other side of the car to where the blind man was
already starting to get out. This blind man, feature this, he was wearing
140 a full beard! A beard on a blind man! Too much, I say. The blind man
reached into the back seat and dragged out a suitcase. My wife took his
arm, shut the car door, and, talking all the way, moved him down the
drive and then up the steps to the front porch. I turned off the TV.
I finished my drink, rinsed the glass, dried my hands. Then I went to
the door.

My wife said, "I want you to meet Robert. Robert, this is my husband. I've told you all about him." She was beaming. She had this blind
man by his coat sleeve.

The blind man let go of his suitcase and up came his hand.

150   I took it. He squeezed hard, held my hand, and then he let it go.

"I feel like we've already met," he boomed.

"Likewise," I said. I didn't know what else to say. Then I said, "Welcome. I've heard a lot about you." We began to move then, a little group, from the porch into the living room, my wife guiding him by the arm. The blind man was carrying his suitcase in his other hand. My wife said things like, "To your left here, Robert. That's right. Now watch it, there's a chair. That's it. Sit down right here. This is the sofa. We just bought this sofa two weeks ago."

160 I started to say something about the old sofa. I'd liked that old sofa. But I didn't say anything. Then I wanted to say something else, small-talk, about the scenic ride along the Hudson. How going *to* New York, you should sit on the right-hand side of the train, and coming *from* New York, the left-hand side.

"Did you have a good train ride?" I said. "Which side of the train did you sit on, by the way?"

"What a question, which side!" my wife said. "What's it matter which side?" she said.

"I just asked," I said.

"Right side," the blind man said. "I hadn't been on a train in nearly 170 forty years. Not since I was a kid. With my folks. That's been a long time. I'd nearly forgotten the sensation. I have winter in my beard now," he said. "So I've been told, anyway. Do I look distinguished, my dear?" the blind man said to my wife.

"You look distinguished, Robert," she said. "Robert," she said. "Robert, it's just so good to see you."

My wife finally took her eyes off the blind man and looked at me. I had the feeling she didn't like what she saw. I shrugged.

I've never met, or personally known, anyone who was blind. This blind man was late forties, a heavy-set, balding man with stooped 180 shoulders, as if he carried great weight there. He wore brown slacks, brown shoes, a light-brown shirt, a tie, a sports coat. Spiffy. He also had this full beard. But he didn't use a cane and he didn't wear dark glasses. I'd always thought dark glasses were a must for the blind. Fact was, I wished he had a pair. At first glance, his eyes looked like anyone else's eyes. But if you looked close, there was something different about them. Too much white in the iris, for one thing, and the pupils seemed to move around in the sockets without his knowing it or being able to stop it. Creepy. As I stared at his face, I saw the left pupil turn in toward his nose while the other made an effort to keep in one place. But it was only 190 an effort, for that eye was on the roam without his knowing it or want-ing it to be.

I said, "Let me get you a drink. What's your pleasure? We have a little of everything. It's one of our pastimes."

"Bub, I'm a Scotch man myself," he said fast enough in this big voice.

"Right," I said. Bub! "Sure you are. I knew it."

He let his fingers touch his suitcase, which was sitting alongside the sofa. He was taking his bearings. I didn't blame him for that.

"I'll move that up to your room," my wife said.

200   "No, that's fine," the blind man said loudly. "It can go up when I go up."

"A little water with the Scotch?" I said.

"Very little," he said.

"I knew it," I said.

He said, "Just a tad. The Irish actor, Barry Fitzgerald? I'm like that fellow. When I drink water, Fitzgerald said, I drink water. When I drink whiskey, I drink whiskey." My wife laughed. The blind man brought his hand up under his beard. He lifted his beard slowly and let it drop.

I did the drinks, three big glasses of Scotch with a splash of water in
210   each. Then we made ourselves comfortable and talked about Robert's travels. First the long flight from the West Coast to Connecticut, we covered that. Then from Connecticut up here by train. We had another drink concerning that leg of the trip.

I remembered having read somewhere that the blind didn't smoke because, as speculation had it, they couldn't see the smoke they exhaled. I thought I knew that much and that much only about blind people. But this blind man smoked his cigarette down to the nubbin and then lit another one. This blind man filled his ashtray and my wife emptied it.

When we sat down at the table for dinner, we had another drink.
220   My wife heaped Robert's plate with cube steak, scalloped potatoes, green beans. I buttered him up two slices of bread. I said, "Here's bread and butter for you." I swallowed some of my drink. "Now let us pray," I said, and the blind man lowered his head. My wife looked at me, her mouth agape. "Pray the phone won't ring and the food doesn't get cold," I said.

We dug in. We ate everything there was to eat on the table. We ate like there was no tomorrow. We didn't talk. We ate. We scarfed. We grazed that table. We were into serious eating. The blind man had right away located his foods, he knew just where everything was on his plate.
230   I watched with admiration as he used his knife and fork on the meat. He'd cut two pieces of meat, fork the meat into his mouth, and then go all out for the scalloped potatoes, the beans next, and then he'd tear off a hunk of buttered bread and eat that. He'd follow this up with a big drink of milk. It didn't seem to bother him to use his fingers once in a while, either.

We finished everything, including half a strawberry pie. For a few moments, we sat as if stunned. Sweat beaded on our faces. Finally, we got up from the table and left the dirty plates. We didn't look back. We took ourselves into the living room and sank into our places again.
240   Robert and my wife sat on the sofa. I took the big chair. We had us two or three more drinks while they talked about the major things that had come to pass for them in the past ten years. For the most part, I just listened. Now and then I joined in. I didn't want him to think I'd left the room, and I didn't want her to think I was feeling left out. They talked of things that had happened to them—to them!—these past ten years. I

waited in vain to hear my name on my wife's sweet lips: "And then my dear husband came into my life"—something like that. But I heard nothing of the sort. More talk of Robert. Robert had done a little of everything, it seemed, a regular blind jack-of-all-trades. But most recently he
250 and his wife had had an Amway distributorship, from which, I gathered, they'd earned their living, such as it was. The blind man was also a ham radio operator. He talked in his loud voice about conversations he'd had with fellow operators in Guam, in the Philippines, in Alaska, and even in Tahiti. He said he'd have a lot of friends there if he ever wanted to go visit those places. From time to time, he'd turn his blind face toward me, put his hand under his beard, ask me something. How long had I been in my present position? (Three years.) Did I like my work? (I didn't.) Was I going to stay with it? (What were the options?) Finally, when I thought he was beginning to run down, I got up and
260 turned on the TV.

My wife looked at me with irritation. She was heading toward a boil. Then she looked at the blind man and said, "Robert, do you have a TV?"

The blind man said, "My dear, I have two TVs. I have a color set and a black-and-white thing, an old relic. It's funny, but if I turn the TV on, and I'm always turning it on, I turn on the color set. It's funny, don't you think?"

I didn't know what to say to that. I had absolutely nothing to say to that. No opinion. So I watched the news program and tried to listen
270 to what the announcer was saying.

"This is a color TV," the blind man said. "Don't ask me how, but I can tell."

"We traded up a while ago," I said.

The blind man had another taste of his drink. He lifted his beard, sniffed it, and let it fall. He leaned forward on the sofa. He positioned his ashtray on the coffee table, then put the lighter to his cigarette. He leaned back on the sofa and crossed his legs at the ankles.

My wife covered her mouth, and then she yawned. She stretched. She said, "I think I'll go upstairs and put on my robe. I think I'll change
280 into something else. Robert, you make yourself comfortable," she said.

"I'm comfortable," the blind man said.

"I want you to feel comfortable in this house," she said.

"I am comfortable," the blind man said.

After she'd left the room, he and I listened to the weather report and then to the sports roundup. By that time, she'd been gone so long I didn't know if she was going to come back. I thought she might have gone to bed. I wished she'd come back downstairs. I didn't want to be left alone with a blind man. I asked him if he wanted another drink, and he said sure. Then I asked if he wanted to smoke some dope with me. I said I'd
290 just rolled a number. I hadn't, but I planned to do so in about two shakes.

"I'll try some with you," he said.

"Damn right," I said. "That's the stuff."

I got our drinks and sat down on the sofa with him. Then I rolled us two fat numbers. I lit one and passed it. I brought it to his fingers. He took it and inhaled.

"Hold it as long as you can," I said. I could tell he didn't know the first thing.

My wife came back downstairs wearing her pink robe and her pink slippers.

300   "What do I smell?" she said.

"We thought we'd have us some cannabis," I said.

My wife gave me a savage look. Then she looked at the blind man and said, "Robert, I didn't know you smoked."

He said, "I do now, my dear. There's a first time for everything. But I don't feel anything yet."

"This stuff is pretty mellow," I said. "This stuff is mild. It's dope you can reason with," I said. "It doesn't mess you up."

"Not much it doesn't, bub," he said, and laughed.

My wife sat on the sofa between the blind man and me. I passed her
310 the number. She took it and toked and then passed it back to me. "Which way is this going?" she said. Then she said, "I shouldn't be smoking this. I can hardly keep my eyes open as it is. That dinner did me in. I shouldn't have eaten so much."

"It was the strawberry pie," the blind man said. "That's what did it," he said, and he laughed his big laugh. Then he shook his head.

"There's more strawberry pie," I said.

"Do you want some more, Robert?" my wife said.

"Maybe in a little while," he said.

We gave our attention to the TV. My wife yawned again. She said,
320 "Your bed is made up when you feel like going to bed, Robert. I know you must have had a long day. When you're ready to go to bed, say so." She pulled his arm. "Robert?"

He came to and said, "I've had a real nice time. This beats tapes, doesn't it?"

I said, "Coming at you," and I put the number between his fingers. He inhaled, held the smoke, and then let it go. It was like he'd been doing it since he was nine years old.

"Thanks, bub," he said. "But I think this is all for me. I think I'm beginning to feel it," he said. He held the burning roach out for my wife.

330   "Same here," she said. "Ditto. Me, too." She took the roach and passed it to me. "I may just sit here for a while between you two guys with my eyes closed. But don't let me bother you, okay? Either one of you. If it bothers you, say so. Otherwise, I may just sit here with my eyes closed until you're ready to go to bed," she said. "Your bed's made up, Robert, when you're ready. It's right next to our room at the top of the stairs. We'll show you up when you're ready. You wake me up now, you guys, if I fall asleep." She said that and then she closed her eyes and went to sleep.

The news program ended. I got up and changed the channel. I sat
340 back down on the sofa. I wished my wife hadn't pooped out. Her head
lay across the back of the sofa, her mouth open. She'd turned so that her
robe had slipped away from her legs, exposing a juicy thigh. I reached to
draw her robe back over her, and it was then that I glanced at the blind
man. What the hell! I flipped the robe open again.

"You say when you want some strawberry pie," I said.

"I will," he said.

I said, "Are you tired? Do you want me to take you up to your bed?
Are you ready to hit the hay?"

"Not yet," he said. "No, I'll stay up with you, bub. If that's all right.
350 I'll stay up until you're ready to turn in. We haven't had a chance to talk.
Know what I mean? I feel like me and her monopolized the evening." He
lifted his beard and he let it fall. He picked up his cigarettes and his
lighter.

"That's all right," I said. Then I said, "I'm glad for the company."

And I guess I was. Every night I smoked dope and stayed up as long
as I could before I fell asleep. My wife and I hardly ever went to bed at
the same time. When I did go to sleep, I had these dreams. Sometimes
I'd wake up from one of them, my heart going crazy.

Something about the church and the Middle Ages was on the TV.
360 Not your run-of-the-mill TV fare. I wanted to watch something else. I
turned to the other channels. But there was nothing on them, either. So
I turned back to the first channel and apologized.

"Bub, it's all right," the blind man said. "It's fine with me. Whatever
you want to watch is okay. I'm always learning something. Learning
never ends. It won't hurt me to learn something tonight. I got ears," he
said.

We didn't say anything for a time. He was leaning forward with his
head turned at me, his right ear aimed in the direction of the set. Very
disconcerting. Now and then his eyelids drooped and then they
370 snapped open again. Now and then he put his fingers into his beard and
tugged, like he was thinking about something he was hearing on the
television.

On the screen, a group of men wearing cowls was being set upon
and tormented by men dressed in skeleton costumes and men dressed
as devils. The men dressed as devils wore devil masks, horns, and long
tails. This pageant was part of a procession. The Englishman who was
narrating the thing said it took place in Spain once a year. I tried to explain to the blind man what was happening.

"Skeletons," he said. "I know about skeletons," he said, and he
380 nodded.

The TV showed this one cathedral. Then there was a long, slow look at
another one. Finally, the picture switched to the famous one in Paris, with
its flying buttresses and its spires reaching up to the clouds. The camera
pulled away to show the whole of the cathedral rising above the skyline.

There were times when the Englishman who was telling the thing would shut up, would simply let the camera move around over the cathedrals. Or else the camera would tour the countryside, men in fields walking behind oxen. I waited as long as I could. Then I felt I had to say something. I said, "They're showing the outside of this cathedral now.
390 Gargoyles. Little statues carved to look like monsters. Now I guess they're in Italy. Yeah, they're in Italy. There's paintings on the walls of this one church."

"Are those fresco paintings, bub?" he asked, and he sipped from his drink.

I reached for my glass. But it was empty. I tried to remember what I could remember. "You're asking me are those frescoes?" I said. "That's a good question. I don't know."

The camera moved to a cathedral outside Lisbon. The differences in the Portuguese cathedral compared with the French and Italian were not
400 that great. But they were there. Mostly the interior stuff. Then something occurred to me, and I said, "Something has occurred to me. Do you have any idea what a cathedral is? What they look like, that is? Do you follow me? If somebody says cathedral to you, do you have any notion what they're talking about? Do you know the difference between that and a Baptist church, say?"

He let the smoke dribble from his mouth. "I know they took hundreds of workers fifty or a hundred years to build," he said. "I just heard the man say that, of course. I know generations of the same families worked on a cathedral. I heard him say that, too. The men who began
410 their life's work on them, they never lived to see the completion of their work. In that wise, bub, they're no different from the rest of us, right?" He laughed. Then his eyelids drooped again. His head nodded. He seemed to be snoozing. Maybe he was imagining himself in Portugal. The TV was showing another cathedral now. This one was in Germany. The Englishman's voice droned on. "Cathedrals," the blind man said. He sat up and rolled his head back and forth. "If you want the truth, bub, that's about all I know. What I just said. What I heard him say. But maybe you could describe one to me? I wish you'd do it. I'd like that. If you want to know, I really don't have a good idea."
420   I stared hard at the shot of the cathedral on the TV. How could I even begin to describe it? But say my life depended on it. Say my life was being threatened by an insane guy who said I had to do it or else.

I stared some more at the cathedral before the picture flipped off into the countryside. There was no use. I turned to the blind man and said, "To begin with, they're very tall." I was looking around the room for clues. "They reach way up. Up and up. Toward the sky. They're so big, some of them, they have to have these supports. To help hold them up, so to speak. These supports are called buttresses. They remind me of viaducts, for some reason. But maybe you don't know viaducts, either? Sometimes the
430 cathedrals have devils and such carved into the front. Sometimes lords and ladies. Don't ask me why this is," I said.

He was nodding. The whole upper part of his body seemed to be moving back and forth.

"I'm not doing so good, am I?" I said.

He stopped nodding and leaned forward on the edge of the sofa. As he listened to me, he was running his fingers through his beard. I wasn't getting through to him, I could see that. But he waited for me to go on just the same. He nodded, like he was trying to encourage me. I tried to think what else to say. "They're really big," I said. "They're
440 massive. They're built of stone. Marble, too, sometimes. In those olden days, when they built cathedrals, men wanted to be close to God. In those olden days, God was an important part of everyone's life. You could tell this from their cathedral-building. I'm sorry," I said, "but it looks like that's the best I can do for you. I'm just no good at it."

"That's all right, bub," the blind man said. "Hey, listen. I hope you don't mind my asking you: Can I ask you something? Let me ask you a simple question, yes or no. I'm just curious and there's no offense. You're my host. But let me ask if you are in any way religious? You don't mind my asking?"
450 I shook my head. He couldn't see that, though. A wink is the same as a nod to a blind man. "I guess I don't believe in it. In anything. Sometimes it's hard. You know what I'm saying?"

"Sure, I do," he said.

"Right," I said.

The Englishman was still holding forth. My wife sighed in her sleep. She drew a long breath and went on with her sleeping.

"You'll have to forgive me," I said. "But I can't tell you what a cathedral looks like. It just isn't in me to do it. I can't do any more than I've done."
460 The blind man sat very still, his head down, as he listened to me. I said, "The truth is, cathedrals don't mean anything special to me. Nothing. Cathedrals. They're something to look at on late-night TV. That's all they are."

It was then that the blind man cleared his throat. He brought something up. He took a handkerchief from his back pocket. Then he said, "I get it, bub. It's okay. It happens. Don't worry about it," he said. "Hey, listen to me. Will you do me a favor? I got an idea. Why don't you find us some heavy paper? And a pen. We'll do something. We'll draw one together. Get us a pen and some heavy paper. Go on, bub, get the stuff,"
470 he said.

So I went upstairs. My legs felt like they didn't have any strength in them. They felt like they did after I'd done some running. In my wife's room, I looked around. I found some ballpoints in a little basket on her table. And then I tried to think where to look for the kind of paper he was talking about.

Downstairs, in the kitchen, I found a shopping bag with onion skins in the bottom of the bag. I emptied the bag and shook it. I brought it into the living room and sat down with it near his legs. I moved some

things, smoothed the wrinkles from the bag, spread it out on the coffee
480 table.

The blind man got down from the sofa and sat next to me on the carpet.

He ran his fingers over the paper. He went up and down the sides of the paper. The edges, even the edges. He fingered the corners.

"All right," he said. "All right, let's do her."

He found my hand, the hand with the pen. He closed his hand over my hand. "Go ahead, bub, draw," he said. "Draw. You'll see. I'll follow along with you. It'll be okay. Just begin now like I'm telling you. You'll see. Draw," the blind man said.

490   So I began. First I drew a box that looked like a house. It could have been the house I lived in. Then I put a roof on it. At either end of the roof, I drew spires. Crazy.

"Swell," he said. "Terrific. You're doing fine," he said. "Never thought anything like this could happen in your lifetime, did you, bub? Well, it's a strange life, we all know that. Go on now. Keep it up."

I put in windows with arches. I drew flying buttresses. I hung great doors. I couldn't stop. The TV station went off the air. I put down the pen and closed and opened my fingers. The blind man felt around over the paper. He moved the tips of his fingers over the paper, all over what
500 I had drawn, and he nodded.

"Doing fine," the blind man said.

I took up the pen again, and he found my hand. I kept at it. I'm no artist. But I kept drawing just the same.

My wife opened up her eyes and gazed at us. She sat up on the sofa, her robe hanging open. She said, "What are you doing? Tell me, I want to know."

I didn't answer her.

The blind man said, "We're drawing a cathedral. Me and him are working on it. Press hard," he said to me. "That's right. That's good," he
510 said. "Sure. You got it, bub. I can tell. You didn't think you could. But you can, can't you? You're cooking with gas now. You know what I'm saying? We're going to really have us something here in a minute. How's the old arm?" he said. "Put some people in there now. What's a cathedral without people?"

My wife said "What's going on? Robert, what are you doing? What's going on?"

"It's all right," he said to her. "Close your eyes now," the blind man said to me.

I did it. I closed them just like he said.

520   "Are they closed?" he said. "Don't fudge."

"They're closed," I said.

"Keep them that way," he said. He said, "Don't stop now. Draw."

So we kept on with it. His fingers rode my fingers as my hand went over the paper. It was like nothing else in my life up to now.

Then he said, "I think that's it. I think you got it," he said. "Take a look. What do you think?"

But I had my eyes closed. I thought I'd keep them that way for a little longer. I thought it was something I ought to do.

"Well?" he said. "Are you looking?"

530   My eyes were still closed. I was in my house. I knew that. But I didn't feel like I was inside anything.

"It's really something," I said.

MAXINE HONG KINGSTON (1940–)
The Wild Man of the Green Swamp
(1977)

For eight months in 1975, residents on the edge of Green Swamp, Florida, had been reporting to the police that they had seen a Wild Man. When they stepped toward him, he made strange noises as in a foreign language and ran back into the saw grass. At first, authorities said the Wild Man was a mass hallucination. Man-eating animals lived in the swamp, and a human being could hardly find a place to rest without sinking. Perhaps it was some kind of a bear the children had seen.

In October, a game officer saw a man crouched over a small fire, but as he approached, the figure ran away. It couldn't have been a bear be-
10 cause the Wild Man dragged a burlap bag after him. Also, the fire was obviously manmade.

The fish-and-game wardens and the sheriff's deputies entered the swamp with dogs but did not search for long; no one could live in the swamp. The mosquitoes alone would drive him out.

The Wild Man made forays out of the swamp. Farmers encountered him taking fruit and corn from the turkeys. He broke into a house trailer, but the occupant came back, and the Wild Man escaped out a window. The occupant said that a bad smell came off the Wild Man. Usually, the only evidence of him were his abandoned campsites. At one
20 he left the remains of a four-foot-long alligator, of which he had eaten the feet and tail.

In May a posse made an air and land search; the plane signaled down to the hunters on the ground, who circled the Wild Man. A fish-and-game warden "brought him down with a tackle," according to the news. The Wild Man fought, but they took him to jail. He looked Chinese, so they found a Chinese in town to come translate.

The Wild Man talked a lot to the translator. He told him his name. He said he was thirty-nine years old, the father of seven children, who were in Taiwan. To support them, he had shipped out on a Liberian freighter.
30 He had gotten very homesick and asked everyone if he could leave the ship and go home. But the officers would not let him off. They sent messages to China to find out about him. When the ship landed, they took

him to the airport and tried to put him on an airplane to some foreign place. Then, he said, the white demons took him to Tampa Hospital, which is for insane people, but he escaped, just walked out and went into the swamp.

The interpreter asked how he lived in the swamp. He said he ate snakes, turtles, armadillos, and alligators. The captors could tell how he lived when they opened up his bag, which was not burlap but a pair of
40 pants with the legs knotted. Inside, he had carried a pot, a piece of sharpened tin, and a small club, which he had made by sticking a railroad spike into a section of aluminum tubing.

The sheriff found the Liberian freighter that the Wild Man had been on. The ship's officers said that they had not tried to stop him from going home. His shipmates had decided that there was something wrong with his mind. They had bought him a plane ticket and arranged his passport to send him back to China. They had driven him to the airport, but there he began screaming and weeping and would not get on the plane. So they had found him a doctor, who sent him to Tampa Hospital.

50   Now the doctors at the jail gave him medicine for the mosquito bites, which covered his entire body, and medicine for his stomachache. He was getting better, but after he'd been in jail for three days, the U.S. Border Patrol told him they were sending him back. He became hysterical. That night, he fastened his belt to the bars, wrapped it around his neck, and hung himself.

In the newspaper picture he did not look very wild, being led by the posse out of the swamp. He did not look dirty, either. He wore a checkered shirt unbuttoned at the neck, where his white undershirt showed; his shirt was tucked into his pants; his hair was short. He was su-
60 rounded by men in cowboy hats. His fingers stretching open, his wrists pulling apart to the extent of the handcuffs, he lifted his head, his eyes screwed shut, and cried out.

There was a Wild Man in our slough too, only he was a black man. He wore a shirt and no pants, and some mornings when we walked to school, we saw him asleep under the bridge. The police came and took him away. The newspaper said he was crazy; it said the police had been on the lookout for him for a long time, but we had seen him every day.

JAMAICA KINCAID (1949–   )

Girl
(1978)

Wash the white clothes on Monday and put them on the stone heap; wash the color clothes on Tuesday and put them on the clothesline to dry; don't walk barehead in the hot sun; cook pumpkin fritters in very hot sweet oil; soak your little cloths right after you take them off; when buying cotton to make yourself a nice blouse, be sure that it doesn't have gum on it, because that way it won't hold up well after a wash; soak salt fish overnight before you cook it; is it true that you sing benna in Sunday school?; al-

ways eat your food in such a way that it won't turn someone else's stomach; on Sundays try to walk like a lady and not like the slut you are
10 so bent on becoming; don't sing benna in Sunday school; you mustn't speak to wharf-rat boys, not even to give directions; don't eat fruits on the street—flies will follow you; *but I don't sing benna on Sundays at all and never in Sunday school;* this is how to sew on a button; this is how to make a buttonhole for the button you have just sewed on; this is how to hem a dress when you see the hem coming down and so to prevent yourself from looking like the slut I know you are so bent on becoming; this is how you iron your father's khaki shirt so that it doesn't have a crease; this is how you iron your father's khaki pants so that they don't have a crease; this is how you grow okra—far from the house, because okra tree harbors
20 red ants; when you are growing dasheen, make sure it gets plenty of water or else it makes your throat itch when you are eating it; this is how you sweep a corner; this is how you sweep a whole house; this is how you sweep a yard; this is how you smile to someone you don't like too much; this is how you smile to someone you don't like at all; this is how you smile to someone you like completely; this is how you set a table for tea; this is how you set a table for dinner; this is how you set a table for dinner with an important guest; this is how you set a table for lunch; this is how you set a table for breakfast; this is how to behave in the presence of men who don't know you very well, and this way they won't recognize imme-
30 diately the slut I have warned you against becoming; be sure to wash every day, even if it is with your own spit; don't squat down to play marbles—you are not a boy, you know; don't pick people's flowers—you might catch something; don't throw stones at blackbirds, because it might not be a blackbird at all; this is how to make a bread pudding; this is how to make doukona; this is how to make pepper pot; this is how to make a good medicine for a cold; this is how to make a good medicine to throw away a child before it even becomes a child; this is how to catch a fish; this is how to throw back a fish you don't like, and that way something bad won't fall on you; this is how to bully a man; this is how a man bul-
40 lies you; this is how to love a man, and if this doesn't work there are other ways, and if they don't work don't feel too bad about giving up; this is how to spit up in the air if you feel like it, and this is how to move quick so that it doesn't fall on you; this is how to make ends meet; always squeeze bread to make sure it's fresh; *but what if the baker won't let me feel the bread?;* you mean to say that after all you are really going to be the kind of woman who the baker won't let near the bread?

IAN FRAZIER (1951–   )

The Killion
(1985)

At a little after noon on Friday, August 6, Marcie Chang, anchorwoman on TV 8's *Newsbeaters* evening news show, picked up her envelope at the pay window on the studio's fifth floor, bought a ham-salad sandwich and

a cup of coffee from the lunch wagon in the hall, and took the elevator back to her office on the tenth floor. Sitting down at her desk, she tore open the envelope, which contained the first payment of the lucrative new contract that the station had offered her in the spring. She took one look at the check and collapsed. She was dead before her face hit the desk top. A few minutes later, TV reporter Kerri Corcoran, a colleague and friend,
10 came into Marcie's office, saw her, looked at the check she still held in her hand, and crumpled, lifeless, to the floor. The same fate met the receptionist who came to Marcie's office to find out why she wasn't answering her phone, and the building security guard, who was summoned by the cleaning woman after she had noticed the pile of bodies.

Nor was that the end. In quick succession, three police officers, a fireman, a newspaper reporter, and a pathologist from Mount Sinai were added to the death list. Alarmed public-health officials called on the Institute for Catastrophe Control in Princeton. With grim predictability, two of the institute's top scientists soon showed the seriousness of the
20 challenge when they, too, were felled. Within forty-eight hours, scientists from the institute who had taken over the case were fairly certain that the fatal agent was the check that Marcie had picked up that Wednesday afternoon. They examined it through heavily tinted safety glasses, in sections, with no one scientist viewing the entire check. Within another forty-eight hours, Dr. Leo Wiedenthal, director of the institute, knew what he had on his hands. In a statement released to the press, he said that there was no evidence of a supertoxin or highly contagious disease on the fatal paycheck. Rather, he said, "Marcie Chang and the eleven other victims almost certainly died as a result of what they *saw* on the
30 check. Through a computer error, Marcie's check was made out to an extremely high number. Apparently, the computer made Marcie's check out to the sum of one killion dollars. The killion, as every mathematician knows, is a number so big that it kills you."

Since the days of Archimedes, man has known that numbers could attain great size. The Greeks could count up to a million, and the Romans, in their turn, made it to a billion and a trillion. Then man had to wait almost fifteen centuries, until the gilded arms of the Renaissance had flung open the shutters of the Dark Ages, before he could move on to a billion trillion, a million billion trillion, and, finally, a zillion. In 1702, Sir Isaac
40 Newton, father of the theory of universal gravitation, experimented with numbers as high as a million billion trillion zillion, at one point even getting up to a bazillion. These experiments convinced him of the theoretical possibility of the existence of the killion. He stopped his experiments abruptly when, as the numbers approached one killion, he found himself becoming very sick. The German mathematician Karl Friedrich Gauss, hearing about Newton's discovery from someone he met at a party, was so upset by the thought of a killion that he made up his own numbers, called Gaussian numbers. These were numbers that could get big, but not that big. Unfortunately, Gauss's brave attempt to develop a risk-free numerical
50 system wound up on the scrap heap of failed theories. In the early twenti-

eth century, Albert Einstein made some calculations that brought him right to the very threshold of the killion. But here even Einstein halted. Probably the smartest scientist who ever lived, Einstein also had a great, abiding affection for life. After the invention of the computer, it was Einstein who insisted that each one be equipped with a governor that would shut it off automatically if it ever approached a killion. Were it not for Einstein's farsightedness, the dawn of the computer age might have had frightening consequences for mankind.

So what went wrong in the affair of Marcie Chang's deadly paycheck? 60 Why did the network computer, running a routine payroll program, make an error that no computer had ever made before? To understand this question, it is important to understand how a computer works. People unfamiliar with computers sometimes find it helpful to think of them as fairly good-sized, complicated things. Computers range in size from as small as a motel ice bucket to as large as an entertainment complex like New Jersey's Meadowlands, including the parking lot. Inside, a computer will have a short red wire hooked to a terminal at one end and to another terminal at the other end. Then there will be a blue wire also hooked to terminals at either end, and then a green wire, and then a yellow wire, 70 then an orange wire, then a pink wire, and so on.

This particular computer was so big that when expert technicians began to disassemble it to find out what was the matter with it, they soon had more wires, terminals, and other parts lying around than they knew what to do with. The technicians spread the parts all over the floor of an unused equipment shed, and finally they found one that they identified as the governor—the little safety device that could trace its lineage back to Einstein's terrifying vision on that rainy February afternoon in Munich so many years ago. When they examined it closely, they discovered the problem. It was completely covered with gray stuff, kind of similar to the 80 gray stuff that collects on rotary hot-dog grills. There was so much gray stuff that the little armature that was supposed to fit into a V-shaped groove on this other armature couldn't fit in at all. No one knew where the gray stuff could have come from, so there was nowhere to fix the blame. That did not change the fact that a small amount of gray stuff you could blow from your palm with one light breath had cost twelve human lives.

In the aftermath of the tragedy, many people asked, "How can such tragedies be prevented in the future?" Well, you could give your paycheck to the bank teller every week without looking at it—taking such risks is 90 what bank tellers are paid for. But then you would never know how much money you had. You could move to a country where people have never heard of computers. But that might be awfully far away, and it might be years before you felt comfortable there. You could vacuum computers at least three times a week to remove any foreign matter. But, on the other hand, what if that didn't work?

One hard, indisputable truth remains: There is nothing anybody can do about the killion. It is not a person, or a product, or an institution, and

so need answer to no one. It will always be out there, in the far range of mathematics, where space bends and parallel lines converge, and I don't
100 know what all. In the end, the best you can really do is hope that if the killion gets anyone, the person it gets won't be you.

LORRIE MOORE (1957–   )
How to Be the Other Woman
(1988)

Meet in expensive beige raincoats, on a pea-soupy night. Like a detective movie. First, stand in front of Florsheim's Fifty-seventh Street window, press your face close to the glass, watch the fake velvet Hummels inside revolving around the wing tips; some white shoes, like your father wears, are propped up with garlands on a small mound of chemical snow. All the stores have closed. You can see your breath on the glass. Draw a peace sign. You are waiting for a bus.

He emerges from nowhere, looks like Robert Culp, the fog rolling, then parting, then sort of closing up again behind him. He asks you for
10 a light and you jump a bit, startled, but you give him your "Lucky's Lounge—Where Leisure Is a Suit" matches. He has a nice chuckle, nice fingernails. He lights the cigarette, cupping his hands around the end, and drags deeply, like a starving man. He smiles as he exhales, returns you the matches, looks at your face, says: "Thanks."

He then stands not far from you, waiting. Perhaps for the same bus. The two of you glance furtively at each other, shifting feet. Pretend to contemplate the chemical snow. You are two spies glancing quickly at watches, necks disappearing in the hunch of your shoulders, collars upturned and slowly razoring the cab and store-lit fog like sharkfins. You begin to circle,
20 gauging each other in primordial sniffs, eyeing, sidling, keen as Basil Rathbone.

A bus arrives. It is crowded, everyone looking laughlessly into one another's underarms. A blonde woman in barrettes steps off, holding her shoes in one hand.

You climb on together, grab adjacent chrome posts, and when the bus hisses and rumbles forward, you take out a book. A minute goes by and he asks what you're reading. It is *Madame Bovary* in a Doris Day biography jacket. Try to explain about binding warpage. He smiles, interested.

Return to your book. Emma is opening her window, thinking of
30 Rouen.

"What weather," you hear him sigh, faintly British or uppercrust Delaware.

Glance up. Say: "It is fit for neither beast nor vegetable."

It sounds dumb. It makes no sense.

But it is how you meet.

At the movies he is tender, caressing your hand beneath the seat.

At concerts he is sweet and attentive, buying cocktails, locating the ladies' lounge when you can't find it.

At museums he is wise and loving, leading you slowly through the
40 Etruscan cinerary urns with affectionate gestures and an art history
minor from Columbia. He is kind; he laughs at your jokes.

After four movies, three concerts, and two-and-a-half museums, you
sleep with him. It seems the right number of cultural events. On the
stereo you play your favorite harp and oboe music. He tells you his wife's
name. It is Patricia. She is an intellectual property lawyer. He tells you he
likes you a lot. You lie on your stomach, naked and still too warm. When
he says, "How do you feel about that?" don't say "Ridiculous" or "Get the
hell out of my apartment." Prop your head up with one hand and say: "It
depends. What is intellectual property law?"
50 He grins. "Oh, you know. Where leisure is a suit."

Give him a tight, wiry little smile.

"I just don't want you to feel uncomfortable about this," he says.

Say: "Hey. I am a very cool person. I am tough." Show him your bicep.

When you were six you thought *mistress* meant to put your shoes on
the wrong feet. Now you are older and know it can mean many things,
but essentially it means to put your shoes on the wrong feet.

You walk differently. In store windows you don't recognize yourself;
you are another woman, some crazy interior display lady in glasses
stumbling frantic and preoccupied through the mannequins. In public
60 restrooms you sit dangerously flat against the toilet seat, a strange flesh
sundae of despair and exhilaration, murmuring into your bluing thighs:
"Hello, I'm Charlene. I'm a mistress."

It is like having a book out from the library.

It is like constantly having a book out from the library.

You meet frequently for dinner, after work, split whole liters of the
house red, then wamble the two blocks east, twenty blocks south to
your apartment and lie sprawled on the living room floor with your expensive beige raincoats still on.

He is a systems analyst—you have already exhausted this joke—but
70 what he really wants to be, he reveals to you, is an actor.

"Well, how did you become a systems analyst?" you ask, funny you.

"The same way anyone becomes anything," he muses. "I took courses
and sent out resumes." Pause. "Patricia helped me work up a great resume. Too great."

"Oh." Wonder about mistress courses, certification, resumes. Perhaps
you are not really qualified.

"But I'm not good at systems work," he says, staring through and beyond, way beyond, the cracked ceiling. "Figuring out the cost-effectiveness
of two hundred people shuffling five hundred pages back and forth across
80 a new four-and-a-half-by-three-foot desk. I'm not an organized person, like
Patricia, for instance. She's just incredibly organized. She makes lists for
everything. It's pretty impressive."

Say flatly, dully: "What?"

"That she makes lists."

"That she makes lists? You like that?"

"Well, yes. You know, what she's going to do, what she has to buy, names of clients she has to see, et cetera."

"Lists?" you murmur hopelessly, listlessly, your expensive beige rain-coat still on. There is a long, tired silence. Lists? You stand up, brush off
90 your coat, ask him what he would like to drink, then stump off to the kitchen without waiting for the answer.

At one-thirty, he gets up noiselessly except for the soft rustle of his dressing. He leaves before you have even quite fallen asleep, but before he does, he bends over you in his expensive beige raincoat and kisses the ends of your hair. Ah, he kisses your hair.

CLIENTS TO SEE
Birthday snapshots
Scotch tape
Letters to TD and Mom

100   Technically, you are still a secretary for Karma-Kola, but you wear your Phi Beta Kappa key around your neck on a cheap gold chain, hop-ing someone will spot you for a promotion. Unfortunately, you have lost the respect of all but one of your co-workers and many of your superi-ors as well, who are working in order to send their daughters to univer-sities so they won't have to be secretaries, and who, therefore, hold you in contempt for having a degree and being a failure anyway. It is like having a degree in failure. Hilda, however, likes you. You are young and remind her of her sister, the professional skater.

"But I hate to skate," you say.

110   And Hilda smiles, nodding. "Yup, that's exactly what my sister says sometimes and in that same way."

"What way?"

"Oh, I don't know," says Hilda. "Your bangs parted on the side or something."

Ask Hilda if she will go to lunch with you. Over Reuben sandwiches ask her if she's ever had an affair with a married man. As she attempts, mid-bite, to complete the choreography of her chomp, Russian dressing spurts out onto her hands.

"Once," she says. "That was the last lover I had. That was over two
120 years ago."

Say: "Oh my god," as if it were horrible and tragic, then try to miti-gate that rudeness by clearing your throat and saying, "Well, actually, I guess that's not so bad."

"No," she sighs good-naturedly. "His wife had Hodgkin's disease, or so everyone thought. When they came up with the correct diagnosis,

something that wasn't nearly so awful, he went back to her. Does that
make sense to you?"

"I suppose," say doubtfully.

"Yeah, maybe you're right." Hilda is still cleaning Reuben off the
130 backs of her hands with a napkin. "At any rate, who are you involved
with?"

"Someone who has a wife that makes lists. She has List-maker's
disease."

"What are you going to do?"

"I don't know."

"Yeah," says Hilda. "That's typical."

CLIENTS TO SEE
Tomatoes, canned
Health food toothpaste
140   Health food deodorant

Vit. C on sale, Rexall
Check re: other shoemaker, 32nd St.

"Patricia's really had quite an interesting life," he says, smoking a
cigarette.

"Oh, really?" you say, stabbing one out in the ashtray.

Make a list of all the lovers you've ever had.

Warren Lasher
Ed "Rubberhead" Catapano
Charles Deats or Keats
150   Alfonse

Tuck it in your pocket. Leave it lying around, conspicuously. Somehow
you lose it. Make "mislaid" jokes to yourself. Make another list.

Whisper, "Don't go yet," as he glides out of your bed before sunrise
and you lie there on your back cooling, naked between the sheets and
smelling of musky, oniony sweat. Feel gray, like an abandoned locker
room towel. Watch him as he again pulls on his pants, his sweater, his
socks and shoes. Reach out and hold his thigh as he leans over and
kisses you quickly, telling you not to get up, that he'll lock the door
when he leaves. In the smoky darkness, you see him smile weakly, guilt-
160 ily, and attempt a false, jaunty wave from the doorway. Turn on your
side, toward the wall, so you don't have to watch the door close. You
hear it thud nonetheless, the jangle of keys and snap of the bolt lock, the
footsteps loud, then fading down the staircase, the clunk of the street

door, then nothing, all his sounds blending with the city, his face passing namelessly uptown in a bus or a badly heated cab, the room, the whole building you live in, shuddering at the windows as a truck roars by toward the Queensboro Bridge.

Wonder who you are.

"Hi, this is Attila," he says in a false deep voice when you pick up
170 your office phone.

Giggle. Like an idiot. Say: "Oh. Hi, Hun."

Hilda turns to look at you with a what's-with-you look on her face. Shrug your shoulders.

"Can you meet me for lunch?"

Say: "Meet? I'm sorry, I don't eat meat."

"Cute, you're cute," he says, not laughing, and at lunch he gives you his tomatoes.

Drink two huge glasses of wine and smile at all his office and mother-in-law stories. It makes his eyes sparkle and crinkle at the corners,
180 his face pleased and shining. When the waitress clears the plates away, there is a silence where the two of you look down then back up again.

"You get more beautiful every day," he says to you, as you hold your wine glass over your nose, burgundy rushing down your throat. Put your glass down. Redden. Smile. Fiddle with your Phi Beta Kappa key.

When you get up to leave, take deep breaths. In front of the restaurant, where you will stride off in different directions, don't give him a kiss in the noontime throng. Patricia's office is nearby and she likes to go to the bank right around now; his back will stiffen and his eyes dart around like a crazy person's. Instead, do a quick shuffle-ball-chain like
190 you saw Barbra Streisand do in a movie once. Wave gigantically and say: "Till we eat again."

In your office building the elevator is slow and packed and you forget to get off at the tenth floor and have to ride all the way back down again from the nineteenth. Five minutes after you arrive dizzily back at your desk, the phone rings.

"Meet me tomorrow at seven," he says, "in front of Florsheim's and I'll carry you off to my castle. Patricia is going to a copyright convention."

Wait freezing in front of Florsheim's until seven-twenty. He finally dashes up, gasping apologies (he just now got back from the airport), his
200 coat flying open, and he takes you in tow quickly uptown toward the art museums. He lives near art museums. Ask him what a copyright convention is.

"Where leisure is a suit *and* a suite," he drawls, long and smiling, quickening his pace and yours. He kisses your temple, brushes hair off your face.

You arrive at his building in twenty minutes.

"So, this is it?" The castle doorman's fly is undone. Smile politely. In the elevator, say: "The unexamined fly is not worth zipping."

The elevator has a peculiar rattle, for all eight floors, like someone
210 obsessively clearing her throat.

When he finally gets the apartment door unlocked, he shows you into an L-shaped living room bursting with plants and gold-framed posters announcing exhibitions you are too late for by six years. The kitchen is off to one side—tiny, digital, spare, with a small army of chrome utensils hanging belligerent and clean as blades on the wall. Walk nervously around like a dog sniffing out the place. Peek into the bedroom: in the center, like a giant bloom, is a queen-sized bed with a Pennsylvania Dutch spread. A small photo of a woman in ski garb is propped on a nightstand. It frightens you.

220 Back in the living room, he mixes drinks with Scotch in them. "So, this is it," you say again with a forced grin and an odd heaving in your rib cage. Light up one of his cigarettes.

"Can I take your coat?"

Be strange and awkward. Say: "I like beige. I think it is practical."

"What's wrong with you?" he says, handing you your drink.

Try to decide what you should do:

1. rip open the front of your coat, sending the buttons torpedoing across the room in a series of pops into the asparagus fern;
2. go into the bathroom and gargle with hot tap water;
230 3. go downstairs and wave down a cab for home.

He puts his mouth on your neck. Put your arms timidly around him. Whisper into his ear: "There's a woman, uh, another woman in your room."

When he is fast asleep upon you, in the middle of the night, send your left arm out slowly toward the nightstand like a mechanical limb programmed for a secret intelligence mission, and bring the ski garb picture back close to your face in the dark and try to study the features over his shoulder. She seems to have a pretty smile, short hair, no eyebrows, tough flaring nostrils, body indecipherably ensconced in nylon
240 and down and wool.

Slip carefully out, like a shoe horn, from beneath his sleeping body— he grunts groggily—and go to the closet. Open it with a minimum of squeaking and stare at her clothes. A few suits. Looks like beige blouses and a lot of brown things. Turn on the closet light. Look at the shoes. They are all lined up in neat, married pairs on the closet floor. Black pumps, blue sneakers, brown moccasins, brown T-straps. They have been to an expensive college, say, in Massachusetts. Gaze into her shoes. Her feet are much larger than yours. They are like small cruise missiles.

Inside the caves of those shoes, eyes form and open their lids,
250 stare up at you, regard you, wink at you from the insoles. They are

half-friendly, conspiratorial, amused at this reconnaissance of yours, like little smiling men from the open hatches of a fleet of military submarines. Turn off the light and shut the door quickly, before they start talking or dancing or something. Scurry back to the bed and hide your face in his armpit.

In the morning he makes you breakfast. Something with eggs and mushrooms and hot sauce.

Use his toothbrush. The red one. Gaze into the mirror at a face that looks too puffy to be yours. Imagine using her toothbrush by mistake.
260 Imagine a wife and a mistress sharing the same toothbrush forever and ever, never knowing. Look into the medicine cabinet:

Midol
dental floss
Tylenol
Merthiolate
package of eight emory boards
razors and cartridges
two squeezed in the middle toothpaste tubes: Crest *and* Sensodyne
Band-Aids
270   hand lotion
rubbing alcohol
three small bars of Cashmere Bouquet stolen from a hotel

On the street, all over, you think you see her, the boring hotel-soap stealer. Every woman is her. You smell Cashmere Bouquet all over the place. That's her. Someone waiting near you for the downtown express: yup, that's her. A woman waiting behind you in a deli near Marine Midland who has smooth, hand-lotioned hands and looks like she skis: good god, what if that is her. Break out in cold sweats. Stare into every pair of flared nostrils with clinical curiosity and unbridled terror. Scrutinize
280 feet. Glance sidelong at pumps. Then look quickly away, like a woman, some other woman, who is losing her mind.

Alone on lunch hours or after work, continue to look every female over the age of twelve straight in the nose and straight in the shoes. Feel your face aquiver and twice bolt out of Bergdorf's irrationally when you are sure it is her at the skirt sale rack choosing brown again, a Tylenol bottle peeking out from the corner of her purse. Sit on a granite wall in the GM plaza and catch your breath. Listen to an old man singing "Frosty the Snowman." Lose track of time.

"You're late," Hilda turns and whispers at you. "Carlyle's been back
290 here twice already asking where you were and if the market survey report has been typed up yet."

Mutter: "Shit." You are only on the T's: Tennessee Karma-Kola consumption per square dollar-mile of investment market. Figures for July 1980–October 1981.

Texas—Fiscal Year 1980
Texas—Fiscal Year 1981
Utah.

It is like typing a telephone directory. Get tears in your eyes.

CLIENTS TO SEE

300
1. Fallen in love(?) Out of control. Who is this? Who am I? And who is this wife with the skis and the nostrils and the Tylenol and does she have orgasms?
2. Reclaim yourself. Pieces have fluttered away.
3. Everything you do is a masochistic act. Why?
4. Don't you like yourself? Don't you deserve better than all of this?
5. Need: something to lift you from your boots out into the sky, something to make you like little things again, to whirl around the curves of your ears and muss up your hair and call you every single day.

310
6. A drug.
7. A man.
8. A religion.
9. A good job. Revise and send out resumes.
10. Remember what Mrs. Kloosterman told the class in second grade: Just be glad you have legs.

"What are you going to do for Christmas?" he says, lying supine on your couch.

"Oh. I don't know. See my parents in New Jersey, I guess." Pause. "Wanna come? Meet my folks?"

320 A kind, fatherly, indulgent smile. "Charlene," he purrs, sitting up to pat your hand, your silly ridiculous little hand.

He gives you a pair of leather slippers. They were what you wanted. You give him a book about cars.

"Ma, open the red one first. The other package goes with it."

"A coffee grinder, why thank you, dear." She kisses you wetly on the cheek, a Christmas mist in her eyes. She thinks you're wonderful. She's truly your greatest fan. She is aging and menopausal. She stubbornly thinks you're an assistant department head at Karma-Kola. She wants so badly, so earnestly, to be you.

330 "And this bag is some exotic Colombian bean, and this is a chocolate-flavored decaf."

Your father fidgets in the corner, looking at his watch, worrying that your mom should be checking the crown roast.

"Decaf bean," he says. "That's for me?"
Say: "Yeah, Dad. That's for you."

"Who is he?" says your mom, later, in the kitchen after you've washed the dishes.
"He's a systems analyst."
"What do they do?"
340   "Oh . . . they get married a lot. They're usually always married."
"Charlene, are you having an affair with a married man?"
"Ma, do you have to put it that way?"
"You are asking for big trouble," she says, slowly, and resumes polishing silver with a vehement energy.
Wonder why she always polishes the silver *after* meals.
Lean against the refrigerator and play with the magnets.
Say, softly, carefully: "I know, Mother, it's not something you would do."
She looks up at you, her mouth trembling, pieces of her brown-gray
350   hair dangling in her salty eyes, pink silverware cream caking onto her hands, onto her wedding ring. She stops, puts a spoon down, looks away and then hopelessly back at you, like a very young girl, and, shaking her head, bursts into tears.

"I missed you," he practically shouts, ebullient and adolescent, pacing about the living room with a sort of bounce, like a child who is up way past his bedtime and wants to ask a question. "What did you do at home?" He rubs your neck.
"Oh, the usual holiday stuff with my parents. On New Year's Eve I went to a disco in Morristown with my cousin Denise, but I dressed
360   wrong. I wore the turtleneck and plaid skirt my mother gave me, because I wanted her to feel good, and my slip kept showing."
He grins and kisses your cheek, thinking this sweet.
Continue: "There were three guys, all in purple shirts and paper hats, who kept coming over and asking me to dance. I don't think they were together or brothers or anything. But I danced, and on 'New York City Girl,' that song about how jaded and competent urban women are, I went crazy dancing and my slip dropped to the floor. I tried to pick it up, but finally just had to step out of it and jam it in my purse. At the stroke of midnight, I cried."
370   "I'll bet you suffered terribly," he says, clasping you around the small of your back.
Say: "Yes, I did."

———————

"I'm thinking of telling Patricia about us."
Be skeptical. Ask: "What will you say?"
He proceeds confidently: "I'll go, 'Dear, there's something I have to tell you.'"

"And she'll look over at you from her briefcase full of memoranda and say: 'Hmmmmmm?'"

"And I'll say, 'Dear, I think I'm falling in love with another woman, 380 and I *know* I'm having sex with her.'"

"And she'll say, 'Oh my god, what did you say?'"

"And I'll say: 'Sex.'"

"And she'll start weeping inconsolably and *then* what will you do?"

There is a silence, still as the moon. He shifts his legs, seems confused. "I'll . . . tell her I was just kidding." He squeezes your hand.

Shave your legs in the bathroom sink. Philosophize: you are a mistress, part of a great hysterical you mean historical tradition. Wives are like cockroaches. Also part of a great historical tradition. They will survive you after a nuclear attack—they are tough and hardy and travel in 390 packs—but right now they're not having any fun. And when you look in the bathroom mirror, you spot them scurrying, up out of reach behind you.

An hour of gimlets after work, a quick browse through Barnes and Noble, and he looks at his watch, gives you a peck, and says: "Good night. I'll call you soon."

Walk out with him. Stand there, shivering, but do not pout. Say: "Call you 'later' would sound better than 'soon.' 'Soon' always means just the opposite."

He smiles feebly. "I'll phone you in a few days."

400   And when he is off, hurrying up Third Avenue, look down at your feet, kick at a dirty cigarette butt, and in your best juvenile mumble, say: "Fuck you, jack."

Some nights he says he'll try to make it over, but there's no guarantee. Those nights, just in case, spend two hours showering, dressing, applying makeup unrecognizably, like someone in drag, and then, as it is late, and you have to work the next day, climb onto your bed like that, wearing perfume and an embarrassing, long, flowing, lacy bathrobe that is really not a bathrobe at all, but a "hostess loungecoat." With the glassed candle by your bed lit and burning away, doze off and on, arranged with excruciat-410 ing care on top of the covers, the window lamp on in the living room, the door unlocked for him in case he arrives in a passionate flurry, forgetting his key. Six blocks from Fourteenth Street: you are risking your life for him, spread out like a ridiculous cake on the bed, waiting with the door unlocked, thinking you hear him on the stairs, but no. You should have a corsage, you think to yourself. You should have a goddamned orchid pinned to the chest of your long flowing hostess coat, then you would be appropriately absurd. Think: What has happened to me? Why am I lying like this on top of my covers with too much Jontue and mascara and jewelry, pretending casually that this is how I always go to bed, while a

420 pervert with six new steak knives is about to sneak through my unlocked
door. Remember: at Blakely Falls High, Willis Holmes would have done
anything to be with you. You don't have to put up with this: you were
second runner-up at the Junior Prom.

A truck roars by.

Some deaf and dumb kids, probably let out from a dance at the
school nearby, are gathered downstairs below your window, hooting and
howling, making unearthly sounds. You guess they are laughing and
having fun, but they can't hear themselves, and at night the noises are
scary, animal-like.

430   Your clock-radio reads 1:45.

Wonder if you are getting old, desperate. Believe that you have really
turned into another woman:

your maiden aunt Phyllis;

some vaporish cocktail waitress;

a glittery transvestite who has wandered, lost, up from the Village.

When seven consecutive days go by that you do not hear from him,
send witty little postcards to all your friends from college. On the
eighth day, when finally he calls you at the office, murmuring lascivious
things in German, remain laconic. Say: *"Ja . . . nein . . . ja."*

440   At lunch regard your cream of cauliflower soup with a pinched
mouth and ask what on earth he and his wife *do* together. Sound irritated. He shrugs and says, "Dust, eat, bicker about the shower curtain.
Why do you ask?"

Say: "Gee, I don't know. What an outrageous question, huh?"

He gives you a look of sympathy that could bring a dead cat back to
life. "You're upset because I didn't call you." He reaches across the table
to touch your fingers. Pull your hand away. Say: "Don't flatter yourself." Look slightly off to one side. Put your hand over your eyes like
you have a headache. Say: "God, I'm sorry."

450   "It's okay," he says.

And you think: Something is backward here. Reversed. Wrong. Like
the something that is wrong in "What is wrong with this picture?" in
kids' magazines in dentists' offices. Toothaches. Stomachaches. God, the
soup. Excuse yourself and hurry toward the women's room. Slam the
stall door shut. Lean back against it. Stare into the throat of the toilet.

Hilda is worried about you and wants to fix you up with a cousin of
hers from Brooklyn.

Ask wearily: "What's his name?"

She looks at you, frowning. "Mark. He's a banker. And what the hell
460 kind of attitude is that?"

Mark orders you a beer in a Greek coffee shop near the movie theater. "So, you're a secretary."

Squirm and quip: "More like a sedentary," and look at him in surprise and horror when he guffaws and snorts way too loudly.

Say: "Actually, what I really should have been is a dancer. Everybody has always said that."

Mark smiles. He likes the idea of you being a dancer.

Look at him coldly. Say: "No, nobody has ever said that. I just made it up."

470   All through the movie you forget to read the subtitles, thinking instead about whether you should sleep with Mark the banker. Glance at him out of the corner of your eye. In the dark, his profile seems important and mysterious. Sort of. He catches you looking at him and turns and winks at you. Good god. He seems to be investing something in all of this. Bankers. Sigh. Stare straight ahead. Decide you just don't have the energy, the interest.

"I saw somebody else."

"Oh?"

"A banker. We went to a Godard movie."

480   "Well . . . good."

"Good?"

"I mean for you, Charlene. You should be doing things like that once in a while."

"Yeah. He's real rich."

"Did you have fun?"

"No."

"Did you sleep with him?"

"No."

He kisses you, almost gratefully, on the ear. Fidget. Twitch. Lie. Say: 490 "I mean, yes."

He nods. Looks away. Says nothing.

———————————

Cut up an old calendar into week-long strips. Place them around your kitchen floor, a sort of bar graph on the linoleum, representing the number of weeks you have been a mistress: thirteen. Put X's through all the national holidays.

Go out for a walk in the cold. Three little girls hanging out on the stoop are laughing and calling to strange men on the street. "Hi! Hi, Mister!" Step around them. Think: They have never had orgasms.

A blonde woman in barrettes passes you in stockinged feet, holding 500 her shoes.

There are things you have to tell him.

CLIENTS TO SEE

1. This affair is demeaning.
2. Violates decency. Am I just some scampish tart, some tartish scamp?
3. No emotional support here.
4. Why do you never say "I love you" or "Stay in my arms forever my little tadpole" or "Your eyes set me on fire my sweet nubkin"?

510 The next time he phones, he says: "I was having a dream about you and suddenly I woke up with a jerk and felt very uneasy."

Say: "Yeah, I hate to wake up with jerks."

He laughs, smooth, beautiful, and tenor, making you feel warm inside of your bones. And it hits you; maybe it all boils down to this: people will do anything, anything, for a really nice laugh.

Don't lose your resolve. Fumble for your list. Sputter things out as convincingly as possible.

Say: "I suffer indignities at your hands. And agonies of duh feet. I don't know why I joke. I hurt."

"That is why."

520 "What?"

"That is why."

"But you don't really care." Wince. It sounds pitiful.

"But I do."

For some reason this leaves you dumbfounded.

He continues: "You know my situation . . . or maybe you don't." Pause. "What can I do, Charlene? Stand on my goddamned head?"

Whisper: "Please. Stand on your goddamned head."

"It is ten o'clock," he says. "I'm coming over. We need to talk."

What he has to tell you is that Patricia is not his wife. He is sepe-
530 rated from his wife; her name is Carrie. You think of a joke you heard once: What do you call a woman who marries a man with no arms and no legs? Carrie. Patricia is the woman he lives with.

"You mean, I'm just another one of the fucking gang?"

He looks at you, puzzled. "Charlene, what I've always admired about you, right from when I first met you, is your strength, your independence."

Say: "That line is old as boots."

Tell him not to smoke in your apartment. Tell him to get out.

At first he protests. But slowly, slowly, he leaves, pulling up the col-
540 lar on his expensive beige raincoat, like an old and haggard Robert Culp.

Slam the door like Bette Davis.

Love drains from you, takes with it much of your blood sugar and water weight. You are like a house slowly losing its electricity, the fans slowing, the lights dimming and flickering; the clocks stop and go and stop.

At Karma-Kola the days are peg-legged and aimless, collapsing into one another with the comic tedium of old clowns, nowhere fast.

In April you get a raise. Celebrate by taking Hilda to lunch at the Plaza.

Write for applications to graduate schools.

550   Send Mark the banker a birthday card.

Take long walks at night in the cold. The blonde in barrettes scuttles timelessly by you, still carrying her shoes. She has cut her hair.

He calls you occasionally at the office to ask how you are. You doodle numbers and curlicues on the corners of the Rolodex cards. Fiddle with your Phi Beta Kappa key. Stare out the window. You always, always, say: "Fine."

PART TWO

POETRY

Chapter Ten

Introduction to Poetry

COMMON TERMS OF LITERARY DISCOURSE ON POETRY

One famous line of verse in a much-anthologized poem by Archibald MacLeish asserts: "A poem should not mean, but be." This line raises basic issues: Why should we *talk* about poetry at all? Shouldn't we just enjoy it? One answer to such common questions begins by noting how much in fact we *like* to discuss not only the people, places, and things we enjoy, but also how much they mean to us. It may be true that a poem will exist whatever we say (or do not say) about its meaning and technique, but people for thousands of years have found their own existences made richer by reading and discussing poetry.

As with the introduction to fiction, this section aims to give you some ways of talking about your literary experience in order to enhance that experience. But since the techniques and forms of poetic activity have produced so many technical words over the centuries, only basic terms will be given here to avoid confusing you through an overabundance of new terminology all at once. For example, there are so many differing ideas about **prosody** alone—the study of the rhythms and sounds of poetry—that no more than a beginning may be made within the scope of an introduction like this one. However, you will find many more useful names for prosody—and for many other ways of analyzing poetic activity—defined in the glossary at the end of this book. Your instructor will no doubt teach you many others as well.

As is the case for a reader of fiction, all the elements of a poem may act on the reader of poetry simultaneously, but it is only possible to speak of them one at a time. Which should a discussion focus on first? It is customary to begin by trying to describe our general impressions by characterizing the **voice** we imagine hearing in the poem—the poem's **speaker**. Like the narrator of a story, the speaker or **persona** invented by the poet may be characterized by the values and assumptions that seem to define why and how what is said gets said.

Consider, for instance, the different voices you hear in the two poems that follow. Each is an **elegy**—a poem on the occasion of a death.

BEN JONSON (1572–1637)

On My First Daughter

Here lies to each her parents' ruth,
Mary, the daughter of their youth:
Yet, all heaven's gifts, being heaven's due,
It makes the father, less, to rue.
5 At six months' end, she parted hence
With safety of her innocence;
Whose soul heaven's Queen (whose name she bears)
In comfort of her mother's tears,
Hath placed amongst her virgin-train:
10 Where, while that severed doth remain,
This grave partakes the fleshly birth.
Which cover lightly, gentle earth.

In trying to describe the speaker's **attitude**, we might first note what subjects or themes make the focus of his attention throughout the poem. He talks about important subjects, such as religion, and seems to adopt a dignified and lofty **tone of voice**. Further, his manner of speaking seems hesitant and almost awkward, partly due to the way the rather short lines are themselves frequently brought up short by rhyming every two lines—**couplets**. Yet despite the hesitation, the dignity in his voice comes from his confidence in claiming to understand exactly what has happened to his daughter after her death. Mary, the mother of Christ, has made Mary, the child, one of her attendants, and that glorious position is a comfort to her human mother. But the certainty of religious conviction does *not* stop the parents from feeling a grief that is made all the more poignant by their believing that, logically, they should not feel any sorrow at all, since their girl is presumably better off and happier in heaven. The emotional struggle within the speaker's voice seems most poignant at the end of the poem, where the father's rational expression of comfort to himself and his wife breaks down into an irrational plea to the earth to spare the child's body pain, though he "knows" that body can no longer feel anything at all.

The **dramatic situation** then—a father struggling to express both his religious convictions and his natural feelings that cannot quite be comforted by those convictions—tends to create the impression of an underlying helpless agony in the tone of the speaker's voice. Such a tone might be opposed in imagination to the stolid, stiff and merely elevated tone we would have heard had the last lines not been there to add depth to our perception of how the speaker sounds throughout the poem as a whole.

To refine your sense of the tone of voice you hear in any poem it often helps to proceed by comparison and contrast. Consider the following, more contemporary elegy.

GWENDOLYN BROOKS (1917–   )

Of DeWitt Williams on His Way to Lincoln Cemetery

He was born in Alabama.
He was bred in Illinois.
He was nothing but a
Plain black boy.

5 Swing low sweet sweet chariot.
Nothing but a plain black boy.

Drive him past the Pool Hall.
Drive him past the Show.
Blind within his casket,
10 But maybe he will know.

Down through forty-seventh Street:
Underneath the L,
And—Northwest Corner, Prairie,
That he loved so well.

15 Don't forget the Dance Halls—
Warwick and Savoy,
Where he picked his women, where
He drank his liquid joy.

Born in Alabama.
20 Bred in Illinois.
He was nothing but a
Plain black boy.

Swing low swing low sweet sweet chariot.
Nothing but a plain black boy.

Certainly this poem presents a different dramatic situation from Jonson's, and the speaker's voice takes on a different sound in the face of death. The speaker's **attitude** toward the life lamented might be summed up as "What a waste!" The voice may sound *bitter*—and its drama operates differently from the ways in which Jonson combines in his voice the expression of a lofty and logical confident mind with a tender and irrational breaking heart. For one thing, there seems to be a great deal of

irony in the speaker's tone. This is partly created by a tension in the poem's **diction** or word choice. Are words such as "Lincoln," "Alabama," and "Illinois" to be read **literally**—simply as place names—or **figuratively**—as **symbolic** expressions of themes of freedom and slavery? Similarly the words that make up the refrain "Nothing but a plain black boy" are repeated so often and so intensely that we begin to hear further reverberations of meaning that each word takes on when understood in different senses.

In what senses, for example, could DeWitt Williams be called a "boy?" Literally, he was apparently old enough to go into bars. But does the speaker consider that in doing so Williams acted childishly by seeking a life solely in pleasure—that (ironically) he behaved figuratively like a boy though he was literally a man? "Boy" is also a figurative term of racial insult used to belittle grown men. Does the speaker suggest that prejudice has become the ironic result of the "freedom" symbolized by his own progress north and the country's progress toward emancipation under President Lincoln? Where is freedom to be found? Slaves, by singing spirituals like "Swing Low Sweet Chariot," used to pray for freedom and emancipation through death and for the heaven promised beyond death. What use of legal freedom has Williams made? Where did he find his "heaven?" Whose fault is the wasted life bitterly lamented here?

All these questions are charged with importance by the repetition of the refrain "Nothing but a plain black boy." But the sound of the poem through its rhythms further reinforces and intensifies the significance and emphasis given to these words. **Rhythm** in English poetry is created by the patterned alternation of stressed and unstressed syllables. These patterns are created in turn not only by the facts that every polysyllabic word has an accented syllable and that we stress important words as we speak, but also by the context of expectation that poems can set up within themselves. In a prose sentence, the words "plain black boy" would take on a different degree of emphasis from that they take on given the rhythmic context of the poem. For example, compare how the words in the poem sound to the way they sound in the following sentence. "In his childhood, DeWitt Williams—a plain black boy with no fancy ideas or pretensions—used to love to go on picnics with his aunts and uncles."

The same words within the rhythmic context of the poem take on an entirely different rhythmic emphasis. For one thing, because the first two lines have three stresses each, we expect each subsequent line to have three stresses. And since the third line has the same rhythm as the first two, we hear a continuation of the rhythmic pattern. But because the fourth line has only three words in three syllables, we can only give the line three stresses if *each word* receives a stress. This pattern explains the emphasis that most readers give the words of the fourth line and its subsequent repetitions in different rhythmic environments throughout the poem. In this and other ways, the poet achieves the "music" and other sound effects of verse by manipulating the reader's sense of rhythmic expectations—by setting patterns and modulating them.

Over time, certain patterns gain particular associations of sound. For example, Shakespeare's noble characters speak in **blank verse**, which means "unrhymed iambic pentameter." Explaining what these words mean leads us to some technical matters of *meter*.

Meter basically means *measure* and the *meter* part of the word *pentameter* measures "length of line." **Penta** means *five* as in the five-sided figure of a pentagon. *Iambic* refers to a pattern of rhythm in a poetic **foot**, and five such feet measure a line of "iambic pentameter"—or a line five "feet" long in which each foot has an iambic pattern.

Here are the terms for line lengths:

monometer	one foot	**pentameter**	five feet
dimeter	two feet	**hexameter**	six feet
trimeter	three feet	**heptameter**	seven feet
tetrameter	four feet	**octameter**	eight feet

But what of the feet that make up the lines? Ben Jonson's poem is written in iambic tetrameter. The iambic pattern describes an unstress–stress rhythm as in:

      1   2   3   4

Here **lies**/ to **each**/ her **par**/ents **ruth**.

A **trochaic** foot is made up of two units but in a reverse pattern—stress–unstress as in Brooks' trochaic trimeter:

      1   2   3

Drive him / **past** the / **Pool** Hall

Other rhythmic feet have three units:

dactyls: stress–unstress–unstress:
Each of us / **Lov**-ing and / **ten**-derly
anapests: unstress–unstress–stress:
In the **moon**- / light the **eve**- / ning was **still**

The more **regular** a verse pattern, the more often the feet in a line are of the same type. At the other extreme, **free verse** (or **vers libre**) depends on rhythms that vary without any apparent sustained regularity. Yet, regularity may be overdone. Unmodulated regularity leads to **doggerel** like the simple regular rhythms of "Jack and Jill / Went up the hill." Poets often achieve comic effects with such deliberately clumsy rhythms, but in serious verse the verse rhythms are delicately varied, and their variety makes them often harder to analyze or **scan** than the textbook examples given above.

In regular verse, the regularities of rhythm in units of foot and line are further built up into larger units like the **couplets** of Jonson's poem and the generally four-line **stanzas** of Brooks' poem, in which the second and the fourth lines rhyme.

A **sonnet** is a still larger unit and consists of fourteen lines. For example, the **Shakespearean** sonnets appearing later in this section take the form of three **quatrains** (or four-line stanzas)—which rhyme on the first and third and second and fourth lines—and conclude with a couplet. The usual notation gives a new letter for each new rhyme and repeats that letter as often as the rhyme occurs. For example, a Shakespearean sonnet could be described through notation as having the following **rhyme scheme**:

a
b
a
b

octave

c
d
c
d
_____

e
f
e
f

sestet

g
g

As the diagram shows, the sonnet is organized in another way in addition to its rhyme scheme—into **octave**, the first eight lines, and **sestet**, the last six. The result of having all these patterning devices—in foot, line, stanza, and sonnet units—is the variety in sound pattern that contributes to the "musical" pleasures of verse.

Other heightened uses of the resources of language make their contributions too. Examples include patterns of repeated consonants, or **alliteration**, as in "black boy" or repeated vowel sounds (**assonance**) as in "Alabama." **Metaphors** such as "liquid joy" and **similes** such as "a joy like liquid" are examples of the **figurative language** that helps make poetry vivid through the use of **images** and **symbols**.

At this point, you have in hand some of the terms critics use when talking about poetry in all its forms, from short **lyrics** that express the feelings or thoughts of one speaker, through **dramatic monologues** and longer **narrative** poems that tell a larger story, up to the **epic**—traditionally the grandest and largest form of poetry—whose concerns are the great legends which express the values and assumptions of a civilization and whose composition calls out the greatest powers and talents of a poet.

Your specific critical vocabulary for poetry will enable you to describe some of the ways in which poetry differs from the narratives of fiction. But poetry, like imaginative prose, is concerned with the meaning of life, and the critical approaches introduced in the section on fiction are also used to explore meaning in poetry. In the following sections, you will find two differing critical approaches to each of five featured poems by major poets. By understanding how critics explore the larger issues of poetry and by going through the suggested questions and exercises, you will build on the critical skills practiced in the first part of this book.

Chapter Eleven

Approaches to Alexander Pope's *The Rape of the Lock*

ALEXANDER POPE (1688–1744) was born the son of a Roman Catholic linen merchant in the City of London in 1688. He spent his formative years reading the classics, writing poetry, and studying Greek, French, and Italian. In 1709 his *Pastorals* were published, after which he became friends with famous writers of the period: Jonathan Swift, John Gay, and John Arbuthnot. In 1714 the friends established the Scriblerus Club, an organization whose aim was to combat pedantry and "false tastes in learning." The group disbanded after less than a year, but the spirit of their alliance resurfaced in Pope's *The Dunciad* (1728), in which he attacked his literary enemies. After his father's death in 1718, Pope moved with his mother to Twickenham on the Thames; this estate inspired Pope's nickname, "The Wasp of Twickenham." He remained there until his death in 1744. Among his greatest poems are *An Essay on Criticism* (1711), *Eloisa to Abelard* (1717), *An Essay on Man* (1733–34), and his *Epistle to Dr. Arbuthnot* (1735). In addition to writing poetry, Pope also translated Homer's *Iliad* (1715–20) and *Odyssey* (1725–26), and edited a bestselling edition of Shakespeare (1725).

The Rape of the Lock is one of Pope's most popular works. The mock-heroic poem is based on an actual incident: In 1711 Pope's friend John Caryll asked him to write a humorous poem to reunite two fashionable but feuding families, the Petres and the Fermors, after Robert Lord Petre cut off a lock of Arabella Fermor's hair. Pope satirizes not only this event but also the traditional components of an epic (prayers, laments, feasts, sacrifices, and so on) as well as the traditional epic style (invocations, similes, exclamations, and so on). The first version of the poem, consisting of only two cantos, was published in 1712; the final five-canto version was published in 1714.

ALEXANDER POPE

The Rape of the Lock

AN HEROI-COMICAL POEM[1]

(1712, 1714)

Nolueram, Belinda, tuos violare capillos;
sed juvat hoc precibus me tribuisse tuis.[2]
—*MARTIAL*

Canto I

What dire offense from amorous causes springs,
What mighty contests rise from trivial things,
I sing—This verse to Caryll, Muse! is due:
This, even Belinda may vouchsafe to view:
5 Slight is the subject, but not so the praise,
If she inspire, and he approve my lays.
   Say what strange motive, Goddess! could compel
A well-bred lord to assault a gentle belle?
Oh, say what stranger cause, yet unexplored,
10 Could make a gentle belle reject a lord?
In tasks so bold can little men engage,
And in soft bosoms dwells such mighty rage?
   Sol through white curtains shot a timorous ray,
And oped those eyes that must eclipse the day.[3]
15 Now lapdogs give themselves the rousing shake,
And sleepless lovers just at twelve awake:
Thrice rung the bell, the slipper knocked the ground,[4]
And the pressed watch returned a silver sound.[5]
Belinda still her downy pillow pressed,
20 Her guardian Sylph[6] prolonged the balmy rest:
'Twas he had summoned to her silent bed
The morning dream that hovered o'er her head.

---

[1] Based on an actual incident. A young man, Lord Petre, had sportively cut off a lock of a Miss Arabella Fermor's hair. She and her family were angered by the prank, and Pope's friend John Caryll (line 3), a relative of Lord Petre's, asked the poet to turn the incident into jest, so that good relations (and possibly negotiations toward a marriage between the principals) might be resumed. Pope responded by treating the incident in a mock epic or "heroi-comical poem." The epic conventions first encountered are the immediate statement of the topic, which the poet says he will "sing" as if in oral recitation, and the request to the Muse (line 7) to grant him the necessary insight.

[2] "I did not want, Belinda, to violate your locks, but it pleases me to have paid this tribute to your prayers." Miss Fermor did not in fact request the poem.

[3] The eyes of lovely young women—though Belinda herself is still asleep.

[4] These are two ways of summoning servants.

[5] In the darkened beds, one discovered the approximate time by a watch which chimed the hour and quarter-hour when the stem was pressed.

[6] Air-spirit. He accounts for himself in the lines below.

A youth more glittering than a birthnight beau[7]
(That even in slumber caused her cheek to glow)
25 Seemed to her ear his winning lips to lay,
And thus in whispers said, or seemed to say:
"Fairest of mortals, thou distinguished care
Of thousand bright inhabitants of air!
If e'er one vision touched thy infant thought,
30 Of all the nurse and all the priest have taught,
Of airy elves by moonlight shadows seen,
The silver token, and the circled green,[8]
Or virgins visited by angel powers,
With golden crowns and wreaths of heavenly flowers,
35 Hear and believe! thy own importance know,
Nor bound thy narrow views to things below.
Some secret truths, from learned pride concealed,
To maids alone and children are revealed:
What though no credit doubting wits may give?
40 The fair and innocent shall still believe.
Know, then, unnumbered spirits round thee fly,
The light militia of the lower sky:
These, though unseen, are ever on the wing,
Hang o'er the box, and hover round the Ring.[9]
45 Think what an equipage thou hast in air,
And view with scorn two pages and a chair.°   *sedan chair*
As now your own, our beings were of old,
And once enclosed in woman's beauteous mold;
Thence, by a soft transition, we repair
50 From earthly vehicles[1] to these of air.
Think not, when woman's transient breath is fled,
That all her vanities at once are dead:
Succeeding vanities she still regards,
And though she plays no more, o'erlooks the cards.
55 Her joy in gilded chariots,° when alive,   *carriages*
And love of ombre,[2] after death survive.
For when the Fair in all their pride expire,
To their first elements their souls retire:[3]

---

[7] Courtier dressed for a royal birthday celebration.

[8] The silver token is the coin left by a fairy or elf, and the circled green is a ring of bright green grass, supposedly by a dancing circle of fairies.

[9] The box is a theater box; the Ring, the circular carriage course in Hyde Park.

[1] Mediums of existence, with a side glance at the fondness of young women for riding in carriages.

[2] A popular card game, pronounced *omber.*

[3] Namely, to fire, water, earth, and air, the four elements of the old cosmology and the several habitats (in the Rosicrucian myths upon which Pope embroiders) of four different kinds of "spirit." Envisaging these spirits as the transmigrated souls of different kinds of women, Pope causes termagants (scolds) to become fire-spirits or Salamanders (line 60); irresolute women to become water-spirits or Nymphs (line 62); prudes, or women who

The sprites of fiery termagants in flame
60 Mount up, and take a Salamander's name.
Soft yielding minds to water glide away,
And sip, with Nymphs, their elemental tea.[4]
The graver prude sinks downward to a Gnome,
In search of mischief still on earth to roam.
65 The light coquettes in Sylphs aloft repair,
And sport and flutter in the fields of air.
    "Know further yet; whoever fair and chaste
Rejects mankind, is by some Sylph embraced:
For spirits, freed from mortal laws, with ease
70 Assume what sexes and what shapes they please.[5]
What guards the purity of melting maids,
In courtly balls, and midnight masquerades,
Safe from the treacherous friend, the daring spark,
The glance by day, the whisper in the dark,
75 When kind occasion prompts their warm desires,
When music softens, and when dancing fires?
'Tis but their Sylph, the wise Celestials know,
Though Honor is the word with men below.
    "Some nymphs there are, too conscious of their face,
80 For life predestined to the Gnomes' embrace.
These swell their prospects and exalt their pride,
When offers are disdained, and love denied:
Then gay ideas° crowd the vacant brain,   *imaginings*
While peers, and dukes, and all their sweeping train,
85 And garters, stars, and coronets[6] appear,
And in soft sounds, 'your Grace' salutes their ear.
'Tis these that early taint the female soul,
Instruct the eyes of young coquettes to roll,
Teach infant cheeks a bidden blush to know,
90 And little hearts to flutter at a beau.
    "Oft, when the world imagine women stray,
The Sylphs through mystic mazes guide their way,
Through all the giddy circle they pursue,
And old impertinence expel by new.
95 What tender maid but must a victim fall
To one man's treat, but for another's ball?
When Florio speaks what virgin could withstand,
If gentle Damon did not squeeze her hand?

---

delight in rejection and negation, to become earth-spirits or Gnomes (line 64); and coquettes to become air-spirits or Sylphs. Since "nymph" could designate either a water-
spirit or (in literary usage) a young lady, Pope permits his water-spirits to claim tea as
their native element (line 62) and to keep their former company at tea-parties.
    [4] Pronounced *tay.*
    [5] Like Milton's angels (*Paradise Lost* I.423 ff.).
    [6] Insignia of rank and court status.

With varying vanities, from every part,
100 They shift the moving toyshop of their heart;
Where wigs with wigs, with sword-knots sword-knots strive,[7]
Beaux banish beaux, and coaches coaches drive.
This erring mortals levity may call;
Oh, blind to truth! the Sylphs contrive it all.
105   "Of these am I, who thy protection claim,
A watchful sprite, and Ariel is my name.
Late, as I ranged the crystal wilds of air,
In the clear mirror of thy ruling star
I saw, alas! some dread event impend,
110 Ere to the main this morning sun descend,
But Heaven reveals not what, or how, or where:
Warned by the Sylph, O pious maid, beware!
This to disclose is all thy guardian can:
Beware of all, but most beware of Man!"
115   He said; when Shock,[8] who thought she slept too long,
Leaped up, and waked his mistress with his tongue.
'Twas then, Belinda, if report say true,
Thy eyes first opened on a billet-doux;[9]
Wounds, charms, and ardors were no sooner read,
120 But all the vision vanished from thy head.
     And now, unveiled, the toilet stands displayed,
Each silver vase in mystic order laid.
First, robed in white, the nymph intent adores,
With head uncovered, the cosmetic powers.
125 A heavenly image in the glass[1] appears;
To that she bends, to that her eyes she rears.
The inferior priestess, at her altar's side,
Trembling begins the sacred rites of pride.
Unnumbered treasures ope at once, and here
130 The various offerings of the world appear;
From each she nicely culls with curious toil,
And decks the goddess with the glittering spoil.
This casket India's glowing gems unlocks,
And all Arabia[2] breathes from yonder box.
135 The tortoise here and elephant unite,
Transformed to combs, the speckled and the white.

---

[7]Sword-Knots are ribbons tied to hilts. The verbal repetition and the tangled syntax recall descriptions of the throng and press of battle appearing in English translations of classical epic.

[8]A name for lapdogs (like "Poll" for parrots); they looked like little "shocks" of hair.

[9]A love letter. The affected language of the fashionable love letter is exhibited in the next line.

[1]The mirror. Her image is the object of veneration, the "goddess" named later. Belinda presides over the appropriate rites. Betty, her maid, is the "inferior priestess."

[2]Source of perfumes.

Here files of pins extend their shining rows,
Puffs, powders, patches, Bibles, billet-doux.
Now awful Beauty put on all its arms;
140 The fair each moment rises in her charms,
Repairs her smiles, awakens every grace,
And calls forth all the wonders of her face;
Sees by degrees a purer blush arise,
And keener lightnings quicken in her eyes.
145 The busy Sylphs surround their darling care,
These set the head, and those divide the hair,
Some fold the sleeve, whilst others plait the gown;
And Betty's praised for labors not her own.

Canto II

Not with more glories, in the ethereal plain,
The sun first rises o'er the purpled main,
Than, issuing forth, the rival of his beams[3]
Launched on the bosom of the silver Thames.
5 Fair nymphs and well-dressed youths around her shone,
But every eye was fixed on her alone.
On her white breast a sparkling cross she wore,
Which Jews might kiss, and infidels adore.
Her lively looks a sprightly mind disclose,
10 Quick as her eyes, and as unfixed as those:
Favors to none, to all she smiles extends;
Oft she rejects, but never once offends.
Bright as the sun, her eyes the gazers strike,
And, like the sun, they shine on all alike.
15 Yet graceful ease, and sweetness void of pride,
Might hide her faults, if belles had faults to hide:
If to her share some female errors fall,
Look on her face, and you'll forget 'em all.
This nymph, to the destruction of mankind,
20 Nourished two locks which graceful hung behind
In equal curls, and well conspired to deck
With shining ringlets the smooth ivory neck.
Love in these labyrinths his slaves detains,
And mighty hearts are held in slender chains.
25 With hairy springes° we the birds betray,   *snares*
Slight lines of hair surprise the finny prey,
Fair tresses man's imperial race ensnare,
And beauty draws us with a single hair.
The adventurous Baron the bright locks admired,

---

[3]i.e., Belinda. She is en route to Hampton Court, a royal palace some twelve miles up the river Thames from London.

30 He saw, he wished, and to the prize aspired.
   Resolved to win, he meditates the way,
   By force to ravish, or by fraud betray;
   For when success a lover's toil attends,
   Few ask if fraud or force attained his ends.
35   For this, ere Phoebus rose, he had implored
   Propitious Heaven, and every power adored,
   But chiefly Love—to Love an altar built,
   Of twelve vast French romances, neatly gilt.
   There lay three garters, half a pair of gloves,
40 And all the trophies of his former loves.
   With tender billet-doux he lights the pyre,
   And breathes three amorous sighs to raise the fire.
   Then prostrate falls, and begs with ardent eyes
   Soon to obtain, and long possess the prize:
45 The powers gave ear, and granted half his prayer,
   The rest the winds dispersed in empty air.
     But now secure the painted vessel glides,
   The sunbeams trembling on the floating tides,
   While melting music steals upon the sky,
50 And softened sounds along the waters die.
   Smooth flow the waves, the zephyrs gently play,
   Belinda smiled, and all the world was gay.
   All but the Sylph—with careful thoughts oppressed,
   The impending woe sat heavy on his breast.
55 He summons straight his denizens° of air;   *inhabitants*
   The lucid squadrons round the sails repair:°   *assemble*
   Soft o'er the shrouds aërial whispers breathe
   That seemed but zephyrs to the train beneath.
   Some to the sun their insect-wings unfold,
60 Waft on the breeze, or sink in clouds of gold.
   Transparent forms too fine for mortal sight,
   Their fluid bodies half dissolved in light,
   Loose to the wind their airy garments flew,
   Thin glittering textures of the filmy dew,[4]
65 Dipped in the richest tincture of the skies,
   Where light disports in ever-mingling dyes,
   While every beam new transient colors flings,
   Colors that change whene'er they wave their wings.
   Amid the circle, on the gilded mast,
70 Superior by the head was Ariel placed;
   His purple° pinions opening to the sun,   *brilliant*
   He raised his azure wand, and thus begun:
     "Ye Sylphs and Sylphids, to your chief give ear!

---

[4] The supposed material of spider webs.

Fays, Fairies, Genii, Elves, and Daemons, hear!
75 Ye know the spheres and various tasks assigned
By laws eternal to the aërial kind.
Some in the fields of purest ether play,
And bask and whiten in the blaze of day.
Some guide the course of wandering orbs on high,
80 Or roll the planets through the boundless sky.
Some less refined, beneath the moon's pale light
Pursue the stars that shoot athwart the night,
Or suck the mists in grosser air below,
Or dip their pinions in the painted bow,°   *rainbow*
85 Or brew fierce tempests on the wintry main,
Or o'er the glebe° distill the kindly rain.   *farmland*
Others on earth o'er human race preside,
Watch all their ways, and all their actions guide:
Of these the chief the care of nations own,
90 And guard with arms divine the British Throne.
    "Our humbler province is to tend the Fair,
Not a less pleasing, though less glorious care:
To save the powder from too rude a gale,
Nor let the imprisoned essences exhale;
95 To draw fresh colors from the vernal flowers;
To steal from rainbows e'er they drop in showers
A brighter wash;° to curl their waving hairs,   *(cosmetic) wash*
Assist their blushes, and inspire their airs;
Nay oft, in dreams invention we bestow,
100 To change a flounce, or add a furbelow.
    "This day black omens threat the brightest fair,
That e'er deserved a watchful spirit's care;
Some dire disaster, or by force or slight,
But what, or where, the Fates have wrapped in night:
105 Whether the nymph shall break Diana's law,[5]
Or some frail china jar receive a flaw,
Or stain her honor or her new brocade,
Forget her prayers, or miss a masquerade,
Or lose her heart, or necklace, at a ball;
110 Or whether Heaven has doomed that Shock must fall.
Haste, then, ye spirits! to your charge repair:
The fluttering fan be Zephyretta's care;
The drops° to thee, Brillante, we consign;   *earrings*
And, Momentilla, let the watch be thine;
115 Do thou, Crispissa,[6] tend her favorite Lock;
Ariel himself shall be the guard of Shock.

---

[5] Of chastity.
[6] To "crisp" is to curl (hair).

"To fifty chosen Sylphs, of special note,
We trust the important charge, the petticoat;
Oft have we known that sevenfold fence to fail,
120 Though stiff with hoops, and armed with ribs of whale.
Form a strong line about the silver bound,
And guard the wide circumference around.
"Whatever spirit, careless of his charge,
His post neglects, or leaves the fair at large,
125 Shall feel sharp vengeance soon o'ertake his sins,
Be stopped in vials, or transfixed with pins,
Or plunged in lakes of bitter washes lie,
Or wedged whole ages in a bodkin's° eye;   *large needle's*
Gums and pomatums shall his flight restrain,
130 While clogged he beats his silken wings in vain,
Or alum styptics with contracting power
Shrink his thin essence like a riveled° flower: *shriveled*
Or, as Ixion⁷ fixed, the wretch shall feel
The giddy motion of the whirling mill,°   *cocoa-mill*
135 In fumes of burning chocolate shall glow,
And tremble at the sea that froths below!"
He spoke; the spirits from the sails descend;
Some, orb in orb, around the nymph extend;
Some thread the mazy ringlets of her hair;
140 Some hang upon the pendants of her ear:
With beating hearts the dire event they wait,
Anxious, and trembling for the birth of Fate.

Canto III

Close by those meads, forever crowned with flowers,
Where Thames with pride surveys his rising towers,
There stands a structure of majestic frame,⁸
Which from the neighboring Hampton takes its name.
5 Here Britain's statesmen oft the fall foredoom
Of foreign tyrants and of nymphs at home;
Here thou, great Anna! whom three realms obey,
Dost sometimes counsel take—and sometimes tea.
Hither the heroes and the nymphs resort,
10 To taste awhile the pleasures of a court;
In various talk the instructive hours they passed,
Who gave the ball, or paid the visit last;
One speaks the glory of the British Queen,
And one describes a charming Indian screen;
15 A third interprets motions, looks, and eyes;
At every word a reputation dies.

---

⁷For an affront to Juno, Ixion was bound eternally to a turning wheel.
⁸Hampton Court.

Snuff, or the fan, supply each pause of chat,
With singing, laughing, ogling, and all that.
   Meanwhile, declining from the noon of day,
20 The sun obliquely shoots his burning ray;
The hungry judges soon the sentence sign,
And wretches hang that jurymen may dine;
The merchant from the Exchange° returns in peace,   *stock market*
And the long labors of the toilet cease.
25 Belinda now, whom thirst of fame invites,
Burns to encounter two adventurous knights,
At ombre⁹ singly to decide their doom,
And swells her breast with conquests yet to come.
Straight the three bands prepare in arms° to join,   *combat*
30 Each band the number of the sacred nine.
Soon as she spreads her hand, the aërial guard
Descend, and sit on each important card:
First Ariel perched upon a Matadore,
Then each according to the rank they bore;
35 For Sylphs, yet mindful of their ancient race,
Are, as when women, wondrous fond of place.
   Behold, four Kings in majesty revered,
With hoary whiskers and a forky beard;
And four fair Queens whose hands sustain a flower,
40 The expressive emblem of their softer power;
Four Knaves in garbs succinct,¹ a trusty band,
Caps on their heads, and halberts in their hand;
And parti-colored troops, a shining train,
Draw forth to combat on the velvet plain.
45   The skillful nymph reviews her force with care;
"Let Spades be trumps!" she said, and trumps they were.
   Now move to war her sable Matadores,

---

⁹This game is like three-handed bridge with some features of poker added. From a deck lacking 8's, 9's and 10's, nine cards are dealt to each player (line 30) and the rest put in a central pool. A declarer called the *Ombre* (Spanish *hombre*, man) commits himself to taking more tricks than either of his opponents individually; hence Belinda would "encounter two knights *singly*." Declarer, followed by the other players, then selects discards and replenishes his hand with cards drawn sight unseen from the pool (line 45). He proceeds to name his trumps (line 46). The three principal trumps, called *Matadors* (line 47), always include the black aces. When spades are declared, the Matadors are, in order of value, the ace of spades (called *Spadille*, line 49), the deuce of spades (called *Manille*, line 51), and the ace of clubs (called *Basto*, line 53). The remaining spades fill out the trump suit. In the game here described, Belinda leads out her high trumps (lines 49–56), but the suit breaks badly (line 54); the Baron retains the queen (line 67), with which he presently trumps her king of clubs (line 69). He then leads high diamonds until she is on the verge of a set (called *Codille*, line 92). But she makes her bid at the last trick (line 94), taking his ace of hearts with her king (line 95), this being, in ombre, the highest card in the heart suit. The game is played on a green velvet cloth (line 44).
  ¹Hemmed up short, not flowing.

In show like leaders of the swarthy Moors.
Spadillio first, unconquerable lord!
50 Led off two captive trumps, and swept the board.
As many more Manillio forced to yield,
And marched a victor from the verdant field.
Him Basto followed, but his fate more hard
Gained but one trump and one plebeian card.
55 With his broad saber next, a chief in years,
The hoary Majesty of Spades appears,
Puts forth one manly leg, to sight revealed,
The rest his many-colored robe concealed.
The rebel Knave, who dares his prince engage,
60 Proves the just victim of his royal rage.
Even mighty Pam,[2] that kings and queens o'erthrew
And mowed down armies in the fights of loo,
Sad chance of war! now distitute of aid,
Falls undistinguished by the victor Spade.
65   Thus far both armies to Belinda yield;
Now to the Baron fate inclines the field.
His warlike amazon her host invades,
The imperial consort of the crown of Spades.
The Club's black tyrant first her victim died,
70 Spite of his haughty mien and barbarous pride.
What boots the regal circle on his head,
His giant limbs, in state unwieldy spread?
That long behind he trails his pompous robe.
And of all monarchs only grasps the globe?
75   The Baron now his Diamonds pours apace;
The embroidered King who shows but half his face,
And his refulgent Queen, with powers combined
Of broken troops in easy conquest find.
Clubs, Diamonds, Hearts, in wild disorder seen,
80 With throngs promiscuous strew the level green.
Thus when dispersed a routed army runs,
Of Asia's troops, and Afric's sable sons,
With like confusion different nations fly,
Of various habit,° and of various dye,°   *dress   /   color*
85 The pierced battalions disunited fall
In heaps on heaps; one fate o'erwhelms them all.
   The Knave of Diamonds tries his wily arts,
And wins (oh, shameful chance!) the Queen of Hearts.
At this, the blood the virgin's cheek forsook,
90 A livid paleness spreads o'er all her look;
She sees, and trembles at the approaching ill,
Just in the jaws of ruin, and Codille,

---

[2] The jack of clubs, paramount trump in the game of loo.

And now (as oft in some distempered state)
On one nice trick depends the general fate.
95 An Ace of Hearts steps forth: the King unseen
Lurked in her hand, and mourned his captive Queen.
He springs to vengeance with an eager pace,
And falls like thunder on the prostrate Ace.
The nymph exulting fills with shouts the sky,
100 The walls, the woods, and long canals[3] reply.
    O thoughtless mortals! ever blind to fate,
Too soon dejected, and too soon elate:
Sudden these honors shall be snatched away,
And cursed forever this victorious day.
105   For lo! the board with cups and spoons is crowned,
The berries crackle, and the mill turns round;[4]
On shining altars of Japan[5] they raise
The silver lamp; the fiery spirits blaze:
From silver spouts the grateful liquors glide,
110 While China's earth[6] receives the smoking tide.
At once they gratify their scent and taste,
And frequent cups prolong the rich repast.
Straight hover round the fair her airy band;
Some, as she sipped, the fuming liquor fanned,
115 Some o'er her lap their careful plumes displayed,
Trembling, and conscious of the rich brocade.
Coffee (which makes the politician wise,
And see through all things with his half-shut eyes)
Sent up in vapors to the Baron's brain
120 New stratagems, the radiant Lock to gain.
Ah, cease, rash youth! desist ere 'tis too late,
Fear the just Gods, and think of Scylla's fate![7]
Changed to a bird, and sent to flit in air,
She dearly pays for Nisus' injured hair!
125   But when to mischief mortals bend their will,
How soon they find fit instruments of ill!
Just then, Clarissa drew with tempting grace
A two-edged weapon from her shining case:
So ladies in romance assist their knight,
130 Present the spear, and arm him for the fight.
He takes the gift with reverence, and extends

---

[3] Passages between avenues of trees.
[4] As coffee beans are roasted and ground.
[5] Lacquered tables.
[6] Ceramic cups.
[7] Scylla cut from the head of her father Nisus the lock of hair on which his life depended and gave it to her love Minos of Crete, who was Scylla's enemy. For this she was turned into a sea-bird relentlessly pursued by an eagle.

The little engine on his fingers' ends;
This just behind Belinda's neck he spread,
As o'er the fragrant steams she bends her head.
135 Swift to the Lock a thousand sprites repair,
A thousand wings, by turns, blow back the hair,
And thrice they twitched the diamond in her ear,
Thrice she looked back, and thrice the foe drew near.
Just in that instant, anxious Ariel sought
140 The close recesses of the virgin's thought;
As on the nosegay in her breast reclined,
He watched the ideas rising in her mind,
Sudden he viewed, in spite of all her art,
An earthly lover lurking at her heart.
145 Amazed, confused, he found his power expired,[8]
Resigned to fate, and with a sigh retired.
   The Peer now spreads the glittering forfex° wide,   *scissors*
To enclose the Lock; now joins it, to divide.
Even then, before the fatal engine closed,
150 A wretched Sylph too fondly interposed;
Fate urged the shears, and cut the Sylph in twain
(But airy substance soon unites again):[9]
The meeting points the sacred hair dissever
From the fair head, forever, and forever!
155   Then flashed the living lightning from her eyes,
And screams of horror rend the affrighted skies.
Not louder shrieks to pitying heaven are cast,
When husbands, or when lapdogs breathe their last;
Or when rich china vessels fallen from high,
160 In glittering dust and painted fragments lie!
"Let wreaths of triumph now my temples twine,"
The victor cried, "the glorious prize is mine!
While fish in streams, or birds delight in air,
Or in a coach and six the British Fair,
165 As long as *Atalantis*[1] shall be read,
Or the small pillow grace a lady's bed,
While visits shall be paid on solemn days,
When numerous wax-lights in bright order blaze,[2]
While nymphs take treats, or assignations give,
170 So long my honor, name, and praise shall live!
What Time would spare, from Steel receives its date,°   *termination*
And monuments, like men, submit to fate!

---

[8] Belinda, being strongly attracted to the Baron (line 144), can no longer merely coquette. She hence passes beyond Ariel's control.

[9] Again as with Milton's angels (*Paradise Lost* VI.329–31).

[1] A set of memoirs which, under thin disguise, recounted actual scandals.

[2] Attending the formal evening visits of the previous line.

Steel could the labor of the Gods destroy,[3]
And strike to dust the imperial towers of Troy;
175 Steel could the works of mortal pride confound,
And hew triumphal arches to the ground.
What wonder then, fair nymph! thy hairs should feel,
The conquering force of unresisted Steel?"

Canto IV

But anxious cares the pensive nymph oppressed,
And secret passions labored in her breast.
Not youthful kings in battle seized alive,
Not scornful virgins who their charms survive,
5 Not ardent lovers robbed of all their bliss,
Not ancient ladies when refused a kiss,
Not tyrants fierce that unrepenting die,
Not Cynthia when her manteau's[4] pinned awry,
E'er felt such rage, resentment, and despair,
10 As thou, sad virgin! for thy ravished hair.
   For, that sad moment, when the Sylphs withdrew
And Ariel weeping from Belinda flew,
Umbriel,[5] a dusky, melancholy sprite
As ever sullied the fair face of light,
15 Down to the central earth, his proper scene,
Repaired to search the gloomy Cave of Spleen.[6]
   Swift on his sooty pinions flits the Gnome,
And in a vapor reached the dismal dome.
No cheerful breeze this sullen region knows,
20 The dreaded east is all the wind that blows.
Here in a grotto, sheltered close from air,
And screened in shades from day's detested glare,
She sighs forever on her pensive bed,
Pain at her side, and Megrim° at her head.   *migraine*
25   Two handmaids wait the throne: alike in place,
But differing far in figure and in face.
Here stood Ill-Nature like an ancient maid,
Her wrinkled form in black and white arrayed;
With store of prayers for mornings, nights, and noons,

---

[3] Troy (named in the next line) was built by Apollo and Poseidon.
[4] i.e., robe is.
[5] Suggesting *umbra,* shadow; and *umber,* brown. The final *el* of this name is a further reminiscence of Milton's angels: Gabriel, Abdiel, Zophiel.
[6] This journey is formally equivalent to Odysseus' and Aeneas' visits to the underworld. "Spleen" refers to the human organ, the supposed seat of melancholy; hence to melancholy itself. Believed to be induced by misty weather such as the east wind brings (lines 18–20), the condition was also called the "vapors." In its severer manifestations it tends toward madness; in its milder forms, it issues in peevishness and suspicion.

30 Her hand is filled; her bosom with lampoons.°   *slanders*
 There Affectation, with a sickly mien,
Shows in her cheek the roses of eighteen,
Practiced to lisp, and hang the head aside,
Faints into airs, and languishes with pride,
35 On the rich quilt sinks with becoming woe,
Wrapped in a gown, for sickness and for show.
The fair ones feel such maladies as these,
When each new nightdress gives a new disease.
 A constant vapor o'er the palace flies,
40 Strange phantoms rising as the mists arise;
Dreadful as hermit's dreams in haunted shades,
Or bright as visions of expiring maids.
Now glaring fiends, and snakes on rolling spires,°   *coils*
Pale specters, gaping tombs, and purple fires;
45 Now lakes of liquid gold, Elysian scenes,
And crystal domes, and angels in machines.[7]
 Unnumbered throngs on every side are seen
Of bodies changed to various forms by Spleen.
Here living teapots stand, one arm held out,
50 One bent; the handle this, and that the spout:
A pipkin[8] there, like Homer's tripod, walks;
Here sighs a jar, and there a goose pie talks;
Men prove with child, as powerful fancy works,
And maids, turned bottles, call aloud for corks.
55 Safe passed the Gnome through this fantastic band,
A branch of healing spleenwort[9] in his hand.
Then thus addressed the Power: "Hail, wayward Queen!
Who rule the sex to fifty from fifteen:
Parent of vapors and of female wit,
60 Who give the hysteric or poetic fit,
On various tempers act by various ways,
Make some take physic, others scribble plays;
Who cause the proud their visits to delay,
And send the godly in a pet to pray.
65 A nymph there is that all thy power disdains,
And thousands more in equal mirth maintains.
But oh! if e'er thy Gnome could spoil a grace,
Or raise a pimple on a beauteous face,
Like citron-waters° matrons' cheeks inflame,   *orange brandy*

---

 [7] These images are both 1) the hallucinations of insane melancholy and 2) parodies of
stage properties and effects.
 [8] An earthen pot; it walks like the three-legged stools which Vulcan made for the gods
in *Iliad* XVIII.
 [9] A kind of fern, purgative of spleen; suggesting the golden bough which Aeneas bore
as a passport to Hades in *Aeneid* VI.

70 Or change complexions at a losing game;
   If e'er with airy horns I planted heads,[1]
   Or rumpled petticoats, or tumbled beds,
   Or caused suspicion when no soul was rude,
   Or discomposed the headdress of a prude,
75 Or e'er to costive lapdog gave disease,
   Which not the tears of brightest eyes could ease,
   Hear me, and touch Belinda with chagrin:°   *annoyance*
   That single act gives half the world the spleen."
      The Goddess with a discontented air
80 Seems to reject him though she grants his prayer.
   A wondrous bag with both her hands she binds,
   Like that where once Ulysses held the winds;[2]
   There she collects the force of female lungs,
   Sighs, sobs, and passions, and the war of tongues.
85 A vial next she fills with fainting fears,
   Soft sorrows, melting griefs, and flowing tears.
   The Gnome rejoicing bears her gifts away,
   Spreads his black wings, and slowly mounts to day.
      Sunk in Thalestris'[3] arms the nymph he found,
90 Her eyes dejected and her hair unbound.
   Full o'er their heads the swelling bag he rent,
   And all the Furies issued at the vent.
   Belinda burns with more than mortal ire,
   And fierce Thalestris fans the rising fire.
95 "O wretched maid!" she spreads her hands, and cried
   (While Hampton's echoes, "Wretched maid!" replied),
   "Was it for this you took such constant care
   The bodkin,° comb, and essence to prepare?   *hairpin*
   For this your locks in paper durance bound,
100 For this with torturing irons wreathed around?
   For this with fillets° strained your tender head,   *bands*
   And bravely bore the double loads of lead?[4]
   Gods! shall the ravisher display your hair,
   While the fops envy, and the ladies stare!
105 Honor forbid! at whose unrivaled shrine
   Ease, pleasure, virtue, all, our sex resign.
   Methinks already I your tears survey,
   Already hear the horrid things they say,
   Already see you a degraded toast,
110 And all your honor in a whisper lost!

---

[1] i.e., made men imagine they were being cuckolded.
[2] Aeolus, the wind god, enabled Odysseus so to contain all adverse winds in *Odyssey* X.
[3] The name of an Amazon.
[4] The means by which Belinda's locks were fashioned into a ringlet: lead strips held her curl papers in place.

How shall I, then, your helpless fame defend?
'Twill then be infamy to seem your friend!
And shall this prize, the inestimable prize,
Exposed through crystal to the gazing eyes,
115 And heightened by the diamond's circling rays,
On that rapacious hand forever blaze?
Sooner shall grass in Hyde Park Circus[5] grow,
And wits take lodgings in the sound of Bow;[6]
Sooner let earth, air, sea, to chaos fall,
120 Men, monkeys, lapdogs, parrots, perish all!"
    She said; then raging to Sir Plume repairs,
And bids her beau demand the precious hairs
(Sir Plume of amber snuffbox justly vain,
And the nice° conduct° of a clouded cane).   *precise / handling*
125 With earnest eyes, and round unthinking face,
He first the snuffbox opened, then the case,
And thus broke out—"My Lord, why, what the devil!
Zounds! damn the lock! 'fore Gad, you must be civil!
Plague on't! 'tis past a jest—nay prithee, pox!
130 Give her the hair"—he spoke, and rapped his box.
    "It grieves me much," replied the Peer again,
"Who speaks so well should ever speak in vain.
But by this Lock, this sacred Lock I swear
(Which never more shall join its parted hair;
135 Which never more its honors shall renew,
Clipped from the lovely head where late it grew),
That while my nostrils draw the vital air,
This hand, which won it, shall forever wear."
He spoke, and speaking, in proud triumph spread
140 The long-contended honors° of her head.   *ornaments*
    But Umbriel, hateful Gnome, forbears not so;
He breaks the vial whence the sorrows flow.
Then see! the nymph is beauteous grief appears,
Her eyes half languishing, half drowned in tears;
145 On her heaved bosom hung her drooping head,
Which with a sigh she raised, and thus she said:
    "Forever cursed be this detested day,
Which snatched my best, my favorite curl away!
Happy! ah, ten times happy had I been,
150 If Hampton Court these eyes had never seen!
Yet am not I the first mistaken maid,
By love of courts to numerous ills betrayed.
Oh, had I rather unadmired remained

---

[5] The fashionable carriage course (the "Ring" of I.44).
[6] i.e., the sound of the bells of Bowchurch in the unfashionable commercial section of London.

In some lone isle, or distant northern land;
155 Where the gilt chariot never marks the way,
Where none learn ombre, none e'er taste bohea!°   *fine tea*
There kept my charms concealed from mortal eye,
Like roses that in deserts bloom and die.
What moved my mind with youthful lords to roam?
160 Oh, had I stayed, and said my prayers at home!
'Twas this the morning omens seemed to tell,
Thrice from my trembling hand the patch box[7] fell;
The tottering china shook without a wind,
Nay, Poll sat mute, and Shock as most unkind!
165 A Sylph too warned me of the threats of fate,
In mystic visions, now believed too late!
See the poor remnants of these slighted hairs!
My hands shall rend what e'en thy rapine spares.
These in two sable ringlets taught to break,
170 Once gave new beauties to the snowy neck;
The sister lock now sits uncouth, alone,
And in its fellow's fate foresees its own;
Uncurled it hangs, the fatal shears demands,
And tempts once more thy sacrilegious hands.
175 Oh, hadst thou, cruel! been content to seize
Hairs less in sight, or any hairs but these!"

Canto V

She said: the pitying audience melt in tears.
But Fate and Jove had stopped the Baron's ears.
In vain Thalestris with reproach assails,
For who can move when fair Belinda fails?
5 Not half so fixed the Trojan could remain,
While Anna begged and Dido raged in vain.[8]
Then grave Clarissa graceful waved her fan;
Silence ensued, and thus the nymph began:
"Say why are beauties praised and honored most,
10 The wise man's passion, and the vain man's toast?
Why decked with all that land and sea afford,
Why angels called, and angel-like adored?
Why round our coaches crowd the white-gloved beaux,
Why bows the side box from its inmost rows?
15 How vain are all these glories, all our pains,
Unless good sense preserve what beauty gains;
That men may say when we the front box grace,

---

[7] A box for ornamental patches to accent the face.
[8] Aeneas was determined to leave Carthage for Italy, though the enamored queen Dido raved and her sister Anna pleaded with him to stay.

'Behold the first in virtue as in face!'
Oh! if to dance all night, and dress all day,
20 Charmed the smallpox, or chased old age away,
Who would not scorn what housewife's cares produce,
Or who would learn one earthly thing of use?
To patch, nay ogle, might become a saint,
Nor could it sure be such a sin to paint.
25 But since, alas! frail beauty must decay,
Curled or uncurled, since locks will turn to gray;
Since painted, or not painted, all shall fade,
And she who scorns a man must die a maid;
What then remains but well our power to use,
30 And keep good humor still whate'er we lose?
And trust me, dear, good humor can prevail
When airs, and flights, and screams, and scolding fail.
Beauties in vain their pretty eyes may roll;
Charms strike the sight, but merit wins the soul."[9]
35   So spoke the dame, but no applause ensued;
Belinda frowned, Thalestris called her prude.
"To arms, to arms!" the fierce virago cries,
And swift as lightning to the combat flies.
All side in parties, and begin the attack;
40 Fans clap, silks rustle, and tough whalebones crack;
Heroes' and heroines' shouts confusedly rise,
And bass and treble voices strike the skies.
No common weapons in their hands are found,
Like Gods they fight, nor dread a mortal wound.
45   So when bold Homer makes the Gods engage,
And heavenly breasts with human passions rage;
'Gainst Pallas, Mars; Latona, Hermes arms;[1]
And all Olympus rings with loud alarms:
Jove's thunder roars, heaven trembles all around,
50 Blue Neptune storms, the bellowing deeps resound:
Earth shakes her nodding towers, the ground gives way,
And the pale ghosts start at the flash of day!
   Triumphant Umbriel on a sconce's height
Clapped his glad wings, and sat to view the fight:
55 Propped on the bodkin spears, the sprites survey
The growing combat, or assist the fray.
   While through the press enraged Thalestris flies,
And scatters death around from both her eyes,
A beau and witling perished in the throng,

---

[9] Clarissa's address parallels a speech in *Iliad* XII, wherein Sarpedon tells Glaucus that, as leaders of the army, they must justify their privilege by extraordinary prowess.

[1] Mars arms against Pallas, and Hermes against Latona in *Iliad* XX. The tangled syntax is supposed to mirror the press of battle.

60 One died in metaphor, and one in song.
   "O cruel nymph! a living death I bear,"
   Cried Dapperwit, and sunk beside his chair.
   A mournful glance Sir Fopling upwards cast,
   "Those eyes are made so killing"—was his last.
65 Thus on Maeander's flowery margin lies
   The expiring swan, and as he sings he dies.
      When bold Sir Plume had drawn Clarissa down,
   Chloe stepped in, and killed him with a frown;
   She smiled to see the doughty hero slain,
70 But, at her smile, the beau revived again.
      Now Jove suspends his golden scales in air,[2]
   Weighs the men's wits against the lady's hair;
   The doubtful beam long nods from side to side;
   At length the wits mount up, the hairs subside.
75   See, fierce Belinda on the Baron flies,
   With more than usual lightning in her eyes;
   Nor feared the chief the unequal fight to try,
   Who sought no more than on his foe to die.
      But this bold lord with manly strength endued,
80 She with one finger and a thumb subdued:
   Just where the breath of life his nostrils drew,
   A charge of snuff the wily virgin threw;
   The Gnomes direct, to every atom just,
   The pungent grains of titillating dust.
85 Sudden, with starting tears each eye o'erflows,
   And the high dome re-echoes to his nose.
      "Now meet thy fate," incensed Belinda cried,
   And drew a deadly bodkin[3] from her side.
   (The same, his ancient personage to deck,
90 Her great-great-grandsire wore about his neck,
   In three seal rings; which after, melted down,
   Formed a vast buckle for his widow's gown:
   Her infant grandame's whistle next it grew,
   The bells she jingled, and the whistle blew;
95 Then in a bodkin graced her mother's hairs,
   Which long she wore, and now Belinda wears.)
      "Boast not my fall," he cried, "insulting foe!
   Thou by some other shalt be laid as low.
   Nor think to die dejects my lofty mind:
100 All that I dread is leaving you behind!
   Rather than so, ah, let me still survive,
   And burn in Cupid's flames—but burn alive."

---

[2] He so weighs the fortunes of war in classical epic.

[3] Here an ornamental hairpin. Its history suggests that of Agamemnon's scepter in *Iliad* II. "Seal rings" (line 91) are for impressing seals on letters and legal documents.

"Restore the Lock!" she cries; and all around
"Restore the Lock!" the vaulted roofs rebound.
105 Not fierce Othello in so loud a strain
Roared for the handkerchief that caused his pain.[4]
But see how oft ambitious aims are crossed,
And chiefs contend till all the prize is lost!
The lock, obtained with guilt, and kept with pain,
110 In every place is sought, but sought in vain:
With such a prize no mortal must be blessed,
So Heaven decrees! with Heaven who can contest?
Some thought it mounted to the lunar sphere,
Since all things lost on earth are treasured there.
115 There heroes' wits are kept in ponderous vases,
And beaux' in snuffboxes and tweezer cases.
There broken vows and deathbed alms are found,
And lovers' hearts with ends of riband bound,
The courtier's promises, and sick man's prayers,
120 The smiles of harlots, and the tears of heirs,
Cages for gnats, and chains to yoke a flea,
Dried butterflies, and tomes of casuistry.
But trust the Muse—she saw it upward rise,
Though marked by none but quick, poetic eyes
125 (So Rome's great founder to the heavens withdrew,
To Proculus alone confessed in view);
A sudden star, it shot through liquid° air,   *clear*
And drew behind a radiant trail of hair.
Not Berenice's locks first rose so bright,
130 The heavens bespangling with disheveled light.
The Sylphs behold it kindling as it flies,
And pleased pursue its progress through the skies.
This the beau monde shall from the Mall survey,
And hail with music its propitious ray.
135 This the blest lover shall for Venus take,
And send up vows from Rosamonda's Lake.
This Partridge soon shall view in cloudless skies,
When next he looks through Galileo's eyes;
And hence the egregious wizard shall foredoom
140 The fate of Louis, and the fall of Rome.
Then cease, bright nymph! to mourn thy ravished hair,
Which adds new glory to the shining sphere!
Not all the tresses that fair head can boast,
Shall draw such envy as the Lock you lost.
145 For, after all the murders of your eye,
When, after millions slain, yourself shall die:
When those fair suns shall set, as set they must,

---

[4] In *Othello* III.iv.

And all those tresses shall be laid in dust,
This Lock the Muse shall consecrate to fame,
150 And 'midst the stars inscribe Belinda's name.

ACCOUNT: KATE BEAIRD MEYERS ON
A READER-RESPONSE APPROACH TO
THE RAPE OF THE LOCK

Meyers says that even recent critical methods like Reader-Response Approaches to the poem have commonly tended to reinforce the traditional meaning of Pope's mock epic. The basic trouble behind all such results is that by imagining "the reader" as a single ideal, critics fail to take account of the fact that a reader may be of one gender or another. And when the male perspective on the poem is automatically attributed to women readers, it "*immasculates*" them. That is, just as to *e*masculate a man is to take away his maleness, to *im*masculate a woman is to attribute male qualities to her. But by *refusing* to take on an attributed male identity, the response of female readers "produces a considerably different story than the traditional one and reveals a new layer in an already multilayered text."

The idea of the "immasculated" female reader is first illustrated by the intentions of the letter to Arabella Fermor that precedes the poem and makes the true beginning of the work as a whole. In that letter, Pope assumes that Arabella will adopt a "masculinist" reading, and that she will therefore share in his laughter at "the little unguarded follies" of the female sex. Meyers says:

> Pope's duplicity is apparent from the first sentence. His claim that the poem is written for Arabella is false. The person to whom Pope actually addresses the poem is his friend John Caryll (see 1.3). Arabella's story, told to Pope by Caryll, may have "inspired" the poem, but it is Caryll and other males who are his "intended readers" (see 1.6). Pope's antifeminism appears full-blown in the second sentence: The poem is intended to "divert a few young ladies, who have good sense and good humor enough to laugh not only at their sex's little unguarded follies, but at their own." The choice of "divert" is perfect: Pope hopes to divert attention away from his act of misogynous judgment and focus it on what he calls the "folly" of female *nature*. Like the more or less formalist readers with whom reader-response criticism argues, Pope attempts to present activity and relationship as some reified, unchanging "nature."

From Kate Beaird Meyers, "Feminist Hermeneutics and Reader-Response: The Role of Gender in Reading *The Rape of the Lock.*" *The New Orleans Review*, 15, no. 4 (1988) 43–50.

Meyers says that at this point in the poem begins for her what Stanley Fish, the Reader-Response theorist, has called the "succession of decisions" by which she will "resist" the text and become an "unintended reader." For example, Pope's linking of Belinda to the Sylphs may be read by a resisting reader as a threat to women that male society will afford them protection only as long as they cooperated in maintaining their chastity. That is, "the woman who strays loses the protection of the same society that led her astray in the first place."

Pope wants to preserve the social status quo (Meyers says) because (ironically) he fears the power of women's "otherness"—of her link to the dark forces of "nature" that are opposed to Pope's patriarchal "civilization":

> The site of her chastity is a dark place that men can only visit, leaving fragments of themselves and getting momentary pleasure in return. Woman's "chastity" represents a gap in her access to the mysterious powers of Nature. As long as she is kept chaste, the object of male desire, woman cannot know her own innate power as subject.

By looking at the poem in the way that these examples suggest, the "immasculated reader" may be "de-immasculated" and find her allegiance, not with the hero in restoring order and in disapproving of Belinda, but in "identifying herself" with Belinda, the "other" against whom Pope seems to be writing. To read with Belinda may be difficult, but the patriarchal, "negative satirical reading" of Pope's poem *can* be resisted:

> A feminist re-reading of *The Rape of the Lock* exposes a sub-text layered in between the primary story and the epic form of the discourse, a sub-text that articulates female power in its very otherness. Belinda, whose locks give her a great deal of power, is raped (with scissors) by a "hero" who lacks power. By figuratively castrating Belinda—the "other" who (at least in Western culture) should *lack* power—the "hero" regains control of his society.

Such a reading casts a new light on many aspects of the poem. For example, the grotesque nature of the poem's mock violence comes, in part, from a reversal. Belinda has been taught that the penis is the only recognized sexual organ of value, so she makes use of every means to appropriate that organ for herself. Her own powers of sexuality are figured in her locks, and "rather than one sex organ, Belinda has grown two." Further, in using the scissors, the Baron employs

> an instrument that unites in its design the phallus (closed) and the vagina (opened). Imitating his version of the female power he so fears— the woman who can cut him off from Nature, just by closing her legs together—the Baron "spreads the glitt'ring *Forfex* wide,/T'inclose the

Lock; now joins it, to divide" (3.147–48). In a sort of reverse rape, the hero castrates the too-powerful female returning her to a position of powerlessness.

Meyers says that this resistant reading of the poem as a story of reverse penis envy "turns all the violence and almost palpable misogyny of the poem back on itself." Yet by translating the warfare that makes the subject of the traditional epic into the sexual warfare of this *mock* epic, Pope suggests a possible positive Feminist re-reading, a "utopian" one that substitutes the powers of love for the powers of killing in the way Blake's myths were later to do. Meyers concludes that, for any reading of the poem:

> Sexual difference must be acknowledged as legitimate grounds for literary interpretation; the power of validation must be distributed equally among all participants.

In other words, a female reader such as Pope seems at first to imagine—an "immasculated" female—must not be allowed to define the ideal of female response to the poem. Readings like that Meyers has performed—readings she calls de-immasculated ones—must also be acknowledged as equally valid responses to the mock-epic product of Pope's imagination.

ACCOUNT: TOM BOWDEN ON A MARXIST APPROACH TO *THE RAPE OF THE LOCK*

Bowden posits that the perpetual war of the sexes figured and parodied in Pope's poem has its origins in an economic system of commodification—a system that turns unique, valuable, and invisible qualities like honor into commodities that may be exchanged for others:

> [T]o be reproducible is to be replaceable; to be replaceable is to be commodified, subject to the forces of the marketplace. And when people live as products of commodification, like brocades and china, then no substantive difference between people and store-bought goods prevails, so that a reproducible commodity representing a specialized activity (such as a Lord or a Lady) collapses psychological motivation. One simply does or does not commit specific acts because such acts exist strictly inside or outside of one's specialization and so simply are or are not done.

From Tom Bowden, "Postmodern Pope: *The Rape of the Lock*; Or, Have a Nice Day." *The New Orleans Review* 15, no. 4 (1988) 60–67.

But Pope's satire also implies a lost world that truly distinguished between honor and hair. In such a world, actions "are or are not done" out of a non-commercial code of values. With the loss of such a code come other losses such as Belinda's lack of distinction between flirtatiousness and disdain. A world that mechanizes human life erases the differences between the material and the non-material, between the "use-value" and "exchange value" of physical objects and the metaphysical aspects of life.

The poem itself wonderfully counterfeits bad poetry in some of its clunky lines and exaggerated images, showing that bad poetry is itself mechanically reproducible. More surprising, Pope takes his own translation of Sarpedon's speech to Glaucus in the *Iliad* and (with only minor changes) transforms high drama into parody. In this way he gives equal exchange-value to the two poetic performances by "turning his twenty-five line passage into a tradable commodity":

> In theory at least, Pope could manufacture passage after similar, equivalent, and exchangeable passage, and by so doing blur the distinction between and the significance of both context and the forms of literary genres (tragedy and parody in this case), and imply the paradoxical simultaneity of contrary interpretation of those passages, resulting in a literature of ambivalence.

By making everything "exchangeable," the characters in *The Rape of the Lock* are denied uniqueness and individuality. Viewed as objects to be acted on, they are reduced to their exchange value. To the commodified world of the poem, Bowden says, it ultimately does not really matter that the Baron cuts off Belinda's lock because—in a world where honor is no longer an individual matter but a matter of exchange value—*any* Baron could cut off *any* lock with the same effects:

> In *The Rape of the Lock*, a system of commodification controls and makes a product of Belinda, preying upon and encouraging her ignorance and vanity. Narrating a situation in which divine intervention will supposedly protect her from the men lured to her by her coiffure and dress, Pope creates a character who resists that intervention, for whom a stained honor means less than a stained brocade because honor is invisible.

For the Baron, Belinda is a prize to be possessed like any other commodity. Love has nothing to do with such a process of possession in a world where hair matters more than honor. And by the end of the poem, the battle of the sexes is "reified" (that is, turned into a *thing* in itself) when a constellation in the heavens appears in the shape of Belinda's lock. Bowden describes the process at work as follows:

> Pope maintains the blur between person and marketable object, between material object and non-material ideals in the following passages:

On her white Breast a sparkling Cross she wore,
Which Jews might kiss, and infidels adore.

(2.7–8)

But what, or where, the Fates have wrapt in Night.
Whether the Nymph shall break *Diana's* law,
Or some frail *China* jar receive a Flaw,
Or stain her Honour or her new Brocade,
Or lose her Heart, or Necklace, at a Ball;
Or whether Heav'n has doom'd that *Shock* must fall.

(2.104–10)

Bowden says that the joke of Pope's mock epic tells us his characters do not distinguish between kissing a cross and kissing a breast, and that for Belinda no meaningful difference exists between missing a dance and forgetting to pray.

In a world without meaningful differences, the enhancements of Belinda's beauty, such as jewelry and makeup, are indistinguishable from the effects of that beauty. And, being themselves products of consumption, the enhancements cumulatively increase the value of the commodity she represents. Yet all the adornments may be purchased by *anyone*, and so the Baron's treatment of love as the collection of trophies makes the masculine equivalent of the world's basic confusion between unique values and exchange values.

> Belinda may assign commodities to herself to shape her physical and figurative appearance to others, her commodities acting as signs telling others how to read her, engendering product recognition. By assigning commodities to herself, she wishes to assimilate as much as possible those products in hopes of reifying and making visible an array of absent or invisible qualities with which she desires associations—a certain way of life and economic standing and a fine sense of taste and discrimination.

By looking at the poem in a Marxist way, Bowden points to economic underpinnings that he says support what might seem only a tale of social frivolity. Or rather, he suggests a way that frivolity may be seen to take on a very serious meaning in the poem. That is, frivolous social actions become a sign and symbol of an economic set of values that has come to pervade the whole of society.

SUGGESTIONS FOR DISCUSSION AND WRITING

1. Pope's poem is "mock heroic" in spirit. How does his versification contribute to that spirit? How do you **scan** the first two lines? What kind of **meter** does the poet use? What kind of **feet** are employed and how many appear in each line? How are the lines organized by **rhyme scheme**? How do you have to pronounce "amorous" (1.1) and "trivial" (1.2) to keep the lines **regular**? How regular are the first ten lines? Locate Pope's modulations. What uses do Meyers and Bowden make of the mockery created in their new analyses?

2. Characterize the **tone of voice** employed by Pope's **narrator** or **speaker**. What is the **dramatic situation** announced at the beginning of the poem and played out within it? How do Pope's **images** work in the beginning to create his comic manner? How does his **irony** say one thing and mean another? Find two examples of irony in the early part of the poem and explain exactly how each invites the reader to respond. Is irony the same as mockery for the two critics?

3. Both Meyers and Bowden agree that, as a subject, the mock epic substitutes the **figurative** "war" of the sexes for the **literal** wars that make the subject of the traditional **epic** like *The Iliad*, *The Aneiad*, or *Paradise Lost*. Yet they disagree to some extent on the results of Pope's substitution. Pick a passage from the poem that concerns itself in some way with warfare and write a brief essay comparing and contrasting the interpretations that you think Meyers and Bowden would each make of the passage.

4. Look at Thomas Gray's "Ode. . . ." (p. 467). This poem also might be seen to concern itself with the themes of women and "commodification." Though not about war, it too is written in a mock-heroic style. How do you think Meyers and Bowden would each interpret that poem? Make some notes for class discussion or for an essay. Compare Gray's versification, his speaker, and any other aspects that seem pertinent to their equivalents in Pope's poem.

5. Pick another critical approach and make some notes for class discussion or for an essay in which you explore a passage within *The Rape of the Lock* by its aid. What, for example, might a structuralist like Todorov (see p. 174) make of a poem that revolves so importantly around the presence or absence of a lock of hair?

Chapter Twelve

Approaches to William Wordsworth's "A Slumber Did My Spirit Seal"

WILLIAM WORDSWORTH (1770–1850) was born in the beautiful Lake District of England in 1770. As a boy, Wordsworth loved to roam the countryside; his fascination with nature continued throughout his life and his poetry. Although his parents died when Wordsworth was quite young, his education was provided for: In 1787 he entered Cambridge. After graduating, Wordsworth visited France, where he sympathized with the Revolution. He fell in love with a young Frenchwoman, Anette Vallon, who later bore him a child. The Reign of Terror, however, prevented him from returning to France, and the two were never married. He settled in Dorsetshire with his sister Dorothy and eventually relocated to Grasmere, in the Lake District, where he lived for the rest of his life. His friendship with Samuel Taylor Coleridge resulted in their joint publication in 1798 of *Lyrical Ballads*, one of the first landmarks of English Romanticism. "A Slumber Did My Spirit Seal," one of the so-called "Lucy" poems, first appeared in *Lyrical Ballads*.

WILLIAM WORDSWORTH
A Slumber Did My Spirit Seal
(1800)

A slumber did my spirit seal;
   I had no human fears—
She seemed a thing that could not feel
   The touch of earthly years.

5 No motion has she now, no force;
   She neither hears nor sees;
Rolled round in earth's diurnal course,
   With rocks, and stones, and trees.

ACCOUNT: GEOFFREY HARTMAN ON A PSYCHOANALYTIC APPROACH TO "A SLUMBER DID MY SPIRIT SEAL"

According to Hartman, one of Freud's great virtues is that he neither curses nor blesses the knowledge brought to the surface by his interpretations of the subconscious in general or of dreams in particular. This is true even though the dream language is often "ordinary"—one of his own dreams was partially about noodles and overcoats, for example—while *the language by which the dream was interpreted* is "hieratic," that is, a language supposedly more important because it seems "scientific" through its use of many Latin and Greek terms, with their implied greater status and importance. Freud refuses to "evaluate" his results, even though the knowledge obtained is sometimes frightening.*

Hartman says that Wordsworth's poem operates in a similar way. It too refuses to overvalue through language any one of the psychological discoveries it records, even though some of them are very threatening and potentially embarrassing. Hartman says:

> "A slumber did my spirit seal." After that line one would expect a dream vision. The formula is, I fell asleep, and behold! Yet here is no vision, or not in the expected sense. The boundary between slumber and vision is elided. That the poet had no human fears, that he experienced a curious anesthesia vis-a-vis the girl's mortality or his own, may be what he names a slumber. As out of Adam's first sleep an Eve arose, so out of this sealed but not unconscious spirit a womanly image arises with the same idolatrous charm. Wordsworth's image seems to come from within: It is a delusive daydream, yet still a revision of that original vision.

Similarly, the second stanza does not express disillusionment when the calm of the first stanza is changed to something else. "Both transitions, the passage from slumber to dream, and the breaking of the dream are described without surprise or shock."

Yet, for all this calm on the tonal level, there is still a strong "displacement" on the structural level: The speaker's slumber has (in Freudian terms) been "transferred," and *sleep* becomes intensified in the *death* of the girl.

Hartman goes on to look at some reactions to the poem by other readers. He says that Coleridge thought the poem to be really an imaginary epitaph written for Wordsworth's sister, Dorothy, with whom William was very close. More recently, F. W. Bateson seized on this remark to claim that the poem (and all the "Lucy" poems) "arose from

* "One Interpreter's Freud" *Raritan Review* (Fall 1984)

incestuous emotions and expressed a death wish by the brother against the sister." Of this contention, Hartman says:

> But the question for literary criticism, even as it engages with psycho-analysis, is why such a wish, at once idealizing and deadly, and as if fulfilled in the second stanza, does not disturb the poet's language more. Even if the death did not occur except in idea, one might expect the spirit to awake, and to wonder what kind of deception it had practiced on itself. Yet though the poem can be said to approach mute-ness—if we interpret the blank between the stanzas as another elision, a lesion in fact—Wordsworth keeps speech going without a trace of guilty knowledge. The eyes of the spirit may be open, but the diction remains unperturbed.

How can this be? How can the poem maintain such a calm in the face of such shocking subjects? Hartman says the answer partly lies in the euphemistic qualities of ordinary language: "Slumber" is a possible euphemism for "death," for example. Similarly, it is no surprise that epitaphs (if the poem is an imaginary epitaph) commonly carry words of consolation or elevation:

> Here, however, not all the words are consoling. They approach a negative that could foreclose the poem: "No...No...Neither...Nor..." Others even show Wordsworth's language penetrated by an inappropriate subliminal punning. So "diurnal" divides into "die" and "urn," and "course" may recall the older pronunciation of "corpse." Yet these condensations are troublesome rather than expressive: The power of the second stanza resides predominantly in the euphemistic displacement of *grave* by an image of *gravitation* ("Rolled round in earth's diurnal course"). And though there is no agreement on the tone of this stanza, it is clear that a subvocal word is uttered without being written out. It is a word that rhymes with "fears" and "years" and "hears" but which is closed off by the very last syllable of the poem: "trees." Read *tears*, and the animating, cosmic metaphor comes alive, the poet's lament echoes through nature as in pastoral elegy. "Tears," however, must give way to what is written to a dull yet definitive sound, the anagram "trees."

Another fact that the "ordinary" language of the poem may keep us from seeing directly is how close the poem in some ways is to the more "elevated" traditions of pastoral elegy in which rocks, woods, and streams are called upon to join in mourning and to weep for the loss of the beloved.

But Hartman suggests a reason for the absence of explicit grief here. He proposes that Wordsworth found the ecstatic *feelings* that nature evoked in him to do the *work* of mourning that a special "higher" language of mourning might do for others:

Whether beautiful or frightening, they sustain and nourish him as intimations of immortality; and though Wordsworth can be called the first ego psychologist, the first careful observer of the growth of a mind, he shows the disruptive strength of those ecstatic memories as they threaten the maturing poet who must respect their drive. If there is a death wish in the Lucy poems, it is insinuated by nature itself and asks lover or growing child not to give up earlier yearnings—to die rather than become an ordinary mortal.

In Wordsworth's manner of expressing "thoughts too deep for tears" by giving them language that does them justice without judging them or making one thought seem more important than another, Hartman finds Wordsworth's manner as a psychoanalytic interpreter to rival that of Freud. He sees both men as psychoanalysts who explore the "dark" regions of mind and emotion without feeling the need to claim special importance either for those regions or for their own explorations. They avoid those kinds of claims by avoiding an overvaluation of any given mode of language that would describe their discoveries—thus, they neither bless nor curse them.

ACCOUNT: J. HILLIS MILLER ON A POST-STRUCTURALIST APPROACH TO "A SLUMBER DID MY SPIRIT SEAL"

Miller begins by saying that a deconstructive reading is one that will show how, in any work of literature, metaphysical assumptions are both present in the text and at the same time undermined by the play of the figures of speech that express those assumptions. To read by following out the implications of figures of speech or "tropes" is therefore a process that truly "boggles the mind" by creating contradictory meanings. Further, such contradictions are *not* resolvable by the usual methods of rationality, including that whereby opposites are dialectically resolved into a "synthesis."

Wordsworth's poem at first seems to be organized around many of the opposites that are traditionally resolvable, and in fact the poem gives the illusion of reconciling them. We see among other oppositions:

slumber as against waking; male as against female; sealed up as against open; seeming as against being; ignorance as against knowledge; past as against present; inside as against outside; light as against darkness in the "diurnal" course of the earth; subject or consciousness, "spirit" as against object, the natural world of stones and trees; feeling as "touch" as against feeling as emotion, "fears"; "human fears" as against—what?— perhaps inhuman fears; "thing" in its meaning of "girl," young virgin, as against "thing" in the sense of physical object; years as against days; hearing as against seeing; motion as against force; self-propulsion as against exterior compulsion. . . .*

The words of the poem are not the only oppositions that seem to promise a resolution. The organization of the poem in the two opposed stanzas, the alternating rhyme scheme, the oppositional form of the sentences (no . . . not—no . . . neither . . . nor), the shift of narrative time for the speaker between stanzas from the past to the present—all these elements seem to confirm a meaning that the speaker claims to have discovered:

> The speaker has moved across the line from innocence to knowledge through the experience of Lucy's death. The poem expresses both eloquently restrained grief for that death and the calm of mature knowledge. Before, he was innocent. His spirit was sealed from knowledge as though he were asleep, closed in on himself. His innocence took the form of an ignorance of the fact of death. Lucy seemed so much alive, such an invulnerable vital young thing, that she could not possibly be touched by time, reach old age, and die. Her seeming immortality reassured the speaker of his own, and so he did not anticipate with fear his own death. He had no human fears. To be human is to be mortal, and the most specifically human fear, it may be, is the fear of death.

So far in his reading, Miller generally concurs with many other readers. But, he says, other elements are at work within the text of this "apparently simple" poem. A sexual drama or allegory is figured in the two senses of "thing" available in the meanings of "sweet young thing" or young virgin, and thing in the sense of an "inanimate object"—which in death she becomes. It is as if death were her only deflowerer—"to be touched by earthly years is a way to be sexually penetrated while still remaining a virgin."

Further, Miller says, nature is frequently personified both as a male punishing spirit and a female nurturing one throughout Wordsworth's poetry. Wordsworth's own mother died young when he was eight, and one might see Lucy's "imagined death as a reenactment of the death of the mother"—as a loss of "that direct filial bond to nature."

The speaker's identity also "occilates" widely in mutually contradictory ways: The speaker was "sealed," as she was in her virginity; now he knows; now he is as unsealed as she, for example. Miller goes on to say:

> Male and female, however, come together in the earth, and so Lucy and the speaker are "the same," though the poet is also the perpetually excluded difference from Lucy, an unneeded increment like an abandoned child. The two women, mother and child, have jumped over the male

---

* "On Edge: The Crossways of Contemporary Criticism" *Bulletin of The American Academy of Arts and Sciences* (32) (Jan. 1979)

generation in the middle. They have erased its power of mastery, its power of logical understanding, which is the male power *par excellence.* In expressing this, the poem leaves its reader with no possibility of moving through or beyond or standing outside in sovereign control. The reader is caught in an unstillible occilation unsatisfying to the mind and incapable of being grounded in anything outside the activity of the poem itself.

Miller offers several other examples of the ways categories of meaning "shimmer" into contradictory relations. But the final and most basic level of contradiction enacted by the figures of speech in the poem is one that Miller says all Wordsworth's poetry and the entire Western tradition follows: "the repeated occidental drama of the lost sun." Since the root of the word *Lucy* means "light," the loss of light figuratively expresses the lost "light" or "sun" or "fixed point" or "ground" or "logos"—the axiomatic beginning necessary to Western rational thought.

In the loss of any firm grounding the poem necessarily takes on a structure of chiasmas [a:b—b:a]. This is the perpetual reversal of properties in crisscross substitutions I have tried to identify. The senses of the poem continually cross over the borders set up by the words if they are taken to refer to fixed "things," whether material or subjective. The words waver in their meaning. Each word in itself becomes the dwelling place of contradictory senses, as though host and parasite were together in the same house. . . . As groundless, the movement is, precisely, alogical.

It is in this way that Miller shows the deconstructive illumination of factors in the human condition that are *not* poetically reconciled—and may perhaps not finally be reconcilable at all. Darkness and light, for example, change positions in the poem and seem to move toward the common ground of a synthesis. But they never do reach that point, and the result is an instability that further energizes the poem's language. That language thereby continues to "boggle the mind" by creating irreconcilable, contradictory meanings.

SUGGESTIONS FOR DISCUSSION AND WRITING

1. "A Slumber Did My Spirit Seal" is from a book by Wordsworth and Coleridge called *Lyrical Ballads* and is written in **ballad meter** like some early poems in the collection here and like the poems of Emily Dickinson included later. **Scan** the two **quatrains** of Wordsworth's poem to find out how ballad meter (or **common meter**) operates.

2. Does the **speaker** of this poem sound like the speakers in the other poems by Wordsworth? What is the **tone of voice** you hear in

this poem and elsewhere? Are the **images** drawn from the same kinds of experience? Is there any **irony** in Wordsworth's tone here or elsewhere? Are the **dramatic situations** of the poems similar? Be sure to explain your answers and to support them with the evidence of examples.

3. Both Hartman and Miller seem to agree in seeing the poem as an expression of loss. How might the poem be seen as providing *comfort* to the speaker in his imagination of what death *would be* like for him or for the "she" of the poem? For example, neither figure within the poem seems upset emotionally. But how are they described as feeling? What is the "life" of the universe described here? How is it different from, and how does it resemble, human life with its "fears" and wakenings as well as slumbers? How might either Miller or Hartman respond to the issue?

4. Look at "Design" by Robert Frost (p. 512). Compare and contrast the implications for the meaning of "nature" and "life" and "the way things are in the universe" with Wordsworth's imagination of these concepts. Make some notes for discussion or for an essay on how you think Hartman would read Frost's poem psychoanalytically. Do the same for Miller's deconstructive approach.

5. Pick another critical approach and make some notes for discussion or for an essay on Wordsworth's poem as an **elegy**. For example, how might a Feminist critic respond to the images of *passivity* that define the position of the female figure in the poem?

MORE POEMS BY WILLIAM WORDSWORTH

She Dwelt Among the Untrodden Ways
(1800)

She dwelt among the untrodden ways
  Beside the springs of Dove.
A Maid whom there were none to praise
  And very few to love;

5 A violet by a mossy stone
  Half hidden from the eye!
—Fair as a star, when only one
  Is shining in the sky.

She lived unknown, and few could know
10   When Lucy ceased to be;
  But she is in her grave, and, oh,
    The difference to me!

She Was a Phantom of Delight
(1807)

She was a Phantom of delight
When first she gleamed upon my sight;
A lovely Apparition, sent
To be a moment's ornament;
5 Her eyes as stars of Twilight fair;
Like Twilight's, too, her dusky hair;
But all things else about her drawn
From May-time and the cheerful Dawn;
A dancing Shape, an Image gay,
10 To haunt, to startle, and way-lay.

I saw her upon nearer view,
A Spirit, yet a Woman too!
Her household motions light and free,
And steps of virgin-liberty;
15 A countenance in which did meet
Sweet records, promises as sweet;
A Creature not too bright or good
For human nature's daily food;
For transient sorrows, simple wiles,
20 Praise, blame, love, kisses, tears, and smiles.

And now I see with eye serene
The very pulse of the machine;
A Being breathing thoughtful breath,
A Traveller between life and death;
25 The reason firm, the temperate will,
Endurance, foresight, strength, and skill;
A perfect Woman, nobly planned,
To warn, to comfort, and command;
And yet a Spirit still, and bright
30 With something of angelic light.

I Wandered Lonely As a Cloud
(1807)

I wandered lonely as a cloud
That floats on high o'er vales and hills,
When all at once I saw a crowd,
A host, of golden daffodils;
5 Beside the lake, beneath the trees,
Fluttering and dancing in the breeze.

Continuous as the stars that shine
And twinkle on the milky way,
They stretched in never-ending line
10 Along the margin of a bay:
Ten thousand saw I at a glance,
Tossing their heads in sprightly dance.

The waves beside them danced; but they
Outdid the sparkling waves in glee;
15 A poet could not but be gay,
In such a jocund company;
I gazed—and gazed—but little thought
What wealth the show to me had brought:

For oft, when on my couch I lie
20 In vacant or in pensive mood,
They flash upon that inward eye
Which is the bliss of solitude;
And then my heart with pleasure fills,
And dances with the daffodils.

The Solitary Reaper
(1807)

Behold her, single in the field,
Yon solitary Highland Lass!
Reaping and singing by herself;
Stop here, or gently pass!
5 Alone she cuts and binds the grain,
And sings a melancholy strain;
O Listen! for the Vale profound
Is overflowing with the sound.

No Nightingale did ever chaunt
10 More welcome notes to weary bands
Of travelers in some shady haunt,
Among Arabian Sands;
A voice so thrilling ne'er was heard
In springtime from the Cuckoo bird,
15 Breaking the silence of the seas
Among the farthest Hebrides.

Will no one tell me what she sings?—
Perhaps the plaintive numbers flow
For old, unhappy, far-off things,
20 And battles long ago;

Or is it some more humble lay,
Familiar matter of today?
Some natural sorrow, loss, or pain,
That has been, and may be again?

25 Whate'er the theme, the Maiden sang
As if her song could have no ending;
I saw her singing at her work,
And o'er the sickle bending—
I listened, motionless and still;
30 And, as I mounted up the hill,
The music in my heart I bore,
Long after it was heard no more.

The World Is Too Much with Us
(1807)

The world is too much with us; late and soon,
Getting and spending, we lay waste our powers;
Little we see in Nature that is ours;
We have given our hearts away, a sordid boon!
5 This Sea that bares her bosom to the moon,
The winds that will be howling at all hours,
And are up-gathered now like sleeping flowers,
For this, for everything, we are out of tune;
It moves us not.—Great God! I'd rather be
10 A Pagan suckled in a creed outworn;
So might I, standing on this pleasant lea,
Have glimpses that would make me less forlorn;
Have sight of Proteus rising from the sea;
Or hear old Triton blow his wreathéd horn.

Ode
Intimations of Immortality from Recollections of
Early Childhood
(1807)

The Child is father of the Man;
And I could wish my days to be
Bound each to each by natural piety.

1
There was a time when meadow, grove, and stream,
The earth, and every common sight,
To me did seem
Appareled in celestial light,

5 The glory and the freshness of a dream.
It is not now as it hath been of yore—
        Turn whereso'er I may,
            By night or day,
The things which I have seen I now can see no more.

2

10   The Rainbow comes and goes,
            And lovely is the Rose,
            The Moon doth with delight
Look round her when the heavens are bare,
            Waters on a starry night
15   Are beautiful and fair;
        The sunshine is a glorious birth;
        But yet I know, where'er I go,
That there hath passed away a glory from the earth.

3

Now, while the birds thus sing a joyous song,
20   And while the young lambs bound
            As to the tabor's sound,
To me alone there came a thought of grief:
A timely utterance gave that thought relief,
            And I again am strong:
25 The cataracts blow their trumpets from the steep;
No more shall grief of mine the season wrong;
I hear the Echoes through the mountains throng,
The Winds come to me from the fields of sleep,
            And all the earth is gay;
30   Land and sea
        Give themselves up to jollity,
            And with the heart of May
        Doth every Beast keep holiday—
            Thou Child of Joy,
35 Shout round me, let me hear thy shouts, thou happy
    Shepherd-boy!

4

Ye blesséd Creatures, I have heard the call
    Ye to each other make; I see
The heavens laugh with you in your jubilee;
40   My heart is at your festival,
            My head hath its coronal,
The fullness of your bliss, I feel—I feel it all.
            Oh, evil day! if I were sullen
            While Earth herself is adorning,

45   This sweet May morning,
        And the Children are culling
            On every side,
        In a thousand valleys far and wide,
        Fresh flowers; while the sun shines warm,
50 And the Babe leaps up on his Mother's arm—
        I hear, I hear, with joy I hear!
        —But there's a Tree, of many, one,
    A single Field which I have looked upon,
    Both of them speak of something that is gone:
55   The Pansy at my feet
            Doth the same tale repeat:
    Whither is fled the visionary gleam?
    Where is it now, the glory and the dream?

                    5
    Our birth is but a sleep and a forgetting:
60 The Soul that rises with us, our life's Star,
        Hath had elsewhere its setting,
        And cometh from afar:
        Not in entire forgetfulness,
        And not in utter nakedness,
65 But trailing clouds of glory do we come
        From God, who is our home:
    Heaven lies about us in our infancy!
    Shades of the prison-house begin to close
        Upon the growing Boy
70   But he
    Beholds the light, and whence it flows,
        He sees it in his joy;
    The Youth, who daily farther from the east
        Must travel, still is Nature's Priest,
75   And by the vision splendid
        Is on his way attended;
    At length the Man perceives it die away,
    And fade into the light of common day.

                    6
    Earth fills her lap with pleasures of her own;
80 Yearnings she hath in her own natural kind,
    And, even with something of a Mother's mind,
        And no unworthy aim,
        The homely Nurse doth all she can
    To make her foster child, her Inmate Man,
85   Forget the glories he hath known,
    And that imperial palace whence he came.

7

Behold the Child among his newborn blisses,
A six-years' Darling of a pygmy size!
See, where 'mid work of his own hand he lies,
90 Fretted by sallies of his mother's kisses,
With light upon him from his father's eyes!
See, at his feet, some little plan or chart,
Some fragment from his dream of human life,
Shaped by himself with newly-learnéd art;
95   A wedding or a festival,
          A mourning or a funeral;
            And this hath now his heart,
            And unto this he frames his song;
              Then will he fit his tongue
100 To dialogues of business, love, or strife;
              But it will not be long
              Ere this be thrown aside,
              And with new joy and pride
The little Actor cons another part;
105 Filling from time to time his "humorous stage"
With all the Persons, down to palsied Age,
That Life brings with her in her equipage;
              As if his whole vocation
              Were endless imitation.

8

110 Thou, whose exterior semblance doth belie
              Thy Soul's immensity;
Thou best Philosopher, who yet dost keep
Thy heritage, thou Eye among the blind,
That, deaf and silent, read'st the eternal deep,
115 Haunted forever by the eternal mind—
              Mighty Prophet! Seer blest!
              On whom those truths do rest,
Which we are toiling all our lives to find,
In darkness lost, the darkness of the grave;
120 Thou, over whom thy Immortality
Broods like the Day, a Master o'er a Slave,
A Presence which is not to be put by;
Thou little Child, yet glorious in the might
Of heaven-born freedom on thy being's height,
125 Why with such earnest pains dost thou provoke
The years to bring the inevitable yoke,
Thus blindly with thy blessedness at strife?
Full soon thy Soul shall have her earthly freight,
And custom lie upon thee with a weight,
130 Heavy as frost, and deep almost as life!

9

O joy! that in our embers
Is something that doth live,
That nature yet remembers
What was so fugitive!
135 The thought of our past years in me doth breed
Perpetual benediction: not indeed
For that which is most worthy to be blest;
Delight and liberty, the simple creed
Of Childhood, whether busy or at rest,
140 With new-fledged hope still fluttering in his breast—
Not for these I raise
The song of thanks and praise;
But for those obstinate questionings
Of sense and outward things,
145 Fallings from us, vanishings;
Blank misgivings of a Creature
Moving about in worlds not realized,
High instincts before which our mortal Nature
Did tremble like a guilty Thing surprised;
150 But for those first affections,
Those shadowy recollections,
Which, be they what they may,
Are yet the fountain light of all our day,
Are yet a master light of all our seeing;
155 Uphold us, cherish, and have power to make
Our noisy years seem moments in the being
Of the eternal Silence: truths that wake,
To perish never;
Which neither listlessness, nor mad endeavor,
160 Nor Man nor Boy,
Nor all that is at enmity with joy,
Can utterly abolish or destroy!
Hence in a season of calm weather
Though inland far we be,
165 Our souls have sight of that immortal sea
Which brought us hither,
Can in a moment travel thither,
And see the Children sport upon the shore,
And hear the mighty waters rolling evermore.

10

170 Then sing, ye Birds, sing, sing a joyous song!
And let the young Lambs bound
As to the tabor's sound!
We in thought will join your throng,
Ye that pipe and ye that play,

175   Ye that through your hearts today
         Feel the gladness of the May!
    What though the radiance which was once so bright
    Be now forever taken from my sight,
         Though nothing can bring back the hour
180 Of splendor in the grass, of glory in the flower;
         We will grieve not, rather find
         Strength in what remains behind;
         In the primal sympathy
         Which having been must ever be;
185   In the soothing thoughts that spring
         Out of human suffering;
         In the faith that looks through death,
    In years that bring the philosophic mind.

11

    And O, ye Fountains, Meadows, Hills, and Groves,
190 Forebode not any severing of our loves!
    Yet in my heart of hearts I feel your might;
    I only have relinquished one delight
    To live beneath your more habitual sway.
    I love the Brooks which down their channels fret,
195 Even more than when I tripped lightly as they;
    The innocent brightness of a newborn Day
         Is lovely yet;
    The clouds that gather round the setting sun
    Do take a sober coloring from an eye
200 That hath kept watch o'er man's mortality;
    Another race hath been, and other palms are won.
    Thanks to the human heart by which we live,
    Thanks to its tenderness, its joys, and fears,
    To me the meanest flower that blows can give
205 Thoughts that do often lie too deep for tears.

It Is a Beauteous Evening
(1807)

    It is a beauteous evening, calm and free,
    The holy time is quiet as a Nun
    Breathless with adoration; the broad sun
    Is sinking down in its tranquility;
5   The gentleness of heaven broods o'er the Sea:
    Listen! the mighty Being is awake,
    And doth with his eternal motion make
    A sound like thunder—everlastingly.
    Dear Child! dear Girl! that walkest with me here,

10 If thou appear untouched by solemn thought,
Thy nature is not therefore less divine:
Thou liest in Abraham's bosom all the year,
And worship'st at the Temple's inner shrine,
God being with thee when we know it not.

London, 1802
(1807)

Milton! thou shouldst be living at this hour:
England hath need of thee: she is a fen
Of stagnant waters: altar, sword, and pen,
Fireside, the heroic wealth of hall and bower,
5 Have forfeited their ancient English dower
Of inward happiness. We are selfish men;
Oh! raise us up, return to us again;
And give us manners, virtue, freedom, power.
Thy soul was like a Star, and dwelt apart;
10 Thou hadst a voice whose sound was like the sea:
Pure as the naked heavens, majestic, free,
So didst thou travel on life's common way,
In cheerful godliness; and yet thy heart
The lowliest duties on herself did lay.

My Heart Leaps Up
(1807)

My heart leaps up when I behold
  A rainbow in the sky:
So was it when my life began;
So is it now I am a man;
5 So be it when I shall grow old,
  Or let me die!
The child is father of the Man;
And I could wish my days to be
Bound each to each by natural piety.

Chapter Thirteen

Approaches to Emily Dickinson's "My Life Had Stood—A Loaded Gun"

EMILY DICKINSON (1830–1886) was the daughter of Edward Dickinson, a lawyer, treasurer of Amherst College, and (for one term) a United States Congressman. With the exception of a brief, unhappy period spent at nearby Mount Holyoke Female Seminary, she passed her entire life in Amherst, Massachusetts. As Dickinson grew older, she spent more and more time in seclusion; we are told that she dressed only in white and rarely came down from her room to receive visitors. She died in 1886.

Although Dickinson wrote over a thousand poems, only seven were published in her lifetime; her skill as a poet only fully became known after her death, when the remainder of her work was discovered in her attic. Beginning in the late nineteenth century, more and more posthumous editions of her poetry were compiled by her friends and relatives; in 1955, Thomas H. Johnson's three-volume edition of the *Poems* was released.

"My Life Had Stood—A Loaded Gun" is typical of Dickinson's style in that it consists of four-line stanzas, is written in a terse, stacatto rhythm, and is strewn with dashes and seemingly odd capitalizations. The poem is believed to have been written some time around 1863.

EMILY DICKINSON
My Life Had Stood—A Loaded Gun
(1863)

My Life had stood—A Loaded Gun—
In Corners—till a Day
The Owner passed—identified—
And carried Me away—

5 And now We roam in Sovreign Woods—
And now We hunt the Doe—
And every time I speak for Him—
The Mountains straight reply—

And do I smile, such cordial light
10 Upon the Valley glow—
It is as a Vesuvian face
Had let its pleasure through—

And when at Night—Our good Day done—
I guard My Master's Head—
15 'Tis better than the Eider-Duck's
Deep Pillow—to have shared—

To foe of His—I'm deadly foe—
None stir the second time—
On whom I lay a Yellow Eye—
20 Or an emphatic Thumb—

Though I than He—may longer live
He longer must—than I—
For I have but the power to kill,
Without—the power to die—

ACCOUNT: HELMUT BONHEIM ON A STRUCTURALIST APPROACH TO "MY LIFE HAD STOOD—A LOADED GUN"

Bonheim begins by noting that while newer approaches to narrative structure have so far been mainly applied to prose works, they might also profitably be applied to narrative poems such as the piece in question:

> "My life had stood a loaded gun" begins with the typical elements of narrative exposition: a prior state of things is postulated (anteriority). This state continues for an unspecified length of time (habituality). Then a particular moment is named ("till a day/The owner passed"), and this shifting of chronological gears gets the plot underway:

> My Life had stood—A Loaded Gun—
> In Corners, till a Day
> The Owner passed—identified—
> And carried Me away—

> This stanza, a single sentence, establishes a good part of the vital data we need if we want to interpret the remainder of the narrative.

From Helmut Bonheim, "Narrative Technique in Emily Dickinson's 'My Life Had Stood—A Loaded Gun'" *The Journal of Narrative Technique* 18, (1988), 258–268.

For Bonheim, the narrator (and central character) of the fictional world belongs to the age-old technique called "prosopopoei" in which an inanimate object such as a coin or a goose quill tells a story. We progressively learn about the positive and negative qualities of that narrator in ways that may be charted with reference to the stanzas:

stanza 1	stanza 2	stanzas 3 & 4
+object	+object	+lethal
−person	+person	+servant
+passive	−passive	+subservient
−sentient	+sentient	+lover
−expressive	+expressive	+female

The progress of positive qualities in the structure of the poem roughly shown in the chart has more subtle manifestations. For example:

> The gun going off was personified in stanza 2 as "I speak"—but in stanza 3 the explosion is conveyed by the more insidious "I smile." Gradually we see that the owner of the gun is also its lover. The gun going off is not painful: rather it creates "pleasure"—a Freudian narratologist would surely point out the orgastic image. In stanza 4 the togetherness of hunger and gun becomes more clearly an odd kind of love affair: the gun, conventionally a male object, is now the female partner of a love relationship. It is totally loyal and subservient, and apparently glad without reservation to be "used" by the master (this is the term with which Emily Dickinson refers in three of her letters [about 1859–1865] to the man in her abortive attachment to a member of the other sex who has identified her as his property.

But male and female roles do not entirely clarify the poem. Bonheim says that the relations of the poem are full of ironies and plays of opposites, such as in the fatal "speak to him" of stanza 2 and the deadly smile of pleasure on the "Vesuvian face." These ambiguities carry over into the relations of a "master" and a gun. Though sometimes spoken of as female, it finds a gun-like satisfaction in guarding rather than sleeping with the master.

Still, Bonheim says, the two characters of the poem (gun and master) do tend to join at its end:

> The unification of the two characters, now become loyal friends or lovers, is emphasized once more in stanza 5:

> To foe of His—I'm deadly foe—
> None stir the second time—

On whom I lay a Yellow Eye—
Or an emphatic Thumb—

> The connotations of the images shift from stanzas 2 to 5: from hunt-
> ing to war; from "hunt the doe" in stanza 2 to killing the "deadly foe" in
> stanza 5. . . . The masochistic self-abasement of the persona has a corol-
> lary characteristic: the sadistic pleasure in being fatal to others.

The "coda" of the poem also takes the form of a paradox and the
"rhetorical fireworks" of the poem peak at its end. The puzzling meaning of the last stanza may perhaps be better seen, Bonheim says, by for-
mulating it this way:

For I have but the art to kill = (I am with the power to make die)
   Without the power to die. = (I am without the power to . . . die)

The speaker may seem to lament the facts so expressed, yet one implication of being without the power to die is a god-like immortality. In
this reading the status of the gun as character is radically changed:

> Put in rhetorical terms, the metaphor of *gun = subservient being* turns
> into its reverse, *gun = omnipotent being.* Thus the poem's central meta-
> phor, if we want to take it at all seriously, shows itself to be a metaphor
> gone off the tracks, a *catachresis.* . . . The allegorical equation no longer
> works. Why?

Bonheim answers his question in two ways: 1) The conceit of the
poem may have become too cumbersome to make sense for the poet any
longer—the overextended metaphor breaks down into nonsense; 2) the
illogicality of death is apparent in many other of Dickinson's poems—for
example, "I heard a fly buzz when I died" and "Because I could not stop
for death." Or perhaps the odd jolts to logic are intended to foster an
atmosphere of fantasy or of weirdness *within* the everyday world of the
poem's images.

Bonheim ends by analyzing some of the ways in which the rhetorical
structure of the poem's conclusion enforces the notion of contradiction
or paradox. For example, the form taken by the grammar makes the
rhetorical figure of the "antimetabole" in the climax of the poem. That
is, a grammatical sequence is first given and then immediately reversed
in the pattern a-b-c-d : d-c-b-a.

> . . . for instance in stanza 6, line 1:

1. personal pronoun   I
2. conjunction   than
3. auxiliary   may
4. adverb   longer

reversed into stanza 6, line 2:

4. adverb   longer
3. auxiliary   must
2. conjunction   than
1. personal pronoun I

Bonheim concludes that, without attention to the carefully plotted narrative structures behind its paradoxes, the poem might tend to seem merely "an unsystematic sequence of utterances, pretty and unproblematic." However, with the structures in mind, the poem appears "a narrative puzzle in lyric form." Such a structure, he says, makes the typical shape of Emily Dickinson's best poetry.

ACCOUNT: ADRIENNE RICH ON A FEMINIST APPROACH TO "MY LIFE HAD STOOD—A LOADED GUN"

In one of her letters, Emily Dickinson wrote that she had heard the poems of Walt Whitman (the other "odd" and powerful poetic genius of her time) were "disgraceful." Rich says that the anecdote reminds us about the various pressures any nineteenth-century poet might feel from society to meet its expectations of what a poet should be like. Female poets all the more especially were expected to content themselves with "delicacies" in verse, and when Emily Dickinson is seen as merely eccentric or quaint, it seems similarly a way of dismissing a troublesome originality rather than dealing with it.

Rich says that Emily Dickinson might be better seen as too *strong* for her environment rather than too delicate for it. The masculine images in her poems are images of power, but they should not be simply seen as images of lovers or of God. Similarly, the idiosyncrasies of her diction and punctuation (and the admitted existence of some of her purposefully "cute" or "arch" poems) have led some readers to condescend to the power of her originality in all its manifestations—to imagine her as an eternal little girl, though she was all of fifty-five when she died. More recent critics, however, "have gradually begun to approach the poet in terms of her greatness, rather than her Littleness."

Dickinson's biographer tells us that she felt herself possessed by a demonic force, particularly during her most active years as a poet, 1861 and 1862. Rich proposes a way of viewing Dickinson's problem of creating a poetic expression for this force:

From "Vesuvius at Home: The Power of Emily Dickinson," in *On Lies, Secrets, and Selected Prose 1968–1978*, Norton 1979.

> I suggest that a woman's poetry about her relationship to her daemon—
> her own active, creative power—has in patriarchal culture used the lan-
> guage of heterosexual love or patriarchal theology.

In other words, the images of masculine power in her poetry—given the
implications of language and poetry in Emily Dickinson's time and social structure—are really metaphors for ways of expressing her relation
to her own poetry and the imaginative act of its creation.

Dickinson wrote three hundred and sixty five poems during "the
year of her fullest power." Rich asks, what did it *feel* like to be possessed
of or by such a poetic force as that number suggests? For Rich, "My Life
Had Stood—A Loaded Gun" is a poem that stands as the source of her
sense of how Dickinson felt in relation to the overwhelming power of a
poetic muse that seemed to come from outside her own being:

> There is one poem which is the real "onlie begetter" of my thoughts
> here about Dickinson; a poem I have mused over, repeated to myself,
> taken into myself over many years. I think it is a poem about posses-
> sion by the daemon, about the dangers and risks of such possession if
> you are a woman, about the knowledge that power in a woman can
> seem destructive, and that you cannot live without the daemon once it
> has possessed you.

Rich says that the poet sees herself in the poem as split—but not between masculine and feminine identities. Rather, the division is one between hunter and gun—"an object condemned to remain inactive until
the hunter—the *owner*—takes possession of it." In other words, the poet
feels her personal talents are like a loaded gun. They are only *potentially*
powerful for poetry until inspiration or something like a muse comes to
her. For a gun, this something is an owner or a master or a hunter—all
masculine metaphors.

The female consciousness of power in the poem lies in the extreme
ambivalence felt toward it, particularly toward its destructive qualities.
The final stanza desperately attempts in its verbal balance to resolve
this ambiguity, but Rich sees it not as a resolution but as an extension of
ambivalence:

> The poet experiences herself as loaded gun, imperious energy; yet with-
> out the Owner, the possessor, she is merely lethal. Should that possession
> abandon her—but the thought is unthinkable: "He longer *must*—than I."
> The pronoun is masculine; the antecedent is what Keats called "The
> Genius of Poetry."

In other words, for a female poet in Dickinson's time and place, the
"muse" or "daemon" of poetry takes on a masculine identity to express
through the language of heterosexual love the creative force of an overwhelming poetic power.

SUGGESTIONS FOR DISCUSSION AND WRITING

1. Emily Dickinson writes in **meters** influenced by the hymns of the Congregational Church in which she was raised. Like many of those hymns, "My Life Had Stood—A Loaded Gun" is written in what is called **common meter** or **ballad meter. Scan** the first four lines of the poem to identify how a **ballad stanza** works prosodically.

2. What are some of the implications of the **image** of a "loaded gun"? For example, the image implies "potential." What *kinds* of potential and what *else* does the image imply as a **metaphor** or **symbol** for the life of a person? What do Bonheim and Rich see as the potential powers of life?

3. Both Rich and Bonheim emphasize a direct relation of the poem's **persona** to the life of the poet. In what ways do they differ on the nature of the poet expressed by the poem? Since the technique of comparison and contrast is so commonly helpful, try imagining that Dickinson the poet was **satirizing** the persona of her **speaker**. What values and assumptions might form the basis of such a satire?

4. Look at Ezra Pound's "The River Merchant's Wife: A Letter" (p. 520) and compare and contrast the ways in which the relationships of each poem are created by its particular uses of language. On what might Bonheim and Rich focus in this poem?

5. Both Rich and Bonheim see "My Life Had Stood—A Loaded Gun" as representative of Dickinson's poetry as a whole. Make some notes for discussion or for an essay on the other poems by Emily Dickinson included here, with a view toward showing the extent to which that poem is or is not a good representation of her poetic practice. Pick one poem and carefully say as much as you can, in particular about what you think Rich would point out about it as a feminist critic. Do the same for Bonheim as a structuralist.

6. Pick another critical approach and make some notes for discussion or for an essay on "My Life Had Stood—A Loaded Gun." For example, how might a Marxist critic view the relations of people to things imagined in the poem?

MORE POEMS BY EMILY DICKINSON

Success Is Counted Sweetest
(ca 1862)

Success is counted sweetest
By those who ne'er succeed.
To comprehend a nectar
Requires sorest need.

5 Not one of all the purple Host
Who took the Flag today
Can tell the definition
So clear of Victory

As he defeated—dying—
10 On whose forbidden ear
The distant strains of triumph
Burst agonized and clear!

After Great Pain
(ca 1862)

After great pain, a formal feeling comes—
The Nerves sit ceremonious, like Tombs—
The stiff Heart questions was it He, that bore,
And Yesterday, or Centuries before?

5 The Feet, mechanical, go round—
Of Ground, or Air, or Ought—
A Wooden way
Regardless grown,
A Quartz contentment, like a stone—

10 This is the Hour of Lead—
Remembered, if outlived,
As Freezing persons, recollect the Snow—
First—Chill—then Stupor—then the letting go—

I Heard a Fly Buzz
(ca 1862)

I heard a Fly buzz—when I died—
The Stillness in the Room
Was like the Stillness in the Air—
Between the Heaves of Storm—

5 The Eyes around—had wrung them dry—
And Breaths were gathering firm
For that last Onset—when the King
Be witnessed—in the Room—

I willed my Keepsakes—Signed away
10 What portion of me be
Assignable—and then it was
There interposed a Fly—

With Blue—uncertain stumbling Buzz—
Between the light—and me—
15 And then the Windows failed—and then
I could not see to see—

Because I Could Not Stop for Death
(ca 1863)

Because I could not stop for Death—
He kindly stopped for me—
The Carriage held but just Ourselves—
And Immortality.

5 We slowly drove—He knew no haste
And I had put away
My labor and my leisure too,
For His Civility—

We passed the School, where Children strove
10 At Recess—in the Ring—
We passed the Fields of Gazing Grain—
We passed the Setting Sun—

Or rather—He passed Us—
The Dews drew quivering and chill—
15 For only Gossamer, my Gown—
My Tippet—only Tulle—

We paused before a House that seemed
A Swelling of the Ground—
The Roof was scarcely visible—
20 The Cornice—in the Ground—

Since then—'tis Centuries—and yet
Feels shorter than the Day
I first surmised the Horses' Heads
Were toward Eternity—

There's a Certain Slant of Light
(ca 1861)

There's a certain Slant of light,
Winter Afternoons—
That oppresses, like the Heft
Of Cathedral Tunes—

5 Heavenly Hurt, it gives us—
We can find no scar,
But internal difference,
Where the Meanings, are—

None may teach it—Any—
10 'Tis the Seal Despair—
An imperial affliction
Sent us of the Air—

When it comes, the Landscape listens—
Shadows—hold their breath—
15 When it goes, 'tis like the Distance
On the look of Death—

I Like to See It Lap The Miles
(ca 1862)

I like to see it lap the Miles—
And lick the Valleys up—
And stop to feed itself at Tanks—
And then—prodigious step

5 Around a Pile of Mountains—
And supercilious peer
In Shanties—by the sides of Roads—
And then a Quarry pare

To fit its Ribs
10 And crawl between
Complaining all the while
In horrid—hooting stanza—
Then chase itself down Hill—

And neigh like Boanerges—
15 Then—punctual as a Star
Stop—docile and omnipotent
At its own stable door—

Wild Nights
(ca 1861)

Wild Nights—Wild Nights!
Were I with thee
Wild Nights should be
Our luxury!

5 Futile—the Winds—
To a Heart in port—
Done with the Compass—
Done with the Chart!

Rowing in Eden—
10 Ah, the Sea!
Might I but moor—Tonight—
In Thee!

Chapter Fourteen

Approaches to William Butler Yeats' "Among School Children"

WILLIAM BUTLER YEATS (1865–1939), poet and playwright, was born in Dublin, the son of the well-known Irish painter John Butler Yeats. He was schooled in Dublin and London, and studied painting for a period of three years. In 1916, he became a leader of the Irish Renaissance, promoting the belief that the Irish poet's task was to communicate simply and directly with the Irish people. *The Wind Among the Reeds* (1899) and *In the Seven Woods* (1903) are collections which represent this period of Yeats' career. In 1888, Yeats met and fell in love with Maud Gonne, a crusading Irish Nationalist who drew Yeats into the world of Irish politics and became a central subject of his poetry. In 1899, Yeats founded the Irish National Theatre, which in 1904 moved to the celebrated Abbey Theatre in Dublin.

Yeats did not subscribe to an orthodox religion, but was instead interested in magic and occult philosophy. In 1917, he married Georgie Hyde Lees, a spiritualist medium with whose help he composed *A Vision* (1937), which he believed to have been dictated by spirits through his wife. After the establishment of the Irish Free State, Yeats served, from 1922 to 1928, as a senator and as a school inspector. Yeats is widely regarded as one of the greatest poets of the twentieth century; he was awarded the Nobel Prize in Literature in 1923. He died in 1939.

WILLIAM BUTLER YEATS
Among School Children
(1927)

I

I walk through the long schoolroom questioning;
A kind old nun in a white hood replies;
The children learn to cipher and to sing,
To study reading-books and history,
5 To cut and sew, be neat in everything
In the best modern way—the children's eyes
In momentary wonder stare upon
A sixty-year-old smiling public man.

II

I dream of a Ledaean body, bent
10 Above a sinking fire, a tale that she
   Told of a harsh reproof, or trivial event
   That changed some childish day to tragedy—
   Told, and it seemed that our two natures blent
   Into a sphere from youthful sympathy,
15 Or else, to alter Plato's parable,
   Into the yolk and white of the one shell.

III

And thinking of that fit of grief or rage
I look upon one child or t'other there
And wonder if she stood so at that age—
20 For even daughters of the swan can share
   Something of every paddler's heritage—
   And had that color upon cheek or hair,
   And thereupon my heart is driven wild:
   She stands before me as a living child.

IV

25 Her present image floats into the mind—
   Did Quattrocento finger fashion it
   Hollow of cheek as though it drank the wind
   And took a mess of shadows for its meat?
   And I though never of Ledaean kind
30 Had pretty plumage once—enough of that,
   Better to smile on all that smile, and show
   There is a comfortable kind of old scarecrow.

V

What youthful mother, a shape upon her lap
Honey of generation had betrayed,
35 And that must sleep, shriek, struggle to escape
   As recollection or the drug decide,
   Would think her son, did she but see that shape
   With sixty or more winters on its head,
   A compensation for the pang of his birth,
40 Or the uncertainty of his setting forth?

VI

Plato thought nature but a spume that plays
Upon a ghostly paradigm of things;
Solider Aristotle played the taws
Upon the bottom of a king of kings;
45 World-famous golden-thighed Pythagoras
   Fingered upon a fiddle-stick or strings

What a star sang and careless Muses heard:
Old clothes upon old sticks to scare a bird.

VII
Both nuns and mothers worship images,
50 But those the candles light are not as those
That animate a mother's reveries,
But keep a marble or a bronze repose.
And yet they too break hearts—O Presences
That passion, piety or affection knows,
55 And that all heavenly glory symbolize—
O self-born mockers of man's enterprise;

VIII
Labor is blossoming or dancing where
The body is not bruised to pleasure soul,
Nor beauty born out of its own despair,
60 Nor blear-eyed wisdom out of midnight oil.
O chestnut-tree, great-rooted blossomer,
Are you the leaf, the blossom or the bole?
O body swayed to music, O brightening glance,
How can we know the dancer from the dance?

ACCOUNT: CLEANTH BROOKS ON A NEW CRITICAL APPROACH TO "AMONG SCHOOL CHILDREN"

Like Wordsworth's "Intimations" ode (see p. 409), "Among School Children" is a poem that "meditates on what has been gained and what lost in the process of growing up." Yet Brooks says that, while Wordsworth is more direct in his approach to the theme, Yeats relies on his imagery more fully to *dramatize* that theme. Brooks finds that within an apparently rambling "stream of consciousness," all the poem's images become symbols that contribute to its magnificent ending:

[T]he very inconsequence of some of the reflection—the apparent aimlessness itself of the progression—are brought to bear upon the final statement. If they account for it, in a sense they also guarantee its validity. For they suggest that it is not a "loaded" statement prepared beforehand, and forced upon the occasion; but rather a statement which the impact of the opening scene has precipitated out of the experience of a lifetime.

Brooks illustrates his point by noting that the poem opens with a humdrum scene couched in sing-song rhythms. Yet this first moment prepares us (by contrast) for the rich verse of the world of thought and recollection announced by "I dream of a Ledaean body." The heroic world has nothing apparently to do with the everyday world of the school inspector that Yeats was, and the gawking children he saw, yet the two worlds are connected by the poem. The meditation on the parable of the egg as a symbol of sympathy's ability to join opposites without destroying their individuality connects the staring children and the old man to the "shape" they were both once—formless, but full of potential yet to be realized:

> As shape, it is pure potentiality—plastic enough to be molded even to a mother's dream. But the reality, whatever it will come to be, will deny the mother's dream.

Yet, Brooks asks, "How is the formless given form?" Put another way, what are the relations of the abstract ideal and the concrete reality? Yeats' meditation continues as three great philosophers are surveyed through striking symbols that dramatize their views. Yet Yeats insists on a still wider range of reference and, in the "Presences" he addresses, evokes a symbol for *all* ideals:

> It is to the "presences" that he addresses the vision of totality of being and unity of being which occupies the last stanza. What is drudgery becomes "blossoming or dancing where/The body is not bruised to pleasure soul." In the total activity, one can separate the actor from the action only by an act of abstraction. What is the tree—leaf, blossom, or bole? When the dance is completed, has not the dancer ceased to be a dancer? Yet, is the last line a powerful insight or an obvious quibble? Does this whole last stanza, with all its power and beauty, constitute the poet's refutation to Plato and all cruel idealism? Or, does it mark a desertion of—or a transcendence of—the common sense world in which we feel we have so little difficulty in distinguishing dancers from the dances in which they engage?

In the way it dramatizes the issues, Yeats' poem is like the chestnut tree. His entire poem enacts the issues it raises in ways that resemble the symbol of the tree that embodies the ending. That is, just as the poem seems to manifest itself and to blossom without effort, so the blossoms of the chestnut tree grow out of its roots and earlier material. Yeats thereby seems to affirm the concrete natural world of growth and death over the timeless, ageless world of art and the ideal—the world of Keats' urn.

Yet Yeats' mind was even more fully dramatic than the poem. The same year in which he wrote "Among School Children" saw him compose "Sailing to Byzantium" (see p. 437). This poem entertains the same questions; yet, in it, Yeats makes his greatest *tribute* to the world of the ideal and his greatest apparent *questioning* of the world of natural process. As Kenneth Burke has pointed out, the two poems thus balance one another.

As to the question of *which* world—the world of the material or the world of the eternal—it is that Yeats finally affirms in "Among School Children," Brooks concludes that:

> Yeats chooses both and neither. One cannot know the world of being save through the world of becoming, though one must remember that the world of becoming is a meaningless flux apart from the world of being which it implies. . . . [*both* poems make] a recognition of the problem which the reflective human being can never escape—the dilemma which is the ground of the philosophic problem; and the "solution" which is reached in neither case *solves* the problem. The poet in both cases comes to terms with the situation—develops an attitude toward the situation which everywhere witnesses to the insolubility of the problem. As I. A. Richards has suggested of Wordsworth's "Ode," so here: "Among School Children" (or for that matter, "Sailing to Byzantium") is finally a poem "about the nature of the human imagination itself."

Thus, Brooks sees the human imagination itself as the subject dramatized in the poem. In comparison, note how, in the next approach summarized, Paul de Man sees the poem as a manifestation of something related but different—the nature not of human imagination, but of human *language*.

ACCOUNT: PAUL DE MAN ON A POST-STRUCTURALIST APPROACH TO "AMONG SCHOOL CHILDREN"

De Man uses Yeats' poem to illustrate a characteristic of criticism that seems to him to have been overlooked. When criticism becomes concerned with *form* in literature, it seems inevitably to become reductive of the literary experience in one way or another. When form is considered to be the mere "external trappings" of literature's meaning, it comes to seem "superficial and expendable." But (on the other hand) when criticism focuses on the *importance* of form (as he says the New Criticism does, for example), the referential meaning of the poem—its relation to the world outside literature—tends to become reduced to insignificance or irrelevance. Thus, the "inside" of literature and the "outside" it refers to tend to be at odds throughout the history of criticism. De Man proposes to try to find an alternative to the "inside/

Paul de Man, "Seminology and Rhetoric" from *Allegories of Reading* (New Haven, CT: Yale University Press, 1979).

outside" model of criticizing literature by exploring the differences between two other relevant categories—*rhetoric* (which he limits here to figures of speech and the figurative relations they create among words) and *grammar* (which assumes a literal relation among the meanings of words). The two methods of analyzing language come together in the figure of the so-called "rhetorical question," and de Man illustrates how the combination works with an example from a situation comedy in the "subliterature" of TV.

A wife asks her husband whether he wants his bowling shoes laced over or under. He impatiently replies, "What's the difference?" She then goes on in a patient and plodding manner to explain the difference between lacing over and lacing under. In other words, the joke involves the wife's seeing the question literally, as meaning what its grammar says, while the husband uses his words figuratively, as a rhetorical question that means the opposite of what it says, i.e., that the difference has no interest or importance at all.

In reading literature (the most intensely figurative of language's manifestations), the same qualities that make the basis of the joke often create problems of interpretation:

> The grammatical model of the question becomes rhetorical not when we have, on the one hand, a literal meaning and on the other hand a figural meaning, but when it is impossible to decide by grammatical or other linguistic devices which of the two meanings (that can be entirely incompatible) prevails. Rhetoric radically suspends logic and opens up vertiginous possibilities of referential aberration. And although it would perhaps be somewhat more remote from common usage, I would not hesitate to equate the rhetorical, figural potentiality of language with literature itself.

De Man goes on to explore "Among School Children" by beginning with its final question:

> O chestnut-tree, great-rooted blossomer,
> Are you the leaf, the blossom or the bole?
> O, body swayed to music, O brightening glance,
> How can we know the dancer from the dance?

De Man allows that, on the one hand, if the last line is read as a rhetorical question to mean we *cannot* know the parts separate from the whole, it is possible to make an extended reading of the entire poem from first line to last that fully and consistently accounts for all the poem's details. But on the other hand, reading the question only grammatically, "asking with some urgency" how we can possibly make very real and very necessary distinctions between creator and created, also supplies a full reading of the poem with an entirely different theme and a meaning that may perhaps be of even greater complexity:

The oneness of trunk, leaf, and blossom, for example, that would have appealed to Goethe, would find itself replaced by the much less reassuring Tree of Life from the Mabinogion that appears in the poem "Vacillation," in which the fiery blossom and the earthly leaf are held together, as well as apart, by the crucified and castrated god, Attis, of whose body it can hardly be said that it is not "bruised to pleasure soul." This hint should suffice to suggest that two entirely coherent but entirely incompatible readings can be made to hinge on one line whose grammatical structure is devoid of ambiguity, but whose rhetorical mode turns the mood as well as the mode of the entire poem upside down.

De Man concludes that the result here is not a case of two different side-by-side interpretations existing at the reader's preference:

> The two readings have to engage each other in direct confrontation for the one reading is precisely the error denounced by the other; none can exist in the other's absence. There can be no dance without a dancer, no sign without a referent. On the other hand, the authority of the meaning engendered by the grammatical structure is fully obscured by the duplicity of a figure that cries out for the differentiation that it conceals.

In other words, de Man's conclusion to his analysis (in one of the first important essays in this country to use the approach of deconstruction) is that the very *language* that expresses meaning in literature will, in its most intense manifestations, *refuse* to let us know what it means.

SUGGESTIONS FOR DISCUSSION AND WRITING

1. For each critic, Yeats' poem presents a grand philosophical meditation. What **meter** does he employ for such a great task? How do you **scan** the poem? What is its **rhyme scheme**? In the first ten lines, how many lines are entirely **regular**? How many have more than one modulated **foot**?

2. How would you compare and contrast the manner of the **speaker** and that of the figure of Yeats as a **character** within the **narrative** of the poem? How are they similar? How do they differ? Is the contrast between the "public man" and the man who "dreams" **ironic**? Is this difference like the differences examined by Brooks and de Man? Explain.

3. Both Brooks and de Man see the poem as struggling with alternatives. What are the alternatives for each critic? How do they differ? How are they similar?

4. Brooks compares "Among School Children" to Yeats' "Sailing To Byzantium." Make some notes for discussion or for an essay on how you think de Man would analyze that poem from a deconstructionist point

of view. How do the alternatives of each critic apply to this poem? In what ways does it in fact seem to "balance" "Among School Children?" Is the contrast between the two ways of looking at life also present in Wordsworth's "Ode"?

5. Pick another critical approach and make some notes for discussion or for an essay on "Among School Children." What, for example, might a psychoanalytic critic say about the **images** Yeats uses and the "dream" he describes?

MORE POEMS BY WILLIAM BUTLER YEATS

The Lake Isle of Innisfree
(1892)

I will arise and go now, and go to Innisfree,
And a small cabin build there, of clay and wattles made:
Nine bean-rows will I have there, a hive for the honey-bee,
And live alone in the bee-loud glade.

5 And I shall have some peace there, for peace comes dropping slow,
Dropping from the veils of the morning to where the cricket sings;
There midnight's all a glimmer, and noon a purple glow,
And evening full of the linnet's wings.
I will arise and go now, for always night and day
10 I hear lake water lapping with low sounds by the shore;
While I stand on the roadway, or on the pavements grey,
I hear it in the deep heart's core.

The Rose of the World
(1892)

Who dreamed that beauty passes like a dream?
For these red lips, with all their mournful pride,
Mournful that no new wonder may betide,
Troy passed away in one high funeral gleam,
5 And Usna's children died.

We and the labouring world are passing by:
Amid men's souls, that waver and give place
Like the pale waters in their wintry race,
Under the passing stars, foam of the sky,
10 Lives on this lonely face.

Bow down, archangels, in your dim abode:
Before you were, or any hearts to beat,
Weary and kind one lingered by His seat;
He made the world to be a grassy road
15 Before her wandering feet.

The Wild Swans at Coole
(1917)

The trees are in their autumn beauty,
The woodland paths are dry,
Under the October twilight the water
Mirrors a still sky;
5 Upon the brimming water among the stones
Are nine-and-fifty swans.

The nineteenth autumn has come upon me
Since I first made my count;
I saw, before I had well finished,
10 All suddenly mount
And scatter wheeling in great broken rings
Upon their clamorous wings.

I have looked upon those brilliant creatures,
And now my heart is sore.
15 All's changed since I, hearing at twilight,
The first time on this shore,
The bell-beat of their wings above my head,
Trod with a lighter tread.

Unwearied still, lover by lover,
20 They paddle in the cold
Companionable streams or climb the air;
Their hearts have not grown old;
Passion or conquest, wander where they will,
Attend upon them still.

25 But now they drift on the still water,
Mysterious, beautiful;

Among what rushes will they build,
By what lake's edge or pool
Delight men's eyes when I awake some day
30 To find they have flown away?

The Second Coming
(1921)

Turning and turning in the widening gyre
The falcon cannot hear the falconer;
Things fall apart; the centre cannot hold;
Mere anarchy is loosed upon the world,
5 The blood-dimmed tide is loosed, and everywhere
The ceremony of innocence is drowned;
The best lack all conviction, while the worst
Are full of passionate intensity.

Surely some revelation is at hand;
10 Surely the Second Coming is at hand.
The Second Coming! Hardly are those words out
When a vast image out of *Spiritus Mundi*
Troubles my sight: somewhere in sands of the desert
A shape with lion body and the head of a man,
15 A gaze blank and pitiless as the sun,
Is moving its slow thighs, while all about it
Reel shadows of the indignant desert birds.
The darkness drops again; but now I know
That twenty centuries of stony sleep
20 Were vexed to nightmare by a rocking cradle,
And what rough beast, its hour come round at last,
Slouches towards Bethlehem to be born?

Leda and the Swan
(1924)

A sudden blow: the great wings beating still
Above the staggering girl, her thighs caressed
By the dark webs, her nape caught in his bill,
He holds her helpless breast upon his breast.

5 How can those terrified vague fingers push
The feathered glory from her loosening thighs?
And how can body, laid in that white rush,
But feel the strange heart beating where it lies?

A shudder in the loins engenders there
10 The broken wall, the burning roof and tower
And Agamemnon dead.
                              Being so caught up,
So mastered by the brute blood of the air,
Did she put on his knowledge with his power
15 Before the indifferent beak could let her drop?

Sailing to Byzantium
(1927)

That is no country for old men. The young
In one another's arms, birds in the trees
—Those dying generations—at their song,
The salmon-falls, the mackerel-crowded seas,
5 Fish, flesh, or fowl, commend all summer long
Whatever is begotten, born, and dies.
Caught in that sensual music all neglect
Monuments of unaging intellect.

An aged man is but a paltry thing,
10 A tattered coat upon a stick, unless
Soul clap its hands and sing, and louder sing
For every tatter in its mortal dress,
Nor is there singing school but studying
Monuments of its own magnificence;
15 And therefore I have sailed the seas and come
To the holy city of Byzantium.

Byzantium
(1930)

The unpurged images of day recede;
The Emperor's drunken soldiery are abed;
Night resonance recedes, night-walkers' song
After great cathedral gong;
5 A starlit or a moonlit dome disdains
All that man is,
All mere complexities,
The fury and the mire of human veins.

Before me floats an image, man or shade,
10 Shade more than man, more image than a shade;
For Hades' bobbin bound in mummy-cloth
May unwind the winding path;
A mouth that has no moisture and no breath
Breathless mouths may summon;
15 I hail the superhuman;
I call it death-in-life and life-in-death.

Miracle, bird or golden handiwork,
More miracle than bird or handiwork,
Planted on the star-lit golden bough,
20 Can like the cocks of Hades crow,

Or, by the moon embittered, scorn aloud
In glory of changeless metal
Common bird or petal
And all complexities of mire or blood.

25 At midnight on the Emperor's pavement flit
Flames that no faggot feeds, nor steel has lit,
Nor storm disturbs, flames begotten of flame,
Where blood-begotten spirits come
And all complexities of fury leave,
30 Dying into a dance,
An agony of trance,
An agony of flame that cannot singe a sleeve.

Astraddle on the dolphin's mire and blood,
Spirit after spirit! The smithies break the flood,
35 The golden smithies of the Emperor!
Marbles of the dancing floor
Break bitter furies of complexity,
Those images that yet
Fresh images beget,
40 That dolphin-torn, that gong-tormented sea.

Chapter Fifteen

Approaches to Gwendolyn Brooks' "Gay Chaps at the Bar"

GWENDOLYN BROOKS (1917–   ) was born in Topeka, Kansas. Early in her life, she moved to Chicago's South Side, whose people, along with their language, struggles, and dreams, have been the chief subject of her work. In 1950, Brooks became the first black author to receive the Pulitzer Prize, which she won for *Annie Allen*. In 1953, she published a novel of Chicago, *Maud Martha*, a series of vignettes about a ghetto woman's life. In 1967, she attended a conference for black writers at Fisk University and has since then taught poetry at several colleges and universities. Rather than have her work published by a popular New York publishing house, Brooks instead chose Broadside, a small press in Detroit founded by the black poet Dudley Randall. In 1985, Brooks was appointed Consultant in Poetry to the Library of Congress. Her recent works and collections include *To Disembark* (1981), *Black Love* (1982), *Mayor Harold Washington; and Chicago, The I Will City* (1983), and *The Near Johannesburg Boy, and Other Poems* (1987).

GWENDOLYN BROOKS
Gay Chaps at the Bar
(1945)

gay chaps at the bar

> . . . and guys I knew in the States, young
> officers, return from the front crying and
> trembling. Gay chaps at the bar in Los
> Angeles, Chicago, New York . . .
> Lieutenant William Couch
> in the South Pacific

We knew how to order. Just the dash
Necessary. The length of gaiety in good taste.
Whether the raillery should be slightly iced

And given green, or served up hot and lush.
5 And we knew beautifully how to give to women
The summer spread, the tropics, of our love.
When to persist, or hold a hunger off.
Knew white speech. How to make a look an omen.
But nothing ever taught us to be islands.
10 And smart, athletic language for this hour
Was not in the curriculum. No stout
Lesson showed how to chat with death. We brought
No brass fortissimo, among our talents,
To holler down the lions in this air.

still do I keep my look, my identity . . .

Each body has its art, its precious prescribed
Pose, that even in passion's droll contortions, waltzes,
Or push of pain—or when a grief has stabbed,
Or hatred hacked—is its, and nothing else's.
5 Each body has its pose. No other stock
That is irrevocable, perpetual
And its to keep. In castle or in shack.
With rags or robes. Through good, nothing, or ill.
And even in death a body, like no other
10 On any hill or plain or crawling cot
Or gentle for the lilyless hasty pall
(Having twisted, gagged, and then sweet-ceased to bother),
Shows the old personal art, the look. Shows what
It showed at baseball. What it showed in school.

my dreams, my works, must wait till after hell

I hold my honey and I store my bread
In little jars and cabinets of my will.
I label clearly, and each latch and lid
I bid, Be firm till I return from hell.
5 I am very hungry. I am incomplete.
And none can tell when I may dine again.
No man can give me any word but Wait,
The puny light. I keep eyes pointed in;
Hoping that, when the devil days of my hurt
10 Drag out to their last dregs and I resume
On such legs as are left me, in such heart
As I can manage, remember to go home,
My taste will not have turned insensitive
To honey and bread old purity could love.

looking

You have no word for soldiers to enjoy
The feel of, as an apple, and to chew
With masculine satisfaction. Not "good-by!"
"Come back!" or "careful!" Look, and let him go.
5 "Good-by!" is brutal, and "come back!" the raw
Insistence of an idle desperation
Since could he favor he would favor now.
He will be "careful!" if he has permission.
Looking is better. At the dissolution
10 Grab greatly with the eye, crush in a steel
Of study—Even that is vain. Expression,
The touch or look or word, will little avail.
The brawniest will not beat back the storm
Nor the heaviest haul your little boy from harm.

piano after war

On a snug evening I shall watch her fingers,
Cleverly ringed, declining to clever pink,
Beg glory from the willing keys. Old hungers
Will break their coffins, rise to eat and thank.
5 And music, warily, like the golden rose
That sometimes after sunset warms the west,
Will warm that room, persuasively suffuse
That room and me, rejuvenate a past.
But suddenly, across my climbing fever
10 Of proud delight—a multiplying cry.
A cry of bitter dead men who will never
Attend a gentle maker of musical joy.
Then my thawed eye will go again to ice.
And stone will shove the softness from my face.

mentors

For I am rightful fellow of their band.
My best allegiances are to the dead.
I swear to keep the dead upon my mind,
Disdain for all time to be overglad.
5 Among spring flowers, under summer trees,
By chilling autumn waters, in the frosts
Of supercilious winter—all my days
I'll have as mentors those reproving ghosts.
And at that cry, at that remotest whisper,

10 I'll stop my casual business. Leave the banquet.
Or leave the ball—reluctant to unclasp her
Who may be fragrant as the flower she wears,
Make gallant bows and dim excuses, then quit
Light for the midnight that is mine and theirs.

the white troops had their orders but
the Negroes looked like men

They had supposed their formula was fixed.
They had obeyed instructions to devise
A type of cold, a type of hooded gaze.
But when the Negroes came they were perplexed.
5 These Negroes looked like men. Besides, it taxed
Time and the temper to remember those
Congenital iniquities that cause
Disfavor of the darkness. Such as boxed
Their feelings properly, complete to tags—
10 A box for dark men and a box for Other—
Would often find the contents had been scrambled.
Or even switched. Who really gave two figs?
Neither the earth nor heaven ever trembled.
And there was nothing startling in the weather.

firstly inclined to take what it is told

Thee sacrosanct, Thee sweet, Thee crystalline,
With the full jewel wile of mighty light—
With the narcotic milk of peace for men
Who find Thy beautiful center and relate
5 Thy round command, Thy grand, Thy mystic good—
Thee like the classic quality of a star:
A little way from warmth, a little sad,
Delicately lovely to adore—
I had been brightly ready to believe.
10 For youth is a frail thing, not unafraid.
Firstly inclined to take what it is told.
Firstly inclined to lean. Greedy to give
Faith tidy and total. To a total God.
With billowing heartiness no whit withheld.

"God works in a mysterious way"

But often now the youthful eye cuts down its
Own dainty veiling. Or submits to winds.

And many an eye that all its age had drawn its
Beam from a Book endures the impudence
5 Of modern glare that never heard of tact
Or timeliness, or Mystery that shrouds
Immortal joy: it merely can direct
Chancing feet across dissembling clods.
Out from Thy shadows, from Thy pleasant meadows,
10 Quickly, in undiluted light. Be glad, whose
Mansions are bright, to right Thy children's air.
If Thou be more than hate or atmosphere
Step forth in splendor, mortify our wolves.
Or we assume a sovereignty ourselves.

love note
I: surely

Surely you stay my certain own, you stay
My you. All honest, lofty as a cloud.
Surely I could come now and find you high,
As mine as you ever were; should not be awed.
5 Surely your word would pop as insolent
As always: "Why, of course I love you, dear."
Your gaze, surely, ungauzed as I could want.
Your touches, that never were careful, what they were.
Surely—But I am very off from that.
10 From surely. From indeed. From the decent arrow
That was my clean naïveté and my faith.
This morning men deliver wounds and death.
They will deliver death and wounds tomorrow.
And I doubt all. You. Or a violet.

love note
II: flags

Still, it is dear defiance now to carry
Fair flags of you above my indignation,
Top, with a pretty glory and a merry
Softness, the scattered pound of my cold passion.
5 I pull you down my foxhole. Do you mind?
You burn in bits of saucy color then.
I let you flutter out against the pained
Volleys. Against my power crumpled and wan.
You, and the yellow pert exuberance
10 Of dandelion days, unmocking sun:
The blowing of clear wind in your gay hair;
Love changeful in you (like a music, or

Like a sweet mournfulness, or like a dance,
Or like the tender struggle of a fan).

the progress

And still we wear our uniforms, follow
The cracked cry of the bugles, comb and brush
Our pride and prejudice, doctor the sallow
Initial ardor, wish to keep it fresh.
5 Still we applaud the President's voice and face.
Still we remark on patriotism, sing,
Salute the flag, thrill heavily, rejoice
For death of men who too saluted, sang.
But inward grows a soberness, an awe,
10 A fear, a deepening hollow through the cold.
For even if we come out standing up
How shall we smile, congratulate: and how
Settle in chairs? Listen, listen. The step
Of iron feet again. And again wild.

ACCOUNT: GLADYS MARGARET WILLIAMS ON A MULTICULTURAL APPROACH TO "GAY CHAPS AT THE BAR"

Williams begins by inquiring about the interest that Brooks shows in the sonnet form itself and the relation of that form to other cultural expressions. What technical characteristics and advantages does the sonnet offer to Brooks as a poet? For one thing, the form allows for a short and coolly intense expression—the qualities also found in many of the poet's poems that are not sonnets:

> Her sensitivity to the authenticity and force of the Afro-American folk forms she learned as a child may be responsible for this penchant. Certainly the blues, the spirituals, and the folk seculars make their impressions quickly. They, like the sonnet, share a sense of intimacy, of a poet-singer speaking-singing directly to another. Several of the folk forms, like the sonnet, are lyric cries. Emotions seem to be poured into and overflowing the sonnet, blues, spirituals.

While the longstanding high cultural status of the sonnet gives it a reputation for complexity, and the popular folk forms appear simple, the two modes are not really opposed in this way. For the folk forms were created by a people that had to mask its true feelings and hence led to "a

Gladys Margaret Williams, "Gwendolyn Brooks's Way With the Sonnet" *CLA Journal*, 26 (1982–83), 215–240.

language of accommodation and concealment, a language of ironic double-ness, a language whose messages were intended to be received one way by outsiders and in another way by insiders." Perhaps the poet's under-standing of the folk forms thereby led her to an appreciation of how to accommodate old poetic forms like the sonnet to her own new ends, giv-ing "restraint and distance to the nearly unbearable ethnic experience, turning screams and bitter anguish into high art."

The war sonnets were in fact written about a world that required this kind of art, for in World War II the Navy still automatically consigned what it then called Negroes to menial duties, and it was only with reluc-tance that the Army Air Corps trained Negro officers as combat pilots and navigators. Even these men were housed separately in the South, and they were policed at Tuskegee by the Alabama State Police.

Williams says that it is against such a background that the sonnet se-ries must be read. In the first sonnet, for example, the apparent confi-dence in the attitudes of the young men toward their abilities and powers must be read against not only the dangers they face but the problematics of the patriotism that brings them to those dangers—an issue examined further and in greater depth in later sonnets.

In "The white troops . . .," for example, the white men were follow-ing orders, and the poem describes in rigid and fixed rhythms how "their formula was fixed," but:

> Things shake loose when the Negroes come. The contents of boxes, one marked "dark men" and one marked "Other," are scrambled. The col-loquialism in line twelve is brilliant. Negroes are men, not denizens of the netherworld who disturb the universe when they appear. The change in language from formality to naturalness *is* meaning in the only Gay Chaps sonnet in which Brooks writes outside the gay chaps as personae.

Similarly the "Liberty" that Williams sees as the apostrophized *Thou* in a later sonnet may appear either in a corrupted or uncorrupted mode. If true liberty is not the issue, the gay chaps themselves, it is implied, will fight to make it one. "Blinded by 'a modern glare' and energized by their own frustrated power, they will overwhelm Liberty in her corrupt mani-festation." Williams concludes that it is in touches like these that Brooks supplies the texture of social context for the soldiers in the poem:

> The unmasking of the gay chaps has been so well done, the fleshing of the faces and states of being so clearly and surely achieved that Brooks has directed readers to her valuation of the social context which has made the gay chaps the men they are. We deny the truth of that valua-tion at our personal—and national—peril.

That is, Brooks has merged these several modes of being and identity—personal, racial, social, national—by merging uses of language. Her sonnet form may similarly be supported by many other folk forms that supply the necessary complexity of expression to a complex content.

ACCOUNT: MARIA K. MOOTRY ON A NEW CRITICAL READING OF "GAY CHAPS AT THE BAR"

Mootry sees the sonnet sequence as reflective of a modernist impulse. Using "vivid personal landscapes, narrative and epigraph," Brooks creates in an indirect and understated way a "collage-like assemblage by adding to them visual prosody and shifting voice." Mootry suggests that, given the setting of World War II, such techniques are necessary for "a responsible art" that can combat fascism, while simultaneously expressing a love for and critique of American democracy:

> It is from this perspective that "Gay Chaps" may be seen as a collage with a modernist aesthetic of indeterminacy, fragmentation, multi-locused meaning, and difficulty of interpretation.

Mootry sees the "interplay" of sequence title, dedication, and epigraph at the beginning of the sequence as offering a good example of Brooks' "visual prosody" by setting a pattern of repetition and variation of themes in both "heroic" and "ordinary" modes:

> Comparable to the scraps of news copy typical of plastic collage, this fragment from a friend's letter injects a private, almost confessional, voice into the collage of sounds that will structure the text. It also undercuts the bold "public" ethos suggested by the title. Further, the identification of the letter writer's location (i.e., 'LIEUTENANT WILLIAM COUCH/in the South Pacific') elliptically establishes the text's shifting geographical imagery. The non-Western, the tropical and the exotic are juxtaposed with the American, the urban, the commonplace. Such protean landscape imagery matches the voices that will reverberate throughout the sonnets.

Allusions to popular culture in the context of altered Shakespearean and Petrarchean forms give another layer to the texture as do the opening phrases that begin, often *in medias res*, to set up a series of implied relationships. Those relationships are themselves fragmentary and tentative as implied by the use of the word "still" in the last two sonnets or by beginning with "But" in an earlier one.

Similarly, the variations of voice—from first-person to impersonal narrative—work contrapuntally, yet at the same time they establish an element of continuity among the sonnets. There are apostrophic addresses to absent friends and lovers as in "love note I: surely" and "love note II: flags." In the first and last sonnets, the "we" that speak collectively for the "Gay Chaps" act as a unifying sound for the sequence.

From Maria K. Mootry, "The Step of Iron Feet: Creative Practice in the War Sonnets of Melvin B. Tolson and Gwendolyn Brooks," *Obsidian II*, 2, no. 3 (1987), 69–87.

Other patterns present themselves simultaneously. In "love note II: flags," for example, Brooks joins the female icon with patriotic symbols, particularly the flag, thus creating an interplay between reality and illusion:

> Here the woman–flag equation achieves surprising meaning when the soldier makes the equivocal gesture of taking the flag he has carried with 'dear defiance,' and pulling it 'down' into the foxhole, then releasing it to flutter again 'crumpled and wan' against his 'passion.' Her womanness is associated, as in tradition, with the lovely, the privileged, the changeful, the weak, but it is also a symbol the Black soldier must appropriate even as he defends it. Brooks thus suggests that an 'illicit' sexual act if not a love affair, is necessary between a Black man and his 'fair' democracy. . . . The soldier's love–doubt relation with a vacillating America is seen when he describes the flag–woman to herself: The blowing of clear wind in your gay hair;/Love changeful in you. . . ."

Mootry notes that sound images also make a theme that works in a collage-like way. Sounds also form patterns of true and false, reality and illusion, and the mute soldiers of the first sonnet are true to the enormity of their situation ("We brought/No brass fortissimo, among our talents,/To holler down the lions in this air." Their silence contrasts to the "banal phrases uttered by well meaning civilians" like "come back" and "careful" in the fourth sonnet:

> Thus, from the "cracked cry of bugles" to the "step of iron feet" a collage of sounds and silence reifies the soldiers' metaphysical and sociopolitical condition. In the sound image of the iron feet, Brooks sets up a brilliant final "equivocal vibration." Are these the marking boots of democracy or of Nazi Germany? Or are they the home-grown sound of American racism? The step of iron feet becomes a somber pun, suggesting even the iron feet of metrical convention, the tyranny of poetic practice to match the tyranny of political relations.

In these ways, the poet's modernist impulse is adapted to a phase of modern life in a country whose culture is also in many ways like a collage. In using the poetic equivalent of collage, Brooks "insisted on seeking a creative practice" that would make her technique accountable to her ideas as she wished her society would be accountable to its citizens.

SUGGESTIONS FOR DISCUSSION AND WRITING

1. Compare and contrast Brooks' sonnets with the more traditional examples of Shakespeare (see p. 455). How does the **meter** differ? Does

Brooks use **vers libre**? How do you scan the "rigid rhythms" mentioned by Mootry as describing the white troops?

2. Characterize the **tones of voice** created by Brooks for different personae in different poems. How do they differ? How are they similar—in **diction**, for example? How does the **dramatic situation** differ in each poem? What **metaphors** does Brooks use, and how are they related to the **dramatic situation** of her **setting** for the **sonnet sequence**?

3. Both Mootry and Williams see the dramatic tensions of the poems informed by issues of race. How are those tensions also informed by the issue of the threat of sudden death? Find some moments when death seems to be the main theme, explicit or implicit, and describe the ways in which Brooks uses language to create that theme.

4. Given the conventions of diction at the time, in the poems "Gay" means "lighthearted" and has no connotations of homosexuality. Find some other poems in the collection that convey a feeling of lightheartedness and compare and contrast the ways Brooks and the poet you choose create this effect. Include Wordsworth's "I Wandered Lonely as a Cloud" in your discussion.

5. Pick another critical approach and make some notes for discussion or for an essay on how it illuminates one or more of the sonnets. For example, how might a psychoanalytic approach read the images in "love note II: flags?"

MORE POEMS BY GWENDOLYN BROOKS

the ballad of chocolate Mabbie

It was Mabbie without the grammar school gates.
And Mabbie was all of seven.
And Mabbie was cut from a chocolate bar.
And Mabbie thought life was heaven.

5 The grammar school gates were the pearly gates,
For Willie Boone went to school.
When she sat by him in history class
Was only her eyes were cool.

It was Mabbie without the grammar school gates
10 Waiting for Willie Boone.
Half hour after the closing bell!
He would surely be coming soon.

Oh, warm is the waiting for joys, my dears!
And it cannot be too long.
15 Oh, pity the little poor chocolate lips
That carry the bubble of song!

Out came the saucily bold Willie Boone.
It was woe for our Mabbie now.
He wore like a jewel a lemon-hued lynx
20 With sand-waves loving her brow.

It was Mabbie alone by the grammar school gates.
Yet chocolate companions had she:
Mabbie on Mabbie with hush in the heart.
Mabbie on Mabbie to be.

A Lovely Love

Let it be alleys. Let it be a hall
Whose janitor javelins epithet and thought
To cheapen hyacinth darkness that we sought
And played we found, rot, make the petals fall.
5 Let it be stairways, and a splintery box
Where you have thrown me, scraped me with your kiss,
Have honed me, have released me after this
Cavern kindness, smiled away our shocks.
That is the birthright of our lovely love
10 In swaddling clothes. Not like that Other one.
Not lit by any fondling star above.
Not found by any wise men, either. Run.
People are coming. They must not catch us here
Definitionless in this strict atmosphere.

We Real Cool

**The Pool Players.
Seven at the Golden Shovel.**

We real cool. We
Left school. We

Lurk late. We
Strike straight. We

Sing sin. We
Thin gin. We

Jazz June. We
Die soon.

A Collection of Poems

Westron winde, when will thou blow,
The smalle raine downe can raine?
Crist, if my love wer in my armis,
And I in my bed againe.

ANONYMOUS

Sir Patrick Spens
(Sixteenth Century)

1

The king sits in Dumferling town,
  Drinking the blude-reid° wine: *blood-red*
"Oh whar will I get guid sailor,
  To sail this ship of mine?"

2

5 Up and spak an eldern knicht,
  Sat at the king's richt knee:
"Sir Patrick Spens is the best sailor
  That sails upon the sea."

3

The king has written a braid° letter   *broad*
10 And signed it wi' his hand,
And sent it to Sir Patrick Spens,
  Was walking on the sand.

4

The first line that Sir Patrick read,
  A loud lauch° lauched he;   *laugh*
15 The next line that Sir Patrick read,
  The tear blinded his ee.°   *eye*

5

"O wha is this has done this deed,
  This ill deed done to me,
To send me out this time o' the year,
20   To sail upon the sea?

6

"Mak haste, mak haste, my mirry men all,
  Our guid ship sails the morn."
"O say na sae,° my master dear,   *so*
  For I fear a deadly storm.

7

25 "Late, late yestre'en I saw the new moon
  Wi' the auld moon in hir arm,
And I fear, I fear, my dear master,
  That we will come to harm."

8

O our Scots nobles were richt laith°   *loath*
30   To weet° their cork-heeled shoon,°   *wet / shoes*
But lang or° a' the play were played   *before*
  Their hats they swam aboon.

9

O lang, lang may their ladies sit,
  Wi' their fans into their hand,
35 Or ere they see Sir Patrick Spens
  Come sailing to the land.

10

O lang, lang may the ladies stand
  Wi' their gold kems° in their hair,   *combs*
Waiting for their ain dear lords,
40   For they'll see them na mair.

11

Half o'er, half o'er to Aberdour
  It's fifty fadom deep,
And there lies guid Sir Patrick Spens
  Wi' the Scots lords at his feet.

SIR THOMAS WYATT (1503?–1542)

The Lover Showeth How He Is Forsaken of Such as He Sometime Enjoyed
(1557)

They flee from me that sometime did me seek,
  With naked foot stalking in my chamber.
I have seen them gentle, tame and meek,
  That now are wild and do not remember
5 That sometime they put themselves in danger
    To take bread at my hand; and now they range
    Busily seeking with a continual change.

Thanked be fortune, it hath been otherwise
  Twenty times better; but once, in special,
10 In thin array, after a pleasant guise,
  When her loose gown from her shoulders did fall,
  And she me caught in her arms long and small,
    Therewith all sweetly did me kiss,
    And softly said: "Dear heart, how like you this?"

15 It was no dream; I lay broad waking:
  But all is turned thorough my gentleness
Into a strange fashion of forsaking;
  And I have leave to go of her goodness;
  And she also to use new-fangleness.
20   But since that I so kindely° am served,   *naturally*
    I fain would know what she hath deserved.

CHRISTOPHER MARLOWE (1564–1593)

The Passionate Shepherd to His Love
(1599, 1600)

Come live with me and be my love,
And we will all the pleasures prove°   *try*
That valleys, groves, hills, and fields,
Woods, or steepy mountain yields.

5 And we will sit upon the rocks,
Seeing the shepherds feed their flocks,
By shallow rivers to whose falls
Melodious birds sing madrigals.

And I will make thee beds of roses
10 And a thousand fragrant posies,

A cap of flowers, and a kirtle
Embroidered all with leaves of myrtle;

A gown made of the finest wool
Which from our pretty lambs we pull;
15 Fair lined slippers for the cold,
With buckles of the purest gold;

A belt of straw and ivy buds,
With coral clasps and amber studs:
And if these pleasures may thee move,
20 Come live with me, and be my love.

The shepherds' swains shall dance and sing
For thy delight each May morning:
If these delights thy mind may move,
Then live with me and be my love.

EDMUND SPENSER (1552?–1599)

from Amoretti/*Sonnet 75*
(1595)

One day I wrote her name upon the strand,
But came the waves and washéd it away:
Agayne I wrote it with a second hand,°   *a second time*
But came the tyde, and made my paynes his pray.
5 "Vayne man," sayd she, "that doest in vaine assay,
A mortall thing so to immortalize,
For I my selve shall lyke to this decay,
And eek° my name bee wypéd out lykewize."   *also*
"Not so," quod° I, "let baser things devize°   *quoth* / *plan*
10 To dy in dust, but you shall live by fame:
My verse your vertues rare shall eternize,
And in the hevens wryte your glorious name.
Where whenas death shall all the world subdew,
Our love shall live, and later life renew."

SIR PHILIP SIDNEY (1554–1586)

from Astrophel and Stella/*Sonnet 31*
(1582)

With how sad steps, Oh Moon, thou climb'st the skies,
How silently, and with how wan a face!
What, may it be that even in heav'nly place
That busy archer° his sharp arrows tries?   *Cupid*

5 Sure, if that long-with-love-acquainted eyes
  Can judge of love, thou feel'st a lover's case;
  I read it in thy looks: thy languished grace,
  To me that feel the like, thy state descries.
  Then even of fellowship, Oh Moon, tell me,
10 Is constant love deemed there but want of wit?
  Are beauties there as proud as here they be?
  Do they above love to be loved, and yet
  Those lovers scorn whom that love doth possess?
  Do they call virtue there ungratefulness?

MICHAEL DRAYTON (1563–1631)

from Idea/Sonnet 61
(1619)

Since there's no help, come let us kiss and part;
Nay, I have done, you get no more of me,
And I am glad, yea glad with all my heart
That thus so cleanly I myself can free;
5 Shake hands forever, cancel all our vows,
And when we meet at any time again,
Be it not seen in either of our brows
That we one jot of former love retain.
Now at the last gasp of love's latest breath,
10 When, his pulse failing, passion speechless lies,
When faith is kneeling by his bed of death,
And innocence is closing up his eyes,
   Now if thou wouldst, when all have given him over,
   From death to life thou mightst him yet recover.

SIR WALTER RALEGH (ca. 1552–1618)

The Nymph's Reply to the Shepherd[1]
(1600)

If all the world and love were young,
And truth in every shepherd's tongue,
These pretty pleasures might me move
To live with thee and be thy love.

5 Time drives the flocks from field to fold
When rivers rage and rocks grow cold,
And Philomel° becometh dumb;   *the nightingale*
The rest complains of cares to come.

---

[1]Written in reply to Christopher Marlowe's *The Passionate Shepherd to His Love.*

The flowers do fade, and wanton fields
10 To wayward winter reckoning yields;
A honey tongue, a heart of gall,
Is fancy's spring, but sorrow's fall.

Thy gowns, thy shoes, thy beds of roses,
Thy cap, thy kirtle,° and thy posies   *long dress*
15 Soon break, soon wither, soon forgotten—
In folly ripe, in reason rotten.

Thy belt of stray and ivy buds,
Thy coral clasps and amber studs,
All these in me no means can move
20 To come to thee and be thy love.

But could youth last and love still breed,
Had joys no date nor age no need,
Then these delights my mind might move
To live with thee and be thy love.

WILLIAM SHAKESPEARE (1564–1616)

Sonnet 18: Shall I Compare Thee to a Summer's Day?
(1609)

Shall I compare thee to a summer's day?
Thou art more lovely and more temperate.
Rough winds do shake the darling buds of May,
And summer's lease hath all too short a date.
5 Sometime too hot the eye of heaven shines,
And often is his gold complexion dimmed;
And every fair from fair sometime declines,
By chance, or nature's changing course, untrimmed;
But thy eternal summer shall not fade
10 Nor lose possession of that fair thou ow'st,°   *beauty you possess*
Nor shall Death brag thou wand'rest in his shade
When in eternal lines to time thou grow'st.
   So long as men can breathe or eyes can see,
   So long lives this, and this gives life to thee.

Sonnet 29: When, in Disgrace with Fortune and Men's Eyes
(1609)

When, in disgrace with Fortune and men's eyes,
I all alone beweep my outcast state,
And trouble deaf heaven with my bootless cries,
And look upon myself and curse my fate,
5 Wishing me like to one more rich in hope,
Featured like him, like him with friends possessed,
Desiring this man's art, and that man's scope,
With what I most enjoy contented least;
Yet in these thoughts myself almost despising,
10 Haply I think on thee, and then my state,
Like to the lark at break of day arising
From sullen earth, sings hymns at heaven's gate;
   For thy sweet love rememb'red such wealth brings
   That then I scorn to change my state with kings.

Sonnet 130: My Mistress' Eyes Are Nothing Like the Sun
(1609)

My mistress' eyes are nothing like the sun;
Coral is far more red than her lips' red;
If snow be white, why then her breasts are dun;
If hairs be wires, black wires grow on her head.
5 I have seen roses damasked,° red and white,   *variegated*
But no such roses see I in her cheeks;
And in some perfumes is there more delight
Than in the breath that from my mistress reeks.
I love to hear her speak, yet well I know
10 That music hath a far more pleasing sound;
I grant I never saw a goddess go;°   *walk*
My mistress, when she walks, treads on the ground.
And yet, by heaven, I think my love as rare
As any she belied with false compare.

JOHN DONNE (1572–1631)

The Good-Morrow
(1633)

I wonder, by my troth, what thou and I
Did, till we loved? were we not weaned till then?
But sucked on country pleasures, childishly?

Or snorted we in the Seven Sleepers' den?[1]
5 'Twas so; but° this, all pleasures fancies be.   *except for*
If ever any beauty I did see,
Which I desired, and got, 'twas but a dream of thee.

And now good-morrow to our waking souls,
Which watch not one another out of fear;
10 For love, all love of other sights controls,
And makes one little room an everywhere.
Let sea-discoverers to new worlds have gone,
Let maps° to others, worlds on worlds have shown,   *sky charts*
Let us possess one world, each hath one, and is one.

15 My face in thine eye, thine in mine appears,
And true plain hearts do in the faces rest;
Where can we find two better hemispheres,
Without sharp north, without declining west?
Whatever dies was not mixed equally;[2]
20 If our two loves be one, or, thou and I
Love so alike that none do slacken, none can die.

The Flea
(1633)

Mark but this flea, and mark in this,
How little that which thou deny'st me is;
Me it sucked first, and now sucks thee,
And in this flea, our two bloods mingled be;[1]
5 Confess it, this cannot be said
A sin, or shame, or loss of maidenhead,
    Yet this enjoys before it woo,
    And pampered swells with one blood made of two,
    And this, alas, is more than we would do.

10 Oh stay, three lives in one flea spare,
Where we almost, nay more than married are.
This flea is you and I, and this
Our marriage bed, and marriage temple is;
Though parents grudge, and you, we'are met,
15 And cloistered in these living walls of jet.

---

[1] Seven early Christians, immured in the persecution of A.D. 249, were believed to have slept for nearly two centuries.

[2] In earlier medicine, death was often considered the result of an imbalance in the body's elements.

[1] It was commonly thought that during sexual intercourse the blood of the lovers mingled—a notion derived from Aristotle.

Though use make you apt to kill me,
Let not to this, self murder added be,
And sacrilege, three sins in killing three.

Cruel and sudden, hast thou since
20 Purpled thy nail, in blood of innocence?
In what could this flea guilty be,
Except in that drop which it sucked from thee?
Yet thou triumph'st, and say'st that thou
Find'st not thyself, nor me the weaker now;
25   'Tis true, then learn how false, fears be;
Just so much honour, when thou yield'st to me,
Will waste, as this flea's death took life from thee.

The Ecstasy

(1633)

Where, like a pillow on a bed,
    A pregnant bank swelled up to rest
The violet's reclining head,
    Sat we two, one another's best.
5 Our hands were firmly cémented
    With a fast balm, which thence did spring.
Our eye-beams twisted, and did thread
    Our eyes upon one double string;
So to'intergraft our hands, as yet
10   Was all the means to make us one;
And pictures in our eyes to get°   beget
    Was all our propagation.
As 'twixt two equal armies, Fate
    Suspends uncertain victory,
15 Our souls (which to advance their state,
    Were gone out) hung 'twixt her and me.
And whilst our souls negotiate there,
    We like sepulchral statues lay;
All day the same our postures were,
20   And we said nothing all the day.
If any, so by love refined
    That he soul's language understood,
And by good love were grown all mind,
    Within convenient distance stood,
25 He (though he knew not which soul spake,
    Because both meant, both spake the same)
Might thence a new concoction[1] take,

---

[1] Mixture of diverse elements refined by heat (alchemical term).

And part far purer than he came.
This ecstasy doth unperplex,
30   We said, and tell us what we love;
We see by this it was not sex;
  We see we saw not what did move;
But as all several° souls contain   *separate*
  Mixture of things, they know not what,
35 Love these mixed souls doth mix again,
  And makes both one, each this and that.
A single violet transplant,
  The strength, the colour, and the size
(All which before was poor, and scant)
40   Redoubles still, and multiplies.
When love, with one another so
  Interinanimates two souls,
That abler soul, which thence doth flow,
  Defects of loneliness controls.
45 We then, who are this new soul, know,
  Of what we are composed, and made,
For, th' atomies° of which we grow,   *atoms*
  Are souls, whom no change can invade.
But O alas, so long, so far
50   Our bodies why do we forbear?
They're ours, though they're not we; we are
  Th' intelligences, they the spheres.[2]
We owe them thanks because they thus,
  Did us to us at first convey,
55 Yielded their forces, sense, to us,
  Nor are dross to us, but allay.°   *alloy*
On man heaven's influence works not so
  But that it first imprints the air,[3]
So soul into the soul may flow,
60   Though it to body first repair.
As our blood labors to beget
  Spirits as like souls as it can,[4]
Because such fingers need to knit
  That subtle knot which makes us man:
65 So must pure lovers' souls descend

---

[2] The nine orders of angels ("intelligences") were believed to govern the nine spheres of Ptolemaic astronomy.

[3] Influences from the heavenly bodies were conceived of as being transmitted through the medium of the air; also, angels were thought to assume bodies of air in their dealings with men.

[4] "Spirits" were vapors believed to permeate the blood and to mediate between the body and the soul.

To' affections, and to faculties
    Which sense may reach and apprehend;
      Else a great Prince in prison lies.
    To'our bodies turn we then, that so
70   Weak men on love revealed may look;
    Love's mysteries in souls do grow,
      But yet the body is his book.
    And if some lover, such as we,
      Have heard this dialogue of one,
75 Let him still mark us; he shall see
    Small change when we're to bodies gone.

BEN JONSON (1573–1637)

On My First Son
(1616)

Farewell, thou child of my right hand,[1] and joy;
My sin was too much hope of thee, loved boy:
Seven years thou'wert lent to me, and I thee pay,
Exacted by thy fate, on the just day.[2]
5 O could I lose all father now! for why
Will man lament the state he should envý,
To have so soon 'scaped world's and flesh's rage,
And, if no other misery, yet age?
Rest in soft peace, and asked, say, "Here doth lie
10 Ben Jonson his best piece of poetry."
For whose sake henceforth all his vows be such
As what he loves may never like too much.

ROBERT HERRICK (1591–1674)

Delight in Disorder
(1648)

A sweet disorder in the dress
Kindles in clothes a wantonness.
A lawn about the shoulders thrown
Into a fine distractiön;
5 An erring lace, which here and there
Enthralls the crimson stomacher;[1]
A cuff neglectful, and thereby
Ribbons to flow confusedly;

---

[1] A literal translation of the Hebrew *Benjamin,* the boy's name.
[2] Jonson's son died on his seventh birthday in 1603.
[1] An ornamental piece worn under the open (and often laced) front of a bodice.

A winning wave, deserving note,
10 In the tempestuous petticoat;
A careless shoestring, in whose tie
I see a wild civility;
Do more bewitch me than when art
Is too precise in every part.

To the Virgins, to Make Much of Time
(1648)

Gather ye rosebuds while ye may,
Old time is still a-flying;
And this same flower that smiles today
Tomorrow will be dying.

5 The glorious lamp of heaven, the sun,
The higher he's a-getting,
The sooner will his race be run,
And nearer he's to setting.

That age is best which is the first,
10 When youth and blood are warmer;
But being spent, the worse, and worst
Times still succeed the former.

Then be not coy, but use your time,
And, while ye may, go marry;
15 For, having lost but once your prime,
You may forever tarry.

GEORGE HERBERT (1593–1633)
Easter Wings
(1633)

Lord, who createdst man in wealth and store,°   *abundance*
Though foolishly he lost the same,
Decaying more and more
Till he became
5   Most poor:
With thee
O let me rise
As larks, harmoniously,
And sing this day thy victories:
10 Then shall the fall further the flight in me.

My tender age in sorrow did begin;
   And still with sicknesses and shame
      Thou didst so punish sin,
        That I became
15   Most thin.
        With thee
      Let me combine,
   And feel this day thy victory;
   For, if I imp° my wing on thine,   *graft*
20 Affliction shall advance the flight in me.

Virtue
(1633)

Sweet day, so cool, so calm, so bright,
   The bridal of the earth and sky:
The dew shall weep thy fall tonight;
    For thou must die.

5 Sweet rose, whose hue, angry and brave,
   Bids the rash gazer wipe his eye:
Thy root is ever in its grave,
    And thou must die.

Sweet spring, full of sweet days and roses,
10   A box where sweets° compacted lie;   *perfumes*
My music shows ye have your closes,[1]
    And all must die.

Only a sweet and virtuous soul,
   Like seasoned timber, never gives;
15 But though the whole world turn to coal,[2]
   Then chiefly lives.

JOHN MILTON (1608–1664)
When I Consider How My Light Is Spent[1]
(1652)

When I consider how my light is spent
Ere half my days, in this dark world and wide,

---

[1] A close is a cadence, the conclusion of a musical strain.
[2] An allusion to Judgment Day, when the world will end in a general conflagration.
[1] Milton had become totally blind in 1651.

And that one talent which is death to hide[2]
Lodged with me useless, though my soul more bent
5 To serve therewith my Maker, and present
My true account, lest he returning chide;
"Doth God exact day-labor, light denied?"
I fondly° ask; but Patience to prevent   *foolishly*
That murmur, soon replies, "God doth not need
10   Either man's work or his own gifts; who best
Bear his mild yoke, they serve him best. His state
Is kingly. Thousands at his bidding speed
And post o'er land and ocean without rest:
They also serve who only stand and wait."

RICHARD LOVELACE (1618–1658)

To Lucasta, Going to the Wars
(1649)

Tell me not, sweet, I am unkind
That from the nunnery
Of thy chaste breast and quiet mind,
To war and arms I fly.

5 True, a new mistress now I chase,
The first foe in the field;
And with a stronger faith embrace
A sword, a horse, a shield.

Yet this inconstancy is such
10 As you too shall adore;
I could not love thee, dear, so much,
Loved I not honor more.

To Althea, from Prison
(1649)

When Love with unconfinéd wings
Hovers within my gates,
And my divine Althea brings
To whisper at the grates;
5 When I lie tangled in her hair
And fettered to her eye,

---

[2] An allusion to the parable of the talents, in which the servant who buried the single talent his lord had given him, instead of investing it, was deprived of all he had and cast "into outer darkness" at the lord's return (Matthew xxv.14–30).

The gods[1] that wanton in the air
Know no such liberty.

When flowing cups run swiftly round,
10 With no allaying Thames,[2]
Our careless heads with roses bound,
Our hearts with loyal flames;
When thirsty grief in wine we steep,
When healths and draughts go free,
15 Fishes, that tipple in the deep,
Know no such liberty.

When, like committed° linnets, I   *caged*
With shriller throat shall sing
The sweetness, mercy, majesty,
20 And glories of my King;
When I shall voice aloud how good
He is, how great should be,
Enlargéd winds, that curl the flood,
Know no such liberty.

25 Stone walls do not a prison make,
Nor iron bars a cage;
Minds innocent and quiet take
That for an hermitage.
If I have freedom in my love,
30 And in my soul am free,
Angels alone, that soar above,
Enjoy such liberty.

ANDREW MARVELL (1621–1678)

To His Coy Mistress
(1681)

Had we but world enough, and time,
This coyness, lady, were no crime.
We would sit down, and think which way
To walk, and pass our long love's day.
5 Thou by the Indian Ganges' side
Shoudst rubies[1] find; I by the tide
Of Humber[2] would complain. I would

---

[1] Most 17th-century versions read "birds" for "gods."
[2] i.e., without dilution (the Thames River flows through London).
[1] Rubies are talismans, preserving virginity.
[2] The Humber flows through Marvell's native town of Hull.

Love you ten years before the flood,
And you should, if you please, refuse
10 Till the conversion of the Jews.[3]
My vegetable[4] love should grow
Vaster than empires and more slow;
An hundred years should go to praise
Thine eyes, and on thy forehead gaze;
15 Two hundred to adore each breast,
But thirty thousand to the rest;
An age at least to every part,
And the last age should show your heart.
For, lady, you deserve this state,°   *dignity*
20 Nor would I love at lower rate.
    But at my back I always hear
Time's wingéd chariot hurrying near;
And yonder all before us lie
Deserts of vast eternity.
25 Thy beauty shall no more be found;
Nor, in thy marble vault, shall sound
My echoing song; then worms shall try
That long-preserved virginity,
And your quaint° honor turn to dust,   *over-subtle*
30 And into ashes all my lust:
The grave's a fine and private place,
But none, I think, do there embrace.
    Now therefore, while the youthful hue
Sits on thy skin like morning glow,
35 And while thy willing soul transpires°   *breathes out*
At every pore with instant fires,
Now let us sport us while we may,
And now, like amorous birds of prey,
Rather at once our time devour
40 Than languish in his slow-chapped° power.   *slow-jawed*
Let us roll all our strength and all
Our sweetness up into one ball,
And tear our pleasures with rough strife
Thorough the iron gates[5] of life:
45 Thus, though we cannot make our sun
Stand still,[6] yet we will make him run.

---

[3] To occur, as tradition had it, at the end of recorded history.

[4] A technical term: "possessing, like plants, the power of growth but not of consciousness"; in context, "being magnified without conscious nurture."

[5] The obscurity "iron gates" suggests that the "ball" of line 42 has become a missile from a siege gun, battering its way into a citadel.

[6] We lack, that is, the power of Zeus, who, to prolong his enjoyment of the mortal Alcmena, arrested the diurnal course and created a week-long night.

JONATHAN SWIFT (1667–1745)

A Description of the Morning
(1709)

    Now hardly here and there a hackney-coach[1]
    Appearing, showed the ruddy morn's approach.
    Now Betty from her master's bed had flown,
    And softly stole to discompose her own;
5 The slip-shod 'prentice from his master's door
    Had pared the dirt and sprinkled round the floor.
    Now Moll had whirled her mop with dext'rous airs,
    Prepared to scrub the entry and the stairs.
    The youth with broomy stumps began to trace
10 The kennel-edge,[2] where wheels had worn the place.
    The small-coal man[3] was heard with cadence deep,
    Till drowned in shriller notes of chimney-sweep:
    Duns° at his lordship's gate began to meet;   *bill collectors*
    And brickdust Moll[4] had screamed through half the street.
15 The turnkey° now his flock returning sees,   *jailer*
    Duly let out a-nights to steal for fees:
    The watchful bailiffs[5] take their silent stands,
    And schoolboys lag with satchels in their hands.

SAMUEL JOHNSON (1709–1784)

On the Death of Dr. Robert Levet
(1783)

    Condemned to Hope's delusive mine,
        As on we toil from day to day,
    By sudden blasts, or slow decline,
        Our social comforts drop away.

5 Well tried through many a varying year,
        See Levet to the grave descend;
    Officious,° innocent, sincere,   *dutiful*
        Of every friendless name the friend.

---

[1] A horse-drawn carriage, for hire.
[2] Curb of the road.
[3] Seller of charcoal.
[4] A woman selling powdered brick (used for cleaning knives).
[5] i.e., sheriff's deputies.

Yet still he fills Affection's eye,
10   Obscurely wise, and coarsely kind;
Nor, lettered Arrogance, deny
    Thy praise to merit unrefined.

When fainting Nature called for aid,
    And hovering Death prepared the blow,
15 His vigorous remedy displayed
    The power of art without the show.

In Misery's darkest cavern known,
    His useful care was ever nigh,
Where hopeless Anguish poured his groan,
20   And lonely Want retired to die.

No summons mocked by chill delay,
    No petty gain disdained by pride,
The modest wants of every day
    The toil of every day supplied.

25 His virtues walked their narrow round,
    Nor made a pause, nor left a void;
And sure the Eternal Master found
    The single talent[1] well employed.

The busy day, the peaceful night,
30   Unfelt, uncounted, glided by;
His frame was firm, his powers were bright,
    Though now his eightieth year was nigh.

Then with no throbbing fiery pain,
    No cold gradations of decay,
35 Death broke at once the vital chain,
    And freed his soul the nearest way.

THOMAS GRAY (1716–1771)

Ode: On the Death of a Favorite Cat, Drowned in a Tub of Goldfishes
(1748)

'Twas on a lofty vase's side,
    Where China's gayest art had dyed

---

[1] An allusion to the portion of wealth given in trust in the parable of the talents, Matthew xxv.14–30.

The azure flowers that blow;°   *bloom*
Demurest of the tabby kind,
5 The pensive Selima, reclined,
Gazed on the lake below.

Her conscious tail her joy declared;
The fair round face, the snowy beard,
The velvet of her paws,
10 Her coat, that with the tortoise vies,
Her ears of jet, and emerald eyes,
She saw; and purred applause.

Still had she gazed; but 'midst the tide
Two angel forms were seen to glide,
15   The genii° of the stream: *guardian spirits*
Their scaly armor's Tyrian hue
Through richest purple to the view
Betrayed a golden gleam.[1]

The hapless nymph with wonder saw:
20 A whisker first and then a claw,
With many an ardent wish,
She stretched in vain to reach the prize.
What female heart can gold despise?
What cat's averse to fish?

25 Presumptuous maid! with looks intent
Again she stretched, again she bent,
Nor knew the gulf between.
(Malignant Fate sat by and smiled)
The slippery verge her feet beguiled,
30   She tumbled headlong in.

Eight times emerging from the flood
She mewed to every watery god,
Some speedy aid to send.
No dolphin came, no Nereid stirred;[2]
35 Nor cruel Tom, nor Susan heard;
A favorite has no friend!

---

[1]"Tyrian" and (in classical reference) "purple" cover a considerable spectrum, including crimson. The fish are seen, through red highlights, as golden.

[2]A dolphin appeared to save the singer Arion when he was cast overboard. Nereids are sea-nymphs.

From hence, ye beauties, undeceived,
  Know, one false step is ne'er retrieved,
    And be with caution bold.
40 Not all that tempts your wandering eyes
  And heedless hearts, is lawful prize;
    Nor all that glisters, gold.

Elegy Written in a Country Churchyard
(ca 1742–50)

The curfew tolls the knell of parting day,
  The lowing herd wind slowly o'er the lea,
The plowman homeward plods his weary way,
  And leaves the world to darkness and to me.

5 Now fades the glimmering landscape on the sight,
  And all the air a solemn stillness holds,
Save where the beetle wheels his droning flight,
  And drowsy tinklings lull the distant folds;

Save that from yonder ivy-mantled tower
10 The moping owl does to the moon complain
Of such, as wandering near her secret bower,
  Molest her ancient solitary reign.

Beneath those rugged elms, that yew tree's shade,
  Where heaves the turf in many a moldering heap,
15 Each in his narrow cell forever laid,
  The rude° forefathers of the hamlet sleep.   *rustic*

The breezy call of incense-breathing morn,
  The swallow twittering from the straw-built shed,
The cock's shrill clarion, or the echoing horn,°   *hunting horn*
20 No more shall rouse them from their lowly bed.

For them no more the blazing hearth shall burn,
  Or busy housewife ply her evening care;
No children run to lisp their sire's return,
  Or climb his knees the envied kiss to share.

25 Oft did the harvest to their sickle yield,
  Their furrow oft the stubborn glebe° has broke;   *soil*
How jocund did they drive their team afield!
  How bowed the woods beneath their sturdy stroke!

Let not Ambition mock their useful toil,
30   Their homely joys, and destiny obscure;
Nor Grandeur hear with a disdainful smile
The short and simple annals of the poor.

The boast of heraldry,[1] the pomp of power,
And all that beauty, all that wealth e'er gave,
35 Awaits alike the inevitable hour.
The paths of glory lead but to the grave.

Nor you, ye proud, impute to these the fault,
If Memory o'er their tomb no trophies[2] raise,
Where through the long-drawn aisle and fretted°   ornamented
vault
40   The pealing anthem swells the note of praise.

Can storied urn[3] or animated° bust   lifelike
Back to its mansion call the fleeting breath?
Can Honor's voice provoke° the silent dust,   call forth
Or Flattery soothe the dull cold ear of Death?

45 Perhaps in this neglected spot is laid
Some heart once pregnant with celestial fire;
Hands that the rod of empire might have swayed,
Or waked to ecstasy the living lyre.

But Knowledge to their eyes her ample page
50   Rich with the spoils of time did ne'er unroll;
Chill Penury repressed their noble rage,
And froze the genial current of the soul.

Full many a gem of purest ray serene,
The dark unfathomed caves of ocean bear:
55 Full many a flower is born to blush unseen,
And waste its sweetness on the desert air.

Some village Hampden,[4] that with dauntless breast
The little tyrant of his fields withstood;
Some mute inglorious Milton here may rest,
60   Some Cromwell guiltless of his country's blood.

---

[1] i.e., noble family.

[2] Memorials to military heroes; typically, statuary representations of arms captured in battle.

[3] Funeral urn with descriptive epitaph.

[4] Leader of the opposition to Charles I in the controversy over ship money; killed in battle in the Civil Wars.

The applause of listening senates to command,
  The threats of pain and ruin to despise,
To scatter plenty o'er a smiling land,
  And read their history in a nation's eyes,

65 Their lot forbade: nor circumscribed alone
  Their growing virtues, but their crimes confined;
Forbade to wade through slaughter to a throne,
  And shut the gates of mercy on mankind,

The struggling pangs of conscious truth to hide,
70 To quench the blushes of ingenuous shame,
Or heap the shrine of Luxury and Pride
  With incense kindled at the Muse's flame.

Far from the madding° crowd's ignoble strife,   *milling*
  Their sober wishes never learned to stray;
75 Along the cool sequestered vale of life
  They kept the noiseless tenor of their way.

Yet even these bones from insult to protect
  Some frail memorial still erected nigh,
With uncouth rhymes and shapeless sculpture decked,
80 Implores the passing tribute of a sigh.

Their name, their years, spelt by the unlettered Muse,
  The place of fame and elegy supply:
And many a holy text around she strews,
  That teach the rustic moralist to die.

85 For who to dumb Forgetfulness a prey,
  This pleasing anxious being e'er resigned,
Left the warm precincts of the cheerful day,
  Nor cast one longing lingering look behind?

On some fond breast the parting soul relies,
90 Some pious drops the closing eye requires;
Even from the tomb the voice of Nature cries,
  Even in our ashes live their wonted fires.

For thee, who mindful of the unhonored dead
  Dost in these lines their artless tale relate;
95 If chance, by lonely contemplation led,
  Some kindred spirit shall inquire thy fate,

Haply some hoary-headed swain may say,
  "Oft have we seen him at the peep of dawn

Brushing with hasty steps the dews away
100   To meet the sun upon the upland lawn.

"There at the foot of yonder nodding beech
    That wreathes its old fantastic roots so high,
His listless length at noontide would he stretch,
    And pore upon the brook that babbles by.

105 "Hard by yon wood, now smiling as in scorn,
    Muttering his wayward fancies he would rove,
Now drooping, woeful wan, like one forlorn,
    Or crazed with care, or crossed in hopeless love.

"One morn I missed him on the customed hill,
110   Along the heath and near his favorite tree;
Another came; nor yet beside the rill,
    Nor up the lawn, nor at the wood was he;

"The next with dirges due in sad array
    Slow through the churchway path we saw him borne.
115 Approach and read (for thou canst read) the lay,
    Graved on the stone beneath yon aged thorn."

The Epitaph

Here rests his head upon the lap of Earth
    A youth to Fortune and to Fame unknown.
Fair Science° frowned not on his humble birth,   *Learning*
120   *And Melancholy marked him for her own.*

Large was his bounty, and his soul sincere,
    Heaven did a recompense as largely send:
He gave to Misery all he had, a tear,
    He gained from Heaven ('twas all he wished) a friend.

125 *No farther seek his merits to disclose,*
    Or draw his frailties from their dread abode
(There they alike in trembling hope repose),
    The bosom of his Father and his God.

WILLIAM BLAKE (1757–1827)

The Lamb
(1789)

Little Lamb, who made thee?
Dost thou know who made thee?
Gave the life & bid thee feed,

By the stream & o'er the mead;
5 Gave thee clothing of delight,
Softest clothing wooly bright;
Gave thee such a tender voice,
Making all the vales rejoice!
　　Little Lamb who made thee?
10　　Dost thou know who made thee?

　　Little Lamb I'll tell thee,
　　Little Lamb I'll tell thee!
He° is callèd by thy name,　　　　　　　　　　*Christ*
For he calls himself a Lamb:
15 He is meek & he is mild,
He became a little child:
I a child & thou a lamb,
We are callèd by his name.
　　Little Lamb God bless thee.
20　　Little Lamb God bless thee.

Holy Thursday [I.]
(1789)

'Twas on a Holy Thursday, their innocent faces clean,
The children walking two & two, in red & blue & green,
Grey headed beadles° walkd before with wands as　　*parish officials*
　　white as snow,
5 Till into the high dome of Paul's they like Thames' waters flow.

O what a multitude they seemd, these flowers of London town!
Seated in companies they sit with radiance all their own.
The hum of multitudes was there, but multitudes of lambs,
Thousands of little boys & girls raising their innocent hands.

10 Now like a mighty wind they raise to heaven the voice of song,
Or like harmonious thunderings the seats of heaven among.
Beneath them sit the aged men, wise guardians of the poor;
Then cherish pity, lest you drive an angel from your door.

The Tyger
(1794)

Tyger! Tyger! burning bright
In the forests of the night,
What immortal hand or eye
Could frame thy fearful symmetry?

5 In what distant deeps or skies
  Burnt the fire of thine eyes?
  On what wings dare he aspire?
  What the hand, dare seize the fire?

  And what shoulder, & what art,
10 Could twist the sinews of thy heart?
  And when thy heart began to beat,
  What dread hand? & what dread feet?

  What the hammer? what the chain?
  In what furnace was thy brain?
15 What the anvil? what dread grasp
  Dare its deadly terrors clasp?

  When the stars threw down their spears,
  And water'd heaven with their tears,
  Did he smile his work to see?
20 Did he who made the Lamb make thee?

  Tyger! Tyger! burning bright
  In the forests of the night,
  What immortal hand or eye
  Dare frame thy fearful symmetry?

Holy Thursday [II.]
(1794)

  Is this a holy thing to see,
  In a rich and fruitful land,
  Babes reducd to misery,
  Fed with cold and usurous hand?

5 Is that trembling cry a song?
  Can it be a song of joy?
  And so many children poor?
  It is a land of poverty!

  And their sun does never shine,
10 And their fields and bleak & bare,
  And their ways are fill'd with thorns;
  It is eternal winter there.

  For where-e'er the sun does shine,
  And where-e'er the rain does fall,
15 Babe can never hunger there,
  Nor poverty the mind appall.

ROBERT BURNS (1759–1796)

To a Mouse

On Turning Her Up in Her Nest with the Plough, November, 1785

(1785, 1786)

Wee, sleekit,° cow'rin, tim'rous beastie,   *sleek*
O, what a panic's in they breastie!
Thou need na start awa sae hasty,
    Wi' bickering° brattle!°   *hurried / scamper*
5 I wad be laith to rin an' chase thee,
    Wi' murd'ring pattle!°   *plowstaff ("paddle")*

I'm truly sorry man's dominion
Has broken Nature's social union,
An' justifies that ill opinion
10   Which makes thee startle
At me, thy poor earth-born companion,
    An' fellow-mortal!

I doubt na, whiles,° but thou may thieve;   *sometimes*
What then? poor beastie, thou maun° live!   *must*
15 A daimen° icker° in a thrave°   *random / corn-ear / shock*
    'S a sma' request:
I'll get a blessin wi' the lave,°   *rest*
    And never miss't!

Thy wee bit housie, too, in ruin!
20 Its silly° wa's the win's are strewin!   *frail*
An' naething, now, to big° a new ane,   *build*
    O' foggage° green!   *mosses*
An' bleak December's winds ensuin,
    Baith snell° an' keen!   *bitter*

25 Thou saw the fields laid bare and waste,
An' weary winter comin fast,
An' cozie here, beneath the blast,
    Thou thought to dwell,
Till crash! the cruel coulter° past   *plowshare*
30   Out thro' thy cell.

That wee bit heap o' leaves an' stibble°   *stubble*
Has cost thee mony a weary nibble!
Now thou's turned out, for a' thy trouble,
    But° house or hald,°   *without / home ("hold")*
35 To thole° the winter's sleety dribble,   *endure*
    An' cranreuch° cauld!   *hoarfrost*

But, Mousie, thou art no thy lane,°   *not alone*
In proving foresight may be vain:
The best laid schemes o' mice an' men
10   Gang° aft a-gley.°   *go / astray*
An' lea'e us nought but grief an' pain
For promised joy.

Still thou art blest, compared wi' me!
The present only toucheth thee:
15 But och! I backward cast my e'e
On prospects drear!
An' forward, tho' I canna see,
I guess an' fear!

A Red, Red Rose
(1796)

O my luve's like a red, red rose,
That's newly sprung in June;
O my luve's like the melodie
That's sweetly played in tune.

5 As fair art thou, my bonnie lass,
So deep in luve am I;
And I will luve thee still, my dear,
Till a' the seas gang dry.

Till a' the seas gang dry, my dear,
10   And the rocks melt wi' the sun:
O I will love thee still, my dear,
While the sands o' life shall run.

And fare thee weel, my only luve,
And fare thee weel awhile!
15 And I will come again, my luve,
Though it were ten thousand mile.

SAMUEL TAYLOR COLERIDGE (1772–1834)

Kubla Khan
Or a Vision in a Dream. A Fragment
(1797–98)

In Xanadu did Kubla Khan
A stately pleasure dome decree:
Where Alph, the sacred river, ran

Through caverns measureless to man
5   Down to a sunless sea.
So twice five miles of fertile ground
With walls and towers were girdled round:
And there were gardens bright with sinuous rills,
Where blossomed many an incense-bearing tree;
10 And here were forests ancient as the hills,
Enfolding sunny spots of greenery.

But oh! that deep romantic chasm which slanted
Down the green hill athwart a cedarn cover!
A savage place! as holy and enchanted
15 As e'er beneath a waning moon was haunted
By woman wailing for her demon lover!
And from this chasm, with ceaseless turmoil seething,
As if this earth in fast thick pants were breathing,
A mighty fountain momently was forced:
20 Amid whose swift half-intermitted burst
Huge fragments vaulted like rebounding hail,
Or chaffy grain beneath the thresher's flail:
And 'mid these dancing rocks at once and ever
It flung up momently the sacred river.
25 Five miles meandering with a mazy motion
Through wood and dale the sacred river ran,
Then reached the caverns measureless to man,
And sank in tumult to a lifeless ocean:
And 'mid this tumult Kubla heard from far
30 Ancestral voices prophesying war!

The shadow of the dome of pleasure
Floated midway on the waves;
Where was heard the mingled measure
From the fountain and the caves.
35 It was a miracle of rare device,
A sunny pleasure dome with caves of ice!

A damsel with a dulcimer
In a vision once I saw:
It was an Abyssinian maid,
40   And on her dulcimer she played,
Singing of Mount Abora.
Could I revive within me
Her symphony and song,
To such a deep delight 'twould win me,
45 That with music loud and long,
I would build that dome in air,
That sunny dome! those caves of ice!

And all who heard should see them there,
And all should cry, Beware! Beware!
50 His flashing eyes, his floating hair!
Weave a circle round him thrice,
And close your eyes with holy dread,
For he on honey-dew hath fed,
And drunk the milk of Paradise.

GEORGE GORDON, LORD BYRON (1788–1824)

She Walks in Beauty
(1815)

1

She walks in beauty, like the night
   Of cloudless climes and starry skies;
And all that's best of dark and bright
   Meet in her aspect and her eyes:
5 Thus mellowed to that tender light
   Which heaven to gaudy day denies.

2

One shade the more, one ray the less,
   Had half impaired the nameless grace
Which waves in every raven tress,
10   Or softly lightens o'er her face;
Where thoughts serenely sweet express
   How pure, how dear their dwelling place.

3

And on that cheek, and o'er that brow,
   So soft, so calm, yet eloquent,
15 The smiles that win, the tints that glow,
   But tell of days in goodness spent,
A mind at peace with all below,
   A heart whose love is innocent!

The Destruction of Sennacherib
(1815)

The Assyrian came down like the wolf on the fold,
And his cohorts were gleaming in purple and gold;
And the sheen of their spears was like stars on the sea,
When the blue wave rolls nightly on deep Galilee.

5 Like the leaves of the forest when Summer is green,
That host with their banners at sunset were seen:
Like the leaves of the forest when Autumn hath blown,
That host on the morrow lay withered and strown.

For the Angel of Death spread his wings on the blast,
10 And breathed in the face of the foe as he passed;
And the eyes of the sleepers waxed deadly and chill,
And their hearts but once heaved, and for ever grew still!

And there lay the steed with his nostril all wide,
But through it there rolled not the breath of his pride:
15 And the foam of his gasping lay white on the turf,
And cold as the spray of the rock-beating surf.

And there lay the rider distorted and pale,
With the dew on his brow and the rust on his mail;
And the tents were all silent, the banners alone,
20 The lances unlifted, the trumpet unblown.

And the widows of Ashur are loud in their wail,
And the idols are broke in the temple of Baal;
And the might of the Gentile, unsmote by the sword,
Hath melted like snow in the glance of the Lord!

PERCY BYSSHE SHELLEY (1792–1822)

Ozymandias[1]
(1818)

I met a traveler from an antique land
Who said: Two vast and trunkless legs of stone
Stand in the desert . . . Near them, on the sand,
Half sunk, a shattered visage lies, whose frown,
5 And wrinkled lip, and sneer of cold command,
Tell that its sculptor well those passions read
Which yet survive, stamped on these lifeless things,
The hand that mocked them, and the heart that fed:
And on the pedestal these words appear:
10 "My name is Ozymandias, king of kings:
Look on my works, ye Mighty, and despair!"
Nothing beside remains. Round the decay
Of that colossal wreck, boundless and bare
The lone and level sands stretch far away.

---

[1]Greek name for the Egyptian monarch Ramses II (13th century B.C.), who is said to have erected a huge statue of himself.

Ode to the West Wind
(1820)

1

O wild West Wind, thou breath of Autumn's being,
Thou, from whose unseen presence the leaves dead
Are driven, like ghosts from an enchanter fleeing,

Yellow, and black, and pale, and hectic red,
5 Pestilence-stricken multitudes: O thou,
Who chariotest to their dark wintry bed

The wingéd seeds, where they lie cold and low,
Each like a corpse within its grave, until
Thine azure sister of the Spring shall blow

10 Her clarion[1] o'er the dreaming earth, and fill
(Driving sweet buds like flocks to feed in air)
With living hues and odors plain and hill:

Wild Spirit, which art moving everywhere;
Destroyer and preserver; hear, oh, hear!

2

15 Thou on whose stream, mid the steep sky's commotion,
Loose clouds like earth's decaying leaves are shed,
Shook from the tangled boughs of Heaven and Ocean,

Angels[2] of rain and lightning: there are spread
On the blue surface of thine aëry surge,
20 Like the bright hair uplifted from the head

Of some fierce Maenad,[3] even from the dim verge
Of the horizon to the zenith's height,
The locks of the approaching storm. Thou dirge

Of the dying year, to which this closing night
25 Will be the dome of a vast sepulcher,
Vaulted with all thy congregated might

Of vapors, from whose solid atmosphere
Black rain, and fire, and hail will burst: oh, hear!

---

[1] Melodious trumpet-call.
[2] In Greek derivation, messengers or divine messengers.
[3] Frenzied dancer, worshipper of Dionysus, a god of wine and fertility.

3

Thou who didst waken from his summer dreams
30 The blue Mediterranean, where he lay,
Lulled by the coil of his crystálline streams,

Beside a pumice isle in Baiae's bay,[4]
And saw in sleep old palaces and towers
Quivering within the wave's intenser day,

35 All overgrown with azure moss and flowers
So sweet, the sense faints picturing them! Thou
For whose path the Atlantic's level powers

Cleave themselves into chasms, while far below
The sea-blooms and the oozy woods which wear
40 The sapless foliage of the ocean, know

Thy voice, and suddenly grow gray with fear,
And tremble and despoil themselves: oh, hear!

4

If I were a dead leaf thou mightest bear;
If I were a swift cloud to fly with thee;
45 A wave to pant beneath thy power, and share

The impulse of thy strength, only less free
Than thou, O uncontrollable! If even
I were as in my boyhood, and could be

The comrade of thy wanderings over Heaven,
50 As then, when to outstrip thy skyey speed
Scarce seemed a vision; I would ne'er have striven

As thus with thee in prayer in my sore need.
Oh, lift me as a wave, a leaf, a cloud!
I fall upon the thorns of life! I bleed!

55 A heavy weight of hours has chained and bowed
One too like thee: tameless, and swift, and proud.

5

Make me thy lyre,[5] even as the forest is:
What if my leaves are falling like its own!
The tumult of thy mighty harmonies

---

[4] Near Naples, Italy.
[5] Small harp traditionally used to accompany songs and recited poems.

60 Will take from both a deep, autumnal tone,
   Sweet though in sadness. Be thou, Spirit fierce,
   My spirit! Be thou me, impetuous one!

   Drive my dead thoughts over the universe
   Like withered leaves to quicken a new birth!
65 And, by the incantation of this verse,

   Scatter, as from an unextinguished hearth
   Ashes and sparks, my words among mankind!
   Be through my lips to unawakened earth

   The trumpet of a prophecy! O Wind,
70 If Winter comes, can Spring be far behind?

JOHN KEATS (1795–1821)
When I Have Fears
(1818)

When I have fears that I may cease to be
    Before my pen has gleaned my teeming brain,
Before high-piléd books, in charact'ry,°   *written symbols*
    Hold like rich garners the full-ripened grain;
5 When I behold, upon the night's starred face,
    Huge cloudy symbols of a high romance,
And think that I may never live to trace
    Their shadows, with the magic hand of chance;
And when I feel, fair creature of an hour,
10   That I shall never look upon thee more,
Never have relish in the faery° power   *magical*
    Of unreflecting love!—then on the shore
Of the wide world I stand alone, and think
Till Love and Fame to nothingness do sink.

Ode to a Nightingale
(1819)

1

My heart aches, and a drowsy numbness pains
    My sense, as though of hemlock[1] I had drunk,
Or emptied some dull opiate to the drains
    One minute past, and Lethe-wards[2] had sunk:

---

[1] Opiate made from a poisonous herb.
[2] Toward the river Lethe, whose waters in Hades bring the dead forgetfulness.

5 'Tis not through envy of thy happy lot,
　　But being too happy in thine happiness—
　　　That thou, light-wingéd Dryad of the trees,
　　　　In some melodious plot
　　Of beechen green, and shadows numberless,
10　　　Singest of summer in full-throated ease.

2

　　O, for a draught of vintage! that hath been
　　　Cooled a long age in the deep-delvéd earth,
　　Tasting of Flora³ and the country green,
　　　Dance, and Provençal song,⁴ and sunburnt mirth!
15 O for a beaker full of the warm South,
　　　Full of the true, the blushful Hippocrene,⁵
　　　　With beaded bubbles winking at the brim,
　　　　　And purple-stainéd mouth;
　　That I might drink, and leave the world unseen,
20　　　And with thee fade away into the forest dim:

3

　　Fade far away, dissolve, and quite forget
　　　What thou among the leaves hast never known,
　　The weariness, the fever, and the fret
　　　Here, where men sit and hear each other groan;
25 Where palsy shakes a few, sad, last gray hairs,
　　　Where youth grows pale, and specter-thin, and dies,
　　　　Where but to think is to be full of sorrow
　　　　　And leaden-eyed despairs,
　　Where Beauty cannot keep her lustrous eyes,
30　　　Or new Love pine at them beyond tomorrow.

4

　　Away! away! for I will fly to thee,
　　　Not charioted by Bacchus and his pards,⁶
　　But on the viewless° wings of Poesy,　　　　　　　　　*invisible*
　　　Though the dull brain perplexes and retards:
35 Already with thee! tender is the night,
　　　And haply the Queen-Moon is on her throne,
　　　　Clustered around by all her starry Fays;°　　　　　*fairies*
　　　　　But here there is no light,
　　Save what from heaven is with the breezes blown
40　　　Through verdurous glooms and winding mossy ways.

---

³ Roman goddess of springtime and flowers.
⁴ Of the late-medieval troubadours of Provence, in southern France.
⁵ The fountain of the Muses (goddesses of poetry and the arts) on Mt. Helicon in Greece; its waters induce poetic inspiration.
⁶ "Bacchus": god of wine, often depicted in a chariot drawn by leopards ("pards").

5

I cannot see what flowers are at my feet,
  Nor what soft incense hangs upon the boughs,
But, in embalméd° darkness, guess each sweet   *perfumed*
  Wherewith the seasonable month endows
45 The grass, the thicket, and the fruit tree wild;
  White hawthorn, and the pastoral eglantine;[7]
    Fast fading violets covered up in leaves;
      And mid-May's eldest child,
  The coming musk-rose, full of dewy wine,
50   The murmurous haunt of flies on summer eves.

6

Darkling° I listen; and for many a time   *in darkness*
  I have been half in love with easeful Death,
Called him soft names in many a muséd rhyme,
  To take into the air my quiet breath;
55 Now more than ever seems it rich to die,
  To cease upon the midnight with no pain,
    While thou art pouring forth thy soul abroad
      In such an ecstasy!
Still wouldst thou sing, and I have ears in vain—
60   To thy high requiem become a sod.

7

Thou wast not born for death, immortal Bird!
  No hungry generations tread thee down;
The voice I hear this passing night was heard
  In ancient days by emperor and clown:
65 Perhaps the selfsame song that found a path
  Through the sad heart of Ruth,[8] when, sick for home,
    She stood in tears amid the alien corn;
      The same that ofttimes hath
Charmed magic casements, opening on the foam
70   Of perilous seas, in faery lands forlorn.

8

Forlorn! the very word is like a bell
  To toll me back from thee to my sole self!
Adieu! the fancy cannot cheat so well
  As she is famed to do, deceiving elf.
75 Adieu! adieu! thy plaintive anthem fades
  Past the near meadows, over the still stream,

---

[7] Sweetbrier; wood roses.
[8] In the Old Testament, a woman of great loyalty and modesty who, as a stranger in Judah, won a husband while gleaning in the barley-fields ("the alien corn," line 67).

Up the hill side; and now 'tis buried deep
   In the next valley-glades:
Was it a vision, or a waking dream?
80   Fled is that music:—Do I wake or sleep?

Ode on a Grecian Urn
(1819)

1

Thou still unravished bride of quietness,
   Thou foster child of silence and slow time,
Sylvan historian, who canst thus express
   A flowery tale more sweetly than our rhyme:
5 What leaf-fringed legend haunts about thy shape
   Of deities or mortals, or of both,
      In Tempe or the dales of Arcady?[1]
What men or gods are these? What maidens loath?
What mad pursuit? What struggle to escape?
10   What pipes and timbrels? What wild ecstasy?

2

Heard melodies are sweet, but those unheard
   Are sweeter; therefore, ye soft pipes, play on;
Not to the sensual ear, but, more endeared,
   Pipe to the spirit ditties of no tone:
15 Fair youth, beneath the trees, thou canst not leave
   Thy song, nor ever can those trees be bare;
      Bold Lover, never, never canst thou kiss,
Though winning near the goal—yet, do not grieve;
   She cannot fade, though thou hast not thy bliss,
20   Forever wilt thou love, and she be fair!

3

Ah, happy, happy boughs! that cannot shed
   Your leaves, nor ever bid the Spring adieu;
And, happy melodist, unweariéd,
   Forever piping songs forever new;
25 More happy love! more happy, happy love!
   Forever warm and still to be enjoyed,
      Forever panting, and forever young;
All breathing human passion far above,
   That leaves a heart high-sorrowful and cloyed,
30   A burning forehead, and a parching tongue.

---

[1] Tempe and Arcady (or Arcadia), in Greece, are traditional symbols of perfect pastoral landscapes.

4

Who are these coming to the sacrifice?
　　To what green altar, O mysterious priest,
Lead'st thou that heifer lowing at the skies,
　　And all her silken flanks with garlands dressed?
35 What little town by river or sea shore,
　　Or mountain-built with peaceful citadel,
　　　Is emptied of this folk, this pious morn?
And, little town, thy streets forevermore
　　Will silent be; and not a soul to tell
40　　Why thou art desolate, can e'er return.

5

O Attic² shape! Fair attitude! with brede°　　　　*woven pattern*
　　Of marble men and maidens overwrought,
With forest branches and the trodden weed;
　　Thou, silent form, dost tease us out of thought
45 As doth eternity: Cold Pastoral!
　　When old age shall this generation waste,
　　　Thou shalt remain, in midst of other woe
Than ours, a friend to man, to whom thou say'st,
　　"Beauty is truth, truth beauty,"³—that is all
50　　Ye know on earth, and all ye need to know.

ELIZABETH BARRETT BROWNING (1806–1861)

Sonnet 14: If Thou Must Love Me
(1850)

If thou must love me, let it be for nought
Except for love's sake only. Do not say
"I love her for her smile—her look—her way
Of speaking gently,—for a trick of thought
5 That falls in well with mine, and certes brought
A sense of pleasant ease on such a day"—
For these things in themselves, Belovèd, may
Be changed, or change for thee,—and love, so wrought,
May be unwrought so. Neither love me for
10 Thine own dear pity's wiping my cheeks dry,—
A creature might forget to weep, who bore
Thy comfort long, and lose thy love thereby!

---

²Greek, especially Athenian.
　³The quotation marks around this phrase are absent from some other versions also having good authority. This discrepancy has led some readers to ascribe only this phrase to the voice of the Urn; others ascribe to the Urn the whole of the two concluding lines.

But love me for love's sake, that evermore
Thou mayst love on, through love's eternity.

EDGAR ALLAN POE (1809–1849)
To Helen
(1823)

Helen, thy beauty is to me
  Like those Nicean barks of yore,
That gently, o'er a perfumed sea,
  The weary, way-worn wanderer bore
5 To his own native shore.

On desperate seas long wont to roam,
  Thy hyacinth hair,[1] thy classic face,
Thy Naiad airs have brought me home
  To the glory that was Greece
10 And the grandeur that was Rome.

Lo! in yon brilliant window-niche
  How statue-like I see thee stand!
  The agate lamp within thy hand,
Ah! Psyche,° from the regions which   *lover of Cupid*
15 Are Holy Land!

The Raven
(1844–1849)

Once upon a midnight dreary, while I pondered, weak and weary,
Over many a quaint and curious volume of forgotten lore—
While I nodded, nearly napping, suddenly there came a tapping,
As of some one gently rapping, rapping at my chamber door.
5 "'T is some visitor," I muttered, "tapping at my chamber door—
                Only this and nothing more."

Ah, distinctly I remember it was in the bleak December;
And each separate dying ember wrought its ghost upon the floor.
Eagerly I wished the morrow;—vainly I had sought to borrow
10 From my books surcease of sorrow—sorrow for the lost Lenore—
For the rare and radiant maiden whom the angels name Lenore—
                Nameless *here* for evermore.

---

[1] Presumably, hair like that of the slain youth Hyacinthus, beloved of Apollo.

And the silken, sad, uncertain rustling of each purple curtain
Thrilled me—filled me with fantastic terrors never felt before;
15 So that now, to still the beating of my heart, I stood repeating
"'T is some visiter entreating entrance at my chamber door—
Some late visiter entreating entrance at my chamber door;—
This it is and nothing more."

Presently my soul grew stronger; hesitating then no longer,
20 "Sir," said I, "or Madam, truly your forgiveness I implore;
But the fact is I was napping, and so gently you came rapping,
And so faintly you came tapping, tapping at my chamber door,
That I scarce was sure I heard you"—here I opened wide the door; —
Darkness there and nothing more.

25 Deep into that darkness peering, long I stood there wondering, fearing,
Doubting, dreaming dreams no mortal ever dared to dream before;
But the silence was unbroken, and the stillness gave no token,
And the only word there spoken was the whispered word, "Lenore!"
This I whispered, and an echo murmured back the word "Lenore!"
30   Merely this and nothing more.

Back into the chamber turning, all my soul within me burning,
Soon again I heard a tapping somewhat louder than before.
"Surely," said I, "surely that is something at my window lattice;
Let me see, then, what thereat is, and this mystery explore—
35 Let my heart be still a moment and this mystery explore;—
'T is the wind and nothing more!"

Open here I flung the shutter, when, with many a flirt and flutter
In there stepped a stately Raven of the saintly days of yore.
Not the least obeisance made he; not a minute stopped or stayed he;
40 But, with mien of lord or lady, perched above my chamber door—
Perched upon a bust of Pallas just above my chamber door—
Perched, and sat, and nothing more.

Then this ebony bird beguiling my sad fancy into smiling,
By the grave and stern decorum of the countenance it wore,
45 "Though thy crest be shorn and shaven, thou," I said, "art sure no craven,
Ghastly grim and ancient Raven wandering from the Nightly shore—
Tell me what thy lordly name is on the Night's Plutonian shore!"
Quoth the Raven, "Nevermore."

Much I marvelled this ungainly fowl to hear discourse so plainly,
50 Though its answer little meaning—little relevancy bore;
For we cannot help agreeing that no living human being
Ever yet was blessed with seeing bird above his chamber door—
Bird or beast upon the sculptured bust above his chamber door,
With such name as "Nevermore."

55 But the Raven, sitting lonely on the placid bust, spoke only
   That one word, as if his soul in that one word he did outpour.
   Nothing farther then he uttered—not a feather then he fluttered—
   Till I scarcely more than muttered "Other friends have flown before—
   On the morrow *he* will leave me, as my hopes have flown before."
60   Then the bird said "Nevermore."

   Startled at the stillness broken by reply so aptly spoken,
   "Doubtless," said I, "what it utters is its only stock and store—
   Caught from some unhappy master whom unmerciful Disaster
   Followed fast and followed faster till his songs one burden bore—
65 Till the dirges of his Hope that melancholy burden bore
                          Of 'Never—nevermore.'"

   But the Raven still beguiling all my fancy into smiling,
   Straight I wheeled a cushioned seat in front of bird, and bust and door;
   Then, upon the velvet sinking, I betook myself to linking
70 Fancy unto fancy, thinking what this ominous bird of yore—
   What this grim, ungainly, ghastly, gaunt, and ominous bird of yore
                          Meant in croaking "Nevermore."

   This I sat engaged in guessing, but no syllable expressing
   To the fowl whose fiery eyes now burned into my bosom's core;
75 This and more I sat divining, with my head at ease reclining
   On the cushion's velvet lining that the lamp-light gloated o'er,
   But whose velvet violet lining with the lamp-light gloating o'er,
                          She shall press, ah, nevermore!

   Then, methought, the air grew denser, perfumed from an unseen censer
80 Swung by Seraphim whose foot-falls tinkled on the tufted floor.
   "Wretch," I cried, "thy God hath lent thee—by these angels he hath
       sent thee
   Respite—respite and nepenthe from thy memories of Lenore;
   Quaff, oh quaff this kind nepenthe and forget this lost Lenore!"
85   Quoth the Raven "Nevermore."

   "Prophet!" said I, "thing of evil! prophet still, if bird or devil!—
   Whether Tempter sent, or whether tempest tossed thee here ashore,
   Desolate yet all undaunted, on this desert land enchanted—
   On this home of Horror haunted—tell me truly, I implore—
90 Is there—*is* there balm in Gilead?—tell me—tell me, I implore!"
                          Quoth the Raven "Nevermore."

   "Prophet!" said I, "thing of evil!—prophet still, if bird or devil!
   By that Heaven that bends above us—by that God we both adore—
   Tell this soul with sorrow laden if, within the distant Aidenn,

95 It shall clasp a sainted maiden whom the angels name Lenore—
  Clasp a rare and radiant maiden whom the angels name Lenore."
                                        Quoth the Raven "Nevermore."

"Be that word our sign of parting, bird or fiend!" I shrieked,
      upstarting—
100 "Get thee back into the tempest and the Night's Plutonian shore!
  Leave no black plume as a token of that lie thy soul hath spoken!
  Leave my loneliness unbroken!—quit the bust above my door!
  Take thy beak from out my heart, and take thy form from off my
      door!"
105   Quoth the Raven "Nevermore."

And the Raven, never flitting, still is sitting, *still* is sitting
  On the pallid bust of Pallas just above my chamber door;
  And his eyes have all the seeming of a demon's that is dreaming,
  And the lamp-light o'er him streaming throws his shadow on the
110   floor;
  And my soul from out that shadow that lies floating on the floor
                                        Shall be lifted—nevermore!

ROBERT BROWNING (1812–1889)

My Last Duchess
Ferrara
(1842)

  That's my last duchess painted on the wall,
  Looking as if she were alive. I call
  That piece a wonder, now: Frà Pandolf's hands
  Worked busily a day, and there she stands.
5 Will't please you sit and look at her? I said
  "Frà Pandolf" by design, for never read
  Strangers like you that pictured countenance,
  The depth and passion of its earnest glance,
  But to myself they turned (since none puts by
10 The curtain I have drawn for you, but I)
  And seemed as they would ask me, if they durst,
  How such a glance came there; so, not the first
  Are you to turn and ask thus. Sir, 'twas not
  Her husband's presence only, called that spot
15 Of joy into the Duchess' cheek: perhaps
  Frà Pandolf chanced to say "Her mantle laps
  "Over my lady's wrist too much," or "Paint
  "Must never hope to reproduce the faint
  "Half-flush that dies along her throat": such stuff
20 Was courtesy, she thought, and cause enough
  For calling up that spot of joy. She had

A heart—how shall I say?—too soon made glad,
Too easily impressed; she liked whate'er
She looked on, and her looks went everywhere.
25 Sir, 'twas all one! My favor at her breast,
The dropping of the daylight in the West,
The bough of cherries some officious fool
Broke in the orchard for her, the white mule
She rode with round the terrace—all and each
30 Would draw from her alike the approving speech,
Or blush, at least. She thanked men—good! but thanked
Somehow—I know not how—as if she ranked
My gift of a nine-hundred-years-old name
With anybody's gift. Who'd stoop to blame
35 This sort of trifling? Even had you skill
In speech—which I have not—to make your will
Quite clear to such an one, and say, "Just this
"Or that in you disgusts me; here you miss,
"Or there exceed the mark"—and if she let
40 Herself be lessoned so, nor plainly set
Her wits to yours, forsooth, and made excuse,
—E'en then would be some stooping; and I choose
Never to stoop. Oh sir, she smiled, no doubt,
Whene'er I passed her; but who passed without
45 Much the same smile? This grew; I gave commands;
Then all smiles stopped together. There she stands
As if alive. Will't please you rise? We'll meet
The company below, then. I repeat,
The Count your master's known munificence
50 Is ample warrant that no just pretense
Of mine for dowry will be disallowed;
Though his fair daughter's self, as I avowed
At starting, is by object. Nay, we'll go
Together down, sir. Notice Neptune, though,
55 Taming a sea-horse, thought a rarity,
Which Claus of Innsbruck cast in bronze for me!

WALT WHITMAN (1819–1892)

Crossing Brooklyn Ferry
(1856)

1

Flood-tide below me! I see you face to face!
Clouds of the west—sun there half an hour high—I see you also face
  to face.
Crowds of men and women attired in the usual costumes, how curious
5   you are to me!

On the ferry-boats the hundreds and hundreds that cross, returning
    home, are more curious to me than you suppose,
And you that shall cross from shore to shore years hence are more to
    me, and more in my meditations, than you might suppose.

2

10 The impalpable sustenance of me from all things at all hours of the
    day,
The simple, compact, well-join'd scheme, myself disintegrated, every
    one disintegrated yet part of the scheme,
The similitudes of the past and those of the future,
15 The glories strung like beads on my smallest sights and hearings, on
    the walk in the street and the passage over the river,
The current rushing so swiftly and swimming with me far away,
The others that are to follow me, the ties between me and them,
The certainty of others, the life, love, sight, hearing of others.

20 Others will enter the gates of the ferry and cross from shore to shore,
Others will watch the run of the flood-tide,
Others will see the shipping of Manhattan north and west, and the
    heights of Brooklyn to the south and east,
Others will see the islands large and small;
25 Fifty years hence, others will see them as they cross, the sun half an
    hour high,
A hundred years hence, or ever so many hundred years hence, others
    will see them,
Will enjoy the sunset, the pouring-in of the flood-tide, the falling-back
30   to the sea of the ebb-tide.

3

It avails not, time nor place—distance avails not,
I am with you, you men and women of a generation, or ever so many
    generations hence,
Just as you feel when you look on the river and sky, so I felt,
35 Just as any of you is one of a living crowd, I was one of a crowd,
Just as you are refresh'd by the gladness of the river and the bright
    flow, I was refresh'd,
Just as you stand and lean on the rail, yet hurry with the swift
    current, I stood yet was hurried,
40 Just as you look on the numberless masts of ships and the
    thick-stemm'd pipes of steamboats, I look'd.

I too many and many a time cross'd the river of old,
Watched the Twelfth-month° sea-gulls, saw them high in   *December*
    the air floating with motionless wings, oscillating their bodies,
45 Saw how the glistening yellow lit up parts of their bodies and
    left the rest in strong shadow,

Saw the slow-wheeling circles and the gradual edging toward the
    south,
Saw the reflection of the summer sky in the water,
50 Had my eyes dazzled by the shimmering track of beams,
Look'd at the fine centrifugal spokes of light round the shape of my
    head in the sunlit water,
Look'd on the haze on the hills southward and south-westward,
Look'd on the vapor as it flew in fleeces tinged with violet,
55 Look'd toward the lower bay to notice the vessels arriving,
Saw their approach, saw aboard those that were near me,
Saw the white sails of schooners and sloops, saw the ships at anchor,
The sailors at work in the rigging or out astride the spars,
The round masts, the swinging motion of the hulls, the slender
60   serpentine pennants,
The large and small steamers in motion, the pilots in their
    pilot-houses,
The white wake left by the passage, the quick tremulous whirl of the
    wheels,
65 The flags of all nations, the falling of them at sunset,
The scallop-edged waves in the twilight, the ladled cups, the
    frolicsome crests and glistening,
The stretch afar growing dimmer and dimmer, the gray walls of the
    granite storehouses by the docks,
70 On the river the shadowy group, the big steam-tug closely flank'd on
    each side by the barges, the hay-boat, the belated lighter,[1]
On the neighboring shore the fires from the foundry chimneys
    burning high and glaringly into the night,
Casting their flicker of black contrasted with wild red and yellow
75   light over the tops of houses, and down into the clefts of streets.

4

These and all else were to me the same as they are to you,
I loved well those cities, loved well the stately and rapid river,
The men and women I saw were all near to me,
Others the same—others who look back on me because I look'd
80   forward to them,
(The time will come, though I stop here to-day and to-night.)

5

What is it then between us?
What is the count of the scores or hundreds of years between us?

Whatever it is, it avails not—distance avails not, and place avails not,
85 I too lived, Brooklyn of ample hills was mine,

---

[1] Barge used for loading and unloading ships.

I too walk'd the streets of Manhattan island, and bathed in the waters
    around it,
I too felt the curious abrupt questionings stir within me,
In the day among crowds of people sometimes they came upon me,
90 In my walks home late at night or as I lay in my bed they came upon
    me,
I too had been struck from the float forever held in solution,
I too had receiv'd identity by my body,
That I was I knew was of my body, and what I should be I knew I
95   should be of my body.

6

It is not upon you alone the dark patches fall,
The dark threw its patches down upon me also,
The best I had done seem'd to me blank and suspicious,
My great thoughts as I supposed them, were they not in reality
100   meager?
Nor is it you alone who know what it is to be evil,
I am he who knew what it was to be evil,
I too knitted the old knot of contrariety,
Blabb'd, blush'd, resented, lied, stole, grudg'd,
105 Had guile, anger, lust, hot wishes I dared not speak,
Was wayward, vain, greedy, shallow, sly, cowardly, malignant,
The wolf, the snake, the hog, not wanting in me,
The cheating look, the frivolous word, the adulterous wish, not
    wanting,
110 Refusals, hates, postponements, meanness, laziness, none of these
    wanting,
Was one with the rest, the days and haps of the rest,
Was call'd by my nighest name by clear loud voices of young men as
    they saw me approaching or passing,
115 Felt their arms on my neck as I stood, or the negligent leaning of their
    flesh against me as I sat,
Saw many I loved in the street or ferry-boat or public assembly, yet
    never told them a word,
Lived the same life with the rest, the same old laughing, gnawing,
120   sleeping,
Play'd the part that still looks back on the actor or actress,
The same old role, the role that is what we make it, as great as we
    like,
Or as small as we like, or both great and small.

7

125 Closer yet I approach you,
What thought you have of me now, I had as much of you—I laid in
    my stores in advance,
I consider'd long and seriously of you before you were born.

Who was to know what should come home to me?
130 Who knows but I am enjoying this?
Who knows, for all the distance, but I am as good as looking at you
   now, for all you cannot see me?

8

Ah, what can ever be more stately and admirable to me than
   mast-hemm'd Manhattan?
135 River and sunset and scallop-edg'd waves of flood-tide?
The sea-gulls oscillating their bodies, the hay-boat in the twilight, and
   the belated lighter?
What gods can exceed these that clasp me by the hand, and with
   voices I love call me promptly and loudly by my nighest name as I
140   approach?
What is more subtle than this which ties me to the woman or man
   that looks in my face?
Which fuses me into you now, and pours my meaning into you?

We understand then do we not?
145 What I promis'd without mentioning it, have you not accepted?
What the study could not teach—what the preaching could not
   accomplish is accomplish'd, is it not?

9

Flow on, river! flow with the flood-tide, and ebb with the ebb-tide!
Frolic on, crested and scallop-edg'd waves!
150 Gorgeous clouds of the sunset! drench with your splendor me, or the
   men and women generations after me!
Cross from shore to shore, countless crowds of passengers!
Stand up, tall masts of Mannahatta![2] stand up, beautiful hills of
   Brooklyn!
155 Throb, baffled and curious brain! throw out questions and answers!
Suspend here and everywhere, eternal float of solution!
Gaze, loving and thirsting eyes, in the house or street or public
   assembly!
Sound out, voices of young men! loudly and musically call me by my
160   nighest name!
Live, old life! play the part that looks back on the actor or actress!
Play the old role, the role that is great or small according as one
   makes it!
Consider, you who peruse me, whether I may not in unknown ways be
165   looking upon you;
Be firm, rail over the river, to support those who lean idly, yet haste
   with the hasting current;
Fly on, sea birds! fly sideways, or wheel in large circles high in the air;

---

[2] Variant for the Indian word normally spelled Manhattan.

Receive the summer sky, you water, and faithfully hold it till all
170   downcast eyes have time to take it from you!
Diverge, fine spokes of light, from the shape of my head, or any one's
    head, in the sunlit water!
Come on, ships from the lower bay! pass up or down, white-sail'd
    schooners, sloops, lighters!
175 Flaunt away, flags of all nations! be duly lower'd at sunset!
Burn high your fires, foundry chimneys! cast black shadows at
    nightfall! cast red and yellow light over the tops of the houses!
Appearances, now or henceforth, indicate what you are,
You necessary film, continue to envelop the soul,
180 About my body for me, and your body for you, be hung our divinest
    aromas,
Thrive, cities—bring your freight, bring your shows, ample and
    sufficient rivers,
Expand, being than which none else is perhaps more spiritual,
185 Keep your places, objects than which none else is more lasting.

You have waited, you always wait, you dumb, beautiful ministers,
We receive you with free sense at last, and are insatiate henceforward,
Not you any more shall be able to foil us, or withhold yourselves from
    us,
190 We use you, and do not cast you aside—we plant you permanently
    within us,
We fathom you not—we love you—there is perfection in you also,
You furnish your parts toward eternity,
Great or small, you furnish your parts toward the soul.

Cavalry Crossing a Ford
(1865)

A line in long array, where they wind betwixt green islands;
They take a serpentine course—their arms flash in the sun—hark to
    the musical clank;
Behold the silvery river—in it the splashing horses, loitering, stop to
5   drink;
Behold the brown-faced men—each group, each person, a picture—the
    negligent rest on the saddles;
Some emerge on the opposite bank—others are just entering the
    ford—while,
10 Scarlet, and blue, and snowy white,
The guidon[1] flags flutter gaily in the wind.

---

[1] A guidon is a guide-flag carried by a cavalry troop.

When Lilacs Last in the Dooryard Bloom'd
(1865–66)

1

When lilacs last in the dooryard bloom'd,
And the great star early droop'd in the western sky in the night,
I mourn'd, and yet shall mourn with ever-returning spring.
Ever-returning spring, trinity sure to me you bring,
5 Lilac blooming perennial and drooping star in the west,
And thought of him I love.

2

O powerful western fallen star!
O shades of night—O moody, tearful night!
O great star disappear'd—O the black murk that hides the star!
10 O cruel hands that hold me powerless—O helpless soul of me!
O harsh surrounding cloud that will not free my soul.

3

In the dooryard fronting an old farm-house near the white-wash'd
        palings,
Stands the lilac-bush tall-growing with heart-shaped leaves of rich
15   green,
With many a pointed blossom rising delicate, with the perfume strong
        I love,
With every leaf a miracle—and from this bush in the dooryard,
With delicate-color'd blossoms and heart-shaped leaves of rich green,
20 A sprig with its flower I break.

4

In the swamp in secluded recesses,
A shy and hidden bird is warbling a song.

Solitary the thrush,
The hermit withdrawn to himself, avoiding the settlements,
25 Sings by himself a song.

Song of the bleeding throat,
Death's outlet song of life, (for well dear brother I know,
If thou wast not granted to sing thou would'st surely die.)

5

Over the breast of spring, the land, amid cities,
30 Amid lanes and through old woods, where lately the violets peep'd
        from the ground, spotting the gray debris,
Amid the grass in the fields each side of the lanes, passing the endless
        grass,

Passing the yellow-spear'd wheat, every grain from its shroud in the
35   dark-brown fields uprisen,
Passing the apple-tree blows of white and pink in the orchards,
Carrying a corpse to where it shall rest in the grave,
Night and day journeys a coffin.

6

40 Coffin that passes through lanes and streets,[1]
Through day and night with the great cloud darkening the land,
With the pomp of the inloop'd flags with the cities draped in black,
With the show of the States themselves as of crape-veil'd women
    standing,
45 With processions long and winding and the flambeaus of the night,
With the countless torches lit, with the silent sea of faces and the
    unbared heads,
With the waiting depot, the arriving coffin, and the sombre faces,
With dirges through the night, with the thousand voices rising strong
50   and solemn,
With all the mournful voices of the dirges pour'd around the coffin,
The dim-lit churches and the shuddering organs—where amid these
    you journey,
With the tolling tolling bells' perpetual clang,
55 Here, coffin that slowly passes,
I give you my sprig of lilac.

7

(Nor for you, for one alone,
Blossoms and branches green to coffins all I bring,
For fresh as the morning, thus would I chant a song for you O sane
60   and sacred death.

All over bouquets of roses,
O death, I cover you over with roses and early lilies,
But mostly and now the lilac that blooms the first,
Copious I break, I break the sprigs from the bushes,
65 With loaded arms I come, pouring for you,
For you and the coffins all of you O death.)

8

O western orb sailing the heaven,
Now I know what you must have meant as a month since I walk'd,
As I walk'd in silence the transparent shadowy night,
70 As I saw you had something to tell as you bent to me night after
    night,

---

[1]The funeral cortège of Lincoln traveled from Washington to Springfield, Illinois, stopping at cities and towns all along the way for the people to honor the murdered President.

As you droop'd from the sky low down as if to my side, (while the
    other stars all look'd on,)
As we wander'd together the solemn night, (for something I know not
75   what kept me from sleep,)
As the night advanced, and I saw on the rim of the west how full you
    were of woe,
As I stood on the rising ground in the breeze in the cool transparent
    night,
80 As I watch'd where you pass'd and was lost in the netherward black of
    the night,
As my soul in its trouble dissatisfied sank, as where you sad orb,
Concluded, dropt in the night, and was gone.

9

Sing on there in the swamp,
85 O singer bashful and tender, I hear your notes, I hear your call,
I hear, I come presently, I understand you,
But a moment I linger, for the lustrous star has detain'd me,
The star my departing comrade holds and detains me.

10

O how shall I warble myself for the dead one there I loved?
90 And how shall I deck my song for the large sweet soul that has gone?
And what shall my perfume be for the grave of him I love?

Sea-winds blown from east and west,
Blown from the Eastern sea and blown from the Western sea, till there
    on the prairies meeting,
95 These and with these and the breath of my chant,
I'll perfume the grave of him I love.

11

O what shall I hang on the chamber walls?
And what shall the pictures be that I hang on the walls,
To adorn the burial-house of him I love?

100 Pictures of growing spring and farms and homes,
    With the Fourth-month eve at sundown, and the gray smoke lucid and
    bright,
    With floods of the yellow gold of the gorgeous, indolent, sinking sun,
    burning, expanding the air,
105 With the fresh sweet herbage under foot, and the pale green leaves of
    the trees prolific,
    In the distance the flowing glaze, the breast of the river, with a
    wind-dapple here and there,
    With ranging hills on the banks, with many a line against the sky, and
110   shadows,

And the city at hand with dwellings so dense, and stacks of
    chimneys,
And all the scenes of life and the workshops, and the workmen
    homeward returning.

12

115 Lo, body and soul—this land,
My own Manhattan with spires, and the sparkling and hurrying tides,
    and the ships,
The varied and ample land, the South and the North in the light,
    Ohio's shores and flashing Missouri,
120 And ever the far-spreading prairies cover'd with grass and corn.

Lo, the most excellent sun so calm and haughty,
The violet and purple morn with just-felt breezes,
The gentle soft-born measureless light,
The miracle spreading bathing all, the fulfill'd noon,
125 The coming eve delicious, the welcome night and the stars,
Over my cities shining all, enveloping man and land.

13

Sing on, sing on you gray-brown bird,
Sing from the swamps, the recesses, pour your chant from the bushes,
Limitless out of the dusk, out of the cedars and pines.

130 Sing on dearest brother, warble your reedy song,
Loud human song, with voice of uttermost woe.

O liquid and free and tender!
O wild and loose to my soul—O wondrous singer!
You only I hear—yet the star holds me, (but will soon depart,)
135 Yet the lilac with mastering odor holds me.

14

Now while I sat in the day and look'd forth,
In the close of the day with its light and the fields of spring, and the
    farmers preparing their crops,
In the large unconscious scenery of my land with its lakes and forests,
140 In the heavenly aerial beauty, (after the perturb'd winds and the
    storms,)
Under the arching heavens of the afternoon swift passing, and the
    voices of children and women.
The many-moving sea-tides, and I saw the ships how they sail'd,
145 And the summer approaching with richness, and the fields all busy
    with labor,
And the infinite separate houses, how they all went on, each with its
    meals and minutia of daily usages,

And the streets how their throbbings throbb'd, and the cities pent—lo,
150   then and there,
Falling upon them all and among them all, enveloping me with the
        rest,
Appear'd the cloud, appear'd the long black trail,
And I knew death, its thought, and the sacred knowledge of death.

155 Then with the knowledge of death as walking one side of me,
And the thought of death close-walking the other side of me,
And I in the middle as with companions, and as holding the hands of
        companions,
I fled forth to the hiding receiving night that talks not,
160 Down to the shores of the water, the path by the swamp in the
        dimness,
To the solemn shadowy cedars and ghostly pines so still.

And the singer so shy to the rest receiv'd me,
The gray-brown bird I know receiv'd us comrades three,
165 And he sang the carol of death, and a verse for him I love.

From deep secluded recesses,
From the fragrant cedars and the ghostly pines so still,
Came the carol of the bird.

And the charm of the carol rapt me,
170 As I held as if by their hands my comrades in the night,
And the voice of my spirit tallied the song of the bird.

Come lovely and soothing death,
Undulate round the world, serenely arriving, arriving,
In the day, in the night, to all, to each,
175 *Sooner or later delicate death.*

Prais'd be the fathomless universe,
For life and joy, and for objects and knowledge curious,
And for love, sweet love—but praise! praise! praise!
For the sure-enwinding arms of cool-enfolding death.

180 *Dark mother always gliding near with soft feet,*
Have none chanted for thee a chant of fullest welcome?
Then I chant it for thee, I glorify thee above all,
I bring thee a song that when thou must indeed come, come unfalteringly.

Approach strong deliveress,
185 *When it is so, when thou hast taken them I joyously sing the dead,*
Lost in the loving floating ocean of thee,
Laved in the flood of thy bliss O death.

From me to thee glad serenades,
Dances for thee I propose saluting thee, adornments and feastings for thee,
190 *And the sights of the open landscape and the high-spread sky are fitting,*
And life and the fields, and the huge and thoughtful night.

The night in silence under many a star,
The ocean shore and the husky whispering wave whose voice I know,
And the soul turning to thee O vast and well-veil'd death,
195 *And the body gratefully nestling close to thee.*

Over the tree-tops I float thee a song,
Over the rising and sinking waves, over the myriad fields and the prairies
wide,
Over the dense-pack'd cities all and the teeming wharves and ways,
200 *I float this carol with joy, with joy to thee O death.*

15

To the tally of my soul,
Loud and strong kept up the gray-brown bird,
With pure deliberate notes spreading filling the night.

Loud in the pines and cedars dim,
205 Clear in the freshness moist and the swamp-perfume,
And I with my comrades there in the night.

While my sight that was bound in my eyes unclosed,
As to long panoramas of visions.

And I saw askant the armies,
210 I saw as in noiseless dreams hundreds of battle-flags,
Borne through the smoke of the battles and pierc'd with missiles I saw
them,
And carried hither and yon through the smoke, and torn and bloody,
And at last but a few shreds left on the staffs, (and all in silence,)
215 And the staffs all splinter'd and broken.

I saw battle-corpses, myriads of them,
And the white skeletons of young men, I saw them,
I saw the debris and debris of all the slain soldiers of the war,
But I saw they were not as was thought,
220 They themselves were fully at rest, they suffer'd not,
The living remain'd and suffer'd, the mother suffer'd,
And the wife and the child and the musing comrade suffer'd,
And the armies that remain'd suffer'd.

16

Passing the visions, passing the night,
225 Passing, unloosing the hold of my comrades' hands,
Passing the song of the hermit bird and the tallying song of my soul,
Victorious song, death's outlet song, yet varying ever-altering song,
As low and wailing, yet clear the notes, rising and falling, flooding
    the night,
230 Sadly sinking and fainting, as warning and warning, and yet again
    bursting with joy,
Covering the earth and filling the spread of the heaven,
As that powerful psalm in the night I heard from recesses,
Passing, I leave thee lilac with heart-shaped leaves,
235 I leave thee there in the door-yard, blooming, returning with spring.

I cease from my song for thee,
From my gaze on thee in the west, fronting the west, communing with
    thee,
O comrade lustrous with silver face in the night.

240 Yet each to keep and all, retrievements out of the night,
The song, the wondrous chant of the gray-brown bird,
And the tallying chant, the echo arous'd in my soul,
With the lustrous and drooping star with the countenance full of woe,
With the holders holding my hand nearing the call of the bird,
245 Comrades mine and I in the midst, and their memory ever to keep, for
    the dead I loved so well,
For the sweetest, wisest soul of all my days and lands—and this for
    his dear sake,
Lilac and star and bird twined with the chant of my soul,
250 There in the fragrant pines and the cedars dusk and dim.

CHRISTINA ROSSETTI (1830–1894)

Song
(1848)

When I am dead, my dearest,
    Sing no sad songs for me;
Plant thou no roses at my head,
    Nor shady cypress tree:
5 Be the green grass above me
    With showers and dewdrops wet;
And if thou wilt, remember,
    And if thou wilt, forget.

I shall not see the shadows,
10   I shall not feel the rain;

I shall not hear the nightingale
   Sing on, as if in pain:
And dreaming through the twilight
   That doth not rise nor set,
15 Haply I may remember,
   And haply may forget.

LEWIS CARROLL (1832–1898)

The White Knight's Song
Haddock's Eyes or *The Aged Aged Man* or *Ways and Means* or *A-Sitting On A Gate*
(1871)

I'll tell thee everything I can;
   There's little to relate.
I saw an aged, aged man,
   A-sitting on a gate.
5 "Who are you, aged man?" I said.
   "And how is it you live?"
And his answer trickled through my head
   Like water through a sieve.

He said "I look for butterflies
10   That sleep among the wheat;
I make them into mutton-pies,
   And sell them in the street.
I sell them unto men," he said,
   "Who sail on stormy seas;
15 And that's the way I get my bread—
   A trifle, if you please."

But I was thinking of a plan
   To dye one's whiskers green,
And always use so large a fan
20   That it could not be seen.
So, having no reply to give
   To what the old man said,
I cried, "Come, tell me how you live!"
   And thumped him on the head.

25 His accents mild took up the tale;
   He said, "I go my ways,
And when I find a mountain-rill,
   I set it in a blaze;
And thence they make a stuff they call

30   Rowland's Macassar Oil—[1]
      Yet twopence-halfpenny is all
         They give me for my toil."

      But I was thinking of a way
         To feed oneself on batter,
35 And so go on from day to day
      Getting a little fatter.
   I shook him well from side to side,
      Until his face was blue;
   "Come, tell me how you live," I cried
40   "And what it is you do!"

      He said, "I hunt for haddocks' eyes
         Among the heather bright,
      And work them into waistcoat-buttons
         In the silent night.
45 And these I do not sell for gold
      Or coin of silvery shine,
   But for a copper halfpenny,
      And that will purchase nine.

      "I sometimes dig for buttered rolls,
50   Or set limed twigs for crabs;
   I sometimes search the grassy knolls
      For wheels of hansom-cabs.
   And that's the way" (he gave a wink)
      "By which I get my wealth—
55 And very gladly will I drink
      Your Honor's noble health."

      I heard him then, for I had just
         Completed my design
      To keep the Menai bridge[2] from rust
60   By boiling it in wine.
   I thanked him much for telling me
      The way he got his wealth,
   But chiefly for his wish that he
      Might drink my noble health.

65 And now, if e'er by chance I put
      My fingers into glue,
   Or madly squeeze a right-hand foot
      Into a left-hand shoe,

---

[1] A patented hairdressing.
[2] A large bridge in Wales.

Or if I drop upon my toe
70   A very heavy weight,
I weep, for it reminds me so
Of that old man I used to know—
Whose look was mild, whose speech was slow,
Whose hair was whiter than the snow,
75 Whose face was very like a crow,
With eyes, like cinders, all aglow,
Who seemed distracted with his woe,
Who rocked his body to and fro,
And muttered mumblingly and low,
80 As if his mouth were full of dough,
Who snorted like a buffalo—
That summer evening long ago
    A-sitting on a gate.

Jabberwocky
(1871)

'Twas brillig, and the slithy toves
    Did gyre and gimble in the wabe:
All mimsy were the borogoves,
    And the mome raths outgrabe.

5 "Beware the Jabberwock, my son!
    The jaws that bite, the claws that catch!
Beware the Jubjub bird, and shun
    The frumious Bandersnatch!"

He took his vorpal sword in hand:
10   Long time the manxome foe he sought—
So rested he by the Tumtum tree,
    And stood awhile in thought.

And, as in uffish thought he stood,
    The Jabberwock, with eyes of flame,
15 Came whiffling through the tulgey wood,
    And burbled as it came!

One, two! One, two! And through and through
    The vorpal blade went snicker-snack!
He left it dead, and with its head
20   He went galumphing back.

"And hast thou slain the Jabberwock?
    Come to my arms, my beamish boy!

O frabjous day! Callooh! Callay!"
  He chortled in his joy.

25 'Twas brillig, and the slithy toves
    Did gyre and gimble in the wabe:
  All mimsy were the borogoves,
    And the mome raths outgrabe.

THOMAS HARDY (1840–1928)

The Darkling Thrush
(1900)

I leant upon a coppice gate
  When Frost was specter-gray,
And Winter's dregs made desolate
  The weakening eye of day.
5 The tangled bine-stems scored the sky
  Like strings of broken lyres,
And all mankind that haunted nigh
  Had sought their household fires.

The land's sharp features seemed to be
10   The Century's corpse outleant,
His crypt the cloudy canopy,
  The wind his death-lament.
The ancient pulse of germ and birth
  Was shrunken hard and dry,
15 And every spirit upon earth
  Seemed fervorless as I.

At once a voice rose among
  The bleak twigs overhead
In a full-hearted evensong
20   Of joy illimited;
An aged thrush, frail, gaunt, and small,
  In blast-beruffled plume,
Had chosen thus to fling his soul
  Upon the growing gloom.

25 So little cause for carolings
  Of such ecstatic sound
Was written on terrestrial things
  Afar or nigh around,
That I could think there trembled through
30   His happy good-night air
Some blessed Hope, whereof he knew
  And I was unaware.

The Convergence of the Twain
Lines on the Loss of the Titanic[1]
(1912)

1

In a solitude of the sea
Deep from human vanity,
And the Pride of Life that planned her, stilly couches she.

2

Steel chambers, late the pyres
5   Of her salamandrine fires,[2]
Cold currents thrid,° and turn to rhythmic tidal lyres.   *thread*

3

Over the mirrors meant
To glass the opulent
The sea-worm crawls—grotesque, slimed, dumb, indifferent.

4

10   Jewels in joy designed
To ravish the sensuous mind
Lie lightless, all their sparkles bleared and black and blind.

5

Dim moon-eyed fishes near
Gaze at the gilded gear
15 And query: "What does this vaingloriousness down here?"

6

Well: while was fashioning
This creature of cleaving wing,
The Immanent Will that stirs and urges everything

7

Prepared a sinister mate
20   For her—so gaily great—
A Shape of Ice, for the time far and dissociate.

---

[1] The White Star liner R.M.S. *Titanic* was sunk, with great loss of life, as the result of collision with an iceberg on its maiden voyage from Southampton to New York on April 15, 1912.

[2] The ship's fires, which burn though immersed in water, are compared to the salamander, a lizard-like creature which according to fable could live in the midst of fire.

8

And as the smart ship grew
In stature, grace, and hue,
In shadowy silent distance grew the Iceberg too.

9

25   Alien they seemed to be:
No mortal eye could see
The intimate welding of their later history,

10

Or sign that they were bent
By paths coincident
30 On being anon twin halves of one august event,

11

Till the Spinner of the Years
Said "Now!" And each one hears,
And consummation comes, and jars two hemispheres.

GERARD MANLEY HOPKINS (1844–1889)

The Windhover[1]

To Christ Our Lord

(1877)

I caught this morning morning's minion,° kingdom of   *darling, favorite*
    daylight's dauphin,[2] dapple-dawn-drawn Falcon, in
    his riding
  Of the rolling level underneath him steady air, and
5   striding
High there, how he rung upon the rein of a wimpling° wing   *rippling*
In his ecstasy! then off, off forth on swing,
  As a skate's heel sweeps smooth on a bow-bend: the hurl and
    gliding
10   Rebuffed the big wind. My heart in hiding
Stirred for a bird,—the achieve of, the mastery of the thing!

---

[1] "A name for the kestrel [a species of small hawk], from its habit of hovering or hang-ing with its head to the wind" [O.E.D.].

[2] The eldest son of the king of France was called the *dauphin;* hence, the word here means heir to a splendid, kingly condition.

Brute beauty and valour and act, oh, air, pride, plume, here
　　Buckle!³ AND the fire that breaks from thee then, a billion
Times told lovelier, more dangerous, O my chevalier!⁴

15　　No wonder of it: shéer plód makes plough down sillion°　　　*furrow*
Shine, and blue-bleak embers, ah my dear,
　　Fall, gall themselves, and gash gold-vermilion.

*Pied Beauty*¹
(1877)

Glory be to God for dappled things—
　　For skies of couple-colour as a brinded° cow;　　　*streaked, brindled*
　　　For rose-moles all in stipple upon trout that swim;
Fresh-firecoal chestnut-falls;² finches' wings;
5　　Landscape plotted and pieced—fold, fallow, and plough;³
　　　And áll trádes, their gear and tackle and trim.
All things counter, original, spare, strange;
　　Whatever is fickle, freckled (who knows how?)
　　　With swift, slow; sweet, sour; adazzle, dim;
10 He fathers-forth whose beauty is past change:
　　　　　　　　　　　　Praise him.

A. E. HOUSMAN (1859–1936)
Loveliest of Trees, the Cherry Now
(1896)

　　　Loveliest of trees, the cherry now
　　　Is hung with bloom along the bough,
　　　And stands about the woodland ride
　　　Wearing white for Eastertide.

　　5 Now, of my threescore years and ten,
　　　Twenty will not come again,

---

³The word "buckle" brings to a single focus the several elements of line 8, in both their literal sense, as descriptive of a single, sudden movement of the airborne bird, and in their symbolic sense as descriptive of Christ and with further reference to the poet himself and the lesson he draws from his observation. It may be read either as indicative or imperative, and in one or another of its possible meanings: "to fasten," "to join closely," "to equip for battle," "to grapple with, engage," but also "to cause to bend, give way, crumple."

⁴Knight, nobleman, champion.

¹Having two or more colors, in patches or blotches.

²W. H. Gardner cites a note from Hopkins's *Journals:* "Chestnuts as bright as coals or spots of vermilion."

³The land makes a pattern of varicolored patches by reason of its several uses, as for pasture, or being left fallow for a season, or being plowed and sown.

And take from seventy springs a score,
It only leaves me fifty more.

And since to look at things in bloom
10 Fifty springs are little room,
About the woodlands I will go
To see the cherry hung with snow.

To an Athlete Dying Young
(1896)

The time you won your town the race
We chaired you through the market-place;
Man and boy stood cheering by,
And home we brought you shoulder-high.

5 Today, the road all runners come,
Shoulder-high we bring you home,
And set you at your threshold down,
Townsman of a stiller town.

Smart lad, to slip betimes away
10 From fields where glory does not stay
And early through the laurel grows
It withers quicker than the rose.

Eyes the shady night has shut
Cannot see the record cut,
15 And silence sounds no worse than cheers
After earth has stopped the ears:

Now you will not swell the rout
Of lads that wore their honors out,
Runners whom renown outran
20 And the name died before the man.

So set, before its echoes fade,
The fleet foot on the sill of shade,
And hold to the low lintel up
The still-defended challenge-cup.

25 And round that early-laureled head
Will flock to gaze the strengthless dead,
And find unwithered on its curls
The garland briefer than a girl's.

ROBERT FROST (1874–1963)

Stopping by Woods on a Snowy Evening
(1923)

Whose woods these are I think I know.
His house is in the village, though;
He will not see me stopping here
To watch his woods fill up with snow.

5 My little horse must think it queer
To stop without a farmhouse near
Between the woods and frozen lake
The darkest evening of the year.

He gives his harness bells a shake
10 To ask if there is some mistake.
The only other sound's the sweep
Of easy wind and downy flake.

The woods are lovely, dark and deep.
But I have promises to keep,
15 And miles to go before I sleep,
And miles to go before I sleep.

Design
(1936)

I found a dimpled spider, fat and white,
On a white heal-all,[1] holding up a moth
Like a white piece of rigid satin cloth—
Assorted characters of death and blight
5 Mixed ready to begin the morning right,
Like the ingredients of a witches' broth—
A snow-drop spider, a flower like a froth,
And dead wings carried like a paper kite.

What had that flower to do with being white,
10 The wayside blue and innocent heal-all?
What brought the kindred spider to that height,
Then steered the white moth thither in the night?
What but design of darkness to appall?—
If design govern in a thing so small.

---

[1] One of a variety of plants thought to have curative powers.

WALLACE STEVENS (1879–1955)

Disillusionment of Ten O'Clock
(1923)

The houses are haunted
By white night-gowns.
None are green,
Or purple with green rings,
5 Or green with yellow rings,
Or yellow with blue rings.
None of them are strange,
With socks of lace
And beaded ceintures.
10 People are not going
To dream of baboons and periwinkles.
Only, here and there, an old sailor,
Drunk and asleep in his boots,
Catches tigers
15 In red weather.

Sunday Morning
(1915)

1

Complacencies of the peignoir, and late
Coffee and oranges in a sunny chair,
And the green freedom of a cockatoo
Upon a rug mingle to dissipate
5 The holy hush of ancient sacrifice.
She dreams a little, and she feels the dark
Encroachment of that old catastrophe,
As a calm darkens among water-lights.
The pungent oranges and bright, green wings
10 Seem things in some procession of the dead,
Winding across wide water, without sound.
The day is like wide water, without sound,
Stilled for the passing of her dreaming feet
Over the seas, to silent Palestine,
15 Dominion of the blood and sepulchre.

2

Why should she give her bounty to the dead?
What is divinity if it can come
Only in silent shadows and in dreams?
Shall she not find in comforts of the sun,
20 In pungent fruit and bright, green wings, or else

In any balm or beauty of the earth,
Things to be cherished like the thought of heaven?
Divinity must live within herself:
Passions of rain, or moods in falling snow;
25 Grievings in loneliness, or unsubdued
Elations when the forest blooms; gusty
Emotions on wet roads on autumn nights;
All pleasures and all pains, remembering
The bough of summer and the winter branch.
30 These are the measures destined for her soul.

3

Jove in the clouds had his inhuman birth.
No mother suckled him, no sweet land gave
Large-mannered motions to his mythy mind
He moved among us, as a muttering king,
35 Magnificent, would move among his hinds,
Until our blood, commingling, virginal,
With heaven, brought such requital to desire
The very hinds discerned it, in a star.
Shall our blood fail? Or shall it come to be
40 The blood of paradise? And shall the earth
Seem all of paradise that we shall know?
The sky will be much friendlier then than now,
A part of labor and a part of pain,
And next in glory to enduring love,
45 Not this dividing and indifferent blue.

4

She says, "I am content when wakened birds,
Before they fly, test the reality
Of misty fields, by their sweet questionings;
But when the birds are gone, and their warm fields
50 Return no more, where, then, is paradise?"
There is not any haunt of prophecy,
Nor any old chimera of the grave,
Neither the golden underground, nor isle
Melodious, where spirits gat them home,
55 Nor visionary south, nor cloudy palm
Remote on heaven's hill, that has endured
As April's green endures; or will endure
Like her remembrance of awakened birds,
Or her desire for June and evening, tipped
60 By the consummation of the swallow's wings.

5

She says, "But in contentment I still feel
The need of some imperishable bliss."

Death is the mother of beauty; hence from her,
Alone, shall come fulfilment to our dreams
65 And our desires. Although she strews the leaves
Of sure obliteration on our paths,
The path sick sorrow took, the many paths
Where triumph rang its brassy phrase, or love
Whispered a little out of tenderness,
70 She makes the willow shiver in the sun
For maidens who were wont to sit and gaze
Upon the grass, relinquished to their feet.
She causes boys to pile new plums and pears
On disregarded plate.[1] The maidens taste
75 And stray impassioned in the littering leaves.

6

Is there no change of death in paradise?
Does ripe fruit never fall? Or do the boughs
Hang always heavy in that perfect sky,
Unchanging, yet so like our perishing earth,
80 With rivers like our own that seek for seas
They never find, the same receding shores
That never touch with inarticulate pang?
Why set the pear upon those river-banks
Or spice the shores with odors of the plum?
85 Alas, that they should wear our colors there,
The silken weavings of our afternoons,
And pick the strings of our insipid lutes!
Death is the mother of beauty, mystical,
Within whose burning bosom we devise
90 Our earthly mothers waiting, sleeplessly.

7

Supple and turbulent, a ring of men
Shall chant in orgy on a summer morn
Their boisterous devotion to the sun,
Not as a god, but as a god might be,
95 Naked among them, like a savage source.
Their chant shall be a chant of paradise,
Out of their blood, returning to the sky;
And in their chant shall enter, voice by voice,
The windy lake wherein their lord delights,
100 The trees, like serafin,° and echoing hills,   *celestial beings*
That choir among themselves long afterward.
They shall know well the heavenly fellowship

---

[1] "Plate is used in the sense of so-called family plate. Disregarded refers to the disuse into which things fall that have been possessed for a long time. I mean, therefore, that death releases and renews" [*Letters of Wallace Stevens*, New York, 1966, pp. 183–184].

Of men that perish and of summer morn.
And whence they came and whither they shall go
105 The dew upon their feet shall manifest.

8

She hears, upon that water without sound,
A voice that cries, "The tomb in Palestine
Is not the porch of spirits lingering.
It is the grave of Jesus, where he lay."
110 We live in an old chaos of the sun,
Or old dependency of day and night,
Or island solitude, unsponsored, free,
Of that wide water, inescapable.
Deer walk upon our mountains, and the quail
115 Whistle about us their spontaneous cries;
Sweet berries ripen in the wilderness;
And, in the isolation of the sky,
At evening, casual flocks of pigeons make
Ambiguous undulations as they sink,
120 Downward to darkness, on extended wings.

WILLIAM CARLOS WILLIAMS (1883–1963)

The Red Wheelbarrow
(1923)

so much depends
upon

a red wheel
barrow

5 glazed with rain
water

beside the white
chickens.

This Is Just to Say
(1934)

I have eaten
the plums
that were in
the icebox

5 and which
  you were probably
  saving
  for breakfast

  Forgive me
10 they were delicious
   so sweet
   and so cold

D. H. LAWRENCE (1885–1930)

Snake
(1923)

A snake came to my water-trough
On a hot, hot day, and I in pajamas for the heat,
To drink there.

In the deep, strange-scented shade of the great dark carob-tree
5 I came down the steps with my pitcher
And must wait, must stand and wait, for there he was at the trough
    before me.

He reached down from a fissure in the earth-wall in the gloom
And trailed his yellow-brown slackness soft-bellied down, over the
10   edge of the stone trough
And rested his throat upon the stone bottom,
And where the water had dripped from the tap, in a small clearness,
He sipped with his straight mouth,
Softly drank through his straight gums, into his slack long body,
15 Silently.

Someone was before me at my water-trough,
And I, like a second comer, waiting.

He lifted his head from his drinking, as cattle do,
And looked at me vaguely, as drinking cattle do,
20 And flickered his two-forked tongue from his lips, and mused a
    moment,
And stooped and drank a little more,
Being earth-brown, earth-golden from the burning bowels of the earth
On the day of Sicilian July, with Etna smoking.

25 The voice of my education said to me
He must be killed,

For in Sicily the black, black snakes are innocent, the gold are
    venomous.

And voices in me said, If you were a man
30 You would take a stick and break him now, and finish him off.

But must I confess how I liked him,
How glad I was he had come like a guest in quiet, to drink at my
    water-trough

And depart peaceful, pacified, and thankless,
35 Into the burning bowels of this earth?

Was it cowardice, that I dared not kill him?
Was it perversity, that I longed to talk to him?
Was it humility, to feel so honored?
I felt so honored.

40 And yet those voices:
If you were not afraid, you would kill him!

And truly I was afraid, I was most afraid,
But even so, honored still more
That he should seek my hospitality
45 From out the dark door of the secret earth.

He drank enough
And lifted his head, dreamily, as one who has drunken,
And flickered his tongue like a forked night on the air, so black,
Seeming to lick his lips,
50 And looked around like a god, unseeing, into the air,
And slowly turned his head,
And slowly, very slowly, as if thrice adream,
Proceeded to draw his slow length curving round
And climb again the broken bank of my wall-face.

55 And as he put his head into that dreadful hole,
And as he slowly drew up, snake-easing his shoulders, and entered
    farther,
A sort of horror, a sort of protest against his withdrawing into that
    horrid black hole,
60 Deliberately going into the blackness, and slowly drawing himself
    after,
Overcame me now his back was turned.

I looked round, I put down my pitcher,
I picked up a clumsy log
65 And threw it at the water-trough with a clatter.

I think it did not hit him,
But suddenly that part of him that was left behind convulsed in
    undignified haste.
Writhed like lightning, and was gone
70 Into the black hole, the earth-lipped fissure in the wall-front,
At which, in the intense still noon, I stared with fascination.

And immediately I regretted it.
I thought how paltry, how vulgar, what a mean act!
I despised myself and the voices of my accursed human education.

75 And I thought of the albatross
And I wished he would come back, my snake.

For he seemed to me again like a king,
Like a king in exile, uncrowned in the underworld,
Now due to be crowned again.

80 And so, I missed my chance with one of the lords
Of life.
And I have something to expiate;
A pettiness.

Piano
(1918)

Softly, in the dusk, a woman is singing to me;
Taking me back down the vista of years, till I see
A child sitting under the piano, in the boom of the tingling strings
And pressing the small, poised feet of a mother who smiles as she sings.

5 In spite of myself, the insidious mastery of song
Betrays me back, till the heart of me weeps to belong
To the old Sunday evenings at home, with winter outside
And hymns in the cozy parlor, the tinkling piano our guide.

So now it is vain for the singer to burst into clamor
10 With the great black piano appassionato. The glamour
Of childish days is upon me, my manhood is cast
Down in the flood of remembrance, I weep like a child for the past.

EZRA POUND (1885–1972)

Portrait d'une Femme[1]

(1912)

Your mind and you are our Sargasso Sea,[2]
London has swept about you this score years
And bright ships left you this or that in fee:
Ideas, old gossip, oddments of all things,
5 Strange spars of knowledge and dimmed wares of price.
Great minds have sought you—lacking someone else.
You have been second always. Tragical?
No. You preferred it to the usual thing:
One dull man, dulling and uxorious,
10 One average mind—with one thought less, each year.
Oh, you are patient, I have seen you sit
Hours, where something might have floated up.
And now you pay one. Yes, you richly pay.
You are a person of some interest, one comes to you
15 And takes strange gain away:
Trophies fished up; some curious suggestion;
Fact that leads nowhere; and a tale or two,
Pregnant with mandrakes,[3] or with something else
That might prove useful and yet never proves,
20 That never fits a corner or shows use,
Or finds its hour upon the loom of days:
The tarnished, gaudy, wonderful old work;
Idols and ambergris[4] and rare inlays,
These are your riches, your great store; and yet
25 For all this sea-hoard of deciduous things,
Strange woods half sodden, and new brighter stuff:
In the slow float of differing light and deep,
No! there is nothing! In the whole and all,
Nothing that's quite your own.
                    Yet this is you.

The River-Merchant's Wife: a Letter

(1915)

While my hair was still cut straight across my forehead
I played about the front gate, pulling flowers.

---

[1] Portrait of a Lady.

[2] A region of the North Atlantic partially covered with accumulations of floating gulfweed. In legend, it collects the wrecks of ships from all oceans.

[3] A plant, of narcotic properties, and sometimes believed to be aphrodisiac, whose forked root was traditionally thought to resemble the human body.

[4] Secretion of the whale, used in perfumery.

You came by on bamboo stilts, playing horse,
You walked about my seat, playing with blue plums.
5 And we went on living in the village of Chokan:
Two small people, without dislike or suspicion.

At fourteen I married My Lord you.
I never laughed, being bashful.
Lowering my head, I looked at the wall.
10 Called to, a thousand times, I never looked back.

At fifteen I stopped scowling,
I desired my dust to be mingled with yours
Forever and forever and forever.
Why should I climb the look out?

15 At sixteen you departed,
You went into far Ku-to-yen, by the river of swirling eddies,
And you have been gone five months.
The monkeys make sorrowful noise overhead.

You dragged your feet when you went out.
20 By the gate now, the moss is grown, the different mosses,
Too deep to clear them away!
The leaves fall early this autumn, in wind.
The paired butterflies are already yellow with August
Over the grass in the West garden;
25 They hurt me. I grow older.
If you are coming down through the narrows of the river Kiang,
Please let me know beforehand,
And I will come out to meet you
          As far as Cho-fu-Sa.

H. D. (HILDA DOOLITTLE) (1886–1961)

Oread[1]
(1914)

> Whirl up, sea—
> whirl your pointed pines,
> splash your great pines
> on our rocks,
> 5 hurl your green over us,
> cover us with your pools of fir.

---

[1] Mountain nymph.

Heat
(1914)

O wind, rend open the heat,
cut apart the heat,
rend it to tatters.
Fruit cannot drop
5 through this thick air—
fruit cannot fall into heat
that presses up and blunts
the points of pears
and rounds the grapes.

10 Cut the heat—
plough through it,
turning it on either side
of your path.

T. S. ELIOT (1888–1965)

The Love Song of J. Alfred Prufrock
(1917)

S'io credesse che mia risposta fosse
A persona che mai tornasse al mondo,
Questa fiamma staria senza più scosse.
Ma perciocche giammai di questo fondo
Non tornò vivo alcun, s'i'odo il vero,
Senza tema d'infamia ti rispondo.[1]

Let us go then, you and I,
When the evening is spread out against the sky
Like a patient etherized upon a table;
Let us go, through certain half-deserted streets,
5 The muttering retreats
Of restless nights in one-night cheap hotels
And sawdust restaurants with oyster-shells:
Streets that follow like a tedious argument
Of insidious intent

---

[1] Dante, *Inferno*, XXVII.61–66. These words are spoken by Guido da Montefeltro, whom Dante and Virgil have encountered in the Eighth Chasm, that of the False Counselors, where each spirit is concealed within a flame which moves as the spirit speaks: "If I thought my answer were given/to anyone who would ever return to the world,/this flame would stand still without moving any further./But since never from this abyss/has anyone ever returned alive, if what I hear is true,/without fear of infamy I answer thee."

10 To lead you to an overwhelming question. . .
   Oh, do not ask, "What is it?"
   Let us go and make our visit.

   In the room the women come and go
   Talking of Michelangelo.

15 The yellow fog that rubs its back upon the window-panes
   The yellow smoke that rubs its muzzle on the window-panes
   Licked its tongue into the corners of the evening,
   Lingered upon the pools that stand in drains,
   Let fall upon its back the soot that falls from chimneys,
20 Slipped by the terrace, made a sudden leap,
   And seeing that it was a soft October night,
   Curled once about the house, and fell asleep.

   And indeed there will be time
   For the yellow smoke that slides along the street,
25 Rubbing its back upon the window-panes;
   There will be time, there will be time
   To prepare a face to meet the faces that you meet;
   There will be time to murder and create,
   And time for all the works and days² of hands
30 That lift and drop a question on your plate;
   Time for you and time for me,
   And time yet for a hundred indecisions,
   And for a hundred visions and revisions,
   Before the taking of a toast and tea.

35 In the room the women come and go
   Talking of Michelangelo.

   And indeed there will be time
   To wonder, "Do I dare?" and, "Do I dare?"
   Time to turn back and descend the stair,
40 With a bald spot in the middle of my hair—
   [They will say: "How his hair is growing thin!"]
   My morning coat, my collar mounting firmly to the chin,
   My necktie rich and modest, but asserted by a simple pin—
   [They will say: "But how his arms and legs are thin!"]
45 Do I dare
   Disturb the universe?
   In a minute there is time
   For decisions and revisions which a minute will reverse.

---

²Possibly alludes to the title of a didactic work on the seasonal pursuits of country life, *Works and Days,* by the Greek poet Hesiod (eighth century B.C.).

For I have known them all already, known them all:
50 Have known the evenings, mornings, afternoons,
  I have measured out my life with coffee spoons;
  I know the voices dying with a dying fall
  Beneath the music from a farther room.
    So how should I presume?

55 And I have known the eyes already, known them all—
  The eyes that fix you in a formulated phrase,
  And when I am formulated, sprawling on a pin,
  When I am pinned and wriggling on the wall,
  Then how should I begin
60 To spit out all the butt-ends of my days and ways?
    And how should I presume?

  And I have known the arms already, known them all—
  Arms that are braceleted and white and bare
  [But in the lamplight, downed with light brown hair!]
65 Is it perfume from a dress
  That makes me so digress?
  Arms that lie along a table, or wrap about a shawl.
    And should I then presume?
    And how should I begin?

           . . . . .

70 Shall I say, I have gone at dusk through narrow streets
  And watched the smoke that rises from the pipes
  Of lonely men in shirt-sleeves, leaning out of windows? . . .

  I should have been a pair of ragged claws
  Scuttling across the floors of silent seas.

           . . . . .

75 And the afternoon, the evening, sleeps so peacefully!
  Smoothed by long fingers,
  Asleep . . . tired . . . or it malingers,
  Stretched on the floor, here beside you and me.
  Should I, after tea and cakes and ices,
80 Have the strength to force the moment to its crisis?

  But though I have wept and fasted, wept and prayed,
  Though I have seen my head [grown slightly bald] brought in upon a
      platter,[3]
  I am no prophet—and here's no great matter;

---

[3]See the story of the martyrdom of St. John the Baptist (Matthew xiv.1–12), whose head
was presented to Salome on a plate at the order of the tetrarch Herod.

85 I have seen the moment of my greatness flicker,
And I have seen the eternal Footman hold my coat, and snicker,
And in short, I was afraid.

And would it have been worth it, after all,
After the cups, the marmalade, the tea,
90 Among the porcelain, among some talk of you and me,
Would it have been worth while,
To have bitten off the matter with a smile,
To have squeezed the universe into a ball
To roll it toward some overwhelming question,
95 To say: "I am Lazarus,[4] come from the dead,
Come back to tell you all, I shall tell you all"—
If one, settling a pillow by her head,
    Should say: "That is not what I meant at all.
    That is not it, at all."

100 And would it have been worth it, after all,
Would it have been worth while,
After the sunsets and the dooryards and the sprinkled streets,
After the novels, after the teacups, after the skirts that trail along the
        floor—
105 And this, and so much more?—
It is impossible to say just what I mean!
But as if a magic lantern threw the nerves in patterns on a screen:
Would it have been worth while
If one, settling a pillow or throwing off a shawl,
110 And turning toward the window, should say:
    "That is not it at all,
    That is not what I meant, at all."

                    · · · · ·

No! I am not Prince Hamlet, nor was meant to be;
115 Am an attendant lord, one that will do
To swell a progress,[5] start a scene or two,
Advise the prince; no doubt, an easy tool,
Deferential, glad to be of use,
Politic, cautious, and meticulous;
120 Full of high sentence,° but a bit obtuse;   *sententiousness*
At times, indeed, almost ridiculous—
Almost, at times, the Fool.

I grow old . . . I grow old . . .
I shall wear the bottoms of my trousers rolled.

---

[4] See John xi, and xii.1–2.
[5] In Elizabethan sense: state journey.

125 Shall I part my hair behind? Do I dare to eat a peach?
I shall wear white flannel trousers, and walk upon the beach.
I have heard the mermaids singing, each to each.

I do not think that they will sing to me.
I have seen them riding seaward on the waves
130 Combing the white hair of the waves blown back
When the wind blows the water white and black.

We have lingered in the chambers of the sea
By sea-girls wreathed with seaweed red and brown
Till human voices wake us, and we drown.

Macavity: the Mystery Cat
(1939)

Macavity's a Mystery Cat: he's called the Hidden Paw—
For he's the master criminal who can defy the Law.
He's the bafflement of Scotland Yard, the Flying Squad's despair:
For when they reach the scene of crime—*Macavity's not there!*

5 Macavity, Macavity, there's no one like Macavity,
He's broken every human law, he breaks the law of gravity.
His powers of levitation would make a fakir stare,
And when you reach the scene of crime—*Macavity's not there!*
You may seek him in the basement, you may look up in the air—
10 But I tell you once and once again, *Macavity's not there!*

Macavity's a ginger cat, he's very tall and thin;
You would know him if you saw him, for his eyes are sunken in.
His brow is deeply lined with thought, his head is highly domed;
His coat is dusty from neglect, his whiskers are uncombed.
15 He sways his head from side to side, with movements like a snake;
And when you think he's half asleep, he's always wide awake.

Macavity, Macavity, there's no one like Macavity,
For he's a fiend in feline shape, a monster of depravity.
You may meet him in a by-street, you may see him in the square—
20 But when a crime's discovered, then *Macavity's not there!*

He's outwardly respectable. (They say he cheats at cards.)
And his footprints are not found in any file of Scotland Yard's.
And when the larder's looted, or the jewel-case is rifled,
Or when the milk is missing, or another Peke's been stifled,
25 Or the greenhouse glass is broken, and the trellis past repair—
Ay, there's the wonder of the thing! *Macavity's not there!*

And when the Foreign Office find a Treaty's gone astray,
Or the Admiralty lose some plans and drawings by the way,
There may be a scrap of paper in the hall or on the stair—
30 But it's useless to investigate—*Macavity's not there!*
And when the loss has been disclosed, the Secret Service say:
"It *must* have been Macavity!"—but he's a mile away.
You'll be sure to find him resting, or a-licking of his thumbs,
Or engaged in doing complicated long division sums.

35 Macavity, Macavity, there's no one like Macavity,
There never was a Cat of such deceitfulness and suavity.
He always has an alibi, and one or two to spare:
At whatever time the deed took place—MACAVITY WASN'T THERE!
And they say that all the Cats whose wicked deeds are widely known
40 (I might mention Mungojerrie, I might mention Griddlebone)
Are nothing more than agents for the Cat who all the time
Just controls their operations: the Napoleon of Crime!

JOHN CROWE RANSOM (1888–1974)
Bells for John Whiteside's Daughter
(1924)

There was such speed in her little body,
And such lightness in her footfall,
It is no wonder her brown study
Astonishes us all.

5 Her wars were bruited in our high window.
We looked among orchard trees and beyond
Where she took arms against her shadow,
Or harried unto the pond

The lazy geese, like a snow cloud
10 Dripping their snow on the green grass,
Tricking and stopping, sleepy and proud,
Who cried in goose, Alas,

For the tireless heart within the little
Lady with rod that made them rise
15 From their noon apple-dreams and scuttle
Goose-fashion under the skies!

But now go the bells, and we are ready,
In one house we are sternly stopped
To say we are vexed at her brown study,
20 Lying so primly propped.

EDNA ST. VINCENT MILLAY (1892–1950)

Love Is Not All: It Is Not Meat nor Drink
(1931)

Love is not all: it is not meat nor drink
Nor slumber nor a roof against the rain;
Nor yet a floating spar to men that sink
And rise and sink and rise and sink again;
5 Love can not fill the thickened lung with breath,
Nor clean the blood, nor set the fractured bone;
Yet many a man is making friends with death
Even as I speak, for lack of love alone.
It well may be that in a difficult hour,
10 Pinned down by pain and moaning for release,
Or nagged by want past resolution's power,
I might be driven to sell your love for peace,
Or trade the memory of this night for food.
It well may be. I do not think I would.

I, Being Born a Woman and Distressed
(1923)

I, being born a woman and distressed
By all the needs and notions of my kind,
Am urged by your propinquity to find
Your person fair, and feel a certain zest
5 To bear your body's weight upon my breast:
So subtly is the fume of life designed,
To clarify the pulse and cloud the mind,
And leave me once again undone, possessed.
Think not for this, however, the poor treason
10 Of my stout blood against my staggering brain,
I shall remember you with love, or season
My scorn with pity,—let me make it plain:
I find this frenzy insufficient reason
For conversation when we meet again.

E. E. CUMMINGS (1894–1963)

Portrait

Buffalo Bill's
defunct
       who used to
       ride a watersmooth-silver
5   stallion
and break onetwothreefourfive pigeonsjustlikethat
                                      Jesus

he was a handsome man
                              and what i want to know is
10 how do you like your blueeyed boy
   Mister Death

old age sticks

old age sticks
up Keep
Off
signs)&

5 youth yanks them
down(old
age
cries No

Tres)&(pas)
10 youth laughs
(sing
old age

scolds Forbid
den Stop
15 Must
n't Don't

&)youth goes
right on
gr
20 owing old

HART CRANE (1899–1932)
Proem: To Brooklyn Bridge
(1930)

How many dawns, chill from his rippling rest
The seagull's wings shall dip and pivot him,
Shedding white rings of tumult, building high
Over the chained bay waters Liberty—

5 Then, with inviolate curve, forsake our eyes
As apparitional as sails that cross
Some page of figures to be filed away;
—Till elevators drop us from our day . . .

I think of cinemas, panoramic sleights
10 With multitudes bent toward some flashing scene
Never disclosed, but hastened to again,
Foretold to other eyes on the same screen;

And Thee,[1] across the harbor, silver-paced
As though the sun took step of thee, yet left
15 Some motion ever unspent in thy stride—
Implicitly thy freedom staying thee!

Out of some subway scuttle, cell or loft
A bedlamite° speeds to thy parapets,   *madman*
Tilting there momently, shrill shirt ballooning,
20 A jest falls from the speechless caravan.

Down Wall, from girder into street noon leaks,
A rip-tooth of the sky's acetylene,
All afternoon the cloud-flown derricks turn . . .
Thy cables breathe the North Atlantic still.

25 And obscure as that heaven of the Jews,
Thy guerdon . . . Accolade thou dost bestow
Of anonymity time cannot raise:
Vibrant reprieve and pardon thou dost show.

O harp and altar, of the fury fused,
30 (How could mere toil align thy choiring strings!)
Terrific threshold of the prophet's pledge,
Prayer of pariah, and the lover's cry—

Again the traffic lights that skim thy swift
Unfractioned idiom, immaculate sigh of stars,
35 Beading thy path—condense eternity:
And we have seen night lifted in thine arms.

Under thy shadow by the piers I waited;
Only in darkness is thy shadow clear.
The City's fiery parcels all undone,
40 Already snow submerges an iron year . . .

O Sleepless as the river under thee,
Vaulting the sea, the prairies' dreaming sod,
Unto us lowliest sometime sweep, descend
And of the curveship lend a myth to God.

---

[1] i.e., Brooklyn Bridge.

OGDEN NASH (1902–1971)

Very Like a Whale
(1934)

One thing that literature would be greatly the better for
Would be a more restricted employment by authors of simile and
    metaphor.
Authors of all races, be they Greeks, Romans, Teutons or Celts,
5 Can't seem just to say that anything is the thing it is but have to
    go out of their way to say that it is like something else.
What does it mean when we are told
That the Assyrian came down like a wolf on the fold?[1]
In the first place, George Gordon Byron had had enough experience
10 To know that it probably wasn't just one Assyrian, it was a lot of
    Assyrians.
However, as too many arguments are apt to induce apoplexy and thus
    hinder longevity,
We'll let it pass as one Assyrian for the sake of brevity.
15 Now then, this particular Assyrian, the one whose cohorts were
    gleaming in purple and gold,
Just what does the poet mean when he says he came down like a wolf
    on the fold?
In heaven and earth more than is dreamed of in our philosophy there
20   are a great many things,
But I don't imagine that among them there is a wolf with purple and
    gold cohorts or purple and gold anythings.
No, no, Lord Byron, before I'll believe that this Assyrian was actually
    like a wolf I must have some kind of proof;
25 Did he run on all fours and did he have a hairy tail and a big red
    mouth and big white teeth and did he say Woof woof?
Frankly I think it very unlikely, and all you were entitled to say, at the
    very most,
Was that the Assyrian cohorts came down like a lot of Assyrian
30   cohorts about to destroy the Hebrew host.
But that wasn't fancy enough for Lord Byron, oh dear me no, he had
    to invent a lot of figures of speech and then interpolate them,
With the result that whenever you mention Old Testament soldiers
    to people they say Oh yes, they're the ones that a lot of wolves
35   dressed up in gold and purple ate them.
That's the kind of thing that's being done all the time by poets, from
    Homer to Tennyson;
They're always comparing ladies to lilies and veal to venison,
And they always say things like that the snow is a white blanket after
40   a winter storm.

---

[1] See "The Destruction of Sennacherib" on page 478.

Oh it is, is it, all right then, you sleep under a six-inch blanket of
   snow and I'll sleep under a half-inch blanket of unpoetical blanket
   material and we'll see which one keeps warm,
And after that maybe you'll begin to comprehend dimly
45 What I mean by too much metaphor and simile.

LANGSTON HUGHES (1902–1967)

Night Funeral in Harlem
(1951)

Night funeral
in Harlem:

Where did they get
Them two fine cars?

5 Insurance man, he did not pay—
His insurance lapsed the other day—
Yet they got a satin box
For his head to lay.

Night funeral
5   in Harlem:

Who was it sent
That wreath of flowers?

Them flowers came
from that poor boy's friends—
15 They'll want flowers, too,
When they meet their ends.

Night funeral
in Harlem:

Who preached that
Black boy to his grave?

Old preacher-man
Preached that boy away—
Charged Five Dollars
His girl friend had to pay:

25   Night funeral
in Harlem.

When it was all over
And the lid shut on his head
and the organ had done played
30 and the last prayers been said
and six pallbearers
Carried him out for dead
And off down Lenox Avenue
That long black hearse sped,
35   The street light
At his corner
Shined just like a tear—

That boy that they was mournin'
Was so dear, so dear
40 To them folks that brought the flowers,

To that girl who paid the preacher-man—
It was all their tears that made
That poor boy's
Funeral grand.

45   Night funeral
in Harlem.

Harlem
(1951)

What happens to a dream deferred?

Does it dry up
like a raisin in the sun?
Or fester like a sore—
6 And then run?
Does it stink like rotten meat?
Or crust and sugar over—
like a syrupy sweet?

Maybe it just sags
10 like a heavy load.

Or does it explode?

Same in Blues
(1951)

I said to my baby,
Baby, take it slow.

I can't, she said, I can't!
I got to go!

5   *There's a certain*
        amount of traveling
        in a dream deferred.

Lulu said to Leonard,
I want a diamond ring.
10 Leonard said to Lulu,
You won't get a goddam thing!

        A certain
        amount of nothing
        in a dream deferred.

15 Daddy, daddy, daddy,
All I want is you.

You can have me, baby—
But my lovin' days is through.

        A certain
20   *amount of impotence*
        in a dream deferred.

Three parties
On my party line—
But that third party,
25 Lord, ain't mine!

        There's liable
        to be confusion
        in a dream deferred.

From river to river
30 Uptown and down,
There's liable to be confusion
when a dream gets kicked around.

ROBERT BLY (1926–   )

For My Son Noah, Ten Years Old
(1981)

Night and day arrive, and day after day goes by,
and what is old remains old, and what is young remains young, and
    grows old.

The lumber pile does not grow younger, nor the two-by-fours lose
5   their darkness,
but the old tree goes on, the barn stands without help so many years;
the advocate of darkness and night is not lost.

The horse steps up, swings on one leg, turns its body,
the chicken flapping claws onto the roost, its wings whelping and
10   walloping,
but what is primitive is not to be shot out into the night and the dark.
And slowly the kind man comes closer, loses his rage, sits down at
    table.

ROBERT CREELEY (1926–)

Kore[1]

As I was walking
   I came upon
chance walking
   the same road upon.

5 As I sat down
   by chance to move
later
   if and as I might,

light the wood was,
10   light and green,
and what I saw
   before I had not seen.

It was a lady
   accompanied
15 by goat men
   leading her.

Her hair held earth.
   Her eyes were dark.
A double flute
20   made her move.

"O love,
   where are you
leading
   me now?"

---

[1] Persephone. In Greek mythology, daughter of Zeus and Demeter, wife of Hades, ruler of the underworld. She spent two-thirds of the year in the underworld as the goddess of death, the rest in the upper world with her mother who presided over the fertility of the earth.

ALLEN GINSBERG (1926–   )

A Supermarket in California
(1955)

What thoughts I have of you tonight, Walt Whitman, for I walked down the sidestreets under the trees with a headache self-conscious looking at the full moon.

In my hungry fatigue, and shopping for images, I went into the
5 neon fruit supermarket, dreaming of your enumerations!

What peaches and what penumbras![1] Whole families shopping at night! Aisles full of husbands! Wives in the avocados, babies in the tomatoes!—and you, Garcia Lorca,[2] what were you doing down by the watermelons?

10   I saw you, Walt Whitman, childless, lonely old grubber, poking among the meats in the refrigerator and eyeing the grocery boys.

I heard you asking questions of each: Who killed the pork chops? What price bananas? Are you my Angel?

I wandered in and out of the brilliant stacks of cans following
15 you, and followed in my imagination by the store detective.

We strode down the open corridors together in our solitary fancy tasting artichokes, possessing every frozen delicacy, and never passing the cashier.

Where are we going, Walt Whitman? The doors close in an hour.
20 Which way does your beard point tonight?

(I touch your book and dream of our odyssey[3] in the supermarket and feel absurd.)

Will we walk all night through solitary streets? The trees add shade to shade, lights out in the houses, we'll both be lonely.

25   Will we stroll dreaming of the lost America of love past blue automobiles in driveways, home to our silent cottage?

Ah, dear father, graybeard, lonely old courage-teacher, what America did you have when Charon quit poling his ferry and you got out on a smoking bank and stood watching the boat disappear on the
30 black waters of Lethe?[4]

---

[1] *Penumbra:* a space of partial illumination (as in an eclipse) between the shadow and the light.

[2] Spanish poet and playwright.

[3] Wandering journey—from the *Odyssey* of Homer, an epic that describes the wanderings of Odysseus.

[4] In Greek mythology, Charon is the ferryman who brings souls across the river Lethe (forgetfulness) to the underworld.

ANNE SEXTON (1928–1974)

Cinderella

You always read about it:
the plumber with twelve children
who wins the Irish Sweepstakes.
From toilets to riches.
5 That story.

Or the nursemaid,
some luscious sweet from Denmark
who captures the oldest son's heart.
From diapers to Dior.
10 That story.

Or a milkman who serves the wealthy,
eggs, cream, butter, yogurt, milk,
the white truck like an ambulance
who goes into real estate
15 and makes a pile.
From homogenized to martinis at lunch.

Or the charwoman
who is on the bus when it cracks up
and collects enough from the insurance.
20 From mops to Bonwit Teller.
That story.

Once
the wife of a rich man was on her deathbed
and she said to her daughter Cinderella:
25 Be devout. Be good. Then I will smile
down from heaven in the seam of a cloud.
The man took another wife who had
two daughters, pretty enough
but with hearts like blackjacks.
30 Cinderella was their maid.
She slept on the sooty hearth each night
and walked around looking like Al Jolson.
Her father brought presents home from town,
jewels and gowns for the other women
35 but the twig of a tree for Cinderella.
She planted that twig on her mother's grave
and it grew to a tree where a white dove sat.
Whenever she wished for anything the dove
would drop it like an egg upon the ground.
40 The bird is important, my dears, so heed him.

Next came the ball, as you all know.
It was a marriage market.
The prince was looking for a wife.
All but Cinderella were preparing
45 and gussying up for the big event.
Cinderella begged to go too.
Her stepmother threw a dish of lentils
into the cinders and said: Pick them
up in an hour and you shall go.
50 The white dove brought all his friends;
all the warm wings of the fatherland came,
and picked up the lentils in a jiffy.
No, Cinderella, said the stepmother,
you have no clothes and cannot dance.
55 That's the way with stepmothers.

Cinderella went to the tree at the grave
and cried forth like a gospel singer:
Mama! Mama! My turtledove,
send me to the prince's ball!
60 The bird dropped down a golden dress
and delicate little gold slippers.
Rather a large package for a simple bird.
So she went. Which is no surprise.
Her stepmother and sisters didn't
65 recognize her without her cinder face
and the prince took her hand on the spot
and danced with no other the whole day.

As nightfall came she thought she'd better
get home. The prince walked her home
70 and she disappeared into the pigeon house
and although the prince took an axe and broke
it open she was gone. Back to her cinders.
These events repeated themselves for three days.
However on the third day the prince
75 covered the palace steps with cobbler's wax
and Cinderella's gold shoe stuck upon it.
Now he would find whom the shoe fit
and find his strange dancing girl for keeps.
He went to their house and the two sisters
80 were delighted because they had lovely feet.
The eldest went into a room to try the slipper on
but her big toe got in the way so she simply
sliced it off and put on the slipper.
The prince rode away with her until the white dove

85 told him to look at the blood pouring forth.
   That is the way with amputations.
   They don't just heal up like a wish.
   The other sister cut off her heel
   but the blood told as blood will.
90 The prince was getting tired.
   He began to feel like a shoe salesman.
   But he gave it one last try.
   This time Cinderella fit into the shoe
   like a love letter into its envelope.

95 At the wedding ceremony
   the two sisters came to curry favor
   and the white dove pecked their eyes out.
   Two hollow spots were left
   like soup spoons.

100 Cinderella and the prince
    lived, they say, happily ever after,
    like two dolls in a museum case
    never bothered by diapers or dust,
    never arguing over the timing of an egg,
105 never telling the same story twice,
    never getting a middle-aged spread,
    their darling smiles pasted on for eternity.
    Regular Bobbsey Twins.
    That story.

ADRIENNE RICH (1929–   )

Diving into the Wreck
(1973)

First having read the book of myths,
and loaded the camera,
and checked the edge of the knife-blade,
I put on
5 the body-armor of black rubber
the absurd flippers
the grave and awkward mask.
I am having to do this
not like Cousteau with his
10 assiduous team
aboard the sun-flooded schooner
but here alone.

There is a ladder.
The ladder is always there
15 hanging innocently
close to the side of the schooner.
We know what it is for,
we who have used it.
otherwise
20 it is a piece of maritime floss
some sundry equipment.

I go down.
Rung after rung and still
the oxygen immerses me
25 the blue light
the clear atoms
of our human air.
I go down.
My flippers cripple me,
30 I crawl like an insect down the ladder
and there is no one
to tell me when the ocean
will begin.

First the air is blue and then
35 it is bluer and then green and then
black I am blacking out and yet
my mask is powerful
it pumps my blood with power
the sea is another story
40 the sea is not a question of power
I have to learn alone
to turn my body without force
in the deep element.

And now: it is easy to forget
45 what I came for
among so many who have always
lived here
swaying their crenellated fans
between the reefs
50 and besides
you breathe differently down here.

I came to explore the wreck.
The words are purposes.

The words are maps.
55 I came to see the damage that was done
and the treasures that prevail.
I stroke the beam of my lamp
slowly along the flank
of something more permanent
60 than fish or weed

the thing I came for:
the wreck and not the story of the wreck
the thing itself and not the myth
the drowned face always staring
65 toward the sun
the evidence of damage
worn by salt and sway into this threadbare beauty
the ribs of the disaster
curving their assertion
70 among the tentative haunters.

This is the place.
And I am here, the mermaid whose dark hair
streams black, the merman in his armored body.
We circle silently
75 about the wreck
we dive into the hold.
I am she: I am he

whose drowned face sleeps with open eyes
whose breasts still bear the stress
80 whose silver, copper, vermeil cargo lies
obscurely inside barrels
half-wedged and left to rot
we are the half-destroyed instruments
that once held to a course
85 the water-eaten log
the fouled compass

We are, I am, you are
by cowardice or courage
the one who find our way
90 back to this scene
carrying a knife, a camera
a book of myths
in which
our names do not appear.

GARY SNYDER (1930–   )

Hay for the Horses

He had driven half the night
From far down San Joaquin
Through Mariposa, up the
Dangerous mountain roads,
5 And pulled in at eight a.m.,
With his big truckload of hay
        behind the barn.
With winch and ropes and hooks
We stacked the bales up clean
10 To splintery redwood rafters
High in the dark, flecks of alfalfa
Whirling through shingle-cracks of light,
Itch of haydust in the
        sweaty shirt and shoes.
15 At lunchtime under black oak
Out in the hot corral,
—The old mare nosing lunchpails,
Grasshoppers crackling in the weeds—
"I'm sixty-eight" he said,
20 "I first bucked hay when I was seventeen.
I thought, that day I started,
I sure would hate to do this all my life.
And dammit, that's just what
I've gone and done."

SYLVIA PLATH (1932–1963)

Daddy
(1962)

You do not do, you do not do
Any more, black shoe
In which I have lived like a foot
For thirty years, poor and white,
5 Barely daring to breathe or Achoo.

Daddy, I have had to kill you.
You died before I had time—
Marble-heavy, a bag full of God,
Ghastly statue with one gray toe
10 Big as a Frisco seal

And a head in the freakish Atlantic
Where it pours bean green over blue
In the waters off beautiful Nauset.
I used to pray to recover you.
15 Ach, du.[1]

In the German tongue, in the Polish town[2]
Scraped flat by the roller
Of wars, wars, wars.
But the name of the town is common.
20 My Polack friend

Says there are a dozen or two.
So I never could tell where you
Put your foot, your root,
I never could talk to you.
25 The tongue stuck in my jaw.

It stuck in a barb wire snare.
Ich, ich, ich, ich,[3]
I could hardly speak.
I thought every German was you.
30 And the language obscene

An engine, an engine
Chuffing me off like a Jew.
A Jew to Dachau, Auschwitz, Belsen.
I began to talk like a Jew.
35 I think I may well be a Jew.

The snows of the Tyrol, the clear beer of Vienna
Are not very pure or true.
With my gypsy ancestress and my weird luck
And my Taroc pack and my Taroc pack[4]
40 I may be a bit of a Jew.

I have always been scared of *you,*
With your Luftwaffe,[5] your gobbledygoo.
And your neat moustache

---

[1] "Oh, you" (German).

[2] Grabow, in Poland, Otto Plath's birthplace.

[3] "I, I, I, I" (German).

[4] Taroc (or tarot), from Italian *tarocco,* a pack of cards used for fortunetelling (as, for example, in T. S. Eliot's "The Waste Land," lines 43–59).

[5] Air Force (German).

And your Aryan eye, bright blue.
45 Panzer-man, panzer-man,[6] O You—

Not God but a swastika
So black no sky could squeak through.
Every woman adores a Fascist,
The boot in the face, the brute
50 Brute heart of a brute like you.

You stand at the blackboard, daddy,
In the picture I have of you,
A cleft in your chin instead of your foot
But no less a devil for that, no not
55 Any less the black man who

Bit my pretty red heart in two.
I was ten when they buried you.
At twenty I tried to die
And get back, back, back to you.
60 I thought even the bones would do.

But they pulled me out of the sack,
And they stuck me together with glue,
And then I knew what to do.
I made a model of you,
65 A man in black with a Meinkampf[7] look

And a love of the rack and the screw.
And I said I do, I do.
So daddy, I'm finally through.
The black telephone's off at the root,
70 The voices just can't worm through.

If I've killed one man, I've killed two—
The vampire who said he was you
And drank my blood for a year,
Seven years, if you want to know.
75 Daddy, you can lie back now.

There's a stake in your fat black heart
And the villagers never liked you.
They are dancing and stamping on you.
They always *knew* it was you.
80 Daddy, daddy, you bastard, I'm through.

---

[6] Armor (German), especially, during World War II, as in armored tank and the soldiers (panzer troops) who manned them.

[7] From *Mein Kampf* ("My Battle"), the title of Hitler's book about his life and political aims.

SHARON OLDS (1942–   )

Armor
(1983)

Just about at the triple-barreled pistol
I can't go on. I sink down
as if shot, beside the ball of its butt
larded with mother-of-pearl. My son
5 leaves me on the bench, and goes on. Hand on
hip, he gazes at a suit of armor,
blue eyes running over the silver,
looking for a slit. He shakes his head,
hair greenish as the gold velvet
10 cod-skirt hanging before him in volutes
at a metal groin. Next, I see him
facing a case of shields, fingering
the sweater over his heart, and then
for a long time I don't see him, as a mother will
15 lose her son in war. I sit
and think about men. Finally Gabe
comes back, sated, so fattened with gore
his eyelids bulge. We exit under the
huge tumescent jousting irons,
20 their pennants a faded rose, like the mist
before his eyes. He slips his hand
lightly in mine, and says *Not one of those
suits is really safe.* But when we
get to the wide museum steps
25 railed with gold like the descent from heaven,
he can't resist,
and before my eyes, down the stairs,
over and over, clutching his delicate
unprotected chest, Gabriel
30 dies, and dies.

MARK LEIGH GIBBONS (1943–1981)

How I Love My Life
(1982)

Each morning I awake amid the soothing aftertaste of
    dreams in which I am peacefully omnipotent
    and am pleasantly surprised that my wakeful
    life is so much like my dreams.

5 My wives and children are singing aubades by the
    mist-shrouded pool in the orchid conservatory;
    they beam like little suns when they see me.

For breakfast each wonderful day I eat only my favorite
foods. This morning an ellipsoidal, roseate mango—
10   perfectly ripe. Its juices gush cool sweetness on
my lips and tongue but never drip on my shirt or
make my hands sticky.

My newspapers (decorated with delicate graphics) are filled
with amusing and informative feature stories and
15   news articles praising all my friends for what they
are doing. What I said and did yesterday is the subject
of a special, dedicatory editorial. The weather report
is always just as I had hoped.

What a surprise! My dressing room has been redecorated in
20   transparent pastel materials; the floor is opalescent
and the curtains are fashioned of living flowers that
move aside as I walk through them.

All my favorite costumes are still there though—and even
some new fashions with which I'll set the pace. But
25   not today; for this morning, in disguise I'm to
distribute gifts among the citizens I'll talk with
while pretending I am a visitor from another planet.
They appreciate my wisdom and are grateful for
my generosity.

30 My bowel movement was vastly pleasureable. My hair falls
gracefully in place over my tanned shoulders. Eyes
and teeth gleam. I laugh when I again remember that
though forty I still look eighteen.

Two birds of paradise drape my cloak on my arm; my pet dogs
35   open the door and the happy servants sing praise as
I step to the rigged catamaran and begin a brisk
sail to the city gleaming in the distance.

Not merely pleasure, but arousing adventure awaits my
many disguises. Thrilling danger that ends in safety
40   and honor! Brilliant abstract conceptions and
immortal witticisms! Consuming love affairs that end
in friendship just as other love affairs begin!
Every thought and action to be proud of! How I love
my life!

ALICE WALKER (1944–   )

Chic Freedom's Reflection
(for Marilyn Pryce)
(1968)

One day
Marilyn marched

beside me (demon-
stration)
5 and we ended up
at county farm
no phone
no bail
something about
10 "traffic vio-
lation"
which irrelevance
Marilyn dismissed
with a shrug
15   *She*
had just got
        back
from
        Paris France
20   In
            the
        Alabama
            hell
            she
25   smell-
                ed
        so
        wonderful
like spring
30 & love
        &
freedom

        She
    wore a
35 SNCC pin
right between
her breasts
    near her
        heart

<pre>
40 & with a chic
        (on "jail?")
    accent
        & nod of
    condescent
45   to frumpy
        work-house
            hags
    powdered her nose
        tip-
50   toe
    in a badge.
</pre>

SHERELY WILLIAMS (1944–   )

Say Hello to John
(1975)

I swear I ain't done what Richard
told me bout jumpin round and stuff.
And he knew I wouldn't do nothin to make the baby
come, just joke, say I'mo cough

5 this child up one day.
So in the night when I felt the water tween
my legs, I thought it was pee and I laid
there wonderin if maybe I was in a dream.

Then it come to me that my water broke and I went
10 in to tell Ru-ise. *You been havin pains?*
she ask. I hear her fumblin for the light.
Naw, I say. Don't think so. The veins

stand out along her temples. *What time
is it?* Goin on toward four o'clock.
15 *Nigga, I told you:*
You ain't havin no babies, not

in the middle of the night.
Get yo ass back to bed.
That ain't nothin but pee. And what
20 I know bout havin kids cept what she said?

Second time it happen, even she
got to admit this mo'n pee.
And the pain when it come, wa'n't bad
least no mo'n I eva expect to see

25 again. I remember the doctor smilin,
sayin, Shel, you got a son.
His bright black face above me
sayin, Say hello to John.

CAROLYN FORCHÉ (1950–   )

The Colonel
(1978)

What you have heard is true. I was in his house. His wife carried a
tray of coffee and sugar. His daughter filed her nails, his son went
out for the night. There were daily papers, pet dogs, a pistol on the
cushion beside him. The moon swung bare on its black cord over the
5 house. On the television was a cop show. It was in English. Broken
bottles were embedded in the walls around the house to scoop the
kneecaps from a man's legs or cut his hands to lace. On the windows
there were gratings like those in liquor stores. We had dinner, rack of
lamb, good wine, a gold bell was on the table for calling the maid.
10 The maid brought green mangoes, salt, a type of bread. I was asked
how I enjoyed the country. There was a brief commercial in Spanish.
His wife took everything away. There was some talk then of how
difficult it had become to govern. The parrot said hello on the terrace.
The colonel told it to shut up, and pushed himself from the table. My
15 friend said to me with his eyes: say nothing. The colonel returned
with a sack used to bring groceries home. He spilled many human
ears on the table. They were like dried peach halves. There is no other
way to say this. He took one of them in his hands, shook it in our
faces, dropped it into a water glass. It came alive there. I am tired of
20 fooling around he said. As for the rights of anyone, tell your people
they can go fuck themselves. He swept the ears to the floor with his
arm and held the last of his wine in the air. Something for your
poetry, no? he said. Some of the ears on the floor caught this scrap of
his voice. Some of the ears on the floor were pressed to the ground.

LOUISE ERDRICH (1954–   )

Indian Boarding School: The Runaways
(1984)

Home's the place we head for in our sleep.
Boxcars stumbling north in dreams
don't wait for us. We catch them on the run.
The rails, old lacerations that we love,
5 shoot parallel across the face and break
just under Turtle Mountains. Riding scars
you can't get lost. Home is the place they cross.

The lame guard strikes a match and makes the dark
less tolerant. We watch through cracks in boards
10 as the land starts rolling, rolling till it hurts
to be here, cold in regulation clothes.
We know the sheriff's waiting at midrun
to take us back. His car is dumb and warm.
The highway doesn't rock, it only hums
15 like a wing of long insults. The worn-down welts
of ancient punishment lead back and forth.

All runaways wear dresses, long green ones,
the color you would think shame was. We scrub
the sidewalks down because it's shameful work.
20 Our brushes cut the stone in watered arcs
and in the soak frail outlines shiver clear
a moment, things us kids pressed on the dark
face before it hardened, pale, remembering
delicate old injuries, the spines of names and leaves.

CATHY SONG (1955–   )

Lost Sister

1

In China,
even the peasants
named their first daughters
Jade—
5 the stone that in the far fields
could moisten the dry season,
could make men move mountains
for the healing green of the inner hills
glistening like slices of winter melon.

10 And the daughters were grateful:
they never left home.
To move freely was a luxury
stolen from them at birth.
Instead, they gathered patience,
15 learning to walk in shoes
the size of teacups,
without breaking—
the arc of their movements
as dormant as the rooted willow,
20 as redundant as the farmyard hens.
But they traveled far
in surviving,

learning to stretch the family rice,
to quiet the demons,
25 the noisy stomachs.

2

There is a sister
across the ocean,
who relinquished her name,
diluting jade green
30 with the blue of the Pacific.
Rising with a tide of locusts,
she swarmed with others
to inundate another shore.
In America,
35 there are many roads
and women can stride along with men.

But in another wilderness,
the possibilities,
the loneliness,
40 can strangulate like jungle vines.
The meager provisions and sentiments
of once belonging—
fermented roots, Mah-Jongg tiles and firecrackers—
set but a flimsy household
45 in a forest of nightless cities.
A giant snake rattles above,
spewing black clouds into your kitchen.
Dough-faced landlords
slip in and out of your keyholes,
50 making claims you don't understand,
tapping into your communication systems
of laundry lines and restaurant chains.

You find you need China:
your one fragile identification,
55 a jade link
handcuffed to your wrist.
You remember your mother
who walked for centuries,
footless—
60 and like her,
you have left no footprints,
but only because
there is an ocean in between,
the unremitting space of your rebellion.

PART THREE

DRAMA

Chapter Sixteen

Introduction to Drama

COMMON TERMS OF CRITICAL DISCOURSE ON DRAMA

Because of *Hamlet's* familiarity, the general terms used in discussing drama will be introduced here with reference to that great example. Many, if not most, readers of this book have read Shakespeare's play which appears later (see p. 604); other students know at least something about it. As was the case with the general introductions to fiction and poetry, the intention here is not to be exhaustive. Your teacher will no doubt introduce further terms useful in the critical analysis of drama, and the glossary will provide definitions for some of the many special terms that refer to the plays of particular kinds or periods.

Plays are written by **playwrights**—note that spelling which recalls the craftsman and builder rather than the wielder of pen and ink. Plays written *only* to be read are called **closet dramas** from being read in one's closet, an old word for "room," but playwrights who work toward performance must be concerned with the possibilities of gesture and spectacle, with pomp and costume, as well as with poetry or prose. Organizing the many moving parts sustained and connected by the words of a play requires great visual as well as verbal skills—something easy to forget as a reader. Hence, the **stage directions** that give instructions to the actors also help the reader of a play to visualize their movements and gestures. So it is, too, that a visual word **scene** is used to describe the smallest unit of **action** within a play and so it is that scenes are grouped into larger units or main divisions of action called **acts**.

But in the main, many of the critical terms you learned in your studies of fiction and poetry also apply to plays, which often might be said to combine literary elements of both genres. Thus, the **setting** of *Hamlet*, a fortress and seat of government, helps to create its **atmosphere** which includes an embattled kingdom and an embattled prince developed in the **exposition** or early part of the play. **Dialogue** names the verbal interplay between characters like that which opens the play, and **soliloquy** describes the speeches of a character when "solus," solitary or alone. The famous speech "To be or not to be" is an example of a soliloquy.

As with a fiction, a drama usually contains a **protagonist**. While Prince Hamlet is clearly the protagonist of the play, the age-old issue is whether Claudius or King Hamlet or Prince Hamlet himself is the real **antagonist**. Two great **themes** of the play are "investigation" and "fathers and sons," so with regard to these themes, Polonius makes less of an antagonist and more of a contrasting character or **foil** to both Hamlets and to Claudius as well.

The play also generally resembles the movements of fiction in that the **plot** of *Hamlet* may be said to develop through **rising action** to a **climax** focused in a **crisis** which results in a **resolution** leading to **falling action** and a **conclusion** or **dénouement** (French, remember, for "untying the knot"). The conclusion of *Hamlet* marks it as a **tragedy**, while *The Tempest*—with its happier ending in a spirit of reconciliation—is a **comedy**. Shakespeare also wrote **histories**, which, being more or less based on the mixed results of real-life endings, are somewhere outside the classical opposites of tragedy and comedy. Yet in all three modes, techniques like **dramatic irony**—the dramatic opposition of what seems to be and what really is— can inform the action.

Such a general concern as Hamlet's desire for revenge makes for a **unity of action** throughout the play. According to Aristotle, one of the earliest and greatest of critical theorists, unity of action is necessary for all good plays. Some two thousand years later, in the seventeenth century, European thought entered a **neoclassical** period, and theorists then added the **unity of time** and **the unity of place** to make what they called the **classical unities**. In the view of these critics, a play should be probable to increase the power of its illusion; to be probable, its action must roughly conform to the time elapsed in its viewing, and its space must conform to the fixed location of its action as well. As a result, neoclassical theory maintained that a good play should take place in one location on one day. In his plays (as *Hamlet* shows), Shakespeare, like other British playwrights of his time, generally ignores these secondary unities while maintaining the basic unity of action. The other unities are not to be dismissed entirely, however. Great playwrights like Racine and Molière produced their great dramas by working within these artistic disciplines.

When combined with the terms you have already studied, the terms you have just learned will make up most of the vocabulary you will need to discuss the plays of this section. That vocabulary will also enhance your ability to understand critics like Kenneth Burke and Jacques Lacan in the unit on *Hamlet*. In reading *Hamlet*, you will see how all the particular elements of a play, beginning with its setting, *dramatically* combine to present one of the most written-about examples of Western culture.

Chapter Seventeen

Approaches to Sophocles' *Oedipus the King*

SOPHOCLES (496–406 B.C.), regarded (along with Aeschylus and Euripides) as one of the three great Greek tragedians, was born at Kolonos, near Athens. In addition to being a playwright, Sophocles was also an Athenian general and a priest of Asclepius, the Greek god of healing. At the age of twenty-seven, he defeated Aeschylus in a playwright's contest. Further evidence of his outstanding reputation among his contemporaries is the fact that in his play *The Frogs*, Aristophanes ridicules Euripides and Aeschylus but speaks very highly of Sophocles. Although Sophocles wrote over a hundred plays, only seven tragedies and a part of a "satyr" play remain. During his life, Sophocles saw Greece's defeat of the Persian Empire, held the favor of the statesman Pericles, witnessed the building of the Parthenon, and saw his city-state's decline due, in part, to the Peloponnesian Wars.

Sophocles' most popular plays are his three about Oedipus and his children: *Oedipus Rex, Oedipus at Colonus,* and *Antigone.* Sophocles increased the size of the Chorus and partly abandoned the custom of trilogy in favor of single plays (the three Oedipus plays were written over a forty-year period). *Oedipus Rex* is believed to have been first produced in 425 B.C.

SOPHOCLES
Oedipus the King
(c. 430 B.C.)

Translated by Thomas Gould

CHARACTERS

Oedipus,[1] *The King of Thebes*
Priest of Zeus, *Leader of the Suppliants*
Creon, *Oedipus's Brother-in-law*
Chorus, *a Group of Theban Elders*
Choragos, *Spokesman of the Chorus*
Tiresias, *a blind Seer or Prophet*
Jocasta, *The Queen of Thebes*
Messenger, *from Corinth, once a Shepherd*
Herdsman, *once a Servant of Laius*
Second Messenger, *a Servant of Oedipus*

MUTES

Suppliants, *Thebans seeking Oedipus's help*
Attendants, *for the Royal Family*
Servants, *to lead Tiresias and Oedipus*
Antigone, *Daughter of Oedipus and Jocasta*
Ismene, *Daughter of Oedipus and Jocasta*

---

[1]Oedipus: The name may mean "swollen foot." It may refer to the mutilation of Oedipus' feet done by his father, Laius, before the infant was sent to Mount Cithaeron to be put to death by exposure.

The action takes place during the day in front of the royal palace in Thebes. There are two altars (left and right) on the Proscenium and several steps leading down to the Orchestra. As the play opens, Thebans of various ages who have come to beg Oedipus for help are sitting on these steps and in part of the Orchestra. These suppliants are holding branches of laurel or olive which have strips of wool² wrapped around them. Oedipus enters from the palace (the central door of the Skene.)

Prologue

Oedipus: My children, ancient Cadmus'³ newest care,
why have you hurried to those seats, your boughs
wound with the emblems of the suppliant?
The city is weighed down with fragrant smoke,
with hymns to the Healer⁴ and the cries of mourners.
I thought it wrong, my sons, to hear your words
through emissaries, and have come out myself,
I, Oedipus, a name that all men know.

[Oedipus addresses the Priest.]

Old man—for it is fitting that you speak
10 for all—what is your mood as you entreat me,
fear or trust? You may be confident
that I'll do anything. How hard of heart
if an appeal like this did not rouse my pity!
Priest: You, Oedipus, who hold the power here,
you see our several ages, we who sit
before your altars—some not strong enough
to take long flight, some heavy in old age,
the priests, as I of Zeus,⁵ and from our youths
a chosen band. The rest sit with their windings
20 in the markets, at the twin shrines of Pallas,⁶
and the prophetic embers of Ismēnos.⁷
Our city, as you see yourself, is tossed
too much, and can no longer lift its head
above the troughs of billows red with death.
It dies in the fruitful flowers of the soil,
it dies in its pastured herds, and in its women's
barren pangs. And the fire-bearing god⁸

---

²*wool:* Branches wrapped with wool are traditional symbols of prayer or supplication.
³*Cadmus:* Oedipus' great great grandfather (although he does not know this) and the founder of Thebes.   ⁴*Healer:* Apollo, god of prophecy, light, healing, justice, purification, and destruction.   ⁵*Zeus:* father and king of the gods.   ⁶*Pallas:* Athena, goddess of wisdom, arts, crafts, and war.   ⁷*Ismēnos:* a reference to the temple of Apollo near the river Ismēnos in Thebes. Prophecies were made here by "reading" the ashes of the altar fires.   ⁸*fire-bearing god:* contagious fever viewed as a god.

has swooped upon the city, hateful plague,
and he has left the house of Cadmus empty.
30 Black Hades[9] is made rich with moans and weeping.
Not judging you an equal of the gods,
do I and the children sit here at your hearth,
but as the first of men, in troubled times
and in encounters with divinities.
You came to Cadmus' city and unbound
the tax we had to pay to the harsh singer,[10]
did it without a helpful word from us,
with no instruction; with a god's assistance
you raised up our life, so we believe.
40 Again now Oedipus, our greatest power,
we plead with you, as suppliants, all of us,
to find us strength, whether from a god's response,
or learned in some way from another man.
I know that the experienced among men
give counsels that will prosper best of all.
Noblest of men, lift up our land again!
Think also of yourself; since now the land
calls you its Savior for your zeal of old,
oh let us never look back at your rule
50 as men helped up only to fall again!
Do not stumble! Put our land on firm feet!
The bird of omen was auspicious then,
when you brought that luck; be that same man again!
The power is yours; if you will rule our country,
rule over men, not in an empty land.
A towered city or a ship is nothing
if desolate and no man lives within.
Oedipus: Pitiable children, oh I know, I know
the yearnings that have brought you. Yes, I know
60 that you are sick. And yet, though you are sick,
there is not one of you so sick as I.
For your affliction comes to each alone,
for him and no one else, but my soul mourns

---

[9] *Black Hades:* refers to both the underworld where the spirits of the dead go and the god of the underworld.   [10] *harsh singer:* the Sphinx, a monster with a woman's head, a lion's body, and wings. The "tax" that Oedipus freed Thebes from was the destruction of all the young men who failed to solve the Sphinx's riddle and were subsequently devoured. The Sphinx always asked the same riddle: "What goes on four legs in the morning, two legs at noon, and three legs in the evening, and yet is weakest when supported by the largest number of feet?" Oedipus discovered the correct answer—man, who crawls in infancy, walks in his prime, and uses a stick in old age—and thus ended the Sphinx's reign of terror. The Sphinx destroyed herself when Oedipus answered the riddle. Oedipus' reward for freeing Thebes of the Sphinx was the throne and the hand of the recently widowed Jocasta.

for me and for you, too, and for the city.
You do not waken me as from a sleep,
for I have wept, bitterly and long,
tried many paths in the wanderings of thought,
and the single cure I found by careful search
I've acted on: I sent Menoeceus' son,
70 Creon, brother of my wife, to the Pythian
halls of Phoebus,[11] so that I might learn
what I must do or say to save this city.
Already, when I think what day this is,
I wonder anxiously what he is doing.
Too long, more than is right, he's been away.
But when he comes, then I shall be a traitor
if I do not do all that the god reveals.
Priest: Welcome words! But look, those men have signaled
that it is Creon who is now approaching!
80 *Oedipus:* Lord Apollo! May he bring Savior Luck,
a Luck as brilliant as his eyes are now!
Priest: His news is happy, it appears. He comes,
forehead crowned with thickly berried laurel.[12]
Oedipus: We'll know, for he is near enough to hear us.

[Enter Creon along one of the Parados.]

Lord, brother in marriage, son of Menoeceus!
What is the god's pronouncement that you bring?
Creon: It's good. For even troubles, if they chance
to turn out well, I always count as lucky.
Oedipus: But what was the response? You seem to say
90 I'm not to fear—but not to take heart either.
Creon: If you will hear me with these men present,
I'm ready to report—or go inside.

[Creon moves up the steps toward the palace.]

Oedipus: Speak out to all! The grief that burdens me
concerns these men more than it does my life.
Creon: Then I shall tell you what I heard from the god.
The task Lord Phoebus sets for us is clear:
drive out pollution sheltered in our land,
and do not shelter what is incurable.
Oedipus: What is our trouble? How shall we cleanse ourselves?
100 *Creon:* We must banish or murder to free ourselves

---

[11] *Pythian . . . Phoebus:* The temple of Phoebus Apollo's oracle or prophet at Delphi.
[12] *laurel:* Creon is wearing a garland of laurel leaves, sacred to Apollo.

from a murder that blows storms through the city.
Oedipus: What man's bad luck does he accuse in this?
Creon: My Lord, a king named Laius ruled our land
before you came to steer the city straight.
Oedipus: I know. So I was told—I never saw him.
Creon: Since he was murdered, you must raise your hand
against the men who killed him with their hands.
Oedipus: Where are they now? And how can we ever find
the track of ancient guilt now hard to read?
110 *Creon:* In our own land, he said. What we pursue,
that can be caught; but not what we neglect.
Oedipus: Was Laius home, or in the countryside—
or was he murdered in some foreign land?
Creon: He left to see a sacred rite, he said;
He left, but never came home from his journey.
Oedipus: Did none of his party see it and report—
someone we might profitably question?
Creon: They were all killed but one, who fled in fear,
and he could tell us only one clear fact.
120 *Oedipus:* What fact? One thing could lead us on to more
if we could get a small start on our hope.
Creon: He said that bandits chanced on them and killed him—
with the force of many hands, not one alone.
Oedipus: How could a bandit dare so great an act—
unless this was a plot paid off from here!
Creon: We thought of that, but when Laius was killed,
we had no one to help us in our troubles.
Oedipus: It was your very kingship that was killed!
What kind of trouble blocked you from a search?
130 *Creon:* The subtle-singing Sphinx asked us to turn
from the obscure to what lay at our feet.
Oedipus: Then I shall begin again and make it plain.
It was quite worthy of Phoebus, and worthy of you,
to turn our thoughts back to the murdered man,
and right that you should see me join the battle
for justice to our land and to the god.
Not on behalf of any distant kinships,
it's for myself I will dispel this stain.
Whoever murdered him may also wish
140 to punish me—and with the selfsame hand.
In helping him I also serve myself.
Now quickly, children: up from the altar steps,
and raise the branches of the suppliant!
Let someone go and summon Cadmus' people:
say I'll do anything.

[Exit an Attendant along one of the Parados.]

Our luck will prosper
if the god is with us, or we have already fallen.
Priest: Rise, my children; that for which we came,
he has himself proclaimed he will accomplish.
May Phoebus, who announced this, also come
150 as Savior and reliever from the plague.

[*Exit Oedipus and Creon into the Palace. The Priest and the Suppliants exit left and right along the Parados. After a brief pause, the Chorus (including the Choragos) enters the Orchestra from the Parados.*]

Parados

STROPHE 1[13]

Chorus: Voice from Zeus,[14] sweetly spoken, what are you
that have arrived from golden
Pytho[15] to our shining
Thebes? I am on the rack, terror
   shakes my soul.
Delian Healer,[16] summoned by "iē!"
I await in holy dread what obligation, something new
or something back once more with the revolving years,
   you'll bring about for me.
160 Oh tell me, child of golden Hope,
   deathless Response!

ANTISTROPHE 1

I appeal to you first, daughter of Zeus,
   deathless Athena,
   and to your sister who protects this land,
Artemis,[17] whose famous throne is the whole circle
   of the marketplace,
and Phoebus, who shoots from afar: iō!
Three-fold defenders against death, appear!
If ever in the past, to stop blind ruin
170   sent against the city,
you banished utterly the fires of suffering,
   come now again!

---

[13] *Strophe, Antistrophe:* probably refer to the direction in which the Chorus danced while reciting specific stanzas. Strophe may have indicated dance steps to stage left, antistrophe to stage right.   [14] *Voice from Zeus:* a reference to Apollo's prophecy. Zeus taught Apollo how to prophesy.   [15] *Pytho:* Delphi.   [16] *Delian Healer:* Apollo.   [17] *Artemis:* goddess of virginity, childbirth, and hunting.

Strophe 2

Ah! Ah! Unnumbered are the miseries
I bear. The plague claims all
our comrades. Nor has thought found yet a spear
by which a man shall be protected. What our glorious
earth gives birth to does not grow. Without a birth
from cries of labor
   do the women rise.
180 One person after another
   you may see, like flying birds,
faster than indomitable fire, sped
to the shore of the god that is the sunset.[18]

Antistrophe 2

And with their deaths unnumbered dies the city.
Her children lie unpitied on the ground,
spreading death, unmourned.
Meanwhile young wives, and gray-haired mothers with them,
on the shores of the altars, from this side and that,
suppliants from mournful trouble,
190   cry out their grief.
A hymn to the Healer shines,
   the flute a mourner's voice.
Against which, golden goddess, daughter of Zeus,
   send lovely Strength.

Strophe 3

Causing raging Ares[19]—who,
   armed now with no shield of bronze,
burns me, coming on amid loud cries—
to turn his back and run from my land,
with a fair wind behind, to the great
200   hall of Amphitritē,[20]
or to the anchorage that welcomes no one,
Thrace's troubled sea!
If night lets something get away at last,
   it comes by day.
Fire-bearing god . . . . . .
   you who dispense the might of lightning,
Zeus! Father! Destroy him with your thunderbolt!

   [Enter Oedipus from the palace.]

---

[18] *god . . . sunset:* Hades, god of the underworld.   [19] *Ares:* god of war and destruction.
[20] *Amphitritē:* the Atlantic Ocean.

ANTISTROPHE 3

Lycēan Lord![21] From your looped
  bowstring, twisted gold,
210 I wish indomitable missiles might be scattered
and stand forward, our protectors; also fire-bearing
radiance of Artemis, with which
  she darts across the Lycian mountains.
I call the god whose head is bound in gold,
with whom this country shares its name,
Bacchus,[22] wine-flushed, summoned by "euoi!,"
  Maenads' comrade,
to approach ablaze
  with gleaming . . . . . .
220 pine, opposed to that god-hated god.

EPISODE 1

Oedipus: I hear your prayer. Submit to what I say
and to the labors that the plague demands
and you'll get help and a relief from evils.
I'll make the proclamation, though a stranger
to the report and to the deed. Alone,
had I no key, I would soon lose the track.
Since it was only later that I joined you,
to all the sons of Cadmus I say this:
whoever has clear knowledge of the man
230 who murdered Laius, son of Labdacus,
I command him to reveal it all to me—
nor fear if, to remove the charge, he must
accuse himself: his fate will not be cruel—
he will depart unstumbling into exile.
But if you know another, or a stranger,
to be the one whose hand is guilty, speak:
I shall reward you and remember you.
But if you keep your peace because of fear,
and shield yourself or kin from my command,
240 hear you what I shall do in that event:
I charge all in this land where I have throne
and power, shut out that man—no matter who—
both from your shelter and all spoken words,
nor in your prayers or sacrifices make
him partner, nor allot him lustral[23] water.
All men shall drive him from their homes: for he

---

[21] *Lycēan Lord:* Apollo.   [22] *Bacchus:* Dionysus, god of fertility and wine.   [23] *lustral:*
purifying.

is the pollution that the god-sent Pythian
response has only now revealed to me.
In this way I ally myself in war
250 with the divinity and the deceased.[24]
And this curse, too, against the one who did it,
whether alone in secrecy, or with others:
may he wear out his life unblest and evil!
I pray this, too: if he is at my hearth
and in my home, and I have knowledge of him,
may the curse pronounced on others come to me.
All this I lay to you to execute,
for my sake, for the god's, and for this land
nor ruined, barren, abandoned by the gods.
260 Even if no god had driven you to it,
you ought not to have left this stain uncleansed,
the murdered man a nobleman, a king!
You should have looked! But now, since, as it happens,
It's I who have the power that he had once,
and have his bed, and a wife who shares our seed,
and common bond had we had common children
(had not his hope of offspring had bad luck—
but as it happened, luck lunged at his head);
because of this, as if for my own father,
270 I'll fight for him, I'll leave no means untried,
to catch the one who did it with his hand,
for the son of Labdacus, of Polydōrus,
of Cadmus before him, and of Agēnor.[25]
This prayer against all those who disobey:
the gods send out no harvest from their soil,
nor children from their wives. Oh, let them die
victims of this plague, or of something worse.
Yet for the rest of us, people of Cadmus,
we the obedient, may Justice, our ally,
280 and all the gods, be always on our side!
Choragos: I speak because I feel the grip of your curse:
the killer is not I. Nor can I point
to him. The one who set us to this search,
Phoebus, should also name the guilty man.
Oedipus: Quite right, but to compel unwilling gods—
no man has ever had that kind of power.
Choragos: May I suggest to you a second way?
Oedipus: A second or a third—pass over nothing!
Choragos: I know of no one who sees more of what
290 Lord Phoebus sees than Lord Tiresias.

---

[24] *the deceased:* Laius.   [25] *Son . . . Agēnor:* refers to Laius by citing his genealogy.

My Lord, one might learn brilliantly from him.
Oedipus: Nor is this something I have been slow to do.
At Creon's word I sent an escort—twice now!
I am astonished that he has not come.
Choragos: The old account is useless. It told us nothing.
Oedipus: But tell it to me. I'll scrutinize all stories.
Choragos: He is said to have been killed by travelers.
Oedipus: I have heard, but the one who did it no one sees.
Choragos: If there is any fear in him at all,
300 he won't stay here once he has heard that curse.
Oedipus: He won't fear words: he had no fear when he did it.

[Enter Tiresias from the right, led by a Servant and two of Oedipus' Attendants.]

Choragos: Look there! There is the man who will convict him!
It's the god's prophet they are leading here,
one gifted with the truth as no one else.
Oedipus: Tiresias, master of all omens—
public and secret, in the sky and on the earth—
your mind, if not your eyes, sees how the city
lives with a plague, against which Thebes can find
no Saviour or protector, Lord, but you.
310 For Phoebus, as the attendants surely told you,
returned this answer to us: liberation
from the disease would never come unless
we learned without a doubt who murdered Laius—
put them to death, or sent them into exile.
Do not begrudge us what you may learn from birds
or any other prophet's path you know!
Care for yourself, the city, care for me,
care for the whole pollution of the dead!
We're in your hands. To do all that he can
320 to help another is man's noblest labor.
Tiresias: How terrible to understand and get
no profit from the knowledge! I knew this,
but I forgot, or I had never come.
Oedipus: What's this? You've come with very little zeal.
Tiresias: Let me go home! If you will listen to me,
You will endure your troubles better—and I mine.
Oedipus: A strange request, not very kind to the land
that cared for you—to hold back this oracle!
Tiresias: I see your understanding comes to you
330 inopportunely. So that won't happen to me . . .
Oedipus: Oh, by the gods, if you understand about this,
don't turn away! We're on our knees to you.
Tiresias: None of you understands! I'll never bring
my grief to light—I will not speak of yours.

Oedipus: You know and won't declare it! Is your purpose
to betray us and to destroy this land!
Tiresias: I will grieve neither of us. Stop this futile
cross-examination. I'll tell you nothing!
Oedipus: Nothing? You vile traitor! You could provoke
340 a stone to anger! You still refuse to tell?
Can nothing soften you, nothing convince you?
Tiresias: You blamed anger in me—you haven't seen.
Can nothing soften you, nothing convince you?
Oedipus: Who wouldn't fill with anger, listening
to words like yours which now disgrace this city?
Tiresias: It will come, even if my silence hides it.
Oedipus: If it will come, then why won't you declare it?
Tiresias: I'd rather say no more. Now if you wish,
respond to that with all your fiercest anger!
350 *Oedipus:* Now I am angry enough to come right out
with this conjecture: you, I think, helped plot
the deed; you did it—even if your hand,
cannot have struck the blow. If you could see,
I should have said the deed was yours alone.
Tiresias: Is that right! Then I charge you to abide
by the decree you have announced: from this day
say no word to either these or me,
for you are the vile polluter of this land!
Oedipus: Aren't you appalled to let a charge like that
360 come bounding forth? How will you get away?
Tiresias: You cannot catch me. I have the strength of truth.
Oedipus: Who taught you this? Not your prophetic craft!
Tiresias: You did. You made me say it. I didn't want to.
Oedipus: Say what? Repeat it so I'll understand.
Tiresias: I made no sense? Or are you trying me?
Oedipus: No sense I understood. Say it again!
Tiresias: I say you are the murderer you seek.
Oedipus: Again that horror! You'll wish you hadn't said that.
Tiresias: Shall I say more, and raise your anger higher?
370 *Oedipus:* Anything you like! Your words are powerless.
Tiresias: You live, unknowing, with those nearest to you
in the greatest shame. You do not see the evil.
Oedipus: You won't go on like that and never pay!
Tiresias: I can if there is any strength in truth.
Oedipus: In truth, but not in you! You have no strength,
blind in your ears, your reason, and your eyes.
Tiresias: Unhappy man! Those jeers you hurl at me
before long all these men will hurl at you.
Oedipus: You are the child of endless night; it's not
380 for me or anyone who sees to hurt you.
Tiresias: It's not my fate to be struck down by you.
Apollo is enough. That's his concern.

Oedipus: Are these inventions Creon's or your own?
Tiresias: No, your affliction is yourself, not Creon.
Oedipus: Oh success!—in wealth, kingship, artistry,
in any life that wins much admiration—
the envious ill will stored up for you!
to get at my command, a gift I did not
seek, which the city put into my hands,
390 my loyal Creon, colleague from the start,
longs to sneak up in secret and dethrone me.
So he's suborned this fortuneteller—schemer!
deceitful beggar-priest!—who has good eyes
for gains alone, though in his craft he's blind.
Where were your prophet's powers ever proved?
Why, when the dog who chanted verse[26] was here,
did you not speak and liberate this city?
Her riddle wasn't for a man chancing by
to interpret; prophetic art was needed,
400 but you had none, it seems—learned from birds
or from a god. I came along, yes I,
Oedipus the ignorant, and stopped her—
by using thought, not augury from birds.
And it is I whom you now wish to banish,
so you'll be close to the Creontian throne.
You—and the plot's concocter—will drive out
pollution to your grief: you look quite old
or you would be the victim of that plot!
Choragos: It seems to us that this man's words were said
410 in anger, Oedipus, and yours as well.
Insight, not angry words, is what we need,
the best solution to the god's response.
Tiresias: You are the king, and yet I am your equal
in my right to speak. In that I too am Lord.
for I belong to Loxias,[27] not you.
I am not Creon's man. He's nothing to me.
Hear this, since you have thrown my blindness at me:
Your eyes can't see the evil to which you've come,
nor where you live, nor who is in your house.
420 Do you know your parents? Not knowing, you are
their enemy, in the underworld and here.
A mother's and a father's double-lashing
terrible-footed curse will soon drive you out.
Now you can see, then you will stare into darkness.
What place will not be harbor to your cry,
or what Cithaeron[28] not reverberate

---

[26] *dog . . . verse:* The Sphinx.   [27] *Loxias:* Apollo.   [28] *Cithaeron:* reference to the mountain on which Oedipus was to be exposed as an infant.

when you have heard the bride-song in your palace
to which you sailed? Fair wind to evil harbor!
Nor do you see how many other woes
430 will level you to yourself and to your children.
So, at my message, and at Creon, too,
splatter muck! There will never be a man
ground into wretchedness as you will be.
Oedipus: Am I to listen to such things from him!
May you be damned! Get out of here at once!
Go! Leave my palace! Turn around and go!

[*Tiresias begins to move away from Oedipus.*]

Tiresias: I wouldn't have come had you not sent for me.
Oedipus: I did not know you'd talk stupidity,
or I wouldn't have rushed to bring you to my house.
440 *Tiresias:* Stupid I seem to you, yet to your parents
who gave you natural birth I seemed quite shrewd.
Oedipus: Who? Wait! Who is the one who gave me birth?
Tiresias: This day will give you birth,[29] and ruin too.
Oedipus: What murky, riddling things you always say!
Tiresias: Don't you surpass us all at finding out?
Oedipus: You sneer at what you'll find has brought me greatness.
Tiresias: And that's the very luck that ruined you.
Oedipus: I wouldn't care, just so I saved the city.
Tiresias: In that case I shall go. Boy, lead the way!
450 *Oedipus:* Yes, let him lead you off. Here, underfoot,
you irk me. Gone, you'll cause no further pain.
Tiresias: I'll go when I have said what I was sent for.
Your face won't scare me. You can't ruin me.
I say to you, the man whom you have looked for
as you pronounced your curses, your decrees
on the bloody death of Laius—he is here!
A seeming stranger, he shall be shown to be
a Theban born, though he'll take no delight
in that solution. Blind, who once could see,
460 a beggar who was rich, through foreign lands
he'll go and point before him with a stick.
To his beloved children, he'll be shown
a father who is also brother; to the one
who bore him, son and husband; to his father,
his seed-fellow and killer. Go in
and think this out; and if you find I've lied,
say then I have no prophet's understanding!

[*Exit Tiresias, led by a Servant. Oedipus exits into the palace with his Attendants.*]

---

[29] *give you birth:* that is, identify your parents.

Stasimon 1

STROPHE 1

Chorus: Who is the man of whom the inspired
    rock of Delphi[30] said
470 he has committed the unspeakable
    with blood-stained hands?
Time for him to ply a foot
mightier than those of the horses
    of the storm in his escape;
upon him mounts and plunges the weaponed
son of Zeus,[31] with fire and thunderbolts,
and in his train the dreaded goddesses
of Death, who never miss.

ANTISTROPHE 1

The message has just blazed,
480   gleaming from the snows
of Mount Parnassus: we must track
    everywhere the unseen man.
He wanders, hidden by wild
forests, up through caves
    and rocks, like a bull,
anxious, with an anxious foot, forlorn.
He puts away from him the mantic[32] words come from earth's
navel,[33] at its center, yet these live
forever and still hover round him.

STROPHE 2

490 Terribly he troubles me,
    the skilled interpreter of birds![34]
I can't assent, nor speak against him.
    Both paths are closed to me.
I hover on the wings of doubt,
    not seeing what is here nor what's to come.
What quarrel started in the house of Labdacus[35]
or in the house of Polybus,[36]
    either ever in the past
    or now, I never
500 heard, so that . . . with this fact for my touchstone
    I could attack the public

---

[30] *rock of Delphi:* Apollo's oracle at Delphi.   [31] *son of Zeus:* Apollo.   [32] *mantic:* prophetic.
[33] *earth's navel:* Delphi.   [34] *interpreter of birds:* Tiresias. The Chorus is troubled by his accusations.   [35] *house of Labdacus:* the line of Laius.   [36] *Polybus:* Oedipus' foster father.

fame of Oedipus, by the side of the Labdaceans
an ally, against the dark assassination.

ANTISTROPHE 2

No, Zeus and Apollo
   understand and know things
mortal; but that another man
   can do more as a prophet than I can—
for that there is no certain test,
   though, skill to skill,
510 one man might overtake another.
No, never, not until
   I see the charges proved,
when someone blames him shall I nod assent.
For once, as we all saw, the winged maiden[37] came
against him: he was seen then to be skilled,
   proved, by that touchstone, dear to the people. So,
never will my mind convict him of the evil.

Episode 2

[Enter Creon from the right door of the skene and speaks to the Chorus.]

Creon: Citizens, I hear that a fearful charge
is made against me by King Oedipus!
520 I had to come. If, in this crisis,
he thinks that he has suffered injury
from anything that I have said or done,
I have no appetite for a long life—
bearing a blame like that! It's no slight blow
the punishment I'd take from what he said:
it's the ultimate hurt to be called traitor
by the city, by you, by my own people!
Choragos: The thing that forced that accusation out
could have been anger, not the power of thought.
530 *Creon:* But who persuaded him that thoughts of mine
had led the prophet into telling lies?
Choragos: I do not know the thought behind his words.
Creon: But did he look straight at you? Was his mind right
when he said that I was guilty of this charge?
Choragos: I have no eyes to see what rulers do.
But here he comes himself out of the house.

[Enter Oedipus from the palace.]

---

[37] *winged maiden:* The Sphinx.

Oedipus: What? You here? And can you really have
the face and daring to approach my house
when you're exposed as its master's murderer
540 and caught, too, as the robber of my kingship?
Did you see cowardice in me, by the gods,
or foolishness, when you began this plot?
Did you suppose that I would not detect
your stealthy moves, or that I'd not fight back?
It's your attempt that's folly, isn't it—
tracking without followers or connections,
kingship which is caught with wealth and numbers?
Creon: Now wait! Give me as long to answer back!
Judge me for yourself when you have heard me!
550 *Oedipus:* You're eloquent, but I'd be slow to learn
from you, now that I've seen your malice toward me.
Creon: That I deny. Hear what I have to say.
Oedipus: Don't you deny it! You are the traitor here!
Creon: If you consider mindless willfulness
a prized possession, you are not thinking sense.
Oedipus: If you think you can wrong a relative
and get off free, you are not thinking sense.
Creon: Perfectly just, I won't say no. And yet
what is this injury you say I did you?
560 *Oedipus:* Did you persuade me, yes or no, to send
someone to bring that solemn prophet here?
Creon: And I still hold to the advice I gave.
Oedipus: How many years ago did your King Laius . . .
Creon: Laius! Do what? Now I don't understand.
Oedipus: Vanish—victim of a murderous violence?
Creon: That is a long count back into the past.
Oedipus: Well, was this seer then practicing his art?
Creon: Yes, skilled and honored just as he is today.
Oedipus: Did he, back then, ever refer to me?
570 *Creon:* He did not do so in my presence ever.
Oedipus: You did inquire into the murder then.
Creon: We had to, surely, though we discovered nothing.
Oedipus: But the "skilled" one did not say this then? Why not?
Creon: I never talk when I am ignorant.
Oedipus: But you're not ignorant of your own part.
Creon: What do you mean? I'll tell you if I know.
Oedipus: Just this: if he had not conferred with you
he'd not have told about my murdering Laius.
Creon: If he said that, you are the one who knows.
580 But now it's fair that you should answer me.
Oedipus: Ask on! You won't convict me as the killer.
Creon: Well then, answer. My sister is your wife?
Oedipus: Now there's a statement that I can't deny.

Creon: You two have equal power in this country?
Oedipus: She gets from me whatever she desires.
Creon: And I'm a third? The three of us are equals?
Oedipus: That's where you're treacherous to your kinship!
Creon: But think about this rationally, as I do.
First look at this: do you think anyone
590 prefers the anxieties of being king
to untroubled sleep—if he has equal power?
I'm not the kind of man who falls in love
with kingship. I am content with a king's power.
And so would any man who's wise and prudent.
I get all things from you, with no distress;
as king I would have onerous duties, too.
How could the kingship bring me more delight
than this untroubled power and influence?
I'm not misguided yet to such a point
600 that profitable honors aren't enough.
As it is, all wish me well and all salute;
those begging you for something have me summoned,
for their success depends on that alone.
Why should I lose all this to become king?
A prudent mind is never traitorous.
Treason's a thought I'm not enamored of;
nor could I join a man who acted so.
In proof of this, first go yourself to Pytho[38]
and ask if I brought back the true response.
610 Then, if you find I plotted with that portent
reader,[39] don't have me put to death by your vote
only—I'll vote myself for my conviction.
Don't let an unsupported thought convict me!
It's not right mindlessly to take the bad
for good or to suppose the good are traitors.
Rejecting a relation who is loyal
is like rejecting life, our greatest love.
In time you'll know securely without stumbling,
for time alone can prove a just man just,
620 though you can know a bad man in a day.
Choragos: Well said, to one who's anxious not to fall.
Swift thinkers, Lord, are never safe from stumbling.
Oedipus: But when a swift and secret plotter moves
against me, I must make swift counterplot.
If I lie quiet and await his move,
he'll have achieved his aims and I'll have missed.
Creon: You surely cannot mean you want me exiled!
Oedipus: Not exiled, no. Your death is what I want!

---

[38] *Pytho:* Delphi.   [39] *portent reader:* Apollo's oracle or prophet.

Creon: If you would first define what envy is . . .
630 *Oedipus:* Are you still stubborn? Still disobedient?
Creon: I see you cannot think!
Oedipus: For me I can.
Creon: You should for me as well!
Oedipus: But you're a traitor!
Creon: What if you're wrong?
Oedipus: Authority must be maintained.
Creon: Not if the ruler's evil.
Oedipus: Hear that, Thebes!
Creon: It is my city too, not yours alone!
Choragos: Please don't, my Lords! Ah, just in time, I see
Jocasta there, coming from the palace.
With her help you must settle your quarrel.

[*Enter Jocasta from the Palace.*]

Jocasta: Wretched men! What has provoked this ill-
640 advised dispute? Have you no sense of shame,
with Thebes so sick, to stir up private troubles?
Now go inside! And Creon, you go home!
Don't make a general anguish out of nothing!
Creon: My sister, Oedipus your husband here
sees fit to do one of two hideous things:
to have me banished from the land—or killed!
Oedipus: That's right: I caught him, Lady, plotting harm
against my person—with a malignant science.
Creon: May my life fail, may I die cursed, if I
650 did any of the things you said I did!
Jocasta: Believe his words, for the god's sake, Oedipus,
in deference above all to his oath
to the gods. Also for me, and for these men!

Kommos[40]

Strophe 1

Chorus: Consent, with will and mind,
my king, I beg of you!
Oedipus: What do you wish me to surrender?
Chorus: Show deference to him who was not feeble in time past
and is now great in the power of his oath!
Oedipus: Do you know what you're asking?
Chorus: Yes.
Oedipus: Tell me then.

---

[40] *Kommos:* a dirge or lament sung by the Chorus and one or more of the chief characters.

660 ***Chorus:*** Never to cast into dishonored guilt, with an unproved
assumption, a kinsman who has bound himself by curse.
Oedipus: Now you must understand, when you ask this,
you ask my death or banishment from the land.

STROPHE 2

Creon: No, by the god who is the foremost of all gods,
the Sun! No! Godless,
    friendless, whatever death is worst of all,
let that be my destruction, if this
    thought ever moved me!
But my ill-fated soul
670   this dying land
wears out—the more if to these older troubles
she adds new troubles from the two of you!
Oedipus: Then let him go, though it must mean my death,
or else disgrace and exile from the land.
My pity is moved by your words, not by his—
he'll only have my hate, wherever he goes.
Creon: You're sullen as you yield; you'll be depressed
when you've passed through this anger. Natures like yours
are hardest on themselves. That's as it should be.
Oedipus: Then won't you go and let me be?
680 ***Creon:***   I'll go.
Though you're unreasonable, they know I'm righteous.

                                                    [Exit Creon.]

ANTISTROPHE 1

Chorus: Why are you waiting, Lady?
Conduct him back into the palace!
Jocasta: I will, when I have heard what chanced.
Chorus: Conjectures—words alone, and nothing based on thought.
But even an injustice can devour a man.
Jocasta: Did the words come from both sides?
Chorus: Yes.
Jocasta: What was said?
690 ***Chorus:*** To me it seems enough! enough! the land already troubled,
that this should rest where it has stopped.
Oedipus: See what you've come to in your honest thought,
in seeking to relax and blunt my heart?

ANTISTROPHE 2

Chorus: I have not said this only once, my Lord.
That I had lost my sanity,

without a path in thinking—
be sure this would be clear
   if I put you away
who, when my cherished land
700   wandered crazed
with suffering, brought her back on course.
Now, too, be a lucky helmsman!

Jocasta: Please, for the god's sake, Lord, explain to me
the reason why you have conceived this wrath?
Oedipus: I honor you, not them,[41] and I'll explain
to you how Creon has conspired against me.
Jocasta: All right, if that will explain how the quarrel started.
Oedipus: He says I am the murderer of Laius!
Jocasta: Did he claim knowledge or that someone told him?
710 *Oedipus:* Here's what he did: he sent that vicious seer
so he could keep his own mouth innocent.
Jocasta: Ah then, absolve yourself of what he charges!
Listen to this and you'll agree, no mortal
is ever given skill in prophecy.
I'll prove this quickly with one incident.
It was foretold to Laius—I shall not say
by Phoebus himself, but by his ministers—
that when his fate arrived he would be killed
by a son who would be born to him and me.
720 And yet, so it is told, foreign robbers
murdered him, at a place where three roads meet.
As for the child I bore him, not three days passed
before he yoked the ball-joints of its feet,[42]
then cast it, by others' hands, on a trackless mountain.
That time Apollo did not make our child
a patricide, or bring about what Laius
feared, that he be killed by his own son.
That's how prophetic words determined things!
Forget them. The things a god must track
730 he will himself painlessly reveal.
Oedipus: Just now, as I was listening to you, Lady,
what a profound distraction seized my mind!
Jocasta: What made you turn around so anxiously?
Oedipus: I thought you said that Laius was attacked
and butchered at a place where three roads meet.
Jocasta: That is the story, and it is told so still.
Oedipus: Where is the place where this was done to him?
Jocasta: The land's called Phocis, where a two-forked road
comes in from Delphi and from Daulia.
740 *Oedipus:* And how much time has passed since these events?

---

[41] *them:* the Chorus.   [42] *ball-joints of its feet:* the ankles.

Jocasta: Just prior to your presentation here
as king this news was published to the city.
Oedipus: Oh, Zeus, what have you willed to do to me?
Jocasta: Oedipus, what makes your heart so heavy?
Oedipus: No, tell me first of Laius' appearance,
what peak of youthful vigor he had reached.
Jocasta: A tall man, showing his first growth of white.
He had a figure not unlike your own.
Oedipus: Alas! It seems that in my ignorance
750 I laid those fearful curses on myself.
Jocasta: What is it, Lord? I flinch to see your face.
Oedipus: I'm dreadfully afraid the prophet sees.
But I'll know better with one more detail.
Jocasta: I'm frightened too. But ask: I'll answer you.
Oedipus: Was his retinue small, or did he travel
with a great troop, as would befit a prince?
Jocasta: There were just five in all, one a herald.
There was a carriage, too, bearing Laius.
Oedipus: Alas! Now I see it! But who was it,
760 Lady, who told you what you know about this?
Jocasta: A servant who alone was saved unharmed.
Oedipus: By chance, could he be now in the palace?
Jocasta: No, he is not. When he returned and saw
you had the power of the murdered Laius,
he touched my hand and begged me formally
to send him to the fields and to the pastures,
so he'd be out of sight, far from the city.
I did. Although a slave, he well deserved
to win this favor, and indeed far more.
770 *Oedipus:* Let's have him called back in immediately.
Jocasta: That can be done, but why do you desire it?
Oedipus: I fear, Lady, I have already said
too much. That's why I wish to see him now.
Jocasta: Then he shall come; but it is right somehow
that I, too, Lord, should know what troubles you.
Oedipus: I've gone so deep into the things I feared
I'll tell you everything. Who has a right
greater than yours, while I cross through this chance?
Polybus of Corinth was my father,
780 my mother was the Dorian Meropē.
I was first citizen, until this chance
attacked me—striking enough, to be sure,
but not worth all the gravity I gave it.
This: at a feast a man who'd drunk too much
denied, at the wine, I was my father's son.
I was depressed and all that day I barely
held it in. Next day I put the question

to my mother and father. They were enraged
at the man who'd let this fiction fly at me.
790 I was much cheered by them. And yet it kept
grinding into me. His words kept coming back.
Without my mother's or my father's knowledge
I went to Pytho. But Phoebus sent me away
dishonoring my demand. Instead, other
wretched horrors he flashed forth in speech.
He said that I would be my mother's lover,
show offspring to mankind they could not look at,
and be his murderer whose seed I am.[43]
When I heard this, and ever since, I gauged
800 the way to Corinth by the stars alone,
running to a place where I would never see
the disgrace in the oracle's words come true.
But I soon came to the exact location
where, as you tell of it, the king was killed.
Lady, here is the truth. As I went on,
when I was just approaching those three roads,
a herald and a man like him you spoke of
came on, riding a carriage drawn by colts.
Both the man out front and the old man himself[44]
810 tried violently to force me off the road.
The driver, when he tried to push me off,
I struck in anger. The old man saw this, watched
me approach, then leaned out and lunged down
with twin prongs[45] at the middle of my head!
He got more than he gave. Abruptly—struck
once by the staff in this my hand—he tumbled
out, head first, from the middle of the carriage.
And then I killed them all. But if there is
a kinship between Laius and this stranger,
820 who is more wretched than the man you see?
Who was there born more hated by the gods?
For neither citizen nor foreigner
may take me in his home or speak to me.
No, they must drive me off. And it is I
who have pronounced these curses on myself!
I stain the dead man's bed with these my hands,
by which he died. Is not my nature vile?
Unclean?—if I am banished and even
in exile I may not see my own parents,
830 or set foot in my homeland, or else be yoked
in marriage to my mother, and kill my father,

---

[43] *be . . . am:* that is, murder my father. [44] *old man himself:* Laius. [45] *lunged . . .
prongs:* Laius strikes Oedipus with a two-pronged horse goad or whip.

Polybus, who raised me and gave me birth?
If someone judged a cruel divinity
did this to me, would he not speak the truth?
You pure and awful gods, may I not ever
see that day, may I be swept away
from men before I see so great and so
calamitous a stain fixed on my person!
Choragos: These things seem fearful to us, Lord, and yet,
840 until you hear it from the witness, keep hope!
Oedipus: That is the single hope that's left to me,
to wait for him, that herdsman—until he comes.
Jocasta: When he appears, what are you eager for?
Oedipus: Just this: if his account agrees with yours
then I shall have escaped this misery.
Jocasta: But what was it that struck you in my story?
Oedipus: You said he spoke of robbers as the ones
who killed him. Now: if he continues still
to speak of many, then I could not have killed him.
850 One man and many men just do not jibe.
But if he says one belted man, the doubt
is gone. The balance tips toward me. I did it.
Jocasta: No! He told it as I told you. Be certain.
He can't reject that and reverse himself.
The city heard these things, not I alone.
But even if he swerves from what he said,
he'll never show that Laius' murder, Lord,
occurred just as predicted. For Loxias
expressly said my son was doomed to kill him.
860 The boy—poor boy—he never had a chance
to cut him down, for he was cut down first.
Never again, just for some oracle
will I shoot frightened glances right and left.
Oedipus: That's full of sense. Nonetheless, send a man
to bring that farm hand here. Will you do it?
Jocasta: I'll send one right away. But let's go in.
Would I do anything against your wishes?

[Exit Oedipus and Jocasta through the central door into the palace.]

Stasimon 2

Strophe 1

Chorus: May there accompany me
the fate to keep a reverential purity in what I say,
870 in all I do, for which the laws have been set forth
and walk on high, born to traverse the brightest,

highest upper air; Olympus[46] only
is their father, nor was it
mortal nature
that fathered them, and never will
oblivion lull them into sleep;
the god in them is great and never ages.

ANTISTROPHE 1

The will to violate, seed of the tyrant,
if it has drunk mindlessly of wealth and power,
880 without a sense of time or true advantage,
mounts to a peak, then
plunges to an abrupt . . . destiny,
where the useful foot
is of no use. But the kind
of struggling that is good for the city
I ask the god never to abolish.
The god is my protector: never will I give that up.

STROPHE 2

But if a man proceeds disdainfully
    in deeds of hand or word
890 and has no fear of Justice
    or reverence for shrines of the divinities
(may a bad fate catch him
    for his luckless wantonness!),
if he'll not gain what he gains with justice
and deny himself what is unholy,
or if he clings, in foolishness, to the untouchable
(what man, finally, in such an action, will have strength
enough to fend off passion's arrows from his soul?),
if, I say, this kind of
900   deed is held in honor—
why should I join the sacred dance?

ANTISTROPHE 2

No longer shall I visit and revere
    Earth's navel, [47] the untouchable,
nor visit Abae's[48] temple,
    or Olympia,[49]

---

[46] *Olympus:* Mount Olympus, home of the gods, treated as a god. [47] *Earth's navel:* Delphi. [48] *Abae:* a town in Phocis where there was another oracle of Apollo. [49] *Olympia:* site of the oracle of Zeus.

if the prophecies are not matched by events
    for all the world to point to.
No, you who hold the power, if you are rightly called
Zeus the king of all, let this matter not escape you
910 and your ever-deathless rule,
    for the prophecies to Laius fade . . .
and men already disregard them;
nor is Apollo anywhere
    glorified with honors.
Religion slips away.

Episode 3

[Enter Jocasta from the palace carrying a branch wound with wool and a jar of incense. She is attended by two women.]

Jocasta: Lords of the realm, the thought has come to me
to visit shrines of the divinities
with suppliant's branch in hand and fragrant smoke.
For Oedipus excites his soul too much
920 with alarms of all kinds. He will not judge
the present by the past, like a man of sense.
He's at the mercy of all terror-mongers.

[Jocasta approaches the altar on the right and kneels.]

Since I can do no good by counseling,
Apollo the Lycēan!—you are the closest—
I come a suppliant, with these my vows,
for a cleansing that will not pollute him.
For when we see him shaken we are all
afraid, like people looking at their helmsman.

[Enter a Messenger along one of the Parados. He sees Jocasta at the altar and then addresses the Chorus.]

Messenger: I would be pleased if you would help me, stranger.
930 Where is the palace of King Oedipus?
Or tell me where he is himself, if you know.
Chorus: This is his house, stranger. He is within.
This is his wife and mother of his children.
Messenger: May she and her family find prosperity,
if, as you say, her marriage is fulfilled.
Jocasta: You also, stranger, for you deserve as much
for your gracious words. But tell me why you've come.
What do you wish? Or what have you to tell us?
Messenger: Good news, my Lady, both for your house and
    husband.

940 *Jocasta:* What is your news? And who has sent you to us?
Messenger: I come from Corinth. When you have heard my
news
you will rejoice, I'm sure—and grieve perhaps.
Jocasta: What is it? How can it have this double power?
Messenger: They will establish him their king, so say the people of the
land of Isthmia.[50]
Jocasta: But is old Polybus not still in power?
Messenger: He's not, for death has clasped him in the tomb.
Jocasta: What's this? Has Oedipus' father died?
Messenger: If I have lied then I deserve to die.
950 *Jocasta:* Attendant! Go quickly to your master,
and tell him this.

[*Exit an Attendant into the palace.*]

Oracles of the gods!
Where are you now? The man whom Oedipus
fled long ago, for fear that he should kill him—
he's been destroyed by chance and not by him!

[*Enter Oedipus from the palace.*]

Oedipus: Darling Jocasta, my beloved wife,
Why have you called me from the palace?
Jocasta: First hear what this man has to say. Then see
what the god's grave oracle has come to now!
Oedipus: Where is he from? What is this news he brings me?
960 *Jocasta:* From Corinth. He brings news about your father:
that Polybus is no more! that he is dead!
Oedipus: What's this, old man? I want to hear you say it.
Messenger: If this is what must first be clarified,
please be assured that he is dead and gone.
Oedipus: By treachery or by the touch of sickness?
Messenger: Light pressures tip agéd frames into their sleep.
Oedipus: You mean the poor man died of some disease.
Messenger: And of the length of years that he had tallied.
Oedipus: Aha! Then why should we look to Pytho's vapors,[51]
970 or to the birds that scream above our heads?[52]
If we could really take those things for guides,
I would have killed my father. But he's dead!
He is beneath the earth, and here am I,
who never touched a spear. Unless he died

---

[50] *land of Isthmia:* Corinth, which was on an isthmus.   [51] *Pytho's vapors:* the prophecies of
the oracle at Delphi.   [52] *birds . . . heads:* the prophecies derived from interpreting the
flights of birds.

of longing for me and I "killed" him that way!
No, in this case, Polybus, by dying, took
the worthless oracle to Hades with him.
Jocasta: And wasn't I telling you that just now?
Oedipus: You were indeed. I was misled by fear.
980 *Jocasta:* You should not care about this anymore.
Oedipus: I must care. I must stay clear of my mother's bed.
Jocasta: What's there for man to fear? The realm of chance
prevails. True foresight isn't possible.
His life is best who lives without a plan.
This marriage with your mother—don't fear it.
How many times have men in dreams, too, slept
with their own mothers! Those who believe such things
mean nothing endure their lives most easily.
Oedipus: A fine, bold speech, and you are right, perhaps,
990 except that my mother is still living,
so I must fear her, however well you argue.
Jocasta: And yet your father's tomb is a great eye.
Oedipus: Illuminating, yes. But I still fear the living.
Messenger: Who is the woman who inspires this fear?
Oedipus: Meropē, Polybus' wife, old man.
Messenger: And what is there about her that alarms you?
Oedipus: An oracle, god-sent and fearful, stranger.
Messenger: Is it permitted that another know?
Oedipus: It is. Loxias once said to me
1000 I must have intercourse with my own mother
and take my father's blood with these my hands.
So I have long lived far away from Corinth.
This has indeed brought much good luck, and yet,
to see one's parents' eyes is happiest.
Messenger: Was it for this that you have lived in exile?
Oedipus: So I'd not be my father's killer, sir.
Messenger: Had I not better free you from this fear,
my Lord? That's why I came—to do you service.
Oedipus: Indeed, what a reward you'd get for that!
1010 *Messenger:* Indeed, this is the main point of my trip,
to be rewarded when you get back home.
Oedipus: I'll never rejoin the givers of my seed![53]
Messenger: My son, clearly you don't know what you're doing.
Oedipus: But how is that, old man? For the gods' sake, tell me!
Messenger: If it's because of them you won't go home.
Oedipus: I fear that Phoebus will have told the truth.
Messenger: Pollution from the ones who gave you seed?

---

[53] *givers of my seed:* that is, my parents. Oedipus still thinks Meropē and Polybus are his parents.

Oedipus: That is the thing, old man, I always fear.

Messenger: Your fear is groundless. Understand that.

1020 *Oedipus:* Groundless? Not if I was born their son.

Messenger: But Polybus is not related to you.

Oedipus: Do you mean Polybus was not my father?

Messenger: No more than I. We're both the same to you.

Oedipus: Same? One who begot me and one who didn't?

Messenger: He didn't beget you any more than I did.

Oedipus: But then, why did he say I was his son?

Messenger: He got you as a gift from my own hands.

Oedipus: He loved me so, though from another's hands?

Messenger: His former childlessness persuaded him.

1030 *Oedipus:* But had you bought me, or begotten me?

Messenger: Found you. In the forest hallows of Cithaeron.

Oedipus: What were you doing traveling in that region?

Messenger: I was in charge of flocks which grazed those mountains.

Oedipus: A wanderer who worked the flocks for hire?

Messenger: Ah, but that day I was your savior, son.

Oedipus: From what? What was my trouble when you took me?

Messenger: The ball-joints of your feet might testify.

Oedipus: What's that? What makes you name that ancient trouble?

Messenger: Your feet were pierced and I am your rescuer.

1040 *Oedipus:* A fearful rebuke those tokens left for me!

Messenger: That was the chance that names you who you are.

Oedipus: By the gods, did my mother or my father do this?

Messenger: That I don't know. He might who gave you to me.

Oedipus: From someone else? You didn't chance on me?

Messenger: Another shepherd handed you to me.

Oedipus: Who was he? Do you know? Will you explain!

Messenger: They called him one of the men of—was it Laius?

Oedipus: The one who once was king here long ago?

Messenger: That is the one! The man was shepherd to him.

1050 *Oedipus:* And is he still alive so I can see him?

Messenger: But you who live here ought to know that best.

Oedipus: Does any one of you now present know
about the shepherd whom this man has named?
Have you seen him in town or in the fields? Speak out!
The time has come for the discovery!

Choragos: The man he speaks of, I believe, is the same
as the field hand you have already asked to see.
But it's Jocasta who would know this best.

Oedipus: Lady, do you remember the man we just

1060 now sent for—is that the man he speaks of?

Jocasta: What? The man he spoke of? Pay no attention!
His words are not worth thinking about. It's nothing.

Oedipus: With clues like this within my grasp, give up?
Fail to solve the mystery of my birth?

Jocasta: For the love of the gods, and if you love your life,
give up this search! My sickness is enough.
Oedipus: Come! Though my mothers for three generations
were in slavery, you'd not be lowborn!
Jocasta: No, listen to me! Please! Don't do this thing!
1070 *Oedipus:* I will not listen; I will search out the truth.
Jocasta: My thinking is for you—it would be best.
Oedipus: This "best" of yours is starting to annoy me.
Jocasta: Doomed man! Never find out who you are!
Oedipus: Will someone go and bring that shepherd here?
Leave her to glory in her wealthy birth!
Jocasta: Man of misery! No other name
shall I address you by, ever again.

> *[Exit Jocasta into the palace after a long pause.]*

Choragos: Why has your lady left, Oedipus,
hurled by a savage grief? I am afraid
1080 disaster will come bursting from this silence.
Oedipus: Let it burst forth! However low this seed
of mine may be, yet I desire to see it.
She, perhaps—she has a woman's pride—
is mortified by my base origins.
But I who count myself the child of Chance,
the giver of good, shall never know dishonor.
She is my mother,[54] and the months my brothers
who first marked out my lowness, then my greatness.
I shall not prove untrue to such a nature
1090 by giving up the search for my own birth.

Stasimon 3

STROPHE

Chorus: If I have mantic power
and excellence in thought,
by Olympus,
   you shall not, Cithaeron, at tomorrow's
full moon,
fail to hear us celebrate you as the countryman
of Oedipus, his nurse and mother,
or fail to be the subject of our dance,
   since you have given pleasure
1100 to our king.
Phoebus, whom we summon by "iē!,"
may this be pleasing to you!

---

[54] *She . . . mother:* Chance is my mother.

ANTISTROPHE

Who was your mother, son?
which of the long-lived nymphs
after lying with Pan,[55]
    the mountain roaming . . . Or was it a bride
of Loxias?[56]
For dear to him are all the upland pastures.
Or was it Mount Cyllēnē's lord,[57]
1110 or the Bacchic god,[58]
    dweller of the mountain peaks,
who received you as a joyous find
from one of the nymphs of Helicon,
the favorite sharers of his sport?

Episode 4

Oedipus: If someone like myself, who never met him,
may calculate—elders, I think I see
the very herdsman we've been waiting for.
His many years would fit that man's age,
and those who bring him on, if I am right,
1120 are my own men. And yet, in real knowledge,
you can outstrip me, surely: you've seen him.

[*Enter the old Herdsman escorted by two of Oedipus' Attendants. At first, the Herdsman will not look at Oedipus.*]

Choragos: I know him, yes, a man of the house of Laius,
a trusty herdsman if he ever had one.
Oedipus: I ask you first, the stranger come from Corinth:
is this the man you spoke of?
Messenger: That's he you see.
Oedipus: Then you, old man. First look at me! Now answer:
did you belong to Laius' household once?
Herdsman: I did. Not a purchased slave but raised in the palace.
Oedipus: How have you spent your life? What is your work?
1130 *Herdsman:* Most of my life now I have tended sheep.
Oedipus: Where is the usual place you stay with them?
Herdsman: On Mount Cithaeron. Or in that district.
Oedipus: Do you recall observing this man there?
Herdsman: Doing what? Which is the man you mean?
Oedipus: This man right here. Have you had dealings with him?
Herdsman: I can't say right away. I don't remember.

---

[55] *Pan:* god of shepherds and woodlands, half man and half goat.   [56] *Loxias:* Apollo.
[57] *Mount Cyllēnē's lord:* Hermes, messenger of the gods.   [58] *Bacchic god:* Dionysus.

Messenger: No wonder, master. I'll bring clear memory
to his ignorance. I'm absolutely sure
he can recall it, the district was Cithaeron,
1140 he with a double flock, and I, with one,
lived close to him, for three entire seasons,
six months along, from spring right to Arcturus.[59]
Then for the winter I'd drive mine to my fold,
and he'd drive his to Laius' pen again.
Did any of the things I say take place?
Herdsman: You speak the truth, though it's from long ago.
Messenger: Do you remember giving me, back then,
a boy I was to care for as my own?
Herdsman: What are you saying? Why do you ask me that?
1150 *Messenger:* There, sir, is the man who was that boy!
Herdsman: Damn you! Shut your mouth! Keep your silence!
Oedipus: Stop! Don't you rebuke his words.
Your words ask for rebuke far more than his.
Herdsman: But what have I done wrong, most royal master?
Oedipus: Not telling of the boy of whom he asked.
Herdsman: He's ignorant and blundering toward ruin.
Oedipus: Tell it willingly—or under torture.
Herdsman: Oh god! Don't—I am old—don't torture me!
Oedipus: Here! Someone put his hands behind his back!
1160 *Herdsman:* But why? What else would you find out, poor man?
Oedipus: Did you give him the child he asks about?
Herdsman: I did. I wish that I had died that day!
Oedipus: You'll come to that if you don't speak the truth.
Herdsman: It's if I speak that I shall be destroyed.
Oedipus: I think this fellow struggles for delay.
Herdsman: No, no! I said already that I gave him.
Oedipus: From your own home, or got from someone else?
Herdsman: Not from my own. I got him from another.
Oedipus: Which of these citizens? What sort of house?
1170 *Herdsman:* Don't—by the gods!—don't, master, ask me more!
Oedipus: It means your death if I must ask again.
Herdsman: One of the children of the house of Laius.
Oedipus: A slave—or born into the family?
Herdsman: I have come to the dreaded thing, and I shall say it.
Oedipus: And I to hearing it, but hear I must.
Herdsman: He was reported to have been—his son.
Your lady in the house could tell you best.
Oedipus: Because she gave him to you?
Herdsman: Yes, my lord.
Oedipus: What was her purpose?

---

[59] *Arcturus:* a star that is first seen in September in the Grecian sky.

Herdsman: I was to kill the boy.
Oedipus: The child she bore?
1180 **Herdsman:**   She dreaded prophecies.
Oedipus: What were they?
Herdsman: The word was that he'd kill his parents.
Oedipus: Then why did you give him up to this old man?
Herdsman: In pity, master—so he would take him home,
to another land. But what he did was save him
for this supreme disaster. If you are the one
he speaks of—know your evil birth and fate!
Oedipus: Ah! All of it was destined to be true!
Oh light, now may I look my last upon you,
shown monstrous in my birth, in marriage monstrous,
1190 a murderer monstrous in those I killed.

[Exit Oedipus, running into the palace.]

Stasimon 4

STROPHE 1

Chorus: Oh generations of mortal men,
while you are living, I will
   appraise your lives at zero!
What man
comes closer to seizing lasting blessedness
than merely to seize its semblance,
and after living in this semblance, to plunge?
With your example before us,
with your destiny, yours,
1200   suffering Oedipus, no mortal
can I judge fortunate.

ANTISTROPHE 1

For he,[60] outranging everybody,
shot his arrow[61] and became the lord
   of wide prosperity and blessedness,
oh Zeus, after destroying
the virgin with the crooked talons,[62]
singer of oracles; and against death,
in my land, he arose a tower of defense.
From which time you were called my king

---

[60] *he:* Oedipus.   [61] *shot his arrow:* took his chances; made a guess at the Sphinx's riddle.
[62] *virgin . . . talons:* the Sphinx.

1210 and granted privileges supreme—in mighty
Thebes the ruling lord.

STROPHE 2

But now—whose story is more sorrowful than yours?
Who is more intimate with fierce calamities,
with labors, now that your life is altered?
Alas, my Oedipus, whom all men know:
one great harbor[63]—
one alone sufficed for you,
as son and father,
when you tumbled,[64] plowman[65] of the woman's chamber.
1220 How, how could your paternal
furrows, wretched man,
endure you silently so long.

ANTISTROPHE 2

Time, all-seeing, surprised you living an unwilled life
and sits from of old in judgment on the marriage, not a marriage,
where the begetter is the begot as well.
Ah, son of Laius . . . ,
would that—oh, would that
I had never seen you!
I wail, my scream climbing beyond itself
1230 from my whole power of voice. To say it straight:
from you I got new breath—
but I also lulled my eye to sleep.[66]

Exodos

[Enter the Second Messenger from the palace.]

Second Messenger: You who are first among the citizens,
what deeds you are about to hear and see!
What grief you'll carry, if, true to your birth,
you still respect the house of Labdacus!
Neither the Ister nor the Phasis river
could purify this house, such suffering
does it conceal, or soon must bring to light—
1240 willed this time, not unwilled. Griefs hurt worst
which we perceive to be self-chosen ones.

---

[63] *one great harbor:* metaphorical allusion to Jocasta's body.   [64] *tumbled:* were born and had
sex.   [65] *plowman:* Plowing is used here as a sexual metaphor.   [66] *I . . . sleep:* I failed to
see the corruption you brought.

Choragos: They were sufficient, the things we knew before,
to make us grieve. What can you add to those?
Second Messenger: The thing that's quickest said and quickest heard:
our own, our royal one, Jocasta's dead.
Choragos: Unhappy queen! What was responsible?
Second Messenger: Herself. The bitterest of these events
is not for you, you were not there to see,
but yet, exactly as I can recall it,
1250 you'll hear what happened to that wretched lady.
She came in anger through the outer hall,
and then she ran straight to her marriage bed,
tearing her hair with the fingers of both hands.
Then, slamming shut the doors when she was in,
she called to Laius, dead so many years,
remembering the ancient seed which caused
his death, leaving the mother to the son
to breed again an ill-born progeny.
She mourned the bed where she, alas, bred double—
1260 husband by husband, children by her child.
From this point on I don't know how she died,
for Oedipus then burst in with a cry,
and did not let us watch her final evil.
Our eyes were fixed on him. Wildly he ran
to each of us, asking for his spear
and for his wife—no wife: where he might find
the double mother-field, his and his children's.
He raved, and some divinity then showed him—
for none of us did so who stood close by.
1270 With a dreadful shout—as if some guide were leading—
he lunged through the double doors; he bent the hollow
bolts from the sockets, burst into the room,
and there we saw her, hanging from above,
entangled in some twisted hanging strands.
He saw, was stricken, and with a wild roar
ripped down the dangling noose. When she, poor woman,
lay on the ground, there came a fearful sight:
he snatched the pins of worked gold from her dress,
with which her clothes were fastened: these he raised
1280 and struck into the ball-joints of his eyes.[67]
He shouted that they would no longer see
the evils he had suffered or had done,
see in the dark those he should not have seen,
and know no more those he once sought to know.
While chanting this, not once by many times
he raised his hand and struck into his eyes.

---

[67] *ball-joints of his eyes:* his eyeballs, Oedipus blinds himself in both eyes at the same time.

Blood from his wounded eyes poured down his chin,
not freed in moistening drops, but all at once
a stormy rain of black blood burst like hail.
1290 These evils, coupling them, making them one,
have broken loose upon both man and wife.
The old prosperity that they had once
was true prosperity, and yet today,
mourning, ruin, death, disgrace, and every
evil you could name—not one is absent.
Choragos: Has he allowed himself some peace from all this grief?
Second Messenger: He shouts that someone slide the bolts and show
to all the Cadmeians the patricide,
his mother's—I can't say it, it's unholy—
1300 so he can cast himself out of the land,
not stay and curse his house by his own curse.
He lacks the strength, though, and he needs a guide,
for his is a sickness that's too great to bear.
Now you yourself will see: the bolts of the doors
are opening. You are about to see
a vision even one who hates must pity.

[*Enter the blinded Oedipus from the palace, led in by a household Servant.*]

Choragos: This suffering sends terror through men's eyes,
terrible beyond any suffering
my eyes have touched. Oh man of pain,
1310 what madness reached you? Which god from far off,
surpassing in range his longest spring,
    struck hard against your god-abandoned fate?
Oh man of pain,
I cannot look upon you—though there's so much
I would ask you, so much to hear,
so much that holds my eyes—
    so awesome the convulsions you send through me.
Oedipus: Ah! Ah! I am a man of misery.
Where am I carried? Pity me! Where
1320 is my voice scattered abroad on wings?
    Divinity, where has your lunge transported me?
Choragos: To something horrible, not to be heard or seen.

Kommos

STROPHE 1

Oedipus: Oh, my cloud
of darkness, abominable, unspeakable as it attacks me,
not to be turned away, brought by an evil wind!

Alas!
Again alas! Both enter me at once:
the sting of the prongs,[68] the memory of evils!
Chorus: I do not marvel that in these afflictions
1330 you carry double griefs and double evils.

ANTISTROPHE 1

Oedipus: Ah, friend,
so you at least are there, resolute servant!
Still with a heart to care for me, the blind man.
Oh! Oh!
I know that you are there. I recognize
even inside my darkness, that voice of yours.
Chorus: Doer of horror, how did you bear to quench
your vision? What divinity raised your hand?

STROPHE 2

Oedipus: It was Apollo there, Apollo, friends,
1340 who brought my sorrows, vile sorrows to their perfection,
    these evils that were done to me.
But the one who struck them with his hand,
    that one was none but I, in wretchedness.
For why was I to see
when nothing I could see would bring me joy?
Chorus: Yes, that is how it was.
Oedipus: What could I see, indeed,
or what enjoy—what greeting
is there I could hear with pleasure, friends?
1350 Conduct me out of the land
        as quickly as you can!
Conduct me out, my friends,
    the man utterly ruined,
supremely cursed,
    the man who is by gods
the most detested of all men!
Chorus: Wretched in disaster and in knowledge:
oh, I could wish you'd never come to know!

ANTISTROPHE 2

Oedipus: May he be destroyed, whoever freed the savage shackles
1360 from my feet when I'd been sent to the wild pasture,
        whoever rescued me from murder

---

[68] *prongs:* refers to both the whip that Laius used and the two gold pins Oedipus used to
blind himself.

and became my savior—
   a bitter gift:
if I had died then,
I'd not have been such grief to self and kin.
Chorus: I also would have had it so.
Oedipus: I'd not have returned to be my father's
murderer; I'd not be called by men
my mother's bridegroom.
1370 Now I'm without a god,
      child of a polluted parent,
fellow progenitor with him
   who gave me birth in misery.
If there's an evil that
   surpasses evils, that
has fallen to the lot of Oedipus.

Choragos: How can I say that you have counseled well?
Better not to be than live a blind man.
Oedipus: That this was not the best thing I could do—
1380 don't tell me that, or advise me any more!
Should I descend to Hades and endure
to see my father with these eyes? Or see
my poor unhappy mother? For I have done,
to both of these, things too great for hanging.
Or is the sight of children to be yearned for,
to see new shoots that sprouted as these did?
Never, never with these eyes of mine!
Nor city, nor tower, nor holy images
of the divinities! For I, all-wretched,
1390 most nobly raised—as no one else in Thebes—
deprived myself of these when I ordained
that all expel the impious one—god-shown
to be polluted, and the dead king's son![69]
Once I exposed this great stain upon me,
could I have looked on these with steady eyes?
No! No! And if there were a way to block
the source of hearing in my ears, I'd gladly
have locked up my pitiable body,
so I'd be blind and deaf. Evils shut out—
1400 that way my mind could live in sweetness.
Alas, Cithaeron,[70] why did you receive me?
Or when you had me, not killed me instantly?
I'd not have had to show my birth to mankind.

---

[69] *I . . . son:* Oedipus refers to his own curse against the murderer as well as his sins of
patricide and incest.   [70] *Cithaeron:* the mountain on which the infant Oedipus was supposed to be exposed.

Polybus, Corinth, halls—ancestral,
they told me—how beautiful was your ward,
a scar that held back festering disease!
Evil my nature, evil my origin.
You, three roads, and you, secret ravine,
you oak grove, narrow place of those three paths
1410 that drank my blood[71] from these hands, from him
who fathered me, do you remember still
the things I did to you? When I'd come here,
what I then did once more? Oh marriages! Marriages!
You gave us life and when you'd planted us
you sent the same seed up, and then revealed
fathers, brothers, sons, and kinsman's blood,
and brides, and wives, and mothers, all the most
atrocious things that happen to mankind!
One should not name what never should have been.
1420 Somewhere out there, then, quickly, by the gods,
cover me up, or murder me, or throw me
to the ocean where you will never see me more!

[*Oedipus moves toward the Chorus and they back away from him.*]

Come! Don't shrink to touch this wretched man!
Believe me, do not be frightened! I alone
of all mankind can carry these afflictions.

[*Enter Creon from the palace with Attendants.*]

Choragos: Tell Creon what you wish for. Just when we need him
he's here. He can act, he can advise you.
He's now the land's sole guardian in your place.
Oedipus: Ah! Are there words that I can speak to him?
1430 What ground for trust can I present? It's proved
that I was false to him in everything.
Creon: I have not come to mock you, Oedipus,
nor to reproach you for your former falseness.
You men, if you have no respect for sons
of mortals, let your awe for the all-feeding
flames of lordy Hēlius[72] prevent
your showing unconcealed so great a stain,
abhorred by earth and sacred rain and light.
Escort him quickly back into the house!
1440 If blood kin only see and hear their own
afflictions, we'll have no impious defilement.

---

[71] *my blood:* that is, the blood of my father, Laius.   [72] *Hēlius:* the sun.

Oedipus: By the gods, you've freed me from one terrible fear,
so nobly meeting my unworthiness:
grant me something—not for me; for you!
Creon: What do you want that you should beg me so?
Oedipus: To drive me from the land at once, to a place
where there will be no man to speak to me!
Creon: I would have done just that—had I not wished
to ask first of the god what I should do.
1450 *Oedipus:* His answer was revealed in full—that I,
the patricide, unholy, be destroyed.
Creon: He said that, but our need is so extreme,
it's best to have sure knowledge what must be done.
Oedipus: You'll ask about a wretched man like me?
Creon: Is it not time you put your trust in the god?
Oedipus: But I bid you as well, and shall entreat you.
Give her who is within what burial
you will—you'll give your own her proper rites;
but me—do not condemn my fathers' land
1460 to have me dwelling here while I'm alive,
but let me live on mountains—on Cithaeron
famed as mine, for my mother and my father,
while they yet lived, made it my destined tomb,
and I'll be killed by those who wished my ruin!
And yet I know: no sickness will destroy me,
nothing will: I'd never have been saved
when left to die unless for some dread evil.
Then let my fate continue where it will!
As for my children, Creon, take no pains
1470 for my sons—they're men and they will never lack
the means to live, wherever they may be—
but my two wretched, pitiable girls,
who never ate but at my table, never
were without me—everything that I
would touch, they'd always have a share of it—
please care for them! Above all, let me touch
them with my hands and weep aloud my woes!
Please, my Lord!
Please, noble heart! Touching with my hands,
1480 I'd think I held them as when I could see.

[*Enter Antigone and Ismene from the palace with Attendants.*]

What's this?
Oh gods! Do I hear, somewhere, my two dear ones
sobbing? Has Creon really pitied me
and sent to me my dearest ones, my children?
Is that it?

Creon: Yes, I prepared this for you, for I knew
you'd feel this joy, as you have always done.
Oedipus: Good fortune, then, and, for your care, be guarded
far better by divinity than I was!
1490 Where are you, children? Come to me! Come here
to these my hands, hands of your brother, hands
of him who gave you seed, hands that made
these once bright eyes to see now in this fashion.

[*Oedipus embraces his daughters.*]

He, children, seeing nothing, knowing nothing,
he fathered you where his own seed was plowed.
I weep for you as well, though I can't see you,
imagining your bitter life to come,
the life you will be forced by men to live.
What gatherings of townsmen will you join,
1500 what festivals, without returning home
in tears instead of watching holy rites?
And when you've reached the time for marrying,
where, children, is the man who'll run the risk
of taking on himself the infamy
that will wound you as it did my parents?
What evil is not here? Your father killed
his father, plowed the one who gave him birth,
and from the place where he was sown, from there
he got you, from the place he too was born.
1510 These are the wounds: then who will marry you?
No man, my children. No, it's clear that you
must wither in dry barrenness, unmarried.

[*Oedipus addresses Creon.*]

Son of Menoeceus! You are the only father
left to them—we two who gave them seed
are both destroyed: watch that they don't become
poor, wanderers, unmarried—they are your kin.
Let not my ruin be their ruin, too!
No, pity them! You see how young they are,
bereft of everyone, except for you.
1520 Consent, kind heart, and touch me with your hand!

[*Creon grasps Oedipus' right hand.*]

You, children, if you had reached an age of sense,
I would have counseled much. Now, pray you may live

always where it's allowed, finding a life
better than his was, who gave you seed.
Creon: Stop this now. Quiet your weeping. Move away, into the house.
Oedipus: Bitter words, but I obey them.
Creon: There's an end to all things.
Oedipus: I have first this request.
Creon: I will hear it.
Oedipus: Banish me from my homeland.
Creon: You must ask that of the god.
Oedipus: But I am the gods' most hated man!
Creon: Then you will soon get what you want.
Oedipus: Do you consent?
1530 *Creon:*   I never promise when, as now, I'm ignorant.
Oedipus: Then lead me in.
Creon: Come. But let your hold fall from your children.
Oedipus: Do not take them from me, ever!
Creon: Do not wish to keep all of the power.
You had power, but that power did not follow you through life.

[*Oedipus' daughters are taken from him and led into the palace by Attendants. Oedipus is led into the palace by a Servant. Creon and the other Attendants follow. Only the Chorus remains.*]

Chorus: People of Thebes, my country, see: here is that Oedipus—
he who "knew" the famous riddle, and attained the highest power,
whom all citizens admired, even envying his luck!
See the billows of wild troubles which he has entered now!
Here is the truth of each man's life: we must wait, and see his end,
scrutinize his dying day, and refuse to call him happy
1540 till he has crossed the border of his life without pain.

[*Exit the Chorus along each of the Parados.*]

ACCOUNT: CLEANTH BROOKS AND ROBERT B. HEILMAN ON A NEW CRITICAL APPROACH TO *OEDIPUS THE KING*

While modern audiences familiar with the detective story have little difficulty in appreciating the brilliant handling of the plot of the play and its suspense, the problem of the drama's moral meaning remains. "How can Oedipus be guilty of something he did unwittingly?"

From Cleanth Brooks and Robert B. Heilman, *Understanding Drama* (New York: Henry Holt, 1948), 573–583.

Brooks and Heilman begin their analysis by rejecting the appropriateness here of one meaning often associated with Greek tragedy. They deny that Oedipus exemplifies *hubris*—that is, that Oedipus is "too sure of himself, too confident in his own powers and unmindful of the gods." The two critics object to this common view of the play on the grounds, first of all, of the general *modesty* of Oedipus' character and his unquestioned *faith* in the gods—though he does not necessarily believe in the human interpreters of the gods or in the impossibility of human self-help.

Brooks and Heilman suggest a view of the play that locates its meaning elsewhere than in personal pride:

> Perhaps the easiest way for a modern audience to approach the play is to look at it as a *critique of the claims of rationalism.* We live in a period in which the claims of a complete rationalism have been energetically urged, and one in which the methods of rationalism have been pursued with an apparently overwhelming success. If the play bears upon the problem of rationalism in any fashion, then it may yield something for us at once—whatever our final judgment of the play turns out to be.

The critics begin to support their claim with a consideration of the character of Oedipus. Since the original audience of the play knew well the whole cycle of myth on which the play was based, it would have known that Oedipus, by his earlier answering of the riddle of the sphinx, had given "an impressive demonstration of the power of the unaided human mind to dispel the darkness of irrationality." Yet this play dramatizes another fact: The human intellect has its limitations. "Fate is finally inscrutable."

Oedipus begins this play completely in character as a believer in reason by eagerly responding to the appeal of the people and proclaiming his belief in the positive results of a full and rational investigation of the city's trouble. His accompanying skepticism about needing the gods before self-help has been attempted seems perfectly natural, and it surely appears as an act of mere complacency rather than one filled with *"hubris."* Again it is on his *own* powers that Oedipus here relies, the powers that had successfully defeated the sphinx—the powers of reason.

His very diligence in pursuing an objective and fully unprejudiced investigation as suggested by human reason—his taunting of Tiresias for being a mystery monger, for example—make it manifest that Oedipus' very virtues are hurrying him toward the disaster that the audience knows awaits him, and the catastrophe is itself the answer to a new riddle. Significantly, the Chorus here supports this critical view from within the play by the song that refers to Oedipus' victory over the sphinx.

However, the hero's reputation for reason and logic does not keep Creon from pointing out that he is not *wise.* Oedipus "does not realize that in human affairs the simplest, or even the apparently most logical explanation of the facts is not necessarily the true one."

The irony of the messenger's news shows the limits of Oedipus' rationality:

> The Messenger endeavors to reassure him by telling him that Merope was never his mother, nor Polybus his father. But, eager as he is to give Oedipus joy and make possible his return to Corinth, the Messenger has failed to understand the earlier conversation, or else is very shortsighted and clumsy. By telling Oedipus that Polybus and Merope are not his parents, he does not invalidate the curse—he actually gives it a new vitality. For the prophecy has failed only if Polybus was the father of Oedipus. If he was not, then Oedipus may yet kill, or may already have killed, his father: the death of Polybus now proves nothing. In the same way, Oedipus has now been freed from fear of Merope—*but only at the price of having to fear every other woman old enough to be his mother.* Thus the Messenger, whose first words have filled Oedipus with a sense of triumph and exultation, ironically goes on to open up the abyss beneath Oedipus's feet.

When the messenger identifies the shepherd who gave him the infant Oedipus as one belonging to Laius' house, the truth is sufficiently revealed to Jocasta, and she attempts to dissuade Oedipus from continuing his rational investigation. But again his faith in the positive power of knowledge through reason prevails, and he declares words that carry a fine irony for the audience: "Nothing can make me other than I am."

The speech of the Chorus that comments on the uncertainties of life and the lack of a necessary connection between human "success" and human happiness sums up various attempts at action, not just by Oedipus, but by all the characters:

> As we have seen, pity, cruelty, foresight, and bravery have all been employed in trying to circumvent fate, and have actually themselves been woven into the web of fate: the cruel decision of Laius and Jocasta to expose the babe, the pity of the Herdsman who found it, the decision of Oedipus to give up his life as a king's son by leaving Corinth—all have played their part in bringing about the fulfillment of the prophecy.

The great virtues of Oedipus—his reasoning and his faith in reasoning's power—are at once his glory and his downfall:

> Since Oedipus has realized, not evaded, his true nature, we can understand how he came to the decisions that he did; that is, we can see from Oedipus's present conduct that those earlier actions were "in character." But by presenting the Oedipus of years later, Sophocles has been able to focus attention, not so much on the problem of action as that of knowledge. That is, Sophocles has chosen for primary emphasis the ironic discrepancy between full knowledge and man's partial knowledge. Oedipus is dramatized for us primarily as thinker rather than as actor, though of course his past actions are necessarily involved.

The problem of reason's proper relation to knowledge makes the theme of the critical analysis here. As you will see in the next account of a Structuralist approach to the play, the subrational powers of myth may be evoked to understand the same problem in a different way.

ACCOUNT: CLAUDE LEVI-STRAUSS ON A STRUCTURALIST APPROACH TO *OEDIPUS THE KING*

In his groundbreaking essay, "The Structural Study of Myth," the famous French anthropologist, Claude Levi-Strauss provides insight not only into Sophocles' play and the cycle of myth to which it belongs, but also into the early interaction between linguistics, anthropology, and literary criticism that opened a major phase of twentieth-century literary theory with the advent of structuralism. The same kinds of analytic models and the same kinds of striking logical insights into apparent logical contradictions that Levi-Strauss displays here were to be played out in many manifestations of the Structuralist and post-Structuralist theory whose critical results in practice are represented elsewhere throughout this text.

Levi-Strauss begins with a basic problem of contradiction that faces any student of myth:

> On the one hand it would seem that in the course of a myth anything is likely to happen. There is no logic, no continuity. Any characteristic can be attributed to any subject; every conceivable relation can be found. With myth, everything becomes possible. But on the other hand, this apparent arbitrariness is belied by the astounding similarity between myths collected in widely different regions. Therefore the problem: If the content of a myth is contingent, how are we going to explain the fact that myths throughout the world are so similar?

The contradictory nature of the problem may in fact help to suggest its solution, since it is the same kind of problem that baffled early students of language. Ancient philosophers noted that definite sounds were linked with definite meanings, but their attempt at an explanation of language was frustrated by the fact that the *same* sounds were equally present in other languages, but they there expressed *different* meanings. Modern linguists like Saussure discovered that it is the *relations among units of sounds* not the units of sound themselves that really produce meaning.

From Claude Levi-Strauss, "The Structural Study of Myth," *Journal of American Folklore*, 78 (1955).

Analogously, the attempt of an investigator like psychologist Carl Jung to find meaning in basic units of mythic constructions he calls "archetypes" may be compared to the unsuccessful attempts to explain language by trying to connect "hard" sounds to hard objects, "liquid" vowels to words describing fluids, and so on. This kind of misconception may be avoided in the study of myth (says Levi-Strauss) just as it was in the study of language, when linguists like Saussure distinguished between the unchanging elements of language such as its grammatical patterns and the constantly changing "contingent" elements such as the particular sequence of words used by a given speaker on a given day. The one element is timeless or "synchronic"; the other unfolds within time as time goes forward and is "diachronic."

In this dual way, myth may be seen to express its meaning *both* in the changing "diachronic" stories actually told *and* in the unchanging "synchronic" "grammar" of these stories seen as parts of a larger myth— the ways in which the patterns within and among the stories are related to one another. Just as two sentences may have the *same* grammar—for example, that of a short declarative sentence with subject, verb, and object— so the same sentence *form* may have different meanings at different times. For example, "Jack loves Jill" and "Jill hates Jack."

Levi-Strauss proposes that the basic elements of myth are not isolated relations but "bundles of such relations." To read a myth properly, then, it is necessary to pay attention not only to a story as it proceeds, but to relations within, between, and among stories. Just as an orchestra score is read from left to right if read "diachronically," so it can also be read at any given moment "synchronically"—that is, reading from top to bottom shows the harmony created by the simultaneous sounding of various notes which are also part of a series continuing in time. To illustrate his method, Levi-Strauss arranges the "relations" in the Oedipus myth into different "bundles" that may be read both diachronically and synchronically. To do so, he includes not only the events dramatized in Sophocles' play, but the actions both before and after those events.

Briefly put, the story of the Oedipus myth may be told diachronically as follows: Cadmus was sent by his parents to seek his sister Europa who had been ravished by Zeus. The Delphic oracle asked him to give up the search and to found a city, which he did at Thebes. Killing a dragon sacred to Ares, the god of war, he sowed its teeth, and armed men called the Spartoi sprang up out of the earth. When he flung a stone among them, they killed one another, except for five who became his allies. Through his son Polydorus, Cadmus fathered the ill-fated line of Oedipus.

After the events of Sophocles' play, one of Oedipus' sons, Etocles, kills another, Polynices, who had tried to conquer the city. As a rebel, Polynices was denied proper burial, but his sister, Antigone, gave him a token funeral, though she was punished by being buried alive for her defiance.

This is the way we might *tell* the myth, says Levi-Strauss, and we can read it in this way in the *rows* of the following chart, moving through the rows one at a time and proceeding from top row to bottom row. But to *understand* the myth we should read the *columns* which place the basic relations into bundles.

Cadmus seeks his sister Europa, ravished by Zeus			
		Cadmus kills the dragon	
	The Spartoi kill one another		
			Labdacus (Laius' father) - *lame* (?)
	Oedipus kills his father, Laius		Laius (Oedipus' father - *left-sided* (?)
		Oedipus kills the sphinx	
Oedipus marries his mother, Jocasta			Oedipus - *swollen-foot* (?)
	Etocles kills his brother, Polynices		
Antigone buries her brother, Polynices, despite prohibition			

Levi-Strauss explains his chart as follows:

> All the relations belonging to the same column exhibit one common feature which it is our task to discover. For instance, all the events grouped in the first column on the left have something to do with blood relations which are overemphasized, that is, are more intimate than they should be. Let us say, then, that the first column has as its common feature the *overrating of blood relations*. It is obvious that the second column expresses the same thing, but inverted: *underrating blood relations*. The third column refers to monsters being slain. As to the fourth, a few words of clarification are needed.

Understanding the fourth column is problematic because of the nature of Greek proper names, but one reasonable interpretation suggests itself: "All the hypothetical meanings (which may well remain hypothetical) refer to *difficulties in walking straight and standing upright."*

After reading the columns, we can also read the relations between and among columns. The overrating/underrating makes an obvious logical contrast, but what of the two remaining columns? Column three refers to killing monsters, and dragons are associated with the earth. A dragon must be slain before men can be born from the earth, while the sphinx will not permit men to live.

Levi-Strauss explains that the basic origin of human life is a puzzle addressed by many cultures. We see vegetable life springing from the earth and vegetable matter decays back into earth; so do human bodies. May these facts not suggest that the ultimate origin of people *is* the earth? In Judeo-Christian cultures, for example, God created Adam from clay.

On the other hand, we know from experience that people in the present are born from the union of men and women. In column three, the earth-related monsters are overcome by men, and so Levi-Strauss reads that column as a *denial* of the origin of humans from the earth. The myth, therefore, by including *both* aspects of human knowledge about the origins of human life (born from the earth; born from two people), all human knowledge on a subject (though contradictory in itself) may be accommodated by one myth.

Further, one of the worldwide features of myths that *do* show people springing from the earth is the initial difficulty that all the new creatures have in walking. This common theme suggests that column four *affirms* the individual origin in the earth or "autochthonous" origin of mankind, just as column three denies it. Turning back to the myth as a whole:

> We may now see what it means. The myth has to do with the inability, for a culture which holds the belief that mankind is autochthonous (see, for instance, Pausanias, VIII, xxix, 4: plants provide a *model* for humans), to find a satisfactory transition between this theory and the knowledge that human beings are actually born from the union of man and woman. Although the problem obviously cannot be solved, the Oedipus myth provides a kind of logical tool which relates the original problem—born from one or born from two?—to the derivative problem: born from different or born from same? By a correlation of this type, the overrating of blood relations is to the underrating of blood relations as the attempt to escape autochthony is to the impossibility to succeed in it.

One of the implications of this way of looking at myth as a whole has to do with the way "earlier" or "later" versions of a myth are neither more nor less the "true" version, since "if myth is made up of *all* its variants, structural analysis should take all of them into account." One surprising corollary of this implication is the way Levi-Strauss sees Freud's concept of the "Oedipal Complex" as only *the latest variation on the myth itself.* In other words, Freud sees the overvaluing by the child of one of its parents and the attempt to eliminate or undervalue the importance of the other parent as still one more attempt to solve the problem: "born of one or born of two?"

Levi-Strauss makes an analysis that not only illuminates the issues within and around Sophocles play, but shows how myth—like drama—is *dramatic.* That is, both forms of human expression are less concerned with delivering a "message" than with dramatizing perhaps intractable questions about the meaning of human life. In this way, and on his own terms, the critical analysis produced by Levi-Strauss is itself a great "myth."

SUGGESTIONS FOR DISCUSSION AND WRITING

1. The title of the play gives Oedipus a title as a king. What about his speeches in the beginning establish a regal nature in the character? What notions of his power are played off in **dramatic irony** against his powerlessness? Explain and exemplify your answers. How do the two critical approaches you have read resemble each other and differ from one another with regard to the theme of power?

2. Are the speeches of the other characters "in character" for you? Pick a character and analyze the particular manner and content of that figure. What is the function of the other characters according to each of the critical approaches?

3. How (if at all) do the notions of right and wrong held by the characters in the play seem to differ from your own notions? What is the difference between shame and guilt for the characters? For you? In what ways are the two opposites, glory and shame, a function of power in the play? In what ways are they a function of justice? How do the two critical approaches view the moral issues of the play?

4. *Oedipus the King* is one of the early great plays in the Western tradition. What, if anything, about that tradition do you find continued in *Hamlet*, waiving the issue of Shakespeare's knowing or not knowing the earlier drama? How, for example, are guilt and shame treated similarly? How are they treated differently? Explain and exemplify your answers.

5. Make some notes for discussion or for an essay in which you address the problem of *properly valuing* what Levi-Strauss calls "blood relations" by comparing and contrasting *Oedipus the King* in this regard with any other play included here—*Hamlet*, for example. Similarly, make some notes on what Brooks and Heilman see as the problem of the limits of rationality in *Hamlet* or another play.

6. Make some notes for discussion or for an essay in which you use another critical approach to understand *Oedipus the King*. For example, how might a Reader-Response critic distinguish between the reactions of an audience in ancient Greece and the reactions of an audience today on the issue of guilt versus shame in the play?

Chapter Eighteen

Approaches to William Shakespeare's *Hamlet*

WILLIAM SHAKESPEARE (1564–1616) is a man about whom we know only a little even though his works have been studied more than any other writer's. We do know that Shakespeare was born in Stratford-on-Avon, a small village located in southern England. His father was a glovemaker and also served as high bailiff of the town. As a boy, Shakespeare probably attended the King Edward IV Grammar School, where he learned Latin, some Greek, and read the works of Roman dramatists. At the age of eighteen, he married Anne Hathaway, who was eight years his senior. In 1583, she bore him a daughter, Susana; 1585 saw the birth of twins, Hamnet (who died in boyhood) and Judith. Very little is known of Shakespeare's activities between 1585 and 1592; there is some speculation that he may have taught school during this period, but it is most likely that he spent this time establishing himself as an actor in London. In 1594, Shakespeare appears in records as a member of a theatrical company, The Lord Chamberlain's Men, later renamed The King's Men in honor of their patron, King James I. Shakespeare wrote some thirty-six plays for this company, for which it is also believed he served as a supporting player. (When the plague closed the theatres from 1592 to 1594, it is believed that Shakespeare wrote his famous *Sonnets*, published only in 1609.) The company prospered and moved to the Globe Theatre in 1599; in 1608, the Blackfriar's Theatre was also purchased. Shakespeare died in 1616 and is buried at Stratford-on-Avon. *Hamlet* is believed to have been composed in 1601.

WILLIAM SHAKESPEARE
Hamlet, Prince of Denmark
(1601)

DRAMATIS PERSONAE

Claudius, *King of Denmark*

Hamlet, *son to the late, and nephew to the present king*

Polonius, *lord chamberlain*

Horatio, *friend to Hamlet*

Laertes, *son to Polonius*

Voltimand
Cornelius } *courtiers*
Rosencrantz

Guildenstern
Osric } *courtiers*
A Gentleman

A Priest

Marcellus } *officers*
Bernardo

Francisco, *a soldier*

Reynaldo, *servant to Polonius*

Players

Two Clowns, *grave-diggers*
Fortinbras, Prince of Norway
A Captain
English Ambassadors
Gertrude, Queen of Denmark, *and*
   mother to **Hamlet**

Ophelia, *daughter to Polonius*
Lords, Ladies, Officers, Soldiers,
   Sailors, Messengers, and other
   Attendants
Ghost of Hamlet's Father

Scene: Denmark.

Act I

Scene I. Elsinore. A platform° before the castle.

Enter Bernardo and Francisco, two sentinels.

Bernardo: Who's there?
Francisco: Nay, answer me:° stand, and unfold yourself.
Bernardo: Long live the king!°
Francisco: Bernardo?
Bernardo: He.
Francisco: You come most carefully upon your hour.
Bernardo: 'Tis now struck twelve; get thee to bed, Francisco.
Francisco: For this relief much thanks: 'tis bitter cold,
And I am sick at heart.
Bernardo: Have you had quiet guard?
10 **Francisco:**   Not a mouse stirring.
Bernardo: Well, good night.
If you do meet Horatio and Marcellus,
The rivals° of my watch, bid them make haste.

Enter Horatio and Marcellus.

Francisco: I think I hear them. Stand, ho! Who is there?
Horatio: Friends to this ground.
Marcellus: And liegemen to the Dane.
Francisco: Give you° good night.
Marcellus: O, farewell, honest soldier:
Who hath reliev'd you?
Francisco: Bernardo hath my place.
Give you good night.   *Exit Francisco.*
Marcellus: Holla! Bernardo!
Bernardo: Say,

ACT I. SCENE I.   *platform:* A level space on the battlements of the royal castle at Elsinore, a
Danish seaport; now Helsingör.   2 *me:* This is emphatic, since Francisco is the sentry.
3 *Long live the king:* Either a password or greeting; Horatio and Marcellus use a different
one in line 15.   13 *rivals:* Partners.   16 *Give you:* God give you.

What, is Horatio there?
Horatio: A piece of him.
20 *Bernardo:* Welcome, Horatio: welcome, good Marcellus.
Marcellus: What, has this thing appear'd again to-night?
Bernardo: I have seen nothing.
Marcellus: Horatio says 'tis but our fantasy,
And will not let belief take hold of him
Touching this dreaded sight, twice seen of us:
Therefore I have entreated him along
With us to watch the minutes of this night;
That if again this apparition come,
He may approve° our eyes and speak to it.
Horatio: Tush, tush, 'twill not appear.
30 *Bernardo:*   Sit down awhile;
And let us once again assail your ears,
That are so fortified against our story
What we have two nights seen.
Horatio: Well, sit we down,
And let us hear Bernardo speak of this.
Bernardo: Last night of all,
When yond same star that's westward from the pole°
Had made his course t' illume that part of heaven
Where now it burns, Marcellus and myself,
The bell then beating one,—

Enter Ghost.

40 *Marcellus:* Peace, break thee off; look, where it comes again!
Bernardo: In the same figure, like the king that's dead.
Marcellus: Thou art a scholar;° speak to it, Horatio.
Bernardo: Looks 'a not like the king? mark it, Horatio.
Horatio: Most like: it harrows° me with fear and wonder.
Bernardo: It would be spoke to.°
Marcellus: Speak to it, Horatio.
Horatio: What art thou that usurp'st this time of night,
Together with that fair and warlike form
In which the majesty of buried Denmark°
Did sometimes march? by heaven I charge thee, speak!
Marcellus: It is offended.
50 *Bernardo:*   See, it stalks away!
Horatio: Stay! speak, speak! I charge thee, speak!   *Exit Ghost.*
Marcellus: 'Tis gone, and will not answer.

---

29 *approve:* Corroborate.   36 *pole:* Polestar.   42 *scholar:* Exorcisms were performed in
Latin, which Horatio as an educated man would be able to speak.   44 *harrows:* Lacerates
the feelings.   45 *It . . . to:* A ghost could not speak until spoken to.   48 *buried Den-*
mark: the buried king of Denmark.

Bernardo: How now, Horatio! you tremble and look pale:
Is not this something more than fantasy?
What think you on 't?
Horatio: Before my God, I might not this believe
Without the sensible and true avouch
Of mine own eyes.
Marcellus: Is it not like the king?
Horatio: As thou art to thyself:
60 Such was the very armour he had on
When he the ambitious Norway combated;
So frown'd he once, when, in an angry parle,
He smote° the sledded Polacks° on the ice.
'Tis strange.
Marcellus: Thus twice before, and jump° at this dead hour,
With martial stalk hath he gone by our watch.
Horatio: In what particular thought to work I know not;
But in the gross and scope° of my opinion,
This bodes some strange eruption to our state.
70 *Marcellus:* Good now,° sit down, and tell me, he that knows,
Why this same strict and most observant watch
So nightly toils° the subject° of the land,
And why such daily cast° of brazen cannon,
And foreign mart° for implements of war;
Why such impress° of shipwrights, whose sore task
Does not divide the Sunday from the week;
What might be toward, that this sweaty haste
Doth make the night joint-labourer with the day:
Who is't that can inform me?
Horatio: That can I;
80 At least, the whisper goes so. Our last king,
Whose image even but now appear'd to us,
Was, as you know, by Fortinbras of Norway,
Thereto prick'd on° by a most emulate° pride,
Dar'd to the combat; in which our valiant Hamlet—
For so this side of our known world esteem'd him—
Did slay this Fortinbras; who, by a seal'd compact,
Well ratified by law and heraldry,°
Did forfeit, with his life, all those his lands
Which he stood seiz'd° of, to the conqueror:
90 Against the which, a moiety competent°
Was gaged by our king; which had return'd

63 *smote:* Defeated; *sledded Polacks:* Polanders using sledges.   65 *jump:* Exactly.   68 *gross and scope:* General drift.   70 *Good now:* An expression denoting entreaty or expostulation.   72 *toils:* Causes or makes to toil; *subject:* people, subjects.   73 *cast:* Casting, founding.   74 *mart:* Buying and selling, traffic.   75 *impress:* Impressment.   83 *prick'd on:* Incited; *emulate:* Rivaling.   87 *law and heraldry:* Heraldic law, governing combat. 89 *seiz'd:* Possessed.   90 *moiety competent:* Adequate or sufficient portion.

To the inheritance of Fortinbras,
Had he been vanquisher; as, by the same comart,°
And carriage° of the article design'd,
His fell to Hamlet. Now, sir, young Fortinbras,
Of unimproved° mettle hot and full,°
Hath in the skirts of Norway here and there
Shark'd up° a list of lawless resolutes,°
For food and diet,° to some enterprise
100 That hath a stomach in't; which is no other—
As it doth well appear unto our state—
But to recover of us, by strong hand
And terms compulsatory, those foresaid lands
So by his father lost: and this, I take it,
Is the main motive of our preparations,
The source of this our watch and the chief head
Of this post-haste and romage° in the land.
Bernardo: I think it be no other but e'en so:
Well may it sort° that this portentous figure
110 Comes armed through our watch; so like the king
That was and is the question of these wars.
Horatio: A mote° it is to trouble the mind's eye.
In the most high and palmy state° of Rome,
A little ere the mightiest Julius fell,
The graves stood tenantless and the sheeted dead
Did squeak and gibber in the Roman streets:
As stars with trains of fire° and dews of blood,
Disasters° in the sun; and the moist star°
Upon whose influence Neptune's empire° stands
120 Was sick almost to doomsday with eclipse:
And even the like precurse° of fear'd events,
As harbingers preceding still the fates
And prologue to the omen coming on,
Have heaven and earth together demonstrated
Unto our climatures and countrymen.—

Enter Ghost.

But soft, behold! lo, where it comes again!
I'll cross° it, though it blast me. Stay, illusion!
If thou hast any sound, or use of voice,

---

93 *comart:* Joint bargain.   94 *carriage:* Import, bearing.   96 *unimproved:* Not turned to account; *hot and full:* Full of fight.   98 *Shark'd up:* Got together in haphazard fashion; *resolutes:*
Desperadoes.   99 *food and diet:* No pay but their keep.   107 *romage:* Bustle, commotion.   109 *sort:* Suit.   112 *mote:* Speck of dust.   113 *palmy state:* Triumphant sovereignty.   117 *stars . . . fire:* i.e., comets.   118 *Disasters:* Unfavorable aspects; *moist star:*
The moon, governing tides.   119 *Neptune's empire:* The sea.   121 *precurse:* Heralding.
127 *cross:* Meet, face; thus bringing down the evil influence on the person who crosses it.

Speak to me!   *It° spreads his arms.*
130 If there be any good thing to be done,
That may to thee do ease and grace to me,
Speak to me!
If thou art privy to thy country's fate,
Which, happily, foreknowing may avoid,
O, speak!
Or if thou hast uphoarded in thy life
Extorted treasure in the womb of earth,
For which, they say, you spirits oft walk in death,   *The cock crows.*
Speak of it:° stay, and speak! Stop it, Marcellus.
140 *Marcellus:* Shall I strike at it with my partisan?°
Horatio: Do, if it will not stand.
Bernardo: 'Tis here!
Horatio: 'Tis here!
Marcellus: 'Tis gone!   *(Exit Ghost.)*
We do it wrong, being so majestical,
To offer it the show of violence;
For it is, as the air, invulnerable,
And our vain blows malicious mockery.
Bernardo: It was about to speak, when the cock crew.°
Horatio: And then it started like a guilty thing
Upon a fearful summons. I have heard,
150 The cock, that is the trumpet to the morn,
Doth with his lofty and shrill-sounding throat
Awake the god of day; and, at his warning,
Whether in sea or fire, in earth or air,
Th' extravagant and erring° spirit hies
To his confine:° and of the truth herein
This present object made probation.°
Marcellus: It faded on the crowing of the cock.
Some say that ever 'gainst° that season comes
Wherein our Saviour's birth is celebrated,
160 The bird of dawning singeth all night long:
And then, they say, no spirit dare stir abroad;
The nights are wholesome; then no planets strike,°
No fairy takes, nor witch hath power to charm,
So hallow'd and so gracious° is that time.

---

129 *It:* The Ghost, or perhaps Horatio.   133–139 *If . . . it:* Horatio recites the traditional reasons why ghosts might walk.   140 *partisan:* Long-handled spear with a
blade having lateral projections.   147 *cock crew:* According to traditional ghost lore,
spirits returned to their confines at cockcrow.   154 *extravagant and erring:* Wandering.
Both words mean the same thing.   155 *confine:* Place of confinement.   156 *probation:* Proof, trial.   158 *'gainst:* Just before.   162 *planets strike:* It was thought that
planets were malignant and might strike travelers by night.   164 *gracious:* Full of
goodness.

Horatio: So have I heard and do in part believe it.
But, look, the morn, in russet mantle clad,
Walks o'er the dew of yon high eastward hill:
Break we our watch up; and by my advice,
Let us impart what we have seen to-night
170 Unto young Hamlet; for, upon my life,
This spirit, dumb to us, will speak to him.
Do you consent we shall acquaint him with it,
As needful in our loves, fitting our duty?
Marcellus: Let's do 't, I pray; and I this morning know
Where we shall find him most conveniently.   *Exeunt.*

Scene II. A room of state in the castle.

Flourish. Enter Claudius, King of Denmark, Gertrude the Queen, Councilors,
Polonius and his Son Laertes, Hamlet, cum aliis° including Voltimand and Cornelius.

King: Though yet of Hamlet our dear brother's death
The memory be green, and that it us befitted
To bear our hearts in grief and our whole kingdom
To be contracted in one brow of woe,
Yet so far hath discretion fought with nature
That we with wisest sorrow think on him,
Together with remembrance of ourselves.
Therefore our sometime sister, now our queen,
Th' imperial jointress° to this warlike state,
10 Have we, as 'twere with a defeated joy,—
With an auspicious and a dropping eye,
With mirth in funeral and with dirge in marriage,
In equal scale weighing delight and dole,—
Taken to wife: nor have we herein barr'd
Your better wisdoms, which have freely gone
With this affair along. For all, our thanks.
Now follows, that° you know, young Fortinbras,
Holding a weak supposal° of our worth,
Or thinking by our late dear brother's death
20 Our state to be disjoint° and out of frame,°
Colleagued° with this dream of his advantage,°
He hath not fail'd to pester us with message,
Importing° the surrender of those lands
Lost by his father, with all bands of law,
To our most valiant brother. So much for him.

SCENE II.   *cum aliis:* With others.   9 *jointress:* Woman possessed of a jointure, or, joint
tenancy of an estate.   17 *that:* That which.   18 *weak supposal:* Low estimate.   20 *dis-*
joint: Distracted, out of joint; *frame:* Order.   21 *Colleagued:* added to; *dream . . .*
advantage: Visionary hope of success.   23 *Importing:* Purporting, pertaining to.

Now for ourself and for this time of meeting:
Thus much the business is: we have here writ
To Norway, uncle of young Fortinbras,—
Who, impotent and bed-rid, scarcely hears
30 Of this his nephew's purpose,—to suppress
His further gait° herein; in that the levies,
The lists and full proportions, are all made
Out of his subject:° and we here dispatch
You, good Cornelius, and you, Voltimand,
For bearers of this greeting to old Norway;
Giving to you no further personal power
To business with the king, more than the scope
Of these delated° articles allow.
Farewell, and let your haste commend your duty.
40 **Cornelius:**
Voltimand: In that and all things will we show our duty.
King: We doubt it nothing: heartily farewell.

(Exeunt Voltimand and Cornelius.)

And now, Laertes, what's the news with you?
You told us of some suit; what is't, Laertes?
You cannot speak of reason to the Dane,°
And lose your voice:° what wouldst thou beg, Laertes,
That shall not be my offer, not thy asking?
The head is not more native° to the heart,
The hand more instrumental° to the mouth,
Than is the throne of Denmark to thy father.
What wouldst thou have, Laertes?
50 **Laertes:**   My dread lord,
Your leave and favour to return to France;
From whence though willingly I came to Denmark,
To show my duty in your coronation,
Yet now, I must confess, that duty done,
My thoughts and wishes bend again toward France
And bow them to your gracious leave and pardon.°
King: Have you your father's leave? What says Polonius?
Polonius: He hath, my lord, wrung from me my slow leave
By laboursome petition, and at last
60 Upon his will I seal'd my hard consent:
I do beseech you, give him leave to go.

---

31 *gait:* Proceeding.   33 *Out of his subject:* At the expense of Norway's subjects (collectively).   38 *delated:* Expressly stated.   44 *the Dane:* Danish king.   45 *lose your voice:*
Speak in vain.   47 *native:* Closely connected, related.   48 *instrumental:* Serviceable.
56 *leave and pardon:* Permission to depart.

King: Take thy fair hour, Laertes; time be thine,
And thy best graces spend it at thy will!
But now, my cousin° Hamlet, and my son,—
Hamlet (aside): A little more than kin, and less than kind!°
King: How is it that the clouds still hang on you?
Hamlet: Not so, my lord; I am too much in the sun.°
Queen: Good Hamlet, cast thy nighted colour off,
And let thine eye look like a friend on Denmark.
70 Do not for ever with thy vailed lids
Seek for thy noble father in the dust:
Thou know'st 'tis common; all that lives must die,
Passing through nature to eternity.
Hamlet: Ay, madam, it is common.°
Queen:　　　　If it be,
Why seems it so particular with thee?
Hamlet: Seems, madam! nay, it is; I know not "seems."
'Tis not alone my inky cloak, good mother,
Nor customary suits° of solemn black,
Nor windy suspiration° of forc'd breath,
80 No, nor the fruitful river in the eye,
Nor the dejected 'haviour of the visage,
Together with all forms, moods, shapes of grief,
That can denote me truly: these indeed seem,
For they are actions that a man might play:
But I have that within which passeth show;
These but the trappings and the suits of woe.
King: 'Tis sweet and commendable in your nature, Hamlet,
To give these mourning duties to your father:
But, you must know, your father lost a father;
90 That father lost, lost his, and the survivor bound
In filial obligation for some term
To do obsequious° sorrow: but to persever
In obstinate condolement° is a course
Of impious stubbornness; 'tis unmanly grief;
It shows a will most incorrect° to heaven,
A heart unfortified, a mind impatient,
An understanding simple and unschool'd:

---

64 *cousin:* Any kin not of the immediate family.　　65 *A little . . . kind:* My relation to you
has become more than kinship warrants; it has also become unnatural.　　67 *I am . . .*
sun: The senses seem to be: I am too much out of doors, I am too much in the sun of your
grace (ironical), I am too much of a son to you. Possibly an allusion to the proverb "Out of
heaven's blessing into the warm sun"; i.e., Hamlet is out of house and home in being deprived of the kingship.　　74 *Ay . . . common:* It is common, but it hurts nevertheless;
possibly a reference to the commonplace quality of the queen's remark.　　78 *customary*
suits: Suits prescribed by custom for mourning.　　79 *windy suspiration:* Heavy sighing.
92 *obsequious:* Dutiful.　　93 *condolement:* Sorrowing.　　95 *incorrect:* Untrained, uncorrected.

For what we know must be and is as common
As any the most vulgar thing° to sense,
100 Why should we in our peevish opposition
Take it to heart? Fie! 'tis a fault to heaven,
A fault against the dead, a fault to nature,
To reason most absurd; whose common theme
Is death of fathers, and who still hath cried,
From the first corse till he that died to-day,
"This must be so." We pray you, throw to earth
This unprevailing° woe, and think of us
As of a father: for let the world take note,
You are the most immediate° to our throne;
110 And with no less nobility° of love
Than that which dearest father bears his son,
Do I impart° toward you. For your intent
In going back to school in Wittenberg,°
It is most retrograde° to our desire:
And we beseech you, bend you° to remain
Here, in the cheer and comfort of our eye,
Our chiefest courtier, cousin, and our son.
Queen: Let not thy mother lose her prayers, Hamlet:
I pray thee, stay with us; go not to Wittenberg.
120 *Hamlet:* I shall in all my best obey you, madam.
King: Why, 'tis a loving and a fair reply:
Be as ourself in Denmark. Madam, come;
This gentle and unforc'd accord of Hamlet
Sits smiling to my heart: in grace whereof,
No jocund health that Denmark drinks to-day,
But the great cannon to the clouds shall tell,
And the king's rouse° the heaven shall bruit again,°
Re-speaking earthly thunder. Come away.

Flourish. Exeunt all but Hamlet.

Hamlet: O, that this too too sullied flesh would melt,
130 Thaw and resolve itself into a dew!
Or that the Everlasting had not fix'd
His canon 'gainst self-slaughter! O God! God!
How weary, stale, flat and unprofitable,
Seem to me all the uses of this world!
Fie on't! ah fie! 'tis an unweeded garden,

---

99 *vulgar thing:* Common experience.   107 *unprevailing:* Unavailing.   109 *most immedi-*
ate: Next in succession.   110 *nobility:* High degree.   112 *impart:* The object is apparently *love* (l. 110).   113 *Wittenberg:* Famous German university founded in 1502.   114
retrograde: Contrary.   115 *bend you:* Incline yourself; imperative.   127 *rouse:* Draft of
liquor; *bruit again:* Echo.

That grows to seed; things rank and gross in nature
Possess it merely.° That it should come to this!
But two months dead: nay, not so much, not two:
So excellent a king; that was, to this,
140 Hyperion° to a satyr; so loving to my mother
That he might not beteem° the winds of heaven
Visit her face too roughly. Heaven and earth!
Must I remember? why, she would hang on him,
As if increase of appetite had grown
By what it fed on: and yet, within a month—
Let me not think on't—Frailty, thy name is woman!—
A little month, or ere those shoes were old
With which she followed my poor father's body,
Like Niobe,° all tears:—why she, even she—
150 O God! a beast, that wants discourse of reason,°
Would have mourn'd longer—married with my uncle,
My father's brother, but no more like my father
Than I to Hercules: within a month:
Ere yet the salt of most unrighteous tears
Had left the flushing in her galled° eyes,
She married. O, most wicked speed, to post
With such dexterity° to incestuous sheets!
It is not nor it cannot come to good:
But break, my heart; for I must hold my tongue.

Enter Horatio, Marcellus, and Bernardo.

Horatio: Hail to your lordship!
160 ***Hamlet:***   I am glad to see you well:
Horatio!—or I do forget myself.
Horatio: The same, my lord, and your poor servant ever.
Hamlet: Sir, my good friend; I'll change that name with you:°
And what make you from Wittenberg, Horatio?
Marcellus?
Marcellus: My good lord—
Hamlet: I am very glad to see you. Good even, sir.
But what, in faith, make you from Wittenberg?
Horatio: A truant disposition, good my lord.
170 ***Hamlet:*** I would not hear your enemy say so,
Nor shall you do my ear that violence,

---

137 *merely:* Completely, entirely.   140 *Hyperion:* God of the sun in the older regime of
ancient gods.   141 *beteem:* Allow.   149 *Niobe:* Tantalus's daughter, who boasted that
she had more sons and daughters than Leto; for this Apollo and Artemis slew her children. She was turned into stone by Zeus on Mount Sipylus.   150 *discourse of reason:* Process or faculty of reason.   155 *galled:* Irritated.   157 *dexterity:* Facility.   163 *I'll . . .
you:* I'll be your servant, you shall be my friend; also explained as "I'll exchange the name
of friend with you."

To make it truster of your own report
Against yourself: I know you are no truant.
But what is your affair in Elsinore?
We'll teach you to drink deep ere you depart.
Horatio: My lord, I came to see your father's funeral.
Hamlet: I prithee, do not mock me, fellow-student;
I think it was to see my mother's wedding.
Horatio: Indeed, my lord, it follow'd hard° upon.
180 *Hamlet:* Thrift, thrift, Horatio! the funeral bak'd meats°
Did coldly furnish forth the marriage tables.
Would I had met my dearest° foe in heaven
Or ever I had seen that day, Horatio!
My father!—methinks I see my father.
Horatio: Where, my lord!
Hamlet: In my mind's eye, Horatio.
Horatio: I saw him once; 'a° was a goodly king.
Hamlet: 'A was a man, take him for all in all,
I shall not look upon his like again.
Horatio: My lord, I think I saw him yesternight.
190 *Hamlet:* Saw? who?
Horatio: My lord, the king your father.
Hamlet: The king my father!
Horatio: Season your admiration° for a while
With an attent ear, till I may deliver,
Upon the witness of these gentlemen,
This marvel to you.
Hamlet: For God's love, let me hear.
Horatio: Two nights together had these gentlemen,
Marcellus and Bernardo, on their watch,
In the dead waste and middle of the night,
Been thus encount'red. A figure like your father,
200 Armed at point exactly, cap-a-pe,°
Appears before them, and with solemn march
Goes slow and stately by them: thrice he walk'd
By their oppress'd° and fear-surprised eyes,
Within his truncheon's° length; whilst they, distill'd°
Almost to jelly with the act° of fear,
Stand dumb and speak not to him. This to me
In dreadful secrecy impart they did;
And I with them the third night kept the watch:
Where, as they had deliver'd, both in time,

---

179 *hard:* Close.   180 *bak'd meats:* Meat pies.   182 *dearest:* Direst. The adjective *dear* in
Shakespeare has two different origins: O.E. *deore,* "beloved," and O.E. *deor,* "fierce."
Dearest is the superlative of the second.   186 *'a:* He.   192 *Season your admiration:* Restrain your astonishment.   200 *cap-a-pe:* From head to foot.   203 *oppress'd:* Distressed.
204 *truncheon:* Officer's staff; *distill'd:* Softened, weakened.   205 *act:* Action.

210 Form of the thing, each word made true and good,
The apparition comes: I knew your father;
These hands are not more like.
Hamlet: But where was this?
Marcellus: My lord, upon the platform where we watch'd.
Hamlet: Did you not speak to it?
Horatio: My lord, I did;
But answer made it none: yet once methought
It lifted up it° head and did address
Itself to motion, like as it would speak;
But even then the morning cock crew loud,
And at the sound it shrunk in haste away,
And vanish'd from our sight.
220 *Hamlet:*   'Tis very strange.
Horatio: As I do live, my honour'd lord, 'tis true;
And we did think it writ down in our duty
To let you know of it.
Hamlet: Indeed, indeed, sirs, but this troubles me.
Hold you the watch to-night?
Marcellus:
Bernardo: We do, my lord.
Hamlet: Arm'd, say you?
Marcellus:
Bernardo: Arm'd, my lord.
Hamlet: From top to toe?
Marcellus:
Bernardo: My lord, from head to foot.
Hamlet: Then saw you not his face?
230 *Horatio:* O, yes, my lord; he wore his beaver° up.
Hamlet: What, look'd he frowningly?
Horatio: A countenance more in sorrow than in anger.
Hamlet: Pale or red?
Horatio: Nay, very pale.
Hamlet: And fix'd his eyes upon you?
Horatio: Most constantly.
Hamlet: I would I had been there.
Horatio: It would have much amaz'd you.
Hamlet: Very like, very like. Stay'd it long?
Horatio: While one with moderate haste might tell a hundred.
Marcellus:
Bernardo: Longer, longer.
Horatio: Not when I saw't.
240 *Hamlet:*   His beard was grizzled,—no?
Horatio: It was, as I have seen it in his life,
A sable° silver'd.

---

216 *it:* Its.   230 *beaver:* Visor on the helmet.   242 *sable:* Black color.

Hamlet: I will watch to-night;
Perchance 'twill walk again.
Horatio: I warr'nt it will.
Hamlet: If it assume my noble father's person,
I'll speak to it, though hell itself should gape
And bid me hold my peace. I pray you all,
If you have hitherto conceal'd this sight,
Let it be tenable in your silence still;
And whatsoever else shall hap to-night,
250 Give it an understanding, but no tongue:
I will requite your loves. So, fare you well:
Upon the platform, 'twixt eleven and twelve,
I'll visit you.
All: Our duty to your honour.
Hamlet: Your loves, as mine to you: farewell.

Exeunt (all but Hamlet).

My father's spirit in arms! all is not well;
I doubt° some foul play: would the night were come!
Till then sit still, my soul: foul deeds will rise,
Though all the earth o'erwhelm them, to men's eyes.   *Exit.*

Scene III. A room in Polonius's house.

Enter Laertes and Ophelia, his Sister.

Laertes: My necessaries are embark'd: farewell:
And, sister, as the winds give benefit
And convoy is assistant,° do not sleep,
But let me hear from you.
Ophelia: Do you doubt that?
Laertes: For Hamlet and the trifling of his favour,
Hold it a fashion° and a toy in blood,°
A violet in the youth of primy° nature,
Forward,° not permanent, sweet, not lasting,
The perfume and suppliance of a minute;°
No more.
Ophelia: No more but so?
10 *Laertes:*   Think it no more:
For nature, crescent,° does not grow alone
In thews° and bulk, but, as this temple° waxes,

---

256 *doubt:* Fear.   SCENE III. 3 *convoy is assistant:* Means of conveyance are available.
6 *fashion:* Custom, prevailing usage; *toy in blood:* Passing amorous fancy.   7 *primy:* In its
prime.   8 *Forward:* Precocious.   9 *suppliance of a minute:* Diversion to fill up a minute.
11 *crescent:* Growing, waxing.   12 *thews:* Bodily strength; *temple:* Body.

The inward service of the mind and soul
Grows wide withal. Perhaps he loves you now,
And now no soil° nor cautel° doth besmirch
The virtue of his will: but you must fear,
His greatness weigh'd,° his will is not his own;
For he himself is subject to his birth:
He may not, as unvalued persons do,
20 Carve for himself; for on his choice depends
The safety and health of this whole state;
And therefore must his choice be circumscrib'd
Unto the voice and yielding° of that body
Whereof he is the head. Then if he says he loves you,
It fits your wisdom so far to believe it
As he in his particular act and place
May give his saying deed;° which is no further
Than the main voice of Denmark goes withal.
Then weigh what loss your honour may sustain,
30 If with too credent° ear you list his songs,
Or lose your heart, or your chaste treasure open
To his unmast'red° importunity.
Fear it, Ophelia, fear it, my dear sister,
And keep you in the rear of your affection,
Out of the shot and danger of desire.
The chariest° maid is prodigal enough,
If she unmask her beauty to the moon:
Virtue itself 'scapes not calumnious strokes:
The canker galls the infants of the spring,°
40 Too oft before their buttons° be disclos'd,°
And in the morn and liquid dew° of youth
Contagious blastments° are most imminent.
Be wary then; best safety lies in fear:
Youth to itself rebels, though none else near.
Ophelia: I shall the effect of this good lesson keep,
As watchman to my heart. But, good my brother,
Do not, as some ungracious° pastors do,
Show me the steep and thorny way to heaven;
Whiles, like a puff'd° and reckless libertine,
50 Himself the primrose path of dalliance treads,
And recks° not his own rede.°

---

15 *soil:* blemish; *cautel:* Crafty device.   17 *greatness weigh'd:* High position considered.
23 *voice and yielding:* Assent, approval.   27 *deed:* Effect.   30 *credent:* Credulous.
32 *unmast'red:* unrestrained.   36 *chariest:* Most scrupulously modest.   39 *The
canker . . . spring:* The cankerworm destroys the young plants of spring.   40 *buttons:*
buds; *disclos'd:* opened.   41 *liquid dew:* i.e., time when dew is fresh.   42 *blastments:*
Blights.   47 *ungracious:* Graceless.   49 *puff'd:* Bloated.   51 *recks:* Heeds; *rede:* Counsel.

Enter Polonius.

Laertes: O, fear me not.
I stay too long: but here my father comes.
A double° blessing is a double grace;
Occasion° smiles upon a second leave.
Polonius: Yet here, Laertes? aboard, aboard, for shame!
The wind sits in the shoulder of your sail,
And you are stay'd for. There; my blessing with thee!
And these few precepts° in thy memory
Look thou character.° Give thy thoughts no tongue,
60 Nor any unproportion'd° thought his act.
Be thou familiar, but by no means vulgar.°
Those friends thou hast, and their adoption tried,
Grapple them to thy soul with hoops of steel;
But do not dull thy palm with entertainment
Of each new-hatch'd, unfledg'd° comrade. Beware
Of entrance to a quarrel, but being in,
Bear't that th' opposed may beware of thee.
Give every man thy ear, but few thy voice;
Take each man's censure, but reserve thy judgement.
70 Costly thy habit as thy purse can buy,
But not express'd in fancy;° rich, not gaudy;
For the apparel oft proclaims the man,
And they in France of the best rank and station
Are of a most select and generous chief in that.°
Neither a borrower nor a lender be;
For loan oft loses both itself and friend,
And borrowing dulleth edge of husbandry.°
This above all: to thine own self be true,
And it must follow, as the night the day,
80 Thou canst not then be false to any man.
Farewell: my blessing season° this in thee!
Laertes: Most humbly do I take my leave, my lord.
Polonius: The time invites you; go; your servants tend.
Laertes: Farewell, Ophelia; and remember well
What I have said to you.
Ophelia: 'Tis in my memory lock'd,
And you yourself shall keep the key of it.
Laertes: Farewell.   *Exit Laertes.*
Polonius: What is 't, Ophelia, he hath said to you?

---

53 *double:* i.e., Laertes has already bade his father good-by.   54 *Occasion:* Opportunity.   58 *precepts:* Many parallels have been found to the series of maxims which follows, one of the closer being that in Lyly's *Euphues.*   59 *character:* Inscribe.   60 *unproportion'd:* Inordinate.   61 *vulgar:* Common.   65 *unfledg'd:* Immature.   71 *express'd in fancy:* Fantastical in design.   74 *Are . . . that: Chief* is usually taken as a substantive meaning "head," "eminence."   77 *husbandry:* Thrift.   81 *season:* Mature.

Ophelia: So please you, something touching the Lord Hamlet.
90 *Polonius:* Marry, well bethought:
'Tis told me, he hath very oft of late
Given private time to you; and you yourself
Have of your audience been most free and bounteous:
If it be so, as so't is put on° me,
And that in way of caution, I must tell you,
You do not understand yourself so clearly
As it behooves my daughter and your honour.
What is between you? give me up the truth.
Ophelia: He hath, my lord, of late made many tenders°
100 Of his affection to me.
Polonius: Affection! pooh! you speak like a green girl,
Unsifted° in such perilous circumstance.
Do you believe his tenders, as you call them?
Ophelia: I do not know, my lord, what I should think.
Polonius: Marry, I will teach you: think yourself a baby;
That you have ta'en these tenders° for true pay,
Which are not sterling.° Tender° yourself more dearly;
Or—not to crack the wind° of the poor phrase,
Running it thus—you'll tender me a fool.°
110 *Ophelia:* My lord, he hath importun'd me with love
In honourable fashion.
Polonius: Ay, fashion° you may call it; go to, go to.
Ophelia: And hath given countenance° to his speech, my lord,
With almost all the holy vows of heaven.
Polonius: Ay, springes° to catch woodcocks.° I do know,
When the blood burns, how prodigal the soul
Lends the tongue vows: these blazes, daughter,
Giving more light than heat, extinct in both,
Even in their promise, as it is a-making,
120 You must not take for fire. From this time
Be somewhat scanter of your maiden presence;
Set your entreatments° at a higher rate
Than a command to parley.° For Lord Hamlet,
Believe so much in him,° that he is young,
And with a larger tether may he walk
Than may be given you: in few,° Ophelia,
Do not believe his vows; for they are brokers;°

---

94 *put on:* Impressed on.   99, 103 *tenders:* Offers.   102 *Unsifted:* Untried.   106 *ten-*
ders: Promises to pay.   107 *sterling:* Legal currency; *Tender:* Hold.   108 *crack the wind:*
i.e., run it until it is broken-winded.   109 *tender . . . fool:* Show me a fool (for a daughter).   112 *fashion:* Mere form, pretense.   113 *countenance:* Credit, support.   115
springes: Snares; *woodcocks:* Birds easily caught, type of stupidity.   122 *entreatments:*
Conversations, interviews.   123 *command to parley:* Mere invitation to talk.   124
so . . . him: This much concerning him.   126 *in few:* Briefly. 127 *brokers:* Go-betweens,
procurers.

Not of that dye° which their investments° show,
But mere implorators° of unholy suits,
130 Breathing° like sanctified and pious bawds,
The better to beguile. This is for all:
I would not, in plain terms, from this time forth,
Have you so slander° any moment leisure,
As to give words or talk with the Lord Hamlet.
Look to 't, I charge you: come your ways.
Ophelia: I shall obey, my lord.   *Exeunt.*

Scene IV. The platform.

Enter Hamlet, Horatio, and Marcellus.

Hamlet: The air bites shrewdly; it is very cold.
Horatio: It is a nipping and an eager air.
Hamlet: What hour now?
Horatio: I think it lacks of twelve.
Marcellus: No, it is struck.
Horatio: Indeed? I heard it not: then it draws near the season
Wherein the spirit held his wont to walk.

A flourish of trumpets, and two pieces go off.

What does this mean, my lord?
Hamlet: The king doth wake° to-night and takes his rouse,°
Keeps wassail,° and the swagg'ring up-spring° reels;°
10 And, as he drains his draughts of Rhenish° down,
The kettle-drum and trumpet thus bray out
The triumph of his pledge.°
Horatio: Is it a custom?
Hamlet: Ay, marry, is 't:
But to my mind, though I am native here
And to the manner born,° it is a custom
More honour'd in the breach than the observance.
This heavy-headed revel east and west
Makes us traduc'd and tax'd of other nations:
They clepe° us drunkards, and with swinish phrase°
20 Soil our addition;° and indeed it takes
From our achievements, though perform'd at height,

---

128 *dye:* Color or sort; *investments:* Clothes.   129 *implorators of:* Solicitors of.   130
Breathing: Speaking.   133 *slander:* Bring disgrace or reproach upon.   SCENE IV. 8
wake: Stay awake, hold revel; *rouse:* Carouse, drinking bout.   9 *wassail:* Carousal; *up-spring:* Last and wildest dance at German merry-makings; *reels:* Reels through.   10
Rhenish: Rhine wine.   12 *triumph . . . pledge:* His glorious achievement as a drinker.
15 *to . . . born:* Destined by birth to be subject to the custom in question.
19 *clepe:* Call; *with swinish phrase:* By calling us swine.   20 *addition:* Reputation.

The pith and marrow of our attribute.°
So, oft it chances in particular men,
That for some vicious mole of nature° in them,
As, in their birth—wherein they are not guilty,
Since nature cannot choose his origin—
By the o'ergrowth of some complexion,
Oft breaking down the pales° and forts of reason,
Or by some habit that too much o'er-leavens°
30 The form of plausive° manners, that these men,
Carrying, I say, the stamp of one defect,
Being nature's livery,° or fortune's star,°—
Their virtues else—be they as pure as grace,
As infinite as man may undergo—
Shall in the general censure take corruption
From that particular fault: the dram of ev'
Doth all the noble substance of a doubt
To his own scandal.

     Enter Ghost.

Horatio: Look, my lord, it comes!
Hamlet: Angels and ministers of grace° defend us!
40 Be thou a spirit of health or goblin damn'd,
Bring with thee airs from heaven or blasts from hell,
Be thy intents wicked or charitable,
Thou com'st in such a questionable° shape
That I will speak to thee: I'll call thee Hamlet,
King, father, royal Dane: O, answer me!
Let me not burst in ignorance; but tell
Why thy canoniz'd° bones, hearsed° in death,
Have burst their cerements;° why the sepulchre,
Wherein we saw thee quietly interr'd,
50 Hath op'd his ponderous and marble jaws,
To cast thee up again. What may this mean,
That thou, dead corse, again in complete steel
Revisits thus the glimpses of the moon,°
Making night hideous; and we fools of nature°

---

22 *attribute:* Reputation.   24 *mole of nature:* Natural blemish in one's constitution.   28
pales: Palings (as of a fortification).   29 *o'er-leavens:* Induces a change throughout (as
yeast works in bread).   30 *plausive:* Pleasing.   32 *nature's livery:* Endowment from nature; *fortune's star:* The position in which one is placed by fortune, a reference to astrology. The two phrases are aspects of the same thing.   36–38 *the dram . . . scandal:* A
famous crux: *dram of eale* has had various interpretations, the preferred one being probably, "a dram of evil."   39 *ministers of grace:* Messengers of God.   43 *questionable:* Inviting question or conversation.   47 *canoniz'd:* Buried according to the canons of the
church; *hearsed:* Coffined.   48 *cerements:* Grave-clothes.   53 *glimpses of the moon:* The
earth by night.   54 *fools of nature:* Mere men, limited to natural knowledge.

So horridly to shake our disposition
With thoughts beyond the reaches of our souls?
Say, why is this? wherefore? what should we do?

Ghost beckons Hamlet.

Horatio: It beckons you to go away with it,
As if it some impartment° did desire
To you alone.
60 *Marcellus:*   Look, with what courteous action
It waves you to a more removed° ground:
But do not go with it.
Horatio: No, by no means.
Hamlet: It will not speak; then I will follow it.
Horatio: Do not, my lord!
Hamlet: Why, what should be the fear?
I do not set my life at a pin's fee;
And for my soul, what can it do to that,
Being a thing immortal as itself?
It waves me forth again: I'll follow it.
Horatio: What if it tempt you toward the flood, my lord,
70 Or to the dreadful summit of the cliff
That beetles o'er° his base into the sea,
And there assume some other horrible form,
Which might deprive your sovereignty of reason°
And draw you into madness? think of it:
The very place puts toys of desperation,°
Without more motive, into every brain
That looks so many fathoms to the sea
And hears it roar beneath.
Hamlet: It waves me still.
Go on; I'll follow thee.
Marcellus: You shall not go, my lord.
80 *Hamlet:*   Hold off your hands!
Horatio: Be rul'd; you shall not go.
Hamlet: My fate cries out,
And makes each petty artere° in this body
As hardy as the Nemean lion's° nerve.°
Still am I call'd. Unhand me, gentlemen.

---

59 *impartment:* Communication.   61 *removed:* Remote.   71 *beetles o'er:* Overhangs
threateningly.   73 *deprive . . . reason:* Take away the sovereignty of your reason. It was
thought that evil spirits would sometimes assume the form of departed spirits in order to
work madness in a human creature.   75 *toys of desperation:* Freakish notions of suicide.
82 *artere:* Artery.   83 *Nemean lion's:* The Nemean lion was one of the monsters slain by
Hercules; *nerve:* Sinew, tendon. The point is that the arteries which were carrying the spirits out into the body were functioning and were as stiff and hard as the sinews of the lion.

By heaven, I'll make a ghost of him that lets° me!
I say, away! Go on; I'll follow thee.   *Exeunt Ghost and Hamlet.*
Horatio: He waxes desperate with imagination.
Marcellus: Let's follow; 'tis not fit thus to obey him.
Horatio: Have after. To what issue° will this come?
90 *Marcellus:* Something is rotten in the state of Denmark.
Horatio: Heaven will direct it.°
Marcellus: Nay, let's follow him.   *Exeunt.*

Scene V. Another part of the platform.

   Enter Ghost and Hamlet.

Hamlet: Whither wilt thou lead me? speak; I'll go no further.
Ghost: Mark me.
Hamlet: I will.
Ghost: My hour is almost come,
When I to sulphurous and tormenting flames
Must render up myself.
Hamlet: Alas, poor ghost!
Ghost: Pity me not, but lend thy serious hearing
To what I shall unfold.
Hamlet: Speak; I am bound to hear.
Ghost: So art thou to revenge, when thou shalt hear.
Hamlet: What?
10 *Ghost:* I am thy father's spirit.
Doom'd for a certain term to walk the night,
And for the day confin'd to fast° in fires,
Till the foul crimes done in my days of nature
Are burnt and purg'd away. But that I am forbid
To tell the secrets of my prison-house,
I could a tale unfold whose lightest word
Would harrow up thy soul, freeze thy young blood,
Make thy two eyes, like stars, start from their spheres,°
Thy knotted° and combined° locks to part
20 And each particular hair to stand an end,
Like quills upon the fretful porpentine:°
But this eternal blazon° must not be
To ears of flesh and blood. List, list, O, list!
If thou didst ever thy dear father love—
Hamlet: O God!

---

85 *lets:* Hinders.   89 *issue:* Outcome.   91 *it:* i.e., the outcome.   SCENE V.   12 *fast:*
Probably, do without food. It has been sometimes taken in the sense of doing general
penance.   18 *spheres:* Orbits.   19 *knotted:* Perhaps intricately arranged; *combined:* Tied,
bound.   21 *porpentine:* Porcupine.   22 *eternal blazon:* Promulgation or proclamation of
eternity, revelation of the hereafter.

Ghost: Revenge his foul and most unnatural° murder.
Hamlet: Murder!
Ghost: Murder most foul, as in the best it is;
But this most foul, strange and unnatural.
30 *Hamlet:* Haste me to know't, that I, with wings as swift
As meditation or the thoughts of love,
May sweep to my revenge.
Ghost: I find thee apt;
And duller shouldst thou be than the fat weed°
That roots itself in ease on Lethe wharf,°
Wouldst thou not stir in this. Now, Hamlet, hear:
'Tis given out that, sleeping in my orchard,
A serpent stung me; so the whole ear of Denmark
Is by a forged process of my death
Rankly abus'd: but know, thou noble youth,
40 The serpent that did sting thy father's life
Now wears his crown.
Hamlet: O my prophetic soul!
My uncle!
Ghost: Ay, that incestuous, that adulterate° beast,
With witchcraft of his wit, with traitorous gifts,—
O wicked wit and gifts, that have the power
So to seduce!—won to his shameful lust
The will of my most seeming-virtuous queen:
O Hamlet, what a falling-off was there!
From me, whose love was of that dignity
50 That it went hand in hand even with the vow
I made to her in marriage, and to decline
Upon a wretch whose natural gifts were poor
To those of mine!
But virtue, as it never will be moved,
Though lewdness court it in a shape of heaven,
So lust, though to a radiant angel link'd,
Will sate itself in a celestial bed,
And prey on garbage.
But, soft! methinks I scent the morning air;
60 Brief let me be. Sleeping within my orchard,
My custom always of the afternoon,
Upon my secure° hour thy uncle stole,
With juice of cursed hebona° in a vial,

---

26 *unnatural:* i.e., pertaining to fratricide.   33 *fat weed:* Many suggestions have been offered as to the particular plant intended, including asphodel; probably a general figure for plants growing along rotting wharves and piles.   34 *Lethe wharf:* Bank of the river of forgetfulness in Hades.   43 *adulterate:* Adulterous.   62 *secure:* Confident, unsuspicious.   63 *hebona:* Generally supposed to mean henbane, conjectured *hemlock; ebenus,* meaning "yew."

And in the porches of my ears did pour
The leperous° distilment; whose effect
Holds such an enmity with blood of man
That swift as quicksilver it courses through
The natural gates and alleys of the body,
And with a sudden vigour it doth posset°
70 And curd, like eager° droppings into milk,
The thin and wholesome blood: so did it mine;
And a most instant tetter bark'd about,
Most lazar-like,° with vile and loathsome crust,
All my smooth body.
Thus was I, sleeping, by a brother's hand
Of life, of crown, of queen, at once dispatch'd:°
Cut off even in the blossoms of my sin,
Unhous'led,° disappointed,° unanel'd,°
No reck'ning made, but sent to my account
80 With all my imperfections on my head:
O, horrible! O, horrible! most horrible!°
If thou hast nature in thee, bear it not;
Let not the royal bed of Denmark be
A couch for luxury° and damned incest.
But, howsomever thou pursues this act,
Taint not thy mind,° nor let thy soul contrive
Against thy mother aught: leave her to heaven
And to those thorns that in her bosom lodge,
To prick and sting her. Fare thee well at once!
90 The glow-worm shows the matin° to be near,
And 'gins to pale his uneffectual fire:°
Adieu, adieu, adieu! remember me.   *Exit.*
Hamlet: O all you host of heaven! O earth! what else?
And shall I couple° hell? O, fie! Hold, hold, my heart;
And you, my sinews, grow not instant old,
But bear me stiffly up. Remember thee!
Ay, thou poor ghost, whiles memory holds a seat
In this distracted globe.° Remember thee!
Yea, from the table of my memory
100 I'll wipe away all trivial fond records,
All saws° of books, all forms, all pressures° past,

---

65 *leperous:* Causing leprosy.   69 *posset:* Coagulate, curdle.   70 *eager:* Sour, acid.   73
lazar-like: Leperlike.   76 *dispatch'd:* Suddenly bereft.   78 *Unhous'led:* Without having
received the sacrament; *disappointed:* Unready, without equipment for the last journey;
unanel'd: Without having received extreme unction.   81 *O . . . horrible:* Many editors
give this line to Hamlet; Garrick and Sir Henry Irving spoke it in that part.   84 *luxury:*
Lechery. 86 *Taint . . . mind:* Probably, deprave not thy character, do nothing except in the
pursuit of a natural revenge.   90 *matin:* Morning.   91 *uneffectual fire:* Cold light.
94 *couple:* Add.   98 *distracted globe:* Confused head.   101 *saws:* Wise sayings; *pressures:*
Impressions stamped.

That youth and observation copied there;
And thy commandment all alone shall live
Within the book and volume of my brain,
Unmix'd with baser matter: yes, by heaven!
O most pernicious woman!
O villain, villain, smiling, damned villain!
My tables,°—meet it is I set it down,
That one may smile, and smile, and be a villain;
110 At least I am sure it may be so in Denmark: *(Writing.)*
So, uncle, there you are. Now to my word;°
It is "Adieu, adieu! remember me,"
I have sworn't.

Enter Horatio and Marcellus.

Horatio: My lord, my lord—
Marcellus: Lord Hamlet,—
Horatio: Heavens secure him!
Hamlet: So be it!
Marcellus: Hillo, ho, ho,° my lord!
Hamlet: Hillo, ho, ho, boy! come, bird, come.
Marcellus: How is't, my noble lord?
Horatio: What news, my lord?
Hamlet: O, wonderful!
Horatio: Good my lord, tell it.
120 *Hamlet:* No; you will reveal it.
Horatio: Not I, my lord, by heaven.
Marcellus: Nor I, my lord.
Hamlet: How say you, then; would heart of man once think it?
But you'll be secret?
Horatio:
Marcellus: Ay, by heaven, my lord.
Hamlet: There's ne'er a villain dwelling in all Denmark
But he's an arrant° knave.
Horatio: There needs no ghost, my lord, come from the grave
To tell us this.
Hamlet: Why, right; you are in the right;
And so, without more circumstance at all,
I hold it fit that we shake hands and part:
130 You, as your business and desire shall point you;
For every man has business and desire,
Such as it is; and for my own poor part,
Look you, I'll go pray.
Horatio: These are but wild and whirling words, my lord.

---

108 *tables:* Probably a small portable writing-tablet carried at the belt. 111 *word:* Watch-
word.   116 *Hillo, ho, ho:* A falconer's call to a hawk in air.   125 *arrant:* Thoroughgoing.

Hamlet: I am sorry they offend you, heartily;
Yes, 'faith, heartily.
Horatio: There's no offence, my lord.
Hamlet: Yes, by Saint Patrick,° but there is, Horatio,
And much offence too. Touching this vision here,
It is an honest° ghost, that let me tell you:
140 For your desire to know what is between us,
O'ermaster 't as you may. And now, good friends,
As you are friends, scholars and soldiers,
Give me one poor request.
Horatio: What is 't, my lord? we will.
Hamlet: Never make known what you have seen to-night.
Horatio:
Marcellus: My lord, we will not.
Hamlet: Nay, but swear't.
Horatio: In faith,
My lord, not I.
Marcellus: Nor I, my lord, in faith.
Hamlet: Upon my sword.°
Marcellus: We have sworn, my lord, already.
Hamlet: Indeed, upon my sword, indeed.   *Ghost cries under the stage.*
Ghost: Swear.
150 *Hamlet:* Ah, ha, boy! say'st thou so? art thou there, truepenny?°
Come on—you hear this fellow in the cellarage—
Consent to swear.
Horatio: Propose the oath, my lord.
Hamlet: Never to speak of this that you have seen,
Swear by my sword.
Ghost (beneath): Swear.
Hamlet: Hic et ubique?° then we'll shift our ground.
Come hither, gentlemen,
And lay your hands again upon my sword:
Swear by my sword,
160 Never to speak of this that you have heard.
Ghost (beneath): Swear by his sword.
Hamlet: Well said, old mole! canst work i' th' earth so fast?
A worthy pioner!° Once more remove, good friends.
Horatio: O day and night, but this is wondrous strange!
Hamlet: And therefore as a stranger give it welcome.
There are more things in heaven and earth, Horatio,
Than are dreamt of in your philosophy.
But come;

---

137 *Saint Patrick:* St. Patrick was keeper of Purgatory and patron saint of all blunders and confusion.   139 *honest:* i.e., a real ghost and not an evil spirit.   147 *sword:* i.e., the hilt in the form of a cross.   150 *truepenny:* Good old boy, or the like. 156 *Hic et ubique?:* Here and everywhere?   163 *pioner:* Digger, miner.

Here, as before, never, so help you mercy,
170 How strange or odd soe'er I bear myself,
As I perchance hereafter shall think meet
To put an antic° disposition on,
That you, at such times seeing me, never shall,
With arms encumb'red° thus, or this head-shake,
Or by pronouncing of some doubtful phrase,
As "Well, well, we know," or "We could, an if we would,"
Or "If we list to speak," or "There be, an if they might,"
Or such ambiguous giving out,° to note°
That you know aught of me: this not to do,
180 So grace and mercy at your most need help you,
Swear.
Ghost (beneath): Swear.
Hamlet: Rest, rest, perturbed spirit! *(They swear.)* So, gentlemen,
With all my love I do commend me to you:
And what so poor a man as Hamlet is
May do, t' express his love and friending° to you,
God willing, shall not lack. Let us go in together;
And still your fingers on your lips, I pray.
The time is out of joint: O cursed spite,
190 That ever I was born to set it right!
Nay, come, let's go together.   *Exeunt.*

Act II

Scene I. A room in Polonius's house.

Enter old Polonius with his man Reynaldo.

Polonius: Give him this money and these notes, Reynaldo.
Reynaldo: I will, my lord.
Polonius: You shall do marvellous wisely, good Reynaldo,
Before you visit him, to make inquire
Of his behaviour.
Reynaldo: My lord, I did intend it.
Polonius: Marry, well said; very well said. Look you, sir,
Inquire me first what Danskers° are in Paris;
And how, and who, what means, and where they keep,°
What company, at what expense; and finding
10 By this encompassment° and drift° of question

---

172 *antic:* Fantastic.   174 *encumb'red:* Folded or entwined.   178 *giving out:* Profession
of knowledge; *to note:* To give a sign.   186 *friending:* Friendliness.   ACT II. SCENE I.   7
Danskers: Danke was a common variant for "Denmark"; hence "Dane."   8 *keep:*
Dwell.   10 *encompassment:* Roundabout talking; *drift:* Gradual approach or course.

That they do know my son, come you more nearer
Than your particular demands will touch it:°
Take° you, as 'twere, some distant knowledge of him;
As thus, "I know his father and his friends,
And in part him": do you mark this, Reynaldo?
Reynaldo: Ay, very well, my lord.
Polonius: "And in part him; but" you may say "not well:
But, if 't be he I mean, he's very wild;
Addicted so and so": and there put on° him
20 What forgeries° you please; marry, none so rank
As may dishonour him; take heed of that;
But, sir, such wanton,° wild and usual slips
As are companions noted and most known
To youth and liberty.
Reynaldo:　　　　　　　As gaming, my lord.
Polonius: Ay, or drinking, fencing,° swearing, quarrelling,
Drabbing;° you may go so far.
Reynaldo: My lord, that would dishonour him.
Polonius: 'Faith, no; as you may season it in the charge.
You must not put another scandal on him,
30 That he is open to incontinency;°
That's not my meaning: but breathe his faults so quaintly°
That they may seem the taints of liberty,°
The flash and outbreak of a fiery mind,
A savageness in unreclaimed° blood,
Of general assault.°
Reynaldo:　　　　　　　But, my good lord,—
Polonius: Wherefore should you do this?
Reynaldo:　　　　　　　Ay, my lord,
I would know that.
Polonius:　　　　　　　Marry, sir, here's my drift;
And, I believe, it is a fetch of wit:°
You laying these slight sullies on my son,
40 As 'twere a thing a little soil'd i' th' working,
Mark you,
Your party in converse, him you would sound,
Having ever° seen in the prenominate° crimes
The youth you breathe of guilty, be assur'd

11–12 *come . . . it:* i.e., you will find out more this way than by asking pointed questions.　　13 *Take:* Assume, pretend.　　19 *put on:* Impute to.　　20 *forgeries:* Invented tales.　　22 *wanton:* Sportive, unrestrained.　　25 *fencing:* Indicative of the ill repute of professional fencers and fencing schools in Elizabethan times.　　26 *Drabbing:* Associating with immoral women.　　30 *incontinency:* Habitual loose behavior.　　31 *quaintly:* Delicately, ingeniously.　　32 *taints of liberty:* Blemishes due to freedom.　　34 *unreclaimed:* Untamed.　　35 *general assault:* Tendency that assails all untrained youth.　　38 *fetch of wit:* Clever trick.　　43 *ever:* At any time; *prenominate:* Before-mentioned.

He closes with you in this consequence;°
"Good sir," or so, or "friend," or "gentleman,"
According to the phrase or the addition
Of man and country.
Reynaldo: Very good, my lord.
Polonius: And then, sir, does 'a this—'a does—what was I about to say?
50 By the mass, I was about to say something: where did I leave?
Reynaldo: At "closes in the consequence," at "friend or so," and
"gentleman."
Polonius: At "closes in the consequence," ay, marry;
He closes thus: "I know the gentleman;
I saw him yesterday, or t' other day,
Or then, or then; with such, or such; and, as you say,
There was 'a gaming; there o'ertook in 's rouse;°
There falling out at tennis"; or perchance,
"I saw him enter such a house of sale,"
60 Videlicet,° a brothel, or so forth.
See you now;
Your bait of falsehood takes this carp of truth:
And thus do we of wisdom and of reach,°
With windlasses° and with assays of bias,°
By indirections° find directions° out:
So by my former lecture° and advice,
Shall you my son. You have me, have you not?
Reynaldo: My lord, I have.
Polonius: God bye ye;° fare ye well.
Reynaldo: Good my lord!
70 *Polonius:* Observe his inclination in yourself.°
Reynaldo: I shall, my lord.
Polonius: And let him ply his music.°
Reynaldo: Well, my lord.
Polonius: Farewell!   *Exit Reynaldo.*

Enter Ophelia.

          How now, Ophelia! what's the matter?
Ophelia: O, my lord, my lord, I have been so affrighted!
Polonius: With what, i' th' name of God?

---

45 *closes . . . consequence:* Agrees with you in this conclusion.   57 *o'ertook in 's rouse:*
Overcome by drink.   60 *Videlicet:* Namely.   63 *reach:* Capacity, ability.   64 *wind-
lasses:* i.e., circuitous paths; *assays of bias:* Attempts that resemble the course of the bowl,
which, being weighted on one side, has a curving motion.   65 *indirections:* Devious
courses; *directions:* Straight courses, i.e., the truth.   66 *lecture:* Admonition.   68 *bye ye:*
Be with you.   70 *Observe . . . yourself:* In your own person, not by spies; or conform
your own conduct to his inclination; or test him by studying yourself.   72 *ply his music:*
Probably to be taken literally.

Ophelia: My lord, as I was sewing in my closet,°
Lord Hamlet, with his doublet° all unbrac'd;°
No hat upon his head; his stockings foul'd,
Ungart'red, and down-gyved° to his ankle;
80 Pale as his shirt; his knees knocking each other;
And with a look so piteous in purport
As if he had been loosed out of hell
To speak of horrors,—he comes before me.
Polonius: Mad for thy love?
Ophelia: My lord, I do not know;
But truly, I do fear it.
Polonius: What said he?
Ophelia: He took me by the wrist and held me hard;
Then goes he to the length of all his arm;
And, with his other hand thus o'er his brow,
He falls to such perusal of my face
90 As 'a would draw it. Long stay'd he so;
At last, a little shaking of mine arm
And thrice his head thus waving up and down,
He rais'd a sigh so piteous and profound
As it did seem to shatter all his bulk°
And end his being: that done, he lets me go:
And, with his head over his shoulder turn'd,
He seem'd to find his way without his eyes;
For out o' doors he went without their helps,
And, to the last, bended their light on me.
100 *Polonius:* Come, go with me: I will go seek the king.
This is the very ecstasy of love,
Whose violent property° fordoes° itself
And leads the will to desperate undertakings
As oft as any passion under heaven
That does afflict our natures. I am sorry.
What, have you given him any hard words of late?
Ophelia: No, my good lord, but, as you did command,
I did repel his letters and denied
His access to me.
Polonius: That hath made him mad.
110 I am sorry that with better heed and judgement
I had not quoted° him: I fear'd he did but trifle,
And meant to wrack thee; but, beshrew my jealousy!°
By heaven, it is as proper to our age
To cast beyond° ourselves in our opinions

---

76 *closet:* Private chamber.   77 *doublet:* close-fitting coat; *unbrac'd:* Unfastened. 79 *down-gyved:* Fallen to the ankles (like gyves or fetters).   94 *bulk:* Body.   102 *property:* Nature; *fordoes:* Destroys.   111 *quoted:* Observed.   112 *beshrew my jealousy:* Curse my suspicions.   114 *cast beyond:* Overshoot, miscalculate.

As it is common for the younger sort
To lack discretion. Come, go we to the king:
This must be known; which, being kept close, might move
More grief to hide than hate to utter love.°
Come.   *Exeunt.*

Scene II. A room in the castle.

   Flourish. Enter King and Queen, Rosencrantz, and Guildenstern with others.

King: Welcome, dear Rosencrantz and Guildenstern!
Moreover that° we much did long to see you,
The need we have to use you did provoke
Our hasty sending. Something have you heard
Of Hamlet's transformation; so call it,
Sith° nor th' exterior nor the inward man
Resembles that it was. What it should be,
More than his father's death, that thus hath put him
So much from th' understanding of himself,
10 I cannot dream of: I entreat you both,
That, being of so young days° brought up with him,
And sith so neighbour'd to his youth and haviour,
That you vouchsafe your rest° here in our court
Some little time: so by your companies
To draw him on to pleasures, and to gather,
So much as from occasion you may glean,
Whether aught, to us unknown, afflicts him thus,
That, open'd, lies within our remedy.
   Queen: Good gentlemen, he hath much talk'd of you;
20 And sure I am two men there are not living
To whom he more adheres. If it will please you
To show us so much gentry° and good will
As to expend your time with us awhile,
For the supply and profit° of our hope,
Your visitation shall receive such thanks
As fits a king's remembrance.
   Rosencrantz: Both your majesties
Might, by the sovereign power you have of us,
Put your dread pleasures more into command
Than to entreaty.
   Guildenstern: But we both obey,

117–118 *might . . . love:* i.e., I might cause more grief to others by hiding the knowledge
of Hamlet's love to Ophelia than hatred to me and mine by telling of it.   SCENE II. 2
Moreover that: Besides the fact that.   6 *Sith:* Since.   11 *of . . . days:* From such early
youth.   13 *vouchsafe your rest:* Please to stay.   22 *gentry:* Courtesy.   24 *supply and
profit:* Aid and successful outcome.

30 And here give up ourselves, in the full bent°
To lay our service freely at your feet,
To be commanded.
King: Thanks, Rosencrantz and gentle Guildenstern.
Queen: Thanks, Guildenstern and gentle Rosencrantz:
And I beseech you instantly to visit
My too much changed son. Go, some of you,
And bring these gentlemen where Hamlet is.
Guildenstern: Heavens make our presence and our practices
Pleasant and helpful to him!
Queen: Ay, amen!

Exeunt Rosencrantz and Guildenstern with some Attendants. Enter Polonius.

40 *Polonius:* Th' ambassadors from Norway, my good lord,
Are joyfully return'd.
King: Thou still hast been the father of good news.
Polonius: Have I, my lord? I assure my good liege,
I hold my duty, as I hold my soul,
Both to my God and to my gracious king:
And I do think, or else this brain of mine
Hunts not the trail of policy so sure
As it hath us'd to do, that I have found
The very cause of Hamlet's lunacy.
50 *King:* O, speak of that; that do I long to hear.
Polonius: Give first admittance to th' ambassadors;
My news shall be the fruit to that great feast.
King: Thyself do grace to them, and bring them in.   (*Exit Polonius.*)
He tells me, my dear Gertrude, he hath found
The head and source of all your son's distemper.
Queen: I doubt° it is no other but the main;°
His father's death, and our o'erhasty marriage.
King: Well, we shall sift him.

Enter Ambassadors Voltimand and Cornelius, with Polonius.

           Welcome, my good friends!
Say, Voltimand, what from our brother Norway?
60 *Voltimand:* Most fair return of greetings and desires.
Upon our first, he sent out to suppress
His nephew's levies; which to him appear'd
To be a preparation 'gainst the Polack;
But, better look'd into, he truly found
It was against your highness: whereat griev'd,

---

30 *in . . . bent:* To the utmost degree of our mental capacity.   56 *doubt:* Fear; *main:*
Chief point, principal concern.

That so his sickness, age and impotence
Was falsely borne in hand,° sends out arrests
On Fortinbras; which he, in brief, obeys;
Receives rebuke from Norway, and in fine°
70 Makes vow before his uncle never more
To give th' assay° of arms against your majesty.
Whereon old Norway, overcome with joy,
Gives him three score thousand crowns in annual fee,
And his commission to employ those soldiers,
So levied as before, against the Polack:
With an entreaty, herein further shown, *(giving a paper.)*
That it might please you to give quiet pass
Through your dominions for this enterprise,
On such regards of safety and allowance°
As therein are set down.
80 *King:*   It likes° us well;
And at our more consider'd° time we'll read,
Answer, and think upon this business.
Meantime we thank you for your well-took labour:
Go to your rest; at night we'll feast together:
Most welcome home!   *Exeunt Ambassadors.*
Polonius: This business is well ended.
My liege, and madam, to expostulate
What majesty should be, what duty is,
Why day is day, night night, and time is time,
Were nothing but to waste night, day and time.
90 Therefore, since brevity is the soul of wit,°
And tediousness the limbs and outward flourishes,°
I will be brief: your noble son is mad:
Mad call I it; for, to define true madness
What is 't but to be nothing else but mad?
But let that go.
Queen: More matter, with less art.
Polonius: Madam, I swear I use no art at all.
That he is mad, 'tis true: 'tis true 'tis pity;
And pity 'tis 'tis true: a foolish figure;°
But farewell it, for I will use no art.
100 Mad let us grant him, then: and now remains
That we find out the cause of this effect,
Or rather say, the cause of this defect,
For this effect defective comes by cause:

---

67 *borne in hand:* Deluded.   69 *in fine:* In the end.   71 *assay:* Assault, trial (of arms).   79 *safety and allowance:* Pledges of safety to the country and terms of permission for the troops to pass.   80 *likes:* Pleases.   81 *consider'd:* Suitable for deliberation. 90 *wit:* Sound sense or judgment.   91 *flourishes:* Ostentation, embellishments.   98 *figure:* Figure of speech.

Thus it remains, and the remainder thus.
Perpend.°
I have a daughter—have while she is mine—
Who, in her duty and obedience, mark,
Hath given me this: now gather, and surmise. *(Reads the letter.)* "To the
celestial and my soul's idol, the most
110 beautified Ophelia,"—
 That's an ill phrase, a vile phrase; "beautified" is a vile phrase: but
  you shall hear. Thus: *(Reads.)*
"In her excellent white bosom, these, & c."
Queen: Came this from Hamlet to her?
Polonius: Good madam, stay awhile; I will be faithful.   *(Reads.)*

    "Doubt thou the stars are fire;
       Doubt that the sun doth move;
     Doubt truth to be a liar;
        But never doubt I love.

120   "O dear Ophelia, I am ill at these numbers;° I have not art to
   reckon° my groans: but that I love thee best, O most best, believe it.
   Adieu.
          "Thine evermore, most dear lady, whilst this machine° is to him,
                                                              HAMLET."
This, in obedience, hath my daughter shown me,
And more above,° hath his solicitings,
As they fell out° by time, by means° and place,
All given to mine ear.
King: But how hath she
Receiv'd his love?
Polonius: What do you think of me?
130 *King:* As of a man faithful and honourable.
Polonius: I would fain prove so. But what might you think,
When I had seen this hot love on the wing—
As I perceiv'd it, I must tell you that,
Before my daughter told me—what might you,
Or my dear majesty your queen here, think,
If I had play'd the desk or table-book,°
Or given my heart a winking,° mute and dumb,
Or look'd upon this love with idle sight;
What might you think? No, I went round to work,
140 And my young mistress thus I did bespeak:°

---

105 *Perpend:* Consider.   120 *ill . . . numbers:* Unskilled at writing verses.   121 *reckon:*
Number metrically, scan.   123 *machine:* Bodily frame.   126 *more above:* Moreover.
127 *fell out:* Occurred; *means:* Opportunities (of access).   136 *play'd . . . table-book:* i.e.,
remained shut up, concealed this information.   137 *given . . . winking:* Given my heart
a signal to keep silent.   140 *bespeak:* Address.

"Lord Hamlet is a prince, out of thy star;°
This must not be": and then I prescripts gave her,
That she should lock herself from his resort,
Admit no messengers, receive no tokens.
Which done, she took the fruits of my advice;
And he, repelled—a short tale to make—
Fell into a sadness, then into a fast,
Thence to a watch,° thence into a weakness,
Thence to a lightness,° and, by this declension,°
150 Into the madness wherein now he raves,
And all we mourn for.
King: Do you think 'tis this?
Queen: It may be, very like.
Polonius: Hath there been such a time—I would fain know that—
That I have positively said "'Tis so,"
When it prov'd otherwise?
King: Not that I know.
Polonius (pointing to his head and shoulder): Take this from this, if
     this be otherwise:
If circumstances lead me, I will find
Where truth is hid, though it were hid indeed
Within the centre.°
160 *King:*   How may we try it further?
Polonius: You know, sometimes he walks four hours together
Here in the lobby.
Queen: So he does indeed.
Polonius: At such a time I'll loose my daughter to him:
Be you and I behind an arras° then;
Mark the encounter: if he love her not
And be not from his reason fall'n thereon,°
Let me be no assistant for a state,
But keep a farm and carters.
King: We will try it.

     Enter Hamlet reading on a book.

Queen: But, look, where sadly the poor wretch comes reading.
170 *Polonius:* Away, I do beseech you both, away:

          Exeunt King and Queen with Attendants.

I'll board° him presently. O, give me leave.
How does my good Lord Hamlet?

---

141 *out . . . star:* Above thee in position.   148 *watch:* State of sleeplessness.   149 *light-*
ness: Lightheadedness; *declension:* Decline, deterioration.   160 *centre:* Middle point of
the earth.   164 *arras:* Hanging, tapestry.   166 *thereon:* On that account.   171 *board:*
Accost.

Hamlet: Well, God-a-mercy.

Polonius: Do you know me, my lord?

Hamlet: Excellent well; you are a fishmonger.°

Polonius: Not I, my lord.

Hamlet: Then I would you were so honest a man.

Polonius: Honest, my lord!

Hamlet: Ay, sir; to be honest, as this world goes, is to be one man
180   picked out of ten thousand.

Polonius: That's very true, my lord.

Hamlet: For if the sun breed maggots in a dead dog, being a good
      kissing carrion,°—Have you a daughter?

Polonius: I have, my lord.

Hamlet: Let her not walk i' the sun:° conception° is a blessing: but as
      your daughter may conceive—Friend, look to 't.

Polonius (aside): How say you by° that? Still harping on my daughter:
      yet he knew me not at first; 'a said I was a fishmonger: 'a is far gone,
      far gone: and truly in my youth I suffered much extremity for love;
190   very near this. I'll speak to him again. What do you read, my lord?

Hamlet: Words, words, words.

Polonius: What is the matter,° my lord?

Hamlet: Between who?°

Polonius: I mean, the matter that you read, my lord.

Hamlet: Slanders, sir: for the satirical rogue says here that old men
      have grey beards, that their faces are wrinkled, their eyes purging°
      thick amber and plum-tree gum and that they have a plentiful
      lack of wit, together with most weak hams: all which, sir, though I
      most powerfully and potently believe, yet I hold it not honesty° to
200   have it thus set down, for yourself, sir, should be old as I am, if
      like a crab you could go backward.

Polonius (aside): Though this be madness, yet there is method in
      't.—Will you walk out of the air, my lord?

Hamlet: Into my grave.

Polonius: Indeed, that's out of the air. *(Aside.)* How pregnant
      sometimes his replies are! a happiness° that often madness hits on,
      which reason and sanity could not so prosperously° be delivered
      of. I will leave him, and suddenly contrive the means of meeting
      between him and my daughter.—My honourable lord, I will most
210   humbly take my leave of you.

Hamlet: You cannot, sir, take from me any thing that I will more
      willingly part withal: except my life, except my life, except my life.

---

175 *fishmonger:* An opprobrious expression meaning "bawd," "procurer."   183 *good kiss-*
ing carrion: i.e., a good piece of flesh for kissing (?).   185 *i' the sun:* In the sunshine of
princely favors; *conception:* Quibble on "understanding" and "pregnancy."   188 *by:*
Concerning.   192 *matter:* Substance.   193 *Between who:* Hamlet deliberately takes *mat-*
ter as meaning "basis of dispute"; modern usage demands *whom* instead of *who.*   196
purging: discharging.   199 *honesty:* Decency.   206 *happiness:* Felicity of expression.
207 *prosperously:* Successfully.

Enter Guildenstern and Rosencrantz.

Polonius: Fare you well, my lord.

Hamlet: These tedious old fools!

Polonius: You go to seek the Lord Hamlet; there he is.

Rosencrantz (to Polonius): God save you, sir!   *(Exit Polonius.)*

Guildenstern: My honoured lord!

Rosencrantz: My most dear lord!

Hamlet: My excellent good friends! How dost thou, Guildenstern? Ah,
220 Rosencrantz! Good lads, how do ye both?

Rosencrantz: As the indifferent° children of the earth.

Guildenstern: Happy, in that we are not over-happy;
On Fortune's cap we are not the very button.

Hamlet: Nor the soles of her shoe?

Rosencrantz: Neither, my lord.

Hamlet: Then you live about her waist, or in the middle of her favours?

Guildenstern: 'Faith, her privates° we.

Hamlet: In the secret parts of Fortune? O, most true; she is a
strumpet. What's the news?

230 *Rosencrantz:* None, my lord, but that the world's grown honest.

Hamlet: Then is doomsday near: but your news is not true. Let me
question more in particular: what have you, my good friends,
deserved at the hands of Fortune, that she sends you to prison
hither?

Guildenstern: Prison, my lord!

Hamlet: Denmark's a prison.

Rosencrantz: Then is the world one.

Hamlet: A goodly one; in which there are many confines,° wards and
dungeons, Denmark being one o' the worst.

240 *Rosencrantz:* We think not so, my lord.

Hamlet: Why, then, 'tis none to you; for there is nothing either good
or bad, but thinking makes it so: to me it is a prison.

Rosencrantz: Why then, your ambition makes it one; 'tis too narrow
for your mind.

Hamlet: O God, I could be bounded in a nutshell and count myself a
king of infinite space, were it not that I have bad dreams.

Guildenstern: Which dreams indeed are ambition, for the very
substance of the ambitious° is merely the shadow of a dream.

Hamlet: A dream itself is but a shadow.

250 *Rosencrantz:* Truly, and I hold ambition of so airy and light a quality
that it is but a shadow's shadow.

Hamlet: Then are our beggars bodies, and our monarchs and

---

221 *indifferent:* Ordinary.   227 *privates:* i.e., ordinary men (with sexual pun on *private
parts*).   238 *confines:* Places of confinement.   247–248 *very . . . ambitious:* That seemingly most substantial thing which the ambitious pursue.

outstretched heroes the beggars' shadows. Shall we to the court?
for, by my fay,° I cannot reason.°

Rosencrantz: ⎱
Guildenstern: ⎰ We'll wait upon° you.

Hamlet: No such matter: I will not sort° you with the rest of my
servants, for, to speak to you like an honest man, I am most
dreadfully attended.° But, in the beaten way of friendship,° what
make you at Elsinore?

260 *Rosencrantz:* To visit you, my lord: no other occasion.

Hamlet: Beggar that I am, I am ever poor in thanks; but I thank you:
and sure, dear friends, my thanks are too dear a° halfpenny. Were
you not sent for? Is it your own inclining? Is it a free visitation?
Come, come, deal justly with me: come, come; nay, speak.

Guildenstern: What should we say, my lord?

Hamlet: Why, any thing, but to the purpose. You were sent for; and
there is a kind of confession in your looks which your modesties
have not craft enough to colour: I know the good king and queen
have sent for you.

270 *Rosencrantz:* To what end, my lord?

Hamlet: That you must teach me. But let me conjure° you, by the
rights of our fellowship, by the consonancy of our youth,° by the
obligation of our ever-preserved love, and by what more dear a
better proposer° could charge you withal, be even and direct with
me, whether you were sent for, or no?

Rosencrantz (aside to Guildenstern): What say you?

Hamlet (aside): Nay, then, I have an eye of you.—If you love me, hold
not off.

Guildenstern: My lord, we were sent for.

280 *Hamlet:* I will tell you why; so shall my anticipation prevent your
discovery,° and your secrecy to the king and queen moult no
feather. I have of late—but wherefore I know not—lost all my
mirth, forgone all custom of exercises; and indeed it goes so
heavily with my disposition that this goodly frame, the earth,
seems to me a sterile promontory, this most excellent canopy, the
air, look you, this brave o'erhanging firmament, this majestical
roof fretted° with golden fire, why, it appeareth nothing to me but
a foul and pestilent congregation of vapours. What a piece of work
is a man! how noble in reason! how infinite in faculties!° in form
290   and moving how express° and admirable! in action how like an

---

254 *fay:* Faith; *reason:* Argue;   255 *wait upon:* Accompany.   256 *sort:* Class.
258 *dreadfully attended:* Poorly provided with servants; *in the . . . friendship:* As a matter
of course among friends.   262 *a:* i.e., at a.   271 *conjure:* Adjure, entreat.   272 *consonancy of our youth:* The fact that we are of the same age.   274 *better proposer:* One more
skillful in finding proposals.   281 *prevent your discovery:* Forestall your disclosure.   287 *fretted:* Adorned.   289 *faculties:* Capacity.   290 *express:* Well-framed (?),
exact (?).

angel! in apprehension° how like a god! the beauty of the world!
the paragon of animals! And yet, to me, what is this quintessence°
of dust? man delights not me: no, nor woman neither, though by
your smiling you seem to say so.

Rosencrantz: My lord, there was no such stuff in my thoughts.

Hamlet: Why did you laugh then, when I said "man delights not me"?

Rosencrantz: To think, my lord, if you delight not in man, what
lenten° entertainment the players shall receive from you: we coted°
them on the way; and hither are they coming, to offer you service.

300 *Hamlet:* He that plays the king shall be welcome; his majesty shall
have tribute of me; the adventurous knight shall use his foil and
target;° the lover shall not sigh gratis; the humorous man° shall
end his part in peace; the clown shall make those laugh whose
lungs are tickle o' the sere;° and the lady shall say her mind
freely, or the blank verse shall halt for 't.° What players are they?

Rosencrantz: Even those you were wont to take delight in, the
tragedians of the city.

Hamlet: How chances it they travel? their residence,° both in
reputation and profit, was better both ways.

310 *Rosencrantz:* I think their inhibition° comes by the means of the late
innovation.°

Hamlet: Do they hold the same estimation they did when I was in the
city? are they so followed?

Rosencrantz: No, indeed, are they not.

Hamlet: How comes it? do they grow rusty?

Rosencrantz: Nay, their endeavour keeps in the wonted pace: but there
is, sir, an aery° of children, little eyases,° that cry out on the top
of question,° and are most tyrannically° clapped for 't: these are
now the fashion, and so berattle° the common stages°—so they call

320 them—that many wearing rapiers° are afraid of goose-quills° and
dare scarce come thither.

---

291 *apprehension:* Understanding.   292 *quintessence:* The fifth essence of ancient philosophy, supposed to be the substance of the heavenly bodies and to be latent in all
things.   298 *lenten:* Meager; *coted:* Overtook and passed beyond.   302 *foil and target:*
Sword and shield; *humorous man:* Actor who takes the part of the humor characters.
304 *tickle o' the sere:* Easy on the trigger.   304–305 *the lady . . . for 't:* The lady (fond of
talking) shall have opportunity to talk, blank verse or no blank verse.   308 *residence:*
Remaining in one place.   310 *inhibition:* Formal prohibition (from acting plays in the
city or, possibly, at court).   311 *innovation:* The new fashion in satirical plays performed
by boy actors in the "private" theaters.   315–335 *How . . . load too:* The passage is the
famous one dealing with the War of the Theatres (1599–1602); namely, the rivalry between
the children's companies and the adult actors.   313 *aery:* Nest.   313 *eyases:* Young
hawks.   313–314 *cry . . . question:* Speak in a high key dominating conversation; clamor
forth the height of controversy; probably "excel" (cf. l. 471); perhaps intended to decry
leaders of the dramatic profession.   318 *tyrannically:* Outrageously.   319 *berattle:* Be-
rate; *common stages:* Public theaters.   320 *many wearing rapiers:* Many men of fashion,
who were afraid to patronize the common players for fear of being satirized by the poets
who wrote for the children; *goose-quills:* i.e., pens of satirists.

Hamlet: What, are they children? who maintains 'em? how are they
escoted?° Will they pursue the quality° no longer than they can
sing?° will they not say afterwards, if they should grow
themselves to common° players—as it is most like, if their means
are no better—their writers do them wrong, to make them exclaim
against their own succession?°

Rosencrantz: 'Faith, there has been much to do on both sides; and the
nation holds it no sin to tarre° them to controversy: there was, for
330   a while, no money bid for argument,° unless the poet and the
player went to cuffs° in the question.°

Hamlet: Is't possible?

Guildenstern: O, there has been much throwing about of brains.

Hamlet: Do the boys carry it away?°

Rosencrantz: Ay, that they do, my lord; Hercules and his load too.°

Hamlet: It is not very strange; for my uncle is king of Denmark, and
those that would make mows° at him while my father lived, give
twenty, forty, fifty, a hundred ducats° a-piece for his picture in
little.° 'Sblood, there is something in this more than natural, if
340   philosophy could find it out.

A flourish of trumpets within.

Guildenstern: There are the players.

Hamlet: Gentlemen, you are welcome to Elsinore. Your hands, come
then: the appurtenance of welcome is fashion and ceremony: let me
comply° with you in this garb,° lest my extent° to the players,
which, I tell you, must show fairly outwards, should more appear
like entertainment than yours. You are welcome: but my
uncle-father and aunt-mother are deceived.

Guildenstern: In what, my dear lord?

Hamlet: I am but mad north-north-west:° when the wind is southerly
350   I know a hawk from a handsaw.°

Enter Polonius.

Polonius: Well be with you, gentlemen!

---

323 *escoted:* Maintained; *quality:* Acting profession.   *323–324 no longer . . . sing:* i.e., until their voices change.   325 *common:* Regular, adult.   327 *succession:* future careers.
329 *tarre:* Set on (as dogs).   330 *argument:* Probably, plot for a play.   331 *went to cuffs:*
Came to blows; *question:* Controversy.   334 *carry it away:* Win the day.   335 *Hercules . . .*
load: Regarded as an allusion to the sign of the Globe Theatre, which was Hercules bearing the world on his shoulder.   337 *mows:* Grimaces.   338 *ducats:* Gold coins worth 9s.
4d.   339 *in little:* In miniature.   344 *comply:* Observe the formalities of courtesy; *garb:*
Manner; *extent:* Showing of kindness.   349 *I am . . . north-north-west:* I am only partly
mad, i.e., in only one point of the compass.   350 *handsaw:* A proposed reading of *hern-*
shaw would mean "heron"; *handsaw* may be an early corruption of *hernshaw.* Another view
regards *hawk* as the variant of *hack,* a tool of the pickax type, and *handsaw* as a saw operated by hand.

Hamlet: Hark you, Guildenstern; and you too: at each ear a hearer: that great baby you see there is not yet out of his swaddling-clouts.°

Rosencrantz: Happily he is the second time come to them; for they say an old man is twice a child.

Hamlet: I will prophesy he comes to tell me of the players; mark it.—You say right, sir: o' Monday morning;° 'twas then indeed.

Polonius: My lord, I have news to tell you.

360 *Hamlet:* My lord, I have news to tell you. When Roscius° was an actor in Rome,—

Polonius: The actors are come hither, my lord.

Hamlet: Buz, buz!°

Polonius: Upon my honour,—

Hamlet: Then came each actor on his ass,—

Polonius: The best actors in the world, either for tragedy, comedy, history, pastoral, pastoral-comical, historical-pastoral, tragical-historical, tragical-comical-historical-pastoral, scene individable,° or poem unlimited:° Seneca° cannot be too heavy,

370 nor Plautus° too light. For the law of writ and the liberty,° these are the only men.

Hamlet: O Jephthah, judge of Israel,° what a treasure hadst thou!

Polonius: What a treasure had he, my lord?

Hamlet: Why,
"One fair daughter, and no more,
  The which he loved passing well."

Polonius (aside): Still on my daughter.

Hamlet: Am I not i' the right, old Jephthah?

Polonius: If you call me Jephthah, my lord, I have a daughter that I

380 love passing° well.

Hamlet: Nay, that follows not.

Polonius: What follows, then, my lord?

Hamlet: Why,
        "As by lot, God wot,"
and then, you know,
        "It came to pass, as most like° it was,"—
the first row° of the pious chanson° will show you more; for look, where my abridgement comes.°

---

354 *swaddling-clouts:* Cloths in which to wrap a newborn baby.   358 *o' Monday morning:* Said to mislead Polonius.   360 *Roscius:* A famous Roman actor.   363 *Buz, buz:* An interjection used at Oxford to denote stale news.   369 *scene individable:* A play observing the unity of place; *poem unlimited:* A play disregarding the unities of time and place; *Seneca:* Writer of Latin tragedies, model of early Elizabethan writers of tragedy; *Plautus:* Writer of Latin comedy.   370 *law . . . liberty:* Pieces written according to rules and without rules, i.e., "classical" and "romantic" dramas.   372 *Jephthah . . . Israel:* Jephthah had to sacrifice his daughter; see Judges 11.   380 *Passing:* surpassingly.   386 *like:* Probable.   387 *row:* Stanza; *chanson:* Ballad.   388 *abridgement comes:* Opportunity comes for cutting short the conversation.

Enter the Players.

You are welcome, masters; welcome, all. I am glad to see thee well.
390   Welcome, good friends. O, old friend! why, thy face is valanced°
since I saw thee last: comest thou to beard me in Denmark? What,
my young lady and mistress! By'r lady, your ladyship is nearer to
heaven than when I saw you last, by the altitude of a chopine.°
Pray God, your voice, like a piece of uncurrent° gold, be not
cracked within the ring.° Masters, you are all welcome. We'll e'en
to 't like French falconers, fly at any thing we see: we'll have a
speech straight: come, give us a taste of your quality; come, a
passionate speech.
    First Player: What speech, my good lord?
400 *Hamlet:* I heard thee speak me a speech once, but it was never acted;
or, if it was, not above once; for the play, I remember, pleased not
the million; 'twas caviary to the general:° but it was—as I received
it, and others, whose judgements in such matters cried in the top
of° mine—an excellent play, well digested in the scenes, set down
with as much modesty as cunning.° I remember, one said there
were no sallets° in the lines to make the matter savoury, nor no
matter in the phrase that might indict° the author of affectation;
but called it an honest method, as wholesome as sweet, and by
very much more handsome than fine.° One speech in 't I chiefly
410   loved: 'twas Æneas' tale to Dido;° and thereabout of it especially,
where he speaks of Priam's slaughter: if it live in your memory,
begin at this line: let me see, let me see—
"The rugged Pyrrhus,° like th' Hyrcanian beast,°"—
'tis not so:—it begins with Pyrrhus—
"The rugged Pyrrhus, he whose sable arms,
Black as his purpose, did the night resemble
When he lay couched in the ominous horse,°
Hath now this dread and black complexion smear'd
With heraldry more dismal; head to foot
420 Now is he total gules;° horridly trick'd°

---

390 *valanced:* Fringed (with a beard).   393 *chopine:* Kind of shoe raised by the thickness
of the heel; worn in Italy, particularly at Venice.   394 *uncurrent:* Not passable as lawful
coinage.   395 *cracked within the ring:* In the center of coins were rings enclosing the
sovereign's head; if the coin was cracked within this ring, it was unfit for currency.
402 *caviary to the general:* Not relished by the multitude.   403–404 *cried in the top of:*
Spoke with greater authority than.   405 *cunning:* Skill.   406 *sallets:* Salads: here, spicy
improprieties.   407 *indict:* Convict.   408-409 *as wholesome . . . fine:* Its beauty was
not that of elaborate ornament, but that of order and proportion.   410 *AEneas' tale to
Dido:* The lines recited by the player are imitated from Marlowe and Nashe's *Dido Queen of
Carthage* (II. i. 214 ff.). They are written in such a way that the conventionality of the play
within a play is raised above that of ordinary drama.   413 *Pyrrhus:* A Greek hero in the
Trojan War; *Hyrcanian beast:* The tiger; see Virgil, *Aeneid*, IV. 266.   417 *ominous horse:*
Trojan horse.   420 *gules:* Red, a heraldic term; *trick'd:* Spotted, smeared.

With blood of fathers, mothers, daughters, sons,
Bak'd and impasted° with the parching streets,
That lend a tyrannous and a damned light
To their lord's murder: roasted in wrath and fire,
And thus o'er-sized° with coagulate gore,
With eyes like carbuncles, the hellish Pyrrhus
Old grandsire Priam seeks."
So, proceed you.
Polonius: 'Fore God, my lord, well spoken, with good accent and good
430   discretion.
First Player: "Anon he finds him
Striking too short at Greeks; his antique sword,
Rebellious to his arm, lies where it falls,
Repugnant° to command: unequal match'd,
Pyrrhus at Priam drives; in rage strikes wide;
But with the whiff and wind of his fell sword
Th' unnerved father falls. Then senseless Ilium,°
Seeming to feel this blow, with flaming top
Stoops to his base, and with a hideous crash
440 Takes prisoner Pyrrhus' ear: for, lo! his sword
Which was declining on the milky head
Of reverend Priam, seem'd i' th' air to stick:
So, as a painted tyrant,° Pyrrhus stood,
And like a neutral to his will and matter,°
Did nothing.
But, as we often see, against° some storm,
A silence in the heavens, the rack° stand still,
The bold winds speechless and the orb below
As hush as death, anon the dreadful thunder
450 Doth rend the region,° so, after Pyrrhus' pause,
Aroused vengeance sets him new a-work;
And never did the Cyclops' hammers fall
On Mars's armour forg'd for proof eterne°
With less remorse than Pyrrhus' bleeding sword
Now falls on Priam.
Out, out, thou strumpet, Fortune! All you gods,
In general synod,° take away her power;
Break all the spokes and fellies° from her wheel,
And bowl the round nave° down the hill of heaven,
460 As low as to the fiends!"
Polonius: This is too long.

---

422 *impasted:* Made into a paste.   425 *o'er-sized:* Covered as with size or glue.   434 *Re-*
pugnant: Disobedient.   437 *Then senseless Ilium:* Insensate Troy.   443 *painted tyrant:*
Tyrant in a picture.   444 *matter:* Task.   446 *against:* Before.   447 *rack:* Mass of clouds.
450 *region:* Assembly.   453 *proof eterne:* External resistance to assault.   457 *synod:* Assembly.   458 *fellies:* Pieces of wood forming the rim of a wheel.   459 *nave:* Hub.

Hamlet: It shall to the barber's, with your beard. Prithee, say on: he's for a jig° or a tale of bawdry,° or he sleeps: say on: come to Hecuba.°

First Player: "But who, ah woe! had seen the mobled° queen—"

Hamlet: "The mobled queen?"

Polonius: That's good; "mobled queen" is good.

First Player: "Run barefoot up and down, threat'ning the flames
With bisson rheum;° a clout° upon that head

470   Where late the diadem stood, and for a robe,
About her lank and all o'er-teemed° loins,
A blanket, in the alarm of fear caught up;
Who this had seen, with tongue in venom steep'd,
'Gainst Fortune's state would treason have pronounc'd:°
But if the gods themselves did see her then
When she saw Pyrrhus make malicious sport
In mincing with his sword her husband's limbs,
The instant burst of clamour that she made,
Unless things mortal move them not at all,

480   Would have made milch° the burning eyes of heaven,
And passion in the gods."

Polonius: Look, whe'r he has not turned° his colour and has tears in 's eyes. Prithee, no more.

Hamlet: 'Tis well; I'll have thee speak out the rest soon. Good my lord, will you see the players well bestowed? Do you hear, let them be well used; for they are the abstract° and brief chronicles of the time: after your death you were better have a bad epitaph than their ill report while you live.

Polonius: My lord, I will use them according to their desert.

490 *Hamlet:* God's bodykins,° man, much better: use every man after his desert, and who shall 'scape whipping? Use them after your own honour and dignity: the less they deserve, the more merit is in your bounty. Take them in.

Polonius: Come, sirs.

Hamlet: Follow him, friends: we'll hear a play tomorrow. *(Aside to First Player.)* Dost thou hear me, old friend; can you play the Murder of Gonzago?

First Player: Ay, my lord.

Hamlet: We'll ha 't to-morrow night. You could, for a need, study a

500   speech of some dozen or sixteen lines,° which I would set down and insert in 't, could you not?

---

463 *jig:* Comic performance given at the end or in an interval of a play; *bawdry:* Indecency.   464 *Hecuba:* Wife of Priam, king of Troy.   465 *mobled:* Muffled.   469 *bisson rheum:* Blinding tears; *clout:* Piece of cloth.   471 *o'er-teemed:* Worn out with bearing children.   474 *pronounc'd:* Proclaimed.   480 *milch:* Moist with tears.   482 *turned:* Changed.   486 *abstract:* Summary account.   490 *bodykins:* Diminutive form of the oath "by God's body."   500 *dozen or sixteen lines:* Critics have amused themselves by trying to locate Hamlet's lines. Lucianus's speech III. ii. 226–231 is the best guess.

First Player: Ay, my lord.

Hamlet: Very well. Follow that lord; and look you mock him not.—My good friends, I'll leave you till night: you are welcome to Elsinore.

Exeunt Polonius and Players.

Rosencrantz: Good my lord!   (*Exeunt Rosencrantz and Guildenstern.*)

Hamlet: Ay, so, God bye to you.—Now I am alone.

O, what a rogue and peasant° slave am I!

Is it not monstrous that this player here,

But in a fiction, in a dream of passion,

510 Could force his soul so to his own conceit

That from her working all his visage wann'd,°

Tears in his eyes, distraction in 's aspect,

A broken voice, and his whole function suiting

With forms to his conceit?° and all for nothing!

For Hecuba!

What's Hecuba to him, or he to Hecuba,

That he should weep for her? What would he do,

Had he the motive and the cue for passion

That I have? He would drown the stage with tears

520 And cleave the general ear with horrid speech,

Make mad the guilty and appal the free,

Confound the ignorant, and amaze indeed

The very faculties of eyes and ears.

Yet I,

A dull and muddy-mettled° rascal, peak,°

Like John-a-dreams,° unpregnant of° my cause,

And can say nothing; no, not for a king.

Upon whose property° and most dear life

A damn'd defeat was made. Am I a coward?

530 Who calls me villain? breaks my pate across?

Plucks off my beard, and blows it in my face?

Tweaks me by the nose? gives me the lie i' th' throat,

As deep as to the lungs? who does me this?

Ha!

'Swounds, I should take it: for it cannot be

But I am pigeon-liver'd° and lack gall

To make oppression bitter, or ere this

---

507 *peasant:* Base.   511 *wann'd:* Grew pale.   513–514 *his whole . . . conceit:* His whole being responded with forms to suit his thought.   525 *muddy-mettled:* Dull-spirited; *peak:* Mope, pine.   526 *John-a-dreams:* An expression occurring elsewhere in Elizabethan literature to indicate a dreamer; *unpregnant of:* Not quickened by.   528 *property:* Proprietorship (of crown and life).   536 *pigeon-liver'd:* The pigeon was supposed to secrete no gall; if Hamlet, so he says, had had gall, he would have felt the bitterness of oppression, and avenged it.

I should have fatted all the region kites°
With this slave's offal: bloody, bawdy villain!
540 Remorseless, treacherous, lecherous, kindless° villain!
O, vengeance!
Why, what an ass am I! This is most brave,
That I, the son of a dear father murder'd,
Prompted to my revenge by heaven and hell,
Must, like a whore, unpack my heart with words,
And fall a-cursing, like a very drab,°
A stallion!°
Fie upon 't! foh! About,° my brains! Hum, I have heard
That guilty creatures sitting at a play
550 Have by the very cunning of the scene
Been struck so to the soul that presently
They have proclaim'd their malefactions;
For murder, though it have no tongue, will speak
With most miraculous organ. I'll have these players
Play something like the murder of my father
Before mine uncle: I'll observe his looks:
I'll tent° him to the quick: if 'a do blench,°
I know my course. The spirit that I have seen
May be the devil:° and the devil hath power
560 T' assume a pleasing shape; yea, and perhaps
Out of my weakness and my melancholy,
As he is very potent with such spirits,°
Abuses me to damn me: I'll have grounds
More relative° than this:° the play's the thing
Wherein I'll catch the conscience of the king.   *Exit.*

Act III

Scene I. A room in the castle.

Enter King, Queen, Polonius, Ophelia, Rosencrantz, Guildenstern, Lords.

King: And can you, by no drift of conference,°
Get from him why he puts on this confusion,
Grating so harshly all his days of quiet
With turbulent and dangerous lunacy?
Rosencrantz: He does confess he feels himself distracted;
But from what cause 'a will by no means speak.

---

538 *region kites:* Kites of the air.   540 *kindless:* Unnatural.   546 *drab:* Prostitute.   547
stallion: Prostitute (male or female).   548 *About:* About it, or turn thou right
about.   557 *tent:* Probe; *blench:* Quail, flinch.   559 *May be the devil:* Hamlet's suspicion
is properly grounded in the belief of the time.   562 *spirits:* Humors.   564 *relative:*
Closely-related, definite; *this:* i.e., the ghost's story.   ACT III. SCENE I.   1 *drift of confer-*
ence: Device of conversation.

Guildenstern: Nor do we find him forward° to be sounded,
But, with a crafty madness, keeps aloof,
When we would bring him on to some confession
Of his true state.
10 *Queen:*　　　　　Did he receive you well?
Rosencrantz: Most like a gentleman.
Guildenstern: But with much forcing of his disposition.°
Rosencrantz: Niggard of question;° but, of our demands,
Most free in his reply.
Queen:　　　　　Did you assay° him
To any pastime?
Rosencrantz: Madam, it so fell out, that certain players
We o'er-raught° on the way: of these we told him;
And there did seem in him a kind of joy
To hear of it: they are here about the court,
20 And, as I think, they have already order
This night to play before him.
Polonius:　　　　　'Tis most true:
And he beseech'd me to entreat your majesties
To hear and see the matter.
King: With all my heart; and it doth much content me
To hear him so inclin'd.
Good gentlemen, give him a further edge,°
And drive his purpose into these delights.
Rosencrantz: We shall, my lord.　　　(*Exeunt Rosencrantz and Guildenstern.*)
King:　　　　　Sweet Gertrude, leave us too;
For we have closely° sent for Hamlet hither,
30 That he, as 'twere by accident, may here
Affront° Ophelia:
Her father and myself, lawful espials,°
Will so bestow ourselves that, seeing, unseen,
We may of their encounter frankly judge,
And gather by him, as he is behav'd,
If 't be th' affliction of his love or no
That thus he suffers for.
Queen:　　　　　I shall obey you.
And for your part, Ophelia, I do wish
That your good beauties be the happy cause
40 Of Hamlet's wildness:° so shall I hope your virtues
Will bring him to his wonted way again,
To both your honours.
Ophelia:　　　　　Madam, I wish it may.　　　(*Exit Queen.*)

---

7 *forward:* Willing.　　12 *forcing of his disposition:* i.e., against his will.　　13 *Niggard of question:* Sparing of conversation.　　14 *assay:* Try to win.　　17 *o'er-raught:* Overtook. 26 *edge:* Incitement.　　29 *closely:* Secretly.　　31 *Affront:* Confront.　　32 *lawful espials:* Legitimate spies.　　40 *wildness:* Madness.

Polonius: Ophelia, walk you here. Gracious,° so please you,
We will bestow ourselves. *(To Ophelia.)* Read on this book;
That show of such an exercise° may colour°
Your loneliness. We are oft to blame in this,—
'Tis too much prov'd—that with devotion's visage
And pious action we do sugar o'er
The devil himself.
King: *(aside)* O, 'tis too true!
50 How smart a lash that speech doth give my conscience!
The harlot's cheek, beautied with plast'ring art,
Is not more ugly to° the thing° that helps it
Than is my deed to my most painted word:
O heavy burthen!
Polonius: I hear him coming: let's withdraw, my lord.

(Exeunt King and Polonius.)

    Enter Hamlet.

Hamlet: To be, or not to be: that is the question:
Whether 'tis nobler in the mind to suffer
The slings and arrows of outrageous fortune,
Or to take arms against a sea° of troubles,
60 And by opposing end them? To die: to sleep;
No more; and by a sleep to say we end
The heart-ache and the thousand natural shocks
That flesh is heir to, 'tis a consummation
Devoutly to be wish'd. To die, to sleep;
To sleep: perchance to dream: ay, there's the rub;
For in that sleep of death what dreams may come
When we have shuffled° off this mortal coil,°
Must give us pause: there's the respect°
That makes calamity of so long life;°
70 For who would bear the whips and scorns of time,°
Th' oppressor's wrong, the proud man's contumely,
The pangs of despis'd° love, the law's delay,
The insolence of office° and the spurns°
That patient merit of th' unworthy takes,
When he himself might his quietus° make

---

43 *Gracious:* Your grace (addressed to the king).   45 *exercise:* Act of devotion (the book she reads is one of devotion); *colour:* Give a plausible appearance to.   52 *to:* Compared to; *thing:* i.e., the cosmetic.   59 *sea:* The mixed metaphor of this speech has often been commented on; a later emendation *siege* has sometimes been spoken on the stage.   67 *shuffled:* Sloughed, cast; *coil:* Usually means "turmoil"; here, possibly "body" (conceived of as wound about the soul like rope); *clay, soil, veil,* have been suggested as emendations.   68 *respect:* Consideration.   69 *of . . . life:* So long-lived.   70 *time:* The world.   72 *despis'd:* Rejected.   73 *office:* Office-holders; *spurns:* Insults.   75 *quietus:* Acquittance; here, death.

With a bare bodkin?° who would fardels° bear,
To grunt and sweat under a weary life,
But that the dread of something after death,
The undiscover'd country from whose bourn°
80 No traveller returns, puzzles the will
And makes us rather bear those ills we have
Than fly to others that we know not of?
Thus conscience° does make cowards of us all;
And thus the native hue° of resolution
Is sicklied o'er° with the pale cast° of thought,
And enterprises of great pitch° and moment°
With this regard° their currents° turn awry,
And lose the name of action—Soft you now!
The fair Ophelia! Nymph, in thy orisons°
Be all my sins rememb'red.
90 *Ophelia:*   Good my lord,
How does your honour for this many a day?
Hamlet: I humbly thank you; well, well, well.
Ophelia: My lord, I have remembrances of yours,
That I have longed long to re-deliver;
I pray you, now receive them.
Hamlet: No, not I;
I never gave you aught.
Ophelia: My honour'd lord, you know right well you did;
And, with them, words of so sweet breath compos'd
As made the things more rich: their perfume lost,
100 Take these again; for to the noble mind
Rich gifts wax poor when givers prove unkind.
There, my lord.
Hamlet: Ha, ha! are you honest?
Ophelia: My lord?
Hamlet: Are you fair?
Ophelia: What means your lordship?
Hamlet: That if you be honest and fair, your honesty° should admit no
    discourse to° your beauty.
Ophelia: Could beauty, my lord, have better commerce° than with
110   honesty?

---

76 *bare bodkin:* Mere dagger; *bare* is sometimes understood as "unsheathed"; *fardels:* Burdens.   79 *bourn:* Boundary.   83 *conscience:* Probably, inhibition by the faculty of reason restraining the will from doing wrong.   84 *native hue:* Natural color; metaphor derived from the color of the face.   85 *sicklied o'er:* Given a sickly tinge; *cast:* Shade of color.   86 *pitch:* Height (as of a falcon's flight); *moment:* Importance.   87 *regard:* Respect, consideration; *currents:* Courses.   89 *orisons:* Prayers.   103–8 *are you . . . beauty: Honest* meaning "truthful" (l. 103) and "chaste" (l. 107), and *fair* meaning "just, honorable" (l. 105) and "beautiful" (l. 107) are not mere quibbles; the speech has the irony of a *double entendre.*   107 *your honesty:* Your chastity.   108 *discourse to:* Familiar intercourse with.   109 *commerce:* Intercourse.

Hamlet: Ay, truly; for the power of beauty will sooner transform honesty from what it is to a bawd than the force of honesty can translate beauty into his likeness: this was sometime a paradox, but now the time° gives it proof. I did love you once.

Ophelia: Indeed, my lord, you made me believe so.

Hamlet: You should not have believed me; for virtue cannot so inoculate° our old stock but we shall relish of it:° I loved you not.

Ophelia: I was the more deceived.

Hamlet: Get thee to a nunnery: why wouldst thou be a breeder of
120   sinners? I am myself indifferent honest;° but yet I could accuse me of such things that it were better my mother had not borne me: I am very proud, revengeful, ambitious, with more offences at my beck° than I have thoughts to put them in, imagination to give them shape, or time to act them in. What should such fellows as I do crawling between earth and heaven? We are arrant knaves, all; believe none of us. Go thy ways to a nunnery. Where's your father?

Ophelia: At home, my lord.

Hamlet: Let the doors be shut upon him, that he may play the fool no where but in 's own house. Farewell.

130 *Ophelia:* O, help him, you sweet heavens!

Hamlet: If thou dost marry, I'll give thee this plague for thy dowry: be thou as chaste as ice, as pure as snow, thou shalt not escape calumny. Get thee to a nunnery, go; farewell. Or, if thou wilt needs marry, marry a fool; for wise men know well enough what monsters° you make of them. To a nunnery, go, and quickly too. Farewell.

Ophelia: O heavenly powers, restore him!

Hamlet: I have heard of your° paintings too, well enough; God hath given you one face, and you make yourselves another: you jig,°
140   you amble, and you lisp; you nick-name God's creatures, and make your wantonness your ignorance.° Go to, I'll no more on 't; it hath made me mad. I say, we will have no moe marriage: those that are married already, all but one,° shall live; the rest shall keep as they are. To a nunnery, go.

Exit.

Ophelia: O, what a noble mind is here o'er-thrown!
The courtier's, soldier's, scholar's, eye, tongue, sword;

---

114 *the time:* The present age.   117 *inoculate:* Graft (metaphorical); *but . . . it:* i.e., That we do not still have about us a taste of the old stock; i.e., retain our sinfulness.   120 *indifferent honest:* Moderately virtuous.   123 *beck:* Command.   135 *monsters:* An allusion to the horns of a cuckold.   138 *your:* Indefinite use.   139 *jig:* Move with jerky motion; probably allusion to the *jig,* or song and dance, of the current stage.   140–141 *make . . . ignorance:* i.e., excuse your wantonness on the ground of your ignorance.   143 *one:* i.e., The king.

that will themselves laugh, to set on some quantity of barren°
spectators to laugh too; though, in the mean time, some necessary
question of the play be then to be considered: that's villanous, and
shows a most pitiful ambition in the fool that uses it. Go, make
you ready.

Exeunt Players.
Enter Polonius, Guildenstern, and Rosencrantz.

How now, my lord! will the king hear this piece of work?
Polonius: And the queen too, and that presently.
40 *Hamlet:* Bid the players make haste.   *(Exit Polonius.)*
Will you two help to hasten them?
Rosencrantz: ⎫
            ⎬ We will, my lord.
Guildenstern: ⎭   *Exeunt they two.*
Hamlet: What ho! Horatio!

Enter Horatio.

Horatio: Here, sweet lord, at your service.
Hamlet: Horatio, thou art e'en as just° a man
As e'er my conversation cop'd withal.
Horatio: O, my dear lord,—
Hamlet: Nay, do not think I flatter;
For what advancement may I hope from thee
50 That no revenue hast but thy good spirits,
To feed and clothe thee? Why should the poor be flatter'd?
No, let the candied tongue lick absurd pomp,
And crook the pregnant° hinges of the knee
Where thrift° may follow fawning. Dost thou hear?
Since my dear soul was mistress of her choice
And could of men distinguish her election,
S' hath seal'd thee for herself; for thou hast been
As one, in suff'ring all, that suffers nothing,
A man that fortune's buffets and rewards
60 Hast ta'en with equal thanks: and blest are those
Whose blood and judgment are so well commeddled,
That they are not a pipe for fortune's finger
To sound what stop° she please. Give me that man
That is not passion's slave, and I will wear him
In my heart's core, ay, in my heart of heart,
As I do thee.—Something too much of this.—
There is a play to-night before the king;
One scene of it comes near the circumstance

---

33 *barren:* i.e., of wit.   47 *just:* Honest, honorable.   53 *pregnant:* Pliant.   54 *thrift:*
profit.   63 *stop:* Hole in a wind instrument for controlling the sound.

Which I have told thee of my father's death:
70 I prithee, when thou seest that act afoot,
Even with the very comment of thy soul°
Observe my uncle: if his occulted° guilt
Do not itself unkennel in one speech,
It is a damned° ghost that we have seen,
And my imaginations are as foul
As Vulcan's stithy.° Give him heedful note;
For I mine eyes will rivet to his face,
And after we will both our judgements join
In censure of his seeming.°
80 **Horatio:**   Well, my lord:
If 'a steal aught the whilst this play is playing,
And 'scape detecting, I will pay the theft.

*Enter trumpets and kettledrums, King, Queen, Polonius, Ophelia, Rosencrantz,
Guildenstern, and others.*

Hamlet: They are coming to the play; I must be idle:° Get you a place.
King: How fares our cousin Hamlet?
Hamlet: Excellent, i' faith; of the chameleon's dish:° I eat the air,
   promise-crammed: you cannot feed capons so.
King: I have nothing with° this answer, Hamlet; these words are not
   mine.°
Hamlet: No, nor mine now. *(To Polonius.)* My lord, you played once i'
90   the university, you say?
Polonius: That did I, my lord; and was accounted a good actor.
Hamlet: What did you enact?
Polonius: I did enact Julius Caesar: I was killed i' the Capitol; Brutus
   killed me.
Hamlet: It was a brute part of him to kill so capital a calf there. Be
   the players ready?
Rosencrantz: Ay, my lord; they stay upon your patience.
Queen: Come hither, my dear Hamlet, sit by me.
Hamlet: No, good mother, here's metal more attractive.
100 **Polonius (to the king):** O, ho! do you mark that?
Hamlet: Lady, shall I lie in your lap?

(Lying down at Ophelia's feet.)

---

71 *very . . . soul:* Inward and sagacious criticism.   72 *occulted:* Hidden.   74 *damned:*
In league with Satan.   76 *stithy:* Smithy, place of *stiths* (anvils).   79 *censure . . .
seeming:* Judgment of his appearance or behavior.   83 *idle:* Crazy, or not attending to
anything serious.   85 *chameleon's dish:* Chameleons were supposed to feed on air. (Hamlet deliberately misinterprets the king's "fares" as "feeds.")   87 *have . . . with:* Make
nothing of.   87–88 *are not mine:* Do not respond to what I asked.

Ophelia: No, my lord.
Hamlet: I mean, my head upon your lap?
Ophelia: Ay, my lord.
Hamlet: Do you think I meant country° matters?
Ophelia: I think nothing, my lord.
Hamlet: That's a fair thought to lie between maids' legs.
Ophelia: What is, my lord?
Hamlet: Nothing.
110 *Ophelia:* You are merry, my lord.
Hamlet: Who, I?
Ophelia: Ay, my lord.
Hamlet: O God, your only° jig-maker.° What should a man do but be
merry? for, look you, how cheerfully my mother looks, and my
father died within's two hours.
Ophelia: Nay, 'tis twice two months, my lord.
Hamlet: So long? Nay then, let the devil wear black, for I'll have a suit
of sables.° O heavens! die two months ago, and not forgotten yet?
Then there's hope a great man's memory may outlive his life half
120 a year: but, by 'r lady, 'a must build churches, then; or else shall 'a
suffer not thinking on,° with the hobbyhorse, whose epitaph is
"For, O, for, O, the hobbyhorse is forgot."°

The trumpets sound. Dumb show follows.

*Enter a King and a Queen very lovingly; the Queen embracing him, and he her. She
kneels, and makes show of protestation unto him. He takes her up, and declines his
head upon her neck: he lies him down upon a bank of flowers: she, seeing him asleep,
leaves him. Anon comes in another man, takes off his crown, kisses it, pours poison
in the sleeper's ears, and leaves him. The Queen returns; finds the King dead, makes
passionate action. The Poisoner, with some three or four come in again, seem to
condole with her. The dead body is carried away. The Poisoner wooes the Queen with
gifts: she seems harsh awhile, but in the end accepts love. (Exeunt.)*

Ophelia: What means this, my lord?
Hamlet: Marry, this is miching mallecho;° it means mischief.
Ophelia: Belike this show imports the argument of the play.

Enter Prologue.

Hamlet: We shall know by this fellow: the players cannot keep
counsel; they'll tell all.

---

105 *country:* With a bawdy pun.   113 *your only:* Only your; *jig-maker:* Composer of jigs
(song and dance).   117–118 *suit of sables:* Garments trimmed with the fur of the sable,
with a quibble on *sable* meaning "black."   121 *suffer . . . on:* Undergo oblivion.   122
"For . . . forgot:" Verse of a song occurring also in *Love's Labour's Lost,* III. i. 30. The hobbyhorse was a character in the Morris Dance.   124 *miching mallecho:* Sneaking mischief.

Ophelia: Will 'a tell us what this show meant?
Hamlet: Ay, or any show that you'll show him: be not you ashamed to
130   show, he'll not shame to tell you what it means.
Ophelia: You are naught, you are naught:° I'll mark the play.
Prologue: For us, and for our tragedy,
Here stooping° to your clemency,
We beg your hearing patiently.   *(Exit.)*
Hamlet: Is this a prologue, or the posy° of a ring?
Ophelia: 'Tis brief, my lord.
Hamlet: As woman's love.

Enter two Players as King and Queen.

Player King: Full thirty times hath Phoebus' cart gone round
Neptune's salt wash° and Tellus'° orbed ground,
140   And thirty dozen moons with borrowed° sheen
About the world have times twelve thirties been,
Since love our hearts and Hymen° did our hands
Unite commutual° in most sacred bands.
Player Queen: So many journeys may the sun and moon
Make us again count o'er ere love be done!
But, woe is me, you are so sick of late,
So far from cheer and from your former state,
That I distrust° you. Yet, though I distrust,
Discomfort you, my lord, it nothing must:
150   For women's fear and love holds quantity;°
In neither aught, or in extremity.
Now, what my love is, proof hath made you know;
And as my love is siz'd, my fear is so:
Where love is great, the littlest doubts are fear;
Where little fears grow great, great love grows there.
Player King: 'Faith, I must leave thee, love, and shortly too;
My operant° powers their functions leave° to do:
And thou shalt live in this fair world behind,
Honour'd, belov'd; and haply one as kind
160   For husband shalt thou—
Player Queen: O, confound the rest!
Such love must needs be treason in my breast:
In second husband let me be accurst!
None wed the second but who kill'd the first.
Hamlet (aside): Wormwood, wormwood.

---

131 *naught:* Indecent.   133 *stooping:* Bowing.   135 *posy:* Motto.   139 *salt wash:* The
sea; *Tellus:* Goddess of the earth (*orbed ground*).   140 *borrowed:* i.e., reflected.   142 *Hy-*
men: God of matrimony.   143 *commutual:* Mutually.   148 *distrust:* Am anxious about.
150 *holds quantity:* Keeps proportion between.   157 *operant:* Active; *leave:* Cease.

Player Queen: The instances that second marriage move
Are base respects of thrift, but none of love:
A second time I kill my husband dead,
When second husband kisses me in bed.

170 *Player King:* I do believe you think what now you speak;
But what we do determine oft we break.
Purpose is but the slave to memory,
Of violent birth, but poor validity:
Which now, like fruit unripe, sticks on the tree;
But fall, unshaken, when they mellow be.
Most necessary 'tis that we forget
To pay ourselves what to ourselves is debt:
What to ourselves in passion we propose,
The passion ending, doth the purpose lose.

180 The violence of either grief or joy
Their own enactures° with themselves destroy:
Where joy most revels, grief doth most lament;
Grief joys, joy grieves, on slender accident.
This world is not for aye,° nor 'tis not strange
That even our loves should with our fortunes change;
For 'tis a question left us yet to prove,
Whether love lead fortune, or else fortune love.
The great man down, you mark his favourite flies;
The poor advanc'd makes friends of enemies.

190 And hitherto doth love on fortune tend;
For who° not needs shall never lack a friend,
And who in want a hollow friend doth try,
Directly seasons° him his enemy.
But, orderly to end where I begun,
Our wills and fates do so contrary run
That our devices still are overthrown;
Our thoughts are ours, their ends° none of our own:
So think thou wilt no second husband wed;
But die thy thoughts when thy first lord is dead.

200 *Player Queen:* Nor earth to me give food, nor heaven light!
Sport and repose lock from me day and night!
To desperation turn my trust and hope!
An anchor's° cheer° in prison be my scope!
Each opposite° that blanks° the face of joy
Meet what I would have well and it destroy!
Both here and hence pursue me lasting strife,
If, once a widow, ever I be wife!

---

181 *enactures:* Fulfillments.   184 *aye:* Ever.   191 *who:* Whoever.   193 *seasons:* Matures,
ripens.   197 *ends:* Results.   203 *An anchor's:* An anchorite's; *cheer:* Fare; sometimes
printed as *chair.*   204 *opposite:* Adverse thing; *blanks:* Causes to *blanch* or grow pale.

Hamlet: If she should break it now!
Player King: 'Tis deeply sworn. Sweet, leave me here awhile;
210 My spirits grow dull, and fain I would beguile
The tedious day with sleep.   *(Sleeps.)*
Player Queen: Sleep rock thy brain.
And never come mischance between us twain!   *Exit.*
Hamlet: Madam, how like you this play?
Queen: The lady doth protest too much, methinks.
Hamlet: O, but she'll keep her word.
King: Have you heard the argument? Is there no offence in 't?
Hamlet: No, no, they do but jest, poison in jest; no offence i' the world.
King: What do you call the play?
220 *Hamlet:* The Mouse-trap. Marry, how? Tropically.° This play is the
image of a murder done in Vienna: Gonzago° is the duke's name;
his wife, Baptista: you shall see anon; 't is a knavish piece of
work: but what o' that? your majesty and we that have free souls,
it touches us not: let the galled jade° winch,° our withers° are
unwrung.°

Enter Lucianus.

This is one Lucianus, nephew to the king.
Ophelia: You are as good as a chorus,° my lord.
Hamlet: I could interpret between you and your love, if I could see
the puppets dallying.°
230 *Ophelia:* You are keen, my lord, you are keen.
Hamlet: It would cost you a groaning to take off my edge.
Ophelia: Still better, and worse.°
Hamlet: So you mistake° your husbands. Begin, murderer; pox,° leave
thy damnable faces, and begin. Come: the croaking raven doth bellow
for revenge.
Lucianus: Thoughts black, hands apt, drugs fit, and time agreeing;
Confederate° season, else no creature seeing;
Thou mixture rank, of midnight weeds collected,
With Hecate's° ban° thrice blasted, thrice infected,

---

220 *Tropically:* Figuratively, *trapically* suggests a pun on *trap* in *Mouse-trap* (1. 211).   221
Gonzago: In 1538 Luigi Gonzago murdered the Duke of Urbano by pouring poisoned lotion
in his ears.   224 *galled jade:* Horse whose hide is rubbed by saddle or harness; *winch:*
Wince; *withers:* The part between the horse's shoulder blades.   225 *unwrung:* Not wrung
or twisted.   227 *chorus:* In many Elizabethan plays the action was explained by an actor
known as the "chorus"; at a puppet show the actor who explained the action was known
as an "interpreter," as indicated by the lines following.   229 *dallying:* With sexual suggestion, continued in *keen* (sexually aroused), *groaning* (i.e., in pregnancy), and *edge* (i.e.,
sexual desire or impetuosity).   232 *Still . . . worse:* More keen, less decorous.   233
mistake: Err in taking; *pox:* An imprecation.   237 *Confederate:* Conspiring (to assist the
murderer).   239 *Hecate:* The goddess of witchcraft; *ban:* Curse.

240 Thy natural magic and dire property,
On wholesome life usurp immediately.

Pours the poison into the sleeper's ears.

Hamlet: 'A poisons him i' the garden for his estate. His name's
Gonzago: the story is extant, and written in very choice Italian: you
shall see anon how the murderer gets the love of Gonzago's wife.
Ophelia: The king rises.
Hamlet: What, frighted with false fire!°
Queen: How fares my lord?
Polonius: Give o'er the play.
King: Give me some light: away!
250 *Polonius:* Lights, lights, lights!   *Exeunt all but Hamlet and Horatio.*
Hamlet: Why, let the strucken deer go weep,
   The hart ungalled play;
  For some must watch, while some must sleep:
   Thus runs the world away.°

Would not this,° sir, and a forest of feathers°—if the rest of my
fortunes turn Turk with° me—with two Provincial roses° on
my razed° shoes, get me a fellowship in a cry° of players,° sir?
Horatio: Half a share.°
Hamlet: A whole one, I.
260 For thou dost know, O Damon dear,
This realm dismantled° was
Of Jove himself; and now reigns here
  A very, very°—pajock.°
Horatio: You might have rhymed.
Hamlet: O good Horatio, I'll take the ghost's word for a thousand
pound.
Didst perceive?
Horatio: Very well, my lord.
Hamlet: Upon the talk of the poisoning?
270 *Horatio:* I did very well note him.
Hamlet: Ah, ha! Come, some music! come, the recorders!°

---

246 *false fire:* Fireworks, or a blank discharge. 251–254 *Why . . . away:* Probably from
an old ballad, with allusion to the popular belief that a wounded deer retires to weep and
die. Cf. *As You Like It,* II, i. 66. 255 *this:* i.e., the play; *feathers:* Allusion to the plumes
which Elizabethan actors were fond of wearing. 256 *turn Turk with:* Go back on; *two
Provincial roses:* Rosettes of ribbon like the roses of Provins near Paris, or else the roses of
Provence; *razed:* Cut, slashed (by way of ornament). 257 *fellowship . . . players:* Part-
nership in a theatrical company; *cry:* Pack (as of hounds). 258 *Half a share:* Allusion to
the custom in dramatic companies of dividing the ownership into a number of shares
among the householders. 260–263 *For . . . very:* Probably from an old ballad having to
do with Damon and Pythias. 261 *dismantled:* Stripped, divested. 263 *pajock:* Peacock
(a bird with a bad reputation). Possibly the word was *patchock,* diminutive of *patch,* clown.
271 *recorders:* Wind instruments of the flute kind.

For if the king like not the comedy,
Why then, belike, he likes it not, perdy.°
Come, some music!

Enter Rosencrantz and Guildenstern.

Guildenstern: Good my lord, vouchsafe me a word with you.
Hamlet: Sir, a whole history.
Guildenstern: The king, sir,—
Hamlet: Ay, sir, what of him?
Guildenstern: Is in his retirement marvellous distempered.
280 *Hamlet:* With drink, sir?
Guildenstern: No, my lord, rather with choler.°
Hamlet: Your wisdom should show itself more richer to signify this
    to his doctor; for, for me to put him to his purgation would
    perhaps plunge him into far more choler.
Guildenstern: Good my lord, put your discourse into some frame° and
    start not so wildly from my affair.
Hamlet: I am tame, sir: pronounce.
Guildenstern: The queen, your mother, in most great affliction of
    spirit, hath sent me to you.
290 *Hamlet:* You are welcome.
Guildenstern: Nay, good my lord, this courtesy is not of the right
    breed. If it shall please you to make me a wholesome° answer, I
    will do your mother's commandment; if not, your pardon and my
    return shall be the end of my business.
Hamlet: Sir, I cannot.
Guildenstern: What, my lord?
Hamlet: Make you a wholesome answer; my wit's diseased: but, sir,
    such answer as I can make, you shall command; or, rather, as you
    say, my mother: therefore no more, but to the matter:° my mother,
300   you say,—
Rosencrantz: Then thus she says; your behaviour hath struck her into
    amazement and admiration.
Hamlet: O wonderful son, that can so 'stonish a mother! But is there
    no sequel at the heels of this mother's admiration? Impart.
Rosencrantz: She desires to speak with you in her closet, ere you go
    to bed.
Hamlet: We shall obey, were she ten times our mother. Have you any
    further trade with us?
Rosencrantz: My lord, you once did love me.
310 *Hamlet:* And do still, by these pickers and stealers.°

---

273 *perdy:* Corruption of *par dieu.*   281 *choler:* Bilious disorder, with quibble on the sense
"anger."   285 *frame:* Order.   292 *wholesome:* Sensible.   299 *matter:* Matter in hand.
310 *pickers and stealers:* Hands, so called from the catechism "to keep my hands from picking and stealing."

.

Rosencrantz: Good my lord, what is your cause of distemper? you do, surely, bar the door upon your own liberty, if you deny your griefs to your friend.

Hamlet: Sir, I lack advancement.

Rosencrantz: How can that be, when you have the voice° of the king himself for your succession in Denmark?

Hamlet: Ay, sir, but "While the grass grows,"°—the proverb is something musty.

Enter the Players with recorders.

O, the recorders! let me see one. To withdraw° with you—why do you
320 go about to recover the wind° of me, as if you would drive me into a toil?°

Guildenstern: O, my lord, if my duty be too bold, my love is too unmannerly.°

Hamlet: I do not well understand that. Will you play upon this pipe?

Guildenstern: My lord, I cannot.

Hamlet: I pray you.

Guildenstern: Believe me, I cannot.

Hamlet: I beseech you.

Guildenstern: I know no touch of it, my lord.

330 *Hamlet:* 'Tis as easy as lying: govern these ventages° with your fingers and thumb, give it breath with your mouth, and it will discourse most eloquent music. Look you, these are the stops.

Guildenstern: But these cannot I command to any utterance of harmony; I have not the skill.

Hamlet: Why, look you now, how unworthy a thing you make of me! You would play upon me; you would seem to know my stops; you would pluck out the heart of my mystery; you would sound me from my lowest note to the top of my compass:° and there is much music, excellent voice, in this little organ;° yet cannot you make it
340 speak. 'Sblood, do you think I am easier to be played on than a pipe? Call me what instrument you will, though you can fret° me, you cannot play upon me.

Enter Polonius.

God bless you, sir!

Polonius: My lord, the queen would speak with you, and presently.

---

315 *voice:* Support.   317 *"While . . . grows:"* The rest of the proverb is "the silly horse starves." Hamlet may be destroyed while he is waiting for the succession to the king-dom.   319 *withdraw:* Speak in private.   320 *recover the wind:* Get to the windward side.   321 *toil:* Snare.   322–323 *if . . . unmannerly:* If I am using an unmannerly bold-ness, it is my love which occasions it.   330 *ventages:* Stops of the recorders.   338 *com-pass:* Range of voice.   339 *organ:* Musical instrument, i.e., the pipe.   341 *fret:* Quibble on meaning "irritate" and the piece of wood, gut, or metal which regulates the fingering.

Hamlet: Do you see yonder cloud that 's almost in shape of a camel?
Polonius: By the mass, and 'tis like a camel, indeed.
Hamlet: Methinks it is like a weasel.
Polonius: It is backed like a weasel.
Hamlet: Or like a whale?
350 *Polonius:* Very like a whale.
Hamlet: Then I will come to my mother by and by. *(Aside.)* They fool
me to the top of my bent.°—I will come by and by.°
Polonius: I will say so.   *(Exit.)*
Hamlet: By and by is easily said.
Leave me, friends.   *(Exeunt all but Hamlet.)*
'Tis now the very witching time° of night,
When churchyards yawn and hell itself breathes out
Contagion to this world: now could I drink hot blood,
And do such bitter business as the day
360 Would quake to look on. Soft! now to my mother.
O heart, lose not thy nature; let not ever
The soul of Nero° enter this firm bosom:
Let me be cruel, not unnatural:
I will speak daggers to her, but use none;
My tongue and soul in this be hypocrites;
How in my words somever she be shent,°
To give them seals° never, my soul, consent!   *Exit.*

Scene III. A room in the castle.

   Enter King, Rosencrantz, and Guildenstern.

King: I like him not, nor stands it safe with us
To let his madness range. Therefore prepare you;
I your commission will forthwith dispatch,°
And he to England shall along with you:
The terms° of our estate° may not endure
Hazard so near us as doth hourly grow
Out of his brows.°
Guildenstern: We will ourselves provide:
Most holy and religious fear it is
To keep those many many bodies safe
10 That live and feed upon your majesty.
Rosencrantz: The single and peculiar° life is bound,
With all the strength and armour of the mind,

---

352 *top of my bent:* Limit of endurance, i.e., extent to which a bow may be bent; *by and by:*
Immediately.   356 *witching time:* i.e., time when spells are cast.   362 *Nero:* Murderer
of his mother, Agrippina.   366 *shent:* Rebuked.   367 *give them seals:* Confirm with
deeds.   Scene III. 3 *dispatch:* Prepare.   5 *terms:* Condition, circumstances; *estate:*
State.   7 *brows:* Effronteries.   11 *single and peculiar:* Individual and private.

To keep itself from noyance;° but much more
That spirit upon whose weal depend and rest
The lives of many. The cess° of majesty
Dies not alone; but, like a gulf,° doth draw
What's near it with it: it is a massy wheel,
Fix'd on the summit of the highest mount,
To whose huge spokes ten thousand lesser things
20 Are mortis'd and adjoin'd; which, when it falls,
Each small annexment, petty consequence,
Attends° the boist'rous ruin. Never alone
Did the king sigh, but with a general groan.
King: Arm° you, I pray you, to this speedy voyage;
For we will fetters put about this fear,
Which now goes too free-footed.
Rosencrantz: We will haste us.

Exeunt Rosencrantz and Guildenstern.

Enter Polonius.

Polonius: My lord, he's going to his mother's closet:
Behind the arras° I'll convey° myself,
To hear the process;° I'll warrant she'll tax him home:°
30 And, as you said, and wisely was it said,
'Tis meet that some more audience than a mother,
Since nature makes them partial, should o'erhear
The speech, of vantage.° Fare you well, my liege:
I'll call upon you ere you go to bed,
And tell you what I know.
King: Thanks, dear my lord.

Exit Polonius.

O, my offence is rank, it smells to heaven;
It hath the primal eldest curse° upon't,
A brother's murder. Pray can I not,
Though inclination be as sharp as will:°
40 My stronger guilt defeats my strong intent;
And, like a man to double business bound,
I stand in pause where I shall first begin,
And both neglect. What if this cursed hand

---

13 *noyance:* Harm.   15 *cess:* Decease.   16 *gulf:* Whirlpool.   22 *Attends:* Participates
in.   24 *Arm:* Prepare.   28 *arras:* Screen of tapestry placed around the walls of household apartments; *convey:* Implication of secrecy, *convey* was often used to mean "steal."
29 *process:* Proceedings; *tax him home:* Reprove him severely.   33 *of vantage:* From an advantageous place.   37 *primal eldest curse:* The curse of Cain, the first to kill his brother.
39 *sharp as will:* i.e., his desire is as strong as his determination.

Were thicker than itself with brother's blood,
Is there not rain enough in the sweet heavens
To wash it white as snow? Whereto serves mercy
But to confront° the visage of offence?
And what's in prayer but this two-fold force,
To be forestalled° ere we come to fall,
50 Or pardon'd being down? Then I'll look up;
My fault is past. But, O, what form of prayer
Can serve my turn? "Forgive me my foul murder"?
That cannot be: since I am still possess'd
Of those effects for which I did the murder,
My crown, mine own ambition° and my queen.
May one be pardon'd and retain th' offence?°
In the corrupted currents° of this world
Offence's gilded hand° may shove by justice,
And oft 'tis seen the wicked prize° itself
60 Buys out the law: but 'tis not so above;
There is no shuffling,° there the action lies°
In his true nature; and we ourselves compell'd,
Even to the teeth and forehead° of our faults,
To give in evidence. What then? what rests?°
Try what repentance can: what can it not?
Yet what can it when one can not repent?
O wretched state! O bosom black as death!
O limed° soul, that, struggling to be free,
Art more engag'd!° Help, angels! Make assay!°
70 Bow, stubborn knees; and, heart with strings of steel,
Be soft as sinews of the new-born babe!
All may be well.   *(He kneels.)*

Enter Hamlet.

Hamlet: Now might I do it pat,° now he is praying;
And now I'll do't. And so 'a goes to heaven;
And so am I reveng'd. That would be scann'd:°
A villain kills my father; and for that,
I, his sole son, do this same villain send
To heaven.
Why, this is hire and salary, not revenge.
80 'A took my father grossly, full of bread;°

---

47 *confront:* Oppose directly.   49 *forestalled:* Prevented.   55 *ambition:* i.e., realization of
ambition.   56 *offence:* Benefit accruing from offense.   57 *currents:* Courses.   58
gilded hand: Hand offering gold as a bribe.   59 *wicked prize:* Prize won by wickedness.
61 *shuffling:* Escape by trickery; *lies:* Is sustainable.   63 *teeth and forehead:* Very face.
64 *rests:* Remains.   68 *limed:* Caught as with birdlime.   69 *engag'd:* Embedded; *assay:*
Trial.   73 *pat:* Opportunely.   75 *would be scann'd:* Needs to be looked into.   80 *full
of bread:* Enjoying his worldly pleasures (see Ezekiel 16:49).

With all his crimes broad blown,° as flush° as May;
And how his audit stands who knows save heaven?
But in our circumstance and course° of thought,
'Tis heavy with him: and am I then reveng'd,
To take him in the purging of his soul,
When he is fit and season'd for his passage?°
No!
Up, sword; and know thou a more horrid hent:°
When he is drunk asleep,° or in his rage,
90 Or in th' incestuous pleasure of his bed;
At game, a-swearing, or about some act
That has no relish of salvation in't;
Then trip him, that his heels may kick at heaven,
And that his soul may be as damn'd and black
As hell, whereto it goes. My mother stays:
This physic° but prolongs thy sickly days. *Exit.*
King: *(Rising)* My words fly up, my thoughts remain below:
Words without thoughts never to heaven go. *Exit.*

Scene IV. The Queen's closet.

Enter Queen Gertrude and Polonius.

Polonius: 'A will come straight. Look you lay° home to him:
Tell him his pranks have been too broad° to bear with,
And that your grace hath screen'd and stood between
Much heat° and him. I'll sconce° me even here.
Pray you, be round° with him.
Hamlet (within): Mother, mother, mother!
Queen: I'll warrant you,
Fear me not: withdraw, I hear him coming.

(Polonius hides behind the arras.)

Enter Hamlet.

Hamlet: Now, mother, what's the matter?
Queen: Hamlet, thou hast thy father much offended.
10 **Hamlet:** Mother, you have my father° much offended.
Queen: Come, come, you answer with an idle tongue.
Hamlet: Go, go, you question with a wicked tongue.

---

81 *broad blown:* In full bloom; *flush:* Lusty.   83 *in . . . course:* As we see it in our mortal situation.   86 *fit . . . passage:* i.e., reconciled to heaven by forgiveness of his sins.   88 *hent:* Seizing; or more probably, occasion of seizure.   89 *drunk asleep:* In a drunken sleep.   96 *physic:* Purging (by prayer).   SCENE IV. 1 *lay:* Thrust.   2 *broad:* Unrestrained.   4 *Much heat:* i.e., the king's anger; *sconce:* Hide.   5 *round:* Blunt.   9–10 *thy father, my father:* i.e., Claudius, the elder Hamlet.

Queen: Why, how now, Hamlet!
Hamlet: What's the matter now?
Queen: Have you forgot me?
Hamlet: No, by the rood,° not so:
You are the queen, your husband's brother's wife;
And—would it were not so!—you are my mother.
Queen: Nay, then, I'll set those to you that can speak.
Hamlet: Come, come, and sit you down; you shall not budge;
You go not till I set you up a glass
20 Where you may see the inmost part of you.
Queen: What wilt thou do? thou wilt not murder me?
Help, help, ho!
Polonius (behind): What, ho! help, help; help!
Hamlet (drawing): How now! a rat? Dead, for a ducat, dead!

(Makes a pass through the arras.)

Polonius (behind): O, I am slain!   (*Falls and dies.*)
Queen: O me, what hast thou done?
Hamlet: Nay, I know not:
Is it the king?
Queen: O, what a rash and bloody deed is this!
Hamlet: A bloody deed! almost as bad, good mother,
30 As kill a king, and marry with his brother.
Queen: As kill a king!
Hamlet: Ay, lady, it was my word.

(Lifts up the arras and discovers Polonius.)

Thou wretched, rash, intruding fool, farewell!
I took thee for thy better: take thy fortune;
Thou find'st to be too busy is some danger.
Leave wringing of your hands: peace! sit you down,
And let me wring your heart; for so I shall,
If it be made of penetrable stuff,
If damned custom have not braz'd° it so
That it be proof and bulwark against sense.
40 *Queen:* What have I done, that thou dar'st wag thy tongue
In noise so rude against me?
Hamlet: Such an act
That blurs the grace and blush of modesty,
Calls virtue hypocrite, takes off the rose
From the fair forehead of an innocent love
And sets a blister° there, makes marriage-vows
As false as dicers' oaths: O, such a deed

---

14 *rood:* Cross.   38 *braz'd:* Brazened, hardened.   45 *sets a blister:* Brands as a harlot.

As from the body of contraction° plucks
The very soul, and sweet religion° makes
A rhapsody° of words: heaven's face does glow
50 O'er this solidity and compound mass
With heated visage, as against the doom
Is thought-sick at the act.°
Queen: Ay me, what act,
That roars so loud, and thunders in the index?°
Hamlet: Look here, upon this picture, and on this.
The counterfeit presentment° of two brothers.
See, what a grace was seated on this brow;
Hyperion's° curls; the front° of Jove himself;
An eye like Mars, to threaten and command;
A station° like the herald Mercury
60 New-lighted on a heaven-kissing hill;
A combination and a form indeed,
Where every god did seem to set his seal,
To give the world assurance° of a man:
This was your husband. Look you now, what follows:
Here is your husband; like a mildew'd ear,°
Blasting his wholesome brother. Have you eyes?
Could you on this fair mountain leave to feed,
And batten° on this moor?° Ha! have you eyes?
You cannot call it love; for at your age
70 The hey-day° in the blood is tame, it's humble,
And waits upon the judgement: and what judgement
Would step from this to this? Sense, sure, you have,
Else could you not have motion;° but sure, that sense
Is apoplex'd;° for madness would not err,
Nor sense to ecstasy was ne'er so thrall'd°
But it reserv'd some quantity of choice,°
To serve in such a difference. What devil was't
That thus hath cozen'd° you at hoodman-blind?°
Eyes without feeling, feeling without sight,

---

47 *contraction:* The marriage contract.   48 *religion:* Religious vows.   49 *rhapsody:* Senseless string.   49–52 *heaven's . . . act:* Heaven's face blushes to look down upon this world, compounded of the four elements, with hot face as though the day of doom were near, and thought-sick at the deed (i.e., Gertrude's marriage).   53 *index:* Prelude or preface.   55 *counterfeit presentment:* Portrayed representation.   57 *Hyperion:* The sun god; *front:* Brow.   59 *station:* Manner of standing.   63 *assurance:* Pledge, guarantee.   65 *mildew'd ear:* See Genesis 41:5–7.   68 *batten:* Grow fat; *moor:* Barren upland.   70 *hey-day:* State of excitement.   72–73 *Sense . . . motion:* Sense and motion are functions of the middle or sensible soul, the possession of sense being the basis of motion.   74 *apoplex'd:* Paralyzed. Mental derangement was thus of three sorts: apoplexy, ecstasy, and diabolic possession.   75 *thrall'd:* Enslaved.   76 *quantity of choice:* Fragment of the power to choose.   78 *cozen'd:* Tricked, cheated; *hoodman-blind:* Blindman's buff.

80 Ears without hands or eyes, smelling sans° all,
Or but a sickly part of one true sense
Could not so mope.°
O shame! where is thy blush? Rebellious hell,
If thou canst mutine° in a matron's bones,
To flaming youth let virtue be as wax,
And melt in her own fire: proclaim no shame
When the compulsive ardour gives the charge,°
Since frost itself as actively doth burn
And reason pandars will.°
Queen: O Hamlet, speak no more:
90 Thou turn'st mine eyes into my very soul;
And there I see such black and grained° spots
As will not leave their tint.
Hamlet: Nay, but to live
In the rank sweat of an enseamed° bed,
Stew'd in corruption, honeying and making love
Over the nasty sty,—
Queen: O, speak to me no more;
These words, like daggers, enter in mine ears;
No more, sweet Hamlet!
Hamlet: A murderer and a villain;
A slave that is not twentieth part the tithe
Of your precedent lord;° a vice of kings;°
100 A cutpurse of the empire and the rule,
That from a shelf the precious diadem stole,
And put it in his pocket!
Queen: No more!

    Enter Ghost.

Hamlet: A king of shreds and patches,°—
Save me, and hover o'er me with your wings,
You heavenly guards! What would your gracious figure?
Queen: Alas, he's mad!
Hamlet: Do you not come your tardy son to chide,
That, laps'd in time and passion,° lets go by

---

80 *sans:* Without.   82 *mope:* Be in a depressed, spiritless state, act aimlessly.   84 *mu-*
tine: Mutiny, rebel.   92 *gives the charge:* Delivers the attack.   94 *reason pandars will:*
The normal and proper situation was one in which reason guided the will in the direction
of good; here, reason is perverted and leads in the direction of evil.   96 *grained:* Dyed in
grain.   98 *enseamed:* Loaded with grease, greased.   104 *precedent lord:* i.e., the elder
Hamlet; *vice of kings:* Buffoon of kings; a reference to the Vice, or clown, of the morality
plays and interludes.   108 *shreds and patches:* i.e., motley, the traditional costume of the
Vice.   113 *laps'd . . . passion:* Having suffered time to slip and passion to cool; also explained as "engrossed in casual events and lapsed into mere fruitless passion, so that he
no longer entertains a rational purpose."

Th' important° acting of your dread command?
110 O, say!
 Ghost: Do not forget: this visitation
Is but to whet thy almost blunted purpose.
But, look, amazement° on thy mother sits:
O, step between her and her fighting soul:
Conceit in weakest bodies strongest works:
Speak to her, Hamlet.
 Hamlet: How is it with you, lady?
 Queen: Alas, how is 't with you,
That you do bend your eye on vacancy
And with th' incorporal° air do hold discourse?
120 Forth at your eyes your spirits wildly peep;
And, as the sleeping soldiers in th' alarm,
Your bedded° hair, like life in excrements,°
Start up, and stand an° end. O gentle son,
Upon the heat and flame of thy distemper
Sprinkle cool patience. Whereon do you look?
 Hamlet: On him, on him! Look you, how pale he glares!
His form and cause conjoin'd,° preaching to stones,
Would make them capable.—Do not look upon me;
Lest with this piteous action you convert
130 My stern effects:° then what I have to do
Will want true colour;° tears perchance for blood.
 Queen: To whom do you speak this?
 Hamlet: Do you see nothing there?
 Queen: Nothing at all; yet all that is I see.
 Hamlet: Nor did you nothing hear?
 Queen: No, nothing but ourselves.
 Hamlet: Why, look you there! look, how it steals away!
My father, in his habit as he liv'd!
Look, where he goes, even now, out at the portal!   *Exit Ghost.*
 Queen: This is the very coinage of your brain:
This bodiless creation ecstasy
Is very cunning in.
140 *Hamlet:*   Ecstasy!
My pulse, as yours, doth temperately keep time,
And makes us healthful music: it is not madness
That I have utt'red: bring me to the test,
And I the matter will re-word,° which madness

---

114 *important:* Urgent. 118 *amazement:* Frenzy, distraction. 119 *incorporal:* Immaterial. 122 *bedded:* Laid in smooth layers; *excrements:* The hair was considered an excrement or voided part of the body. 123 *an:* On. 127 *conjoin'd:* United. 129–130 *convert . . . effects:* Divert me from my stern duty. For *effects,* possibly *affects* (affections of the mind). 131 *want true colour:* Lack good reason so that (with a play on the normal sense of *colour*) I shall shed tears instead of blood. 144 *re-word:* Repeat in words.

Would gambol° from. Mother, for love of grace,
Lay not that flattering unction° to your soul,
That not your trespass, but my madness speaks:
It will but skin and film the ulcerous place,
Whiles rank corruption, mining° all within,
150 Infects unseen. Confess yourself to heaven;
Repent what's past; avoid what is to come;°
And do not spread the compost° on the weeds,
To make them ranker. Forgive me this my virtue;°
For in the fatness° of these pursy° times
Virtue itself of vice must pardon beg,
Yea, curb° and woo for leave to do him good.
Queen: O Hamlet, thou hast cleft my heart in twain.
Hamlet: O, throw away the worser part of it,
And live the purer with the other half.
160 Good night: but go not to my uncle's bed;
Assume a virtue, if you have it not.
That monster, custom, who all sense doth eat,
Of habits devil, is angel yet in this,
That to the use of actions fair and good
He likewise gives a frock or livery,
That aptly is put on. Refrain to-night,
And that shall lend a kind of easiness
To the next abstinence: the next more easy;
For use almost can change the stamp of nature,
170 And either . . . the devil, or throw him out°
With wondrous potency. Once more, good night:
And when you are desirous to be bless'd,°
I'll blessing beg of you. For this same lord,   *(Pointing to Polonius.)*
I do repent: but heaven hath pleas'd it so,
To punish me with this and this with me,
That I must be their scourge and minister.
I will bestow him, and will answer well
The death I gave him. So, again, good night.
I must be cruel, only to be kind:
180 Thus bad begins and worse remains behind.
One word more, good lady.
Queen: What shall I do?
Hamlet: Not this, by no means, that I bid you do:
Let the bloat° king tempt you again to bed;

---

145 *gambol:* Skip away.   146 *unction:* Ointment used medicinally or as a rite; suggestion
that forgiveness for sin may not be so easily achieved.   149 *mining:* Working under the
surface.   151 *what is to come:* i.e., the sins of the future.   152 *compost:* Manure.   153
this my virtue: My virtuous talk in reproving you.   154 *fatness:* Grossness; *pursy:* Short-
winded, corpulent.   156 *curb:* Bow, bend the knee.   170 Defective line usually
emended by inserting *master* after *either.*   172 *be bless'd:*   Become blessed, i.e., repentant.   183 *bloat:* Bloated.

Pinch wanton on your cheek; call you his mouse;
And let him, for a pair of reechy° kisses,
Or paddling in your neck with his damn'd fingers,
Make you to ravel all this matter out,
That I essentially° am not in madness,
But mad in craft. 'Twere good you let him know;
190 For who, that's but a queen, fair, sober, wise,
Would from a paddock,° from a bat, a gib,°
Such dear concernings° hide? who would do so?
No, in despite of sense and secrecy,
Unpeg the basket on the house's top,
Let the birds fly, and, like the famous ape,°
To try conclusions,° in the basket creep,
And break your own neck down.
Queen: Be thou assur'd, if words be made of breath,
And breath of life, I have no life to breathe
200 What thou hast said to me.
Hamlet: I must to England; you know that?
Queen: Alack,
I had forgot: 'tis so concluded on.
Hamlet: There's letters seal'd: and my two schoolfellows,
Whom I will trust as I will adders fang'd,
They bear the mandate; they must sweep my way,°
And marshal me to knavery. Let it work;
For 'tis the sport to have the enginer°
Hoist° with his own petar:° and 't shall go hard
But I will delve one yard below their mines,
210 And blow them at the moon: O, 'tis most sweet,
When in one line two crafts° directly meet.
This man shall set me packing:°
I'll lug the guts into the neighbour room.
Mother, good night. Indeed this counsellor
Is now most still, most secret and most grave,
Who was in life a foolish prating knave.

---

185 *reechy:* Dirty, filthy.   188 *essentially:* In my essential nature.   191 *paddock:* Toad; *gib:* Tomcat.   192 *dear concernings:* Important affairs.   195 *the famous ape:* A letter from Sir John Suckling seems to supply other details of the story, otherwise not identified: "It is the story of the jackanapes and the partridges; thou starest after a beauty till it be lost to thee, then let'st out another, and starest after that till it is gone too."   196 *conclusions:* Experiments.   205 *sweep my way:* Clear my path.   207 *enginer:* Constructor of military works, or possibly, artilleryman.   208 *Hoist:* Blown up; *petar:* Defined as a small engine of war used to blow in a door or make a breach, and as a case filled with explosive materials.   211 *two crafts:* Two acts of guile, with quibble on the sense of "two ships."   212 *set me packing:* Set me to making schemes, and set me to lugging (him), and, also, send me off in a hurry.

Come, sir, to draw° toward an end with you.
Good night, mother.

Exeunt severally; Hamlet dragging in Polonius.

Act IV

Scene I. A room in the castle.

Enter King and Queen, with Rosencrantz and Guildenstern.

King: There's matter in these sighs, these profound heaves:
You must translate: 'tis fit we understand them.
Where is your son?
Queen: Bestow this place on us a little while.

(Exeunt Rosencrantz and Guildenstern.)

Ah, mine own lord, what have I seen to-night!
King: What, Gertrude? How does Hamlet?
Queen: Mad as the sea and wind, when both contend
Which is the mightier: in his lawless fit,
Behind the arras hearing something stir,
10 Whips out his rapier, cries, "A rat, a rat!"
And, in this brainish° apprehension,° kills
The unseen good old man.
King: O heavy dead!
It had been so with us, had we been there:
His liberty is full of threats to all;
To you yourself, to us, to every one.
Alas, how shall this bloody deed be answer'd?
It will be laid to us, whose providence°
Should have kept short,° restrain'd and out of haunt,°
This mad young man: but so much was our love,
20 We would not understand what was most fit;
But, like the owner of a foul disease,
To keep it from divulging,° let it feed
Even on the pith of life. Where is he gone?
Queen: To draw apart the body he hath kill'd:
O'er whom his very madness, like some ore
Among a mineral° of metals base,
Shows itself pure; 'a weeps for what is done.

---

217 *draw:* Come, with quibble on literal sense.   ACT IV. SCENE I.   11 *brainish:* Head-
strong, passionate; *apprehension:* Conception, imagination.   17 *providence:* Foresight.
18 *short:* i.e., on a short tether; *out of haunt:* Secluded. 22 *divulging:* Becoming evident.
26 *mineral:* Mine.

King: O Gertrude, come away!
The sun no sooner shall the mountains touch,
30 But we will ship him hence: and this vile deed
We must, with all our majesty and skill,
Both countenance and excuse. Ho, Guildenstern!

Enter Rosencrantz and Guildenstern.

Friends both, go join you with some further aid:
Hamlet in madness hath Polonius slain,
And from his mother's closet hath he dragg'd him:
Go seek him out; speak fair, and bring the body
Into the chapel. I pray you, haste in this.

(Exeunt Rosencrantz and Guildenstern.)

Come, Gertrude, we'll call up our wisest friends;
And let them know, both what we mean to do,
40 And what's untimely done . . .°
Whose whisper o'er the world's diameter,°
As level° as the cannon to his blank,°
Transports his pois'ned shot, may miss our name,
And hit the woundless° air. O, come away!
My soul is full of discord and dismay.   *Exeunt.*

Scene II. Another room in the castle.

Enter Hamlet.

Hamlet: Safely stowed.
Rosencrantz:
Guildenstern: *(within)* Hamlet! Lord Hamlet!
Hamlet: But soft, what noise? who calls on Hamlet? O, here they come.

Enter Rosencrantz and Guildenstern.

Rosencrantz: What have you done, my lord, with the dead body?
Hamlet: Compounded it with dust, whereto 'tis kin.
Rosencrantz: Tell us where 'tis, that we may take it thence
And bear it to the chapel.
Hamlet: Do not believe it.
Rosencrantz: Believe what?

---

40 Defective line; some editors add: *so, haply, slander;* others add: *for, haply, slander;* other
conjectures.   41 *diameter:* Extent from side to side.   42 *level:* Straight; *blank:* White
spot in the center of a target.   44 *woundless:* Invulnerable.

10 **Hamlet:** That I can keep your counsel° and not mine own. Besides, to
be demanded of a sponge! what replication° should be made by the
son of a king?

Rosencrantz: Take you me for a sponge, my lord?

Hamlet: Ay, sir, that soaks up the king's countenance, his rewards, his
authorities.° But such officers do the king best service in the end: he
keeps them, like an ape an apple, in the corner of his jaw; first
mouthed, to be last swallowed: when he needs what you have
gleaned, it is but squeezing you, and, sponge, you shall be dry again.

Rosencrantz: I understand you not, my lord.

20 **Hamlet:** I am glad of it: a knavish speech sleeps in a foolish ear.

Rosencrantz: My lord, you must tell us where the body is, and go
with us to the king.

Hamlet: The body is with the king, but the king is not with the body.°
The king is a thing—

Guildenstern: A thing, my lord!

Hamlet: Of nothing: bring me to him. Hide fox, and all after.°   *Exeunt.*

Scene III. Another room in the castle.

Enter King, and two or three.

King: I have sent to seek him, and to find the body.
How dangerous is it that this man goes loose!
Yet must not we put the strong law on him:
He's lov'd of the distracted° multitude,
Who like not in their judgement, but their eyes;
And where 'tis so, th' offender's scourge° is weigh'd,°
But never the offence. To bear all smooth and even,
This sudden sending him away must seem
Deliberate pause:° diseases desperate grown
10 By desperate appliance are reliev'd,
Or not at all.

Enter Rosencrantz, (Guildenstern), and all the rest.

How now! what hath befall'n?

Rosencrantz: Where the dead body is bestow'd, my lord,
We cannot get from him.

SCENE II.   10 *keep your counsel:* Hamlet is aware of their treachery but says nothing about
it.   11 *replication:* Reply.   15 *authorities:* Authoritative backing.   23 *The body . . .
body:* There are many interpretations; possibly, "The body lies in death with the king, my
father; but my father walks disembodied"; or "Claudius has the bodily possession of kingship, but kingliness, or justice of inheritance, is not with him."   26 *Hide . . . after:* An
old signal cry in the game of hide-and-seek.   SCENE III.   4 *distracted:* i.e., without power
of forming logical judgments.   6 *scourge:* Punishment; *weigh'd:* Taken into consideration.
9 *Deliberate pause:* Considered action.

King: But where is he?

Rosencrantz: Without, my lord; guarded, to know your pleasure.

King: Bring him before us.

Rosencrantz: Ho! bring in the lord.

They enter with Hamlet.

King: Now, Hamlet, where's Polonius?

Hamlet: At supper.

King: At supper! where?

20 *Hamlet:* Not where he eats, but where 'a is eaten: a certain
    convocation of politic° worms° are e'en at him. Your worm is your
    only emperor for diet: we fat all creatures else to fat us, and we
    fat ourselves for maggots: your fat king and your lean beggar is
    but variable service,° two dishes, but to one table: that's the end.

King: Alas, alas!

Hamlet: A man may fish with the worm that hath eat of a king, and
    eat of the fish that hath fed of that worm.

King: What dost thou mean by this?

Hamlet: Nothing but to show you how a king may go a progress°
30   through the guts of a beggar.

King: Where is Polonius?

Hamlet: In heaven; send thither to see: if your messenger find him
    not there, seek him i' the other place yourself. But if indeed you
    find him not within this month, you shall nose him as you go up
    the stairs into the lobby.

King (to some Attendants): Go seek him there.

Hamlet: 'A will stay till you come.   *(Exeunt Attendants.)*

King: Hamlet, this deed, for thine especial safety,—

Which we do tender,° as we dearly grieve

40 For that which thou hast done,—must send thee hence

With fiery quickness: therefore prepare thyself;

The bark is ready, and the wind at help,

Th' associates tend, and everything is bent

For England.

Hamlet: For England!

King: Ay, Hamlet.

Hamlet: Good.

King: So is it, if thou knew'st our purposes.

Hamlet: I see a cherub° that sees them. But, come; for England!
    Farewell, dear mother.

King: Thy loving father, Hamlet.

---

21 *convocation . . . worms:* Allusion to the Diet of Worms (1521); *politic:* Crafty.   24 *variable service:* A variety of dishes.   29 *progress:* Royal journey of state.   39 *tender:* Regard, hold dear.   46 *cherub:* Cherubim are angels of knowledge.

Hamlet: My mother: father and mother is man and wife; man and
50   wife is one flesh; and so, my mother. Come, for England!   *Exit.*
King: Follow him at foot;° tempt him with speed aboard;
Delay it not; I'll have him hence to-night:
Away! for every thing is seal'd and done
That else leans on th' affair: pray you, make haste.

(Exeunt all but the King.)

And, England, if my love thou hold'st at aught—
As my great power thereof may give thee sense,
Since yet thy cicatrice° looks raw and red
After the Danish sword, and thy free awe°
Pays homage to us—thou mayst not coldly set
60 Our sovereign process; which imports at full,
By letters congruing to that effect,
The present death of Hamlet. Do it, England;
For like the hectic° in my blood he rages,
And thou must cure me: till I know 'tis done,
Howe'er my haps,° my joys were ne'er begun.   *Exit.*

Scene IV. A plain in Denmark.

Enter Fortinbras with his Army over the stage.

Fortinbras: Go, captain, from me greet the Danish king;
Tell him that, by his license,° Fortinbras
Craves the conveyance° of a promis'd march
Over his kingdom. You know the rendezvous.
If that his majesty would aught with us,
We shall express our duty in his eye;°
And let him know so.
Captain: I will do't, my lord.
Fortinbras: Go softly° on.   *(Exeunt all but Captain.)*

Enter Hamlet, Rosencrantz, Guildenstern, &c.

Hamlet: Good sir, whose powers are these?
10 *Captain:* They are of Norway, sir.
Hamlet: How purpos'd, sir, I pray you?
Captain: Against some part of Poland.
Hamlet: Who commands them, sir?
Captain: The nephew to old Norway, Fortinbras.

---

51 *at foot:* Close behind, at heel.   57 *cicatrice:* Scar.   58 *free awe:* Voluntary show of respect. 63 *hectic:* Fever.   65 *haps:* Fortunes.   SCENE IV. 2 *license:* Leave.   3 *con-*
veyance: Escort, convoy.   6 *in his eye:* In his presence.   8 *softly:* Slowly.

Hamlet: Goes it against the main° of Poland, sir,
Or for some frontier?
Captain: Truly to speak, and with no addition,
We go to gain a little patch of ground
That hath in it no profit but the name.
20 To pay five ducats, five, I would not farm it;°
Nor will it yield to Norway or the Pole
A ranker rate, should it be sold in fee.°
Hamlet: Why, then the Polack never will defend it.
Captain: Yes, it is already garrison'd.
Hamlet: Two thousand souls and twenty thousand ducats
Will not debate the question of this straw:°
This is th' imposthume° of much wealth and peace,
That inward breaks, and shows no cause without
Why the man dies. I humbly thank you, sir.
Captain: God be wi' you, sir.   *(Exit.)*
30 *Rosencrantz:*   Will 't please you go, my lord?
Hamlet: I'll be with you straight. Go a little before.

(Exeunt all except Hamlet.)

How all occasions° do inform against° me,
And spur my dull revenge! What is a man,
If his chief good and market of his time°
Be but to sleep and feed? a beast, no more.
Sure, he that made us with such large discourse,
Looking before and after, gave us not
That capability and god-like reason
To fust° in us unus'd. Now, whether it be
40 Bestial oblivion, or some craven scruple
Of thinking too precisely on th' event,
A thought which, quarter'd, hath but one part wisdom
And ever three parts coward, I do not know
Why yet I live to say "This thing 's to do";
Sith I have cause and will and strength and means
To do 't. Examples gross as earth exhort me:
Witness this army of such mass and charge
Led by a delicate and tender prince,
Whose spirit with divine ambition puff'd
50 Makes mouths at the invisible event,
Exposing what is mortal and unsure

---

15 *main:* Country itself.   20 *farm it:* Take a lease of it.   22 *fee:* Fee simple.   26 *debate
. . . straw:* Settle this trifling matter.   27 *imposthume:* Purulent abscess or swelling.
32 *occasions:* Incidents, events; *inform against:* generally defined as "show," "betray," (i.e.,
his tardiness); more probably *inform* means "take shape," as in *Macbeth,* II. i. 48.   34
market of his time: The best use he makes of his time, or, that for which he sells his time.
39 *fust:* Grow moldy.

To all that fortune, death and danger dare,
Even for an egg-shell. Rightly to be great
Is not to stir without great argument,
But greatly to find quarrel in a straw
When honour's at the stake. How stand I then,
That have a father kill'd, a mother stain'd,
Excitements of° my reason and my blood,
And let all sleep? while, to my shame, I see
60 The imminent death of twenty thousand men,
That, for a fantasy and trick° of fame,
Go to their graves like beds, fight for a plot°
Whereon the numbers cannot try the cause,
Which is not tomb enough and continent
To hide the slain? O, from this time forth,
My thoughts be bloody, or be nothing worth!   *Exit.*

Scene V. Elsinore. A room in the castle.

    Enter Horatio, Queen Gertrude, and a Gentleman.

Queen: I will not speak with her.
Gentleman: She is importunate, indeed distract:
Her mood will needs be pitied.
Queen: What would she have?
Gentleman: She speaks much of her father; she says she hears
There's tricks° i' th' world; and hems, and beats her heart;°
Spurns enviously at straws;° speaks things in doubt,
That carry but half sense: her speech is nothing,
Yet the unshaped° use of it doth move
The hearers to collection;° they yawn° at it,
10 And botch° the words up fit to their own thoughts;
Which, as her winks, and nods, and gestures yield° them,
Indeed would make one think there might be thought,
Though nothing sure, yet much unhappily.°
Horatio: 'Twere good she were spoken with: for she may strew
Dangerous conjectures in ill-breeding minds.°
Queen: Let her come in.   *(Exit Gentleman.)*
(Aside.) To my sick soul, as sin's true nature is,
Each toy seems prologue to some great amiss:°

---

58 *Excitements of:* Incentives to.   61 *trick:* Toy, trifle.   62 *plot:* i.e., of ground.
Scene V.   5 *tricks:* Deceptions; *heart:* i.e., breast.   6 *Spurns . . . straws:* Kicks spitefully
at small objects in her path.   8 *unshaped:* Unformed, artless.   9 *collection:* Inference, a
guess at some sort of meaning; *yawn:* Wonder.   10 *botch:* Patch.   11 *yield:* Deliver,
bring forth (her words).   13 *much unhappily:* Expressive of much unhappiness.   15 *ill-
breeding minds:* Minds bent on mischief.   18 *great amiss:* Calamity, disaster.

So full of artless jealousy is guilt,
20 It spills itself in fearing to be spilt.°

Enter Ophelia (distracted).

Ophelia: Where is the beauteous majesty of Denmark?
Queen: How now, Ophelia!
Ophelia (she sings):

How should I your true love know
    From another one?
By his cockle hat° and staff,
    And his sandal shoon.°

Queen: Alas, sweet lady, what imports this song?
Ophelia: Say you? nay, pray you mark.

(Song) He is dead and gone, lady,
30   He is dead and gone;
        At his head a grass-green turf,
        At his heels a stone.

O, ho!
Queen: Nay, but, Ophelia—
Ophelia: Pray you, mark

(Sings.) White his shroud as the mountain snow,—

Enter King.

Queen: Alas, look here, my lord.
Ophelia (Song):

    Larded° all with flowers;
Which bewept to the grave did not go
40   With true-love showers.

King: How do you, pretty lady?
Ophelia: Well, God 'ild° you! They say the owl° was a baker's daughter.
    Lord, we know what we are, but know not what we may be. God be
    at your table!

19–20 *So . . . spilt:* Guilt is so full of suspicion that it unskillfully betrays itself in fearing
to be betrayed.   25 *cockle hat:* Hat with cockleshell stuck in it as a sign that the wearer
has been a pilgrim to the shrine of St. James of Compostella. The pilgrim's garb was a
conventional disguise for lovers.   26 *shoon:* Shoes.   38 *Larded:* Decorated.   42 *God
'ild:* God yield or reward; *owl:* Reference to a monkish legend that a baker's daughter was
turned into an owl for refusing bread to the Saviour.

King: Conceit upon her father.

Ophelia: Pray let's have no words of this; but when they ask you what
it means, say you this:

(Song) To-morrow is Saint Valentine's day,
　　　All in the morning bedtime,
50　　　And I a maid at your window,
　　　To be your Valentine.°
　　Then up he rose, and donn'd his clothes,
　　　And dupp'd° the chamber-door;
　　Let in the maid, that out a maid
　　　Never departed more.

King: Pretty Ophelia!

Ophelia: Indeed, la, without an oath, I'll make an end on 't:

(Sings.) By Gis° and by Saint Charity,
　　　Alack, and fie for shame!
60　　Young men will do 't, if they come to 't;
　　　By cock,° they are to blame.
　　Quoth she, before you tumbled me,
　　　You promis'd me to wed.
　　So would I ha' done, by yonder sun,
　　　An thou hadst not come to my bed.

King: How long hath she been thus?

Ophelia: I hope all will be well. We must be patient: but I cannot
choose but weep, to think they would lay him i' the cold ground.
My brother shall know of it: and so I thank you for your good
70　counsel. Come, my coach! Good night, ladies; good night, sweet
ladies; good night, good night.　　　　　　　　　　　*(Exit.)*

King: Follow her close; give her good watch, I pray you.　*(Exit Horatio.)*
O, this is the poison of deep grief; it springs
All from her father's death. O Gertrude, Gertrude,
When sorrows come, they come not single spies,
But in battalions. First, her father slain:
Next your son gone; and he most violent author
Of his own just remove: the people muddied,
Thick and unwholesome in their thoughts and whispers,
80 For good Polonius' death; and we have done but greenly,°
In hugger-mugger° to inter him: poor Ophelia
Divided from herself and her fair judgement,

---

51 *Valentine:* This song alludes to the belief that the first girl seen by a man on the
morning of this day was his valentine or true love.　　53 *dupp'd:* Opened.　　58 *Gis:*
Jesus.　　61 *cock:* Perversion of "God" in oaths.　　80 *greenly:* Foolishly.　　81 *hugger-
mugger:* Secret haste.

Without the which we are pictures, or mere beasts:
Last, and as much containing as all these,
Her brother is in secret come from France;
Feeds on his wonder, keeps himself in clouds,°
And wants not buzzers° to infect his ear
With pestilent speeches of his father's death;
Wherein necessity, of matter beggar'd,°
90 Will nothing stick° our person to arraign
In ear and ear.° O my dear Gertrude, this,
Like to a murd'ring-piece,° in many places
Gives me superfluous death.   *A noise within.*
Queen: Alack, what noise is this?
King: Where are my Switzers?° Let them guard the door.

Enter a Messenger.

What is the matter?
Messenger: Save yourself, my lord:
The ocean, overpeering° of his list,°
Eats not the flats with more impiteous haste
Than young Laertes, in a riotous head,
O'erbears your officers. The rabble call him lord;
100 And, as the world were now but to begin,
Antiquity forgot, custom not known,
The ratifiers and props of every word,°
They cry "Choose we: Laertes shall be king":
Caps, hands, and tongues, applaud it to the clouds:
"Laertes shall be king, Laertes king!"   *A noise within.*
Queen: How cheerfully on the false trail they cry!
O, this is counter,° you false Danish dogs!
King: The doors are broke.

Enter Laertes with others.

Laertes: Where is this king? Sirs, stand you all without.
Danes: No, let's come in.
110 *Laertes:*   I pray you, give me leave.
Danes: We will, we will.   *(They retire without the door.)*
Laertes: I thank you: keep the door. O thou vile king,
Give me my father!
Queen: Calmly, good Laertes.

---

86 *in clouds:* Invisible.   87 *buzzers:* Gossipers.   89 *of matter beggar'd:* Unprovided with facts.   90 *nothing stick:* Not hesitate.   91 *In ear and ear:* In everybody's ears. 92 *murd'ring-piece:* Small cannon or mortar; suggestion of numerous missiles fired. 94 *Switzers:* Swiss guards, mercenaries.   96 *overpeering:* Overflowing; *list:* Shore. 102 *word:* Promise.   107 *counter:* A hunting term meaning to follow the trail in a direction opposite to that which the game has taken.

Laertes: That drop of blood that's calm proclaims me bastard,
Cries cuckold to my father, brands the harlot
Even here, between the chaste unsmirched brow
Of my true mother.
King: What is the cause, Laertes,
That thy rebellion looks so giant-like?
Let him go, Gertrude; do not fear our person:
120 There's such divinity doth hedge a king,
That treason can but peep to° what it would,°
Acts little of his will. Tell me, Laertes,
Why thou art thus incens'd. Let him go, Gertrude.
Speak, man.
Laertes: Where is my father?
King: Dead.
Queen: But not by him.
King: Let him demand his fill.
Laertes: How came he dead? I'll not be juggled with:
To hell, allegiance! vows, to the blackest devil!
Conscience and grace, to the profoundest pit!
130 I dare damnation. To this point I stand,
That both the worlds I give to negligence,°
Let come what comes; only I'll be reveng'd
Most thoroughly for my father.
King: Who shall stay you?
Laertes: My will,° not all the world's:
And for my means, I'll husband them so well,
They shall go far with little.
King: Good Laertes,
If you desire to know the certainty
Of your dear father, is 't writ in your revenge,
That, swoopstake,° you will draw both friend and foe,
140 Winner and loser?
Laertes: None but his enemies.
King: Will you know them then?
Laertes: To his good friends thus wide I'll ope my arms;
And like the kind life-rend'ring pelican,°
Repast° them with my blood.
King: Why, now you speak
Like a good child and a true gentleman.
That I am guiltless of your father's death,
And am most sensibly in grief for it,

---

121 *peep to:* i.e., look at from afar off; *would:* Wishes to do.   131 *give to negligence:* He despises both the here and the hereafter.   134 *My will:* He will not be stopped except by his own will.   139 *swoopstake:* Literally, drawing the whole stake at once, i.e., indiscriminately.   143 *pelican:* Reference to the belief that the pelican feeds its young with its own blood.   144 *Repast:* Feed.

It shall as level to your judgement 'pear
As day does to your eye.

A noise within: "Let her come in."

150 **Laertes:** How now! what noise is that?

Enter Ophelia.

O heat,° dry up my brains! tears seven times salt,
Burn out the sense and virtue of mine eye!
By heaven, thy madness shall be paid with weight,
Till our scale turn the beam. O rose of May!
Dear maid, kind sister, sweet Ophelia!
O heavens! is 't possible, a young maid's wits
Should be as mortal as an old man's life?
Nature is fine in love, and where 'tis fine,
It sends some precious instance of itself
160 After the thing it loves.
Ophelia (Song): They bore him barefac'd on the bier;
Hey non nonny, nonny, hey nonny;
And in his grave rain'd many a tear—
Fare you well, my dove!
Laertes: Hadst thou thy wits, and didst persuade revenge,
It could not move thus.
Ophelia (Sings):

You must sing a-down a-down,
An you call him a-down-a.

O, how the wheel° becomes it! It is the false steward,°
170   that stole his master's daughter.
Laertes: This nothing's more than matter.
Ophelia: There's rosemary,° that's for remembrance; pray you, love,
    remember: and there is pansies,° that's for thoughts.
Laertes: A document° in madness, thoughts and remembrance fitted.
Ophelia: There's fennel° for you, and columbines:° there's rue° for
    you; and here's some for me: we may call it herb of grace o'

---

151 *heat:* Probably the heat generated by the passion of grief.   169 *wheel:* Spinning wheel
as accompaniment to the song refrain; *false steward:* The story is unknown.   172 *rosemary:* Used as a symbol of remembrance both at weddings and at funerals.   173 *pansies:*
Emblems of love and courtship. Cf. French *pensées.*   174 *document:* Piece of instruction
or lesson.   175 *fennel:* Emblem of flattery; *columbines:* Emblem of unchastity (?) or in-
gratitude (?); *rue:* Emblem of repentance. It was usually mingled with holy water and then
known as *herb of grace.* Ophelia is probably playing on the two meanings of *rue,*
"repentant" and "even for ruth (pity)"; the former signification is for the queen, the latter
for herself.

Sundays: O, you must wear your rue with a difference. There's a
daisy:° I would give you some violets,° but they withered all when
my father died: they say 'a made a good end,—

180   *(Sings.)* For bonny sweet Robin is all my joy.°

Laertes: Thought° and affliction, passion, hell itself,
She turns to favour and to prettiness.

Ophelia (Song):

And will 'a not come again?°
And will 'a not come again?
   No, no, he is dead:
   Go to thy death-bed:
He never will come again.
His beard was as white as snow,
All flaxen was his poll:°

190   He is gone, he is gone,
   And we cast away° moan;
God ha' mercy on his soul!

And of all Christian souls, I pray God. God be wi' you.   *(Exit.)*

Laertes: Do you see this, O God?

King: Laertes, I must commune with your grief,
Or you deny me right.° Go but apart,
Make choice of whom your wisest friends you will,
And they shall hear and judge 'twixt you and me:
If by direct or by collateral° hand

200 They find us touch'd,° we will our kingdom give,
Our crown, our life, and all that we call ours,
To you in satisfaction; but if not,
Be you content to lend your patience to us,
And we shall jointly labour with your soul
To give it due content.

Laertes: Let this be so;
His means of death, his obscure funeral—
No trophy, sword, nor hatchment° o'er his bones,
No noble rite nor formal ostentation—
Cry to be heard, as 'twere from heaven to earth,
That I must call 't in question.

210 *King:*   So you shall;
And where th' offence is let the great axe fall.
I pray you, go with me.   *Exeunt.*

---

177 *daisy:* Emblem of dissembling, faithlessness; *violets:* Emblems of faithfulness.   180
For . . . joy: Probably a line from a Robin Hood ballad.   181 *Thought:* Melancholy
thought.   184 *And . . . again:* This song appeared in the songbooks as "The Merry
Milkmaids' Dumps."   189 *poll:* Head.   191 *cast away:* Shipwrecked.   196 *right:* My
rights.   199 *collateral:* Indirect.   200 *touch'd:* Implicated.   207 *hatchment:* Tablet displaying the armorial bearings of a deceased person.

Scene VI. Another room in the castle.

Enter Horatio and others.

Horatio: What are they that would speak with me?
Gentleman: Sea-faring men, sir: they say they have letters for you.
Horatio: Let them come in. *(Exit Gentleman.)*
    I do not know from what part of the world
    I should be greeted, if not from lord Hamlet.

Enter Sailors.

First Sailor: God bless you, sir.
Horatio: Let him bless thee too.
First Sailor: 'A shall sir, an 't please him. There's a letter for you, sir;
    it comes from the ambassador that was bound for England; if your
10   name be Horatio, as I am let to know it is.
Horatio (Reads): "Horatio, when thou shalt have overlooked this, give
    these fellows some means° to the king: they have letters for him. Ere
    we were two days old at sea, a pirate of very warlike appointment
    gave us chase. Finding ourselves too slow of sail, we put on a
    compelled valour, and in the grapple I boarded them: on the instant
    they got clear of our ship; so I alone became their prisoner. They
    have dealt with me like thieves of mercy:° but they knew what they
    did; I am to do a good turn for them. Let the king have the letters I
    have sent; and repair thou to me with as much speed as thou
20   wouldest fly death. I have words to speak in thine ear will make
    thee dumb; yet are they much too light for the bore° of the matter.
    These good fellows will bring thee where I am. Rosencrantz and
    Guildenstern hold their course for England: of them I have much to
    tell thee. Farewell.

                    "He that thou knowest thine, Hamlet."

Come, I will give you way for these your letters;
And do 't the speedier, that you may direct me
To him from whom you brought them.   *Exeunt.*

Scene VII. Another room in the castle.

Enter King and Laertes.

King: Now must your conscience° my acquittance seal,
And you must put me in your heart for friend,
Sith you have heard, and with a knowing ear,

SCENE VI.   12 *means:* Means of access.   17 *thieves of mercy:* Merciful thieves.   21 *bore:*
Caliber, importance.   SCENE VII.   1 *conscience:* Knowledge that this is true.

That he which hath your noble father slain
Pursued my life.
Laertes: It well appears: but tell me
Why you proceeded not against these feats,
So criminal and so capital° in nature,
As by your safety, wisdom, all things else,
You mainly° were stirr'd up.
King: O, for two special reasons;
10 Which may to you, perhaps, seem much unsinew'd,°
But yet to me th' are strong. The queen his mother
Lives almost by his looks; and for myself—
My virtue or my plague, be it either which—
She's so conjunctive° to my life and soul,
That, as the star moves not but in his sphere,°
I could not but by her. The other motive,
Why to a public count° I might not go,
Is the great love the general gender° bear him;
Who, dipping all his faults in their affection,
20 Would, like the spring° that turneth wood to stone,
Convert his gyves° to graces; so that my arrows,
Too slightly timber'd° for so loud° a wind,
Would have reverted to my bow again,
And not where I had aim'd them.
Laertes: And so have I a noble father lost;
A sister driven into desp'rate terms,°
Whose worth, if praises may go back° again,
Stood challenger on mount° of all the age°
For her perfections: but my revenge will come.
30 ***King:*** Break not your sleeps for that: you must not think
That we are made of stuff so flat and dull
That we can let our beard be shook with danger
And think it pastime. You shortly shall hear more:
I lov'd your father, and we love ourself;
And that, I hope, will teach you to imagine—

Enter a Messenger with letters.

How now! what news?
Messenger: Letters, my lord, from Hamlet:

---

7 *capital:* Punishable by death.   9 *mainly:* Greatly.   10 *unsinew'd:* Weak.   14 *conjunctive:* Conformable (the next line suggesting planetary conjunction).   15 *sphere:* The hollow sphere in which, according to Ptolemaic astronomy, the planets were supposed to move.   17 *count:* Account, reckoning.   18 *general gender:* Common people.   20 *spring:* i.e., one heavily charged with lime.   21 *gyves:* Fetters; here, faults, or possibly, punishments inflicted (on him).   22 *slightly timber'd:* Light; *loud:* Strong.   26 *terms:* State, condition.   27 *go back:* i.e., to Ophelia's former virtues.   28 *on mount:* Set up on high, *mounted* (on horseback); *of all the age:* Qualifies *challenger* and not *mount.*

These to your majesty; this to the queen.°

King: From Hamlet! who brought them?

Messenger: Sailors, my lord, they say; I saw them not:

40 They were given me by Claudio;° he receiv'd them
Of him that brought them.

King: Laertes, you shall hear them.
Leave us.   *(Exit Messenger.)*

(Reads.) "High and mighty, You shall know I am set naked° on your
kingdom. To-morrow shall I beg leave to see your kingly eyes:
when I shall, first asking your pardon thereunto, recount the
occasion of my sudden and more strange return.

                                               "Hamlet."

What should this mean? Are all the rest come back?
Or is it some abuse, and no such thing?

Laertes: Know you the hand?

King: 'Tis Hamlet's character. "Naked!"

50 And in a postscript here, he says "alone."
Can you devise° me?

Laertes: I 'm lost in it, my lord. But let him come;
It warms the very sickness in my heart,
That I shall live and tell him to his teeth,
"Thus didst thou."

King: If it be so, Laertes—
As how should it be so? how otherwise?°—
Will you be rul'd by me?

Laertes: Ay, my lord;
So you will not o'errule me to a peace.

King: To thine own peace. If he be now return'd,

60 As checking at° his voyage, and that he means
No more to undertake it, I will work him
To an exploit, now ripe in my device,
Under the which he shall not choose but fall:
And for his death no wind of blame shall breathe,
But even his mother shall uncharge the practice°
And call it accident.

Laertes: My lord, I will be rul'd;
The rather, if you could devise it so
That I might be the organ.°

---

37 *to the queen:* One hears no more of the letter to the queen.   40 *Claudio:* This character
does not appear in the play. 43 *naked:* Unprovided (with retinue).   51 *devise:* Explain
to.   56 *As . . . otherwise?:* How can this (Hamlet's return) be true? (yet) how otherwise than true (since we have the evidence of his letter)? Some editors read *How should it
not be so,* etc., making the words refer to Laertes's desire to meet with Hamlet.   60
checking at: Used in falconry of a hawk's leaving the quarry to fly at a chance bird, turn
aside.   65 *uncharge the practice:* Acquit the stratagem of being a plot.   68 *organ:* Agent,
instrument.

King: It falls right.
You have been talk'd of since your travel much,
70 And that in Hamlet's hearing, for a quality
Wherein, they say, you shine: your sum of parts
Did not together pluck such envy from him
As did that one, and that, in my regard,
Of the unworthiest siege.°
Laertes: What part is that, my lord?
King: A very riband in the cap of youth,
Yet needful too; for youth no less becomes
The light and careless livery that it wears
That settled age his sables° and his weeds,
Importing health and graveness. Two months since,
80 Here was a gentleman of Normandy:—
I have seen myself, and serv'd against, the French,
And they can well° on horseback: but this gallant
Had witchcraft in 't; he grew unto his seat;
And to such wondrous doing brought his horse,
As had he been incorps'd and demi-natur'd°
With the brave beast: so far he topp'd° my thought,
That I, in forgery° of shapes and tricks,
Come short of what he did.
Laertes: A Norman was 't?
King: A Norman.
Laertes: Upon my life, Lamord.°
90 *King:*   The very same.
Laertes: I know him well: he is the brooch indeed
And gem of all the nation.
King: He made confession° of you,
And gave you such a masterly report
For art and exercise° in your defence°
And for your rapier most especial,
That he cried out, 'twould be a sight indeed,
If one could match you: the scrimers° of their nation,
He swore, had neither motion, guard, nor eye,
100 If you oppos'd them. Sir, this report of his
Did Hamlet so envenom with his envy
That he could nothing do but wish and beg
Your sudden coming o'er, to play° with you.
Now, out of this,—
Laertes: What out of this, my lord?

---

74 *siege:* Rank.   78 *sables:* Rich garments.   82 *can well:* Are skilled.   85 *incorps'd and
demi-natur'd:* Of one body and nearly of one nature (like the centaur).   86 *topp'd:* Surpassed.   87 *forgery:* Invention.   90 *Lamord:* This refers possibly to Pietro Monte, instructor to Louis XII's master of the horse.   93 *confession:* Grudging admission of
superiority.   95 *art and exercise:* Skillful exercise; *defence:* Science of defense in sword
practice.   98 *scrimers:* Fencers.   103 *play:* Fence.

King: Laertes, was your father dear to you?
Or are you like the painting of a sorrow,
A face without a heart?
Laertes: Why ask you this?
King: Not that I think you did not love your father;
But that I know love is begun by time;
110 And that I see, in passages of proof,°
Time qualifies the spark and fire of it.
There lives within the very flame of love
A kind of wick or snuff that will abate it;
And nothing is at a like goodness still;
For goodness, growing to a plurisy,°
Dies in his own too much:° that we would do,
We should do when we would; for this "would" changes
And hath abatements° and delays as many
As there are tongues, are hands, are accidents;°
120 And then this "should" is like a spendthrift° sigh,
That hurts by easing. But, to the quick o' th' ulcer:°—
Hamlet comes back: what would you undertake,
To show yourself your father's son in deed
More than in words?
Laertes: To cut his throat i' th' church.
King: No place, indeed, should murder sanctuarize;°
Revenge should have no bounds. But, good Laertes,
Will you do this, keep close within your chamber.
Hamlet return'd shall know you are come home:
We'll put on those shall praise your excellence
130 And set a double varnish on the fame
The Frenchman gave you, bring you in fine together
And wager on your heads: he, being remiss,
Most generous and free from all contriving,
Will not peruse the foils; so that, with ease,
Or with a little shuffling, you may choose
A sword unbated,° and in a pass of practice°
Requite him for your father.
Laertes: I will do 't:
And, for that purpose, I'll anoint my sword.
I bought an unction of a mountebank,°
140 So mortal that, but dip a knife in it,
Where it draws blood no cataplasm° so rare,

---

110 *passages of proof:* Proved instances.   115 *plurisy:* Excess, plethora.   116 *in his own too much:* Of its own excess.   118 *abatements:* Diminutions.   119 *accidents:* Occurrences, incidents.   120 *spendthrift:* An allusion to the belief that each sigh cost the heart a drop of blood.   121 *quick o' th' ulcer:* Heart of the difficulty.   125 *sanctuarize:* Protect from punishment; allusion to the right of sanctuary with which certain religious places were invested.   136 *unbated:* Not blunted, having no button; *pass of practice:* Treacherous thrust.   139 *mountebank:* Quack doctor.   141 *cataplasm:* Plaster or poultice.

Collected from all simples° that have virtue
Under the moon,° can save the thing from death
That is but scratch'd withal: I'll touch my point
With this contagion, that, if I gall° him slightly,
It may be death.
King: Let's further think of this;
Weigh what convenience both of time and means
May fit us to our shape:° if this should fail,
And that our drift look through our bad performance,°
150 'Twere better not assay'd: therefore this project
Should have a back or second, that might hold,
If this should blast in proof.° Soft! let me see:
We'll make a solemn wager on your cunnings:°
I ha 't:
When in your motion you are hot and dry—
As make your bouts more violent to that end—
And that he calls for drink, I'll have prepar'd him
A chalice° for the nonce, whereon but sipping,
If he by chance escape your venom'd stuck,°
160 Our purpose may hold there. But stay, what noise?

     Enter Queen.

Queen: One woe doth tread upon another's heel,
So fast they follow: your sister's drown'd, Laertes.
Laertes: Drown'd! O, where?
Queen: There is a willow° grows askant° the brook,
That shows his hoar° leaves in the glassy stream;
There with fantastic garlands did she make
Of crow-flowers,° nettles, daisies, and long purples°
That liberal° shepherds give a grosser name,
But our cold maids do dead men's fingers call them:
170 There, on the pendent boughs her crownet° weeds
Clamb'ring to hang, an envious sliver° broke;
When down her weedy° trophies and herself
Fell in the weeping brook. Her clothes spread wide;
And, mermaid-like, awhile they bore her up:
Which time she chanted snatches of old lauds;°

---

142 *simples:* Herbs.   143 *Under the moon:* i.e., when collected by moonlight to add to
their medicinal value.   145 *gall:* Graze, wound.   148 *shape:* Part we propose to act.
149 *drift . . . performance:* Intention be disclosed by our bungling.   152 *blast in proof:*
Burst in the test (like a cannon).   153 *cunnings:* Skills.   158 *chalice:* Cup.   159 *Stuck:*
Thrust (from *stoccado*).   164 *willow:* For its significance of forsaken love; *askant:* Aslant.
165 *hoar:* White (i.e., on the underside).   167 *crow-flowers:* Buttercups; *long purples:* Early
purple orchis.   168 *liberal:* Probably, free-spoken.   170 *crownet:* Coronet; made into a
chaplet.   171 *sliver:* Branch.   172 *weedy:* i.e., of plants.   175 *lauds:* Hymns.

As one incapable° of her own distress,
Or like a creature native and indued°
Upon that element: but long it could not be
Till that her garments, heavy with their drink,
180 Pull'd the poor wretch from her melodious lay
To muddy death.
Laertes: Alas, then, she is drown'd?
Queen: Drown'd, drown'd.
Laertes: Too much of water hast thou, poor Ophelia,
And therefore I forbid my tears: but yet
It is our trick;° nature her custom holds,
Let shame say what it will: when these are gone,
The woman will be out.° Adieu, my lord:
I have a speech of fire, that fain would blaze,
But that this folly drowns it.   *Exit.*
King: Let's follow, Gertrude:
190 How much I had to do to calm his rage!
Now fear I this will give it start again;
Therefore let's follow.   *Exeunt.*

Act V

Scene I. A churchyard.

Enter two Clowns° (with spades, &c.).

First Clown: Is she to be buried in Christian burial when she wilfully
    seeks her own salvation?
Second Clown: I tell thee she is; therefore make her grave straight:°
    the crowner° hath sat on her, and finds it Christian burial.
First Clown: How can that be, unless she drowned herself in her own
    defence?
Second Clown: Why, 'tis found so.
First Clown: It must be "se offendendo";° it cannot be else. For here
    lies the point: if I drown myself wittingly,° it argues an act: and an
10   act hath three branches;° it is, to act, to do, and to perform: argal,°
    she drowned herself wittingly.
Second Clown: Nay, but hear you, goodman delver,°—

---

176 *incapable:* Lacking capacity to apprehend.   177 *indued:* Endowed with qualities fitting her for living in water.   185 *trick:* Way.   186–187 *when . . . out:* When my tears
are all shed, the woman in me will be satisfied.   ACT V. SCENE I. *Clowns:* The word
clown was used to denote peasants as well as humorous characters; here applied to the
rustic type of clown.   3 *straight:* Straightway, immediately; some interpret "from east to
west in a direct line, parallel with the church."; *crowner:* Coroner.   8 *"se offendendo:"* For
se defendendo, term used in verdicts of justifiable homicide.   9 *wittingly:* Intentionally.
10 *three branches:* Parody of legal phraseology; *argal:* Corruption of *ergo,* therefore.   12
delver: Digger.

First Clown: Give me leave. Here lies the water; good: here stands the
   man; good: if the man go to this water, and drown himself, it is,
   will he, nill he, he goes,—mark you that; but if the water come to
   him and drown him, he drowns not himself: argal, he that is not
   guilty of his own death shortens not his own life.
Second Clown: But is this law?
First Clown: Ay, marry, is 't; crowner's quest° law.
20 *Second Clown:* Will you ha' the truth on 't? If this had not been a
   gentlewoman, she should have been buried out o' Christian burial.
First Clown: Why, there thou say'st:° and the more pity that great
   folk should have countenance° in this world to drown or hang
   themselves, more than their even° Christian. Come, my spade.
   There is no ancient gentlemen but gardeners, ditchers, and
   grave-makers: they hold up° Adam's profession.
Second Clown: Was he a gentleman?
First Clown: 'A was the first that ever bore arms.
Second Clown: Why, he had none.
30 *First Clown:* What, art a heathen? How dost thou understand the
   Scripture? The Scripture says "Adam digged": could he dig
   without arms? I'll put another question to thee: if thou answerest
   me not to the purpose, confess thyself°—
Second Clown: Go to.°
First Clown: What is he that builds stronger than either the mason,
   the shipwright, or the carpenter?
Second Clown: The gallows-maker; for that frame outlives a thousand
   tenants.
First Clown: I like thy wit well, in good faith: the gallows does well;
40   but how does it well? It does well to those that do ill: now thou
   dost ill to say the gallows is built stronger than the church: argal,
   the gallows may do well to thee. To 't again, come.
Second Clown: "Who builds stronger than a mason, a shipwright, or a
   carpenter?"
First Clown: Ay, tell me that, and unyoke.°
Second Clown: Marry, now I can tell.
First Clown: To 't.
Second Clown: Mass,° I cannot tell.

   Enter Hamlet and Horatio at a distance.

First Clown: Cudgel thy brains no more about it, for your dull ass
50   will not mend his pace with beating; and, when you are asked

---

19 *quest:* Inquest.   22 *there thou say'st:* That's right.   23 *countenance:* Privilege.   24
even: Fellow.   26 *hold up:* Maintain, continue.   33 *confess thyself:* "And be hanged"
completes the proverb.   34 *Go to:* Perhaps, "begin," or some other form of concession.
45 *unyoke:* After this great effort you may unharness the team of your wits.   48 *mass:*
By the Mass.

this question next, say "a grave-maker": the houses he makes lasts till doomsday. Go, get thee in, and fetch me a stoup° of liquor.

(Exit Second Clown.) Song. (He digs.)

In youth, when I did love, did love,
   Methought it was very sweet,
To contract—O—the time, for—a—my behove,°
   O, methought, there—a—was nothing—a—meet.

Hamlet: Has this fellow no feeling of his business, that 'a sings at
   gravemaking?
Horatio: Custom hath made it in him a property of easiness.°
60 *Hamlet:* 'Tis e'en so: the hand of little employment hath the daintier
   sense.
First Clown (Song):

But age, with his stealing steps,
   Hath claw'd me in his clutch,
And hath shipped me into the land
   As if I had never been such.   *(Throws up a skull.)*

Hamlet: That skull had a tongue in it, and could sing once: how the
   knave jowls° it to the ground, as if 'twere Cain's jaw-bone,° that
   did the first murder! This might be the pate of a politician,° which
   this ass now o'er-reaches;° one that would circumvent God, might
70   it not?
Horatio: It might, my lord.
Hamlet: Or of a courtier; which could say "Good morrow, sweet lord!
   How dost thou, sweet lord?" This might be my lord such-a-one,
   that praised my lord such-a-one's horse, when he meant to beg it;
   might it not?
Horatio: Ay, my lord.
Hamlet: Why, e'en so: and now my Lady Worm's; chapless,° and
   knocked about the mazzard° with a sexton's spade: here's fine
   revolution, an we had the trick to see 't. Did these bones cost no
80   more the breeding, but to play at loggats° with 'em? mine ache to
   think on 't.

---

52 *stoup:* Two-quart measure.   55 *behove:* Benefit.   59 *property of easiness:* A peculiarity that now is easy.   67 *jowls:* Dashes; *Cain's jaw-bone:* Allusion to the old tradition that Cain slew Abel with the jawbone of an ass.   68 *politician:* Schemer, plotter.   69 *o'er-reaches:* Quibble on the literal sense and the sense "circumvent."   77 *chapless:* Having no lower jaw.   78 *mazzard:* Head.   80 *loggats:* A game in which six sticks are thrown to lie as near as possible to a stake fixed in the ground, or block of wood on a floor.

First Clown (Song):

A pick-axe, and a spade, a spade,
  For and° a shrouding sheet:
O, a pit of clay for to be made
  For such a guest is meet.   *(Throws up another skull.)*

Hamlet: There's another: why may not that be the skull of a lawyer?
    Where be his quiddities° now, his quillities,° his cases, his
    tenures,° and his tricks? why does he suffer this mad knave now
    to knock him about the sconce° with a dirty shovel, and will not
90   tell him of his action of battery? Hum! This fellow might be in 's
    time a great buyer of land, with his statutes,° his recognizances,°
    his fines, his double vouchers,° his recoveries:° is this the fine° of
    his fines, and the recovery of his recoveries, to have his fine pate
    full of fine dirt? will his vouchers vouch him no more of his
    purchases, and double ones too, than the length and breadth of a
    pair of indentures?° The very conveyances of his lands will
    scarcely lie in this box; and must the inheritor° himself have no
    more, ha?
Horatio: Not a jot more, my lord.
100 *Hamlet:* Is not parchment made of sheep-skins?
Horatio: Ay, my lord, and of calf-skins° too.
Hamlet: They are sheep and calves which seek out assurance in that.°
    I will speak to this fellow. Whose grave's this, sirrah?
First Clown: Mine, sir.

(Sings.) O, a pit of clay for to be made
      For such a guest is meet.

Hamlet: I think it be thine, indeed; for thou liest in 't.
First Clown: You lie out on 't, sir, and therefore 't is not yours: for my
    part, I do not lie in 't, yet it is mine.
110 *Hamlet:* Thou dost lie in 't, to be in 't and say it is thine: 'tis for the
    dead, not for the quick; therefore thou liest.
First Clown: 'Tis a quick lie, sir; 'twill away again, from me to you.
Hamlet: What man dost thou dig it for?
First Clown: For no man, sir.
Hamlet: What woman, then?

---

83 *For and:* And moreover.   87 *quiddities:* Subtleties, quibbles; *quillities:* Verbal niceties,
subtle distinctions.   88 *tenures:* The holding of a piece of property or office or the conditions or period of such holding.   89 *sconce:* Head.   91 *statutes, recognizances:* Legal
terms connected with the transfer of land.   92 *vouchers:* Persons called on to warrant a
tenant's title; *recoveries:* Process for transfer of entailed estate.   92 *fine:* The four uses of
this word are as follows: (1) end, (2) legal process, (3) elegant, (4) small.   96 *indentures:*
Conveyances or contracts.   97 *inheritor:* Possessor, owner.   101 *calfskins:* Parchments.
102 *assurance in that:* Safety in legal parchments.

First Clown: For none, neither.

Hamlet: Who is to be buried in 't?

First Clown: One that was a woman, sir; but, rest her soul, she's dead.

Hamlet: How absolute° the knave is! we must speak by the card,° or
120   equivocation° will undo us. By the Lord, Horatio, these three years
I have taken note of it; the age is grown so picked° that the toe of
the peasant comes so near the heel of the courtier, he galls° his
kibe.° How long hast thou been a grave-maker?

First Clown: Of all the day i' the year, I came to 't that day that our
last king Hamlet overcame Fortinbras.

Hamlet: How long is that since?

First Clown: Cannot you tell that? Every fool can tell that: it was the
very day that young Hamlet was born; he that is mad, and sent
into England.

130 *Hamlet:* Ay, marry, why was he sent into England?

First Clown: Why, because 'a was mad: 'a shall recover his wits there;
or, if 'a do not, 'tis no great matter there.

Hamlet: Why?

First Clown: 'Twill not be seen in him there; there the men are as
mad as he.

Hamlet: How came he mad?

First Clown: Very strangely, they say.

Hamlet: How strangely?

First Clown: Faith, e'en with losing his wits.

140 *Hamlet:* Upon what ground?

First Clown: Why, here in Denmark: I have been sexton here, man and
boy, thirty years.°

Hamlet: How long will a man lie i' the earth ere he rot?

First Clown: Faith, if 'a be not rotten before 'a die—as we have many
pocky° corses now-a-days, that will scarce hold the laying in—'a
will last you some eight year or nine year: a tanner will last you
nine year.

Hamlet: Why he more than another?

First Clown: Why, sir, his hide is so tanned with his trade, that 'a will
150   keep out water a great while; and your water is a sore decayer of
your whoreson dead body. Here's a skull now hath lain you i' th'
earth three and twenty years.

Hamlet: Whose was it?

First Clown: A whoreson mad fellow's it was: whose do you think it
was?

Hamlet: Nay, I know not.

---

119 *absolute:* Positive, decided; *by the card:* With precision, i.e., by the mariner's card on which the points of the compass were marked. 120 *equivocation:* Ambiguity in the use of terms. 121 *picked:* Refined, fastidious. 122 *galls:* Chafes. 123 *kibe:* Chilblain. 142 *thirty years:* This statement with that in line 152 shows Hamlet's age to be thirty years. 145 *pocky:* Rotten, diseased.

First Clown: A pestilence on him for a mad rogue! 'a poured a flagon
of Rhenish on my head once. This same skull, sir, was Yorick's skull,
the king's jester.

160 **Hamlet:** This?

First Clown: E'en that.

Hamlet: Let me see. *(Takes the skull.)* Alas, poor Yorick! I knew him,
Horatio: a fellow of infinite jest, of most excellent fancy: he hath
borne me on his back a thousand times; and now, how abhorred in
my imagination it is! My gorge rises at it. Here hung those lips
that I have kissed I know not how oft. Where be your gibes now?
Your gambols? Your songs? Your flashes of merriment, that were
wont to set the table on a roar? Not one now, to mock your own
grinning? Quite chap-fallen? Now get you to my lady's chamber,
170   and tell her, let her paint an inch thick, to this favour she must
come; make her laugh at that. Prithee, Horatio, tell me one thing.

Horatio: What's that, my lord?

Hamlet: Dost thou think Alexander looked o' this fashion i' the earth?

Horatio: E'en so.

Hamlet: And smelt so? pah!   *(Puts down the skull.)*

Horatio: E'en so, my lord.

Hamlet: To what base uses we may return, Horatio! Why may not
imagination trace the noble dust of Alexander, till 'a find it stopping
a bunghole?

180 **Horatio:** 'Twere to consider too curiously,° to consider so.

Hamlet: No, faith, not a jot; but to follow him thither with modesty
enough, and likelihood to lead it: as thus: Alexander died,
Alexander was buried, Alexander returneth into dust; the dust
is earth; of earth we make loam;° and why of that loam,
whereto he was converted, might they not stop a beer-barrel?
Imperious° Caesar, dead and turn'd to clay,
Might stop a hole to keep the wind away:
O, that that earth, which kept the world in awe,
Should patch a wall t'expel the winter's flaw!°
190 But soft! but soft awhile! here comes the king,

*Enter King, Queen, Laertes, and the Corse of Ophelia, in procession, with Priest,
Lords, etc.*

The queen, the courtiers: who is this they follow?
And with such maimed rites? This doth betoken
The corse they follow did with desp'rate hand
Fordo° its° own life: 'twas of some estate.
Couch° we awhile, and mark.   *(Retiring with Horatio.)*

---

180 *curiously:* Minutely.   184 *loam:* Clay paste for brickmaking.   186 *Imperious:* Imperial.   189 *flaw:* Gust of wind.   194 *Fordo:* Destroy; *it:* Its.   195 *Couch:* Hide, lurk.

Laertes: What ceremony else?
Hamlet: That is Laertes,
A very noble youth: mark.
Laertes: What ceremony else?
200 *First Priest:* Her obsequies have been as far enlarg'd°
As we have warranty: her death was doubtful;
And, but that great command o'ersways the order,
She should in ground unsanctified have lodg'd
Till the last trumpet; for charitable prayers,
Shards,° flints and pebbles should be thrown on her:
Yet here she is allow'd her virgin crants,°
Her maiden strewments° and the bringing home
Of bell and burial.°
Laertes: Must there no more be done?
210 *First Priest:*   No more be done:
We should profane the service of the dead
To sing a requiem and such rest to her
As to peace-parted° souls.
Laertes: Lay her i' th' earth:
And from her fair and unpolluted flesh
May violets spring! I tell thee, churlish priest,
A minist'ring angel shall my sister be,
When thou liest howling.°
Hamlet: What, the fair Ophelia!
220 *Queen:* Sweets to the sweet: farewell!

(*Scattering flowers.*)

I hop'd thou shouldst have been my Hamlet's wife;
I thought thy bride-bed to have deck'd, sweet maid,
And not have strew'd thy grave.
Laertes: O, treble woe
Fall ten times treble on that cursed head,
Whose wicked deed thy most ingenious sense°
Depriv'd thee of! Hold off the earth awhile,
Till I have caught her once more in mine arms:

(*Leaps into the grave.*)

Now pile your dust upon the quick and dead,
230 Till of this flat a mountain you have made,

---

200 *enlarg'd:* Extended, referring to the fact that suicides are not given full burial rites.   205 *Shards:* Broken bits of pottery.   206 *crants:* Garlands customarily hung upon the biers of unmarried women.   207 *strewments:* Traditional strewing of flowers. 207–208 *bringing . . . burial:* The laying to rest of the body, to the sound of the bell. 213 *peace-parted:* Allusion to the text "Lord, now lettest thou thy servant depart in peace." 218 *howling:* i.e., in hell.   226 *ingenious sense:* Mind endowed with finest qualities.

T' o'ertop old Pelion,° or the skyish head
Of blue Olympus.
Hamlet: (*Advancing*) What is he whose grief
Bears such an emphasis? whose phrase of sorrow
Conjures the wand'ring stars,° and makes them stand
Like wonder-wounded hearers? This is I,
Hamlet the Dane.   (*Leaps into the grave.*)
Laertes: The devil take thy soul!   (*Grappling with him.*)
Hamlet: Thou pray'st not well.
240 I prithee, take thy fingers from my throat;
For, though I am not splenitive° and rash,
Yet have I in me something dangerous,
Which let thy wisdom fear: hold off thy hand.
King: Pluck them asunder.
Queen: Hamlet, Hamlet!
All: Gentlemen,—
Horatio: Good my lord, be quiet.

The Attendants part them, and they come out of the grave.

Hamlet: Why, I will fight with him upon this theme
Until my eyelids will no longer wag.°
250 *Queen:* O my son, what theme?
Hamlet: I lov'd Ophelia: forty thousand brothers
Could not, with all their quantity° of love,
Make up my sum. What wilt thou do for her?
King: O, he is mad, Laertes.
Queen: For love of God, forbear° him.
Hamlet: 'Swounds,° show me what thou'lt do:
Woo't° weep? woo't fight? woo't fast? woo't tear thyself?
Woo't drink up eisel?° eat a crocodile?
I'll do't. Dost thou come here to whine?
260 To outface me with leaping in her grave?
Be buried quick with her, and so will I:
And, if thou prate of mountains, let them throw
Millions of acres on us, till our ground,
Singeing his pate against the burning zone,°
Make Ossa like a wart! Nay, an thou'lt mouth,
I'll rant as well as thou.

---

231 *Pelion:* Olympus, Pelion, and Ossa are mountains in the north of Thessaly.   235
wand'ring stars: Planets.   241 *splenitive:* Quick-tempered.   249 *wag:* Move (not used lu-
dicrously).   252 *quantity:* Some suggest that the word is used in a deprecatory sense (little bits, fragments).   255 *forbear:* Leave alone.   256 *'Swounds:* Oath, "God's wounds."
257 *Woo 't:* Wilt thou.   258 *eisel:* Vinegar. Some editors have taken this to be the name of
a river, such as the Yssel, the Weissel, and the Nile.   264 *burning zone:* Sun's orbit.

Queen: This is mere madness:
And thus awhile the fit will work on him;
Anon, as patient as the female dove.
270 When that her golden couplets° are disclos'd,
His silence will sit drooping.
Hamlet: Hear you, sir;
What is the reason that you use me thus?
I lov'd you ever: but it is no matter;
Let Hercules himself do what he may,
The cat will mew and dog will have his day.
King: I pray thee, good Horatio, wait upon him.

Exit Hamlet and Horatio.

(*To Laertes.*) Strengthen your patience in° our last night's speech;
We'll put the matter to the present push.°
280 Good Gertrude, set some watch over your son.
This grave shall have a living° monument:
An hour of quiet shortly shall we see;
Till then, in patience our proceeding be.   *Exeunt.*

Scene II. A hall in the castle.

Enter Hamlet and Horatio.

Hamlet: So much for this, sir: now shall you see the other;
You do remember all the circumstance?
Horatio: Remember it, my lord!
Hamlet: Sir, in my heart there was a kind of fighting,
That would not let me sleep: methought I lay
Worse than the mutines° in the bilboes.° Rashly,°
And prais'd be rashness for it, let us know,
Our indiscretion sometime serves us well,
When our deep plots do pall:° and that should learn us
10 There's a divinity that shapes our ends,
Rough-hew° them how we will,—
Horatio: That is most certain.
Hamlet: Up from my cabin,
My sea-gown° scarf'd about me, in the dark
Grop'd I to find out them; had my desire,

---

270 *golden couplets:* The pigeon lays two eggs; the young when hatched are covered with golden down.   278 *in:* By recalling.   279 *present push:* Immediate test.   281 *living:* Lasting; also refers (for Laertes's benefit) to the plot against Hamlet.   Scene II. 6 *mutines:* Mutineers; *bilboes:* Shackles; *Rashly:* Goes with line 12.   9 *pall:* Fail.   11 *Rough-hew:* Shape roughly; it may mean "bungle."   13 *sea-gown:* "A sea-gown, or a coarse, high-collered, and short-sleeved gowne, reaching down to the mid-leg, and used most by seamen and saylors" (Cotgrave, quoted by Singer).

Finger'd° their packet, and in fine° withdrew
To mine own room again; making so bold,
My fears forgetting manners, to unseal
Their grand commission; where I found, Horatio,—
O royal knavery!—an exact command,
20 Larded° with many several sorts of reasons
Importing Denmark's health and England's too,
With, ho! such bugs° and goblins in my life,°
That, on the supervise,° no leisure bated,°
No, not to stay the grinding of the axe,
My head should be struck off.
Horatio: Is 't possible?
Hamlet: Here's the commission: read it at more leisure.
But wilt thou hear me how I did proceed?
Horatio: I beseech you.
Hamlet: Being thus be-netted round with villanies,—
30 Ere I could make a prologue to my brains,
They had begun the play°—I sat me down,
Devis'd a new commission, wrote it fair:
I once did hold it, as our statists° do,
A baseness to write fair° and labour'd much
How to forget that learning, but, sir, now
It did me yeoman's° service: wilt thou know
Th' effect of what I wrote?
Horatio: Ay, good my lord.
Hamlet: An earnest conjuration from the king,
As England was his faithful tributary,
40 As love between them like the palm might flourish,
As peace should still her wheaten garland° wear
And stand a comma° 'tween their amities,
And many such-like 'As'es° of great charge,°
That, on the view and knowing of these contents,
Without debatement further, more or less,
He should the bearers put to sudden death,
Not shriving-time° allow'd.
Horatio: How was this seal'd?
Hamlet: Why, even in that was heaven ordinant.°
I had my father's signet in my purse,

---

15 *Finger'd:* Pilfered, filched; *in fine:* Finally.   20 *Larded:* Enriched.   22 *such . . . life:*
Such imaginary dangers if I were allowed to live; *bugs:* Bugbears.   23 *supervise:* Perusal;
leisure bated: Delay allowed.   30–31 *prologue . . . play:* i.e., before I could begin to think,
my mind had made its decision.   33 *statists:* Statesmen.   34 *fair:* In a clear hand.
36 *yeoman's:* i.e., faithful.   41 *wheaten garland:* Symbol of peace.   42 *comma:* Smallest
break or separation. Here *amity* begins and *amity* ends the period, and *peace* stands between like a dependent clause. The comma indicates continuity, link.   43 *'As'es:* The
"whereases" of a formal document, with play on the word *ass; charge:* Import, and burden.
47 *shriving-time:* Time for absolution. 48 *ordinant:* Directing.

50 Which was the model of that Danish seal;
Folded the writ up in the form of th' other,
Subscrib'd it, gave 't th' impression, plac'd it safely,
The changeling never known. Now, the next day
Was our sea-fight; and what to this was sequent°
Thou know'st already.
Horatio: So Guildenstern and Rosencrantz go to 't.
Hamlet: Why, man, they did make love to this employment;
They are not near my conscience; their defeat
Does by their own insinuation° grow:
60 'Tis dangerous when the baser nature comes
Between the pass° and fell incensed° points
Of mighty opposites.
Horatio: Why, what a king is this!
Hamlet: Does it not, think thee, stand° me now upon—
He that hath kill'd my king and whor'd my mother,
Popp'd in between th' election° and my hopes,
Thrown out his angle° for my proper life,
And with such coz'nage°—is 't not perfect conscience,
To quit° him with this arm: and is't not to be damn'd,
To let this canker° of our nature come
70 In further evil?
Horatio: It must be shortly known to him from England
What is the issue of the business there.
Hamlet: It will be short: the interim is mine;
And a man's life's no more than to say "One."
But I am very sorry, good Horatio,
That to Laertes I forgot myself;
For, by the image of my cause, I see
The portraiture of his: I'll court his favours:
But, sure, the bravery° of his grief did put me
80 Into a tow'ring passion.
Horatio: Peace! who comes here?

Enter a Courtier (Osric).

Osric: Your lordship is right welcome back to Denmark.
Hamlet: I humbly thank you, sir. *(To Horatio.)* Dost know this
    water-fly?°
Horatio: No, my good lord.
Hamlet: Thy state is the more gracious; for 'tis a vice to know him.

---

54 *sequent:* Subsequent.   59 *insinuation:* Interference.   61 *pass:* Thrust; *fell incensed:*
Fiercely angered.   63 *stand:* Become incumbent.   65 *election:* The Danish throne was
filled by election.   66 *angle:* Fishing line.   67 *coz'nage:* Trickery.   68 *quit:* Repay.
69 *canker:* Ulcer, or possibly the worm which destroys buds and leaves.   79 *bravery:*
Bravado.   83 *water-fly:* Vain or busily idle person.

He hath much land, and fertile: let a beast be lord of beasts,° and
his crib shall stand at the king's mess:° 'tis a chough;° but, as I
say, spacious in the possession of dirt.

Osric: Sweet lord, if your lordship were at leisure, I should impart a
90   thing to you from his majesty.

Hamlet: I will receive it, sir, with all diligence of spirit. Put your
bonnet to his right use; 'tis for the head.

Osric: I thank you lordship, it is very hot.

Hamlet: No, believe me, 'tis very cold; the wind is northerly.

Osric: It is indifferent° cold, my lord, indeed.

Hamlet: But yet methinks it is very sultry and hot for my complexion.

Osric: Exceedingly, my lord; it is very sultry,—as 'twere,—I cannot tell
how. But, my lord, his majesty bade me signify to you that 'a has
laid a great wager on your head: sir, this is the matter,—

100 *Hamlet:* I beseech you, remember°—

> *(Hamlet moves him to put on his hat.)*

Osric: Nay, good my lord; for mine ease,° in good faith. Sir, here is
newly come to court Laertes; believe me, an absolute gentleman,
full of most excellent differences, of very soft° society and great
showing:° indeed, to speak feelingly° of him, he is the card° or
calendar of gentry,° for you shall find in him the continent of
what part a gentleman would see.

Hamlet: Sir, his definement° suffers no perdition° in you; though, I
know, to divide him inventorially° would dozy° the arithmetic of
memory, and yet but yaw° neither, in respect of his quick sail. But,
110   in the verity of extolment, I take him to be a soul of great article;°
and his infusion° of such dearth and rareness,° as, to make true
diction of him, his semblable° is his mirror; and who else would
trace° him, his umbrage,° nothing more.

Osric: Your lordship speaks most infallibly of him.

Hamlet: The concernancy,° sir? why do we wrap the gentleman in our
more rawer breath?°

Osric: Sir?

86–87 *lord of beasts:* Cf. Genesis 1:26, 28; *his crib . . . mess:* He shall eat at the king's table,
i.e., be one of the group of persons (usually four) constituting a *mess* at a banquet.   87
chough: Probably, chattering jackdaw; also explained as *chuff,* provincial boor or churl.
95 *indifferent:* Somewhat.   100 *remember:* i.e., remember thy courtesy; conventional
phrase for "Be covered."   101 *mine ease:* Conventional reply declining the invitation of
"Remember thy courtesy."   103 *soft:* Gentle; *showing:* Distinguished appearance.   104
feelingly: With just perception; *card:* Chart, map.   105 *gentry:* Good breeding.   107 *de-
finement:* Definition; *perdition:* Loss, diminution.   108 *divide him inventorially:* i.e., enumerate his graces; *dozy:* Dizzy.   109 *yaw:* To move unsteadily (of a ship).   110 *article:*
Moment or importance; *infusion:* Infused temperament, character imparted by na-
ture.   111 *dearth and rareness:* Rarity.   112 *semblable:* True likeness.   113 *trace:* Follow; *umbrage:* Shadow.   115 *concernancy:* Import.   116 *breath:* Speech.

Horatio (aside to Hamlet): Is 't not possible to understand in another tongue?° You will do 't, sir, really.

120 *Hamlet:* What imports the nomination° of this gentleman?

Osric: Of Laertes?

Horatio (aside to Hamlet): His purse is empty already; all 's golden words are spent.

Hamlet: Of him, sir.

Osric: I know you are not ignorant—

Hamlet: I would you did, sir; yet, in faith, if you did, it would not much approve° me. Well, sir?

Osric: You are not ignorant of what excellence Laertes is—

Hamlet: I dare not confess that, lest I should compare with him in
130   excellence; but, to know a man well, were to know himself.°

Osric: I mean, sir, for his weapon; but in the imputation° laid on him by them, in his meed° he's unfellowed.

Hamlet: What's his weapon?

Osric: Rapier and dagger.

Hamlet: That's two of his weapons: but, well.

Osric: The king, sir, hath wagered with him six Barbary horses: against the which he has impawned,° as I take it, six French rapiers and poniards, with their assigns, as girdle, hangers,° and so: three of the carriages, in faith, are very dear to fancy,° very
140   responsive° to the hilts, most delicate° carriages, and of very liberal conceit.°

Hamlet: What call you the carriages?

Horatio (aside to Hamlet): I knew you must be edified by the margent° ere you had done.

Osric: The carriages, sir, are the hangers.

Hamlet: The phrase would be more german° to the matter, if we could carry cannon by our sides: I would it might be hangers till then. But, on: six Barbary horses against six French swords, their assigns, and three liberal-conceited carriages; that's the French bet
150   against the Danish. Why is this "impawned," as you call it?

Osric: The king, sir, hath laid, that in a dozen passes between yourself and him, he shall not exceed you three hits: he hath laid on twelve for nine; and it would come to immediate trial, if your lordship would vouchsafe the answer.

Hamlet: How if I answer "no"?

118–119 *Is 't . . . tongue?:* i.e., can one converse with Osric only in this outlandish jargon?   120 *nomination:* Naming.   127 *approve:* Command.   130 *but . . . himself:* But to know a man as excellent were to know Laertes.   131 *imputation:* Reputation.   132 *meed:* Merit.   137 *he has impawned:* He has wagered.   138 *hangers:* Straps on the sword belt from which the sword hung.   139 *dear to fancy:* Fancifully made.   140 *responsive:* Probably, well balanced, corresponding closely.   140 *delicate:* i.e., in workmanship.   141 *liberal conceit:* Elaborate design.   144 *margent:* Margin of a book, place for explanatory notes.   146 *german:* Germain, appropriate.

Osric: I mean, my lord, the opposition of your person in trial.

Hamlet: Sir, I will walk here in the hall: if it please his majesty, it is
the breathing time° of day with me; let the foils be brought, the
gentleman willing, and the king hold his purpose, I will win for him
160   as I can; if not, I will gain nothing but my shame and the odd hits.

Osric: Shall I re-deliver you e'en so?

Hamlet: To this effect, sir; after what flourish your nature will.

Osric: I commend my duty to your lordship.

Hamlet: Yours, yours. (*Exit Osric.*) He does well to commend it
himself; there are no tongues else for 's turn.

Horatio: This lapwing° runs away with the shell on his head.

Hamlet: 'A did comply, sir, with his dug,° before 'a sucked it. Thus
has he—and many more of the same breed that I know the drossy°
age dotes on—only got the tune° of the time and out of an habit of
170   encounter;° a kind of yesty° collection, which carries them through
and through the most fann'd and winnowed° opinions; and do but
blow them to their trial, the bubbles are out.°

Enter a Lord.

Lord: My lord, his majesty commended him to you by young Osric,
who brings back to him, that you attend him in the hall: he sends
to know if your pleasure hold to play with Laertes, or that you
will take longer time.

Hamlet: I am constant to my purposes; they follow the king's
pleasure; if his fitness speaks, mine is ready; now or whensoever,
provided I be so able as now.

180 *Lord:* The king and queen and all are coming down.

Hamlet: In happy time.°

Lord: The queen desires you to use some gentle entertainment to
Laertes before you fall to play.

Hamlet: She well instructs me.   (*Exit Lord.*)

Horatio: You will lose this wager, my lord.

Hamlet: I do not think so; since he went into France, I have been in
continual practice; I shall win at the odds. But thou wouldst not
think how ill all 's here about my heart: but it is no matter.

Horatio: Nay, good my lord,—

190 *Hamlet:* It is but foolery; but it is such a kind of gain-giving,° as
would perhaps trouble a woman.

---

158 *breathing time:* Exercise period.   166 *lapwing:* Peewit; noted its wiliness in drawing a
visitor away from its nest and its supposed habit of running about when newly hatched
with its head in the shell; possibly an allusion to Osric's hat.   167 *did comply . . . dug:*
Paid compliments to his mother's breast.   168 *drossy:* Frivolous.   169 *tune:* Temper,
mood.   169–170 *habit of encounter:* Demeanor of social intercourse; *yesty:* Frothy.   171
fann'd and winnowed: Select and refined.   172 *blow . . . out:* i.e., put them to the test,
and their ignorance is exposed.   181 *In happy time:* A phrase of courtesy.   190 *gain-
giving:* Misgiving.

Horatio: If your mind dislike any thing, obey it: I will forestal their
   repair hither, and say you are not fit.
Hamlet: Not a whit, we defy augury: there's a special providence in the
   fall of a sparrow. If it be now, 'tis not to come; if it be not to come, it
   will be now; if it be not now, yet it will come: the readiness is all:°
   since no man of aught he leaves knows, what is 't to leave betimes?
   Let be.

*A table prepared. Enter Trumpets, Drums, and Officers with cushions; King,
Queen, Osric, and all the State; foils, daggers, and wine borne in; and Laertes.*

King: Come, Hamlet, come, and take this hand from me.

The King puts Laertes's hand into Hamlet's.

200 **Hamlet:** Give me your pardon, sir: I have done you wrong;
   But pardon 't as you are a gentleman.
   This presence° knows,
   And you must needs have heard, how I am punish'd
   With a sore distraction. What I have done,
   That might your nature, honour and exception°
   Roughly awake, I here proclaim was madness.
   Was 't Hamlet wrong'd Laertes? Never Hamlet:
   If Hamlet from himself be ta'en away,
   And when he's not himself does wrong Laertes,
210 Then Hamlet does it not, Hamlet denies it.
   Who does it, then? His madness: if 't be so,
   Hamlet is of the faction that is wrong'd;
   His madness is poor Hamlet's enemy.
   Sir, in this audience,
   Let my disclaiming from a purpos'd evil
   Free me so far in your most generous thoughts,
   That I have shot mine arrow o'er the house,
   And hurt my brother.
Laertes: I am satisfied in nature,°
   Whose motive, in this case, should stir me most
220 To my revenge: but in my terms of honour
   I stand aloof; and will no reconcilement,
   Till by some elder masters, of known honour,
   I have a voice° and precedent of peace,
   To keep my name ungor'd. But till that time,
   I do receive your offer'd love like love,
   And will not wrong it.

---

196 *all:* All that matters.   202 *presence:* Royal assembly.   205 *exception:* Disapproval.
218 *nature:* i.e., he is personally satisfied, but his honor must be satisfied by the rules of
the code of honor.   223 *voice:* Authoritative pronouncement.

Hamlet: I embrace it freely;
And will this brother's wager frankly play.
Give us the foils. Come on.
Laertes: Come, one for me.
Hamlet: I'll be your foil,° Laertes: in mine ignorance
230 Your skill shall, like a star i' th' darkest night,
Stick fiery off° indeed.
Laertes: You mock me, sir.
Hamlet: No, by this hand.
King: Give them the foils, young Osric. Cousin Hamlet,
You know the wager?
Hamlet: Very well, my lord;
Your grace has laid the odds o' th' weaker side.
King: I do not fear it; I have seen you both;
But since he is better'd, we have therefore odds.
Laertes: This is too heavy, let me see another.
Hamlet: This likes me well. These foils have all a length?

They prepare to play.

240 *Osric:* Ay, my good lord.
King: Set me the stoups of wine upon that table.
If Hamlet give the first or second hit,
Or quit in answer of the third exchange,
Let all the battlements their ordnance fire;
The king shall drink to Hamlet's better breath;
And in the cup an union° shall he throw,
Richer than that which four successive kings
In Denmark's crown have worn. Give me the cups;
And let the kettle° to the trumpet speak,
250 The trumpet to the cannoneer without,
The cannons to the heavens, the heavens to earth,
"Now the king drinks to Hamlet." Come begin:

Trumpets the while.

And you, the judges, bear a wary eye.
Hamlet: Come on, sir.
Laertes: Come, my lord.   *(They play.)*
Hamlet: One.
Laertes: No.
Hamlet: Judgement.
Osric: A hit, a very palpable hit.

---

229 *foil:* Quibble on the two senses: "background which sets something off," and "blunted rapier for fencing."   231 *Stick fiery off:* Stand out brilliantly.   246 *union:* Pearl.
249 *kettle:* Kettledrum.

Drum, trumpets, and shot. Flourish. A piece goes off.

Laertes: Well; again.

260 **King:** Stay; give me drink. Hamlet, this pearl° is thine;
Here's to thy health. Give him the cup.
Hamlet: I'll play this bout first; set it by awhile.
Come. *(They play.)* Another hit; what say you?
Laertes: A touch, a touch, I do confess 't.
King: Our son shall win.
Queen: He's fat,° and scant of breath.
Here, Hamlet, take my napkin, rub thy brows:
The queen carouses° to thy fortune, Hamlet.
Hamlet: Good madam!
King: Gertrude, do not drink.
270 **Queen:** I will, my lord; I pray you, pardon me. *(Drinks.)*
King (aside): It is the poison'd cup: it is too late.
Hamlet: I dare not drink yet, madam; by and by.
Queen: Come, let me wipe thy face.
Laertes: My lord, I'll hit him now.
King: I do not think 't.
Laertes (aside): And yet 'tis almost 'gainst my conscience.
Hamlet: Come, for the third, Laertes: you but dally;
I pray you, pass with your best violence;
I am afeard you make a wanton° of me.
Laertes: Say you so? come on.   *(They play.)*
280 **Osric:** Nothing, neither way.
Laertes: Have at you now!

*Laertes wounds Hamlet; then, in scuffling, they change rapiers,° and Hamlet
wounds Laertes.*

King: Part them; they are incens'd.
Hamlet: Nay, come again.   *(The Queen falls.)*
Osric: Look to the queen there, ho!
Horatio: They bleed on both sides. How is it, my lord?
Osric: How is 't, Laertes?
Laertes: Why, as a woodcock° to mine own springe,° Osric;
I am justly kill'd with mine own treachery.
Hamlet: How does the queen?

---

260 *pearl:* i.e., the poison.   265 *fat:* Not physically fit, out of training. Some earlier editors speculated that the term applied to the corpulence of Richard Burbage, who originally played the part, but the allusion now appears unlikely. *Fat* may also suggest "sweaty."   267 *carouses:* Drinks a toast.   278 *wanton:* Spoiled child.   281 *in scuffling, they change rapiers:* According to a widespread stage tradition, Hamlet receives a scratch, realizes that Laertes's sword is unbated, and accordingly forces an exchange.   286 *woodcock:* As type of stupidity or as decoy; *springe:* Trap, snare.

King: She swounds° to see them bleed.
Queen: No, no, the drink, the drink,—O my dear Hamlet,—
The drink, the drink! I am poison'd.   *(Dies.)*
290 *Hamlet:* O villany! Ho! let the door be lock'd:
Treachery! Seek it out.   *(Laertes falls.)*
Laertes: It is here, Hamlet: Hamlet, thou art slain;
No med'cine in the world can do thee good;
In thee there is not half an hour of life;
The treacherous instrument is in thy hand,
Unbated° and envenom'd: the foul practice
Hath turn'd itself on me; lo, here I lie,
Never to rise again: thy mother's poison'd:
I can no more: the king, the king's to blame.
300 *Hamlet:* The point envenom'd too!
Then, venom, to thy work.   *(Stabs the King.)*
All: Treason! treason!
King: O, yet defend me, friends; I am but hurt.
Hamlet: Here, thou incestuous, murd'rous, damned Dane,
Drink off this potion. Is thy union here?
Follow my mother.   *(King dies.)*
Laertes: He is justly serv'd;
It is a poison temper'd° by himself.
Exchange forgiveness with me, noble Hamlet:
Mine and my father's death come not upon thee,
310 Nor thine on me!   *(Dies.)*
Hamlet: Heaven make thee free of it! I follow thee.
I am dead, Horatio. Wretched queen, adieu!
You that look pale and tremble at this chance,
That are but mutes° or audience to this act,
Had I but time—as this fell sergeant,° Death,
Is strict in his arrest—O, I could tell you—
But let it be. Horatio, I am dead;
Thou livest; report me and my cause aright
To the unsatisfied.
Horatio: Never believe it:
320 I am more an antique Roman° than a Dane:
Here 's yet some liquor left.
Hamlet: As th' art a man,
Give me the cup: let go, by heaven, I'll ha 't.
O God! Horatio, what a wounded name,
Things standing thus unknown, shall live behind me!
If thou didst ever hold me in thy heart,
Absent thee from felicity awhile,

---

288 *swounds:* Swoons.   296 *Unbated:* Not blunted with a button.   307 *temper'd:* Mixed.
314 *mutes:* Performers in a play who speak no words.   315 *sergeant:* Sheriff's officer.
320 *Roman:* It was the Roman custom to follow masters in death.

And in this harsh world draw thy breath in pain,
To tell my story.   *A march afar off.*
          What warlike noise is this?
Osric: Young Fortinbras, with conquest come from Poland,
To the ambassadors of England gives
330 This warlike volley.
Hamlet: O, I die, Horatio;
The potent poison quite o'er-crows° my spirit:
I cannot live to hear the news from England;
But I do prophesy th' election lights
On Fortinbras: he has my dying voice;
So tell him, with th' occurrents,° more and less,
Which have solicited.° The rest is silence.   *(Dies.)*
Horatio: Now cracks a noble heart. Good night, sweet prince;
And flights of angels sing thee to thy rest!
Why does the drum come hither?   *(March within.)*

Enter Fortinbras, with the English Ambassadors and others.

340 *Fortinbras:* Where is this sight?
Horatio: What is it you would see?
If aught of woe or wonder, cease your search.
Fortinbras: This quarry° cries on havoc.° O proud Death,
What feast is toward in thine eternal cell,
That thou so many princes at a shot
So bloodily hast struck?
First Ambassador: The sight is dismal;
And our affairs from England come too late:
The ears are senseless that should give us hearing,
To tell him his commandment is fulfill'd,
That Rosencrantz and Guildenstern are dead:
350 Where should we have our thanks?
Horatio: Not from his mouth,°
Had it th' ability of life to thank you:
He never gave commandment for their death.
But since, so jump° upon this bloody question,°
You from the Polack wars, and you from England,
Are here arriv'd, give order that these bodies
High on a stage° be placed to the view;
And let me speak to th' yet unknowing world
How these things came about: so shall you hear
Of carnal, bloody, and unnatural acts,
360 Of accidental judgements, casual slaughters,

---

331 *o'er-crows:* Triumphs over.   335 *occurrents:* Events, incidents.   336 *solicited:* Moved, urged.   342 *quarry:* Heap of dead; *cries on havoc:* Proclaims a general slaughter.   350 *his mouth:* i.e., the king's.   353 *jump:* Precisely; *question:* Dispute.   356 *stage:* Platform.

Of deaths put on by cunning and forc'd cause,
And, in this upshot, purposes mistook
Fall'n on th' inventors' heads: all this can I
Truly deliver.
Fortinbras: Let us haste to hear it,
And call the noblest to the audience.
For me, with sorrow I embrace my fortune:
I have some rights of memory° in this kingdom,
Which now to claim my vantage doth invite me.
Horatio: Of that I shall have also cause to speak,
370 And from his mouth whose voice will draw on more:°
But let this same be presently perform'd,
Even while men's minds are wild; lest more mischance,
On° plots and errors, happen.
Fortinbras: Let four captains
Bear Hamlet, like a soldier, to the stage;
For he was likely, had he been put on,
To have prov'd most royal: and, for his passage,°
The soldiers' music and the rites of war
Speak loudly for him.
Take up the bodies: such a sight as this
380 Becomes the field,° but here shows much amiss.
Go, bid the soldiers shoot.

*Exeunt marching, bearing off the dead bodies; after which a peal of ordnance is
shot off.*

ACCOUNT: KENNETH BURKE ON A
RHETORICAL/READER-RESPONSE
APPROACH TO *HAMLET*

Burke begins by noting that it is not until the fourth scene of the
first act that Hamlet meets the ghost of his father. The audience has
been waiting for the encounter (consciously or unconsciously), and now
the promised moment is at hand.

Hamlet has earlier arranged with Horatio to come at night to see
the ghost; it is now night and he has come. Midnight has just struck, and
Horatio confirms that it is now the time "Wherein the spirit held his
wont to walk." Just this moment of completed preparation, a sound is
heard offstage—but it is *not* the sound of the ghost.

---

367 *of memory:* Traditional, remembered.   370 *voice . . . more:* Vote will influence still
others.   373 *On:* On account of, or possibly, on top of, in addition to.   376 *passage:*
Death.   380 *field:* i.e., of battle.
From *Counterstatement* © 1931, 1953 (University of California Press, 1968).

Rather, we hear "A flourish of trumpets, and ordnance shot off within." Burke emphasizes that we have been prepared for the ghost, but there is no ghost. Further, the sounds are in fact those associated with the king's carousal, and the imagined joy elsewhere sets off and highlights by contrast the gloom and isolation of Hamlet's own situation.

Still, the trumpets suggest a topic for conversation. Hamlet begins to unfold his views of the excessive drinking that, he says, harms the reputation of his country abroad, in spite of the many virtues of the Danes. Hamlet is talking intelligently and rather argumentatively on this topic, when in the midst of his speech: "Look, my lord, it comes!" The ghost has appeared at the one moment when the scene did *not* lead us to expect it.

But now that the surprise has occurred, we expect something else—a response from Hamlet. And the style of that response makes an immediate and striking contrast to the style of his discourse on drink, just as the images of light had contrasted to the gloom of the scene earlier. Rather than the sober, reasoning manner in which Hamlet has been expressing himself, Burke says that Shakespeare's "floodgates are unloosed," and we hear the "grandiose, full-throated and full-voweled" burst of poetry in a style all the richer for its difference from the immediate context of style:

> Angels and ministers of grace defend us!
> Be thou a spirit of health or goblin damned,
> Bring with thee airs from heaven or blasts from hell . . .

Yet while this burst of speech and action has satisfied one part of our desire to see the confrontation, another appetite has been whetted, and we now want Hamlet to learn the details of the murder from the ghost. Yet Shakespeare characteristically delays the satisfaction of this desire too, and we must wait for "Scene V.—Another Part of the Platform."

Burke has analyzed this scene so closely, he says, because it illustrates so well the relations of psychology and aesthetic form while also illustrating how the one is defined in terms of the other:

> That is, the psychology here is not the psychology of the *hero,* but the psychology of the *audience.* And by that distinction, form would be the psychology of the audience. Or, seen from another angle, form is the creation of an appetite in the mind of the auditor, and the adequate satisfying of that appetite. This satisfaction—so complicated is the human mechanism—at times involves a temporary set of frustrations, but in the end these frustrations prove to be simply a more involved kind of satisfaction, and furthermore serve to make the satisfaction of fulfillment more intense. If, in a work of art, the poet says something, let us say, about a meeting, writes in such a way that we desire to observe that meeting, and then, if he places that meeting before us—that is form. While obviously, that is also the psychology of the audience, since it involves desires and their appeasements.

Burke says that the connection between psychology and aesthetic form needs particular attention in modern criticism, since a great deal of contemporary psychology in its quite proper aspiration toward becoming a science has become a "body of information." Yet this development has unfortunately led to looking at psychology in art as the purveying of information. Information "while intrinsically interesting is not intrinsically valuable." Burke says:

> Consider, for instance, the speech of Mark Antony, the "Brutus is an honourable man." Imagine in the same place a very competently developed thesis on human conduct, with statistics, intelligence tests, definitions; imagine it as the finest thing of the sort ever written, and as really being at the roots of an understanding of Brutus. Obviously the play would simply stop until Antony had finished. For in the case of Antony's speech, the value lies in the fact that his words are shaping the future of the audience's desires, not the desires of the Roman populace, but the desires of the pit. This is the psychology of form as distinguished from the psychology of information.

Burke allows that the distinction is absolutely clear-cut only in extreme cases which may not exist in literature. But he points out an example in *Hamlet*—how the play stops in its development when Hamlet gives his advice to the players. That speech is intrinsically very interesting, but contributes little to the psychology of form. The expectation of Hamlet's movement toward revenge is delayed without any very enhancing purpose, in contrast to the *effective* delays in the scene on the platform.

Burke does not deny the place of information in art, but says that he only wishes to restore it to its proper minor place—"seen as merely one out of many possible elements of style":

> One reason why music can stand repetition so much more sturdily than correspondingly good prose is that music, of all the arts, is by its nature least suited to the psychology of information, and has remained closer to the psychology of form. Here form cannot atrophy. Every dissonant chord cries out for resolution, and whether the musician resolves or refuses to resolve this dissonance into the chord which the body cries for, he is dealing in human appetites.

Burke says that the aesthetic value of information is lost once the information has been imparted, and we know it. Yet the satisfactions of aesthetic desire do not depend on mysteries of information (as, say, detective novels do), for we can re-read and even memorize an example like the exchange between Hamlet and Guildenstern (when Hamlet offers him the pipe to play on) without any loss of enjoyment. We may even fairly gloat with satisfaction knowing how the retort is to develop out of the metaphor of the pipe all the while as we await Hamlet's conclusion:

Why, look you now, how unworthy a thing you make of me. You would play upon me, you would seem to know my stops; you would pluck out the heart of my mystery; you would sound me from my lowest note to the top of my compass; and there is much music, excellent voice, in this little organ, yet cannot you make it speak. 'Sblood, do you think I am easier to be played on than a pipe? Call me what instrument you will, though you can fret me, you cannot play upon me.

Burke concludes that it is right that art should be called a "waking dream." However, he says, modern criticism mistakenly tends to attribute the dream to the artist:

It is rather the audience which dreams, while the artist oversees the conditions which determine this dream. He is the manipulator of blood, brains, heart, and bowels which, while we sleep, dictate the mould of our desires. This is of course, the real meaning of artistic felicity—an exaltation at the correctness of the procedure, so that we enjoy the steady march of doom in a Racinian tragedy with exactly the same equipment as that which produces our delight with Benedick's "Peace! I'll stop your mouth. (*Kisses her*)" which terminates the imbroglio of *Much Ado About Nothing*.

Burke goes on to call the proper management of the audience's psychology "Eloquence." He posits, first, that a desire for what he calls form exists within the entire human race, and, second, that a greater degree of eloquence more fully satisfies this human "racial appetite":

The distinction between the psychology of information and the psychology of form involves a definition of aesthetic truth. It is here precisely to combat the deflection which the strength of science has caused to our tastes, that we must examine the essential breach between scientific and artistic truth. Truth in art is not the discovery of facts, not an addition to human knowledge in the scientific sense of the word. It is, rather, the exercise of human propriety, the formulation of symbols which rigidify our sense of poise and rhythm. Artistic truth is the externalization of taste.

ACCOUNT: JACQUES LACAN ON A PSYCHOANALYTIC APPROACH TO *HAMLET*

Lacan begins by stating that his purpose is to show the tragedy of desire in *Hamlet*, with "desire" being understood in psychoanalytic terms:

From Jacques Lacan, "Desire and the Interpretation of Desire in *Hamlet*" in *Literature and Psychoanalysis: The Question of Reading Otherwise* (Baltimore: The John Hopkins University Press, 1982), 11–52.

> We distort this desire and confuse it with other terms if we fail to lo-
> cate it in reference to a set of co-ordinates that, as Freud showed, estab-
> lish the subject in a certain position of dependence upon the signifier.
> The signifier is not a reflection, a product pure and simple of what are
> called interhuman relationships—all psychoanalytic experience indi-
> cates the contrary.

That is, if Hamlet's (the subject's) desire were simply a matter of
"interhuman relationships," Ophelia would simply be the "object" of that
desire, and in that case Hamlet's difficulties would not be what they are.

But in fact, the source of his trouble is in his unconscious. For Lacan,
the desire of the unconscious functions like a language. In particular, the
unconscious operates in the same way that Ferdinand Saussaure says that
language operates. (See A Brief Introduction to Structuralist Criticism,
p. 136.) That is, the unconscious desires an object known by a "sign," and
in   Hamlet's case, the sign is "Ophelia." But a sign is made up of a signifier and a signified. The question is, what is the signified of desire for
Hamlet, what is the complex set of things that "Ophelia" signifies for
Hamlet's unconscious?

The issue for the play, therefore, is not so much Ophelia as a person,
but Ophelia as the signifier of what Hamlet unconsciously desires. In dramatizing the issue, Shakespeare's treatment of the character Ophelia
marks a shift that distinguishes his play from previous treatments of the
same story. For Shakespeare, Ophelia becomes one of the main elements
in the drama of Hamlet as a man who has "lost the way of his desire."

In Lacan's terminology, desire is always an issue involving the
"Other," which is in general the realm of all that is not constructed as
part of the Self in the unconscious. An object of fantasy stands for what a
subject has been deprived of. Lacan calls this desired thing the "phallus,"
but his term should not be confused with a name for the male sex organ.
Lacan uses it to refer to the object of desire for any subject (male or female), whatever or whoever the desired thing may be. Yet looking at the
origin and development of desire, we see that the "primordial" subject of
demand for the Self is the Mother. Given his terminology, Lacan's first analytic point is to remark the degree to which the play is dominated by the
Mother as Other. Hamlet's basic desire or demand of his mother is manifested in his own inability to choose between the two clearly distinct figures of his idealized father and despicable uncle. He wants *her* to choose.
But Gertrude does not distinguish these men. By seeing them purely as
objects of sexual enjoyment, she refuses to make the choice in the ideal
terms that Hamlet would have her use. Instead, she returns to Claudius's
bed, and Hamlet's own desire for revenge must fail because it is so dependent on the desire of this Other.

Lacan says that in its most basic form, neurotic behavior shows the
subject trying to get his or her sense of time *in* or *from* the object. Hamlet, for example, is not only dependent on his mother's desire, but is constantly suspended in the time of the Other until the very end of the

story. This dependence is seen in his inability to kill Claudius at prayer in the midst of his avowed guilt. For Hamlet, here (as always until the end) it is either too early or too late: "Whatever Hamlet may do, he will do it only at the hour of the Other." In other examples, Hamlet stays in Denmark at the hour of his parents; he suspends his crime at the hour of others; he leaves for England at the hour of his stepfather; and finally, in the hour of Ophelia, in the hour of her suicide, his tragedy of desire will run its course.

Lacan says that Hamlet's situation as the man who has lost the way of his desire is representative of the modern hero's relation to his fate: Unlike Oedipus, Hamlet *knows*. Out of this knowledge he must feign the opposite of knowledge—madness—and this is the typical strategy of the modern hero.

What, then, is the function of the character of Ophelia? Lacan begins to answer by pointing out that her very name is *O phallos*, the very sign of the phallus itself! We first encounter her as she reports her clinical observations of Hamlet's strange behavior on seeing the ghost. But while Polonius concludes from this behavior that Hamlet is in love, it is precisely *after* this point Ophelia ceases to be loved by Hamlet ("I did love you once"). From this point until the end of the play, Hamlet's behavior toward Ophelia continues to be cruelly aggressive. This happens because his unconscious has cast Ophelia as the signifier of the phallus that he is attempting to reject, and his rejection is focused on childbearing as representative of all, in his mother and elsewhere, that he condemns.

Lacan had earlier said that in sadistic fantasy, the sadist's interest in the humiliated party depends on the ability to imagine being submitted to the same humiliation himself. This condition is satisfied here, since Ophelia never knows what Hamlet wants, and Hamlet himself never knows what he wants. Further:

> The object of desire is essentially different from the object of any need [in French, *besoin*]. Something becomes an object in desire when it takes the place of what by its very nature becomes concealed from the subject.

Hamlet loves Ophelia and yet contests for her only *after* her death, when she ceases to be "the very symbol of the rejection of his desire":

> I loved Ophelia. Forty thousand brothers
> Could not with all their quantity of love
> Make up the sum. What wilt thou do for her?
> (act V, sc. 1)

So Hamlet begins his challenge to Laertes. Characteristically, only at the point that Ophelia becomes impossible for Hamlet can she once more become the object of his desire. This paradox becomes more understandable when we remember the complaint with which Hamlet begins the play—that his mother has remarried with undue haste. Lacan says that this in part explains Hamlet's treatment of Ophelia. "Ophelia appears as a victim offered in expiation of that primordial offense of insufficient Mourning." Hamlet responds to the offense with revenge when he makes the same thing happen to Polonius's family by hiding the body of Polonius.

Lacan says that Mourning is a ritual-value overlooked by modern society in its overriding concern with use-values and exchange-values. [The "use-value" of an expensive car, for example, is perhaps the same as the use-value of a less expensive car, but their "exchange-values" may be wildly different.] The whole strange ritualistic nature of Hamlet's playing out of desire may be traced to the neglected ritual-value of mourning, according to Lacan.

Thus, the play proceeds because of a neglected point of honor:

> Until the last term, until the final hour, Hamlet's hour, in which he is mortally wounded before he wounds his enemy, the tragedy follows its course and attains completion at the hour of the Other. . . .

But while Hamlet ultimately rushes into the rigged contest arranged at the hour of the Other, something else now characterizes him. What has changed at the end of the play is the energy with which he acts. Why? The prizes of the contest—precious objects, sword fittings, and so on—have existence only as luxuries—that is, *purely* as objects of desire rather than use. In other words, they are signifiers purely of honor.

Lacan says of Hamlet that in the contest, "He stakes his resolution against the things that interest him least in the world, and he does this in order to win for somebody else." Hamlet's fight, then, is a fight for honor. Just as the prizes are purely luxuries and therefore signs only of prestige, so Hamlet fights for pure prestige, for being totally committed to one's word as a man of honor. He fights Laertes, his ego ideal, the one he admires most and his mirror image. The rivalry means that the phallus will appear only with the disappearance of the subject Hamlet himself—only *then* in his death will he become manifested as a brave man and resolute killer—that is, as the man of honor (as defined by ritual-value) that he has really desired to be all along.

SUGGESTIONS FOR DISCUSSION AND WRITING

1. Does it seem to you that both Lacan and Burke find **unity of action** in the play? Where and how do they point to what this term names? Do they both find the same unity? What does each see as the essential **dramatic situation** in the play? Which critic focuses on the first **act** most? Which on the last? Is the focus a function of the method?

Does the **rising action** appeal to one critic more than the other? What of the **falling action**?

2. Characterize at some length a **dramatic irony** to which each critic points. How do the **images** of the **dialogue** contribute to the creation of the irony? Take, for example, a conversation between Polonius and Hamlet.

3. Both Burke and Lacan are interested in psychology in the play. Where does each locate the actions of psychology? Do they ever focus on the same sense of the process? Explain your answer. Would Burke count Lacan as contributing to "information"? Why or why not?

4. Write out some notes toward a psychoanalytic examination of the first scene of *The Tempest* as you imagine Burke would make it. Do the same thing for Lacan and the last scene of that play.

5. Pick a scene in which Ophelia is the subject for Hamlet whether or not she is on stage. Pick a critical approach that is not psychoanalytic or rhetorical and make some notes for a discussion or for an essay in which you analyze the scene by its methods. How, for example, might a Feminist critic analyze the speech?

Chapter Nineteen

Approaches to William Shakespeare's *The Tempest*

(For a brief biography of Shakespeare, see the introduction to Hamlet, *p. 604)* Shakespeare's plays are generally divided into three categories: the histories (such as *Henry IV, Henry V, Richard III*), the tragedies (such as *Hamlet, Macbeth, Othello*), and the comedies (such as *As You Like It, A Midsummer Night's Dream, Twelfth Night*). Many critics and readers have created a fourth category: the romances. The four plays which are labeled thus are *Pericles, The Winter's Tale, Cymbeline,* and *The Tempest,* for they do not easily fit any of the three basic categories.

The romances may be described as tragicomedies, for they are comic yet serious, frivolous yet highly symbolic. Further, the romances were clearly experimental works in which Shakespeare toyed with both language and music; the songs and masques of these plays are among the best in Shakespeare and are striking in performance. The plots of these plays hinge upon what many would call contrived coincidences, and the characters are usually faced with great dangers in the form of the elements or wild animals. The romances also treat the theme of parent–child relationships, specifically, the bond between father and daughter. In *The Tempest,* Shakespeare explores this bond through the characters of Prospero and Miranda.

WILLIAM SHAKESPEARE
The Tempest
(1611)

Edited by Robert Langbaum

CHARACTERS

Alonso, king of Naples	*Master of a ship*
Sebastian, his brother	*Boatswain*
Prospero, the right duke of Milan	*Mariners*
Antonio, his brother, the usurping duke of Milan	*Miranda,* daughter to Prospero
	Ariel, an airy spirit
Ferdinand, son to the king of Naples	*Iris*
Gonzalo, an honest old councilor	*Ceres*
Adrian and *Francisco,* lords	*Juno* [presented by] spirits
Caliban, a savage and deformed slave	*Nymphs*
Trinculo, a jester	*Reapers*
Stephano, a drunken butler	*Other spirits attending on Prospero*

Scene: An uninhabited island.

Act I

Scene I. [On a ship at sea.]

A tempestuous noise of thunder and lightning heard. Enter a Shipmaster and a Boatswain.

Master: Boatswain!
Boatswain: Here, master. What cheer?
Master: Good°, speak to th' mariners! Fall to't yarely°, or we run
   ourselves aground. Bestir, bestir!   *Exit.*

Enter Mariners.

Boatswain: Heigh, my hearts! Cheerly, cheerly, my hearts! Yare, yare!
   Take in the topsail! Tend to th' master's whistle! Blow till thou
   burst thy wind, if room enough°!

Enter Alonso, Sebastian, Antonio, Ferdinand, Gonzalo, and others.

Alonso: Good boatswain, have care. Where's the master? Play the
   men°.
10 **Boatswain:** I pray now, keep below.
Antonio: Where is the master, bos'n?
Boatswain: Do you not hear him? You mar our labor. Keep your
   cabins; you do assist the storm.
Gonzalo: Nay, good, be patient.
Boatswain: When the sea is. Hence! What care these roarers for the
   name of king? To cabin! Silence! Trouble us not!
Gonzalo: Good, yet remember whom thou hast aboard.
Boatswain: None that I more love than myself. You are a councilor;
   if you can command these elements to silence and work the peace
20   of the present°, we will not hand° a rope more. Use your
   authority. If you cannot, give thanks you have lived so long, and
   make yourself ready in your cabin for the mischance of the hour,
   if it so hap. Cheerly, good hearts! Out of our way, I say.   *Exit.*

Gonzalo: I have great comfort from this fellow. Methinks he hath no
   drowning mark upon him; his complexion is perfect gallows°.

I.i. 3 *Good:* good fellow.   3 *yarely:* briskly.   6–7 *Blow . . . enough:* The storm can blow and split itself as long as there is open sea, without rocks, to maneuver in.   8–9 *Play the men:* Act like men.   19–20 *work . . . present:* restore the present to peace (because as a councilor his job is to quell disorder).   20 *hand:* handle.   24–25 *no drowning . . . gallows:* alluding to the proverb, "He that's born to be hanged need fear no drowning."

Stand fast, good Fate, to his hanging! Make the rope of his destiny
our cable, for our own doth little advantage°. If he be not born to
be hanged, our case is miserable.   *Exit [with the rest].*

Enter Boatswain.

Boatswain: Down with the topmast! Yare! Lower, lower! Bring her to
30   try with main course°! (*A cry within.*) A plague upon this howling!
They are louder than the weather or our office°.

Enter Sebastian, Antonio, and Gonzalo.

Yet again? What do you here? Shall we give o'er° and drown? Have
you a mind to sink?
Sebastian: A pox o' your throat, you bawling, blasphemous,
incharitable dog!
Boatswain: Work you, then.
Antonio: Hang, cur! Hang, you whoreson, insolent noisemaker! We are
less afraid to be drowned than thou art.
Gonzalo: I'll warrant him for° drowning, though the ship were no
40   stronger than a nutshell and as leaky as an unstanched° wench.
Boatswain: Lay her ahold, ahold! Set her two courses°! Off to sea
again! Lay her off°!

Enter Mariners wet.

Mariners: All lost! To prayers, to prayers! All lost!   *[Exeunt.]°*
Boatswain: What, must our mouths be cold?
Gonzalo: The king and prince at prayers! Let's assist them,
For our case is as theirs.
Sebastian: I am out of patience.
Antonio: We are merely° cheated of our lives by drunkards.
This wide-chopped° rascal—would thou mightst lie drowning
The washing of ten tides°!
Gonzalo: He'll be hanged yet,
50 Though every drop of water swear against it
And gape at wid'st to glut him.

---

27 *doth little advantage:* gives us little advantage.   29–30 *Bring . . . course:* Heave to, under the mainsail.   30–31 *They . . . office:* These passengers make more noise than the
tempest or than we do at our work.   32 *give o'er:* give up trying to run the ship.   39
warrant him for: guarantee him against.   40 *unstanched:* wide-open.   41 *Lay . . .
courses:* the ship is still being blown dangerously close to shore, and so the boatswain orders that the foresail be set in addition to the mainsail; but the ship still moves toward
shore.   42 *Lay her off:* i.e., away from the shore.   43 *Exeunt:* Latin, "They go out," a
direction indicating that all or some characters leave the stage.   47 *merely:* completely.   48 *wide-chopped:* big-mouthed.   49 *ten tides:* pirates were hanged on the shore
and left there until three tides had washed over them.

A confused noise within: "Mercy on us!"
"We split, we split!" "Farewell, my wife and children!"
"Farewell, brother!" "We split, we split, we split!"

[Exit Boatswain.]

Antonio: Let's all sink wi' th' king.
Sebastian: Let's take leave of him.

Exit [with Antonio].

Gonzalo: Now would I give a thousand furlongs of sea for an acre of
60   barren ground—long heath°, brown furze, anything. The wills
   above be done, but I would fain die a dry death.   *Exit.*

Scene II. [The island. In front of Prospero's cell.]

Enter Prospero and Miranda.

Miranda: If by your art, my dearest father, you have
Put the wild waters in this roar, allay them.
The sky, it seems, would pour down stinking pitch
But that the sea, mounting to th' welkin's cheek°,
Dashes the fire out. O, I have suffered
With those that I saw suffer! A brave° vessel
(Who had no doubt some noble creature in her)
Dashed all to pieces! O, the cry did knock
Against my very heart! Poor souls, they perished!
10 Had I been any god of power, I would
Have sunk the sea within the earth or ere
It should the good ship to have swallowed and
The fraughting° souls within her.
Prospero: Be collected.
No more amazement°. Tell your piteous heart
There's no harm done.
Miranda: O, woe the day!
Prospero: No harm.
I have done nothing but in care of thee,
Of thee my dear one, thee my daughter, who
Art ignorant of what thou art, naught knowing
Of whence I am, nor that I am more better
20 Than Prospero, master of a full poor cell,
And thy no greater father°.

---

56 *heath:* heather.   I.ii. 4 *welkin's cheek:* face of the sky.   6 *brave:* fine, gallant (the word
often has this meaning in the play).   13 *fraughting:* forming her freight.   14 *amazement:*
consternation.   21 *thy . . . father:* thy father, no greater than the Prospero just described.

Miranda: More to know
Did never meddle° with my thoughts.
Prospero: 'Tis time
I should inform thee farther. Lend thy hand
And pluck my magic garment from me. So.

[*Lays down his robe.*]

Lie there, my art. Wipe thou thine eyes; have comfort.
The direful spectacle of the wrack, which touched
The very virtue° of compassion in thee,
I have with such provision° in mine art
So safely ordered that there is no soul—
30 No, not so much perdition° as an hair
Betid° to any creature in the vessel
Which thou heard'st cry, which thou saw'st sink. Sit down;
For thou must now know farther.
Miranda: You have often
Begun to tell me what I am; but stopped
And left me to a bootless inquisition,
Concluding, "Stay; not yet."
Prospero: The hour's now come;
The very minute bids thee ope thine ear.
Obey, and be attentive. Canst thou remember
A time before we came until this cell?
40 I do not think thou canst, for then thou wast not
Out° three years old.
Miranda: Certainly, sir, I can.
Prospero: By what? By any other house or person?
Of anything the image tell me that
Hath kept with thy remembrance.
Miranda: 'Tis far off,
And rather like a dream than an assurance
That my remembrance warrants°. Had I not
Four or five women once that tended me?
Prospero: Thou hadst, and more, Miranda. But how is it
That this lives in thy mind? What see'st thou else
50 In the dark backward and abysm of time?
If thou rememb'rest aught ere thou cam'st here,
How thou cam'st here thou mayst.
Miranda: But that I do not.
Prospero: Twelve year since, Miranda, twelve year since,
Thy father was the Duke of Milan° and

---

22 *meddle:* mingle.   27 *virtue:* essence.   28 *provision:* foresight.   30 *perdition:* loss.
31 *Betid:* happened.   41 *Out:* fully.   46 *remembrance warrants:* memory guarantees.
54 *Milan:* pronounced "Mílan."

A prince of power.
Miranda: Sir, are not you my father?
Prospero: Thy mother was a piece° of virtue, and
She said thou wast my daughter; and thy father
Was Duke of Milan; and his only heir
And princess, no worse issued.°
Miranda: O the heavens!
60 What foul play had we that we came from thence?
Or blessèd was't we did?
Prospero: Both, both, my girl!
By foul play, as thou say'st, were we heaved thence,
But blessedly holp° hither.
Miranda: O, my heart bleeds
To think o' th' teen that I have turned you to°,
Which is from° my remembrance! Please you, farther.
Prospero: My brother and thy uncle, called Antonio—
I pray thee mark me—that a brother should
Be so perfidious—he whom next thyself
Of all the world I loved, and to him put
70 The manage of my state°, as at that time
Through all the signories° it was the first,
And Prospero the prime duke, being so reputed
In dignity, and for the liberal arts
Without a parallel. Those being all my study,
The government I cast upon my brother
And to my state grew stranger, being transported
And rapt in secret studies. Thy false uncle—
Dost thou attend me?
Miranda: Sir, most heedfully.
Prospero: Being once perfected° how to grant suits,
80 How to deny them, who t' advance, and who
To trash for overtopping,° new-created
The creatures that were mine, I say—or changed 'em,
Or else new-formed 'em°—having both the key°
Of officer and office, set all hearts i' th' state
To what tune pleased his ear, that now he was
The ivy which had hid my princely trunk
And sucked my verdure out on't. Thou attend'st not?
Miranda: O, good sir, I do.

---

56 *piece:* masterpiece.   59 *no worse issued:* of no meaner lineage than he.   63 *holp:* helped.
64 *teen . . . to:* sorrow I have caused you to remember.   65 *from:* out of.   70 *manage . . .
state:* management of my domain.   71 *signories:* lordships (of Italy).   79 *perfected:*
grown skillful.   81 *trash for overtopping:* (1) check the speed of (as of hounds) (2) cut
down to size (as of over-tall trees) the aspirants for political favor who are growing too
bold.   81–83 *new-created . . . 'em:* he recreated my following—either exchanging my adherents for his own, or else transforming my adherents into different people.   83 *key:* a
pun leading to the musical metaphor.

Prospero: I pray thee mark me.
I thus neglecting worldly ends, all dedicated
90 To closeness° and the bettering of my mind—
With that which, but by being so retired,
O'erprized all popular rate, in my false brother
Awaked an evil nature°, and my trust,
Like a good parent°, did beget of him
A falsehood in its contrary as great
As my trust was, which had indeed no limit,
A confidence sans bound. He being thus lorded—
Not only with what my revenue° yielded
But what my power might else exact, like one
100 Who having into truth—by telling of it°—
Made such a sinner of his memory
To° credit his own lie, he did believe
He was indeed the duke, out o' th' substitution
And executing th' outward face of royalty
With all prerogative°. Hence his ambition growing—
Dost thou hear?
Miranda: Your tale, sir, would cure deafness.
Prospero: To have no screen between this part he played
And him he played it for, he needs will be
Absolute Milan°. Me (poor man) my library
110 Was dukedom large enough. Of temporal royalties
He thinks me now incapable; confederates
(So dry° he was for sway) wi' th' King of Naples
To give him annual tribute, do him homage,
Subject his coronet to his crown, and bend
The dukedom, yet unbowed (alas, poor Milan!),
To most ignoble stooping.
Miranda: O the heavens!
Prospero: Mark his condition°, and th' event°, then tell me
If this might be a brother.
Miranda: I should sin
To think but nobly of my grandmother.
Good wombs have borne bad sons.
120 *Prospero:*   Now the condition.
This King of Naples, being an enemy

---

90 *closeness:* seclusion.   91–93 *With . . . nature:* with that dedication to the mind which,
were it not that it kept me from exercising the duties of my office would surpass in value
all ordinary estimate, I awakened evil in my brother's nature.   94 *good parent:* alluding
to the proverb cited by Miranda in line 120.   98 *revenue:* pronounced "revènue."   99–
100 *like . . . it:* like one who really had these things—by repeatedly saying he had them
("into"—unto).   102 *To:* as to.   103–05 *out . . . prerogative:* as a result of his acting as
my substitute and performing the outward functions of royalty with all its prerogatives.
109 *Absolute Milan:* Duke of Milan in fact.   112 *dry:* thirsty.   117 *condition:* terms of
his pact with Naples; *event:* outcome.

To me inveterate, hearkens my brother's suit;
Which was, that he, in lieu o' th' premises°
Of homage and I know not how much tribute,
Should presently extirpate me and mine
Out of the dukedom and confer fair Milan,
With all the honors, on my brother. Whereon,
A treacherous army levied, one midnight
Fated to th' purpose, did Antonio open
130 The gates of Milan; and, i' th' dead of darkness,
The ministers° for th' purpose hurried thence
Me and thy crying self.
Miranda: Alack, for pity!
I, not rememb'ring how I cried out then,
Will cry it o'er again; it is a hint°
That wrings mine eyes to't.
Prospero: Hear a little further,
And then I'll bring thee to the present business
Which now's upon's; without the which this story
Were most impertinent°.
Miranda: Wherefore did they not
That hour destroy us?
Prospero: Well demanded, wench.
140 My tale provokes that question. Dear, they durst not,
So dear the love my people bore me; nor set
A mark so bloody on the business; but,
With colors fairer, painted their foul ends.
In few°, they hurried us aboard a bark;
Bore us some leagues to sea, where they prepared
A rotten carcass of a butt°, not rigged,
Nor tackle, sail, nor mast; the very rats
Instinctively have quit it. There they hoist us,
To cry to th' sea that roared to us; to sigh
150 To th' winds, whose pity, sighing back again,
Did us but loving wrong.
Miranda: Alack, what trouble
Was I then to you!
Prospero: O, a cherubin
Thou wast that did preserve me! Thou didst smile,
Infusèd with a fortitude from heaven,
When I have decked° the sea with drops full salt,
Under my burden groaned; which° raised in me
An undergoing stomach°, to bear up

---

123 *in . . . premises:* in return for the guarantees.   131 *ministers:* agents.   134 *hint:*
occasion.   138 *impertinent:* inappropriate.   144 *few:* few words.   146 *butt:* tub.
155 *decked:* covered (wept salt tears into the sea).   156 *which:* Miranda's smile.
157 *undergoing stomach:* spirit of endurance.

Against what should ensue.
Miranda: How came we ashore?
Prospero: By providence divine.
160 Some food we had, and some fresh water, that
A noble Neapolitan, Gonzalo,
Out of his charity, who being then appointed
Master of this design, did give us, with
Rich garments, linens, stuffs, and necessaries
Which since have steaded° much. So, of his gentleness,
Knowing I loved my books, he furnished me
From mine own library with volumes that
I prize above my dukedom.
Miranda: Would I might
But ever see that man!
Prospero: Now I arise.
170 Sit still, and hear the last of our sea sorrow.
Here in this island we arrived; and here
Have I, thy schoolmaster, made thee more profit
Than other princess' can°, that have more time
For vainer hours, and tutors not so careful.
Miranda: Heavens thank you for't! And now I pray you, sir—
For still 'tis beating in my mind—your reason
For raising this sea storm?
Prospero: Know thus far forth.
By accident most strange, bountiful Fortune
(Now my dear lady)° hath mine enemies
180 Brought to this shore; and by my prescience
I find my zenith° doth depend upon
A most auspicious star, whose influence
If now I court not, but omit°, my fortunes
Will ever after droop. Here cease more questions.
Thou art inclined to sleep. 'Tis a good dullness,
And give it way. I know thou canst not choose.

    [*Miranda sleeps.*]

Come away°, servant, come! I am ready now.
Approach, my Ariel! Come!

    Enter Ariel.

Ariel: All hail, great master! Grave sir, hail! I come
190 To answer thy best pleasure; be't to fly,

---

165 *steaded:* been of use.   173 *princess' can:* princesses can have.   179 *Now . . . lady:*
i.e., formerly my foe, now my patroness.   181 *zenith:* apex of fortune.   183 *omit:* neglect.   187 *Come away:* come from where you are; come here.

To swim, to dive into the fire, to ride
On the curled clouds. To thy strong bidding task°
Ariel and all his quality.°
Prospero: Hast thou, spirit,
Performed, to point°, the tempest that I bade thee?
Ariel: To every article.
I boarded the king's ship. Now on the beak°,
Now in the waist°, the deck°, in every cabin,
I flamed amazement°. Sometime I'd divide
And burn in many places; on the topmast,
200 The yards, and boresprit° would I flame distinctly°,
Then meet and join. Jove's lightnings, the precursors
O' th' dreadful thunderclaps, more momentary
And sight-outrunning were not. The fire and cracks
Of sulfurous roaring the most mighty Neptune
Seem to besiege, and make his bold waves tremble;
Yea, his dread trident shake.
Prospero: My brave spirit!
Who was so firm, so constant, that this coil°
Would not infect his reason?
Ariel: Not a soul
But felt a fever of the mad and played
210 Some tricks of desperation. All but mariners
Plunged in the foaming brine and quit the vessel,
Then all afire with me. The king's son Ferdinand,
With hair up-staring° (then like reeds, not hair),
Was the first man that leapt; cried, "Hell is empty,
And all the devils are here!"
Prospero: Why, that's my spirit!
But was not this nigh shore?
Ariel: Close by, my master.
Prospero: But are they, Ariel, safe?
Ariel: Not a hair perished.
On their sustaining° garments not a blemish,
But fresher than before; and as thou bad'st me,
220 In troops I have dispersed them 'bout the isle.
The king's son have I landed by himself,
Whom I left cooling of the air with sighs
In an odd angle of the isle, and sitting,
His arms in this sad knot.

   [Illustrates with a gesture.]

---

192 *task:* tax to the utmost.   193 *quality:* cohorts (Ariel is leader of a band of spirits).   194 *to point:* in every detail.   196 *beak:* prow.   197 *waist:* amidships.   197 *deck:* poop.   198 *flamed amazement:* struck terror by appearing as (Saint Elmo's) fire. 200 *boresprit:* bowsprit; 200 *distinctly:* in different places.   207 *coil:* uproar.   213 *up-staring:* standing on end.   218 *sustaining:* buoying them up.

Prospero: Of the king's ship,
The mariners, say how thou hast disposed,
And all the rest o' th' fleet.
Ariel: Safely in harbor
Is the king's ship; in the deep nook where once
Thou call'dst me up at midnight to fetch dew
From the still-vexed Bermoothes°, there she's hid;
230 The mariners all under hatches stowed,
Who, with a charm joined to their suff'red° labor,
I have left asleep. And for the rest o'th' fleet,
Which I dispersed, they all have met again,
And are upon the Mediterranean flote°
Bound sadly home for Naples,
Supposing that they saw the king's ship wracked
And his great person perish.
Prospero: Ariel, thy charge
Exactly is performed; but there's more work.
What is the time o' th' day?
Ariel: Past the mid season°.
240 *Prospero:* At least two glasses.° The time 'twixt six and now
Must by us both be spent most preciously.
Ariel: Is there more toil? Since thou dost give me pains°,
Let me remember° thee what thou hast promised,
Which is not yet performed me.
Prospero: How now? Moody?
What is't thou canst demand?
Ariel: My liberty.
Prospero: Before the time be out? No more!
Ariel: I prithee,
Remember I have done thee worthy service,
Told thee no lies, made thee no mistakings, served
Without or grudge or grumblings. Thou did promise
To bate me° a full year.
250 *Prospero:*   Dost thou forget
From what a torment I did free thee?
Ariel: No.
Prospero: Thou dost; and think'st it much to tread the ooze
Of the salt deep,
To run upon the sharp wind of the North,
To do me business in the veins° o' th' earth
When it is baked° with frost.
Ariel: I do not, sir.

---

229 *Bermoothes:* Bermudas.   231 *suff'red:* undergone.   234 *flote:* sea.   239 *mid season:*
noon.   240 *two glasses:* two o'clock.   242 *pains:* hard tasks.   243 *remember:* remind.
250 *bate me:* reduce my term of service.   255 *veins:* streams.   256 *baked:* caked.

Prospero: Thou liest, malignant thing! Hast thou forgot
The foul witch Sycorax°, who with age and envy°
Was grown into a hoop? Hast thou forgot her?
Ariel: No, sir.
260 *Prospero:*   Thou hast. Where was she born? Speak!
Tell me!
Ariel: Sir, in Argier°.
Prospero: O, was she so? I must
Once in a month recount what thou hast been,
Which thou forget'st. This damned witch Sycorax,
For mischiefs manifold, and sorceries terrible
To enter human hearing, from Argier,
Thou know'st, was banished. For one thing she did
They would not take her life. Is not this true?
Ariel: Ay, sir.
270 *Prospero:* This blue-eyed° hag was hither brought with child
And here was left by th' sailors. Thou, my slave,
As thou report'st thyself, wast then her servant.
And, for thou wast a spirit too delicate
To act her earthy and abhorred commands,
Refusing her grand hests°, she did confine thee,
By help of her more potent ministers°,
And in her most unmitigable rage,
Into a cloven pine; within which rift
Imprisoned thou didst painfully remain
280 A dozen years; within which space she died
And left thee there, where thou didst vent thy groans
As fast as millwheels strike. Then was this island
(Save for the son that she did litter here,
A freckled whelp, hagborn) not honored with
A human shape.
Ariel: Yes, Caliban her son.
Prospero: Dull thing, I say so! He, that Caliban
Whom now I keep in service. Thou best know'st
What torment I did find thee in; thy groans
Did make wolves howl and penetrate the breasts
290 Of ever-angry bears. It was a torment
To lay upon the damned, which Sycorax
Could not again undo. It was mine art,
When I arrived and heard thee, that made gape
The pine, and let thee out.
Ariel: I thank thee, master.

---

258 *Sycorax:* name not found elsewhere; probably derived from Greek *sys,* "sow," and *korax,* which means both "raven"—see line 324—and "hook"—hence perhaps "hoop;" *envy:* malice.   262 *Argier:* Algiers.   270 *blue-eyed:* referring to the livid color of the eyelid, a sign of pregnancy.   275 *hests:* commands.   276 *her . . . ministers:* her agents, spirits more powerful than thou.

Prospero: If thou more murmur'st, I will rend an oak
And peg thee in his° knotty entrails till
Thou hast howled away twelve winters.
Ariel: Pardon, master.
I will be correspondent° to command
And do my spiriting gently°.
Prospero: Do so; and after two days
I will discharge thee.
300 *Ariel:*   That's my noble master!
What shall I do? Say what? What shall I do?
Prospero: Go make thyself like a nymph o' th' sea. Be subject
To no sight but thine and mine, invisible
To every eyeball else°. Go take this shape
And hither come in't. Go! Hence with diligence!   *Exit [Ariel].*
Awake, dear heart, awake! Thou hast slept well.
Awake!
Miranda: The strangeness of your story put
Heaviness in me.
Prospero: Shake it off. Come on.
310 We'll visit Caliban, my slave, who never
Yields us kind answer.
Miranda: 'Tis a villain, sir,
I do not love to look on.
Prospero: But as 'tis,
We cannot miss° him. He does make our fire,
Fetch in our wood, and serves in offices
That profit us. What, ho! Slave! Caliban!
Thou earth, thou! Speak!
Caliban [Within.]:   There's wood enough within.
Prospero: Come forth, I say! There's other business for thee.
Come, thou tortoise! When°?

    Enter Ariel like a water nymph.

Fine apparition! My quaint° Ariel,
Hark in thine ear. [*Whispers.*]
320 *Ariel:*   My lord, it shall be done.   *Exit.*
Prospero: Thou poisonous slave, got by the devil himself
Upon thy wicked dam, come forth!

---

296 *his:* its.   298 *correspondent:* obedient.   299 *do . . . gently:* render graciously my
services as a spirit.   303–304 *invisible . . . else:* Ariel is invisible to everyone in the play
except   Prospero;   Henslowe's   *Diary,*   an   Elizabethan   stage   account,
lists "a robe for to go invisible."   313 *miss:* do without.   318 *When:* expression of impatience.   319 *quaint:* ingenious.

Enter Caliban.

Caliban: As wicked dew as e'er my mother brushed
With raven's feather from unwholesome fen
Drop on you both! A southwest blow on ye
And blister you all o'er!
Prospero: For this, be sure, tonight thou shalt have cramps,
Side-stitches that shall pen thy breath up. Urchins°
Shall, for that vast of night that they may work°,
330 All exercise on thee; thou shalt be pinched
As thick as honeycomb, each pinch more stinging
Than bees that made 'em.
Caliban: I must eat my dinner.
This island's mine by Sycorax my mother,
Which thou tak'st from me. When thou cam'st first,
Thou strok'st me and made much of me; wouldst give me
Water with berries in't; and teach me how
To name the bigger light, and how the less,
That burn by day and night. And then I loved thee
And showed thee all the qualities o' th' isle,
340 The fresh springs, brine pits, barren place and fertile.
Cursed be I that did so! All the charms
Of Sycorax—toads, beetles, bats, light on you!
For I am all the subjects that you have,
Which first was mine own king; and here you sty me
In this hard rock, whiles you do keep from me
The rest o' th' island.
Prospero: Thou most lying slave,
Whom stripes° may move, not kindness! I have used thee
(Filth as thou art) with humane care, and lodged thee
In mine own cell till thou didst seek to violate
350 The honor of my child.
Caliban: O ho, O ho! Would't had been done!
Thou didst prevent me; I had peopled else
This isle with Calibans.
Miranda:°   Abhorrèd slave,
Which any print of goodness wilt not take,
Being capable of all ill°! I pitied thee,
Took pains to make thee speak, taught thee each hour
One thing or other. When thou didst not, savage,
Know thine own meaning, but wouldst gabble like
A thing most brutish, I endowed thy purposes

---

328 *Urchins:* goblins in the shape of hedgehogs.   329 *vast . . . work:* the long, empty stretch of night during which malignant spirits are allowed to be active.   347 *stripes:* lashes.   353 *Miranda:* many editors transfer this speech to Prospero as inappropriate to Miranda.   355 *capable . . . ill:* susceptible only to evil impressions.

360 With words that made them known. But thy vile race,
    Though thou didst learn, had that in't which good natures
    Could not abide to be with. Therefore wast thou
    Deservedly confined into this rock, who hadst
    Deserved more than a prison.
    Caliban: You taught me language, and my profit on't
    Is, I know how to curse. The red plague rid° you
    For learning me your language!
    Prospero: Hagseed, hence!
    Fetch us in fuel. And be quick, thou'rt best°,
    To answer other business. Shrug'st thou, malice?
370 If thou neglect'st or dost unwillingly
    What I command, I'll rack thee with old° cramps,
    Fill all thy bones with aches°, make thee roar
    That beasts shall tremble at thy din.
    Caliban: No, pray thee.

        [Aside.]

    I must obey. His art is of such pow'r
    It would control my dam's god, Setebos,
    And make a vassal of him.
    Prospero: So, slave; hence!   *Exit Caliban.*
        Enter Ferdinand; and Ariel (invisible), playing and singing.

                          Ariel's song.
    Ariel: Come unto these yellow sands,
                             And then take hands.
                         Curtsied when you have and kissed
380   The wild waves whist°,
                         Foot it featly° here and there;
                         And, sweet sprites, the burden bear.
                             Hark, hark!

    Burden, dispersedly°. Bow, wow!
                 The watchdogs bark.

    Burden, dispersedly°. Bow, wow!

                     Hark, hark! I hear
                     The strain of strutting chanticleer
                         Cry cock-a-diddle-dow.

---

366 *rid:* destroy.   368 *thou'rt best:* you'd better.   371 *old:* plenty of (with an additional suggestion, "such as old people have").   372 *aches:* pronounced "aitches."
379–80 *kissed . . . whist:* when you have, through the harmony of kissing in the dance,
kissed the wild waves into silence (?) when you have kissed in the dance, the wild waves
being silenced (?).   381 *featly:* nimbly.   384 *Burden, dispersedly:* an undersong, coming from all parts of the stage; it imitates the barking of dogs and perhaps at the end the
crowing of a cock.

390 *Ferdinand:* Where should this music be? I' th' air or th' earth?
It sounds no more; and sure it waits upon
Some god o' th' island. Sitting on a bank,
Weeping again the King my father's wrack,
This music crept by me upon the waters,
Allaying both their fury and my passion°
With its sweet air. Thence I have followed it,
Or it hath drawn me rather; but 'tis gone.
No, it begins again.

Ariel's song.

   Ariel: Full fathom five thy father lies;
400   Of his bones are coral made;
       Those are pearls that were his eyes;
        Nothing of him that doth fade
       But doth suffer a sea change
       Into something rich and strange.
       Sea nymphs hourly ring his knell:

Burden. Ding-dong.

   Hark! Now I hear them—ding-dong bell.

Ferdinand: The ditty does remember my drowned father.
This is no mortal business, nor no sound
410 That the earth owes°. I hear it now above me.
Prospero: The fringèd curtains of thine eye advance°
And say what thou see'st yond.
Miranda: What is't? A spirit?
Lord, how it looks about! Believe me, sir,
It carries a brave form. But 'tis a spirit.
Prospero: No, wench; it eats, and sleeps, and hath such senses
As we have, such. This gallant which thou see'st
Was in the wrack; and, but he's something stained
With grief (that's beauty's canker), thou mightst call him
A goodly person. He hath lost his fellows
And strays about to find 'em.
420 *Miranda:*   I might call him
A thing divine; for nothing natural
I ever saw so noble.
Prospero [Aside.]: It goes on, I see,
As my soul prompts it. Spirit, fine spirit, I'll free thee
Within two days for this.
Ferdinand: Most sure, the goddess
On whom these airs attend! Vouchsafe my prayer
May know if you remain° upon this island,

---

395 *passion:* grief. 410 *owes:* owns. 411 *advance:* raise. 425–26 *Vouchsafe . . .*
remain: may my prayer induce you to inform me whether you dwell.

And that you will some good instruction give
How I may bear me° here. My prime request,
Which I do last pronounce, is (O you wonder!)
If you be maid or no?
430 *Miranda:*   No wonder, sir,
But certainly a maid.
Ferdinand: My language? Heavens!
I am the best of them that speak this speech,
Were I but where 'tis spoken.
Prospero: How? The best?
What wert thou if the King of Naples heard thee?
Ferdinand: A single° thing, as I am now, that wonders
To hear thee speak of Naples. He does hear me;
And that he does I weep. Myself am Naples,
Who with mine eyes, never since at ebb, beheld
The king my father wracked.
Miranda: Alack, for mercy!
440 *Ferdinand:* Yes, faith, and all his lords, the Duke of Milan
And his brave son° being twain.°
Prospero [Aside.]:   The Duke of Milan
And his more braver daughter could control° thee,
If now 'twere fit to do't. At the first sight
They have changed eyes°. Delicate Ariel,
I'll set thee free for this. [*To Ferdinand.*] A word, good sir.
I fear you have done yourself some wrong°. A word!
Miranda: Why speaks my father so ungently? This
Is the third man that e'er I saw; the first
That e'er I sighed for. Pity move my father
To be inclined my way!
450 *Ferdinand:*   O, if a virgin,
And your affection not gone forth, I'll make you
The queen of Naples.
Prospero: Soft, sir! One word more.

    [*Aside.*]

They are both in either's pow'rs. But this swift business
I must uneasy make, lest too light winning
Make the prize light. [*To Ferdinand.*] One word more! I charge thee
That thou attend me. Thou dost here usurp
The name thou ow'st° not, and hast put thyself
Upon this island as a spy, to win it

---

428 *bear me:* conduct myself.   435 *single:* (1) solitary (2) helpless.   441 *son:* the only
time Antonio's son is mentioned; *twain:* two (of these lords).   442 *control:* refute.   444
changed eyes: i.e., fallen in love.   446 *done . . . wrong:* said what is not so.   457 *ow'st:*
ownest.

From me, the lord on't.
Ferdinand: No, as I am a man!
460 **Miranda:** There's nothing ill can dwell in such a temple.
If the ill spirit have so fair a house,
Good things will strive to dwell with't.
Prospero: Follow me.

[To Miranda.]

Speak not you for him; he's a traitor. [*To Ferdinand.*] Come!
I'll manacle thy neck and feet together;
Sea water shalt thou drink; thy food shall be
The fresh-brook mussels, withered roots, and husks
Wherein the acorn cradled. Follow!
Ferdinand: No.
I will resist such entertainment till
Mine enemy has more pow'r.

He draws, and is charmed from moving.

Miranda: O dear father,
470 Make not too rash a trial of him, for
He's gentle and not fearful°.
Prospero: What, I say,
My foot my tutor°? [*To Ferdinand.*] Put thy sword up, traitor—
Who mak'st a show but dar'st not strike, thy conscience
Is so possessed with guilt! Come, from thy ward°!
For I can here disarm thee with this stick°
And make thy weapon drop.
Miranda: Beseech you, father!
Prospero: Hence! Hang not on my garments.
Miranda: Sir, have pity.
I'll be his surety.
Prospero: Silence! One word more
Shall make me chide thee, if not hate thee. What,
480 An advocate for an impostor? Hush!
Thou think'st there is no more such shapes as he,
Having seen but him and Caliban. Foolish wench!
To th' most of men this is a Caliban,
And they to him are angels.
Miranda: My affections
Are then most humble. I have no ambition
To see a goodlier man.
Prospero [To Ferdinand.]: Come on, obey!

---

471 *gentle . . . fearful:* of noble birth and no coward.   472 *My . . . tutor?:* am I to be instructed by my inferior?   474 *ward:* fighting posture.   475 *stick:* his wand.

Thy nerves° are in their infancy again
And have no vigor in them.
Ferdinand: So they are.
490 My spirits, as in a dream, are all bound up.
My father's loss, the weakness which I feel,
The wrack of all my friends, not this man's threats
To whom I am subdued, are but light to me,
Might I but through my prison once a day
Behold this maid. All corners else o' th' earth
Let liberty make use of. Space enough
Have I in such a prison.
Prospero [Aside.]: It works. [*To Ferdinand.*] Come on.

     [*To Ariel.*]

Thou hast done well, fine Ariel! [*To Ferdinand.*] Follow me.
[*To Ariel.*] Hark what thou else shalt do me.
500 ***Miranda:***   Be of comfort.
My father's of a better nature, sir,
Than he appears by speech. This is unwonted
Which now came from him.
Prospero: Thou shalt be as free
As mountain winds; but then° exactly do
All points of my command.
Ariel: To th' syllable.
Prospero [To Ferdinand.]:
Come, follow. [*To Miranda.*] Speak not for him.   *Exeunt.*

Act II

Scene I. [Another part of the island.]

     Enter Alonso, Sebastian, Antonio, Gonzalo, Adrian, Francisco, and others.

Gonzalo: Beseech you, sir, be merry. You have cause
(So have we all) of joy; for our escape
Is much beyond our loss. Our hint of° woe
Is common; every day some sailor's wife,
The master of some merchant°, and the merchant,
Have just our theme of woe. But for the miracle,
I mean our preservation, few in millions
Can speak like us. Then wisely, good sir, weigh
Our sorrow with° our comfort.
Alonso: Prithee, peace.

---

488 *nerves:* sinews.   504 *then:* till then.   II.i. 3 *hint of:* occasion for.   5 *master . . .*
merchant: captain of some merchant ship.   9 *with:* against.

10 *Sebastian [Aside to Antonio.]:* He receives comfort like cold porridge°.
Antonio [Aside to Sebastian.]: The visitor° will not give him o'er so.°
Sebastian: Look, he's winding up the watch of his wit; by and by it
    will strike.
Gonzalo: Sir—
Sebastian [Aside to Antonio.]: One. Tell°.
Gonzalo: When every grief is entertained, that's° offered
Comes to th' entertainer—
Sebastian: A dollar.
Gonzalo: Dolor comes to him, indeed. You have spoken truer than you
20   purposed.
Sebastian: You have taken it wiselier° than I meant you should.
Gonzalo: Therefore, my lord—
Antonio: Fie, what a spendthrift is he of his tongue!
Alonso: I prithee, spare°.
Gonzalo: Well, I have done. But yet—
Sebastian: He will be talking.
Antonio: Which, of he or Adrian, for a good wager, first° begins to
    crow?
Sebastian: The old cock°.
Antonio: The cock'rel°.
30 *Sebastian:* Done! The wager?
Antonio: A laughter°.
Sebastian: A match!
Adrian: Though this island seem to be desert—
Antonio: Ha, ha, ha!
Sebastian: So, you're paid.
Adrian: Uninhabitable and almost inaccessible—
Sebastian: Yet—
Adrian: Yet—
Antonio: He could not miss't.
40 *Adrian:* It must needs be of subtle, tender, and delicate temperance°.
Antonio: Temperance was a delicate wench.
Sebastian: Ay, and a subtle, as he most learnedly delivered.
Adrian: The air breathes upon us here most sweetly.
Sebastian: As if it had lungs, and rotten ones.
Antonio: Or as 'twere perfumed by a fen.
Gonzalo: Here is everything advantageous to life.
Antonio: True; save means to live.
Sebastian: Of that there's none, or little.

---

10 *He . . . porridge:* "He" is Alonso; pun on "peace," for porridge contained peas.   11
visitor: spiritual comforter.   11 *give . . . so:* release him so easily.   15 *One. Tell:* He has
struck one. Keep count.   16 *that's:* that which is.   21 *wiselier:* i.e., understood my
pun.   24 *spare:* spare your words.   27 *Which . . . first:* let's wager which of the two, Gonzalo or Adrian, will first.   28 *old cock:* Gonzalo.   29 *cock'rel:* young cock; i.e.,
Adrian.   31 *laughter:* the winner will have the laugh on the loser.   40 *temperance:* climate
(in the next line, a girls' name).

Gonzalo: How lush and lusty the grass looks! How green!

50 *Antonio:* The ground indeed is tawny.

Sebastian: With an eye° of green in't.

Antonio: He misses not much.

Sebastian: No; he doth but mistake the truth totally.

Gonzalo: But the rarity of it is—which is indeed almost beyond credit—

Sebastian: As many vouched rarities are.

Gonzalo: That our garments, being, as they were, drenched in the sea, hold, notwithstanding, their freshness and glosses, being rather new-dyed than stained with salt water.

60 *Antonio:* If but one of his pockets could speak, would it not say he lies°?

Sebastian: Ay, or very falsely pocket up his report°.

Gonzalo: Methinks our garments are now as fresh as when we put them on first in Afric, at the marriage of the king's fair daughter Claribel to the King of Tunis.

Sebastian: 'Twas a sweet marriage, and we prosper well in our return.

Adrian: Tunis was never graced before with such a paragon to° their queen.

Gonzalo: Not since widow Dido's time.

70 *Antonio:* Widow? A pox o' that! How came that "widow" in? Widow Dido!

Sebastian: What if he had said "widower Aeneas"° too? Good Lord, how you take it!

Adrian: "Widow Dido," said you? You make me study of that. She was of Carthage, not of Tunis.

Gonzalo: This Tunis, sir, was Carthage.

Adrian: Carthage?

Gonzalo: I assure you, Carthage.

Antonio: His word is more than the miraculous harp°.

80 *Sebastian:* He hath raised the wall and houses too.

Antonio: What impossible matter will he make easy next?

Sebastian: I think he will carry this island home in his pocket and give it his son for an apple.

Antonio: And, sowing the kernels of it in the sea, bring forth more islands.

Gonzalo: Ay!

Antonio: Why, in good time°.

---

51 *eye:* spot (also perhaps Gonzalo's eye).   60–61 *If . . . lies:* i.e., the insides of Gonzalo's pockets are stained.   62 *Ay . . . report:* unless the pocket were, like a false knave, to receive without resentment the imputation that it is unstained.   67 *to:* for.   70–72 *Widow Dido . . ."widower Aeneas":* the point of the joke is that Dido was a widow, but one does not ordinarily think of her in that way; and the same with Aeneas.   70 *miraculous harp:* of Amphion, which raised only the *walls* of Thebes; whereas Gonzalo has rebuilt the whole ancient city of Carthage by identifying it mistakenly with modern Tunis.   86 *Why . . . time:* hearing Gonzalo reaffirm his false statement about Tunis and Carthage, Antonio suggests that Gonzalo will indeed, at the first opportunity, carry this island home in his pocket.

Gonzalo [To Alonso.]: Sir, we were talking that our garments seem now
　　as fresh as when we were at Tunis at the marriage of your daughter,
　　who is now queen.
90 *Antonio:* And the rarest that e'er came there.
Sebastian: Bate°, I beseech you, widow Dido.
Antonio: O, widow Dido? Ay, widow Dido!
Gonzalo: Is not, sir, my doublet as fresh as the first day I wore it? I
　　mean, in a sort°.
Antonio: That "sort" was well fished for.
Gonzalo: When I wore it at your daughter's marriage.
Alonso: You cram these words into mine ears against
The stomach of my sense°. Would I had never
Married my daughter there! For, coming thence,
100 My son is lost; and, in my rate°, she too,
Who is so far from Italy removed
I ne'er again shall see her. O thou mine heir
Of Naples and of Milan, what strange fish
Hath made his meal on thee?
Francisco:　　　　　　　Sir, he may live.
I saw him beat the surges under him
And ride upon their backs. He trod the water,
Whose enmity he flung aside, and breasted
The surge most swol'n that met him. His bold head
'Bove the contentious waves he kept, and oared
110 Himself with his good arms in lusty stroke
To th' shore, that o'er his° wave-worn basis bowed°,
As stooping to relieve him. I not doubt
He came alive to land.
Alonso:　　　　　　No, no, he's gone.
Sebastian [To Alonso.]: Sir, you may thank yourself for this great loss,
That would not bless our Europe with your daughter,
But rather loose her to an African,
Where she, at least, is banished from your eye
Who hath cause to wet the grief on't.
Alonso:　　　　　　　　　Prithee, peace.
Sebastian: You were kneeled to and importuned otherwise
120 By all of us; and the fair soul herself
Weighed, between loathness and obedience, at
Which end o' th' beam should bow°. We have lost your son,
I fear, forever. Milan and Naples have
Moe° widows in them of this business' making
Than we bring men to comfort them.

---

91 *Bate:* except.　　94 *in a sort:* so to speak.　　97–98 *against . . . sense:* though my mind
(or feelings) have no appetite for them.　　100 *rate:* opinion.　　111 *his:* its; *wave-worn
basis bowed:* the image is of a guardian cliff on the shore.　　121–22 *Weighed . . .
bow:* Claribel's unwillingness to marry was outweighed by her obedience to her father.
124 *Moe:* more.

The fault's your own.
Alonso: So is the dear'st° o' th' loss.
Gonzalo: My Lord Sebastian,
The truth you speak doth lack some gentleness,
And time to speak it in. You rub the sore
When you should bring the plaster.
130 *Sebastian:*   Very well.
Antonio: And most chirurgeonly°.
Gonzalo [To Alonso.]: It is foul weather in us all, good sir,
When you are cloudy.
Sebastian [Aside to Antonio.]: Foul weather?
Antonio [Aside to Sebastian.]:   Very foul.
Gonzalo: Had I plantation° of this isle, my lord—
Antonio: He'd sow't with nettle seed.
Sebastian: Or docks, or mallows.
Gonzalo: And were the king on't, what would I do?
Sebastian: Scape being drunk for want of wine.
Gonzalo: I' th' commonwealth I would by contraries°
Execute all things. For no kind of traffic°
140 Would I admit; no name of magistrate;
Letters° should not be known; riches, poverty
And use of service°, none; contract, succession°,
Bourn°, bound of land, tilth°, vineyard, none;
No use of metal, corn, or wine, or oil;
No occupation; all men idle, all;
And women too, but innocent and pure;
No sovereignty.
Sebastian: Yet he would be king on't.
Antonio: The latter end of his commonwealth forgets the beginning.
Gonzalo: All things in common nature should produce
150 Without sweat or endeavor. Treason, felony,
Sword, pike, knife, gun, or need of any engine°
Would I not have; but nature should bring forth,
Of it° own kind, all foison°, all abundance,
To feed my innocent people.
Sebastian: No marrying 'mong his subjects?
Antonio: None, man, all idle—whores and knaves.
Gonzalo: I would with such perfection govern, sir,
T' excel the Golden Age.
Sebastian [Loudly.]:   Save his majesty!
Antonio [Loudly.]: Long live Gonzalo!
Gonzalo: And—do you mark me, sir?

---

126 *dear'st:* intensifies the meaning of the noun.   131 *chirurgeonly:* like a surgeon.
134 *plantation:* colonization (Antonio then puns by taking the word in its other
sense).   138 *contraries:* in contrast to the usual customs.   139 *traffic:* trade.   141
Letters: learning.   142 *service:* servants; *succession:* inheritance.   143 *Bourn:* boundary;
tilth: agriculture.   151 *engine:* weapon.   153 *it:* its; *foison:* abundance.

160 *Alonso:* Prithee, no more. Thou dost talk nothing to me.
  Gonzalo: I do well believe your highness; and did it to minister
     occasion° to these gentlemen, who are of such sensible° and
     nimble lungs that they always use to laugh at nothing.
  Antonio: 'Twas you we laughed at.
  Gonzalo: Who in this kind of merry fooling am nothing to you; so
     you may continue, and laugh at nothing still.
  Antonio: What a blow was there given!
  Sebastian: And° it had not fall'n flatlong°.
  Gonzalo: You are gentlemen of brave mettle; you would lift the moon
170   out of her sphere if she would continue in it five weeks without
     changing.

    Enter Ariel [invisible] playing solemn music.

  Sebastian: We would so, and then go a-batfowling°.
  Antonio: Nay, good my lord, be not angry.
  Gonzalo: No, I warrant you; I will not adventure my discretion so
     weakly°. Will you laugh me asleep? For I am very heavy.
  Antonio: Go sleep, and hear us.

    [All sleep except Alonso, Sebastian, and Antonio.]

  Alonso: What, all so soon asleep? I wish mine eyes
  Would, with themselves, shut up my thoughts. I find
  They are inclined to do so.
  Sebastian: Please you, sir,
180 Do not omit° the heavy offer of it.
  It seldom visits sorrow; when it doth,
  It is a comforter.
  Antonio: We two, my lord,
  Will guard your person while you take your rest,
  And watch your safety.
  Alonso: Thank you. Wondrous heavy.

                                [Alonso sleeps. Exit Ariel.]

  Sebastian: What a strange drowsiness possesses them!
  Antonio: It is the quality o' th' climate.
  Sebastian: Why
  Doth it not then our eyelids sink? I find not

161–162 *minister occasion:* afford opportunity.   162 *sensible:* sensitive.   168 *And:* if;
flatlong: with the flat of the sword.   172 *We . . . a-batfowling:* We would use the moon
for a lantern in order to hunt birds at night by attracting them with a light and beating
them down with bats; i.e., in order to gull simpletons like you (?).   174–75 *adven-*
ture . . . weakly: risk my reputation for good sense because of your weak wit.   180
omit: neglect.

Myself disposed to sleep.
Antonio: Nor I: my spirits are nimble.
They fell together all, as by consent.
190 They dropped as by a thunderstroke. What might,
Worthy Sebastian—O, what might?—No more!
And yet methinks I see it in thy face,
What thou shouldst be. Th' occasion speaks° thee, and
My strong imagination sees a crown
Dropping upon thy head.
Sebastian: What? Art thou waking?
Antonio: Do you not hear me speak?
Sebastian: I do; and surely
It is a sleepy language, and thou speak'st
Out of thy sleep. What is it thou didst say?
This is a strange repose, to be asleep
200 With eyes wide open; standing, speaking, moving,
And yet so fast asleep.
Antonio: Noble Sebastian,
Thou let'st thy fortune sleep—die, rather; wink'st°
Whiles thou art waking.
Sebastian: Thou dost snore distinctly;
There's meaning in thy snores.
Antonio: I am more serious than my custom. You
Must be so too, if heed° me; which to do
Trebles thee o'er°.
Sebastian: Well, I am standing water.
Antonio: I'll teach you how to flow.
Sebastian: Do so. To ebb
Hereditary sloth instructs me.
Antonio: O,
210 If you but knew how you the purpose cherish
Whiles thus you mock it; how, in stripping it,
You more invest it°! Ebbing men, indeed,
Most often do so near the bottom run
By their own fear or sloth.
Sebastian: Prithee, say on.
The setting of thine eye and cheek proclaim
A matter° from thee; and a birth, indeed,
Which throes thee much° to yield.
Antonio: Thus, sir:
Although this lord of weak remembrance°, this

---

193 *speaks:* speaks to.   202 *wink'st:* dost shut thine eyes.   206 *if heed:* if you
heed.   207 *Trebles thee o'er:* makes thee three times what thou now art.   211–212 *in stripping . . . invest it:* in stripping the purpose off you, you clothe yourself with it all the
more.   216 *matter:* matter of importance.   217 *throes thee much:* costs thee much
pain.   218 *remembrance:* memory.

Who shall be of as little memory°
220 When he is earthed°, hath here almost persuaded
(For he's a spirit of persuasion, only
Professes to persuade°) the king his son's alive,
'Tis as impossible that he's undrowned
As he that sleeps here swims.
Sebastian: I have no hope
That he's undrowned.
Antonio: O, out of that no hope
What great hope have you! No hope that way is
Another way so high a hope that even
Ambition cannot pierce a wink beyond,
But doubt discovery there°. Will you grant with me
That Ferdinand is drowned?
Sebastian: He's gone.
230 **Antonio:**   Then tell me,
Who's the next heir of Naples?
Sebastian: Claribel.
Antonio: She that is Queen of Tunis; she that dwells
Ten leagues beyond man's life°; she that from Naples
Can have no note—unless the sun were post°;
The man i' th' moon's too slow—till newborn chins
Be rough and razorable°; she that from whom
We all were sea-swallowed°, though some cast° again,
And, by that destiny, to perform an act
Whereof what's past is prologue, what to come,
In yours and my discharge.
240 **Sebastian:**   What stuff is this? How say you?
'Tis true my brother's daughter's Queen of Tunis;
So is she heir of Naples; 'twixt which regions
There is some space.
Antonio: A space whose ev'ry cubit
Seems to cry out, "How shall that Claribel
Measure us back to Naples? Keep in Tunis,
And let Sebastian wake!" Say this were death
That now hath seized them, why, they were no worse
Than now they are. There be that can rule Naples
As well as he that sleeps; lords that can prate
250 As amply and unnecessarily

---

219 *of . . . memory:* as little remembered. 220 *earthed:* buried. 221–22 *only . . . persuade:* his only profession is to persuade. 228–29 *Ambition . . . there:* the eye of ambition can reach no further, but must even doubt the reality of what it discerns thus far. 233 *Ten . . . life:* it would take a lifetime to get within ten leagues of the place. 234 *post:* messenger. 235–36 *till . . . razorable:* till babies just born be ready to shave. 236–37 *she . . . sea-swallowed:* she who is separated from Naples by so dangerous a sea that we were ourselves swallowed up by it. 237 *cast:* cast upon the shore (with a suggestion of its theatrical meaning that leads to the next metaphor).

As this Gonzalo; I myself could make
A chough° of as deep chat. O, that you bore
The mind that I do! What a sleep were this
For your advancement! Do you understand me?
Sebastian: Methinks I do.
Antonio: And how does your content
Tender° your own good fortune?
Sebastian: I remember
You did supplant your brother Prospero.
Antonio: True.
And look how well my garments sit upon me,
Much feater° than before. My brother's servants
260 Were then my fellows; now they are my men.
Sebastian: But, for your conscience—
Antonio: Ay, sir, where lies that? If 'twere a kibe°,
'Twould put me to my slipper; but I feel not
This deity in my bosom. Twenty consciences
That stand 'twixt me and Milan, candied be they
And melt, ere they molest! Here lies your brother,
No better than the earth he lies upon—
If he were that which now he's like, that's dead°—
Whom I with this obedient steel (three inches of it)
270 Can lay to bed forever; whiles you, doing thus,
To the perpetual wink° for aye might put
This ancient morsel, this Sir Prudence, who
Should not upbraid our course. For all the rest,
They'll take suggestion as a cat laps milk;
They'll tell the clock° to any business that
We say befits the hour.
Sebastian: Thy case, dear friend,
Shall be my precedent. As thou got'st Milan,
I'll come by Naples. Draw thy sword. One stroke
Shall free thee from the tribute which thou payest,
And I the king shall love thee.
280 *Antonio:*   Draw together;
And when I rear my hand, do you the like,
To fall it on Gonzalo. [*They draw.*]
Sebastian: O, but one word!

---

252 *chough:* jackdaw (a bird that can be taught to speak a few words).   256 *Tender:* regard (i.e., Do you like your good fortune?).   259 *feater:* more becomingly.   262 *kibe:*
chilblain on the heel.   268 *that's dead:* that is, if he were dead.   271 *wink:* eye-
shut.   275 *tell the clock:* say yes.

Enter Ariel [invisible] with music and song.

Ariel: My master through his art foresees the danger
That you, his friend, are in, and sends me forth
(For else his project dies) to keep them living.

Sings in Gonzalo's ear.

> While you here do snoring lie,
> Open-eyed conspiracy
>   His time doth take.
> If of life you keep a care,
> Shake off slumber and beware.
>   Awake, awake!

290

Antonio: Then let us both be sudden.
Gonzalo [Wakes.]:   Now good angels
Preserve the king!

[The others wake.]

Alonso: Why, how now? Ho, awake! Why are you drawn?
Wherefore this ghastly looking?
Gonzalo: What's the matter?
Sebastian: Whiles we stood here securing your repose,
Even now, we heard a hollow burst of bellowing
Like bulls, or rather lions. Did't not wake you?
It struck mine ear most terribly.
Alonso: I heard nothing.
300 *Antonio:* O, 'twas a din to fright a monster's ear,
To make an earthquake! Sure it was the roar
Of a whole herd of lions.
Alonso: Heard you this, Gonzalo?
Gonzalo: Upon mine honor, sir, I heard a humming,
And that a strange one too, which did awake me.
I shaked you, sir, and cried. As mine eyes opened,
I saw their weapons drawn. There was a noise,
That's verily°. 'Tis best we stand upon our guard,
Or that we quit this place. Let's draw our weapons.
Alonso: Lead off this ground, and let's make further search
For my poor son.
310 *Gonzalo:*   Heavens keep him from these beasts!
For he is, sure, i' th' island.
Alonso: Lead away.

---

307 *verily:* the truth.

Ariel: Prospero my lord shall know what I have done.
So, king, go safely on to seek thy son.   *Exeunt.*

Scene II. [Another part of the island.]

   Enter Caliban with a burden of wood. A noise of thunder heard.

Caliban: All the infections that the sun sucks up
From bogs, fens, flats, on Prosper fall, and make him
By inchmeal° a disease! His spirits hear me,
And yet I needs must curse. But they'll nor pinch,
Fright me with urchin shows°, pitch me i' th' mire,
Nor lead me, like a firebrand°, in the dark
Out of my way, unless he bid 'em. But
For every trifle are they set upon me;
Sometime like apes that mow° and chatter at me,
10 And after bite me; then like hedgehogs which
Lie tumbling in my barefoot way and mount
Their pricks at my footfall; sometime am I
All wound with adders, who with cloven tongues
Do hiss me into madness.

   Enter Trinculo.

                    Lo, now, lo!
Here comes a spirit of his, and to torment me
For bringing wood in slowly. I'll fall flat.
Perchance he will not mind me.

   [Lies down.]
Trinculo: Here's neither bush nor shrub to bear off° any weather at all,
   and another storm brewing; I hear it sing i' th' wind. Yond same
20   black cloud, yond huge one, looks like a foul bombard° that would
   shed his liquor. If it should thunder as it did before, I know not
   where to hide my head. Yond same cloud cannot choose but fall
   by pailfuls. What have we here? A man or a fish? Dead or alive?
   A fish! He smells like a fish; a very ancient and fishlike smell; a
   kind of not of the newest Poor John°. A strange fish! Were I in
   England now, as once I was, and had but this fish painted°, not
   a holiday fool there but would give a piece of silver. There would
   this monster make a man°; any strange beast there makes a man.

II.ii. 3 *By inchmeal:* inch by inch.   5 *urchin shows:* impish apparitions.   6 *like a fire-*
brand: in the form of a will-o'-the-wisp.   9 *mow:* make faces.   18 *bear off:* ward
off.   20 *bombard:* large leather jug.   25 *Poor John:* dried hake.   26 *painted:* i.e., as a
sign hung outside a booth at a fair.   27–28 *make a man:* pun: make a man's fortune.

When they will not give a doit° to relieve a lame beggar, they will
30   lay out ten to see a dead Indian. Legged like a man! And his fins
like arms! Warm, o' my troth! I do now let loose my opinion, hold
it no longer. This is no fish, but an islander, that hath lately
suffered by a thunderbolt. [*Thunder.*] Alas, the storm is come
again! My best way is to creep under his gaberdine; there is no
other shelter hereabout. Misery acquaints a man with strange
bedfellows. I will here shroud till the dregs of the storm be past.

[Creeps under Caliban's garment.]

Enter Stephano, singing, [a bottle in his hand.]

Stephano: I shall no more to sea, to sea;
                    Here shall I die ashore.
This is a very scurvy tune to sing at a man's funeral.
40 Well, here's my comfort.

[Drinks.]

                The master, the swabber, the boatswain, and I,
                    The gunner, and his mate,
                Loved Moll, Meg, and Marian, and Margery,
                    But none of us cared for Kate.
                    For she had a tongue with a tang,
                    Would cry to a sailor, "Go hang!"
                She loved not the savor of tar nor of pitch;
                    Yet a tailor might scratch her where'er she did itch.
                    Then to sea, boys, and let her go hang!
50   This is a scurvy tune too; but here's my comfort.

[Drinks.]

Caliban: Do not torment me! O!
Stephano: What's the matter? Have we devils here? Do you put tricks
upon's with savages and men of Inde, ha? I have not 'scaped
drowning to be afeard now of your four legs. For it hath been
said, "As proper a man as ever went on four legs cannot make him
give ground"; and it shall be said so again, while Stephano
breathes at' nostrils°.
Caliban: The spirit torments me. O!
Stephano: This is some monster of the isle, with four legs, who hath
60   got, as I take it, an ague. Where the devil should he learn our
language? I will give him some relief, if it be but for that. If I can

---

29 *doit:* smallest coin.   56–57 *at' nostrils:* at the nostrils.

recover° him, and keep him tame, and get to Naples with him,
he's a present for any emperor that ever trod on neat's leather°.

Caliban: Do not torment me, prithee; I'll bring my wood home faster.

Stephano: He's in his fit now and does not talk after the wisest. He
shall taste of my bottle; if he have never drunk wine afore, it will
go near to remove his fit. If I can recover him and keep him tame,
I will not take too much° for him. He shall pay for him that hath
him, and that soundly.

70 *Caliban:* Thou dost me yet but little hurt. Thou wilt anon°; I know it
by thy trembling°. Now Prosper works upon thee.

Stephano: Come on your ways, open your mouth; here is that which
will give language to you, cat°. Open your mouth. This will shake
your shaking, I can tell you, and that soundly. [*Gives Caliban drink.*]
You cannot tell who's your friend. Open your chaps° again.

Trinculo: I should know that voice. It should be—but he is drowned;
and these are devils. O, defend me!

Stephano: Four legs and two voices—a most delicate monster! His
forward voice now is to speak well of his friend; his backward
80   voice is to utter foul speeches and to detract. If all the wine in
my bottle will recover him, I will help his ague. Come! [*Gives
drink.*] Amen! I will pour some in thy other mouth.

Trinculo: Stephano!

Stephano: Doth thy other mouth call me? Mercy, mercy! This is a
devil, and no monster. I will leave him; I have no long spoon°.

Trinculo: Stephano! If thou beest Stephano, touch me and speak to
me; for I am Trinculo—be not afeard—thy good friend Trinculo.

Stephano: If thou beest Trinculo, come forth. I'll pull thee by the lesser
legs. If any be Trinculo's legs, these are they. [*Draws him out from
90   under Caliban's garment.*] Thou art very Trinculo indeed! How cam'st
thou to be the siege° of this mooncalf°? Can he vent Trinculos?

Trinculo: I took him to be killed with a thunderstroke. But art thou
not drowned, Stephano? I hope now thou art not drowned. Is the
storm overblown? I hid me under the dead mooncalf's gaberdine
for fear of the storm. And art thou living, Stephano? O Stephano,
two Neapolitans scaped!

Stephano: Prithee do not turn me about; my stomach is not constant.

Caliban [Aside.]: These be fine things, and if° they be not sprites.
That's a brave god and bears celestial liquor.

100 I will kneel to him.

Stephano: How didst thou scape? How cam'st thou hither? Swear by
this bottle how thou cam'st hither. I escaped upon a butt of sack

---

61 *recover:* cure.   63 *neat's leather:* cowhide.   67–68 *not . . . much:* too much will not
be enough.   70 *anon:* soon.   71 *trembling:* Trinculo is shaking with fear.   73 *cat:* alluding to the proverb "Liquor will make a cat talk."   75 *chaps:* jaws.   85 *long spoon:*
alluding to the proverb "He who sups with (i.e., from the same dish as) the devil must
have a long spoon."   91 *siege:* excrement; *mooncalf:* monstrosity.   98 *and if:* if.

which the sailors heaved o'erboard—by this bottle which I made
of the bark of a tree with mine own hands since I was cast ashore.
Caliban: I'll swear upon that bottle to be thy true subject, for the
liquor is not earthly.
Stephano: Here! Swear then how thou escap'dst.
Trinculo: Swum ashore, man, like a duck. I can swim like a duck, I'll
be sworn.
110 *Stephano:* Here, kiss the book. [*Gives him drink.*] Though thou canst
swim like a duck, thou art made like a goose.
Trinculo: O Stephano, hast any more of this?
Stephano: The whole butt, man. My cellar is in a rock by th' seaside,
where my wine is hid. How now, mooncalf? How does thine ague?
Caliban: Hast thou not dropped from heaven?
Stephano: Out o' th' moon, I do assure thee. I was the Man i' th'
Moon when time was°.
Caliban: I have seen thee in her, and I do adore thee.
My mistress showed me thee, and thy dog, and thy bush°.
120 *Stephano:* Come, swear to that; kiss the book. [*Gives him drink.*] I will
furnish it anon with new contents. Swear.

[*Caliban drinks.*]

Trinculo: By this good light, this is a very shallow monster! I afeard
of him? A very weak monster! The Man i' th' Moon? A most poor
credulous monster! Well drawn°, monster, in good sooth!
Caliban: I'll show thee every fertile inch o' th' island;
And I will kiss thy foot. I prithee, be my god.
Trinculo: By this light, a most perfidious and drunken monster!
When's god's asleep, he'll rob his bottle.
Caliban: I'll kiss thy foot. I'll swear myself thy subject.
130 *Stephano:* Come on then. Down, and swear!
Trinculo: I shall laugh myself to death at this puppyheaded monster.
A most scurvy monster! I could find in my heart to beat him—
Stephano: Come, kiss.
Trinculo: But that the poor monster's in drink. An abominable
monster!
Caliban: I'll show thee the best springs; I'll pluck thee berries;
I'll fish for thee, and get thee wood enough.
A plague upon the tyrant that I serve!
I'll bear him no more sticks, but follow thee,
Thou wondrous man.
140 *Trinculo:* A most ridiculous monster, to make a wonder of a poor
drunkard!

---

117 *when time was:* once upon a time.   118–19 *thee . . . bush:* the Man in the Moon was
banished there, according to legend, for gathering brushwood with his dog on Sunday.
124 *Well drawn:* a good pull at the bottle.

Caliban: I prithee let me bring thee where crabs° grow;
And I with my long nails will dig thee pignuts°,
Show thee a jay's nest, and instruct thee how
To snare the nimble marmoset. I'll bring thee
To clust'ring filberts, and sometimes I'll get thee
Young scamels° from the rock. Wilt thou go with me?
Stephano: I prithee now, lead the way without any more talking.
    Trinculo, the king and all our company else being drowned, we
150   will inherit here. Here, bear my bottle. Fellow Trinculo, we'll fill
him by and by again.

Caliban sings drunkenly.

Caliban: Farewell, master; farewell, farewell!
Trinculo: A howling monster! A drunken monster!
Caliban: No more dams° I'll make for fish,
        Nor fetch in firing
        At requiring,
        Nor scrape trenchering°, nor wash dish.
         'Ban, 'Ban, Ca—Caliban
        Has a new master. Get a new man!
160 Freedom, high day! High day, freedom! Freedom, high day, freedom!
Stephano: O brave monster! Lead the way.   *Exeunt.*

Act III

Scene I. [In front of Prospero's cell.]

Enter Ferdinand, bearing a log.

Ferdinand: There be some sports are painful, and their labor
Delight in them sets off°; some kinds of baseness
Are nobly undergone, and most poor matters
Point to rich ends. This my mean task
Would be as heavy to me as odious, but
The mistress which I serve quickens° what's dead
And makes my labors pleasures. O, she is
Ten times more gentle than her father's crabbed;
And he's composed of harshness. I must remove
10 Some thousands of these logs and pile them up,
Upon a sore injunction°. My sweet mistress
Weeps when she sees me work, and says such baseness

---

142 *crabs:* crabapples.   143 *pignuts:* earthnuts.   147 *scamels:* perhaps a misprint for
"seamels" or "seamews," a kind of sea bird.   154 *dams:* to catch fish and keep
them.   157 *trenchering:* trenchers, wooden plates.   III.i. 2 *sets off:* cancels.   6 *quick-*
ens: brings to life.   11 *sore injunction:* severe command.

Had never like executor. I forget°;
But these sweet thoughts do even refresh my labors,
Most busiest when I do it°.

Enter Miranda; and Prospero [behind, unseen].

Miranda: Alas, now pray you,
Work not so hard! I would the lightning had
Burnt up those logs that you are enjoined to pile!
Pray set it down and rest you. When this burns,
'Twill weep° for having wearied you. My father
20 Is hard at study; pray now rest yourself;
He's safe for these three hours.
Ferdinand: O most dear mistress,
The sun will set before I shall discharge
What I must strive to do.
Miranda: If you'll sit down,
I'll bear your logs the while. Pray give me that;
I'll carry it to the pile.
Ferdinand: No, precious creature,
I had rather crack my sinews, break my back,
Than you should such dishonor undergo
While I sit lazy by.
Miranda: It would become me
As well as it does you; and I should do it
30 With much more ease; for my good will is to it,
And yours it is against.
Prospero [Aside.]:   Poor worm, thou art infected!
This visitation° shows it.
Miranda: You look wearily.
Ferdinand: No, noble mistress, 'tis fresh morning with me
When you are by at night°. I do beseech you,
Chiefly that I might set it in my prayers,
What is your name?
Miranda: Miranda. O my father,
I have broke your hest° to say so!
Ferdinand: Admired Miranda°!
Indeed the top of admiration, worth
What's dearest to the world! Full many a lady
40 I have eyed with best regard, and many a time
Th' harmony of their tongues hath into bondage

---

13 *forget:* i.e., my task.   15 *Most . . . it:* i.e., my thoughts are busiest when I am (the
Folio's "busie lest" has been variously emended; "it" may refer to "task," line 4, the understood object in line 13).   19 *weep:* i.e., exude resin.   32 *visitation:* (1) visit (2) attack
of plague (referring to metaphor of "infected").   34 *at night:* i.e., even at night when I
am very tired.   37 *hest:* command; *Admired Miranda: admired* means "to be wondered
at," the Latin *Miranda* means "wonderful."

Brought my too diligent ear. For several virtues
Have I liked several women; never any
With so full soul but some defect in her
Did quarrel with the noblest grace she owed°,
And put it to the foil°. But you, O you,
So perfect and so peerless, are created
Of every creature's best.
Miranda: I do not know
One of my sex; no woman's face remember,
50 Save, from my glass, mine own. Nor have I seen
More that I may call men than you, good friend,
And my dear father. How features are abroad
I am skilless° of; but, by my modesty
(The jewel in my dower), I would not wish
Any companion in the world but you;
Nor can imagination form a shape,
Besides yourself, to like of°. But I prattle
Something too wildly, and my father's precepts
I therein do forget.
Ferdinand: I am, in my condition,
60 A prince, Miranda; I do think, a king
(I would not so), and would no more endure
This wooden slavery than to suffer
The fleshfly blow my mouth. Hear my soul speak!
The very instant that I saw you, did
My heart fly to your service; there resides,
To make me slave to it; and for your sake
Am I this patient log-man.
Miranda: Do you love me?
Ferdinand: O heaven, O earth, bear witness to this sound,
And crown what I profess with kind event°
70 If I speak true! If hollowly, invert
What best is boded me° to mischief! I,
Beyond all limit of what else i' th' world,
Do love, prize, honor you.
Miranda: I am a fool
To weep at what I am glad of.
Prospero [Aside.]:   Fair encounter
Of two most rare affections! Heavens rain grace
On that which breeds between 'em!
Ferdinand: Wherefore weep you?
Miranda: At mine unworthiness, that dare not offer
What I desire to give, and much less take

---

45 *owed:* owned.   46 *put . . . foil:* defeated it.   53 *skilless:* ignorant.   57 *like of:* like.
69 *event:* outcome.   71 *What . . . me:* whatever good fortune fate has in store for me.

What I shall die to want°. But this is trifling°;
80 And all the more it seeks to hide itself,
The bigger bulk it shows. Hence, bashful cunning,
And prompt me, plain and holy innocence!
I am your wife, if you will marry me;
If not, I'll die your maid. To be your fellow°
You may deny me; but I'll be your servant,
Whether you will or no.
Ferdinand: My mistress, dearest,
And I thus humble ever.
Miranda: My husband then?
Ferdinand: Ay, with a heart as willing
As bondage e'er of freedom°. Here's my hand.
90 *Miranda:* And mine, with my heart in't; and now farewell
Till half an hour hence.
Ferdinand: A thousand thousand!

Exeunt [Ferdinand and Miranda in different directions].

Prospero: So glad of this as they I cannot be,
Who are surprised withal°; but my rejoicing
At nothing can be more. I'll to my book;
For yet ere suppertime must I perform
Much business appertaining°.   *Exit.*

Scene II. [Another part of the island.]

Enter Caliban, Stephano, and Trinculo.

Stephano: Tell not me! When the butt is out, we will drink water; not
a drop before. Therefore bear up and board 'em°! Servant monster,
drink to me.
Trinculo: Servant monster? The folly of this island! They say there's
but five upon this isle; we are three of them. If th' other two be
brained like us, the state totters.
Stephano: Drink, servant monster, when I bid thee; thy eyes are
almost set in thy head.
Trinculo: Where should they be set else? He were a brave monster
10   indeed if they were set in his tail.
Stephano: My man-monster hath drowned his tongue in sack. For my
part, the sea cannot drown me. I swam, ere I could recover the shore,

---

79 *to want:* if I lack; *trifling:* i.e., to speak in riddles like this.   84 *fellow:* equal.   89 *of freedom:* i.e., to win freedom.   93 *withal:* by it.   96 *appertaining:* i.e., to my plan.
III.ii. 2 *bear . . . 'em:* i.e., drink up.

five-and-thirty leagues off and on, by this light. Thou shalt be my
lieutenant, monster, or my standard°.

Trinculo: Your lieutenant, if you list°; he's no standard.

Stephano: We'll not run°, Monsieur Monster.

Trinculo: Nor go° neither; but you'll lie° like dogs, and yet say nothing
neither.

Stephano: Mooncalf, speak once in thy life, if thou beest a good
mooncalf.

20 *Caliban:* How does thy honor? Let me lick thy shoe. I'll not serve him;
he is not valiant.

Trinculo: Thou liest, most ignorant monster; I am in case° to justle°
a constable. Why, thou deboshed° fish thou, was there ever man a
coward that hath drunk so much sack as I today? Wilt thou tell
a monstrous lie, being but half a fish and half a monster?

Caliban: Lo, how he mocks me! Wilt thou let him, my lord?

Trinculo: "Lord" quoth he? That a monster should be such a natural°!

Caliban:
Lo, lo, again! Bite him to death, I prithee.

Stephano: Trinculo, keep a good tongue in your head. If you prove

30   mutineer—the next tree°! The poor monster's my subject, and he
shall not suffer indignity.

Caliban: I thank my noble lord. Wilt thou be pleased
To hearken once again to the suit I made to thee?

Stephano: Marry°, will I. Kneel and repeat it; I will stand, and so
shall Trinculo.

Enter Ariel, invisible.

Caliban: As I told thee before, I am subject to a tyrant,
A sorcerer, that by his cunning hath
Cheated me of the island.

Ariel: Thou liest.

Caliban: Thou liest, thou jesting monkey thou!

40 I would my valiant master would destroy thee.
I do not lie.

Stephano: Trinculo, if you trouble him any more in's tale, by this
hand, I will supplant some of your teeth.

Trinculo: Why, I said nothing.

Stephano: Mum then, and no more. Proceed.

---

14 *standard:* standard-bearer, ensign (pun, for Caliban is so drunk he cannot stand).   15
if you list: if it please you (with pun on *list* as pertaining to a ship that leans over to one
side).   16–17 *run, lie:* with puns on secondary meanings: "make water," "excrete."   17
go: walk.   22 *case:* fit condition; *justle:* jostle.   23 *deboshed:* debauched.   27 *natural:*
idiot.   30 *the next tree:* i.e., you will be hanged.   34 *Marry:* an expletive, from "By the
Virgin Mary."

Caliban: I say by sorcery he got this isle;
From me he got it. If thy greatness will
Revenge it on him—for I know thou dar'st,
But this thing° dare not—
50 *Stephano:* That's most certain.
Caliban: Thou shalt be lord of it, and I'll serve thee.
Stephano: How now shall this be compassed?
Canst thou bring me to the party?
Caliban: Yea, yea, my lord! I'll yield him thee asleep,
Where thou mayst knock a nail into his head.
Ariel: Thou liest; thou canst not.
Caliban: What a pied° ninny's this! Thou scurvy patch°!
I do beseech thy greatness, give him blows
And take his bottle from him. When that's gone,
60 He shall drink naught but brine, for I'll not show him
Where the quick freshes° are.
Stephano: Trinculo, run into no further danger! Interrupt the monster
    one word further and, by this hand, I'll turn my mercy out o'
    doors and make a stockfish° of thee.
Trinculo: Why, what did I? I did nothing. I'll go farther off.
Stephano: Didst thou not say he lied?
Ariel: Thou liest.
Stephano: Do I so? Take thou that! [*Strikes Trinculo.*] As you like this,
    give me the lie another time.
70 *Trinculo:* I did not give the lie. Out o' your wits, and hearing too? A
    pox o' your bottle! This can sack and drinking do. A murrain° on
    your monster, and the devil take your fingers!
Caliban: Ha, ha, ha!
Stephano: Now forward with your tale. [*To Trinculo.*] Prithee, stand
    further off.
Caliban: Beat him enough. After a little time
I'll beat him too.
Stephano: Stand farther. Come, proceed.
Caliban: Why, as I told thee, 'tis a custom with him
I' th' afternoon to sleep. There thou mayst brain him,
80 Having first seized his books, or with a log
Batter his skull, or paunch° him with a stake,
Or cut his wezand° with thy knife. Remember
First to possess his books; for without them
He's but a sot°, as I am, nor hath not
One spirit to command. They all do hate him
As rootedly as I. Burn but his books.

---

49 *this thing:* Trinculo.   57 *pied:* referring to Trinculo's parti-colored jester's costume;
patch: clown.   61 *quick freshes:* living springs of fresh water.   64 *stockfish:* dried cod,
softened by beating.   71 *murrain:* plague (that infects cattle).   81 *paunch:* stab in the
belly.   82 *wezand:* windpipe.   84 *sot:* fool.

He has brave utensils° (for so he calls them)
Which, when he has a house, he'll deck withal.
And that most deeply to consider is
90 The beauty of his daughter. He himself
Calls her a nonpareil. I never saw a woman
But only Sycorax my dam and she;
But she as far surpasseth Sycorax
As great'st does least.
Stephano: Is it so brave a lass?
Caliban: Ay, lord. She will become thy bed, I warrant,
And bring thee forth brave brood.
Stephano: Monster, I will kill this man. His daughter and I will be
    king and queen—save our graces!—and Trinculo and thyself shall
    be viceroys. Dost thou like the plot, Trinculo?
100 *Trinculo:* Excellent.
Stephano: Give me thy hand. I am sorry I beat thee; but while thou
    liv'st, keep a good tongue in thy head.
Caliban: Within this half hour will he be asleep.
Wilt thou destroy him then?
Stephano: Ay, on mine honor.
Ariel: This will I tell my master.
Caliban: Thou mak'st me merry; I am full of pleasure.
Let us be jocund. Will you troll the catch°
You taught me but whilere°?
Stephano: At thy request, monster, I will do reason, any reason°. Come
110   on, Trinculo, let us sing.

    [*Sings.*]

                    Flout 'em and scout° 'em
                    And scout 'em and flout 'em!
                    Thought is free.

Caliban: That's not the tune.

    Ariel [plays the tune on a tabor° and pipe].

Stephano: What is this same?
Trinculo: This is the tune of our catch, played by the picture of
    Nobody°.
Stephano: If thou beest a man, show thyself in thy likeness. If thou
    beest a devil, take't as thou list.

---

87 *brave utensils:* fine furnishings (pronounced "utensils").   107 *troll the catch:* sing the
round.   108 *but whilere:* just now.   109 *reason, any reason:* i.e., anything within reason.   111 *scout:* jeer at.   114 *tabor:* small drum worn at the side.   117 *Nobody:* alluding to the picture of No-body—a man all head, legs, and arms, but without trunk—on the
title page of the anonymous comedy *No-body and Some-body.*

120 *Trinculo:* O, forgive me my sins!
Stephano: He that dies pays all debts. I defy thee. Mercy upon us!
Caliban: Art thou afeard?
Stephano: No, monster, not I.
Caliban: Be not afeard; the isle is full of noises,
Sounds and sweet airs that give delight and hurt not.
Sometimes a thousand twangling instruments
Will hum about mine ears; and sometime voices
That, if I then had waked after long sleep,
Will make me sleep again; and then, in dreaming,
The clouds methought would open and show riches
130 Ready to drop upon me, that, when I waked,
I cried to dream again.
Stephano: This will prove a brave kingdom to me, where I shall have
    my music for nothing.
Caliban: When Prospero is destroyed.
Stephano: That shall be by and by; I remember the story.
Trinculo: The sound is going away; let's follow it, and after do our
    work.
Stephano: Lead, monster; we'll follow. I would I could see this taborer;
    he lays it on.
Trinculo [To Caliban.]: Wilt come°? I'll follow Stephano.   *Exeunt.*

Scene III. [Another part of the island.]

   Enter Alonso, Sebastian, Antonio, Gonzalo, Adrian, Francisco, &c.

Gonzalo: By'r Lakin°, I can go no further, sir;
My old bones aches. Here's a maze trod indeed
Through forthrights and meanders°. By your patience,
I needs must rest me.
Alonso: Old lord, I cannot blame thee,
Who am myself attached° with weariness
To th' dulling of my spirits. Sit down and rest.
Even here I will put off my hope, and keep it
No longer for my flatterer. He is drowned
Whom thus we stray to find; and the sea mocks
10 Our frustrate search on land. Well, let him go.
Antonio [Aside to Sebastian.]: I am right glad that he's so out of hope.
Do not for one repulse forgo the purpose
That you resolved t' effect.
Sebastian [Aside to Antonio.]:   The next advantage
Will we take throughly°.

---

140 *Wilt come:* Caliban lingers because the other two are being distracted from his purpose
by the music.   III.iii. 1 *By'r Lakin:* by our Lady.   3 *forthrights and meanders:* straight
and winding paths.   5 *attached:* seized.   14 *throughly:* thoroughly.

Antonio [Aside to Sebastian.]:   Let it be tonight;
For, now they are oppressed with travel, they
Will not nor cannot use such vigilance
As when they are fresh.
Sebastian [Aside to Antonio.]:   I say tonight. No more.

> *Solemn and strange music; and Prospero on the top° (invisible). Enter several strange shapes, bringing in a banquet; and dance about it with gentle actions of salutations; and, inviting the king [Alonso] Ec. to eat, they depart.*

Alonso: What harmony is this? My good friends, hark!
Gonzalo: Marvelous sweet music!
20 *Alonso:* Give us kind keepers°, heavens! What were these?
Sebastian: A living drollery°. Now I will believe
That there are unicorns; that in Arabia
There is one tree, the phoenix' throne; one phoenix
At this hour reigning there.
Antonio: I'll believe both;
And what does else want credit°, come to me,
And I'll be sworn 'tis true. Travelers ne'er did lie,
Though fools at home condemn 'em.
Gonzalo: If in Naples
I should report this now, would they believe me
If I should say I saw such islanders?
30 (For certes these are people of the island)
Who, though they are of monstrous shape, yet note,
Their manners are more gentle, kind, than of
Our human generation you shall find
Many—nay, almost any.
Prospero [Aside.]:   Honest lord,
Thou hast said well; for some of you there present
Are worse than devils.
Alonso: I cannot too much muse°
Such shapes, such gesture, and such sound, expressing
(Although they want the use of tongue) a kind
Of excellent dumb discourse.
Prospero [Aside.]:   Praise in departing°.
Francisco: They vanished strangely.
40 *Sebastian:*   No matter, since
They have left their viands behind; for we have stomachs.
Will't please you taste of what is here?
Alonso: Not I.

---

17 *the top:* upper stage (or perhaps a playing area above it).   20 *kind keepers:* guardian
angels.   21 *drollery:* puppet show.   25 *credit:* believing.   36 *muse:* wonder at.   39
Praise in departing: Save your praise for the end.

Gonzalo: Faith, sir, you need not fear. When we were boys,
Who would believe that there were mountaineers
Dewlapped° like bulls, whose throats had hanging at 'em
Wallets of flesh? Or that there were such men
Whose heads stood in their breasts? Which now we find
Each putter-out of five for one° will bring us
Good warrant of.
Alonso:　　　　I will stand to, and feed;
50 Although my last, no matter, since I feel
The best is past. Brother, my lord the duke,
Stand to, and do as we.

　　　Thunder and lightning. Enter Ariel, like a harpy; claps his wings upon the table;
　　　and with a quaint device° the banquet vanishes.

Ariel: You are three men of sin, whom destiny—
That hath to instrument° this lower world
And what is in't—the never-surfeited sea
Hath caused to belch up you and on this island,
Where man doth not inhabit, you 'mongst men
Being most unfit to live. I have made you mad;
And even with suchlike valor° men hang and drown
Their proper selves. [*Alonso, Sebastian, &c. draw their swords.*] You fools!
60　　I and my fellows
Are ministers of Fate. The elements,
Of whom your swords are tempered°, may as well
Wound the loud winds, or with bemocked-at stabs
Kill the still-closing° waters, as diminish
One dowle° that's in my plume°. My fellow ministers
Are like invulnerable. If you could hurt°,
Your swords are now too massy° for your strengths
And will not be uplifted. But remember
(For that's my business to you) that you three
70 From Milan did supplant good Prospero;
Exposed unto the sea, which hath requit it°,
Him and his innocent child; for which foul deed
The pow'rs, delaying, not forgetting, have
Incensed the seas and shores, yea, all the creatures,
Against your peace. Thee of thy son, Alonso,

---

45 *Dewlapped:* with skin hanging from the neck (like mountaineers with goiter). 48 *putter-out . . . one:* traveler who insures himself by depositing a sum of money to be repaid fivefold if he returns safely (i.e., any ordinary traveler will confirm nowadays those reports we used to think fanciful). 52 *quaint device:* ingenious device (of stage mechanism). 54 *to instrument:* as its instrument. 59 *suchlike valor:* i.e., the courage that comes of madness. 62 *tempered:* composed. 64 *still-closing:* ever closing again (as soon as wounded). 65 *dowle:* bit of down; *plume:* plumage. 66 *If . . . hurt:* even if you could hurt us. 67 *massy:* heavy. 71 *requit it:* avenged that crime.

They have bereft; and do pronounce by me
Ling'ring perdition (worse than any death
Can be at once) shall step by step attend
You and your ways; whose wraths to guard you from,
80 Which here, in this most desolate isle, else falls
Upon your heads, is nothing but heart's sorrow°
And a clear life ensuing.

*He vanishes in thunder; then, to soft music, enter the Shapes again, and dance
with mocks and mows°, and carrying out the table.*

Prospero: Bravely the figure of this harpy hast thou
Performed, my Ariel; a grace it had, devouring°.
Of my instruction hast thou nothing bated°
In what thou hadst to say. So, with good life°
And observation strange°, my meaner ministers°
Their several kinds have done°. My high charms work,
And these, mine enemies, are all knit up
90 In their distractions. They now are in my pow'r;
And in these fits I leave them, while I visit
Young Ferdinand, whom they suppose is drowned,
And his and mine loved darling.   *[Exit above.]*
Gonzalo: I' th' name of something holy, sir, why stand you
In this strange stare?
Alonso: O, it is monstrous, monstrous!
Methought the billows spoke and told me of it;
The winds did sing it to me; and the thunder,
That deep and dreadful organ pipe, pronounced
The name of Prosper; it did bass my trespass°.
100 Therefore my son i' th' ooze is bedded; and
I'll seek him deeper than e'er plummet sounded
And with him there lie mudded.   *Exit.*
Sebastian: But one fiend at a time,
I'll fight their legions o'er°!
Antonio: I'll be thy second.

Exeunt [Sebastian and Antonio].

Gonzalo: All three of them are desperate; their great guilt,
Like poison given to work a great time after,

---

81 *nothing . . . sorrow:* only repentance (will protect you from the wrath of these powers).   82 *mocks and mows:* mocking gestures and grimaces.   84 *devouring:* i.e., in making
the banquet disappear.   85 *bated:* omitted.   86 *good life:* good lifelike acting.   87 *observation strange:* remarkable attention to my wishes; *meaner ministers:* i.e., inferior to Ariel.   88
Their . . . done: have acted the parts their natures suited them for.   99 *bass my trespass:* i.e.,
made me understand my trespass by turning it into music for which the thunder provided the
bass part.   103 *o'er:* one after another to the last.

Now 'gins to bite the spirits. I do beseech you,
That are of suppler joints, follow them swiftly
110 And hinder them from what this ecstasy°
May now provoke them to.
Adrian: Follow, I pray you.   *Exeunt omnes°.*

Act IV

Scene I. [In front of Prospero's cell.]

Enter Prospero, Ferdinand, and Miranda.

Prospero: If I have too austerely punished you,
Your compensation makes amends; for I
Have given you here a third of mine own life,
Or that for which I live; who once again
I tender to thy hand. All thy vexations
Were but my trials of thy love, and thou
Hast strangely° stood the test. Here, afore heaven,
I ratify this my rich gift. O Ferdinand,
Do not smile at me that I boast her off°,
10 For thou shalt find she will outstrip all praise
And make it halt° behind her.
Ferdinand: I do believe it
Against an oracle°.
Prospero: Then, as my gift, and thine own acquisition
Worthily purchased, take my daughter. But
If thou dost break her virgin-knot before
All sanctimonious° ceremonies may
With full and holy rite be minist'red,
No sweet aspersion° shall the heavens let fall
To make this contact grow°; but barren hate,
20 Sour-eyed distain, and discord shall bestrew
The union of your bed with weeds so loathly
That you shall hate it both. Therefore take heed,
As Hymen's lamps shall light you°.
Ferdinand: As I hope
For quiet days, fair issue, and long life,
With such love as 'tis now, the murkiest den,
The most opportune° place, the strong'st suggestion

---

110 *ecstasy:* madness.   112 *Exeunt omnes:* "They all go out."   IV.i. 7 *strangely:* wonderfully.   9 *boast her off:* includes perhaps the idea of showing her off.   11 *halt:* limp.
12 *Against an oracle:* though an oracle should declare otherwise.   16 *sanctimonious:*
holy.   18 *aspersion:* blessing (like rain on crops).   19 *grow:* become fruitful.   23 *As
Hymen's . . . you:* i.e., as earnestly as you pray that the torch of the god of marriage shall
burn without smoke (a good omen for wedded happiness).   26 *opportune:* pronounced
"oppórtune."

Our worser genius can°, shall never melt
Mine honor into lust, to take away
The edge° of that day's celebration
30 When I shall think or Phoebus' steeds are foundered°
Or Night kept chained below°.
Prospero: Fairly spoke.
Sit then and talk with her; she is thine own.
What, Ariel°! My industrious servant, Ariel!

   [Enter Ariel.]

Ariel: What would my potent master? Here I am.
Prospero: Thou and thy meaner fellows your last service
Did worthily perform; and I must use you
In such another trick. Go bring the rabble°,
O'er whom I give thee pow'r, here to this place.
Incite them to quick motion; for I must
40 Bestow upon the eyes of this young couple
Some vanity of° mine art. It is my promise,
And they expect it from me.
Ariel: Presently?
Prospero: Ay, with a twink.
Ariel: Before you can say "Come" and "Go,"
And breathe twice and cry, "So, so,"
Each one, tripping on his toe,
Will be here with mop and mow°.
Do you love me, master? No?
Prospero: Dearly, my delicate Ariel. Do not approach
Till thou dost hear me call.
50 *Ariel:*   Well; I conceive°.   *Exit.*
Prospero: Look thou be true°. Do not give dalliance
Too much the rein; the strongest oaths are straw
To th' fire i' th' blood. Be more abstemious,
Or else good night your vow!
Ferdinand: I warrant you, sir.
The white cold virgin snow upon my heart°
Abates the ardor of my liver°.
Prospero: Well.
Now come, my Ariel; bring a corollary°

---

27 *Our . . . can:* our evil spirit can offer.   29 *edge:* keen enjoyment.   30 *foundered:* lamed.   30–31 *or Phoebus' . . . below:* i.e., that either day will never end or night will never come.   33 *What, Ariel:* summoning Ariel.   37 *rabble:* "thy meaner fellows."   41 *vanity of:* illusion conjured up by.   47 *mop and mow:* gestures and grimaces. 50 *conceive:* understand.   51 *be true:* Prospero appears to have caught the lovers in an embrace.   55 *white . . . heart:* her pure white breast on mine (?).   56 *liver:* supposed seat of sexual passion.   57 *corollary:* surplus (of spirits).

Rather than want a spirit. Appear, and pertly!
No tongue! All eyes! Be silent.

Soft music. Enter Iris°.

60 **Iris:** Ceres, most bounteous lady, thy rich leas°
Of wheat, rye, barley, fetches°, oats, and peas;
Thy turfy mountains, where live nibbling sheep,
And flat meads thatched with stover°, them to keep;
Thy banks with pionèd and twillèd brims°,
Which spongy April at thy hest betrims
To make cold nymphs chaste crowns; and thy broom groves,
Whose shadow the dismissèd bachelor loves,
Being lasslorn; thy pole-clipt vineyard°;
And thy sea-marge, sterile and rocky-hard,
70 Where thou thyself dost air°—the queen o' th' sky°,
Whose wat'ry arch and messenger am I,
Bids thee leave these, and with her sovereign grace,

Juno descends°.

Here on this grass plot, in this very place,
To come and sport; her peacocks fly amain°.
Approach, rich Ceres, her to entertain.

Enter Ceres.

Ceres: Hail, many-colored messenger, that ne'er
Dost disobey the wife of Jupiter,
Who, with thy saffron wings, upon my flow'rs
Diffusest honey drops, refreshing show'rs,
80 And with each end of thy blue bow dost crown
My bosky° acres and my unshrubbed down,
Rich scarf to my proud earth. Why hath thy queen
Summoned me hither to this short-grassed green?
Iris: A contract of true love to celebrate
And some donation freely to estate°
On the blessed lovers.

---

59 *Iris:* goddess of the rainbow and Juno's messenger.   60 *leas:* meadows.   61 *fetches:*
vetch (a kind of forage).   63 *meads . . . stover:* meadows covered with a kind of grass
used for winter fodder.   64 *pionèd . . . brims:* obscure; may refer to the trenched and
ridged edges of banks that have been repaired after the erosions of winter.   68 *pole-clipt
vineyard:* i.e., vineyard whose vines grow neatly around (embrace) poles (though possibly
the word is "poll-clipped," i.e., pruned).   70 *air:* take the air; *queen o' th' sky:* Juno.
72 This direction seems to come too soon, but the machine may have lowered her very
slowly.   74 *amain:* swiftly (peacocks, sacred to Juno, drew her chariot).   81 *bosky:*
shrubbed.   85 *estate:* bestow.

Ceres: Tell me, heavenly bow,
If Venus or her son, as thou dost know,
Do now attend the queen? Since they did plot
The means that dusky Dis my daughter got°,
90 Her and her blind boy's scandaled° company
I have forsworn.
Iris: Of her society
Be not afraid; I met her deity
Cutting the clouds towards Paphos°, and her son
Dove-drawn with her. Here thought they to have done
Some wanton charm upon this man and maid,
Whose vows are, that no bed-right shall be paid
Till Hymen's torch be lighted. But in vain;
Mars's hot minion is returned again°,
Her waspish-headed son° has broke his arrows,
100 Swears he will shoot no more, but play with sparrows
And be a boy right out°.

[Juno alights.]

Ceres: Highest queen of state,
Great Juno, comes; I know her by her gait.
Juno: How does my bounteous sister? Go with me
To bless this twain, that they may prosperous be
And honored in their issue.

They sing.

Juno: Honor, riches, marriage blessing,
Long continuance, and increasing,
Hourly joys be still° upon you!
Juno sings her blessings on you.
110 *[Ceres]:*   Earth's increase, foison° plenty,
Barns and garners never empty,
Vines with clust'ring bunches growing,
Plants with goodly burden bowing;
Spring come to you at the farthest
In the very end of harvest°.
Scarcity and want shall shun you,
Ceres' blessing so is on you.

---

89 *dusky . . . got:* alluding to the abduction of Proserpine by Pluto (Dis), god of the underworld.   90 *scandaled:* scandalous.   93 *Paphos:* in Cyprus, center of Venus' cult.
98 *Mars's . . . again:* Mars' lustful mistress (Venus) is on her way back to Paphos.
99 *waspish-headed son:* Cupid is irritable and stings with his arrows.   101 *boy right out:*
an ordinary boy.   108 *still:* ever.   110 *foison:* abundance.   114–15 *Spring . . .
harvest:* i.e., May there be no winter in your lives.

Ferdinand: This is a most majestic vision, and
Harmonious charmingly. May I be bold
To think these spirits?
120 *Prospero:*   Spirits, which by mine art
I have from their confines called to enact
My present fancies.
Ferdinand: Let me live here ever!
So rare a wond'red° father and a wise
Makes this place Paradise.

> *Juno and Ceres whisper, and send Iris on employment.*

Prospero: Sweet now, silence!
Juno and Ceres whisper seriously.
There's something else to do. Hush and be mute,
Or else our spell is marred.
Iris: You nymphs, called Naiades, of the windring° brooks,
With your sedged crowns and ever-harmless looks,
130 Leave your crisp° channels, and on this green land
Answer your summons; Juno does command.
Come, temperate nymphs, and help to celebrate
A contract of true love; be not too late.

> *Enter certain Nymphs.*

You sunburned sicklemen, of August weary,
Come hither from the furrow and be merry.
Make holiday; your rye-straw hats put on,
And these fresh nymphs encounter everyone
In country footing°.

> *Enter certain Reapers, properly habited. They join with the Nymphs in a graceful*
> *dance; towards the end whereof Prospero starts suddenly and speaks°; after which,*
> *to a strange, hollow, and confused noise, they heavily° vanish.*

Prospero [Aside.]: I had forgot that foul conspiracy
140 Of the beast Caliban and his confederates
Against my life. The minute of their plot
Is almost come. [*To the Spirits.*] Well done! Avoid°! No more!
Ferdinand: This is strange. Your father's in some passion
That works him strongly.
Miranda: Never till this day

---

123 *wond'red:* possessed of wonders; i.e., both wonderful and wonder-working, and therefore to be wondered at.   128 *windring:* winding and wandering (?).   130 *crisp:* rippling.   138 *footing:* dance.   138 *speaks:* breaking the spell, which depends on silence;
heavily: reluctantly.   142 *Avoid:* Begone!

Saw I him touched with anger so distempered°.
Prospero: You do look, my son, in a movèd sort°,
As if you were dismayed; be cheerful, sir.
Our revels now are ended. These our actors,
As I foretold you, were all spirits and
150 Are melted into air, into thin air;
And, like the baseless fabric of this vision,
The cloud-capped towers, the gorgeous palaces,
The solemn temples, the great globe itself,
Yea, all which it inherit°, shall dissolve,
And, like this insubstantial pageant faded,
Leave not a rack° behind. We are such stuff
As dreams are made on, and our little life
Is rounded with a sleep. Sir, I am vexed.
Bear with my weakness; my old brain is troubled.
160 Be not disturbed with my infirmity.
If you be pleased, retire into my cell
And there repose. A turn or two I'll walk
To still my beating mind.
Ferdinand, Miranda: We wish your peace.

Exit [Ferdinand, with Miranda].

Prospero: Come with a thought! I thank thee°, Ariel. Come.

Enter Ariel.

Ariel: Thy thoughts I cleave to. What's thy pleasure?
Prospero: Spirit,
We must prepare to meet with Caliban.
Ariel: Ay, my commander. When I presented° Ceres,
I thought to have told thee of it, but I feared
Lest I might anger thee.
170 *Prospero:* Say again, where didst thou leave these varlets°?
Ariel: I told you, sir, they were red-hot with drinking;
So full of valor that they smote the air
For breathing in their faces, beat the ground
For kissing of their feet; yet always bending°
Towards their project. Then I beat my tabor;
At which like unbacked° colts they pricked their ears,
Advanced° their eyelids, lifted up their noses
As they smelt music. So I charmed their ears

---

145 *distempered:* violent.   146 *movèd sort:* troubled state.   154 *it inherit:* occupy
it.   156 *rack:* wisp of cloud.   164 *I thank thee:* i.e., for the masque (?).   167 *presented:*
acted the part of (?) introduced (?).   170 *varlets:* ruffians.   174 *bending:* directing their
steps.   176 *unbacked:* unbroken.   177 *Advanced:* lifted up.

That calflike they my lowing followed through
180 Toothed briers, sharp furzes, pricking goss°, and thorns,
Which ent'red their frail shins. At last I left them
I' th' filthy mantled° pool beyond your cell,
There dancing up to th' chins, that the foul lake
O'erstunk their feet.
Prospero: This was well done, my bird.
Thy shape invisible retain thou still.
The trumpery° in my house, go bring it hither
For stale° to catch these thieves.
Ariel: I go, I go. *Exit.*
Prospero: A devil, a born devil, on whose nature
Nurture can never stick; on whom my pains,
190 Humanely taken, all, all lost, quite lost!
And as with age his body uglier grows,
So his mind cankers. I will plague them all,
Even to roaring.

Enter Ariel, loaden with glistering apparel, &c.

Come, hang them on this line°.

[Prospero and Ariel remain, invisible.] Enter Caliban, Stephano, and Trinculo, all wet.

Caliban: Pray you tread softly, that the blind mole may not
Hear a foot fall. We now are near his cell.
Stephano: Monster, your fairy, which you say is a harmless fairy, has
done little better than played the Jack° with us.
Trinculo: Monster, I do smell all horse piss, at which my nose is in
great indignation.
200 *Stephano:* So is mine. Do you hear, monster? If I should take a
displeasure against you, look you—
Trinculo: Thou wert but a lost monster.
Caliban: Good my lord, give me thy favor still.
Be patient, for the prize I'll bring thee to
Shall hoodwink° this mischance. Therefore speak softly.
All's hushed as midnight yet.
Trinculo: Ay, but to lose our bottles in the pool—
Stephano: There is not only disgrace and dishonor in that, monster,
but an infinite loss.
210 *Trinculo:* That's more to me than my wetting. Yet this is your
harmless fairy, monster.

---

180 *goss:* gorse.　182 *filthy mantled:* covered with filthy scum. 186 *trumpery:* the
"glistering apparel" mentioned in the next stage direction.　187 *stale:* decoy.　193 *line:*
lime tree (linden).　197 *Jack:* (1) knave (2) jack-o'-lantern, will-o'-the-wisp.　205 *hood-
wink:* put out of sight.

Stephano: I will fetch off my bottle, though I be o'er ears° for my
labor.

Caliban: Prithee, my king, be quiet. See'st thou here?
This is the mouth o' th' cell. No noise, and enter.
Do that good mischief which may make this island
Thine own forever, and I, thy Caliban,
For aye thy footlicker.

Stephano: Give me thy hand. I do begin to have bloody thoughts.

Trinculo: O King Stephano! O peer°! O worthy Stephano, look what a
220   wardrobe here is for thee!

Caliban: Let it alone, thou fool! It is but trash.

Trinculo: O, ho, monster! We know what belongs to a frippery°.
O King Stephano!

Stephano: Put off that gown, Trinculo! By this hand, I'll have that
gown!

Trinculo: Thy grace shall have it.

Caliban: The dropsy drown this fool! What do you mean
To dote thus on such luggage°? Let't alone,
And do the murder first. If he awake,
From toe to crown he'll fill our skins with pinches,
230 Make us strange stuff.

Stephano: Be you quiet, monster. Mistress line, is not this my jerkin°?
[*Takes it down.*] Now is the jerkin under the line°. Now, jerkin, you
are like to lose your hair and prove a bald jerkin°.

Trinculo: Do, do°! We steal by line and level°, and't like° your grace.

Stephano: I thank thee for that jest. Here's a garment for't. Wit shall not
go unrewarded while I am king of this country. "Steal by line and
level" is an excellent pass of pate°. There's another garment for't.

Trinculo: Monster, come put some lime° upon your fingers, and away
240   with the rest.

Caliban: I will have none on't. We shall lose our time
And all be turned to barnacles°, or to apes
With foreheads villainous low.

Stephano: Monster, lay-to your fingers; help to bear this away where
my hogshead of wine is, or I'll turn you out of my kingdom. Go
to, carry this.

---

212 *o'er ears:* i.e., over my ears in water.   219 *peer:* alluding to the song "King Stephen
was and a worthy peer; / His breeches cost him but a crown," quoted in *Othello*
II.iii.   222 *frippery:* old-clothes shop; i.e., we are good judges of castoff clothes.   227
luggage: useless encumbrances.   231 *jerkin:* kind of jacket.   232 *under the line:* pun: (1)
under the lime tree (2) under the equator.   233 *bald jerkin:* sailors proverbially lost their
hair from fevers contracted while crossing the equator.   234 *Do, do:* Fine, fine!   234
by . . . level: by plumb line and carpenter's level; i.e., according to rule (with pun on
line).   234 *and't like:* if it please.   237 *pass of pate:* sally of wit.   239 *lime:* bird lime
(which is sticky; thieves have sticky fingers).   242 *barnacles:* kind of geese supposed to
have developed from shellfish.

Trinculo: And this.
Stephano: Ay, and this.

A noise of hunters heard. Enter divers Spirits in shape of dogs and hounds, hunting them about; Prospero and Ariel setting them on.

Prospero: Hey, Mountain, hey!
250 **Ariel:** Silver! There it goes, Silver!
Prospero: Fury, Fury! There, Tyrant, there! Hark, hark!

[Caliban, Stephano, and Trinculo are driven out.]

Go, charge my goblins that they grind their joints
With dry convulsions°, shorten up their sinews
With agèd° cramps, and more pinch-spotted make them
Than pard or cat o' mountain°.
Ariel: Hark, they roar!
Prospero: Let them be hunted soundly. At this hour
Lies at my mercy all mine enemies.
Shortly shall all my labors end, and thou
Shalt have the air at freedom. For a little,
260 Follow, and do me service.   *Exeunt.*

Act V

Scene I. [In front of Prospero's cell.]

Enter Prospero in his magic robes, and Ariel.

Prospero: Now does my project gather to a head.
My charms crack not, my spirits obey, and Time
Goes upright with his carriage°. How's the day?
Ariel: On the sixth hour, at which time, my lord,
You said our work should cease.
Prospero: I did say so
When first I raised the tempest. Say, my spirit,
How fares the king and's followers?
Ariel: Confined together
In the same fashion as you gave in charge,
Just as you left them—all prisoners, sir,
10 In the line grove which weather-fends° your cell.
They cannot budge till your release°. The king,

---

253 *dry convulsions:* such as come when the joints are dry from old age.   254 *agèd:* i.e., such as old people have.   255 *pard . . . mountain:* leopard or catamount.   V.i. 2–3 *Time . . . carriage:* time does not stoop under his burden (because there is so little left to do). 10 *weather-fends:* protects from the weather.   11 *till your release:* until released by you.

His brother, and yours abide all three distracted,
And the remainder mourning over them,
Brimful of sorrow and dismay; but chiefly
Him that you termed, sir, the good old Lord Gonzalo.
His tears runs down his beard like winter's drops
From eaves of reeds°. Your charm so strongly works 'em,
That if you now beheld them, your affections
Would become tender.

Prospero: Dost thou think so, spirit?

Ariel: Mine would, sir, were I human.

20 *Prospero:*   And mine shall.
Hast thou, which art but air, a touch, a feeling
Of their afflictions, and shall not myself
One of their kind, that relish all as sharply,
Passion° as they, be kindlier moved than thou art?
Though with their high wrongs I am struck to th' quick,
Yet with my nobler reason 'gainst my fury
Do I take part. The rarer action is
In virtue than in vengeance. They being penitent,
The sole drift of my purpose doth extend
30 Not a frown further. Go, release them, Ariel.
My charms I'll break, their senses I'll restore,
And they shall be themselves.

Ariel: I'll fetch them, sir.   *Exit.*

Prospero: Ye elves of hills, brooks, standing lakes, and groves,
And ye that on the sands with printless foot
Do chase the ebbing Neptune, and do fly him°
When he comes back; you demi-puppets that
By moonshine do the green sour ringlets° make,
Whereof the ewe not bites; and you whose pastime
Is to make midnight mushrumps°, that rejoice
40 To hear the solemn curfew; by whose aid
(Weak masters° though ye be) I have bedimmed
The noontide sun, called forth the mutinous winds,
And 'twixt the green sea and the azured vault
Set roaring war; to the dread rattling thunder
Have I given fire and rifted Jove's stout oak
With his own bolt; the strong-based promontory
Have I made shake and by the spurs° plucked up
The pine and cedar; graves at my command
Have waked their sleepers, oped, and let 'em forth
50 By my so potent art. But this rough magic

---

17 *eaves of reeds:* i.e., a thatched roof.   24 *Passion:* verb.   35 *fly him:* fly with him.
37 *green sour ringlets:* "fairy rings," little circles of rank grass supposed to be formed by
the dancing of fairies.   39 *mushrumps:* mushrooms.   41 *masters:* masters of supernatural power.   47 *spurs:* roots.

I here abjure; and when I have required°
Some heavenly music (which even now I do)
To work mine end upon their senses that°
This airy charm is for, I'll break my staff,
Bury it certain fathoms in the earth,
And deeper than did ever plummet sound
I'll drown my book.

Solemn music.

Here enters Ariel before; then Alonso, with a frantic gesture, attended by Gonzalo;
Sebastian and Antonio in like manner, attended by Adrian and Francisco. They all
enter the circle which Prospero had made, and there stand charmed; which Prospero
observing, speaks.

A solemn air, and° the best comforter
To an unsettled fancy, cure thy brains,
60 Now useless, boiled within thy skull! There stand,
For you are spell-stopped.
Holy Gonzalo, honorable man,
Mine eyes, ev'n sociable to the show of thine,
Fall fellowly drops°. The charm dissolves apace;
And as the morning steals upon the night,
Melting the darkness, so their rising senses
Begin to chase the ignorant fumes that mantle
Their clearer reason. O good Gonzalo,
My true preserver, and a loyal sir
70 To him thou follow'st, I will pay thy graces
Home° both in word and deed. Most cruelly
Didst thou, Alonso, use me and my daughter.
Thy brother was a furtherer in the act.
Thou art pinched for't now, Sebastian. Flesh and blood,
You, brother mine, that entertained ambition,
Expelled remorse° and nature°; whom, with Sebastian
(Whose inward pinches therefore are most strong),
Would here have killed your king, I do forgive thee,
Unnatural though thou art. Their understanding
80 Begins to swell, and the approaching tide
Will shortly fill the reasonable shore,
That now lies foul and muddy. Not one of them
That yet looks on me or would know me. Ariel,
Fetch me the hat and rapier in my cell.

---

51 *required:* asked for.   53 *their senses that:* the senses of those whom.   58 *and:* which
is.   63–64 *sociable . . . drops:* associating themselves with the (tearful) appearance of
your eyes, shed tears in sympathy.   70–71 *pay . . . Home:* repay thy favors thoroughly.   76 *remorse:* pity; *nature:* natural feeling.

I will discase° me, and myself present
As I was sometime Milan. Quickly, spirit!
Thou shalt ere long be free.   *[Exit Ariel and returns immediately.]*

Ariel sings and helps to attire him:

Ariel: Where the bee sucks, there suck I;
              In a cowslip's bell I lie;
90   There I couch when owls do cry.
              On the bat's back I do fly
              After summer merrily.
              Merrily, merrily shall I live now
              Under the blossom that hangs on the bough.

Prospero: Why, that's my dainty Ariel! I shall miss thee,
But yet thou shalt have freedom; so, so, so.
To the king's ship, invisible as thou art!
There shalt thou find the mariners asleep
Under the hatches. The master and the boatswain
100 Being awake, enforce them to this place,
And presently°, I prithee.
Ariel: I drink the air before me, and return
Or ere your pulse twice beat.   *Exit.*
Gonzalo: All torment, trouble, wonder, and amazement
Inhabits here. Some heavenly power guide us
Out of this fearful country!
Prospero: Behold, sir king,
The wronged Duke of Milan, Prospero.
For more assurance that a living prince
Does now speak to thee, I embrace thy body,
110 And to thee and thy company I bid
A hearty welcome.
Alonso: Whe'r° thou be'st he or no,
Or some enchanted trifle° to abuse me,
As late I have been, I not know. Thy pulse
Beats, as of flesh and blood; and, since I saw thee,
Th' affliction of my mind amends, with which,
I fear, a madness held me. This must crave°
(And if this be at all°) a most strange story.
Thy dukedom I resign and do entreat
Thou pardon me my wrongs. But how should Prospero
Be living and be here?
120 *Prospero:*   First, noble friend,

---

85 *discase:* disrobe.   101 *presently:* immediately.   111 *Whe'r:* whether.   112 *trifle:*
apparition.   116 *crave:* require (to account for it).   117 *And . . . all:* if this is really
happening.

Let me embrace thine age, whose honor cannot
Be measured or confined.
Gonzalo: Whether this be
Or be not, I'll not swear.
Prospero: You do yet taste
Some subtleties° o' th' isle, that will not let you
Believe things certain. Welcome, my friends all.

[*Aside to Sebastian and Antonio.*]

But you, my brace of lords, were I so minded,
I here could pluck his highness' frown upon you,
And justify° you traitors. At this time
I will tell no tales.
Sebastian [Aside.]:   The devil speaks in him.
Prospero: No.
130 For you, most wicked sir, whom to call brother
Would even infect my mouth, I do forgive
Thy rankest fault—all of them; and require
My dukedom of thee, which perforce I know
Thou must restore.
Alonso: If thou beest Prospero,
Give us particulars of thy preservation;
How thou hast met us here, whom three hours since
Were wracked upon this shore; where I have lost
(How sharp the point of this remembrance is!)
My dear son Ferdinand.
Prospero: I am woe° for't, sir.
140 *Alonso:* Irreparable is the loss, and Patience
Says it is past her cure.
Prospero: I rather think
You have not sought her help, of whose soft grace
For the like loss I have her sovereign aid
And rest myself content.
Alonso: You the like loss?
Prospero: As great to me, as late°, and supportable°
To make the dear° loss, have I means much weaker
Than you may call to comfort you; for I
Have lost my daughter.
Alonso: A daughter?
O heavens, that they were living both in Naples,
150 The king and queen there! That they were, I wish

---

124 *subtleties:* deceptions (referring to pastries made to look like something else—e.g.,
castles made out of sugar).   128 *justify:* prove.   139 *woe:* sorry.   145 *As . . . late:* as
great to me as your loss, and as recent; *supportable:* pronounced "súpportable."   146
dear: intensifies the meaning of the noun.

Myself were mudded in that oozy bed
Where my son lies. When did you lose your daughter?
Prospero: In this last tempest. I perceive these lords
At this encounter do so much admire°
That they devour their reason, and scarce think
Their eyes do offices° of truth, their words
Are natural breath. But, howsoev'r you have
Been justled from your senses, know for certain
That I am Prospero, and that very duke
160 Which was thrust forth of Milan, who most strangely
Upon this shore, where you were wracked, was landed
To be the lord on't. No more yet of this;
For 'tis a chronicle of day by day,
Not a relation for a breakfast, nor
Befitting this first meeting. Welcome, sir;
This cell's my court. Here have I few attendants,
And subjects none abroad°. Pray you look in.
My dukedom since you have given me again,
I will requite you with as good a thing,
170 At least bring forth a wonder to content ye
As much as me my dukedom.

   Here Prospero discovers° Ferdinand and Miranda playing at chess.

Miranda: Sweet lord, you play me false.
Ferdinand: No, my dearest love,
I would not for the world.
Miranda: Yes, for a score of kingdoms you should wrangle,
And I would call it fair play°.
Alonso: If this prove
A vision of the island, one dear son
Shall I twice lose.
Sebastian: A most high miracle!
Ferdinand: Though the seas threaten, they are merciful.
I have cursed them without cause. [*Kneels.*]
Alonso: Now all the blessings
180 Of a glad father compass thee about!
Arise, and say how thou cam'st here.
Miranda: O, wonder!
How many goodly creatures are there here!
How beauteous mankind is! O brave new world

---

154 *admire:* wonder.   156 *do offices:* perform services.   167 *abroad:* on the island.   171 *discovers:* reveals (by opening a curtain at the back of the stage).   174–75 *for
. . . play:* i.e., if we were playing for stakes just short of the world, you would protest as now;
but then, the issue being important, I would call it fair play, so much do I love you (?).

That has such people in't!
Prospero: 'Tis new to thee.
Alonso: What is this maid with whom thou wast at play?
Your eld'st° acquaintance cannot be three hours.
Is she the goddess that hath severed us
And brought us thus together?
Ferdinand: Sir, she is mortal;
But by immortal providence she's mine.
190 I chose her when I could not ask my father
For his advice, nor thought I had one. She
Is daughter to this famous Duke of Milan,
Of whom so often I have heard renown
But never saw before; of whom I have
Received a second life; and second father
This lady makes him to me.
Alonso: I am hers.
But, O, how oddly will it sound that I
Must ask my child forgiveness!
Prospero: There, sir, stop.
Let us not burden our remembrance with
A heaviness that's gone.
200 *Gonzalo:*   I have inly wept,
Or should have spoke ere this. Look down, you gods,
And on this couple drop a blessèd crown!
For it is you that have chalked forth the way
Which brought us hither.
Alonso: I say amen, Gonzalo.
Gonzalo: Was Milan thrust from Milan that his issue
Should become kings of Naples? O, rejoice
Beyond a common joy, and set it down
With gold on lasting pillars. In one voyage
Did Claribel her husband find at Tunis,
210 And Ferdinand her brother found a wife
Where he himself was lost; Prospero his dukedom
In a poor isle; and all of us ourselves
When no man was his own.
Alonso [To Ferdinand and Miranda.]: Give me your hands.
Let grief and sorrow still° embrace his heart
That doth not wish you joy.
Gonzalo: Be it so! Amen!

Enter Ariel, with the Master and Boatswain amazedly following.

O, look, sir; look, sir! Here is more of us!
I prophesied if a gallows were on land,

---

186 *eld'st:* longest.   214 *still:* forever.

This fellow could not drown. Now, blasphemy,
That swear'st grace o'erboard°, not an oath on shore?
220 Hast thou no mouth by land? What is the news?
Boatswain: The best news is that we have safely found
Our king and company; the next, our ship,
Which, but three glasses° since, we gave out split,
Is tight and yare° and bravely rigged as when
We first put out to sea.
Ariel [Aside to Prospero.]:   Sir, all this service
Have I done since I went.
Prospero [Aside to Ariel.]:   My tricksy spirit!
Alonso: These are not natural events; they strengthen
From strange to stranger. Say, how came you hither?
Boatswain: If I did think, sir, I were well awake,
230 I'd strive to tell you. We were dead of sleep
And (how we know not) all clapped under hatches;
Where, but even now, with strange and several° noises
Of roaring, shrieking, howling, jingling chains,
And moe° diversity of sounds, all horrible,
We were awaked; straightway at liberty;
Where we, in all our trim, freshly beheld
Our royal, good, and gallant ship, our master
Cap'ring to eye° her. On a trice, so please you,
Even in a dream, were we divided from them
And were brought moping° hither.
240 *Ariel [Aside to Prospero.]:*   Was't well done?
Prospero [Aside to Ariel.]: Bravely, my diligence. Thou shalt be free.
Alonso: This is as strange a maze as e'er men trod,
And there is in this business more than nature
Was ever conduct° of. Some oracle
Must rectify our knowledge.
Prospero: Sir, my liege,
Do not infest your mind with beating on
The strangeness of this business. At picked leisure,
Which shall be shortly, single I'll resolve you
(Which to you shall seem probable) of every
250 These happened accidents°; till when, be cheerful
And think of each thing well. [*Aside to Ariel.*] Come hither, spirit.
Set Caliban and his companions free.
Untie the spell. [*Exit Ariel.*] How fares my gracious sir?

---

219 *That . . . o'erboard:* that (at sea) swearest enough to cause grace to be withdrawn from
the ship.   223 *glasses:* hours.   224 *yare:* shipshape.   232 *several:* various.   234
moe: more.   238 *Cap'ring to eye:* dancing to see.   240 *moping:* in a daze.   244 *conduct:*
conductor. 248–50 *single . . . accidents:* I myself will solve the problems (and my story will
make sense to you) concerning each and every incident that has happened.

There are yet missing of your company
Some few odd lads that you remember not.

Enter Ariel, driving in Caliban, Stephano, and Trinculo, in their stolen apparel.

Stephano: Every man shift for all the rest, and let no man take care
    for himself; for all is but fortune. Coragio°, bully-monster, coragio!
Trinculo: If these be true spies which I wear in my head, here's a
    goodly sight.
260 **Caliban:** O Setebos°, these be brave spirits indeed!
How fine my master is! I am afraid
He will chastise me.
Sebastian: Ha, ha!
What things are these, my Lord Antonio?
Will money buy 'em?
Antonio: Very like. One of them
Is a plain fish and no doubt marketable.
Prospero: Mark but the badges° of these men, my lords,
Then say if they be true°. This misshapen knave,
His mother was a witch, and one so strong
That could control the moon, make flows and ebbs,
270 And deal in her command without her power°.
These three have robbed me, and this demi-devil
(For he's a bastard one) had plotted with them
To take my life. Two of these fellows you
Must know and own; this thing of darkness I
Acknowledge mine.
Caliban: I shall be pinched to death.
Alonso: Is not this Stephano, my drunken butler?
Sebastian: He is drunk now. Where had he wine?
Alonso: And Trinculo is reeling ripe. Where should they
Find this grand liquor that hath gilded 'em?
280 How cam'st thou in this pickle?
Trinculo: I have been in such a pickle, since I saw you last, that I fear
    me will never out of my bones. I shall not fear flyblowing°.
Sebastian: Why, how now, Stephano?
Stephano: O, touch me not! I am not Stephano, but a cramp.
Prospero: You'd be king o' the isle, sirrah?
Stephano: I should have been a sore° one then.
Alonso: This is a strange thing as e'er I looked on.
Prospero: He is as disproportioned in his manners

---

257 *Coragio:* courage (Italian).   260 *Setebos:* the god of Caliban's mother.   266 *badges:*
worn by servants to indicate to whose service they belong; in this case, the stolen clothes
are badges of their rascality.   267 *true:* honest.   270 *deal . . . power:* i.e., dabble in the
moon's realm without the moon's legitimate authority.   282 *flyblowing:* pickling preserves meat from flies.   286 *sore:* (1) tyrannical (2) aching.

As in his shape. Go, sirrah, to my cell;
290 Take with you your companions. As you look
   To have my pardon, trim it handsomely.
   Caliban: Ay, that I will; and I'll be wise hereafter,
   And seek for grace. What a thrice-double ass
   Was I to take this drunkard for a god
   And worship this dull fool!
   Prospero: Go to! Away!
   Alonso: Hence, and bestow your luggage where you found it.
   Sebastian: Or stole it rather.   [*Exeunt Caliban, Stephano, and Trinculo.*]
   Prospero: Sir, I invite your highness and your train
   To my poor cell, where you shall take your rest
300 For this one night; which, part of it, I'll waste°
   With such discourse as, I not doubt, shall make it
   Go quick away—the story of my life,
   And the particular accidents° gone by
   Since I came to this isle. And in the morn
   I'll bring you to your ship, and so to Naples,
   Where I have hope to see the nuptial
   Of these our dear-beloved solemnizèd°;
   And thence retire me to my Milan, where
   Every third thought shall be my grave.
310 *Alonso:*   I long
   To hear the story of your life, which must
   Take° the ear strangely.
   Prospero: I'll deliver° all;
   And promise you calm seas, auspicious gales,
   And sail so expeditious that shall catch°
   Your royal fleet far off. [*Aside to Ariel.*] My Ariel, chick,
   That is thy charge. Then to the elements
   Be free, and fare thou well! [*To the others.*] Please you, draw near.

                                            Exeunt omnes.

Epilogue

   Spoken by Prospero:

   Now my charms are all o'erthrown,
   And what strength I have's mine own,
   Which is most faint. Now 'tis true
   I must be here confined by you,
   Or sent to Naples. Let me not,
   Since I have my dukedom got

---

300 *waste:* spend.   303 *accidents:* incidents.   307 *solemnizèd:* pronounced "solémn-
izèd."   311 *Take:* captivate; *deliver:* tell.   313 *catch:* catch up with.

And pardoned the deceiver, dwell
In this bare island by your spell;
But release me from my bands°
10 With the help of your good hands°.
Gentle breath° of yours my sails
Must fill, or else my project fails,
Which was to please. Now I want°
Spirits to enforce, art to enchant;
And my ending is despair
Unless I be relieved by prayer°,
Which pierces so that it assaults
Mercy itself and frees all faults.
As you from crimes would pardoned be,
20 Let your indulgence set me free.   *Exit.*

ACCOUNT: ROB NIXON ON A MULTICULTURAL APPROACH TO *THE TEMPEST*

Nixon begins by pointing out that from the late 1950s until the early 1970s both Africa and the Caribbean saw an era of anticolonial sentiment and the formation of many new governments in former European colonies. During this period, intellectuals in these former colonies often used *The Tempest* as a text to oppose colonialism and to expose the ways in which they saw its culture cooperating in that oppressive process. By using a play by an author like Shakespeare, whose culturally valuable status was unquestioned, they were able both to command attention and to question the idea of static values possessed by the conquerors and (perhaps) transmitted to the conquered. Instead, they sought to show that cultural values really came out of social process.

Many of the writers knew in advance that any "tampering" with a sacred text by a sacred writer would be denounced as a vulgar error by critics whose point of view remained in the European tradition. But they hoped to show thereby (among other things) the way the dominant culture claims to itself, as if by Divine Right, the office of assigning the values of nobility and vulgarity. Following the rejection of European traditions, the dual process in the former colonies of attempting to retrieve suppressed traditions and to invent new ones made use of *The Tempest* in many ways.

Epi. 9 *bands:* bonds.   10 *hands:* i.e., applause to break the spell.   11 *Gentle breath:* i.e., favorable comment.   13 *want:* lack.   16 *prayer:* i.e., this petition.

From Rob Nixon, "Caribbean and African Appropriations of *The Tempest*," *Critical Inquiry* 13 (1986–87), 557–578.

First of all, Shakespeare could stand as a symbol for the European culture that had been foisted upon the colonized peoples in the name of educating them:

> Given the resistance during decolonialization to this kind of cultural de-
> pendency, those writers who took up *The Tempest* from the standpoint of
> the colonial subject did so in a manner that was fraught with complexity.
> On the one hand, they hailed Caliban and identified themselves with
> him; on the other, they were intolerant of received colonial definitions of
> Shakespeare's value. They found the European play compelling, but in-
> sisted on engaging with it on their own terms.

The intellectuals were not the first to read the play as supplying the terms for a discussion of colonialism. In the nineteenth century, Daniel Wilson had used the notion of Social Darwinism to write *Caliban: The Missing Link* (1873), and in the early twentieth century, the French social scientist Octave Mannoni saw in the play symbols for a psychology of colonialism:

> Mannoni's account of the psychological climate of colonialism is ad-
> vanced through an opposition between the Prospero (or inferiority) com-
> plex and the Caliban (or dependence) complex.

Mannoni claimed that Europeans from a highly competitive society need to feel highly regarded by others and are driven to seek out peoples where their technology is regarded with worship as magic. Primitive peoples, on the other hand, depend on the security of authority in "tribal" cultures and transfer that sense of dependence to the European when the tribal culture is destroyed. Caliban wants "not to win his freedom, for he could not support freedom, but to have a new master whose 'footlicker' he can become." In this way, Shakespeare is seen by Mannoni to dramatize "a mutual sense of a trust betrayed: Prospero is a fickle dissembler, Caliban an ingrate."

The new intellectuals sought to rehabilitate this idea of a Caliban who could not live on his own and substituted a rebel with a noble urge to eject the invading Prospero from an island that was Caliban's by right of birth. They resented the idea of discounting European blame for exploiting the colonies, and the first Caribbean writer to champion Caliban was George Lamming in *The Pleasures of Exile,* a nonfiction book begun in 1959. Lamming takes up Caliban's famous remarks: "You taught me language; and my profit on't / Is, I know how to curse." Nixon says:

> As a writer by vocation, he [Lamming] is especially alert to the way
> colonialism has generated linguistic discrimination, to whom as a West
> Indian born into English, he is branded a second class speaker of his
> first language.

Lamming himself curses or abuses colonialism with the language it taught him to use—the language that by extension includes *The Tempest*.

The process was carried further by Césaire's *Une Témpête* (1969) where the new aesthetic concept of negritude is explored. There, Caliban is seen as the superior rebel, while Prospero is "the complete totalitarian," and Caliban's cursing serves to break out of the prison imposed by his master's language. Césaire says that Caliban's superiority "even in Shakespeare's version" is further shown in a more basic way:

> Caliban can still *participate* in a world of marvels, whereas his master can merely "create" them through his acquired knowledge.

Nixon says *Une Témpête* opposes the materialist Prospero to an animistic Caliban "empowered by a culture that coexists empathetically with nature." The culture of slaves need not be an enslaved culture, and the idea of negritude urged that colonial subjects look to "cultural forms dating back to before that wracking sea change which was the Middle Passage."

Césaire makes his Ariel and Caliban enact the debate of the late fifties and sixties over "evolutionary" versus "revolutionary" change. Ariel is a mulatto who shuns violence while "the success of Caliban's uncompromising strategies is imminent at the end of the drama." Of Césaire's play, Nixon concludes that:

> This renovation of the play for black cultural ends was doubly impertinent: Besides treating a classic sacrilegiously, it implicitly lampooned the educational practice, so pervasive in the colonies, of distributing only bowdlerized versions of Shakespeare, of watering him down "for the natives." *Une Témpête* can thus be read as parodying this habit by indicating how the bard might have looked were he indeed made fit reading for a subject people.

The years 1968–1971 saw a succession of essayists, novelists, poets, and dramatists use Shakespeare's play in one way or another to attack colonialism. But, Nixon says, it was a Cuban, Fernández Retamar, who most specifically found his nation's revolutionary experience of decolonialization in the play. Retamar saw that:

> Oppositional appropriations of *The Tempest* could be enabling because "to assume our condition as Caliban implies rethinking our history from the *other* side, from the viewpoint of the *other* protagonist."

In other words, the play could be used to redefine which was the "right" and which the "wrong" side of the struggle from the point of view of those whose ancestors were colonized. For Retamar, as a part of the Cuban Communist Revolution, the issue of the struggle was predominantly one of class. For example, "The lofty Ariel is representative of the intellectual who must choose between collaborating with Prospero and deliberately allying himself with Caliban, the exploited proletarian who is to advance revolutionary change."

The backdrop of Lemuel Johnson's volume of poems *Highlife for Caliban* reflects a neocolonial spirit and marks the end of the use of the play for decolonizing culture:

> Caliban is now head of state, but his nationalistic ideals have become corrupted and enfeebled by power. By the same token, he has experienced the gulf between formal independence and authentic autonomy, as his nation remains in Prospero's cultural and economic thrall and the final exorcism of the master seems improbable. This condition is psychologically dissipating, for "it is the neocolonial event that finally divests Caliban of that which had kept him whole—a dream of revenge against Prospero. But how shall he now revenge himself upon himself?"

Nixon says that the value of *The Tempest* "faded as the plot ran out." The play has no sixth act to reflect an "era of 'imperialism without colonies.'" But between the late fifties and early seventies, the play was competed for as a highly regarded vehicle by both colonizers and colonized:

> Writers and intellectuals from the colonies appropriated *The Tempest* in a way that was outlandish in the original sense of the word. They reaffirmed the play's importance from outside its central tradition, not passively or obsequiously, but through what may best be described as a series of insurrectional endorsements. For in that turbulent and intensely reactive phase of Caribbean and African history, *The Tempest* came to serve as a Trojan horse, whereby cultures barred from the citadel of "universal" Western values could win entry and assail those global pretensions from within.

In this way, Nixon sees the play as something that exists in history and is therefore affected by historical changes. These changes include one culture's reaction to its being imagined by another.

ACCOUNT: MARJORIE GARBER ON A STRUCTURALIST APPROACH TO *THE TEMPEST*

Garber begins by agreeing with the critic Northrup Frye, a pioneer of Structural Analysis, when he says that the critical "scaffolding" (or technical terminologies and diagrams) may be needed in the kind of approach

---

From Marjorie Garber, "The Eye of the Storm: Structure and Myth in Shakespeare's *Tempest* in *William Shakespeare and* The Tempest, ed., Harold Bloom (New York: Cheelsear House, 1988), 43–63).

structuralists favor. But such aids should not be confused by either proponents or opponents of the method with the literary structure itself—the meaning experienced by readers and audiences. Garber says:

> In fact, structuralist literary criticism is neither the heresy nor the revealed truth it is sometimes thought to be. Rather, it is another way of looking at the details of a literary work, and putting them together in a persuasive, illuminating way. In other words, properly used it is a kind of close reading, which focuses the reader's attention upon significant comparisons, contrasts, and patterns which more impressionistic methods sometimes neglect, in a way that places a strong emphasis upon the process of reading itself.

Garber next poses a problem: Except for *Love's Labour's Lost, The Tempest* is the only Shakespearean play without a source for its plot. Yet the experience of the play is oddly like that of recognition. It *seems* familiar: Like the Mariners in act V, we seem to have slept and dreamed all this before. In the rest of her essay, Garber tries to account for this feeling by exploring "the kindred realms of structure and myth."

Many of the themes of the play lend themselves to binary or polar opposites, so that they might be represented as parallel lines with subhuman behavior at one pole and superhuman behavior at the other—with humans somewhere in the middle. Thus, considering the play as dramatizing actions of the human mind, Caliban would signify the libido or id—the dark but necessary part of every mind. He lusts after Miranda and would rape her; yet Prospero says he performs useful functions, and "We cannot miss him." Ariel, at the other pole, embodies:

> . . . the imagination, the spirit of music, art and the fleeting capacities of genius, which can be captured briefly, but must always be let go. Again Prospero delimits and animates the spectrum: It is, in a sense *his* mind that we see expanded and mirrored upon the stage.

Considered as reflections of the macrocosm of the universe rather than the microcosm of man, Ariel and Caliban stand for opposite classical elements, air and fire versus earth and water, with man again necessarily combining the extremes in his physical makeup. A third line of approach might oppose spirit and beast, with man's soul and body once more in the middle.

Many extremes—god/beast, song/curse, fire/water, and freedom/bondage—make the structural elements in the design of the play. Yet the extremes are not left in isolation—the binary opposition between Caliban and Ariel soon gives way to god/man, beast/man in Ferdinand and Caliban:

> [B]oth are suitors to Miranda; and, most importantly, both participate in a central pattern which, as we shall see, can most easily be described

in terms of the binarism freedom/bondage. Similarly, there is a useful comparison to be made between Caliban and Miranda, both nurtured on the island, both pupils of Prospero, but radically opposed, of course, on the axis of nature and nurture, or original sin and grace.

Other binary oppositions include two groups of conspirators, high and low, courtiers and servants; two kinds of magic, the black of Sycorax and the white of Prospero; high freedom through government, low freedom through liquor—among many others. Garber says that the multiplications of structures of this kind help to answer her original question:

> We are now, perhaps, in a position to see more clearly why *The Tempest* evokes in its audience a feeling so much akin to recognition, why our acceptance of the fable it has to tell is so complete, and why its events and actions, though they have no known source, appear to be so familiar. For one thing, the play is constructed along parallel axes in such a way that its themes, subjects, and contexts can all be translated into systems with the coordinates god/man/beast. It thus possesses an inherent and pervasive unity far beyond the neoclassical unities of time, place, and action. We are in effect seeing the same story told over and over again, simultaneously—or, to put it in other terms, the action of the play is at the same time synchronic and diachronic.

Yet, Garber says, it remains to explore the *deep structure* of the play to get at the universality of its basic fable. Told in these terms:

> We discover that the play is about a human artist-magician whose time is divided between the locking up of monster-men (Caliban, the high and low conspirators), and the freeing of godlike men (Ferdinand, Miranda, Prospero himself, even by license Ariel). The degree of success and failure he brings to these two tasks determines the possibility of his own escape, and is related to his acknowledgment of his own humanity and mortality.

Garber finds the same pattern in the age-old myth of Daedalus, who built the original labyrinth to imprison a beast and who then fashions wings for himself and his son Icarus to escape his own prison. Beneath this pattern is the still deeper notion of humanity's attempt to discover what it is by exploring what it is not. The story of Daedalus and Icarus is a story of failed education and filial disobedience: Daedalus warns his son not to soar too high, but the boy fails to accept a distinction between himself and the gods, and he falls in punishment when the wax sealing his wings is melted by the sun. Prospero seeks to teach a similar lesson. Because Miranda sees Ferdinand as a god, Prospero is constantly concerned to display his mortality. The theme has its parodic expression in Caliban's worship of Stephano, whom he discovers as a false god.

Prospero himself, like Daedalus, is open to the vanities of power, and his original exile and near defeat result directly from his raptness in his magic studies.

Daedalus built the labyrinth to enclose the Minotaur, the monster, half man and half beast, who preys on virgins as Caliban wishes to do. Further, Caliban's encloser is an artist like Daedalus, the prototypical artist of antiquity. Twice in the play characters are led in mystifying wandering as in a maze, and they use the very word themselves.

Garber says that the Daedalus fable works like the other structures of the play to invite approval of the Renaissance "middle way" as a model for human behavior, since human beings were themselves perceived as a middle way in God's creation between mortal animals and the immortal angels. It is man's task and the effort of his education through knowledge to use his freedom of choice:

> For *The Tempest* affirms the necessity of a choice, not of bestiality of godhead, but of something, everything, in between—a choice, as Wallace Stevens wrote, "not between, but of."

By focusing on the choices within the play, Garber shows what she sees as its basic structure. On that opposition, she says, Shakespeare builds the manifold patterns of the play as a whole.

SUGGESTIONS FOR DISCUSSION AND WRITING

1. The play begins with a literal storm and is called by one name for a storm. In what **figurative** senses might the story be described as a "tempest"? Be sure to consider Ariel's song about a "sea change" in your answer. What uses might a Multicultural critic make of the metaphor of storm or tempest? A Structuralist critic?

2. Prospero as a **character** seems much more decisive than Hamlet, but are there any moments when he seems at a loss in spite of his powers? How has he lost his kingdom originally? Do you see a comparable behavior as a constant in his character? What views might a Multicultural critic take of this aspect of Prospero's character? A Structuralist critic?

3. *The Tempest* is a play about family relations. In what ways might a Multicultural critic analyze the different family relations (including Caliban and his mother) that figure in the play? How might a Structuralist critic view the issues?

4. Both *Oedipus Rex* and *The Tempest* are analyzed in this book by Structuralist critics. How do their approaches differ and how are they the same? Do any of Levi-Strauss's insights illuminate *The Tempest* for you?

Do any of Garber's structural units illuminate *Oedipus Rex?* Explain and exemplify your answers.

5. Pick another critical approach and make some notes for discussion or for an essay on a conflict in the play. How, for example, might a Psychoanalytic critic see Shakespeare using the play to explore his own situation? For example, both Shakespeare and Prospero create powerful illusions. How else are they similar figures?

Chapter Twenty

Approaches to Henrik Ibsen's *A Doll House*

HENRIK IBSEN (1828–1906) was born in Skien, a seaport in Norway. During Ibsen's childhood, his father faced severe financial troubles, and the family was reduced from their comfortable middle-class status to poverty. In his adolescence, Ibsen was apprenticed to a druggist, but quickly abandoned medicine to work in the theatre. In 1851, he was named manager and official playwright of the National Theatre at Bergen. During this period, he wrote four plays based on Norwegian folklore and history, including *Lady Inger of Ostrat* (1855). When the King refused to give Ibsen any more grants to continue writing, he left Norway and lived in Italy and Germany for twenty-seven years. There, Ibsen wrote most of his popular plays such as *A Doll House* (1879), *Ghosts* (1881), *An Enemy of the People* (1882), *The Wild Duck* (1884), and *Hedda Gabler* (1890). His last two plays are highly symbolic treatments of spiritually dead characters: *John Gabriel Borkman* (1896) and *When We Dead Awaken* (1899).

Regarded as one of the fathers of modern drama, Ibsen brought the issues and ideas of his time onto the stage, often resulting in great controversy. *A Doll House* is no exception; Nora's actions sparked a great amount of debate and fervor when the play was first produced.

HENRIK IBSEN
A Doll House
(1879)

Translated by Rolf Fjelde

CHARACTERS

Torvald Helmer, *a lawyer*

Nora, *his wife*

Dr. Rank

Mrs. Linde

Nils Krogstad, *a bank clerk*

The Helmers' three small children

Anne-Marie, *their nurse*

Helene, *a maid*

A Delivery Boy

The action takes place in Helmer's residence.

Act I

A comfortable room, tastefully but not expensively furnished. A door to the right in the back wall leads to the entryway; another to the left leads to Helmer's study. Between these doors, a piano. Midway in the left-hand wall a door, and further back a window. Near the window a round table with an armchair and a small sofa. In the right-hand wall, toward the rear, a door, and nearer the foreground a porcelain stove with two armchairs and a rocking chair beside it. Between the stove and the side door, a small table. Engravings on the walls. An étagère with china figures and other small art objects; a small bookcase with richly bound books; the floor carpeted; a fire burning in the stove. It is a winter day.

A bell rings in the entryway; shortly after we hear the door being unlocked. Nora comes into the room, humming happily to herself; she is wearing street clothes and carries an armload of packages, which she puts down on the table to the right. She has left the hall door open; and through it a Delivery Boy is seen, holding a Christmas tree and a basket, which he gives to the Maid who let them in.

Nora: Hide the tree well, Helene. The children mustn't get a glimpse of it till this evening, after it's trimmed. (*To the Delivery Boy, taking out her purse.*) How much?
Delivery Boy: Fifty, ma'am.
Nora: There's a crown. No, keep the change. (*The Boy thanks her and leaves. Nora shuts the door. She laughs softly to herself while taking off her street things. Drawing a bag of macaroons from her pocket, she eats a couple, then steals over and listens at her husband's study door.*) Yes, he's home. (*Hums again as she moves to the table right.*)
10 *Helmer:* (*from the study*) Is that my little lark twittering out there?
Nora: (*busy opening some packages*) Yes, it is.
Helmer: Is that my squirrel rummaging around?
Nora: Yes!
Helmer: When did my squirrel get in?
Nora: Just now. (*Putting the macaroon bag in her pocket and wiping her mouth.*) Do come in, Torvald, and see what I've bought.
Helmer: Can't be disturbed. (*After a moment he opens the door and peers in, pen in hand.*) Bought, you say? All that there? Has the little spendthrift been out throwing money around again?
20 *Nora:* Oh, but Torvald, this year we really should let ourselves go a bit. It's the first Christmas we haven't had to economize.
Helmer: But you know we can't go squandering.
Nora: Oh yes, Torvald, we can squander a little now. Can't we? Just a tiny, wee bit. Now that you've got a big salary and are going to make piles and piles of money.
Helmer: Yes—starting New Year's. But then it's a full three months till the raise comes through.
Nora: Pooh! We can borrow that long.
Helmer: Nora! (*Goes over and playfully takes her by the ear.*) Are your
30   scatterbrains off again? What if today I borrowed a thousand

crowns, and you squandered them over Christmas week, and then on New Year's Eve a roof tile fell on my head, and I lay there—

Nora: (*putting her hand on his mouth*) Oh! Don't say such things!

Helmer: Yes, but what if it happened—then what?

Nora: If anything so awful happened, then it just wouldn't matter if I had debts or not.

Helmer: Well, but the people I'd borrowed from?

Nora: Them? Who cares about them! They're strangers.

Helmer: Nora, Nora, how like a woman! No, but seriously, Nora, you
40   know what I think about that. No debts! Never borrow! Something of freedom's lost—and something of beauty, too—from a home that's founded on borrowing and debt. We've made a brave stand up to now, the two of us; and we'll go right on like that the little while we have to.

Nora: (*going toward the stove*) Yes, whatever you say, Torvald.

Helmer: (*following her*) Now, now, the little lark's wings mustn't droop. Come on, don't be a sulky squirrel. (*Taking out his wallet.*) Nora, guess what I have here.

Nora: (*turning quickly*) Money!

50 *Helmer:* There, see. (*Hands her some notes.*) Good grief, I know how costs go up in a house at Christmastime.

Nora: Ten—twenty—thirty—forty. Oh, thank you, Torvald; I can manage no end on this.

Helmer: You really will have to.

Nora: Oh yes, I promise I will! But come here so I can show you everything I bought. And so cheap! Look, new clothes for Ivar here—and a sword. Here a horse and a trumpet for Bob. And a doll and a doll's bed here for Emmy; they're nothing much, but she'll tear them to bits in no time anyway. And here I have dress
60   material and handkerchiefs for the maids. Old Anne-Marie really deserves something more.

Helmer: And what's in that package there?

Nora: (*with a cry*) Torvald, no! You can't see that till tonight!

Helmer: I see. But tell me now, you little prodigal, what have you thought of for yourself?

Nora: For myself? Oh, I don't want anything at all.

Helmer: Of course you do. Tell me just what—within reason—you'd most like to have.

Nora: I honestly don't know. Oh, listen, Torvald—

70 *Helmer:* Well?

Nora: (*fumbling at his coat buttons, without looking at him*) If you want to give me something, then maybe you could—you could—

Helmer: Come on, out with it.

Nora: (*hurriedly*) You could give me money, Torvald. No more than you think you can spare; then one of these days I'll buy something with it.

Helmer: But Nora—

Nora: Oh, please, Torvald darling, do that! I beg you, please. Then I
could hang the bills in pretty gilt paper on the Christmas tree.
80   Wouldn't that be fun?

Helmer: What are those little birds called that always fly through
their fortunes?

Nora: Oh yes, spendthrifts; I know all that. But let's do as I say,
Torvald; then I'll have time to decide what I really need most.
That's very sensible, isn't it?

Helmer: (*smiling*) Yes, very—that is, if you actually hung onto the
money I give you, and you actually used it to buy yourself
something. But it goes for the house and for all sorts of foolish
things, and then I only have to lay out some more.

90 *Nora:* Oh, but Torvald—

Helmer: Don't deny it, my dear little Nora. (*Putting his arm around her
waist.*) Spendthrifts are sweet, but they use up a frightful amount
of money. It's incredible what it costs a man to feed such birds.

Nora: Oh, how can you say that! Really, I save everything I can.

Helmer: (*laughing*) Yes, that's the truth. Everything you can. But that's
nothing at all.

Nora: (*humming, with a smile of quiet satisfaction*) Hm, if you only knew
what expenses we larks and squirrels have, Torvald.

Helmer: You're an odd little one. Exactly the way your father was.
100   You're never at a loss for scaring up money; but the moment you
have it, it runs right out through your fingers; you never know
what you've done with it. Well, one takes you as you are. It's deep
in your blood. Yes, these things are hereditary, Nora.

Nora: Ah, I could wish I'd inherited many of Papa's qualities.

Helmer: And I couldn't wish you anything but just what you are, my
sweet little lark. But wait; it seems to me you have a very—what
should I call it?—a very suspicious look today—

Nora: I do?

Helmer: You certainly do. Look me straight in the eye.

110 *Nora:* (*looking at him*) Well?

Helmer: (*shaking an admonitory finger*) Surely my sweet tooth hasn't
been running riot in town today, has she?

Nora: No. Why do you imagine that?

Helmer: My sweet tooth really didn't make a little detour through the
confectioner's?

Nora: No, I assure you, Torvald—

Helmer: Hasn't nibbled some pastry?

Nora: No, not at all.

Helmer: Nor even munched a macaroon or two?

120 *Nora:* No, Torvald, I assure you, really—

Helmer: There, there now. Of course I'm only joking.

Nora: (*going to the table, right*) You know I could never think of going
against you.

Helmer: No, I understand that; and you *have* given me your word.

(*Going over to her.*) Well, you keep your little Christmas secrets to yourself, Nora darling. I expect they'll come to light this evening, when the tree is lit.

Nora: Did you remember to ask Dr. Rank?

Helmer: No. But there's no need for that; it's assumed he'll be dining
130   with us. All the same, I'll ask him when he stops by here this morning. I've ordered some fine wine. Nora, you can't imagine how I'm looking forward to this evening.

Nora: So am I. And what fun for the children, Torvald!

Helmer: Ah, it's so gratifying to know that one's gotten a safe, secure job, and with a comfortable salary. It's a great satisfaction, isn't it?

Nora: Oh, it's wonderful!

Helmer: Remember last Christmas? Three whole weeks before, you shut yourself in every evening till long after midnight, making flowers for the Christmas tree, and all the other decorations to
140   surprise us. Ugh, that was the dullest time I've ever lived through.

Nora: It wasn't at all dull for me.

Helmer: (*smiling*) But the outcome *was* pretty sorry, Nora.

Nora: Oh, don't tease me with that again. How could I help it that the cat came in and tore everything to shreds.

Helmer: No, poor thing, you certainly couldn't. You wanted so much to please us all, and that's what counts. But it's just as well that the hard times are past.

Nora: Yes, it's really wonderful.

Helmer: Now I don't have to sit here alone, boring myself, and you
150   don't have to tire your precious eyes and your fair little delicate hands—

Nora: (*clapping her hands*) No, is it really true, Torvald, I don't have to? Oh, how wonderfully lovely to hear! (*Taking his arm.*) Now I'll tell you just how I've thought we should plan things. Right after Christmas—(*The doorbell rings.*) Oh, the bell. (*Straightening the room up a bit.*) Somebody would have to come. What a bore!

Helmer: I'm not at home to visitors, don't forget.

Maid: (*from the hall doorway*) Ma'am, a lady to see you—

Nora: All right, let her come in.

160 *Maid:* (*to Helmer*) And the doctor's just come too.

Helmer: Did he go right to my study?

Maid: Yes, he did.

Helmer goes into his room. The Maid shows in Mrs. Linde, dressed in traveling clothes, and shuts the door after her.

Mrs. Linde: (*in a dispirited and somewhat hesitant voice*) Hello, Nora.

Nora: (*uncertain*) Hello—

Mrs. Linde: You don't recognize me.

Nora: No, I don't know—but wait, I think—(*Exclaiming.*) What! Kristine! Is it really you?

Mrs. Linde: Yes, it's me.

Nora: Kristine! To think I didn't recognize you. But then, how could I?
170   (*More quietly.*) How you've changed, Kristine!

Mrs. Linde: Yes, no doubt I have. In nine—ten long years.

Nora: Is it so long since we met! Yes, it's all of that. Oh, these last
     eight years have been a happy time, believe me. And so now
     you've come in to town, too. Made the long trip in the winter.
     That took courage.

Mrs. Linde: I just got here by ship this morning.

Nora: To enjoy yourself over Christmas, of course. Oh, how lovely!
     Yes, enjoy ourselves, we'll do that. But take your coat off. You're
     not still cold? (*Helping her.*) There now, let's get cozy here by the
180   stove. No, the easy chair there! I'll take the rocker here. (*Seizing
     her hands.*) Yes, now you have your old look again; it was only in
     that first moment. You're a bit more pale, Kristine—and maybe a
     bit thinner.

Mrs. Linde: And much, much older, Nora.

Nora: Yes, perhaps a bit older; a tiny, tiny bit; not much at all.
     (*Stopping short; suddenly serious.*) Oh, but thoughtless me, to sit
     here, chattering away. Sweet, good Kristine, can you forgive me?

Mrs. Linde: What do you mean, Nora?

Nora: (*softly*) Poor Kristine, you've become a widow.

190 *Mrs. Linde:* Yes, three years ago.

Nora: Oh, I knew it, of course: I read it in the papers. Oh, Kristine,
     you must believe me; I often thought of writing you then, but I
     kept postponing it, and something always interfered.

Mrs. Linde: Nora dear, I understand completely.

Nora: No, it was awful of me, Kristine. You poor thing, how much you
     must have gone through. And he left you nothing?

Mrs. Linde: No.

Nora: And no children?

Mrs. Linde: No.

200 *Nora:* Nothing at all, then?

Mrs. Linde: Not even a sense of loss to feed on.

Nora: (*looking incredulously at her*) But Kristine, how could that be?

Mrs. Linde: (*smiling wearily and smoothing her hair*) Oh, sometimes it
     happens, Nora.

Nora: So completely alone. How terribly hard that must be for you. I
     have three lovely children. You can't see them now; they're out
     with the maid. But now you must tell me everything—

Mrs. Linde: No, no, no, tell me about yourself.

Nora: No, you begin. Today I don't want to be selfish. I want to think
210   only of you today. But there *is* something I must tell you. Did you
     hear of the wonderful luck we had recently?

Mrs. Linde: No, what's that?

Nora: My husband's been made manager in the bank, just think!

Mrs. Linde: Your husband? How marvelous!

Nora: Isn't it? Being a lawyer is such an uncertain living, you know, especially if one won't touch any cases that aren't clean and decent. And of course Torvald would never do that, and I'm with him completely there. Oh, we're simply delighted, believe me! He'll join the bank right after New Year's and start getting a huge
220 salary and lots of commissions. From now on we can live quite differently—just as we want. Oh, Kristine, I feel so light and happy! Won't it be lovely to have stacks of money and not a care in the world?

Mrs. Linde: Well, anyway, it would be lovely to have enough for necessities.

Nora: No, not just for necessities, but stacks and stacks of money!

Mrs. Linde: (*smiling*) Nora, Nora, aren't you sensible yet? Back in school you were such a free spender.

Nora: (*with a quiet laugh*) Yes, that's what Torvald still says. (*Shaking*
230 *her finger.*) But "Nora, Nora" isn't as silly as you all think. Really, we've been in no position for me to go squandering. We've had to work, both of us.

Mrs. Linde: You too?

Nora: Yes, at odd jobs—needlework, crocheting, embroidery, and such—(*casually*) and other things too. You remember that Torvald left the department when we were married? There was no chance of promotion in his office, and of course he needed to earn more money. But that first year he drove himself terribly. He took on all kinds of extra work that kept him going morning and night. It
240 wore him down, and then he fell deathly ill. The doctors said it was essential for him to travel south.

Mrs. Linde: Yes, didn't you spend a whole year in Italy?

Nora: That's right. It wasn't easy to get away, you know. Ivar had just been born. But of course we had to go. Oh, that was a beautiful trip, and it saved Torvald's life. But it cost a frightful sum, Kristine.

Mrs. Linde: I can well imagine.

Nora: Four thousand, eight hundred crowns it cost. That's really a lot of money.

Mrs. Linde: But it's lucky you had it when you needed it.
250 *Nora:* Well, as it was, we got it from Papa.

Mrs. Linde: I see. It was just about the time your father died.

Nora: Yes, just about then. And, you know, I couldn't make that trip out to nurse him. I had to stay here, expecting Ivar any moment, and with my poor sick Torvald to care for. Dearest Papa, I never saw him again, Kristine. Oh, that was the worst time I've known in all my marriage.

Mrs. Linde: I know how you loved him. And then you went off to Italy?

Nora: Yes. We had the means now, and the doctors urged us. So we
260 left a month after.

Mrs. Linde: And your husband came back completely cured?

Nora: Sound as a drum!

Mrs. Linde: But—the doctor?

Nora: Who?

Mrs. Linde: I thought the maid said he was a doctor, the man who came in with me.

Nora: Yes, that was Dr. Rank—but he's not making a sick call. He's our closest friend, and he stops by at least once a day. No, Torvald hasn't had a sick moment since, and the children are fit and strong, and I
270   am, too. (*Jumping up and clapping her hands.*) Oh, dear God, Kristine, what a lovely thing to live and be happy! But how disgusting of me—I'm talking of nothing but my own affairs. (*Sits on a stool close by Kristine, arms resting across her knees.*) Oh, don't be angry with me! Tell me, is it really true that you weren't in love with your husband? Why did you marry him, then?

Mrs. Linde: My mother was still alive, but bedridden and helpless—and I had my two younger brothers to look after. In all conscience, I didn't think I could turn him down.

Nora: No, you were right there. But was he rich at the time?

280 *Mrs. Linde:* He was very well off, I'd say. But the business was shaky, Nora. When he died, it all fell apart, and nothing was left.

Nora: And then—?

Mrs. Linde: Yes, so I had to scrape up a living with a little shop and a little teaching and whatever else I could find. The last three years have been like one endless workday without a rest for me. Now it's over, Nora. My poor mother doesn't need me, for she's passed on. Nor the boys, either; they're working now and can take care of themselves.

Nora: How free you must feel—

290 *Mrs. Linde:* No—only unspeakably empty. Nothing to live for now. (*Standing up anxiously.*) That's why I couldn't take it any longer out in that desolate hole. Maybe here it'll be easier to find something to do and keep my mind occupied. If I could only be lucky enough to get a steady job, some office work—

Nora: I told you about the trip to Italy. Torvald never would have lived if he hadn't gone south—

Mrs. Linde: Of course; your father gave you the means—

Nora: (*smiling*) That's what Torvald and all the rest think, but—

Mrs. Linde: But—?

300 *Nora:* Papa didn't give us a pin. I was the one who raised the money.

Mrs. Linde: You? That whole amount?

Nora: Four thousand, eight hundred crowns. What do you say to that?

Mrs. Linde: But Nora, how was it possible? Did you win the lottery?

Nora: (*disdainfully*) The lottery? Pooh! No art to that.

Mrs. Linde: But where did you get it from then?

Nora: (*humming, with a mysterious smile*) Hmm, tra-la-la-la.

Mrs. Linde: Because you couldn't have borrowed it.

Nora: No? Why not?

Mrs. Linde: A wife can't borrow without her husband's consent.

310 **Nora:** (*tossing her head*) Oh, but a wife with a little business sense, a wife who knows how to manage—

Mrs. Linde: Nora, I simply don't understand—

Nora: You don't have to. Whoever said I *borrowed* the money? I could have gotten it other ways. (*Throwing herself back on the sofa.*) I could have gotten it from some admirer or other. After all, a girl with my ravishing appeal—

Mrs. Linde: You lunatic.

Nora: I'll bet you're eaten up with curiosity, Kristine.

Mrs. Linde: Now listen here, Nora—you haven't done something

320   indiscreet?

Nora: (*sitting up again*) Is it indiscreet to save your husband's life?

Mrs. Linde: I think it's indiscreet that without his knowledge you—

Nora: But that's the point: he mustn't know! My Lord, can't you understand? He mustn't ever know the close call he had. It was to *me* the doctors came to say his life was in danger—that nothing could save him but a stay in the south. Didn't I try strategy then! I began talking about how lovely it would be for me to travel abroad like other young wives; I begged and I cried; I told him please to remember my condition, to be kind and indulge me; and

330   then I dropped a hint that he could easily take out a loan. But at that, Kristine, he nearly exploded. He said I was frivolous, and it was his duty as man of the house not to indulge me in whims and fancies—as I think he called them. Aha, I thought, now you'll just have to be saved—and that's when I saw my chance.

Mrs. Linde: And your father never told Torvald the money wasn't from him?

Nora: No, never. Papa died right about then. I'd considered bringing him into my secret and begging him never to tell. But he was too sick at the time—and then, sadly, it didn't matter.

340 **Mrs. Linde:** And you've never confided in your husband since?

Nora: For heaven's sake, no! Are you serious? He's so strict on that subject. Besides—Torvald, with all his masculine pride—how painfully humiliating for him if he ever found out he was in debt to me. That would just ruin our relationship. Our beautiful, happy home would never be the same.

Mrs. Linde: Won't you ever tell him?

Nora: (*thoughtfully, half smiling*) Yes—maybe sometime, years from now, when I'm no longer so attractive. Don't laugh! I only mean when Torvald loves me less than now, when he stops enjoying my

350   dancing and dressing up and reciting for him. Then it might be wise to have something in reserve—(*Breaking off.*) How ridiculous! That'll never happen—Well, Kristine, what do you think of my big secret? I'm capable of something too, hm? You can imagine, of course, how this thing hangs over me. It really hasn't been easy meeting the payments on time. In the business world there's what

they call quarterly interest and what they call amortization, and these are always so terribly hard to manage. I've had to skimp a little here and there, wherever I could, you know. I could hardly spare anything from my house allowance, because Torvald has to
360   live well. I couldn't let the children go poorly dressed; whatever I got for them, I felt I had to use up completely—the darlings!

Mrs. Linde: Poor Nora, so it had to come out of your own budget, then?

Nora: Yes, of course. But I was the one most responsible, too. Every time Torvald gave me money for new clothes and such, I never used more than half; always bought the simplest, cheapest outfits. It was a godsend that everything looks so well on me that Torvald never noticed. But it did weigh me down at times, Kristine. It *is* such a joy to wear fine things. You understand.

370 *Mrs. Linde:* Oh, of course.

Nora: And then I found other ways of making money. Last winter I was lucky enough to get a lot of copying to do. I locked myself in and sat writing every evening till late in the night. Ah, I was tired so often, dead tired. But still it was wonderful fun, sitting and working like that, earning money. It was almost like being a man.

Mrs. Linde: But how much have you paid off this way so far?

Nora: That's hard to say, exactly. These accounts, you know, aren't easy to figure. I only know that I've paid out all I could scrape together. Time and again I haven't known where to turn. (*Smiling.*)
380   Then I'd sit here dreaming of a rich old gentleman who had fallen in love with me—

Mrs. Linde: What! Who is he?

Nora: Oh, really! And that he'd died, and when his will was opened, there in big letters it said, "All my fortune shall be paid over in cash, immediately, to that enchanting Mrs. Nora Helmer."

Mrs. Linde: But Nora dear—who *was* this gentleman?

Nora: Good grief, can't you understand? The old man never existed; that was only something I'd dream up time and again whenever I was at my wits' end for money. But it makes no difference now;
390   the old fossil can go where he pleases for all I care; I don't need him or his will—because now I'm free. (*Jumping up.*) Oh, how lovely to think of that, Kristine! Carefree! To know you're carefree, utterly carefree; to be able to romp and play with the children, and to keep up a beautiful, charming home—everything just the way Torvald likes it! And think, spring is coming, with big blue skies. Maybe we can travel a little then. Maybe I'll see the ocean again. Oh yes, it *is* so marvelous to live and be happy!

(*The front doorbell rings.*)

Mrs. Linde: (*rising*) There's the bell. It's probably best that I go.

Nora: No, stay. No one's expected. It must be for Torvald.

400 **Maid:** (*from the hall doorway*) Excuse me, ma'am—there's a gentleman here to see Mr. Helmer, but I didn't know—since the doctor's with him—

Nora: Who is the gentleman?

Krogstad: (*from the doorway*) It's me, Mrs. Helmer.

Mrs. Linde starts and turns away toward the window.

Nora: (*stepping toward him, tense, her voice a whisper*) You? What is it? Why do you want to speak to my husband?

Krogstad: Bank business—after a fashion. I have a small job in the investment bank, and I hear now your husband is going to be our chief—

410 **Nora:** In other words, it's—

Krogstad: Just dry business, Mrs. Helmer. Nothing but that.

Nora: Yes, then please be good enough to step into the study. (*She nods indifferently as she sees him out by the hall door, then returns and begins stirring up the stove.*)

Mrs. Linde: Nora—who was that man?

Nora: That was a Mr. Krogstad—a lawyer.

Mrs. Linde: Then it really was him.

Nora: Do you know that person?

Mrs. Linde: I did once—many years ago. For a time he was a law clerk

420 in our town.

Nora: Yes, he's been that.

Mrs. Linde: How he's changed.

Nora: I understand he had a very unhappy marriage.

Mrs. Linde: He's a widower now.

Nora: With a number of children. There now, it's burning. (*She closes the stove door and moves the rocker a bit to one side.*)

Mrs. Linde: They say he has a hand in all kinds of business.

Nora: Oh? That may be true: I wouldn't know. But let's not think about business. It's so dull.

Dr. Rank enters from Helmer's study.

430 **Rank:** (*still in the doorway*) No, no, really—I don't want to intrude, I'd just as soon talk a little while with your wife. (*Shuts the door, then notices Mrs. Linde.*) Oh, beg pardon. I'm intruding here too.

Nora: No, not at all. (*Introducing him.*) Dr. Rank, Mrs. Linde.

Rank: Well now, that's a name much heard in this house. I believe I passed the lady on the stairs as I came.

Mrs. Linde: Yes, I take the stairs very slowly. They're rather hard on me.

Rank: Uh-hm, some touch of internal weakness?

Mrs. Linde: More overexertion, I'd say.

Rank: Nothing else? Then you're probably here in town to rest up in a

440 round of parties?

Mrs. Linde: I'm here to look for work.

Rank: Is that the best cure for overexertion?

Mrs. Linde: One has to live, Doctor.

Rank: Yes, there's a common prejudice to that effect.

Nora: Oh, come on, Dr. Rank—you really do want to live yourself.

Rank: Yes, I really do. Wretched as I am, I'll gladly prolong my torment indefinitely. All my patients feel like that. And it's quite the same, too, with the morally sick. Right at this moment there's one of those moral invalids in there with Helmer—

450 *Mrs. Linde:* (*softly*) Ah!

Nora: Who do you mean?

Rank: Oh, it's a lawyer, Krogstad, a type you wouldn't know. His character is rotten to the root—but even he began chattering all-importantly about how he had to *live.*

Nora: Oh? What did he want to talk to Torvald about?

Rank: I really don't know. I only heard something about the bank.

Nora: I didn't know that Krog—that this man Krogstad had anything to do with the bank.

Rank: Yes, he's gotten some kind of berth down there. (*To Mrs. Linde.*)
460   I don't know if you also have, in your neck of the woods, a type of person who scuttles about breathlessly, sniffing out hints of moral corruption, and then maneuvers his victim into some sort of key position where he can keep an eye on him. It's the healthy these days that are out in the cold.

Mrs. Linde: All the same, it's the sick who most need to be taken in.

Rank: (*with a shrug*) Yes, there we have it. That's the concept that's turning society into a sanatorium.

Nora, lost in her thoughts, breaks out into quiet laughter and claps her hands.

Rank: Why do you laugh at that? Do you have any real idea of what society is?

470 *Nora:* What do I care about dreary old society? I was laughing at something quite different—something terribly funny. Tell me, Doctor—is everyone who works in the bank dependent now on Torvald?

Rank: Is that what you find so terribly funny?

Nora: (*smiling and humming*) Never mind, never mind! (*Pacing the floor.*) Yes, that's really immensely amusing: that we—that Torvald has so much power now over all those people. (*Taking the bag out of her pocket.*) Dr. Rank, a little macaroon on that?

Rank: See here, macaroons! I thought they were contraband here.

480 *Nora:* Yes, but these are some that Kristine gave me.

Mrs. Linde: What? I—?

Nora: Now, now, don't be afraid. You couldn't possibly know that Torvald had forbidden them. You see, he's worried they'll ruin my teeth. But hmp! Just this once! Isn't that so, Dr. Rank? Help yourself! (*Puts a macaroon in his mouth.*) And you too, Kristine. And I'll also have one, only a little one—or two, at the most. (*Walking about again.*) Now I'm really tremendously happy. Now there's just one last thing in the world that I have an enormous desire to do.

490 *Rank:* Well! And what's that?

Nora: It's something I have such a consuming desire to say so Torvald could hear.

Rank: And why can't you say it?

Nora: I don't dare. It's quite shocking.

Mrs. Linde: Shocking?

Rank: Well, then it isn't advisable. But in front of us you certainly can. What do you have such a desire to say so Torvald could hear?

Nora: I have such a huge desire to say—to hell and be damned!

Rank: Are you crazy?

500 *Mrs. Linde:* My goodness, Nora!

Rank: Go on, say it. Here he is.

Nora: (*hiding the macaroon bag*) Shh, shh, shh!

Helmer comes in from his study, hat in hand, overcoat over his arm.

Nora: (*going toward him*) Well, Torvald dear, are you through with him?

Helmer: Yes, he just left.

Nora: Let me introduce you—this is Kristine, who's arrived here in town.

Helmer: Kristine—? I'm sorry, but I don't know—

Nora: Mrs. Linde, Torvald dear. Mrs. Kristine Linde.

Helmer: Of course. A childhood friend of my wife's, no doubt?

510 *Mrs. Linde:* Yes, we knew each other in those days.

Nora: And just think, she made the long trip down here in order to talk with you.

Helmer: What's this?

Mrs. Linde: Well, not exactly—

Nora: You see, Kristine is remarkably clever in office work, and so she's terribly eager to come under a capable man's supervision and add more to what she already knows—

Helmer: Very wise, Mrs. Linde.

Nora: And then when she heard that you'd become a bank manager—

520 the story was wired out to the papers—then she came in as fast as she could and—Really, Torvald, for my sake you can do a little something for Kristine, can't you?

Helmer: Yes, it's not at all impossible. Mrs. Linde, I suppose you're a widow?

Mrs. Linde: Yes.

Helmer: Any experience in office work?

Mrs. Linde: Yes, a good deal.

Helmer: Well, it's quite likely that I can make an opening for you—

Nora: (*clapping her hands*) You see, you see!

530   *Helmer:* You've come at a lucky moment, Mrs. Linde.

Mrs. Linde: Oh, how can I thank you?

Helmer: Not necessary. (*Putting his overcoat on.*) But today you'll have to excuse me—

Rank: Wait, I'll go with you. (*He fetches his coat from the hall and warms it at the stove.*)

Nora: Don't stay out long, dear.

Helmer: An hour; no more.

Nora: Are you going too, Kristine?

Mrs. Linde: (*putting on her winter garments*) Yes, I have to see about a
540   room now.

Helmer: Then perhaps we can all walk together.

Nora: (*helping her*) What a shame we're so cramped here, but it's quite impossible for us to—

Mrs. Linde: Oh, don't even think of it! Good-bye, Nora dear, and thanks for everything.

Nora: Good-bye for now. Of course you'll be back this evening. And you too, Dr. Rank. What? If you're well enough? Oh, you've got to be! Wrap up tight now.

In a ripple of small talk the company moves out into the hall; children's voices are heard outside on the steps.

Nora: There they are! There they are! (*She runs to open the door. The*
550   *children come in with their nurse, Anne-Marie.*) Come in, come in! (*Bends down and kisses them.*) Oh, you darlings—! Look at them, Kristine. Aren't they lovely!

Rank: No loitering in the draft here.

Helmer: Come, Mrs. Linde—this place is unbearable now for anyone but mothers.

Dr. Rank, Helmer, and Mrs. Linde go down the stairs. Anne-Marie goes into the living room with the children. Nora follows, after closing the hall door.

Nora: How fresh and strong you look. Oh, such red cheeks you have! Like apples and roses. (*The children interrupt her throughout the following.*) And it was so much fun? That's wonderful. Really? You pulled both Emmy and Bob on the sled? Imagine, all together! Yes,
560   you're a clever boy, Ivar. Oh, let me hold her a bit, Anne-Marie. My sweet little doll baby! (*Takes the smallest from the nurse and dances with her.*) Yes, yes, Mama will dance with Bob as well. What? Did you throw snowballs? Oh, if I'd only been there! No, don't bother, Anne-Marie—I'll undress them myself. Oh yes, let me. It's such fun. Go in and rest; you look half frozen. There's hot coffee waiting for you on the stove. (*The nurse goes into the room to the left. Nora takes the children's winter things off, throwing them about, while the children talk to*

her all at once.) Is that so? A big dog chased you? But it didn't bite?
No, dogs never bite little, lovely doll babies. Don't peek in the
570   packages, Ivar! What is it? Yes, wouldn't you like to know. No, no,
it's an ugly something. Well? Shall we play? What shall we play?
Hide-and-seek? Yes, let's play hide-and-seek. Bob must hide first.
I must? Yes, let me hide first. (*Laughing and shouting, she and the
children play in and out of the living room and the adjoining room to the
right. At last Nora hides under the table. The children come storming in,
search, but cannot find her, then hear her muffled laughter, dash over to
the table, lift the cloth up and find her. Wild shouting. She creeps forward
as if to scare them. More shouts. Meanwhile, a knock at the hall door; no
one has noticed it. Now the door half opens, and Krogstad appears. He
580   waits a moment; the game goes on.*)

Krogstad: Beg pardon, Mrs. Helmer—

Nora: (*with a strangled cry, turning and scrambling to her knees*) Oh!
What do you want?

Krogstad: Excuse me. The outer door was ajar; it must be someone
forgot to shut it—

Nora: (*rising*) My husband isn't home, Mr. Krogstad.

Krogstad: I know that.

Nora: Yes—then what do you want here?

Krogstad: A word with you.

590 *Nora:* With—? (*To the children, quietly.*) Go in to Anne-Marie. What? No,
the strange man won't hurt Mama. When he's gone, we'll play some
more. (*She leads the children into the room to the left and shuts the door
after them. Then, tense and nervous*) You want to speak to me?

Krogstad: Yes, I want to.

Nora: Today? But it's not yet the first of the month—

Krogstad: No, it's Christmas Eve. It's going to be up to you how
merry a Christmas you have.

Nora: What is it you want? Today I absolutely can't—

Krogstad: We won't talk about that till later. This is something else.
600   You do have a moment to spare, I suppose?

Nora: Oh yes, of course—I do, except—

Krogstad: Good. I was sitting over at Olsen's Restaurant when I saw
your husband go down the street—

Nora: Yes?

Krogstad: With a lady.

Nora: Yes. So?

Krogstad: If you'll pardon my asking: wasn't that lady a Mrs. Linde?

Nora: Yes.

Krogstad: Just now come into town?

610 *Nora:* Yes, today.

Krogstad: She's a good friend of yours?

Nora: Yes, she is. But I don't see—

Krogstad: I also knew her once.

Nora: I'm aware of that.

Krogstad: Oh? You know all about it. I thought so. Well, then let me ask you short and sweet: is Mrs. Linde getting a job in the bank?

Nora: What makes you think you can cross-examine me, Mr. Krogstad—you, one of my husband's employees? But since you ask, you might as well know—yes, Mrs. Linde's going to be taken on at

620   the bank. And I'm the one who spoke for her, Mr. Krogstad. Now you know.

Krogstad: So I guessed right.

Nora: (*pacing up and down*) Oh, one does have a tiny bit of influence, I should hope. Just because I am a woman, don't think it means that—When one has a subordinate position, Mr. Krogstad, one really ought to be careful about pushing somebody who—hm—

Krogstad: Who has influence?

Nora: That's right.

Krogstad: (*in a different tone*) Mrs. Helmer, would you be good enough

630   to use your influence on my behalf?

Nora: What? What do you mean?

Krogstad: Would you please make sure that I keep my subordinate position in the bank?

Nora: What does that mean? Who's thinking of taking away your position?

Krogstad: Oh, don't play the innocent with me. I'm quite aware that your friend would hardly relish the chance of running into me again; and I'm also aware now whom I can thank for being turned out.

Nora: But I promise you—

640 *Krogstad:* Yes, yes, yes, to the point: there's still time, and I'm advising you to use your influence to prevent it.

Nora: But Mr. Krogstad, I have absolutely no influence.

Krogstad: You haven't? I thought you were just saying—

Nora: You shouldn't take me so literally. I! How can you believe that I have any such influence over my husband?

Krogstad: Oh, I've known your husband from our student days. I don't think the great bank manager's more steadfast than any other married man.

Nora: You speak insolently about my husband, and I'll show you the

650   door.

Krogstad: The lady has spirit.

Nora: I'm not afraid of you any longer. After New Year's, I'll soon be done with the whole business.

Krogstad: (*restraining himself*) Now listen to me, Mrs. Helmer. If necessary, I'll fight for my little job in the bank as if it were life itself.

Nora: Yes, so it seems.

Krogstad: It's not just a matter of income; that's the least of it. It's something else—All right, out with it! Look, this is the thing.

660   You know, just like all the others, of course, that once, a good many years ago, I did something rather rash.

Nora: I've heard rumors to that effect.

Krogstad: The case never got into court; but all the same, every door was closed in my face from then on. So I took up those various activities you know about. I had to grab hold somewhere; and I dare say I haven't been among the worst. But now I want to drop all that. My boys are growing up. For their sakes, I'll have to win back as much respect as possible here in town. That job in the bank was like the first rung in my ladder. And now your husband
670   wants to kick me right back down in the mud again.

Nora: But for heaven's sake, Mr. Krogstad, it's simply not in my power to help you.

Krogstad: That's because you haven't the will to—but I have the means to make you.

Nora: You certainly won't tell my husband that I owe you money?

Krogstad: Hm—what if I told him that?

Nora: That would be shameful of you. (*Nearly in tears.*) This secret—my joy and my pride—that he should learn it in such a crude and disgusting way—learn it from you. You'd expose me to
680   the most horrible unpleasantness—

Krogstad: Only unpleasantness?

Nora: (*vehemently*) But go on and try. It'll turn out the worse for you, because then my husband will really see what a crook you are, and then you'll *never* be able to hold your job.

Krogstad: I asked if it was just domestic unpleasantness you were afraid of?

Nora: If my husband finds out, then of course he'll pay what I owe at once, and then we'd be through with you for good.

Krogstad: (*a step closer*) Listen, Mrs. Helmer—you've either got a very
690   bad memory, or else no head at all for business. I'd better put you a little more in touch with the facts.

Nora: What do you mean?

Krogstad: When your husband was sick, you came to me for a loan of four thousand, eight hundred crowns.

Nora: Where else could I go?

Krogstad: I promised to get you that sum—

Nora: And you got it.

Krogstad: I promised to get you that sum, on certain conditions. You were so involved in your husband's illness, and so eager to finance
700   your trip, that I guess you didn't think out all the details. It might just be a good idea to remind you. I promised you the money on the strength of a note I drew up.

Nora: Yes, and that I signed.

Krogstad: Right. But at the bottom I added some lines for your father to guarantee the loan. He was supposed to sign down there.

Nora: Supposed to? He did sign.

Krogstad: I left the date blank. In other words, your father would have dated his signature himself. Do you remember that?

Nora: Yes, I think—

710 *Krogstad:* Then I gave you the note for you to mail to your father. Isn't that so?

Nora: Yes.

Krogstad: And naturally you sent it at once—because only some five, six days later you brought me the note, properly signed. And with that, the money was yours.

Nora: Well, then; I've made my payments regularly, haven't I?

Krogstad: More or less. But—getting back to the point—those were hard time for you then, Mrs. Helmer.

Nora: Yes, they were.

720 *Krogstad:* Your father was very ill, I believe.

Nora: He was near the end.

Krogstad: He died soon after?

Nora: Yes.

Krogstad: Tell me, Mrs. Helmer, do you happen to recall the date of your father's death? The day of the month, I mean.

Nora: Papa died the twenty-ninth of September.

Krogstad: That's quite correct; I've already looked into that. And now we come to a curious thing—(*taking out a paper*) which I simply cannot comprehend.

730 *Nora:* Curious thing? I don't know—

Krogstad: This is the curious thing: that your father co-signed the note for your loan three days after his death.

Nora: How—? I don't understand.

Krogstad: Your father died the twenty-ninth of September. But look. Here your father dated his signature October second. Isn't that curious, Mrs. Helmer? (*Nora is silent.*) Can you explain it to me? (*Nora remains silent.*) It's also remarkable that the words "October second" and the year aren't written in your father's hand, but rather in one that I think I know. Well, it's easy to understand.

740   Your father forgot perhaps to date his signature, and then someone or other added it, a bit sloppily, before anyone knew of his death. There's nothing wrong in that. It all comes down to the signature. And there's no question about *that*, Mrs. Helmer. It really *was* your father who signed his own name here, wasn't it?

Nora: (*after a short silence, throwing her head back and looking squarely at him*) No, it wasn't. *I* signed Papa's name.

Krogstad: Wait, now—are you fully aware that this is a dangerous confession?

Nora: Why? You'll soon get your money.

750 *Krogstad:* Let me ask you a question—why didn't you send the paper to your father?

Nora: That was impossible. Papa was so sick. If I'd asked him for his signature, I also would have had to tell him what the money was for. But I couldn't tell him, sick as he was, that my husband's life was in danger. That was just impossible.

Krogstad: Then it would have been better if you'd given up the trip abroad.

Nora: I couldn't possibly. The trip was to save my husband's life. I couldn't give that up.

760 *Krogstad:* But didn't you ever consider that this was a fraud against me?

Nora: I couldn't let myself be bothered by that. You weren't any concern of mine. I couldn't stand you, with all those cold complications you made, even though you knew how badly off my husband was.

Krogstad: Mrs. Helmer, obviously you haven't the vaguest idea of what you've involved yourself in. But I can tell you this: it was nothing more and nothing worse than I once did—and it wrecked my whole reputation.

770 *Nora:* You? Do you expect me to believe that you ever acted bravely to save your wife's life?

Krogstad: Laws don't inquire into motives.

Nora: Then they must be very poor laws.

Krogstad: Poor or not—if I introduce this paper in court, you'll be judged according to law.

Nora: This I refuse to believe. A daughter hasn't a right to protect her dying father from anxiety and care? A wife hasn't a right to save her husband's life? I don't know much about laws, but I'm sure that somewhere in the books these things are allowed. And you

780 don't know anything about it—you who practice the law? You must be an awful lawyer, Mr. Krogstad.

Krogstad: Could be. But business—the kind of business we two are mixed up in—don't you think I know about that? All right. Do what you want now. But I'm telling you *this:* if I get shoved down a second time, you're going to keep me company. (*He bows and goes out through the hall.*)

Nora: (*pensive for a moment, then tossing her head*) Oh, really! Trying to frighten me! I'm not so silly as all that. (*Begins gathering up the children's clothes, but soon stops.*) But—? No, but that's impossible! I

790 did it out of love.

The Children: (*in the doorway, left*) Mama, that strange man's gone out the door.

Nora: Yes, yes, I know it. But don't tell anyone about the strange man. Do you hear? Not even Papa!

The Children: No, Mama. But now will you play again?

Nora: No, not now.

The Children: Oh, but Mama, you promised.

Nora: Yes, but I can't now. Go inside; I have too much to do. Go in, go in, my sweet darlings. (*She herds them gently back in the room and*

800 *shuts the door after them. Settling on the sofa, she takes up a piece of embroidery and makes some stitches, but soon stops abruptly.*) No! (*Throws the work aside, rises, goes to the hall door and calls out.*)

Helene! Let me have the tree in here. (*Goes to the table, left, opens the table drawer, and stops again.*) No, but that's utterly impossible!

Maid: (*with the Christmas tree*) Where should I put it, ma'am?

Nora: There. The middle of the floor.

Maid: Should I bring anything else?

Nora: No, thanks. I have what I need.

The Maid, who has set the tree down, goes out.

Nora: (*absorbed in trimming the tree*) Candles here—and flowers here.
810 That terrible creature! Talk, talk, talk! There's nothing to it at all.
The tree's going to be lovely. I'll do anything to please you,
Torvald. I'll sing for you, dance for you—

Helmer comes in from the hall, with a sheaf of papers under his arm.

Nora: Oh! You're back so soon?

Helmer: Yes. Has anyone been here?

Nora: Here? No.

Helmer: That's odd. I saw Krogstad leaving the front door.

Nora: So? Oh yes, that's true. Krogstad was here a moment.

Helmer: Nora, I can see by your face that he's been here, begging you
to put in a good word for him.

820 **Nora:** Yes.

Helmer: And it was supposed to seem like your own idea? You were
to hide it from me that he'd been here. He asked you that, too,
didn't he?

Nora: Yes, Torvald, but—

Helmer: Nora, Nora, and you could fall for that? Talk with that sort of
person and promise him anything? And then in the bargain, tell
me an untruth.

Nora: An untruth—?

Helmer: Didn't you say that no one had been here? (*Wagging his*
830 *finger.*) My little songbird must never do that again. A songbird
needs a clean beak to warble with. No false notes. (*Putting his arm
about her waist.*) That's the way it should be, isn't it? Yes, I'm sure
of it. (*Releasing her.*) And so, enough of that. (*Sitting by the stove.*)
Ah, how snug and cozy it is here. (*Leafing among his papers.*)

Nora: (*busy with the tree, after a short pause*) Torvald!

Helmer: Yes.

Nora: I'm so much looking forward to the Stenborgs' costume party,
day after tomorrow.

Helmer: And I can't wait to see what you'll surprise me with.

840 **Nora:** Oh, that stupid business!

Helmer: What?

Nora: I can't find anything that's right. Everything seems so
ridiculous, so inane.

Helmer: So my little Nora's come to *that* recognition?

Nora: (*going behind his chair, her arms resting on its back*) Are you very busy, Torvald?

Helmer: Oh—

Nora: What papers are those?

Helmer: Bank matters.

850 *Nora:* Already?

Helmer: I've gotten full authority from the retiring management to make all necessary changes in personnel and procedure. I'll need Christmas week for that. I want to have everything in order by New Year's.

Nora: So that was the reason this poor Krogstad—

Helmer: Hm.

Nora: (*still leaning on the chair and slowly stroking the nape of his neck*) If you weren't so very busy, I would have asked you an enormous favor, Torvald.

860 *Helmer:* Let's hear. What is it?

Nora: You know, there isn't anyone who has your good taste—and I want so much to look well at the costume party. Torvald, couldn't you take over and decide what I should be and plan my costume?

Helmer: Ah, is my stubborn little creature calling for a lifeguard?

Nora: Yes, Torvald, I can't get anywhere without your help.

Helmer: All right—I'll think it over. We'll hit on something.

Nora: Oh, how sweet of you. (*Goes to the tree again. Pause.*) Aren't the red flowers pretty—? But tell me, was it really such a crime that this Krogstad committed?

870 *Helmer:* Forgery. Do you have any idea what that means?

Nora: Couldn't he have done it out of need?

Helmer: Yes, or thoughtlessness, like so many others. I'm not so heartless that I'd condemn a man categorically for just one mistake.

Nora: No, of course not, Torvald!

Helmer: Plenty of men have redeemed themselves by openly confessing their crimes and taking their punishment.

Nora: Punishment—?

Helmer: But now Krogstad didn't go that way. He got himself out by

880 sharp practices, and that's the real cause of his moral breakdown.

Nora: Do you really think that would—?

Helmer: Just imagine how a man with that sort of guilt in him has to lie and cheat and deceive on all sides, has to wear a mask even with the nearest and dearest he has, even with his own wife and children. And with the children, Nora—that's where it's most horrible.

Nora: Why?

Helmer: Because that kind of atmosphere of lies infects the whole life of a home. Every breath the children take in is filled with the

890 germs of something degenerate.

Nora: (*coming closer behind him*) Are you sure of that?

Helmer: Oh, I've seen it often enough as a lawyer. Almost everyone who goes bad early in life has a mother who's a chronic liar.

Nora: Why just—the mother?

Helmer: It's usually the mother's influence that's dominant, but the father's works in the same way, of course. Every lawyer is quite familiar with it. And still this Krogstad's been going home year in, year out, poisoning his own children with lies and pretense; that's why I call him morally lost. (*Reaching his hands out toward her.*) So
900   my sweet little Nora must promise me never to plead his cause. Your hand on it. Come, come, what's this? Give me your hand. There, now. All settled. I can tell you it'd be impossible for me to work alongside of him. I literally feel physically revolted when I'm anywhere near such a person.

Nora: (*withdraws her hand and goes to the other side of the Christmas tree*) How hot it is here! And I've got so much to do.

Helmer: (*getting up and gathering his papers*) Yes, and I have to think about getting some of these read through before dinner. I'll think about your costume, too. And something to hang on the tree in
910   gilt paper, I may even see about that. (*Putting his hand on her head.*) Oh you, my darling little songbird. (*He goes into his study and closes the door after him.*)

Nora: (*softly, after a silence*) Oh, really! It isn't so. It's impossible. It must be impossible.

Anne-Marie: (*in the doorway, left*) The children are begging so hard to come in to Mama.

Nora: No, no, no, don't let them in to me! You stay with them, Anne-Marie.

Anne-Marie: Of course, ma'am. (*Closes the door.*)

920 **Nora:** (*pale with terror*) Hurt my children—! Poison my home? (*A moment's pause; then she tosses her head.*) That's not true. Never. Never in all the world.

Act II

Same room. Beside the piano the Christmas tree now stands stripped of ornaments, burned-down candle stubs on its ragged branches. Nora's street clothes lie on the sofa. Nora, alone in the room, moves restlessly about; at last she stops at the sofa and picks up her coat.

Nora: (*dropping the coat again*) Someone's coming! (*Goes toward the door, listens.*) No—there's no one. Of course—nobody's coming today, Christmas Day—or tomorrow, either. But maybe—(*Opens the door and looks out.*) No, nothing in the mailbox. Quite empty. (*Coming forward.*) What nonsense! He won't do anything serious. Nothing terrible could happen. It's impossible. Why, I have three small children.

Anne-Marie, with a large carton, comes in from the room to the left.

Anne-Marie: Well, at last I found the box with the masquerade clothes.

Nora: Thanks. Put it on the table.

10 **Anne-Marie:** (*does so*) But they're all pretty much of a mess.

Nora: Ahh! I'd love to rip them in a million pieces!

Anne-Marie: Oh, mercy, they can be fixed right up. Just a little patience.

Nora: Yes, I'll go get Mrs. Linde to help me.

Anne-Marie: Out again now? In this nasty weather? Miss Nora will catch cold—get sick.

Nora: Oh, worse things could happen—How are the children?

Anne-Marie: The poor mites are playing with their Christmas presents, but—

20 **Nora:** Do they ask for me much?

Anne-Marie: They're so used to having Mama around, you know.

Nora: Yes. But Anne-Marie, I *can't* be together with them as much as I was.

Anne-Marie: Well, small children get used to anything.

Nora: You think so? Do you think they'd forget their mother if she was gone for good?

Anne-Marie: Oh, mercy—gone for good!

Nora: Wait, tell me, Anne-Marie—I've wondered so often—how could you ever have the heart to give your child over to strangers?

30 **Anne-Marie:** But I had to, you know, to become little Nora's nurse.

Nora: Yes, but how could you *do* it?

Anne-Marie: When I could get such a good place? A girl who's poor and who's gotten in trouble is glad enough for that. Because that slippery fish, he didn't do a thing for me, you know.

Nora: But your daughter's surely forgotten you.

Anne-Marie: Oh, she certainly has not. She's written to me, both when she was confirmed and when she was married.

Nora: (*clasping her about the neck*) You old Anne-Marie, you were a good mother for me when I was little.

40 **Anne-Marie:** Poor little Nora, with no other mother but me.

Nora: And if the babies didn't have one, then I know that you'd—What silly talk! (*Opening the carton.*) Go in to them. Now I'll have to—Tomorrow you can see how lovely I'll look.

Anne-Marie: Oh, there won't be anyone at the party as lovely as Miss Nora. (*She goes off into the room, left.*)

Nora: (*begins unpacking the box, but soon throws it aside*) Oh, if I dared to go out. If only nobody would come. If only nothing would happen here while I'm out. What craziness—nobody's coming. Just don't think. This muff—needs a brushing. Beautiful gloves, beautiful

50 gloves. Let it go. Let it go! One, two, three, four, five, six—(*With a cry.*) Oh, there they are! (*Poises to move toward the door, but remains*

irresolutely standing. Mrs. Linde enters from the hall, where she has removed her street clothes.)

Nora: Oh, it's you, Kristine. There's no one else out there? How good that you've come.

Mrs. Linde: I hear you were up asking for me.

Nora: Yes, I just stopped by. There's something you really can help me with. Let's get settled on the sofa. Look, there's going to be a costume party tomorrow evening at the Stenborgs' right above us, and now Torvald wants me to go as a Neapolitan peasant girl and dance the tarantella that I learned in Capri.

Mrs. Linde: Really, are you giving a whole performance?

Nora: Torvald says yes, I should. See, here's the dress. Torvald had it made for me down there; but now it's all so tattered that I just don't know—

Mrs. Linde: Oh, we'll fix that up in no time. It's nothing more than the trimmings—they're a bit loose here and there. Needle and thread? Good, now we have what we need.

Nora: Oh, how sweet of you!

Mrs. Linde: (*sewing*) So you'll be in disguise tomorrow, Nora. You know what? I'll stop by then for a moment and have a look at you all dressed up. But listen, I've absolutely forgotten to thank you for that pleasant evening yesterday.

Nora: (*getting up and walking about*) I don't think it was as pleasant as usual yesterday. You should have come to town a bit sooner, Kristine—Yes, Torvald really knows how to give a home elegance and charm.

Mrs. Linde: And you do, too, if you ask me. You're not your father's daughter for nothing. But tell me, is Dr. Rank always so down in the mouth as yesterday?

Nora: No, that was quite an exception. But he goes around critically ill all the time—tuberculosis of the spine, poor man. You know, his father was a disgusting thing who kept mistresses and so on—and that's why the son's been sickly from birth.

Mrs. Linde: (*lets her sewing fall to her lap*) But my dearest Nora, how do you know about such things?

Nora: (*walking more jauntily*) Hmp! When you've had three children, then you've had a few visits from—from women who know something of medicine, and they tell you this and that.

Mrs. Linde: (*resumes sewing; a short pause*) Does Dr. Rank come here every day?

Nora: Every blessed day. He's Torvald's best friend from childhood, and *my* good friend, too. Dr. Rank almost belongs to this house.

Mrs. Linde: But tell me—is he quite sincere? I mean, doesn't he rather enjoy flattering people?

Nora: Just the opposite. Why do you think that?

Mrs. Linde: When you introduced us yesterday, he was proclaiming that he'd often heard my name in this house; but later I noticed

that your husband hadn't the slightest idea who I really was. So
100   how could Dr. Rank—?

Nora: But it's all true, Kristine. You see, Torvald loves me beyond
words, and, as he puts it, he'd like to keep me all to himself. For a
long time he'd almost be jealous if I even mentioned any of my old
friends back home. So of course I dropped that. But with Dr. Rank
I talk a lot about such things, because he likes hearing about them.

Mrs. Linde: Now listen, Nora; in many ways you're still like a child. I'm
a good deal older than you, with a little more experience. I'll tell
you something: you ought to put an end to all this with Dr. Rank.

Nora: What should I put an end to?

110 *Mrs. Linde:* Both parts of it, I think. Yesterday you said something
about a rich admirer who'd provide you with money—

Nora: Yes, one who doesn't exist—worse luck. So?

Mrs. Linde: Is Dr. Rank well off?

Nora: Yes, he is.

Mrs. Linde: With no dependents?

Nora: No, no one. But—

Mrs. Linde: And he's over here every day?

Nora: Yes, I told you that.

Mrs. Linde: How can a man of such refinement be so grasping?

120 *Nora:* I don't follow you at all.

Mrs. Linde: Now don't try to hide it, Nora. You think I can't guess
who loaned you the forty-eight hundred crowns?

Nora: Are you out of your mind? How could you think such a thing!
A friend of ours, who comes here every single day. What an
intolerable situation that would have been!

Mrs. Linde: Then it really wasn't him.

Nora: No, absolutely not. It never even crossed my mind for a
moment—And he had nothing to lend in those days; his
inheritance came later.

130 *Mrs. Linde:* Well, I think that was a stroke of luck for you, Nora dear.

Nora: No, it never would have occurred to me to ask Dr. Rank—Still,
I'm quite sure that if I had asked him—

Mrs. Linde: Which you won't, of course.

Nora: No, of course not. I can't see that I'd ever need to. But I'm quite
positive that if I talked to Dr. Rank—

Mrs. Linde: Behind your husband's back?

Nora: I've got to clear up this other thing; *that's* also behind his back.
I've *got* to clear it all up.

Mrs. Linde: Yes, I was saying that yesterday, but—

140 *Nora:* (*pacing up and down*) A man handles these problems so much
better than a woman—

Mrs. Linde: One's husband does, yes.

Nora: Nonsense. (*Stopping.*) When you pay everything you owe, then
you get your note back, right?

Mrs. Linde: Yes, naturally.

Nora: And can rip it into a million pieces and burn it up—that filthy scrap of paper!

Mrs. Linde: (*looking hard at her, laying her sewing aside, and rising slowly*) Nora, you're hiding something from me.

150 *Nora:* You can see it in my face?

Mrs. Linde: Something's happened to you since yesterday morning. Nora, what is it?

Nora: (*hurrying toward her*) Kristine! (*Listening.*) Shh! Torvald's home. Look, go in with the children a while. Torvald can't bear all this snipping and stitching. Let Anne-Marie help you.

Mrs. Linde: (*gathering up some of the things*) All right, but I'm not leaving here until we've talked this out. (*She disappears into the room, left, as Torvald enters from the hall.*)

Nora: Oh, how I've been waiting for you, Torvald dear.

160 *Helmer:* Was that the dressmaker?

Nora: No, that was Kristine. She's helping me fix up my costume. You know, it's going to be quite attractive.

Helmer: Yes, wasn't that a bright idea I had?

Nora: Brilliant! But then wasn't I good as well to give in to you?

Helmer: Good—because you give in to your husband's judgment? All right, you little goose, I know you didn't mean it like that. But I won't disturb you. You'll want to have a fitting, I suppose.

Nora: And you'll be working?

Helmer: Yes. (*Indicating a bundle of papers.*) See. I've been down to the

170   bank. (*Starts toward his study.*)

Nora: Torvald.

Helmer: (*stops*) Yes.

Nora: If your little squirrel begged you, with all her heart and soul, for something—?

Helmer: What's that?

Nora: Then would you do it?

Helmer: First, naturally, I'd have to know what it was.

Nora: Your squirrel would scamper about and do tricks, if you'd only be sweet and give in.

180 *Helmer:* Out with it.

Nora: Your lark would be singing high and low in every room—

Helmer: Come on, she does that anyway.

Nora: I'd be a wood nymph and dance for you in the moonlight.

Helmer: Nora—don't tell me it's that same business from this morning?

Nora: (*coming closer*) Yes, Torvald, I beg you, please!

Helmer: And you actually have the nerve to drag that up again?

Nora: Yes, yes, you've got to give in to me; you *have* to let Krogstad keep his job in the bank.

190 *Helmer:* My dear Nora, I've slated his job for Mrs. Linde.

Nora: That's awfully kind of you. But you could just fire another clerk instead of Krogstad.

Helmer: This is the most incredible stubbornness! Because you go and give an impulsive promise to speak up for him, I'm expected to—

Nora: That's not the reason, Torvald. It's for your own sake. That man does writing for the worst papers; you said it yourself. He could do you any amount of harm. I'm scared to death of him—

Helmer: Ah, I understand. It's the old memories haunting you.

Nora: What do you mean by that?

200 *Helmer:* Of course, you're thinking about your father.

Nora: Yes, all right. Just remember how those nasty gossips wrote in the papers about Papa and slandered him so cruelly. I think they'd have had him dismissed if the department hadn't sent you up to investigate, and if you hadn't been so kind and open-minded toward him.

Helmer: My dear Nora, there's a notable difference between your father and me. Your father's official career was hardly above reproach. But mine is; and I hope it'll stay that way as long as I hold my position.

210 *Nora:* Oh, who can ever tell what vicious minds can invent? We could be so snug and happy now in our quiet, carefree home—you and I and the children, Torvald! That's why I'm pleading with you so—

Helmer: And just by pleading for him you make it impossible for me to keep him on. It's already known at the bank that I'm firing Krogstad. What if it's rumored around now that the new bank manager was vetoed by his wife—

Nora: Yes, what then—?

Helmer: Oh yes—as long as our little bundle of stubbornness gets her way—! I should go and make myself ridiculous in front of the

220 whole office—give people the idea I can be swayed by all kinds of outside pressure. Oh, you can bet I'd feel the effects of that soon enough! Besides—there's something that rules Krogstad right out at the bank as long as I'm the manager.

Nora: What's that?

Helmer: His moral failings I could maybe overlook if I had to—

Nora: Yes, Torvald, why not?

Helmer: And I hear he's quite efficient on the job. But he was a crony of mine back in my teens—one of those rash friendships that crop up again and again to embarrass you later in life. Well, I might as

230 well say it straight out: we're on a first-name basis. And that tactless fool makes no effort at all to hide it in front of others. Quite the contrary—he thinks that entitles him to take a familiar air around me, and so every other second he comes booming out with his "Yes, Torvald!" and "Sure thing, Torvald!" I tell you, it's been excruciating for me. He's out to make my place in the bank unbearable.

Nora: Torvald, you can't be serious about all this.

Helmer: Oh no? Why not?

Nora: Because these are such petty considerations.

240 *Helmer:* What are you saying? Petty? You think I'm petty!

Nora: No, just the opposite, Torvald dear. That's exactly why—

Helmer: Never mind. You call my motives petty; then I might as well be just that. Petty! All right! We'll put a stop to this for good. (*Goes to the hall door and calls.*) Helene!

Nora: What do you want?

Helmer: (*searching among his papers*) A decision. (*The Maid comes in.*) Look here; take this letter; go out with it at once. Get hold of a messenger and have him deliver it. Quick now. It's already addressed. Wait, here's some money.

250 *Maid:* Yes, sir. (*She leaves with the letter.*)

Helmer: (*straightening his papers*) There, now, little Miss Willful.

Nora: (*breathlessly*) Torvald, what was that letter?

Helmer: Krogstad's notice.

Nora: Call it back, Torvald! There's still time. Oh, Torvald, call it back! Do it for my sake—for your sake, for the children's sake! Do you hear, Torvald; do it! You don't know how this can harm us.

Helmer: Too late.

Nora: Yes, too late.

Helmer: Nora dear, I can forgive you this panic, even though basically
260   you're insulting me. Yes, you are! Or isn't it an insult to think that *I* should be afraid of a courtroom hack's revenge? But I forgive you anyway, because this shows so beautifully how much you love me. (*Takes her in his arms.*) This is the way it should be, my darling Nora. Whatever comes, you'll see: when it really counts, I have strength and courage enough as a man to take on the whole weight myself.

Nora: (*terrified*) What do you mean by that?

Helmer: The whole weight, I said.

Nora: (*resolutely*) No, never in all the world.

Helmer: Good. So we'll share it, Nora, as man and wife. That's as it
270   should be. (*Fondling her.*) Are you happy now? There, there, there—not these frightened dove's eyes. It's nothing at all but empty fantasies—Now you should run through your tarantella and practice your tambourine. I'll go to the inner office and shut both doors, so I won't hear a thing; you can make all the noise you like. (*Turning in the doorway.*) And when Rank comes, just tell him where he can find me. (*He nods to her and goes with his papers into the study, closing the door.*)

Nora: (*standing as though rooted, dazed with fright, in a whisper*) He really could do it. He will do it. He'll do it in spite of everything.
280   No, not that, never, never! Anything but that! Escape! A way out—(*The doorbell rings.*) Dr. Rank! Anything but that! *Anything,* whatever it is! (*Her hands pass over her face, smoothing it; she pulls herself together, goes over and opens the hall door. Dr. Rank stands outside, hanging his fur coat up. During the following scene, it begins getting dark.*)

Nora: Hello, Dr. Rank. I recognized your ring. But you mustn't go in to Torvald yet; I believe he's working.

Rank: And you?

Nora: For you, I always have an hour to spare—you know that. (*He has
entered, and she shuts the door after him.*)

Rank: Many thanks. I'll make use of these hours while I can.

Nora: What do you mean by that? While you can?

Rank: Does that disturb you?

Nora: Well, it's such an odd phrase. Is anything going to happen?

Rank: What's going to happen is what I've been expecting so
long—but I honestly didn't think it would come so soon.

Nora: (*gripping his arm*) What is it you've found out? Dr. Rank, you
have to tell me!

Rank: (*sitting by the stove*) It's all over with me. There's nothing to be
done about it.

Nora: (*breathing easier*) Is it you—then—?

Rank: Who else? There's no point in lying to one's self. I'm the most
miserable of all my patients, Mrs. Helmer. These past few days
I've been auditing my internal accounts. Bankrupt! Within a month
I'll probably be laid out and rotting in the churchyard.

Nora: Oh, what a horrible thing to say.

Rank: The thing itself is horrible. But the worst of it is all the other
horror before it's over. There's only one final examination left; when
I'm finished with that, I'll know about when my disintegration will
begin. There's something I want to say. Helmer with his sensitivity
has such a sharp distaste for anything ugly. I don't want him near
my sickroom.

Nora: Oh, but Dr. Rank—

Rank: I won't have him in there. Under no condition. I'll lock my door
to him—As soon as I'm completely sure of the worst, I'll send you
my calling card marked with a black cross, and you'll know then
the wreck has started to come apart.

Nora: No, today you're completely unreasonable. And I wanted you so
much to be in a really good humor.

Rank: With death up my sleeve? And then to suffer this way for
somebody else's sins. Is there any justice in that? And in every
single family, in some way or another, this inevitable retribution of
nature goes on—

Nora: (*her hands pressed over her ears*) Oh, stuff! Cheer up! Please—be
gay!

Rank: Yes, I'd just as soon laugh at it all. My poor, innocent spine,
serving time for my father's gay army days.

Nora: (*by the table, left*) He was so infatuated with asparagus tips and
pâté de foie gras, wasn't that it?

Rank: Yes—and with truffles.

Nora: Truffles, yes. And then with oysters, I suppose?

Rank: Yes, tons of oysters, naturally.

Nora: And then the port and champagne to go with it. It's so sad that
all these delectable things have to strike at our bones.

Rank: Especially when they strike at the unhappy bones that never shared in the fun.

Nora: Ah, that's the saddest of all.

Rank: (*looks searchingly at her*) Hm.

Nora: (*after a moment*) Why did you smile?

340 *Rank:* No, it was you who laughed.

Nora: No, it was you who smiled, Dr. Rank!

Rank: (*getting up*) You're even a bigger tease than I'd thought.

Nora: I'm full of wild ideas today.

Rank: That's obvious.

Nora: (*putting both hands on his shoulders*) Dear, dear Dr. Rank, you'll never die for Torvald and me.

Rank: Oh, that loss you'll easily get over. Those who go away are soon forgotten.

Nora: (*looks fearfully at him*) You believe that?

350 *Rank:* One makes new connections, and then—

Nora: Who makes new connections?

Rank: Both you and Torvald will when I'm gone. I'd say you're well under way already. What was that Mrs. Linde doing here last evening?

Nora: Oh, come—you can't be jealous of poor Kristine?

Rank: Oh yes, I am. She'll be my successor here in the house. When I'm down under, that woman will probably—

Nora: Shh! Not so loud. She's right in there.

Rank: Today as well. So you see.

360 *Nora:* Only to sew on my dress. Good gracious, how unreasonable you are. (*Sitting on the sofa.*) Be nice now, Dr. Rank. Tomorrow you'll see how beautifully I'll dance; and you can imagine then that I'm dancing only for you—yes, and of course for Torvald, too—that's understood. (*Takes various items out of the carton.*) Dr. Rank, sit over here and I'll show you something.

Rank: (*sitting*) What's that?

Nora: Look here. Look.

Rank: Silk stockings.

Nora: Flesh-colored. Aren't they lovely? Now it's so dark here, but
370   tomorrow—No, no, no, just look at the feet. Oh well, you might as well look at the rest.

Rank: Hm—

Nora: Why do you look so critical? Don't you believe they'll fit?

Rank: I've never had any chance to form an opinion on that.

Nora: (*glancing at him a moment*) Shame on you. (*Hits him lightly on the ear with the stockings.*) That's for you. (*Puts them away again.*)

Rank: And what other splendors am I going to see now?

Nora: Not the least bit more, because you've been naughty. (*She hums a little and rummages among her things.*)

380 *Rank:* (*after a short silence*) When I sit here together with you like this, completely easy and open, then I don't know—I simply can't

imagine—whatever would have become of me if I'd never come into this house.

Nora: (*smiling*) Yes, I really think you feel completely at ease with us.

Rank: (*more quietly, staring straight ahead*) And then to have to go away from it all—

Nora: Nonsense, you're not going away.

Rank: (*his voice unchanged*)—and not even be able to leave some poor show of gratitude behind, scarcely a fleeting regret—no more than

390   a vacant place that anyone can fill.

Nora: And if I asked you now for—? No—

Rank: For what?

Nora: For a great proof of your friendship—

Rank: Yes, yes?

Nora: No, I mean—for an exceptionally big favor—

Rank: Would you really, for once, make me so happy?

Nora: Oh, you haven't the vaguest idea what it is.

Rank: All right, then tell me.

Nora: No, but I can't, Dr. Rank—it's all out of reason. It's advice and

400   help, too—and a favor—

Rank: So much the better. I can't fathom what you're hinting at. Just speak out. Don't you trust me?

Nora: Of course. More than anyone else. You're my best and truest friend, I'm sure. That's why I want to talk to you. All right, then, Dr. Rank: there's something you can help me prevent. You know how deeply, how inexpressibly dearly Torvald loves me; he'd never hesitate a second to give up his life for me.

Rank: (*leaning close to her*) Nora—do you think he's the only one—

Nora: (*with a slight start*) Who—?

410 *Rank:* Who'd gladly give up his life for you.

Nora: (*heavily*) I see.

Rank: I swore to myself you should know this before I'm gone. I'll never find a better chance. Yes, Nora, now you know. And also you know now that you can trust me beyond anyone else.

Nora: (*rising, natural and calm*) Let me by.

Rank: (*making room for her, but still sitting*) Nora—

Nora: (*in the hall doorway*) Helene, bring the lamp in. (*Goes over to the stove.*) Ah, dear Dr. Rank, that was really mean of you.

Rank: (*getting up*) That I've loved you just as deeply as somebody else?

420   Was *that* mean?

Nora: No, but that you came out and told me. That was quite unnecessary—

Rank: What do you mean? Have you known—?

The Maid comes in with the lamp, sets it on the table, and goes out again.

Rank: Nora—Mrs. Helmer—I'm asking you: have you known about it?

Nora: Oh, how can I tell what I know or don't know? Really, I don't know what to say—Why did you have to be so clumsy, Dr. Rank! Everything was so good.

Rank: Well, in any case, you now have the knowledge that my body and soul are at your command. So won't you speak out?

430 *Nora:* (*looking at him*) After that?

Rank: Please, just let me know what it is.

Nora: You can't know anything now.

Rank: I have to. You mustn't punish me like this. Give me the chance to do whatever is humanly possible for you.

Nora: Now there's nothing you can do for me. Besides, actually, I don't need any help. You'll see—it's only my fantasies. That's what it is. Of course! (*Sits in the rocker, looks at him, and smiles.*) What a nice one you are, Dr. Rank. Aren't you a little bit ashamed, now that the lamp is here?

440 *Rank:* No, not exactly. But perhaps I'd better go—for good?

Nora: No, you certainly can't do that. You must come here just as you always have. You know Torvald can't do without you.

Rank: Yes, but *you?*

Nora: You know how much I enjoy it when you're here.

Rank: That's precisely what threw me off. You're a mystery to me. So many times I've felt you'd almost rather be with me than with Helmer.

Nora: Yes—you see, there are some people that one loves most and other people that one would almost prefer being with.

450 *Rank:* Yes, there's something to that.

Nora: When I was back home, of course I loved Papa most. But I always thought it was so much fun when I could sneak down to the maids' quarters, because they never tried to improve me, and it was always so amusing, the way they talked to each other.

Rank: Aha, so it's *their* place that I've filled.

Nora: (*jumping up and going to him*) Oh, dear, sweet Dr. Rank, that's not what I mean at all. But you can understand that with Torvald it's just the same as with Papa—

The Maid enters from the hall.

Maid: Ma'am—please! (*She whispers to Nora and hands her a calling card.*)

460 *Nora:* (*glancing at the card*) Ah! (*Slips it into her pocket.*)

Rank: Anything wrong?

Nora: No, no, not at all. It's only some—it's my new dress—

Rank: Really? But—there's your dress.

Nora: Oh, that. But this is another one—I ordered it—Torvald mustn't know—

Rank: Ah, now we have the big secret.

Nora: That's right. Just go in with him—he's back in the inner study. Keep him there as long as—

Rank: Don't worry. He won't get away. (*Goes into the study.*)

470 *Nora:* (*to the Maid*) And he's standing waiting in the kitchen?

Maid: Yes, he came up by the back stairs.

Nora: But didn't you tell him somebody was here?

Maid: Yes, but that didn't do any good.

Nora: He won't leave?

Maid: No, he won't go till he's talked with you, ma'am.

Nora: Let him come in, then—but quietly. Helene, don't breathe a word about this. It's a surprise for my husband.

Maid: Yes, yes, I understand—(*Goes out.*)

Nora: This horror—it's going to happen. No, no, no, it can't happen,
480　　it mustn't. (*She goes and bolts Helmer's door. The Maid opens the hall door for Krogstad and shuts it behind him. He is dressed for travel in a fur coat, boots, and a fur cap.*)

Nora: (*going toward him*) Talk softly. My husband's home.

Krogstad: Well, good for him.

Nora: What do you want?

Krogstad: Some information.

Nora: Hurry up, then. What is it?

Krogstad: You know, of course, that I got my notice.

Nora: I couldn't prevent it, Mr. Krogstad. I fought for you to the bitter
490　　end, but nothing worked.

Krogstad: Does your husband's love for you run so thin? He knows everything I can expose you to, and all the same he dares to—

Nora: How can you imagine he knows anything about this?

Krogstad: Ah, no—I can't imagine it either, now. It's not at all like my fine Torvald Helmer to have so much guts—

Nora: Mr. Krogstad, I demand respect for my husband!

Krogstad: Why, of course—all due respect. But since the lady's keeping it so carefully hidden, may I presume to ask if you're also a bit better informed than yesterday about what you've actually done?

500　*Nora:* More than you ever could teach me.

Krogstad: Yes, I *am* such an awful lawyer.

Nora: What is it you want from me?

Krogstad: Just a glimpse of how you are, Mrs. Helmer. I've been thinking about you all day long. A cashier, a night-court scribbler, a—well, a type like me also has a little of what they call a heart, you know.

Nora: Then show it. Think of my children.

Krogstad: Did you or your husband ever think of mine? But never mind. I simply wanted to tell you that you don't need to take this
510　　thing too seriously. For the present, I'm not proceeding with any action.

Nora: Oh no, really! Well—I knew that.

Krogstad: Everything can be settled in a friendly spirit. It doesn't have to get around town at all; it can stay just among us three.

Nora: My husband must never know anything of this.

Krogstad: How can you manage that? Perhaps you can pay me the balance?

Nora: No, not right now.

Krogstad: Or you know some way of raising the money in a day or
520   two?

Nora: No way that I'm willing to use.

Krogstad: Well, it wouldn't have done you any good, anyway. If you
stood in front of me with a fistful of bills, you still couldn't buy
your signature back.

Nora: Then tell me what you're going to do with it.

Krogstad: I'll just hold onto it—keep it on file. There's no outsider
who'll even get wind of it. So if you've been thinking of taking
some desperate step—

Nora: I have.

530 *Krogstad:* Been thinking of running away from home—

Nora: I have!

Krogstad: Or even of something worse—

Nora: How could you guess that?

Krogstad: You can drop those thoughts.

Nora: How could you guess I was thinking of *that?*

Krogstad: Most of us think about *that* at first. I thought about it too,
but I discovered I hadn't the courage—

Nora: (*lifelessly*) I don't either.

Krogstad: (*relieved*) That's true, you haven't the courage? You too?

540 *Nora:* I don't have it—I don't have it.

Krogstad: It would be terribly stupid, anyway. After that first storm at
home blows out, why, then—I have here in my pocket a letter for
your husband—

Nora: Telling everything?

Krogstad: As charitably as possible.

Nora: (*quickly*) He mustn't ever get that letter. Tear it up. I'll find
some way to get money.

Krogstad: Beg pardon, Mrs. Helmer, but I think I just told you—

Nora: Oh, I don't mean the money I owe you. Let me know how much
550   you want from my husband, and I'll manage it.

Krogstad: I don't want any money from your husband.

Nora: What do you want, then?

Krogstad: I'll tell you what. I want to recoup, Mrs. Helmer; I want to get
on in the world—and there's where your husband can help me. For a
year and a half I've kept myself clean of anything disreputable—all
that time struggling with the worst conditions; but I was satisfied,
working my way up step by step. Now I've been written right off,
and I'm just not in the mood to come crawling back. I tell you, I want
to move on. I want to get back in the bank—in a better position. Your
560   husband can set up a job for me—

Nora: He'll never do that!

Krogstad: He'll do it. I know him. He won't dare breathe a word of
protest. And once I'm in there together with him, you just wait
and see! Inside of a year, I'll be the manager's right-hand man.
It'll be Nils Krogstad, not Torvald Helmer, who runs the bank.

Nora: You'll never see the day!

Krogstad: Maybe you think you can—

Nora: I have the courage now—for *that.*

Krogstad: Oh, you don't scare me. A smart, spoiled lady like you—

570 *Nora:* You'll see; you'll see!

Krogstad: Under the ice, maybe? Down in the freezing, coal-black water? There, till you float up in the spring, ugly, unrecognizable, with your hair falling out—

Nora: You don't frighten me.

Krogstad: Nor do you frighten me. One doesn't do these things, Mrs. Helmer. Besides, what good would it be? I'd still have him safe in my pocket.

Nora: Afterwards? When I'm no longer—?

Krogstad: Are you forgetting that *I'll* be in control then over your final
580 reputation? (*Nora stands speechless, staring at him.*) Good; now I've warned you. Don't do anything stupid. When Helmer's read my letter, I'll be waiting for his reply. And bear in mind that it's your husband himself who's forced me back to my old ways. I'll never forgive him for that. Good-bye, Mrs. Helmer. (*He goes out through the hall.*)

Nora: (*goes to the hall door, opens it a crack, and listens*) He's gone. Didn't leave the letter. Oh no, no, that's impossible too! (*Opening the door more and more.*) What's that? He's standing outside—not going downstairs. He's thinking it over? Maybe he'll—? (*A letter falls in*
590 *the mailbox; then Krogstad's footsteps are heard, dying away down a flight of stairs. Nora gives a muffled cry and runs over toward the sofa table. A short pause.*) In the mailbox. (*Slips warily over to the hall door.*) It's lying there. Torvald, Torvald—now we're lost!

Mrs. Linde: (*entering with the costume from the room, left*) There now, I can't see anything else to mend. Perhaps you'd like to try—

Nora: (*in a hoarse whisper*) Kristine, come here.

Mrs. Linde: (*tossing the dress on the sofa*) What's wrong? You look upset.

Nora: Come here. See that letter? *There!* Look—through the glass in the mailbox.

600 *Mrs. Linde:* Yes, yes, I see it.

Nora: That letter's from Krogstad—

Mrs. Linde: Nora—it's Krogstad who loaned you the money!

Nora: Yes, and now Torvald will find out everything.

Mrs. Linde: Believe me, Nora, it's best for both of you.

Nora: There's more you don't know. I forged a name.

Mrs. Linde: But for heaven's sake—?

Nora: I only want to tell you that, Kristine, so that you can be my witness.

Mrs. Linde: Witness? Why should I—?

610 *Nora:* If I should go out of my mind—it could easily happen—

Mrs. Linde: Nora!

Nora: Or anything else occurred—so I couldn't be present here—

Mrs. Linde: Nora, Nora, you aren't yourself at all!

Nora: And someone should try to take on the whole weight, all of the guilt, you follow me—

Mrs. Linde: Yes, of course, but why do you think—?

Nora: Then you're the witness that it isn't true, Kristine. I'm very much myself; my mind right now is perfectly clear; and I'm telling you: nobody else has known about this; I alone did everything.

620   Remember that.

Mrs. Linde: I will. But I don't understand all this.

Nora: Oh, how could you ever understand it? It's the miracle now that's going to take place.

Mrs. Linde: The miracle?

Nora: Yes, the miracle. But it's so awful, Kristine. It mustn't take place, not for anything in the world.

Mrs. Linde: I'm going right over and talk with Krogstad.

Nora: Don't go near him; he'll do you some terrible harm!

Mrs. Linde: There was a time once when he'd gladly have done

630   anything for me.

Nora: He?

Mrs. Linde: Where does he live?

Nora: Oh, how do I know? Yes. (*Searches in her pocket.*) Here's his card. But the letter, the letter—!

Helmer: (*from the study, knocking on the door*) Nora!

Nora: (*with a cry of fear*) Oh! What is it? What do you want?

Helmer: Now, now, don't be so frightened. We're not coming in. You locked the door—are you trying on the dress?

Nora: Yes, I'm trying it. I'll look just beautiful, Torvald.

640 *Mrs. Linde:* (*who has read the card*) He's living right around the corner.

Nora: Yes, but what's the use? We're lost. The letter's in the box.

Mrs. Linde: And your husband has the key?

Nora: Yes, always.

Mrs. Linde: Krogstad can ask for his letter back unread; he can find some excuse—

Nora: But it's just this time that Torvald usually—

Mrs. Linde: Stall him. Keep him in there. I'll be back as quick as I can. (*She hurries out through the hall entrance.*)

Nora: (*goes to Helmer's door, opens it, and peers in*) Torvald!

650 *Helmer:* (*from the inner study*) Well—does one dare set foot in one's own living room at last? Come on, Rank, now we'll get a look—(*In the doorway.*) But what's this?

Nora: What, Torvald dear?

Helmer: Rank had me expecting some grand masquerade.

Rank: (*in the doorway*) That was my impression, but I must have been wrong.

Nora: No one can admire me in my splendor—not till tomorrow.

Helmer: But Nora dear, you look so exhausted. Have you practiced too hard?

660 ***Nora:*** No, I haven't practiced at all yet.

Helmer: You know, it's necessary—

Nora: Oh, it's absolutely necessary, Torvald. But I can't get anywhere without your help. I've forgotten the whole thing completely.

Helmer: Ah, we'll soon take care of that.

Nora: Yes, take care of me, Torvald, please! Promise me that? Oh, I'm so nervous. That big party—You must give up everything this evening for me. No business—don't even touch your pen. Yes? Dear Torvald, promise?

Helmer: It's a promise. Tonight I'm totally at your service—you little

670 helpless thing. Hm—but first there's one thing I want to—(*Goes toward the hall door.*)

Nora: What are you looking for?

Helmer: Just to see if there's any mail.

Nora: No, no, don't do that, Torvald!

Helmer: Now what?

Nora: Torvald, please. There isn't any.

Helmer: Let me look, though. (*Starts out. Nora, at the piano, strikes the first notes of the tarantella. Helmer, at the door, stops.*) Aha!

Nora: I can't dance tomorrow if I don't practice with you.

680 ***Helmer:*** (*going over to her*) Nora dear, are you really so frightened?

Nora: Yes, so terribly frightened. Let me practice right now; there's still time before dinner. Oh, sit down and play for me, Torvald. Direct me. Teach me, the way you always have.

Helmer: Gladly, if it's what you want. (*Sits at the piano.*)

Nora: (*snatches the tambourine up from the box, then a long, varicolored shawl, which she throws around herself, whereupon she springs forward and cries out*) Play for me now! Now I'll dance!

Helmer plays and Nora dances. Rank stands behind Helmer at the piano and looks on.

Helmer: (*as he plays*) Slower. Slow down.

Nora: Can't change it.

690 ***Helmer:*** Not so violent, Nora!

Nora: Has to be just like this.

Helmer: (*stopping*) No, no, that won't do at all.

Nora: (*laughing and swinging her tambourine*) Isn't that what I told you?

Rank: Let me play for her.

Helmer: (*getting up*) Yes, go on. I can teach her more easily then.

Rank sits at the piano and plays; Nora dances more and more wildly. Helmer has stationed himself by the stove and repeatedly gives her directions; she seems not to hear them; her hair loosens and falls over her shoulders; she does not notice, but goes on dancing. Mrs. Linde enters.

Mrs. Linde: (*standing dumbfounded at the door*) Ah—!

Nora: (*still dancing*) See what fun, Kristine!

Helmer: But Nora darling, you dance as if your life were at stake.

Nora: And it is.

700 *Helmer:* Rank, stop! This is pure madness. Stop it, I say!

Rank breaks off playing, and Nora halts abruptly.

Helmer: (*going over to her*) I never would have believed it. You've forgotten everything I taught you.

Nora: (*throwing away the tambourine*) You see for yourself.

Helmer: Well, there's certainly room for instruction here.

Nora: Yes, you see how important it is. You've got to teach me to the very last minute. Promise me that, Torvald?

Helmer: You can bet on it.

Nora: You mustn't, either today or tomorrow, think about anything else but me; you mustn't open any letters—or the mailbox—

710 *Helmer:* Ah, it's still the fear of that man—

Nora: Oh yes, yes, that too.

Helmer: Nora, it's written all over you—there's already a letter from him out there.

Nora: I don't know. I guess so. But you mustn't read such things now; there mustn't be anything ugly between us before it's all over.

Rank: (*quietly to Helmer*) You shouldn't deny her.

Helmer: (*putting his arm around her*) The child can have her way. But tomorrow night, after you've danced—

Nora: Then you'll be free.

720 *Maid:* (*in the doorway, right*) Ma'am, dinner is served.

Nora: We'll be wanting champagne, Helene.

Maid: Very good, ma'am. (*Goes out.*)

Helmer: So—a regular banquet, hm?

Nora: Yes, a banquet—champagne till daybreak! (*Calling out.*) And some macaroons, Helene. Heaps of them—just this once.

Helmer: (*taking her hands*) Now, now, now—no hysterics. Be my own little lark again.

Nora: Oh, I will soon enough. But go on in—and you, Dr. Rank. Kristine, help me put up my hair.

730 *Rank:* (*whispering, as they go*) There's nothing wrong—really wrong, is there?

Helmer: Oh, of course not. It's nothing more than this childish anxiety I was telling you about. (*They go out, right.*)

Nora: Well?

Mrs. Linde: Left town.

Nora: I could see by your face.

Mrs. Linde: He'll be home tomorrow evening. I wrote him a note.

Nora: You shouldn't have. Don't try to stop anything now. After all, it's a wonderful joy, this waiting here for the miracle.

740 *Mrs. Linde:* What is it you're waiting for?

Nora: Oh, you can't understand that. Go in to them: I'll be along in a moment.

Mrs. Linde goes into the dining room. Nora stands a short while as if composing herself; then she looks at her watch.

Nora: Five. Seven hours to midnight. Twenty-four hours to the midnight after, and then the tarantella's done. Seven and twenty-four? Thirty-one hours to live.

Helmer: (*in the doorway, right*) What's become of the little lark?

Nora: (*going toward him with open arms*) Here's your lark!

Act III

Same scene. The table, with chairs around it, has been moved to the center of the room. A lamp on the table is lit. The hall door stands open. Dance music drifts down from the floor above. Mrs. Linde sits at the table, absently paging through a book, trying to read, but apparently unable to focus her thoughts. Once or twice she pauses, tensely listening for a sound at the outer entrance.

Mrs. Linde: (*glancing at her watch*) Not yet—and there's hardly any time left. If only he's not—(*Listening again.*) Ah, there he is. (*She goes out in the hall and cautiously opens the outer door. Quiet footsteps are heard on the stairs. She whispers:*) Come in. Nobody's here.

Krogstad: (*in the doorway*) I found a note from you at home. What's back of all this?

Mrs. Linde: I just *had* to talk to you.

Krogstad: Oh? And it just *had* to be here in this house?

Mrs. Linde: At my place it was impossible; my room hasn't a private
10 entrance. Come in; we're all alone. The maid's asleep, and the Helmers are at the dance upstairs.

Krogstad: (*entering the room*) Well, well, the Helmers are dancing tonight? Really?

Mrs. Linde: Yes, why not?

Krogstad: How true—why not?

Mrs. Linde: All right, Krogstad, let's talk.

Krogstad: Do we two have anything more to talk about?

Mrs. Linde: We have a great deal to talk about.

Krogstad: I wouldn't have thought so.

20 *Mrs. Linde:* No, because you've never understood me, really.

Krogstad: Was there anything more to understand—except what's all too common in life? A calculating woman throws over a man the moment a better catch comes by.

Mrs. Linde: You think I'm so thoroughly calculating? You think I broke it off lightly?

Krogstad: Didn't you?

Mrs. Linde: Nils—is that what you really thought?

Krogstad: If you cared, then why did you write me the way you did?

Mrs. Linde: What else could I do? If I had to break off with you, then
30 it was my job as well to root out everything you felt for me.

Krogstad: (*wringing his hands*) So that was it. And this—all this, simply for money!

Mrs. Linde: Don't forget I had a helpless mother and two small brothers. We couldn't wait for you, Nils; you had such a long road ahead of you then.

Krogstad: That may be; but you still hadn't the right to abandon me for somebody else's sake.

Mrs. Linde: Yes—I don't know. So many, many times I've asked myself if I did have that right.

40 *Krogstad:* (*more softly*) When I lost you, it was as if all the solid ground dissolved from under my feet. Look at me; I'm a half-drowned man now, hanging onto a wreck.

Mrs. Linde: Help may be near.

Krogstad: It was near—but then you came and blocked it off.

Mrs. Linde: Without my knowing it, Nils. Today for the first time I learned that it's you I'm replacing at the bank.

Krogstad: All right—I believe you. But now that you know, will you step aside?

Mrs. Linde: No, because that wouldn't benefit you in the slightest.

50 *Krogstad:* Not "benefit" me, hm! I'd step aside anyway.

Mrs. Linde: I've learned to be realistic. Life and hard, bitter necessity have taught me that.

Krogstad: And life's taught me never to trust fine phrases.

Mrs. Linde: Then life's taught you a very sound thing. But you do have to trust in actions, don't you?

Krogstad: What does that mean?

Mrs. Linde: You said you were hanging on like a half-drowned man to a wreck.

Krogstad: I've good reason to say that.

60 *Mrs. Linde:* I'm also like a half-drowned woman on a wreck. No one to suffer with; no one to care for.

Krogstad: You made your choice.

Mrs. Linde: There wasn't any choice then.

Krogstad: So—what of it?

Mrs. Linde: Nils, if only we two shipwrecked people could reach across to each other.

Krogstad: What are you saying?

Mrs. Linde: Two on one wreck are at least better off than each on his own.

70 *Krogstad:* Kristine!

Mrs. Linde: Why do you think I came into town?

Krogstad: Did you really have some thought of me?

Mrs. Linde: I have to work to go on living. All my born days, as long as I can remember, I've worked, and it's been my best and my only joy. But now I'm completely alone in the world; it frightens me to be so empty and lost. To work for yourself—there's no joy in that. Nils, give me something—someone to work for.

Krogstad: I don't believe all this. It's just some hysterical feminine urge to go out and make a noble sacrifice.

80 *Mrs. Linde:* Have you ever found me to be hysterical?

Krogstad: Can you honestly mean this? Tell me—do you know everything about my past?

Mrs. Linde: Yes.

Krogstad: And you know what they think I'm worth around here.

Mrs. Linde: From what you were saying before, it would seem that with me you could have been another person.

Krogstad: I'm positive of that.

Mrs. Linde: Couldn't it happen still?

Krogstad: Kristine—you're saying this in all seriousness? Yes, you are!
90 I can see it in you. And do you really have the courage, then—?

Mrs. Linde: I need to have someone to care for; and your children need a mother. We both need each other. Nils, I have faith that you're good at heart—I'll risk everything together with you.

Krogstad: (*gripping her hands*) Kristine, thank you, thank you—Now I know I can win back a place in their eyes. Yes—but I forgot—

Mrs. Linde: (*listening*) Shh! The tarantella. Go now! Go on!

Krogstad: Why? What is it?

Mrs. Linde: Hear the dance up there? When that's over, they'll be coming down.

100 *Krogstad:* Oh, then I'll go. But—it's all pointless. Of course, you don't know the move I made against the Helmers.

Mrs. Linde: Yes, Nils, I know.

Krogstad: And all the same, you have the courage to—?

Mrs. Linde: I know how far despair can drive a man like you.

Krogstad: Oh, if I only could take it all back.

Mrs. Linde: You easily could—your letter's still lying in the mailbox.

Krogstad: Are you sure of that?

Mrs. Linde: Positive. But—

Krogstad: (*looks at her searchingly*) Is that the meaning of it, then?
110 You'll save your friend at any price. Tell me straight out. Is that it?

Mrs. Linde: Nils—anyone who's sold herself for somebody else once isn't going to do it again.

Krogstad: I'll demand my letter back.

Mrs. Linde: No, no.

Krogstad: Yes, of course. I'll stay here till Helmer comes down; I'll tell him to give me my letter again—that it only involves my dismissal—that he shouldn't read it—

Mrs. Linde: No, Nils, don't call the letter back.

Krogstad: But wasn't that exactly why you wrote me to come here?

120 *Mrs. Linde:* Yes, in that first panic. But it's been a whole day and night since then, and in that time I've seen such incredible things in this house. Helmer's got to learn everything; this dreadful secret has to be aired; those two have to come to a full understanding; all these lies and evasions can't go on.

Krogstad: Well, then, if you want to chance it. But at least there's one
  thing I can do, and do right away—

Mrs. Linde: (*listening*) Go now, go, quick! The dance is over. We're not
  safe another second.

Krogstad: I'll wait for you downstairs.

130 *Mrs. Linde:* Yes, please do; take me home.

Krogstad: I can't believe it; I've never been so happy. (*He leaves by way
  of the outer door; the door between the room and the hall stays open.*)

Mrs. Linde: (*straightening up a bit and getting together her street clothes*)
  How different now! How different! Someone to work for, to live
  for—a home to build. Well, it is worth the try! Oh, if they'd only
  come! (*Listening.*) Ah, there they are. Bundle up. (*She picks up her
  hat and coat. Nora's and Helmer's voices can be heard outside; a key
  turns in the lock, and Helmer brings Nora into the hall almost by force.
  She is wearing the Italian costume with a large black shawl about her; he*
140 *has on evening dress, with a black domino open over it.*)

Nora: (*struggling in the doorway*) No, no, no, not inside! I'm going up
  again. I don't want to leave so soon.

Helmer: But Nora dear—

Nora: Oh, I beg you, please, Torvald. From the bottom of my heart,
  please—only an hour more!

Helmer: Not a single minute, Nora darling. You know our agreement.
  Come on, in we go; you'll catch cold out here. (*In spite of her
  resistance, he gently draws her into the room.*)

Mrs. Linde: Good evening.

150 *Nora:* Kristine!

Helmer: Why, Mrs. Linde—are you here so late?

Mrs. Linde: Yes, I'm sorry, but I did want to see Nora in costume.

Nora: Have you been sitting here, waiting for me?

Mrs. Linde: Yes. I didn't come early enough; you were all upstairs;
  and then I thought I really couldn't leave without seeing you.

Helmer: (*removing Nora's shawl*) Yes, take a good look. She's worth
  looking at, I can tell you that, Mrs. Linde. Isn't she lovely?

Mrs. Linde: Yes, I should say—

Helmer: A dream of loveliness, isn't she? That's what everyone thought
160 at the party, too. But she's horribly stubborn—this sweet little
  thing. What's to be done with her? Can you imagine, I almost had
  to use force to pry her away.

Nora: Oh, Torvald, you're going to regret you didn't indulge me, even
  for just a half hour more.

Helmer: There, you see. She danced her tarantella and got a tumultuous
  hand—which was well earned, although the performance may have
  been a bit too naturalistic—I mean it rather overstepped the
  proprieties of art. But never mind—what's important is, she made a
  success, an overwhelming success. You think I could let her stay on
170 after that and spoil the effect? Oh no; I took my lovely little Capri

girl—my capricious little Capri girl, I should say—took her under my arm; one quick tour of the ballroom, a curtsy to every side, and then—as they say in novels—the beautiful vision disappeared. An exit should always be effective, Mrs. Linde, but that's what I can't get Nora to grasp. Phew, it's hot in here. (*Flings the domino on a chair and opens the door to his room.*) Why's it dark in here? Oh yes, of course. Excuse me. (*He goes in and lights a couple of candles.*)

Nora: (*in a sharp, breathless whisper*) So?

Mrs. Linde: (*quietly*) I talked with him.

180 *Nora:* And—?

Mrs. Linde: Nora—you must tell your husband everything.

Nora: (*dully*) I knew it.

Mrs. Linde: You've got nothing to fear from Krogstad, but you have to speak out.

Nora: I won't tell.

Mrs. Linde: Then the letter will.

Nora: Thanks, Kristine. I know now what's to be done. Shh!

Helmer: (*reentering*) Well, then, Mrs. Linde—have you admired her?

Mrs. Linde: Yes, and now I'll say good night.

190 *Helmer:* Oh, come, so soon? Is this yours, this knitting?

Mrs. Linde: Yes, thanks. I nearly forgot it.

Helmer: Do you knit, then?

Mrs. Linde: Oh yes.

Helmer: You know what? You should embroider instead.

Mrs. Linde: Really? Why?

Helmer: Yes, because it's a lot prettier. See here, one holds the embroidery so, in the left hand, and then one guides the needle with the right—so—in an easy, sweeping curve—right?

Mrs. Linde: Yes, I guess that's—

200 *Helmer:* But, on the other hand, knitting—it can never be anything but ugly. Look, see here, the arms tucked in, the knitting needles going up and down—there's something Chinese about it. Ah, that was really a glorious champagne they served.

Mrs. Linde: Yes, good night, Nora, and don't be stubborn any more.

Helmer: Well put, Mrs. Linde!

Mrs. Linde: Good night, Mr. Helmer.

Helmer: (*accompanying her to the door*) Good night, good night. I hope you get home all right. I'd be very happy to—but you don't have far to go. Good night, good night. (*She leaves. He shuts the door after*

210 *her and returns.*) There, now, at last we got her out the door. She's a deadly bore, that creature.

Nora: Aren't you pretty tired, Torvald?

Helmer: No, not a bit.

Nora: You're not sleepy?

Helmer: Not at all. On the contrary, I'm feeling quite exhilarated. But you? Yes, you really look tired and sleepy.

Nora: Yes, I'm very tired. Soon now I'll sleep.

Helmer: See! You see! I was right all along that we shouldn't stay longer.

220 *Nora:* Whatever you do is always right.

Helmer: (*kissing her brow*) Now my little lark talks sense. Say, did you notice what a time Rank was having tonight?

Nora: Oh, was he? I didn't get to speak with him.

Helmer: I scarcely did either, but it's a long time since I've seen him in such high spirits. (*Gazes at her a moment, then comes nearer her.*) Hm—it's marvelous, though, to be back home again—to be completely alone with you. Oh, you bewitchingly lovely young woman!

Nora: Torvald, don't look at me like that!

230 *Helmer:* Can't I look at my richest treasure? At all that beauty that's mine, mine alone—completely and utterly.

Nora: (*moving around to the other side of the table*) You mustn't talk to me that way tonight.

Helmer: (*following her*) The tarantella is still in your blood, I can see—and it makes you even more enticing. Listen. The guests are beginning to go. (*Dropping his voice.*) Nora—it'll soon be quiet through this whole house.

Nora: Yes, I hope so.

Helmer: You do, don't you, my love? Do you realize—when I'm out at
240   a party like this with you—do you know why I talk to you so little, and keep such a distance away; just send you a stolen look now and then—you know why I do it? It's because I'm imagining then that you're my secret darling, my secret young bride-to-be, and that no one suspects there's anything between us.

Nora: Yes, yes; oh, yes, I know you're always thinking of me.

Helmer: And then when we leave and I place the shawl over those fine young rounded shoulders—over that wonderful curving neck—then I pretend that you're my young bride, that we're just coming from the wedding, that for the first time I'm bringing you into my
250   house—that for the first time I'm alone with you—completely alone with you, your trembling young beauty! All this evening I've longed for nothing but you. When I saw you turn and sway in the tarantella—my blood was pounding till I couldn't stand it—that's why I brought you down here so early—

Nora: Go away, Torvald! Leave me alone. I don't want all this.

Helmer: What do you mean? Nora, you're teasing me. You will, won't you? Aren't I your husband—?

A knock at the outside door.

Nora: (*startled*) What's that?

Helmer: (*going toward the hall*) Who is it?

260 *Rank:* (*outside*) It's me. May I come in a moment?

Helmer: (*with quiet irritation*) Oh, what does he want now? (*Aloud.*) Hold on. (*Goes and opens the door.*) Oh, how nice that you didn't just pass us by!

Rank: I thought I heard your voice, and then I wanted so badly to have a look in. (*Lightly glancing about.*) Ah, me, these old familiar haunts. You have it snug and cozy in here, you two.

Helmer: You seemed to be having it pretty cozy upstairs, too.

Rank: Absolutely. Why shouldn't I? Why not take in everything in life? As much as you can, anyway, and as long as you can. The

270 wine was superb—

Helmer: The champagne especially.

Rank: You noticed that too? It's amazing how much I could guzzle down.

Nora: Torvald also drank a lot of champagne this evening.

Rank: Oh?

Nora: Yes, and that always makes him so entertaining.

Rank: Well, why shouldn't one have a pleasant evening after a well-spent day?

Helmer: Well spent? I'm afraid I can't claim that.

280 **Rank:** (*slapping him on the back*) But I can, you see!

Nora: Dr. Rank, you must have done some scientific research today.

Rank: Quite so.

Helmer: Come now—little Nora talking about scientific research!

Nora: And can I congratulate you on the results?

Rank: Indeed you may.

Nora: Then they were good?

Rank: The best possible for both doctor and patient—certainty.

Nora: (*quickly and searchingly*) Certainty?

Rank: Complete certainty. So don't I owe myself a gay evening

290 afterwards?

Nora: Yes, you're right, Dr. Rank.

Helmer: I'm with you—just so long as you don't have to suffer for it in the morning.

Rank: Well, one never gets something for nothing in life.

Nora: Dr. Rank—are you very fond of masquerade parties?

Rank: Yes, if there's a good array of odd disguises—

Nora: Tell me, what should we two go as at the next masquerade?

Helmer: You little featherhead—already thinking of the next!

Rank: We two? I'll tell you what: you must go as Charmed Life—

300 **Helmer:** Yes, but find a costume for *that!*

Rank: Your wife can appear just as she looks every day.

Helmer: That was nicely put. But don't you know what you're going to be?

Rank: Yes, Helmer, I've made up my mind.

Helmer: Well?

Rank: At the next masquerade I'm going to be invisible.

Helmer: That's a funny idea.

Rank: They say there's a hat—black, huge—have you never heard of
310   the hat that makes you invisible? You put it on, and then no one
       on earth can see you.
Helmer: (*suppressing a smile*) Ah, of course.
Rank: But I'm quite forgetting what I came for. Helmer, give me a
       cigar, one of the dark Havanas.
Helmer: With the greatest of pleasure. (*Holds out his case.*)
Rank: Thanks. (*Takes one and cuts off the tip.*)
Nora: (*striking a match*) Let me give you a light.
Rank: Thank you. (*She holds the match for him; he lights the cigar.*) And
       now good-bye.
Helmer: Good-bye, good-bye, old friend.
320 *Nora:* Sleep well, Doctor.
Rank: Thanks for that wish.
Nora: Wish me the same.
Rank: You? All right, if you like—Sleep well. And thanks for the
       light. (*He nods to them both and leaves.*)
Helmer: (*his voice subdued*) He's been drinking heavily.
Nora: (*absently*) Could be. (*Helmer takes his keys from his pocket and goes
       out in the hall.*) Torvald—what are you after?
Helmer: Got to empty the mailbox; it's nearly full. There won't be
       room for the morning papers.
330 *Nora:* Are you working tonight?
Helmer: You know I'm not. Why—what's this? Someone's been at the
       lock.
Nora: At the lock—?
Helmer: Yes, I'm positive. What do you suppose—? I can't imagine one
       of the maids—? Here's a broken hairpin. Nora, it's yours—
Nora: (*quickly*) Then it must be the children—
Helmer: You'd better break them of that. Hm, hm—well, opened it
       after all. (*Takes the contents out and calls into the kitchen.*) Helene!
       Helene, would you put out the lamp in the hall. (*He returns to the
340   room, shutting the hall door, then displays the handful of mail.*) Look
       how it's piled up. (*Sorting through them.*) Now what's this?
Nora: (*at the window*) The letter! Oh, Torvald, no!
Helmer: Two calling cards—from Rank.
Nora: From Dr. Rank?
Helmer: (*examining them*) "Dr. Rank, Consulting Physician." They were
       on top. He must have dropped them in as he left.
Nora: Is there anything on them?
Helmer: There's a black cross over the name. See? That's a gruesome
       notion. He could almost be announcing his own death.
350 *Nora:* That's just what he's doing.
Helmer: What! You've heard something? Something he's told you?
Nora: Yes. That when those cards came, he'd be taking his leave of us.
       He'll shut himself in now and die.

Helmer: Ah, my poor friend! Of course I knew he wouldn't be here much longer. But so soon—And then to hide himself away like a wounded animal.

Nora: If it has to happen, then it's best it happens in silence—don't you think so, Torvald?

Helmer: (*pacing up and down*) He'd grown right into our lives. I simply
360   can't imagine him gone. He with his suffering and loneliness—like a dark cloud setting off our sunlit happiness. Well, maybe it's best this way. For him, at least. (*Standing still.*) And maybe for us too, Nora. Now we're thrown back on each other, completely. (*Embracing her.*) Oh you, my darling wife, how can I hold you close enough? You know what, Nora—time and again I've wished you were in some terrible danger, just so I could stake my life and soul and everything, for your sake.

Nora: (*tearing herself away, her voice firm and decisive*) Now you must read your mail, Torvald.

370 **Helmer:** No, no, not tonight. I want to stay with you, dearest.

Nora: With a dying friend on your mind?

Helmer: You're right. We've both had a shock. There's ugliness between us—these thoughts of death and corruption. We'll have to get free of them first. Until then—we'll stay apart.

Nora: (*clinging about his neck*) Torvald—good night! Good night!

Helmer: (*kissing her on the cheek*) Good night, little songbird. Sleep well, Nora. I'll be reading my mail now. (*He takes the letters into his room and shuts the door after him.*)

Nora: (*with bewildered glances, groping about, seizing Helmer's domino,*
380   *throwing it around her, and speaking in short, hoarse, broken whispers*) Never see him again. Never, never. (*Putting her shawl over her head.*) Never see the children either—them, too. Never, never. Oh, the freezing black water! The depths—down—Oh, I wish it were over—He has it now; he's reading it—now. Oh no, no, not yet. Torvald, good-bye, you and the children—(*She starts for the hall; as she does, Helmer throws open his door and stands with an open letter in his hand.*)

Helmer: Nora!

Nora: (*screams*) Oh—!

390 **Helmer:** What is this? You know what's in this letter?

Nora: Yes, I know. Let me go! Let me out!

Helmer: (*holding her back*) Where are you going?

Nora: (*struggling to break loose*) You can't save me, Torvald!

Helmer: (*slumping back*) True! Then it's true what he writes? How horrible! No, no, it's impossible—it can't be true.

Nora: It *is* true. I've loved you more than all this world.

Helmer: Ah, none of your slippery tricks.

Nora: (*taking one step toward him*) Torvald—!

Helmer: What *is* this you've blundered into!

400 *Nora:* Just let me loose. You're not going to suffer for my sake. You're not going to take on my guilt.

Helmer: No more playacting. (*Locks the hall door.*) You stay right here and give me a reckoning. You understand what you've done? Answer! You understand?

Nora: (*looking squarely at him, her face hardening*) Yes. I'm beginning to understand everything now.

Helmer: (*striding about*) Oh, what an awful awakening! In all these eight years—she who was my pride and joy—a hypocrite, a liar—worse, worse—a criminal! How infinitely disgusting it all is! The shame!

410   (*Nora says nothing and goes on looking straight at him. He stops in front of her.*) I should have suspected something of the kind. I should have known. All your father's flimsy values—Be still! All your father's flimsy values have come out in you. No religion, no morals, no sense of duty—Oh, how I'm punished for letting him off! I did it for your sake, and you repay me like this.

Nora: Yes, like this.

Helmer: Now you've wrecked all my happiness—ruined my whole future. Oh, it's awful to think of. I'm in a cheap little grafter's hands; he can do anything he wants with me, ask for anything,

420   play with me like a puppet—and I can't breathe a word. I'll be swept down miserably into the depths on account of a featherbrained woman.

Nora: When I'm gone from this world, you'll be free.

Helmer: Oh, quit posing. Your father had a mess of those speeches too. What good would that ever do me if you were gone from this world, as you say? Not the slightest. He can still make the whole thing known; and if he does, I could be falsely suspected as your accomplice. They might even think that I was behind it—that I put you up to it. And all that I can thank you for—you that I've

430   coddled the whole of our marriage. Can you see now what you've done to me?

Nora: (*icily calm*) Yes.

Helmer: It's so incredible, I just can't grasp it. But we'll have to patch up whatever we can. Take off the shawl. I said, take if off! I've got to appease him somehow or other. The thing has to be hushed up at any cost. And as for you and me, it's got to seem like everything between us is just as it was—to the outside world, that is. You'll go right on living in this house, of course. But you can't be allowed to bring up the children; I don't dare trust you with them—Oh, to

440   have to say this to someone I've loved so much! Well, that's done with. From now on happiness doesn't matter; all that matters is saving the bits and pieces, the appearance—(*The doorbell rings. Helmer starts.*) What's that? And so late. Maybe the worst—? You think he'd—? Hide, Nora! Say you're sick. (*Nora remains standing motionless. Helmer goes and opens the door.*)

Maid: (*half dressed, in the hall*) A letter for Mrs. Helmer.

Helmer: I'll take it. (*Snatches the letter and shuts the door.*) Yes, it's from him. You don't get it; I'm reading it myself.

Nora: Then read it.

450 **Helmer:** (*by the lamp*) I hardly dare. We may be ruined, you and I. But—I've got to know. (*Rips open the letter, skims through a few lines, glances at an enclosure, then cries out joyfully.*) Nora! (*Nora looks inquiringly at him.*) Nora! Wait—better check it again—Yes, yes, it's true. I'm saved. Nora, I'm saved!

Nora: And I?

Helmer: You too, of course. We're both saved, both of us. Look. He's sent back your note. He says he's sorry and ashamed—that a happy development in his life—oh, who cares what he says! Nora, we're saved! No one can hurt you. Oh, Nora, Nora—but first, this
460   ugliness all has to go. Let me see—(*Takes a look at the note.*) No, I don't want to see it; I want the whole thing to fade like a dream. (*Tears the note and both letters to pieces, throws them into the stove and watches them burn.*) There—now there's nothing left—He wrote that since Christmas Eve you—Oh, they must have been three terrible days for you, Nora.

Nora: I fought a hard fight.

Helmer: And suffered pain and saw no escape but—No, we're not going to dwell on anything unpleasant. We'll just be grateful and keep on repeating: it's over now, it's over! You hear me, Nora? You don't
470   seem to realize—it's over. What's it mean—that frozen look? Oh, poor little Nora, I understand. You can't believe I've forgiven you. But I have, Nora; I swear I have. I know that what you did, you did out of love for me.

Nora: That's true.

Helmer: You loved me the way a wife ought to love her husband. It's simply the means that you couldn't judge. But you think I love you any the less for not knowing how to handle your affairs? No, no—just lean on me; I'll guide you and teach you. I wouldn't be a man if this feminine helplessness didn't make you twice as
480   attractive to me. You mustn't mind those sharp words I said—that was all in the first confusion of thinking my world had collapsed. I've forgiven you, Nora; I swear I've forgiven you.

Nora: My thanks for your forgiveness. (*She goes out through the door, right.*)

Helmer: No, wait—(*Peers in.*) What are you doing in there?

Nora: (*inside*) Getting out of my costume.

Helmer: (*by the open door*) Yes, do that. Try to calm yourself and collect your thoughts again, my frightened little songbird. You can rest easy now; I've got wide wings to shelter you with. (*Walking about
490   close by the door.*) How snug and nice our home is, Nora. You're safe here; I'll keep you like a hunted dove I've rescued out of a hawk's claws. I'll bring peace to your poor, shuddering heart. Gradually it'll happen, Nora; you'll see. Tomorrow all this will look different to

you; then everything will be as it was. I won't have to go on
repeating I forgive you; you'll feel it for yourself. How can you
imagine I'd ever conceivably want to disown you—or even blame you
in any way? Ah, you don't know a man's heart, Nora. For a man
there's something indescribably sweet and satisfying in knowing
he's forgiven his wife—and forgiven her out of a full and open

500   heart. It's as if she belongs to him in two ways now: in a sense he's
given her fresh into the world again, and she's become his wife and
his child as well. From now on that's what you'll be to me—you
little, bewildered, helpless thing. Don't be afraid of anything, Nora;
just open your heart to me, and I'll be conscience and will to you
both—(*Nora enters in her regular clothes.*) What's this? Not in bed?
You've changed your dress?

Nora: Yes, Torvald, I've changed my dress.

Helmer: But why now, so late?

Nora: Tonight I'm not sleeping.

510 *Helmer:* But Nora dear—

Nora: (*looking at her watch*) It's still not so very late. Sit down, Torvald;
we have a lot to talk over. (*She sits at one side of the table.*)

Helmer: Nora—what is this? That hard expression—

Nora: Sit down. This'll take some time. I have a lot to say.

Helmer: (*sitting at the table directly opposite her*) You worry me, Nora.
And I don't understand you.

Nora: No, that's exactly it. You don't understand me. And I've never
understood you either—until tonight. No, don't interrupt. You can
just listen to what I say. We're closing out accounts, Torvald.

520 *Helmer:* How do you mean that?

Nora: (*after a short pause*) Doesn't anything strike you about our
sitting here like this?

Helmer: What's that?

Nora: We've been married now eight years. Doesn't it occur to you
that this is the first time we two, you and I, man and wife, have
ever talked seriously together?

Helmer: What do you mean—seriously?

Nora: In eight whole years—longer even—right from our first
acquaintance, we've never exchanged a serious word on any

530   serious thing.

Helmer: You mean I should constantly go and involve you in problems
you couldn't possibly help me with?

Nora: I'm not talking of problems. I'm saying that we've never sat
down seriously together and tried to get to the bottom of
anything.

Helmer: But dearest, what good would that ever do you?

Nora: That's the point right there: you've never understood me. I've
been wronged greatly, Torvald—first by Papa, and then by you.

Helmer: What! By us—the two people who've loved you more than

540   anyone else?

Nora: (*shaking her head*) You never loved me. You've thought it fun to be in love with me, that's all.

Helmer: Nora, what a thing to say!

Nora: Yes, it's true now, Torvald. When I lived at home with Papa, he told me all his opinions, so I had the same ones too; or if they were different I hid them, since he wouldn't have cared for that. He used to call me his doll-child, and he played with me the way I played with my dolls. Then I came into your house—

Helmer: How can you speak of our marriage like that?

550 *Nora:* (*unperturbed*) I mean, then I went from Papa's hands into yours. You arranged everything to your own taste, and so I got the same taste as you—or I pretended to; I can't remember. I guess a little of both, first one, then the other. Now when I look back, it seems as if I'd lived here like a beggar—just from hand to mouth. I've lived by doing tricks for you, Torvald. But that's the way you wanted it. It's a great sin what you and Papa did to me. You're to blame that nothing's become of me.

Helmer: Nora, how unfair and ungrateful you are! Haven't you been happy here?

560 *Nora:* No, never. I thought so—but I never have.

Helmer: Not—not happy!

Nora: No, only lighthearted. And you've always been so kind to me. But our home's been nothing but a playpen. I've been your doll-wife here, just as at home I was Papa's doll-child. And in turn the children have been my dolls. I thought it was fun when you played with me, just as they thought it fun when I played with them. That's been our marriage, Torvald.

Helmer: There's some truth in what you're saying—under all the raving exaggeration. But it'll all be different after this. Playtime's over; now

570 for the schooling.

Nora: Whose schooling—mine or the children's?

Helmer: Both yours and the children's, dearest.

Nora: Oh, Torvald, you're not the man to teach me to be a good wife to you.

Helmer: And you can say that?

Nora: And I—how am I equipped to bring up children?

Helmer: Nora!

Nora: Didn't you say a moment ago that that was no job to trust me with?

580 *Helmer:* In a flare of temper! Why fasten on that?

Nora: Yes, but you were so very right. I'm not up to the job. There's another job I have to do first. I have to try to educate myself. You can't help me with that. I've got to do it alone. And that's why I'm leaving you now.

Helmer: (*jumping up*) What's that?

Nora: I have to stand completely alone, if I'm ever going to discover myself and the world out there. So I can't go on living with you.

Helmer: Nora, Nora!

Nora: I want to leave right away. Kristine should put me up for the
590   night—

Helmer: You're insane! You've no right! I forbid you!

Nora: From here on, there's no use forbidding me anything. I'll take
with me whatever is mine. I don't want a thing from you, either
now or later.

Helmer: What kind of madness is this!

Nora: Tomorrow I'm going home—I mean, home where I came from.
It'll be easier up there to find something to do.

Helmer: Oh, you blind, incompetent child!

Nora: I must learn to be competent, Torvald.

600 *Helmer:* Abandon your home, your husband, your children! And
you're not even thinking what people will say.

Nora: I can't be concerned about that. I only know how essential this is.

Helmer: Oh, it's outrageous. So you'll run out like this on your most
sacred vows.

Nora: What do you think are my most sacred vows?

Helmer: And I have to tell you that! Aren't they your duties to your
husband and children?

Nora: I have other duties equally sacred.

Helmer: That isn't true. What duties are they?

610 *Nora:* Duties to myself.

Helmer: Before all else, you're a wife and a mother.

Nora: I don't believe in that any more. I believe that, before all else,
I'm a human being, no less than you—or anyway, I ought to try to
become one. I know the majority thinks you're right, Torvald, and
plenty of books agree with you, too. But I can't go on believing
what the majority says, or what's written in books. I have to think
over these things myself and try to understand them.

Helmer: Why can't you understand your place in your own home? On
a point like that, isn't there one everlasting guide you can turn to?
620   Where's your religion?

Nora: Oh, Torvald, I'm really not sure what religion is.

Helmer: What—?

Nora: I only know what the minister said when I was confirmed. He
told me religion was this thing and that. When I get clear and away
by myself, I'll go into that problem too. I'll see if what the minister
said was right, or, in any case, if it's right for me.

Helmer: A young woman your age shouldn't talk like that. If religion
can't move you, I can try to rouse your conscience. You do have
some moral feeling? Or, tell me—has that gone too?

630 *Nora:* It's not easy to answer that, Torvald. I simply don't know. I'm all
confused about these things. I just know I see them so differently
from you. I find out, for one thing, that the law's not at all what I'd
thought—but I can't get it through my head that the law is fair. A

woman hasn't a right to protect her dying father or save her husband's life! I can't believe that.

Helmer: You talk like a child. You don't know anything of the world you live in.

Nora: No, I don't. But now I'll begin to learn for myself. I'll try to discover who's right, the world or I.

640 *Helmer:* Nora, you're sick; you've got a fever. I almost think you're out of your head.

Nora: I've never felt more clearheaded and sure in my life.

Helmer: And—clearheaded and sure—you're leaving your husband and children?

Nora: Yes.

Helmer: Then there's only one possible reason.

Nora: What?

Helmer: You no longer love me.

Nora: No. That's exactly it.

650 *Helmer:* Nora! You can't be serious!

Nora: Oh, this is so hard, Torvald—you've been so kind to me always. But I can't help it. I don't love you any more.

Helmer: (*struggling for composure*) Are you also clearheaded and sure about that?

Nora: Yes, completely. That's why I can't go on staying here.

Helmer: Can you tell me what I did to lose your love?

Nora: Yes, I can tell you. It was this evening when the miraculous thing didn't come—then I knew you weren't the man I'd imagined.

Helmer: Be more explicit; I don't follow you.

660 *Nora:* I've waited now so patiently eight long years—for, my Lord, I know miracles don't come every day. Then this crisis broke over me, and such a certainty filled me: *now* the miraculous event would occur. While Krogstad's letter was lying out there, I never for an instant dreamed that you could give in to his terms. I was so utterly sure you'd say to him: go on, tell your tale to the whole wide world. And when he'd done that—

Helmer: Yes, what then? When I'd delivered my own wife into shame and disgrace—!

Nora: When he'd done that, I was so utterly sure that you'd step
670 forward, take the blame on yourself and say: I am the guilty one.

Helmer: Nora—!

Nora: You're thinking I'd never accept such a sacrifice from you? No, of course not. But what good would my protests be against you? That was the miracle I was waiting for, in terror and hope. And to stave that off, I would have taken my life.

Helmer: I'd gladly work for you day and night, Nora—and take on pain and deprivation. But there's no one who gives up honor for love.

Nora: Millions of women have done just that.

Helmer: Oh, you think and talk like a silly child.

680 **Nora:** Perhaps. But you neither think nor talk like the man I could join myself to. When your big fright was over—and it wasn't from any threat against me, only for what might damage you—when all the danger was past, for you it was just as if nothing had happened. I was exactly the same, your little lark, your doll, that you'd have to handle with double care now that I'd turned out so brittle and frail. (*Gets up.*) Torvald—in that instant it dawned on me that for eight years I've been living here with a stranger, and that I'd even conceived three children—oh, I can't stand the thought of it! I could tear myself to bits.

690 **Helmer:** (*heavily*) I see. There's a gulf that's opened between us—that's clear. Oh, but Nora, can't we bridge it somehow?

Nora: The way I am now, I'm no wife for you.

Helmer: I have the strength to make myself over.

Nora: Maybe—if your doll gets taken away.

Helmer: But to part! To part from you! No, Nora, no—I can't imagine it.

Nora: (*going out, right*) All the more reason why it has to be. (*She reenters with her coat and a small overnight bag, which she puts on a chair by the table.*)

Helmer: Nora, Nora, not now! Wait till tomorrow.

700 **Nora:** I can't spend the night in a strange man's room.

Helmer: But couldn't we live here like brother and sister—

Nora: You know very well how long that would last. (*Throws her shawl about her.*) Good-bye, Torvald. I won't look in on the children. I know they're in better hands than mine. The way I am now, I'm no use to them.

Helmer: But someday, Nora—someday—?

Nora: How can I tell? I haven't the least idea what'll become of me.

Helmer: But you're my wife, now and wherever you go.

Nora: Listen, Torvald—I've heard that when a wife deserts her
710   husband's house just as I'm doing, then the law frees him from all responsibility. In any case, I'm freeing you from being responsible. Don't feel yourself bound, any more than I will. There has to be absolute freedom for us both. Here, take your ring back. Give me mine.

Helmer: That too?

Nora: That too.

Helmer: There it is.

Nora: Good. Well, now it's all over. I'm putting the keys here. The maids know all about keeping up the house—better than I do.
720   Tomorrow, after I've left town, Kristine will stop by to pack up everything that's mine from home. I'd like those things shipped up to me.

Helmer: Over! All over! Nora, won't you ever think about me?

Nora: I'm sure I'll think of you often, and about the children and the house here.

Helmer: May I write you?

Nora: No—never. You're not to do that.

Helmer: Oh, but let me send you—

Nora: Nothing. Nothing.

730 **Helmer:** Or help you if you need it.

Nora: No. I accept nothing from strangers.

Helmer: Nora—can I never be more than a stranger to you?

Nora: (*picking up the overnight bag*) Ah, Torvald—it would take the greatest miracle of all—

Helmer: Tell me the greatest miracle!

Nora: You and I both would have to transform ourselves to the point that—Oh, Torvald, I've stopped believing in miracles.

Helmer: But I'll believe. Tell me! Transform ourselves to the point that—?

740 **Nora:** That our living together could be a true marriage. (*She goes out down the hall.*)

Helmer: (*sinks down on a chair by the door, face buried in his hands*) Nora! Nora! (*Looking about and rising.*) Empty. She's gone. (*A sudden hope leaps in him.*) The greatest miracle—?

(*From below, the sound of a door slamming shut.*)

ACCOUNT: DECLAR KIBERD ON A FEMINIST APPROACH TO *A DOLL HOUSE*

The British playwright, George Bernard Shaw, who was a major force in bringing Ibsen's work to the English-speaking world, wrote in *The Quintessence of Ibsenism* that "All good women are manly and all good men are womanly." Though Shaw in his own work characteristically exaggerated this issue into an occasion for flashy paradoxes (and thereby brought wrong-headed attacks down on both Ibsen and himself), the formulation helps to illuminate the issues of gender for both sexes in *A Doll House*.

Kiberd says that Ibsen contained a deeply passive element that he thought of as feminine in himself, and from his earliest years he was attracted to the kind of self-assured and forceful women his wife represented:

> The dramatist was fully aware of this dimension to his personality and said that "women have something in common with the true artist . . . something that is a good substitute for worldly understanding." Only "something," only "part feminine," for the true artist is an androgynous blend of intellect and intuition, system and instinct.

Declar Kiberd, "Ibsen's Heroines: The New Woman as Rebel," *Men and Feminism in Modern Literature* (New York: St. Martin's, 1985), 61–74.

This "blend" gets at the nature of real women and real men, Kiberd says, because extreme terms like "instinct" are incorrectly thought peculiar to one or another sex. Ibsen dramatizes a *rejection* of such stereotypes of masculinity and femininity. It is the "androgynous" nature of *both* sexes that lies at the bottom of his objections to extreme views on both sides of the Feminist movement of his time:

> There were times when Ibsen feared that feminists were so obsessed with "externals" that they misread *A Doll House* as a play about a woman who slammed a door. It is also a play about the plight of the man who is left behind and it is on his tragedy that the curtain finally falls. The man [Ibsen] who was to die uttering the immortal word "Nevertheless" was not the sort to settle for one side of any story.

Even twenty years after *A Doll House*, in his notes for a new play, Ibsen was still fascinated by the theme of a woman's difficulty in being herself in a society whose laws are created by men: "He realized that men and women are a lot less alike than the law pretends, and a lot more alike than the culture admits":

> The man who lives only by authority, like the woman who lives purely on feelings, can never be whole. Hence the two-dimensional character of Helmer is not a flaw in Ibsen's dramatic techniques, but part of the play's psychological point. Helmer has projected all the emotional aspects of his personality onto Nora, who in turn projects all her own childishness onto her "doll-babies" that "dogs never bite." At the end, it is her fear that she will perpetuate those values if she does not leave.

But the free woman that Nora becomes by the end of the play is latent from its beginning. She is shown to be committed both to the "male" values of work and to the "female" values of self-sacrifice. The previous Christmas, for example, when she worked alone on decorations, she found her task "not dull at all" but satisfying in its sense of self-sufficiency. In this way, Helmer's new prosperity threatens to return her solely to the role of male fetish—an object of possession and pleasure. This stereotyped notion of family life threatens Helmer, as well, who has overworked himself to attain it. He is thereby another victim of the code of specialization by gender.

Nora herself is conscious of her role as childwife. Even in her attempts to save her marriage by working to defray the terrible load of debt, she is preparing herself, Kiberd says, "half consciously" for the moment of self-support. Helmer, on the other hand, thinks that Mrs. Linde is a widow because he assumes that no woman with a husband would work.

The parallel between Krogstad as a criminal and Nora as a woman prepares us for the shock of the ending when Nora leaves her children and gives us a reason for her act—Krogstad too had used his family as an excuse for a deceit which he now forswears. Nora has overcome another deceit—her pretence of the necessity of her own fitness as a mother. If corruption is inherited, she fears to infect her children; if not, she herself grew up without a mother, and she now sees that her servants in fact know more about raising children and running a house than she does:

> Helmer's explosion into recrimination, just after his prayer for the chance to sacrifice himself for Nora, is the deflation of her final illusion. There will be no miracle. With callous pragmatism he points out that her suicide would solve nothing. The only thing for it is to put up a brave front to domestic harmony, despite the fact that Nora will no longer be allowed to bring up the children.

Yet why should Helmer expect a sense of social responsibility in a woman whom he married only as a doll, a "wife and a child," a male fetish? The real challenge of the end of the play, Kiberd says, is to imagine the future virtues of a society in which men and women could properly live with one another:

> In a play where the word "past" is interchangeable with the word "guilt," the idea of an uncertain future has a liberating force, as much because it is uncertain as because it is the future. . . . What if the culture and laws of the future were truly an androgynous blend of male honour and female love, to such a point that it became foolish to equate the one virtue exclusively with either sex?

Kiberd says that, in such a society, couples would live in a marriage of minds with each partner fulfilled. It is on a note of "qualified optimism" about the future possibilities of this kind of marriage that the play ends. Ibsen's play has, therefore, viewed the institution of marriage with suspicions, but not without hope.

ACCOUNT: RICHARD HORNBY ON
A STRUCTURALIST APPROACH TO *A DOLL HOUSE*

A Doll House is the best known of Ibsen's plays and has long been connected by criticism to feminism. But, Hornby says, Ibsen himself disclaimed any connection with the movement in the nineteenth century and insisted the play dealt with human rights, not merely women's rights. Even this way of looking at the play, however, sees it as a kind of social tract, though Ibsen himself was not a social activist and even satirized the idea of democratic movements in *An Enemy of the People*. The issue shows up in an unfortunate way in the critical history of the play:

Richard Hornby, "The Ethical Leap: *A Doll House*" from *Patterns in Ibsen's Middle Plays* (Lewisburg, PA: Bucknell University Press, 1981), 89–119.

A Doll House was championed as a masterpiece of realism and Feminism; then with the passage of time it came to be ridiculed on exactly the same grounds. As realism became passé, *A Doll House* was passed off as being shallow and journalistic. With the gaining of new rights for women in the 1920s, it was criticized in addition for being outdated—a premature judgement, as subsequent events have proved.

Should the play be criticized for being both too realistic and not realistic enough? Hornby says that the answer lies in the part realism plays in Ibsen's work: He used the new realism for his own poetic ends. That is, he remained the symbolist of his earlier play, *Peer Gynt*, but came to use the material and events of middle-class life for his symbols, where he had formerly used trolls, fantastic journeys, legendary animals, and so on. Further, unlike ordinary realistic playwrights, Ibsen was concerned not with trends and general social issues and typical people but with individuals and exceptional cases.

For example, while Nora, in realistic terms, is an exceptional, free-willed character, she is also treated symbolically. She is established at the beginning of the play (in the terms of the philosopher Kierkegaard) as an "Aesthetic" character as opposed to an "Ethical" character. But *during* the play, she becomes dramatically transformed from the one to the other—while other characters are similarly transformed in one direction or the other.

From her entrance, Nora takes on Aesthetic qualities:

> . . . she comes in humming and carrying Christmas gifts for her children. A delivery boy follows with a Christmas tree. Nora pays him, adding a large tip (which she can hardly afford, we soon discover). As soon as he leaves she reaches into her pocket for some macaroons, which she eats greedily. Hearing her moving about, her husband, Helmer, calls to her from his study, "Is that my little lark twittering out there?" He is in the habit, it appears, of calling her by the names of small animals as terms of endearment; he later repeatedly calls her a bird, a squirrel, a dove, a lark. Nora's love of music, her extravagance, her appetite, her association with animals, are all strongly reminiscent of Peer Gynt, as are her love of family (she dissembled to protect her dying father from anguish, as Peer did to comfort his dying mother in the scene where he pretends to drive her to heaven), her trip south, her ability to lie unselfconsciously, her sexuality, her dancing the Tarantella.

Helmer, in the first two acts, contrasts to Nora in being an Ethical character. His high standards make them live frugally and force the forgery; he loves to preach morals—to others—and turns every scene until the last into a little moral lesson: "against debt, against extravagance, against lying, against hypocrisy." But when the disaster comes, it turns out Helmer is not so concerned with Nora's character as with his own *career:*

The irony is that he is "swept down miserably into the depths" not socially but morally. The word *puppet* is not in the original Norwegian, but it is appropriate at this point: Now he is the "doll" of the house. His moral downfall parallels Nora's moral rise, although in Nora's case it is a genuine change while in his it is merely an unmasking: He has been a hypocrite all along.

Just as Helmer and Nora reflect each other in reverse, the other characters in the play can be arranged in the Kierkegaardian scheme and are transformed in the course of the play from one type into another:

AESTHETIC	IRONIC	ETHICAL
Nora (Acts 1, 2 beginning of 3)		Nora (end of 3)
Helmer (end of 3)		Helmer (1, 2 beginning of 3)
	(Helmer throughout)	
Krogstad (1, 2 beginning of 3)		Krogstad (end of 3)
Dr. Rank (middle of 2, 3)		Dr. Rank (1, beginning of 2)
Mrs. Linde (before play)		Mrs. Linde (during play)

Krogstad's position is clarified by this system, though his transformation, like Nora's, may seem stagy in its abruptness and weak motivation. Like Nora, he makes a "sudden leap into the ethical" and mirrors Nora's change like a Shakespearean subplot.

Mrs. Linde also displays the same pattern. She had married a man she did not love and so lived in a "doll house." She now has become obsessed with living for duty—she has *already* made the ethical leap and so proves to Nora that a woman can function on her own and be true to her own nature. One example is seen in the love scene between Mrs. Linde and Krogstad: Mrs. Linde does not flirt or even mention marriage, but remains straightforward—unlike Nora and her behavior with Dr. Rank. Even the minor character of Dr. Rank shows a similar transformation when, in reaction to facing death, he tries to embrace the aesthetic life and to get all the pleasure he can "by attempting to make love to Nora, going to parties, drinking, smoking fine cigars. . . ." Finally he hides himself "like a wounded animal."

Hornby's analysis shows that Ibsen's social drama:

[J]ust as it is never a profession of a simple social thesis, so too it is not merely the depiction of a single hero or heroine. *A Doll House* is a study of the relation between the aesthetic and ethical levels of life, of the way in which people in moments of crisis choose one or the other or attempt to cling to both.

Thus the structure of the play illuminates a transformation of character. At the same time, it illuminates Ibsen's philosophical views on what "character" means.

SUGGESTIONS FOR DISCUSSION AND WRITING

---

1. Some translators render the title of the play as *A Doll's House* and some as *A Doll House*. What difference in implications do you see between the two titles, particularly for the play's **dramatic irony**? Which title would you choose as most in keeping with the spirit of the play? Be sure to explain and to support your answer. How might each of the critics represented here react to the two titles, and why?

2. Find, if you can, **images** in the play that seem to contradict Shaw's claim that "all good women are manly and all good men are womanly." Find, if you can, some images that support Shaw's claim. Do you locate a moment of **crisis** in the play? Are the images before and after that moment of a different sort? Is the style of **dialogue** in the characters different after the crisis? The quotation by Shaw is from the Structuralist account. What might a feminist account make of it?

3. How do the two critics account differently for the same evidence in the play? How, especially, do they account for changes in style or content in the language of the characters? Does either critic contradict the other? Explain your answer.

4. Both critics summarized here deal with the issue of Ibsen's relation to feminism. Which account seems most convincing to you *based on the evidence of the play?* Explain your answer.

5. Pick another critical approach and make some notes for discussion or for an essay on how Nora leaving her children creates a dramatic effect in the play. For example, what might a psychoanalytic critic make of her motives? In making your analysis, be sure to explain your position with regard to the motives Kiberd and Hornby propose.

Chapter Twenty-One

Approaches to Samuel Beckett's *Happy Days*

SAMUEL BECKETT (1906–1989) was born in Dublin, where he attended Trinity College. He taught literature at colleges in Ireland and France and finally settled in Paris in 1937. In Paris, he became a friend of James Joyce and often assisted the almost-blind writer by taking dictation and copying portions of Joyce's books. Beckett's first novel, *Murphy,* was published in 1938.

With a few exceptions, Beckett wrote most of his works after 1939 in French, then translated them into English himself. During World War II, he worked for a time with the French Resistance to German occupation. He also served for a short time with the Irish Red Cross. Between 1947 and 1957, he produced most of the works that made him famous: the novel trilogy *Molloy, Malone Dies,* and *The Unnameable* and the plays *Waiting for Godot* and *Endgame.* Considered milestones in "the theatre of the absurd," these plays present a pessimistic yet comical view of man's condition; the world of these plays is one in which life seems meaningless and chaotic.

SAMUEL BECKETT

Happy Days
A Play in Two Acts
(1961)

CHARACTERS
Winnie, a woman about fifty
Willie, a man about sixty

Act I

Expanse of scorched grass rising centre to low mound. Gentle slopes down to front and either side of stage. Back an abrupter fall to stage level. Maximum of simplicity and symmetry.

Blazing light.

Very pompier trompe-l'oeil backcloth to represent unbroken plain and sky receding to meet in far distance.

Imbedded up to above her waist in exact centre of mound, WINNIE. About fifty, well preserved, blond for preference, plump, arms and shoulders bare, low bodice, big bosom, pearl necklet. She is discovered sleeping, her arms on the ground before her, her head on her arms. Beside her on ground to her left a capacious black bag, shopping variety, and to her right a collapsible collapsed parasol, beak of handle emerging from sheath.

To her right and rear, lying asleep on ground, hidden by mound, WILLIE.

Long pause. A bell rings piercingly, say ten seconds, stops. She does not move. Pause. Bell more piercingly, say five seconds. She wakes. Bell stops. She raises her head, gazes front. Long pause. She straightens up, lays her hands flat on ground, throws back her head and gazes at zenith. Long pause.

Winnie: (*gazing at zenith*). Another heavenly day. (*Pause. Head back level, eyes front, pause. She clasps hands to breast, closes eyes. Lips move in inaudible prayer, say ten seconds. Lips still. Hands remain clasped. Low.*) For Jesus Christ sake Amen. (*Eyes open, hands unclasp, return to mound. Pause. She clasps hands to breast again, closes eyes, lips move again in inaudible addendum, say five seconds. Low.*) World without end Amen. (*Eyes open, hands unclasp, return to mound. Pause.*) Begin, Winnie. (*Pause.*) Begin your day, Winnie. (*Pause. She turns to bag, rummages in it without moving it from its place, brings out toothbrush,*
10   *rummages again, brings out flat tube of toothpaste, turns back front, unscrews cap of tube, lays cap on ground, squeezes with difficulty small blob of paste on brush, holds tube in one hand and brushes teeth with other. She turns modestly aside and back to her right to spit out behind mound. In this position her eyes rest on WILLIE. She spits out. She cranes a little further back and down. Loud.*) Hoo-oo! (*Pause. Louder.*) Hoo-oo! (*Pause. Tender smile as she turns back front, lays down brush.*) Poor Willie—(*examines tube, smile off*)—running out—(*looks for cap*)—ah well—(*finds cap*)—can't be helped—(*screws on cap*)—just one of those old things—(*lays down tube*)—another of those old
20   things—(*turns towards bag*)—just can't be cured—(*rummages in bag*)—cannot be cured—(*brings out small mirror, turns back front*)—ah yes—(*inspects teeth in mirror*)—poor dear Willie—(*testing upper front teeth with thumb, indistinctly*)—good Lord!—(*pulling back upper lip to inspect gums, do.*)—good God!—(*pulling back corner of mouth, mouth open, do.*)—ah well—(*other corner, do.*)—no worse— (*abandons inspection, normal speech*)—no better, no worse—(*lays down mirror*)—no change—(*wipes fingers on grass*)—no pain—(*looks for toothbrush*)—hardly any—(*takes up toothbrush*)—great thing that—(*examines handle of brush*)—nothing like it—(*examines handle, reads*)
30   reads)—pure . . . what?—(*pause*)— what?—(*lays down brush*)—ah yes—(*turns towards bag*)—poor Willie—(*rummages in bag*)—no zest—(*rummages*)—for anything—(*brings out spectacles in case*)—no interest—(*turns back front*)—in life—(*takes spectacles from case*)—

poor dear Willie—(*lays down case*)—sleep for ever—(*opens spectacles*)—marvellous gift—(*puts on spectacles*)—nothing to touch it—(*looks for toothbrush*)—in my opinion—(*takes up toothbrush*)—always said so—(*examines handle of brush*)—wish I had it—(*examines handle, reads*)—genuine . . . pure . . . what?—(*lays down brush*)—blind next—(*takes off spectacles*)—ah well—(*lays down*

40 *spectacles*)—seen enough—(*feels in bodice for handkerchief*)—I suppose—(*takes out folded handkerchief*)—by now—(*shakes out handkerchief*)—what are those wonderful lines—(*wipes one eye*)—woe woe is me—(*wipes the other*)—to see what I see—(*looks for spectacles*)—ah yes—(*takes up spectacles*)—wouldn't miss it—(*starts polishing spectacles, breathing on lenses*)—or would I?—(*polishes*)—holy light—(*polishes*)—bob up out of dark—(*polishes*)—blaze of hellish light. (*Stops polishing, raises face to sky, pause, head back level, resumes polishing, stops polishing, cranes back to her right and down.*) Hoo-oo! (*Pause. Tender smile as she turns back*

50 *front and resumes polishing. Smile off.*) Marvellous gift—(*stops polishing, lays down spectacles*)—wish I had it—(*folds handkerchief*)—ah well—(*puts handkerchief back in bodice*)—can't complain—(*looks for spectacles*)—no no—(*takes up spectacles*)—mustn't complain—(*holds up spectacles, looks through lens*)—so much to be thankful for—(*looks through other lens*)—no pain—(*puts on spectacles*)—hardly any—(*looks for toothbrush*)—wonderful thing that—(*takes up toothbrush*)—nothing like it—(*examines handle of brush*)—slight headache sometimes—(*examines handle, reads*)—guaranteed . . . genuine . . . pure . . . what?—(*looks closer*)—genuine pure . . . —(*takes*

60 *handkerchief from bodice*)—ah yes—(*shakes out handkerchief*)—occasional mild migraine—(*starts wiping handle of brush*—it comes—(*wipes*)—then goes—(*wiping mechanically*)—ah yes (*wiping*)—many mercies—(*wiping*)—great mercies—(*stops wiping, fixed lost gaze, brokenly*)—prayers perhaps not for naught—(*pause, do.*)—first thing—(*pause, do.*)—last thing—(*head down, resumes wiping, stops wiping, head up, calmed, wipes eyes, folds handkerchief, puts it back in bodice, examines handle of brush, reads*)—fully guaranteed . . . genuine pure . . . —(*looks closer*)—genuine pure . . . (*Takes off spectacles, lays them and brush down, gazes before*

70 *her.*) Old things. (*Pause.*) Old eyes. (*Long pause.*) On, Winnie. (*She casts about her, sees parasol, considers it at length, takes it up and develops from sheath a handle of surprising length. Holding butt of parasol in right hand she cranes back and down to her right to hang over WILLIE.*) Hoo-oo! (*Pause.*) Willie! (*Pause.*) Wonderful gift. (*She strikes down at him with beak of parasol.*) Wish I had it. (*She strikes again. The parasol slips from her grasp and falls behind mound. It is immediately restored to her by WILLIE's invisible hand.*) Thank you, dear. (*She transfers parasol to left hand, turns back front and examines right palm.*) Damp. (*Returns parasol to right hand, examines left palm.*)

80 Ah well, no worse. (*Head up, cheerfully.*) No better, no worse, no

change. (*Pause. Do.*) No pain. (*Cranes back to look down at WILLIE, holding parasol by butt as before.*) Don't go off on me again now dear will you please, I may need you. (*Pause.*) No hurry, no hurry, just don't curl up on me again. (*Turns back front, lays down parasol, examines palms together, wipes them on grass.*) Perhaps a shade off colour just the same. (*Turns to bag, rummages in it, brings out revolver, holds it up, kisses it rapidly, puts it back, rummages, brings out almost empty bottle of red medicine, turns back front, looks for spectacles, puts them on, reads label.*) Loss of spirits . . . lack of keenness . . .

90 want of appetite . . . infants . . . children . . . adults . . . six level . . . tablespoonfuls daily—(*head up, smile*)—the old style!—(*smile off, head down, reads*)—daily . . . before and after . . . meals . . . instantaneous . . . (*looks closer*) . . . improvement. (*Takes off spectacles, lays them down, holds up bottle at arm's length to see level, unscrews cap, swigs it off head well back, tosses cap and bottle away in WILLIE's direction. Sound of breaking glass.*) Ah that's better! (*Turns to bag, rummages in it, brings out lipstick, turns back front, examines lipstick.*) Running out. (*Looks for spectacles.*) Ah well. (*Puts on spectacles, looks for mirror.*) Musn't complain. (*Takes*

100 *up mirror, starts doing lips.*) What is that wonderful line? (*Lips.*) Oh fleeting joys—(*lips*)—oh something lasting woe. (*Lips. She is interrupted by disturbance from WILLIE. He is sitting up. She lowers lipstick and mirror and cranes back and down to look at him. Pause. Top back of WILLIE's bald head, trickling blood, rises to view above slope, comes to rest. WINNIE pushes up her spectacles. Pause. His hand appears with handkerchief, spreads it on skull, disappears. Pause. The hand appears with boater, club ribbon, settles it on head, rakish angle, disappears. Pause. WINNIE cranes a little further back and down.*) Slip on your drawers, dear, before you get singed. (*Pause.*) No? (*Pause.*)

110 Oh I see, you still have some of that stuff left. (*Pause.*) Work it well in, dear. (*Pause.*) Now the other. (*Pause. She turns back front, gazes before her. Happy expression.*) Oh this is going to be another happy day! (*Pause. Happy expression off. She pulls down spectacles and resumes lips. WILLIE opens newspaper, hands invisible. Tops of yellow sheets appear on either side of his head. WINNIE finishes lips, inspects them in mirror held a little further away.*) Ensign crimson. (*WILLIE turns page. WINNIE lays down lipstick and mirror, turns towards bag.*) Pale flag.

WILLIE turns page. WINNIE rummages in bag, brings out small ornate brimless hat with crumpled feather, turns back front, straightens hat, smooths feather, raises it towards head, arrests gesture as WILLIE reads.

Willie: His Grace and Most Reverend Father in God Dr Carolus
120 Hunter dead in tub.

Pause.

Winnie: (*gazing front, hat in hand, tone of fervent reminiscence*). Charlie Hunter! (*Pause.*) I close my eyes—(*she takes off spectacles and does so, hat in one hand, spectacles in other, WILLIE turns page*)—and am sitting on his knees again, in the back garden at Borough Green, under the horse-beech. (*Pause. She opens eyes, puts on spectacles, fiddles with hat.*) Oh the happy memories!

Pause. She raises hat towards head, arrests gesture as WILLIE reads.

Willie: Opening for smart youth.

Pause. She raises hat towards head, arrests gesture, takes off spectacles, gazes front, hat in one hand, spectacles in other.

Winnie: My first ball! (*Long pause.*) My second ball! (*Long pause. Closes eyes.*) My first kiss! (*Pause. WILLIE turns page. WINNIE opens eyes.*)
130   A Mr Johnson, or Johnston, or perhaps I should say John*stone*. Very bushy moustache, very tawny. (*Reverently.*) Almost ginger! (*Pause.*) Within a toolshed, though whose I cannot conceive. We had no toolshed and he most certainly had no toolshed. (*Closes eyes.*) I see the piles of pots. (*Pause.*) The tangles of bast. (*Pause.*) The shadows deepening among the rafters.

Pause. She opens eyes, puts on spectacles, raises hat towards head, arrests gesture as WILLIE reads.

Willie: Wanted bright boy.

Pause. WINNIE puts on hat hurriedly, looks for mirror. WILLIE turns page. WINNIE takes up mirror, inspects hat, lays down mirror, turns towards bag. Paper disappears. WINNIE rummages in bag, brings out magnifying-glass, turns back front, looks for toothbrush. Paper reappears, folded, and begins to fan WILLIE's face, hand invisible. WINNIE takes up toothbrush and examines handle through glass.

Winnie: Fully guaranteed . . . (*WILLIE stops fanning*) . . . genuine pure . . . (*Pause. WILLIE resumes fanning. WINNIE looks closer, reads.*) Fully guaranteed . . . (*WILLIE stops fanning*) . . . genuine
140   pure . . . (*Pause. WILLIE resumes fanning. WINNIE lays down glass and brush, takes handkerchief from bodice, takes off and polishes spectacles, puts on spectacles, looks for glass, takes up and polishes glass, lays down glass, looks for brush, takes up brush and wipes handle, lays down brush, puts handkerchief back in bodice, looks for glass, takes up glass, looks for brush, takes up brush and examines handle through glass.*) Fully guaranteed . . . (*WINNIE stops fanning*) . . . genuine pure . . . (*pause, WILLIE resumes fanning*) . . . hog's (*WILLIE stops fanning, pause*) . . . setae. (*Pause. WINNIE lays down glass and brush,*

paper disappears, WINNIE takes off spectacles, lays them down, gazes
150   *front.*) Hog's setae. (*Pause.*) That is what I find so wonderful, that
not a day goes by—(*smile*)—to speak in the old style—(*smile off*)—hardly a day, without some addition to one's knowledge however trifling, the addition I mean, provided one takes the pains. (*WILLIE's hand reappears with a postcard which he examines close to eyes.*) And if for some strange reason no further pains are possible, why then just close the eyes—(*she does so*)—and wait for the day to come—(*opens eyes*)—the happy day to come when flesh melts at so many degrees and the night of the moon has so many hundred hours. (*Pause.*) That is what I find so comforting when
160   I lose heart and envy the brute beast. (*Turning towards WILLIE.*) I hope you are taking in—(*She sees postcard, bends lower.*) What is that you have there, Willie, may I see? (*She reaches down with hand and WILLIE hands her card. The hairy forearm appears above slope, raised in gesture of giving, the hand open to take back, and remains in this position till card is returned. WINNIE turns back front and examines card.*) Heavens what are they up to! (*She looks for spectacles, puts them on and examines card.*) No but this is just genuine pure filth! (*Examines card.*) Make any nice-minded person want to vomit! (*Impatience of WILLIE's fingers. She looks for glass, takes it up*
170   *and examines card through glass. Long pause.*) What does that creature in the background think he's doing? (*Looks closer.*) Oh no really! (*Impatience of fingers. Last long look. She lays down glass, takes edge of card between right forefinger and thumb, averts head, takes nose between left forefinger and thumb.*) Pah! (*Drops card.*) Take it away! (*WILLIE's arm disappears. His hand reappears immediately, holding card. WINNIE takes off spectacles, lays them down, gazes before her. During what follows WILLIE continues to relish card, varying angles and distance from his eyes.*) Hog's setae. (*Puzzled expression.*) What exactly is a hog? (*Pause. Do.*) A sow of course I know, but a
180   hog . . . (*Puzzled expression off.*) Oh well what does it matter, that is what I always say, it will come back, that is what I find so wonderful, all comes back. (*Pause.*) All? (*Pause.*) No, not all. (*Smile.*) No no. (*Smile off.*) Not quite. (*Pause.*) A part. (*Pause*). Floats up, one fine day, out of the blue. (*Pause.*) That is what I find so wonderful. (*Pause. She turns towards bag. Hand and card disappear. She makes to rummage in bag, arrests gesture.*) No. (*She turns back front. Smile.*) No no. (*Smile off.*) Gently Winnie. (*She gazes front. WILLIE's hand reappears, takes off hat, disappears with hat.*) What then? (*Hand reappears, takes handkerchief from skull, disappears with*
190   *handkerchief. Sharply, as to one not paying attention.*) Winnie! (*WILLIE bows head out of sight.*) What *is* the alternative? (*Pause.*) What *is* the al— (*WILLIE blows nose loud and long, head and hands invisible. She turns to look at him. Pause. Head reappears. Pause. Hand reappears with handkerchief, spreads it on skull, disappears. Pause. Hand reappears with boater, settles it on head, rakish angle, disappears. Pause.*) Would

I had let you sleep on. (*She turns back front. Intermittent plucking at grass, head up and down, to animate following.*) Ah yes, if only I could bear to be alone, I mean prattle away with not a soul to hear. (*Pause.*) Not that I flatter myself you hear much, no Willie, God

200   forbid. (*Pause.*) Days perhaps when you hear nothing. (*Pause.*) But days too when you answer. (*Pause.*) So that I may say at all times, even when you do not answer and perhaps hear nothing, something of this is being heard, I am not merely talking to myself, that is in the wilderness, a thing I could never bear to do—for any length of time. (*Pause.*) That is what enables me to go on, go on talking that is. (*Pause.*) Whereas if you were to die—(*smile*)—to speak in the old style—(*smile off*)—or go away and leave me, then what would I do, what *could* I do, all day long, I mean between the bell for waking and the bell for sleep? (*Pause.*)

210   Simply gaze before me with compressed lips. (*Long pause while she does so. No more plucking.*) Not another word as long as I drew breath, nothing to break the silence of this place. (*Pause.*) Save possibly, now and then, every now and then, a sigh into my looking-glass. (*Pause.*) Or a brief . . . gale of laughter, should I happen to see the old joke again. (*Pause. Smile appears, broadens and seems about to culminate in laugh when suddenly replaced by expression of anxiety.*) My hair! (*Pause.*) Did I brush and comb my hair? (*Pause.*) I may have done. (*Pause.*) Normally I do. (*Pause.*) There is so little one *can* do. (*Pause.*) One does it all. (*Pause.*) All one can.

220   (*Pause.*) Tis only human. (*Pause.*) Human nature. (*She begins to inspect mound, looks up.*) Human weakness. (*She resumes inspection of mound, looks up.*) Natural weakness. (*She resumes inspection of mound.*) I see no comb. (*Inspects.*) Nor any hairbrush. (*Looks up. Puzzled expression. She turns to bag, rummages in it.*) The comb is here. (*Back front. Puzzled expression. Back to bag. Rummages.*) The brush is here. (*Back front. Puzzled expression.*) Perhaps I put them back, after use. (*Pause. Do.*) But normally I do not put things back, after use, no, I leave them lying about and put them back all together, at the end of the day. (*Smile.*) To speak in the old style.

230   (*Pause.*) The sweet old style. (*Smile off.*) And yet . . . I seem . . . to remember . . . (*Suddenly careless.*) Oh well, what does it matter, that is what I always say, I shall simply brush and comb them later on, purely and simply, I have the whole—(*Pause. Puzzled.*) Them? (*Pause.*) Or it? (*Pause.*) Brush and comb it? (*Pause.*) Sounds improper somehow. (*Pause. Turning a little towards WILLIE.*) What would you say, Willie? (*Pause. Turning a little further.*) What would you say, Willie, speaking of your hair, them or it? (*Pause.*) The hair on your head, I mean. (*Pause. Turning a little further.*) The hair on your head, Willie, what would you say speaking of the

240   hair on your head, them or it?

Long pause.

Willie: It.

Winnie: (*turning back front, joyful*). Oh you are going to talk to me today, this is going to be a happy day! (*Pause. Joy off.*) Another happy day. (*Pause.*) Ah well, where was I, hair, yes, later on, I shall be thankful for it later on. (*Pause.*) I have my—(*raises hands to hat*)—yes, on, my hat on—(*lowers hands*)—I cannot take it off now. (*Pause.*) To think there are times one cannot take off one's hat, not if one's life were at stake. Times one cannot put it on, times one cannot take it off. (*Pause.*) How often I have said, Put
250   on your hat now, Winnie, there is nothing else for it, take off your hat now, Winnie, like a good girl, it will do you good, and did not. (*Pause.*) Could not. (*Pause. She raises hand, frees a strand of hair from under hat, draws it towards eye, squints at it, lets it go, hand down.*) Golden you called it, that day, when the last guest was gone—(*hand up in gesture of raising a glass*)—to your golden . . . may it never . . . (*voices breaks*) . . . may it never . . . (*Hand down. Head down. Pause. Low.*) That day. (*Pause. Do.*) What day? (*Pause. Head up. Normal voice.*) What now? (*Pause.*) Words fail, there are times when even they fail. (*Turning a little towards WILLIE.*) Is that
260   not so, Willie? (*Pause. Turning a little further.*) Is not that so, Willie, that even words fail, at times? (*Pause. Back front.*) What is one to do then, until they come again? Brush and comb the hair, if it has not been done, or if there is some doubt, trim the nails if they are in need of trimming, these things tide one over. (*Pause.*) That is what I mean. (*Pause.*) That is all I mean. (*Pause.*) That is what I find so wonderful, that not a day goes by—(*smile*)—to speak in the old style—(*smile off*)—without some blessing—(*WILLIE collapses behind slope, his head disappears, WINNIE turns towards event*)—in disguise. (*She cranes back and down.*) Go back into your hole now,
270   Willie, you've exposed yourself enough. (*Pause.*) Do as I say, Willie, don't lie sprawling there in this hellish sun, go back into your hole. (*Pause.*) Go on now, Willie. (*WILLIE invisible starts crawling left towards hole.*) That's the man. (*She follows his progress with her eyes.*) Not head first, stupid, how are you going to turn? (*Pause.*) That's it . . . right round . . . now . . . back in. (*Pause.*) Oh I know it is not easy, dear, crawling backwards, but it is rewarding in the end. (*Pause.*) You have left your vaseline behind. (*She watches as he crawls back for vaseline.*) The lid! (*She watches as he crawls back towards hole. Irritated.*) Not head first, I tell you! (*Pause.*)
280   More to the right. (*Pause.*) The *right*, I said. (*Pause. Irritated.*) Keep your tail down, can't you! (*Pause.*) Now. (*Pause.*) There! (*All these directions loud. Now in her normal voice, still turned towards him.*) Can you hear me? (*Pause.*) I beseech you, Willie, just yes or no, can you hear me, just yes or nothing.

Pause.

Willie: Yes.

Winnie: (*turning front, same voice*). And now?

Willie: (*irritated*). Yes.

Winnie: (*less loud*). And now?

Willie: (*more irritated*). Yes.

290 **Winnie:** (*still less loud*). And now? (*A little louder.*) And now?

Willie: (*violently*). Yes!

Winnie: (*same voice*). Fear no more the heat o' the sun. (*Pause.*) Did you hear that?

Willie: (*irritated*). Yes.

Winnie: (*same voice*). What? (*Pause.*) What?

Willie: (*more irritated*). Fear no more.

Pause.

Winnie: (*same voice*). No more what? (*Pause.*) Fear no more what?

Willie: (*violently*). Fear no more!

Winnie: (*normal voice, gabbled*). Bless you Willie I do appreciate your
300   goodness I know what an effort it costs you, now you may relax I shall not trouble you again unless I am obliged to, by that I mean unless I come to the end of my own resources which is most unlikely, just to know that in theory you can hear me even though in fact you don't is all I need, just to feel you there within earshot and conceivably on the qui vive is all I ask, not to say anything I would not wish you to hear or liable to cause you pain, not to be just babbling away on trust as it is were not knowing and something gnawing at me. (*Pause for breath.*) Doubt. (*Places index and second finger on heart area, moves them about, brings them to rest.*)
310   Here. (*Moves them slightly.*) Abouts. (*Hand away.*) Oh no doubt the time will come when before I can utter a word I must make sure you heard the one that went before and then no doubt another come another time when I must learn to talk to myself a thing I could never bear to do such wilderness. (*Pause.*) Or gaze before me with compressed lips. (*She does so.*) All day long. (*Gaze and lips again.*) No. (*Smile.*) No no. (*Smile off.*) There is of course the bag. (*Turns towards it.*) There will always be the bag. (*Back front.*) Yes, I suppose so. (*Pause.*) Even when you are gone, Willie. (*She turns a little towards him.*) You *are* going, Willie, aren't you? (*Pause. Louder.*)
320   You *will* be going soon, Willie, won't you? (*Pause. Louder.*) Willie! (*Pause. She cranes back and down to look at him.*) So you have taken off your straw, that is wise. (*Pause.*) You do look snug, I must say, with your chin on your hands and the old blue eyes like saucers in the shadows. (*Pause.*) Can you see me from there I wonder, I still wonder. (*Pause.*) No? (*Back front.*) Oh I know it does not follow when two are gathered together—(*faltering*)—in this way—(*normal*)—that because one sees the other the other sees the

one, life has taught me that . . . too. (*Pause.*) Yes, life I suppose, there is no other word. (*She turns a little towards him.*) Could you
330   see me, Willie, do you think, from where you are, if you were to raise your eyes in my direction? (*Turns a little further.*) Lift up your eyes to me, Willie, and tell me can you see me, do that for me, I'll lean back as far as I can. (*Does so. Pause.*) No? (*Pause.*) Well never mind. (*Turns back painfully front.*) The earth is very tight today, can it be I have put on flesh, I trust not. (*Pause. Absently, eyes lowered.*) The great heat possibly. (*Starts to pat and stroke ground.*) All things expanding, some more than others. (*Pause. Patting and stroking.*) Some less. (*Pause. Do.*) Oh I can well imagine what is passing through your mind, it is not enough to have to
340   listen to the woman, now I must look at her as well. (*Pause. Do.*). Well it is very understandable. (*Pause. Do.*) Most understandable. (*Pause. Do.*) One does not appear to be asking a great deal, indeed at times it would seem hardly possible—(*voice breaks, falls to a murmur*)—to ask less—of a fellow-creature—to put it mildly—whereas actually—when you think about it—look into your heart—see the other—what he needs—peace—to be left in peace—then perhaps the moon—all this time—asking for the moon. (*Pause. Stroking hand suddenly still. Lively.*) Oh I say, what have we here? (*Bending head to ground, incredulous.*) Looks like life
350   of some kind! (*Looks for spectacles, puts them on, bends closer. Pause.*) An emmet! (*Recoils. Shrill.*) Willie, an emmet, a live emmet! (*Seizes magnifying-glass, bends to ground again, inspects through glass.*) Where's it gone? (*Inspects.*) Ah! (*Follows its progress through grass.*) Has like a little white ball in its arms. (*Follows progress. Hand still. Pause.*) It's gone in. (*Continues a moment to gaze at spot through glass, then slowly straightens up, lays down glass, takes off spectacles and gazes before her, spectacles in hand. Finally.*) Like a little white ball.

Long pause. Gesture to lay down spectacles.

Willie: Eggs.
Winnie: (*arresting gesture*). What?

Pause.

360 **Willie:** Eggs. (*Pause. Gesture to lay down glasses.*) Formication.
Winnie: (*arresting gesture*). What?

Pause.

Willie: Formication.

Pause. She lays down spectacles, gazes before her. Finally.

Winnie: (*murmur*). God. (*Pause. WILLIE laughs quietly. After a moment she joins in. They laugh quietly together. WILLIE stops. She laughs on a moment alone. WILLIE joins in. They laugh together. She stops. WILLIE laughs on a moment alone. He stops. Pause. Normal voice.*) Ah well what a joy in any case to hear you laugh again, Willie, I was convinced I never would, you never would. (*Pause.*) I suppose some people might think us a trifle irreverent, but I doubt it. (*Pause.*)

370 How can one better magnify the Almighty than by sniggering with him at his little jokes, particularly the poorer ones? (*Pause.*) I think you would back me up there, Willie. (*Pause.*) Or were we perhaps diverted by two quite different things? (*Pause.*) Oh well, what does it matter, that is what I always say, so long as one . . . you know . . . what is that wonderful line . . . laughing wild . . . something something laughing wild amid severest woe. (*Pause.*) And now? (*Long pause.*) Was I lovable once, Willie? (*Pause.*) Was I ever lovable? (*Pause.*) Do not misunderstand my question, I am not asking you if you loved me, we know all about that, I am

380 asking you if you found me lovable—at one stage. (*Pause.*) No? (*Pause.*) You can't? (*Pause.*) Well I admit it is a teaser. And you have done more than your bit already, for the time being, just lie back now and relax, I shall not trouble you again unless I am compelled to, just to know you are there within hearing and conceivably on the semi-alert is . . . er . . . paradise enow. (*Pause.*) The day is now well advanced. (*Smile.*) To speak in the old style. (*Smile off.*) And yet it is perhaps a little soon for my song. (*Pause.*) To sing too soon is a great mistake, I find. (*Turning towards bag.*) There is of course the bag. (*Looking at bag.*) The bag. (*Back*

390 *front.*) Could I enumerate its contents? (*Pause.*) No. (*Pause.*) Could I, if some kind person were to come along and ask, What all have you got in that big black bag, Winnie? give an exhaustive answer? (*Pause.*) No. (*Pause.*) The depths in particular, who knows what treasures. (*Pause.*) What comforts. (*Turns to look at bag.*) Yes, there is the bag. (*Back front.*) But something tells me, Do not overdo the bag, Winnie, make use of it of course, let it help you . . . along, when stuck, by all means, but cast your mind forward, something tells me, cast your mind forward, Winnie, to the time when words must fail—(*she closes eyes, pause, opens eyes*)—and do not overdo the

400 bag. (*Pause. She turns to look at bag.*) Perhaps just one quick dip. (*She turns back front, closes eyes, throws out left arm, plunges hand in bag and brings out revolver. Disgusted.*) You again! (*She opens eyes, brings revolver front and contemplates it. She weighs it in her palm.*) You'd think the weight of this thing would bring it down among the . . . last rounds. But no. It doesn't. Ever uppermost, like Browning. (*Pause.*) Brownie . . . (*Turning a little towards WILLIE.*) Remember Brownie, Willie? (*Pause.*) Remember how you used to keep on at me to take it away from you? Take it away, Winnie,

410   take it away, before I put myself out of my misery. (*Back front. Derisive.*) *Your* misery! (*To revolver.*) Oh I suppose it's a comfort to know you're there, but I'm tired of you. (*Pause.*) I'll leave you out, that's what I'll do. (*She lays revolver on ground to her right.*) There, that's your home from this day out. (*Smile.*) The old style! (*Smile off.*) And now? (*Long pause.*) Is gravity what it was, Willie, I fancy not. (*Pause.*) Yes, the feeling more and more that if I were not held—(*gesture*)—in this way, I would simply float up into the blue. (*Pause.*) And that perhaps some day the earth will yield and let me go, the pull is so great, yes, crack all round me and let me out. (*Pause.*) Don't you ever have that feeling, Willie, of being

420   sucked up? (*Pause.*) Don't you have to cling on sometimes, Willie? (*Pause. She turns a little towards him.*) Willie.

Pause.

Willie: *Sucked* up?
Winnie: Yes love, up into the blue, like gossamer. (*Pause.*) No? (*Pause.*) You don't? (*Pause.*) Ah well, natural laws, natural laws, I suppose it's like everything else, it all depends on the creature you happen to be. All I can say is for my part is that for me they are not what they were when I was young and . . . foolish and . . . (*faltering, head down*) . . . beautiful . . . possibly . . . lovely . . . in a way . . . to look at. (*Pause. Head up.*) Forgive me, Willie, sorrow

430   keeps breaking in. (*Normal voice.*) Ah well what a joy in any case to know you are there, as usual, and perhaps awake, and perhaps taking all this in, some of all this, what a happy day for me . . . it will have been. (*Pause.*) So far. (*Pause.*) What a blessing nothing grows, imagine if all this stuff were to start growing. (*Pause.*) Imagine. (*Pause.*) Ah yes, great mercies. (*Long pause.*) I can say no more. (*Pause.*) For the moment. (*Pause. Turns to look at bag. Back front. Smile.*) No no. (*Smile off. Looks at parasol.*) I suppose I might—(*takes up parasol*)—yes, I suppose I might . . . hoist this thing now. (*Begins to unfurl it. Following punctuated by mechanical*

440   *difficulties overcome.*) One keeps putting off—putting up—for fear of putting up—too soon—and the day goes by—quite by—without one's having put up—at all. (*Parasol now fully open. Turned to her right she twirls it idly this way and that.*) Ah yes, so little to say, so little to do, and the fear so great, certain days, of finding oneself . . . left, with hours still to run, before the bell for sleep, and nothing more to say, nothing more to do, that the days go by, certain days go by, quite by, the bell goes, and little or nothing said, little or nothing done. (*Raising parasol.*) That is the danger. (*Turning front.*) To be guarded against. (*She gazes front,*

450   *holding up parasol with right hand. Maximum pause.*) I used to perspire freely. (*Pause.*) Now hardly at all. (*Pause.*) The heat is much greater. (*Pause.*) The perspiration much less. (*Pause.*) That is

what I find so wonderful. (*Pause.*) The way man adapts himself.
(*Pause.*) To changing conditions. (*She transfers parasol to left hand.*
Long pause.) Holding up wearies the arm. (*Pause.*) Not if one is
going along. (*Pause.*) Only if one is at rest. (*Pause.*) That is a
curious observation. (*Pause.*) I hope you heard that, Willie, I should
be grieved to think you had not heard that. (*She takes parasol in*
both hands. Long pause.) I am weary, holding it up, and I cannot put
460   it down. (*Pause.*) I am worse off with it up than with it down, and
I cannot put it down. (*Pause.*) Reason says, Put it down, Winnie,
it is not helping you, put the thing down and get on with
something else. (*Pause.*) I cannot. (*Pause.*) I cannot move. (*Pause.*)
No, something must happen, in the world, take place, some
change, I cannot, if I am to move again. (*Pause.*) Willie. (*Mildly.*)
Help. (*Pause.*) No? (*Pause.*) Bid me put this thing down, Willie, I
would obey you instantly, as I have always done, honoured and
obeyed. (*Pause.*) Please, Willie. (*Mildly.*) For pity's sake. (*Pause.*)
No? (*Pause.*) You can't? (*Pause.*) Well I don't blame you, no, it
470   would ill become me, who cannot move, to blame my Willie
because he cannot speak. (*Pause.*) Fortunately I am in tongue
again. (*Pause.*) That is what I find so wonderful, my two lamps,
when one goes out the other burns brighter. (*Pause.*) Oh yes, great
mercies. (*Maximum pause. The parasol goes on fire. Smoke, flames if*
feasible. She sniffs, looks up, throws parasol to her right behind mound,
cranes back to watch it burning. Pause.) Ah earth you old
extinguisher. (*Back front.*) I presume this has occurred before,
though I cannot recall it. (*Pause.*) Can you, Willie? (*Turns a little*
towards him.) Can you recall this having occurred before? (*Pause.*
480   *Cranes back to look at him.*) Do you know what has occurred, Willie?
(*Pause.*) Have you gone off on me again? (*Pause.*) I do not ask if
you are alive to all that is going on, I merely ask if you have not
gone off on me again. (*Pause.*) Your eyes appear to be closed, but
that has no particular significance we know. (*Pause.*) Raise a
finger, dear, will you please, if you are not quite senseless. (*Pause.*)
Do that for me, Willie please, just the little finger, if you are still
conscious. (*Pause. Joyful.*) Oh all five, you are a darling today, now
I may continue with an easy mind. (*Back front.*) Yes, what ever
occurred that did not occur before and yet . . . I wonder, yes, I
490   confess I wonder. (*Pause.*) With the sun blazing so much fiercer
down, and hourly fiercer, is it not natural things should go on fire
never known to do so, in this way I mean, spontaneous like.
(*Pause.*) Shall I myself not melt perhaps in the end, or burn, oh I
do not mean necessarily burst into flames, no, just little by little
be charred to a black cinder, all this—(*ample gesture of*
arms)—visible flesh. (*Pause.*) On the other hand, did I ever know a
temperate time? (*Pause.*) No. (*Pause.*) I speak of temperate times
and torrid times, they are empty words. (*Pause.*) I speak of when
I was not yet caught—in this way—and had my legs and had the

500 use of my legs, and could seek out a shady place, like you, when I was tired of the sun, or a sunny place when I was tired of the shade, like you, and they are all empty words. (*Pause.*) It is no hotter today than yesterday, it will be no hotter tomorrow than today, how could it, and so on back into the far past, forward into the far future. (*Pause.*) And should one day the earth cover my breasts, then I shall never have seen my breasts, no one ever seen by breasts. (*Pause.*) I hope you caught something of that, Willie, I should be sorry to think you had caught nothing of all that, it is not every day I rise to such heights. (*Pause.*) Yes, something seems

510 to have occurred, something has seemed to occur, and nothing has occurred, nothing at all, you are quite right, Willie. (*Pause.*) The sunshade will be there again tomorrow, beside me on this mound, to help me through the day. (*Pause. She takes up mirror.*) I take up this little glass, I shiver it on a stone—(*does so*)—I throw it away—(*does so far behind her*)—it will be in the bag again tomorrow, without a scratch, to help me through the day. (*Pause.*) No, one can do nothing. (*Pause.*) That is what I find so wonderful, the way things . . . (*voice breaks, head down*) . . . things . . . so wonderful. (*Long pause, head down. Finally turns, still bowed, to bag,*

520 *brings out unidentifiable odds and ends, stuffs them back, fumbles deeper, brings out finally musical-box, winds it up, turns it on, listens for a moment holding it in both hands, huddled over it, turns back front, straightens up and listens to tune, holding box to breast with both hands. It plays the Waltz Duet "I love you so" from* The Merry Widow. *Gradually happy expression. She sways to the rhythm. Music stops. Pause. Brief burst of hoarse song without words—musical-box tune—from* WILLIE. *Increase of happy expression. She lays down box.*) Oh this will have been a happy day! (*She claps hands.*) Again, Willie, again! (*Claps.*) Encore, Willie, please! (*Pause. Happy*

530 *expression off.*) No? You won't do that for me? (*Pause.*) Well it is very understandable, very understandable. One cannot sing just to please someone, however much one loves them, no, song must come from the heart, that is what I always say, pour out from the inmost, like a thrush. (*Pause.*) How often I have said, in evil hours, Sing now, Winnie, sing your song, there is nothing else for it, and did not. (*Pause.*) Could not. (*Pause.*) No, like the thrush, or the bird of dawning, with no thought of benefit, to oneself or anyone else. (*Pause.*) And now? (*Long pause. Low.*) Strange feeling. (*Pause. Do.*) Strange feeling that someone is looking at me. I am clear, then

540 dim, then gone, then dim again, then clear again, and so on, back and forth, in and out of someone's eye. (*Pause. Do.*) Strange? (*Pause. Do.*) No, here all is strange. (*Pause. Normal voice.*) Something says, Stop talking now, Winnie, for a minute, don't squander all your words for the day, stop talking and do something for a change, will you? (*She raises hands and holds them open before her eyes. Apostrophic.*) Do something! (*She closes hands.*) What claws!

(*She turns to bag, rummages in it, brings out finally a nailfile, turns back front and begins to file nails. Files for a time in silence, then the following punctuated by filing.*) There floats up—into my thoughts—
550   a Mr Shower—a Mr and perhaps a Mrs Shower—no—they are holding hands—his fiancée then more likely—or just some—loved one. (*Looks closer at nails.*) Very brittle today. (*Resumes filing.*) Shower—Shower—does the name mean anything—to you, Willie—evoke any reality, I mean—for you, Willie—don't answer if you don't—feel up to it—you have done more—than your bit—already—Shower—Shower. (*Inspects filed nails.*) Bit more like it. (*Raises head, gazes front.*) Keep yourself nice, Winnie, that's what I always say, come what may, keep yourself nice. (*Pause. Resumes filing.*) Yes—Shower—Shower—(*stops filing, raises head, gazes front, pause*)—
560   or Cooker, perhaps I should say Cooker. (*Turning a little towards WILLIE.*) Cooker, Willie, does Cooker strike a chord? (*Pause. Turns a little further. Louder.*) Cooker, Willie, does Cooker ring a bell, the name Cooker? (*Pause. She cranes back to look at him. Pause.*) Oh, really! (*Pause.*) Have you no handkerchief, darling? (*Pause.*) Have you no delicacy? (*Pause.*) Oh, Willie, you're not eating it! Spit it out, dear, spit it out! (*Pause. Back front.*) Ah well, I suppose it's only natural. (*Break in voice.*) Human. (*Pause. Do.*) What *is* one to do? (*Head down. Do.*) All day long. (*Pause. Do.*) Day after day. (*Pause. Head up. Smile. Calm.*) The old style! (*Smile off.*
570   *Resumes nails.*) No, done him. (*Passes on to next.*) Should have put on my glasses. (*Pause.*) Too late now. (*Finishes left hand, inspects it.*) Bit more human. (*Starts right hand. Following punctuated as before.*) Well anyway—this man Shower—or Cooker—no matter—and the woman—hand in hand—in the other hands bags—kind of big brown grips—standing there gaping at me—and at last this man Shower—or Cooker—ends in er anyway—stake my life on that—What's she doing? he says—What's the idea? he says—stuck up to her diddies in the bleeding ground—coarse fellow—What does it mean? he says—What's it meant to mean?—and so on—lot
580   more stuff like that—usual drivel—Do you hear me? he says—I do, she says, God help me—What do you mean, he says, God help you? (*Stops filing, raises head, gazes front.*) And you, she says, what's the idea of you, she says, what are you meant to mean? It is because you're still on your two flat feet, with your old ditty full of tinned muck and changes of underwear, dragging me up and down this fornicating wilderness, coarse creature, fit mate—(*with sudden violence*)—let go of my hand and drop for God's sake, she says, drop! (*Pause. Resumes filing.*) Why doesn't he dig her out? he says—referring to you, my dear—What good is she to him like
590   that?—What good is he to her like that?—and so on—usual tosh—Good! she says, have a heart for God's sake—Dig her out, he says, dig her out, no sense in her like that—Dig her out with what? she says—I'd dig her out with my bare hands, he

says—must have been man and—wife. (*Files in silence.*) Next thing they're away—hand in hand—and the bags—dim—then gone—last human kind—to stray this way. (*Finishes right hand, inspects it, lays down file, gazes front.*) Strange thing, time like this, drift up into the mind. (*Pause.*) Strange? (*Pause.*) No, here all is strange. (*Pause.*) Thankful for it in any case. (*Voice breaks.*) Most thankful. (*Head*

600   *down. Pause. Head up. Calm.*) Bow and raise the head, bow and raise, always that. (*Pause.*) And now? (*Long pause. Starts putting things back in bag, toothbrush last. This operation, interrupted by pauses as indicated, punctuates following.*) It is perhaps a little soon—to make ready—for the night—(*stops tidying, head up, smile*)—the old style!—(*smile off, resumes tidying*)—and yet I do—make ready for the night—feeling it at hand—the bell for sleep—saying to myself—Winnie—it will not be long now, Winnie—until the bell for sleep. (*Stops tidying, head up.*) Sometimes I am wrong. (*Smile.*) But not often. (*Smile off.*) Sometimes all is over, for the day, all

610   done, all said, all ready for the night, and the day not over, far from over, the night not ready, far, far from ready. (*Smile.*) But not often. (*Smile off.*) Yes, the bell for sleep, when I feel it at hand, and so make ready for the night—(*gesture*)—in this way, sometimes I am wrong—(*smile*)—but not often. (*Smile off. Resumes tidying.*) I used to think—I say I used to think—that all these things—put back into the bag—if too soon—put back too soon—could be taken out again—if necessary—if needed—and so on—indefinitely—back into the bag—back out of the bag—until the bell—went. (*Stops tidying, head up, smile.*) But no. (*Smile broader.*) No no. (*Smile off.*

620   *Resumes tidying.*) I suppose this—might seem strange—this— what shall I say—this what I have said—yes—(*she takes up revolver*)—strange—(*she turns to put revolver in bag*)—were it not—(*about to put revolver in bag she arrests gesture and turns back front*)—were it not—(*she lays down revolver to her right, stops tidying, head up*)—that all seems strange. (*Pause.*) Most strange. (*Pause.*) Never any change. (*Pause.*) And more and more strange. (*Pause. She bends to mound again, takes up last object, i.e., toothbrush, and turns to put it in bag when her attention is drawn to disturbance from WILLIE. She cranes back and to her right to see. Pause.*) Weary of your hole,

630   dear? (*Pause.*) Well I can understand that. (*Pause.*) Don't forget your straw. (*Pause.*) Not the crawler you were, poor darling. (*Pause.*) No, not the crawler I gave my heart to. (*Pause.*) The hands and knees, love, try the hands and knees. (*Pause.*) The knees! The knees! (*Pause.*) What a curse, mobility! (*She follows with eyes his progress towards her behind mound, i.e., towards place he occupied at beginning of act.*) Another foot, Willie, and you're home. (*Pause as she observes last foot.*) Ah! (*Turns back front laboriously, rubs neck.*) Crick in my neck admiring you. (*Rubs neck.*) But it's worth it, well worth it. (*Turning slightly towards him.*) Do you know what I dream

640   sometimes? (*Pause.*) What I dream sometimes, Willie. (*Pause.*) That you'll come round and live this side where I could see you. (*Pause. Back front.*) I'd be a different woman. (*Pause.*) Unrecognizable. (*Turning slightly towards him.*) Or just now and then, come round this side just every now and then and let me feast on you. (*Back front.*) But you can't, I know. (*Head down.*) I know. (*Pause. Head up.*) Well anyway—(*looks at toothbrush in her hand*)—can't be long now—(*looks at brush*)—until the bell. (*Top back of WILLIE's head appears above slope. WINNIE looks closer at brush.*) Fully guaranteed . . . (*head up*) . . . what's this it was? (*WILLIE's hand appears with*

650   *handkerchief, spreads it on skull, disappears.*) Genuine pure . . . fully guaranteed . . . (*WILLIE's hand appears with boater, settles it on head, rakish angle, disappears*) . . . genuine pure . . . ah! hog's setae. (*Pause.*) What is a hog exactly? (*Pause. Turns slightly towards WILLIE.*) What exactly is a hog, Willie, do you know, I can't remember. (*Pause. Turning a little further, pleading.*) What *is* a hog, Willie, please!

Pause.

Willie: Castrated male swine. (*Happy expression appears on WINNIE's face.*) Reared for slaughter.

Happy expression increases. WILLIE opens newspaper, hands invisible. Tops of yellow sheets appear on either side of his head. WINNIE gazes before her with happy expression.

Winnie: Oh this *is* a happy day! This will have been another happy

660   day! (*Pause.*) After all. (*Pause.*) So far.

Pause. Happy expression off. WILLIE turns page. Pause. He turns another page. Pause.

Willie: Opening for smart youth.

Pause. WINNIE takes off hat, turns to put it in bag, arrests gesture, turns back front. Smile.

Winnie: No. (*Smile broader.*) No no. (*Smile off. Puts on hat again, gazes front, pause.*) And now? (*Pause.*) Sing. (*Pause.*) Sing your song, Winnie. (*Pause.*) No? (*Pause.*) Then pray. (*Pause.*) Pray your prayer, Winnie.

Pause. WILLIE turns page. Pause.

Willie: Wanted bright boy.

Pause. WINNIE gazes before her. WILLIE turns page. Pause. Newspaper disappears. Long pause.

Pray your old prayer, Winnie.

Long pause.

Curtain

Act II

Scene as before.

WINNIE imbedded up to neck, hat on head, eyes closed. Her head, which she can no longer turn, nor bow, nor raise, faces front motionless throughout act. Movements of eyes as indicated.

Bag and parasol as before. Revolver conspicuous to her right on mound.

Long pause.

Bell rings loudly. She opens eyes at once. Bell stops. She gazes front. Long pause.

Winnie: Hail, holy light. (*Long pause. She closes her eyes. Bell rings loudly. She opens eyes at once. Bell stops. She gazes front. Long smile. Smile off. Long pause.*) Someone is looking at me still. (*Pause.*) Caring for me still. (*Pause.*) That is what I find so wonderful. (*Pause.*) Eyes on my eyes. (*Pause.*) What is that unforgettable line? (*Pause. Eyes right.*) Willie. (*Pause. Louder.*) Willie. (*Pause. Eyes front.*) May one still speak of time? (*Pause.*) Say it is a long time now, Willie, since I saw you. (*Pause.*) Since I heard you. (*Pause.*) May one? (*Pause.*) One does. (*Smile.*) The old style! (*Smile off.*)
10   There is so little one can speak of. (*Pause.*) One speaks of it all. (*Pause.*) All one can. (*Pause.*) I used to think . . . (*pause*) . . . I say I used to think that I would learn to talk alone. (*Pause.*) By that I mean to myself, the wilderness. (*Smile.*) But no. (*Smile broader.*) No no. (*Smile off.*) Ergo you are there. (*Pause.*) Oh no doubt you are dead, like the others, no doubt you have died, or gone away and left me, like the others, it doesn't matter, you are there. (*Pause. Eyes left.*) The bag too is there, the same as ever, I can see it. (*Pause. Eyes right. Louder.*) The bag is there, Willie, as good as ever, the one you gave me that day . . . to go to market.
20   (*Pause. Eyes front.*) That day. (*Pause.*) What day? (*Pause.*) I used to pray. (*Pause.*) I say I used to pray. (*Pause.*) Yes, I must confess I did. (*Smile.*) Not now. (*Smile broader.*) No no. (*Smile off. Pause.*) Then . . . now . . . what difficulties here, for the mind. (*Pause.*) To have been always what I am—and so changed from what I

was. (*Pause.*) I am the one, I say the one, then the other. (*Pause.*) Now the one, then the other. (*Pause.*) There is so little one can say, one says it all. (*Pause.*) All one can. (*Pause.*) And no truth in it anywhere. (*Pause.*) My arms. (*Pause.*) My breasts. (*Pause.*) What arms? (*Pause.*) What breasts? (*Pause.*) Willie. (*Pause.*) What Willie?

30 (*Sudden vehement affirmation.*) My Willie! (*Eyes right, calling.*) Willie! (*Pause. Louder.*) Willie! (*Pause. Eyes front.*) Ah well, not to know, not to know for sure, great mercy, all I ask. (*Pause.*) Ah yes . . . then . . . now . . . beechen green . . . this . . . Charlie . . . kisses . . . this . . . all that . . . deep trouble for the mind. (*Pause.*) But it does not trouble mine. (*Smile.*) Not now. (*Smile broader.*) No no. (*Smile off. Long pause. She closes eyes. Bell rings loudly. She opens eyes. Pause.*) Eyes float up that seem to close in peace . . . to see . . . in peace. (*Pause.*) Not mine. (*Smile.*) Not now. (*Smile broader.*) No no. (*Smile off. Long pause.*) Willie. (*Pause.*)

40 Do you think the earth has lost its atmosphere, Willie? (*Pause.*) Do you, Willie? (*Pause.*) You have no opinion? (*Pause.*) Well that is like you, you never had any opinion about anything. (*Pause.*) It's understandable. (*Pause.*) Most. (*Pause.*) The earthball. (*Pause.*) I sometimes wonder. (*Pause.*) Perhaps not quite all. (*Pause.*) There always remains something. (*Pause.*) Of everything. (*Pause.*) Some remains. (*Pause.*) If the mind were to go. (*Pause.*) It won't of course. (*Pause.*) Not quite. (*Pause.*) Not mine. (*Smile*) Not now. (*Smile broader.*) No no. (*Smile off. Long pause.*) It might be the eternal cold. (*Pause.*) Everlasting perishing cold. (*Pause.*) Just

50 chance, I take it, happy chance. (*Pause.*) Oh yes, great mercies, great mercies. (*Pause.*) And now? (*Long pause.*) The face. (*Pause.*) The nose. (*She squints down.*) I can see it . . . (*squinting down*) . . . the tip . . . the nostrils . . . breath of life . . . that curve you so admired . . . (*pouts*) . . . a hint of lip . . . (*pouts again*) . . . if I pout them out . . . (*sticks out tongue*) . . . the tongue of course . . . you so admired . . . if I stick it out . . . (*sticks it out again*) . . . the tip . . . (*eyes up*) . . . suspicion of brow . . . eyebrow . . . imagination possibly . . . (*eyes left*) . . . cheek . . . no . . . (*eyes right*) . . . no . . . (*distends cheeks*)

60 . . . even if I puff them out . . . (*eyes left, distends cheeks again*) . . . no . . . no damask. (*Eyes front.*) That is all. (*Pause.*) The bag of course . . . (*eyes left*) . . . a little blurred perhaps . . . but the bag. (*Eyes front. Offhand.*) The earth of course and sky. (*Eyes right.*) The sunshade you gave me . . . that day . . . (*pause*) . . . that day . . . the lake . . . the reeds. (*Eyes front. Pause.*) What day? (*Pause.*) What reeds? (*Long pause. Eyes close. Bell rings loudly. Eyes open. Pause. Eyes right.*) Brownie of course. (*Pause.*) You remember Brownie, Willie, I can see him. (*Pause.*) Brownie is there, Willie, beside me. (*Pause. Loud.*) Brownie is

70 there, Willie. (*Pause. Eyes front.*) That is all. (*Pause.*) What would I do without them. (*Pause.*) What would I do without them, when

words fail? (*Pause.*) Gaze before me, with compressed lips. (*Long pause while she does so.*) I cannot. (*Pause.*) Ah yes, great mercies, great mercies. (*Long pause. Low.*) Sometimes I hear sounds. (*Listening expression. Normal voice.*) But not often. (*Pause.*) They are a boon, sounds are a boon, they help me . . . through the day. (*Smile*) The old style! (*Smile off.*) Yes, those are happy days, when there are sounds. (*Pause.*) When I hear sounds. (*Pause.*) I used to think . . . (*pause*) . . . I say I used to think they were in my

80   head. (*Smile.*) But no. (*Smile broader.*) No no. (*Smile off.*) That was just logic. (*Pause.*) Reason. (*Pause.*) I have not lost my reason. (*Pause.*) Not yet. (*Pause.*) Not all. (*Pause.*) Some remains. (*Pause.*) Sounds. (*Pause.*) Like little . . . sunderings, little falls . . . apart. (*Pause. Low.*) It's things, Willie. (*Pause. Normal voice.*) In the bag, outside the bag. (*Pause.*) Ah yes, things have their life, that is what I always say, *things* have a life. (*Pause.*) Take my looking-glass, it doesn't need me. (*Pause.*) The bell. (*Pause.*) It hurts like a knife. (*Pause.*) A gouge. (*Pause.*) One cannot ignore it. (*Pause.*) How often . . . (*pause*) . . . I say how often I have said,

90   Ignore it, Winnie, ignore the bell, pay no heed, just sleep and wake, sleep and wake, as you please, open and close the eyes, as you please, or in the way you find most helpful. (*Pause.*) Open and close the eyes, Winnie, open and close, always that. (*Pause.*) But no. (*Smile.*) Not now. (*Smile broader.*) No no. (*Smile off. Pause.*) What now? (*Pause.*) What now, Willie? (*Long pause.*) There is my story of course, when all else fails. (*Pause.*) A life. (*Smile.*) A long life. (*Smile off.*) Beginning in the womb, where life used to begin, Mildred has memories, she will have memories, of the womb, before she dies, the mother's womb. (*Pause.*) She is now four or

100   five already and has recently been given a big waxen dolly. (*Pause.*) Fully clothed, complete outfit. (*Pause.*) Shoes, socks, undies, complete set, frilly frock, gloves. (*Pause.*) White mesh. (*Pause.*) A little white straw hat with a chin elastic. (*Pause.*) Pearly necklet. (*Pause.*) A little picture-book with legends in real print to go under her arm when she takes her walk. (*Pause.*) China blue eyes that open and shut. (*Pause. Narrative.*) The sun was not well up when Milly rose, descended the steep . . . (*pause*) . . . slipped on her nightgown, descended all alone the steep wooden stairs, backwards on all fours, though she had been forbidden to do

110   so, entered the . . . (*pause*) . . . tiptoed down the silent passage, entered the nursery and began to undress Dolly. (*Pause.*) Crept under the table and began to undress Dolly. (*Pause.*) Scolding her . . . the while. (*Pause.*) Suddenly a mouse—(*Long pause.*) Gently, Winnie. (*Long pause. Calling.*) Willie! (*Pause. Louder.*) Willie! (*Pause. Mild reproach.*) I sometimes find your attitude a little strange, Willie, all this time, it is not like you to be wantonly cruel. (*Pause.*) Strange? (*Pause.*) No. (*Smile.*) Not here. (*Smile broader.*) Not now. (*Smile off.*) And yet . . . (*Suddenly anxious.*) I do

hope nothing is amiss. (*Eyes right, loud.*) Is all well, dear? (*Pause.*
120 *Eyes front. To herself.*) God grant he did not go in head foremost!
(*Eyes right, loud.*) You're not stuck, Willie? (*Pause. Do.*) You're not
jammed, Willie? (*Eyes front, distressed.*) Perhaps he is crying out
for help all this time and I do not hear him! (*Pause.*) I do of
course hear cries. (*Pause.*) But they are in my head surely. (*Pause.*)
Is it possible that . . . (*Pause. With finality.*) No no, my head was
always full of cries. (*Pause.*) Faint confused cries. (*Pause.*) They
come. (*Pause.*) Then go. (*Pause.*) As on a wind. (*Pause.*) That is
what I find so wonderful. (*Pause.*) They cease. (*Pause.*) Ah yes,
great mercies, great mercies. (*Pause.*) The day is now well
130 advanced. (*Smile. Smile off.*) And yet it is perhaps a little soon for
my song. (*Pause.*) To sing too soon is fatal, I always find. (*Pause.*)
On the other hand it is possible to leave it too late. (*Pause.*) The
bell goes for sleep and one has not sung. (*Pause.*) The whole day
has flown—(*smile, smile off*)—flown by, quite by, and no song of
any class, kind or description. (*Pause.*) There is a problem here.
(*Pause.*) One cannot sing . . . just like that, no. (*Pause.*) It bubbles
up, for some unknown reason, the time is ill chosen, one chokes it
back. (*Pause.*) One says, Now is the time, it is now or never, and
one cannot. (*Pause.*) Simply cannot sing. (*Pause.*) Not a note.
140 (*Pause.*) Another thing, Willie, while we are on this subject.
(*Pause.*) The sadness after long. (*Pause.*) Have you run across that,
Willie? (*Pause.*) In the course of your experience. (*Pause.*) No?
(*Pause.*) Sadness after intimate sexual intercourse one is familiar
with of course. (*Pause.*) You would concur with Aristotle there,
Willie, I fancy. (*Pause.*) Yes, that one knows and is prepared to
face. (*Pause.*) But after song . . . (*Pause.*) It does not last of course.
(*Pause.*) That is what I find so wonderful. (*Pause.*) It wears away.
(*Pause.*) What are those exquisite lines? (*Pause.*) Go forget me why
should something o'er that something shadow fling . . . go forget
150 me . . . why should sorrow . . . brightly smile . . . go forget me
. . . never hear me . . . sweetly smile . . . brightly sing . . .
(*Pause. With a sigh.*) One loses one's classics. (*Pause.*) Oh not all.
(*Pause.*) A part. (*Pause.*) A part remains. (*Pause.*) That is what I
find so wonderful, a part remains, of one's classics, to help one
through the day. (*Pause.*) Oh yes, many mercies, many mercies.
(*Pause.*) And now? (*Pause.*) And now, Willie? (*Long pause.*) I call
to the eye of the mind . . . Mr. Shower—or Cooker. (*She closes her
eyes. Bell rings loudly. She opens her eyes. Pause.*) Hand in hand, in
the other hands bags. (*Pause.*) Getting on . . . in life. (*Pause.*) No
160 longer young, not yet old. (*Pause.*) Standing there gaping at me.
(*Pause.*) Can't have been a bad bosom, he says, in its day. (*Pause.*)
Seen worse shoulders, he says, in my time. (*Pause.*) Does she feel
her legs? he says. (*Pause.*) Is there any life in her legs? he says.
(*Pause.*) Has she anything on underneath? he says. (*Pause.*) Ask
her, he says, I'm shy. (*Pause.*) Ask her what? she says. (*Pause.*)

Is there any life in her legs. (*Pause.*) Has she anything on underneath. (*Pause.*) Ask her yourself, she says. (*Pause. With sudden violence.*) Let go of me for Christ sake and drop! (*Pause. Do.*) Drop dead! (*Smile.*) But no. (*Smile broader.*) No no. (*Smile off.*)

170   I watch them recede. (*Pause.*) Hand in hand—and the bags. (*Pause.*) Dim. (*Pause.*) Then gone. (*Pause.*) Last human kind—to stray this way. (*Pause.*) Up to date. (*Pause.*) And now? (*Pause. Low.*) Help. (*Pause. Do.*) Help, Willie. (*Pause. Do.*) No? (*Long pause. Narrative.*) Suddenly a mouse . . . (*Pause.*) Suddenly a mouse ran up her little thigh and Mildred, dropping Dolly in her fright, began to scream—(*WINNIE gives a sudden piercing scream*)—and screamed and screamed—(*WINNIE screams twice*)—screamed and screamed and screamed and screamed till all came running, in their night attire, papa, mamma, Bibby and . . . old Annie, to

180   see what was the matter . . . (*pause*) . . . what on earth could possibly be the matter. (*Pause.*) Too late. (*Pause.*) Too late. (*Long pause. Just audible.*) Willie. (*Pause. Normal voice.*) Ah well, not long now, Winnie, can't be long now, until the bell for sleep. (*Pause.*) Then you may close your eyes, then you *must* close your eyes—and keep them closed. (*Pause.*) Why say that again? (*Pause.*) I used to think . . . (*pause*) . . . I say I used to think there was no difference between one fraction of a second and the next (*Pause.*) I used to say . . . (*pause*) . . . I say I used to say, Winnie, you are changeless, there is never any difference between

190   one fraction of a second and the next. (*Pause.*) Why bring that up again? (*Pause.*) There is so little one can bring up, one brings up all. (*Pause.*) All one can. (*Pause.*) My neck is hurting me. (*Pause. With sudden violence.*) My neck is hurting me! (*Pause.*) Ah that's better. (*With mild irritation.*) Everything within reason. (*Long pause.*) I can do no more. (*Pause.*) Say no more. (*Pause.*) But I must say more. (*Pause.*) Problem here. (*Pause.*) No, something must move, in the world, I can't any more. (*Pause.*) A zephyr. (*Pause.*) A breath. (*Pause.*) What are those immortal lines? (*Pause.*) It might be the eternal dark. (*Pause.*) Black night without end. (*Pause.*) Just

200   chance, I take it, happy chance. (*Pause.*) Oh yes, abounding mercies. (*Long pause.*) And now? (*Pause.*) And now, Willie? (*Long pause.*) That day. (*Pause.*) The pink fizz. (*Pause.*) The flute glasses. (*Pause.*) The last guest gone. (*Pause.*) The last bumper with the bodies nearly touching. (*Pause.*) The look. (*Long pause.*) What day? (*Long pause.*) What look? (*Long pause.*) I hear cries. (*Pause.*) Sing. (*Pause.*) Sing your old song, Winnie. *Long pause. Suddenly alert expression. Eyes switch right. WILLIE's head appears to her right round corner of mound. He is on all fours, dressed to kill—top hat, morning coat, striped trousers, etc., white gloves in hand. Very long bushy white*

210   *Battle of Britain moustache. He halts, gazes front, smooths moustache. He emerges completely from behind mound, turns to his left, halts, looks up at WINNIE. He advances on all fours toward centre, halts, turns head front, gazes front, strokes moustache, straightens tie, adjusts hat,*

advances a little further, halts, takes off hat and looks up at WINNIE.
He is now not far from centre and within her field of vision. Unable to
sustain effort of looking up he sinks head to ground.

Winnie: (*mondaine*). Well this is an unexpected pleasure! (*Pause.*)
Reminds me of the day you came whining for my hand. (*Pause.*)
I worship you, Winnie, be mine. (*He looks up.*) Life a mockery

220 without Win. (*She goes off into a giggle.*) What a get up, you do look
a sight! (*Giggles.*) Where are the flowers? (*Pause.*) That smile today.
(*WILLIE sinks head.*) What's that on your neck, an anthrax? (*Pause.*)
Want to watch that, Willie, before it gets a hold on you. (*Pause.*)
Where were you all this time? (*Pause.*) What were you doing all this
time? (*Pause.*) Changing? (*Pause.*) Did you not hear me screaming for
you? (*Pause.*) Did you get stuck in your hole? (*Pause. He looks up.*)
That's right, Willie, look at me. (*Pause.*) Feast your old eyes, Willie.
(*Pause.*) Does anything remain? (*Pause.*) Any remains? (*Pause.*) No?
(*Pause.*) I haven't been able to look after it, you know. (*He sinks his*

230 *head.*) You are still recognizable, in a way. (*Pause.*) Are you thinking
of coming to live this side now . . . for a bit maybe? (*Pause.*) No?
(*Pause.*) Just a brief call? (*Pause.*) Have you gone deaf, Willie?
(*Pause.*) Dumb? (*Pause.*) Oh I know you were never one to talk, I
worship you Winnie be mine and then nothing from that day forth
only tidbits from Reynolds' News. (*Eyes front. Pause.*) Ah well, what
matter, that's what I always say, it will have been a happy day, after
all, another happy day. (*Pause.*) Not long now, Winnie. (*Pause.*) I hear
cries. (*Pause.*) Do you ever hear cries, Willie? (*Pause.*) No? (*Eyes back*
on WILLIE.) Willie. (*Pause.*) Look at me again, Willie. (*Pause.*) Once

240 more, Willie, (*He looks up. Happily.*) Ah! (*Pause. Shocked.*) What ails
you, Willie, I never saw such an expression! (*Pause.*) Put on your hat,
dear, it's the sun, don't stand on ceremony, I won't mind. (*He drops*
hat and gloves and starts to crawl up mound towards her. Gleeful.) Oh I
say, this is terrific! (*He halts, clinging to mound with one hand, reaching*
up with the other.) Come on, dear, put a bit of jizz into it, I'll cheer
you on. (*Pause.*) Is it me you're after, Willie . . . or is it something
else? (*Pause.*) Do you want to touch my face . . . again? (*Pause.*) Is it
a kiss you're after, Willie . . . or is it something else? (*Pause.*) There
was a time when I could have given you a hand. (*Pause.*) And then a

250 time before that again when I did give you a hand. (*Pause.*) You
were always in dire need of a hand, Willie. (*He slithers back to foot of*
mound and lies with face to ground.) Brrum! (*Pause. He rises to hands*
and knees, raises his face towards her.) Have another go, Willie, I'll
cheer you on. (*Pause.*) Don't look at me like that! (*Pause. Vehement.*)
Don't look at me like that! (*Pause. Low.*) Have you gone off your
head, Willie? (*Pause. Do.*) Out of your poor old wits, Willie?

Pause.

Willie: (*just audible*). Win.

Pause. WINNIE's eyes front. Happy expression appears, grows.

Winnie: Win! (*Pause.*) Oh this *is* a happy day, this will have been another happy day! (*Pause.*) After all. (*Pause.*) So far.

Pause. She hums tentatively beginning of song, then sings softly, musical-box tune.

260
Though I say not
What I may not
Let you hear,
Yet the swaying
Dance is saying,
Love me dear!
Every touch of fingers
Tells me what I know,
Says for you,
It's true, it's true,
270
You love me so!

Pause. Happy expression off. She closes her eyes. Bell rings loudly. She opens her eyes. She smiles, gazing front. She turns her eyes, smiling, to WILLIE, still on his hands and knees looking up at her. Smile off. They look at each other. Long pause.

Curtain

ACCOUNT: STEPHEN WATT ON A MARXIST APPROACH TO *HAPPY DAYS*

According to Watt, most Marxist criticism has tended to dismiss Beckett's dramas as merely "ahistorical, allegorical, bourgeois work." Watt thinks, however, that the time has come to reassess such a position.

In *Happy Days*, Winnie's memories of the back garden in Borough Green act like Nell's recollections of Lake Como in Beckett's *End Game* to suggest what the critic Northrop Frye has called "a green world"— that is, a land of heart's desire somehow outside the material, social, and political realities that elsewhere impinge on human life. Such "green worlds" abound in literature—the forest of Arden in Shakespeare's *As You Like It* and Gonzalo's republic in *The Tempest* make two of many examples.

By its nature, the green world is one "immune to the very predicaments of Beckett's characters." Those predicaments include the social

Stephen Watt, "Beckett by Way of Baudrillard: Toward a Political Reading of Samuel Beckett's Drama" pp. 103–123 in Katherine H. Burkman, ed., *Myth and Ritual in the Plays of Samuel Beckett* (Rutherford, NJ: Fairleigh Dickinson University Press, 1987). © 1987 by Associated University Presses, Inc. 440 Forsgate Drive, Cranbury, NJ 08512.

and political hierarchies that oppose ideals of equality and community, and Beckett often explores a clash between the human values associated with "nature" and those associated with "social status":

> In fact this opposition—the desire to acquire, regain, or maintain a defined location in a social hierarchy and the opposing impulse symbolized by the green world to escape from such a hierarchy—emerges in *Gadded, End Game, Happy Days,* and others.

Looking further into the opposition between the two "worlds," Watt examines the function of material objects in Beckett's drama in general, and *Happy Days* in particular, in the light of ideas about economic consumption formulated by the French Marxist critic, Jean Baudrillard. For Baudrillard, no material objects are consumed simply because of their real use to the consumer, their "use-value." A cheap car, for example, will produce transportation more or less equal to that of an expensive car. But if use-value is not the point of consumption, it follows that objects of pure wealth cannot be desired because they have (like money or gold) an "exchange-value" in that they can be traded for objects that have use-value. If neither use-value nor exchange-value is what people really desire to consume, what then are we to make of the human *motive* for gaining greater and greater wealth (or the accumulation of more and more exchange-values)?

Baudrillard explains the economic consumption of material objects by claiming that what is really being consumed is *ideas* about their worth and particularly about the social status their consumption is supposed to convey. Buying an expensive car, for example, may be considered as buying not transportation but a *sign* of wealth in general. Hence, what one really consumes is the *prestige* that supposedly attaches to wealth, not the material objects that classical economics has traditionally defined as the ultimate constituents of wealth:

> This "logic" manifests itself time and time again in Beckett's plays, revealing its ideological genesis in class consciousness, prestige, the family, and other all-too-familiar values and institutions. One political or social critique *within* a Beckett play, then, is located in the ideological value attached to the commodification and encoding of objects (including costumes and properties) in *Happy Days, Waiting for Godot, End Game,* and others. These same values, not nature, God, or other origins of the characters' predicaments in existential explanations, also form an absolute horizon which the Beckettian subject cannot transcend.

In this way, Winnie's dreams of a garden are (like her pearls) a confirmation of her social and political status, and the "green world" in such a case turns out to be confusingly indistinguishible from the values that the green world is usually felt to oppose in literature (values of hierarchy in power and wealth, for example). Winnie says her memories help to get her through the day, yet, as she also says, "things have their life" and:

> I take up this little glass, I shiver it on a stone—(*does so*)—I throw it away—(*does so, far behind her*)—it will be in the bag tomorrow, without a scratch, to help me through the day.

By her dependence for help on the eternal existence of objects of consumption (dramatized most fully in her bag), Winnie is the more pathetic in act two when she cannot form through means other than those of vision and language a relation to any objects at all, however much they may have defined her in act one. Watt says:

> What I am proposing here is that act 2 of *Happy Days*, because in it any sense of an object's utility is exploded by Winnie's immobility and consequent inability to "use" anything, betrays the fetishized nature of all objects in Beckett's plays.

That is, all Winnie's few possessions (for example) are really "fetishes" that represent socially produced *ideas* of what it is to be a woman, just as her memories of a green world do. And Beckett's dramatization of this fact of similarity, therefore, is one representative instance of what makes him a political writer. He shows just how politically and socially constituted are *all* the values by which people live, even those associated with the stories people make up about "nature." And finally, Watt says, it is Beckett's constant "demystification of the fictions" by which people live—including the fiction that the "green world" is somehow in opposition to the material world of social and political relations—that makes him (in Marxist terms) a "responsible" writer.

ACCOUNT: PHYLLIS CAREY ON A POST-STRUCTURALIST APPROACH TO *HAPPY DAYS*

Carey begins by observing that, throughout his works, Beckett explores different aspects of the relations of people to machines in both crude and subtle ways. In *Happy Days*, his concern is both to reveal what can be seen as "mechanical" in human actions and also to explore what about human beings works against the mechanical.

Phyllis Carey, "The Ritual of Human Techne in *Happy Days*" in *Myth and Ritual in the Plays of Samuel Beckett* ed., Katherine H. Burkman (Rutherford, NJ: Fairleigh Dickinson University Press, 1987), pp. 144–150. © 1987 by Associated University Presses, Inc. 440 Forsgate Drive, Cranbury, NJ 08512.

Beckett's depiction of Winnie undercuts the human propensity to follow established patterns of behavior, the mechanical rituals of habit. At the same time, *Happy Days* discloses the impotence of ritual as magic—as an attempt to coerce through incantation. In the artistic shaping of the whole, nevertheless, Beckett suggests the potency of aesthetic ritual as an agent of revelation.

In early drafts, Beckett made use of allusions to a rocket to account for the exhausted, devastated landscape of the play, and thereby suggested one potentially destructive relation of people to machines. Yet, the play more subtlely dramatizes a world as seen from a mechanical perspective. Winnie's attempts to accommodate herself to the perceived mechanical nature of life comes itself to seem mechanical. Her gestures, like brushing her teeth and unfurling her parasol, are presented as the rituals by which she gets through the day, the ceremonies that help her to avoid confronting the real horror of her situation.

That situation seems mechanical in that it is entropic, or always running down in a direction from a potential for action to a static condition. In act one she is imbedded up to her waist; by act two she can only move her eyes. When she unfurls her parasol, she cannot close it, and it eventually consumes itself in flame, as if the process of inevitable, entropic decay in the material world were speeded up in a fast-forward image of any mechanical creation's eventual destruction.

All the objects Winnie manipulates in act one or gazes at in act two become aspects of the metaphor "human-as-machine." Yet, if *everything* exists for mechanical exploitation, objects themselves lose their distinction as objects and become what Martin Heidegger called *Bestand* or "standing reserve." That is, objects themselves are not seen as unique but as things that can be substituted for one another or ordered in the way any other set of objects may be ordered. The contents of Winnie's bag, her language, and her gestures are all portrayed in this way.

Yet, the tendency humans seem to have for imagining a mechanical world and then mechanically adapting themselves to it is not the whole story:

> That other visions of human existence are possible is suggested in *Happy Days* both by the incantatory quality of Winnie's ritual of saying and her frequent allusions to literature, and by Beckett's structuring of the ritual of the play to point beyond human words and gestures. It becomes clear that the action of the play takes place primarily not in Winnie's ever-decreasing gestures but in the interplay of language and silence.

Winnie's mechanical clichés ("another heavenly [or happy] day" and "wonderful"), for example, not only contrast to the life represented in the play, but become increasingly devoid of any meaning at all by their dulling repetition. Her verbal efforts also reveal a desperate effort to "transform sound into meaning" and thereby control her world by understanding it.

Through the incantatory, magical aspect of Winnie's words as ritual, Beckett "discloses" what has been lost in human worship of technology. The related human method of attempting to control the world through "techne"—that is, ordering it through language and meaning expressed in ritual—makes another subject Beckett explores here. For example, "Winnie's allusions to her 'classics,' moreover, reveal the impotency of the mythology that would inform the ritual of her existence."

Carey says that ritual is usually created to recognize the existence of past lives in the present; but here, "Winnie experiences the radical dichotomy between the 'old style' and her present experience." Beckett shows the old kind of ritual to be exhausted, but he also structures the relations of the visual, language, and silence to disclose other possibilities:

> By gradually emptying words of their significance through repetition, distortion, misapplications, and clichés and by restricting Winnie's movements to her eyes, Beckett focuses the audience's attention more and more on two elements: seeing and silence. What *Happy Days* becomes, aesthetically, it would seem is a ritualistic prelude designed to prepare the audience for a moment of silent mediation when Winnie and Willie look at each other in the *'Long Pause'* that concludes the play.

Carey suggests that in this conclusion and in the preparation for it throughout the rest of the play, Beckett attempts to reawaken us to awe and terror, the wonder and the horror of being human. At the same time, he reveals the basis and content of our "primordial techne"—the humanly invented metaphors by which we invent and shape our world and which in turn shape our responses to it.

SUGGESTIONS FOR DISCUSSION AND WRITING

1. Most students find Beckett's play a very strange one. What makes it so from its beginning? In what ways do even the Showers within the play find it strange, and how do they mimic the responses of the audience? Pick another play you have read in this book and compare and contrast its opening to the beginning of *Happy Days*, with particular regard to **setting, dramatic situation, dialogue, and images.** In what differing and similar ways does each account you have read attempt to explain the strangeness of the play?

2. How do the concepts of **rising action, crisis, dénouement,** and **falling action** illuminate the plot of this play? Can you see any ways in which our expectation of a play whose **plot** might be named by these terms

makes a part of our experience of the play? Explain and exemplify your answer. How does each account take the plot into consideration?

3. Both critics are concerned with making sense out of the apparent nonsense of the play. Pick a moment that neither analyzes. Explain as fully as you can what is "nonsensical" or "absurd" about that moment, being sure to make clear your standards of "sense" and "the normal." Now explain how, if at all, this moment illuminates any part of life for you.

4. Make some notes for discussion or for an essay comparing the critical approaches of Watt and Carey. Where do the Marxist and Poststructuralist approaches agree in their results? Where do they disagree? For example, would Watt consider Carey's category of "mechanical" to be related to his idea of "fetishes"? Would Carey consider Watt's "green world" to be part of humanity's "primordial techne"?

5. Pick another critical approach and from its point of view make some notes for discussion or for an essay on an aspect of the play. For example, what might a Feminist critic make of the relations of Winnie and Willie? What of Winnie's attitude toward her own conditions, toward its changes, and toward "happiness"? How would you compare *Happy Days* to "The Yellow Wallpaper"?

A Collection of Plays

SUSAN GLASPELL (1882–1948)
Trifles
(1916)

CHARACTERS

George Henderson, *county attorney*   **Mrs. Peters**
Henry Peters, *sheriff*   **Mrs. Hale**
Lewis Hale, *a neighboring farmer*

Scene.

The kitchen in the now abandoned farmhouse of John Wright, a gloomy kitchen, and left without having been put in order—unwashed pans under the sink, a loaf of bread outside the breadbox, a dish towel on the table—other signs of incompleted work. At the rear the outer door opens and the Sheriff comes in followed by the County Attorney and Hale. The Sheriff and Hale are men in middle life, the County Attorney is a young man; all are much bundled up and go at once to the stove. They are followed by two women—the Sheriff's wife first; she is a slight wiry woman, a thin nervous face. Mrs. Hale is larger and would ordinarily be called more comfortable looking, but she is disturbed now and looks fearfully about as she enters. The women have come in slowly, and stand close together near the door.

County Attorney: (*rubbing his hands*) This feels good. Come up to the fire, ladies.
Mrs. Peters: (*after taking a step forward*) I'm not—cold.
Sheriff: (*unbuttoning his overcoat and stepping away from the stove as if to mark the beginning of official business*) Now, Mr. Hale, before we move things about, you explain to Mr. Henderson just what you saw when you came here yesterday morning.
County Attorney: By the way, has anything been moved? Are things just as you left them yesterday?
10 **Sheriff:** (*looking about*) It's just the same. When it dropped below zero last night I thought I'd better send Frank out this morning to

make a fire for us—no use getting pneumonia with a big case on,
but I told him not to touch anything except the stove—and you
know Frank.

County Attorney: Somebody should have been left here yesterday.

Sheriff: Oh—yesterday. When I had to send Frank to Morris Center for
that man who went crazy—I want you to know I had my hands full
yesterday. I knew you could get back from Omaha by today and as
long as I went over everything here myself—

20 *County Attorney:* Well, Mr. Hale, tell just what happened when you
came here yesterday morning.

Hale: Harry and I had started to town with a load of potatoes. We
came along the road from my place and as I got here I said, "I'm
going to see if I can't get John Wright to go in with me on a party
telephone." I spoke to Wright about it once before and he put me
off, saying folks talked too much anyway, and all he asked was
peace and quiet—I guess you know about how much he talked
himself; but I thought maybe if I went to the house and talked
about it before his wife, though I said to Harry that I didn't know
30   as what his wife wanted made much difference to John—

County Attorney: Let's talk about that later, Mr. Hale. I do want to
talk about that, but tell now just what happened when you got to
the house.

Hale: I didn't hear or see anything; I knocked at the door, and still it
was all quiet inside. I knew they must be up, it was past eight
o'clock. So I knocked again, and I thought I heard somebody say,
"Come in." I wasn't sure, I'm not sure yet, but I opened the
door—this door (*Indicating the door by which the two women are still
standing.*) and there in that rocker—(*Pointing to it.*) sat Mrs. Wright.

They all look at the rocker.

40 *County Attorney:* What—was she doing?

Hale: She was rockin' back and forth. She had her apron in her hand
and was kind of—pleating it.

County Attorney: And how did she—look?

Hale: Well, she looked queer.

County Attorney: How do you mean—queer?

Hale: Well, as if she didn't know what she was going to do next. And
kind of done up.

County Attorney: How did she seem to feel about your coming?

Hale: Why, I don't think she minded—one way or other. She didn't pay
50   much attention. I said, "How do, Mrs. Wright, it's cold, ain't it?"
And she said, "Is it?"—and went on kind of pleating at her apron.
Well, I was surprised; she didn't ask me to come up to the stove, or
to set down, but just sat there, not even looking at me, so I said, "I
want to see John." And then she—laughed. I guess you would call it
a laugh. I thought of Harry and the team outside, so I said a little

sharp: "Can't I see John?" "No," she says, kind o' dull like. "Ain't he home?" says I. "Yes," says she, "he's home." "Then why can't I see him?" I asked her, out of patience. "'Cause he's dead," says she. "*Dead?*" says I. She just nodded her head, not getting a bit excited,

60   but rockin' back and forth. "Why—where is he?" says I, not knowing what to say. She just pointed upstairs—like that. (*Himself pointing to the room above.*) I got up, with the idea of going up there. I walked from there to here—then I says, "Why, what did he die of?" "He died of a rope round his neck," says she, and just went on pleatin' at her apron. Well, I went out and called Harry. I thought I might—need help. We went upstairs and there he was lyin'—

County Attorney: I think I'd rather have you go into that upstairs, where you can point it all out. Just go on now with the rest of the story.

70 **Hale:** Well, my first thought was to get that rope off. It looked . . . (*Stops, his face twitches.*) . . . but Harry, he went up to him, and he said, "No, he's dead all right, and we'd better not touch anything." So we went back down stairs. She was still sitting that same way. "Has anybody been notified?" I asked. "No," says she, unconcerned. "Who did this, Mrs. Wright?" said Harry. He said it businesslike—and she stopped pleatin' of her apron. "I don't know," she says. "You don't *know?*" says Harry. "No," says she. "Weren't you sleepin' in the bed with him?" says Harry. "Yes," says she, "but I was on the inside." "Somebody slipped a rope

80   round his neck and strangled him and you didn't wake up?" says Harry. "I didn't wake up," she said after him. We must'a looked as if we didn't see how that could be, for after a minute she said, "I sleep sound." Harry was going to ask her more questions but I said maybe we ought to let her tell her story first to the coroner, or the sheriff, so Harry went fast as he could to Rivers' place, where there's a telephone.

County Attorney: And what did Mrs. Wright do when she knew that you had gone for the coroner?

Hale: She moved from that chair to this one over here (*Pointing to a*
90   *small chair in the corner.*) and just sat there with her hands held together and looking down. I got a feeling that I ought to make some conversation, so I said I had come in to see if John wanted to put in a telephone, and at that she started to laugh, and then she stopped and looked at me—scared. (*The County Attorney, who has had his notebook out, makes a note.*) I dunno, maybe it wasn't scared. I wouldn't like to say it was. Soon Harry got back, and then Dr. Lloyd came, and you, Mr. Peters, and so I guess that's all I know that you don't.

County Attorney: (*looking around*) I guess we'll go upstairs first—and
100   then out to the barn and around there. (*To the Sheriff.*) You're convinced that there was nothing important here—nothing that would point to any motive.

Sheriff: Nothing here but kitchen things.

The County Attorney, after again looking around the kitchen, opens the door of a cupboard closet. He gets up on a chair and looks on a shelf. Pulls his hand away, sticky.

County Attorney: Here's a nice mess.

The women draw nearer.

Mrs. Peters: (*to the other woman*) Oh, her fruit; it did freeze. (*To the County Attorney.*) She worried about that when it turned so cold. She said the fire'd go out and her jars would break.

Sheriff: Well, can you beat the women! Held for murder and worryin' about her preserves.

110 **County Attorney:** I guess before we're through she may have something more serious than preserves to worry about.

Hale: Well, women are used to worrying over trifles.

The two women move a little closer together.

County Attorney: (*with the gallantry of a young politician*) And yet, for all their worries, what would we do without the ladies? (*The women do not unbend. He goes to the sink, takes a dipperful of water from the pail and pouring it into a basin, washes his hands. Starts to wipe them on the roller towel, turns it for a cleaner place.*) Dirty towels! (*Kicks his foot against the pans under the sink.*) Not much of a housekeeper, would you say, ladies?

120 **Mrs. Hale:** (*stiffly*) There's a great deal of work to be done on a farm.

County Attorney: To be sure. And yet (*With a little bow to her*) I know there are some Dickson county farmhouses which do not have such roller towels.

He gives it a pull to expose its full length again.

Mrs. Hale: Those towels get dirty awful quick. Men's hands aren't always as clean as they might be.

County Attorney: Ah, loyal to your sex, I see. But you and Mrs. Wright were neighbors. I suppose you were friends, too.

Mrs. Hale: (*shaking her head*) I've not seen much of her of late years. I've not been in this house—it's more than a year.

130 **County Attorney:** And why was that? You didn't like her?

Mrs. Hale: I liked her all well enough. Farmers' wives have their hands full, Mr. Henderson. And then—

County Attorney: Yes—?

Mrs. Hale: (*looking about*) It never seemed a very cheerful place.

County Attorney: No—it's not cheerful. I shouldn't say she had the homemaking instinct.

Mrs. Hale: Well, I don't know as Wright had, either.

County Attorney: You mean that they didn't get on very well?

Mrs. Hale: No, I don't mean anything. But I don't think a place'd be
140   any cheerfuller for John Wright's being in it.

County Attorney: I'd like to talk more of that a little later. I want to
get the lay of things upstairs now.

He goes to the left, where three steps lead to a stair door.

Sheriff: I suppose anything Mrs. Peters does'll be all right. She was to
take in some clothes for her, you know, and a few little things. We
left in such a hurry yesterday.

County Attorney: Yes, but I would like to see what you take, Mrs.
Peters, and keep an eye out for anything that might be of use to us.

Mrs. Peters: Yes, Mr. Henderson.

The women listen to the men's steps on the stairs, then look about the kitchen.

Mrs. Hale: I'd hate to have men coming into my kitchen, snooping
150   around and criticising.

*She arranges the pans under sink which the County Attorney had shoved out of
place.*

Mrs. Peters: Of course it's no more than their duty.

Mrs. Hale: Duty's all right, but I guess that deputy sheriff that came
out to make the fire might have got a little of this on. (*Gives the
roller towel a pull.*) Wish I'd thought of that sooner. Seems mean
to talk about her for not having things slicked up when she had
to come away in such a hurry.

Mrs. Peters: (*who has gone to a small table in the left rear corner of the
room, and lifted one end of a towel that covers a pan*) She had bread
set.

Stands still.

160 **Mrs. Hale:** (*eyes fixed on a loaf of bread beside the breadbox, which is on a
low shelf at the other side of the room. Moves slowly toward it.*) She
was going to put this in there. (*Picks up loaf, then abruptly drops it.
In a manner of returning to familiar things.*) It's a shame about her
fruit. I wonder if it's all gone. (*Gets up on the chair and looks.*) I
think there's some here that's all right, Mrs. Peters. Yes—here;
(*Holding it toward the window*) this is cherries, too. (*Looking again.*)
I declare I believe that's the only one. (*Gets down, bottle in her hand.
Goes to the sink and wipes it off on the outside.*) She'll feel awful bad
after all her hard work in the hot weather. I remember the
170   afternoon I put up my cherries last summer.

She puts the bottle on the big kitchen table, center of the room. With a sigh, is about to sit down in the rocking-chair. Before she is seated realizes what chair it is; with a slow look at it, steps back. The chair which she has touched rocks back and forth.

Mrs. Peters: Well, I must get those things from the front room closet. (*She goes to the door at the right, but after looking into the other room, steps back.*) You coming with me, Mrs. Hale? You could help me carry them.

They go in the other room; reappear, Mrs. Peters carrying a dress and skirt, Mrs. Hale following with a pair of shoes.

Mrs. Peters: My, it's cold in there.

She puts the clothes on the big table, and hurries to the stove.

Mrs. Hale: (*examining her skirt*) Wright was close. I think maybe that's why she kept so much to herself. She didn't even belong to the Ladies Aid. I suppose she felt she couldn't do her part, and then you don't enjoy things when you feel shabby. She used to wear
180 pretty clothes and be lively, when she was Minnie Foster, one of the town girls singing in the choir. But that—oh, that was thirty years ago. This all you was to take in?

Mrs. Peters: She said she wanted an apron. Funny thing to want, for there isn't much to get you dirty in jail, goodness knows. But I suppose just to make her feel more natural. She said they was in the top drawer in this cupboard. Yes, here. And then her little shawl that always hung behind the door. (*Opens stair door and looks.*) Yes, here it is.

Quickly shuts door leading upstairs.

Mrs. Hale: (*abruptly moving toward her*) Mrs. Peters?
190 **Mrs. Peters:** Yes, Mrs. Hale?

Mrs. Hale: Do you think she did it?

Mrs. Peters: (*in a frightened voice*) Oh, I don't know.

Mrs. Hale: Well, I don't think she did. Asking for an apron and her little shawl. Worrying about her fruit.

Mrs. Peters: (*starts to speak, glances up, where footsteps are heard in the room above. In a low voice.*) Mr. Peters says it looks bad for her. Mr. Henderson is awful sarcastic in a speech and he'll make fun of her sayin' she didn't wake up.

Mrs. Hale: Well, I guess John Wright didn't wake when they was
200 slipping that rope under his neck.

Mrs. Peters: No, it's strange. It must have been done awful crafty and still. They say it was such a—funny way to kill a man, rigging it all up like that.

Mrs. Hale: That's just what Mr. Hale said. There was a gun in the house. He says that's what he can't understand.

Mrs. Peters: Mr. Henderson said coming out that what was needed for the case was a motive; something to show anger, or—sudden feeling.

Mrs. Hale: (*who is standing by the table*) Well, I don't see any signs of
210   anger around here. (*She puts her hand on the dish towel which lies on the table, stands looking down at table, one half of which is clean, the other half messy.*) It's wiped to here. (*Makes a move as if to finish work, then turns and looks at loaf of bread outside the breadbox. Drops towel. In that voice of coming back to familiar things.*) Wonder how they are finding things upstairs. I hope she had it a little more red-up* up there. You know, it seems kind of *sneaking.* Locking her up in town and then coming out here and trying to get her own house to turn against her!

Mrs. Peters: But Mrs. Hale, the law is the law.

220 **Mrs. Hale:** I s'pose 'tis. (*Unbuttoning her coat.*) Better loosen up your things, Mrs. Peters. You won't feel them when you go out.

Mrs. Peters takes off her fur tippet, goes to hang it on hook at back of room, stands looking at the under part of the small corner table.

Mrs. Peters: She was piecing a quilt.

She brings the large sewing basket and they look at the bright pieces.

Mrs. Hale: It's log cabin pattern. Pretty, isn't it? I wonder if she was goin' to quilt it or just knot it?

Footsteps have been heard coming down the stairs. The Sheriff enters followed by Hale and the County Attorney.

Sheriff: They wonder if she was going to quilt it or just knot it!

The men laugh; the women look abashed.

County Attorney: (*rubbing his hands over the stove*) Frank's fire didn't do much up there, did it? Well, let's go out to the barn and get that cleared up.

The men go outside.

Mrs. Hale: (*resentfully*) I don't know as there's anything so strange,
230   our takin' up our time with little things while we're waiting for

---

* (slang) spruced up.

them to get the evidence. (*She sits down at the big table smoothing out a block with decision.*) I don't see as it's anything to laugh about.

Mrs. Peters: (*apologetically*) Of course they've got awful important things on their minds.

Pulls up a chair and joins Mrs. Hale at the table.

Mrs. Hale: (*examining another block*) Mrs. Peters, look at this one. Here, this is the one she was working on, and look at the sewing! All the rest of it has been so nice and even. And look at this! It's all over the place! Why, it looks as if she didn't know what she was about!

After she has said this they look at each other, then start to glance back at the door. After an instant Mrs. Hale has pulled at a knot and ripped the sewing.

240 **Mrs. Peters:** Oh, what are you doing, Mrs. Hale?

Mrs. Hale: (*mildly*) Just pulling out a stitch or two that's not sewed very good. (*Threading a needle.*) Bad sewing always made me fidgety.

Mrs. Peters: (*nervously*) I don't think we ought to touch things.

Mrs. Hale: I'll just finish up this end. (*Suddenly stopping and leaning forward.*) Mrs. Peters?

Mrs. Peters: Yes, Mrs. Hale?

Mrs. Hale: What do you suppose she was so nervous about?

Mrs. Peters: Oh—I don't know. I don't know as she was nervous. I sometimes sew awful queer when I'm just tired. (*Mrs. Hale starts to*
250   *say something, looks at Mrs. Peters, then goes on sewing.*) Well, I must get these things wrapped up. They may be through sooner than we think. (*Putting apron and other things together.*) I wonder where I can find a piece of paper, and string.

Mrs. Hale: In that cupboard, maybe.

Mrs. Peters: (*looking in cupboard*) Why, here's a birdcage. (*Holds it up.*) Did she have a bird, Mrs. Hale?

Mrs. Hale: Why, I don't know whether she did or not—I've not been here for so long. There was a man around last year selling canaries cheap, but I don't know as she took one; maybe she did. She used
260   to sing real pretty herself.

Mrs. Peters: (*glancing around*) Seems funny to think of a bird here. But she must have had one, or why would she have a cage? I wonder what happened to it.

Mrs. Hale: I s'pose maybe the cat got it.

Mrs. Peters: No, she didn't have a cat. She's got that feeling some people have about cats—being afraid of them. My cat got in her room and she was real upset and asked me to take it out.

Mrs. Hale: My sister Bessie was like that. Queer, ain't it?

Mrs. Peters: (*examining the cage*) Why, look at this door. It's broke. One
270   hinge is pulled apart.

Mrs. Hale: (*looking too*) Looks as if someone must have been rough with it.

Mrs. Peters: Why, yes.

She brings the cage forward and puts it on the table.

Mrs. Hale: I wish if they're going to find any evidence they'd be about it. I don't like this place.

Mrs. Peters: But I'm awful glad you came with me, Mrs. Hale. It would be lonesome for me sitting here alone.

Mrs. Hale: It would, wouldn't it? (*Dropping her sewing.*) But I tell you what I do wish, Mrs. Peters. I wish I had come over sometimes
280   when *she* was here. I—(*Looking around the room*)—wish I had.

Mrs. Peters: But of course you were awful busy, Mrs. Hale—your house and your children.

Mrs. Hale: I could've come. I stayed away because it weren't cheerful—and that's why I ought to have come. I—I've never liked this place. Maybe because it's down in a hollow and you don't see the road. I dunno what it is but it's a lonesome place and always was. I wish I had come over to see Minnie Foster sometimes. I can see now—

Shakes her head.

Mrs. Peters: Well, you mustn't reproach yourself, Mrs. Hale. Somehow
290   we just don't see how it is with other folks until—something comes up.

Mrs. Hale: Not having children makes less work—but it makes a quiet house, and Wright out to work all day, and no company when he did come in. Did you know John Wright, Mrs. Peters?

Mrs. Peters: Not to know him; I've seen him in town. They say he was a good man.

Mrs. Hale: Yes—good; he didn't drink, and kept his word as well as most, I guess, and paid his debts. But he was a hard man, Mrs. Peters. Just to pass the time of day with him—(*shivers*). Like a raw
300   wind that gets to the bone. (*Pauses, her eye falling on the cage.*) I should think she would 'a wanted a bird. But what do you suppose went with it?

Mrs. Peters: I don't know, unless it got sick and died.

She reaches over and swings the broken door, swings it again. Both women watch it.

Mrs. Hale: You weren't raised round here, were you? (*Mrs. Peters shakes her head.*) You didn't know—her?

Mrs. Peters: Not till they brought her yesterday.

Mrs. Hale: She—come to think of it, she was kind of like a bird herself—real sweet and pretty, but kind of timid and—fluttery.

How—she—did—change. (*Silence; then as if struck by a happy*
310   *thought and relieved to get back to everyday things.*) Tell you what,
        Mrs. Peters, why don't you take the quilt in with you? It might
        take up her mind.
Mrs. Peters: Why, I think that's a real nice idea, Mrs. Hale. There
        couldn't possibly be any objection to it, could there? Now, just
        what would I take? I wonder if her patches are in here—and her
        things.

They look in the sewing basket.

Mrs. Hale: Here's some red. I expect this has got sewing things in it.
        (*Brings out a fancy box.*) What a pretty box. Looks like something
        somebody would give you. Maybe her scissors are in here. (*Opens*
320   *box. Suddenly puts her hand to her nose.*) Why—(*Mrs. Peters bends*
        nearer, then turns her face away.) There's something wrapped up in
        this piece of silk.
Mrs. Peters: Why, this isn't her scissors.
Mrs. Hale: (*lifting the silk*) Oh, Mrs. Peters—it's—

Mrs. Peters bends closer.

Mrs. Peters: It's the bird.
Mrs. Hale: (*jumping up*) But, Mrs. Peters—look at it! Its neck! Look at
        its neck! It's all—other side *to.*
Mrs. Peters: Somebody—wrung—its—neck.

Their eyes meet. A look of growing comprehension, of horror. Steps are heard
outside. Mrs. Hale slips box under quilt pieces, and sinks into her chair. Enter
Sheriff and County Attorney. Mrs. Peters rises.

County Attorney: (*as one turning from serious things to little pleasantries*)
330   Well, ladies, have you decided whether she was going to quilt it or
        knot it?
Mrs. Peters: We think she was going to—knot it.
County Attorney: Well, that's interesting, I'm sure. (*Seeing the*
        birdcage.) Has the bird flown?
Mrs. Hale: (*putting more quilt pieces over the box*) We think the—cat got it.
County Attorney: (*preoccupied*) Is there a cat?

Mrs. Hale glances in a quick covert way at Mrs. Peters.

Mrs. Peters: Well, not *now.* They're superstitious, you know. They
        leave.
County Attorney: (*to Sheriff Peters, continuing an interrupted conversation*)
340   No sign at all of anyone having come from the outside. Their own
        rope. Now let's go up again and go over it piece by piece. (*They start*
        upstairs.) It would have to have been someone who knew just the—

Mrs. Peters sits down. The two women sit there not looking at one another, but as if peering into something and at the same time holding back. When they talk now it is in the manner of feeling their way over strange ground, as if afraid of what they are saying, but as if they can not help saying it.

Mrs. Hale: She liked the bird. She was going to bury it in that pretty box.

Mrs. Peters: (*in a whisper*) When I was a girl—my kitten—there was a boy took a hatchet, and before my eyes—and before I could get there—(*covers her face an instant*). If they hadn't held me back I would have—(*catches herself, looks upstairs where steps are heard, falters weakly*)—hurt him.

350 **Mrs. Hale:** (*with a slow look around her*) I wonder how it would seem never to have had any children around. (*Pause.*) No, Wright wouldn't like the bird—a thing that sang. She used to sing. He killed that, too.

Mrs. Peters: (*moving uneasily*) We don't know who killed the bird.

Mrs. Hale: I knew John Wright.

Mrs. Peters: It was an awful thing was done in this house that night, Mrs. Hale. Killing a man while he slept, slipping a rope around his neck that choked the life out of him.

Mrs. Hale: His neck. Choked the life out of him.

Her hand goes out and rests on the birdcage.

360 **Mrs. Peters:** (*with rising voice*) We don't know who killed him. We don't know.

Mrs. Hale: (*her own feeling not interrupted*) If there'd been years and years of nothing, then a bird to sing to you, it would be awful—still, after the bird was still.

Mrs. Peters: (*something within her speaking*) I know what stillness is. When we homesteaded in Dakota, and my first baby died—after he was two years old, and me with no other then—

Mrs. Hale: (*moving*) How soon do you suppose they'll be through, looking for the evidence?

370 **Mrs. Peters:** I know what stillness is. (*Pulling herself back.*) The law has got to punish crime, Mrs. Hale.

Mrs. Hale: (*not as if answering that*) I wish you'd seen Minnie Foster when she wore a white dress with blue ribbons and stood up there in the choir and sang. (*A look around the room.*) Oh, I *wish* I'd come over here once in a while! That was a crime! That was a crime! Who's going to punish that?

Mrs. Peters: (*looking upstairs*) We mustn't—take on.

Mrs. Hale: I might have known she needed help! I know how things can be—for women. I tell you, it's queer, Mrs. Peters. We live
380   close together and we live far apart. We all go through the same things—it's all just a different kind of the same thing. (*Brushes*

her eyes; noticing the bottle of fruit, reaches out for it.) If I was you I wouldn't tell her her fruit was gone. Tell her it *ain't*. Tell her it's all right. Take this in to prove it to her. She—she may never know whether it was broke or not.

Mrs. Peters: (*takes the bottle, looks about for something to wrap it in; takes petticoat from the clothes brought from the other room, very nervously begins winding this around the bottle. In a false voice*) My, it's a good thing the men couldn't hear us. Wouldn't they just laugh! Getting
390   all stirred up over a little thing like a—dead canary. As if that could have anything to do with—with—wouldn't they *laugh!*

The men are heard coming down stairs.

Mrs. Hale: (*under her breath*) Maybe they would—maybe they wouldn't.

County Attorney: No, Peters, it's all perfectly clear except a reason for doing it. But you know juries when it comes to women. If there was some definite thing. Something to show—something to make a story about—a thing that would connect up with this strange way of doing it—

The women's eyes meet for an instant. Enter Hale from outer door.

Hale: Well, I've got the team around. Pretty cold out there.

County Attorney: I'm going to stay here a while by myself. (*To the*
400   *Sheriff.*) You can send Frank out for me, can't you? I want to go over everything. I'm not satisfied that we can't do better.

Sheriff: Do you want to see what Mrs. Peters is going to take in?

The County Attorney goes to the table, picks up the apron, laughs.

County Attorney: Oh, I guess they're not very dangerous things the ladies have picked out. (*Moves a few things about, disturbing the quilt pieces which cover the box. Steps back.*) No, Mrs. Peters doesn't need supervising. For that matter, a sheriff's wife is married to the law. Ever think of it that way, Mrs. Peters?

Mrs. Peters: Not—just that way.

Sheriff: (*chuckling*) Married to the law. (*Moves toward the other room.*) I
410   just want you to come in here a minute, George. We ought to take a look at these windows.

County Attorney: (*scoffingly*) Oh, windows!

Sheriff: We'll be right out, Mr. Hale.

Hale goes outside. The Sheriff follows the County Attorney into the other room. Then Mrs. Hale rises, hands tight together, looking intensely at Mrs. Peters, whose eyes make a slow turn, finally meeting Mrs. Hale's. A moment Mrs. Hale holds her, then her own eyes point the way to where the box is concealed. Suddenly Mrs. Peters throws back quilt pieces and tries to put the box in the bag she is wearing.

It is too big. She opens box, starts to take bird out, cannot touch it, goes to pieces, stands there helpless. Sound of a knob turning in the other room. Mrs. Hale snatches the box and puts it in the pocket of her big coat. Enter County Attorney and Sheriff.

County Attorney: *(facetiously)* Well, Henry, at least we found out that she was not going to quilt it. She was going to—what is it you call it, ladies?

Mrs. Hale: *(her hand against her pocket)* We call it—knot it, Mr.
420   Henderson.

ZORA NEALE HURSTON (1891–1960)
The First One
A Play in One Act

PERSONS

Noah, His Wife, Their Sons: Shem, Japheth, Ham; Eve, Ham's Wife; the Sons' wives and children (6 or 7).

Time: Three Years after the Flood

Place: Valley of Ararat

Setting: Morning in the Valley of Ararat. The Mountain is in the near distance. Its lower slopes grassy with grazing herds. The very blue sky beyond that. These together form the background. On the left downstage is a brown tent. A few shrubs are scattered here and there over the stage indicating the temporary camp. A rude altar is built center stage. A shepherd's crook, a goat skin water bottle, a staff and other evidences of nomadic life lie about the entrance to the tent. To the right stretches a plain clad with bright flowers. Several sheep or goat skins are spread about on the ground upon which the people kneel or sit whenever necessary.

Action: Curtain rises on an empty stage. It is dawn. A great stillness, but immediately Noah enters from the tent and ties back the flap. He is clad in a loose-fitting dingy robe tied about the waist with a strip of goat hide. Stooped shoulders, flowing beard. He gazes about him. His gaze takes in the entire stage.

Noah: *(fervently)* Thou hast restored the Earth, Jehovah, it is good. *(Turns to the tent.)* My sons! Come, deck the altar for the sacrifices to Jehovah. It is the third year of our coming to this valley to give thanks offering to Jehovah that he spared us.

(Enter Japheth bearing a haunch of meat and Shem with another. The wife of Noah and those of Shem and Japheth follow laying on sheaves of grain and fruit [dates and figs]. They are all middle-aged and clad in dingy garments.)

Noah: And where is Ham—son of my old age? Why does he not come with his wife and son to the sacrifice?

Mrs. Noah: He arose before the light and went. (*She shades her eyes with one hand and points toward the plain with the other.*) His wife, as ever, went with him.

10 *Shem:* (*impatiently*) This is the third year that we have come here to this Valley to commemorate our delivery from the flood. Ham knows the sacrifice is made always at sunrise. See! (*He points to rising sun.*) He should be here.

Noah: (*lifts his hand in a gesture of reproval*) We shall wait. The sweet singer, the child of my loins after old age had come upon me is warm to my heart—let us wait.

(*There is off-stage, right, the twanging of a rude stringed instrument and laughter. Ham, his wife and son come dancing on down-stage right. He is in his early twenties. He is dressed in a very white goat-skin with a wreath of shiny green leaves about his head. He has the rude instrument in his hands and strikes it. His wife is clad in a short blue garment with a girdle of shells. She has a wreath of scarlet flowers about her head. She has black hair, is small, young and lithe. She wears anklets and wristlets of the same red flowers. Their son about three years old wears nothing but a broad band of leaves and flowers about his middle. They caper and prance to the altar. Ham's wife and son bear flowers. A bird is perched on Ham's shoulder.*)

Noah: (*extends his arms in greeting*) My son, thou art late. But the sunlight comes with thee. (*Ham gives bird to Mrs. Noah, then embraces Noah.*)

20 *Ham:* (*rests his head for a moment on Noah's shoulder*) We arose early and went out on the plain to make ready for the burnt offering before Jehovah.

Mrs. Shem: (*tersely*) But you bring nothing.

Ham: See thou! We bring flowers and music to offer up. I shall dance before Jehovah and sing joyfully upon the harp that I made of the thews of rams. (*He proudly displays the instrument and strums once or twice.*)

Mrs. Shem: (*clapping her hands to her ears*) Oh, Peace! Have we not enough of thy bawling and prancing all during the year? Shem

30 and Japheth work always in the fields and vineyards, while you do naught but tend the flock and sing!

Mrs. Japheth: (*looks contemptuously at both Ham and Noah*) Still, thou art beloved of thy father . . . he gives thee all his vineyards for thy singing, but Japheth must work hard for his fields.

Mrs. Shem: And Shem—

Noah: (*angrily*) Peace! Peace! Are lust and strife *again* loose upon the Earth? Jehovah might have destroyed us all. Am I not Lord of the world? May I not bestow where I will? Besides, the world is great. Did I not give food, and plenty to the thousands upon thousands

40   that the waters licked up? Surely there is abundance for us and
        our seed forever. Peace! Let us to the sacrifice.

        *(Noah goes to the heaped up altar. Ham exits to the tent hurriedly and returns
        with a torch and hands it to Noah who applies it to the altar. He kneels at the altar
        and the others kneel in a semi-circle behind him at a little distance. Noah makes
        certain ritualistic gestures and chants.)*

Noah: "Oh Mighty Jehovah, who created the Heaven and the firmaments
        thereof, the Sun and Moon, the stars, the Earth and all else besides—
Others: I am here
        I am here, O, Jehovah
        I am here. This is thy Kingdom, and I am here

        (A deep silence falls for a moment.)

Noah: Jehovah, who saw evil in the hearts of men, who opened upon
        them the windows of Heaven and loosed the rain upon
        them—And the fountains of the great deep were broken up—
50 **Others:** *(repeat chant)*
Noah: Jehovah who dried up the floods and drove the waters of the
        sea again to the deeps—who met Noah in the Vale of Ararat and
        made covenant with Noah, His servant, that no more would he
        smite the Earth—And Seed time and Harvest, Cold and Heat,
        Summer and Winter, day and night shall not cease forever, and set
        His rainbow as a sign.
Noah and Others: We are here O Jehovah
        We are here
        We are here
60   This is Thy Kingdom
        And we are here.

        *(Noah arises, makes obeisance to the smoking altar, then turns and blesses the
        others.)*

Noah: Noah alone, whom the Lord found worthy; Noah whom He
        made lord of the Earth, blesses you and your seed forever. *(At a
        gesture from him all arise. The women take the meat from the altar and
        carry it into the tent.)* Eat, drink and make a joyful noise before
        Him. For He destroyed the Earth, but spared us. *(Women re-enter
        with bits of roast meat—all take some and eat. All are seated on the
        skins.)*
Mrs. Noah: *(feelingly)* Yes, three years ago, all was water, *water,*
70   WATER! The deeps howled as one beast to another. *(She shudders.)*
        In my sleep, even now, I am in that Ark again being borne here,
        there on the great bosom.

Mrs. Ham: *(wide-eyed)* And the dead! Floating, floating all about us—
We were one little speck of life in a world of death! *(The bone slips from her hand.)* And there, close beside the Ark, close with her face upturned as if begging for shelter—my *mother!* *(She weeps, Ham comforts her.)*

Mrs. Shem: *(eating vigorously)* She would not repent. Thou art as thy mother was—a seeker after beauty of raiment and laughter. God
80   is just. She would not repent.

Mrs. Ham: But the unrepentant are no less loved. And why must Jehovah hate beauty?

Noah: Speak no more of the waters. Oh, the strength of the waters! The voices and the death of it! Let us have the juice of the grape to make us forget. Where once was death in this Valley there is now life abundant of beast and herbs. *(He waves towards the scenery.)* Jehovah meets us here. Dance! Be glad! Bring wine! Ham smite thy harp of ram's thews and sing!

(Mrs. Noah gathers all the children and exits to the tent. Shem, Japheth, their wives and children eat vigorously. Mrs. Ham exits, left. Ham plays on his harp and capers about singing. Mrs. Ham re-enters with goatskin of wine and a bone cup. She crosses to where Noah reclines on a large skin. She kneels and offers it to him. He takes the cup—she pours for him. Ham sings—

Ham: "I am as a young ram in the Spring
90   Or a young male goat
The hills are beneath my feet
And the young grass.
Love rises in me like the flood
And ewes gather round me for food."

(His wife joins in the dancing. Noah cries "Pour" and Mrs. Ham hurries to fill his cup again. Ham joins others on the skins. The others have horns suspended from their girdles. Mrs. Ham fills them all. Noah cries "pour" again and she returns to him. She turns to fill the others' cups.

Noah: *(rising drunkenly)* Pour again, Eve, and Ham sing on and dance and drink—drown out the waters of the flood if you can. *(His tongue grows thick. Eve fills his cup again. He reels drunkenly toward the tent door, slopping the liquor out of the cup as he walks.)* Drink wine, forget
100   water—it means death, *death!* And bodies floating, face up! *(He stares horrified about himself and creeps stealthily into the tent, but sprawls just inside the door so that his feet are visible. There is silence for a moment, the others are still eating. They snatch tid-bits from each other.)*

Japheth: *(shoves his wife)* Fruit and herbs, woman! *(He thrusts her impatiently forward with his foot. She exits left.)*

Shem: *(to his wife)* More wine!

Mrs. Shem: *(irritated)* See you not that there is plenty still in the
  bottle?

*(He seizes it and pours. Ham snatches it away and pours. Shem tries to get it back
but Ham prevents him. Re-enter Mrs. Japheth with figs and apples. Everybody
grabs. Ham and Shem grab for the same one, Ham gets it.)*

Mrs. Shem: *(significantly)* Thus he seizes all else that he desires. Noah
110   would make him lord of the Earth because he sings and capers. *(Ham
  is laughing drunkenly and pelting Mrs. Shem with fruit skins and withered
  flowers that litter the ground. This infuriates her.)*
Noah: *(calls from inside the tent)* Eve, wine, quickly! I'm sinking down
  in the WATER! Come drown the WATER with wine.

*(Eve exits to him with the bottle. Ham arises drunkenly and starts toward the tent
door.)*

Ham: *(thickly)* I go to pull our father out of the water, or to drown with
  him in it. *(Ham is trying to sing and dance.)* "I am as a young goat in
  the sp—sp—sp—. *(He exits to the tent laughing. Shem and Japheth
  sprawl out in the skins. The wives are showing signs of surfeit. Ham is
  heard laughing raucously inside the tent. He re-enters still laughing.)*
120 **Ham:** *(in the tent door)* Our Father has stripped himself, showing all
  his wrinkles. Ha! Ha! He's as no young goat in the spring. Ha! Ha!
  *(Still laughing, he reels over to the altar and sinks down behind it still
  laughing.)* The old Ram, Ha! Ha! Ha! He has had no spring for
  years! Ha! Ha! *(He subsides into slumber. Mrs. Shem looks about her
  exultantly.)*
Mrs. Shem: Ha! The young goat has fallen into a pit! *(She shakes her
  husband.)* Shem! Shem! Rise up and become owner of Noah's
  vineyards as well as his flocks! *(Shem kicks weakly at her.)* Shem!
  Fool! Arise! Thou art thy father's first born. *(She pulls him protesting
130   to his feet.)* Do stand up and regain thy birthright from *(she points
  to the altar)* that dancer who plays on his harp of ram thews, and
  decks his brow with bay leaves. Come!
Shem: *(brightens)* How?
His Wife: Did he not go into the tent and come away laughing at thy
  father's nakedness? Oh *(she beats her breast)* that I should live to
  see a father so mocked and shamed by his son to whom he has
  given all his vineyards! *(She seizes a large skin from the ground.)*
  Take this and cover him and tell him of the wickedness of thy
  brother.
140 **Mrs. Japheth:** *(arising takes hold of the skin also)* No, my husband shall
  also help to cover Noah, our father. Did I not also hear? Think
  your Shem and his seed shall possess both flocks and vineyard

while Japheth ànd his seed have only the fields? (*She arouses Japheth, he stands.*)

Shem: He shall share—

Mrs. Shem: (*impatiently*) Then go in (*the women release the skin to the men*) quickly, lest he wake sober, then will he not believe one word against Ham who needs only to smile to please him. (*The men lay the skin across their shoulders and back over to the tent and cover Noah.*
150   *They motion to leave him.*)

Mrs. Shem: Go back, fools, and wake him. You have done but half.

(*They turn and enter the tent and both shake Noah. He sits up and rubs his eyes. Mrs. Shem and Mrs. Japheth commence to weep ostentatiously.*)

Noah: (*peevishly*) Why do you disturb me, and why do the women weep? I thought all sorrow and all cause for weeping was washed away by the flood. (*He is about to lie down again but the men hold him up.*)

Shem: Hear, father, thy age has been scoffed, and thy nakedness made a thing of shame here in the midst of the feasting where all might know—thou the Lord of all under Heaven, hast been mocked.

Mrs. Shem: And we weep in shame, that thou our father should have thy nakedness uncovered before us.

160 **Noah:** (*struggling drunkenly to his feet*) Who, *who* has done this thing?

Mrs. Shem: (*timidly crosses and kneels before Noah*) We fear to tell thee, lord, lest thy love for the doer of this iniquity should be so much greater than the shame, that thou should slay us for telling thee.

Noah: (*swaying drunkenly*) Say it, woman, shall the lord of the Earth be mocked? Shall his nakedness be uncovered and he be shamed before his family?

Shem: Shall the one who has done this thing hold part of thy goods after thee? How wilt thou deal with them? Thou hast been wickedly shamed.

170 **Noah:** No, he shall have no part in my goods—his goods shall be parcelled out among the others.

Mrs. Shem: Thou art wise, father, thou art just!

Noah: He shall be accursed. His skin shall be black! Black as the nights, when the waters brooded over the Earth!

(*Enter Mrs. Noah from tent, pauses by Noah.*)

Mrs. Noah: (*catches him by the arm*) Cease! Whom dost thou curse?

Noah: (*shaking his arm free. The others also look awed and terrified and also move to stop him. All rush to him. Mrs. Noah attempts to stop his mouth with her hand. He shakes his head to free his lips and goes in a drunken fury*) Black! He and his seed forever. He shall serve his brothers
180   and they shall rule over him—Ah—Ah—. (*He sinks again to the ground. There is a loud burst of drunken laughter from behind the altar.*)

Ham: Ha! Ha! I am as a young ram—Ha! Ha!

Mrs. Noah: (to Mrs. Shem) Whom cursed Noah?

Mrs. Shem: Ham—Ham mocked his age. Ham uncovered his nakedness, and Noah grew wrathful and cursed him. Black! He could not mean *black.* It is enough that he should lose his vineyards. (*There is absolute silence for a while. Then realization comes to all. Mrs. Noah rushes in the tent to her husband, shaking him violently.*)

Mrs. Noah: (voice from out of tent) Noah! Arise! Thou art no lord of the
190   Earth, but a drunkard. Thou hast cursed my son. Oh water, Shem! Japheth! Cold water to drive out the wine. Noah! (*She sobs.*) Thou must awake and unsay thy curse. Thou must! (*She is sobbing and rousing him. Shem and Japheth seize a skin bottle from the ground by the skin door and dash off right. Mrs. Noah wails and the other women join in. They beat their breasts. Enter Eve through the tent. She looks puzzled.*)

Mrs. Ham: Why do you wail? Are all not happy today?

Mrs. Noah: (pityingly) Come, Eve. Thou art but a child, a heavy load awaits thee. (*Eve turns and squats beside her mother-in-law.*)

Eve: (caressing Mrs. Noah) Perhaps the wine is too new. Why do you
200   shake our father?

Mrs. Noah: Not the wine of grapes, but the wine of sorrow bestirs me thus. Turn thy comely face to the wall, Eve. Noah has cursed thy husband and his seed forever to be black, and to serve his brothers and they shall rule over him. (*Re-enter the men with the water bottle running. Mrs. Noah seizes it and pours it in his face. He stirs.*) See, I must awaken him that he may unspeak the curse before it be too late.

Eve: But Noah is drunk—surely Jehovah hears not a drunken curse. Noah would not curse Ham if he knew. Jehovah knows Noah loves Ham more than all. (*She rushes upon Noah and shakes him violently.*)
210   Oh, awake thou (*she shrieks*) and uncurse thy curse. (*All are trying to rouse Noah. He sits, opens his eyes wide and looks about him. Mrs. Noah caresses him.*)

Mrs. Noah: Awake, my lord, and unsay thy curse.

Noah: I am awake, but I know of no curse. Whom did I curse?

Mrs. Noah and Eve: Ham, lord of the Earth. (*He rises quickly to his feet and looks bewildered about.*)

Japheth: (falls at his feet) Our father, and lord of all under Heaven, you cursed away his vineyards, but we do not desire them. You cursed him to be black—he and his seed forever, and that his seed shall be
220   our servants forever, but we desire not their service. Unsay it all.

Noah: (rushes down stage to the footlights, center. He beats his breast and bows his head to the ground.) Oh, that I had come alive out of my mother's loins! Why did not the waters of the flood bear me back to the deeps! Oh Ham, my son!

Eve: (rushing down to him) Unspeak the Curse! Unspeak the Curse!

Noah: (in prayerful attitude) Jehovah, by our covenant in this Valley, record not my curses on my beloved Ham. Show me once again the sign of covenant—the rainbow over the Vale of Ararat.

Shem: *(strikes his wife)* It was thou, covetous woman, that has brought
230 this upon us.

Mrs. Shem: *(weeping)* Yes, I wanted the vineyards for thee, Shem,
because at night as thou slept on my breast I heard thee sob for
them. I head thee murmur "Vineyards" in thy dreams.

Noah: Shem's wife is but a woman.

Mrs. Noah: How rash thou art, to curse unknowing in thy cups the
son of thy loins.

Noah: Did not Jehovah repent after he had destroyed the world? Did
He not make all flesh? Their evils as well as their good? Why did
He not with His flood of waters wash out the evil from men's
240 hearts, and spare the creatures He had made, or else destroy us
all, *all?* For in sparing one, He has preserved all the wickedness
that He creates abundantly, but punishes terribly. No, He
destroyed them because vile as they were it was His handiwork,
and it shamed and reproached Him night and day. He could not
bear to look upon the thing He had done, so He destroyed them.

Mrs. Noah: Thou canst not question.

Noah: *(weeping)* Where is my son?

Shem: *(pointing)* Asleep behind the altar.

Noah: If Jehovah keeps not the covenant this time, if he spare not my
250 weakness, then I pray that Ham's heart remains asleep forever.

Mrs. Shem: *(beseeching)* O Lord of the Earth, let his punishment be
mine. We coveted his vineyards, but the curse is too awful for
him. He is drunk like you—save him, Father Noah.

Noah: *(exultantly)* Ah, the rainbow! The promise! Jehovah will meet
me! He will set His sign in the Heavens! Shem hold thou my right
hand and Japheth bear up my left arm.

(Noah approaches the altar and kneels. The two men raise his hands aloft.)

Our Jehovah who carried us into the ark—

Sons: Victory, O Jehovah! The Sign.

Others: *(beating their breasts)* This is Thy Kingdom and we are here.
260 **Noah:** Who saved us from the Man of the Waters.

Sons: Victory, O Jehovah! The Sign.

Others: We belong to Thee, Jehovah, we belong to Thee.

*(There is a sudden, loud raucous laugh from behind the altar. Ham sings brokenly,
"I am a young ram in the Spring.")*

Noah: *(hopefully)* Look! Look! To the mountain—do ye see colors
appear?

Mrs. Noah: None but what our hearts paint for us—ah, false
hope.

Noah: Does the sign appear, I seem to see a faint color just above the
mountain. *(Another laugh from Ham.)*

Eve: None, none yet. (*Beats her breast violently, speaks rapidly.*) Jehovah, we
270   belong to *Thee*, we belong to *Thee*.
Mrs. Noah and Eve: Great Jehovah! Hear us. We are here in Thy
Valley. We who belong to Thee!

(*Ham slowly rises. He stands and walks around the altar to join the others, and
they see that he is black. They shrink back terrified. He is laughing happily. Eve
approaches him timidly as he advances around the end of the altar. She touches his
hand, then his face. She begins kissing him.*)

Ham: Why do you all pray and weep?
Eve: Look at thy hands, thy feet. Thou art cursed black by thy
Father. (*She exits weeping left.*)
Ham: (*gazing horrified at his hands*) Black! (*He appears stupefied. All
shrink away from him as if they feared his touch. He approaches each in
turn. He is amazed. He lays his hand upon Shem.*)
Shem: (*shrinking*) Away! Touch me not!
280 *Ham:* (*approaches his mother. She does not repel him but averts her face.*)
Why does my mother turn away?
Mrs. Noah: So that my baby may not see the flood that hath broken
the windows of my soul and loosed the fountains of my heart.

(*There is a great clamor off stage and Eve re-enters left with her boy in her arms
weeping and all the other children in pursuit jeering and pelting him with things.
The child is also black. Ham looks at his child and falls at Noah's feet.*)

Ham: (*beseeching in agony*) Why Noah, my father and lord of the Earth,
why?
Noah: (*sternly*) Arise, Ham. Thou art black. Arise and go out from
among us that we may see thy face no more, lest by lingering the
curse of thy blackness come upon all my seed forever.

(*Ham grasps his father's knees. Noah repels him sternly, pointing away right. Eve
steps up to Ham and raises him with her hand. She displays both anger and scorn.*)

Eve: Ham, my husband, Noah is right. Let us go before you awake
290   and learn to despise your father and your God. Come away Ham,
beloved, come with me, where thou canst never see these faces
again, where never thy soft eyes can harden by looking too oft
upon the fruit of their error, where never thy happy voice can
learn to weep. Come with me to where the sun shines forever,
to the end of the Earth, beloved the sunlight of all my years. (*She
kisses his mouth and forehead. She crosses to door of tent and picks up a
water bottle. Ham looks dazedly about him. His eyes light on the harp
and he smilingly picks it up and takes his place beside Eve.*)
Ham: (*lightly cynical to all*) Oh, remain with your flocks and fields and
300   vineyards, to covet, to sweat, to die and know no peace. I go to the

sun. (*He exits right across the plain with his wife and child trudging beside him. After he is off-stage comes the strumming of the harp and Ham's voice happily singing: "I am as a young ram in the Spring." It grows fainter and fainter until it is heard no more. The sun is low in the west. Noah sits looking tragically stern. All are ghastly calm. Mrs. Noah kneels upon the altar facing the mountain and she sobs continually.*

We belong to Thee, O Jehovah
We belong to Thee.
She keeps repeating this to a slow curtain).

Curtain

FEDERICO GARCÍA LORCA (1899–1936)
The Love of Don Perlimplín and Belisa in the Garden
An Erotic Lace-Paper Valentine in Four Scenes
Chamber Version
(1936)

Translated from the Spanish by James Graham-Lujan and Richard L. O'Connell

CHARACTERS

Don Perlimplín	**Mother of Belisa**
Belisa	**First Sprite**
Marcolfa	**Second Sprite**

Prologue

House of Don Perlimplín. Green walls; chairs and furniture painted black. At the rear, a deep window with balcony through which Belisa's balcony may be seen. A sonata is heard. Perlimplín wears a green cassock and a white wig full of curls. Marcolfa, the servant, wears the classic striped dress.

Perlimplín: Yes?
Marcolfa: Yes.
Perlimplín: But why "yes"?
Marcolfa: Just because yes.
Perlimplín: And if I should say no?
Marcolfa: (*acidly*) No?
Perlimplín: No.
Marcolfa: Tell me, Master, the reason for that "no."
Perlimplín: You tell me, you persevering domestic, the reasons for that
10 "yes."

(*Pause.*)

Marcolfa: Twenty and twenty are forty . . .
Perlimplín: (listening) Proceed.
Marcolfa: And ten, fifty.
Perlimplín: Go ahead.
Marcolfa: At fifty years one is no longer a child.
Perlimplín: Of course!
Marcolfa: I may die any minute.
Perlimplín: Good Lord!
Marcolfa: (weeping) And what will happen to you all alone in the
20   world?
Perlimplín: What will happen?
Marcolfa: That's why you have to marry.
Perlimplín: (distracted) Yes?
Marcolfa: (sternly) Yes.
Perlimplín: (miserably) But Marcolfa . . . why "yes"? When I was a
child a woman strangled her husband. He was a shoemaker. I
can't forget it. I've always said I wouldn't marry. My books are
enough for me. What good will marriage do me?
Marcolfa: Marriage holds great charms, Master. It isn't what it appears
30   on the outside. It's full of hidden things . . . things which it
would not be becoming for a servant to mention. You see that . . .
Perlimplín: That what?
Marcolfa: That I have blushed.

(Pause. A piano is heard.)

Voice of Belisa (within, singing): Ah love, ah love.
Tight in my thighs imprisoned
There swims like a fish the sun.
Warm water in the rushes.
Ah love.
40   Morning cock, the night is going!
Don't let it vanish, no!

Marcolfa: My master will see the reason I have.
Perlimplín: (scratching his head) She sings prettily.
Marcolfa: She is the woman for my master. The fair Belisa.
Perlimplín: Belisa . . . but wouldn't it be better . . . ?
Marcolfa: No. Now come. *(She takes him by the hand and goes toward the
balcony.)* Say, "Belisa."
Perlimplín: Belisa . . .
Marcolfa: Louder.
50 *Perlimplín:* Belisa!

*(The balcony of the house opposite opens and Belisa appears, resplendent in her
loveliness. She is half naked.)*

Belisa: Who calls?

(Marcolfa hides behind the window curtains.)

Marcolfa: Answer!
Perlimplín: *(trembling)* I was calling.
Belisa: Yes?
Perlimplín: Yes.
Belisa: But why, "yes"?
Perlimplín: Just because yes.
Belisa: And if I should say no?
Perlimplín: I would be sorry, because . . . we have decided that I
60   want to marry.
Belisa: *(laughs)* Marry whom?
Perlimplín: You.
Belisa: *(serious)* But . . . *(calling)* Mamá! Mamá-á-á!
Marcolfa: This is going well.

*(Enter the Mother wearing a great eighteenth-century wig full of birds, ribbons
and glass beads.)*

Belisa: Don Perlimplín wants to marry me. What must I do?
Mother: The very best of afternoons to you, my charming little
      neighbor. I always said to my poor little girl that you have the
      grace and elegance of that great lady who was your mother, whom
      I did not have the pleasure of knowing.
70 *Perlimplín:* Thank you.
Marcolfa: *(furiously, from behind the curtain)* I have decided that we are
      going . . .
Perlimplín: We have decided that we are going . . .
Mother: To contract matrimony. Is that not so?
Perlimplín: That is so.
Belisa: But, Mamá, what about me?
Mother: You are agreeable, naturally. Don Perlimplín is a fascinating
      husband.
Perlimplín: I hope to be one, madam.
80 *Marcolfa:* *(calling to Don Perlimplín)* This is almost settled.
Perlimplín: Do you think so?

(They whisper together.)

Mother: *(to Belisa)* Don Perlimplín has many lands. On these are many
      geese and sheep. The sheep are taken to market. At the market
      they give money for them. Money produces beauty . . . and
      beauty is sought after by all men.
Perlimplín: Then . . .

Mother: Ever so thrilled . . . Belisa . . . go inside. It isn't well for a maiden to hear certain conversations.

Belisa: Until later. (*She leaves.*)

90 *Mother:* She is a lily. You've seen her face? (*Lowering her voice.*) But if you should see further! Just like sugar. But, pardon. I need not call these things to the attention of a person as modern and competent as you. . . .

Perlimplín: Yes?

Mother: Why, yes. I said it without irony.

Perlimplín: I don't know how to express our gratitude.

Mother: Oh, "our gratitude." What extraordinary delicacy! The gratitude of your heart and your self . . . I have sensed it. I have sensed it . . . in spite of the fact that it is twenty years since I

100 have had relations with a man.

Marcolfa: (*aside*) The wedding.

Perlimplín: The wedding . . .

Mother: Whenever you wish. Though . . . (*She brings out a handkerchief and weeps.*) . . . to every mother . . . until later! (*Leaves.*)

Marcolfa: At last!

Perlimplín: Oh, Marcolfa, Marcolfa! Into what world are you going to thrust me?

Marcolfa: Into the world of matrimony.

Perlimplín: And if I should be frank, I would say that I feel thirsty.

110 Why don't you bring me some water? (*Marcolfa approaches him and whispers in his ear.*) Who could believe it?

(*The piano is heard. The stage is in darkness. Belisa opens the curtains of her balcony, almost naked, singing languidly.*)

Belisa: Ah love, ah love.
Tight in my warm thighs imprisoned,
There swims like a fish the sun.

Marcolfa: Beautiful maiden.

Perlimplín: Like sugar . . . white inside. Will she be capable of strangling me?

Marcolfa: Woman is weak if frightened in time.

120 *Belisa:* Ah love, ah love.
Morning cock, the night is going!
Don't let it vanish, no!

Perlimplín: What does she mean, Marcolfa? What does she mean? (*Marcolfa laughs.*) What is happening to me? What is it?

(*The piano goes on playing. Past the balcony flies a band of black paper birds.*)

Curtain

Scene One

Don Perlimplín's room. At the center there is a great bed topped by a canopy with plume ornaments. In the back wall there are six doors. The first one on the right serves as entrance and exit for Don Perlimplín. It is the wedding night. Marcolfa, with a candelabrum in her hand, speaks at the first door on the left side.

Marcolfa: Good night.
Belisa: *(offstage)* Good night, Marcolfa.

(Don Perlimplín enters, magnificently dressed.)

Marcolfa: May my master have a good wedding night.
Perlimplín: Good night, Marcolfa. (*Marcolfa leaves. Perlimplín tiptoes toward the room in front and looks from the door.*) Belisa, in all that froth of lace you look like a wave, and you give me the same fear of the sea that I had as a child. Since you came from the church my house is full of secret whispers, and the water grows warm by itself in the glasses. Oh! Perlimplín . . . Where are you,
10   Perlimplín?

(Leaves on tiptoe. Belisa appears, dressed in a great sleeping garment adorned with lace. She wears an enormous headdress which launches cascades of needlework and lace down to her feet. Her hair is loose and her arms bare.)

Belisa: The maid perfumed this room with thyme and not with mint as I ordered . . . (*Goes toward the bed.*) Nor did she put on the fine linen which Marcolfa has. (*At this moment there is a soft music of guitars. Belisa crosses her hands over her breast.*) Ah! Whoever seeks me ardently will find me. My thirst is never quenched, just as the thirst of the gargoyles who spurt water in the fountains is never quenched. (*The music continues.*) Oh, what music! Heavens, what music! Like the soft warm downy feathers of a swan! Oh! Is it I? Or is it the music?

(She throws a great cape of red velvet over her shoulders and walks about the room. The music is silent and five whistles are heard.)

20 **Belisa:** Five of them!

(Perlimplín appears.)

Perlimplín: Do I disturb you?
Belisa: How could that be possible?
Perlimplín: Are you sleepy?
Belisa: *(ironically)* Sleepy?
Perlimplín: The night has become a little chilly.

(Rubs his hands. Pause.)

Belisa: *(with decision)* Perlimplín.
Perlimplín: *(trembling)* What do you want?
Belisa: *(vaguely)* It's a pretty name, "Perlimplín."
Perlimplín: Yours is prettier, Belisa.
30 **Belisa:** *(laughing)* Oh! Thank you!

(Short pause.)

Perlimplín: I wanted to tell you something.
Belisa: And that is?
Perlimplín: I have been late in deciding . . . but . . .
Belisa: Say it.
Perlimplín: Belisa, I love you.
Belisa: Oh, you little gentleman! That's your duty.
Perlimplín: Yes?
Belisa: Yes.
Perlimplín: But why "yes"?
40 **Belisa:** *(coyly)* Because.
Perlimplín: No.
Belisa: Perlimplín!
Perlimplín: No, Belisa, before I married you, I didn't love you.
Belisa: *(jokingly)* What are you saying?
Perlimplín: I married . . . for whatever reason, but I didn't love you.
    I couldn't have imagined your body until I saw it through the
    keyhole when you were putting on your wedding dress. And then
    it was that I felt love come to me. Then! Like the deep thrust of a
    lancet in my throat.
50 **Belisa:** *(intrigued)* But, the other women?
Perlimplín: What women?
Belisa: Those you knew before.
Perlimplín: But are there other women?
Belisa: *(getting up)* You astonish me!
Perlimplín: The first to be astonished was I. *(Pause. The five whistles are
    heard.)* What's that?
Belisa: The clock.
Perlimplín: Is it five?
Belisa: Bedtime.
60 **Perlimplín:** Do I have your permission to remove my coat?
Belisa: Of course *(yawning)* little husband. And put out the light, if
    that is your wish.

(Perlimplín puts out the light.)

Perlimplín: *(in a low voice)* Belisa.
Belisa: *(loudly)* What, child?
Perlimplín: *(whispering)* I've put the light out.

Belisa: *(jokingly)* I see that.
Perlimplín: *(in a much lower voice)* Belisa . . .
Belisa: *(in a loud voice)* What, enchanter?
Perlimplín: I adore you!

(The five whistles are heard much louder and the bed is uncovered. Two Sprites, entering from opposite sides of the stage, run a curtain of misty gray. The theater is left in darkness. Flutes sound with a sweet, sleepy tone. The Sprites should be two children. They sit on the prompt box facing the audience.)

70 **First Sprite:** And how goes it with you in this tiny darkness?
Second Sprite: Neither well nor badly, little friend.
First Sprite: Here we are.
Second Sprite: And how do you like it? It's always nice to cover other people's failings . . .
First Sprite: And then to let the audience take care of uncovering them.
Second Sprite: Because if things are not covered up with all possible precautions . . .
First Sprite: They would never be discovered.
80 **Second Sprite:** And without this covering and uncovering . . .
First Sprite: What would the poor people do?
Second Sprite: *(looking at the curtain)* There must not even be a slit.
First Sprite: For the slits of today are darkness tomorrow.

(They laugh.)

Second Sprite: When things are quite evident . . .
First Sprite: Man figures that he has no need to discover them . . . in them secrets he already knew.
Second Sprite: And he goes to dark things to discover them . . . in them secrets he already knew.
First Sprite: But that's what we're here for. We Sprites!
90 **Second Sprite:** Did you know Perlimplín?
First Sprite: Since he was a child.
Second Sprite: And Belisa?
First Sprite: Very well. Her room exhaled such intense perfume that I once fell asleep and awoke between her cat's claws.

(They laugh.)

Second Sprite: This affair was . . .
First Sprite: Oh, of course!
Second Sprite: All the world thought so.
First Sprite: And the gossip must have turned then to more mysterious things.

100 ***Second Sprite:*** That's why our efficient and most sociable screen
      should not be opened yet.
 First Sprite: No, don't let them find out.
 Second Sprite: The soul of Perlimplín, tiny and frightened like
      a newborn duckling, becomes enriched and sublime at these
      moments.

 (They laugh.)

 First Sprite: The audience is impatient.
 Second Sprite: And with reason. Shall we go?
 First Sprite: Let's go. I feel a fresh breeze on my back already.
 Second Sprite: Five cool camellias of the dawn have opened in the
110   walls of the bedroom.
 First Sprite: Five balconies upon the city.

 (They rise and throw on some great blue hoods.)

 Second Sprite: Don Perlimplín, do we help or hinder you?
 First Sprite: Help: because it is not fair to place before the eyes of the
      audience the misfortune of a good man.
 Second Sprite: That's true, little friend, for it's not the same to say: "I
      have seen," as "It is said."
 First Sprite: Tomorrow the whole world will know about it.
 Second Sprite: And that's what we wish.
 First Sprite: One word of gossip and the whole world knows.
120 ***Second Sprite:*** Sh . . .

 (Flutes begin to sound.)

 First Sprite: Shall we go through this tiny darkness?
 Second Sprite: Let us go now, little friend.
 First Sprite: Now?
 Second Sprite: Now.

 *(They open the curtain. Don Perlimplín appears on the bed, with two enormous
 gilded horns. Belisa is at his side. The five balconies at the back of the stage are
 wide open, and through them the white light of dawn enters.)*

 Perlimplín: *(awakening)* Belisa! Belisa! Answer me!
 Belisa: *(pretending to awaken)* Perlimplinpinito . . . what do you want?
 Perlimplín: Tell me quickly.
 Belisa: What do you want me to tell you? I fell asleep long before you
      did.
130 ***Perlimplín:*** *(leaps from the bed. He has on his cassock)* Why are the
      balconies open?
 Belisa: Because this night the wind has blown as never before.

Perlimplín: Why do the balconies have five ladders that reach to the ground?

Belisa: Because that is the custom in my mother's country.

Perlimplín: And whose are those five hats which I see under the balconies?

Belisa: (*leaping from the bed*) The little drunkards who come and go. Perlimplinillo! Love!

(*Perlimplín looks at her, staring stupefied.*)

140 *Perlimplín:* Belisa! Belisa! And why not? You explain everything so well. I am satisfied. Why couldn't it have been like that?

Belisa: (*coyly*) I'm not a little fibber.

Perlimplín: And I love you more every minute!

Belisa: That's the way I like it.

Perlimplín: For the first time in my life I am happy! (*He approaches and embraces her, but, in that instant, turns brusquely from her.*) Belisa, who has kissed you? Don't lie, for I know!

Belisa: (*gathering her hair and throwing it over her shoulder*) Of course you know! What a playful little husband I have! (*In a low voice.*)
150 You! You have kissed me!

Perlimplín: Yes, I have kissed you . . . but . . . if someone else had kissed you . . . if someone else had kissed you . . . do you love me?

Belisa: (*lifting a naked arm*) Yes, little Perlimplín.

Perlimplín: Then, what do I care? (*He turns and embraces her.*) Are you Belisa?

Belisa: (*coyly, and in a low voice*) Yes! Yes! Yes!

Perlimplín: It almost seems like a dream!

Belisa: (*recovering*) Look, Perlimplín, close the balconies because before
160 long people will be getting up.

Perlimplín: What for? Since we have both slept enough, we shall see the dawn. Don't you like that?

Belisa: Yes, but . . .

(*She sits on the bed.*)

Perlimplín: I have never seen the sunrise. (*Belisa, exhausted, falls on the pillows of the bed*). It is a spectacle which . . . this may seem an untruth . . . thrills me! Don't you like it? (*Goes toward the bed.*) Belisa, are you asleep?

Belisa: (*in her dreams*) Yes.

(*Perlimplín tiptoes over and covers her with the red cape. An intense golden light enters through the balconies. Bands of paper birds cross them amidst the ringing of the morning bells. Perlimplín has seated himself on the edge of the bed.*)

Perlimplín: Love, love
Love, love
170   that here lies wounded.
So wounded by love's going;
so wounded,
dying of love.
Tell every one that it was just
the nightingale.
A surgeon's knife with four sharp edges;
the bleeding throat—forgetfulness.
Take me by the hands, my love,
for I come quite badly wounded,
180   so wounded by love's going.
So wounded!
Dying of love!

Curtain

Scene Two

Perlimplín's dining room. The perspectives are deliciously wrong. All the objects on the table are painted as in a primitive Last Supper.

Perlimplín: Then you will do as I say?
Marcolfa: (*crying*) Don't worry, master.
Perlimplín: Marcolfa, why do you keep on crying?
Marcolfa: Your Grace knows. On your wedding night five men entered your bedroom through the balconies. Five! Representatives of the five races of the earth. The European, with his beard—the Indian—the Negro—the Yellow Man—and the American. And you unaware of it all.
Perlimplín: That is of no importance.
10 *Marcolfa:* Just imagine: yesterday I saw her with another one.
Perlimplín: (*intrigued*) Really?
Marcolfa: And she didn't even hide from me.
Perlimplín: But I am happy, Marcolfa.
Marcolfa: The master astonishes me.
Perlimplín: You have no idea how happy I am. I have learned many things and above all I can imagine many others.
Marcolfa: My master loves her too much.
Perlimplín: Not as much as she deserves.
Marcolfa: Here she comes.
20 *Perlimplín:* Please leave.

(*Marcolfa leaves and Perlimplín hides in a corner. Enter Belisa dressed in a red dress of eighteenth-century style. The skirt, at the back, is slit, allowing silk stockings to be seen. She wears huge earrings and a red hat trimmed with big ostrich plumes.*)

Belisa: Again I have failed to see him. In my walk through the park they were all behind me except him. His skin must be dark, and his kisses must perfume and burn at the same time—like saffron and cloves. Sometimes he passes underneath my balconies and moves his hand slowly in a greeting that makes my breasts tremble.

Perlimplín: Ahem!

Belisa: (*turning*) Oh! What a fright you gave me.

Perlimplín: (*approaching her affectionately*) I observe you were speaking
30   to yourself.

Belisa: (*distastefully*) Go away!

Perlimplín: Shall we take a walk?

Belisa: No.

Perlimplín: Shall we go to the confectioner's?

Belisa: I said No!

Perlimplín: Pardon.

(*A letter rolled about a stone falls through the balcony. Perlimplín picks it up.*)

Belisa: Give that to me.

Perlimplín: Why?

Belisa: Because it's for me.

40 *Perlimplín:* (*jokingly*) And who told you that?

Belisa: Perlimplín! Don't read it!

Perlimplín: (*jokingly severe*) What are you trying to say?

Belisa: (*weeping*) Give me that letter!

Perlimplín: (*approaching her*) Poor Belisa! Because I understand your feelings I give you this paper which means so much to you. (*Belisa takes the note and hides it in her bosom.*) I can see things. And even though it wounds me deeply, I understand you live in a drama.

Belisa: (*tenderly*) Perlimplín!

Perlimplín: I know that you are faithful to me, and that you will
50   continue to be so.

Belisa: (*fondly*) I've never known any man other than my Perlimplinillo.

Perlimplín: That's why I want to help you as any good husband should when his wife is a model of virtue. . . . Look. (*He closes the door and adopts a mysterious air.*) I know everything! I realized immediately. You are young and I am old . . . What can we do about it! But I understand perfectly. (*Pause. In a low voice.*) Has he come by here today?

Belisa: Twice.

60 *Perlimplín:* And has he signaled to you?

Belisa: Yes . . . but in a manner that's a little disdainful . . . and that hurts me!

Perlimplín: Don't be afraid. Two weeks ago I saw that young man for the first time. I can tell you with all sincerity that his beauty dazzled me. I have never seen another man in whom manliness and delicacy meet in a more harmonious fashion. Without knowing why, I thought of you.

Belisa: I haven't seen his face . . . but . . .

Perlimplín: Don't be afraid to speak to me. I know you love

70   him . . . and I love you now as if I were your father. I am far from that foolishness: therefore . . .

Belisa: He writes me letters.

Perlimplín: I know that.

Belisa: But he doesn't let me see him.

Perlimplín: That's strange.

Belisa: And it even seems . . . as though he scorns me.

Perlimplín: How innocent you are!

Belisa: But there's no doubt he loves me as I wish. . . .

Perlimplín: (*intrigued*) How is that?

80 *Belisa:* The letters I have received from other men . . . and which I didn't answer because I had my little husband, spoke to me of ideal lands—of dreams and wounded hearts. But these letters from him . . . they . . .

Perlimplín: Speak without fear.

Belisa: They speak about me . . . about my body . . .

Perlimplín: (*stroking her hair*) About your body!

Belisa: "What do I want your soul for?" he tells me. "The soul is the patrimony of the weak, of crippled heroes and sickly people. Beautiful souls are at death's door, leaning upon whitest hairs and

90   lean hands. Belisa, it is not your soul that I desire, but your white and soft trembling body."

Perlimplín: Who could that beautiful youth be?

Belisa: No one knows.

Perlimplín: (*inquisitive*) No one?

Belisa: I have asked all my friends.

Perlimplín: (*inscrutably and decisively*) And if I should tell you I know him?

Belisa: Is that possible?

Perlimplín: Wait. (*Goes to the balcony.*) Here he is.

100 *Belisa:* (*running*) Yes?

Perlimplín: He has just turned the corner.

Belisa: (*choked*) Oh!

Perlimplín: Since I am an old man, I want to sacrifice myself for you. This that I do no one ever did before. But I am already beyond the world and the ridiculous morals of its people. Good-by.

Belisa: Where are you going?

Perlimplín: (*at the door, grandiosely*) Later you will know everything. Later.

Curtain

Scene Three

A grove of cypresses and orange trees. When the curtain rises, Marcolfa and Perlimplín appear in the garden.

Marcolfa: Is it time yet?

Perlimplín: No, it isn't time yet.

Marcolfa: But what has my master thought?

Perlimplín: Everything he hadn't thought before.

Marcolfa: (weeping) It's my fault!

Perlimplín: Oh, if you only knew what gratitude there is in my heart for you!

Marcolfa: Before this, everything went smoothly. In the morning, I would take my master his coffee and milk and grapes. . . .

10 *Perlimplín:* Yes . . . the grapes! The grapes! But . . . I? It seems to me that a hundred years have passed. Before, I could not think of the extraordinary things the world holds. I was merely on the threshold. On the other hand . . . today! Belisa's love has given me a precious wealth that I ignored before . . . don't you see? Now I can close my eyes and . . . I can see what I want. For example, my mother, when she was visited by the elves. Oh, you know how elves are . . . tiny. It's marvelous! They can dance upon my little finger.

Marcolfa: Yes, yes, the elves, the elves, but . . . how about this other?

20 *Perlimplín:* The other? Ah! *(With satisfaction.)* What did you tell my wife?

Marcolfa: Even though I'm not very good at these things, I told her what the master had instructed me to say . . . that that young man . . . would come tonight at ten o'clock sharp to the garden, wrapped, as usual, in his red cape.

Perlimplín: And she?

Marcolfa: She became as red as a geranium, put her hands to her heart, and kissed her lovely braids passionately.

Perlimplín: (enthusiastic) So she got red as a geranium, eh? And, what did she say?

30

Marcolfa: She just sighed; that's all. But, oh! such a sigh!

Perlimplín: Oh, yes! As no woman ever sighed before! Isn't that so?

Marcolfa: Her love must border on madness.

Perlimplín: (vibrantly) That's it! What I need is for her to love that youth more than her own body. And there is no doubt that she loves him.

Marcolfa: (weeping) It frightens me to hear you . . . but how is it possible? Don Perlimplín, how is it possible that you yourself should encourage your wife in the worst of sins?

40 *Perlimplín:* Because Perlimplín has no honor and wants to amuse himself! Now do you see? Tonight the new and unknown lover of

my lady Belisa will come. What should I do but sing? (*Singing.*)
Don Perlimplín has no honor! Has no honor!

Marcolfa: Let my master know that from this moment on I consider
myself dismissed from his service. We servants also have a sense
of shame.

Perlimplín: Oh, innocent Marcolfa! Tomorrow you will be as free as a
bird. Wait until tomorrow. Now go and perform your duty. You
will do what I have told you?

50 *Marcolfa:* (*leaving, drying her tears*) What else is there for me to do?
What else?

Perlimplín: Good, that's how I like it.

(*A sweet serenade begins to sound. Don Perlimplín hides behind some rosebushes.*)

Voices: Upon the banks of the river
the passing night has paused to bathe.
The passing night has paused to bathe.
And on the breasts of Belisa
the flowers languish of their love.
The flowers languish of their love.

Perlimplín: The flowers languish of their love.

Voices: The naked night stands there singing,
60   singing on the bridge of March.
Singing on the bridge of March.
Belisa, too, bathes her body
with briny water and spikenard.
With briny water and spikenard.

Perlimplín: The flowers languish of their love!

Voices: The night of anise and silver
on all the roofs glows and shines.
On all the roofs glows and shines.
70   The silver of streams and of mirrors
and anise white of your thighs.
And anise white of your thighs.

Perlimplín: The flowers languish of their love!

(*Belisa appears in the garden splendidly dressed. The moon lights the stage.*)

Belisa: What voices fill with sweet harmony the air of this fragment of
the night? I have felt your warmth and your weight, delicious
youth of my soul. Oh! The branches are moving . . .

(A man dressed in a red cape appears and crosses the garden cautiously.)

Belisa: Sh! Here! Here! (*The man signals with his hand that he will return immediately.*) Oh! Yes . . . come back my love! Like a jasmine floating and without roots, the sky will fall over my moistening shoulders. Night! My night of mint and lapis lazuli . . .

80

(Perlimplín appears.)

Perlimplín: *(surprised)* What are you doing here?
Belisa: I was walking.
Perlimplín: Only that?
Belisa: In the clear night.
Perlimplín: *(severely)* What were you doing here?
Belisa: *(surprised)* Don't you know?
Perlimplín: I don't know anything.
Belisa: You sent me the message.
Perlimplín: *(with ardent desire)* Belisa . . . are you still waiting for

90   him?
Belisa: With more ardor than ever.
Perlimplín: *(severely)* Why?
Belisa: Because I love him.
Perlimplín: Well, he will come.
Belisa: The perfume of his flesh passes beyond his clothes. I love him! Perlimplín, I love him! It seems to me that I am another woman!
Perlimplín: That is my triumph.
Belisa: What triumph?
Perlimplín: The triumph of my imagination.
100 **Belisa:** It's true that you helped me love him.
Perlimplín: As now I will help you mourn him.
Belisa: *(puzzled)* Perlimplín! What are you saying?

(The clock sounds ten. A nightingale sings.)

Perlimplín: It is the hour.
Belisa: He should be here this instant.
Perlimplín: He's leaping the walls of my garden.
Belisa: Wrapped in his red cape.
Perlimplín: *(drawing a dagger)* Red as his blood.
Belisa: *(holding him)* What are you going to do?
Perlimplín: *(embracing her)* Belisa, do you love him?
110 **Belisa:** *(forcefully)* Yes!
Perlimplín: Well, since you love him so much, I don't want him ever to leave you. And in order that he should be completely yours, it has come to me that the best thing would be to stick this dagger in his gallant heart. Would you like that?

Belisa: For God's sake, Perlimplín!

Perlimplín: Then, dead, you will be able to caress him in your bed—so handsome and well groomed—without the fear that he should cease to love you. He will love you with the infinite love of the dead, and I will be free of this dark little nightmare of your
120 magnificent body. (*Embracing her.*) Your body . . . that I will never decipher! (*Looking into the garden.*) Look where he comes. Let go, Belisa. Let go! (*He exits running.*)

Belisa: (*desperately*) Marcolfa! Bring me the sword from the dining room; I am going to run my husband's throat through. (*Calling.*)

Don Perlimplín
Evil husband!
If you kill him,
I'll kill you!

(*A man wrapped in a large red cape appears among the branches. He is wounded and stumbling.*)

Belisa: My love! . . . Who has wounded you in the breast? (*The man hides his face in his cape. The cape must be enormous and cover him to the feet. She embraces him.*) Who opened your veins so that you fill my garden with blood? Love, let me look at your face for an instant. Oh! Who has killed you . . . Who?

130 *Perlimplín:* (*uncovering himself*) Your husband has just killed me with this emerald dagger. (*He shows the dagger stuck in his chest.*)

Belisa: (*frightened*) Perlimplín!

Perlimplín: He ran away through the fields and you will never see him again. He killed me because he knew I loved you as no one else. . . . While he wounded me he shouted: "Belisa has a soul now!" Come near. (*He has stretched out on the bench.*)

Belisa: Why is this? And you are truly wounded.

Perlimplín: Perlimplín killed me. . . . Ah, Don Perlimplín! Youngish old man, manikin without strength, you couldn't enjoy the body of Belisa . . . the body of Belisa was for younger muscles and warm
140 lips. . . . I, on the other hand, loved your body only . . . your body! But he has killed me . . . with this glowing branch of precious stones.

Belisa: What have you done?

Perlimplín: (*near death*) Don't you understand? I am my soul and you are your body. Allow me this last moment, since you have loved me so much, to die embracing it.

(*Belisa, half naked, draws near and embraces him.*)

Belisa: Yes . . . but the young man? Why have you deceived me?

Perlimplín: The young man?

(Closes his eyes. The stage is left in magical light. Marcolfa enters.)

Marcolfa: Madam . . .

150 **Belisa:** *(weeping)* Don Perlimplín is dead!

Marcolfa: I knew it! Now his shroud will be the youthful red suit in which he used to walk under his own balconies.

Belisa: *(weeping)* I never thought he was so devious.

Marcolfa: You have found out too late. I shall make him a crown of flowers like the noonday sun.

Belisa: *(confused, as if in another world)* Perlimplín, what have you done, Perlimplín?

Marcolfa: Belisa, now you are another woman. You are dressed in the most glorious blood of my master.

160 **Belisa:** But who was this man? Who was he?

Marcolfa: The beautiful adolescent whose face you never will see.

Belisa: Yes, yes, Marcolfa—I love him—I love him with all the strength of my flesh and my soul—but where is the young man in the red cape? Dear God, where is he?

Marcolfa: Don Perlimplín, sleep peacefully. . . . Do you hear? Don Perlimplín. . . . Do you hear her?

(The bells sound.)

Curtain

Appendix I:
Four Critical Essays on
Poe and Hawthorne

CRITICAL ESSAYS

Throughout the book critics have been represented by accounts or summaries of their work. In this section, students can work directly with the essays of four critics who take four different approaches as follows:

On Poe's "Purloined Letter" (p. 198)

1. Marie Bonaparte, the French psychoanalyst who studied with Sigmund Freud, analyzes the story from a Psychoanalytic point of view.
2. Joseph G. Kronick, a professor at Louisiana State University and an expert on Southern Literature, uses many of the approaches of Reader-Response theory to analyze the story.

On Hawthorne's "The Birthmark" (p. 212)

1. Eric Mottram, author of books on subjects ranging from Ezra Pound to detective fiction, gives a contemporary Marxist approach that employs elements of recent Lacanian methods.
2. Noted Feminist critic, Judith Fetterley, author of *The Resisting Reader: A Feminist Approach to American Fiction,* offers a Feminist reading of the story.

Each essay begins with a headnote that sets the critical context, and the essays are followed by writing exercises that show the student several ways to make use of their interaction with critical documents.

MARIE BONAPARTE
"The Purloined Letter": A Psychoanalytic Approach

In The Life and Works of Edgar Allan Poe (1933), Marie Bonaparte treats Poe's writing as a Freudian case history. For her, the poet's motivating fantasy is a desire for his dead mother that, along with the fear of castration it causes, dominates his writing. Poe's images disguise and combine his covert meaning. Bonaparte analyzes "The Purloined Letter" along with others of his stories that she calls "Tales About Mother." The following excerpt begins just after she has discussed "The Black Cat" where she says the image of a chimney stands for "the dread cloaca of the mother."

Other tales by Poe also express, though in different and less aggressive fashion, regret for the missing maternal penis, with reproach for its loss. First among these, strange though it seem, is "The Purloined Letter."[1]

The reader will remember that, in this story, the Queen of France, like Elizabeth Arnold,[2] is in possession of dangerous and secret letters, whose writer is unknown. A wicked minister, seeking a political advantage and to strengthen his power, steals one of these letters under the Queen's eyes, which she is unable to prevent owing to the King's presence. This letter must at all costs be recovered. Every attempt by the police fails. Fortunately Dupin is at hand. Wearing dark spectacles with which he can look about him, while his own eyes are concealed, he makes an excuse to call on the minister, and discovers the letter openly displayed in a card-rack, hung "from a little brass knob just beneath the middle of the mantelpiece."

By a further subterfuge, he possesses himself of the compromising letter and leaves a similar one in its place. The Queen, who will have the original restored to her, is saved.

Let us first note that this letter, very symbol of the maternal penis, also "hangs" over the fireplace, in the same manner as the female penis, if it existed, would be hung over the cloaca which is here represented— as in the foregoing tales—by the general symbol of fireplace or chimney. We have here, in fact, what is almost an anatomical chart, from which not even the clitoris (or brass knob) is omitted. Something very different, however, should be hanging from that body!

The struggle between Dupin and the minister who once did Dupin an "ill turn"—a struggle in which the latter is victorious—represents, in effect, the Oedipal struggle between father and son, though on an archaic, pregenital and phallic level, to seize possession, not of the mother herself, but of a part; namely, her penis.

From *The Life and Works of Edgar Allen Poe: A Psycho-Analytic Interpretation,* by Marie Bonaparte, trans. John Rodker (London: Imago Publishing Co., 1933; 1949), 483–85. Reprinted by permission of Chatto & Windus.

[1] *The Purloined Letters: The Gift,* 1845.

[2] Elizabeth Arnold, Poe's actress mother who died when Poe was three years old, left behind a packet of letters—practically her only legacy to her son.—ED.

We have here an illustration of that "partial love" and desire, not for the whole of the loved being but for an organ, which characterises one stage of infantile libidinal development.[3]

Yet though the minister, impressive father-figure and "man of genius" as he is, is outwitted by the ratiocinatory and so more brilliant son, he presents one outstanding characteristic which recalls that very "son" for he, too, is a poet! He is a composite figure, combining characteristics of the two "wicked" fathers; first of Elizabeth Arnold's unknown lover, her castrator in the child's eyes, and then of John Allan.

For did not John Allan, too, appear to the child as the ravisher castrator of a woman, Frances, Edgar's beloved and ailing "Ma"?[4] More still, had he not impugned his true mother's virtue and injured her reputation, as the blackmailing minister planned to do with the Queen's?

The minister also reminds us of John Allan by his unscrupulous ambition. And it was John Allan again, who, to Poe as a child, represented that *"monstrum horrendum*—an unprincipled man of genius," not far removed from the "criminal" of "vast intelligence" figured in "The Man of the Crowd." So does the father often appear to the small boy, at once admired and hated.

Most striking of all, the minister exhibits Poe's outstanding feature, his poetic gift. And here Poe, in fact, identifies himself with the hated though admired father by that same gift of identification whose praises he sings in "The Purloined Letter" as being the one, supremely effective way of penetrating another's thoughts and feelings.

Poe, impotent and a poet, could never so wholly identify himself with the Orang-Outang in "The Murders in the Rue Morgue," for there the father conquers the mother only by reason of his overwhelming strength. But, in his unconscious, Poe could achieve this with the minister for, though the latter, once more, triumphs by superior strength, this time it is of the intellect.

As to the King whom the Queen deceives, he must again be David Poe, Elizabeth's husband. Small wonder that Dupin, embodying the son, should declare his "political sympathies" with the lady! Finally, in return for a cheque of 50,000 francs, leaving to the Prefect of Police the fabulous reward, Dupin restores the woman her symbolic letter or missing penis. Thus, once more, we meet the equation gold = penis. The mother gives her son gold in exchange for the penis he restores.

So too, in "The Gold Bug," the treasure would seem to be bestowed by the mother, on the son, in return for the penis he restores to her. In our analysis of the tale it was too soon to emphasize the equivalence gold = penis: the point had not been reached at which we could offer an explanation. But now that we know the unconscious significance of the

---

[3] Cf. Abraham, *A Short Study of the Development of the Libido.*

[4] John and Frances Allan adopted the young Edgar after his mother's death.—ED.

From ed. Jefferson Humphries, *Southern Literature and Literary Theory* (University of Georgia Press) 1990 pp. 206–225.

hanging-theme, we will recall the strange means devised by Captain Kidd to lead to his treasure. A plumb-line, *hung* through a hollow eye-socket, gives the position from which measurements should be made to reveal its presence. This is, indeed, strangely reminiscent of the gouged-out eye, symbolising castration, and the hanging theme, symbolising rephallisation. Both relate to the dead mother, whose skull thus, clearly, guards the treasure.

This theme of the castrated mother, so familiar to infantile ways of thinking and the unconscious throughout life, though far removed from consciousness and adult ways of thought, is thus found at the root of some of Poe's best-known tales.

It is time, however, to leave these tales which revolve round so many avatars of the mother. As was to be expected, in almost all the tales we have so far analysed, the son's relation to the mother is the main theme. Nevertheless, in some—as in the Marchese Mentoni on his palace steps, old Berlifitzing in his castle, or Mr. Windenough and the surgeon in "Loss of Breath"—we already catch fleeting glimpses of the father. In "The Murders in the Rue Morgue," the father, killer and castrator, as the anthropoid ape is, even, the main character. But it is in "The Man of the Crowd" that, for the first time in Poe's work, the father's figure fills the stage in all his tragic grandeur. Even the mother and victim remains hid in the mystery shrouding the crime. Indeed, we might well be asked why we included this tale in the "Tales of the Mother" at all, were it not that the deeper logic of Poe's inspiration determined that place, since its main theme, in fact, is the father's relation *to the mother.*

The tales which now remain to be studied [in the essay's original setting] are almost all variants on another main theme: that of the son's relation to the father. We shall now see these two protagonists at grips; hate being uppermost first, then love.

JOSEPH G. KRONICK
"Edgar Allan Poe: The Error of Reading and The Reading of Error": A Reader-Response Approach

In this essay, Kronick surveys some of the ways Poe has been read in general and in particular. He also traces the theme of "error" both in critical appreciations and in Poe's works themselves: "Error in Poe is always an error of intentionality—either the critic attacks Poe for failing to achieve the effects he seems to have intended, such as humor or horror, or the critic defends Poe for having anticipated the interpretations his texts have elicited."

In a famous letter to Evert A. Duyckink, Melville expresses his grudging admiration for Emerson, who, despite his "oracular gibberish," can be counted as one of the "thought-divers": "I love all men who *dive*. Any fish can swim near the surface, but it takes a great whale to go down stairs five miles or more; & if he dont attain the bottom, why, all the lead in Galena can't fashion the plumet that will. I'm not talking of Mr. Emerson now—but of the whole corps of thought-divers, that have been diving & coming up again with blood-shot eyes since the world began."[1] Although "blood-shot eyes" may have figured in contemporary portraits of a haggard Edgar Allan Poe, he never, so he tells us, chose to search the depths for truth: "As regards the greater truths, men oftener err by seeking them at the bottom than at the top; the depth lies in the huge abysses where wisdom is sought—not in the palpable palaces where she is found."[2] For Melville, we discover truth only by diving deep, but for Poe, deep leads unto deep and not to truth. This contrast between depth and surface may serve as some indication of what distinguishes Poe from his northern contemporaries, but critical discussion of symbolism and, more recently, of the hieroglyphic has erased this difference.[3]

Poe has long been the other of American literature—he is either the protosymbolist who has returned to us via the translations of Baudelaire, Mallarmé, and Valéry, or the poet of the unconscious who has anatomized that part of the psyche few writers ever admitted existed. Roy Harvey Pearce aptly describes Poe as "a kind of cultural hero of the imagination."[4] When he is not being defended as a founder of modernism or as the dark genius of American literature, he is attacked for the crudity of both his style and thought. The vigor of Poe's defenders and detractors has assured his status as a major writer, but it has taken poststructuralists to secure for Poe a place in the American renaissance. The way for this revision, however, was prepared by F. O. Matthiessen's and Charles Feidelson's theories of symbolism. Although Matthiessen hardly mentions Poe in *The American Renaissance*, he says that Poe is closer to his American contemporaries than to Baudelaire precisely because he shared with Emerson and Hawthorne the "loosely Platonic" concept that in poetry the word is to the idea as the body is to the soul.[5] Feidelson, who gives a little more attention to Poe in his *Symbolism and American Literature*, also says Poe's idea of literature was basically the same as Emerson's, Hawthorne's, and Melville's, but whereas transcendentalism is a kind of "materialistic idealism," Poe sought to rarefy or idealize matter, instead of beginning with the Christian concept of spirit.[6]

---

[1] Herman Melville, *The Confidence-Man: His Masquerade,* ed. Hershel Parker (New York: Norton, 1971), 257.

[2] Edgar Allan Poe, *Essays and Reviews,* ed. G. R. Thompson (New York: Library of America, 1984), 2:8. Hereafter this volume will be cited in the text, as will volume I, *Poetry and Tales,* ed. Patrick Quinn (New York: Library of America, 1984).

[3] The figure of the hieroglyphic in Poe has received its most extensive treatment in John T. Irwin, *American Hieroglyphics: The Symbol of the Egyptian Hieroglyphics in the American Renaissance* (New Haven: Yale University Press, 1980).

[4] Roy Harvey Pearce, *The Continuity of American Poetry* (Princeton: Princeton University Press, 1961), 142.

[5] F. O. Matthiessen, *The American Renaissance: Art and Expression in the Age of Emerson and Whitman* (London: Oxford University Press, 1941), 242–43.

[6] Charles Feidelson, Jr., *Symbolism and American Literature* (Chicago: University of Chicago Press, 1953), 36.

Following Matthiessen's and Feidelson's pioneering work, John Irwin's *American Hieroglyphics* succeeds in assimilating Poe into the American renaissance by substituting the Saussurian concept of the sign for Matthiessen's Coleridgean notion of the symbol. Poe now joins Emerson, Whitman, Melville, and Hawthorne in their attempts to discover the origin of man by deciphering the origin of language. The hieroglyph is central to Irwin's study "because in pictographic writing the shape of a sign is in a sense a double of the physical shape of the object it represents."[7] Irwin's examination of the mirroring of the self in the hieroglyph reorients us toward a semiological reading of nineteenth-century American literature.

We have come more and more to think of the writers of nineteenth-century America as telling us that the self is a product of language. The self has been dislodged from its principal place as the origin of the work or as that which we can identify as consciousness and is now seen as a product of the play of signifiers in a text without a determinable signified. If we reject the phenomenological description of consciousness as the self-presence of the speaking subject, then in the writerly text, we may conclude that the self becomes an activity of writing, and the pure auto-affection of consciousness is opened to the temporal and spatial play of signs that function in the total absence of the subject.[8] The play of signifiers opens a space in writing wherein the author declares his absence.[9] And we confirm his absence whenever we read his tales: "Ye who read are still among the living; but I who write shall have long since gone my way into the region of shadows" (1:218).

The receptivity of Poe's texts to poststructuralist readings may rest largely on his insistence on their textuality. Poe's love of cryptography, literary hoaxes, and puzzles opens his texts to pyrotechnical displays of interpretive skills, for Poe remains a writer who draws many of his readers not because they like or admire him but because his texts are so malleable for the close interpreter. This quality may explain the hold Poe's texts have exerted on his French readers from Baudelaire to Lacan and Derrida. Barbara Johnson has investigated the triad of Poe, Lacan, and Derrida within the framework of psychoanalysis and has argued that the disagreement over the meaning of "The Purloined Letter" reveals that the meaning of a message is so "traversed by its own otherness to itself" that any reading must be in a sense narcissistic—the

---

[7] Irwin, *American Hieroglyphics*, 61.

[8] I refer to Jacques Derrida's critique of Husserl in *Speech and Phenomena*, trans. David B. Allison (Evanston, Ill.: Northwestern University Press, 1973), 78.

[9] The concept of the absence of the author has been treated in various ways by Derrida, Roland Barthes, and Michel Foucault. See, for instance, Jacques Derrida, "Signature Event Context," in *Margins of Philosophy*, trans. Alan Bass (Chicago: University of Chicago Press, 1982), 307–30. See also Michel Foucault, "What Is an Author?" and Roland Barthes, "From Work to Text," in *Textual Strategies: Perspectives in Post-Structuralist Criticism*, ed. and trans. Josué V. Harari (Ithaca: Cornell University Press, 1979), 73–81 and 141–60.

reader can find only the message that he or she sends.[10] The intensity of these readers, however, makes them liable to blindness, as was that other Parisian interpreter, the prefect of police in the Dupin tales: "'He impaired his vision by holding the object too close. He might see perhaps, one or two points with unusual clearness, but in so doing he, necessarily, lost sight of the matter as a whole'" (1:412). Poe offers a sure remedy for this failing—be superficial. If critics have not heeded this advice to seek for clues in obvious places, it is not because they have been inattentive to the surface of Poe's texts.

Various psychoanalytic and poststructuralist readings have focused almost entirely on the interrelationship of signifiers in Poe's text to the exclusion of any signified content. This transformation of Poe's works into texts, to borrow Roland Barthes's distinction,[11] has produced readings striking not only for their theoretical insights but also for their avoidance of those questions that have plagued Poe criticism, that is, the uncertainty of his intentions and his so-called execrable style. The questions of style and intention would seem to throw us back into the uncertain theoretical position of pre–New Critical interpretation, but Shoshana Felman has suggested that "the critical discourse surrounding Poe, is indeed one of the most visible ('self-evident') *effects* of Poe's poetic signifier, of his text." Felman rightly points out that the question of effects is a question of the place of the analyst or interpreter in the text: "the very position of the interpreter—of the analyst—turns out to be not *outside*, but *inside* the text."[12] Felman's essay is a subtle and valuable one, but it may be said that she reaches conclusions not only shared by many of Poe's critics but, as she argues so well, one already anticipated by Poe, even down to the unreadability of the analytical.

There are certain mysteries, Poe says, that are like "a certain German book . . . 'er lasst sich nicht lesen'—it does not permit itself to be read" (1:388). The question of the unreadability of the Poe text is a question of superficiality. It is the superficiality, the very overdeterminedness, of his tales that renders them opaque. For the psychoanalytic critic, this unreadability is the negative moment wherein depth is restored to the text as a projection of the reader. In making the interpretation, rather than the text, the object of analysis, the critic beats Poe at his own game—the critic now asserts that all interpretations of Poe err by being superficial, but in their very superficiality they register the effects of Poe's signifiers. Depth now is shifted from the text to the reader, who in turn ascribes it to the text. The psychoanalytic critic reinscribes the interpretation and returns it to its source: the reader. We discover in Poe's texts and their scenes of misreading that error makes interpretation possible: "Deprived of

---

[10] Barbara Johnson, "The Frame of Reference: Poe, Lacan, Derrida," *Yale French Studies* 55/56 (1977): 503.

[11] Barthes, "From Work to Text."

[12] Shoshana Felman, "On Reading Poetry: Reflections on the Limits and Possibilities of Psychoanalytic Approaches," in *The Literary Freud: Mechanisms of Defense and the Poetic Will*, ed. Joseph M. Smith (New Haven: Yale University Press, 1980), 147, 145.

ordinary resources, the analyst throws himself into the spirit of his opponent, identifies himself therewith, and not unfrequently sees thus, at a glance, the sole methods (sometimes indeed absurdly simple ones) by which he may seduce into error or hurry into miscalculation" (1:398). By identifying the interpretation with the text, the reader is seduced into the error of profundity. The text that generates the interpretation is only known by the effects it produces. The reader, however, identifies the effect with the author and ultimately errs by his ingenuity: "The analytical power should not be confounded with simple ingenuity; for while the analyst is necessarily ingenious, the ingenious man is often remarkably incapable of analysis" (1:399).

Error in Poe is always an error of intentionality—either the critic attacks Poe for failing to achieve the effects he seems to have intended, such as humor or horror, or the critic defends Poe for having anticipated the interpretations his texts have elicited. In one case, the reader confounds Poe's texts with their effects, and in the other, the reader confounds the effects with his own ingenious interpretation. In both cases, the effect is an interpretation, and this interpretation is a product of the error of profundity, the confusion of significance with depth. But in erring, the interpreter confirms the truth of Poe's texts—understanding is not only impossible but also unproductive, for misreading alone generates textuality. The reader errs by his or her ingenuity because Poe's texts are analytical, not ingenious. To analyze is not to uncover or bring to light what is hidden; it means to expose what lies in plain view—that is, the impenetrability of the familiar. To read Poe, then, is to confound the familiar with the hidden.

Poe's tales are filled with clues that reflect both upon himself as writer and on the reader as well. In tale after tale, Poe incorporates within his stories their own misreading. As Patrick Quinn has pointed out, much of "The Fall of the House of Usher" concerns the narrator's failure to interpret the clues laid out before him in this doppelgänger. The doubling in this story extends beyond the incestuous pairing of Roderick and Madeline Usher to the narrator, who "is at the same time both the author of the story and, as spectator of its events, the audience as well."[13] Unlike Roderick, whose desire for his sister reflects a desire for self-possession, the narrator is incapable of reflection—that is, the story he tells escapes him or passes beyond his vision.

The image of this failure of vision comes in the beginning when he admits he cannot explain the horror he feels upon seeing the House of Usher: "I was forced to fall back upon the unsatisfactory conclusion, that while, beyond doubt, there *are* combinations of very simple natural objects which have the power of thus affecting us, still the analysis of this power lies among considerations beyond our depth" (1:317). The very familiarity of this arrangement places the scene beyond the understanding,

---

[13] Patrick F. Quinn, *The French Face of Edgar Poe* (Carbondale: Southern Illinois University Press, 1957), 237.

but, the narrator goes on to say, an aesthetic rearrangement brings the natural within the realm of understanding: "It was possible, I reflected, that a mere different arrangement of the particulars of the scene, of the details of the picture, would be sufficient to modify, or perhaps to annihilate its capacity for sorrowful impression" (1:317–18). Only by disordering the scene through aesthetic representation can the narrator control its effects. This reflection on the affective properties of a "scene" or "picture" leads to a reflection to the second degree—the narrator proceeds to the tarn and looks down into the reflection in the water and gazes "with a shudder even more thrilling than before—upon the remodelled and inverted images of the grey sedge, and the ghostly tree-stems, and the vacant eye-like windows" (1:318). Reflection leads to reflection, but the narrator's blindness produces no insight; his eyes, like those of the windows, are vacant. Distinctly missing from this image, however, is the face of the narrator, which we can expect is reflected in the water. The text is certainly overdetermined. The narrator enters upon a highly artificial scene only to call it natural and then transforms this artifice into a second artifice. The inverted image found in the tarn foreshadows the inverted relation between the House and its inhabitants and between the incestuous twins as well. Finally, we get further doublings in the inclusion of the previously published poem, "The Haunted Palace," which is said to be an impromptu composition, and in the "Mad Trist" of Sir Launcelot Canning, a nonexistent book from which the narrator reads only to hear echoes in the house of the ludicrous tale before him.

Lost in this seemingly unending series of reflections, the narrator can never resolve the events into a discernible meaning. Nor can we agree with Quinn that the reader can decipher the clues that escape the frightened narrator, for whatever naturalistic or symbolic reading we can come up with, the tale's multiple scenes of reflection are tropes for the very misreading it attributes to the narrator. The readers participate in the deception when they attempt to fix the tale within one of the several perspectives offered in the text.

The scene of reading receives its most explicit treatment in "The Purloined Letter" and the passage on the game of odd and even. The game, we will recall, consists of guessing whether an opponent has an odd or even number of marbles hidden in his hand. This guessing game is perfected by a boy who invariably succeeds by identifying himself with his opponent. As the narrator says, "'It is merely . . . an identification of the reasoner's intellect with that of the opponent.'" The narrator, being a man of average intellect—he is smarter than the prefect of police but not as smart as Dupin—has not quite fathomed the significance of Dupin's story. The identification is not strictly with the intellect but with the expression of the opponent. Dupin quotes the boy himself: "'When I wish to find out how wise, or how stupid, or how good, or how wicked is any one, or what are his thoughts at the moment, I fashion the expression of my face, as accurately as possible, in accordance with the expression of his, and then wait to see what thoughts or sentiments arise in my mind or heart, as if to match or correspond with the expression'" (1:689–90). It is by imitating the expression of the other that the boy achieves understanding. By means of his wholly superficial imitation, thoughts and sentiments lying within or behind the expression spontaneously arise within the imitator.

The process would seem to be a paradigmatic example of the hermeneutic principle that understanding means understanding the expression, not some hypostasized interior that exists independent of the expression. This promise of complete understanding, however, exceeds anything the hermeneutician would claim as possible. Richard Wilbur correctly remarks that Dupin, despite his "analytical genius," really bases his solutions on "poetic intuition."[14] But applying the boy's description of his method to Dupin's solution of the mystery, we might say that his intuition is more properly phenomenological—he intuits the intention of his opponent in a wholly sensuous way.

The importance of the superficiality of this method underlies Dupin's explanation of the prefect's failure to discover the letter: "For its practical value it [the boy's method] depends upon this . . . and the Prefect and his cohort fail so frequently, first, by default of this identification, and, secondly, by ill-admeasurement, or rather through non-admeasurement, of the intellect with which they are engaged. They consider only their *own* ideas of ingenuity; and, in searching for anything hidden, advert only to the modes in which *they* would have hidden it" (1:690). Failure to identify is a failure to imitate. The prefect can identify only with what resembles him; the other or the different escapes the range of his understanding because he has not learned the art of mimicry. It is, of course, tempting to see in this passage on identification with the other a metaphor for various models of psychoanalytic reading. I would, however, agree with Bloom that such "Freudian translations are in his case merely redundant."[15] (We might note that in dismissing Freudian readings of Poe as redundant, Bloom at once hits upon a feature of Derrida's reading of Poe—all interpretation is redundant or a repetition of a pre-text—and yet fails to grasp it.) But the question of identification can be put within a hermeneutic framework as well, and in light of Poe's penchant for cryptography and the various tropes for reading in "The Purloined Letter," this approach seems to have a certain "authorization."

The failure of the prefect, therefore, is a failure to "read" his opponent. He has been too ingenious and not analytical enough. Confronted with a text, he projects an understanding that he possesses but which does not correspond to that of the text. The Minister D., of course, has anticipated how the police will act and so is able to circumvent their efforts to recover the letter. We are within the hermeneutic circle. All efforts to understand a text, according to Heidegger, involve an act of

---

[14] Richard Wilbur, "The Poe Mystery Case," in *Responses, Prose Pieces: 1953–1976* (New York: Harcourt Brace Jovanovich, 1976), 134.

[15] Harold Bloom, "Inescapable Poe," *New York Review of Books,* Oct. 11, 1984, 24.

projecting a meaning onto the text, and this meaning is revised through the course of time. Gadamer describes the hermeneutic circle succinctly: "The process that Heidegger describes is that every revision of the fore-project is capable of projecting before itself a new project of meaning, that rival projects can emerge side by side until it becomes clearer what the unity of meaning is, that interpretation begins with fore-conceptions that are replaced by more suitable ones."[16] The police project upon the minister a certain mode of behavior that corresponds with what experience has taught them to expect. But having made this projection, they do not revise it when their interpretation fails. Indeed, they simply repeat the error, assuming that their theory must be right and that the error lies in the execution. The police fail, not because they offer the wrong interpretation, but because they fail to understand what is being interpreted. Heidegger writes, "Any interpretation which is to contribute understanding, must already have understood what is to be interpreted."[17] The police believe that they are confronted by an intellect that is no different from theirs: "They consider only their *own* ideas of ingenuity; and, in searching for anything hidden, advert only to the modes in which *they* would have hidden it" (1:690). Their error lies in their ingenuity; they fail because they are confronted with an intellect that is either above or *below* their own. The prefect says, the minister is "a poet, which I take to be only one remove from a fool" (1:684). The prefect's error is to think the minister is only one remove from a fool, for, as we shall see, if he recognized that D. is a fool, he could have solved the case himself.

Dupin explains his success in retrieving the letter by referring back to his joke that the truth is "A little *too* self-evident" (1:681). As self-evident truth, the mystery bears its solution in its face, so to speak—it is the evidence of its own truth or solution. The prefect insists that the surface hides a mystery that he must explore to the depths. Dupin corrects this mistake by describing another scene of misreading. In a passage where Dupin begins to sound like Emerson, he elaborates his own theory of correspondence: "'The material world . . . abounds with very strict analogies to the immaterial; and thus some color of truth has been given to the rhetorical dogma, that metaphor, or simile, may be made to strengthen an argument, as well as to embellish a description'" (1:694). Metaphor is here defined in quite traditional terms as the material embodiment of the intellectual or nonmaterial idea. What is curious, however, is Dupin's second illustrative example. Following an analysis of the principle of the *vis inertia* in physics and metaphysics, he speaks of a "'game of puzzles . . . which is played upon a map.'" The object of this game is to find a given word on a map that an opponent has selected

---

[16] Hans-Georg Gadamer, *Truth and Method,* trans. Garrett Barden and John Cumming (New York: Crossroad, 1982), 236.

[17] Martin Heidegger, *Being and Time,* trans. John Macquarrie and Edward Robinson (New York: Harper and Row, 1962), 194.

from the various names of countries, cities, rivers, mountains, and so on. The novice invariably chooses an obscure or minutely printed name, whereas the experienced player chooses names so large as to stretch across the map and thereby escape the notice of the opponent. Dupin next proceeds to explicate this metaphor: "'the physical oversight is precisely analogous with the moral inapprehension by which the intellect suffers to pass unnoticed those considerations which are too obtrusively and too palpably self-evident. But this is a point, it appears, somewhat above or beneath the understanding of the Prefect'" (1:694). The misreading of the map proves analogous to a moral misreading. The moralist, like the novice, believes truth is found in some *recherché* corner. Dupin confirms that this is the source of the prefect's error when he says that the prefect fails to entertain the possibility that the '"Minister had deposited the letter immediately beneath the nose of the whole world, by way of best preventing any portion of the world from perceiving it'" (1:694–95).

Let us return to the game of odd and even, the foolishness of poets, and the problem of expression. The boy, we will recall, adopts his expression to the expression of his opponents. He says that the simpleton behaves in the most obvious fashion. If the boy guesses even, the simpleton, Dupin says, possesses the "'amount of cunning . . . just sufficient to make him have them odd upon the second'" (1:689). A simpleton of a degree above the first would reason his opponent would anticipate this and keep the number even. If we turn now to the minister, we find he is said to be extremely clever. The scene of the crime is another scene of reading, but this one yields knowledge. Caught off guard by her husband and then by the minister, the personage leaves a letter on a table with only the address showing. The prefect says, the minister's '"lynx eye immediately perceives the paper, recognizes the handwriting of the address, observes the confusion of the personage addressed, and fathoms the secret'" (1:682). The personage, unlike Dupin and the minister, betrays herself because she believes that what lies in plain sight will be discovered. On the basis of the handwriting and the expression of the personage, the minister discovers the letter's contents.

The minister, as is well known, foils the police's search by leaving the letter exposed in a card-rack. The prefect errs, according to Dupin, '"by being too deep or too shallow, for the matter in hand'" (1:689). It is at this point in the story that Dupin tells of the game of odd and even. The boy succeeds by being as deep or as shallow as his opponent. But his method itself is shallow or superficial, even if it produces deep thoughts. The prefect knows D. to be a poet and one remove from a fool, and had he been willing to think like a fool, as I have said, he would have succeeded. Dupin knows D. to be both a poet and a mathematician, and being both poet and something of a mathematician himself, he knows how D. thinks.

I would like to turn now to Dupin's spotting of the letter in the cardrack. What stands out in this scene is that D. has, after all, made an attempt to hide the letter. Spotting the card-rack with a solitary letter, Dupin sees "'This last was much soiled and crumpled. It was torn nearly in two, across the middle—as if a design, in the first instance, to tear it entirely up as worthless, had been altered, or stayed, in the second. It had a large black seal, bearing the D____ cipher very conspicuously, and was addressed, in a diminutive female hand, to D____, the minister, himself. It was thrust carelessly, and even, as it seemed, contemptuously, into one of the upper divisions of the rack'" (1:695). Dupin has no trouble recognizing this as the letter by virtue of the "radicalness" of its differences from the original description of the stolen letter. The first letter had a red seal "'with the decal of the S____ family.'" It was also addressed to the personage and was written in a large, bold hand. Finally, the soiled appearance of the minister's letter seems a little too deliberate because its condition is "'so inconsistent with the *true* methodical habits of D____'" (1:696). I describe this scene at length because it is significant for a few basic reasons. First, the minister attempts to disguise the letter. Second, Dupin recognizes the letter by virtue of its difference—he recognizes its identity because the letter no longer resembles itself. Finally, the soiled appearance of the letter betrays the minister because he, we might say, no longer resembles himself, since his habits are methodical, not slovenly. Dupin's analytical skills are like those of the boy's, but only up to a certain point. He knows in principle how the minister's genius will work and suspects the letter will be in the open. If we think of Dupin as identifying with the expression of D., then we might conclude that he recognizes the letter when he sees that it is hidden differently from the way he—that is, Dupin as the double of the minister—would have hidden it. It is the moment when identity confronts radical difference within itself that recognition emerges. If the minister were true to his genius, he would not have made any alteration in the letter and would have left it as he first found it for all to see. He fails, in other words, not because he suffers a lapse in ingenuity but for not being, if I may say so, stupid enough, for only a complete idiot or a genius would leave the letter for all to see. And if this is the case, then according to "The Purloined Letter," there is nothing to distinguish a genius from an idiot. If he had been a better poet and, therefore, a bigger fool, the minister would have succeeded. But Dupin, who a number of critics have identified as D.'s double, perhaps D.'s brother or even D. himself, cannot be duped.[18] By identifying himself with D., he thinks whatever D. thinks. The question here concerns the identity between subject and object. That Dupin succeeds in his investigation by uncovering difference within identity subverts the speculative ideal of absolute identity between subject and object.

Gadamer describes this ideal in a discussion of Hegel and self-consciousness: "Everything that is alive nourishes itself on what is

---

[18] See, for instance, Wilbur, "The Poe Mystery Case," 135–37. David Ketterer suggests that Dupin and D. are brothers in *The Rationale of Deception in Poe* (Baton Rouge: Louisiana State University Press, 1979), 252–54.

alien to it. The fundamental fact of being alive is assimilation. Differentiation, then, is at the same time non-differentiation. The alien is appropriated. . . . this structure of what is alive has its correlative in the nature of self-consciousness. Its being consists in its being able to make everything the object of its knowledge, and yet in everything that it knows, it knows itself. Thus as knowledge it is a differentiation from itself and, at the same time, as self-consciousness, it is an overlapping of and return to self."[19] Since D. H. Lawrence, readers have been quick to point out the vampirish elements in Poe—his characters frequently are described as nourishing themselves by assimilating, and destroying, others. The appropriation of the alien—that is, the negative moment of knowledge wherein perception of the alien leads to the perception of oneself as differentiated from the other—is the origin of self-consciousness. The negative moment of differentiation, says Gadamer, is overcome by self-consciousness and the return of the differentiated self to its self. Poe's debt to the German Romantics, so well documented by Henry A. Pochmann and G. R. Thompson, makes him a good candidate for employing a reflective model of self-consciousness.[20] But Poe seems at various points to deny that such a return to the self is possible. Although Dupin discovers the letter in D.'s possession and returns it to the personage, he fails to possess his other, D., and thereby fails to possess himself. In recognizing the letter, Dupin comes to recognize that he is not himself—he is neither Dupin nor D. but the reader whose identity is determined by the radical difference of the letter. He thus signs the letter "Atreus": "—un dessein si funeste, / S'il n'est digne d'Atree, est digne de Thyeste" (1:698). It was Thyestes who seduced the wife of Atreus, who then slew Thyestes' sons and served them to their father for a meal. If we can assume that Dupin plays Atreus to D.'s Thyestes, then D.'s design is worthy of Thyestes, but Dupin's is worthy of Atreus, for he has the final revenge.[21]

This reading of "The Purloined Letter" can make no claim to completeness, and this is hardly the first reading to suggest the tale is an allegory of reading. In various ways, the truth is taken to function at a performative level—the reader, as Barbara Johnson says, "is in fact one of its effects. The text's 'truth' is what puts the status of the reader in question."[22] The letter dictates whatever can be said about it. Perhaps the ultimate power of the tale is that its control over theoretical discourse remains hidden behind the rather pyrotechnical displays of reading of which the tale has been the occasion. Allen Tate has warned, "All

---

[19] Gadamer, *Truth and Method,* 223.

[20] See Henry A. Pochmann, *German Culture in America: 1600–1900* (Madison: University of Wisconsin Press, 1957), 388–408, and G. R. Thompson, *Poe's Fiction: Romantic Irony in the Gothic Tales* (Madison: University of Wisconsin Press, 1973).

[21] For a discussion of the doublings of the signature in "The Purloined Letter," see Joseph N. Riddel, "The 'Crypt' of Edgar Poe," *Boundary 2 7* (Spring 1979): 139–40.

[22] For essays on "The Purloined Letter" as an allegory of reading, see Johnson, "The Frame of Reference"; Felman, "On Reading Poetry"; and Riddel, "The 'Crypt' of Edgar Poe."

readers of Poe, of the work or of the life, and the rare reader of both, are peculiarly liable to the vanity of discovery."[23] Readers of Poe are frequently guilty of believing themselves not only to have discovered what previous readers have passed over but also things Poe himself hardly foresaw. This can hold true of the critic who admires Poe, such as Irwin, and the critic who does not, such as Bloom. Two questions remain: is Poe conscious of the effects his stories produce? and have his critics been too profound?

The most egregious error of missing what lies in plain view occurs in *Arthur Gordon Pym.* On the island of Tsalal, Pym and his companion, Peters, discover themselves wandering in chasms that Peters says resemble an alphabetic script, but Pym takes the chips of marl that precisely fit the indentures as proof they were naturally produced (1:1167). The self-evident sign of human labor—the very sign that the indentures were chipped out of the rocks—leads Pym into error. He errs by being literally too deep—he wanders in the chasms of writing and, therefore, cannot perceive the traces of language all around him. This error remains unsolved by Pym and Peters, but an interpretation is offered by an unnamed person, whom we are directed to identify with Poe, since he has been mentioned in Pym's preface as the author of the first chapters of the narrative. Poe, then, corrects Pym's error by deciphering the mysterious writing he identifies as a conglomeration of Ethiopian, Arabic, and Egyptian words. He translates the figures as "To be shady," "To be white," and "The region of the south" (1:1181). Tsalal is the shady region where nothing white is found, and the south is the region of white. Although this may be coded allegory of antebellum America, it is but another of Poe's puzzles created for the express purpose of being deciphered. Pym's error generates another text, the interpretive note. Poe posits the mystery beneath our noses so that he may interpret it. The error, then, lies in attributing profundity to the author who deciphers a mystery he himself has created.

In an early Dupin tale, "The Murders in the Rue Morgue," Dupin says, "'Thus there is such a thing as being too profound. Truth is not always in a well. In fact, as regards the more important knowledge, I do believe she is invariably superficial. . . . By undue profundity we perplex and enfeeble thought'" (1:412). Poe repeatedly returns to this concept not only in the tales of ratiocination but also in such pieces as "The Poetic Principle," which begins with the declaration, "I have no design to be either thorough or profound" (2:71). The question of profundity is also a question of effects; Poe claims in several places, including a review he wrote of his *Tales* in 1845, that his first aim "is for a novel effect" (2:873). He explains this aim at greater length in the famous essays "The Poetic Principle" and "The Philosophy of Composition."

---

[23] Allen Tate, "The Angelic Imagination: Poe as God," *Essays of Four Decades* (Chicago: Swallow Press, 1968), 433.

"The Murders in the Rue Morgue" is an illustration of a series of propositions on the nature of analysis. The solution to the murder is offered as an illustration of Dupin's analytical skills, but we are told that analytical mental features are "little susceptible of analysis. We appreciate them only in their effects" (1:397). The explanation of Dupin's method, which the prologue tells us appears as if it were intuition and not analysis, can be found in Poe's "A Few Words on Secret Writing": "The reader should bear in mind that the basis of the whole art of solution, as far as regards these matters, is found in the general principles of the formation of language itself, and this is altogether independent of the particular laws which govern any cipher, or the construction of its key. The difficulty of reading a cryptographical puzzle is by no means always in accordance with the labor or ingenuity with which it has been constructed. . . . this complexity is only in shadow. It has no substance whatever. It appertains merely to the formation, and has no bearing upon the solution, of the cipher" (2:1280). The best of cryptograms would not be recognized as such: "Experience shows that the most cunningly constructed cryptography, if suspected, can and will be unriddled" (2:1283). The difficulty of the cryptogram ultimately rests on its appearance as something other than a cryptogram. It is not at all a matter of the ingenuity with which the cryptogram has been constructed. The solution of the cipher, then, rests upon the recognition of it as a cipher. The most difficult cipher is one that is taken to be something other than a cipher. This conforms to the logic of "The Purloined Letter." The prefect errs by being too profound—he thinks the letter has been ingeniously hidden and that, in order to find it, he must expend an equal amount of ingenuity. But the expenditure is unequal—the minister uses nearly no ingenuity at all. The little he does use leads to his downfall. Dupin recognizes the letter because he can see from its appearance that it is cunningly disguised; in other words, he sees it is a cipher. His replacement perfectly resembles the disguised letter and will, therefore, escape the attention of D., who will eventually find that his letter has been replaced by a riddle, one whose manuscript provides the solution.

The crucial advice, however, is to base the solution on the "general principles of the formation of language itself" and not on any "particular laws which govern any cipher, or the construction of its key." Poe's advice is quite sound and fits in rather neatly with hermeneutical principles. If the cipher is a language, it must be understandable and, as Poe says, a certain order must be agreed upon between those communicating by the cipher. There must, therefore, be rules governing the cipher's construction but *not* for its solution: there are not rules for the solution of cipher, and anyone in search of them "will find nothing upon record which he does not in his own intellect possess" (2:1291). The cipher would be worthless if each message required an individual key for its solution—the cipher would be no cipher at all. The cipher, consequently, must conform to a general rule of customary usage, which means, says Gadamer, "that we cannot arbitrarily change the meaning of words if there is to be language."[24] And the cipher, like a made-up language, must follow some order in its renaming of words so that understanding remains possible. "Language," Gadamer writes, "has no independent life apart from the world that comes to language within it."[25] The world is available to us in language, and language, in turn, has no life apart from the world that is re-presented in it. Language, according to Gadamer, is in its very essence human. Turning back to Poe on ciphers, we find that he applies this principle to secret writing: "it may be roundly asserted that human ingenuity cannot concoct a cipher which human ingenuity cannot resolve" (2:1278). Although Poe never says so explicitly, his comments on the solving of ciphers rest upon the principle that language, because it is by definition human, is always understandable, and because ciphers must conform to the general principle of the formation of language, they will always be solved. This also explains why Dupin has no trouble solving the mystery concerning the language spoken by the murderer of Madame and Mademoiselle L'Espanaye: the fact that no one could understand it meant it was spoken by an animal, not a person.

Poe's skill as a cryptographer comes into play in many, if not all, of his tales. Ever since Baudelaire, readers have said all of Poe's writings are autobiographical, and critics have attempted to decode Poe's "secret autobiography."[26] Testing the analytical skills of his readers in these cryptograms, Poe inscribes his name or those of his contemporaries in various tales, or readers exercise their ingenuity looking for meanings hidden behind the signifiers of the text. Yet as many readers note, Poe's texts appear so willfully overdetermined that he seems to be declaring that his tales are ciphers, which, according to his principle, would be as good as giving the solution away at the start of the game.

"The Gold-Bug" is a curious and, yet, obvious case in point. Louis Renza has discussed how the second part of the story, wherein the code is deciphered, displaces the first narrative concerning the gold-bug. This displacement, he says, mimics a critical reading of the first part and forces the "reader to adopt a reflective relation to the narrative as a whole." Legrand's pretended illness is a further doubling of this reflective relation in which the "aesthetic effect has become retroactively and irrecoverably, lost or sabotaged by its production of the reader's self-conscious relation to it."[27] The doubling of the interpreter's self-conscious relation to the text can be found in most romantic literature, from Shelley's *Triumph of Life* to Melville's *Confidence Man*. Renza, like so many of Poe's readers restores depth to Poe's superficial texts by applying a self-reflexive model of reading. Once again, the buried meaning becomes the

---

[24] Gadamer, *Truth and Method*, 367.

[25] Ibid., 401.

[26] The phrase "secret autobiography" comes from Louis A. Renza, "Poe's Secret Autobiography," in *The American Renaissance Reconsidered*, ed. Walter Benn Michaels and Donald E. Pease (Baltimore: Johns Hopkins University Press, 1985), 58–89.

[27] Ibid., 66.

reflective consciousness produced by the text: "this lost aesthetic relation to the narrative becomes the tale's *still* buried treasure."[28]

Poe's use of cryptography and the transformation of a narrative into
a critical explication of a code makes "The Gold-Bug" one of the more
heavy-handed examples of the romantic allegory of reading. The story
opens with Legrand telling of his discovery of a gold-bug that he has
temporarily lent to someone. In place of showing the bug to the narrator,
he draws it. He is insulted when the narrator says he sees the picture of a
skull, not of an insect. The scene is one of either a misreading or a misrep-
resentation. When later in the story we discover the paper is a parchment
containing a picture of a skull, we realize that the first misreading resulted from a substitution of one image for another. As the story deals
with cryptography, it is not out of place to note how the tale turns upon
the relation of signifier to signified. The connection of the two signifiers—the bug and the skull—is metonymic or simply contingent. After
Legrand had been bitten by the bug, the freed slave, Jupiter, picked it up
with the parchment he had found on the shore where the bug was discovered. The bug, then, serves as a false sign for the narrator-interpreter. We
look for meaning in the bug and seek some connection between the bug
and the skull, expecting a signifier to point toward a signified. The connection, however, is at best metonymic. The bug that bites Legrand is the
occasion for the discovery of the parchment with the drawing of the skull.
Legrand plays a game and transforms the metonymy into a metaphor.
Having been bitten by what Jupiter insists is a gold-bug, he pretends to be
struck mad with desire for some gold he believes is hidden.

The narrator-interpreter seeks, according to the principle of cryptography, a signifier that would translate the encoded signifier. Because he
finds no relation between the gold-bug and the skull, he believes Legrand
is mad. Legrand, however, recognizes the arbitrary relation between the
signifiers and proceeds to create the interpretable story of the gold-bug by
pretending to be mad. The fiction, then, is a double—there is Legrand's
pretended madness and the double signifier. The signifier, consequently,
is a fiction or, perhaps more accurately, a trope. The gold-bug has an interpretable meaning only by virtue of Legrand's providing the metaphor of
being bitten by a gold-bug.

Legrand discovers that the parchment, when held to heat, has a secret
writing. This invisible writing is the perfect cipher because it does not appear to be a message at all, not even a coded one. It is discovered by accident, and once the discovery is made, Legrand easily deciphers the secret.

The fiction of the signifier is repeated at the level of the narrative. Just
as there is no connection between the two signifiers, there is also a dis-
junction between the story proper and the decipherment of the code. The
latter usurps the place of the former. The narrator proves to have failed in
his interpretation. The double signifier and the superfluous mysteries
point to the ultimate fictionality of any interpretation. Understanding

---

[28] Ibid.

rests upon the substitution of metaphor for metonymy. No one would accuse the narrator of undue profundity—the conclusion he draws from Legrand's behavior is quite sensible. The deception is deliberate and passes unnoticed because the narrator has no reason to suspect Legrand. The narrator cannot solve this mystery because it rests not on contingency but upon an error—Legrand is insulted when he believes the narrator has mistaken his drawing of the bug for that of a skull. The error is Legrand's and not the narrator's, but this error leads to Legrand's chance discovery of the parchment and the decipherment of the code.

The question still remains concerning Poe's crypts—do they lie in the plays on names and the hidden details in the story or are they in the scene of misreading? The source lies in errors. The paper with a drawing of a bug turns out to be a parchment with a drawing of a skull. The metamorphosis takes place for the purpose of the story. In "The Purloined Letter," Dupin recognizes the disguised letter and describes both sides, which is impossible without actually turning it over himself. Julian Symons cites Laura Riding's objection to Dupin's solution in "The Murders in the Rue Morgue": the ape could not possibly climb out of the window and fasten it by the secret catch.[29] The errors seem to be gratuitous. Poe aims at one level at a purely mechanical analysis of evidence leading to the solution of the puzzle or mystery. To make the solution work, however, he must either reconstruct the mystery, which he literally does with the newspaper accounts in "The Mystery of Marie Roget," or introduce discrepancies, as in "The Murders in the Rue Morgue" and "The Purloined Letter," or finally, join two systematic narratives by an implausible series of accidents, as in "The Gold-Bug." Are we left with concluding that Poe is a careless artist, as bad in the construction of his plots as he is in his various styles? Harold Bloom has been the most recent of a number of critics who say "yes."

Those who praise Poe are those who find him an ingenious writer who anticipates any possible interpretation. Those who condemn him point to the sloppy construction of plots and his execrable style. I would suggest that the former have been too profound to understand Poe, while the latter, if not superficial, have focused on the apparent deficiencies of Poe's surface. Poe characterizes these readings in his *Marginalia:* "In reading some books we occupy ourselves chiefly with the thoughts of the author; in perusing others, exclusively with our own. . . . there are two classes of suggestive books—the positively and the negatively suggestive. The former suggest by what they say; the latter by what they might and should have said. It makes little difference, after all. In either case the true book-purpose is answered" (2:1338). Poe's detractors have occupied themselves with Poe's thoughts. Yvor Winters, for instance, criticizes him for his "childish view of intellectuality, on the one hand, and the unoriented emotionalism of the tale of

---

[29] Julian Symons, *The Tell-Tale Heart: The Life and Works of Edgar Allan Poe* (1978; repr. New York: Penguin Books, 1981), 224.

effect on the other."[30] His defenders have been preoccupied with their own thoughts. Hence, they are forever finding in the tales the doubling of the reader or the narrator. John Irwin finds "the indeterminate status of nature's script" in *Arthur Gordon Pym* acted out by the interpreter who attributes to the author his ingenious archaeological uncovering of "resemblance between *tkl* and *Tekeli-li*": "Such an interpretation may simply be a self-projection that creates the illusion of depth, a shadow mistaken for a body."[31] Even if it is an illusion, depth has been restored to the text as a function of the interpretive act.

In a letter about "The Murders in the Rue Morgue," Poe suggests a third mode of reading: "You are right about the hair-splitting of my French Friend:—that is all done for effect. These tales of ratiocination owe most of their popularity to being something in a new key. I do not mean to say that they are not ingenious—but people think them more ingenious than they are—on account of their method and *air* of method. In the 'Murders in the Rue Morgue,' for instance, where is the ingenuity of unravelling a web which you yourself (the author) have woven for the express purpose of unravelling? The reader is made to confound the ingenuity of the suppositious Dupin with that of the writer of the story."[32] The tales are, in fact, ciphers—they are mechanically constructed to appear as ingenious webs of mystery so that the reader will attribute the ingenuity of the character to the author. Because of their "*air* of method," the reader thinks them more ingenious than they are, but the ingenuity does not lie in the complexity of the puzzle to be solved but in their effect.

When Poe tells his correspondent that there is no ingenuity at all; he merely follows his own rules for composition laid out for all to see in "The Philosophy of Composition": "Nothing is more clear than that every plot, worth the name, must be elaborated to its *dénouement* before any thing be attempted with the pen. It is only with the *dénouement* constantly in view that we can give a plot its indispensable air of consequence, or causation, by making the incidents, and especially the tone at all points, tend to the development of the intention" (2:13). The *dénouement* of the tale of ratiocination is the effect of attributing ingenuity to the author. To achieve this end, he tells his tale in order that the reader will mistake Dupin's ingenuity for Poe's. But there is no trick to Poe at all. He merely follows the rules for constructing a cryptograph. And if we recall that no rule is necessary for solving a cryptograph—whatever the reader needs, he already possesses—then we may conclude that not only is the author's ingenuity an illusion but so is the reader's, for the answer lies in any reader's mind

---

[30] Yvor Winters, *In Defense of Reason* (Chicago: Swallow Press, 1947), 255.

[31] Irwin, *American Hieroglyphics*, 234.

[32] John Ward Ostrom, ed., *The Letters of Edgar Allan Poe*, new ed., 2 vols. (New York: Gordian Press, 1966), 2:328.

From "Power and Law in Hawthorne's Fictions" in *Nathaniel Hawthorne: New Critical Essays*, ed. A. Robert Lee (London: Vision Press Ltd; Totowa, N.J.: Barnes & Noble Books, 1982). Copyright 1982 by Vision Press Ltd. Reprinted by permission.

because the rules for the solution are grounded in language. The error, then, consists in attributing ingenuity to anyone, whether it be the author, the text, or the reader. Interpretation requires no thought, for even language does not think for us—thought is an effect of language, and this is why error alone produces interpretation. Error opens up the identity of language and thought to the radical difference between signifier and signified that alone makes reading a forever erring task.

ERIC MOTTRAM
"Power and Law in Hawthorne's Fictions": A Marxist Approach

Mottram draws on recent tendencies in criticism to make use of more than one theoretical approach to a text. In the following essay, he uses the work of recent Marxist theorists who use the version of Freud associated with Lacan, an account of whose study of *Hamlet* appears earlier in the book (p. 715). In general, Mottram works to explain why people accept or even desire their own oppression, and he makes an analogy: As for psychoanalytic theory, consciousness represents the repression of libidinal desires, so ideology manifests the repression of our social relations.

Frankenstein creates a monster and becomes himself monstrous; the two figures are popularly taken as one. Aylmer becomes monstrous by manipulating his wife before the laughing "underworker," the shaggy, smoky and earthy Aminadab. Hawthorne writes guardedly of the possibility that "the Eve of Powers" might be converted to "a monster." Intellectuality and sexuality are shown in dubious relationship as the Aylmer house is turned into a laboratory, as other fictional nineteenth-century houses are turned into asylums or houses of correction or assignation. The wife becomes a patient first, and then a victim murdered for scientific curiosity and erotic self-satisfaction. The repressed returns in the disguise of science, and the professional gets away with it once again: it is the continual theme of Hawthorne's fictions of professionals. Here and in "Rappaccini's Daughter" the Renaissance seventeenth-century scientist returns as the nineteenth-century inventor manipulating energy, human and nonhuman, for and against the social, ambivalently a figure of exploitation and enterprise (the business man is not fully used until Dreiser's Cowperwood). The scientist inventor, supposedly the generative centre of technological progress and trade, is morally negated. The relationships of desire to production, of desire to public and private interests, and therefore to law, are repeatedly proposed in Hawthorne's fictions. But in both "The Birthmark" and "Rappaccini's Daughter" the victim is a woman. Hawthorne's contemporary, Karl Marx, wrote in the 1844 *Economic and Philosophic Manuscripts*:

> The direct, natural and necessary relation of person to person is the relation of man to woman. . . . It therefore reveals the extent to which man's natural behaviour has become human . . . the extent to which man's

need has become a human need; the extent to which, therefore, the other person as a person has become for him a need—the extent to which he in his individual existence is at the same time a social being.[1]

Hawthorne repeatedly collapses and reinstates, sometimes in variable forms, male dominance figures parallel to the partial emergence, and sometimes the total suppression, of female figures. Obedience and disobedience between men and women fascinate him; for him, the cannibal and vampire steal energy, take over, expropriate wherever the class structure permits it. But his sense of the inevitable action of predatory will is that it cannot be halted, let alone eradicated, because it is "evil." He asks the crucial questions: What is control, what is counter-control, and who operates their system? What values conflict? What is the nature of alienation and its relations with isolation and community? But he asks them in a particular structure of actual and imagined inheritance, still thinking of the production of relationships as a theological theatre rather than a political factory. "Historical fixatives" control his ethics or "traditional bonds"; he feels bound to confront the American seventeenth-century origins with mid-nineteenth century industrial capitalist democracy in terms of an unchanging, unchangeable manichean battle.[2] Deleuze and Guattari put the force of the secular instances in such fictions in post-Reichian terms:

> The strength of Reich consists in having shown how psychic repression depended on social repression . . . social repression needs psychic repression precisely in order to form docile subjects and ensure the reproduction of the social formation, including its repressive structures . . . civilization must be understood in terms of a social repression inherent in a given form of social production.[3]

Hawthorne comes near to asking his questions of repression within the crucial question—particularly in *The Scarlet Letter* and *The Marble Faun*—how does it come about that we desire our own repression? But his questions are taken up with a constant reminder that Americans are helpless, that Emerson's characteristic dicta of self-reliance are mistaken. Helplessness is a main source for gothic, horror and science fiction systems, the oscillations between voluntary and involuntary behaviours. Seventeenth-century New England society can be used as the instance of a group which knows it is corrupt but knows, too, that, short of prayer, penitence and Jeremiads, it is condemned to the manichean battlefield, the prior inhuman system of God and Devil. Life polarized into punishment and blessing, confession and concealment,

[1] Karl Marx, *Economic and Philosophic Manuscripts of 1844* (London: Lawrence and Wishart, 1961), 101.
[2] G. Deleuze and F. Guattari, *Anti-Oedipus* (New York: Viking Press, 1977), 256.
[3] Ibid., 118.

marks the presence of the repressed in continuous dialectic with the public surfaces, partly euphoric drive and partly exhausting depression. "Confidence in America" could be the endlessly punning title of the history of New World fictions. Confidence is undermined in Hawthorne's contribution by his fast conviction that the Unpardonable Sin is utterly wrong and inevitable. His work is therefore a criticism of *all* manipulative power between human beings. Since religion and capitalism (imply) manipulation, his work has to be a criticism of the American structure itself (in 1981, we have President Reagan attacking Communists for not believing in an afterlife). So that the inevitability of America as a euphoric prophecy, reaching fulfilment in the mid-nineteenth century, is confronted with the regressiveness of the manichean permanence. Hawthorne moves out from concepts he hardly changes; it is both a strength and an inhibition. His characters are liable to be obliterated by an ideological scheme in which they have to be exemplary. This is his peculiar legalism, his own totalitarian pattern, which, curiously and especially in *The Marble Faun,* needs the Unpardonable Sin just as he defined it in his *American Notebooks*—"want of love and reverence for the Human Soul; in consequence of which the investigator pried into its dark depths, not with a hope or purpose of making it better, but from a cold philosophical curiosity . . . the separation of the intellect from the heart." But what exactly are the risks? The desires of the heart are notoriously as possibly cruel as the desires of intellect may be beneficent. Hawthorne's framework of enquiry initiates but clings to a prohibitive social ethos. The preface to his children's *Wonder-Book* (1851) asks "Is not the human heart deeper than any system of philosophy?" But what does "deeper" [imply] as value? A spatialization of ethical images does not make the differentiations any the more "natural." "System" apparently must be a surface action in its artifice. It is a fatal and mistaken separation, since theory and coherence are as "deep" a need as automatic feeling, and both are equally liable to be programmatic.

But Hawthorne properly resists an over-interiorization of behaviour motivations and sequences. He knows that the so-called individual is, as Marx postulates it, "a social product (as is even the language in which the thinker is active): my *own* existence *is* social activity. . . . The Individual's manifestations of life—even if they may not appear in the direct form of *communal* manifestations of life carried out in association with others—*are* therefore an expression and confirmation of social life."[4] But the effect of using "Puritan seventeenth-century New England" (his own artefact, in fact) as an exemplary field of events, images and explanations through which to compose nineteenth-century fictions is to universalize that field by dehistoricizing it—as if the theocratic state were *the* archetype: just as Freud creates a universal Law of the Father out of parts of an Oedipus story in one ancient Greek writer, refusing to describe "the unconscious" as an historically determined phenomenon,

---

[4] K. Marx and F. Engels, *Collected Works,* vol. 3 (London: Lawrence and Wishart, 1975), 298–99.

variable in different societies with differing modes of production. De-historicization is mystification. Hawthorne resorts to an onward-going explanatory scheme—in effect, an ideology—of good and evil which is a manichean structure beyond dialectical change, a diachrony carried forward in a vocabulary of inheritance and inevitability, partly Christian, partly medieval, and partly heretical. It is hardly surprising that the nineteenth-century and the seventeenth-century intervention into this scheme is the woman who will not submit to male usage, unlike Aylmer's Georgiana and Rappaccini's Beatrice. Psychological analysis is a politics rather than a science. The anxiety over Mesmerism everywhere in Hawthorne has to be poised between fear of hypnotic domination and submission from one man (a singular source of energy control) and a sense that something beneficial might come from it.

Mesmerism is the type of all procedures that control subliminally, whether through religion or education or psychological persuasion within desire and the erotic. Hawthorne is well aware that interference with another self [implies] the presence of the Unpardonable Sin immediately the process becomes sheer usage for production—a perverse desire to move in on someone's life and use it, perhaps to use it up. The popular seventeenth-century context for Ethan Brand is male witchcraft. But Brand himself believes that the Devil can only use "half-way sinners." His full sin is to have sacrificed everything to the claims of "an intellect," "a high state of enthusiasm" (Hawthorne uses the term in the late seventeenth-century and Augustan usage). A girl, Esther (from the same source as Hester), is "made the subject of a psychological experiment" through which she is "wasted, absorbed and perhaps annihilated"—or, as William Burroughs would say, "assimilated." Brand's "powers," his "star-lit eminence" in the intellectual world, are detached from that "moral nature" which is the basis of "brotherhood." But Hawthorne withdraws from the actual processes of experimental control. The fiction remains visual and theoretical, a discourse on an abstract theme. The erotic desire at its centre is barely hinted. But at least the story reaches towards a point where we can say "psychoanalysis is a soul murder."[5] The detective story, like science fiction and fantastic fiction, must be a book of philosophy.[6]

Hawthorne is haunted by a further seventeenth-century image-event—the ability of Comus to change men into beasts in "the forest" (his name means "revelry" and he is the son of Bacchus or Dionysus, the enemy of Christ, and Circe), a figure of Control by total transformation. But Hawthorne's mode is not Milton's (the redemptive Lady channel is not available to him) but a different enquiry into the verbal and visual forms and the political-religious dogmas of Control. The manner of transformation may be visually symbolic but, like the burning A and its

[5] G. Deleuze, "Four Perspectives On Psychoanalysis," *Language, Sexuality and Subversion,* ed. P. Foss and M. Morris (Darlington, Australia, 1978). Working Papers Collection, 138.

[6] Colin Gordon, "The Subtracting Machine," *I & C: Power and Desire—Diagrams of the Social,* no. 8 (Oxford: I & C Publications, 1981), 34.

several interpretations, its effects are concrete enough. Hawthorne explores how much and what should be repressed by oppression to produce a society, and asks long before *Civilization and its Discontents.* "Young Goodman Brown" proposes that Christ and the Devil may control equally well in terms of daily co-ordinated moral living in a town, and that dogmatic exclusivity may produce deadly isolation. The Mars/ Indian leader at the head of the rebel Comus rout looks directly at Robin, and his gaze is the challenge of counter-control from revolt in the State. The rout may be docile, but it is the American future. Power operates on the frontier crossings of legality, crime and sin. Transgression and innovation move together. In the words of Deleuze and Guattari (*Anti-Oedipus*):

> We docile subjects say to ourselves: so that's what I wanted! Will it ever be suspected that the law discredits—and has an interest in discrediting and disgracing—the person it presumes to be guilty, the person the law wants to be guilty and wants to be made to feel guilty? One acts as if it were possible to conclude directly from psychic repression the nature of the repressed, and from the prohibition the nature of what is prohibited . . . what really takes place is that the law prohibits something that is perfectly fictitious in the order of desire or of the "instincts," so as to persuade its subjects that they had this intention corresponding to this fiction. This is indeed the only way the law has of getting a grip on intention, of making the unconscious guilty.

This is the casual plot of Hester Prynne's obedience and disobedience between the law of marriage and transcendental law of erotic desire, with "a consecration of its own" (chapter 17). Hawthorne is further to dramatize the transmission of repression, from the seventeenth century to the nineteenth, from Europe to New England, in the palimpsest of his Rome, in *Blithedale* with its Fourierism and Mesmerism and Benthamite panopticon, in all those who use "natural science" to tamper with the human body and soul. The Devil is the repressed working through the ages and needs human souls, and working especially in the utopian ambivalences of Westervelt and Hollingsworth, the classic double figure of repression/ oppression in *The Blithedale Romance.* Woody Allen's self-lacerating comedy takes up guilt and neurosis into an anti-intellectual series of routines; his standard figures are sceptical and paralyzed into indecision and endless verbalizations. Hawthorne's professionals are decisive in control but still neurotic, and equally cut off from the masses. The ritual sacrifice of intellectuals and artists lies well within the traditions of the Paleface, in Rahv's terms, and the celebrated thin pale face of the American intellectual.[7]

---

[7] Philip Rahv, "Paleface and Redskin," *Image and Idea* (New York: New Directions, 1957).

In fact the repressed returns in Hawthorne's fictions largely if not altogether through the Comus intellectual with or without his rout, or her dark erotic pressures. And there is an accurate sense that energies are repressed in American as in any other Western culture, at least since the Salem witch-hunts. Sexual energy, and its transference into creativity, is repressed towards the ideal which haunts nineteenth-century American fiction: the robot, the automaton, the slave without human limitations which interfere with productivity, who is so totally balanced that he can be used as an it. The woman is repressed towards subordinate passivity and away from assertion, creativity and organizational responsibility. Children's impishness is interpreted as devilry and educated out, for future labour usefulness. In America the repressed appears as the Indian, the Black Man in the forest, wilderness and wildness, the Devil, uncontrolled libido in any form—so that religious and capitalist relationships can be imposed. Sects flourish but they are rarely liberatory. Hawthorne can easily use the seventeenth century as a continuous present in which the repressed returns, since what is feared continually is the coherence of a particularly thrustful energy imaged as the Adversary. Certain salient sections of that past are given key powers, certain events become metonymic instances. The resulting fiction is employed to analyze the nineteenth-century lacks and suppressions, especially the deterioration of professionals in law, science, the church, and so on, which erodes confidence in society. What thrusts past the censor, what threatens normality, is presented as monstrous, a villain, the natural threatening state forms. The overwhelming emphasis on self-reliance, individual enterprise and personal aggressiveness is countered by the chances of being transformed in this process into a criminal, a sinner, a monster or a deprived recluse at the very moment of self-realization. Brand commits suicide in the Devil's fire, and Clifford Pyncheon emerges from false imprisonment as an enfeebled eccentric. A man may live with a snake in his body or facially concealed beneath a long black veil. A woman may be turned into an adulteress just as a black woman is turned into a negress. Innocence is everywhere emergent as experience because of the determinate need to conquer energy. Women and sexuality are nervously shown by Hawthorne moving against their relegation in Christian capitalist society to the utilitarian and subordinate, to the reality principle which devours pleasure. Pearl's position proposes that the innocence of children may no longer be assumed (the educational system had long ago given up such a belief). "Possession" haunts Hawthorne's pages as a challenge to both reason and innocence and is signalled by displays of intellectual and physical passion. It is "Rome" in *The Marble Faun* to such an extent that "New England" becomes a shadowy place for the chastened American lovers to return to. In Hawthorne's fictions heroes and heroines have all but vanished as figures of dominant revolutionary apparatus. Threats to the State and to the family, the nucleus of the State, have to be put down as "Merry England," maypoles and garlanded lords of misrule are put down. But the threats remain. All Endicott can do is have the May Lord's hair cropped and throw a wreath of roses over his head.

Some of the reasons are clear. The creative/subversive must somehow be given permission: the dilemma of the State. Within Hawthorne's critique of the exceptional man or woman lies a fear that the masses may produce nothing new, do not produce through disobedience or breaking laws. The power of the social group in "My Kinsman, Major Molineaux" and "The Artist of the Beautiful" is clear: the rout may have destructive leadership. Lonely work is fearful to the mob, but that is a major source of change. The rout's leader in "Molineaux" is the figure of choice in lawbreaking to which Robin is invited to contribute his energy for a new stage in social production—in effect, the future of New England and of the United States lies with the Mars/Indian at the head of a lynch mob. And here the tar-and-feathering is laid on the governor rather than Southern blacks or the keepers in "The System of Doctor Tarr and Professor Fether." Nostalgia for a feudal order in hierarchy, a class-structured unity, confronts the new, the forward movement in revolt. Within the writing confidence of the tale, the author is puzzled by the possibility of two orders of control in conflict which seems to be inevitable. But he finely shows how they lie on either side of the moment where the paradigm is forcibly changing. The fiction is generated from and generates the question so frequently posed in Hawthorne's career: where does change come from? The individual and the masses conflict precisely here. Hawthorne's thought is not evolutionary, as Whitman's is, nor is it an organicist longing for the unity in which "the everlasting universe of Things/Flows through the Mind . . . from secret springs."[8]

So he works within fictional methods which are voyeuristic and manichean. An obsessive basis in the visual, the placing of crucial events within the single perception, demands a voyeuristic mode, and the fiction becomes spectatorist. The complete oeuvre is an equivalent of a panopticon, with Hollingsworth, the author, at its centre, gazing into each cell holding its captive. Or Henry Ford dreaming of being able to survey each assembly-line operative, and then follow him home. Hollingsworth the egotistic reformer has to be defeated and converted to love of a passive woman. Following a leader almost certainly means you yield to him or her. The continuing power of this programme, within the manichean control system, is still highly valid in the polarizations of Mailer's *Why Are We in Vietnam?* in 1967, where the plot includes, essentially, the reaches of cosmic energy, still imaged as the divine or the satanic into the human brain, "in the deep of its mysterious unwindings" "the deep mystery which is whatever is electricity." This is no great distance from that Poe-like entry in the *American Notebooks:* "questions as to unsettled points of History, and Mysteries of Nature, to be asked of a mesmerized person." Like Mailer, Hawthorne

---

[8] Shelley, "Mont Blanc."

grasped the need of the fantastic mode in order to work in these inter-faces between possibility, probability and the present:

> In a world which is indeed our world, the one we know, a world without devils, sylphides, or vampires, there recurs an event which cannot be explained by the laws of this same familiar world. The person who experiences the event must opt for one of two possible solutions: either he is the victim of an illusion of the senses, of a product of the imagination—and laws of the world then remain what they are; or else the event has indeed taken place, it is an integral part of reality—but then this reality is controlled by laws unknown to us. Either the devil is an illusion, an imaginary being; or else he really exists, precisely like the other living beings—with this reservation, that we encounter him infrequently.
>
> The fantastic occupies the duration of this uncertainty. Once we choose one answer or the other, we leave the fantastic for a neighbouring genre, the uncanny or the marvellous. The fantastic is that hesitation experienced by a person who knows only the laws of nature confronting an apparently supernatural event.[9]

But in fact it may be possible, and Hawthorne certainly found it possible, to oscillate between a secular and a theological usage of what Todorov calls "illusion," "supernatural." Inside these defining procedures lies, therefore, a further decision: the writer may hesitate or he may not, and his reader may hesitate or not, according to prior belief, knowledge and experience. Science fiction and science non-fiction may be experienced as possible or improbable or probable accordingly. The "fantastic" uses "the laws of nature" to extrapolate a fiction from scientific hypotheses as well as scientific discovery. The writer may compose to a formulaic procedure which produces money-spinners out of tidy moral plots or shiver-causing plots of indecision. In the nineteenth century, the nature of already rapidly accelerating cultural change could frequently be experienced as "fantastic"—and the decision to place it theologically or not would have to follow. Ignorance and indecision are made within apparent knowledge and decisions. Fictional products imitate. "The wonderful world around us in harmony" of the Romantics may be poisonous and incurably so, or at least governed, as Rappaccini's garden is, by the Roman god of change (and Hawthorne uses the language of "adultery" for the hybrids there—"no longer of God's making, but the monstrous offspring of man's depraved fancy, glowing with only an evil mockery of beauty"). Legalistic Nature is the fiction of the Law of the State. Fallout kills Lucy in Cumbria. The apparently inexplicable may be an apparent killer in the real world, and without "hesitation." Explanations may "hesitate" but existential and manmade events happen to real people. You have to believe it, as today's Americans say, to counter the fantastic. Laws kill in the hands

---

[9] Tzvetan Todorov, *The Fantastic: A Structural Approach to a Literary Genre* (Ithaca, New York: Cornell University Press, 1975), 25.

of class, caste and intellect or brute force. The victim's innocence may be proved later by other laws. The event is not fantastic unless you believe in singular god-permitted control which is infallible everywhere and at all times—so that you can shift between centuries without shifting gear.

Who in fact "hesitates" between descriptions of events? Todorov gives the formula which sums up the spirit of the fantastic as "I nearly reached the point of believing."[10] Total faith or total incredulity would lead beyond the fantastic: it is hesitation that sustains life, he says. Or in Kuhn's terms, the paradigmatic closure is penetrated, and only then generates. But Hester Prynne's risk in sexuality is fantastic only to the unpassionate and the timid, the forever obedient and the academic in whatever class of caste, the utterly law-abiding. Decisions about her action lie between reading fiction and the reader's life praxis. He who hesitates may well be lost, as Miles Coverdale is, rather than sustained. And sustained where? In *The Scarlet Letter* Hester survives in an Atlantic shore cottage—"within the verge of the peninsular, but not in close vicinity to any other habitation"—in order to become a new social power in a tired and hesitant community. But the penalty would have otherwise been worse—Edmund Wilson quotes Sophocles in his essay on the "Philoctetes": "Everything becomes disgusting when you are false to your own nature and behave in an unbecoming way." The hero with a suppurating wound is abandoned on his peninsula—"exacerbated by hardship and chagrin"—but becomes sacred, acquires superhuman powers and "is destined to be purged of his guilt." And Gide's version says: "I have come to know more of the secrets of life than my masters had ever revealed to me."[11]

So the monster created by a society or by and through its invented gods—and this is a major basis of all fiction since Defoe, and cuts across the genres—elicits sympathy because he or she or it is the form of the repressed and oppressed. The illegal becomes a category of necessity and therefore strangely legal.

Fear in the legal citizen relates to power, control, authority, the State, the gods, all forms of the One and its agents and agencies. The practical counter is in the matter-of-factness of Mistress Hibbins, who knows what Hester has been up to. In one of the few comic scenes in the book (chapter 22):

> "Fie, woman, fie!" cried the old lady, shaking her finger at Hester. "Dost think I have been to the forest so many times, and have yet no skill to judge who else has been there? . . . Thou wearest (the token) openly; so there need be no question about that. But this minister! Let me tell thee, in thine ear! When the Black Man sees one of his own servants, signed and sealed, so shy of owning to the bond as is the Reverend Mr. Dimmesdale, he hath a way of ordering matters so that the mark shall be disclosed in open daylight to the eyes of all the world!"

---

[10] Ibid., 31.

[11] Edmund Wilson, *The Wound and the Bow* (London: Methuen, 1961), 254–55.

So Arthur's A may be psychosomatic or it may be diabolic. But more important is that this passage indicates another judge, outside the law and inside the community. What is more, it is a woman to whom Hawthorne gives central words on the way the repressed inevitably returns. And she speaks without hesitation. If, as Todorov believes, quoting Lovecraft, "a tale is fantastic if the reader experiences an emotion of profound fear and terror, the presence of unsuspected worlds and powers," Mistress Hibbins partly allays those fears in her familiarity with "the forest" as a daily pattern, as daily as the Church, and she certainly is not perplexed.

Hawthorne understood something of how laws exemplify active ideology—in Colin Sumner's terms:

> As the (passive) reflections of certain social relations, ideologies can become embodied in laws which, when applied, involve their intrinsic ideologies as (active) determinants of other social relations. The legal process also admirably illustrates the theoretical point that, once embodied, ideologies to not *necessarily* (re-)structure our practice; sometimes they need reinforcement to make them effective. . . . New ideologies, new uses for old ideologies, old ideologies—all are thoroughly social products.[12]
>
> A legal enactment is a hybrid form combining power and ideology; an ideological formation sanctioned, according to fixed and hallowed procedures for the creation of Law, by the instituted executors of social power. . . . An ideology of legality develops which celebrates and elevates The Law to an exalted status as the expression of unity in the nation.[13]

Curiously, Hawthorne felt the need to "establish a theatre, a little removed from the highway of ordinary travel, where the creatures of his brain may play their phantasmagorical antics, without exposing them to too close a comparison with the actual events of real lives." In fact, his patterns of guilt, shame, power and law dramatize the real. . . .

JUDITH FETTERLEY
"Women Beware Science: 'The Birthmark'": A Feminist Approach

In her book *The Resisting Reader*, Judith Fetterley argues that, in American literature, American experience is male experience which can cause female readers self-doubt and

---

[12] Colin Sumner, *Reading Ideologies* (London, New York and San Francisco: Academic Press, 1979), 22–23.

[13] Ibid., 293.

From *The Resisting Reader: A Feminist Approach to American Fiction*, by Judith Fetterley (Bloomington and London: Indiana University Press, 1978). Copyright 1978 by Judith Fetterley. Reprinted by permission.

self-hatred. It is such readings that they should "resist," and Fetterley attempts to show how this might be done in her analysis of Hawthorne's tale, which she sees as a manifestation of sexual politics in which hatred is disguised as love, neurosis as science, murder as idealization, and success as failure.

The scientist Aylmer in Nathaniel Hawthorne's "The Birthmark" provides another stage in the psychological history of the American protagonist. Aylmer is Irving's Rip and Anderson's boy discovered in that middle age which Rip evades and the boy rejects. Aylmer is squarely confronted with the realities of marriage, sex, and women. There are compensations, however, for as an adult he has access to a complex set of mechanisms for accomplishing the great American dream of eliminating women. It is testimony at once to Hawthorne's ambivalence, his seeking to cover with one hand what he uncovers with the other; and to the pervasive sexism of our culture that most readers would describe "The Birthmark" as a story of failure rather than as the success story it really is—the demonstration of how to murder your wife and get away with it. It is, of course, possible to read "The Birthmark" as a story of misguided idealism, a tale of the unhappy consequences of man's nevertheless worthy passion for perfecting and transcending nature; and this is the reading usually given it.[1] This reading, however, ignores the significance of

---

[1] See, for example, Cleanth Brooks and Robert Penn Warren, *Understanding Fiction* (New York: Appleton-Century-Crofts, 1943), 103–6: "We are not, of course, to conceive of Aylmer as a monster, a man who would experiment on his own wife for his own greater glory. Hawthorne does not mean to suggest that Aylmer is depraved and heartless. . . . Aylmer has not realized that perfection is something never achieved on earth and in terms of mortality"; Richard Harter Fogle, *Hawthorne's Fiction: The Light and the Dark,* rev. ed. (Norman, Okla.: University of Oklahoma Press, 1964), 117–31; Robert Heilman, "Hawthorne's 'The Birthmark': Science as Religion," *South Atlantic Qarterly* 48 (1949): 575–83: "Aylmer, the overweening scientist, resembles less the villain than the tragic hero: in his catastrophic attempt to improve on human actuality there is not only pride and a deficient sense of reality but also disinterested aspiration"; F. O. Matthiessen, *American Renaissance* (New York: Oxford University Press, 1941), 253–55; Arlin Turner, *Nathaniel Hawthorne* (New York: Holt, Rinehart, and Winston, 1961), 88, 98, 132: "In 'The Birthmark' he applauded Aylmer's noble pursuit of perfection, in contrast to Aminadab's ready acceptance of earthiness, but Aylmer's achievement was tragic failure because he had not realized that perfection is not of this world." The major variation in these readings occurs as a result of the degree to which individual critics see Hawthorne as critical of Aylmer. Still, those who see Hawthorne as critical locate the source of his criticism in Aylmer's idealistic pursuit of perfection—e.g., Millicent Bell, *Hawthorne's View of the Artist* (New York: State University of New York, 1962), 182–85: "Hawthorne, with his powerful Christian sense of the inextricable mixture of evil in the human compound, regards Aylmer as a dangerous perfectibilitarian"; William Bysshe Stein, *Hawthorne's Faust* (Gainesville: University of Florida Press, 1953), 91–92: "Thus the first of Hawthorne's Fausts, in a purely symbolic line of action sacrifices his soul to conquer nature, the universal force of which man is but a tool." Even Simon Lesser (*Fiction and the Unconscious* [1957; reprint, New York: Vintage-Random, 1962], 87–90 and 94–98), who is clearly aware of the sexual implications of the story, subsumes his analysis under the reading of misguided idealism and in so doing provides a fine instance of phallic criticism in action:

The ultimate purpose of Hawthorne's attempt to present Aylmer in balanced perspective is to quiet our fears so that the wishes which motivate his experiment, which are

the form idealism takes in the story. It is not irrelevant that "The Birthmark" is about a man's desire to perfect his wife, not is it accidental that the consequence of this idealism is the wife's death. In fact, "The Birthmark" provides a brilliant analysis of the sexual politics of idealization and a brilliant exposure of the mechanisms whereby hatred can be disguised as love, neurosis can be disguised as science, murder can be disguised as idealization, and success can be disguised as failure. Thus, Hawthorne's insistence in his story on the metaphor of disguise serves as both warning and clue to a feminist reading.

Even a brief outline is suggestive. A man, dedicated to the pursuit of science, puts aside his passion in order to marry a beautiful woman. Shortly after the marriage he discovers that he is deeply troubled by a tiny birthmark on her left cheek. Of negligible importance to him before marriage, the birthmark now assumes the proportions of an obsession. He reads it as a sign of the inevitable imperfection of all things in nature and sees in it a challenge to man's ability to transcend nature. So nearly perfect as she is, he would have her be completely perfect. In pursuit of this lofty aim, he secludes her in chambers that he has converted for the purpose, subjects her to a series of influences, and finally presents her with a potion which, as she drinks it, removes at last the hated birthmark but kills her in the process. At the end of the story Georgiana is both perfect and dead.

One cannot imagine this story in reverse—that is, a woman's discovering an obsessive need to perfect her husband and deciding to perform experiments on him—nor can one imagine the story being about a man's conceiving such an obsession for another man. It is woman, and specifically woman as wife, who elicits the obsession with imperfection and the compulsion to achieve perfection, just as it is man, and specifically man as husband, who is thus obsessed and compelled. In addition, it is clear from the summary that the imagined perfection is purely physical. Aylmer is not concerned with the quality of Georgiana's character or with the state of her soul, for he considers her "fit for heaven without tasting death." Rather, he is absorbed in her physical appearance, and

---

also urgent, can be given their opportunity. Aylmer's sincerity and idealism give us a sense of kinship with him. We see that the plan takes shape gradually in his mind, almost against his conscious intention. We are reassured by the fact that he loves Georgiana and feels confident that his attempt to remove the birthmark will succeed. Thus at the same time that we recoil we can identify with Aylmer and through him act out some of our secret desires. . . . The story not only gives expression to impulses which are ordinarily repressed; it gives them a sympathetic hearing—an opportunity to show whether they can be gratified without causing trouble or pain. There are obvious gains in being able to conduct tests of this kind with no more danger and no greater expenditure of effort than is involved in reading a story.

The one significant dissenting view is offered by Frederick C. Crews, *The Sins of the Fathers: Hawthorne's Psychological Themes* (New York: Oxford University Press, 1966), whose scattered comments on the story focus on the specific form of Aylmer's idealism and its implication for his secret motives.

perfection for him is equivalent to physical beauty. Georgiana is an ex-
emplum of woman as beautiful object, reduced to and defined by her
body. And finally, the conjunction of perfection and nonexistence, while
reminding us of Anderson's story in which the good girl is the one you
never see, develops what is only implicit in that story: namely, that the
only good woman is a dead one and that the motive underlying the desire to perfect is the need to eliminate. "The Birthmark" demonstrates
the fact that the idealization of women has its source in a profound hostility toward women and that it is at once a disguise for this hostility
and the fullest expression of it.

The emotion that generates the drama of "The Birthmark" is revulsion. Aylmer is moved not by the vision of Georgiana's potential perfection but by his horror at her present condition. His revulsion for the
birthmark is insistent: he can't bear to see it or touch it; he has nightmares about it; he has to get it out. Until she is "fixed," he can hardly
bear the sight of her and must hide her away in secluded chambers
which he visits only intermittently, so great is his fear of contamination.
Aylmer's compulsion to perfect Georgiana is a result of his horrified
perception of what she actually is, and all his lofty talk about wanting
her to be perfect so that just this once the potential of Nature will be
fulfilled is but a cover for his central emotion of revulsion. But Aylmer
is a creature of disguise and illusion. In order to persuade this beautiful
woman to become his wife, he "left his laboratory to the care of an assistant, cleared his fine countenance from the furnace smoke, washed
the stains of acid from his fingers." Best not to let her know who he really is or what he really feels, lest she might say before the marriage instead of after, "You cannot love what shocks you!" In the chambers
where Aylmer secludes Georgiana, "airy figures, absolutely bodiless
ideas, and forms of unsubstantial beauty" come disguised as substance
in an illusion so nearly perfect as to "warrant the belief that her husband possessed sway over the spiritual world." While Aylmer does
not really possess sway over the spiritual world, he certainly controls
Georgiana and he does so in great part because of his mastery of the art
of illusion.

If the motive force for Aylmer's action in the story is repulsion, it
is the birthmark that is the symbolic location of all that repels him.
And it is important that the birthmark is just that: a birth *mark*, that is,
something physical; and a *birth* mark, that is, something not acquired
but inherent, one of Georgiana's givens, in fact equivalent to her.[2] The
close connection between Georgiana and her birthmark is continually
emphasized. As her emotions change, so does the birthmark, fading or

---

[2] In the conventional reading of the story Georgiana's birthmark is seen as the symbol of
original sin—see, for example, Heilman, "Hawthorne's 'The Birthmark,'" 579; Bell,
Hawthorne's View of the Artist, 185. But what this reading ignores are, of course, the implications of the fact that the symbol of original sin is female and that the story only "works"
because men have the power to project that definition onto women.

deepening in response to her feelings and providing a precise clue to her state of mind. Similarly, when her senses are aroused, stroked by the influences that pervade her chamber, the birthmark throbs sympathetically. In his efforts to get rid of the birthmark Aylmer has "administered agents powerful enough to do aught except change your entire physical system," and these have failed. The object of Aylmer's obsessive revulsion, then, is Georgiana's "physical system," and what defines this particular system is the fact that it is female. It is Georgiana's female physiology, which is to say her sexuality, that is the object of Aylmer's relentless attack. The link between Georgiana's birthmark and her sexuality is implicit in the birthmark's role as her emotional barometer, but one specific characteristic of the birthmark makes the connection explicit: the hand which shaped Georgiana's birth has left its mark on her in *blood*. The birthmark is redolent with references to the particular nature of female sexuality; we hardly need Aylmer's insistence on seclusion, with its reminiscences of the treatment of women when they are "unclean," to point us in this direction. What repels Aylmer is Georgiana's sexuality; what is imperfect in her is the fact that she is female; and what perfection means is elimination.

In Hawthorne's analysis the idealization of women stems from a vision of them as hideous and unnatural; it is a form of compensation, an attempt to bring them up to the level of nature. To symbolize female physiology as a blemish, a deformity, a birthmark suggests that women are in need of some such redemption. Indeed, "The Birthmark" is a parable of woman's relation to the cult of female beauty, a cult whose political function is to remind women that they are, in their natural state, unacceptable, imperfect, monstrous. Una Stannard in "The Mask of Beauty" has done a brilliant job of analyzing the implications of this cult:

> Every day, in every way, the billion-dollar beauty business tells women they are monsters in disguise. Every ad for bras tells a woman that her breasts need lifting, every ad for padded bras that what she's got isn't big enough, every ad for girdles that her belly sags and her hips are too wide, every ad for high heels that her legs need propping, every ad for cosmetics that her skin is too dry, too oily, too pale, or too ruddy, or her lips are not bright enough, or her lashes not long enough, every ad for deodorants and perfumes that her natural odors all need disguising, every ad for hair dye, curlers, and permanents that the hair she was born with is the wrong color or too straight or too curly, and lately ads for wigs tell her that she would be better off covering up nature's mistake completely. In this culture women are told they are the fair sex, but at the same time that their "beauty" needs lifting, shaping, dyeing, painting, curling, padding. Women are really being told that "the beauty" is a beast.[3]

---

[3] Vivian Gornick and Barbara K. Moran, eds., *Women in Sexist Society: Studies in Power and Powerlessness* (New York: New American Library, 1971), 192.

The dynamics of idealization are beautifully contained in an analogy which Hawthorne, in typical fashion, remarks on casually: "But it would be as reasonable to say that one of those small blue stains which sometimes occur in the purest statuary marble would convert the Eve of Powers to a monster." This comparison, despite its apparent protest against just such a conclusion, implies that where women are concerned it doesn't take much to convert purity into monstrosity; Eve herself is a classic example of the ease with which such a transition can occur. And the transition is easy because the presentation of woman's image in marble is essentially an attempt to disguise and cover a monstrous reality. Thus, the slightest flaw will have an immense effect, for it serves as a reminder of the reality that produces the continual need to cast Eve in the form of purest marble and women in the molds of idealization.

In exploring the sources of men's compulsion to idealize women Hawthorne is writing a story about the sickness of men, not a story about the flawed and imperfect nature of women. There is a hint of the nature of Aylmer's ailment in the description of his relation to "Mother" Nature, a suggestion that his revulsion for Georgiana has its root in part in a jealousy of the power which her sexuality represents and a frustration in the face of its impenetrable mystery. Aylmer's scientific aspirations have as their ultimate goal the desire to create human life, but "the latter pursuit, however, Aylmer had long laid aside in unwilling recognition of the truth—against which all seekers sooner or later stumble—that our great creative Mother, while she amuses us with apparently working in the broadest sunshine, is yet severely careful to keep her own secrets, and, in spite of her pretended openness, shows us nothing but results. She permits us, indeed, to mar, but seldom to mend, and, like a jealous patentee, on no account to make." This passage is striking for its undercurrent of jealousy, hostility, and frustration toward a specifically female force. In the vision of Nature as playing with man, deluding him into thinking he can acquire her power, and then at the last minute closing him off and allowing him only the role of one who mars, Hawthorne provides another version of woman as enemy, the force that interposes between man and the accomplishment of his deepest desires. Yet Hawthorne locates the source of this attitude in man's jealousy of woman's having something he does not and his rage at being excluded from participating in it.

Out of Aylmer's jealousy at feeling less than Nature and thus less than woman—for if Nature is woman, woman is also Nature and has, by virtue of her biology, a power he does not—comes his obsessional program for perfecting Georgiana. Believing he is less, he has to convince himself he is more: "and then, most beloved, what will be my triumph when I shall have corrected what Nature left imperfect in her fairest work! Even Pygmalion, when his sculptured woman assumed life, felt not greater ecstasy than mine will be." What a triumph indeed to upstage and outdo Nature and make himself superior to her. The function of the fantasy that underlies the myth of Pygmalion, as it underlies the myth of Genesis (making Adam, in the words of Mary Daly, "the first among history's unmarried pregnant males"[4]), is obvious from the reality which it seeks to invert. Such myths are powerful image builders, salving man's injured ego by convincing him that he is not only equal to but better than woman, for he creates in spite of, against, and finally better than nature. Yet Aylmer's failure here is as certain as the failure of his other "experiments," for the sickness which he carries within him makes him able only to destroy, not to create.

If Georgiana is envied and hated because she represents what is different from Aylmer and reminds him of what he is not and cannot be, she is feared for her similarity to him and for the fact that she represents aspects of himself that he finds intolerable. Georgiana is as much a reminder to Aylmer of what he is as of what he is not. This apparently contradictory pattern of double-duty is understandable in the light of feminist analyses of female characters in literature, who frequently function this way. Mirrors for men, they serve to indicate the involutions of the male psyche with which literature is primarily concerned, and their characters and identities shift accordingly. They are projections, not people; and thus coherence of characterization is a concept that often makes sense only when applied to the male characters of a particular work. Hawthorne's tale is a classic example of the woman as mirror, for, despite Aylmer's belief that his response to Georgiana is an objective concern for the intellectual and spiritual problem she presents, it is obvious that his reaction to her is intensely subjective. "Shocks you, my husband?" queries Georgiana, thus neatly exposing his mask, for one is not shocked by objective perceptions. Indeed, Aylmer views Georgiana's existence as a personal insult and threat to him, which, of course, it is, because what he sees in her is that part of himself he cannot tolerate. By the desire she elicits in him to marry her and possess her birthmark, she forces him to confront his own earthiness and "imperfection."

But it is precisely to avoid such a confrontation that Aylmer has fled to the kingdom of science, where he can project himself as a "type of the spiritual element." Unlike Georgiana, in whom the physical and the spiritual are complexly intertwined, Aylmer is hopelessly alienated from himself. Through the figure of Aminadab, the shaggy creature of clay, Hawthorne presents sharply the image of Aylmer's alienation. Aminadab symbolizes that earthly, physical, erotic self that has been split off from Aylmer, that he refuses to recognize as part of himself, and that has become monstrous and grotesque as a result: "With his vast strength, his shaggy hair, his smoky aspect, and the indescribable earthiness that incrusted him, he

---

[4] Daly, *Beyond God the Father: Toward a Philosophy of Women's Liberation* (Boston: Beacon Press, 1973), 195. It is useful to compare Daly's analysis of "Male Mothers" with Mary Ellmann's discussion of the "imagined motherhood of the male" in *Thinking About Women* (New York: Harcourt Brace Jovanovich, 1968), 15ff. It is obvious that this myth is prevalent in patriarchal culture, and it would seem reasonable to suggest that the patterns of cooptation noticed in "Rip Van Winkle" and "I Want to Know Why" are minor manifestations of it. *An American Dream* provides a major manifestation, in fact a tour de force, of the myth of male motherhood.

seemed to represent man's physical nature; while Aylmer's slender figure, and pale, intellectual face, were no less apt a type of the spiritual element." Aminadab's allegorical function is obvious and so is his connection to Aylmer, for while Aylmer may project himself as objective, intellectual, and scientific and while he may pretend to be totally unrelated to the creature whom he keeps locked up in his dark room to do his dirty work, he cannot function without him. It is Aminadab, after all, who fires the furnace for Aylmer's experiments; physicality provides the energy for Aylmer's "science" just as revulsion generates his investment in idealization. Aylmer is, despite his pretenses to the contrary, a highly emotional man: his scientific interests tend suspiciously toward fires and volcanoes; he is given to intense emotional outbursts; and his obsession with his wife's birthmark is a feeling so profound as to disrupt his entire life. Unable to accept himself for what he is, Aylmer constructs a mythology of science and adopts the character of a scientist to disguise his true nature and to hide his real motives, from himself as well as others. As a consequence, he acquires a way of acting out these motives without in fact having to be aware of them. One might describe "The Birthmark" as an exposé of science because it demonstrates the ease with which science can be invoked to conceal highly subjective motives. "The Birthmark" is an exposure of the realities that underlie the scientist's posture of objectivity and rationality and the claims of science to operate in an amoral and value-free world. Pale Aylmer, the intellectual scientist, is a mask for the brutish, earthy, soot-smeared Aminadab, just as the mythology of scientific research and objectivity finally masks murder, disguising Georgiana's death as just one more experiment that failed.

Hawthorne's attitude toward men and their fantasies is more critical than either Irving's or Anderson's. One responds to Aylmer not with pity but with horror. For, unlike Irving and Anderson, Hawthorne has not omitted from his treatment of men an image of the consequences of their ailments for the women who are involved with them. The result of Aylmer's massive self-deception is to live in an unreal world, a world filled with illusions, semblances, and appearances, one which admits of no sunlight and makes no contact with anything outside itself and at whose center is a laboratory, the physical correlative of his utter solipsism. Nevertheless, Hawthorne makes it clear that Aylmer has got someone locked up in that laboratory with him. While "The Birthmark" is by no means explicitly feminist, since Hawthorne seems as eager to be misread and to conceal as he is to read and to reveal, still it is impossible to read his story without being aware that Georgiana is completely in Aylmer's power. For the subject is finally power. Aylmer is able to project himself onto Georgiana and to work out his obsession through her because as woman and as wife she is his possession and in his power; and because as man he has access to the language and structures of that science which provides the mechanisms for such a process and legitimizes it. In addition, since the power of definition and the authority to make those definitions stick is vested in men, Aylmer can endow his illusions with the weight of spiritual aspiration and universal truth.

The implicit feminism in "The Birthmark" is considerable. On one level the story is a study of sexual politics, of the powerlessness of women and of the psychology which results from that powerlessness. Hawthorne dramatizes the fact that woman's identity is a product of men's responses to her: "It must not be concealed, however, that the impression wrought by this fairy sign manual varied exceedingly, according to the difference of temperament in the beholders." To those who love Georgiana, her birthmark is evidence of her beauty; to those who envy or hate her, it is an object of disgust. It is Aylmer's repugnance for the birthmark that makes Georgiana blanch, thus causing the mark to emerge as a sharply-defined blemish against the whiteness of her cheek. Clearly, the birthmark takes on its character from the eye of the beholder. And just as clearly Georgiana's attitude toward her birthmark varies in response to different observers and definers. Her self-image derives from internalizing the attitudes toward her of the man or men around her. Since what surrounds Georgiana is an obsessional attraction expressed as a total revulsion, the result is not surprising: continual self-consciousness that leads to a pervasive sense of shame and a self-hatred that terminates in an utter readiness to be killed. "The Birthmark" demonstrates the consequences to women of being trapped in the laboratory of man's mind, the object of unrelenting scrutiny, examination, and experimentation.

In addition, "The Birthmark" reveals an implicit understanding of the consequences for women of a linguistic system in which the word "man" refers to both male people and all people. Because of the conventions of this system, Aylmer is able to equate his peculiarly male needs with the needs of all human beings, men and women. And since Aylmer can present his compulsion to idealize and perfect Georgiana as a human aspiration, Georgiana is forced to identify with it. Yet to identify with his aspiration is in fact to identify with his hatred of her and his need to eliminate her. Georgiana's situation is a fictional version of the experience that women undergo when they read a story like "Rip Van Winkle." Under the influence of Aylmer's mind, in the laboratory where she is subjected to his subliminal messages, Georgiana is co-opted into a view of herself as flawed and comes to hate herself as an impediment to Aylmer's aspiration; eventually she wishes to be dead rather than to remain alive as an irritant to him and as a reminder of his failure. And as she identifies with him in her attitude toward herself, so she comes to worship him for his hatred of her and for his refusal to tolerate her existence. The process of projection is neatly reversed: he locates in her everything he cannot accept in himself, and she attributes to him all that is good and then worships in him the image of her own humanity.

Through the system of sexual politics that is Aylmer's compensation for growing up, Hawthorne shows how men gain power over women, the power to create and kill, to "mar," "mend," and "make," without ever having to relinquish their image as "nice guys." Under such a system there need be very few power struggles, because women are programmed to deny the validity of their own perceptions and responses and to accept male illusions as truth. Georgiana does faint when she first enters Aylmer's laboratory and sees it for one second with her own eyes; she is also aware that Aylmer is filling her chamber with appearances, not realities; and she is finally aware that his scientific record is in his own terms one of continual failure. Yet so perfect is the program that she comes to respect him even more for these failures and to aspire to be yet another of them.

Hawthorne's unrelenting emphasis on "seems" and his complex use of the metaphors and structures of disguise imply that women are being deceived and destroyed by man's system. And perhaps the most vicious part of this system is its definition of what constitutes nobility in women: "Drink, then, thou lofty creature," exclaims Aylmer with "fervid admiration" as he hands Georgiana the cup that will kill her. Loftiness in women is directly equivalent to the willingness with which they die at the hands of their husbands, and since such loftiness is the only thing about Georgiana which does elicit admiration from Aylmer, it is no wonder she is willing. Georgiana plays well the one role allowed her, yet one might be justified in suggesting that Hawthorne grants her at the end a slight touch of the satisfaction of revenge: "'My poor Aylmer,' she repeated, with a more than human tenderness, you have aimed loftily; you have done nobly. Do not repent that with so high and pure a feeling, you have rejected the best the earth could offer.'" Since dying is the only option, best to make the most of it.

WRITING PROJECTS

1. Write an "account" of one of the critical essays in this appendix: In about 1500 words, represent the spirit and method of the piece without necessarily making all its points or citing all its examples.
2. Write an essay that compares two critical approaches to the same story. How do they differently address the same issues? What, if anything, in the story does either neglect?
3. Find and explore an aspect of either of the stories that seems overlooked by the professional critics but which might be usefully interpreted by the light of any of their methods.
4. Poe and Hawthorne are each represented by two stories in the book. Using one of the approaches to the author represented in this appendix, apply that approach to the *other* story.
5. Using an approach *not* represented by a professional article on either Poe or Hawthorne, write an interpretive essay on one of their stories.
6. Using one of the professional articles as a model, write an essay interpreting a story (or a poem or a play) *not* by Poe or Hawthorne.

Appendix II:
Further Reading in
Critical Theory

The New Criticism

Brooks, Cleanth, and Robert Penn Warren. *Understanding Poetry.* New York: Henry Holt, 1938.

Brooks, Cleanth. *The Well Wrought Urn: Studies in the Structure of Poetry.* New York: Reynal and Hitchcock, 1947.

Eliot, Thomas Stearns. *The Sacred Wood: Essays on Poetry and Criticism.* London: Methuen, 1920.

Empson, William. *Seven Types of Ambiguity.* London: Chatto & Windus, 1930.

Ransom, John Crowe. *The New Criticism.* Norfolk, Conn.: New Directions, 1941.

Tate, Allen. *Reason in Madness: Critical Essays.* New York: G. P. Putnam, 1941.

Wimsatt, William K. *The Verbal Icon: Studies in the Meaning of Poetry.* Lexington: University Press of Kentucky, 1954.

Psychoanalytic Criticism

Bloom, Harold. *The Anxiety of Influence.* New York: Oxford University Press, 1975.

Crews, Frederick. *The Sins of the Fathers: Hawthorne's Psychological Themes.* New York: Oxford University Press, 1966.

Hartman, Geoffrey H., ed. *Psychoanalysis and the Question of the Text: Selected Papers from the English Institute.* Baltimore: Johns Hopkins University Press, 1979.

Kris, Ernst. *Psychoanalytic Explorations in Art.* 1952: New York: Schocken Books, 1964.

Kristeva, Julia. *Desire in Language.* New York: Columbia University Press, 1980.

Lacan, Jacques. "The Seminar on 'The Purloined Letter.'" *Yale French Studies* 48 (1972): 39–72.

Trilling, Lionel. "Art and Neurosis" and "Freud and Literature." *The Liberal Imagination.* New York: Doubleday, 1947.

Wright, Elizabeth. *Psychoanalytic Criticism: Theory in Practice.* New York and London: Methuen, 1984.

Rhetoric and Reader-Response Criticism

Bleich, David. *Readings and Feelings: An Introduction to Subjective Criticism.* New York: Harper and Row, 1977.

Booth, Wayne C. *The Rhetoric of Fiction.* Chicago: University of Chicago Press, 1961.

Burke, Kenneth. *A Rhetoric of Motives.* New York, 1950.

Fish, Stanley. *Is There a Text in This Class?* Cambridge: Harvard University Press, 1980.

Holland, Norman N. *The Dynamics of Literary Response.* New York: Oxford University Press, 1968.

Iser, Wolfgang. *The Act of Reading.* Baltimore: Johns Hopkins University Press, 1978.

Ong, Walter, S. J. *Orality and Literacy.* New York: Methuen, 1982.

Feminist Criticism

Barnes, Annette. "Female Criticism: A Prologue." *The Authority of Experience: Essays in Feminist Criticism.* Ed. Arlyn Diamond and Lee R. Edwards. Amherst: Massachusetts University Press, 1977. 1–15.

Felman, Shoshanna. "Rereading Femininity," in *Yale French Studies* 62 (1981), 19–44.

Gilbert, Sandra M., and Susan Gubar. *The Madwoman in the Attic.* New Haven: Yale University Press, 1979.

Jacobus, Mary, ed. *Women Writing and Writing About Women.* London: Croom Helm, 1979.

Kolodny, Annette. "Some Notes on Defining a 'Feminist Literary Criticism.'" *Critical Inquiry,* 2 (1975), 75–92.

Millett, Kate. *Sexual Politics.* Garden City, NY: Doubleday, 1970.

Showalter, Elaine. *A Literature of Their Own: British Women Novelists from Brontë to Lessing.* Princeton, NJ: Princeton University Press, 1977.

―――, ed., *The New Feminist Criticism.* New York: Pantheon Books, 1985.

Marxist Criticism

Adorno, Theodor W. *Prisms,* trans., Samuel Weber and Shierry Weber. Cambridge: MIT Press, 1983.

Benjamin, Walter. *Illuminations.* New York: Schocken, 1970.

Eagleton, Terry. *Criticism and Ideology.* New York: Schocken, 1978.

Hicks, Granville. *The Great Tradition.* New York: Macmillan, 1933: rev. 1935.

Jameson, Fredric. *Marxism and Form: Twentieth-Century Dialectical Theories of Literature.* Princeton, NJ: Princeton University Press, 1971.

Lentricchia, Frank. *Criticism and Social Change.* Chicago: University of Chicago Press, 1983.

Sartre, Jean-Paul. *What is Literature?* New York: Philosophical Library, 1949.

White, Hayden. *Topics of Discourse: Essays in Cultural Criticism.* Baltimore: Johns Hopkins University Press, 1978.

Williams, Raymond. *Marxism and Literature.* New York: Oxford University Press, 1977.

Racial and Ethnic Criticism

Allen, Paula Gunn. "Introduction." *Studies in American Indian Literature.* New York: MLA, 1983. vii–xiv.

Backus, Joseph M. "'The White Man Will Never Be Alone': The Indian Theme in Standard American Literature Courses." *Studies in American Indian Literature.* Ed. Paula Gunn Allen. New York: MLA, 1983. 259–272.

Baker, Houston A., Jr. *Blues, Ideology, and Afro-American Literature: A Vernacular Theory.* Chicago: University of Chicago Press, 1984.

―――. *Modernism and the Harlem Renaissance.* Chicago: University of Chicago Press, 1987.

Davis, Charles T. "Black Literature and the Critic." *Black is the Color of the Cosmos.* Ed. Henry Louis Gates, Jr. New York: Garland, 1982. 49–62.

Fisher, Dexter. *Minority Language and Literature: Retrospective and Perspective.* New York: MLA, 1977.

Gates, Henry Louis, Jr. *Figures in Black: Words, Signs, and the "Racial" Self.* New York: Oxford University Press, 1987.

————. *The Signifying Monkey: A Theory of Afro-American Literary Criticism.* New York: Oxford University Press, 1988.

————. "Canon Formation, Literary History, and the Afro-American Tradition: From the Seen to the Told." *Afro-American Literary Study in the 1990s.* Ed. Houston A. Baker, Jr., and Patricia Redmond. Chicago: University of Chicago Press, 1989. 14–38.

Graff, Gerald. *Professing Literature: An Institutional History.* Chicago: University of Chicago Press, 1987.

Lincoln, Kenneth. *Native American Renaissance.* Berkeley: University of California Press, 1983.

Miller, J. Hillis. "The Search for Grounds of Literary Study." *Rhetoric and Form: Deconstruction at Yale.* Ed. Robert Con Davis and Ronal Schleifer. Norman: University of Oklahoma Press, 1985. 19–36.

Ohmann, Richard. *English in America.* New York: Oxford University Press, 1976.

Said, Edward. *Orientalism.* New York: Pantheon Books, 1978.

Structuralist Criticism

Barthes, Roland. *Elements of Semiology,* trans. A. Lavers and C. Smith. New York: Hill and Wang, 1977.

Greimas, A. J. *Structural Semantics: An Attempt at a Method,* trans. Daniele McDowell, Ronald Schleifer, and Alan Velie, introduction by Ronald Schleifer. Lincoln: University of Nebraska Press, 1983.

Jameson, Fredric. *The Prison House of Language: A Critical Account of Structuralism and Russian Formalism.* Princeton, NJ: Princeton University Press, 1972.

Lentricchia, Frank. *After the New Criticism.* Chicago: University of Chicago Press, 1980.

Macksey, Richard, and Eugenio Donato, eds. *The Structuralist Controversy.* Baltimore: Johns Hopkins University Press, 1970.

Saussure, Ferdinand de. *Course in General Linguistics,* trans. Wade Baskin. New York: McGraw-Hill, 1966.

Scholes, Robert. *Structuralism in Literature: An Introduction.* New Haven: Yale University Press, 1974.

Todorov, Tzvetan. *The Fantastic: A Structural Approach to a Literary Genre.* trans. R. Howard. Ithaca: Cornell University Press, 1975.

Post-Structuralist Criticism

Barthes, Roland. *S/Z*, trans. Richard Miller. New York: Hill and Wang, 1974.

Culler, Jonathan. *On Deconstruction: Theory and Criticism after Structuralism.* Ithaca: Cornell University Press, 1982.

de Man, Paul. *Allegories of Reading: Figural Language in Rousseau, Nietzsche, Rilke, and Proust.* New Haven: Yale University Press, 1979.

Derrida, Jacques. *Of Grammatology*, trans. Gayatri Spivak. Baltimore: Johns-Hopkins University Press, 1976.

Eco, Umberto. *A Theory of Semiotics.* Bloomington: Indiana University Press, 1976.

Hartman, Geoffrey H. *Criticism in the Wilderness.* New Haven: Yale University Press, 1980.

Johnson, Barbara. *The Critical Difference: Essays in the Contemporary Rhetoric of Reading.* Baltimore: Johns-Hopkins University Press, 1980.

————. "Teaching Deconstructively." *Writing and Reading Differently.* Ed. G. Douglas Atkins and Michael L. Johnson. Lawrence: University Press of Kansas, 1985. 140–148.

Lynn, Steven. "A Passage into Critical Theory." *College English* 52 (1990): 258–271.

Miller, J. Hillis, "Ariadne's Thread: Repetition and the Narrative Line." *Critical Inquiry* 3 (1976) 55–77.

Rorty, Richard. *Consequences of Pragmatism.* Minneapolis: University of Minnesota Press, 1982.

Appendix III:
Glossary of Critical Terms

Here are some of the key terms used throughout this text. A student of criticism who intends to go beyond the introductory level would be well advised to purchase a more complete guide to critical terminology like M. H. Abrams, *A Glossary of Literary Terms* (Fort Worth: Holt, Rinehart and Winston, 1988).

absurd in literature, works whose expressed sense of life is that of the meaningless or the ridiculous as in Franz Kafka's story "The Hunger Artist" (see p. 279) or Samuel Beckett's play *Happy Days*, an example of **the theater of the absurd** (see p. 849).

act a major unit in a play, often subdivided into the smaller units or **scenes.**

action the events of a plot in a drama or narrative.

aesthetic in literature, the qualities of literary beauty considered in themselves and for their own sakes.

allegory a narrative in which some or all of the elements such as **character, plot, and setting** take on another sense in addition to their literal meaning, such as a moral or a political meaning.

alliteration the repetition of sounds in words appearing close together; **assonance** names the repetition of vowel sounds, and **consonance** the repetition of consonant sounds.

allusion a reference in a text to something outside itself, as when Eliot alludes to Shakespeare's *Antony and Cleopatra* in the passage of *The Waste Land* that begins "The Chair she sat in, like a burnished throne . . . ."

ambiguity in literature, the property of containing many possible meanings in a single word, passage, or work.

anachronism a mistake in historical verisimilitude; the reference to a striking clock in Shakespeare's *Julius Caesar* is an example of anachronism, since the play is set in Rome before the invention of clocks that strike.

antagonist the opponent of the **protagonist** or main character in a literary work.

archaism the deliberate use of old fashioned terms—"thee" in a love poem of the twentieth century, for example.

atmosphere the general "feel" of a work of literature created by the setting and point of view; the mood that pervades it. See Introduction to Fiction (p. 6).

Augustan Age in English literature, the **neoclassical period** roughly from the Restoration in 1660 to the rise of the **Romantics** around 1800. Pope's *The Rape of The Lock* (see p. 374) is an example of Augustan poetry.

ballad a longstanding folk form sometimes used by major poets whose four-line stanza alternates four and three stress lines. Wordsworth's "A Slumber Did My Spirit Seal" (see p. 400) is an example of the ballad form.

bathos the opposite of the **sublime**; the deliberate or undeliberate substitution of the low or ridiculous for the noble in sentiment or situation.

blank verse a name for unrhymed iambic pentameter. See p. 370 for a discussion of **meter**.

Bowdlerize to purge editorially from a text that which the editor considers to be indecent material.

burlesque an imitation of a literary work or style that is deliberately ridiculous and makes fun of its model. Pope's *The Rape of the Lock,* for example, is a mock epic and **burlesques** many conventions of the epic such as the battle with supernatural aids for the heroes and heroines. Vladimir Nabokov, author of "Cloud, Castle, Lake" (see p. 301) defined some related terms: "**Satire** is a lesson; **parody** is a game."

canon in literature, the texts considered by a period or a group of critics to be important or major.

carpe diem Latin for "seize the day." A poem that urges its auditor to make the most of life since life is short. See Andrew Marvell's "To His Coy Mistress" (p. 464).

character the "persons" who appear in a literary work. Poorly rendered characters are often described as "flat" and well-rendered ones as "round" by analogy to primitive and more complex painting.

chorus a group of players in Greek tragedies who comment together on the action of the play. See Sophocles' *Oedipus the King* (p. 556) for an example.

cliché an overused or hackneyed expression that calls attention to its exhausted meaning and style.

close reading the critical technique of paying detailed attention to the elements within a literary work as opposed to (say) potential literary influences on the author. Close reading is associated with the New Criticism, but is employed by almost all critics to a degree.

closure a completion or a coming to finality. A book or story that seems to come to an end would be said to manifest closure, while a book or story that seemed simply to stop would not.

comedy loosely, any literary work meant to amuse or having a happy ending.

conceit figures of speech used to make a striking comparison that organizes a literary work or a part of a work. Shakespeare makes fun of the exhausted poetic conceits of his age in "My Mistresses Eyes Are Nothing Like the Sun" (see p. 456).

conflict a common way in which plot produces action.

connotation and denotation *connotation* refers to the flavor of associations of a word or phrase while *denotation* describes the literal or primary reference. The denotation of "wedding" would point to the contractual aspects of the marriage ceremony, while "wedding" includes a connotation of joyous celebration, among other things.

convention literally "a coming together." In literature, the devices which the reader and author agree to allow as part of literary "reality," the remarkable lack of hesitation in the conversations of books as opposed to those in life, for example. Exhausted conventions of one age are often satirized by authors of the next age.

dénouement French for "untying the knot;" the resolution of a plot.

dialectical materialism a Marxian theory that maintains the basis of reality is material and constantly changing in a dialectical process.

dialogue the speech of characters in a work of literature.

diction the word choice of a literary work. For example, a style using "steed" would display a high (or poetic or old-fashioned) level of diction, "nag" would belong to an informal (or slangy or jocular) level of diction.

discourse a connected verbal treatment of a topic as in "critical discourse."

doggerel rough, clumsy verse sometimes deliberately used by skillful poets for comic effects.

dramatic monologue a long speech in verse by a single character, as in Browning's "My Last Duchess" (see p. 490).

elegy in modern times, a term that describes solemn meditations in verse, as Gray's "Elegy" (see p. 469).

empathy or sympathy the literary illusion created in the reader of sharing (**empathy**) or feeling deeply about (**sympathy**) the imaginary feelings of imaginary characters whose identity the reader may claim to share for the moment.

Enlightenment the cultural movement characterized by a faith in reason that generally pervaded Europe in the eighteenth century.

epic also called a heroic poem, such as Homer's *Iliad* or Milton's *Paradise Lost*. Generally considered the most difficult, the greatest, and most glorious of genres. Pope's *The Rape of the Lock* (p. 374) is an example of a mock epic.

epiphany in Christian terms, a manifestation of God's presence; used in a secular sense by James Joyce for a sudden intense revelation of meaning in an apparently commonplace object or event.

essentialism philosophies that see concepts as having an essence or basic nature may be called "essentialist" as opposed to those that see concepts as human constructions of meaning used to mean different things by different people. See the introduction to Structuralism (p. 136).

euphony language pleasing to the ear; **cacophony** is its opposite.

exchange-value the worth of a symbol of value. As opposed to its negligible "use-value," the exchange-value of a bank note is determined by its denomination. A $5 bill will purchase $5 of use-value, but its own use-value in itself is practically nil.

exposition the unfolding of a plot's background and issues.

fabliau a medieval short form in verse with low characters, indecent themes, and satiric intent.

falling action the action in the last part of a plot, leading to its resolution.

figurative language language not literally true, but meant metaphorically, as the lion is literally a beast but only figuratively "the king of beasts." **Similes** call attention to their figurative nature by using "like" or "as," (e.g., "the news came like a thunderbolt"), while **metaphors** also use one area of discourse (politics, monarchy) to describe another (relative prowess among animals) without acknowledging directly their figurative nature. I. A. Richards introduced the term **vehicle** for the figurative area of discourse (e.g., politics, monarchy) and **tenor** for the area of discourse of intended meaning (e.g., relative prowess among animals).

foil a minor character used to bring out the qualities of a major character. In *Hamlet*, Shakespeare partly uses Polonius as a foil to Hamlet in giving the prince an occasion to display wit, bitterness, and so on.

formalist critical theories called formalist are those that pay attention to the form or style of a work as opposed to its ostensible content or that find content expressed most fully in style or form. See the introduction to the New Criticism (p. 29).

free verse in French, *vers libre.* The so-called "open form" of poetry in which no regularity of meter is maintained for more than momentary purposes.

genre loosely, a word for a type or species or subspecies of literature, a literary form. "Drama" would be a genre as opposed to "poetry;" but "comedy" and "tragedy" may be considered genres within drama as "lyric" and "sonnet" are genres within poetry. Some theorists, like Northrop Frye in his *Anatomy of Criticism* (1957), have defined genres more strictly and claimed them to derive from fixed forms that the human imagination takes.

Georgian usually applied to English poets in the reign of George V (1910–1936) and connoting rural subjects treated with delicacy. See for example A. E. Houseman (p. 510).

graveyard poets applied to eighteenth-century English poets who wrote meditative and often melancholy verse. See Thomas Gray's "Elegy" (p. 469).

hegemony a domination or influence by one entity over another. English literature might be said to exemplify a hegemony in terms of American literary education. Feminists claim that literature by males has exercised a hegemony over the literary canon.

heroic couplet two successive rhyming lines of iambic pentameter. A form used throughout much of the history of English poetry for elevated (or mock-elevated) poems. See Pope's *The Rape of the Lock* (p. 374) for an example, and the discussion of meter (p. 370) for a further explanation.

Humanism in the sixteenth century, the word **humanist** was used to name a student of **the humanities**, that is, studies such as grammar, rhetoric, and history as opposed to subjects such as natural philosophy and theology. In the nineteenth century, **humanism** came to describe views of human nature in the tradition of Renaissance humanists, including the view of mankind (opposed to, say, the natural "laws" of science) as of central importance in the universe. The **New Humanists** of the twentieth century like Irving Babbitt were critics of conservative moral and political views who advocated a return to humanistic education and classical values for literary criticism.

imagery verbal activities that evoke sense perceptions, as Wordsworth's "There was a howling in the wind all night."

irony the word comes from a Greek root naming a character in comedy who was a dissembler commonly pretending in his speeches to understand less than he did. From this, **verbal irony** has come to mean in Ruben Brower's phrase "saying one thing and meaning another." For example, see Sir Thomas Wyatt's use of "kindly" (p. 452). **Sarcasm** is thus irony that would be easily understood even by its intended victim; see Sylvia Plath's "Daddy" (p. 542). **Dramatic irony** describes the difference in understanding between audience and character as in *Oedipus the King* (p. 556). **Romantic irony** implies skepticism about *all* values, including those the author may seem to express. See, for example, e. e. cummings (p. 528).

"ivory tower" a term used to describe an attitude toward life that values the contemplative over the active and the aesthetic over the practical.

Jacobean Age the age of James I of England ("Jacobus" in Latin) (1603–25) that included writers such as Shakespeare, Ben Jonson, and John Donne.

lyric originally a song accompanied by a lyre, a harp-like instrument. Now used to describe short poems of intense feeling.

marginality the status of being excluded from consideration as basic or important. See the introduction to Racial and Ethnic Criticism (p. 118).

materialist philosophies that consider the world as only physical without any supernatural aspect are called "materialist."

means of production in economic analysis, the structures (e.g. land, machines) through which goods and services are produced. See Marxist Criticism.

melodrama originally used of plays with music, but now applied generally to crude literary efforts with flat characters and clumsy effects.

metaphor the use of a term from one area of discourse to describe something else: "He's a tiger!" Unlike the **simile**, the metaphor does not signal that its use of language is figurative: "He is like a tiger!" I. A. Richards introduced the terms **vehicle** for the language that conveys the meaning (a ferocious animal) and **tenor** for what is meant (a person with aggressive qualities).

metaphysical poets a term coined by Samuel Johnson to describe poets of the seventeenth century who delighted in philosophical themes and images. See, for example, John Donne (p. 456).

meter originally "measure" and in poetry the measure of poetic rhythms. Meter is generally formed in modern English by the alternation of stressed and unstressed syllables. For a brief introduction, see p. 370.

Middle English period the literature of England between the Norman Conquest (A.D. 1066) used to mark the end of the Old English period, and 1500, the rough date for the beginning of Modern English and its literature.

modernism in literature, the writing of early twentieth-century experimenters like T. S. Eliot (p. 522), Ezra Pound (p. 520), and H. D. (Hilda Doolittle) (p. 521) who reacted against the Romanticism of the nineteenth century and who tended to turn the techniques of literature themselves into literary subjects. **Postmodernism** generally refers to writers after World War II who attempted to adopt the insights and techniques of modernism to their own (in many senses Romantic) reaction against it. See Laurie Moore (p. 350) and Alice Walker (p. 547) for examples in fiction and poetry.

motif a recurring literary theme or pattern.

myth generally, a traditional story that stands as an imaginative or poetic explanation for natural or human behavior. Nowadays, particularly, a *false* explanation is implied; but twentieth-century myth critics like Robert Graves and Northrop Frye have studied myths as a guide to the nature of the human mind and what it accepts as "explanation."

narratology the study of narrative methods and techniques.

narrator the teller of the tale who is best treated as a character within it. See Introduction to Fiction (p. 6) for some of the various kinds of narrators commonly used.

neoclassic See Augustan Age.

novel generally, a long prose fictional form which began to flourish in the eighteenth century and was then "novel," though the word's meaning was early extended and is now applied to a great number of works.

octave the first eight lines of a sonnet, whose last six form the **sestet**.

ode a long, serious, lyric poem. See the two odes by John Keats (pp. 482–485) and the *mock* ode by Thomas Gray (p. 467).

Old English period also called the Anglo-Saxon period after some of the tribes who invaded England after the end of the Roman occupation ca. A.D. 425. The Norman Conquest (1066) roughly marks the end of the period, though Old English continued to be spoken and read among the conquered peoples as Middle English evolved from their interaction with the French-speaking ruling class.

pastoral a **genre** originating in Greek poetry, whose setting is rural and whose themes are basic and unsophisticated, but whose language is delicate and refined.

persona the Latin word for the mask used by actors. Now used especially by critics who consider literature in terms of speech or utterance for the "speaker" of a poem or the "first-person" narrator of a story. See Introduction to Fiction (p. 6).

plot in a literary work, the construction of its action. See Introduction to Fiction (p. 6). The **main plot** may be attended and filled out by various **subplots** secondary to the main action.

point of view the attitude taken toward the events of a literary work by its author or narrator. See Introduction to Fiction (p. 6).

post-modernism the late twentieth-century cultural and literary ethos said to follow that of modernism earlier in the century. While modernists in general attempted to reinstitute an order or orders for the spiritual chaos of modern life, post-modernists claim to subvert all conventional orders in the name of liberation.

pre-Raphaelites a group of English writers and artists in the latter part of the nineteenth century who sought a return to the aesthetic simplicity and purity that they saw as characteristic of Italian painting before the age of Raphael (1483–1520). See Christina Rossetti (p. 503).

problem play a modern type of drama in which the plot reflects a contemporary social problem. The genre is generally understood to have begun with Henrik Ibsen (see p. 789).

prose unmetered speech or writing.

prosody the techniques of poetry generally including meter, figurative language, and the customs of poetic forms. See Introduction to Poetry (p. 366).

protagonist the leading character in a literary work.

realism any literary method, but especially that of the late nineteenth century, that opposes its methods to those of romanticism, idealism, propaganda, or any other method that the realist writer considers distorting of life as it is and should be presented in literature. Still later in the nineteenth century, the proponents of **naturalism** sometimes claimed to be even more "realistic" than realists by treating subjects of a lower order in a manner of "scientific" objectivity that precluded, for example, a "moral" for a story. **Socialist realism** is a word used in **Marxist criticism** as a term of praise for literature that, for example, "realistically" demonstrates the virtues of the proletariat or the vices of the capitalist system.

Renaissance a word meaning originally "rebirth" as in the rebirth of culture after the "dark" ages following the fall of the Roman Empire. The period of European history following the late Middle Ages and preceding the modern period. In English Literature, roughly 1500–1660.

resolution the settling of the plot's issues in its ending.

Restoration in English literary history, the period beginning with the restoration of Charles II to the throne of England in 1660 and conventionally ending in 1700. **The Augustan Age** is sometimes used to refer collectively to **restoration and eighteenth-century literature—1660–1800.**

rhetoric "the art of persuasion," whose formal study has been linked with literary study since the time of Aristotle. See **Rhetoric and Reader-Response Criticism** (p. 69).

rhyme scheme the pattern of rhyming in a poem.

rising action the activities of plot leading to a crisis or climax.

Romantic period the period in English literature dating roughly from the outbreak of the French Revolution (1789) (or the publication of

Lyrical Ballads by Wordsworth and Coleridge in 1798) to the passage of the Reform Bill in 1832, the conventional beginning of **the Victorian era**. See also the poems of Keats, Shelley, and Byron, beginning on p. 478.

satire the literary manner that makes its subject ridiculous in the name of correcting the attitudes of its audience. Vladimir Nabokov says "**Satire** is a lesson; **parody** is a game." Pope's *The Rape of the Lock* (p. 374) is considered a satire; Ian Frazier's "The Killion" (p. 347) is a parody.

scansion the analysis of a poem's meter and its variations in rhythm; to **scan** verse is to make this analysis.

scene a unit of action in a play or (more loosely) any small set of events in a work of literature.

sestet the last six lines of a sonnet whose first eight make its **octave**.

setting the locale in a work of literature. See Introduction to Fiction (p. 6).

simile the explicit use through the words *like* or *as* of figurative language: "He is like a tiger!" See **metaphor**.

speaker a word used to describe the "I" of a poem as a character revealed by the style of language displayed.

soliloquy the moment in drama when a character talks alone aloud.

sonnet a lyric in a single unit of fourteen lines. See Introduction to Poetry (p. 366).

stage directions the instructions by a playwright for stage action, entrances, exits, and the like.

stanza a group of lines in poetry forming a unit by length, rhyme scheme, or the like, and separated visually on the page.

stream of consciousness William James first used this phrase to describe the activity of the mind. It has since been applied to the narrative technique also called **interior monologue** developed most notably by James Joyce. See Introduction to Fiction (p. 6).

symbol a literary device by which one aspect of the work may be seen as the vehicle of a metaphor that expresses a meaning larger or greater than that the aspect apparently claims. In Joyce's story "Araby," the bazaar becomes a positive symbol for the boy in the story and a negative symbol for his older self as narrator.

tone the manner in which a character speaks in literature is called the character's **tone of voice** as if we could hear the intonations and implications of a real speaker.

tragedy generally a literary work with an unhappy conclusion, but more particularly, especially in drama, a work describing an aspect of life when, in Robert Frost's phrase, "something terrible has happened and no one is to blame."

unconscious in psychoanalytic theory the part of the mind unavailable to ordinary self-awareness. For Freud, the unconscious functioned as a struggle between forces; for Lacan it functions like a language as understood by structuralist linguistics.

unities Aristotle spoke of the unity of action as necessary in a drama for verisimilitude. French neo-classic critics added unities of time and place by analogy. These added unities were generally ignored by English playwrights like Shakespeare.

use-value the worth of something in terms of its function as an object of consumption in itself. As opposed its "exchange-value," the use-value of paper money, for example, is practically nil. A bank note worth $100,000.00 might have a use-value of less than a cent, as packing material or the like.

Victorian period The period usually understood to begin in 1832 and end with the death of Queen Victoria in 1901.

voice a term used to describe a literary character or poetic discourse in terms of a style of speech (e.g., boasting) as opposed, say, to moral terms (e.g., prideful).

wit a term that in earlier periods than our own stood not only for quick humor but for intelligence generally. A "wit" was an intellectual as well as a humorous individual. For example, Pope and Swift were **wits** of the Augustan Age.

Credits

DILLION, GEORGE L. "Styles of Reading 'A Rose for Miss Emily,'" from *Poetics Today* 3:2 (1982): 77–88. Reprinted by permission of Duke University Press.

DOOLITTLE, HILDA. "Oread" & "Heat," from *Collected Poems, 1912–1944.* Copyright © 1982 by the Estate of Hilda Doolittle. Reprinted by permission of New Directions Publishing Corporation.

ELIOT, T. S. "The Love Song of J. Alfred Prufrock," from *Collected Poems 1909–1962* by T. S. Eliot. Copyright © 1936 by Harcourt Brace Jovanovich, Inc. Copyright © 1964, 1963 by T. S. Eliot. Reprinted by permission of the publisher.

ELIOT, T. S. "Macavity: The Mystery Cat," from *Old Possum's Book of Practical Cats.* Copyright © 1939 by T. S. Eliot and renewed 1967 by Esme Valerie Eliot. Reprinted by permission of Harcourt Brace Jovanovich, Inc.

ELLISON, RALPH. "King of the Bingo Game," from *Tomorrow V 1944.* Copyright © 1944 by Ralph Ellison. Reprinted by permission of the William Morris Agency, Inc., on behalf of the author.

ERDRICH, LOUISE. "Indian Boarding School: The Runaway," from *Jacklight* poems by Louise Erdrich. Copyright © 1984 by Louise Erdrich. Reprinted by permission of Henry Holt and Company, Inc.

FAULKNER, WILLIAM. "A Rose for Emily," from *Collected Stories* by William Faulkner. Copyright © 1930 and renewed 1958 by William Faulkner. Reprinted by permission of Random House, Inc.

FETTERLEY, JUDITH. "Women Beware Science: 'The Birthmark,'" from *The Resisting Reader* by Judith Fetterley. Copyright © 1978 by Judith Fetterley. Reprinted by permission of the Indiana University Press.

FITZGERALD, ROBERT. "Oedipus Rex." Copyright © 1949 by Harcourt Brace Jovanovich, Inc., and renewed 1977 by Cornelia Fitts and Robert Fitzgerald. Reprinted by permission of the publisher.

FORCHE, CAROLYN. "The Colonel." from *The Country Between Us* by Carolyn Forche. Copyright © 1980 by Carolyn Forche. Reprinted by permission of HarperCollins Publishers.

FRAZIER, IAN. "The Killion," from *Dating Your Mom* by Ian Frazier. Copyright © 1986 by Ian Frazier. Reprinted by permission of Farrar, Straus and Giroux, Inc.

FROST, ROBERT. "Stopping by Woods on a Snowy Evening," and "Design," from *The Poetry of Robert Frost* edited by Edward Connery Lathem. Copyright © 1923, 1969 by Holt, Rinehart and Winston, Inc. Copyright © 1964 by Lesley Frost Ballantine. Copyright © 1936, 1951 by Robert Frost. Reprinted by permission of Henry Holt and Company, Inc.

GARBER, MARJORIE. Quotations from "The Eye of the Storm: Structure and Myth in Shakespeare's *Tempest,*" by Marjorie Garber. Originally published in *Hebrew University Studies in Literature,* 8:1 (Spring 1980). Reprinted by permission of the author.

GIBBONS, MARK L. "How I Love My Life." Used by permission of Gail V. Gibbons Swain.

GINSBERG, ALLEN. "A Supermarket in California," from *Collected Poems: 1947–1980* by Allen Ginsberg. Copyright © 1955 by Allen Ginsberg. Reprinted by permission of HarperCollins Publishers.

HARTMAN, GEOFFERY. "The Interpreter's Freud," from *Raritan: A Quarterly Review,* vol. IV No. 2 (Fall 1984). Copyright © 1984 by Raritan. Reprinted by permission.

HEMINGWAY, ERNEST. "Hills Like White Elephants" from *Men Without Women.* Reprinted with permission of Charles Scribner's Sons, an imprint of Macmillan Publishing Company, from *Men Without Women* by Ernest Hemingway. Copyright © 1927 by Charles Scribner's Sons; renewal copyright © 1955 by Ernest Hemingway.

HORNBY, RICHARD. "The Ethical Leap: A Doll's House," from *Patterns in Ibsen's Middle Plays.* Reprinted by permission of Associated University Presses.

HOUSMAN, A. E. "Loveliest of Trees, the Cherry Now," and "To an Athlete Dying Young," from *A Shropshire Lad*—authorised edition from The Collected Poems of A. E. Housman. Copyright © 1939, 1940, 1965 by Holt, Rinehart and Winston. Copyright © 1967, 1968 by Robert E. Symons. Reprinted by permission of Henry Holt and Company.

HUGHES, LANGSTON. "Harlem," from *The Panther and the Lash: Poems of our Time.* by Langston Hughes. Copyright © 1951 by Langston Hughes. Reprinted by permission of Alfred A. Knopf, Inc.

HUGHES, LANGSTON. "Night Funeral in Harlem," and "Same in Blues," from *Montage of a Dream Deferred* by Langston Hughes. Copyright © 1951 by Langston Hughes; renewed 1979 by George Houston Bass. Reprinted by permission of Harold Ober Associates, Inc.

IBSEN, HENRIK. *A Doll House,* from *The Complete Major Prose of Henrik Ibsen* by Henrik Ibsen, translated by Rolf Fjelde. Translation copyright © 1965, 1970, 1978 by Rolf Fjelde. Reprinted by permission of New American Library, a division of Penguin Books USA Inc.

JACKSON, SHIRLEY. "The Lottery," from *The Lottery and Other Stories* by Shirley Jackson. Copyright © 1948, 1949 by Shirley Jackson. Renewal copyright © 1976, 1977 by Laurence Hyman, Barry Hyman, Mrs. Sarah Webster, and Mrs. Joanne Schnurer. Reprinted by permission of Farrar, Straus and Giroux, Inc.

JOYCE, JAMES. "Araby," from *Dubliners* by James Joyce. Copyright © 1916 by B.W. Heubsch. Definitive text copyright © 1967 by the Estate of James Joyce. Used by permission of Viking Penguin, a division of Penguin Books USA Inc.

KAFKA, FRANZ. "A Hunger Artist," from *Franz Kafka: The Complete Stories* by Franz Kafka, edited by N. Glatzer. Copyright © 1946, 1947, 1948, 1949, 1954, 1958, 1971 by Schocken Books, Inc. Reprinted by permission of Schocken Books, published by

Index

This index includes subject concepts, literary critics, authors and titles of literary works, and first lines of poetry. Page numbers in boldface refer to the text of literary works; page numbers followed by "n" refer to footnotes.